MW00784548

The Penguin Modern Classics Book

Henry Eliot is the author of *The Penguin Classics Book* and presents the podcast *On the Road with Penguin Classics*. He has organized literary tours, including a mass pilgrimage inspired by William Morris, a recreation of Chaucer's *Canterbury Tales*, a Lake Poets walk around Cumbria and a quest for the Holy Grail based on Malory's *Morte D'Arthur*, and he is the author of *Follow This Thread: A Maze Book to Get Lost In* and *Curiocity: An Alternative A to Z of London*.

THE PENGUIN MODERN CLASSICS BOOK

HENRY ELIOT

UK | USA | Canada | Ireland | Australia
India | New Zealand | South Africa

Penguin Books is part of the Penguin Random House
group of companies whose addresses can be found
at global.penguinrandomhouse.com

The authorized representative in the EEA is
Penguin Random House Ireland, Morrison Chambers,
32 Nassau Street, Dublin D02 YH68

First published by Particular Books 2021
002

Text copyright © Henry Eliot, 2021
The moral right of the author has been asserted

Penguin
Random House
UK

Book design by Matthew Young
with help from Theo Inglis

Set in Joanna Nova, Univers Next and Avant Garde Gothic
Printed and bound in Italy by Printer Trento Srl

A CIP catalogue record for this book is available from
the British Library

ISBN: 978-0-241-44160-2

p.1: *Time Transfixed,* 1938 by René Magritte © ADAGP,
Paris and DACS, London 2021, from *The Railway Accident*
(79) by Edward Upward. p.331: photograph, *Sake Pot,*
courtesy of the Mingei International Museum, from
The Beauty of Everyday Things (348) by Soetsu Yanagi.
p.355: photograph, *Prostitute in Zimbabwe* © Trygve
Bolstad / Panos Pictures, from *The House of Hunger* (377)
by Dambudzo Marechera. p.379: drawing by Sidney Nolan
© The Sidney Nolan Trust, all rights reserved, DACS 2021,
from *Voss* (382) by Patrick White. p.393: *Open Range,*
1942 by Maynard Dixon, from *Riders of the Purple Sage*
(411) by Zane Grey.

MIX
Paper from
responsible sources
FSC® C018179

Contents

Preface

The book in your hands contains every title published in the Penguin Modern Classics series between April 1961 – when the series began (ix) – and April 2021. Like its companion volume, *The Penguin Classics Book* (2018), this is a reader's guide to the greatest books ever written, drawing connections across time and space. It aims to be both a trove of literary treasures and a map to inspire future exploration.

The Penguin Classics Book spans 4,000 years – from the *Epic of Gilgamesh* to the poetry of the First World War (60) – and is divided into four epochs: the Ancient World, the Middle Ages, Early Modern Europe and the Industrial Age. This book brings that story up to date, covering the last 100 years or so (578) and presenting a fifth and final epoch: the Modern Age (xviii).

It lists every title that has been published in the Penguin Modern Classics series: more than 1,800 books by more than 600 authors.* Each title is illustrated with its first Modern Classics cover; where more than one edition is listed, the date of the illustrated cover is underlined. Out-of-print editions are indicated with a • red dot.

The reason why a title might no longer be in print with Penguin Modern Classics is that most twentieth-century authors are still within the term of UK copyright – 70 years after death – and during that time the rights to publish their works are controlled by the authors' estates. Publishers vie for these rights, so some authors – such as Ivy Compton-Burnett (104), William Faulkner (433), Graham Greene (88), Ernest Hemingway (428), Aldous Huxley (65), Rosamond Lehmann (77), Thomas Mann (245) and J. D. Salinger (499) – have appeared in Penguin Modern Classics editions in the past but are now no longer part of the series. There are, of course, several notable twentieth-century writers who have never been published as Penguin Modern Classics: Günter Grass, Doris Lessing, Naguib Mahfouz, Toni Morrison and Sylvia Plath, to name a few. But as Paul Valéry (also missing) once said, 'a work is never truly completed'. No doubt, in

How to Use This Book

There are several ways to explore this book: you might read it from cover to cover, in which case you would be travelling around the world, from Ireland (3) to Argentina (572); you might look up authors and titles in the index (592) or explore a decade in the publications timeline (578); you might trace the history of 20th-century cultural movements (xviii); or you could open the book at random, treating it as a literary lucky dip. Or you may wish to consult any of the miniature reading lists that are sprinkled across the pages:

the course of time, these authors will join either Penguin Modern Classics or its parent series, the Penguin Classics.

Both of these series are works in progress, as will be obvious from a quick browse through these pages: the British (22) and US (397) sections are disproportionately large, for example, and some areas, such as India (337), China (346) and, particularly, North Africa (356), are under-represented. Only a fifth of the authors in this book are women and nine in ten of them are white. The task of a classics publisher is to identify these imbalances and redress them, striving always to publish the greatest works of literature from around the world.

A classic text is like a knapped flint: it is an artefact from another age, handled and passed down by generations, but its cutting edge remains sharp and it can still spark a fire. A 'modern' classic has the same power, but it is a product of more recent times: it was written in response to a world we are still experiencing, and it can be all the more challenging and exciting because of it. 'Unlike the

old classic, which was expected to provide answers,' wrote the critic Frank Kermode, a modern classic 'poses a virtually infinite set of questions'. I hope these pages help to raise some of those questions and that these books light the way towards at least some of the answers.

It feels appropriate to be completing this two-volume project in 2021. This is both the 60th anniversary of the Penguin Modern Classics and the 75th anniversary of the Penguin Classics. Together these much-loved series comprise the largest and richest library of classic literature in the world, and I hope they continue to provide you with as much pleasure as they have given me.

Henry Eliot

* The only Modern Classics titles missing from this volume are those which originated overseas – in the Penguin offices in Australia, Canada, India, South Africa and the USA – and which have never been available in the UK, for copyright reasons. There are not many of these, but examples include *The Lost Honor of Katharina Blum* by Heinrich Böll, *The Waste Land and Other Poems* by T. S. Eliot, *Hunger* by Knut Hamsun, *The Sea, The Sea* by Iris Murdoch and *Gravity's Rainbow* by Thomas Pynchon.

The Penguin Modern Classics

1961 • –
(see p.436)

In June 1956, Penguin Books marked its 21st birthday
by publishing *The Penguin Story* by William Emrys
Williams, the editor-in-chief. In the two decades since
Allen Lane founded the company in 1935, Penguin
Books had been transformed from a publisher of
experimentally stylish paperback reprints into a cultural
and educational powerhouse, dominating bookshops
with its fiction titles and its proliferating sub-series,
from Pelican Books (xiii) and Penguin Shakespeare
to Penguin Classics (xiv) and the 'Miscellaneous' series,
in which *The Penguin Story* appeared, rather appropriately,
as number 21. 'If a publisher fails to freshen his list
continually,' Williams advised, '[…] he will forfeit
the support of his better public.'

The Penguin Classics series had been launched in
1946 by E. V. Rieu, with his own translation of Homer's
Odyssey. In ten years, it had grown to comprise 62 titles
of the 'most enduring of the foreign classics, ancient,
medieval and modern'. 'Modern', in this sense, covered
everything from the 16th to the early 20th century,
and the most recent Penguin Classics titles at the
time were *Germinal* (1885) by Émile Zola, *Hedda Gabler*
(1890) by Henrik Ibsen and *The Cherry Orchard* (1904)
by Anton Chekhov. This single series appeared to cover
the literary field adequately. 'We don't want – without
outstandingly good reasons – to start any new series,'
said the Penguin general editor A. S. B. Glover in 1957
– 'such as "Modern Classics".'

1961 • –
(see p.453)

1961 • —
(see p.446)

1961 • —
(see p.107)

Times were changing, however. In January 1961,
Allen Lane appointed the bookseller Tony Godwin as
Penguin's fiction editor, and Godwin went on to succeed
Williams as editor-in-chief. Penguin had always been
famous for its orange fiction and green crime titles, most
of which were paperback reprints of existing hardbacks,
but Godwin foresaw a problem. 'The literary scene is
in peril of being converted into a dustbowl,' he wrote.
'At the moment paperback publishers are cashing in
on the past 60 years of creative writing and publishing.
Unless they take over some of the responsibilities for
discovering and encouraging new talent, the present
literary scene will be denuded within the next decade.'
Godwin's solution was to diversify: he retained orange
covers for contemporary and newly commissioned
fiction, and he introduced a new design to distinguish
the finest literature of recent decades, creating a series
he called 'Penguin Modern Classics'.

Penguin Modern Classics

'This new Penguin series is intended to bring the
very best of modern literature to the reading public,'
ran the advertisement. 'Many are books that people
have heard about but now find out of print or difficult
to obtain. Others are classics which are only just coming
to be recognised as classics. And others have appeared
in the old Penguin fiction covers.' The first five new
titles were issued in April 1961: *The Ides of March* (436)
by Thornton Wilder, *The Heart is a Lonely Hunter* (453)
by Carson McCullers, *Miss Lonelyhearts and A Cool Million*
(446) by Nathanael West, Ronald Firbank's *Valmouth and
Other Stories* (64) and *Enemies of Promise* (107) by Cyril
Connolly. They were given a distinctive colour palette,
combinations of dove grey, orange, black and white,
and they bore a band across the bottom of each cover
with the new series title. The covers were designed by
the Penguin typographer Hans Schmoller, who used
Eric Gill's (96) typeface Joanna. Gill was particularly fond
of Joanna: he named it after his youngest daughter and
selected it to set his monograph *An Essay on Typography*
(96); it is also the typeface used to set this paragraph
and all of the book descriptions in this volume.

Grey

In 1962, Godwin appointed a new art director, Germano Facetti, who set about redesigning all the Penguin series. In October 1963, Facetti addressed the Modern Classics: he retained the predominantly grey colour scheme of Schmoller's design, but reset the covers adapting the 'Marber Grid', which was a cleaner layout that allowed more space for artwork. The Marber Grid had been devised by the Polish designer Romek Marber for the Penguin crime covers, but it was so versatile it had already been adopted for the Pelican series (xiii) and the orange fiction titles too. Facetti wanted to alter

1963 —
(see p.240)

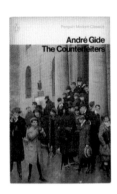

1966
trans. Dorothy Bussy (97),
1931
(see p.165)

the typeface on the cover, but Schmoller persuaded him to stick with Joanna for the time being. The first title in this new look was *Seven Gothic Tales* (240) by Isak Dinesen. Three years later, in March 1966, Facetti got his way: starting with André Gide's *The Counterfeiters* (165), he replaced Joanna with the typeface Helvetica and pushed the title and author name further up the cover. The colour scheme also became looser. The upper panel varied between white, black and grey-green, and in some cases it disappeared altogether when the artwork filled the entire cover.

Orange

Facetti left Penguin in 1972, but his Modern Classics design remained unchanged until February 1982, when the series was given a completely fresh look by the new art director, Cherriwyn Magill. The books were brought out in a larger size – the 'B' format

1969 Modern Classics
1982 Modern Classics *rejacketed*
• —
(see p.9)

1986
• ed. Hans Walter Gabler
pref. Richard Ellmann
(see p.10)

that is still used today – and they had orange-and-white spines and white covers with an inset artwork, centred title and a Penguin logo perched below the overarching series name. The first title to be given this treatment was a rejacketing of *Ulysses* (10) by James Joyce. Magill's design was refined once, in June 1986, when the series title was straightened, and each word separated by a dot. In his book *Penguin By Design* (2005), the typographer Phil Baines describes this period of Penguin's design history, perhaps a little unfairly, as 'the all-time low'.

Penguin Twentieth-Century Classics

The series had its next facelift in May 1989, when it was renamed 'Penguin Twentieth-Century Classics' and the back covers and spines became eau-de-nil, a bright green-blue colour. 'The Penguin Twentieth-Century Classics list offers a wonderfully rich and varied mixture, of tragedy and comedy, of poetry and prose, with some fact and more fiction,' wrote Margaret Drabble (152) in 1992. '[…] The twentieth century itself, in all its aspects, is represented by these handsome and distinctive volumes.' Striking images filled the front covers, with a floating Penguin logo in its own roundel and a moveable white title box with text set in Sabon, a typeface designed by Jan Tschichold, the Penguin typographer who preceded Hans Schmoller. Penguin's catalogue was scoured and many more titles were added to the series in the 1990s.

Silver

At the turn of a new century, however, the Twentieth-Century Classics needed a new name. Editor Simon Winder was brought in to overhaul the series: 'Classics – even modern classics – have suffered from a worthy image,' he said. 'Yet books like *Animal Farm* (84) and *On the Road* (470) are the equivalent of the Beatles' *White Album* or the film *Apocalypse Now*.' In February and March 2000, he introduced 80 fresh titles, including *Money* (160) by Martin Amis, *Two Serious Ladies* (474) by Jane Bowles and *A Month in the Country* (159) by J. L. Carr, aiming to reposition the list as 'a series to be enjoyed, rather than something that is good for you'. The designer Jamie Keenan was commissioned to create a new look: the back cover and spines became glossy silver and the book title and author's name were moved into a silver panel. Three typefaces were used on the cover: Franklin Gothic, Trade Gothic and Clarendon. The Penguin office in the USA decided not to adopt the new design, so the series was labelled 'Penguin Classics' in an attempt to encourage American imports. The design was refined in January 2004: a white band was added between the silver panel and the cover image, with the Penguin logo and the original series name reinstated: 'Modern Classics'. To date the Penguin office in America has not chosen to publish or distribute Modern Classics; they use the black-spined Penguin Classics livery for almost all of their classics, with a few titles still in Twentieth-Century Classics covers.

1975 Penguin Books
1989 Twentieth-Century Classics
• trans. Dmitri Nabokov, Simon Karlinsky & Vladimir Nabokov, 1973
fwd. Vladimir Nabokov, 1973
(see p.305)

1985 Penguin Books
2000 Modern Classics
• —
(see p.160)

2004
intro. Paul O'Keeffe
(see p.63)

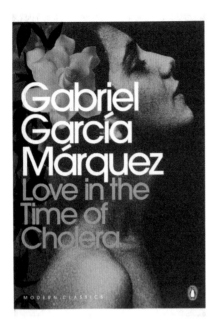

1989 Penguin Books
2007 Modern Classics
trans. Edith Grossman, 1988
(see p.563)

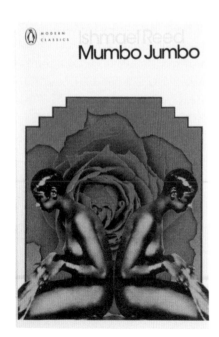

2017
—
(see p.539)

White

Jim Stoddart, the current art director at Penguin Press in the UK, gave Penguin Modern Classics another major makeover in September 2007. The back covers remained silver, but were now matt. The spines became white, matched by narrow white bands along the top and bottom of the covers, and the artwork on the front was superimposed with large silver and white lettering in the typeface Avant Garde, which has now become the 'brand font' of Modern Classics (and has been used to set all the headings in this book). Avant Garde was designed in 1968 by the typographer Herb Lubalin for the masthead of the short-lived New York magazine *Avant Garde*, which was famous for its risqué imagery and strikingly beautiful graphics. *Avant Garde* folded after the editor went to prison for printing an alphabet with letters formed by nude models and Lubalin subsequently worked his titling into a full typeface. Stoddart's design has remained loose: the lettering can be large or small and is sometimes located in a white panel. The first 21st-century title in the series – *Ravelstein* (2000) by Saul Bellow (477) – joined the list in 2008, and Penguin marked the 50th anniversary of Modern Classics in 2011 by publishing a selection of 50 'Mini Moderns'. These miniature books reflected the new design format, with white spines and matt silver covers, and were available singly or in a box set.

2011 Mini Moderns
—
(see p.156)

Eau-de-Nil

In April 2017, the series was given its most recent refinement: the backs, spines, author names and Penguin roundels were coloured eau-de-nil, recalling both the Twentieth-Century Classics of the 1990s and Facetti's early grey-green colour scheme. In 2018, a set of 50 small-format Penguin Moderns was published to celebrate the enduring 'radical spirit of Penguin Modern Classics'. They had striking eau-de-nil covers with Avant Garde typography in large capitals.

2018 Penguin Modern
—
(see p.502)

The Other Penguins

Titles from several other Penguin series have been incorporated into the Penguin Modern Classics series over the years. Here are some to look out for.

1935 Penguin Books
• —

Penguin Books 1935

The 'main' list of Penguin titles, which began as paperback reprints of existing hardbacks and which for many years were colour-coded (27). The first Penguin was *Ariel* by André Maurois, a romantic biography of the poet Percy Bysshe Shelley.

Pelican Books 1937

Penguin's first non-fiction series, which Allen Lane (viii) called 'the true everyman's library of the twentieth century'. There were various Pelican sub-series, including the Pelican Classics, the Pelican History of Art and the Pelican Freud Library (265). The first two Pelicans were the two volumes of George Bernard Shaw's *The Intelligent Woman's Guide to Socialism, Capitalism, Sovietism and Fascism* (4). The series ran until 1990 and was relaunched in 2014.

1937 Pelican Books
• —
(see p.4)

Penguin Specials 1937

A series of original books, commissioned by Penguin, on urgent topical issues. The first Special was *Germany Puts the Clock Back* by Edgar Mowrer.

1937 Penguin Special
• —

Penguin Poets 1941

A dedicated poetry series, which opened with a selection of poems by Tennyson. Poetry had been published previously in both Penguin and Pelican Books. Subsequent sub-series have included Modern Poets (1962), Modern European Poets (1964) and English Poets (1976).

1941 Penguin Poets
• ed. W. E. Williams

1941 Puffin Books
• —

Puffin Books 1941

Story books for children. Puffin Picture Books had launched in 1940, but the first Puffin Story Book – *Worzel Gummidge* by Barbara Euphan Todd – appeared in December 1941. Eleanor Graham, the first editor, aimed to publish 'the best new classics of the new generation'. Kaye Webb (120) was the editor from 1961 to 1979.

1945 Penguin Handbook
• —

Penguin Handbooks
1945

An off-shoot of Penguin Specials (xiii): advice on cookery, gardening, household maintenance and other practical subjects. The first Handbook was *Soft Fruit Growing* by the aptly named Raymond Bush.

1946 Penguin Classics
trans. E. V. Rieu

Penguin Classics

1946

A series of world literature in English translation. The first title was Homer's *Odyssey*, translated by E. V. Rieu, who went on to edit the series for two decades until he was succeeded by Betty Radice. Since 1985, the series has included English-language works and today it forms the largest library of classic literature in the world. See *The Penguin Classics Book* (2018) for more details. The Modern Classics series was temporarily renamed 'Penguin Classics' between 2000 and 2004.

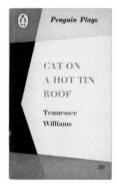

1957 Penguin Plays
—
(see p.456)

Penguin Plays

1957

Plays had appeared previously in the Penguin (xiii), Classics and Shakespeare series: the first was *Seven Famous One-Act Plays* (1937), edited by John Ferguson, which included an adaptation of 'The Monkey's Paw' by W. W. Jacobs (36). The series name 'Penguin Plays' was first used for *Cat on a Hot Tin Roof* (456) by Tennessee Williams.

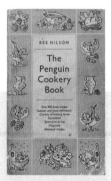

1952 Penguin Handbook
• —

In 1952, Alan Tritton, a member of the British Antarctic Survey, wrote to complain about a Penguin Handbook; he had been disappointed to discover that Bee Nilson's *Penguin Cookery Book* (1952) contained no guidance on cooking penguins. 'The problem about penguin meat is that it is unpalatably fishy, and this taste needs to be removed,' Tritton explained later. 'Our standard recipe was, after evisceration, to fry the breasts in oil with tinned bacon, dried onion, tinned tomatoes, baked beans with touches of curry powder, tomato sauce and Lea & Perrins – this removes the fishiness, thus making a very good meal.'

Peregrine Books

1962

These larger-format academic books, printed on high-quality paper with sewn bindings, were known by the company as 'egghead Penguins'. The first Peregrine was *The Common Pursuit* by F. R. Leavis.

1962 Peregrine Books
● —

Penguin African Library 1962

Non-fiction titles on political and social African issues. Penguin had published a West African Series since 1953, with a device of a penguin under a palm tree, but it was superseded by the African Library. The first title was *African Profiles* by Ronald Segal, who also edited the series.

1962 Penguin African Library
● —

Peacock Books 1962

Young adult titles, the first of which was *National Velvet* by Enid Bagnold. The series was abandoned in 1979, amidst complaints about the inclusion of 'unsuitable' books, such as J. D. Salinger's *The Catcher in the Rye* (499).

1940 Penguin Books
1962 Peacock Books
● —

Australian Penguin Books 1963

Australia had always imported Penguin books, but in 1963 a dedicated Penguin office in Australia began to publish its own titles, with the device of a penguin beneath a pair of crossed boomerangs. The first Australian Penguin was *To the Islands* by Randolph Stow (386).

1962 Australian Penguin Books
● —

Penguin Science Fiction 1963

Penguin had published several works of science fiction, by authors such as Aldous Huxley (65) and John Wyndham (122), before launching this dedicated series, edited by Brian Aldiss (142). The first title was Olaf Stapledon's *Last and First Men*, which was previously published as a Pelican (xiii) in 1937. The series was relaunched in 2020, with Olaf Stapledon's *Star Maker* among the first titles.

1937 Pelican Books
1963 Penguin Science Fiction
—

Penguin English Library 1965

Originally conceived as the 'Penguin English Classics', this series presented great English-language works of literature. The first title was *Wuthering Heights* by Emily Brontë. In 1985, the series was subsumed into Penguin Classics (xiv), but it was relaunched in 2012, with colourful, patterned covers designed by Coralie Bickford-Smith.

1965 Penguin English Library
● ed. David Daiches

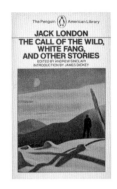

1981 Penguin American
Library
ed. Andrew Sinclair
intro. James Dickey
(see p.405)

Penguin American Library

1981

A short-lived series of American literary classics. It matched the Penguin English Library (xv) editions, but had pink spines instead of orange ones.

1981 King Penguin
• intro. Anthony Powell
(see p.120)

King Penguins

1981

This name had been used previously for a beautiful series of illustrated non-fiction hardbacks. It was revived for this paperback series of contemporary literary fiction and poetry, which transferred to Twentieth-Century Classics in 1989.

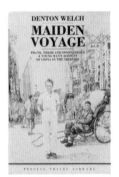

1983 Penguin Travel Library
• —

Penguin Travel Library

1983

A short-lived series of travelogues, most of which were reprints of previous Penguin titles.

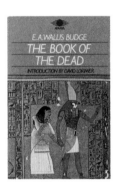

1989 Penguin Arkana
• intro. David Lorrimer

Penguin Arkana

1989

A series of esoteric literature, originally published by Routledge & Kegan Paul. When Penguin took over the series, the first Penguin Arkana title was the Ancient Egyptian *Book of the Dead*, translated by E. A. Wallis Budge.

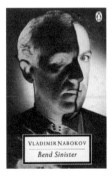

1989 Twentieth-Century
Classics
intro. Vladimir Nabokov, 1964
(see p.309)

Twentieth-Century Classics

1989

This was a rebranding (xi) of the Modern Classics series, between 1989 and 2000. The names 'Modern Classics' and 'Twentieth-Century Classics' are used interchangeably in this volume.

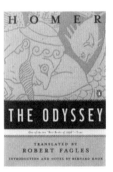

1997 Deluxe Classics
trans. Robert Fagles, 1990
intro. Bernard Knox, 1992

Deluxe Classics

1997

US-originated 'flapped' paperbacks with covers by renowned artists and illustrators. The sub-series Penguin Threads (2011) has covers displaying hand-stitched artworks by Jillian Tamaki and Rachell Sumpter; the inside covers show the reverse sides of the artists' embroidery.

Great Ideas

2004

Pocket-sized editions of political and philosophical texts. Each typographical cover adopts a style that matches the date of the work. By 2010, 100 titles had been published in batches of 20; in 2020, another 20 titles joined the list.

2004 Great Ideas
trans. C. D. N. Costa, 1997

Red Classics

2006

A brief attempt to showcase the more popular titles from the Penguin Classics (xiv) and Modern Classics series, without introductions and notes. 'They're simply wonderful stories,' announced the advertisement.

2006 Red Classics
• trans. Richard Pevear
& Larissa Volokhonsky, 1997
(see p.322)

Clothbound Classics

2008

Beautiful, collectible hardbacks bound in cloth with patterned covers designed by Coralie Bickford-Smith.

2008 Clothbound Classics
trans. Geoffrey Wall, 1992
pref. Michèle Roberts, 2003

Design Classics

2008

A sub-series of Modern Classics, comprising 'pivotal works by creative thinkers whose writings on art, design and the media have changed our vision for ever'.

2008 Design Classics
trans. Patrick Creagh, 1971
(see p.226)

Central European Classics 2010

A one-off sub-series of Modern Classics: ten brightly covered editions that told a story 'from before the First World War to the last years of the Cold War'.

2010 Central European Classics
trans. M & R. Weatherall, 1937
(see p.283)

2010 Central European Classics
trans. Catherine Leach,
Bogdana Carpenter & Madeline
G. Levine, 1968–2001
(see p.287)

The Central European Classics series originated in a visit that editor Simon Winder (xi) made to Krakow in 2009: 'I was talking to a Polish publisher who had known Czesław Miłosz (287) and who berated me for the useless way in which Miłosz was published in English – it was his essays which were so valued and admired in Poland and yet these were virtually unknown in Britain. Suitably shamed I read lots of the essays and, indeed, they were amazing.' A selection under the title *Proud to be a Mammal* (287) became the centrepiece of the new series.

The Modern Age

All that is solid melts into air, all that is holy
is profaned, and man is at last compelled to
face with sober senses, his real conditions of life,
and his relations with his kind.

These words by Karl Marx appear towards the
beginning of *The Communist Manifesto* (1848), the
text that would go on to have a world-shaking
influence on both the politics and the literature
of the 20th century. The philosopher Marshall
Berman described it as 'the archetype of a century
of modernist manifestos and movements [...]
It is the first great modernist work of art.'

   'Workers of the mind, unite!' exclaimed
Filippo Tommaso Marinetti (216) in 1905. Marinetti
published his own manifesto in 1909, on the
front page of *Le Figaro*, announcing a new literary
movement he called 'Futurism' (216). 'There is no
longer any beauty except the struggle,' he declared.
'[...] Poetry must be thought of as a violent
assault upon the forces of the unknown. [...]
Time and Space died yesterday.' Marinetti's
polemic announced the modern age. The world
was changing rapidly and artists and writers were
struggling to keep pace: empires were collapsing,
traditional social structures were evaporating,
culture was fragmenting, war was becoming
mechanized, all that was solid was melting into
air. Marinetti saw that, for the first time in history,
artists would need to reinvent their methods
repeatedly in order to express rapidly evolving
aspects of the human experience.

   Futurism was a facet of the widespread cultural
phenomenon that became known as modernism
(11), and which splintered into movements such
as Expressionism (269), Imagism (61), Dadaism (263),
Surrealism (176) and eventually postmodernism (505).
The story of the modern age is the story of these
complex and contradictory trends and collectives:

formal or informal, each one represents a break
from the past and an attempt to convey a new
vision of the present. There are short pieces about
many of these groups throughout *The Penguin Modern
Classics Book*; they are listed in the box below.

   T. S. Eliot (11) compared the modern age to
a waste land and W. H. Auden (95) dubbed it the
'Age of Anxiety', but as readers we can be more
positive. The last 100 years or so have been one
of the most tumultuous periods of history, but
they have also seen a glorious proliferation of
literature around the world, literature that is more
experimental, more disquieting and more diverse
than humanity has ever before produced. With each
new decade and its associated anxieties, writers take
up the challenge to face the conditions of life and
express new aspects of what it means to be human.
As Marinetti declared at the end of his manifesto:

   Standing tall on the roof of the world, yet again,
   we hurl our defiance at the stars!

Movements

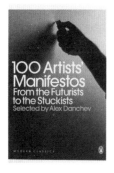

100 ARTISTS' MANIFESTOS
from the Futurists to the Stuckists 1909–2009

Opening with the 'Futurist Manifesto' (216), this anthology covers 100 years –
and 100 manifestos – in the fields of literature, visual art, film, architecture, fashion
and cookery. Drawing mostly on the western aesthetic tradition, it features statements
by feminists, communists, Destructivists, Vorticists (62), Stridentists, Cannibalists
and Stuckists, and writers such as Wyndham Lewis (63), Vladimir Mayakovsky (313),
André Breton (176), Leon Trotsky (322), Guy Debord and Werner Herzog.

2011
ed. Alex Danchev

WHY ARE WE 'ARTISTS'?
100 World Art Manifestos 1909–2012

This volume gathers a remarkably diverse array of manifestos
from around the world, covering Bikyoto in Japan, Iraqi
modernism, the *négritude* movement (558) and Australian
cyberfeminism. It opens with Ananda K. Coomaraswamy's
'Art and Swadeshi' from 1909, an impassioned polemic
expressing the concerns of the Bengal Renaissance (337).

2017
ed. Jessica Lack

1968 Pelican Books
1992 Penguin Books *revised*
2008 Modern Classics
ed. Eric Bentley, 1968–2008
—
Bentley was a British-born
American playwright, scholar
and critic. He was elected to
the American Academy of Arts
and Sciences in 1969.

THE THEORY OF THE MODERN STAGE
from Artaud to Zola: An Introduction to Modern Theatre and Drama 1835–1950

These manifestos by 'ten makers of modern theatre' include Antonin Artaud on
'The Theatre of Cruelty', Bertolt Brecht (255) on 'Experimental Theatre', W. B. Yeats (4)
on 'A People's Theatre', and pieces by Luigi Pirandello (215), George Bernard Shaw (4)
and Konstantin Stanislavski.

EUROPE

THE BRITISH ISLES

Oscar Wilde · **Lord Arthur Savile's Crime and Other Stories**

ISBN 0 14
00.1021 1

Oscar Wilde · The Picture of Dorian Gray

616

BERNARD SHAW

PMC

THE BLACK GIRL IN SEARCH OF GOD AND SOME LESSER TALES

ISBN 0 14
00.8845 8

BERNARD SHAW *The Intelligent Woman's Guide to Socialism, Capitalism, Sovietism and Fascism*

ISBN 0 14
01.8865 7

W. B. YEATS *Writings on Irish Folklore, Legend and Myth*

ISBN 0 14
01.8001 X

W. B. Yeats Selected Poems

PENGUIN CLASSICS

W . B . YEATS Short Fiction

ISBN 0 14
01.8002 8

W. B. YEATS *Selected Plays*

ISBN 0 14
01.8374 4

THE PLAYBOY OF THE WESTERN WORLD AND TWO OTHER IRISH PLAYS · SYNGE, YEATS AND O'CASEY ·

ISBN 0 14
00.8024 4

LADY GREGORY *Selected Writings*

ISBN 0 14
01.8955 6

Ireland

Oscar Wilde 1854–1900

'I find it harder and harder every day to live up to my blue china,' quipped Oscar Fingal O'Flahertie Wills Wilde, surrounded by peacock feathers and *objets d'art* in his student rooms at Oxford. Sparklingly witty and flamboyantly dressed, he became the doyen of the late 19th-century aesthetic movement, a champion of 'art for art's sake'. He achieved literary fame with his short stories, his only novel and his spectacularly successful stage comedies; but when he sued the Marquess of Queensberry for libel, the trial led to his own arrest for acts of gross indecency, and he was sentenced to two years' hard labour in Reading Gaol. After his release, he left Britain and died in Paris at the age of 46. 'Each man kills the things he loves,' wrote Wilde in *The Ballad of Reading Gaol* (1898), a line that Anthony Burgess quoted in *A Clockwork Orange* (148).

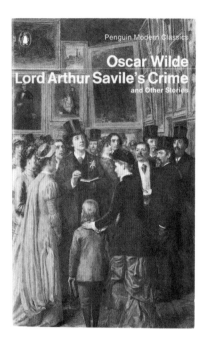

1954 Penguin Books
<u>**1973**</u> Modern Classics
1994 Penguin Classics
Complete Short Fiction
ed. Ian Small, 1994
—
The 1973 cover shows a detail from *A Private View at the Royal Academy, 1881* by William Powell Frith, depicting 'a well-known apostle of the beautiful, with a herd of eager worshippers surrounding him'.

Lord Arthur Savile's Crime
and Other Stories 1888–91

Lord Arthur Savile hasn't committed a crime, but a palm-reader tells him he's destined to commit a murder, so he sets about identifying a suitable victim. Other stories in this volume include 'The Canterville Ghost', about an ineffectual spectre; 'The Happy Prince', about a beneficent statue; and 'The Portrait of Mr. W. H.', which investigates the mysterious dedicatee of Shakespeare's sonnets.

Fin de Siècle

As the 19th century drew to a close, Europe was suffused with malaise. Civilization was slumping into decadence and a growing bourgeoisie, fatted on the proceeds of the Industrial Revolution, led to a corresponding rise in urban squalor and deprivation. 'The nineteenth-century dislike of Realism is the rage of Caliban seeing his own face in a glass,' wrote Oscar Wilde. 'The nineteenth-century dislike of Romanticism is the rage of Caliban not seeing his own face in a glass.' Literature of the period expressed these anxieties through Gothic stories of corruption and decay, in books such as Robert Louis Stevenson's *The Strange Case of Dr Jekyll and Mr Hyde* (1886) and H. G. Wells's *The Time Machine* (26). The new, 20th century demanded a fresh artistic direction, and it was from this impulse that modernism (11) emerged.

The Picture of Dorian Gray 1890

In Wilde's only novel, the beautiful Dorian Gray is led astray by his hedonistic friend Lord Henry Wotton. As Dorian's debaucheries grow increasingly extreme, his appearance remains remarkably unchanged, until a terrible secret is revealed. 'All art is at once surface and symbol,' wrote Wilde in his preface. 'Those who go beneath the surface do so at their peril. Those who read the symbol do so at their peril. It is the spectator, and not life, that art really mirrors.'

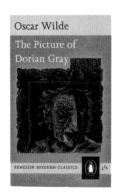

1949 Penguin Books
<u>**1962**</u> Modern Classics
1985 Penguin Classics
● ed. Peter Ackroyd, 1985
2000 Penguin Classics
ed. Robert Mighall, 2000

George Bernard Shaw 1856-1950

Bernard Shaw was a shy Dubliner who moved to London and invented a new persona for himself as a satirist, socialist, arts critic, playwright and wit – qualities encompassed by the eponymous adjective he adopted: 'Shavian'. In 1925, he was awarded the Nobel Prize for Literature (576), and in 1939 he received an Academy Award for the film adaptation of his own play, *Pygmalion* (1913). 'He did his best in redressing the fateful unbalance between truth and reality, in lifting mankind to a higher rung of social maturity,' wrote Thomas Mann (245).

The Black Girl in Search of God
and Some Lesser Tales 1888-1932

Shaw wrote 'The Adventures of the Black Girl in Her Search for God' while visiting South Africa in 1932. The eponymous girl, converted to Christianity by a half-hearted missionary, sets out to find God and meets a series of disappointing male deities, all of whom she whacks with her knobkerrie. Finally, she abandons religion and settles down with a somewhat Shavian red-haired Irish socialist to tend her garden. The story was banned in Ireland. The 'lesser' tales include a game of celestial football, a speaking bust of Shakespeare and an old socialist hero.

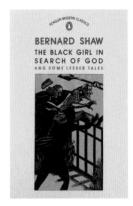

1946 Penguin Books
1986 Modern Classics
● ed. Dan H. Laurence, 1986
—
Many of Shaw's works have been published by Penguin over the years, but only two joined the Modern Classics list. *The Black Girl in Search of God* was first published by Penguin Books in July 1946, as one of a set of ten volumes celebrating Shaw's ninetieth birthday: 100,000 copies of each title were printed, so 1 million books went on sale simultaneously. Every copy sold within six and a half weeks and the accolade of a 'Penguin Million' was later awarded to, among others, Evelyn Waugh (67), H. G. Wells (26), D. H. Lawrence (50), Georges Simenon (201) and Agatha Christie.

1937 Pelican Books
1982 Pelican Books
1995 Twentieth-Century Classics
● intro. Margaret Walters, 1982
—
When Allen Lane (viii) launched the Pelican series of original non-fiction titles in 1937, he invited Shaw to contribute. Shaw expanded *The Intelligent Woman's Guide*, adding topical chapters on 'Sovietism' and 'Fascism', and the complete text was published in two volumes, the first of the Pelican series. Shaw modestly predicted that this sixpenny edition of his book 'would be the salvation of mankind'.

The Intelligent Woman's Guide to Socialism, Capitalism, Sovietism and Fascism 1928, rev. 1937

Shaw's sister-in-law asked him for 'a few of your ideas of socialism' to discuss with her women's study circle. He spent four years working on the response, which he published at the age of 72: *The Intelligent Woman's Guide to Socialism and Capitalism*. He considered it his magnum opus. 'The question of the distribution of wealth and the nature of property has suddenly yawned wide open before us,' he wrote; 'and we all have to open our closed minds accordingly.' The following year, the activist Lilian Le Mesurier responded to Shaw's somewhat condescending title by publishing *The Socialist Woman's Guide to Intelligence: A Reply to Mr. Shaw*.

W. B. Yeats

1865-1939

William Butler Yeats was fascinated by magic. He was a founding member of the Dublin Hermetic Society and Theosophical Lodge, he joined the Ghost Club and the Hermetic Order of the Golden Dawn, and he attended séances. He also became increasingly involved in the Irish nationalist movement, partly through his infatuation with the revolutionary Maud Gonne, to whom he proposed several times. He was a leading figure of the Irish Literary Revival (6) alongside Lady Gregory (0) and J. M. Synge (7). In 1922, he became a senator of the newly founded Irish Free State, and in 1923 he was awarded the Nobel Prize for Literature (576). 'I consider that this honour has come to me less as an individual than as a representative of Irish literature,' he wrote. 'It is part of Europe's welcome to the Free State.'

Writings on Irish Folklore, Legend and Myth 1888–1933

In 1892, Yeats conducted an experiment with his cousin, the witch Lucy Middleton: in a sea cave on the coast of County Sligo, they summoned a group of faery people and conversed with the faery queen, a 'very beautiful tall woman'. He collected this and other supernatural stories in his anthology *The Celtic Twilight* (1893).

1991 Penguin Poets
2000 Modern Classics
ed. Timothy Webb, 1991

Selected Poems 1889–1939

Yeats began writing poetry as a teenager. As his style developed, he drew inspiration from poets ranging from Edmund Spenser and William Blake to Rabindranath Tagore (337) and Ezra Pound (61). In 1917, he purchased an ancient stone tower in Ballylee, County Galway, which became the focus of his most celebrated collection, *The Tower* (1928). 'All art is in the last analysis an endeavour to condense as out of the flying vapour of the world an image of human perfection [...],' he wrote; 'and that is why the labour of the alchemists, who were called artists in their day, is a befitting comparison.' This selection includes 'Who Goes with Fergus?' – a favourite of James Joyce, who set it to music and included snatches in *Ulysses* (10).

1993
ed. Robert Welch
—
When the Penguin Modern Classics series was renamed Penguin Twentieth-Century Classics (xi) in 1989, it was assigned its own ISBN identifier – 018 – for the first time. The first number in the new ISBN sequence was allocated to *Writings on Irish Folklore, Legend and Myth*. Some books took longer to go through the production process than others, however, and many were published out of their numerical order, so this 'first' Twentieth-Century Classic – 978 0 14 001 5 – did not appear until several years after the series name was first used.

1995
• ed. G. J. Watson

Short Fiction 1891–1903

This volume includes Yeats's novella *John Sherman* (1891), in which a man's affections are torn between London and Dublin; 'Red Hanrahan', about an ancient Irish bard; and his companion stories, 'The Tables of the Law' and 'The Adoration of the Magi', of which the poet Edward Thomas wrote: 'Yeats's style is nowhere more admirable [...] it has a simplicity and a subtle and tender rhythm and a spirituality which are unequalled in England today.'

Selected Plays 1900–1939

Yeats co-founded the Abbey Theatre in Dublin with Lady Gregory (6) and it became the centre of the Irish Literary Revival (6). The opening night, 27 December 1904, featured three one-act plays: *On Baile's Strand* by Yeats, *Spreading the News* by Lady Gregory, and *Cathleen ni Houlihan*, which they wrote together. Yeats remained closely involved with the theatre throughout his life. He is best remembered for his five plays about the legendary Irish hero Cúchulainn and for introducing elements of Japanese Nō drama. 'My theatre must be the ancient theatre that can be made by unrolling a carpet,' he wrote, 'or marking out a place with a stick.'

1997
ed. Richard Allen Cave

The Irish Literary Revival

In the late 19th and early 20th centuries, burgeoning Irish nationalism coincided with a growth of interest in the island's history, literature and folklore. This cultural movement was dubbed 'The Celtic Twilight', after the volume of folklore published by W. B. Yeats (4). Yeats, Lady Gregory and the playwright Edward Martyn drew up a manifesto demanding a 'Celtic and Irish school of dramatic literature', and in 1899 they founded the Irish Literary Theatre in Dublin, followed by the Abbey Theatre in 1904. Another key figure of the movement was the writer Æ (George Russell), who encouraged the careers of Frank O'Connor (16), Patrick Kavanagh (15) and P. L. Travers, author of the Mary Poppins books. He appears briefly as a character in *Ulysses* (10). James Joyce mocked the Irish Literary Revival in *Finnegans Wake* (11), calling it the 'cultic twalette'.

THE PLAYBOY OF THE WESTERN WORLD
and Two Other Irish Plays

W. B. Yeats, *The Countess Cathleen*,
J. M. Synge, *The Playboy of the Western World*,
Sean O'Casey, *Cock-a-Doodle Dandy*
1892 – 1949

The Countess Cathleen (1892) is set during a famine: a noblewoman sells her soul to the Devil to save those of her tenant farmers. Riots greeted the opening night of Synge's (7) *The Playboy of the Western World* (1907), in which a young man is adulated for murdering his own 'da': eggs, potatoes and a slice of fruitcake were thrown at the actors. Lady Gregory defended the play, describing the riots as the old battle 'between those who use a toothbrush and those who don't'. *Cock-a-Doodle Dandy* (1949) is about a magical cockerel that grants dark wishes in the parish of Nyadnanave.

1964 Penguin Plays *Classic Irish Drama*
<u>1987</u> Modern Classics
2009 Penguin Classics
intro. W. A. Armstrong, 1964

Lady Gregory 1852 – 1932

Augusta Persse was born while the potato famine was still ravaging western Ireland. Despite little formal education, she taught herself four languages and read voraciously. In 1880 she married Sir William Gregory, former governor of Ceylon, now Sri Lanka. When Sir William died in 1892, Lady Gregory retreated to their country estate, Coole Park, County Galway, where she cultivated a salon of nationalist Irish writers. W. B. Yeats (4) wrote poems about the house, including 'The Wild Swans at Coole', and there is a tree in the former grounds where you can still see the carved initials of Yeats, Synge (7), O'Casey, Shaw (4) and others. Lady Gregory co-founded the Abbey Theatre with Yeats and wrote more than 40 plays herself. Shaw called her 'the greatest living Irishwoman'.

Selected Writings 1892 – 1932

This anthology spans Lady Gregory's extraordinary life and work, from her account of her own childhood, through collections of local folklore and herbal cures, to retellings of Irish sagas, political essays, plays, poems and journals. *Grania* (1912) is a proto-feminist play that addresses female sexuality and gender in a rural community and *A Woman's Sonnets* (1892) are verses sent to the poet Wilfrid Scawen Blunt, with whom she had an affair in Egypt.

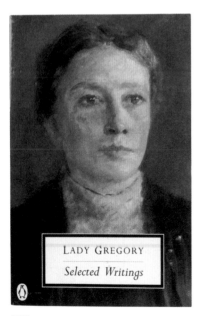

LADY GREGORY
Selected Writings

1995
● ed. Lucy McDiarmid & Maureen Waters

Erskine Childers 1870–1922

Childers was a keen amateur sailor, who learned to handle his 'scrubby little yacht' on the Thames estuary. He was raised in Ireland, though born in London, and spent most of his career as a clerk in the House of Commons. As the First World War approached, he became increasingly politically minded, and in 1914 he and his wife sailed to Dublin overnight, smuggling rifles to Ireland. In 1919, Childers was appointed director of publicity for the First Irish Parliament. He was elected a Sinn Féin member of the Second Dáil, but in 1922 he was arrested, tried, found guilty as a traitor to the new Irish Free State, and executed. His last words to the firing squad were, 'Take a step or two forward, lads, it will be easier that way.' His son, Erskine Hamilton Childers, became the fourth President of Ireland.

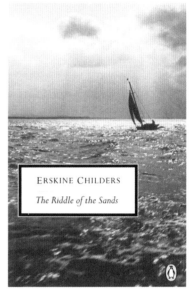

The Riddle of the Sands
A Record of Secret Service 1903

As old friends Carruthers and Davies navigate the shifting sands of the Baltic, they become increasingly drawn into a dangerous and thrilling adventure. 'Vibrant, impassioned, witty, intelligent and shamelessly prejudiced in the manner of its day,' wrote John le Carré (143), 'The Riddle of the Sands remains one of the great foundation stones of the contemporary novel of espionage and adventure with political teeth.'

1952 Penguin Books
1978 Penguin Books
1999 Twentieth-Century Classics
● fwd. Geoffrey Household, 1978
2011 Penguin Classics
intro. Erskine C. Childers, 2011
—
Erskine C. Childers is the great-grandson of the author.

J. M. Synge
1871–1909

John Millington Synge suffered from ill health throughout his life and died at 37. He studied music in Dublin and Germany before becoming the director of the Abbey Theatre in Dublin, working closely with Lady Gregory (6) and W. B. Yeats (4). He fell in love with Molly Allgood, the actress who starred in his masterpiece, *The Playboy of the Western World* (6); they were engaged but never married. With Yeats, Molly completed *Deirdre of the Sorrows*, Synge's last, unfinished play, and starred in the posthumous production of 1910. 'He was a dying man clutching at life,' wrote the poet John Masefield, 'and clutching most wildly at violent life, as the sick man does.'

The Aran Islands 1907

The Oileáin Árann, or 'Aran Islands', are the bleak, rocky remnants of a submerged escarpment off the coast of County Galway. 'There are three islands,' explains Synge: 'Aranmor, the north island, about nine miles long; Inishmaan, the middle island, about three miles and a half across, and nearly round in form; and the south island, Inishere.' In 1895, Yeats (4) suggested that Synge visit the Aran Islands to 'express a life that has never found expression', and Synge began spending his summers there, gathering material for plays such as *In the Shadow of the Glen* (1903), *Riders to the Sea* (1904) and *The Playboy of the Western World* (6), as well as for this book, a poetic prose evocation of the islanders' ancient and vanishing way of life.

1992
ed. Tim Robinson

James Joyce

1882 – 1941

James Augustine Aloysius Joyce met
W.B.Yeats (4) in 1902. 'We have met too
late,' Joyce said, as they parted. 'You are too
old for me to have any effect on you.' Joyce
was born and raised in Dublin, the setting
for all his works, though he spent most of his
adult life abroad. In 1904 he eloped to Europe
with a chambermaid called Nora Barnacle:
initially he taught in Trieste, where Italo
Svevo (214) was one of his pupils. He spent
the First World War writing *Ulysses* (10),
and the rest of his life writing *Finnegans
Wake* (11). He suffered from glaucoma in
his left eye and frequently wore an eyepatch.

Dubliners   1914

'I always write about Dublin,' said Joyce, 'because if
I can get to the heart of Dublin I can get to the heart
of all the cities of the world.' In these fifteen short
stories, the middle-class Dublin protagonists become
gradually older from one story to the next. Each
tale revolves around moments of 'sudden spiritual
transformation' as Joyce put it, and many of the
characters, such as Ignatius Gallaher, Tom Kernan
and Gabriel Conroy, reappear as minor figures in
Ulysses (10). The last and greatest story, 'The Dead',
was adapted into an Academy Award-nominated film
by John Huston, starring his daughter Angelica.

1956 Penguin Books
1961 Modern Classics
1992 Twentieth-Century
Classics
ed. Terence Brown, 1992

Poems and Exiles

1907 – 37

Joyce's first publication was
a volume of 36 love poems
called *Chamber Music* (1907),
a reference, he later joked, to
the sound of urine hitting a
pot. The poems were admired
by Ezra Pound (61), who
praised 'the cross run of
the beat and the word, as
of a stiff wind cutting the
ripple-tops of bright water'.

1992
ed. J.C.C.Mays

In 1927, *Pomes Penyeach* was published, a slim volume
priced at twelve pence, comprising twelve poems and one
'tilly' extra. These and other unpublished and occasional
poems are collected in Mays's edition, including 'Ecce
Puer', written to mark the birth of Joyce's grandson in
1932. *Exiles* (1918) is Joyce's only surviving play, about
ambiguous infidelities and semi-autobiographical
jealousies. Yeats (4) refused to stage it at the Abbey
Theatre; the first critically acclaimed production was
directed by Harold Pinter in 1970.

A Portrait of the Artist as a Young Man

1914 – 15

While attempting to find a publisher for *Dubliners*,
Joyce began work on a coming-of-age novel. *A Portrait
of the Artist as a Young Man* follows the artistic, religious
and intellectual development of Stephen Dedalus, the
pen name that Joyce used for his earliest essays and
stories. 'Once upon a time and a very good time it was
there was a moocow coming
down along the road,' it begins,
'and this moocow that was
coming down along the road
met a nicens little boy named
baby tuckoo.' As Dedalus grows
older, the vocabulary and style
become increasingly mature,
incorporating the interior
monologues, free indirect speech
and streams of consciousness
that would be key features of
Ulysses (10). Dedalus finishes
his self-portrait by promising
to forge the 'uncreated
conscience of my race'.

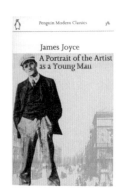

1960 Penguin Books
1964 Modern Classics
1992 Twentieth-Century
Classics
ed. Seamus Deane, 1992

James Joyce Ulysses

1969

The 1969 cover was designed by the
Penguin typographer Hans Schmoller.

Ulysses

1918–22

Ernest Hemingway (428) called it 'a most goddam wonderful book'; Vladimir Nabokov (304) called it a 'divine work of art'; and Virginia Woolf (42) considered it the excrescence of a 'queasy undergraduate scratching his pimples'. T. S. Eliot (11) summarized the legacy of *Ulysses* when he called it 'a book to which we are all indebted, and from which none of us can escape'. Ever since it first appeared in book form, in Paris, on Joyce's 40th birthday, 2 February 1922, *Ulysses* has been a yardstick against which subsequent novelists have measured themselves. The narrative follows the mostly mundane activities of two central characters, Leopold Bloom, a Jewish advertising canvasser, and Stephen Dedalus, the subject of *A Portrait of the Artist as a Young Man* (8), as they wander the streets of Dublin over the course of a single day in 1904. Its highly patterned sections are modelled loosely on episodes from Homer's *Odyssey*, and employ a staggering array of literary techniques and allusions. 'I've put in so many enigmas and puzzles that it will keep the professors busy for centuries,' wrote Joyce gleefully. Its occasional sexual content led to its being banned in many countries, including the USA and the Soviet Union, where the critic Karl Radek called it 'a dung-heap swarming with worms, photographed by a movie-camera through a microscope'. *Ulysses* is set on 16 June, which is celebrated by Joyceans annually as 'Bloomsday'.

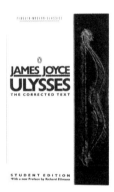

1986
● ed. Hans Walter Gabler

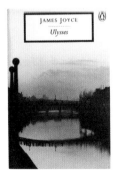

1992
intro. Declan Kiberd

1992 *Annotated Edition*
ed. Declan Kiberd

Ulysses in Penguin

In 1936, the year after he founded Penguin Books, Allen Lane (viii) published the first hardback British edition of *Ulysses* through the Bodley Head. Three decades later, he acquired the paperback rights for £75,000, the highest figure ever paid at the time, and the first Penguin edition of *Ulysses* was published on 23 April 1969, the 50th anniversary of Lane's own publishing career. It was number 3,000 in the Penguin series. In 1986, Penguin published a 'corrected text' edition, compiled by the German academic Hans Walter Gabler, who analysed Joyce's working drafts, fair copies and typescripts in order to 'rebuild *Ulysses* as Joyce wrote it'; it was Penguin number 10,000. Gabler's edition proved controversial, however. Most volubly, an eccentric American scholar called John Kidd denounced Gabler's techniques in a series of scathing articles. In 1992, Penguin reverted to the revised Bodley Head text (1960), with an introduction by Declan Kiberd. A large annotated student edition was published simultaneously, which includes notes and chapter introductions.

More ONE-DAY NOVELS

Finnegans Wake

1939

Written in a unique vocabulary, incorporating 65 languages and thousands of puns, *Finnegans Wake* took Joyce seventeen years to construct. Anthony Burgess (148) praised it as a 'great comic vision', Vladimir Nabokov (304) called it 'a cold pudding' and the psychiatrist Hervey Cleckley described it as 'a 628-page collection of erudite gibberish indistinguishable to most people from the familiar word-salad produced by hebephrenic patients on the back wards of any state hospital'. There is almost no distinguishable plot or characterization, although the book roughly describes a family called Earwicker from Chapelizod, a Dublin suburb. The opening sentence begins on the final page of the book, rendering the entire volume cyclical; Joyce said the 'ideal reader' would have 'ideal insomnia', starting at the beginning again each time they finished. It features ten 100-letter words, such as 'bababadalgharaghtakamminarronnkonnbronntonnerronntuonnthunntrovarrhounawnskawntoohoohoordenenthurnuk'. 'I know it is no more than a game,' wrote Joyce, after working on the *Wake* for several years, 'but it is a game that I have learned to play in my own way. Children may just as well play as not. The ogre will come in any case.'

1992
intro. Seamus Deane
—
The 1992 edition of *Finnegans Wake* is based on the first edition, published by Faber and Faber in London. The 2012 'restored' edition, now out of print, was the product of 30 years' research by two textual scholars, Rose and O'Hanlon, who scoured 20,000 pages of notes, drafts, typescripts and proofs to identify 9,000 minor but 'crucial' corrections.

2012 Hardback Classics
● ed. Danis Rose & John O'Hanlon, 2010

A James Joyce Reader

1907–39

1976 Penguin Books *The Portable James Joyce*
1993 Twentieth-Century Classics
● ed. Harry Levin, 1947

This volume anthologizes the complete texts of *Dubliners* (8), *A Portrait of the Artist as a Young Man* (8), *Exiles* (8), *Chamber Music* (8) and *Pomes Penyeach* (8), with short extracts from *Ulysses* (10) and *Finnegans Wake*. 'The technical and psychological paradox is that Joyce, as his comprehension of ordinary humanity increased, became less comprehensible to the common reader,' wrote the critic Harry Levin in his introduction.

Modernism

The first complete edition of *Ulysses* (10) was published in Paris in February 1922. Eight months later, *The Waste Land* (11) by T. S. Eliot was printed in London. These fragmented, allusive, self-conscious works are considered the literary high-water marks of modernism, the aesthetic movement that swept through the western arts at the start of the 20th century. Inspired by Sigmund Freud's (265) concepts of the mind and the philosopher Henri Bergson's subjective view of time, modernist writers such as Joyce (8), Woolf (42), Eliot and Pound (61) employed stylistic techniques of collage, abstraction and streams of consciousness to mimic the confusing, multifaceted experience of modern life. Modernism was a reaction to the increased urbanization of society and the horrors of mechanized warfare, an attempt to affirm humanity's ability to create and shape our environment through art. 'Make it new!' was Ezra Pound's rallying cry, and despite George Orwell (80) pronouncing the demise of modernism during the Second World War, its spirit continued to influence writers throughout the century.

Robert Tressell 1870–1911

Robert Croker was an Irish signwriter, known as 'the Professor'. He changed his name to Noonan and emigrated to South Africa as a young man, where he worked as an interior decorator and hack journalist and became involved in socialist politics. He then moved to England, where he lodged with his sister in Hastings and developed tuberculosis, before deciding to emigrate to Canada; but he died in Liverpool before he could raise the money for the crossing and before he could find a publisher for his only novel. He took his pseudonym, 'Tressell', from the trestle tables he used while decorating.

1940 Penguin Books
2004 Modern Classics
intro. Tristram Hunt, 2004
–
Tressell's novel was originally called *The Ragged Arsed Philanthropists*. His daughter published it posthumously with an amended title.

The Ragged Trousered Philanthropists
1910, pub. 1914

Frank Owen works for the painting and decorating firm Rushton & Co. He is infuriated by the way his fellow workers submit to the company managers: 'All through the summer the crowd of ragged-trousered philanthropists continued to toil and sweat at their noble and unselfish task of making money for Mr Rushton,' he fumes. This passionate novel has become a key text for the labour movement in Britain. 'There is no finer representation, anywhere in English writing,' wrote the novelist Raymond Williams, 'of a certain rough-edged, mocking, give-and-take conversation between workmen and mates.'

Ernest Shackleton 1874–1922

In 1901 Shackleton joined Captain Scott's *Discovery* expedition to Antarctica and set a new record by marching as far as 82 degrees south in 1902. In 1907 he set a further record, sledging to within 100 nautical miles of the South Pole. He had hopes of being the first explorer to reach the Pole, but these were dashed by the Norwegians in 1911. 'After the conquest of the South Pole by Amundsen,' he wrote, '[...] there remained but one great main object of Antarctic journeyings – the crossing of the South Polar continent from sea to sea.' Accordingly, he embarked on the disastrous *Endurance* expedition of 1914, the subject of his memoir *South* (12). He made a further Antarctic voyage in 1922, during which he died. He is buried at Grytviken, a former whaling station on South Georgia. 'Do not let it be said that Shackleton has failed,' wrote his rival Roald Amundsen. 'No man fails who sets an example of high courage, of unbroken resolution, of unshrinking endurance.'

South
The *Endurance* Expedition 1919

Four days after the First World War was declared, the *Endurance* sailed from Plymouth. In gripping detail, Shackleton describes how the ship was trapped by ice floes in the Weddell Sea and crushed until it sank, marooning 28 men on the sea ice. When the ice broke up they got into three small lifeboats and navigated to Elephant Island, where most of the crew camped on a rocky ledge while Shackleton and a small band completed an 830-mile journey, through the worst seas on the planet, to the coast of South Georgia. From there, he and two others trekked across the island, over mountains that had never been climbed, and made it to Stromness whaling station, from which he was able to rescue the rest of his crew. At times while crossing South Georgia, Shackleton imagined a fourth man walking alongside him and his two companions, a haunting idea that T. S. Eliot incorporated into *The Waste Land* (11). The photographer Frank Hurley's images of the expedition are included in this edition.

Ernest Shackleton South

2002
intro. Fergus Fleming

Elizabeth Bowen

1899–1973

A service is held every year in the little church of St Colman, in Farahy, County Cork, to commemorate Elizabeth Bowen. Bowen's Court used to stand next door, her ancestral home where she entertained Virginia Woolf (42), Eudora Welty (457) and Carson McCullers (453). 'She is what happened after Bloomsbury (44),' writes Victoria Glendinning, her biographer; 'she is the link that connects Virginia Woolf with Iris Murdoch and Muriel Spark (141).' Bowen was married for nearly 30 years but had passionate affairs with, among others, Sean O'Faolain (17) and the American writer May Sarton. She strove to write about 'life with the lid on', and what happens when the lid comes off.

The Collected Stories of Elizabeth Bowen

The Collected Stories 1923–56

Bowen's first publication was a book of short stories called *Encounters* (1923). The 79 stories in this collected edition include love stories, ghost stories, social satire and historical fiction. 'Many of her stories start like Saki (35) and end like Edgar Allan Poe,' writes Peter Ackroyd. 'It is that paradox […] which gives the edge to her writing and contributes to the sharpness of its vision.'

1966 Penguin Books
The Demon Lover and Other Stories
1983 Penguin Books
The Collected Stories
<u>**1985**</u> Modern Classics
• intro. Angus Wilson, 1980
—
The portrait of Bowen on the cover of the 1985 edition is by André Paul Durand. It is part of the National Portrait Gallery collection in London. Durand described Bowen as 'very paintable and very patient'.

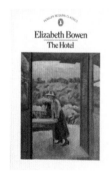

The Hotel 1927

'*The Hotel* is on every level a very good novel,' writes Victoria Glendinning. 'And for a first novel it is extraordinary.' It is set in a stifling hotel drawing room on the Italian Riviera, populated by wealthy Englishwomen.

1943 Penguin Books
<u>**1984**</u> Modern Classics
• —

The Last September 1929

Elizabeth Bowen
The Last September

The 'Big House' of Danielstown is a grand Irish mansion, where late summer sunlight spills across couples flirting on the tennis lawns; but news of the Troubles portends tragedy. This was the novel 'nearest to my heart', wrote Bowen. '[It] had a deep, unclouded, spontaneous source. Though not poetic, it brims up with what could be the stuff of poetry, the sensations of youth.'

1942 Penguin Books
<u>**1982**</u> Modern Classics
• —

Elizabeth Bowen
Friends and Relations

Friends and Relations 1931

Over the course of a single week, two sisters' friendships, relationships and love affairs start to unravel.

1943 Penguin Books
<u>**1982**</u> Modern Classics
• —

To the North 1932

Two young women, Cecilia and Emmeline, are drawn into relationships with very different but equally unsuitable men. 'To the North and The Death of the Heart (14) are among the finest novels of her generation,' wrote V. S. Pritchett (110).

Elizabeth Bowen
To the North

1945 Penguin Books
<u>**1984**</u> Modern Classics
• —

The House in Paris 1935

This is 'the best of Elizabeth Bowen's novels', writes A. S. Byatt in her introduction, 'and a very good novel by any critical standards'. Two children wait in a house in Paris, for reasons that become gradually and dramatically clear. 'Plot might seem to be a matter of choice,' wrote Bowen at the start of 'Notes on Writing a Novel' (1945). 'It is not. The particular plot is something the novelist is driven to: it is what is left after the whittling-away of alternatives.'

The Death of the Heart 1938

Sixteen-year-old Portia Quayne comes to London to live with her older half-brother and his wife. The novel 'reflects the time, the pre-war time with its high tension, its increasing anxieties, and this great stress on individualism', said Bowen in an interview with V. S. Naipaul (555).

Penguin Modern Classics
Elizabeth Bowen
The House in Paris

1946 Penguin Books
1976 Modern Classics
• intro. A. S. Byatt, 1976

The Heat of the Day 1948

In London during the Blitz, Stella Rodney develops a late-flowering love affair with Robert Kelway, who may be a German spy. 'Probably the most intelligent noir ever written,' ran a review in the *Los Angeles Times*. 'The situation is surreal, the psychologizing profound, and the eerie inwardness trapped in Bowen's distinctive prose resonates inside a peculiar silence that fills the reader's heart with dread.'

A World of Love 1955

In the attic of an Irish country house, a young woman discovers a stash of old love letters written to her mother by a long-dead suitor, which leads to her own romantic awakening.

The Little Girls 1964

In 1914, three 11-year-old girls attended St Agatha's day school on the south coast of England. Fifty years later, Dinah tracks down the other two, Clare and Sheila, for reasons that are only gradually revealed.

Eva Trout
or, Changing Scenes 1968

Abandoned by her mother at a young age, Eva is in her mid-twenties when she suddenly inherits a fortune from her wealthy father, fuelling her 'capacity for making trouble, attracting trouble, [and] strewing trouble around her'. *Eva Trout* was shortlisted for the second Booker Prize in 1970.

1962 Penguin Books
1986 Modern Classics
• —

1962 Penguin Books
1987 Modern Classics
• —

1983 Penguin Books
1987 Modern Classics
• —

1982 Penguin Books
1987 Modern Classics
• —

1982 Penguin Books
1987 Modern Classics
• —

Austin Clarke

1896 – 1974

'I load myself with chains and try to get out of them,' Austin Clarke told Robert Frost (415). Clarke is considered to be one the greatest Irish poets of the generation that followed W. B. Yeats (4). He also wrote novels, plays and two volumes of autobiography. He lived in Templeogue, south Dublin, where the River Dodder is now spanned by a commemorative Austin Clarke Bridge.

Selected Poems

1924 – 74

Clarke wrote in English but employed Irish poetic techniques of assonance, alliteration and half-rhyme. He was initially influenced by the Irish Literary Revival (6) but in later years focused on radical politics and sexuality.

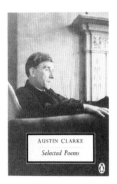

1992
● ed. W. J. McCormack

Patrick Kavanagh 1904 – 1967

Kavanagh was the son of a cobbler and farmer from Mucker, County Monaghan. He left school to work on his father's farm and keep goal for the Iniskeen Gaelic football team. His vernacular verses about rural Ireland, where 'ordinary things wear lovely wings', were noticed by Æ (George Russell) and published in the *Irish Statesman*, and he became one of Ireland's best-loved poets. 'A man (I am thinking of myself) innocently dabbles in words and rhymes,' he once wrote, 'and finds that it is his life.'

1996
ed. Antoinette Quinn

2005
ed. Antoinette Quinn, 2004

1975 Penguin Books
1987 Modern Classics
—
The poet Oliver St John Gogarty objected to a wisecrack in *The Green Fool* about Kavanagh confusing Gogarty's wife for his mistress. He brought a lawsuit against Kavanagh, who was forced to pay £100 and *The Green Fool* was withdrawn from sale.

The Green Fool

1938

'When I was about two years old I was one evening lying in the onion-box that had been converted into a cradle,' wrote Kavanagh at the start of this autobiography. *The Green Fool* evokes his rural upbringing with humour and poignancy.

Tarry Flynn

1948

This semi-autobiographical novel tells the story of a young peasant farmer who longs to write poetry and seduce beautiful women. It was banned briefly by the Irish Censorship Board. A successful stage adaptation was performed at the Abbey Theatre in 1966.

1978 Penguin Books
1987 Modern Classics
—
In 2000, when *Tarry Flynn* was rejacketed, the title was temporarily misspelled on the cover and spine as *Tarry Flyn*.

Poems 1929 – 67

'Indispensable,' wrote Seamus Heaney, about Patrick Kavanagh's *Collected Poems*. '[…] A book that should jolt readers back to an awareness of this poet's place in the twentieth-century pantheon.' From 'On Raglan Road', sung by Van Morrison, Sinéad O'Connor and Ed Sheeran among others, to his epic masterpiece *The Great Hunger*, Kavanagh's poetry is powerfully direct. There is a sculpture of him, sitting on a bench beside the Grand Canal in Dublin, inspired by his lines:

O commemorate me where there is water,
Canal water preferably, so stilly
Greeny at the heart of summer.

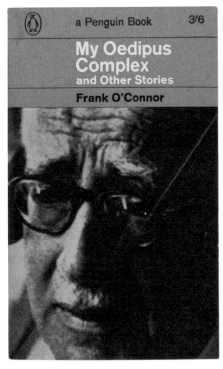

a Penguin Book 3/6

My Oedipus Complex
and Other Stories
Frank O'Connor

1963 • —

1996 Twentieth-Century
Classics
2005 Modern Classics
ed. Julian Barnes, 2005
—
'I first came to Frank
O'Connor by way of a
possessive pronoun,' writes
Julian Barnes. 'The fiction
shelves of a secondhand
bookshop in Dublin proposed
an antique orange Penguin:
author's name in white, title
in black, no strident capitals
on the spine, and the cover
taken up with what was in
those days a come-on – a
blurry author photo. It was
not this, or the distantly
familiar name, that made me
buy it (the original 3/6d now
having become six euros),
but the title: *My Oedipus
Complex and Other Stories*.
It was the slyly inviting "My"
that did it. A lesser writer
might have settled for "The",
and the book would have
stayed on its shelf.'

Frank O'Connor
An Only Child and My Father's Son

2005
• intro. Declan Kiberd

Frank O'Connor
1903 – 1966

'O'Connor is doing for Ireland what Chekhov did for Russia,'
declared W. B. Yeats (4). Michael O'Donovan was born in
County Cork and began preparing a collected edition of his
works at the age of twelve. He spent time in the IRA, in prison
and as a librarian. He later became director of the Abbey
Theatre in Dublin, and wrote short stories under the pseudonym
'Frank O'Connor', as well as novels, plays, essays, poetry
and a biography of the revolutionary leader Michael Collins
called *The Big Fellow* (1937). In 1950 he left Ireland to teach
in America, where many of his short stories were published
in the *New Yorker*. His editor was the novelist William Maxwell,
to whom O'Connor bequeathed his edition of Chekhov, with
its 'turned down corners, turned down sides of pages, coffee
stains, whiskey stains, and perhaps tears'.

My Oedipus Complex
and Other Stories
1931 – 81

'There is in the short story at its most characteristic, something
we do not often find in the novel,' wrote O'Connor – 'an intense
awareness of human loneliness.' This is certainly true of 'Uprooted',
his story about two brothers – a schoolteacher and a priest – who
return home for Easter desperately frustrated and lonely in different
ways. In the title story of this collection, a young boy resents his
father's return from the Second World War and attempts to win
back his mother's attention. Other titles include 'Fish for Friday',
'A Thing of Nothing' and 'The Cornet-Player Who Betrayed Ireland'.

An Only Child and My Father's Son
An Autobiography
1961 – 8

'Frank O'Connor, the Irish writer, tells in one of his books how,
as a boy, he and his friends would make their way across the
countryside, and when they came to an orchard wall that seemed
too high and too doubtful to try and too difficult to permit their
voyage to continue, they took off their hats and tossed them over
the wall – and then they had no choice but to follow them.' These
are the words of President John F. Kennedy, at the dedication
of the Aerospace Medical Health Center in San Antonio in 1963.
'This nation has tossed its cap over the wall of space and we have
no choice but to follow it.' *An Only Child* (1961) describes the
'terrible years' of O'Connor's childhood with his abusive father
and beloved mother. It is dedicated to William Maxwell. *My
Father's Son* (1968) picks up after O'Connor's release from prison,
and describes his life in Dublin and his friendship with W. B. Yeats
(4) in particular. 'His picture of the Dublin literary world is as
lively as a novel,' wrote V. S. Pritchett (110).

Sean O'Faolain 1900–1991

'Sean O'Faolain is not merely one of the finest of Irish short story writers,' writes Susan Hill, 'he is the founding father – after James Joyce (8) and together with Frank O'Connor (16) – of the great and thriving Irish short story tradition.' John Francis Whelan changed his name to Sean O'Faolain after the brutal suppression of the Easter Rising in 1916. He worked as a travelling book salesman before joining the IRA. He wrote short stories, novels, biographies, travel books, literary criticism, and a history of Ireland called *The Irish* (1947). In 1940 he founded a literary periodical called *The Bell*, with contributors including Patrick Kavanagh (15), Frank O'Connor and Flann O'Brien (18).

1982 Penguin Books
1986 Modern Classics
● —
This edition comprises O'Faolain's first three volumes of short stories.

Midsummer Night Madness
and Other Stories 1932–47

The seven tales in O'Faolain's first book, *Midsummer Night Madness and Other Stories* (1932), were based on his experiences in the Irish Civil War. 'One salutes, in these stories, an immense creative humour as broad in speech as Joyce's (8) gloom,' wrote Graham Greene (88).

1983 Penguin Books
1987 Modern Classics
● —
This edition collects O'Faolain's next three volumes of short stories.

The Heat of the Sun
and Other Stories 1958–66

'A Short Story, if it is a good story,' writes O'Faolain, 'is like a child's kite, a small wonder, a brief, bright moment. [...] A Tale is quite different. Like a small plane it is much more free, carries a bit more cargo, roves farther, has time and space for more complex characterization, more changes of mood, more incidents and scenes, even more plot. [...] Compare them with that plane-carrier, the Novel, which can carry as heavy a load as the writer wishes, for as long and over as many seas. [...] Any story, tale or novel that does not levitate a little is, as far as I am concerned, a grounded albatross.'

1986
● —

Foreign Affairs
and Other Stories 1971–82

This edition includes O'Faolain's last volumes of short stories and some that were previously unpublished. Titles include 'Of Sanctity and Whiskey', 'Marmalade' and 'Falling Rocks, Narrowing Road, Cul-de-Sac, Stop'.

1982 Penguin Books
1989 Modern Classics
● —

And Again? 1979

In this fantastical novel, journalist Robert Younger is given a choice: he can live his life all over again, or be run down by a lorry in half an hour's time. The catch is that Younger has to live his life backwards, starting at 65 and growing ever more youthful. 'Without cherished memories,' says Younger at the beginning of the account, 'a man's imagination must fly wild; lose touch with common life; go off its chump.'

Flann O'Brien

1911–1966

Brian O'Nolan had many pen names. At University College Dublin he was 'Brother Barnabus'; in the *Irish Times* he was 'Myles na Gopaleen' and 'An Broc' ('The Badger'); in the *Nationalist and Leinster Times* he was 'George Knowall'; and his English-language novels were published under the pseudonym 'Flann O'Brien'. He was a civil servant and an alcoholic for most of his life. James Joyce (8) once called him 'a real writer, with the true comic spirit'. 'I declare to God,' said O'Nolan, 'if I hear that name Joyce one more time I will surely froth at the gob.'

1967
—

At Swim-Two-Birds

1939

'This is just the book to give your sister if she's a loud, dirty, boozy girl,' wrote Dylan Thomas (98). The title refers to a ford on the River Shannon, reputedly visited by mad King Sweeney, who features as a character in this meta-textual novel. A Dublin student attempts to write a novel about a reclusive novelist, whose novel is repeatedly hijacked by a variety of literary characters. Sean O'Faolain (17) detected 'a general odour of spilt Joyce (8) all over it' but Jorge Luis Borges (572) was more positive: 'At Swim-Two-Birds is not only a labyrinth: it is a discussion of the many ways to conceive of the Irish novel and a repertory of exercises in prose and verse which illustrate or parody all the styles of Ireland.'

Joyce Cary

1888–1957

Cary was born in Londonderry and raised in Donegal. As per Anglo-Irish tradition, he was christened with his mother's surname: Joyce. He studied art in Paris and Edinburgh and joined the Nigerian political service in 1913. During the First World War he fought in the Nigeria Regiment and was wounded at Mora Mountain in northern Cameroon, after which he became a magistrate in the remote Nigerian district of Borgu. In 1920 he left Africa and settled with his wife and family in Oxford, where he spent the rest of his life writing.

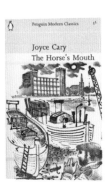 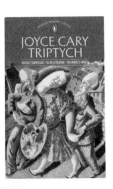

1948 Penguin Books
1964 Modern Classics
● —

1985
● —
This 1985 Penguin edition was the first time the *Triptych* trilogy was published in a single volume.

Mister Johnson 1939

Mister Johnson is the chief clerk in Fada, a small town in colonial Nigeria, and he is full of childlike enthusiasm for the projects and whims of his British masters. Chinua Achebe (359) was inspired to become a novelist after reading *Mister Johnson* and finding its portrait of Nigeria disturbingly two-dimensional.

1962
● —

Triptych

Herself Surprised, To Be a Pilgrim, The Horse's Mouth
1941–4

Inspired by impressionist art, this exuberant 'triptych' of novels is a literary experiment. Each book is told from the point of view of one of three characters: we see how they see themselves and how they are viewed by the other two. *Herself Surprised* (1941) is narrated by the cook Sara Monday and opens with her going to prison. It contains 'more truth of human nature', wrote L. P. Hartley (125), '[than] any novel I have read for a long time'. *To Be a Pilgrim* (1942) is narrated by Tom Wilcher, a retired lawyer, Sara's employer and lover. *The Horse's Mouth* (1944) is narrated by Gulley Jimson, a highly disagreeable painter, who cares only for his art. 'If you like rich writing full of gusto and accurate original character drawing,' wrote John Betjeman (88), 'you will get it from *The Horse's Mouth*. Mr Cary is the right horse.'

The Captive and the Free 1954–7, pub. 1959

Cary's last novel pits the maniacal, manipulative faith healer, the Reverend Walter Preedy, against Harry Hooper, a ruthless journalist who hopes to expose the preacher's chicanery. Caught in the middle is Alice Rodker, whom Preedy seduced as a child. The novel exposes the corruptibility of both religious doctrine and news reporters.

1963 Penguin Books
1985 Modern Classics
• intro. David Cecil, 1963

John Stewart Collis 1900–1984

Collis was born in County Dublin but lived most of his life in England. He wrote biographies of George Bernard Shaw (4), August Strindberg, Leo Tolstoy and other literary figures, although he is best remembered for his accounts of working the land during the Second World War.

The Worm Forgives the Plough

While Following the Plough, Down to Earth
1946–7

'I had hitherto regarded the world too much from the outside,' explained Collis, 'and I wished to become more involved with it.' He volunteered for the Land Army during the Second World War, working on farms in Sussex and Dorset. He describes his incompetent experiences as a new farmhand in *While Following the*

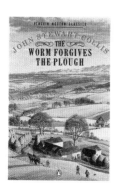

Plough (1946) and *Down to Earth* (1947), while also celebrating the beauty of the natural world. 'Both books are structured as a mosaic of tiny essaylets,' writes Robert Macfarlane, 'riffs, visions, meditations and comic set-pieces.'

1975 Penguin Books
1988 Modern Classics
• —

Mary Lavin

1912–1996

Lavin was born in East Walpole, Massachusetts, the daughter of Irish immigrants. When she was nine years old the family returned to Ireland and she graduated with a degree in literature from University College Dublin. Her first book of stories won the James Tait Black Memorial Prize in 1943, and she went on to write many stories and novels. She won the Katherine Mansfield (388) Prize in 1962 and served as the President of the Irish Academy of Letters. She had the ability 'to illuminate people and places, words and things', wrote William Trevor (21), 'by touching them with the magic of the rarely-gifted storyteller'.

In a Café
Selected Stories

1944–73

Lavin was widowed twice, and much of her best writing deals with women and widowhood. 'Lavin's stories have always given me a feeling of wonder and security,' writes Alice Munro: 'security because of the way the view keeps opening up, with such ease and authority, and wonder because she is, after all, so intrepid, so original and astonishing.'

1981 Penguin Books
Selected Stories
1999 Twentieth-Century Classics
• ed. Elizabeth Peavoy, 1995
fwd. Thomas Kilroy, 1995
—
The poet Elizabeth Peavoy was Lavin's daughter.

19

1980 Modern Classics
2000 Modern Classics *First Love and Other Novellas*
trans. Samuel Beckett, 1967–73
intro. Gerry Dukes, 2000

Samuel Beckett 1906–1989

While living in Paris as a young man, Samuel Barclay Beckett befriended James Joyce (8) and had a brief relationship with Joyce's daughter Lucia; his first publication was an essay in praise of *Finnegans Wake* (11). After the Second World War he had a revelation: 'I realized that Joyce had gone as far as one could in the direction of knowing more. [...] I realized that my own way was in impoverishment, in lack of knowledge and in taking away, in subtracting rather than in adding.' In the following years Beckett produced his greatest works, presenting a bleak, tragicomic view of humanity, unable or unwilling to comprehend its paralysed condition. These works culminated, in 1953, with the huge success of his play *En attendant Godot* (*Waiting for Godot*), which finally secured his international literary reputation. In 1961 he shared the Prix Formentor with Jorge Luis Borges (572), and in 1969 he was awarded the Nobel Prize for Literature (576). He gave away all the prize money and continued to live a simple, private life, writing increasingly minimalist plays. 'He is the most courageous, remorseless writer going,' said Harold Pinter.

The Expelled and Other Novellas

The End, The Expelled, The Calmative, First Love

1946, pub. 1955–70

Beckett composed all four of these elliptical stories in 'a frenzy of writing' between February and December 1946. They are among the first works he wrote in French, and all are written from a first-person perspective. In *The End*, the unnamed narrator is discharged from an institution and walks towards a city; in *The Expelled*, the narrator is thrown out on to the street; in *The Calmative*, the narrator goes on a night-time walk; and in *First Love*, the narrator lurks in a deserted cowshed, recalling a prostitute he once met on a park bench.

Malone Dies

1951

'Nothing is more real than nothing,' scrawls Malone, the naked, bed-bound old man whose pencil-written monologue and memories form the text of this novel. *Malone Dies* is the centrepiece of a loose 'trilogy' of novels, flanked by *Molloy* (1951) and *The Unnameable* (1953). It marks a turning point in Beckett's fiction, in that he dispenses almost entirely with plot and action, stranding the desolate reader inside Malone's expiring skull.

1962
• trans. Samuel Beckett, 1956

The image on the cover of *Malone Dies* is *The Skull* (1923) by Alberto Giacometti, who met Beckett in Paris.

More DEATH

A Death in the Family by James Agee	465
The Death of Virgil by Hermann Broch	272
The Knot of Vipers by François Mauriac	175
The Original of Laura *(Dying is Fun)* by Vladimir Nabokov	311
The Loved One by Evelyn Waugh	70

1982 King Penguin
1996 Twentieth-Century Classics
● intro. Colm Tóibín, 1995
—
The cover shows a portrait of Stuart
by Jack Crabtree.

Francis Stuart 1902–2000

Stuart was born in Queensland, Australia, to Irish parents, and travelled to Ireland as an infant. His novel *The Coloured Dome* (1933) was described by W. B. Yeats (4) as 'more personally and beautifully written than any book of our generation. If luck comes to his aid he will be our great writer.' Stuart married Iseult Gonne, daughter of Maud Gonne, the love of Yeats's life. With her help, he accepted an invitation to visit Nazi Germany, where he remained throughout the Second World War, ill-advisedly broadcasting Nazi propaganda to Ireland. After the war he was interned in Austria and eventually released to London, where he worked as an attendant at the Geological Museum. 'I am in the happy position of not being likely to be forgotten,' he said in 1953, 'never having been known.'

Black List, Section H 1971

Stuart's 'fictional memoir' describes the protagonist's explosive marriage to Iseult Gonne, his involvement in the IRA, his career as a poultry farmer and racehorse owner and his time spent in Nazi Germany. It is 'a book of the finest imaginative distinction', wrote Lawrence Durrell. In his introduction, Colm Tóibín calls it 'an underground masterpiece and one of the most important Irish novels written in the second half of the twentieth century'.

William Trevor

1928–2016

William Trevor was born in County Cork but lived most of his life in Devon. He remained, however, 'Irish in every vein'. After working as a sculptor, a teacher and an advertising copywriter, he wrote dozens of award-winning novels, plays and short stories. He won the Whitbread Novel Prize three times, including for *The Children of Dynmouth*. 'These novels will endure,' wrote Anita Brookner. 'And in every beautiful sentence there is not a word out of place.'

The Children of Dynmouth

1976

In the little town of Dynmouth on the Dorset coast, sinister 15-year-old Timothy Gedge sets out to learn the town's secrets and then use them to his advantage. 'Rereading the book now,' wrote Trevor in his 2001 introduction, 'it seems to reflect, much more than it originally did, the uneasy aftermath of a party that had got out of hand.'

1979 Penguin Books
2001 Modern Classics
● intro. William Trevor, 2001

Britain

Rudyard Kipling 1865–1936

In 1882 Kipling arrived in India aged sixteen to take up the assistant editorship of the Lahore *Civil and Military Gazette*. He had not seen India for more than a decade, but he was born in Bombay, now Mumbai, and Hindi was his first language. He began to contribute short stories to the *Gazette*, and in 1888 he published a selection in a book called *Plain Tales from the Hills*, which instantly made his name around the world. 'In one year,' wrote his father, 'this youngster will have had more said about his work, over a greater extent of the earth's surface, than some of the greatest of England's writers in their whole lives.' He refused a knighthood and the Poet Laureateship, but in 1907 he became the first English-language writer to win the Nobel Prize for Literature (576). Henry James (397) called him 'the most complete man of genius [...] I have ever known'. Towards the end of his life he was increasingly associated with outmoded politics and dubbed, in George Orwell's (80) words, a 'jingo imperialist'. 'It must be nice to inspire affection at short notice,' wrote Kipling to his friend H. Rider Haggard. 'I haven't the gift. Like olives and caviare and asafoetida, I'm an acquired taste.'

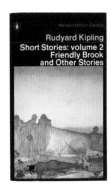

1971 Modern Classics
in two volumes
● ed. Andrew Rutherford
1987 Penguin Books
Selected Stories
1990 Twentieth-Century Classics
● ed. Andrew Rutherford, 1987
2011 Penguin Classics *The Man Who Would be King*
ed. Jan Montefiore, 2011

Stories 1884–1929

Kipling wrote pithy stories about India and England, animals and soldiers, loyalty and grief. He explained his method of editing in *Something of Myself* (25): 'Take of well-ground Indian Ink as much as suffices and a camel-hair brush proportionate to the inter-spaces of your lines. In an auspicious hour, read your final draft and consider faithfully every paragraph, sentence and word, blacking out where requisite. Let it lie by to drain as long as possible. At the end of that time, re-read and you should find that it will bear a second shortening. Finally, read it aloud alone and at leisure. Maybe a shade more brushwork will then indicate or impose itself.'

Poems

1886–1933

Kipling wrote poems as a schoolboy and collaborated with his sister Trix on a slim collection called *Echoes* (1884). He went on to publish five more volumes of verse, the most famous of which was *Barrack-Room Ballads* (1892), and many of his story collections are interspersed with poetry. Peter Keating's selected edition contains about a quarter of his published poems, including 'Gunga Din', 'Mandalay' and 'The Female of the Species'.

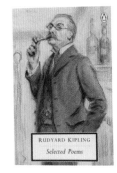

1977 Penguin Poets
Selected Verse
● ed. James Cochrane, 1977
1993 Twentieth-Century Classics *Selected Poems*
2001 Penguin Classics
ed. Peter Keating, 1993

1987 Penguin Classics
1990 Twentieth-Century Classics
● ed. H. R. Woudhuysen, 1987
intro. David Trotter, 1987
2011 Penguin Classics
ed. Kaori Nagai, 2011

Plain Tales from the Hills 1888

'As one turns over the pages of his *Plain Tales from the Hills*,' wrote Oscar Wilde (23), 'one feels as if one were seated under a palm-tree [...]. The bright colours of the bazaars dazzle one's eye.' These 40 stories were published in Calcutta, now Kolkata, in January 1888, one month after Kipling's 22nd birthday. Set against vivid descriptions of Anglo-Indian life, they proved immensely popular and transformed Kipling into an international literary celebrity.

2001
● ed. Craig Raine

1993
• intro. Salman Rushdie

Soldiers Three and In Black and White

1888

Kipling's next story collections were published in Wheeler's Indian Railway Library series and cost one rupee each. *Soldiers Three* enlarged on the escapades of three ordinary soldiers who featured in some of the *Plain Tales from the Hills* (22), and *In Black and White* presents a series of dramatic monologues from Indian points of view. 'The early Kipling is a writer with a storm inside him,' says Salman Rushdie, 'and he creates a mirror-storm of contradictory responses in the reader.'

The Light That Failed

1891

Kipling wrote his first novel after returning to Britain in 1889. The semi-autobiographical story recalls the cruel foster home in Southsea where he lived with his sister Trix and where he became infatuated with Florence Garrard, the model for Maisie in the book. It is a tale of unrequited love and the terror of blindness. He suffered a nervous breakdown after completing it.

1988 Penguin Classics
1989 Twentieth-Century Classics
• ed. Hugh Haughton, 1988

Wee Willie Winkie 1888

Under the Deodars,
The Phantom Rickshaw and Other Tales,
Wee Willie Winkie and Other Stories

These three story collections were also published in Wheeler's Indian Railway Library. *Under the Deodars* has vignettes about English men and women visiting India; *The Phantom Rickshaw* is a collection of mysteries that features 'The Man Who Would Be King'; and all the stories in *Wee Willie Winkie* are about Anglo-Indian children, including 'Baa Baa, Black Sheep'.

1970 Modern Classics
1988 Penguin Classics
1992 Twentieth-Century Classics
• ed. John M. Lyon, 1988

The Jungle Books

1894 – 5

In 1892, Kipling married Carrie Balestier, the sister of an American friend. They settled in Vermont, in 'Bliss Cottage', where Kipling wrote the two *Jungle Books* to entertain their daughter Josephine. They are collections of fables and poems, mostly set in the jungles of Madhya Pradesh. Several follow Mowgli, a lost human child raised by wolves, but there are also stories about the mongoose Rikki-Tikki-Tavi and Kotick, a white seal pup. Kipling's friend Robert Baden-Powell adopted several names from the *Jungle Books* when he founded the Scout movement, and he also borrowed the 'memory game' from *Kim* (24).

1987 Penguin Classics
1989 Twentieth-Century Classics
• ed. Daniel Karlin, 1987
2013 Penguin Classics
ed. Kaori Nagai, 2013

2001
• ed. Thomas Pinney, 2000
—
Kipling completed a stage adaptation of *The Jungle Books* in 1901, intended for performance at the Lyceum Theatre in London. It was never staged, and was considered lost until the American scholar Thomas Pinney discovered the typescript among Kipling's papers in 1998.

1988 Penguin Classics
1990 Twentieth-Century Classics
• ed. Constantine Phipps, 1988

The Day's Work

1898

Kipling wrote these short stories in the years following *The Jungle Books*. They include 'The Devil and the Deep Sea', 'The Maltese Cat' and '.007'.

1987 Penguin Classics
1989 Twentieth-Century
Classics
● ed. Edward W. Said (335),
1987
2011 Penguin Classics
ed. Harish Trivedi, 2011
—
After the First World War,
Kipling befriended a French
soldier, Maurice Hammoneau,
whose life had been saved
by a copy of *Kim*: it had
stopped a bullet in his left
breast pocket.

Kim 1901

In 1899, Kipling's six-year-old daughter Josephine
died of pneumonia. In the wake of this family
tragedy, he began writing his greatest novel: a story
of international espionage and the friendship
between a young British orphan in India, Kimball
O'Hara, and Teshoo Lama, an elderly Tibetan priest
seeking enlightenment.

Just So Stories 1902

The Kiplings and their two surviving children, Elsie
and John, settled in Sussex in 1902. That same year,
Kipling published this collection of stories 'for little
children', which explain how the rhinoceros got
his skin, how the leopard got his spots, and the
origin of armadillos, among other things. The tales
themselves had begun as bedtime stories for his 'best
beloved' Josephine, which had to be recited 'just so'
or else she would correct him. Kipling illustrated
the book himself.

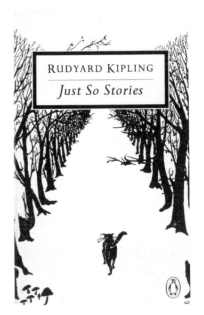

1987 Penguin Classics
1989 Twentieth-Century Classics
● ed. Peter Levi, 1987
2011 Penguin Classics
ed. Judith Plotz, 2011

1987 Penguin Classics
1992 Twentieth-Century
Classics
● ed. Hermione Lee, 1987

Traffics and Discoveries

1904

Many of the stories and
poems in this collection
grew out of Kipling's trips
to Bloemfontein in South
Africa, on holiday with
his family and then to
report on the Second Boer
War, of which he was a
vocal supporter.

Puck of Pook's Hill

1906

Dan and Una are playing in a Sussex
meadow, when suddenly they meet
a 'small, brown, broad-shouldered,
pointy-eared person with a snub
noise, slanting blue eyes, and a grin
that ran right across his freckled
face.' It is Puck, 'the oldest Old
Thing in England', who leads them
on a fantastical time-travelling romp
through episodes of English history.

1987 Penguin Classics
1990 Twentieth-Century
Classics
● ed. Sarah Wintle, 1987

1987 Penguin Classics
1994 Twentieth-Century
Classics
● ed. Paul Driver, 1987

A Diversity of Creatures

1917

Kipling's son John was
killed in the First World
War, at the Battle of Loos in
1915. This diverse collection
of stories and poems
concludes with the chilling
'Mary Postgate', about a
middle-aged woman who
vents her repressed misery
on a German pilot.

Rewards and Fairies

1910

In this sequel to *Puck of Pook's
Hill*, the fantastical adventures
of Dan and Una continue. They
meet a Neolithic farmer, a Sussex
smuggler and Queen Elizabeth I.
'The tales had to be read by children,
before people realized they were
meant for grown-ups,' wrote Kipling,
about both books. *Rewards and
Fairies* includes 'If –', often voted
the nation's favourite poem.

1987 Penguin Classics
1991 Twentieth-Century
Classics
● ed. Roger Lewis, 1987

Debits and Credits 1926

This collection of stories and poems includes 'On the Gate', in which St Peter struggles to process the huge numbers of First World War dead, and 'The Gardener', in which a grieving mother visits her son's war grave and meets a man whom she supposes to be the cemetery gardener.

1987 Penguin Classics
1993 Twentieth-Century Classics
● ed. Sandra Kemp, 1987

Limits and Renewals 1932

Kipling's last collection of stories and poems includes 'Dayspring Mishandled', about a bitter feud between two rival Chaucer scholars; 'Aunt Ellen', about a practical joke; and 'The Woman in His Life', about a man who finds peace through his love for a dog.

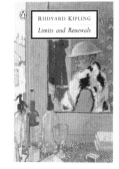

1987 Penguin Classics
1994 Twentieth-Century Classics
● ed. Phillip V. Mallett, 1987

Something of Myself
For My Friends Known and Unknown 1937

Written in the last year of his life and published posthumously, Kipling's memoir describes his childhood in India, his desolate schooldays and his career up to his winning the Nobel Prize for Literature (576) in 1907. 'It does not tell the life story as a continuous narrative,' writes the biographer Richard Holmes, 'but as a series of brilliantly worked fragments, a mosaic of carefully interlocked cameo portraits, memories and anecdotes.'

1977 Modern Classics
1987 Penguin Classics
1992 Twentieth-Century Classics
● ed. Robert Hampson, 1987
intro. Richard Holmes, 1987

George Grossmith 1847–1912

George Grossmith was a court reporter before discovering a talent for acting. He became the principal performer in the Gilbert and Sullivan comic operas, taking roles such as the Major-General in *The Pirates of Penzance* and the Lord High Executioner in the *Mikado*. He wrote hundreds of songs, musical sketches and comic operas himself, and became so famous that he sustained a twelve-year solo tour of Britain and North America.

Weedon Grossmith

1854–1919

Weedon trained as a painter before joining his older brother on the stage. He toured around Britain and North America with a repertory company and wrote novels and plays. At the end of his career, he managed Terry's Theatre in London.

The Diary of a Nobody 1888–92

Charles Pooter is a London clerk with an inflated sense of his own importance and a knack for committing social gaffes. The Grossmith brothers collaborated on instalments of his diary, which spans fifteen months and first appeared as a column in *Punch* magazine. A few years later, they added extra material, including illustrations by Weedon, for its publication in book form. It inspired Anita Loos's *Gentlemen Prefer Blondes* (432) and Evelyn Waugh (67) called it 'the funniest book in the world'.

1945 Penguin Books
1965 Modern Classics
● pref. W. E. Williams, 1945
1999 Penguin Classics
ed. Ed Glinert, 1999

H.G. Wells 1866 – 1946

Herbert George Wells taught biology at Henley House School in northwest London, where A.A. Milne was one of his pupils, and he began writing science fiction stories in his spare time. In 1895, the success of *The Time Machine* secured his reputation and he went on to write novels, essays, histories, biographies, polemic works of social criticism and schemes for world regeneration. The novelist Brian Aldiss (142) called him the 'Shakespeare of science fiction'. He has craters named after him on Mars and the moon.

2016
intro. Matthew Beaumont
—
All Wells's major works are published individually in Penguin Classics, but only a few have appeared in the Modern Classics series.

The Great Science Fiction

The Time Machine,
The Island of Doctor Moreau,
The Invisible Man,
The War of the Worlds,
Short Stories 1888 – 1911

Within these pages lurk murderous troglodytes from the future, monstrous vivisection experiments on remote islands, flesh-eating giant squid, and creatures from other planets. 'I think they will be incorporated, like the fables of Theseus or Ahasuerus, into the general memory of the species,' wrote Jorge Luis Borges (572) about Wells's stories, 'and even transcend the fame of their creator or the extinction of the language in which they were written.'

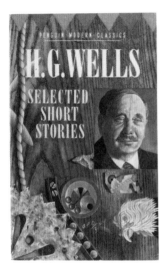

1958 Penguin Books
1988 Modern Classics
2007 Penguin Classics *The Country of the Blind and Other Selected Stories* ed. Patrick Parrinder & Andy Sawyer, 2007
intro. Neil Gaiman, 2007

Selected Short Stories 1894 – 1921

In 1911, Wells wrote that a short story 'may be horrible or pathetic or funny or beautiful or profoundly illuminating, having only this essential, that it should take from fifteen to fifty minutes to read aloud. All the rest is just whatever invention and imagination and the mood can give – a vision of buttered slides on a busy day or of unprecedented worlds. In that spirit of miscellaneous expectation these stories should be received.'

The Island of Doctor Moreau

1896

On an uncharted island in the Pacific, the deranged Doctor Moreau conducts monstrous experiments on live animals. Shipwrecked Edward Prendick is both a guest and a prisoner in the doctor's horrific island laboratory.

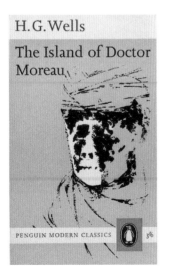

1946 Penguin Books
1962 Modern Classics
2005 Penguin Classics
ed. Steven McLean, 2005
intro. Margaret Atwood, 2005

More TIME-BENDING

'The Curious Case of Benjamin Button'
by F. Scott Fitzgerald   422

And Again?
by Sean O'Faolain   17

The Time Regulation Institute
by Ahmet Hamdi Tanpinar   329

Toward the End of Time
by John Updike   517

Orlando
by Virginia Woolf   44

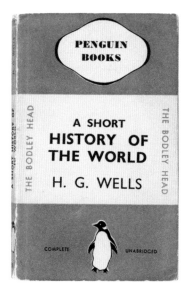

The earliest Penguin Books were colour-coded: orange for fiction, green for crime, dark blue for biographies, cerise for travel and adventure, red for plays, yellow for 'miscellaneous' and later violet for essays and belles-lettres and grey for world affairs. But there was one other colour — lilac. This signified history and was only used twice: for the 1936 edition of *A Short History of the World* and for H. C. Armstrong's *Grey Wolf* in January 1937. After the launch of Pelican Books (xiii) in May 1937, it was never used again.

The New Machiavelli
1911

The life of the MP Richard Remington falls apart when his extramarital affair is exposed to public scandal. This autobiographical novel was based on Wells's own affair with the much younger Amber Reeves and includes a satirical portrait of Beatrice Webb (73). Conrad (28) considered it a 'master-work'.

A Short History of the World 1922

Wells briefly sketches the entire history of the earth, with chapters on 'The Age of Fishes', 'Monkeys, Apes and Sub-men' and 'The First Sea-going Peoples', all the way up to 'The New Overseas Empires of Steamship and Railway'. He finishes by looking to the future, to a time when humans will live 'in a world made more splendid and lovely than any palace or garden that we know, going on from strength to strength in an ever widening circle of adventure and achievement'.

1936 Penguin Books
1937 Pelican Books
1991 Twentieth-Century Classics
2006 Penguin Classics
intro. Norman Stone, 1991
ed. Michael Sherborne, 2006

1946 Penguin Books
1985 Modern Classics
• intro. Melvyn Bragg, 1985
2005 Penguin Classics
ed. Simon J. James & John S. Partington, 2005
intro. Michael Foot (111), 2005

James Frazer 1854–1941

The classicist Sir James George Frazer was commissioned to write entries on 'Totemism' and 'Taboo' for the ninth edition of the *Encyclopaedia Britannica* (1875–89) and a sustained interest in these subjects led to his great work of comparative anthropology, *The Golden Bough*. He spent most of his career as a Fellow at Trinity College, Cambridge.

The Golden Bough
A Study in Magic and Religion 1890–1915, abridged 1922

Frazer's thesis is that human beliefs evolve along similar trajectories around the world: we begin by believing in magic and we practise sacrificial rituals to reflect and encourage seasonal cycles of death and renewal. These rites become formalized as religious traditions before finally we turn to science to explain the world. He took his title from the painting of the same name by J. M. W. Turner, which illustrates the scene in Virgil's *Aeneid* in which Aeneas seeks a golden branch in order to enter the underworld. *The Golden Bough* influenced subsequent writers from T. S. Eliot (11) and Robert Graves (57) to Carl Jung (262), Ernest Hemingway (428) and William Carlos Williams (418).

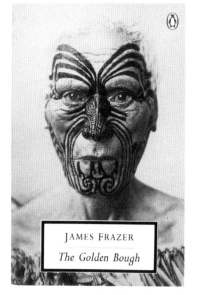

1996
intro. George W. Stocking, Jr.

Frazer wrote and expanded *The Golden Bough* over a period of 25 years, filling twelve volumes in total. This single volume presents the 1922 abridged edition, which Frazer selected with his wife.

Joseph Conrad 1857–1924

Jozéf Teodor Konrad Korzeniowski was born in Russian Poland. His aristocratic parents died of tuberculosis while in exile, leaving 11-year-old Konrad to be raised by an uncle. He ran away to sea as a teenager and spent the next 20 years sailing to the Far East, Australia and up the Congo River, before becoming a British citizen in 1886 and a captain in the British merchant navy. In the 1890s, he retired to Kent, where he married and wrote books for the rest of his life, adopting the anglicized pen name 'Joseph Conrad'. 'He's absolutely the most haunting thing in prose that ever was,' wrote his friend T. E. Lawrence (74): 'I wish I knew how every paragraph he writes [...] goes on sounding in waves, like the note of a tenor bell.'

Almayer's Folly 1895

'In 1889, at the age of thirty-one, [Conrad] came to London for a rest after fifteen years at sea. On this short London holiday he began writing a sea novel, which, after surviving subsequent jungle travel, shipwreck in the Congo, and a railway cloakroom in Berlin, came into the hands of Edward Garnett and through him to a London publisher. The book was *Almayer's Folly*, destined to be the first of a long series of novels and stories, mostly inspired by his experiences of life at sea, which have placed him in the front rank of English literature.' This is the biographical note from the 1976 Penguin edition. *Almayer's Folly* is about the tribulations of a Dutch merchant and his native Malayan wife in the jungles of Borneo.

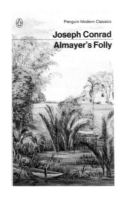

1936 Penguin Books
1976 Modern Classics
• —
George Orwell (80) reviewed the batch of Penguin Books released in March 1936, which included *Almayer's Folly*. 'At present Conrad is out of fashion,' he wrote, 'ostensibly because of his florid style and redundant adjectives (for my part I like a florid style: if your motto is "Cut out the adjectives," why not go a bit further and revert to a system of grunts and squeals, like the animals?), but actually, I suspect, because he was a gentleman, a type hated by the modern intelligentsia.'

1975
• —

An Outcast of the Islands 1896

Conrad's 'special individual gift, as an artist,' wrote the critic Edward Garnett, 'is of so placing a whole scene before the reader that the air, the landscape, the moving people, the houses on the quays, the ships in the harbour, the sounds, the scents, the voices in the air, all fuse in the perfect and dream-like illusion of an unforgettable reality.' *An Outcast of the Islands* was inspired by Conrad's experiences as second mate on a steamer. It is set in a remote Indonesian village in the jungle around Makassar.

Tales of Unrest

1896–8

These are Conrad's earliest short stories. 'The Lagoon', the first he wrote, is 'told in the same breath' as his Malayan novels, but his second, 'An Outpost of Progress', was based on his experiences on the Congo River. He described that story as 'the lightest part of the loot I carried off from Central Africa, the main portion being of course *Heart of Darkness* (29).'

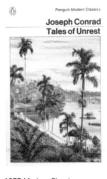

1977 Modern Classics
2007 Penguin Classics *The Secret Sharer and Other Stories*
• ed. J. H. Stape & Allan H. Simmons, 2007
intro. Gail Fraser, 2007

1963 Modern Classics
1990 Twentieth-Century Classics
• ed. Paul Kirschner, 1990
2007 Penguin Classics
ed. J. H. Stape, 2007
—
The 1963 edition comprised *The N—— of the 'Narcissus'*, 'Typhoon', 'Amy Foster', 'Falk' and 'Tomorrow'. The later editions dropped the first of these stories.

Typhoon
and Other Stories 1897–1902

'I have been called a writer of the sea, of the tropics, a descriptive writer – and also a realist,' wrote Conrad. 'But as a matter of fact all my concern has been with the "ideal" value of things, events and people.' These stories describe the dangers that lurk on both land and sea.

Youth and
The End of the Tether 1898–1902

In 'Youth', Conrad introduced his seafaring protagonist Charles Marlow, who recalls a hair-raising voyage to Bangkok at the age of 20. In contrast, *The End of the Tether* (1902) is about an old merchant-service captain approaching blindness and financial ruin.

1975 Modern Classics
1995 Twentieth-Century Classics
• ed. John Lyon, 1995
—
The 1995 edition also includes *Heart of Darkness*, which was first published in book form in 1902 in the same volume as 'Youth' and *The End of the Tether*.

Heart of Darkness 1899

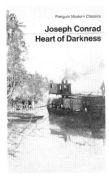

As dusk falls on the lower reaches of the Thames, Charles Marlow describes his experiences on the Congo River. He was sent by a Belgian ivory trading company to investigate the strange behaviour of Mr Kurtz, who was running a trading post deep in the 'heart of Africa'. As Marlow made his way upriver, the stories about Kurtz became wilder and more mysterious until he finally glimpsed the full horror of the situation. *Heart of Darkness* remains Conrad's most enigmatic and popular work, seeming 'to reach into the heart of Conrad himself', as Peter Ackroyd puts it. For many readers today, though, Conrad's treatment of Africa is inescapably racist; in 1975 Chinua Achebe (359) called it 'an offensive and deplorable book'.

1973 Modern Classics
1983 Penguin English Library
1989 Twentieth-Century Classics
• ed. Paul O'Prey, 1983
1995 Twentieth-Century Classics
• ed. Robert Hampson, 1995
2007 Penguin Classics
ed. Owen Knowles, 2007

Nostromo
A Tale of the Seaboard 1904

'No work of European fiction until *Nostromo*,' wrote Edward Said (335), '[...] so piercingly and unsparingly captured the imperialist project in Latin America.' Nostromo is a trustworthy Italian expatriate working for Charles Gould's silver-mining concession in the fictional South American republic of Costaguana. When revolution sweeps the country, however, Gould orders Nostromo to smuggle the silver offshore and the entire boatload of ingots disappears. 'I'd rather have written *Nostromo* than any other novel,' declared F. Scott Fitzgerald (422).

1963 Modern Classics
1983 Penguin English Library
1990 Twentieth-Century Classics
• ed. Martin Seymour-Smith, 1983
2007 Penguin Classics
ed. Véronique Pauly, 2007

Lord Jim
A Tale
1900

Narrated again by Charles Marlow, this is the tale of Jim, a former ship's officer, who is haunted by the fact that he once abandoned ship unnecessarily. He travels the world to escape his cowardly reputation and eventually settles in a remote trading post in the Malay Archipelago, where his magnanimous leadership earns him the title 'tuan Jim', or 'Lord Jim'. The arrival of the marauder Gentleman Brown, however, upsets this island idyll. 'This superb romance [stands] at the head of all his works,' wrote Virginia Woolf (42).

1943 Penguin Books
1962 Modern Classics
1986 Penguin Classics
1989 Twentieth-Century Classics
• ed. Cedric Watts, 1986
2007 Penguin Classics
ed. J. H. Stape, 2007
intro. Allan H. Simmons, 2007

A Personal Record and
The Mirror of the Sea
1906–1912

A Personal Record (1912) is a memoir of Conrad's adventurous life, with anecdotes about smuggling arms and about characters such as his great-uncle, who ate a Lithuanian dog during Napoleon's retreat from Moscow. A few years earlier, in 1906, Conrad had written the autobiographical *Mirror of the Sea* as a reflective tribute to 'the imperishable sea, to the ships that are no more, and to the simple men who have had their day'.

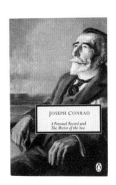

1998
• ed. Mara Kalnins

The Secret Agent
A Simple Tale 1907

Adolf Verloc is a secret
agent, operating from a Soho
pornography shop. When his
anarchist group orders him to
plant a bomb at the Greenwich
Observatory, he delegates
this terrorist act to his wife's
mentally disabled brother, with
disastrous results. 'A brilliant
book,' wrote Malcolm Bradbury,
'one of the greatest works of
modern irony.'

1963 Modern Classics
1984 Penguin English Library
1990 Twentieth-Century
Classics
● ed. Martin Seymour-Smith,
1984
2007 Penguin Classics
ed. Michael Newton, 2007

'Twixt Land and Sea
Three Tales

1910–12, pub. 1912

'The only bond between these
three stories is, so to speak,
geographical,' wrote Conrad, 'for
their scene, be it land, be it sea,
is situated in the same region
which may be called the region
of the Indian Ocean.' Many
consider 'The Secret Sharer'
to be Conrad's best short story.

1943 Penguin Books
1978 Modern Classics
1988 Penguin Classics
1990 Twentieth-Century
Classics
● ed. Boris Ford, 1988

Under Western Eyes 1911

Kirylo Sidorovitch Razumov is a student in St Petersburg, plagued
with guilt after he betrays an anarchist friend to the police, especially
once he visits Geneva and falls in love with the friend's sister, Natalia.
The narrative is pieced together by Natalia's unnamed and unreliable
English teacher. While writing the novel, Conrad had a nervous
breakdown during which he spent several days speaking to the book's
characters in Polish.

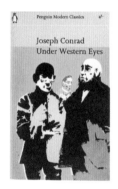

1957 Penguin Books
1964 Modern Classics
1985 Penguin Classics
1990 Twentieth-Century
Classics
● ed. Boris Ford, 1985
1996 Twentieth-Century
Classics
● ed. Paul Kirschner, 1996
2007 Penguin Classics
ed. Stephen Donovan, 2007
intro. Allan H. Simmons, 2007

Within the Tides

1911–14, pub. 1915

'Those who read me know my conviction that the world, the
temporal world, rests on a few very simple ideas,' wrote Conrad
in A Personal Record (29); 'so simple that they must be as old as
the hills. It rests notably, among others, on the idea of Fidelity.'
These four stories all explore notions of loyalty
and betrayal, ranging between Cuba, the Far East
and 18th-century Spain.

1945 Penguin Books
1978 Modern Classics
● —

Chance
A Tale in Two Parts 1913

Chance was Conrad's
first commercial success. The two parts are titled
'The Damsel' and 'The Knight', and are narrated
by a range of characters, including Charles Marlow.
In the first, Flora de Barral, the neglected, dreamy
daughter of a corrupt financier, meets Captain
Anthony. In the second, they embark on married
life, but there are storm clouds on the horizon.
Arnold Bennett (36) called it 'a discouraging book
for a writer because he damn well knows he can't
write as well as this'.

1974
● —

More SHIPS

The Sea is My Brother
by Jack Kerouac 469

The Sea-Wolf
by Jack London 405

Ultramarine
by Malcolm Lowry 101

The Pitards
by Georges Simenon 210

The Voyage Out
by Virginia Woolf 42

Victory
An Island Tale 1915

Axel Heyst lives as a recluse on a remote island in the Malay Archipelago, but when he rescues a young female musician from the advances of a lecherous orchestra conductor he sets in motion a murderous train of events.

1963 Modern Classics
1989 Twentieth-Century Classics
2015 Penguin Classics
ed. Robert Hampson, 1989
intro. John Gray, 2015

The Shadow-Line
A Confession 1917

Conrad wrote *The Shadow-Line* during the First World War, reflecting on the young men heading off to the front. The 'shadow-line' is the border between youth and maturity, which the inexperienced protagonist crosses when he takes over the captaincy of his ship. 'The ship, this ship, our ship, the ship we serve, is the moral symbol of our life,' wrote Conrad. He dedicated *The Shadow-Line* to his son Borys, who fought in the war, 'and all others who like himself have crossed in early youth the shadow-line of their generation'.

1986 Penguin Classics
1990 Twentieth-Century Classics
ed. Jacques Berthoud, 1986

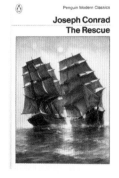

1950 Penguin Books
1978 Modern Classics
• —

The Rescue
A Romance of the Shallows
1920

Conrad began writing *The Rescue* in 1898, and it forms a prequel to the events of *Almayer's Folly* (28) and *An Outcast of the Islands* (28), his first two novels. In the Malay Archipelago, Captain Tom Lingard rescues a stranded English yacht and falls in love with the spirited, beautiful and married Mrs Travers. 'It matters not how often Mr. Conrad tells the story of the man and the brig,' wrote Virginia Woolf (42). 'Out of the million stories that life offers the novelist, this one is founded upon truth. And it is only Mr. Conrad who is able to tell it us.'

A. E. Housman 1859–1936

Alfred Edward Housman left Oxford without a degree and worked for ten years in the Patent Office; but he was a talented classicist and, in 1892, he was appointed Professor of Latin at University College London. Later he became Professor of Latin at Cambridge, and he lived and worked there until he died. Today he is best remembered for his poetry.

Collected Poems and Selected Prose 1896–1936

At the age of 74, Housman delivered a lecture in which he described his writing process: 'Having drunk a pint of beer at luncheon [...] I would go out for a walk of two or three hours. As I went along, thinking of nothing in particular, only looking at things around me and following the progress of the seasons, there would flow into my mind, with sudden and unaccountable emotion, sometimes a line or two of verse, sometimes a whole stanza at once, accompanied, not preceded, by a vague notion of the poem which they were destined to form part of.' He published just two books of poetry in his lifetime; his brother published two posthumous volumes.

1956 Penguin Poets *Collected Poems*
• ed. John Sparrow, 1956
1989 Twentieth-Century Classics
• ed. Christopher Ricks, 1989
2010 Penguin Classics *A Shropshire Lad and Other Poems*
ed. Archie Burnett, 2010
intro. Nick Laird, 2010

The 1989 edition includes Housman's nonsense verse, as well a selection of lectures and letters.

W. Somerset Maugham

1874 – 1965

Maugham's first language was French. He was born in Paris to British parents, who both died before his eleventh birthday. He was then raised by an emotionally distant uncle, the vicar of Whitstable, before studying literature at Heidelberg University and medicine at St Thomas's Hospital in London. After the modest success of his first novel, *Liza of Lambeth*, he abandoned his studies and became a playwright and novelist. During the First World War he drove ambulances for the British Red Cross and also worked as a spy in Switzerland and Russia. Maugham had an affair with Syrie Wellcome, the estranged wife of the pharmaceuticals magnate Henry Wellcome. Syrie divorced Wellcome and married Maugham, but it was not a happy partnership: after twelve acrimonious years they separated, and Maugham spent the rest of his life on the French Riviera, living with first Gerald Haxton and then Alan Searle. 'I tried to persuade myself that I was three-quarters normal and that only a quarter of me was queer,' he once told his nephew – 'whereas really it was the other way around.' In 1947, he instituted the Somerset Maugham literary prize, which is still awarded annually to young writers. Winners have included V. S. Naipaul (555), John le Carré (143), Angela Carter (156) and Martin Amis (160).

Liza of Lambeth

1897

In this tragic tale of adultery, unwanted pregnancy and domestic violence, Maugham drew on his experience as a medical student in Lambeth in south London. 'I saw how men died,' he recalled in *The Summing Up* (34). 'I saw how they bore pain. I saw what hope looked like, fear and relief.'

1967 Penguin Books
1992 Twentieth-Century Classics
● —

Mrs Craddock

1902

After Bertha Ley inherits a fortune, she marries Edward Craddock, a placid man from a lower social class, and they embark on a doomed marriage. Maugham succeeds in 'stripping life to the bone with a thin, sharp knife', wrote the critic Leslie A. Marchand.

1967 Penguin Books
1992 Twentieth-Century Classics
●

The Merry-Go-Round 1904

Miss Mary Ley is Bertha Craddock's spinster aunt. She is too old for love, but she likes to observe the Edwardian marriage merry-go-round.

1972 Penguin Books
1994 Twentieth-Century Classics
● —

The Magician 1908

In 1906, Maugham met the occultist Aleister Crowley in a Parisian restaurant. Crowley became the model for Oliver Haddo, a sinister 'magician' who seduces a young woman in order to pursue his experiments. Crowley wrote a scathing review of *The Magician*, under the pen name 'Oliver Haddo', in which he accused Maugham of plagiarism.

1967 Penguin Books
1992 Twentieth-Century Classics
● —

Maugham first used this symbol on the cover of his fourth novel, *The Hero* (1901). It also appeared on *Mrs Craddock*, which was such a success that he put it on every subsequent book he published. It is a 'sign against the Evil Eye', he explained in *The Summing Up* (34). He painted it outside his villa in southern France, where it can still be seen today.

Of Human Bondage 1915

Maugham's most autobiographical novel revolves around
the club-footed Philip Carey, who is raised by the cruel
vicar of Blackstable, attends university in Heidelberg and
becomes a medical student in London, where he is caught
in a love triangle between the idealistic Fanny and a waitress
called Mildred. 'Fact and fiction are so intermingled in my
work,' wrote Maugham, 'that now, looking back on it, I can
hardly distinguish one from the other.' Theodore Dreiser
(407) compared Of Human Bondage to a Beethoven symphony
and called it 'a novel or biography or autobiography or social
transcript of the utmost importance'.

1963 Penguin Books
1992 Twentieth-Century Classics
• intro. Robert Calder, 1992

1944 Penguin Books
1961 Modern Classics
1993 Twentieth-Century
Classics
• intro. Perry Meisel, 1993

The Moon and Sixpence

1919

Charles Strickland is a middle-aged
stockbroker, who suddenly abandons
his career and his family to pursue
a career as an artist. He struggles in
Paris, before moving to Tahiti, where
he paints voluptuous Polynesian
women and dies of leprosy. Maugham
was inspired to write this novel,
based in part on the life of Paul
Gauguin, after visiting Tahiti in
1914. The title came from a review
of Of Human Bondage, in which
Philip Carey was described as 'so
busy yearning for the moon that he
never saw the sixpence at his feet.'

1963 Penguin Books
1992 Twentieth-Century Classics
• —

1963 Penguin Books
1992 Twentieth-Century Classics
• —

Collected Short Stories

1920–45, pub. 1951

'The first of the stories in this collection, *Rain*, was written
in 1920 in Hong Kong, but I had hit upon the idea for it
during a journey I took in the South Seas during the winter
of 1916,' wrote Maugham in his preface to Volume 1. 'The
last of my stories was written in New York in 1945 from
a brief note that I found by chance among my papers and
which I made as far back as 1901. I do not expect ever to
write another.' Maugham's stories range from London and
Paris to America and the South Pacific. Volume 3 contains
his First World War spy stories, which are thought to have
inspired Ian Fleming (126). 'The short story was Maugham's
true métier,' wrote Anthony Burgess (148), 'and some of the
stories he wrote are among the best in the language.'

1963 Penguin Books
1992 Twentieth-Century Classics
• —

1963 Penguin Books
1992 Twentieth-Century Classics
• —

33

The Painted Veil 1925

Shallow Kitty Fane is stuck in a loveless marriage to a Hong Kong bacteriologist. After her husband exposes her adulterous affair, he forces her to accompany him into the heart of a cholera epidemic. The title comes from Shelley and the premise from a line in Dante's *Divine Comedy*: 'Siena made me, Maremma unmade me: this he knows who after betrothal espoused me with his ring.'

1952 Penguin Books
1992 Twentieth-Century Classics
• —

Cakes and Ale
or, The Skeleton in the Cupboard 1930

Following the death of the author Edward Driffield, his widow approaches a young novelist and invites him to write Driffield's biography. Alroy Kear's research, however, leads to Driffield's first wife, the fascinating Rosie, and the truth about his less respectable days. This was Maugham's favourite of his own novels.

1948 Penguin Books
1993 Twentieth-Century Classics
• —

The Narrow Corner .

1932

When a young Australian accused of murder flees to the Malay Archipelago, a passionate love affair on a remote island leads to disaster. 'Short, therefore, is man's life,' runs the epigraph, taken from the *Meditations* of Marcus Aurelius, 'and narrow is the corner of the earth wherein he dwells.'

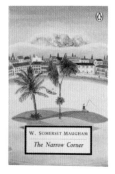

1963 Penguin Books
1993 Twentieth-Century Classics
• —

The Summing Up

1938

Maugham's memoir describes his development as a writer, from his painful childhood and awkward upbringing to his revelatory medical studies and his success as a novelist and playwright. 'I believe the modern writer who has influenced me most is Somerset Maugham,' wrote George Orwell (80) in 1940, 'whom I admire immensely for his power of telling a story straightforwardly and without frills.'

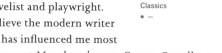

1963 Penguin Books
1992 Twentieth-Century Classics
• —

The Razor's Edge '

1944

Larry Darrell is a traumatized American pilot who travels to India after the First World War in search of enlightenment. Maugham himself is drawn into this quasi-fictional tale of addiction, mysticism, murder and sexual intrigue.

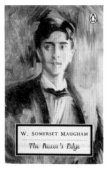

1963 Penguin Books
1992 Twentieth-Century Classics
• intro. Anthony Curtis, 1992

A Writer's Notebook

1892–1949, pub. 1949

Anecdotal and aphoristic, Maugham's notebook, which he kept throughout his life, reveals glimpses of his medical studies, his literary success and his extensive travels. 'I do not publish it because I am so arrogant as to suppose that my every word deserves to be perpetuated,' wrote Maugham in the preface. 'I publish it because I am interested in the technique of literary production and in the process of creation.'

1967 Penguin Books
1993 Twentieth-Century Classics
• —

1985 Penguin Classics
1990 Twentieth-Century Classics
• ed. Dorothy Porter, 1985

George Douglas Brown 1869–1902

Brown was born in Ochiltree, Ayrshire, and raised by a single mother, who worked as a farm labourer. He won a scholarship to Glasgow University and went on to study at Oxford, but returned to Ayrshire to nurse his ailing mother. He then moved to London, where he wrote fiction for magazines and died of pneumonia at the age of 33, at the home of Andrew Melrose, his publisher.

The House with the Green Shutters 1901

John Gourlay is a monstrous man who lives in a big, shuttered house in the centre of the fictional Ayrshire town of Barbie. He has a scatterbrained wife, a feeble son and a nondescript daughter, all of whom he treats diabolically, especially once his livelihood is threatened by the return of a professional rival. This nightmarish domestic drama subverts the previously pastoral tradition of Scottish novels, the 'sentimental slop of Barrie', as Brown put it. There are 'only ten decent folk in the book', he scribbled inside the back cover of his own edition, 'and about thirty brutes, ruffians and fools'. It was much admired by Hugh MacDiarmid (72) and Lewis Grassic Gibbon (100), and it was the first English-language novel that Jorge Luis Borges (572) read.

Saki 1870–1916

Hector Hugh Munro was born in British Burma, where his father was an inspector-general of the Burma police. His mother died after being charged by a cow, so he was raised by quarrelsome maiden aunts in Devon. After a brief spell in the Burma police force, Munro became the foreign correspondent for the *Morning Post*, reporting from the Balkans, Russia and France. Despite being over age, he enlisted as a private soldier in 1914, refused an officer's commission and was shot by a German sniper in 1916. He chose his pen name 'Saki' after the 'Cypress-slender Minister of Wine' in Edward FitzGerald's translation of *The Ruba'iyat of Omar Khayyam*, or possibly after a species of South American monkey, an example of which features in his story 'The Remoulding of Groby Lington'.

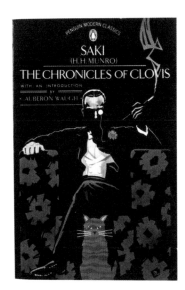

1948 Penguin Books
1986 Modern Classics
• intro. Auberon Waugh, 1986

Stories

1901–16

Saki's witty, macabre stories satirize the hypocrisies of Edwardian England. They feature werewolves, tigers, talking cats and deadly ferrets. His recurring characters include Reginald, a flippant young man who enjoys a prank, and the mischievous Clovis Sangrail, who is also keen on practical jokes and recounting scandalous stories. 'His horror is the correlative of P. G. Wodehouse's (48) humour,' wrote the scholar Angus Ross, 'and is apt to be similarly undervalued.'

1982 Penguin Books
1990 Twentieth-Century Classics
• intro. Noël Coward, 1967
1997 Twentieth-Century Classics
• —

2000
—

As well as short stories, the *Complete Saki* edition also includes plays and three novellas: *The Westminster Alice* (1902), a political parody in the style of *Alice's Adventures in Wonderland*; *The Unbearable Bassington* (1912), a novel of manners; and *When William Came* (1913), a fantasy about England under German occupation.

W. W. Jacobs 1863–1943

William Wymark Jacobs was born in Wapping in London, the son of a wharf manager. He worked as a clerk in the Post Office Savings Bank and wrote successful short stories, commissioned initially by Jerome K. Jerome and published in *The Idler* magazine. His first volume of short stories came out in 1896 and he wrote several more over the following two decades.

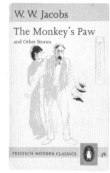

The Monkey's Paw and Other Stories 1901–26

Jacobs was best known in his lifetime for his dockland stories – much admired by P. G. Wodehouse (48) – about life on the wharf-side, with its music halls, magic-lantern shows, threepenny bars and peculiar argot. Today, however, he is best remembered for his tales of the macabre, such as 'The Toll House', 'The Well' and particularly 'The Monkey's Paw', in which a mummified simian paw grants wishes with nightmarishly unintended consequences.

1959 Penguin Books *Selected Short Stories*
1962 Modern Classics
● ed. Denys Kilham Roberts, 1959
—
Several of Jacobs's short-story collections were republished in early Penguin editions, including *Odd Craft* (1903) in 1936, *Deep Waters* (1919) in 1937, *Many Cargoes* (1896) in 1939, *Night Watches* (1914) in 1941 and *The Lady of the Barge* (1902), the collection in which 'The Monkey's Paw' first appeared, in 1943. Denys Kilham Roberts, editor of the *Penguin Parade* miscellanies, made this selection of Jacobs's best stories in 1959.

Arnold Bennett 1867–1931

Bennett had a stammer that was 'painful to watch', according to Somerset Maugham (32), who suffered similarly. 'Except for the stammer which forced him to introspection,' wrote Maugham, 'Arnold would never have become a writer.' Bennett grew up among the potteries of Staffordshire, the son of a draper. At 21, he left home and travelled to London, where he became the assistant editor to the weekly magazine *Woman*, writing reviews, essays and serialized novels. Inspired by his literary heroes, Guy de Maupassant, Gustave Flaubert and Émile Zola, he moved to Paris in 1902 and lived in France for ten years.

The Grand Babylon Hotel
A Fantasia on Modern Themes 1901

When American millionaire Theodore Racksole purchases a luxury hotel on a whim, he and his daughter Nella uncover a thrilling plot involving European aristocrats, mysterious disappearances, false names and murder. The story was first serialized in the *Golden Penny* magazine. 'I imagined a serial,' wrote Bennett, 'of which the interest should gradually close on the reader like a vice until it became intolerable.' The Grand Babylon is modelled on the Savoy Hotel in London and the Savoy Grill still serves the writer's favourite omelette, which is made with smoked haddock, hollandaise sauce and Gruyère cheese, and known as the 'Omelette Arnold Bennett'.

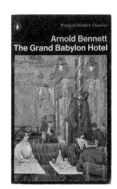

1938 Penguin Books
1954 Penguin Books
1976 Modern Classics
● intro. Frank Swinnerton, 1954

Anna of the Five Towns
1902

Set among the potteries, furnaces and chimneys of Bennett's childhood, this is the story of the spirited Anna Tellwright, who dreams of escaping her miserly father. It is 'deeply moving', writes Margaret Drabble (152), 'original, and dealing with material that I had never encountered in fiction, but only in life'. In reality, there are six towns in the conurbation of Stoke-on-Trent, but Bennett thought 'five towns' sounded better.

1936 Penguin Books
1975 Modern Classics
—

More HOTELS

The Grim Smile of the Five Towns 1907

These short stories expand on life in the Five Towns and the 'singular scenery of coal dust, potsherds, flame and steam'. The longest is 'The Death of Simon Fuge', which 'says as much as a novel', in the opinion of John Wain (124), who also thought it 'the best thing that Arnold Bennett ever did'. H. G. Wells (26) wrote a letter to Bennett after reading *The Grim Smile of the Five Towns*, in which he praised his 'high watermark so far. I've read it and admire and envy a pen so wonderfully under control and now astonishingly expert.'

1946 Penguin Books
1975 Modern Classics
• —

The Old Wives' Tale 1908

In the autumn of 1903, Bennett observed an old woman dining in the Rue de Clichy in Paris. 'She was fat, shapeless, ugly, and grotesque,' he wrote. 'She had a ridiculous voice, and ridiculous gestures. It was easy to see that she lived alone, and that in the long lapse of years she had developed the kind of peculiarity which induces guffaws among the thoughtless.' He then reflected that the woman was 'once young, slim, perhaps beautiful; certainly free from these ridiculous mannerisms. Very probably she is unconscious of her singularities. Her case is a tragedy. One ought to be able to make a heartrending novel out of the history of a woman such as she.' The result was *The Old Wives' Tale* – Bennett's first international success.

1954 Penguin Books
1983 Penguin Classics
1990 Twentieth-Century Classics
2007 Penguin Classics
ed. John Wain (124), 1983

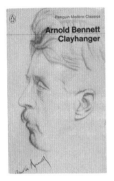

1954 Penguin Books
1975 Modern Classics
1989 Twentieth-Century Classics
• ed. Andrew Lincoln, 1989
—

Clayhanger is the first of a trilogy: the second volume, *Hilda Lessways* (1911), describes Hilda's upbringing, and the third, *These Twain* (1916), is about their married life together.

Clayhanger 1910

Set on the streets of one of the Five Towns, this novel follows Edwin Clayhanger as he tussles with his domineering father, gives up his dream of becoming an architect and pines after the provocative Hilda Lessways.

The Card
A Story of Adventure in the Five Towns 1911

In this comic novel, Denry Machin is the 'card' who hustles his way up the social ladder from washerwoman's son to the youngest ever Mayor of Bursley. Along the way he fakes exam results, capitalizes on shipwrecks, sells chocolate remedies and manages the local football team.

1975
—

Riceyman Steps 1923

Browsing in a Southampton second-hand bookshop one day, Bennett bought a volume about misers for sixpence. Both the book and the shop inspired this novel about a miserly bookseller in Clerkenwell in London, who marries the bubbly owner of the local sweetshop, with disastrous results. The eponymous steps were modelled on a real flight of steps, which still exists, leading from Gwynne Place to Granville Square.

1954 Penguin Books
1991 Twentieth-Century Classics
—

The Journals
1896 – 1929, pub. 1930 – 71

Bennett kept a diary from the moment ('noon precisely') when he finished his first novel in 1896, until his death in 1931. This selection presents a panorama of the places he visited, the writers he met, the books he planned and the fame and fortune he steadily accrued.

1954 Penguin Books
1971 Modern Classics *revised*
• ed. Frank Swinnerton, 1954, 1971

E. M. Forster

1879 – 1970

Edward Morgan Forster was a peripheral member of the Bloomsbury Group (44). 'I write for two reasons,' he said: 'partly to make money and partly to win the respect of people whom I respect.' He wrote five of his six novels before the age of 35, while living with his mother in Surrey. Forster had a long-term relationship with a married policeman called Bob Buckingham, with whose ashes his were mingled. In his obituary, *The Times* celebrated Forster as 'one of the most esteemed English novelists of his time'.

Stories

1903 – 58

In Forster's 26 stories – or 'fantasies', as he preferred to call them – he ranges from England to Italy, Greece and India, indulging in myth and magic, sensuality and sense of place, science fiction and the supernatural. He repeatedly contrasts the delights of the body with inhibiting social conventions. Titles include 'The Celestial Omnibus', 'The Machine Stops' and 'The Purple Envelope'.

1959 Penguin Books
1963 Modern Classics
1976 Modern Classics
1984 Penguin English Library
1986 Penguin Classics
1989 Twentieth-Century Classics
2007 Penguin Classics
ed. Oliver Stallybrass, 1975
intro. Ruth Padel, 2007

Where Angels Fear to Tread

1905

Lilia Herriton, an English widow, is travelling in Italy when she meets a dashing and much younger man, Gino Carella, the son of a dentist. They fall passionately in love, to the horror of Lilia's former in-laws, whose attempts to ameliorate the situation prove disastrous.

The Longest Journey

1907

'*The Longest Journey* is the least popular of my novels,' wrote Forster, 'but the one I am most glad to have written.' Its three sections juxtapose three 'types of existence', which Forster calls 'Cambridge', 'Sawston' and 'Wiltshire'. The first is a sparkling portrait of student days at Cambridge; the second describes the stifling, loveless life of a village schoolmaster; and the third offers a glimmer of redemption among the pagan spirits of Wiltshire.

1954 Penguin Books
1961 Modern Classics
2005 Penguin Classics
Selected Stories
ed. David Leavitt & Mark Mitchell, 2005

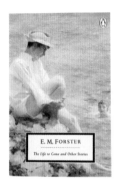

1975 Penguin Books
1987 Penguin Classics
1989 Twentieth-Century Classics
● ed. Oliver Stallybrass, 1972
—
Forster published two volumes of short stories in his lifetime: *The Celestial Omnibus* (1911) and *The Eternal Moment* (1928), a total of twelve stories that compose the *Collected Short Stories* edition. *The Life to Come and Other Stories* was published posthumously in 1972 and gathered fourteen previously uncollected stories, including several works of juvenilia and unpublished works with homosexual themes.

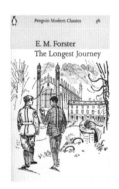

1960 Penguin Books
1964 Modern Classics
1900 Penguin Classics
1989 Twentieth-Century Classics
2006 Penguin Classics
ed. Elizabeth Heine, 1984
intro. Gilbert Adair, 2006

A Room with a View 1908

In a field of violets above Florence, Lucy Honeychurch kisses the unconventional George Emerson under the watchful eye of her prim cousin Charlotte Bartlett. Back in England, Lucy becomes engaged to the supercilious Cecil Vyse, until a chance encounter awakens her true feelings. In 1958, Forster wrote 'A View without a Room', in which he briefly imagined what had happened to the characters in the intervening half century.

1955 Penguin Books
1962 Modern Classics
1978 Modern Classics
1983 Penguin English Library
1986 Penguin Classics
1990 Twentieth-Century Classics
● ed. Oliver Stallybrass, 1978
2000 Modern Classics
2006 Penguin Classics
2018 Penguin Classics
ed. Malcolm Bradbury, 2000
intro. Wendy Moffat, 2018

Howards End 1910

This novel, considered by many to be Forster's masterpiece, centres on Howards End, a country house that is both the scene and the stimulus for much of the narrative. Forster based Howards End on Rooks Nest in Hertfordshire, where he lived as a child after his father died. The wealthy Wilcoxes, the cultured Schlegels and the lowly Basts meet, drift apart and clash in and around the house in a complex pattern of relationships. Forster's famous epigram for the book is 'Only connect…'

1941 Penguin Books
1963 Modern Classics
1983 Penguin English Library
1986 Penguin Classics
1989 Twentieth-Century Classics
● ed. Oliver Stallybrass, 1983
2000 Penguin Classics
ed. David Lodge, 2000

Maurice 1913 – 14, pub. 1971

In 1913, Forster visited the gay-rights activist Edward Carpenter, and the experience prompted him to write *Maurice*, a homosexual love story. 'In Maurice I tried to create a character who was completely unlike myself […],' wrote Forster in 1960: 'someone handsome, healthy, bodily attractive, mentally torpid, not a bad businessman and rather a snob. Into this mixture I dropped an ingredient that puzzles him, wakes him up, torments him and finally saves him.' Forster showed the novel to friends, including Christopher Isherwood (103), but chose never to publish it in his lifetime.

1972 Penguin Books
1985 Modern Classics
● ed. P. N. Furbank, 1971
2005 Penguin Classics
ed. P. N. Furbank, 1971
intro. David Leavitt, 2005

A Passage to India 1924

When Adela Quested has a traumatic experience in the remote and resonant Marabar Caves in northern India, suspicion falls on the charming, well-respected Dr Aziz, and the ensuing scandal raises violent passions in the twilight of the British Raj. The novel was based on Forster's first-hand experience as private secretary to Tukojirao III, the Maharajah of Dewas, in the early 1920s. Its colonial viewpoint has been criticized by Edward Said in *Orientalism* (335), but the novelist Anita Desai calls it Forster's 'great book […] masterly in its prescience and its lucidity'. Forster lived for another 46 years, and never wrote another novel. 'I should have been a more famous writer if I had written or published more,' he wrote, 'but sex has prevented the latter.'

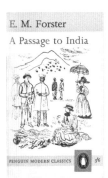

1936 Penguin Books
1961 Modern Classics
1979 Modern Classics
1985 Penguin Classics
1989 Twentieth-Century Classics
2005 Penguin Classics
ed. Oliver Stallybrass, 1979
intro. Pankaj Mishra, 2005

Aspects of the Novel 1927

This analysis of the novel form began as a series of lectures at Cambridge University. Forster decides to abandon chronology and imagines all the great novelists – Austen, Bennett (36), Brontë, Dickens, Dostoyevsky, Henry James (397), etc. – working simultaneously in a circular room, borrowing and sharing the same tools of story, character, plot, pattern and rhythm. 'He says the simple things that clever people don't say,' wrote Virginia Woolf (42); 'I find him the best of critics for that reason.'

1962 Pelican Books
1976 Pelican Books
1990 Twentieth-Century Classics
2005 Penguin Classics
ed. Oliver Stallybrass, 1974
intro. Frank Kermode, 2005

The Prince's Tale
and Other Uncollected Writings 1906 – 63, pub. 1998

This collection of Forster's previously uncollected articles, book reviews, essays, social commentary, memoirs and travel writing incudes his opinions of contemporary writers such as H. G. Wells (26), André Gide (164), Ford Madox Ford (46), Edith Wharton (401) and Virginia Woolf (42). It forms 'a welcome and intimate last experience of a mind full of intelligence, charm and talent', wrote Muriel Spark (141).

1999
● ed. P. N. Furbank, 1998
—
P. N. Furbank, who assembled this collection, was a friend of Forster and the author of *E. M. Forster: A Life* (1977–8), on which he collaborated with Forster himself.

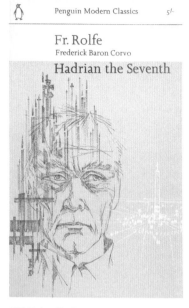

Penguin Modern Classics   5/-

Fr. Rolfe
Frederick Baron Corvo

Hadrian the Seventh

1964 Modern Classics
2018 Penguin Classics
—

Fr. Rolfe
(Frederick Baron Corvo) 1860 – 1913

Frederick William Serafino Austin Lewis Mary Rolfe, known as 'Baron Corvo', or 'Frank English', or occasionally 'A. Crab Maid', was a highly eccentric painter, photographer and novelist. The son of a Dissenting piano manufacturer, he spent his life sponging off a series of beleaguered patrons while writing strange books and attempting to become a Catholic priest. He eventually died of a stroke in his favourite Venetian restaurant. A 'cult of Corvo' began to emerge following the publication of A. J. A. Symons's brilliant biography *The Quest for Corvo* (102).

Hadrian the Seventh 1904

Chain-smoking, soup-eating, cat-loving George Arthur Rose is surprised when the Vatican unexpectedly elects him Pope. Suddenly infallible, he takes the name 'Hadrian VII' and instigates a series of highly controversial reforms, avenging himself on various 'enemies' from his previous life, most of whom are identifiable among Rolfe's own acquaintants. Graham Greene (88) considered it 'a novel of genius'.

M. R. James 1862 – 1936

Montague Rhodes James, known as 'Monty' to his friends, was the youngest child of the rector at Great Livermere in Suffolk. He went to Eton on a scholarship and then King's College, Cambridge, where he became a fellow, junior dean, dean and provost, and vice-chancellor of the university. He was a leading authority on the apocryphal books of the Bible and was director of the Fitzwilliam Museum for fifteen years. In 1918, he returned to Eton as its provost.

The Haunted Dolls' House
and Other Stories 1904 – 31

In the 1890s, James began a tradition of reading a ghost story at Christmas time, in his rooms at King's College, by the light of a single candle. They were subsequently published in four collections and in a complete edition of 1931, for which he wrote five new pieces. Most of them involve bachelor academics and they frequently take place in James's native East Anglia. 'The stories are not only set in, but arise from real localities,' wrote Penelope Fitzgerald – 'respectable hotel rooms, libraries, cathedral cities, modest country houses, seaside towns out of season, dark passages leading to candlelit bedrooms where there is something wrong with the window.' In *The Great Railway Bazaar*, Paul Theroux (543) describes 'The Mezzotint' as 'the most frightening story I know'.

1937 Penguin Books
Ghost Stories of an Antiquary
1959 Penguin Books
More Ghost Stories
1984 Penguin Books
Complete Ghost Stories
2000 Modern Classics
• ed. Penelope Fitzgerald, 2000
2005 Penguin Classics
Count Magnus and Other Ghost Stories, The Complete Ghost Stories, Volume I
ed. S. T. Joshi, 2005
2006 Penguin Classics
The Haunted Dolls' House and Other Stories, The Complete Ghost Stories, Volume II
ed. S. T. Joshi, 2006
—

The novelist Penelope Fitzgerald died in April 2000. One of her last commissions was the introduction to her selection of James's ghost stories, which was published in November that year.

M.R. James
The Haunted Dolls' House and other Stories

G. K. Chesterton

1874 – 1936

Gilbert Keith Chesterton was very tall and extremely portly. When asked, during the First World War, why he was not out at the front, he replied: 'If you go round to the side, you will see that I am.' He assisted the War Propaganda Bureau, alongside Arnold Bennett (36), John Galsworthy (47) and Ford Madox Ford (46). He was a journalist, but he also wrote poetry, essays, biographies, novels and detective stories. Known as 'the Prince of Paradox', he wore a cape and a crumpled hat, carried a swordstick and smoked a cigar. He was received into the Catholic Church in 1922.

The Napoleon of Notting Hill 1904

Chesterton's first novel is set in the distant future of 1984, a time when the monarch is selected at random. Maverick Auberon Quin is proclaimed king and divides London into medieval fiefdoms as a joke, but things get out of hand when Adam Wayne of Notting Hill raises an army to defend his borough's borders with violence. Chesterton used words 'not as neutral rational counters', wrote Anthony Burgess (148), 'but as confetti, bonbons, artillery'.

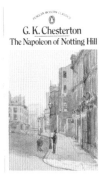

1946 Penguin Books
1982 Modern Classics
• —

The Club of Queer Trades 1905

Rupert Grant, a hapless private detective, pursues mysteries; but in each of these six cases his brother Basil demonstrates that, in fact, no crime has been committed. The stories each feature a figure making his or her living in an unusual way, eventually leading the brothers to the truth behind 'the Club of Queer Trades'.

1946 Penguin Books
1984 Modern Classics
• —

The Man Who Was Thursday
A Nightmare 1908

1937 Penguin Books
1962 Modern Classics
1986 Modern Classics
• intro. Kingsley Amis, 1986
2011 Penguin Classics
ed. Matthew Beaumont, 2011

'The Man Who Was Thursday […] remains the most thrilling book I have ever read,' wrote Kingsley Amis (132). '[It] is not quite a political bad dream, nor a metaphysical thriller, nor a cosmic joke in the form of a spy novel, but it has something of all three.' Gabriel Syme, working for Scotland Yard, infiltrates the Central Anarchist Council, where he is given the codename Thursday. But what appears to be a detective story about espionage and revolutionary politics becomes increasingly fantastical and eventually turns into a religious parable.

Father Brown 1911 – 35

Father Brown is a clumsy Catholic priest with a large umbrella, a face like a Norfolk dumpling and an uncanny insight into the minds of murderers. In stories such as 'The Dagger with Wings', 'The Blast of the Book' and 'The Oracle of the Dog', he uses his brilliant powers of observation to solve crimes. Chesterton 'showed us how to enlarge the boundaries of the detective story', wrote Dorothy L. Sayers, 'by making it deal with real death and real wickedness and real, that is to say, divine judgment'.

1981 Penguin Books
The Penguin Complete Father Brown
2001 Modern Classics
Father Brown
• ed. Ian Ker, 2001
2012 Penguin Classics
The Complete Father Brown Stories
ed. Michael Hurley, 2012

More DETECTIVES

The Ruined Map
by Kobo Abe 352

A Rage in Harlem
by Chester Himes 509

The Drowning Pool
by Ross Macdonald 498

Missing Person
by Patrick Modiano 200

Maigret's First Case
by Georges Simenon 205

Virginia Woolf

1882 – 1941

Virginia Woolf
The Death of the Moth
and Other Essays

PENGUIN MODERN CLASSICS

1961 Modern Classics
*The Death of the Moth
and Other Essays*
● ed. Leonard Woolf, 1942
1992 Twentieth-Century
Classics *A Woman's Essays*
● ed. Rachel Bowlby, 1992
1993 Twentieth-Century
Classics *The Crowded Dance
of Modern Life*
● ed. Rachel Bowlby, 1993
—
The Common Reader was
published by Pelican Books
in 1938.

Adeline Virginia Stephen's mother died when she was thirteen and her older stepsister, Stella, died two years later. Her father, the writer and lexicographer Leslie Stephen, died in 1904 and her favourite brother, Thoby, succumbed to typhoid fever in 1906. She described herself as a 'broken chrysalis' during this 'decade of deaths' and began to experience mental breakdowns and thoughts of suicide, which haunted her throughout her life. In 1904, she moved with her sister Vanessa to the bohemian district of Bloomsbury in London, where she became involved with a group of artists and writers now known as the Bloomsbury Group (44). These included Clive Bell, Vanessa's future husband; Lytton Strachey (64); and Leonard Woolf, whom Virginia married in 1912. The Woolfs founded the Hogarth Press together and published works by T. S. Eliot (11), E. M. Forster (38) and Katherine Mansfield (388) and the first English translations of Freud (265), as well as Woolf's own experimental novels, which soon established her as a leading proponent of modernism (11) in fiction. In 1941, dreading another onset of her illness, she pocketed a large stone and drowned herself in the River Ouse, near her home in Sussex. Today Woolf is considered a seminal figure of 20th-century literature and an inspirational feminist.

Essays 1905 – 41

Woolf wrote essays and reviews throughout her career, often for the *Times Literary Supplement*. She published two collections of essays in her lifetime: *The Common Reader* (1925) and *The Common Reader: Second Series* (1932). When she died, she was preparing a third for publication, which her husband Leonard Woolf edited and published posthumously as *The Death of the Moth* (1942). Her chief themes are writing, feminism and literary critical biography, with titles such as 'How Should One Read a Book?', 'Street Haunting' and 'The Strange Elizabethans'.

1973 Modern Classics
*A Haunted House and
Other Stories*
● ed. Leonard Woolf, 1944
1993 Twentieth-Century
Classics *Selected Short Stories*
2019 Penguin Classics
ed. Sandra Kemp, 1993

Stories 1917 – 39

Woolf's short stories are crucibles for her literary experiments, her 'wild outbursts of freedom' as she once put it. They range from 'A Haunted House', a modernist (11) take on a Gothic genre, to the more traditional 'Solid Objects', the impressionistic 'Kew Gardens', and 'Monday or Tuesday', which is an abstract stream of consciousness, described by Woolf's fellow 'Bloomsberry' Roger Fry as 'more real, or real with a different reality from that which we perceive in daily life'.

The Voyage Out 1915

Woolf's first novel is set on a steamship sailing from London to South America. Among the passengers is the naïve Rachel Vinrace, entranced by a new world of politics and books and the fascinating possibilities of sex, love and marriage. 'It is a strange, tragic, inspired book,' wrote E. M. Forster (38), 'whose scene is a South America not found on any map and reached by a boat which would not float on any sea, an America whose spiritual boundaries touch Xanadu and Atlantis'.

Virginia Woolf
The Voyage Out

1970 Modern Classics
1992 Twentieth-Century Classics
2006 Penguin Classics
ed. Jane Wheare, 1992

Night and Day

1919

Set on the streets of Edwardian London, this social comedy describes the beautiful Katharine Hilbery and her attraction to both the aristocratic poet William Rodney and an ambitious solicitor, Ralph Denham. She compares herself to her friend Mary Datchet, a women's rights campaigner, and her mother, who is struggling to write an ancestral biography. The plot is peppered with references to astronomy, women's suffrage and Shakespeare.

Virginia Woolf
Night and Day

1969 Modern Classics
1992 Twentieth-Century Classics
2016 Penguin Classics
ed. Julia Briggs, 1992

 Penguin Modern Classics   4'6

Virginia Woolf
To the Lighthouse

1964 Modern Classics
1992 Twentieth-Century Classics
2019 Penguin Classics
ed. Stella McNichol, 1992
intro. Hermione Lee, 1992

The artwork on the 1964 cover is by
Duncan Grant, another member of the
Bloomsbury Group (44).

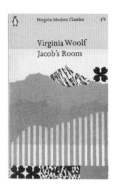

1965 Modern Classics
1992 Twentieth-Century Classics
2006 Penguin Classics ed. Sue Roe, 1992

1964 Modern Classics
1992 Twentieth-Century Classics
2019 Penguin Classics ed. Stella McNichol, 1992 intro. Elaine Showalter, 1992

The Bloomsbury Group

Thoby Stephen introduced his sisters, Vanessa and Virginia (42), to their future husbands, the writers Clive Bell and Leonard Woolf, in 1905. They began to form a loose social group based in Bloomsbury, near the British Museum in London. Other members included E. M. Forster (38), Lytton Strachey (64), John Maynard Keynes, Roger Fry and Duncan Grant. They were influenced by the philosopher G. E. Moore, who wrote that the prime objects in life were 'love, the creation and enjoyment of aesthetic experience and the pursuit of knowledge'. They were a sexually tolerant group about whom Dorothy Parker (419) is said to have quipped, 'they lived in squares, painted in circles and loved in triangles'. The group began to disperse after Strachey's death in 1932.

Jacob's Room 1922

Woolf's third novel is a both an elegy for her brother Thoby and a bold modernist (11) experiment: it presents a portrait of Jacob Flanders, as a boy, as a student at Cambridge and as an adult on the eve of the First World War, but it consists entirely of the impressions of other people. Jacob himself is a silhouette, a gap at the heart of the narrative. 'Perhaps there are analogies in painting,' suggested a bemused reviewer in the *Guardian*. '[…] Perhaps she will yet convince us that this is the way to write novels.'

Mrs Dalloway 1925

Virginia and Leonard Woolf had read Joyce's *Ulysses* (10) and considered it for publication at the Hogarth Press. Like *Ulysses*, the action of *Mrs Dalloway* takes place over the course of a single day in June and is told through streams of consciousness, punctuated here by the leaden chimes of Big Ben. The narrative is shared between the middle-aged Clarissa Dalloway, preparing for a party, and Septimus Smith, a First World War veteran suffering from post-traumatic stress, both of whose memories return to haunt them over the course of the day. The book's working title was *The Hours*, which Michael Cunningham borrowed for his 1998 novel about the afterlife of *Mrs Dalloway*.

← To the Lighthouse 1927

'*To the Lighthouse* is a ghost story,' writes Hermione Lee in her introduction. '[…] It is a lamentation of loss and grief for powerful, loved, dead parents.' The narrative describes two family holidays on the Isle of Skye, ten years apart, but it is based on Woolf's own childhood holidays in Cornwall, near the Godrevy Lighthouse. Mr and Mrs Ramsay are poignant portraits of her own parents, Leslie and Julia Stephen. 'I used to think of him & mother daily,' Woolf wrote in her diary; 'but writing *The Lighthouse* laid them in my mind.'

Orlando
A Biography 1928

Woolf considered this *jeu d'esprit* a 'writer's holiday'. It tells the fantastical story of a young 16th-century nobleman who lives through successive centuries without ageing, becoming a woman in 17th-century Constantinople and publishing a prize-winning novel in 1928. Woolf wrote *Orlando* as a gift for her lover, Vita Sackville-West, the poet, novelist, gardener, and wife of the writer and diplomat Harold Nicolson. Vita's son Nigel called *Orlando* 'the longest and most charming love letter in literature', and it has become a key text in feminist and transgender studies.

1942 Penguin Books
1974 Modern Classics
1993 Twentieth-Century Classics
2019 Penguin Classics ed. Brenda Lyons, 1993 intro. Sandra M. Gilbert, 1993
—
Leonard Woolf was asked if he would like to update Virginia's biographical note for the 1942 Penguin edition of *Orlando*. The one in the 1938 Pelican edition of *The Common Reader* (42) had stated that 'two of the best known of her many books are *Orlando* (an outstanding example of the "stream of consciousness" technique) and *The Waves* (45)'. 'I don't think I have read the note in *The Common Reader* before,' he replied; 'it is rather absurdly inaccurate, for *Orlando* is notable among my wife's books for having absolutely no "stream of consciousness technique" in it at all!'

A Room of One's Own

1929

Woolf developed *A Room of One's Own* from two lectures she delivered under the title 'Woman and Fiction'. This iconic text ranges through the history of literature, discussing Aphra Behn, Jane Austen, Charlotte Brontë and Judith, Shakespeare's imaginary sister. Woolf famously states that 'a woman must have money and a room of her own if she is to write fiction'. The scholar Hermione Lee called *A Room of One's Own* 'probably the most influential piece of non-fictional writing by a woman' in the twentieth century. *Three Guineas* (1938), published nearly a decade after *A Room of One's Own*, is a sequel of sorts, covering the prevention of war and the education of women. It was conceived at the same time as *The Years*.

1945 Penguin Books
1963 Modern Classics
2019 Penguin Classics

–

1993 Twentieth-Century Classics
2019 Penguin Classics
ed. Michèle Barrett, 1993

Michèle Barrett's edition also includes *Three Guineas*.

1951 Penguin Books
1966 Modern Classics
1992 Twentieth-Century Classics
ed. Kate Flint, 1992

The Waves 1931

The Waves follows a group of six friends through childhood, youth and middle age. This is the most experimental of Woolf's works: she abandons plot and dialogue in favour of a poetic, impressionistic evocation of inner experiences, shared and individual, the rhythms of which lap and overlap like waves on a shore. The poet Stephen Spender (95) called it 'a book of great beauty and a prose poem of genius'.

Flush
A Biography 1933

This witty novella is told from the point of view of Flush, the poet Elizabeth Barrett Browning's aristocratic pet cocker spaniel, for whom smells are poetry. Like Barrett Browning, Flush tastes freedom when they elope together to Italy. It is 'a complete success, and exactly what it sets out to be', wrote E. M. Forster (38); 'the material, the method, the length, accord perfectly, it is doggie without being silly, and it does give us, from the altitude of the carpet or the sofa-foot, a peep at high poetic personages, and a new angle on their ways'.

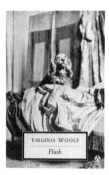

1977 Penguin Books
1995 Twentieth-Century Classics
2000 Modern Classics
● ed. Alison Light, 2000

1968 Modern Classics
1998 Twentieth-Century Classics
2019 Penguin Classics
ed. Jeri Johnson, 1998

The Years 1937

The last novel published in Woolf's lifetime is a family saga that spans 50 years and follows three generations of the Pargiter family as they are forced to transition from late-Victorian drawing rooms to the battlefields of the First World War and beyond. Each chapter takes place in a different year and over the course of a single day. At the time, *The Years* was Woolf's most commercially successful novel. 'Inspired,' wrote the *Times Literary Supplement*; '[...] a brilliant fantasia of all Time's problems, age and youth, change and permanence, truth and illusion.'

Between the Acts 1941

Leonard Woolf published Virginia's final novel shortly after her death. It tells the story of a historical pageant staged in a small English village and the private backstage dramas, which prove to be just as passionate and symbolic as the pageant itself. It is a lyrical meditation on the state of England in the months before the Second World War.

1953 Penguin Books
1974 Modern Classics
1992 Twentieth-Century Classics
2019 Penguin Classics
ed. Stella McNichol, 1992
intro. Gillian Beer, 1992

Ford Madox Ford

1873 – 1939

Ford Hermann Hueffer changed his Germanic-sounding name after the First World War, taking the middle name of his grandfather, the Pre-Raphaelite painter Ford Madox Brown. At 21, Ford eloped with his childhood sweetheart to Winchelsea, where he befriended H. G. Wells (26), Henry James (397) and especially Joseph Conrad (28), with whom he collaborated on several novels. Anthony Burgess (148) called Ford 'the greatest British novelist' of the 20th century. He was also an influential editor, founding the *English Review* in 1908, which saw the first publication of D. H. Lawrence (50), Wyndham Lewis (63) and Norman Douglas (63), and the *Transatlantic Review* in 1924, which featured pieces by James Joyce (8), Gertrude Stein (410), Ernest Hemingway (428), Ezra Pound (61) and Jean Rhys (551), with whom he had an acrimonious affair.

The Good Soldier
A Tale of Passion

1915

'This is the saddest story I have ever heard,' opens *The Good Soldier*, a tale of two couples and the seething miseries that lie beneath seemingly happy appearances. The narrative is unpacked unreliably and out of chronological order by one of the husbands. 'I have always regarded this as my best book,' wrote Ford. William Trevor (21) called it 'a masterpiece'.

1946 Penguin Books
1976 Modern Classics
2002 Modern Classics
2007 Penguin Classics
ed. David Bradshaw, 2002

The Fifth Queen

The Fifth Queen, Privy Seal,
The Fifth Queen Crowned 1906 – 8

This trilogy of historical novels follows the career of the flirtatious Katherine Howard, who becomes the fifth wife of Henry VIII, and tangles with Thomas Cromwell, the Lord Privy Seal, with fatal consequences. It is 'a noble conception,' wrote Joseph Conrad (28) – 'the Swan Song of Historical Romance'.

1999
● intro. A. S. Byatt, 1984

1979
● ed. Michael Killigrew

Memories and Impressions
A Study in Atmospheres

1911, rev. 1937

This miscellany of essays, anecdotes and snippets of autobiography presents a kaleidoscopic self-portrait of Ford, featuring childhood memories of William Morris and Algernon Charles Swinburne, friendships and collaborations with Henry James (397) and Joseph Conrad (28), and encouragement of younger writers such as D. H. Lawrence (50) and Ernest Hemingway (428).

Parade's End

Some Do Not...,
No More Parades,
A Man Could Stand Up –,
The Last Post
1924 – 8

After working for the War Propaganda Bureau, Ford enlisted in the army in 1915 and at the age of 41 fought at the Battle of the Somme and in the Ypres salient. These experiences informed this devastating tetralogy, which is one of the greatest English novels of the First World War. Christopher Tietjens is an awkward Yorkshireman whose world is destroyed by his experiences on the Western Front and the heartlessness of his calculating wife Sylvia.

1948 Penguin Books *in four volumes*
1982 Modern Classics
2012 Modern Classics
2019 Penguin Classics
intro. Julian Barnes, 2012

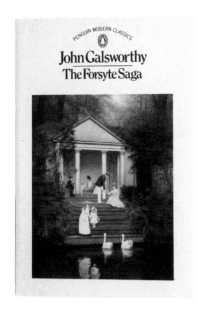

In 1893, Galsworthy was travelling in Australia on behalf of his family's shipping business when he met Joseph Conrad (28), the young first mate of a sailing ship moored in Adelaide. The two men became friends and encouraged each other to pursue writing careers. Galsworthy wrote novels, plays and short stories. He was the first President of International PEN and was awarded the Nobel Prize for Literature (576) in 1932, six weeks before he died.

The Forsyte Saga
The Forsyte Chronicles, Volume 1
The Man of Property, In Chancery, To Let 1906–21

Soames Forsyte is a 'man of property': newly rich, surrounded by possessions, and jealous of his beautiful wife Irene, whom he treats brutally. Galsworthy's painstakingly comprehensive, 50-year family saga sees divorces dragged through the courts of chancery and transgressions passed on to younger generations. The nine novels, multiple 'interludes', and peripheral short stories 'may deal with folk in frock coats, furbelows, and a gilt-edged period', as Galsworthy observed, but they are 'not devoid of the essential heat of conflict'.

1951 Penguin Books
The Man of Property
1965 Modern Classics
● —

1962 Modern Classics
In Chancery
● —

1978 Penguin Books
The Forsyte Saga
1985 Modern Classics
—

A Modern Comedy
The Forsyte Chronicles, Volume 2
The White Monkey, The Silver Spoon, Swan Song
1924–8

Set in the aftermath of the First World War, *A Modern Comedy* focuses on Soames and his daughter Fleur. Unhappily married, she is attracted to her old flame Jon.

1991
● —

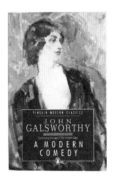

1967 Penguin Books
in three volumes
1980 Penguin Books
1988 Modern Classics
—

The second volume of the Forsyte Chronicles, first collected in 1929, is dedicated to Max Beerbohm (60).

On Forsyte 'Change 1930

These short 'prequel' stories describe the older generation of the Forsytes. 'It is hard to part suddenly and finally from those with whom one has lived so long,' wrote Galsworthy in his foreword; '[…] these footnotes do really, I think, help to fill in and round out the chronicles of the Forsyte family.'

1968 Penguin Books
in three volumes
1990 Twentieth-Century Classics
—

The End of the Chapter
The Forsyte Chronicles, Volume 3
Maid in Waiting, Flowering Wilderness, Over the River
1931–3

The Forsyte Chronicles conclude in the 1930s with these three novels about the Cherrell family, cousins of the Forsytes.

More FAMILY SAGAS

One Hundred Years of Solitude
by Gabriel García Márquez   562

Buddenbrooks
by Thomas Mann   245

The Radetzky March
by Joseph Roth   273

The Family Moskat
by Isaac Bashevis Singer   289

East of Eden
by John Steinbeck   444

P. G. Wodehouse

1881–1975

Pelham Grenville Wodehouse, known as 'Plum', was raised
by an assortment of nannies, aunts and clergymen uncles.
After a short stint in banking, he embarked on a lifetime
of writing stories for magazines, creating timeless comic
creations such as Bertie Wooster and Jeeves, his 'gentleman's
personal gentleman', the loquacious Psmith, Lord Emsworth
of Blandings Castle, the 'Oldest Member' of the golf club
and Mr Mulliner, pub raconteur. He lived in France after 1934
and then in the USA following the Second World War, taking
American citizenship in 1955. During the war, he was captured
by the Germans, interned for a year and induced to make five
broadcasts to the USA. Although the broadcasts were apolitical,
the fact that he made them sparked controversy in Britain
and tarnished his reputation. 'I ought to have had the sense
to see that it was a loony thing to do to use the German radio
for even the most harmless stuff,' he wrote, 'but I didn't.'
Wodehouse died on Long Island, New York, six weeks after
receiving a knighthood. 'One has to regard a man as a Master
who can produce on average three uniquely brilliant and entirely
original similes to every page,' wrote Evelyn Waugh (67).

2002
● intro. Robert McCrum
—
Robert McCrum's
biography of Wodehouse
was published in 2004.

Love Among the Chickens

1906, rev. 1921

Stanley Featherstonehaugh Ukridge is a bungling opportunist who
hatches a get-rich-quick scheme involving a chicken farm in Dorset.
Unfortunately, sickly chickens, bumptious dogs, touchy professors
and angry creditors lead to farcical complications. Wodehouse went
on to write nineteen more stories about Ukridge.

Lord Emsworth Acts for the Best
The Collected Blandings Short Stories

1924–66

Wodehouse set eleven novels and nine short stories at Blandings
Castle, the Shropshire seat of Lord Emsworth. This volume collects
all the stories, including 'Lord Emsworth and the Girl Friend',
which Kipling (22) considered 'one of the most perfect short
stories I have ever read'.

1992
● intro. Frank Muir

Summer Lightning

1929

The third of the Blandings Castle novels sees Lord Emsworth reeling
from the theft of his prize-winning pig, while desperate relatives
go to extreme lengths to prevent the publication of his brother the
Hon. Galahad Threepwood's scandalous memoirs. 'Immortal,' writes
Nick Hornby (162) in his introduction. 'Everything Wodehouse wrote
was of a quality unmatched by any other pretender to his throne.'

1954 Penguin Books
2002 Modern Classics
● intro. Nick Hornby,
2002

Heavy Weather

1933

In this sequel to *Summer Lightning* (48), the publisher Lord Tilbury fights to bring Galahad Threepwood's manuscript to press, while Lord Emsworth suspects his neighbour, Sir Gregory Parsloe-Parsloe, of foul play at the county show.

The Code of the Woosters

1938

The third of the Jeeves and Wooster novels takes place at Totleigh Towers, home of the crotchety Sir Watkyn Bassett. It features newt-fancier Gussie Fink-Nottle, dreamy Madeline Bassett, 'Stiffy' Byng, 'Stinker' Pinker, and the fascist Roderick Spode leading a band of Black Shorts. When Bertie Wooster's Aunt Dahlia persuades him to purloin Sir Watkyn's prized silver cow-creamer, however, only Jeeves can untangle the mess.

1953 Penguin Books
1999 Twentieth-Century Classics
• intro. Joe Keenan, 1999

1966 Penguin Books
2001 Modern Classics
• intro. Anthony Lane, 2001

The Mating Season 1949

'Jeeves and Bertie are as immortal as Don Quixote and Sancho Panza, or Falstaff and Prince Hal,' wrote John Mortimer (139), 'and, quite often, a good deal funnier.' In this instalment, Bertie poses as Gussie Fink-Nottle, as a favour to 'Catsmeat' Potter-Pirbright, while staying with Esmond Haddock at Deverill Hall, but things get complicated when Gussie himself arrives, pretending to be Bertie.

1977 Penguin Books
1999 Twentieth-Century Classics
• intro. Christopher Hitchens, 1999

Edmund Gosse

1849 – 1928

Gosse worked as a librarian in the British Museum and the House of Lords. He was a poet and critic, who popularized the works of W. B. Yeats (4), André Gide (164), James Joyce (8) and particularly Henrik Ibsen, for which he was awarded a Norwegian knighthood.

Father and Son
A Study of Two Temperaments 1907

Gosse's father was an eminent invertebrate zoologist, the inventor of the word 'aquarium' and the 'father of Jamaican ornithology'. He was also a fanatical fundamentalist Christian, a member of the strict Plymouth Brethren. This memoir, sometimes described as the first psychological biography, describes Gosse's dramatic rejection of his faith and his determination to 'fashion his inner life for himself'. George Bernard Shaw (4) called it 'one of the immortal pages in English literature'.

1949 Penguin Books
1973 Modern Classics
1983 Penguin English Library
1986 Penguin Classics
1989 Twentieth-Century Classics
ed. Peter Abbs, 1983

D. H. Lawrence

1885 – 1930

David Herbert Lawrence was born in Nottinghamshire, the son of a barely literate coal miner and a school-teacher. He trained as a teacher himself, between bouts of recurrent pneumonia, and eloped to Germany with Frieda Weekley, the wife of his professor at Nottingham University College. The couple spent a year in Germany and Italy, before returning to England and marrying in 1914, once Frieda had obtained a divorce. After the First World War, they embarked on a 'savage pilgrimage' around the world, from Sicily to Sri Lanka, Australia and eventually New Mexico, where Lawrence bought a ranch in exchange for the manuscript of *Sons and Lovers* (51). They dreamt of founding a utopian community, but after Lawrence suffered a nearly fatal attack of malaria and tuberculosis they returned to Europe and settled in northern Italy, where he wrote *Lady Chatterley's Lover* (56). He died in southern France at the age of 44. 'In my opinion he is the greatest writer of this century,' said Philip Larkin, 'and in many things the greatest writer of all times.'

Starting in 1995, all the Penguin editions of Lawrence were replaced with the newly established texts of the Cambridge Edition of his works. These updated editions were overseen by the advisory editor John Worthen, Professor of D. H. Lawrence Studies at the University of Nottingham.

1945 Penguin Books
1992 Twentieth-Century Classics
1995 Twentieth-Century Classics
ed. John Worthen, 1983
intro. Brian Finney, 1995

1950 Penguin Books
1990 Twentieth-Century Classics
• ed. Richard Aldington, 1950
1996 Twentieth-Century Classics
• ed. Dieter Mehl & Christa Jansohn, 1996
intro. N. H. Reeve, 1996

Stories 1907 – 30

In 1907, Lawrence won a short-story competition in the *Nottinghamshire Guardian*. A few years later, Ford Madox Ford (46) published 'Odour of Chrysanthemums' in the *English Review* and was instrumental in recommending Lawrence's first novel, *The White Peacock* (51), to Heinemann. Lawrence wrote stories throughout his career, set in hayfields, miners' cottages, Bavarian valleys, bohemian Paris and Sicilian palazzi. Some of his best-known titles include 'Love Among the Haystacks', 'The Rocking-Horse Winner' and 'The Prussian Officer'.

1960 Penguin Books
1990 Twentieth-Century Classics
1996 Twentieth-Century Classics
• ed. Bruce Steele, 1996
intro. Michael Bell, 1996

1960 Penguin Books
1990 Twentieth-Century Classics
1996 Twentieth-Century Classics
• ed. John Worthen, 1996
intro. Keith Cushman, 1996

1982 Penguin English Library
1989 Twentieth-Century Classics
• ed. Brian Finney, 1982
2007 Penguin Classics
ed. Sue Wilson, 2007
intro. Louise Welsh, 2007
—
The Prussian Officer (1914) was Lawrence's first collection of short stories, followed by *England, My England* (1922) and several more. *Love Among the Haystacks* (1930) was published posthumously and brought together his uncollected short fiction. Keith Sagar's two-volume 1971 selection saw the first publication of 'The Mortal Coil', which Lawrence himself described as 'a first-class story, one of my purest creations'.

1971 Penguin Books
1992 Twentieth-Century Classics
• ed. Keith Sagar, 1971

1971 Penguin Books
1990 Twentieth-Century Classics
• ed. Keith Sagar, 1971

Three Plays

A Collier's Friday Night, The Daughter-in-Law, The Widowing of Mrs Holroyd 1909 – 14

These early plays were all written while Lawrence was teaching in Croydon. The first two were never published or performed in his lifetime. An amateur production of *The Widowing of Mrs Holroyd* was staged in 1920. 'In my ignorance, I attached no importance to Lawrence until one afternoon at the Stage Society,' wrote George Bernard Shaw (4), 'when I saw a play by him which rushed through in such a torrent of profuse yet vividly effective dialogue, making my own seem archaic in comparison.'

1969 Penguin Plays
1985 Penguin Classics
1991 Twentieth-Century Classics
● intro. Raymond Williams, 1969
—
The cover photograph of the 1991 edition shows a scene from the 1968 Royal Court production of *The Daughter-in-Law* in London.

The White Peacock 1911

Lawrence's first novel was inspired by a painting of a passionate, pastoral embrace by Maurice Greiffenhagen. *An Idyll* is reproduced on the cover of the 1989 Penguin edition: 'it moves me almost as if I were in love myself,' wrote Lawrence. He reworked the manuscript three times. Set in a fictionalized version of Eastwood, Lawrence's home town, it is about a doomed love triangle between the lively Lettie Beardsall and two men, an attractive young farmer and the wealthy son of the local mine owner. 'To think that my son should have written such a story,' exclaimed Lawrence's mother. She died a few weeks after the novel's completion, leading to a year of depression that Lawrence called his 'sick year'.

1950 Penguin Books
● intro. Richard Aldington, 1950
1982 Penguin English Library
1987 Penguin Classics
1989 Twentieth-Century Classics
● ed. Alan Newton, 1982
intro. John Worthen, 1982
1995 Twentieth-Century Classics
● ed. Andrew Robertson, 1995
intro. Michael Black, 1995

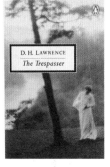

1960 Penguin Books
1989 Twentieth-Century Classics
1994 Twentieth-Century Classics
● ed. Elizabeth Mansfield, 1994
intro. John Turner, 1994

The Trespasser 1912

Lawrence based his second novel on the intimate diaries of a teaching colleague, Helen Corke, who had an extramarital affair that ended with her lover's suicide. The last 50 pages, in the translator Constance Garnett's view, are as good as the work of 'the best Russian school'. Helen Corke eventually published her own version of the original diaries as *Neutral Ground* (1933).

Sons and Lovers 1913

In this highly autobiographical novel, Paul Morel is the son of a Nottinghamshire miner and a suffocating mother, who clings to him as his two lovers attempt to wrestle him away. One of the young women, Miriam, was based on Lawrence's friend Jessie Chambers, with whom he had a brief affair. Chambers was so horrified by her portrayal in the novel she never spoke to Lawrence again after its publication. Anthony Burgess (148) considered it 'Lawrence's masterpiece'.

1948 Penguin Books
1981 Penguin English Library
1986 Penguin Classics
1989 Twentieth-Century Classics
● ed. Keith Sagar, 1981
1994 Twentieth-Century Classics
2006 Penguin Classics
ed. Helen Baron & Carl Baron, 1994
intro. Blake Morrison, 2006

Poems 1913–30

Lawrence began writing poetry using traditional verse forms, but he quickly abandoned them. 'We can get rid of the stereotyped movements and the old hackneyed associations of sound or sense,' he wrote. 'We can break down those artificial conduits and canals through which we do so love to force our utterance. We can break the stiff neck of habit.' Lawrence wrote more than 800 poems, ranging from experiments in Nottingham dialect to Whitmanesque free verse, and from autobiography to poems about fruit, insects and animals. He repeatedly revised his poems, explaining that 'a young man is afraid of his demon and puts his hand over the demon's mouth sometimes'.

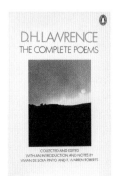

1950 Penguin Poets
Selected Poems
● intro. W. E. Williams, 1950
1973 Penguin Poets
Selected Poems
● ed. Keith Sagar, 1973
1977 Penguin Books
The Complete Poems
1994 Twentieth-Century Classics
● ed. Vivian de Sola Pinto & Warren Roberts, 1964
2008 Penguin Classics
Selected Poems
ed. James Fenton, 2008

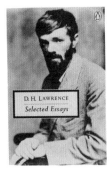

1950 Penguin Books
1992 Twentieth-Century Classics
● ed. Richard Aldington, 1950

2019 Design Classics
Life with a Capital L
ed. Geoff Dyer, 2019

Essays 1913–30

'"Essays" is a poor word for these brilliantly-varied writings,' declared the novelist Richard Aldington in the introduction to his selection, 'since "an essay" unhappily implies something formal and academic and highbrow, whereas Lawrence was always intensely personal and spontaneous, with such a horror of pedantry and the university manner that he vastly preferred to be slangy and jaunty.' Lawrence's non-fiction pieces range across sex and love, to the 'whistling of birds', the art of painting, and John Galsworthy's *Forsyte Saga* (47).

The Rainbow 1915

In 1913, in a cottage in Fiascherino on the Gulf of Spezia, Lawrence began writing a novel called *The Sisters*, which eventually became two novels: *The Rainbow* and *Women in Love*. *The Rainbow* follows three generations of a Nottinghamshire farming family transitioning into the industrial age. It focuses on Ursula Brangwen, who dreams of a fulfilling life, and ends with her vision of a rainbow as 'the earth's new architecture, the old, brittle corruption of houses and factories swept away, the world built up in a living fabric of Truth, fitting to the over-arching heaven'. When *The Rainbow* was published, it was immediately prosecuted for its explicit descriptions of sex; 1,011 copies were seized and burned and it was then unavailable in Britain for eleven years.

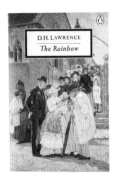

1949 Penguin Books
1981 Penguin English Library
1986 Penguin Classics
1989 Twentieth-Century Classics
● ed. John Worthen, 1981
1995 Twentieth-Century Classics
2000 Modern Classics
2007 Penguin Classics
ed. Mark Kinkead-Weekes, 1989
notes Anne Fernihough, 1995
intro. James Wood, 2007

Women in Love

1917, pub. 1920

Lawrence struggled for three years to find a publisher for *Women in Love*, the sequel to his scandalous *The Rainbow*. The story follows Ursula Brangwen and her sister Gudrun, and their love affairs with the intellectual Rupert Birkin and the industrialist Gerald Crich. The two couples weave a web of relationships, with a strongly implied homosexual attraction between Rupert and Gerald. Lawrence finished writing the book in Cornwall, where he himself may have had a sexual relationship with a local farmer called William. Ursula is based on Frieda, while Gudrun is based on Katherine Mansfield (388). The book's frank sexual vocabulary was denounced by Simone de Beauvoir (187) and described by a contemporary reviewer as 'dirt in heaps – festering, putrid heaps which smell to high Heaven'.

1960 Penguin Books
1982 Penguin English Library
1986 Penguin Classics
1989 Twentieth-Century Classics
● ed. Charles Ross, 1982
1995 Twentieth-Century Classics
2007 Penguin Classics
ed. David Farmer, Lindeth Vasey & John Worthen, 1989
notes Mark Kinead-Weekes, 1995
intro. Amit Chaudhari, 2007

D. H. Lawrence and Italy

Twilight in Italy, *Sea and Sardinia*,
Sketches of Etruscan Places

1916–32

In 1912, Lawrence and Frieda walked across the Alps from
Germany to Italy. Lawrence recorded the experience in a
series of essays, which he published as *Twilight In Italy* (1916).
It 'cannot be read as an ordinary travel book,' wrote Anaïs Nin
(430), 'for Lawrence is again seeking the core of truth, and
his voyage is philosophic, as well as a symbolic and sensuous
one'. *Sea and Sardinia* (1921) is 'perhaps the most charming
of all the books Lawrence ever wrote', according to Anthony
Burgess (148): it is the account of a winter's trip to Sardinia,
made while Lawrence and Frieda were living in Sicily.
Finally, *Sketches of Etruscan Places* (1932) describes a number
of archaeological sites in central Italy, which Lawrence visited
with his friend, the artist Earl Brewster, in April 1927.

1960 Penguin Books
1997 Twentieth-Century
Classics
● ed. Paul Eggert, 1997
intro. Stefania Michelucci,
1997

1944 Penguin Books
1972 Penguin Books
● intro. Anthony Burgess, 1972
1999 Twentieth-Century
Classics
ed. Mara Kalnins, 1997
intro. Jill Franks, 1997

1950 Penguin Books
1990 Twentieth-Century Classics
● intro. Richard Aldington, 1950
1995 Twentieth-Century Classics
● ed. John Worthen, 1995
intro. Carol Siegel, 1995

The Lost Girl

1920

Passionate Alvina Houghton escapes her
suffocating Midlands home, eloping to
Abruzzo with a sensual Italian travelling
performer. In 1920, *The Lost Girl* won the
second James Tait Black Memorial Prize,
the only official award that Lawrence
received in his lifetime.

Mr Noon

1920–21, pub. 1934–84

This unfinished, semi-autobiographical novel was
based on Lawrence's and Frieda's own elopement in 1912.
It follows Gilbert Noon, a schoolteacher, who flees to
Germany and has an affair with the German wife of an
English doctor. It was abandoned by Lawrence and never
published in his lifetime.

1950 Penguin Books
1999 Twentieth-Century
Classics
● ed. Simonetta de Filippis,
1999

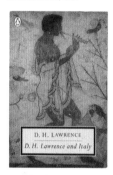

1985 Penguin Travel Library
1997 Twentieth-Century
Classics
● ed. Anthony Burgess, 1985
2007 Penguin Classics
ed. Paul Eggert, Mara Kalnins
& Simonetta de Filippis,
1997–9
intro. Tim Parks, 2007
notes Michael Frederick
Herbert, 2007

Fantasia of the Unconscious and Psychoanalysis and the Unconscious

1921–2

These two essays are a challenge to Freud (265), redefining
the unconscious as 'another word for life'. The theorist
Gilles Deleuze admired the way they challenged Freud's
account of the Oedipus complex. Lawrence 'was a clever
man as well as a man of genius', wrote Aldous Huxley (65),
'[…] a being, somehow of another order, more sensitive,
more highly conscious, more capable of feeling than even
the most gifted of common men'.

1971 Penguin Books
1991 Twentieth-Century Classics
● —

1987 Penguin Books
1996 Twentieth-Century Classics
● ed. Lindeth Vasey, 1996
intro. Peter Preston, 1996
—
The first section of *Mr Noon*
was published in 1934; the
second fragment did not appear
until 1984.

1950 Penguin Books
1989 Twentieth-Century Classics
• intro. Richard Aldington, 1950
1995 Twentieth-Century Classics
• ed. Mara Kalnins, 1995
intro. Steven Vine, 1995

Aaron's Rod 1922

Aaron Sisson abandons his family and his job at the coal mine and sets out on an adventure, paying his way by playing his flute. Once Aaron arrives in Italy, the quality of the writing 'soars [...] to a level more commensurate with Lawrence's genius', according to Richard Aldington. The character James Argyle is based on Lawrence's friend Norman Douglas (63), with whom he fell out as a result.

Kangaroo 1923

Lawrence wrote this autobiographical novel after visiting Thirroul in New South Wales. It is the story of an English writer and his German wife, who visit Australia and become embroiled with a fascist paramilitary group led by a figure known as 'Kangaroo'. One chapter, 'The Nightmare', is based on the harassment Lawrence and Frieda experienced in Cornwall during the First World War.

1950 Penguin Books
1992 Twentieth-Century Classics
• intro. Richard Aldington, 1950
1997 Twentieth-Century Classics
• ed. Bruce Steele, 1997
intro. Macdonald Daly, 1997

1971 Penguin Books
1990 Twentieth-Century Classics
—

Studies in Classic American Literature 1923

'The old American art-speech contains an alien quality, which belongs to the American continent and to nowhere else,' wrote Lawrence. 'There is a new voice in the American classics.' Lawrence describes his fascination with writers including John Fenimore Cooper, Edgar Allan Poe, Nathaniel Hawthorne, Herman Melville and Walt Whitman. In 1943, the American critic Edmund Wilson called it 'one of the few first-rate books that have ever been written on the subject'.

Three Novellas

The Fox, The Captain's Doll,
The Ladybird 1923

Lawrence was the master of the long short story and these three novellas are among his best. They all deal with the impact of the First World War on intimate relationships. In *The Fox*, two young women on a remote farm are approached by a cunning redheaded man; in *The Captain's Doll*, a German countess meets a Scottish soldier in occupied Germany; and, in *The Ladybird*, an Englishwoman becomes entranced by a German prisoner of war in London.

1973 Penguin Books
1989 Twentieth-Century Classics
1994 Twentieth-Century Classics
The Fox, The Captain's Doll,
The Ladybird
2006 Penguin Classics
ed. David Ellis, 1994
intro. Helen Dunmore, 2006

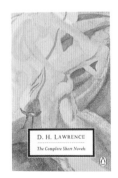

1982 Penguin English Library
1987 Penguin Classics
1990 Twentieth-Century Classics
• ed. Keith Sagar & Melissa Partridge, 1982

The Complete Short Novels also includes *St Mawr* (55), *The Princess* (1925), *The Virgin and the Gipsy* (55) and *The Escaped Cock* (1929). Lawrence summarized this last as 'a story of the Resurrection, where Jesus gets up and feels very sick about everything, and can't stand the old crowd any more – so cuts out – and as he heals up, he begins to find what an astonishing place the phenomenal world is, far more marvellous than any salvation or heaven'.

The Boy in the Bush

with M. L. Skinner 1924

Mollie Skinner was a Western Australian writer from Darlington, near Perth. She met Lawrence in 1922, when he stayed in her guest house, and she showed him her manuscript, entitled *The House of Ellis*. Lawrence took her draft and rewrote it as *The Boy in the Bush*, a novel about a young man who arrives in Australia in 1882 and is transformed and toughened by his experiences of farming, hunting, gold-mining and loving.

1963 Penguin Books
1992 Twentieth-Century Classics
1996 Twentieth-Century Classics
• ed. Paul Eggert, 1996

St Mawr
and Other Stories 1925

The critic F. R. Leavis described *St Mawr* as a 'dramatic poem'. It is the story of a wife in a loveless marriage who develops a passionate emotional bond with a bay stallion. The critic Brenda Maddox called *St Mawr* and *The Princess* 'masterworks of misogyny'.

1997 Twentieth-Century Classics
• ed. Brian Finney, 1983
intro. Charles Rossman, 1997
2006 Penguin Classics
The Woman Who Rode Away, St Mawr, The Princess
ed. Brian Finney, Christa Jansohn & Dieter Mehl, 1983–97
intro. James Lasdun, 2006
notes Paul Poplawski, 2006
—
The 1997 edition includes 'The Overtone', about a stagnant relationship, and two unfinished stories, 'The Wilful Woman' and 'The Flying Fish'; the 2006 edition, introduced by the novelist James Lasdun, includes 'The Woman Who Rode Away' and *The Princess*.

The Plumed Serpent
(Quetzalcoatl) 1926

This controversial novel follows a middle-aged Irish widow, Kate Leslie, on a visit to Mexico. She finds herself drawn to the Aztec cult of Quetzalcoatl, the 'Plumed Serpent', which awakens her sexuality and strips away the layers of her European civilization. *The Plumed Serpent* has been accused of being fascist, racist and sexist; it was disliked by L. P. Hartley (125), praised by Octavio Paz (561), and William S. Burroughs (481) found it inspirational. Lawrence said it was 'nearer to my heart than any other work of mine'.

The Virgin and the Gipsy

1926, pub. 1930

This novella, a forerunner of *Lady Chatterley's Lover* (56), is a story of love between the classes: Yvette, the daughter of an Anglican vicar, has her life transformed by a strong and enigmatic gipsy.

1950 Penguin Books
• intro. Richard Aldington, 1950
1983 Penguin English Library
1985 Penguin Classics
1990 Twentieth-Century Classics
• ed. Ronald G. Walker, 1983
1995 Twentieth-Century Classics
• ed. L. D. Clark & Virginia Crosswhite-Hyde, 1995

1950 Penguin Books
St Mawr and The Virgin and the Gipsy
1990 Twentieth-Century Classics
• intro. Richard Aldington, 1950
1970 Penguin Books
The Virgin and the Gipsi
1990 Twentieth-Century Classics
• —

Regina v. Penguin Books Ltd.

Penguin Books first published *Lady Chatterley's Lover* in the USA in 1946, in a highly abridged edition. When it published the unabridged text, in the UK in 1960, it was prosecuted under the Obscene Publications Act. 'Would you approve of your young sons, young daughters – because girls can read as well as boys – reading this book?' asked the chief prosecutor. '[...] Is it a book that you would even wish your wife or your servants to read?' The new act made exceptions for works that added to 'the public good in the interest of literature', so expert witnesses, including Allen Lane (viii), E. M. Forster (38), Richard Hoggart (136) and the Bishop of Woolwich, were called to testify to the novel's literary credentials. After six days of hearings and three hours of deliberation, the jury returned a unanimous verdict of not guilty, and this landmark case led to greater freedoms for publishing explicit material in the UK. Penguin immediately published a second edition; by the end of 1961 more than 3 million copies had been sold.

More LOVE ACROSS THE CLASS DIVIDE

Lady Chatterley's Lover 1928

Lawrence's last novel was published privately in Florence. It tells the story of Constance, Lady Chatterley, whose emotionally repressed husband, Sir Clifford, has been injured in the First World War, leaving him paralysed from the waist down. Increasingly frustrated, Constance embarks on an affair with their gamekeeper, Oliver Mellors. Their cross-class relationship, the explicit descriptions of sex and Lawrence's use of the words 'fuck' and 'cunt' led to the book being banned in the UK, the USA, Canada, Australia, India and Japan.

1946 Penguin Books (USA)
1960 Penguin Books
1961 Penguin Books
• intro. Richard Hoggart (136), 1961

1990 Twentieth-Century Classics
• intro. Richard Hoggart, 1961
1994 Twentieth-Century Classics
    2006 Penguin Classics
    ed. Michael Squires, 1994
    intro. Doris Lessing, 2006

Squires's edition includes 'A Propos of *Lady Chatterley's Lover*', Lawrence's essay in defence of the book, in which he articulates its purpose: 'I want men and women to be able to think sex, fully, completely, honestly, and cleanly. Even if we can't act sexually to our complete satisfaction, let us at least think sexually, complete and clean.'

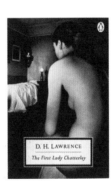

1973 Penguin Books
1989 Twentieth-Century Classics
• fwd. Frieda Lawrence, 1944

1973 Penguin Books
1989 Twentieth-Century Classics
• —

Lawrence wrote his infamous novel three times and published the third version. The initial draft was subsequently published in 1944. 'My favourite is the first draft,' wrote Frieda Lawrence in her foreword. '[...] *The First Lady Chatterley* he wrote as she came out of him, out of his own immediate self.' The second version was published in 1972 as *John Thomas and Lady Jane*.

Apocalypse
and the Writings on Revelation
1930, pub. 1931

Lawrence's last major work is a commentary on the Book of Revelation, incorporating his dying observations on psychology, science, politics, God and man's relationship with the cosmos. It is an optimistic celebration of imaginative and spiritual values.

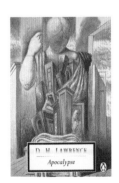

1975 Penguin Books
1990 Twentieth-Century Classics
• ed. Richard Aldington, 1932
1995 Twentieth-Century Classics
ed. Mara Kalnins, 1995

Robert Graves 1895–1985

Graves was bullied at school, so he feigned madness, wrote poetry, took up boxing and went on mountaineering trips with George Mallory, one of his teachers. As a teenager, he went straight from the school playing fields to the trenches of the First World War. His first volume of poetry, *Over the Brazier*, was published in 1916. That same year he was badly wounded during the Battle of the Somme – and he read an announcement of his own death in *The Times* at the age of 21. After the war, he suffered from severe shell shock, but he was determined to become a writer. His first marriage collapsed after six months teaching in Cairo, where he lived with his wife, four children and his mistress, the American poet Laura Riding. The success of his memoir *Goodbye to All That* allowed him to move to the mountain village of Deià on the Spanish island of Mallorca in 1934, where he based himself for most of the rest of his life. He wrote poetry, historical novels, biographies and works of mythography, and he translated several of the early Penguin Classics. He was a 'Renaissance figure', wrote the poet and novelist D. M. Thomas, 'among the most generous, self-willed, unseemly and brilliant writers of our century'.

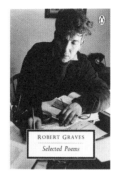

1957 Penguin Poets *Selected Poems*
● ed. Robert Graves, 1957
1986 Penguin Books
1992 Twentieth-Century Classics
● ed. Paul O'Prey, 1986
2003 Modern Classics *The Complete Poems*
ed. Beryl Graves & Dunstan Ward

Selected Poems 1910–75

'A poet's life,' wrote Graves, 'is like Alice falling down the well and clutching at the flowers and things growing out of the walls as she falls past them.' Graves penned more than 1,000 poems over seven decades. They range from 'Georgian' verses (59) and bleakly realist visions of the First World War to lyrically tender love poems, expressing deep melancholy, neurotic anxieties and an irreverent sense of humour. During the Second World War, pursuing a 'sudden overwhelming obsession', he started work on a monumental study of the poetic impulse called *The White Goddess* (1948), inspired by James Frazer's *The Golden Bough* (27). He argues that all true poetry is in subjection to a divine muse. Over the years, he met and adopted several beautiful 'muses', often much younger than himself.

Stories 1913–72

'Pure fiction is beyond my imaginative range,' admitted Graves in 1964. 'I can vouch for that,' confirms his daughter Lucia, 'having myself lived through some of the experiences described in the pieces about our family life in Mallorca.' The 52 semi-fictional stories in this collection also cover life at boarding school, life in the Roman Empire, life in the trenches, life in 1960s New York, and tales of the supernatural. They are 'the product of great imagination', wrote the *Daily Telegraph*, 'and above all of a powerful intellect'.

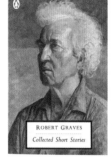

1968 Penguin Books
1991 Twentieth-Century Classics
● ed. Robert Graves, 1964

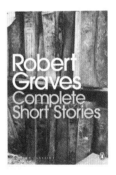

2008
ed. Lucia Graves, 1995
—
Lucia Graves is the second child of Robert and Beryl Graves. She has translated several of her father's works into Spanish, including the *Complete Short Stories*, and she has translated Spanish works into English, including the Penguin Classics edition of Emilia Pardo Bazán's *The House of Ulloa* (with Paul O'Prey) and *The Shadow of the Wind* (2001) by Carlos Ruiz Zafón.

1960 Penguin Books
1961 Modern Classics
2014 Modern Classics
ed. Fran Brearton, 2014
intro. Andrew Motion, 2014

Goodbye to All That 1929

The success of *Goodbye to All That* allowed Graves to emigrate to Mallorca, vowing 'never to make England my home again'. This candid memoir is a 'bitter leave-taking' and cost him his friendship with Siegfried Sassoon. It describes Graves's unhappy schooldays, the horrors of the Western Front, and his tempestuous marriage. It includes a handsome photograph of the Second Battalion Royal Welsh Fusiliers' regimental goat, an acrobatic beast with gilded horns that once leapt over the mess table with a drummer boy on its back.

1941 Penguin Books
2006 Modern Classics
intro. Barry Unsworth, 2006
—
Graves's primary source was *The Twelve Caesars* by Suetonius (2nd century CE), which he translated for Penguin Classics in 1957.

1955 Penguin Books
2006 Modern Classics
intro. John Julius Norwich, 2006

I, Claudius
from the Autobiography of Tiberius Claudius
1934

Stammering, limping Claudius recounts his remarkable trajectory from imbecile to emperor, drawing on decades of corruption, debauchery and insanity at the heart of imperial Rome, from the assassination of Julius Caesar in 44 BCE to the assassination of Caligula in 41 CE. The historical Claudius is known to have written an autobiography, but it has been lost.

Claudius the God
and His Wife Messalina
1935

This sequel continues with Claudius' chronicle of his 'troublesome reign', describing his surprising success in politics, and his friendship with the Jewish king, Herod Agrippa. To his bemusement, he is worshipped as a god during his lifetime at a temple in Colchester. Claudius is unwittingly manipulated by his unscrupulous wives Messalina and Agrippina, and the book concludes with descriptions of his own assassination by poisoned mushroom, by Suetonius, Tacitus, Cassius Dio and Seneca.

1943 Penguin Books
2006 Modern Classics
intro. Barry Unsworth, 2006

1986 Penguin Books
The Claudius Novels
1999 Twentieth-Century Classics
• intro. Nigel Spivey, 1999

Count Belisarius
1938

Belisarius was a 6th-century Byzantine general under the Emperor Justinian, who fought successful campaigns to reconquer North Africa and Italy. This fictional biography, which draws on *The Secret History* by Procopius, is written as if by the eunuch Eugenius, a servant of Antonina, Belisarius' ambitious wife. Winston Churchill loved this book: he told Graves he couldn't put it down.

Sergeant Lamb of the Ninth
1940

'I first came across the name of Sergeant Roger Lamb in 1914, when I was a young officer instructing my platoon in regimental history,' wrote Graves. Roger Lamb was a British soldier who fought during the American War of Independence and distinguished himself by escaping twice from American military prisons. Graves turned this historical footnote into a pair of compelling fictional memoirs, *Sergeant Lamb of the Ninth* and *Proceed, Sergeant Lamb* (1941). He was so engrossed while writing that he often absent-mindedly laid a place for the sergeant at dinner. George Orwell (80) called it 'a pendant to *Goodbye to All That* (57), an act of devotion towards the regiment with which he still feels a tie'.

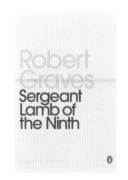

1950 Penguin Books
2012 Modern Classics
—
This and the following books by Graves were all first issued in Penguin Modern Classics with plain covers. This was an experimental way of approaching an author's minor works, but the result was rather drab, and it was not often repeated by the Penguin art department.

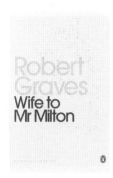

1954 Penguin Books
2011 Modern Classics
—

Wife to Mr Milton
The Story of Marie Powell 1943

These are the fictional journals of Marie Powell, who is sixteen when she is forced to marry the poet John Milton in 1642. As civil war rages around them, Marie feels increasingly stifled by her principled, puritanical and unloving husband. W. H. Auden (95), who went to Oxford, used to enjoy quoting the line about Cambridge, 'where they tune their viol strings always a little sharp'.

The Golden Fleece 1944

This retelling of the story of Jason and the Argonauts reveals the mythical cruise as 'one of the bawdiest, bloodiest, most boisterous expeditions of all time', as *Time* magazine put it.

2011
—

King Jesus 1946

Graves called this novel 'a new solution of the Nativity problem'. Christ is presented as a flawed mortal, the result of a secret marriage, a descendant of Herod and the true King of the Jews.

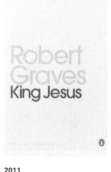

2011
—

Seven Days in New Crete

1949

In this work of science fiction, Edward Venn-Thomas is transported into the future, to the utopian paradise of New Crete. He finds it dull because evil doesn't exist, so he sets about introducing it.

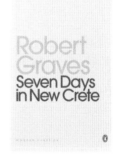

2012
—

Homer's Daughter 1955

Graves recreates the *Odyssey*, imagining its author was a young woman called Nausicaa. It is the story of a 'high-spirited and religious-minded Sicilian girl', he wrote, 'who saves her father's throne from usurpation, herself from a distasteful marriage, and her two younger brothers from butchery by boldly making things happen, instead of sitting still and hoping for the best'.

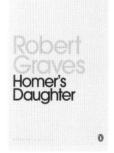

2012
—

In September 1945, Robert Graves wrote a letter to E. V. Rieu, editor of the Penguin Classics series and translator of the *Odyssey*: 'I read somewhere that [Samuel] Butler's theory of the "authoress" has Classical support of which he was unaware: Alexandrian said that "Homer" borrowed most of *The Odyssey* from an Egypto-Greek poetess called Phantasia. There is certainly something in the book which suggests the hand of a predecessor of Aphra Behn, Anita Loos (432), Amanda Ros and who was it wrote *Gone With the Wind*?'

Georgian Poetry

Georgian Poetry was the title of a 1912 anthology, edited by Edward Marsh, designed to show that poetry was 'putting on a new strength and beauty' in the early years of the reign of George V. Four further volumes were published, with poems by D. H. Lawrence (50), Robert Graves (57), G. K. Chesterton (41) and Vita Sackville-West among others. With the emergence of Imagism (61) and modernism (11), however, the term 'Georgian' came to be used pejoratively to describe conservative, conventional poetry about English rural life.

Max Beerbohm 1872–1956

Henry Maximilian Beerbohm was the son of a grain merchant. He made a reputation for himself as a dandy and a humorist in the 1890s: he was a talented caricaturist, and wrote critical and satirical essays much admired by Virginia Woolf (42). When he succeeded George Bernard Shaw (4) as the drama critic for the *Saturday Review*, Shaw referred to him as 'the incomparable Max', a moniker that stuck. In 1910, Beerbohm married the American actress Florence Kahn and they moved to Rapallo on the Italian Riviera, where he lived for the rest of his life, receiving visits from Ezra Pound (61), Somerset Maugham (32) and Truman Capote (463).

Zuleika Dobson
or, An Oxford Love Story 1911

Beerbohm's only novel is set in Edwardian Oxford, where the undergraduates are devastated by the arrival of sexy prestidigitator and former governess, Zuleika Dobson, granddaughter of the Warden of Judas College. The book features the ghosts of historical tourists and a scene in which the stone heads of the 'Emperors' around the Sheldonian Theatre break sweat at the sight of Zuleika. Having wreaked havoc in Oxford, the novel ends with Zuleika catching a train to Cambridge. It is a 'superbly written book', said E. M. Forster (38). '[…] The most consistent achievement of fantasy in our time.'

1952 Penguin Books
1961 Modern Classics
• —

Frances Hodgson Burnett

1849–1924

Frances Hodgson was born into a prosperous family in Manchester, but her father died when she was three and the family slid into poverty. When she was sixteen, they emigrated to a log cabin in rural Tennessee, where Frances ran a 'Select Seminary' of eight pupils, who paid their fees in cabbages, carrots, potatoes and eggs. A year later, she turned her hand to writing, and within fifteen years she was a successful novelist, with a family of her own, living in Washington, DC. She funded the medical degree of her first husband, Swann Burnett, and the acting career of her second, and she bought houses across England for her friends and relations. Today she is best remembered for her three children's books, *Little Lord Fauntleroy* (1886), *A Little Princess* (1905) and *The Secret Garden*.

1951 Puffin Books
1999 Twentieth-Century Classics
2011 Deluxe Classics
ed. Alison Lurie, 1999

The Secret Garden 1911

Ten-year-old orphan Mary Lennox is a 'most disagreeable-looking child' when she arrives at Misselthwaite Manor on the Yorkshire moors, until she discovers a secret walled garden in the grounds. She and her invalid cousin Colin bring the garden back to life, with the help of their friend Dickon; in the process, both of them transform into stronger, more joyful children. Burnett loved gardens: her final, posthumous work, *In the Garden* (1925), celebrated the pleasures of horticulture. *The Secret Garden* is thought to have been an inspiration for works as wide-ranging as *The Four Quartets* (1936–42) by T. S. Eliot (11) and *Lady Chatterley's Lover* by D. H. Lawrence (50).

THE PENGUIN BOOK OF FIRST WORLD WAR POETRY

The First World War produced poems of shattering realism, tenderness and regret, written by the likes of Wilfred Owen, Ivor Gurney, Siegfried Sassoon and Rupert Brooke, as well as Robert Graves (57), Rudyard Kipling (??), Ford Madox Ford (46), Herbert Read (103) and D. H. Lawrence (50), all of whom are represented in this volume. As well as English-language poets, Jon Silkin's expanded second edition includes translations of German, French, Italian and Russian verse, by poets such as Trakl, Apollinaire, Ungaretti and Anna Akhmatova (301).

1979 Penguin Poets
1981 Modern Classics
revised
• ed. Jon Silkin, 1979, 1981
2006 Penguin Classics
ed. George Walter, 2004

Charlotte Mew 1869–1928

When Charlotte Mew's father died, he left four children in straitened circumstances, two of whom were committed to mental institutions. The other two, Charlotte and her artist sister Anne, lived together in London and made a pact never to marry, for fear of passing on insanity to their children. Charlotte had her first story published in *The Yellow Book* in 1894 and published one volume of poetry in her lifetime, *The Farmer's Bride* (1916). It was extremely well received: Virginia Woolf (42) proclaimed Mew 'the greatest living poetess', and Thomas Hardy described her as 'far and away the best living woman poet – who will be read when others are forgotten'. Charlotte cut her hair short and dressed like a male dandy, but when Ann died in 1927, Charlotte sank into a depression and was eventually taken to a nursing home, where she drank disinfectant and died. A second volume of poems, *The Rambling Sailor* (1929), was published posthumously. In all her work, she aimed at 'the heart of hidden things'.

2000
• ed. John Newton

Complete Poems 1912–28

This slim volume includes all of Mew's published poems, including some that she added to the second edition of *The Farmer's Bride* (1921), as well as several earlier and uncollected poems, and a haunting prose poem called 'The Wheat'.

1960 Penguin Books
1983 Modern Classics
• –
Mackenzie's *Carnival* (1912), the tragic love story of a London ballerina and a Cornish farmer, was one of the first batch of ten Penguin books published in 1935.

Compton Mackenzie

1883–1972

Sir Edward Montague Anthony Compton Mackenzie wrote more than 100 books, including *The Monarch of the Glen* (1941) and *Whisky Galore* (1947); he wrote through the night, fuelled by Ovaltine and gramophone records. He also founded and edited the magazine *The Gramophone* and was President of the Croquet Association and the Siamese Cat Club. He lived for many years on the island of Barra in the Outer Hebrides and co-founded the Scottish National Party with his friend Hugh MacDiarmid (72).

Sinister Street 1913–14

This coming-of-age novel follows Michael and Stella Fane, the illegitimate children of wealthy parents, as they grow up and learn to love. It was considered scandalous at the time, but Henry James (397) and Max Beerbohm (60) were admirers, and it was read avidly by George Orwell (80) and Cyril Connolly (107) at school. 'This has always seemed to me one of the best novels of the best period of English writing,' wrote John Betjeman (88) – 'the Edwardian age.'

IMAGIST POETRY 1912–17

Imagism was a brief movement that emerged in 1912 under the guidance of Ezra Pound. Inspired by T. E. Hulme's preference for poetry that was 'dry and hard', the Imagists aimed at brevity and precision, taking traditional Japanese poetry and French Symbolism (303) as their models. It was a reaction against the 'doughy mess' of late-Victorian poetry, as Pound put it: an attempt at 'verbal concentration generating energy'. He published an anthology of Imagist poetry in 1914, before losing interest in favour of Vorticism (62). Three further Imagist anthologies were published in the USA between 1915 and 1917. This selection features all the poets involved in the movement, including Ezra Pound, F. S. Flint, William Carlos Williams (418), Ford Madox Ford (46), James Joyce (8), H. D. (Hilda Doolittle) and D. H. Lawrence (50).

1972 Penguin Poets
1985 Modern Classics
ed. Peter Jones, 1972

John Buchan 1875–1940

Buchan was raised in Pathhead, Fife, and walked six miles every day to attend his local school. He won a scholarship to Oxford, where he was awarded prizes for poetry and history, elected President of the Union and published five books while still a student. As well as penning a series of thrilling novels, or 'shockers' as he called them, Buchan had an active public career: he worked for the government in South Africa, the Intelligence Service during the First World War, was elected the Member of Parliament for the Scottish Universities and appointed Governor-General of Canada in 1935, a post he held until his death in 1940.

Greenmantle 1916

This sequel to *The Thirty-Nine Steps* (1915) is set during the First World War. Richard Hannay is assigned a perilous mission: to enter enemy Turkish territory and stymie a secret German plot. Hannay hurtles from Constantinople to Erzerum, in pursuit of the sinister Colonel von Stumm, the femme fatale Hilda von Einem and the mysterious 'Greenmantle'. Buchan himself was appointed Director of Information in 1917: 'the toughest job I ever took on', he later recalled.

1956 Penguin Books
2001 Modern Classics
● intro. Philip Hensher, 2001
—
Many of Buchan's novels have been published by Penguin Books, including *The Thirty-Nine Steps*, which has had several different editions, but *Greenmantle* is the only title to have appeared in Modern Classics.

Vorticism

Vorticism was an artistic and literary movement founded by Wyndham Lewis (63) and named in 1913 by Ezra Pound (61). Described at the time as 'Cubism charged with electricity', it combined Cubism, Futurism (216) and Expressionism (269), using abstract shapes to critique the machine age. Lewis described it as 'a mental-emotive impulse [...] let loose upon a lot of blocks and lines'. Pound saw the 'Vortex' as the concentrated energy of the avant-garde, blasting away the complacency of established culture. Together they published two issues of a typographically inventive manifesto-magazine (xix) called *Blast: Review of the Great English Vortex* (1914–15). Other Vorticists included T. S. Eliot (11), Jacob Epstein and Henri Gaudier-Brzeska. The group broke up after their only UK exhibition in 1915.

Wyndham Lewis

1882–1957

Percy Wyndham Lewis was born off the coast of Canada, on his father's yacht. He attended a series of English schools and studied at the Slade School of Art in London until he was expelled, after which he led a bohemian life around Europe. He became the founder of Vorticism with Ezra Pound (61), and wrote for Ford Madox Ford's (46) *English Review*. As well as novels, he wrote scathing literary critiques of his contemporaries and friends. His particular targets were D. H. Lawrence (50), the Bloomsbury Group (44) and the 'mirthless formal acrobatics' of his former drinking companion, James Joyce (8).

Lewis was an official war artist for both the Canadian and British governments during the First World War. Later in life he began to lose his eyesight, and by 1953 he was completely blind.

1982
● —
The cover shows a self-portrait by Lewis, painted in 1920.

Tarr 1916–17

Lewis's experimental first novel draws on his life in Paris. He contrasts two struggling artists: the Englishman Tarr, a version of Lewis himself, and the German Kreisler, who eerily prefigures Adolf Hitler: a failed painter with a violently Romantic imagination and protean stores of energy. V. S. Pritchett (110) called *Tarr* 'a considerable comic novel, a masterpiece of the period'.

The Wild Body
A Soldier of Humour and Other Stories 1917–27, pub. 1927

'The Wild Body,' explains Lewis, '[…] is that small, primitive, literally antediluvian vessel in which we set out on our adventures. Or regarded as a brain, it is rather a winged magic horse, that transports us hither and thither, sometimes rushing, as in the Chinese cosmogonies, up and down the outer reaches of space.' Seven stories in this collection involve Ker-Orr, the 'soldier of humour', as he and his wild body wander around the pre-war Breton countryside with a troupe of absurdist (184) circus performers. The volume also includes two essays about the 'system of feeling developed in these tales'.

2004
intro. Paul O'Keeffe

The Apes of God 1930

'It is so immense I have no words for it,' gasped T. S. Eliot (11). Lewis conceived *The Apes of God* as part of a 'megalo-mastodonic masterwork' entitled *The Man of the World*. This satirical novel demolishes the cultural life of London in the 1920s, with stinging, recognizable portraits of Lytton Strachey (64), the literary Sitwell family, Edward Wadsworth (another Vorticist) and many others. Set in the days leading up to the General Strike of 1926, it follows a young simpleton called Dan Boleyn, under the direction of an infatuated 60-year-old albino, as he meets a series of literary charlatans. Chapter titles include 'Dick', 'Lesbian-Ape' and 'Pamela Farnham's Tea-Party'.

1965
● —
Wyndham Lewis illustrated
The Apes of God himself.

The Revenge for Love 1937

In the months before the Spanish Civil War, communist agitator Percy Hardcaster is wounded escaping from a prison in Andalusia and returns to London a hero; but all is not as it seems. This is a nightmarish vision of a world riddled with deceit, false propaganda, and brutal secrets behind smiling masks. 'As I was reading my proofs,' wrote Lewis, 'I realized that the book that is thus to be contemptuously flung upon the market is probably the best work of fiction I have written.'

1972 Modern Classics
2004 Modern Classics
intro. Paul Edwards, 2004

Norman Douglas 1868–1952

In his twenties, Douglas was briefly a diplomat in St Petersburg, until he was sacked amidst a sexual scandal. In 1916 he jumped bail in London on a charge of indecent assault against a 16-year-old boy, and removed himself to Italy and then France as further scandals caught up with him. He wrote several travel books and one successful novel, *South Wind*. His last years were spent on the island of Capri, where he died of a deliberate drugs overdose while suffering from an excruciating illness. His last words are said to have been: 'Get those fucking nuns away from me.'

South Wind 1917

Thomas Heard is an Anglican bishop who visits Nepenthe, a thinly fictionalized version of Capri, on his way home to England from his bishopric in Africa. Almost immediately, he is seduced by the perfumed air and the pleasurable, pagan, hedonistic feelings that overwhelm him. The south wind of the title is the sirocco, said to blow away one's morals. Douglas said that he'd put into *South Wind* all the known sins, as well as some previously unknown ones.

1935 Penguin Books
1962 Modern Classics
1987 Modern Classics
● intro. Norman Lewis, 1987

Lytton Strachey 1880–1932

At Cambridge University, Giles Lytton Strachey befriended Leonard Woolf, Clive Bell and Thoby Stephen, subsequently becoming the linchpin of the Bloomsbury Group (44). He wrote book reviews and contributed to the *Spectator*, before the success of *Eminent Victorians* made his name as a biographer. He was the model for characters in *Maurice* (39) by E. M. Forster, *The Apes of God* (63) by Wyndham Lewis and Virginia Woolf's *The Waves* (45). He had a lifelong platonic relationship with the artist Dora Carrington, who married Strachey's lover Ralph Partridge in order to form a *ménage à trois* at Ham Spray House in Wiltshire.

Eminent Victorians 1918

Strachey pioneered a new form of irreverent biography based around the witty debunking of inflated reputations. His subjects in *Eminent Victorians* are the pompous headmaster Thomas Arnold, the busybody Florence Nightingale, the drunken General Gordon of Khartoum and the ambitious Cardinal Manning. It is 'the work of a great anarch', wrote Cyril Connolly (107).

1948 Penguin Books
1976 Modern Classics
1989 Twentieth-Century Classics
intro. Michael Holroyd, 1986

1971
• —

Queen Victoria 1921

Strachey's second work of Victorian biography focuses on Queen Victoria herself. Virginia Woolf (42), to whom the book is dedicated, wrote: 'In time to come Lytton Strachey's Queen Victoria will be Queen Victoria, just as Boswell's Johnson is now Dr Johnson. The other versions will fade and disappear.'

1950 Penguin Books
1971 Modern Classics
• —

Elizabeth and Essex
A Tragic History 1928

This book was an experiment for Strachey: through psychological detective work and reconstructions bordering on historical fiction, he reveals the complexities of Elizabeth's relationship with one of her favourite and much younger courtiers, who 'satisfied the peculiar cravings of a virgin of sixty-three'.

Ronald Firbank 1886–1926

Arthur Annesley Ronald Firbank wrote just eight novellas and spent most of his life either travelling abroad or sitting in the Café Royal in London. 'He was truly a habitué of that faded, jaded room,' recalled Holt Marvell, a contemporary writer. 'Some days he sat from noon until midnight in his accustomed seat – to the right as you swing through the door. A thin man with a black felt hat. A narrow man and restless – writhing like a basket of serpents.' Firbank was openly gay, extremely shy and had a weak constitution, which he plied with alcohol and cannabis. He was received into the Catholic Church while at university, and died in Rome at the age of 40.

Valmouth
and Other Stories 1919–26
Valmouth, Prancing N—, Concerning the Eccentricities of Cardinal Pirelli

Firbank's plots are wispy and his dialogue fragmentary but the results are stylish. *Valmouth* (1919) is set in a seaside health resort in England, populated by unfeasibly elderly patrons. It was adapted as a stage musical in 1958. *Prancing N—* (1924) is about an ambitious Caribbean family and their attempts to climb the social ladder. *Concerning the Eccentricities of Cardinal Pirelli* (1926) opens with the eponymous prelate christening a dog and ends with him collapsing, naked, while pursuing a choirboy around an altar.

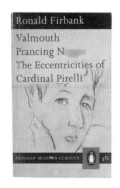

1961
• —

Prancing N— was originally published as *Sorrow in Sunlight* in the UK. It is unclear why the 1961 Penguin edition adopted the US title instead of keeping the original. The portrait sketch on the cover is by Augustus John, whom Firbank befriended at the Eiffel Tower restaurant on the Tottenham Court Road in London.

1986
• intro. John Mortimer (139)

The Flower Beneath the Foot

Being a Record of the Early Life of St Laura de Nazianzi and the Times in which She Lived 1923

In the fabulous kingdom of Pisuerga, somewhere in the Balkans, the unconventional inhabitants worry about fleas at the Ritz in between planning elaborate parties. Characters include His Weariness Prince Yousef, Her Dreaminess the Queen, Countess Medusa Rappa and Dr Cunliffe Babcock. At one point, a Miss Hopkins mentions that she met a writer called Ronald Firbank, who told her that 'writing books was by no means easy'.

Three Novels

The Flower Beneath the Foot, Sorrow in Sunlight, Concerning the Eccentricities of Cardinal Pirelli
1923–6

Firbank's last three novels are 'works of remarkable economy, brilliant humour and disconcerting pathos', writes Alan Hollinghurst. 'Each of Firbank's novels is a daring experiment in style and form. He threw away almost everything he inherited from the Victorian novel, and what he retained he treated in bizarre and unpredictable ways.'

2000
• intro. Alan Hollinghurst

Aldous Huxley 1894–1963

Huxley was known as 'Ogie' as a child, short for 'Ogre', because his head was so large. Before he made his name as a novelist, he worked as a farm labourer at Garsington Manor during the First World War and as a French teacher at Eton, where George Orwell (80) and Steven Runciman (121) were among his pupils. In the 1920s he lived in Italy, where he befriended D. H. Lawrence (50), before spending time in France and eventually moving to California in 1937, where Christopher Isherwood (103) introduced him to Vedanta philosophy and he experimented with vegetarianism, meditation and mescaline. He wrote screenplays and used the pay cheques to transport refugees out of Hitler's Germany. Huxley died from cancer on the same day that C. S. Lewis died, which was also the same day that President John F. Kennedy was assassinated: 22 November 1963.

Crome Yellow 1921

Huxley's first novel is a country-house satire, inspired by Lady Ottoline Morrell's literary parties at Garsington Manor, with recognizable portraits of Bertrand Russell, Norman Douglas (63) and the former Prime Minister H. H. Asquith. T. S. Eliot borrowed the name of Sesostris, the bogus fortune-teller, for *The Waste Land* (11), which was published the following year. It was while working at Garsington that Huxley met his first wife, the Belgian refugee Maria Nys.

Aldous Huxley
Crome Yellow

1936 Penguin Books
1962 Modern Classics
• —

Huxley's Modern Classics covers were illustrated by the muralist Leonard Rosoman, who had made his name painting scenes of firefighting during the Blitz.

Aldous Huxley
Antic Hay

1948 Penguin Books
1962 Modern Classics
• —

Antic Hay 1923

'My men like satyrs grazing on the lawns / Shall with their goat-feet dance the antic hay,' declares Gaveston in Christopher Marlowe's *Edward II* (1592). Set in bohemian London, in the years after the First World War, *Antic Hay* revolves around Theodore Gumbril, inventor of Gumbril's Patent Small-Clothes, and his convoluted quest for love.

Those Barren Leaves 1925

Mrs Aldwinkle gathers a group of would-be intellectuals in an Italian *castello*, including the editor of *The Rabbit Fancier's Gazette*. 'It is brilliant and daring,' wrote Leonard Woolf, 'admirably written, humorous, witty, clever, cultured.' The title comes from Wordsworth: 'Enough of science and of art; / Close up those barren leaves.'

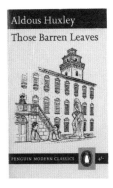

Aldous Huxley
Those Barren Leaves

1951 Penguin Books
1961 Modern Classics
• —

Point Counter Point 1928

This intricate comic novel is constructed out of a series of debates, interwoven like musical counterpoint. Most of the characters are drawn from reality, such as the diabolic Maurice Spandrell, based on Baudelaire; the author Mark Rampion, based on D. H. Lawrence (50); the painter John Bidlake, based on Augustus John; and the writer Philip Quarles, a self-portrait of Huxley himself. While Lord Edward Tantamount dissects tadpoles in his attic laboratory, his wife hosts a party in the great hall below, and the fascist Everard Webley is murdered.

1955 Penguin Books
<u>**1961**</u> Modern Classics
• —

Brief Candles
Four Stories 1930

This collection consists of *After the Fireworks*, a novella about a celebrated author who is doggedly pursued by a younger woman, and three short stories: 'Chawdron', 'The Rest Cure' and 'The Claxtons'.

1965
• —

Brave New World 1932

In Huxley's chilling dystopian vision, genetically calibrated citizens of the 'World State' live in a predetermined social hierarchy based on intelligence. Death is devoid of emotion and peace is maintained through the distribution of a happiness drug. Bernard Marx, a psychologist, comes to resent this bland environment, and attempts to embarrass his superiors by rescuing a naturally born, Shakespeare-quoting man from New Mexico, a 'Savage Reservation'. In his long essay *Brave New World Revisited* (1958), Huxley observed that the fictions in his novel were starting to manifest themselves in reality.

1955 Penguin Books
<u>**1961**</u> Modern Classics
• —

More DYSTOPIAS

The Man in the High Castle
by Philip K. Dick 520

Make Room! Make Room!
by Harry Harrison 530

Nineteen Eighty-Four
by George Orwell 84

Anthem
by Ayn Rand 450

Day of the Oprichnik
by Vladimir Sorokin 318

After Many a Summer 1939

In this nightmarish parable, a Hollywood millionaire sets out to prolong the span of human life indefinitely. He hires the scientist Dr Obispo, who examines long-living carp, crocodiles and parrots before tracing a clue in an 18th century book that leads to a pair of what appear to be 200-year-old apes.

Eyeless in Gaza
1936

In a mosaic of fragmented episodes, we find Anthony Beavis growing up as a vapid socialite before discovering pacifism and seeking a deeper meaning to his life. The title comes from Milton's *Samson Agonistes* (1671). In her memoir *Jigsaw* (261), Sybille Bedford reveals that she and her mother were the basis for the addict Mary Amberley and her daughter; they were Huxley's neighbours in southern France.

1955 Penguin Books
<u>**1962**</u> Modern Classics
• —

1955 Penguin Books
<u>**1961**</u> Modern Classics
• —

Evelyn Waugh 1903–1966

Arthur Evelyn St John Waugh wrote his first short story, 'The Curse of the Horse Race', at the age of seven. As a young man he taught in prep schools, considered becoming a cabinet-maker and attempted suicide on a Welsh beach, an effort that failed due to a shoal of jellyfish. He married Evelyn Gardner in 1928 and they became known as 'He-Evelyn' and 'She-Evelyn', but he filed for divorce the following year and converted to Catholicism. The success of his second novel, *Vile Bodies* (68), allowed him to become a professional writer. He was a proud snob and one of the finest comic novelists in the English language.

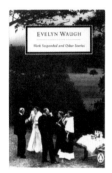
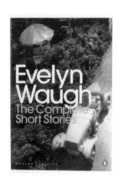

1951 Penguin Books
<u>1989</u> Twentieth-Century
Classics
—

2011
—

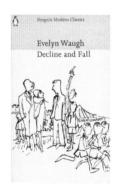

1937 Penguin Books
<u>1964</u> Modern Classics
2001 Modern Classics
● ed. David Bradshaw, 2001
2018 Modern Classics

Decline and Fall

1928, rev. 1962

After Paul Pennyfeather is dragged into a Bollinger Club prank and sent down from Oxford, he takes a position as a schoolmaster at an eccentric Welsh preparatory school. His teaching career culminates at a calamitous sports day, when Lady Circumference's son Tangent is shot in the foot by the starting pistol, and Paul meets the alluring and mysterious Margot Beste-Chetwynde. The title is a reference to Edward Gibbon's *Decline and Fall of the Roman Empire* (1776–88), which Waugh was reading as he worked on the novel. 'Please bear in mind throughout,' wrote Waugh, in his author's note, 'IT IS MEANT TO BE FUNNY.'

A Little Order
Selected Journalism

1921–64

'The aim of this selection is to provide a conspectus of Waughism,' writes the editor, Donat Gallagher; 'of the opinions, attitudes, interests, and styles most representative of the full range of his journalism.' The pieces, on subjects such as Hogarth, Hollywood, P. G. Wodehouse (48) and Graham Greene (88), are arranged under five facets of Waugh's identity: 'Myself', 'Aesthete', 'Man of Letters', 'Conservative' and 'Catholic'.

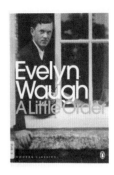

2010
ed. Donat Gallagher, 1977

Stories 1925–63

Waugh's immaculately turned stories include the chilling 'Mr Loveday's Little Outing', about a mild-mannered lunatic, and the novella *Work Suspended* (1939), in which a thriller writer puts his manuscript on hold during the Second World War, and which was itself interrupted by Waugh's own military service. 'Basil Seal Rides Again' details the further adventures of the scurrilous hero of *Black Mischief* (68) and *Put Out More Flags* (69), and 'Charles Ryder's Schooldays' is a posthumously published glimpse of the narrator of *Brideshead Revisited* (69).

Labels
A Mediterranean Journal 1930

Waugh presents an account of his honeymoon cruise with 'She-Evelyn', his wife, around the Mediterranean as far as Egypt. 'I have called this book *Labels*,' wrote Waugh, 'for the reason that all the places I visited on this trip are already fully labelled. [...] I suppose there is no track quite so soundly beaten as the Mediterranean seaboard.' Nonetheless, he makes observations that are 'totally honest, wise as well as clever, and practical', as Kingsley Amis (132) put it.

1985 Penguin Travel Library
<u>1995</u> Twentieth-Century Classics
—

1938 Penguin Books
1961 Modern Classics
1996 Twentieth-Century
Classics
● ed. Richard Jacobs, 1996
2012 Modern Classics
—
The early Modern Classics
editions of Waugh's novels
were illustrated by Quentin
Blake.

Vile Bodies
1930, rev. 1965

'The composition of *Vile Bodies*
was interrupted by a sharp
disturbance in my private life,'
wrote Waugh in his preface,
'and was finished in a very
different mood from that in
which it was begun.' The novel
satirizes twenties' Mayfair, its
lingo, parties, love affairs and
the threat of ennui. Stephen Fry
calls it 'Britain's *Great Gatsby* (424)'
and he adapted it for the screen
as *Bright Young Things* (2003),
the book's original working title.
'I think I can claim that this was
the first English novel in which
dialogue on the telephone plays
a large part,' mused Waugh.

Ninety-Two Days
The Account of a Tropical
Journey through British
Guiana and Part of Brazil
1934

'Who in his senses will read,
still less buy, a travel book of
no scientific value about a place
he has no intention of visiting?'
asks Waugh, at the start of
this chronicle. He describes
a difficult and dangerous journey
through the jungles of South
America, meeting preachers,
ranchers and vagabonds, getting
eaten alive by cabouri flies and
sampling the local *cassiri*, a pink
cocktail made from chewed
cassava root and spittle.

1986 Penguin Travel Library
1995 Twentieth-Century
Classics
● —

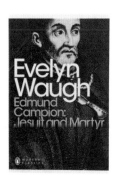

1953 Penguin Books
2012 Modern Classics
—

Edmund Campion
Jesuit and Martyr
1935

This is a biography of the
Elizabethan Jesuit priest who
was arrested for conducting
Catholic services, convicted
of treason and hanged, drawn
and quartered at Tyburn.

1985 Penguin Travel Library
1995 Twentieth-Century
Classics
—

1938 Penguin Books
1961 Modern Classics
2011 Modern Classics
—
The 2011 edition retains
Waugh's own illustrations.

1951 Penguin Books
1961 Modern Classics
1997 Twentieth-Century
Classics
● ed. Robert Murray Davis,
1997
2018 Modern Classics
—

Remote People
A Report from Ethiopia and
British Africa
1931

This travelogue opens with an
account of the 1930 coronation
of Emperor Haile Selassie of
Ethiopia, an event that Waugh
covered as a special correspondent
for *The Times*, and it continues
with descriptions of his journeys
around 'British Africa' and the
Belgian Congo.

Black Mischief
1932, rev. 1962

Inspired by the same trip
that produced *Remote People*,
this novel follows the
Oxford-educated Emperor
Seth, who succeeds to the
throne of the independent
African island state of Azania.
He attempts to reorganize his
country with the aid of his
feckless university friend, the
Minister of Modernization,
Basil Seal. Waugh's apparent
intention – to demonstrate that
African nations are ludicrously
incapable of governing
themselves – today seems both
racist and demonstrably untrue.

A Handful of Dust
1934, rev. 1964

As Waugh's own marriage was
unravelling, he wrote this novel
about Lady Brenda Last, bored
of life at Hetton Abbey and of
her dutiful husband Tony. She
embarks on a shallow love affair,
spending more and more time in
Belgravia, while Tony encounters
a Dickens-obsessed maniac in
the Amazon rainforest. Waugh
took the title from T. S. Eliot's
The Waste Land (11).

1986 Penguin Travel Library
1995 Twentieth-Century
Classics
—

Waugh in Abyssinia 1936

In 1935, Waugh returned to Ethiopia as a reporter, to cover the fighting between Italy and Abyssinia. His account features corrupt officials, Arab spies, and radicals in pyjamas. The first chapter is called 'The Intelligent Woman's Guide to the Ethiopian Question', a parody of George Bernard Shaw's 1928 title (4).

Put Out More Flags

1942, rev. 1967

1943 Penguin Books
1961 Modern Classics
2000 Modern Classics
● intro. Nigel Spivey, 2000
2018 Modern Classics
—

'A drunk military man should order gallons,' runs the Chinese adage, 'and put out more flags in order to increase his military splendour.' Written on a troopship in 1941, and based on Waugh's experiences of the early months of the Second World War, *Put Out More Flags* is a novel about Basil Seal, the upper-class scoundrel from *Black Mischief* (68), who welcomes the war as an opportunity for action, adventure and advancement. It also features returning characters from *Decline and Fall* (67) and *Vile Bodies* (68). It was the only book that Waugh wrote 'purely for pleasure'.

When the Going was Good 1946

1951 Penguin Books
1990 Twentieth-Century
Classics
—

In this travel anthology, Waugh collected 'all that I wish to preserve of the four travel books I wrote between the years 1929 and 1935: *Labels* (67), *Remote People* (68), *Ninety-Two Days* (68) and (a title not of my own choosing) *Waugh in Abyssinia*. [...] I never aspired to being a great traveller. I was simply a young man, typical of my age; we travelled as a matter of course. I rejoice that I went when the going was good.'

1944 Penguin Books
1961 Modern Classics
2000 Modern Classics
● intro. Christopher Hitchens, 2000
2018 Modern Classics
—
'In the pages of *Scoop*, we encounter Waugh at the mid-season point of his perfect pitch,' wrote Christopher Hitchens; 'youthful and limber and light as a feather.'

Scoop
A Novel about Journalists

1938, rev. 1964

Scoop is 'the funniest novel ever written about journalism', declared the *Observer*. The newspaper magnate Lord Copper, owner of the *Daily Beast*, sends William Boot to cover a 'very promising little war' in the African Republic of Ishmaelia, on the strength of a mistaken luncheon-party tip. Despite his inexperience as a foreign correspondent – Boot was previously the author of the *Beast*'s nature column, 'Lush Places' – he does bungle his way into scooping a major story. The novel features a reappearance of Lady Metroland, formerly Margot Beste-Chetwynde in *Decline and Fall* (67). In 2008 an American news website called *The Daily Beast* was launched.

Brideshead Revisited
The Sacred and Profane Memories of Captain Charles Ryder

1945, rev. 1960

1951 Penguin Books
1962 Modern Classics
pref. Evelyn Waugh, 1960
—
Waugh included a cryptic disclaimer: 'I am not I: thou art not he or she: they are not they.'

'I have read *Brideshead Revisited* at least a dozen times and have never failed to be charmed and moved,' wrote Anthony Burgess (148). When Captain Charles Ryder's battalion arrives at its new camp, he discovers they have been stationed at Brideshead Castle, the palatial home of the Flyte family. At Oxford, Charles was besotted by the airy Sebastian Flyte, and later by his sister Julia and the rest of the family. Their house was a paradise and visiting again brings back a torrent of memories. *Brideshead Revisited* proved extraordinarily popular, elevating Waugh to 'an unfamiliar world of fan-mail and press photographers'. It was his first explicitly Catholic novel, an attempt to describe 'the operation of Grace', as he later explained, 'that is to say, the unmerited and unilateral act of love by which God continually calls souls to Himself'.

The Loved One
An Anglo-American Tragedy

1948, rev. 1965

While visiting Hollywood to meet a producer about a proposed film adaptation of *Brideshead Revisited* (69), Waugh made a trip to the Forest Lawn Memorial Park cemetery. In this darkly comic novel, a British pet mortician is inducted into the American art of death at the Whispering Glades Memorial Park, alongside Aimée the corpse beautician – 'the loved one' – and Mr Joyboy the embalmer. The book is dedicated to Nancy Mitford (117).

1951 Penguin Books
1961 Modern Classics
—

Helena 1950

Set in the 4th century CE, this historical novel tells the story of the Empress Helena, mother of Constantine the Great, and her quest to recover the relics of the True Cross. Waugh's daughter Harriet recalled that it was 'the only one of his books that he ever cared to read aloud'.

1963 Penguin Books
1990 Twentieth-Century Classics
—

The Sword of Honour Trilogy

Men at Arms, Officers and Gentlemen, Unconditional Surrender

1952–61, rev. 1965

Sword of Honour was the name Waugh gave to his devastating trilogy of Second World War novels. They are 'unquestionably the finest novels to have come out of the war', wrote Cyril Connolly (107). In *Men at Arms* (1952), an enthusiastic Guy Crouchback takes a commission in the Royal Corps of Halberdiers, but is disappointed by the lack of action during an abortive campaign in West Africa. Guy joins a Commando unit in *Officers and Gentlemen* (1955) and trains on the whisky-soaked Hebridean Isle of Mugg, before taking part in the shattering Battle of Crete. In *Unconditional Surrender* (1961), Guy finally loses the last of his romantic illusions and faces the real horror and futility of war. This last instalment is dedicated to Waugh's daughter Margaret, 'Child of the Locust Years', who was born in 1942.

In 1965, Waugh produced an adapted single-volume edition called *Sword of Honour*. This compilation includes several variations: Waugh changed the ending to leave Guy Crouchback childless, for instance. 'No nippers for Guy,' he wrote to Nancy Mitford (117). Waugh's correspondence with Mitford is published in Modern Classics as *The Letters of Nancy Mitford and Evelyn Waugh* (117).

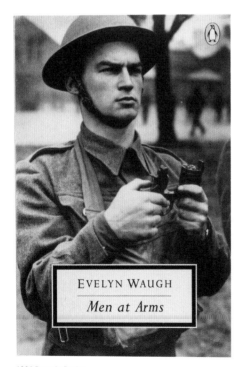

1964 Penguin Books
1990 Twentieth-Century Classics
—

1964 Penguin Books
1990 Twentieth-Century Classics
—

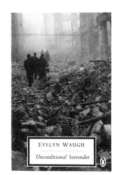

1964 Penguin Books
1990 Twentieth-Century Classics
—

1984 Penguin Books
1991 Twentieth-Century Classics
1999 Twentieth-Century Classics
ed. Angus Calder, 1999

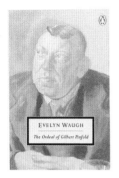

The Ordeal of Gilbert Pinfold
A Conversation Piece 1957

In this semi-autobiographical novel, Waugh depicts a successful novelist afflicted by paranoia and memory loss. Pinfold takes a restorative cruise to Sri Lanka, but the journey aboard the *Caliban* turns into a nightmare of voices and visions. Waugh had experienced similar symptoms on a trip to Sri Lanka in 1954: he was plagued by voices and believed he was possessed by devils.

1962 Penguin Books
1989 Twentieth-Century Classics
• fwd. Richard Jacobs, 1989
2011 Modern Classics

The 1962 and 1989 editions also included the story 'Tactical Exercise' and the fantastical novel *Love Among the Ruins* (1953).

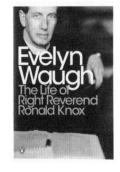

The Life of Right Reverend Ronald Knox
1959

2011
–

Just before his old friend Ronald Knox died in 1957, Waugh asked permission to write his biography. He describes the Oxford chaplain and writer of detective fiction as a 'wit and scholar marked out for popularity and fame; the boon companion of a generation of legendary heroes; the writer of effortless felicity and versatility'. Twenty years later, Knox's niece, the novelist Penelope Fitzgerald, published a new biography of Knox and his three brothers.

A Little Learning
The First Volume of an Autobiography 1964

This is the opening instalment of an autobiography that Waugh never completed. It draws on his early diaries, which he began at the age of seven, describing his childhood in Hampstead, his school years, life at Oxford and the experience of teaching at a prep school in Wales. It is dedicated to his grandchildren.

1983 Penguin Books
1990 Twentieth-Century Classics
–

R. H. Tawney 1880–1962

Richard Henry Tawney was Professor of Economic History at the London School of Economics for eighteen years. He was a social moralist who tutored for the Workers' Educational Association and campaigned for equal opportunities. During the First World War, he was injured on the first day of the Battle of the Somme and lay in no man's land for 30 hours until he could be stretchered out.

Religion and the Rise of Capitalism
A Historical Study 1922, pub. 1926

Tawney's classic study builds on Max Weber's concept of the Protestant work ethic, drawing connections between the emergence of Protestantism and the development of capitalism. 'A society which reverences the attainment of riches as the supreme felicity will naturally be disposed to regard the poor as damned in the next world,' he wrote, 'if only to justify itself for making their life a hell in this.'

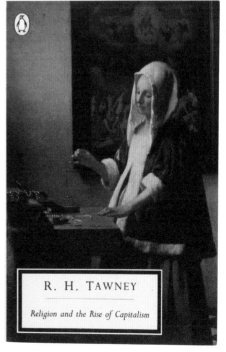

1938 Pelican Books
1984 Peregrine Books
1990 Twentieth-Century Classics
• pref. Charles Gore, 1926

William Gerhardie 1895 – 1977

William Alexander Gerhardi was born in St Petersburg to British parents. He applied for an officer's commission in the First World War and was posted to the British embassy in his home city. He witnessed the Russian Revolution and took part in the British military mission to Siberia during the Russian Civil War, for which he was awarded both an OBE and the imperial Russian Order of St Stanislaus. He moved to England and began publishing novels, later adding an 'e' to the end of his name. 'I have talent,' Evelyn Waugh (67) told Gerhardie, 'but you have genius.'

1942 Penguin Books
1974 Modern Classics *revised*
● pref. Michael Holroyd, 1971
—
Futility was first published with a preface by Edith Wharton (401), after Katherine Mansfield (388) had forwarded Gerhardie's manuscript to the publisher Thomas Cobden-Sanderson. 'It is a living book,' Mansfield enthused. 'What I mean by that is it is warm; one can put it down and it goes on breathing.'

Futility
A Novel on Russian Themes 1922

Gerhardie's first novel is the poignant story of an Englishman raised in Russia, who falls in love with Nina, the second of three beautiful daughters. He has expectations of a fortune, but it does not materialize. 'I'll wait,' he says repeatedly. 'I don't think it can be long now.'

Of Mortal Love 1936

Dinah is a woman 'not meant to live alone' and she cultivates several ardent lovers. The story anatomizes the successive stages of love: desire, fantasy, tenderness and transfiguration. The novelist C. P. Snow called it 'one of the most wonderful books of a generation'.

1982
● —

Hugh MacDiarmid

1892 – 1978

1985 Modern Classics
The Complete Poems
in two volumes
● ed. Michael Grieve
& W. R. Aitken
1994 Twentieth-Century
Classics *Selected Poems*
● ed. Alan Riach
& Michael Grieve, 1992
—
Michael Grieve was a journalist and television producer, the Vice-Chairman of the Scottish National Party, and Hugh MacDiarmid's son.

Christopher Murray Grieve, the son of a postman, was born in the Dumfriesshire weaving town of Langholm. After the First World War, he settled in Montrose, where he published lyrical poetry under the pen name 'Hugh MacDiarmid', catalysing the Scottish Renaissance movement. A lifelong communist, he helped to found the Scottish National Party with Compton Mackenzie (61) in 1928. He lived for a time in a remote croft in the Shetland Islands, before moving to Biggar in Lanarkshire in 1951, to a house with no indoor sanitation or electric lighting. 'For 50 years this man's hot and angry integrity radiated through Scotland,' ran his obituary in the *Scotsman*. 'There is very little written, acted, composed, surmised or demanded in Scotland which does not in some strand descend from the new beginning he made.'

Poems 1923 – 76

MacDiarmid 'has set himself a task which is at once reactionary and revolutionary', wrote John Buchan (62). 'He would treat Scots as a living language and apply it to matters which have been foreign to it since the sixteenth century.' MacDiarmid revived the use of Scots as a literary language in collections such as *Sangschaw* (1925) and *Penny Wheep* (1926), and most notably in his book-length poem *A Drunk Man Looks at the Thistle* (1926). He sought to assimilate the distinctive techniques of modernism (11) with deep-rooted Scottish poetic traditions.

The Scottish Renaissance

In 1922, Hugh MacDiarmid predicted a 'Scottish Renascence as swift and irresistible as was the Belgian Revival between 1880 and 1910'. Inspired by the Irish Literary Revival (6), MacDiarmid championed innovative, rooted Scottish literature, and wrote the first great work of the movement: the long poem *A Drunk Man Looks at the Thistle* (1926). Other writers associated with the Scottish Renaissance include Edwin Muir, Neil M. Gunn, Eric Linklater (96) and, above all, Lewis Grassic Gibbon, whose trilogy, *A Scots Quair* (100), was its greatest achievement.

F. M. Mayor 1872–1932

Flora Macdonald Mayor was the daughter of a Cambridge clergyman. She read history at Newnham College, Cambridge, and became an actress and a writer; her ghost stories were admired by M. R. James (40). When her fiancé, an architect, died of typhoid fever in India, she returned to her family at the age of 30 and lived with siblings for the rest of her life.

The Rector's Daughter 1924

'*The Rector's Daughter* is a masterpiece,' writes Susan Hill. 'It is a blisteringly honest account of middle-aged desire, that most painful of afflictions.' Mary, the daughter of Canon Jocelyn, devotes her life to her father in 'an insignificant village in the Eastern counties', until she meets the powerfully attractive Robert Herbert.

1973 Modern Classics
1992 Twentieth-Century Classics
● intro. Susan Hill, 1992

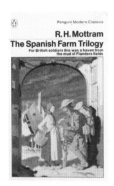

1936 Penguin Books
The Spanish Farm
1979 Modern Classics
● —
When the trilogy was first published in a single volume in 1927, Mottram added three short interstitial chapters, 'D'Archeville', 'The Winner' and 'The Stranger', which are included in this edition.

R. H. Mottram

1883–1971

Ralph Hale Mottram was a bank clerk from Norwich, whose literary ambitions were encouraged by John Galsworthy (47). He went on to become a prolific novelist and was elected Lord Mayor of Norwich in 1953.

The Spanish Farm Trilogy, 1914–1918

The Spanish Farm, Sixty-Four, Ninety-Four, The Crime at Vanderlynden's 1924–7

'The farmer wore a Dutch cap, spoke Flemish by preference, but could only write French,' opens this trilogy. 'His farm was called Ferme l'Espagnole – The Spanish Farm – and stood on French soil.' These three books centre around the titular Nord farm, its inhabitants and the exhausted British soldiers who find an oasis of stability within its sturdy walls. In 1927, the *Times Literary Supplement* called it 'perhaps the most significant work of its kind in English that the War has yet occasioned'.

Beatrice Webb 1858–1943

Beatrice Potter was a socialist campaigner who collaborated with Charles Booth on his influential surveys of London working-class conditions before she married Sidney Webb, with whom she helped to found the London School of Economics, the *New Statesman* and the Fabian Society. The couple were satirized by H. G. Wells in *The New Machiavelli* (27).

My Apprenticeship 1926

Webb describes her Victorian upbringing and her partnerships with Charles Booth and Sidney Webb. Her memoir is 'a unique volume of confessions', wrote George Bernard Shaw (4), 'to say nothing of its record of contacts with all sorts and conditions of men […]. And these are no mere staring and gabbling reminiscences, but judgements and generalizations which give depth to the narrative and value to the time spent in conning it.'

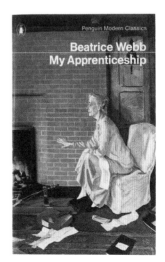

1938 Pelican Books *in two volumes*
1971 Modern Classics
● intro. Brian Jackson, 1970

The cover of the 1971 edition shows a detail from *Sidney and Beatrice Webb* (1928–9) by William Nicholson, which hangs in the Shaw Library at the London School of Economics.

T. E. Lawrence

1888 – 1935

Before the outbreak of the First World War, Thomas Edward Lawrence was in Ottoman Syria, assisting a British Museum excavation on the Euphrates. He signed up and began working for British Intelligence in the Middle East, where he became instrumental in coordinating the revolt of Arab tribesmen against the Ottoman Empire, ultimately leading to the fall of Damascus in 1918. These exploits made him a legendary figure, known as 'Lawrence of Arabia', which was also the title of a major 1962 biopic film. After the war, he worked as the advisor on Arab affairs in the Colonial Office, under Winston Churchill, but became disillusioned with British policy in the Middle East and his own legendary status, so he resigned in 1922. He joined the Royal Air Force secretly, under an assumed name, and served as an ordinary aircraftman until he retired in 1935. Two months later, he died in a motorcycle accident near his home in Dorset, on his way home from sending a telegram to Henry Williamson (77). 'I am not a very tractable person or much of a hero-worshipper,' wrote John Buchan (62), 'but I could have followed Lawrence over the edge of the world.'

1962
—
Seven Pillars of Wisdom was initially published privately in 1926, with illustrations by several artists including Augustus John and Paul Nash. An abridged edition, *Revolt in the Desert*, was published in 1927, but a complete text only became publicly available in 1935, after Lawrence's death. The title comes from the Book of Proverbs (9:1): 'Wisdom hath builded her house, she hath hewn out her seven pillars.'

Seven Pillars of Wisdom
A Triumph   1926, 1935

This is Lawrence's account of the Arab Revolt during the First World War, incorporating essays on military strategy and revealing passages of autobiography. 'It ranks with the greatest books ever written in the English language,' wrote Winston Churchill. 'As a narrative of war and adventure it is unsurpassable.' It had a troubled gestation, partly because Lawrence lost the manuscript in 1919 while changing trains at Reading station. His first draft was edited by his friend George Bernard Shaw (4) and the book opens with a dedicatory love poem addressed 'To S.A.', who was probably Lawrence's one-time companion, Selim Ahmed, a young Syrian boy.

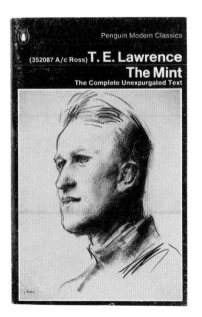

1978
● note A. W. Lawrence, 1936 pref. J. M. Wilson, 1978
—
Professor A. W. Lawrence was an authority on classical sculpture. He was T. E. Lawrence's youngest brother and his literary executor. For the 1955 edition, he revised the text, incorporating handwritten amendments made by Lawrence between 1928 and 1935.

The Mint
by 352087 A/c Ross
1928, pub. 1936, rev. 1955

The title of Lawrence's account of his Royal Air Force training and service compares the recruits to coins, minted from metal blanks in a factory. It is dedicated to the critic Edward Garnett, to whom Lawrence described *The Mint* as 'an iron, rectangular, abhorrent book, one which no man would willingly read'. E. M. Forster (38) was an early admirer of the manuscript, but Lawrence wrote to him, explaining that he could not publish, for 'the horror the fellows with me in the force would feel at my giving them away, at their "off" moments […] *The Mint* shall not be circulated before 1950.' It was not widely available until 1955, when it was published under Lawrence's assumed name, '352087 Aircraftman Ross'.

C. S. Forester

1899 – 1966

After failing his army medical and abandoning his own medical studies, Cecil Louis Troughton Smith turned to writing, under the pseudonym 'Cecil Scott Forester'. He is best known for his eleven Hornblower novels, which follow Horatio Hornblower's career in the Royal Navy of the late 18th and early 19th centuries from midshipman to Admiral of the Fleet. He also wrote *The African Queen* (1935), which was filmed by John Huston in 1951. 'I recommend Forester to every literate I know,' wrote Ernest Hemingway (428).

1955 Penguin Books
2011 Modern Classics
—

1951 Penguin Books
2011 Modern Classics
—

2011 Hardback Classics
2012 Modern Classics
—

Payment Deferred

1926

Debt-ridden bank clerk Mr Marble goes to murderous extremes to pay his family's bills.

Plain Murder 1930

At the Universal Advertising Agency on the Strand in London, a corrupt employee develops a taste for murder.

The Pursued 1935, pub. 2011

When Dot is discovered with her head in the oven, her mother embarks on a meticulous and twisted retribution. Forester wrote *The Pursued* in 1935 but delayed its publication because he was working on a second Hornblower book, and felt it might confuse his readers; it was then lost. 'The lost novel was really lost,' he wrote. 'It is just possible that a typescript still exists, forgotten and gathering dust in a rarely used storeroom in Boston or Bloomsbury.' The typescript of *The Pursued* was indeed rediscovered, in 1999, and bought by the C. S. Forester Society. It was published for the first time, by Penguin, in 2011.

Sylvia Townsend Warner 1893 – 1978

After being expelled from kindergarten, Warner was tutored by various masters at Harrow School, where her father taught history. She worked in a London munitions factory during the First World War and as one of the editors of a ten-volume anthology of *Tudor Church Music* (1922–9). She began writing poetry in the early 1920s, encouraged by T. F. Powys (77). Powys introduced her to the young poet Valentine Ackland, with whom Warner fell in love. The two women became life partners and resided together in Dorset for the rest of their lives. They were active members of the Communist Party and travelled to Barcelona to work for the Red Cross during the Spanish Civil War (232). As well as poetry and novels, Warner wrote short stories, a biography of T. H. White (106) and translations of Proust's essays (168). The novelist Sarah Waters calls her 'one of the great under-read British novelists of the twentieth century'.

1937 Penguin Books
2020 Modern Classics
—
Warner was disappointed by the initial reaction to *Lolly Willowes*. 'I felt as though I had tried to make a sword,' she wrote, 'only to be told what a pretty pattern there was on the blade.'

Lolly Willowes
or, The Loving Huntsman 1926

In Warner's first novel, Laura 'Lolly' Willowes is a gentle, accommodating aunt who lives with her overbearing relations in London. One day, however, she makes a radical decision: she moves to the village of Great Mop in the Chiltern Hills, adopts a stray cat called Vinegar and becomes a witch in the service of Satan, the 'loving huntsman'. The book is 'witty, eerie, tender', wrote John Updike (514); '[…] her prose, in its simple, abrupt evocations, has something preternatural about it'.

1948 Penguin Books
2021 Modern Classics
—

Mr Fortune's Maggot

1927

The Reverend Timothy Fortune, a former clerk at the Hornsey branch of Lloyds Bank, pursues a whimsical 'maggot' and travels to the South Seas as a missionary. After three years on the tropical island of Fanua, however, he has succeeded in making only one convert and he struggles to maintain his own faith.

The True Heart

1929

Warner reimagines the myth of Cupid and Psyche in this Victorian love story. Sixteen-year-old orphan Sukey finds a job as a servant on a remote farm in the Essex Marshes and falls in love with Eric, the gentle son of the rector's wife. When they are separated, Sukey embarks on a quest that involves Queen Victoria herself.

2021
—

2021
—

Summer Will Show

1936

When Sophia Willoughby is forced to pursue her errant husband to Paris, which is in the throes of the 1848 Revolution, she finds herself unexpectedly attracted to his mistress Minna. 'Every page […] contains something brilliant, arresting or amusing,' writes Claire Harman, author of the biography *Sylvia Townsend Warner* (1989).

After the Death of Don Juan

1938

In 18th-century Spain, when the notorious lothario Don Juan disappears, Doña Ana is determined to find out whether or not he has been dragged to Hell by demons. Warner wrote this dark tale after volunteering during the Spanish Civil War (232).

2021
—

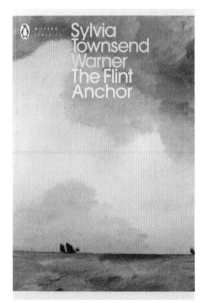

2021
—

The Corner That Held Them

1948

In the 14th century, in a small corner of Norfolk, the nuns of the convent of Oby endure trials of fire, flood, plague, a collapsing spire and an infestation of caterpillars. 'As an act of imagined history this novel has few rivals,' wrote the critic George Steiner, '[…] a work of high, frequent comedy.' This was Warner's own favourite of her novels.

2021
—

The Flint Anchor

1954

John Barnard is a 19th-century Norfolk merchant with an extensive and unhappy family, and Warner follows the dysfunctional Barnards over several decades. It is 'a novel created with solidity and subtlety of feeling', wrote *Atlantic Monthly*, 'a fusion of warmth, wit and quietly biting shrewdness that are reminiscent of Jane Austen'.

T. F. Powys 1875–1953

Theodore Francis Powys was the younger brother of John Cowper Powys (86). He left school at fifteen to manage a farm in Suffolk, which proved a disaster, so he moved to Dorset, where he wrote quietly for the rest of his life.

Mr Weston's Good Wine 1927

When a travelling salesman drives his van into the Dorset village of Folly Down and starts to sell his 'Good Wine', it appears that he may in fact be God. Time stops for the evening and Mr Weston enacts judgement on the sinful village community.

1937 Penguin Books
1976 Modern Classics
• —
The cover shows a detail from *A Village in Heaven* (1937) by Stanley Spencer.

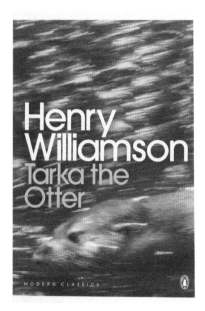

1937 Penguin Books
1949 Puffin Books
2009 Modern Classics
intro. Jeremy Gavron, 2009
—
Williamson included a glossary of local words and phrases, including *oolypuggers*, 'bulrushes'; *pollywiggle*, 'tadpole'; *vuz-peg*, 'hedgehog'; *appledrane*, 'a wasp buzzing inside a ripe apple'; and *quapping*, 'the sound made by a duck with its bill when feeding'.

Henry Williamson

1895–1977

After serving as a machine-gunner and rifleman in the First World War, during which he suffered trench foot, dysentery, anaemia and gassing, Williamson moved to rural north Devon, where he lived and worked as a writer for most of his life. His titles include *The Old Stag* (1926), *Salar the Salmon* (1935) and *Goodbye, West Country* (1937). He was a friend of T. E. Lawrence (74), who loved *Tarka the Otter*.

Tarka the Otter 1927

Tarka learns to fear the bark of hounds, the hunters' cries and the flash of metal traps. Williamson drew on the countryside around him, as well as his own painful war experiences, to paint a portrait of the beautiful yet perilous life of an otter. Tarka was a 'name given to otters many years ago by men dwelling in hut circles on the moor,' he explained. 'It means Little Water Wanderer, or, Wandering as Water.'

Rosamond Lehmann 1901–1990

Rosamond Lehmann was the daughter of Rudolph Lehmann, the founder of *Granta* magazine. She studied at Girton College, Cambridge, and made several translations, including the Penguin Modern Classics edition of Jean Cocteau's *Les Enfants Terribles* (178). 'She uses words with the enjoyment and mastery with which Renoir used paint,' wrote the author and critic Rebecca West. Her brother, John Lehmann, was a poet and the editor of the *Penguin New Writing* series.

Dusty Answer 1927

Set partly at Cambridge, Lehmann's first novel follows the childhood and adolescence of a bisexual girl called Judith Earle. 'This is a remarkable book,' wrote the *Sunday Times*. 'It is not often that one can say with confidence of a first novel by a young writer that it reveals new possibilities for literature. [...] It is the kind of novel that might have been written by Keats if Keats had been a young novelist of to-day.'

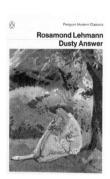

1936 Penguin Books
1981 Modern Classics
• —

1972
• —

The Weather in the Streets

1936

In this semi-autobiographical, fragmentary narrative, Olivia Curtis, a young divorcée, falls in love with a married man. It is one of the first English-language novels to discuss abortion.

The Echoing Grove

1953

'Miss Lehmann has always written brilliantly of women in love,' writes Margaret Drabble (152). In this intricately patterned novel, Dinah Hermann is drawn ineluctably towards her sister's husband, Rickie Masters.

1958 Penguin Books
1981 Modern Classics
• —

Edmund Blunden 1896–1974

Raised in rural Kent, Blunden enlisted at the age of eighteen and served in the Royal Sussex Regiment during the First World War, seeing action in the battles of the Somme, Ypres and Passchendaele. His first poems were published during the war, in Edward Marsh's *Georgian Poetry* (59) anthologies. Afterwards he taught in Japan for some years; he was Professor of English Literature at Hong Kong University and a Fellow of Merton College, Oxford, where he taught Keith Douglas (116).

Undertones of War 1928

Blunden's elegiac wartime memoir describes the horrors of the Western Front through understated prose and poetry. A 'shepherd in a soldier's coat', he contrasts scenes of the natural world with the hideous realities of war.

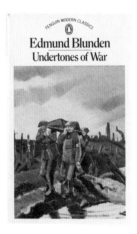

1937 Penguin Books
1982 Modern Classics
2010 Modern Classics
intro. Hew Strachan,
2010

Mary Butts 1890–1937

After studying the occult under Aleister Crowley and experimenting with lesbian relationships, Mary Butts moved to France in 1925. There she befriended Gertrude Stein (410), William Carlos Williams (418) and Ford Madox Ford (46), as well as Jean Cocteau (178), who provided three illustrations for *Armed with Madness*. In 1930 she settled at the tip of Cornwall, with her second husband, where she wrote novels and relied increasingly on alcohol and recreational drugs.

Armed with Madness 1928

2001
• intro. Stephen Heath

Scylla Taverner is 'sometimes a witch and sometimes a bitch'. She and a group of young friends discover an ancient jade cup on the south coast of England, which sparks a modern Grail quest with unexpected and violent results. The *London Review of Books* called it 'a masterpiece of Modernist (11) prose'. 'We need Mary Butts now,' wrote the poet John Ashbery, 'to guide us, "armed with madness", through mazes and forests to the pure sources of storytelling.'

Radclyffe Hall 1880–1943

Marguerite Antonia Radclyffe-Hall's philandering father, Radclyffe Radclyffe-Hall, was known as 'Rat'. After he abandoned the family, Marguerite lived with her violent mother until she inherited her father's estate, funded her own education and travelled to Germany, where she began a lesbian relationship with an older, married woman. She was a poet as well as a novelist and liked to be called 'John'.

2015
intro. Maureen Duffy

The Well of Loneliness 1928

The Well of Loneliness is 'the first long and very serious novel entirely upon the subject of sexual inversion', wrote Radclyffe Hall. It centres around Stephen Gordon, a lesbian woman whose father was hoping for a boy. The *Sunday Express* reviewer called it an 'outrage', writing: 'I would rather give a healthy boy or a healthy girl a phial of prussic acid than this novel.' The book was prosecuted for obscenity and all copies were destroyed. It was not republished in the UK until six years after Radclyffe Hall's death.

Edward Upward 1903–2009

Upward was a school friend of Christopher Isherwood (103). At Cambridge University, they invented the fictional village of Mortmere: 'a sort of anarchist paradise', explained Isherwood, 'in which all accepted moral and social values were turned upside down and inside out, and every kind of extravagant behaviour was possible and usual'. Upward became a schoolmaster and a member of the Communist Party of Great Britain. 'No modern book can be true to life,' he wrote, 'unless it recognizes, more or less clearly, both the decadence of present-day society and the inevitability of revolution.' He retired to the Isle of Wight and died at the age of 105.

1972
● intro. W. H. Sellers

The Railway Accident
and Other Stories 1928–42, pub. 1933–49

'The Railway Accident' is a fantasy story, the only surviving example of the imaginary world of Mortmere. 'I have read it at least half a dozen times,' wrote the poet John Lehmann, the brother of Rosamond (77), 'and each time it seems to me as remarkable, perhaps more remarkable. I would even say it is the most brilliant piece of surrealist (176) prose to have been written in English (if you don't count the Alice stories).' This selection also includes Upward's novella *Journey to the Border* (1938), about a private tutor who tries to escape his job through self-induced insanity.

More SAME-SEX LOVE STORIES

Maurice
by E. M. Forster   39

In the Making
by G. F. Green   124

Death in Venice
by Thomas Mann   245

Olivia
by 'Olivia'   97

Memoirs of Hadrian
by Marguerite Yourcenar   191

SURREALIST POETRY IN ENGLISH 1926–75

Surrealism (176) emerged in France in the 1920s, but the English-speaking world soon embraced the 'kingdom of the irrational'. In 1935, the poet David Gascoyne wrote a manifesto of English Surrealism, relating the movement to 19th-century Romanticism, and the London Surrealist Group was founded that same year. This anthology includes works by Gascoyne as well as by Dylan Thomas (98), Frank O'Hara and many others. It also features English translations of poetry by André Breton (176), Pablo Picasso and Tomas Tranströmer (239) among others.

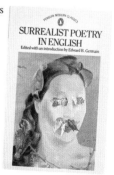

1978 Penguin Poets
English and American Surrealist Poetry
1986 Modern Classics
● ed. Edward B. Germain, 1978

George Orwell

1903 – 1950

Eric Arthur Blair was born in British India, where his father held a post in the Opium Department of the Indian civil service. He went to Eton and then was posted to Burma after flunking his Indian civil service exams. In Burma he worked as an imperial policeman, learned to speak Burmese fluently and was tattooed with blue circles on his knuckles as a protection against snakebite. In 1927, sick with dengue fever, he resigned his post, and later took jobs as a kitchen porter in Paris, a hop picker in Kent, a private tutor, a schoolteacher, and an assistant in a second-hand bookshop, all the while writing essays and articles. He considered various noms de plume, including 'P. S. Burton', 'Kenneth Miles' and 'H. Lewis Allways', but settled on 'George Orwell' as a 'good round English name'; Orwell was the name of his favourite river in Suffolk. He suffered from pneumonia throughout his life and was rejected for military service at the start of the Second World War. He became seriously ill during the winter of 1948–9, while living in a remote farmhouse on the Isle of Jura, and he died of tuberculosis the following year. 'You have made an indelible mark on English literature,' wrote the critic Desmond MacCarthy, in a letter that Orwell received a few days before he died; '[...] you are among the few memorable writers of your generation.' In 2017, a statue of Orwell was unveiled outside BBC Broadcasting House in London, with a line from his preface to *Animal Farm* (84): 'If liberty means anything at all it means the right to tell people what they do not want to hear.'

Orwell in Penguin

'The Penguin books are splendid value for sixpence,' wrote Orwell in March 1936, reviewing what was then the third batch of Penguin books, 'so splendid that if other publishers had any sense they would combine against them and suppress them.' In December 1940, the Penguin paperback edition of *Down and Out in Paris and London* (81) was published. It quickly sold out its initial print run of 55,000 copies and transformed Orwell's reputation. For the last 70 years, he has been one of Penguin's bestselling authors. The current Penguin editions of Orwell are based on the 1986 *Complete Works of George Orwell*, published by Secker & Warburg and edited by the Orwell authority Peter Davison, with his wife Sheila Davison and Ian Angus.

2016
ed. Peter Davison

Seeing Things as They Are
Selected Journalism and Other Writings

1928 – 49

These articles, essays, letters and broadcasts span Orwell's career. There are examples of his schoolboy poetry, an excised passage from *Nineteen Eighty-Four* (84), and reviews of books including J. B. Priestley's *Angel Pavement* (87), Henry Miller's *Tropic of Cancer* (451) and Aldous Huxley's *Brave New World* (66). The title comes from Orwell's essay, 'Why I Write'. 'Desire to see things as they are,' he urges the reader, 'to find out true facts and store them up for the use of posterity.'

Diaries

1931 – 49

Orwell kept diaries throughout his life. Eleven journals and notebooks survive, although a twelfth, and possibly a thirteenth, are lodged in the NKVD archive in Moscow. The selected entries in this volume cover hop picking, his time spent in Wigan, the Second World War, life on Jura and the publication of *Animal Farm* (84) and *Nineteen Eighty-Four* (84).

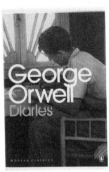

2010
ed. Peter Davison, 2009

1957 Penguin Books
Selected Essays
1962 Penguin Books
Inside the Whale
1991 Twentieth-Century
Classics
● —

1965 Penguin Books
1991 Twentieth-Century
Classics
● —

An Age Like This, 1920–1940
1970 Penguin Books
1993 Twentieth-Century
Classics
● ed. Sonia Orwell & Ian
Angus, 1968

*My Country Right or Left,
1940–1943*
1970 Penguin Books
1993 Twentieth-Century
Classics
● ed. Sonia Orwell & Ian
Angus, 1968

As I Please, 1943–1945
1970 Penguin Books
1993 Twentieth-Century
Classics
● ed. Sonia Orwell & Ian
Angus, 1968

Essays 1931–49

In his lifetime, Orwell was known primarily
for his essays: the critic Irving Howe has
described him as 'the greatest English essayist
since Hazlitt, maybe since Dr Johnson'.
His essays range from literary criticism on
subjects such as Dickens, Rudyard Kipling (22),
W. B. Yeats (4) and Arthur Koestler (278),
to contemporary politics, the qualities
of Englishness, and meditations on the act
of writing itself. 'An anchorman braced in the
middle of the century, Orwell united style
with substance, innocence with experience,'
writes Andrew Motion, the former Poet
Laureate. 'In a style of exemplary purity,
he described the compromised lives we
recognize as our own.'

*In Front of Your Nose,
1945–1950*
1970 Penguin Books
1993 Twentieth-Century
Classics
● ed. Sonia Orwell & Ian
Angus, 1968

1984 Penguin Books
1990 Twentieth-Century
Classics
1994 Twentieth-Century
Classics
2000 Modern Classics *Essays*
intro. Bernard Crick, 1994

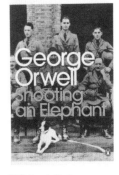

2003 Penguin Books
2009 Modern Classics
intro. Jeremy Paxman, 2009
—
'Shooting an Elephant'
is Orwell's account
of executing an escaped
elephant in Burma, 'solely to
avoid looking a fool'. It was
the opening essay in the first
Penguin New Writing
anthology in 1940.

Down and Out in Paris and London 1933

In the late 1920s, Orwell began to explore the poorer parts
of London, living among the tramps of Limehouse in the
East End and documenting the conditions
of homeless hostels, known as 'spikes'.
In 1928, he moved to Paris, where he worked
as a hotel *plongeur*, occasionally supported
by his aunt Nellie. These experiences led
to his early essay 'The Spike', and a longer
draft called 'A Scullion's Diary', which was
rejected by publishers, including T. S. Eliot (11).
The revised draft was eventually published
by Gollancz as *Down and Out in Paris and London*
and saw the first use of his pseudonym
'George Orwell'.

*Orwell and the
Dispossessed* presents
the complete text of
*Down and Out in Paris
and London* along with a
wealth of other contextual
material by Orwell,
including unpublished
essays, early journalism,
book reviews, poems,
letters and diary entries.

2001 Modern Classics
2020 Penguin Classics
ed. Peter Davison, 2001
intro. Peter Clarke, 2001

1940 Penguin Books
1966 Modern Classics
1989 Twentieth-Century
Classics
ed. Peter Davison, 1989
intro. Dervla Murphy, 1989

Burmese Days 1934

'Orwell's time in Burma marks a key turning point in his life,' writes the journalist Emma Larkin. 'It was during those years that he was transformed from a snobbish public-school boy to a writer of social conscience.' This formative period was the inspiration for *Burmese Days*, Orwell's first novel, in which the teak merchant John Flory becomes increasingly disillusioned by the corruption and bigotry of imperial rule. 'Mr Orwell's indignant and unsparing realism is a sound tonic for us!' wrote John Cowper Powys (86). 'It is convincing realism; and it is as illuminating as it is distressing.'

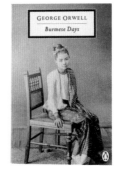

1944 Penguin Books
1989 Twentieth-Century Classics
ed. Peter Davison, 1989
—
In 2013, a new Burmese translation of *Burmese Days* by Maung Myint Kywe won the Burma National Literature Award, the country's highest literary honour.

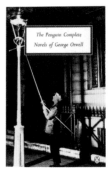

1983 Penguin Books
1990 Twentieth-Century Classics
—
The Complete Novels is a compendium comprising *Animal Farm* (84), *Burmese Days*, *A Clergyman's Daughter*, *Coming Up for Air* (83), *Keep the Aspidistra Flying* and *Nineteen Eighty-Four* (84).

1964 Penguin Books
1990 Twentieth-Century Classics
ed. Peter Davison, 1990

A Clergyman's Daughter 1935

Dorothy Hare is the demure daughter of the rector of Knype Hill, a small village in Suffolk. Her submissive routine is turned upside down, however, when she suffers a bout of amnesia and finds herself penniless in London, unable to remember her own name. Orwell wrote the novel soon after proposing marriage to Brenda Salkeld, the daughter of a Southwold clergyman. She refused his proposal, but remained a friend. Orwell asked her to pray for the book's success, 'by which I mean not less than 4,000 copies. I understand the prayers of clergyman's daughters get special attention in Heaven.' It is Orwell's most stylistically experimental book, heavily influenced by James Joyce (8).

Keep the Aspidistra Flying

1936

Gordon Comstock detests his middle-class world of aspidistras and antimacassars, so he abandons his career in advertising and takes a part-time job in a second-hand bookshop, in order to write a great work of poetry. But his spiral into self-inflicted hardship begins to grind away at his spirit and he becomes increasingly petty, paranoid and incapable of putting pen to paper. The novel is a 'harrowing and stark account of poverty', said Cyril Connolly (107), written in 'clear and violent language, at times making the reader feel he is in a dentist's chair with the drill whirring'.

1962 Penguin Books
1989 Twentieth-Century Classics
ed. Peter Davison, 1989

1962 Penguin Books
1989 Twentieth-Century Classics
ed. Peter Davison, 1989
intro. Richard Hoggart (136), 1989

2001 Modern Classics
2020 Penguin Classics
ed. Peter Davison, 2001
intro. Ben Pimlott, 2001
—
Orwell's England presents *The Road to Wigan Pier* with contextual essays, reviews, letters and poems by Orwell, including 'On a Ruined Farm near the His Master's Voice Gramophone Factory'.

The Road to Wigan Pier 1937

Orwell walked through the industrial Midlands in early 1936, visiting Coventry, Stafford and Macclesfield before arriving at Wigan, northwest of Manchester, where he lodged in dirty rooms above a tripe shop. He visited working-class homes in the area and described the appalling slum housing he encountered. Wigan Pier itself was the site of a former inland wharf on the Liverpool and Leeds Canal, now a 'lunar landscape of slag-heaps'. In the second half of the book, Orwell argues that socialism is an essential requisite for improving housing conditions. As a result of his research, Orwell was put under surveillance by the police's Special Branch, which ended only in 1948, a year before the publication of *Nineteen Eighty-Four* (84).

Homage to Catalonia 1938

On 23 December 1936, Orwell set off to join the civil war in Spain. On the way, he had lunch with Henry Miller (451), who told him that what he was doing was 'sheer stupidity'. Orwell joined the POUM, the Partido Obrero de Unificación Marxista (Workers' Party of Marxist Unification), and was posted to Alcubierre on the Aragon front. His first wife Eileen followed him to Barcelona and brought him packages of tea, chocolate and cigars. He contended with factionalism, distorted propaganda and corruption until May 1937, when he was shot in the throat by a sniper's bullet, which only just missed his carotid artery. He was declared unfit for service, fled Spain amidst accusations of 'rabid Trotskyism' (322) and wrote about the experience in *Homage to Catalonia*. 'The horror of *Homage to Catalonia* is greater than that of *Nineteen Eighty-Four* (84),' wrote Stephen Spender (95): 'but in the earlier book no one can accuse him of having invented tortures; for he is writing of what he has seen.'

1962 Penguin Books
1989 Twentieth-Century Classics
ed. Peter Davison, 1989
intro. Julian Symons, 1989

2001 Modern Classics
2020 Penguin Classics
ed. Peter Davison, 2001
intro. Christopher Hitchens, 2001
—
Orwell in Spain surrounds *Homage to Catalonia* with reviews, letters and associated articles by Orwell such as 'Spilling the Spanish Beans', 'Eye-Witness in Barcelona' and 'Caesarean Section in Spain'.

Coming Up for Air 1939

In this novel, George Bowling feels trapped in middle-class middle age: he's overweight, overdrawn and fed up with family life. As the threat of war looms, he sets off on a nostalgic pilgrimage to the idyllic village on the banks of the Thames where he grew up. Lower Binfield, however, is no longer quite as he remembers.

1962 Penguin Books
1989 Twentieth-Century Classics
ed. Peter Davison, 1989

The Lion and the Unicorn
Socialism and the English Genius 1941

This celebrated essay in three parts was intended to define the political aims of the Second World War. 'As I write,' Orwell opens, 'highly civilized human beings are flying overhead, trying to kill me.' In the view of Arthur Koestler (278), this essay is 'one of the most moving and incisive portraits of the English character'.

1982 Penguin Books
1990 Twentieth-Century Classics
● intro. Bernard Crick, 1982
2018 Modern Classics
—

The War Broadcasts

1941–3, pub. 1985

In 1984 (coincidentally), a cache of previously unknown material was discovered, written by Orwell while he was working for the BBC's Eastern Service. This volume collects his literary talks and adaptations for radio broadcast in India, many of which he recorded himself, on subjects ranging from *Macbeth* and Jonathan Swift to George Bernard Shaw (4), Jack London (404) and H.G. Wells (26).

1987 Penguin Books
1995 Twentieth-Century Classics
● intro. W.J. West, 1985
—
'One phenomenon of the war,' wrote Orwell for one of his wartime broadcasts, 'has been the enormous sale of Penguin Books, Pelican Books and other cheap editions, most of which would have been regarded by the general public as impossibly highbrow a few years back.'

The War Commentaries

1941–3, pub. 1985

Orwell also wrote weekly 'commentaries', recorded by others, which were designed to counter rival German radio stations broadcasting to India. They form a fascinating if propagandistic account of the Second World War.

1987 Penguin Books
1995 Twentieth-Century Classics
● intro. W.J. West, 1985

1963 Modern Classics
1989 Twentieth-Century Classics
ed. Peter Davison, 1989
intro. Malcolm Bradbury, 1989
—
Orwell's preface to *Animal Farm*,
written in 1945, was rediscovered
in 1971 and is included in the
Peter Davison edition.

2001 Modern Classics
2020 Penguin Classics
ed. Peter Davison, 2001
intro. Timothy Garton
Ash, 2001

Orwell and Politics presents
Animal Farm along with
essays, reviews, letters
and poems by Orwell,
including his review
of Hitler's *Mein Kampf*,
and his manifesto, 'If War
Comes, We Shall Resist'.

Animal Farm
A Fairy Story 1945

A group of farm animals overthrow Mr Jones, their human farmer. They establish a free and equal animal society, only to find themselves gradually descending into a dictatorship under the tyrannical pig Napoleon. The book is a thinly veiled satire on Stalinist Russia and Orwell struggled to find a publisher because the Soviet Union was Britain's wartime ally. 'It is the history of a revolution that went wrong,' he wrote – 'and of the excellent excuses that were forthcoming at every step for the perversion of the original doctrine.'

Nineteen Eighty-Four 1949 →

'It was a bright cold day in April, and the clocks were striking thirteen.' Winston Smith is a downtrodden employee of the Ministry for Truth, in London. What was once Great Britain is now Airstrip One, a province of Oceania – a superstate ruled by the totalitarian Inner Party under the figurehead of the ever-watchful Big Brother. Most people accept their oily gin rations, crumbling houses and disease-ridden lives: if they don't, they're crushed by the Thought Police, who employ ubiquitous camera and microphone surveillance. Winston dreams of escaping this sordid existence, a dream that seems less impossible when he meets a partner in 'thoughtcrime'. 'Big Brother', 'thoughtcrime', 'doublethink', 'Newspeak', 'Room 101', 'telescreen', 'memory hole': *Nineteen Eighty-Four* has percolated the English language and provided a grim vocabulary of state oppression. The very word 'Orwellian' has come to describe state surveillance, propaganda and the manipulation of history. *Nineteen Eighty-Four* is 'the book of the twentieth century', wrote the *Independent*: it 'haunts us with an ever-darker relevance'.

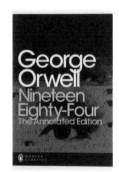

2013 *Annotated Edition*
ed. D. J. Taylor

A Life in Letters 1911–50

'In making this selection I have had two principles in mind,' writes Peter Davison. 'Firstly, that the letters chosen should illustrate Orwell's life and hopes; and secondly that each one should be of interest in its own right.' Taken together, this volume and its companion, *Diaries* (80), compose the autobiography that Orwell never wrote. The letters cover politics, ghosts and gardening, with insights into Orwell's friendships with the likes of T. S. Eliot (11), Arthur Koestler (278), Henry Miller (451) and Steven Runciman (121).

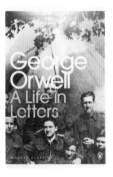

2011
ed. Peter Davison, 2010

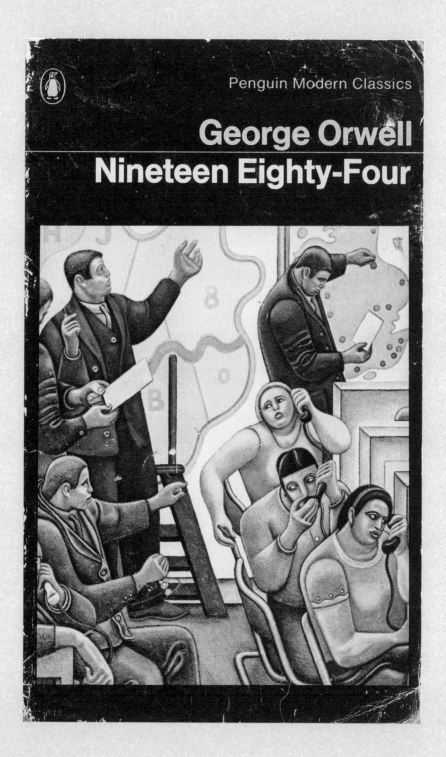

Penguin Modern Classics

George Orwell
Nineteen Eighty-Four

1954 Penguin Books
1969 Modern Classics
1989 Twentieth-Century Classics
• ed. Peter Davison, 1989
intro. Ben Pimlott, 1989

2003 Penguin Books
2013 Modern Classics
2019 Penguin Classics
intro. Thomas Pynchon, 2003

The cover of the 1969 edition shows a detail
from *The Control Room, Civil Defence
Headquarters* (c.1942) by William Roberts.

William Empson 1906–1984

Empson studied mathematics and literature at Cambridge. He turned his undergraduate dissertation into a celebrated work of literary criticism, *Seven Types of Ambiguity* (1930), before leaving Britain to teach in Japan and China. He worked for the BBC in England during the Second World War, befriending George Orwell (80), then returned to Peking National University, where he taught throughout the Chinese civil war and the communist takeover. In 1953, he became Professor of English Literature at the University of Sheffield. He was knighted in 1979.

The Complete Poems 1928–54

Empson's earliest poems were heavily influenced by John Donne, his favourite poet. Subsequent collections were less complex, but nonetheless learned and technically virtuosic. They had an important influence over the poets of 'The Movement' (124).

2001
ed. John Haffenden
—
'If I publish a volume of verse with notes longer than the text, as I want to do, will that be a prose work or a verse one?' Empson asked his publisher in 1930. The same question might be asked of this edition, which has 110 pages of poetry and more than 300 pages of critical apparatus. Like Empson before him, the editor John Haffenden was Professor of English Literature at the University of Sheffield.

Richard Hughes 1900–1976

Hughes dictated stories to his mother before he could hold a pencil. At university he wrote a play that was admired by George Bernard Shaw (4), and he composed the world's first radio drama, *Danger*, which the BBC broadcast in 1924. He was a friend of T. E. Lawrence (74), Robert Graves (57) and Dylan Thomas (98). He liked adventurous travel, and in his late fifties he sailed from Athens to Istanbul in a small open boat.

A High Wind in Jamaica 1929

When the five Bas-Thornton children are kidnapped by Caribbean pirates, they turn out to be far more savage, deranged and treacherous than their captors. This swashbuckling tale plumbs chilling depths as the children swig a cocktail known as 'Hangman's Blood'.

1949 Penguin Books
1971 Modern Classics
• —

John Cowper Powys 1872–1963

John Cowper Powys, the elder brother of T. F. Powys (77), grew up in the West Country and went to Sherborne School in Dorset. He became a poet and a lecturer, touring the USA for 25 years, before moving to North Wales, where he lived for the rest of his life. Margaret Drabble (152) has called him 'a genius – a fearless writer, who writes with reckless passion'.

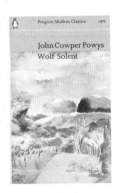

Wolf Solent 1929

This quasi-mystical novel follows Wolf, a young history teacher, as he returns to his roots in the West Country and rediscovers the elemental, sensuous power of the English landscape. 'As I wrote Wolf Solent travelling through all the states of the United States except two,' wrote Powys in his preface, 'I became more and more intensely aware of the hills and valleys, the trees and various flowers, the lanes and hedges and ponds and ditches, of the country round Sherborne. [...] Wolf Solent is a book of Nostalgia, written in a foreign country with the pen of a traveller and the ink-blood of his home.' V. S. Pritchett (110) called it a 'stupendous and rather glorious book [...] as beautiful and strange as an electric storm'.

1964 Modern Classics
2000 Modern Classics
intro. A. N. Wilson, 2000

R. C. Sherriff 1896–1975

Robert Cedric Sherriff worked as a claims adjuster in his father's insurance business, before and after fighting in the First World War, during which he was severely wounded. He was a keen amateur dramatist when he wrote *Journey's End*, a play based on his own letters home from the trenches. Its enormous and unexpected success allowed him to become a full-time writer, and he went on to write novels and screenplays for Hollywood films including *The Invisible Man* (1933), an adaptation of the H. G. Wells story (26), *Goodbye, Mr Chips* (1939) and *The Dam Busters* (1955).

1983 Penguin Plays
1992 Twentieth-Century
Classics
—

Journey's End 1928–9

When newly commissioned Lieutenant Raleigh joins his regiment at the front in 1918, he arrives in the officers' dugout to find his old school friend Stanhope transfigured by trench warfare. After many rejections, *Journey's End* was given a single Sunday evening performance in 1928, with a 21-year-old Laurence Olivier playing Stanhope. George Bernard Shaw (4) was in the audience and convinced the Savoy Theatre to stage a full production. The play became an immediate international success.

More CHICKENS

'The Egg'
by Sherwood Anderson   420

The Ticket That Exploded
by William S. Burroughs   484

Cock-a-Doodle Dandy
by Sean O'Casey   6

Black List, Section H
by Francis Stuart   21

Love Among the Chickens
by P. G. Wodehouse   48

The Hopkins Manuscript 1939

Pompous Edgar Hopkins, once a prize-winning poultry breeder, is writing a manuscript 'by the light of a piece of string [...] pushed through a fragment of bacon fat and arranged in an egg-cup'. He describes the cataclysmic events that unfold in the early 1940s, after the moon is discovered to be on a collision course with the Earth.

2018
—

J. B. Priestley 1894–1984

John Boynton Priestley worked for a Bradford wool firm before the First World War. Afterwards he won a scholarship to Cambridge and found work in London as a literary journalist. His third novel, *The Good Companions*, made his reputation, and he went on to write many other highly successful novels and plays.

1962
● —

The Good Companions

1929

A wealthy spinster decides to bankroll 'the Good Companions', a travelling music-hall troupe formerly known as 'the Dinky Doos'. The eccentric performers enjoy various picaresque adventures in a series of provincial towns.

Angel Pavement

1930

During the Great Depression, the veneer-and-inlay firm of Twigg & Dersingham, 8 Angel Pavement, deep in the City of London, is thrown into disarray by the arrival of a mysterious and progressive new manager.

1948 Penguin Books
1968 Modern Classics
● —

Time and the Conways
and Other Plays 1937–47

Time and the Conways, I Have Been Here Before, An Inspector Calls, The Linden Tree

All these plays experiment with time in different ways. In *Time and the Conways* (1937), Kay Conway dreams about the future of her family; in *I Have Been Here Before* (1937), a young married couple are startled by extreme déjà vu; in *An Inspector Calls* (1945), Priestley's best-known play, a callous middle-class family face the tragic results of their past actions; and in *The Linden Tree* (1947), an ageing history professor struggles with the concept of retirement.

1969 Penguin Plays
1994 Twentieth-Century Classics
2001 Modern Classics *An Inspector Calls and Other Plays*
—

1978 Penguin Books
1985 Modern Classics
● ed. John Guest, 1978

John Betjeman 1906–1984

Betjeman went to Highgate School in north London, where he was taught by T.S.Eliot (11), and then Oxford University, where he was taught by C.S.Lewis. He brought his teddy bear, Archibald Ormsby-Gore, to Oxford, which inspired his contemporary Evelyn Waugh to give Sebastian Flyte a teddy bear called Aloysius in *Brideshead Revisited* (69). Betjeman worked as a film critic for the *Evening Standard* and as an editor at the *Architectural Review*. He instigated the Shell Guides to British counties, wrote the scripts for several BBC television films and co-founded the Victorian Society. He was knighted in 1969 and appointed Poet Laureate in 1972.

The Best of Betjeman 1929–77

This selection compiles the best of Betjeman's wryly comic verse, from his first book, *Mount Zion* (1932), to one of his last, *A Nip in the Air* (1974), but it also features a range of his prose writing, as architectural critic, social historian, railway enthusiast and Christian, as well as the script of his celebrated BBC film *Metro-land* (1973), a poetic celebration of suburban London. It is 'a thoroughly well-rounded portrait of Betjeman the artist and Betjeman the man', wrote the poet Charles Causley. 'It is the portrait of a phenomenon.'

Graham Greene 1904–1991

Henry Graham Greene suffered from depression. At school, he attempted suicide several times, playing Russian roulette, and taking aspirin before jumping into the pool. He later found a way to channel his melancholy, saying that 'the disease is also one's material'. He worked as a sub-editor at *The Times* and later as the film critic and literary editor of the *Spectator*. In 1941, his sister recruited him to MI6 and he worked for British Intelligence in Sierra Leone under the supervision of Kim Philby. Catholicism and espionage are recurring themes in his work. Many of his books are set in hot, colonial outposts, populated by adulterous bureaucrats and known collectively as 'Greeneland'. In 1966, he left England for the south of France. He was a cinematic writer who wrote screenplays, film treatments, and novels that have often been adapted for the screen. 'Graham Greene was in a class by himself,' wrote William Golding (131). 'He will be read and remembered as the ultimate chronicler of twentieth-century man's consciousness and anxiety.'

1971 Penguin Books
1977 Penguin Books *revised*
1994 Twentieth-Century Classics
● —

The Man Within
1929

Greene's first novel is a work of historical fiction, about a band of Sussex smugglers in the 19th century.

Stories

1929–90

Greene's short stories deal with affairs, obsessions, fantasies, myths, fear, pity and violence. There are gurgling stomachs, youthful indiscretions, evil children and a macabre overnight bag.

1986 Penguin Books
1992 Twentieth-Century Classics
● —

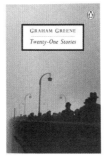

1970 Penguin Books
1977 Penguin Books *revised*
1992 Twentieth-Century Classics
● —

1969 Penguin Books
1975 Penguin Books *revised*
1992 Twentieth-Century Classics
● —

1992 Penguin Books
1999 Twentieth-Century Classics
● —

In Greene's final collection, *The Last Word and Other Stories* (1990), he gathered short works from throughout his career, none of which had appeared in *Collected Short Stories*. The title story describes a meeting between the last Pope and the general who deposed him.

Collected Essays

1929–68, pub. 1969

This volume brings together almost 80 essays, reviews and occasional pieces, with mostly literary subjects, including Frederick Rolfe (102), Norman Douglas (63), Eric Gill (96), Herbert Read (103), François Mauriac (174) and Henry James (397).

1970 Penguin Books
1993 Twentieth-Century Classics
● —

Stamboul Train
An Entertainment

1932

This spy thriller is set on board the Orient Express. It's 'a *tour de force*', wrote L. P. Hartley (125). 'The realist and the romantic struggle with each other in this book, making it a kind of mental battlefield, inducing a sense of breathlessness and urgency. It is a very remarkable piece of work, splendidly written, exciting, disturbing.'

1963 Penguin Books
1975 Penguin Books *revised*
1977 Peacock Books
1992 Twentieth-Century Classics
● —

Initially Greene drew a distinction between his serious novels and his lighter books, which he called 'entertainments'.

It's a Battlefield 1934

In Greene's first overtly political novel, a communist bus-driver faces the death penalty for killing a policeman during a riot. Greene based the writing style on cinematic techniques; but, as yet, it is one of the few novels by him never to have been adapted for the screen.

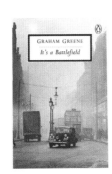

1940 Penguin Books
1976 Penguin Books *revised*
1991 Twentieth-Century Classics
● —

The Third Man
and **The Fallen Idol**

1935–48

Greene wrote 'The Basement Room' in 1935, a short story that became the basis for the film *The Fallen Idol* (1948), directed by Carol Reed; this edition reprints the original tale. In 1948, he wrote a novella that provided the 'raw material' for another collaboration with Reed: *The Third Man* is set in post-war Vienna and centres around the suspicious death of Harry Lime, played by Orson Welles in the Academy Award-winning film of 1949.

1971 Penguin Books
1976 Penguin Books *revised*
1992 Twentieth-Century Classics
● —

England Made Me 1935

1943 Penguin Books
1970 Penguin Books *revised*
1992 Twentieth-Century Classics
● —

Disreputable Anthony Farrant's twin sister secures him a position as the bodyguard for her lover Krogh, a ruthless financier in Sweden.

1963 Penguin Books
1974 Penguin Books *revised*
<u>**1992**</u> Twentieth-Century
Classics
● —

1943 Penguin Books
<u>**1961**</u> Modern Classics
1971 Penguin Books *revised*
1991 Twentieth-Century
Classics
● —

1970–78 Penguin Plays
individual titles
<u>**1985**</u> Penguin Books
1995 Twentieth-Century
Classics
● —

A Gun for Sale
An Entertainment
1936

Greene's first anti-hero is
the disfigured assassin Raven,
who finds himself on the
run for killing a central
European government minister
and tipping the continent
towards war.

Brighton Rock 1938

Pinkie Brown is a teenage,
sociopathic gangster boss,
who seeks vengeance for an
act of betrayal. Like the word
'Brighton' in the eponymous
stick of rock, Pinkie's brutal
nature is engrained, but as a
lapsed Catholic he also believes
in the possibility of redemption
and grace. Greene wrote the
screenplay for the 1948 Boulting
brothers' film adaptation,
starring Richard Attenborough.

The Lawless Roads 1939

In his review of *Wee Willie Winkie* (1937), the film adaptation of the
Kipling short story (23), Greene suggested that the nine-year-old
child star, Shirley Temple, had been uncomfortably sexualized.
He was promptly sued by Twentieth Century Fox and travelled to
Mexico to avoid the trial, which he lost. While in Mexico, he reported
on President Plutarco Elías Calles's anti-Catholic persecutions,
witnessing what he called 'the fiercest persecution of religion
anywhere since the reign of Elizabeth'. One result was this travelogue;
the other was *The Power and the Glory* (91).

The Collected Plays 1939 – 80
*The Living Room, The Potting Shed, The Complaisant Lover,
Carving a Statue, The Return of A. J. Raffles, The Great Jowett,
Yes and No, For Whom the Bell Chimes*

Greene's plays deal with dangerous secrets and fraught
family relationships. In *Carving a Statue* (1964), a father
and son clash over the older man's attempt to sculpt
an image of God.

Journey Without Maps
1936

Greene's first travel book
describes walking across
uncharted terrain in West
Africa, between Sierra Leone
and Liberia. 'His originality lay
in his gifts as a traveller,' wrote
V. S. Pritchett (110). 'He had
the foreign ear and eye for the
strangeness of ordinary life and
its ordinary crises.'

1971 Penguin Books
1980 Penguin Books *revised*
<u>**1991**</u> Twentieth-Century Classics
● —

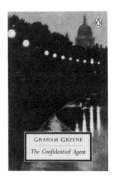

1963 Penguin Books
1971 Penguin Books *revised*
<u>**1992**</u> Twentieth-Century Classics
● —

The Confidential Agent
An Entertainment 1939

D. arrives in London from
a country where civil war is
raging. When he is implicated
in a murder, he's forced to go on
the run. Inspired by the Spanish
Civil War, Greene stoked up on
Benzedrine and wrote the novel
in six weeks.

1947 Penguin Books
1982 Penguin Books *revised*
<u>**1993**</u> Twentieth-Century
Classics
● —

Penguin received a letter
from David Higham,
Graham Greene's literary
agent, in July 1947:
'He is a bit upset – and I dare
say you will be more upset
– to see that on the spine of
your edition of *The Lawless
Roads* his name is misspelt.
Anything that I can tell him?'

Greene in Penguin

It's a Battlefield (89) was the first Greene title to appear in Penguin, in 1940, followed by *England Made Me* (89) and *Brighton Rock* (90) in 1943. Greene was upset by the 1943 *England Made Me* edition: 'the biographical note was horribly chatty and personal and the photograph was quite wildly out of date,' he wrote, and he insisted on no photograph or biographical note in *Brighton Rock*. Between 1970 and 1982, the Bodley Head published the 'Collected Edition' of Graham Greene's works in 22 volumes. Titles which had previously appeared in Penguin were reset and reprinted from these authoritative editions, and new titles were added.

The Power and the Glory 1940

Set in Mexico, *The Power and the Glory* describes a 'whisky priest' in the state of Tabasco, fleeing anti-Catholic purges, and an anonymous, socialist lieutenant committed to hunting him down. It is 'generally agreed to be Graham Greene's masterpiece', wrote John Updike (514) in his introduction. '*The Power and the Glory*'s nameless whisky priest blends seamlessly with his tropical, crooked, anticlerical Mexico. Roman Catholicism is intrinsic to the character and terrain both; Greene's imaginative immersion in both is triumphant.'

1962 Penguin Books
1971 Penguin Books *revised*
1991 Twentieth-Century Classics
● intro. John Updike, 1991

1968 Penguin Books
1994 Twentieth-Century Classics
● —

In Search of a Character
Two African Journals 1941–59, pub. 1961

This volume contains two notebooks: 'Convoy to West Africa' is the account of a voyage from Liverpool to Sierra Leone during the Second World War; and 'Congo Journal' describes Greene's visit to the Yonda leper colony in 1959. He reworked material from the latter in his novel *A Burnt-Out Case* (92).

1963 Penguin Books
1974 Penguin Books *revised*
1993 Twentieth-Century Classics
● —

The Ministry of Fear
An Entertainment 1943

When Arthur Rowe correctly guesses the weight of a cake at a charity fete, he becomes embroiled in a murderous plot and a network of Nazi agents.

The Heart of the Matter
1948

Henry Scobie is a conscientious police officer in West Africa, who descends into a guilt-ridden vortex of adultery, murder and sin, clutching at his Catholic faith. 'If one knew […] the facts,' he wonders, 'would one have to feel pity even for the planets? If one reached what they called the heart of the matter?' The title was inspired by Joseph Conrad's *Heart of Darkness* (29).

1962 Penguin Books
1971 Penguin Books *revised*
1991 Twentieth-Century Classics
● —

The Tenth Man 1944, pub. 1985

In a prison in occupied France, one in every ten men is to be shot by the German guards, and the prisoners draw lots among themselves. Greene wrote this tense novella-length film treatment while under a two-year contract to Metro-Goldwyn-Mayer, but the manuscript lay in their archives until 1983. 'All the Greene hallmarks are there,' writes Penelope Lively (161): 'pace, ingenuity, a sense of profundities suggested but never insisted upon.' 'I prefer it many ways to *The Third Man*,' said Greene.

1985 Penguin Books
1992 Twentieth-Century Classics
● —
This volume includes two other rediscovered film treatments by Greene: 'Jim Braddon and the War Criminal' and 'Nobody to Blame'.

The End of the Affair 1951

This novel, set in London during the Second World War, is about an adulterous author, whose lover leaves him unexpectedly. It is 'one of the most true and moving novels of my time, in anybody's language', wrote William Faulkner (433). Greene was a serial adulterer himself and had left his wife and children in 1947, saying: 'my books are my children'.

1962 Penguin Books
1975 Penguin Books *revised*
1991 Twentieth-Century Classics
• —

Loser Takes All

1955

Bertram is an unambitious assistant accountant until, at the casino in Monte Carlo, his betting system starts unexpectedly and spectacularly to work.

1971 Penguin Books
1977 Penguin Books *revised*
1993 Twentieth-Century Classics
• —

The Quiet American 1955

Alden Pyle, a CIA agent, becomes involved in the French war in Vietnam and entangled with the Vietnamese mistress of the narrator, an English foreign correspondent. The book is based on Greene's own experiences as an MI6 agent in French Indochina.

1962 Penguin Books
1974 Penguin Books *revised*
1991 Twentieth-Century Classics
• —

Our Man in Havana
An Entertainment 1958

James Wormold, a vacuum-cleaner salesman, is recruited by MI6 to work for British Intelligence in Cuba. Greene himself had helped Cuban revolutionaries in 1957, secretly transporting supplies to Fidel Castro's communist rebels, who were hiding in the hills over winter. This black comedy was the last of Greene's books to be labelled an 'entertainment'. It was adapted for the screen in 1959 and as an opera in 1963.

1962 Penguin Books
1971 Penguin Books *revised*
1991 Twentieth-Century Classics
• —

'I learnt later that MI5 suggested to MI6 that they should bring an action against the book for a breach of official secrets,' recalled Greene. 'What secret had I betrayed? Was it the possibility of using bird shit as a secret ink? But luckily C, the head of MI6, had a better sense of humour than his colleague in MI5, and he discouraged him from taking action.'

1963 Penguin Books
1975 Penguin Books *revised*
1991 Twentieth-Century Classics
• —

A Burnt-Out Case 1961

Querry is a celebrated architect suffering from exhaustion and ennui. He travels to the Congo to work in a leper colony, where he is diagnosed as the mental equivalent of a 'burnt-out case': a leper who has gone through all the stages of mutilation. Greene visited several leper communities in the Congo Basin, and dedicated the book to Michel Lechat, the doctor at one such colony in Yonda.

The Comedians 1966

The 'comedians' are three men, Brown, Smith and Jones: a hotelier, a US presidential candidate and a trickster. They meet on a ship bound for the Caribbean island of Haiti, which is controlled by the dictator 'Papa Doc' Duvalier and his sinister secret police. The novel is 'a work of strength and freshness', wrote Sybille Bedford (260), 'and in its core there lies the steel coil of compulsion'.

1967 Penguin Books
1976 Penguin Books *revised*
1991 Twentieth-Century Classics
• —

Travels with My Aunt

1969

In this witty novel, a suburban bank manager embarks on an eccentric and adventurous world tour with his septuagenarian Aunt Augusta, who regales him with stories of former lovers and nefarious exploits.

1971 Penguin Books
1991 Twentieth-Century
Classics
● —

A Sort of Life 1971

An autobiography is only ever 'a sort of life', Greene explains in his preface – 'it may contain less errors of fact than a biography, but it is of necessity even more selective: it begins later and it ends prematurely'. This memoir describes Greene's childhood and ends with the publication of his first novel, *The Man Within* (88); he continued his life story in *Ways of Escape*.

1972 Penguin Books
1993 Twentieth-Century
Classics
● —

The Honorary Consul

1973

Charley Fortnum is a whisky-sodden British honorary consul, based on the Paraná River in Argentina. When he is kidnapped, his captors must negotiate his release with the equally corrupt Argentine authorities.

1974 Penguin Books
1991 Twentieth-Century
Classics
● —

The Human Factor 1978

Greene set out 'to write a novel of espionage free from the conventional violence, which has not, in spite of James Bond (126), been a feature of the British Secret Service'. Maurice Castle is a bureaucrat in the African section at MI6 who attempts to investigate a leak. It is 'as fine a novel as he has ever written', said Anthony Burgess (148) – 'concise, ironic, acutely observant of contemporary life, funny, shocking, above all compassionate'.

1978 Penguin Books
1991 Twentieth-Century
Classics
● —

Doctor Fischer of Geneva
or, The Bomb Party 1980

In this black satire, Dr Fischer is a misanthropic toothpaste millionaire, who devises a deadly party game of Russian-roulette Christmas crackers.

1980 Penguin Books
1992 Twentieth-Century
Classics
●

Ways of Escape 1980

Greene's second volume of biography picks up after *A Sort of Life* and describes his writing career and his journeys across five continents. These travels, he explains, 'as much as the act of writing, were ways of escape'.

1981 Penguin Books
1992 Twentieth-Century
Classics
● —

1983 Penguin Books
1992 Twentieth-Century Classics
● —

Monsignor Quixote

1982

Father Quixote is a Spanish parish priest who thinks he is a direct descendant of Cervantes's fictional hero. When the Pope unexpectedly gives him the title of 'monsignor', his bishop encourages him to take a holiday; so Monsignor Quixote sets off around Spain, in a car he calls 'Rocinante' after Don Quixote's steed, accompanied by a deposed communist mayor as his Sancho Panza.

THE PENGUIN BOOK OF THE BRITISH SHORT STORY
from P. G. Wodehouse to Zadie Smith
1929–2013

British short stories are playful and performative, writes the novelist Philip Hensher, and frequently dependent on comedy. 'From that valuing of comedy comes, I think, a characteristic of the British short story to entwine, reverse, overturn itself and take directions that nobody could foresee.' This volume includes stories by P. G. Wodehouse (48), Graham Greene (88), Roald Dahl (113), Sam Selvon (554), Muriel Spark (141), V. S. Naipaul (555), Jean Rhys (551) and Angela Carter (156).

2016
• ed. Philip Hensher, 2015
—

This is the companion volume to *The Penguin Book of the British Short Story, from Daniel Defoe to John Buchan*, published in Penguin Classics at the same time. Hensher has since published *The Penguin Book of the Contemporary British Short Story* (2018) and *The Golden Age of British Short Stories, 1890–1914* (2020).

1985 Penguin Books
1993 Twentieth-Century Classics
• —

Getting to Know the General
The Story of an Involvement 1984

In 1976, Graham Greene received a mysterious telegram inviting him to Panama, all expenses paid. This is the account of the ensuing adventure and his unexpected friendship with General Omar Torrijos, the Panamanian head of state, who died in an air accident in 1981.

The Captain and the Enemy 1988

Young Victor Baxter is removed from school by an enigmatic stranger known as 'the Captain', who has apparently won him in a game of backgammon. Victor is taken to be the companion of a woman called Liza, for whom he becomes the only contact with the outside world. The novel is 'rich with echoes of Graham Greene's great obsessions', wrote the *New York Times* – 'love, sex, authority, God, the paradoxical natures of truth, honesty, strength, goodness, and evil'.

1989 Penguin Books
1999 Twentieth-Century Classics
• —

Richard Pennington
1904–2003

Richard Pennington was a librarian, who worked variously at the National Liberal Club in London, the University of Queensland in Australia and McGill University in Canada, before retiring to France in 1965 and setting up a small printing press. He has been described as 'a man of dazzling complexity and great charisma who could be charming or disdainful with equal ease'.

1987
• pref. Michael Holroyd, 1985

Peterley Harvest
The Private Diary of David Peterley
1930–39, pub. 1960

Peterley Harvest purports to present a journal of the 1930s by a young man, David Peterley, 'edited' by Richard Pennington. Mysteriously, it was withdrawn from sale within days of its first publication. The book is a riddle and it remains unclear whether its events in London and Czechoslovakia, the love affairs, and the encounters with real figures such as J. B. Priestley (87) and Graham Greene (88) are fictional autobiography or autobiographical fiction. The biographer Michael Holroyd calls it 'a remarkable exercise in ventriloquism'.

E. M. Delafield

1890 – 1943

Edmée Elizabeth Monica de la Pasture used an anglicized pen name, 'Delafield', to distinguish herself from her mother, who was also a novelist. At 21, she entered a nunnery in Belgium, but soon left. She worked as a nurse in Exeter during the First World War and lived most of her life in a small village in Devon, reworking her chaotic home life in delightfully humorous prose.

2014
intro. Rachel Johnson

The Diary of a Provincial Lady

1930 – 40

The Diary of a Provincial Lady,
The Provincial Lady Goes Further,
The Provincial Lady in America,
The Provincial Lady in Wartime

These novellas take the form of a diary, painting a portrait of a large household in a small Devon village, where a long-suffering mother deals with a curmudgeonly husband, difficult children and a petulant cook. In sequels, the Provincial Lady finds a flat in London, travels to America and looks for work at the start of the Second World War. The books, writes Jilly Cooper, are 'incredibly funny, and yet, in a way, as homely and reassuringly familiar as the rattle of pips in a Cox's apple'.

E. F. Benson

1867 – 1940

Edward Frederic Benson's light comic novels caused a stir because his father had been the Archbishop of Canterbury. Benson went on to represent England at figure skating and lived for many years in Henry James's (397) former house in Rye, East Sussex, where he was elected mayor in 1934.

1970 Penguin Books
2004 Modern Classics
intro. Philip Hensher, 2004

Mapp and Lucia

1931

There were six Mapp and Lucia novels, largely set in Tilling, a replica of Rye. In *Mapp and Lucia*, a central instalment, snobbish Mrs Emmeline 'Lucia' Lucas takes a house in Tilling for the summer, bringing her recipe for 'lobster à la Riseholme', and immediately clashes with Miss Elizabeth Mapp in a desperate and hilarious battle of social one-upmanship.

POETRY OF THE THIRTIES
from Auden to Spender 1930 – 39

In the early 1960s, the poet Robin Skelton assembled these poems from 'that period of unease, threatened by war as we are threatened, troubled by social and racial conflicts as we are troubled'. His collection is organized into eight thematic sections, including one on the Spanish Civil War (232), with contributions from poets including John Betjeman (88), William Empson (86), Laurie Lee (114), Louis MacNeice and Dylan Thomas (98), and especially W. H. Auden and Steven Spender, the leading poets of the decade.

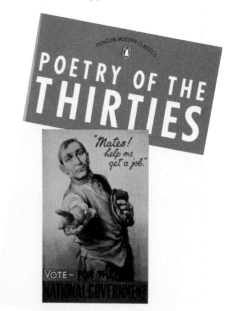

1964 Penguin Poets
1985 Modern Classics
ed. Robin Skelton, 1964
—
Robin Skelton also edited *Poetry of the Forties* (111) for Penguin.

2013
—

Eric Gill

1882 – 1940

Arthur Eric Rowton Gill was a sculptor and type designer, who created faces including Gill Sans, used on the covers of the first Penguin Books, and Joanna (ix), named after his daughter, which was used on the covers of the first Penguin Modern Classics. Gill was a lay member of the Dominican order and wore a monastic habit while he worked. In 1989, it emerged that he had had repeated extramarital affairs, as well as incestuous intercourse with his sisters and teenage daughters, and an 'experimental connection' – as his biographer Fiona MacCarthy put it – with his pet spaniel.

An Essay on Typography

1931

Set in Gill's own Joanna typeface, this essay covers the history, philosophy and practicalities of designing typefaces. 'A good piece of lettering is as beautiful a thing to see as any sculpture or painted picture,' wrote Gill.

Eric Linklater

1899 – 1974

Eric Linklater was the son of an Orcadian master mariner. He went to school in Aberdeen, a city to which he frequently returned: he studied medicine and English at Aberdeen University, where he later taught English Literature and became Rector in 1945. He also served in the Black Watch during the First World War, worked as assistant editor of the *Times of India*, spent two years in the USA as a Commonwealth Fellow at Cornell University and the University of California, Berkeley, and wrote 'instant histories' of the Second World War for the War Office.

Juan in America

1931

Juan, an updated version of Byron's Don Juan, arrives in New York to study at Motley University. Within 24 hours, he has witnessed a suicide, a shoot-out, and yaks making love in Central Park, and he has jumped aboard a train to Chicago, pursuing a glamorous lady whose name he doesn't know. Based on Linklater's own experiences in the USA during Prohibition, the success of this bestseller spawned a flurry of 'an innocent in America' stories. 'Juan in America is a supremely amusing book,' declared the writer and diplomat Harold Nicolson. 'But it is more than that. It is a serious and sympathetic criticism of American conditions. It is a work of outstanding literary skill.'

1956 Penguin Books
1987 Modern Classics
● intro. Michael Parnell, 1987

Linklater's second novel, *Poet's Pub* (1929), was reprinted as one of the first ten Penguin books in 1935: number three in the series. It is now available in Penguin Classics.

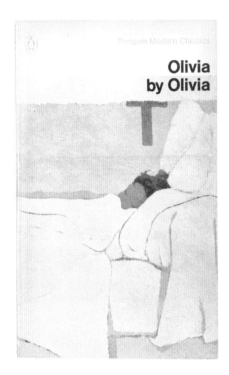

'Olivia'

(Dorothy Bussy) 1865 – 1960

'Olivia' was the pseudonym of Dorothy Bussy, the older sister of Lytton Strachey (64). She was educated at Marie Souvestre's girls' school in Fontainebleau and returned to teach Shakespeare at another of Souvestre's establishments before marrying the French painter Simon Bussy in 1903. She fell desperately in love with André Gide (164), whose works she translated into English.

Olivia 1931 – 3, pub. 1949

Bussy's only novel was published anonymously. The book follows a 16-year-old English schoolgirl's crush on Mlle Julie, a teacher at her French finishing school. Bussy described her book as an account of

1966
• —
Olivia had been the name of one of Dorothy's sisters, who died in infancy.

'the year when I first became conscious of myself, of love and pleasure, of death and pain, and when every reaction to them was as unexpected, as amazing, as involuntary as the experience itself'. It is dedicated to 'the beloved memory of V. W.', Virginia Woolf (42).

James Hanley 1897 – 1985

Hanley was born in Liverpool to Irish parents. His father was a stoker on Cunard liners, and Hanley himself went to sea at the age of seventeen, before jumping ship in Canada to join the Canadian Black Watch. When he returned to Liverpool, he worked as a railway porter, learned the piano, read Russian novels and took up writing. In later years he lived in Wales, where he became a close friend of John Cowper Powys (86). William Faulkner (433) compared Hanley's language to 'a good clean cyclone'.

Boy 1931

In this unremittingly bleak novel, a 13-year-old Liverpool lad runs away to sea to escape his tyrannical father. He cleans the ship's boilers on the way to Alexandria, loses his virginity in an Egyptian brothel and contracts syphilis, in the throes of which he is put down like a sick dog. Hanley wrote Boy in ten days and dedicated it to the writer and heiress Nancy Cunard, who had given him his first typewriter.

1992
• intro. Anthony Burgess, 1989
fwd. Liam Hanley, 1990
—

In 1934, a Lancashire taxi driver and his wife, who had read only the blurb, took Boy to the police in Bury. Hanley's publishers were successfully prosecuted for obscene libel and the book was withdrawn from circulation. The Penguin edition was the first unexpurgated paperback edition since the obscenity trial. 'New readers now have the opportunity to be shocked directly, rather than through notoriety,' wrote Anthony Burgess (148) in his introduction. Liam Hanley, who wrote the foreword, is James Hanley's son.

The Furys 1935

Hanley wrote a series of novels about a poor Anglo-Irish family, the Furys, who lived in a fictionalized version of Liverpool. This is the first instalment, in which Peter Fury returns home during the city's 1911 general transport strike and faces his

1983 King Penguin
1992 Twentieth-Century Classics
• —

mother's disappointment, resentment and anguish. The 'surface is broad, level and simple, almost smooth', wrote Rosamond Lehmann (77). 'The complete world lies bare under a curiously uncoloured light but life informs the whole of it.'

Dylan Thomas

1914–1953

Dylan Marlais Thomas was born in Swansea, South Wales. He worked briefly for the *South Wales Evening Post* before the success of his first poetry book in 1934 allowed him to adopt the lifestyle of a bohemian in London's Fitzrovia, scraping funds together between publications. In 1936, the artist Augustus John introduced him to Caitlin Macnamara, a young blonde dancer at the London Palladium. Within ten minutes, Thomas later recalled, they were having sex. They married the following year, settling in the Carmarthenshire seaside village of Laugharne. Thomas was an extremely popular poet, making frequent broadcasts for the BBC and undertaking several lecture tours of the USA, while cultivating a reputation as a gout-ridden, self-destructive alcoholic.

Dylan Thomas Selected Poems

The New Apocalypse

Inspired by D. H. Lawrence's *Apocalypse* (56), the New Apocalypse was a short-lived poetic movement that was announced in 1939 by an anthology of essays, poems and stories, edited by J. F. Hendry, called *The New Apocalypse*. In his introduction, Hendry explained that 'Apocalyptic writing' occurs 'where expression breaks through the structure of the language to become more organic'. The anthology includes one poem and one story by Dylan Thomas, who later described the group as 'intellectual muckpots leaning on a theory, post-surrealists (176) and orgasmists, tit-in-the-night whistlers and Barkers'. There were two further anthologies, *The White Horseman* (1941) and *The Crown and the Sickle* (1943), but the group had dispersed by the end of the Second World War.

Selected Poems

1931–53

Philip Larkin once wrote to Kingsley Amis (132) saying that no one can 'stick words into us like pins' like Dylan Thomas; Amis, on the other hand, thought that Thomas was 'frothing at the mouth with piss'. Thomas's poems are musical and memorable, with familiar titles such as 'And death shall have no dominion' and 'Do not go gentle into that good night'. 'The world is never the same once a good poem has been added to it,' he said.

2000
• ed. Walford Davies, 1974, 1993

Under Milk Wood
A Play for Voices 1953

This poetic drama, completed just months before Thomas died, has become his best-known work. It depicts a day in the sleepy Welsh seaside village of Llareggub, or 'bugger all' backwards. It opens before dawn with an omniscient narrator watching the characters asleep. We listen to their dreams before they gradually awake and go about their humorous, eccentric and flirtatious business, creating a 'greenleaved sermon on the innocence of men'. Thomas completed *Under Milk Wood* in May 1953, just in time for a full-cast read-through in New York, after being locked in a room until he finished it.

Dylan Thomas Under Milk Wood

2000
• ed. Walford Davies

J. R. Ackerley 1896–1967

Joe Randolph Ackerley was the son of a fruit merchant, the 'Banana King' of London. He had a close and enduring friendship with E. M. Forster (38), who encouraged him to travel to India, where he spent five months in 1923 serving as a private secretary to the Maharajah of Chhatarpur. Ackerley joined the BBC in 1928, soon after its foundation, and worked there for the rest of his career, as an assistant producer for the Talks Department and then as literary editor of the *Listener*, in which he promoted poets including Philip Larkin, W. H. Auden (95) and Stephen Spender (95).

Hindoo Holiday
An Indian Journal 1932, rev. 1952

'About all I knew of [India] when I sailed for it was what I was able to recollect from my schooldays,' recalled Ackerley – 'that there had been a mutiny there, for instance, and that it looked rather like an inverted Matterhorn on the map, pink because we governed it.' He describes his experience of working for the Maharajah of Chhatarpur, lightly fictionalized as 'Chhokrapur', and his fascination with Hindu culture, festivals and language. His Highness the Maharajah Sahib was gay (as was Ackerley), and at the centre of this book is a portrait of a lonely man, who only 'wanted someone to love him'. Ackerley's 'humour is the humour of pity and love', wrote V. S. Pritchett (110). 'He is an artist of understanding.'

1940 Penguin Books
1994 Twentieth-Century Classics
● intro. William Dalrymple, 1994
2009 Modern Classics
—

Stella Gibbons 1902–1989

Gibbons was the daughter of an alcoholic, womanizing London surgeon who died of heart disease, after which Gibbons supported her family by writing. They lived on Hampstead Heath, partly due to its connections with John Keats, a poet she loved. She became famous for her first novel, *Cold Comfort Farm*, the success of which overshadowed her subsequent books, much to Gibbons' annoyance. She called it 'That Book' and 'You Know What' to avoid having to say its title.

1938 Penguin Books
1995 Twentieth-Century Classics
2006 Penguin Classics
2020 Modern Classics
intro. Lynne Truss, 2006

Cold Comfort Farm 1932

The rustic Starkadders of Cold Comfort Farm in Sussex are flabbergasted by the arrival of their sophisticated relative, Flora Poste, who sets about organizing and reforming them all, from remorseful cousin Judith to fiery Amos, lustful Seth, and old Aunt Ada Doom, who once saw 'something nasty in the woodshed'. It satirizes D. H. Lawrence (50) and the copious 'loam and love-child' novels of the 1920s, which Gibbons reviewed for the *Lady*. For the assistance of her own reviewers, she includes a system of asterisks to mark out the 'finer passages', differentiating between literary sections and 'sheer flapdoodle'.

More FEMALE PROTAGONISTS

Zuleika Dobson
by Max Beerbohm — 60

Gilgi, One of Us
by Irmgard Keun — 254

The Rector's Daughter
by F. M. Mayor — 73

Fireflies
by Shiva Naipaul — 556

Novel on Yellow Paper
by Stevie Smith — 108

Lewis Grassic Gibbon

1901–1935

James Leslie Mitchell was born on an Aberdeenshire croft and was laid as a baby in his mother's plaid while she reaped the harvest. He grew up on farms in Kincardineshire, the setting of *A Scots Quair*. At sixteen, he became a junior reporter on the *Aberdeen Journal*, before enrolling as a clerk in the Royal Army Service Corps in 1919 and joining the Royal Air Force a year later. In 1929, he became a full-time writer, occasionally publishing under his mother's maiden name of Gibbon. He wrote seventeen books, including a historical novel about Spartacus, before he died of peritonitis six days shy of his 34th birthday.

A Scots Quair

Sunset Song, Cloud Howe, Grey Granite

1932–4

This trilogy follows Chris Guthrie, a woman driven to extremes of poverty and loneliness, torn between her love of northeast Scotland and her desire to escape her background. It is written as a lyrical stream of consciousness and set against a backdrop of the First World War, the General Strike of 1926 and the hunger marches of the thirties. In *Sunset Song* (1932), Chris grows up in a tragic household and finds love on the eve of the war; in *Cloud Howe* (1933), Chris is married to Robert Colquhoun, a Church of Scotland minister; and in *Grey Granite* (1934), she moves to the city with her son Ewan, who has become a socialist activist. Together these novels are the high point of the Scottish Renaissance (72), marking 'in their different way as great a departure from the run of Scottish novels as James Joyce's *Ulysses* (10) from the run of Irish novels', as Hugh MacDiarmid (72) put it. Ali Smith has called *Sunset Song* an 'unflinching yearn of a book'.

1986 Modern Classics
● intro. David Kerr Cameron, 1986
2007 Penguin Classics *Sunset Song*
ed. William K. Malcolm, 2007
intro. Ali Smith, 2007

Julia Strachey

1901–1979

Julia Strachey was born in India, the daughter of a cryptographer; she was the niece of Lytton Strachey (64) and Dorothy Bussy (97). She was raised in England by various foster-parents, including Bertrand Russell's wife, and worked as a fashion mannequin, a photographer and a publisher's reader.

Cheerful Weather for the Wedding and An Integrated Man

1932–51

Cheerful Weather for the Wedding (1932), Strachey's first novel, was published by Virginia Woolf (42), who said that it was 'astonishingly good – complete and sharp and individual'. It humorously describes a country wedding in Dorset. It is 'a very small book but a very perfect one', wrote the author David Garnett, 'revealing a rich sense of humour and very great literary and dramatic skill'. In *An Integrated Man*, originally published in 1951 as *The Man on the Pier*, Ned falls in love with his friend's wife but resists his own feelings. It is 'an historical novel', wrote the critic John Russell: 'one which brings back to life a whole complex of vanished ways, vanished attitudes, vanished amenities and, some would say, vanished scruples'.

1978
● –

1969
● —
The cover artwork shows
a detail from a 1919 Labour
Party election poster.

Walter Greenwood 1903–1974

Greenwood was born in Salford, Lancashire, the son of a hairdresser. He left school at thirteen and had jobs as a milk-round boy, an office boy, a stable boy, a clerk, a packing-case maker, a signwriter, a driver and a warehouseman; he never earned more than 35 shillings a week. He was unemployed and 'on the dole' at least three times, and it was during one such stint of unemployment that he wrote his first novel, *Love on the Dole*. It was a critical and commercial success, and he went on to write many more books, stage plays and film scripts.

Love on the Dole 1933

Love on the Dole was the first novel to represent the chronic unemployment of the 1930s. Brother and sister Harry and Sally Hardcastle live in a Salford slum: as Harry joins the dole queue, both siblings are gradually crushed by their mounting poverty. The raw narrative caused public outrage and helped lead to social reform.

Malcolm Lowry

1909–1957

Lowry went to sea between school and university, working as a deckhand and coal-trimmer on a ship bound for the Far East. After university, he moved to Paris, where he married his first wife, and then to New York, where he concentrated on literature and alcohol, having arrived, according to legend, with just one football boot and a copy of *Moby-Dick*. He travelled to Mexico, where he drank mescal and his marriage dissolved, before winding up in British Columbia, where he married again and lived in a squatter's shack on the beach outside Vancouver. After the shack burned down, Lowry travelled around the world; he returned to England in 1955, and choked to death in his sleep. He wrote his own poetic epitaph, which was not inscribed on his gravestone:

> Malcolm Lowry
> Late of the Bowery
> His prose was flowery
> And often glowery
> He lived, nightly, and drank, daily,
> And died playing the ukulele.

Ultramarine 1933

Inspired by Lowry's experiences as a deckhand, *Ultramarine* is the story of Dana Hilliot, a teenager who runs away to sea on the freighter *Oedipus Tyrannus*, bound for the Far East. After the book was accepted for publication, the editor's briefcase was stolen along with the only manuscript, so Lowry had to rewrite it.

Hear Us O Lord from Heaven Thy Dwelling Place and Lunar Caustic

1936–54, pub. 1961–3

'Hear Us O Lord' is an ancient fishermen's hymn from the Isle of Man, the tune and lyrics of which are included in this edition. Its words echo through the seven stories in *Hear Us O Lord from Heaven Thy Dwelling Place* (1950–54, pub. 1961), which feature Sigbjørn Wilderness – protagonist of *Dark as the Grave Wherein My Friend is Laid* (102) – on a voyage through the Panama Canal, a description of the wild Pacific coast of Canada, and a steamer full of animals. Lowry had almost completed this manuscript before he died. *Lunar Caustic* (1936–52, pub. 1963) was a neglected work in progress. It is a Surrealist (176) account of Lowry's stay at Bellevue Hospital in New York in 1936, which he described as a 'deliberate pilgrimage' to gather material.

1974 Modern Classics
● intro. Margerie Lowry, 1963
2000 Modern Classics
● intro. Mark Rudman, 2000

1969 Penguin Books *Hear Us
O Lord from Heaven Thy
Dwelling Place*
1979 Modern Classics
with Lunar Caustic
● fwd. Conrad Knickerbocker,
1963
ed. Earle Birney & Margerie
Lowry, 1961–3

1962 Modern Classics
2000 Modern Classics
intro. Michael Schmidt, 2000

1979
• ed. Margerie Lowry, 1970
—
Lowry left *October Ferry to Gabriola* unfinished, but his wife Margerie Lowry assembled and edited the text using his marginal notes and instructions.

Under the Volcano 1940–45, pub. 1947

Lowry's masterpiece takes place on a single day in the life of Geoffrey Firmin, an alcoholic former British consul in Mexico. It is the Day of the Dead, 2 November 1938, in the small town of Quauhnahuac, which lies in the shadow of the volcano Popocatepetl. The book is demented, spiralling deliriously towards a mescal-fuelled climax. 'Under the Volcano eats light like a black hole,' writes the poet and translator Michael Hofmann. 'It is a work of such gravity and connectedness and spectroscopic richness that it is more world than product. [...] It has planetary swagger, it is a planet dancing.'

Dark as the Grave Wherein My Friend is Laid

1946–52, pub. 1968

Sigbjørn Wilderness is a writer unable to write, inept and alcoholic, a cipher for Lowry himself. He is 'a drunk of gargantuan proportions', explained Lowry, 'yet a man who seems never to have let go an almost preternatural degree of self-awareness, even when face down on the floor of a pub or cantina'. The narrative is based on Lowry's own return visit to Mexico in December 1945 with his second wife Margerie, and the ghosts he encountered in Oaxaca.

October Ferry to Gabriola 1946–57, pub. 1970

Lowry's last novel is about Ethan Llewellyn, a once-brilliant lawyer who is sick of the law and haunted by the past. Based on a trip Lowry made in October 1946, it follows Ethan and his wife as they visit Gabriola, an island off the east coast of Vancouver Island. 'It deals with the theme of eviction, which is related to man's dispossession,' wrote Lowry. '[...] This I believe to be a hell of a fine thing.'

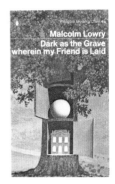

1972 Penguin Books
1975 Modern Classics
• ed. Douglas Day & Margerie Lowry, 1968
—
Douglas Day, who was Lowry's first biographer, discovered the 705-page typescript of *Dark as the Grave* among Lowry's papers at the University of British Columbia.

A. J. A. Symons

1900 – 1941

Alphonse James Albert Symons collected music boxes and rare books and wrote three biographies. He edited an anthology of 1890s verse and founded the Wine and Food Society.

The Quest for Corvo
An Experiment in Biography 1934

In 1925, Symons was given a copy of a neglected masterpiece, Hadrian the Seventh (10), and became captivated by its eccentric author, Frederick Rolfe. This book is the account of Symons's wide-ranging pursuit of increasingly surprising information about Rolfe. It is 'part detective story, part spiritual journey, and part meditation on biography', writes the critic Hermione Lee.

In 1941, Symons wrote to Allen Lane (viii): 'I see from the newspaper that you are going to be married. I hasten to offer you my warmest good wishes for your future happiness. I very much hope that when the war is over you will bring your wife to pay your long delayed visit to this house of lost causes and forgotten tunes. [...] I shall be grateful if you will send me a list of Penguins in print. My brother is a prisoner in Denmark and I want to send him some books for the Prisoners' Library.'
—
1940 Penguin Books
2018 Modern Classics
—

Herbert Read 1893–1968

Read was the son of a Yorkshire farmer. He served as an infantry officer during the First World War and subsequently worked at the Treasury, and then at the Victoria and Albert Museum as the assistant keeper of ceramics and stained glass. He went on to become an anarchist poet and Professor of Fine Arts at Edinburgh University, later lecturing on poetry and art at Cambridge, Liverpool and Harvard universities. He was a champion of Surrealism (176), he inspired the 'New Apocalypse' (98) poets and he co-founded the Institute of Contemporary Arts in London. He was knighted in 1953.

The Green Child 1935

This fantastical novel set in the 19th century opens with the faked assassination of Dr Olivero, President of a South American republic. Olivero is in fact an Englishman called Oliver, who stumbled into dictatorship accidentally, and now yearns for his native Yorkshire. On his return, he follows a stream flowing backwards until he meets Sally, a mysterious 'green child' with transparent flesh. She leads him into a subterraneous world of crystalline philosophers, where he is gradually subsumed into the petrified rockscape. Read was inspired by a 12th-century legend, as well as his own dreams and automatic writing. '*The Green Child* is the kind of book to write if you are going to leave just the one novel behind,' mused the critic Geoffrey Wheatcroft: 'singular, odd, completely original.'

1969
● intro. Graham Greene (88), 1947

Christopher Isherwood 1904–1986

Isherwood lived in London with the violinist André Mangeot, before following his old prep-school friend W. H. Auden (95) to Berlin to teach English. Isherwood lived in Weimar Germany for three years, where he spent time with Stephen Spender (95), fell in love with a German boy and witnessed Hitler's rise to power. In 1939, he emigrated to the USA with Auden and became a scriptwriter, a friend of Truman Capote (463), Aldous Huxley (65) and Dodie Smith, a passionate yoga enthusiast and a lecturer at the University of California, Los Angeles. In 1953, he met the 18-year-old Don Bachardy on the beach at Santa Monica and the pair became on–off partners until Isherwood's death.

Mr Norris Changes Trains 1935

Inspired by Isherwood's experiences in Germany, this novel revolves around the mysterious Arthur Norris, communist and spy, whom the narrator meets while changing trains on the way to Berlin. Norris 'is a true original', wrote the *Daily Telegraph*: 'a flabby rogue without, as one would say, a single redeeming quality, who is nevertheless one of the most delightful persons one has met in fiction for a long time'.

1942 Penguin Books
1961 Modern Classics
● —
The story is narrated by William Bradshaw, a cipher for Isherwood himself, whose full name was Christopher William Bradshaw Isherwood.

Goodbye to Berlin

1939

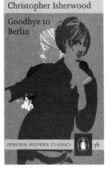

1945 Penguin Books
1962 Modern Classics
• –

This collection of episodes continues and completes Isherwood's portrait of pre-war Berlin, with its tenement boarding houses, dingy nightclubs and glitzy villas. George Orwell (80) called them 'very brilliant sketches of a society in decay'. Isherwood experiments with techniques borrowed from the cinema, with flashbacks, establishing shots, pans and zooms. He introduces the character Sally Bowles, who became the central figure in the play adaptation *I am a Camera* (1951) and the multi-award-winning Broadway musical *Cabaret* (1966). Isherwood chose Sally's surname after meeting Paul Bowles (480).

Prater Violet

1945

1961
• –

This novel, a portrait of the pre-war British film industry, is based on Isherwood's own experiences of the movies. It describes the scripting and shooting of a film, *Prater Violet*, directed by the charismatic and eccentric director Friedrich Bergmann.

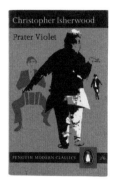

Ivy Compton-Burnett

1884 – 1969

'I have had such an uneventful life that there is little information to give,' wrote Ivy Compton-Burnett, when asked for a biographical paragraph. 'I was educated with my brothers in the country as a child, and later went to Holloway College, and took a degree in Classics. I lived with my family when I was quite young, but for most of my life have had my own flat in London. I see a good deal of a good many friends, not all of them writing people. And there is really no more to say.' Compton-Burnett was one of thirteen children; her favourite brother died of pneumonia; another brother was killed during the First World War; and her two youngest sisters died in a suicide pact on Christmas Day 1917. She lived for much of her life with the historian of English furniture Margaret Jourdain, and wrote chilling novels riddled with malice and violence and populated by late-Victorian and Edwardian aristocrats. The *Times Literary Supplement* described her style as 'Aeschylus [. . .] transposed into the key of Jane Austen'.

1958 Penguin Books
1982 Modern Classics
• –

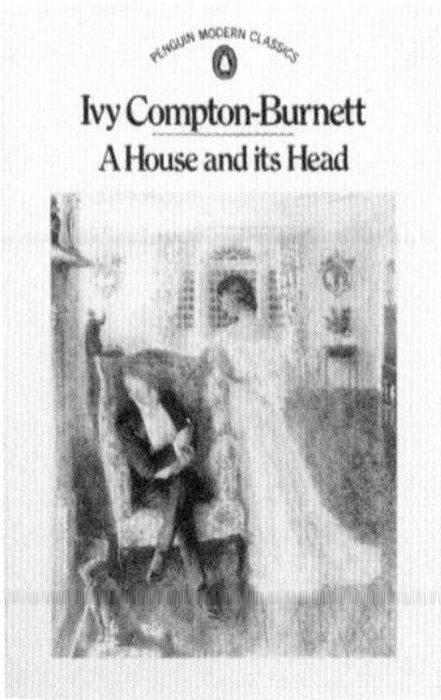

A House and Its Head

1935

This novel, one of Compton-Burnett's own favourites, unpeels an upper-class Victorian family, revealing the writhing jealousies and sexual frustrations below the surface. 'It is as if one's next door neighbour leaned over the garden wall,' ran a review in the *Church Times*, 'and remarked, in the same breath and chatty tone, that he had mown the lawn in the morning and thrust his wife's head in the gas-oven after lunch.'

More DYSFUNCTIONAL FAMILIES

The Sound and the Fury
by William Faulkner 433

Death in Rome
by Wolfgang Koeppen 259

There Once Lived a Mother Who Loved Her Children, Until They Moved Back In
by Ludmilla Petrushevskaya 317

The Man Who Loved Children
by Christina Stead 381

The Flint Anchor
by Sylvia Townsend Warner 76

1962
• —

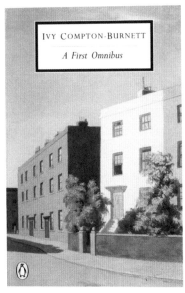

1994
• intro. Hilary Mantel
—

A First Omnibus comprises
A Family and a Fortune,
Parents and Children
and *A God and His Gifts*.
'Ivy Compton-Burnett is one
of the most original, artful and
elegant writers of our century,'
writes Hilary Mantel in her
introduction. '[…] The writing
is pared to the bone, the
technique is a gavotte
on needles.'

A Family and a Fortune
1939

'Well, of course, people are only human,' wrote
Compton-Burnett. '[…] But it really does not
seem much for them to be.' *A Family and a Fortune*
portrays the Gaveston family falling apart after
a large inheritance is announced. It features
the memorable tyrant, Aunt Matty.

Parents and Children
1941

Eleanor and Fulbert Sullivan live in his parents'
rambling but claustrophobic country house with
their nine children, until Fulbert's father sends
him to South America on an ill-fated business
trip. 'To read in these days a page of Compton-
Burnett dialogue,' wrote Elizabeth Bowen (13)
in her review, 'is to think of the sound of glass
being swept up, one of these London mornings
after a blitz.'

The Present and the Past
1953

Nine years after their divorce, Catherine Clare
announces unexpectedly that she is coming back
to live with her ex-husband Cassius, their two
sons and Cassius's second wife. The results of
her arrival are unexpected and extreme.

A God and His Gifts
1963

A God and His Gifts centres around the appalling
Hereward Egerton, who maintains a veneer of
Edwardian respectability while attempting to
seduce his wife's sister and his son's fiancée.

The Last and the First
1969, pub. 1971

Compton-Burnett's
last novel opens with a
dramatic breakfast scene
that initiates a brutal
struggle for dominance
between two aristocratic
female tyrants.

1970
• —

1970
• —

1983
• —

1986
• fwd. Elizabeth Sprigge, 1971
epilogue Charles Burkhart,
1971
—
The novelist Elizabeth Sprigge,
a friend of Compton-Burnett,
helped to edit her manuscript
for this posthumous
publication. 'Unfinished
though it is,' she wrote,
'The Last and the First gives
us one more treasure of
Ivy's superb wit and almost
superhuman perception.'

1971 Pelican Books
1990 Penguin Books
2001 Modern Classics
intro. Ben Rogers, 2001

A. J. Ayer 1910–1989

Alfred Jules 'Freddie' Ayer was an academic philosopher, and worked as a spy during the Second World War. He was a committed humanist, a friend of George Orwell (80) and a fan of Tottenham Hotspur football club, and he was married four times to three women. His first wife, Renée Lees, was the daughter of Thomas Orde-Lees, who accompanied Ernest Shackleton (12) on the *Endurance* expedition. Between 1951 and 1963, Ayer was the editorial advisor for the philosophy titles in the Pelican series (xiii).

Language, Truth and Logic 1936

In this controversial and influential book, Ayer develops the 'verification principle' of logical positivism, which he had encountered in Vienna. A factual proposition is only meaningful, he says, if it can be verified by direct experience, which means that statements about God, for example, are indistinguishable from nonsense. Ayer wrote *Language, Truth and Logic* when he was just 24, and liked to point out that David Hume had been 28 when he published the *Treatise on Human Nature* (1739–40).

T. H. White 1906–1964

Terence Hanbury White, known as 'Tim', was born in Bombay, now Mumbai, the son of an alcoholic policeman. He became a master at Stowe School in Buckinghamshire, where he kept tame grass snakes in the classroom, before leaving to write *The Sword in the Stone* (1938). He spent the Second World War in Ireland, working on the rest of his Arthurian quartet, *The Once and Future King* (1958), and after the war he settled on Alderney in the Channel Islands. He was a solitary man who suffered from periods of intense loneliness. 'It has been my hideous fate to be born with an infinite capacity for love and joy,' he wrote, 'with no hope of using them.'

The Goshawk 1936, pub. 1951

In 1936, White took delivery of a German goshawk and set about taming the feral bird, using a 17th-century austringer's manual. He kept a diary while sharing his home with the ferocious creature and later turned his notes into this classic study of falconry. The writer David Garnett described it as 'the record of an intense clash of wills in which the pride and endurance of the wild raptor are worn down and broken by the almost insane willpower of the schoolmaster falconer. [...] It is strangely like some of the eighteenth-century stories of seduction.'

1963
• —

Cyril Connolly

1903–1974

Connolly was born in Coventry, the son of an army major who was obsessed with molluscs and potted meats. He went to Eton with George Orwell (80), Henry Green (119) and Anthony Powell, and he befriended Graham Greene (88) at Oxford. He became one of the most prominent literary critics of his day, writing for the *New Statesman*, the *Observer* and *The Times*, and co-founding and editing the magazine *Horizon* with Stephen Spender (95). He was the model for the critic Everard Spruce in Evelyn Waugh's *Sword of Honour* (70) and a suburban theatrical impresario in Nancy Mitford's *The Blessing* (117). 'Approaching forty, sense of total failure,' Connolly wrote in *The Unquiet Grave*: '[...] hence the manic-depressiveness of my style, – which is either bright, cruel and superficial; or pessimistic; moth-eaten with self-pity.'

The Rock Pool

1936

In Connolly's only novel, the snobbish Naylor visits a writers' colony on the French Riviera, intending to observe the community like the denizens of a rock pool, but he finds himself drawn into the swindling, vapid lifestyles of the town's inhabitants. The book was rejected by two English publishers, who considered it obscene; it was first published in Paris.

1963
• —

Enemies of Promise

1938, rev. 1948   **1961** • —

In this confessional work, Connolly tried to explain why he was not the successful author that he and his contemporaries had expected him to become. 'Whom the gods wish to destroy they first call promising,' he sighs. He identifies several enemies of literary promise, including journalism, politics, religion, sex, success and above all domesticity, famously identifying the 'pram in the hall' as the 'sombre enemy of good art'.

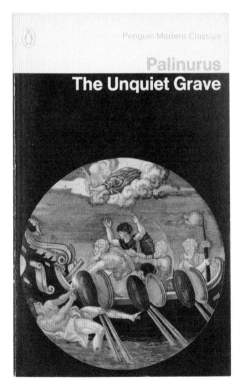

1967
• intro. Cyril Connolly, 1951

The cover artwork shows the Palinurus scene from a Renaissance majolica dish in the Contini Bonacossi Collection at the Uffizi Museum in Florence.

The Unquiet Grave
A Word Cycle by Palinurus

1944, rev. 1945

Connolly published this unusual book under the pseudonym 'Palinurus', the ship's pilot in Virgil's *Aeneid*, who falls asleep and then overboard. For Connolly, Palinurus typifies a 'will-to-failure', an idea that pervades this melancholy florilegium of literary quotations and musings on love, history, nature and art. Ernest Hemingway (428) called it 'a book which, no matter how many readers it will ever have, will never have enough'.

Stevie Smith 1902–1971

When Florence Smith's father ran away to sea, he stayed in touch by writing occasional one-line postcards. She was raised by her aunt Madge ('the Lion') in Palmers Green, north London, where she lived the rest of her life. She became known as 'Stevie', after the jockey Steve Donoghue. She worked as a secretary for some 30 years and suffered from severe depression, although she was apparently consoled by the thought of death. She won the Queen's Gold Medal for poetry in 1969 and had many literary friends, including George Orwell (80), Rosamond Lehmann (77) and Olivia Manning (159).

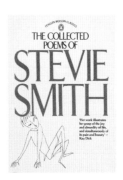

1975 Penguin Books
1985 Modern Classics
● ed. James MacGibbon, 1975

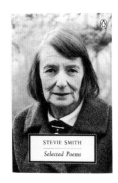

1978 Penguin Poets
1994 Twentieth-Century Classics
ed. James MacGibbon, 1978

1951 Penguin Books
1972 Modern Classics
● postscript Kay Dick, 1971
—
The cover shows a self-portrait of Stevie Smith.

Novel on Yellow Paper
or, Work It Out for Yourself 1936

Smith's first published book presents the random thoughts of a bored secretary called Pompey, who types at random, recording random memories, stories and snippets of gossip. She describes a horrific personal revelation during a visit to Nazi Germany and a painful break-up with a boy called Fred. 'This is a foot-off-the-ground novel that came by the left hand,' explains Pompey. 'And the thoughts come and go and sometimes they do not quite come and I do not pursue them to embarrass them with formality to pursue them into a harsh captivity.'

Poems 1937–71

Smith's poems are bizarre, witty, caustic and sad, and frequently self-illustrated. She had been preoccupied with death since the age of seven, and it is a recurrent theme of her poems, along with loneliness, cruelty, war and religion. Titles include 'Bag-Snatching in Dublin', 'Mother, among the Dustbins', 'To a Dead Vole', 'Souvenir de Monsieur Poop' and perhaps her most famous, 'Not Waving but Drowning'.

Eric Ambler

1909–1998

Ambler's parents worked as 'living marionettes' in southeast London's music halls. He studied engineering and worked for an advertising agency, before moving to Paris and starting to write novels and plays. In the Second World War he joined the army as a private, but transferred to an army film unit in Italy, ending the war as a lieutenant-colonel and assistant director of 'Army Kinematography'. After the war, he wrote screenplays and was nominated for an Academy Award for *The Cruel Sea* (1953). His spy stories are more politically nuanced than those of John Buchan (62) or Ian Fleming (126), and more explicitly opposed to the rising tide of fascism. Graham Greene (88) called Ambler 'unquestionably our finest thriller writer', and John le Carré (143) described him as 'the source on which we all draw'.

Uncommon Danger

1937

Kenton is a cash-strapped freelance journalist, working in Berlin, who catches a train to Austria in order to borrow some money. On the train, he's approached by a stranger, who pays him to smuggle a package over the border. But then the stranger is murdered. It's a 'crackerjack spy story', wrote the *Saturday Review*, 'jammed with action, intrigue, thrills and super-villainy'.

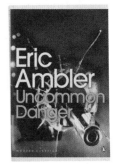

1960 Penguin Books
2009 Modern Classics
intro. Thomas Jones, 2009

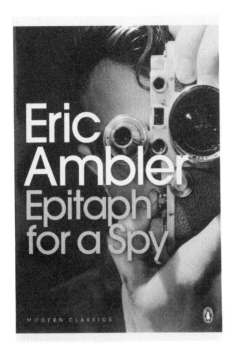

2009
intro. James Fenton

Epitaph for a Spy

1938

Josef Vadassy is a Hungarian refugee taking a long-awaited holiday on the French Riviera. When he takes out his camera for some holiday snaps, however, he is mistaken for a German agent. The only way he can convince the French police of his innocence is to identify which of his fellow hotel guests is the real spy. This is the novel that made Ambler's name.

Cause for Alarm

1938

Nicky Marlow takes a job with an English armaments manufacturer in Italy. When he arrives in the country, he discovers that his predecessor departed under sinister circumstances. As the fascist regime takes hold and Europe rushes towards war, Marlow is approached by secret agents with drastically different agendas.

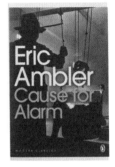

1946 Penguin Books
2009 Modern Classics
intro. John Preston, 2009

The Mask of Dimitrios

1939

In Ambler's masterpiece, Charles Latimer is a crime novelist who becomes intrigued by tales of the Turkish master criminal Dimitrios, whose swollen body has just been fished out of the Bosphorus. Latimer retraces Dimitrios's footsteps across Europe, gathering material for a novel, but soon finds himself drawn into a potentially perilous web of international intrigue. 'Not Le Carré (143), not Deighton (147), not Ludlum,' said *The Times*, 'have surpassed the intelligence, authenticity or engrossing storytelling that established *The Mask of Dimitrios* as the best of its kind.'

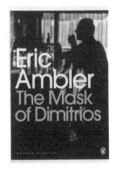

2009
intro. Mark Mazower

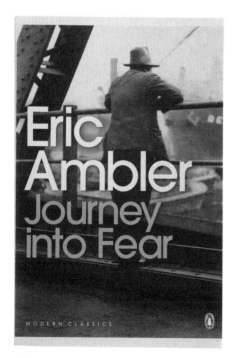

2009
intro. Norman Stone

Journey into Fear

1940

Mr Graham is a mild-mannered engineer and armaments expert taking part in high-level talks with the Turkish government. When he narrowly avoids being shot, however, he escapes from Istanbul on an Italian steamship, but not all of his fellow passengers are as friendly as they appear. The *New Yorker* called it 'one of the best stories you'll ever read'. Orson Welles produced and directed a film adaptation in 1943.

1966 Penguin Books *The Saint and Other Stories*
1973 Penguin Books *Blind Love and Other Stories*
1984 Penguin Books *Collected Stories*
<u>**1991**</u> Twentieth-Century Classics
● pref. V. S. Pritchett, 1982

V. S. Pritchett

1900 – 1997

Victor Sawdon Pritchett was born above a toyshop
in Ipswich. He left school at fifteen and worked
as a clerk in a tannery, a glue salesman and a
journalist. He went on to write novels, biographies
and travelogues, but he was most acclaimed
as a literary critic and as an author of short stories.
He was knighted in 1975.

Collected Stories

1938 – 79

'I love the intricacy of the short form,' wrote Pritchett
in his preface, 'the speed with which it can change from
scene to scene. I have always thought that the writer
of short stories is a mixture of reporter, aphoristic wit,
moralist and poet.' His titles include 'The Wheelbarrow',
'The Skeleton' and 'On the Edge of the Cliff'. 'He is
one of the great pleasure-givers in our language,' said
Eudora Welty (457).

Richard Llewellyn

1906 – 1983

Richard Herbert Vivian Lloyd grew up in
Pembrokeshire and studied hotel management
in Italy. In his spare time he worked for a film unit,
and on his return to England in 1931 he started
work as a director, a production manager and
a screenwriter for Fox-British Pictures. He is best
remembered for his first novel, *How Green Was
My Valley*, which he began drafting in India and
completed in Cardiff. He published under the
pseudonym 'Richard Llewellyn'.

How Green Was My Valley

1939

Huw Morgan grew up in a tough 19th-century mining
community in the South Wales valleys, but his memories
of his youth are infused with tender passions and the
rousing sound of male-voice choirs. 'How green was my
Valley, then,' the novel concludes, 'and the Valley of them
that have gone.' It is 'vivid, eloquent, poetical', wrote the
Times Literary Supplement, 'glowing with an inner flame
of emotion'. The 1941 film adaptation won five Academy
Awards, including Best Picture, beating both *The Maltese
Falcon* and *Citizen Kane*.

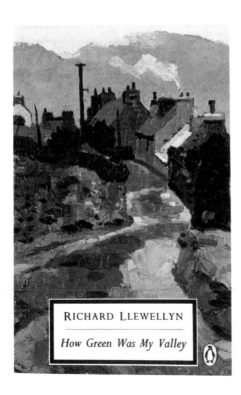

1951
Penguin
Books
<u>**1991**</u>
Twentieth-
Century
Classics
—

Flora Thompson 1876–1947

Flora Jane Timms was born in the hamlet of Juniper Hill in rural Oxfordshire. At fourteen, she became a counter clerk at the post office in Fringford, three miles away, and later married John Thompson, a post-office clerk who was eventually promoted to postmaster. She loved to read and taught herself to write. 'Our literature has had no finer remembrancer in this century,' wrote the novelist John Fowles, 'no observer so genuinely endearing.'

1973 Modern Classics
2008 Modern Classics
● intro. H.J.Massingham, 1945
intro. Richard Mabey, 2008

Lark Rise to Candleford
A Trilogy 1939–43
Lark Rise, Over to Candleford, Candleford Green

These three autobiographical novellas describe a fading way of life in the last decades of the 19th century, as self-sufficient agrarian communities were evolving into commuter villages and suburbs. Writing half a century after the events, Thompson presents lyrical memories of children's games and daily life in the hamlet of Lark Rise, based on Juniper Hill in Oxfordshire, the village of Candleford Green, based on Fringford, and the nearby market town of Candleford, modelled on Buckingham. 'The true successor to *Lark Rise*,' writes Richard Mabey in his introduction, 'is Laurie Lee's luminous account of his childhood, *Cider with Rosie* (114).'

'Cato'

Cato the Younger was a Roman senator, a Stoic and an outspoken critic of political corruption. In 1940, his name was adopted as the pseudonym of three London journalists: Frank Owen, a military historian and editor of the *Evening Standard*; Peter Howard, a columnist for the *Sunday Express* and ex-captain of England's rugby team; and Michael Foot, an *Evening Standard* journalist and future Leader of the Labour Party.

1998
● pref. Michael Foot
intro. John Stevenson

Guilty Men 1940

In the summer of 1940, a month after the evacuation of Dunkirk, 'Cato' published this impassioned polemic, detailing the political mismanagement of the previous decade and singling out a number of 'guilty men', including Ramsay MacDonald, Stanley Baldwin and, above all, Neville Chamberlain. 'It sold like a pornographic classic,' recalled Michael Foot in his preface, 'especially in bookstalls round Leicester Square and especially when regular bookstalls sought to ban it. Being one of the authors, I can testify that the whole affair was contrived in a rush and a rage: our aim was to secure changes in the men running the war.'

POETRY OF THE FORTIES
1940–49

'The forties in England began with war and ended with social revolution,' wrote Robin Skelton in his introduction. 'The social structure which provided the poets of the thirties with their themes of criticism and anxiety was altered, first by violence and then by statute.' In this thematic anthology, he arranged famous names such as R.S.Thomas (119), Keith Douglas (116) and Mervyn Peake (118) alongside less well-known poets, including Ruthven Todd, Francis Scarfe, Demetrios Capetanakis and Emanuel Litvinoff (158).

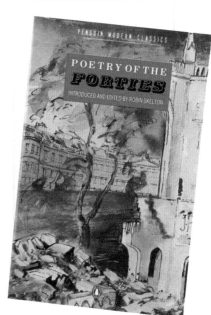

1968 Penguin Poets
1987 Modern Classics
● ed. Robin Skelton, 1968
—
Robin Skelton also edited *Poetry of the Thirties* (95) for Penguin.

Patrick Hamilton 1904–1962

Hamilton's father was a novelist, soldier, theosophist, non-practising barrister, amateur actor and fascist, who inherited a fortune at 21 and married a prostitute who threw herself under a train at Wimbledon station. He then married a dentist's daughter, Hamilton's mother, who copied oil paintings and wrote romantic novels. Hamilton was run over by a car in 1932, which left him with a limp and a withered left arm, and he subsequently became an alcoholic. As well as novels he wrote plays, including *Rope* (1929), which was adapted for the screen by Alfred Hitchcock, and *Gas Light* (1938), which inspired the term 'gaslighting'. Hamilton is 'a marvellous novelist who's grossly neglected', wrote Doris Lessing, who also praised his creation of a 'world of crooks and spivs, blackmailers and bounders, murderers and thieves, and some of the nastiest women in literature'.

Hangover Square
A Story of Darkest Earl's Court 1941

This pitch-black comedy is set in the grimy pubs of west London, in the unsettled months before the Second World War. It centres on George Harvey Bone, who loves the callous Netta, except when something goes click in his head: then he feels like killing her. 'A masterly novel,' ran the *Spectator* review, '[…] you can almost smell the gin.' James Agee (465) called it 'a magnificent thriller'.

1957 Penguin Books
1974 Penguin Books
1985 Modern Classics
● intro. J.B.Priestley, 1974
—
J.B.Priestley (87) described Hamilton as 'the novelist of innocence, appallingly vulnerable, and of malevolence, coming out of some mysterious darkness of evil'.

The Slaves of Solitude 1947

'I think Mr Hamilton is one of the best living novelists, and that this is the best book he has yet written,' said John Betjeman (88). Optimistic Miss Roach escapes the Blitz and finds lodgings in a shabby boarding house in Thames Lockdon, a version of Henley-on-Thames. Among the other inhabitants are the ghastly Mr Thwaites, a Nazi sympathizer, and Miss Roach's awful German friend, Miss Kugelmann.

1999
● intro. Michael Holroyd

The Gorse Trilogy 1951–5
The West Pier, Mr Stimpson and Mr Gorse, Unknown Assailant

These novels chronicle the life of Ernest Ralph Gorse, a suave psychopath and devious sexual predator, who ruthlessly exploits a series of gullible victims. In *The West Pier* (1951), he seduces and destroys the naïve Esther Downes while on holiday in Brighton; Graham Greene (88) called it 'the best novel written about Brighton'. In *Mr Stimpson and Mr Gorse* (1953), Gorse defrauds a snobbish widow; and in *Unknown Assailant* (1955), most of which was dictated while Hamilton was drunk, Gorse exploits an open-hearted barmaid called Ivy.

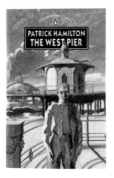

1986 ● —

1992 ● —

More CON ARTISTS

1973 Penguin Books
2010 Modern Classics
fwd. Alex James, 2010
—
Alex James is a pilot,
a cheesemaker and the
bass guitarist in the rock
band Blur. 'I have never
found Dahl to be more
terrifying or harder to
put down than in these
stories,' he writes.

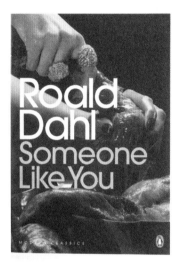

1970 Penguin Books
2009 Modern Classics
fwd. Dom Joly, 2009
—
Dom Joly is a comedian,
journalist, travel writer
and creator of the
hidden-camera show
Trigger Happy TV.

1973 Puffin Books
2011 Deluxe Classics
2014 Modern Classics
intro. Sam Mendes, 2014
—
Sam Mendes directed
the stage musical
adaptation of *Charlie
and the Chocolate Factory*
in 2013. 'Funny, cruel,
naughty, touching,
absurd, astonishingly
imaginative and filled
with chocolate,' he
writes, describing Dahl's
book. 'Well, not real
chocolate, of course.
But sometimes, just
sometimes, words can
be even better.'

Roald Dahl 1916–1990

Dahl was born in Wales to Norwegian parents,
and grew up with tales of trolls, giants and talking
foxes. By the time he was five, his father and his
oldest sister had died. He became a fighter pilot
in the Second World War before working for British
Intelligence in Washington, DC. He began writing
with encouragement from C. S. Forester (75) and
went on to create some of the world's most successful
books for adults and children, which he penned in
Great Missenden, Buckinghamshire, in a replica of
Dylan Thomas's (98) writing shed. When he died,
he was buried with his HB pencils, as well as snooker
cues, a bottle of burgundy, a box of chocolates and
a power saw. 'Children loved his stories and made him
their favourite over a long period of time, so that his
popularity became a phenomenon,' read his obituary
in *The Times*. '[. . .] They will be classics of the future.'

Over to You
Ten Stories of Flyers and Flying
1942–6, pub. 1946

Dahl's earliest stories bring to life his Royal Air Force
experiences, involving enemy parachutists, obese Cairo
prostitutes and a Kenyan cow. 'A Piece of Cake', his first
published story, is an account of crash-landing in the North
African desert, an experience that left him badly injured.

Someone Like You
1948–53, pub. 1953

Dahl's second story collection established him as
a master of the macabre. These eighteen stories include
'Taste' about an overconfident oenophile, 'Skin' about
a tattooed masterpiece and 'Man from the South' about
a pyromaniac gambler.

Charlie and the Chocolate Factory
1964

In this modern fairy tale, starving Charlie Bucket discovers
one of five golden tickets inside his chocolate bar: an
invitation to visit the factory of Willy Wonka, the eccentric
genius chocolatier, who is assisted by his personal army
of diminutive Oompa-Loompas. As a schoolchild, Dahl and
his friends frequently tested new chocolates for the local
Cadbury chocolate factory, and he was once caned for putting
a dead mouse into a jar of gobstoppers.

Laurie Lee 1914–1997

Laurence Lee was born in Stroud in Gloucestershire and grew up in the nearby village of Slad. At nineteen, he left home and walked to London, and then across Spain. He wrote volumes of poetry, documentary film scripts and a trilogy of bestselling autobiographies. 'He had a nightingale inside him,' read his obituary, 'a capacity for sensuous, lyrical precision.'

I Can't Stay Long 1942–75, pub. 1975

This essay collection includes recollections of a Gloucestershire childhood, travel writing about Tuscany, Mexico and the West Indies, and reflections on life, love and death. 'For some considerable time now I have had spread around my workroom floor odd piles and packages of manuscripts,' wrote Lee in his preface. 'At last I thought that the best thing to do was to gather them into a book.'

1977 Penguin Books
2015 Modern Classics
intro. Simon Winchester, 2015

2016
—

Village Christmas
and Other Notes on the English Year
1949–94, pub. 2015

In 2011, Lee's daughter Jessy discovered eight previously unpublished essays among his papers, which have been held at the British Library since 2003. These essays, which include 'A Cold Christmas Walk in the Country', are published in this volume, among 24 others, organized seasonally to give a sense of village life across the year.

1971 Penguin Classics
2014 Modern Classics
intro. Robert Macfarlane, 2014
—
Robert Macfarlane calls this one of 'the two great walks of twentieth-century English literature', the other being by Patrick Leigh Fermor. 'Lee, like Leigh Fermor, believed in walking not only as a means of motion but also as a means of knowing,' writes Macfarlane, 'and this unforgettable book is proof of the truth of that belief.'

As I Walked Out
One Midsummer Morning 1969

Lee's second volume of autobiography describes his leaving home as a teenager and walking to London, where he worked for a year, playing his violin and labouring on building sites. Then he pushed on to Spain, tramping around for a year with a blanket and a violin, until he was evacuated on the eve of the Spanish Civil War.

Cider with Rosie 1959 →

Lee recollects a tranquil, golden childhood in his beautiful Cotswold valley. His poetic autobiography recalls a slower English countryside 'of white narrow roads, rutted by hooves and cartwheels, innocent of oil or petrol', in the decade following the First World War. 'This magical book,' writes Susan Hill in her introduction, 'is a portrait of a place and time past, an elegy, almost a funeral lament.' The book was an instant success and, with the proceeds, Lee was able to buy a cottage of his own in his home village of Slad.

A Moment of War
1991
The final book of Lee's autobiographical trilogy describes crossing the Pyrenees on foot, returning to Spain to join the International Brigade and fight Franco's nationalists. 'It is a wonderful book,' wrote Jan Morris, 'beautiful and terrible in its expressions of all that war means.'

1992 Penguin Books
2014 Modern Classics
intro. Jan Morris, 2014

Down in the Valley
A Writer's Landscape
1994, pub. 2019

In March 1994, in various locations around the Slad Valley, the documentary maker David Parker recorded Lee speaking about his childhood, writing, music, politics, poetry, the local history and landscape. Parker rediscovered the complete recordings in late 2017 in an incorrectly labelled archive box – these are the transcripts.

2020
ed. David Parker, 2019

LAURIE LEE

Cider with Rosie

1962 Penguin Books
1998 Twentieth-Century Classics
• intro. Susan Hill, 1998
ill. John Ward, 1962

The artwork on the cover of the
1998 edition is *On the Way to
Harvest* (1919) by Harold Harvey.

H. E. Bates 1905–1974

Herbert Ernest Bates worked for a local newspaper in his native Northamptonshire and then as a clerk in a leather merchant's warehouse before having his first novel published at the age of 20. He went on to write dozens of short stories, plays, memoirs and novels, including *The Darling Buds of May* (1958) about the irrepressible Larkin family. He was a squadron leader in the Royal Air Force during the Second World War and wrote stories under the pseudonym 'Flying Officer X'.

Fair Stood the Wind for France 1944

John Franklin is the pilot of a Wellington bomber, which crash-lands in occupied France. Franklin and his crew are sheltered by a local mill-owner and his family, who help him escape the German patrols, but Franklin finds himself falling in love with the mill-owner's daughter, Françoise. It is 'perhaps the finest novel of the war', wrote the *Daily Telegraph* at the time; '[…] a fine, lovely book which makes the heart beat with pride'.

1958 Penguin Books
2005 Modern Classics
—

1969
● —
This edition is illustrated with sketches by Keith Douglas himself, and the cover shows one of his paintings: *Shapes of Derelicts*.

Keith Douglas 1920–1944

Douglas's father left home when he was seven. Educated through scholarships, he went to Oxford, where he was taught by Edmund Blunden (78) and developed a reputation as an accomplished poet and artist. He signed up in 1940 and was posted to the Middle East. He took part in the D-Day invasion of Normandy in 1944 and was killed by a mortar three days later at the age of 24.

Alamein to Zem Zem 1944, pub. 1946

In late 1942, Douglas was frustrated at divisional headquarters, 20 miles away from the Battle of El Alamein. He left against orders, drove a truck to the battlefield and lied about his instructions. He joined his regiment, captained a Crusader tank and took part in the campaign across North Africa, from Alamein to Zem Zem, a wadi in Tunisia, where he was wounded in early 1943. He turned his notebooks into this wry document that captures the fear, the exhilaration and the nightmare of desert warfare, in a surreal landscape littered with derelict tanks.

Norman Collins 1907–1982

Collins worked in publishing before moving to the BBC in 1941, where he became director of the Overseas Service and later the Light Programme. He introduced the first daily radio serial, *Dick Barton: Special Agent*, and created *Woman's Hour*, which is still running. In 1947, he was appointed controller of a new medium called 'television'. There were only 31,000 licences in the UK at the time; after three years, there were more than 650,000. He later set up the Independent Television (ITV) network, the first organization to break the BBC's broadcasting monopoly. He wrote sixteen novels and two plays.

London Belongs to Me 1945

'*London Belongs to Me* is the capital's great vernacular novel,' writes Ed Glinert. 'Populist and proletarian, […] it is a work born from the living, beating heart of one of the world's most-used literary settings. Here is a novel packed with memorable period detail, a world of séances, bizarre political societies, smoky Mayfair nightclubs awaiting the next police raid, Nazi spies and stifling petty bourgeois gentility.' The novel opens in 1938, in a boarding house in the down-at-heel district of Kennington, and revolves around a young mechanic accused of murder. 'Real Londoners – some in love, some in debt, some committing murders, some adultery, some trying to get on in the world, some looking forward to a pension, some getting drunk, some losing their jobs, some dying, and some holding up the new baby,' wrote Collins. 'This book is about a few of them.'

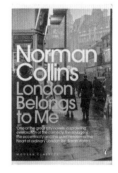

2008
ed. Ed Glinert

Nancy Mitford 1904–1973

Nancy Mitford was the eldest child of the second Baron Redesdale. She grew up with five sisters and one brother in a rambling country house in Oxfordshire, the setting for two of her best-known novels. She became famous as one of the glamorous and controversial 'Mitford sisters', alongside Pamela, Diana, Unity, Jessica and Deborah. She had little formal education, except in horse riding and French, but she began writing 'to relieve the boredom'. In 1935 she married Peter Rodd, but the marriage was not a success. During the war, Nancy worked at Heywood Hill bookshop in London and began an affair with the love of her life, a Free French officer, Gaston Palewski. She moved to Paris after the war to be closer to him, and lived there the rest of her life, although they never had a public relationship. She wrote historical biographies and translated Madame de Lafayette's *Princesse de Clèves* (1678). She died in 1973, with Palewski at her bedside. 'It's very curious, dying,' she wrote to a friend, '& would have many a drôle, amusing & charming side were it not for the pain.'

1949–57 Penguin Books *individual titles*
2000 Modern Classics
intro. Philip Hensher, 2000

Love in a Cold Climate
and Other Novels
The Pursuit of Love, Love in a Cold Climate, The Blessing
1945–51

The first two, largely autobiographical novels in this volume are narrated by Fanny Logan. In *The Pursuit of Love* (1945), Fanny describes her cousin Linda's eccentric, aristocratic upbringing, with coming-out balls and vigorous fox-hunting, followed by misguided attempts at seeking a soulmate. *Love in a Cold Climate* (1949) covers the same period, but this time Fanny describes Polly Hampton, another relation, who returns from India to the 'cold climate' of England and endures a similarly bittersweet series of humorous, romantic escapades. *The Blessing* (1951), which is set in France, is about an English girl who falls in love with a dashing, unfaithful Frenchman.

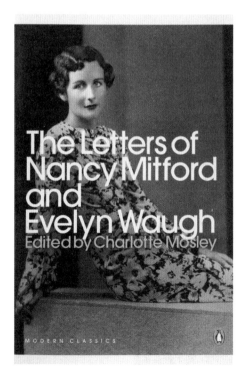

2010 Modern Classics
ed. Charlotte Mosley, 1996

The Letters of Nancy Mitford and Evelyn Waugh
1944–66, pub. 1996

'Both Nancy Mitford and Evelyn Waugh (67) had the gift of writing letters as though they were talking to each other,' writes Charlotte Mosley, Mitford's niece-in-law. 'Reading their correspondence is like overhearing a conversation between two quick-witted, provocative, very funny friends, who know the same people, read the same books, laugh at the same jokes and often share the same prejudices.'

Mervyn Peake 1911–1968

Peake was born in Kuling, China, the son of a missionary doctor. He became
an illustrator, and was commissioned as a war artist to record the devastation
of Germany immediately after the Second World War; one of the locations he
visited and drew was Bergen-Belsen concentration camp. In 1946, he moved with
his family to Sark in the Channel Islands, where he set his novel *Mr Pye* (1953).
As well as novels, he published volumes of poetry, children's books and plays,
and he illustrated many classic titles, including *The Rime of the Ancient Mariner*,
Alice's Adventures in Wonderland and *Treasure Island*. In 1957, the failure of
his play *The Wit to Woo* accelerated his deteriorating health, and in the 1960s
he was overtaken by dementia, for which he was treated unsuccessfully with
electroconvulsive therapy.

1968
● intro. Anthony Burgess
—
The cover of *Titus Groan*
shows Peake's portrait of
Fuchsia, the 15-year-old
daughter of Lord Sepulchrave;
Gormenghast shows a pair
of studies for Steerpike and
Barquentine; and *Titus Alone*
has Irma Prunesquallor,
the sister of the castle doctor.

The Gormenghast Trilogy 1946–59

Peake's Gormenghast novels 'are actual additions to life', wrote C. S. Lewis; 'they give,
like certain rare dreams, sensations we never had before'. Titus Groan (1946) opens with
the birth of Titus, son and heir to Lord Sepulchrave, 76th Earl
of Groan and Lord of Gormenghast Castle, which is a sprawling,
crumbling, cobwebbed kingdom of locked towers and dark
halls. During Titus's birthday celebrations, Steerpike, a young
servant, escapes the heat of the castle kitchens and embarks
on an ambitious and murderous social climb. 'The book is closer
to ancient pagan romance than to traditional British fiction,'
wrote Anthony Burgess (148) in his introduction.

1969
● —

1970
● ed. Langdon Jones
—
After a heavily edited first
edition (1959), *Titus Alone* was
'reconstructed' by Langdon
Jones in 1970. 'Peake seemed
to regard evil and tragedy
as a tangible force,' writes
Jones, 'and the book reflects
a struggle that was taking
place in reality, when Peake
himself was facing a horror
more dreadful and more
protracted than that endured
by Titus, and to which, after
ten years, he succumbed.'

Gormenghast (1950) follows Titus from the age of seven
to seventeen, as he rebels against the taskmaster Barquentine,
the castle's misanthropic master of ritual. Towards the end,
Gormenghast floods and the rising waters lead to a climactic
showdown between Titus and Steerpike. 'Peake is a finer poet
than Edgar Allan Poe,' wrote Robertson Davies (395), 'and he is
therefore able to maintain his world of fantasy brilliantly through
three novels. It is a very, very great work […] a classic of our age.'

In *Titus Alone* (1959), Titus escapes the mad rituals of his ancestral home, but finds
himself in a world that is just as strange and even more frightening. He meets
Muzzlehatch, a melancholic zookeeper in a modern city; the Black Rose, a victim
of the sinister Under-River; and the beautiful, helicopter-flying Cheeta.

2000
● ed. Maeve Gilmore, 1978
intro. John Watney, 1978
—
Maeve Gilmore, Peake's
widow, was also a painter
and a writer. They met at
the Westminster School
of Art and had three children
together. John Watney wrote
a biography of Peake in 1976.

Peake's Progress
Selected Writings and Drawings
1923–60, pub. 1978

This gallimaufry of Peake's poetry, plays, stories, sketches and essays
was collected by his widow Maeve. It features 'Mr Slaughterboard',
'The Rhyme of the Flying Bomb', previously unpublished nonsense
verses, illustrations, a Gormenghast novella called *Boy in Darkness*
(1956), and the full script of his play *The Wit to Woo* (1957) among
many other pieces.

R. S. Thomas 1913–2000

Ronald Stuart Thomas was the son of a sailor. He was ordained in 1937 and worked as a parish priest in the Church of Wales for the next 40 years, publishing many books of poetry. 'He was the Solzhenitsyn (314) of Wales,' wrote the scholar M. Wynn Thomas, 'because he was such a troubler of the Welsh conscience. He was one of the major English language and European poets of the 20th century.'

Selected Poems 1946–95

Thomas made this selection of his poetry himself, shortly before he died in 2000. It spans his career, from his first poetry collection, *The Stones of the Field* (1946), to his last, *No Truce with the Furies* (1995). He writes about the lives of Welsh hill-farmers, the importance of nature and religion, and about family, language, suffering and technology. He is sometimes compared to Robert Frost (415). 'His example reduces most modern verse to footling whimsy,' said Kingsley Amis (132).

2004
—

Julian Maclaren-Ross

1912–1964

James McLaren Ross was the son of a Cuban-Scottish ship merchant and an Anglo-Indian beauty. He was a dandy and raconteur, propping up bohemian London bars with Dylan Thomas (98) and wearing his trademark camel-hair coat, carnation buttonhole and sunglasses. He worked as a vacuum-cleaner salesman in the Sussex seaside town of Bognor Regis before becoming a prolific writer under the name 'Julian Maclaren-Ross'.

Of Love and Hunger 1947

Richard Fanshawe is a vacuum-cleaner salesman, living in a dingy boarding house in a grey seaside town. But things liven up when his friend Roper leaves for a three-month job and asks Fanshawe to 'look after' his sultry wife, Sukie. Played out in smoky pubs and seedy love-nests, Maclaren-Ross's narrative is louche and slangy, peppered with prying landladies and unpaid debts.

2002
intro. D.J. Taylor

1964
● —
Some of Green's other novels have been published in Penguin Twentieth-Century Classics editions in the USA.

Henry Green 1905–1973

Henry Vincent Yorke was the son of a wealthy industrialist. His first novel, *Blindness* (1926), was written at school and published when he was a student at Oxford. After the Second World War, he took over as managing director of the family beer-bottling-machine manufacturing firm. He wrote nine novels under the pseudonym 'Henry Green', including *Living* (1929), *Party Going* (1939) and *Loving* (1945); in *Who's Who*, he described his recreations as 'romancing over the bottle, to a good band'. W. H. Auden (95) considered him 'the best English novelist alive'.

Concluding 1948

This strange novel takes place over the course of a single summer's day at a rural school for teenage girls. The events culminate with the Founder's Ball, after two students go missing and an elderly scientist is kidnapped. No conclusions are reached. 'His novels made more of a stylistic impact upon me than those of any writer living or dead,' wrote John Updike (514).

Jocelyn Brooke

1908 – 1966

Jocelyn Brooke was obsessed with orchids and fireworks. He worked briefly for the family wine business in Folkestone, Kent, before enlisting in the Royal Army Medical Corps and serving as a 'pox wallah' in the Second World War. He later became a full-time writer.

Ronald Searle

1920 – 2011

Searle studied art before enlisting in the Royal Engineers a few months before the Second World War. He was stationed in Singapore when it fell to the Japanese in 1942 and he was held prisoner for three and a half years, spending six months in the Kwai jungle working on the infamous Siam–Burma 'death railway'. After the war, he become a renowned illustrator, with major retrospective exhibitions staged around the world. Reclusive by nature, he separated from his wife Kaye Webb in 1961 and moved first to Paris and later to a picturesque village in Haute-Provence.

Ronald Searle
The Terror of St Trinian's and Other Drawings

The Military Orchid
and Other Novels

The Military Orchid, A Mine of Serpents, The Goose Cathedral 1948 – 50

This loosely semi-autobiographical trilogy follows its narrator as he goes to school, joins the army and struggles with his homosexuality. The 'military orchid' is a species of wild flower, which the narrator seeks in the first volume; a 'mine of serpents' is a guinea box of fireworks; and the 'goose cathedral' is the narrator's name for the grandly Gothic lifeboat station at Seabrook on the Kentish coast, which is transformed into a tearoom. 'Jocelyn Brooke's writing is imaginatively unique,' said Elizabeth Bowen (13).

The Terror of St Trinian's
and Other Drawings 1948 – 59

The ghastly girls of St Trinian's School indulge in torture, witchcraft, seductions and stabbings and sing a school hymn with lyrics by Robert Graves (57). Their teachers glide through the mayhem, gently admonishing mutilation and murder. The drawings in this pictorial anthology are taken from *Hurrah for St Trinian's* (1948), *Back to the Slaughterhouse* (1951), *The Terror of St Trinian's* (1952) and *Souls in Torment* (1953). Also included are drawings from *Merry England, etc.* (1956), the *Molesworth* (125) books and *The Rake's Progress* (1955). As J. G. Ballard wrote, 'Searle has created a unique graphic universe.'

1960 Penguin Books *The Penguin Ronald Searle*
1961 Penguin Books *The St Trinian's Story*
<u>2000</u> Modern Classics
• intro. Nicholas Lezard, 2000

1981 King Penguin *The Orchid Trilogy*
• intro. Anthony Powell, 1981
<u>2002</u> Modern Classics
• pref. Jonathan Hunt, 2002
intro. Anthony Powell, 1981

Kaye Webb

Kaye Webb (1914–1996) edited the Puffin Books series between 1961 and 1979. Webb brought many new writers to Puffin, including Rosemary Sutcliff, Alan Garner, C. S. Lewis, Clive King, Ursula K. Le Guin, Roald Dahl (113) and, briefly, J. R. R. Tolkien. She finally divorced her husband Ronald Searle in 1967, the same year she founded the Puffin Club, a formative literary community for many young readers that she ran until 1981. Webb and Searle collaborated on the Penguin book *Refugees 1960*, a 'report in words and drawings' on camps in Austria, Italy and Greece, which raised money for the UK Committee of the World Refugee Year.

Gilbert Ryle

1900–1976

Ryle was the son of Brighton doctor. He was a philosopher at Oxford University throughout his career and became Waynflete Professor of Metaphysical Philosophy in 1945. He edited the journal *Mind* from 1947 until 1971.

The Concept of Mind 1949

In Ryle's first and most influential book, he challenges Descartes' concept of mind–body dualism, coining the phrase 'the ghost in the machine'. He develops the notion of habitual 'category mistakes' which lead to philosophical nonsense. 'The philosophical arguments which constitute this book,' he wrote, 'are intended not to increase what we know about minds, but to rectify the logical geography of the knowledge which we already possess.'

1963 Peregrine Books
1990 Penguin Books
2000 Modern Classics
intro. Daniel C. Dennett, 2000

1965 Peregrine Books
1971 Pelican Books
1990 Penguin Books
2016 Modern Classics
—

Steven Runciman

1903–2000

Runciman could read Latin by the age of six and Greek by the age of seven. He spent much of his life travelling. At various times, he was Professor of Byzantine Art and History at Istanbul University, a Grand Orator of the Orthodox Church, an honorary Whirling Dervish, Greek Astronomer Royal and Laird of Eigg. According to the historian Andrew Robinson, 'he played piano duets with the last Emperor of China, told tarot cards for King Fuad of Egypt, narrowly missed being blown up by the Germans in the Pera Palace hotel in Istanbul and twice hit the jackpot on slot machines in Las Vegas'. He was knighted in 1958.

A History of the Crusades

The First Crusade, The Kingdom of Jerusalem, The Kingdom of Acre

1951–4

Runciman's three volumes span the origins of the Crusades to the Holy Land in the 11th century and their decline in the 14th, covering the establishment of the kingdom of Jerusalem, the rise of Saladin and the degeneration and final overthrow of the crusader states. 'I believe that the supreme duty of the historian is to write history,' Runciman explained, 'that is to say, to attempt to record in one sweeping sequence the greater events and movements that have swayed the destinies of man.' He presents the Crusades not as romanticized chivalrous endeavours, but as bloody wars of intolerance.

1965 Peregrine Books
1971 Pelican Books
1990 Penguin Books
2016 Modern Classics
—

1965 Peregrine Books
1971 Pelican Books
1990 Penguin Books
2016 Modern Classics
—

John Wyndham 1903 – 1969

John Wyndham Parkes Lucas Benyon Harris turned his hand to farming, law and advertising before he began writing science fiction stories for American magazines. He used various pen names, including 'John Harris', 'John Beynon', 'Wyndham Parkes' and 'Lucas Parkes', but he is most famous for the 'logical fantasy' novels he published under the name 'John Wyndham'.

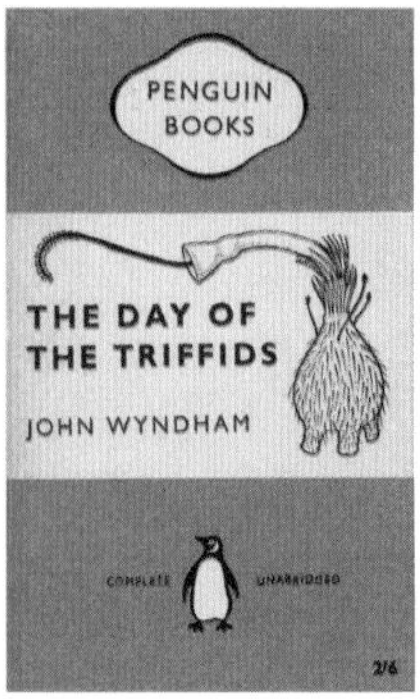

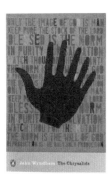

1954 Penguin Books
• –

The Day of the Triffids 1951

Triffids are giant carnivorous plants that can walk, and when all humanity is simultaneously blinded by a green meteor shower they begin devouring the defenceless population. Arthur C. Clarke called *The Day of the Triffids* an 'immortal story'. When Penguin first published the book, Wyndham was consulted on the cover design. 'Regarding the aspect of a Triffid – and I do think it is an excellent idea to have a small illustration of one — I am in some difficulty,' he replied. '[...] In the description I gave them leaves to rustle because I wanted some audible sound of approach. That turns out to have been a mistake pictorially; if they are given many leaves, they invariably start to look domesticated, which isn't what's wanted.' When Wyndham received the 1954 edition, he wrote saying that 'the little drawing has come up well. I imagine it should be well up to its function, which I take to be a pause, a figurative scratch of the head, followed by a "What the ...?" So let us hope a lot of them look inside to find out.'

1958 Penguin Books
2000 Modern Classics
intro. M. John Harrison, 2000

The Chrysalids 1955

In a post-nuclear-holocaust society, deviations from the 'norm' are destroyed. So when young David Strorm discovers that he and other children in Waknuk, Labrador, share mutant telepathic abilities, he must keep his extraordinary powers secret.

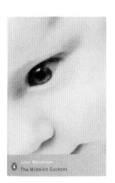

1960 Penguin Books
2000 Modern Classics
• intro. Christopher Priest, 2000

The Midwich Cuckoos 1957

One day, all the child-bearing women in the English village of Midwich find themselves unexpectedly and simultaneously pregnant. They give birth to 'the Children', who have golden hair and golden eyes and the ability to protect themselves through mind control. The story has been filmed twice as *Village of the Damned*, in 1960 and 1995.

More MONSTROUS CHILDREN

The Wild Boys by William S. Burroughs 485

Lord of the Flies by William Golding 131

The Age of the Fish by Ödön von Horváth 277

A High Wind in Jamaica by Richard Hughes 86

The Children of Dynmouth by William Trevor 21

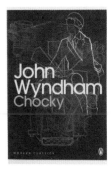

1970 Penguin Books
2010 Modern Classics
intro. Brian Aldiss (142), 2010

Chocky 1968

Eleven-year-old Matthew Gore has an imaginary friend called 'Chocky', a creature who seems to know an unsettling amount about space travel and gravity fields.

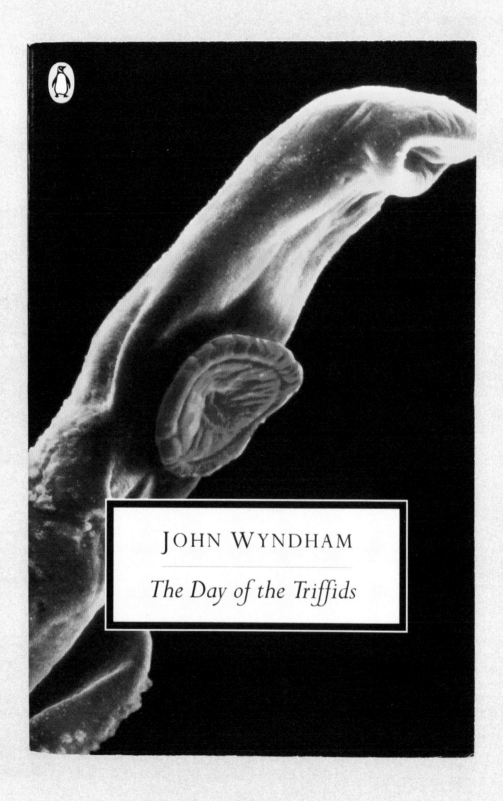

JOHN WYNDHAM

The Day of the Triffids

1999
intro. Barry Langford

The 1999 cover shows a coloured scanning electron micrograph image of a
schistosome, a tiny, tropical parasitic flatworm also known as a 'blood fluke'.

2012
intro. Peter Parker
—
The novelist Candia McWilliam describes *In the Making* as 'pure, tense, and incontrovertibly a modern classic'.

G. F. Green 1911–1977

George Frederick Green was the son of a Derbyshire iron-founder. In the Second World War, he was posted to Sri Lanka, where he edited a magazine called *Veera Lanka* and spent the rest of his time drinking, injecting Benzedrine and conducting homosexual affairs, for which he was court-martialled in 1944 and sentenced to two years in prison. On release, Green had a nervous breakdown. He settled in Somerset and produced novels until he was diagnosed with terminal lung cancer, whereupon he took his own life. Elizabeth Bowen (13) called him 'the most neglected writer of his generation'.

In the Making The Story of a Childhood 1952

This autobiographical novel describes eight-year-old Randal, who falls passionately in love with a charismatic older schoolboy. 'To write about homosexual love as if it were – which in fact it is – normal, is to thread a way through a labyrinth of disasters,' said Green. 'It needs a very pure mind – in the sense of exact, just, full of integrity.'

H. F. M. Prescott 1896–1972

Hilda Frances Margaret Prescott was a historian. 'I became a history addict at the age of eight,' she confessed, 'and from that time lived with a private cinematograph in my head which produced for my benefit the endless number of stories of which history, for me, consisted.'

The Man on a Donkey 1952

This work of historical fiction is set in Tudor England and culminates with the Pilgrimage of Grace, the northern uprising in 1536 against the dissolution of the monasteries by Henry VIII. Prescott's tapestry-like narrative features several historical figures, such as Robert Aske, a Yorkshire squire, and Christabel Cowper, the thunderous Prioress of Marrick.

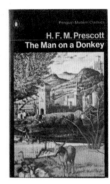

1969
• —

The Movement

'The Movement' was a term coined by the *Spectator* in 1954 to describe a loose group of English poets, including Kingsley Amis (132), D. J. Enright, Thom Gunn, Elizabeth Jennings, Philip Larkin and John Wain. They shared a conservative, anti-romantic sensibility and a preference for conventional forms in poetry. 'The Movement was a reaction against the New Apocalypse (98),' wrote the critic Martin Seymour-Smith, 'a response to the ingenuity of William Empson (86), and a belated, partial recognition of the achievement of Robert Graves (57). [...] Beyond this it amounted to nothing, and it should be noted only as a tendency.'

John Wain 1925–1994

Wain was the son of a dentist from Stoke-on-Trent. Alongside teaching English literature, he was a popular novelist, poet and critic associated with 'The Movement'. He was appointed Professor of Poetry at Oxford University in 1973 and published an acclaimed biography of Samuel Johnson in 1974.

Hurry on Down 1953

A university graduate, Charles Lumley, attempts to break away from his bourgeois background by taking jobs as a window cleaner, a drug runner, a hospital orderly, a chauffeur, a bouncer and a radio comedy writer. Wain described this picaresque novel, which anticipates Kingsley Amis's *Lucky Jim* (132), as 'a youthful firework display'.

The cover of the 1960 edition of *Hurry on Down* was illustrated by Len Deighton (147).

1960 Penguin Books
1979 Penguin Books
1996 Twentieth-Century Classics
• intro. John Wain, 1979

1962 Puffin Books
How to be Topp
<u>1999</u> Twentieth-Century
Classics
intro. Philip Hensher, 1999

Geoffrey Willans 1911–1958

Herbert Geoffrey Willans was born in Smyrna, in Turkey, and educated at Blundells School in Devon. He worked as a school-teacher, served in the naval reserve during the Second World War, and he was also a keen amateur botanist. He spent so much time at Kew Gardens that the staff gave him his own key.

Molesworth

Down with Skool!, How to be Topp, Whizz for Atomms,
Back in the Jug Agane with Ronald Searle 1953–9

Sardonic schoolboy Molesworth, 'the goriller of 3B', invites readers on a tour of his wet and weedy school, St Custard's, promising 'FULL LOWDOWN ON SKOOLS, SWOTS, SNEKES CADS, PRIGS BULIES HEADMASTERS CRIKET FOOPBALL, DIRTY ROTERS, FUNKS, PARENTS, MASTERS WIZARD WHEEZES, WEEDS APLE PIE BEDS AND VARIOUS OTHER CHIZZES – IN FACT THE LOT'. We meet Grimes the headmaster, Grabber the head boy (winner of 'the mrs joyful prize for rafia work') and a blistering array of oiks, uncles and matrons. Most memorable is Molesworth's nemesis Basil Fotherington-Tomas, who likes to skip and speak to the clouds. Willans's words are brilliantly complemented by Ronald Searle's (120) unforgettable illustrations.

'This is me e.g. nigel molesworth the curse of st custard's which is the skool i am at. It is utterly wet and weedy as i shall (i hope) make clear but of course that is the same with all skools.'

L. P. Hartley

1895–1972

Leslie Poles Hartley reviewed books for various publications as well as writing novels himself. He spent much of his time in Venice, where he employed a personal gondolier. He was frequently visited there by his friend, the historian Lord David Cecil. Cecil described Hartley as 'one of the most distinguished of modern novelists; and one of the most original. For the world of his creation is composed of such diverse elements. On the one hand he is a keen and accurate observer of the processes of human thought and feeling; he is also a sharp-eyed chronicler of the social scene. But his picture of both is transformed by the light of a Gothic imagination that reveals itself now in a fanciful reverie, now in the mingled dark and gleam of a mysterious light and a mysterious darkness.'

The Go-Between

1953

'The past is a foreign country: they do things differently there.' Leo Colston, now in his sixties, recalls the summer of 1900, which he spent at Brandham Hall in Norfolk, the home of his school friend Marcus, carrying illicit messages between Marian, Marcus's beautiful sister, and Ted Burgess, a tenant farmer on the estate. It was adapted for the screen in 1971 by Harold Pinter. 'Of all the novels L. P. Hartley has written,' said John Betjeman (88), 'I think *The Go-Between* is the best.'

PENGUIN · MODERN · CLASSICS

L. P. HARTLEY
THE GO-BETWEEN

1958 Penguin Books
<u>1987</u> Modern Classics
1997 Twentieth-Century Classics
ed. Douglas Brooks-Davies, 1997

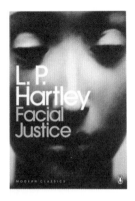

Facial Justice 1953–9, pub. 1960

Following the Third World War, citizens are named after biblical murderers and anything that inspires envy is outlawed. Jael 97 is considered too beautiful, so she is ordered to report to the Ministry of Facial Justice to have her face reconstituted. Anthony Burgess (148) called it 'a brilliant projection of tendencies already apparent in the post-war British welfare state'.

1966 Penguin Books
2014 Modern Classics
intro. John Sutherland, 2014

The Hireling 1957

Leadbitter is a handsome chauffeur, hired to drive the young, widowed Lady Franklin to cathedrals, country houses and beauty spots. The 1973 film adaptation, directed by Alan Bridges, shared the Grand Prix at the Cannes Film Festival.

1964 Penguin Books
1986 Modern Classics
• —

Ian Fleming 1908–1964

Fleming was educated at Eton and the Royal Military College, Sandhurst, leaving the latter after contracting gonorrhoea. In May 1939, he was recruited into Naval Intelligence, rose to the rank of commander and was assigned the codename 17F. After the war, he worked for the *Sunday Times* and took three months' holiday every winter, which he spent in Jamaica writing a new Bond novel at his beach house, Goldeneye. He wrote twelve Bond novels and two collections of short stories, which have sold more than 100 million copies and inspired a legendary series of films. He died on the morning of his son's twelfth birthday; his only children's book, *Chitty Chitty Bang Bang* (1964), was published two months later.

Casino Royale 1953

When Commander James Bond of the Royal Naval Reserve is assigned Double o number seven and a licence to kill, he is dispatched to the casino at Royale-les-Eaux in northern France to ruin a sinister Soviet agent at baccarat, assisted by CIA agent Felix Leiter and Vesper Lynd of MI6, after whom he names his trademark Vesper martini. 'Three measures of Gordon's, one of vodka, half a measure of Kina Lillet,' Bond explains. 'Shake it very well until it's ice-cold, then add a large thin slice of lemon peel.' Raymond Chandler (461) summarized the plot of *Casino Royale* as 'a superb gambling scene, a torture scene which still haunts me, and, of course, a beautiful girl'.

2002 Penguin Books
2004 Modern Classics
• —

2003
• intro. Candia McWilliam

Fleming was a keen birdwatcher. 'James Bond' was the name of an American ornithologist, author of *Birds of the West Indies* (1936).

Fleming in Penguin

The publication of Fleming in Penguin Modern Classics was overseen by Simon Winder, who is still a senior editor at Penguin Books. Winder is also the author of *The Man Who Saved Britain* (2006), an uproarious cultural history of Bond. 'Fleming's books may be a deranged cocktail made from Imperial Leather, fungus-manipulating Chinese super-criminals ("with a brow like Shakespeare and a face like Satan" – stop!), Ruritanian swordsmen and square-jawed Hun-bashers,' he writes, 'but they transmuted into something much more interesting.' As Fleming himself wrote, his books 'may not be Literature with a capital L', but they are thrillers 'designed to be read as literature'.

Live and Let Die 1954

Bond continues to pursue Russian-controlled operatives working for SMERSH, the Soviet counter-intelligence agency. In this instalment he tackles Mr Big, a piratical gold smuggler and leader of the 'Black Widow' voodoo cult in Jamaica. Along the way, he rescues the beautiful fortune-teller Solitaire and escapes through the barracuda-infested waters of Shark Bay.

2002 Penguin Books
2004 Modern Classics
• —

Moonraker 1955

Sir Hugo Drax, a shadowy millionaire, has built a private missile base on the coast of Kent, where he is constructing the Moonraker, a 'super atomic rocket' designed to 'protect' Britain. Bond investigates, assisted by glamorous undercover officer Gala Brand.

Ian Fleming
Moonraker

2002 Penguin Books
2004 Modern Classics
• —

Diamonds are Forever 1956

Bond infiltrates a diamond-smuggling chain that runs from Sierra Leone to Las Vegas. Assisted by icy bombshell Tiffany Case and pursued by US mobsters, as well as a pair of sadistic hitmen, he needs to make an appointment with a dentist. The assassin 'Boofy' Kidd was named after Fleming's friend Arthur Gore, Earl of Arran, known to his friends as 'Boofy'.

2002 Penguin Books
2004 Modern Classics
• —

From Russia with Love
1957

President John F. Kennedy listed *From Russia with Love* as one of his ten favourite books. In this instalment, the Soviet counter-intelligence agency SMERSH instigates a sting operation to assassinate Bond. Irresistible agent Tatiana Romanova is assigned to seduce Bond in Istanbul, while Colonel Rosa Klebb stands ready with her poison-dagger shoes. The action is largely set on the Orient Express.

Ian Fleming
From Russia with Love

2002 Penguin Books
2004 Modern Classics
• —

2002
• intro. Christopher Hitchens

127

Dr No 1958

Investigating the disappearance of MI6 agents in Jamaica, Bond finds himself on the private island of Dr Julius No, a megalomaniac guano miner with bionic hands and a penchant for pain. Along with exotic Honeychile Rider, Bond must survive dragons, centipedes and a sadistic obstacle course that includes a giant squid.

2002 Penguin Books
2004 Modern Classics
• —
Dr No was the first Bond novel to receive mixed reviews: the *New Statesman* criticized what it perceived as 'the sadism of a schoolboy bully, the mechanical, two-dimensional sex-longings of a frustrated adolescent, and the crude, snob-cravings of a suburban adult'. In 1962, it was the basis of the first film in the movie franchise.

2002 Penguin Books
2006 Modern Classics
• —

2002 Penguin Books
2006 Modern Classics
• —

2008
• —

Quantum of Solace (2008) collects the complete set of James Bond short stories. 'I am not surprised that Fleming preferred to write novels,' said Philip Larkin. 'James Bond, unlike Sherlock Holmes, does not fit snugly into the short-story length: there is something grandiose and intercontinental about his adventures that requires elbow-room, and such Bond examples of the form as we have tend to be eccentric or muted.'

Goldfinger 1959

Bond is assigned to monitor Auric Goldfinger, the richest man in England, and he soon uncovers the SMERSH operative's gold-smuggling operations. He must outwit bowler-hatted Oddjob and Pussy Galore (the leader of a gang of lesbian cat-burglars), and navigate a tricky round of golf. Fleming named his villain after the British architect Ernő Goldfinger, whose Brutalist buildings he disliked.

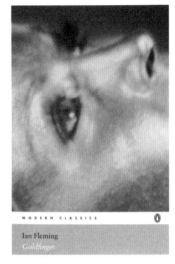

2002 Penguin Books
2004 Modern Classics
• —

Stories 1959–64

For Your Eyes Only (1960) was a short-story collection that included 'From a View to a Kill' and 'Quantum of Solace', as well as Fleming's best stories, 'Risico' and 'The Hildebrand Rarity'. After Fleming died, a posthumous volume was published in 1966, featuring 'Octopussy' and 'The Living Daylights'. These tales take Bond to the Seychelles, American mountain country and Sotheby's auction house, where he bids on a Fabergé egg. Fleming wrote 'Quantum of Solace' as a tribute to Somerset Maugham (32).

Thunderball 1961

Fleming shifts Bond's attention from SMERSH to a new villain: Ernst Stavro Blofeld, leader of the international criminal organization SPECTRE. Blofeld has stolen two atomic weapons and is demanding £100 million or he will destroy a city. Bond is posted to the Bahamas, relying on sultry Domino to get close to Blofeld's right-hand man, Emilio Largo.

2002 Penguin Books
2004 Modern Classics
• —

2009
• intro. Nicholas Lezard

Thunderball is the novelization of an unfilmed screenplay, on which Fleming collaborated with Kevin McClory and Jack Whittingham. *The Blofeld Trilogy* collects all three of the villain's appearances: in *Thunderball*, *On Her Majesty's Secret Service* (129) and *You Only Live Twice* (129). In the books, Blofeld's birthday is 28 May 1908, which was also the day that Fleming was born.

The Spy Who Loved Me

1962

Vivienne Michel, a young Canadian woman, narrates the story of her almost fatal clash with two killers, Sol 'Horror' Horowitz and Sluggsy Morant, and her timely rescue by a suave secret agent, James Bond. Early editions were co-credited to the fictional Vivienne Michel, whose first-person account of 'a night of screaming terror' apparently appeared on Fleming's desk one morning. He subsequently disowned this novel, in which Bond features only briefly.

2002 Penguin Books
2006 Modern Classics
● —

On Her Majesty's Secret Service

1963

Fleming wrote On Her Majesty's Secret Service while the first Bond movie, Dr No (128), was being filmed nearby on Jamaica: Ursula Andress, who plays Honey Ryder in Dr No, appears in On Her Majesty's Secret Service as 'a beautiful movie star'. In this novel, Bond meets Comtesse Teresa 'Tracy' di Vicenzo, a reckless playgirl who loves fast cars. Together they tackle the arch-criminal Blofeld in his Alpine mountain base and, amidst ski chases and rounds of schnapps, they marry.

2002 Penguin Books
2004 Modern Classics
● —

'He was surprised to find that all this nest-building gave him a curious pleasure,' wrote Fleming, 'a feeling that he had at last come to rest and that life would now be fuller, have more meaning, for having someone to share it with.'

You Only Live Twice 1964

'You only live twice,' says Bond, attempting to improvise a haiku: 'Once when you are born / And once when you look death in the face.' Following the success of the Dr No (128) film adaptation, Fleming gave Bond a wry sense of humour for the first time. In this instalment, he is a washed-up amnesiac alcoholic with one final mission: to be trained by Japanese ninjas, infiltrate the 'Garden of Death' and kill Dr Guntram Shatterhand, Blofeld's latest incarnation. He is assisted by the beautiful Kissy Suzuki.

The Man with the Golden Gun

1964, pub. 1965

Fleming's final Bond novel was published eight months after the author's death. A brainwashed Bond attempts to murder M, his boss, before heading to Jamaica to kill the Cuban assassin Francisco 'Pistols' Scaramanga, who likes to fire a gold-plated Colt .45 loaded with silver-jacketed bullets with a solid gold core. In the film adaptation, Scaramanga was played by Fleming's step-cousin, Christopher Lee.

More GOLD

2002 Penguin Books
2006 Modern Classics
● —

The unfinished manuscript of *The Man with the Golden Gun* was given to Kingsley Amis (132) for suggested amendments. None of his suggestions were incorporated, but Amis went on to write the first 'post-Fleming' Bond novel, under the pseudonym 'Robert Markham'. In Amis's *Colonel Sun* (1968), Bond travels to Greece to rescue M from a Chinese villain, assisted by Ariadne Alexandrou. There have been many subsequent Bond novels, by authors including John Gardner, Raymond Benson, Sebastian Faulks, William Boyd and Anthony Horowitz.

2002 Penguin Books
2004 Modern Classics
● —

William Golding

Lord of the Flies

PENGUIN MODERN CLASSICS 2/6

1960 Penguin Books
1962 Modern Classics

The illustration on the cover of the 1962 edition is by the
British printmaker, film director and war artist Anthony Gross.

William Golding

1911 – 1993

Golding was the son of a schoolmaster and became a teacher himself. Many of his novels are visionary fables: in *The Inheritors* (1955) a group of Neanderthals is threatened by *Homo sapiens*; *Pincher Martin* (1956) is about a drowning naval officer clinging to a purgatorial rock; and *The Spire* (1964) is about the spiritual and worldly motives behind the construction of a medieval cathedral tower. Golding's reputation was based, however, on the phenomenal success of his masterpiece and first novel, *Lord of the Flies*. He was awarded the Nobel Prize for Literature (576) in 1983 and knighted in 1988.

← Lord of the Flies 1954

In Golding's first and best-known novel, a party of young British schoolboys survives a plane crash and washes up on a deserted coral island somewhere in the South Pacific. As the boys attempt to govern themselves, their middle-class morals gradually degenerate and they become increasingly competitive, violent and cruel. Simon is a scapegoat, Piggy is a victim and Jack the chorister wrestles power away from the sensible Ralph. Golding's novel reveals our innate capacity for darkness, in direct contrast to R. M. Ballantyne's classic adventure novel *The Coral Island* (1857), in which upstanding boys called Ralph and Jack tackle the dangerous inhabitants of a Pacific island. *Lord of the Flies* is 'a beautiful and desperate book', wrote Stevie Smith (108), 'something quite out of the ordinary'. The title is a translation of 'Beelzebub', one of the names of the Devil.

Elizabeth David 1913 – 1992

The aristocratic Elizabeth Gwynne ran away with a married actor in 1937. They navigated French canals in a small boat, met Norman Douglas (63) in Antibes and had their boat confiscated in Italy. They travelled on to Greece and were evacuated to Egypt, where Gwynne met Olivia Manning (159) and Lawrence Durrell and married the Indian army officer Tony David. The Davids lived in India before separating, and Elizabeth returned to England at the height of food rationing. Inspired by the recipes she had experienced on her travels, she began to write a series of articles and bestselling books, introducing British kitchens to such exotic ingredients as aubergines, basil, garlic, olive oil and pasta. 'She wrote as she cooked,' says Julian Barnes: 'with simplicity, purity, colour, [and] self-effacing authority.' David was made a Fellow of the Royal Society of Literature in 1982.

Italian Food

1954

'The term "Italian" used in relation to food would in fact mean very little to most Italians,' wrote David. 'To them there is Florentine cooking, Venetian cooking, there are the dishes of Genoa, Piedmont, Romagna; of Rome, Naples, and the Abruzzi; of Sardinia and Sicily; of Lombardy, Umbria, and the Adriatic coast.' Based on a year visiting kitchens up and down the length of Italy, David introduces readers to all its various styles of regional cooking. Evelyn Waugh (67) chose *Italian Food* as his book of the year in 1954.

1963 Penguin Handbook
<u>**1999**</u> Twentieth-Century Classics
● fwd. Julia Child, 1999
—
These Twentieth-Century Classics editions carry forewords by the American chef Julia Child, who was inspired by Elizabeth David to introduce Americans to 'the art of French cooking' in 1961, becoming a popular food writer and broadcaster. She attended David's memorial service in 1992.

French Provincial Cooking

1960

'It is difficult [...] to think of any home that can do without Elizabeth David's *French Provincial Cooking*,' wrote the *Observer* in 1960. In this book, her masterpiece, David describes how she discovered her taste for good food and wine while living with a French family in 1930 and studying at the Sorbonne. The social historian Peter Clarke cites the 'seminal influence' of *French Provincial Cooking* on British food culture, especially given 'its enormous sales as a Penguin paperback'.

1964 Penguin Handbook
<u>**1999**</u> Twentieth-Century Classics
● fwd. Julia Child, 1999

1961 Penguin Books
1992 Twentieth-Century Classics
intro. David Lodge, 1992
—

Lucky Jim was one of the first British 'campus novels'. David Lodge, a later exponent of the form, calls it 'a classic comic novel, a seminal campus novel, and a novel which seized and expressed the mood of those who came of age in the 1950s'.

More UNIVERSITIES

Hangsaman
by Shirley Jackson   468

A New Life
by Bernard Malamud   475

All Souls
by Javier Marías   233

Pnin
by Vladimir Nabokov   309

Fortress Besieged
by Qian Zhongshu   347

Kingsley Amis

1922 – 1995

Amis was the son of a Colman's mustard clerk. He loved sex, jazz and James Bond (126). He worked as a lecturer at the University College of Swansea before becoming a full-time writer, producing copious volumes of poems, essays, short stories, literary criticism, and the comic novels for which he's best remembered. He was a serial adulterer, the father of the novelist Martin Amis (160) and a lifelong friend of the poet Philip Larkin. He was knighted in 1990.

Lucky Jim

1954

In Amis's first novel, 'Lucky' Jim Dixon is a lecturer in medieval history at a provincial redbrick university, trying to impress his faculty head, Professor Welch. He ends up delivering a drunken lecture on 'Merrie England' and failing to resist the charms of Christine, Welch's son's girlfriend. Amis dedicated the novel to Philip Larkin, who was living on Dixon Drive in Leicester.

That Uncertain Feeling

1955

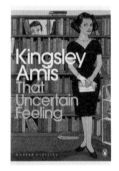

John Lewis is a young librarian, in a Welsh coastal city, who is tempted into adultery with farcical results. Amis 'was a genuine comic writer', declared John Mortimer (139), 'probably the best after P. G. Wodehouse (48)'.

1985 Penguin Books
2013 Modern Classics
—

Complete Stories

1955 – 93

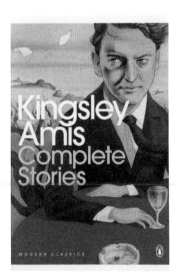

1965 Penguin Books
My Enemy's Enemy
1983 Penguin Books
Collected Short Stories
1994 Penguin Books
Mr Barrett's Secret and Other Stories
2013 Modern Classics
Complete Stories
fwd. Rachel Cusk, 2013

'These stories, spanning Amis's career,' writes Rachel Cusk in her foreword, 'also of course span his interests and preoccupations, his choices and changes of subject matter, his formal experiments, his writerly moods and declensions, his tics and trademarks. There are army stories, literary genre stories (sci-fi, plus a Sherlock Holmes spoof from which Sherlock Holmes is absent), as well as stories about literature (in "Mr Barrett's Secret" Elizabeth Barrett Browning's father discloses his reasons for his estrangement from his daughter after her marriage to the poet); and then there are stories that are more than chips from the work-bench, stories in which Amis's piquancy as an artist, his essence, can be experienced.'

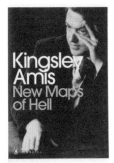

New Maps of Hell
A Survey of Science Fiction
1959, pub. 1960

These lectures, given by Amis at Princeton University in 1959, present a witty overview of science fiction, covering Jules Verne, H. G. Wells (26), John Christopher (135) and John Wyndham (122). J. G. Ballard called it 'the most important and influential critical work' on the genre.

2012
—

Take a Girl Like You 1960

Arrogant schoolmaster Patrick Standish determinedly attempts to seduce the beautiful but stubbornly chaste Jenny Bunn.

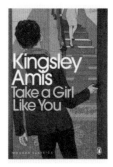

1962 Penguin Books
2013 Modern Classics
—

One Fat Englishman
1963

Roger Micheldene is a gluttonous English publisher, visiting Budweiser University in the USA and attempting to sleep with every woman he meets. The novel is based on Amis's experiences while delivering lectures at Princeton University in 1959.

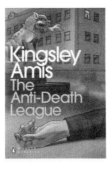

The Anti-Death League
1966

In this surreal comedy, a mysterious secret weapon is tested in a British army camp. The varied cast of characters includes a deranged psychiatrist, an aristocratic nymphomaniac widow, a military chaplain and an officer seconded from the Indian army.

1968 Penguin Books
2012 Modern Classics
—

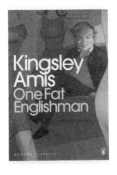

1966 Penguin Books
2011 Modern Classics
intro. David Lodge, 2011
—

Amis took the title from the lipstick message that Hilly, his first wife, drew on his back while he was sleeping on a beach in 1962: '1 FAT ENGLISHMAN I FUCK ANYTHING'. She had just discovered his affair with the novelist Elizabeth Jane Howard.

I Want It Now
1968

TV chat-show host Ronnie Appleyard pursues the androgynous heiress Simona Quick through the swinging sixties and across two continents.

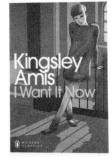

1988 Penguin Books
2012 Modern Classics
—

Girl, 20
1971

Douglas Yandell, a music critic, is enlisted by Kitty Vandervane to control her unfaithful husband, the eminent composer-conductor Sir Roy, but Sir Roy persuades Yandell to be his alibi for his next conquest.

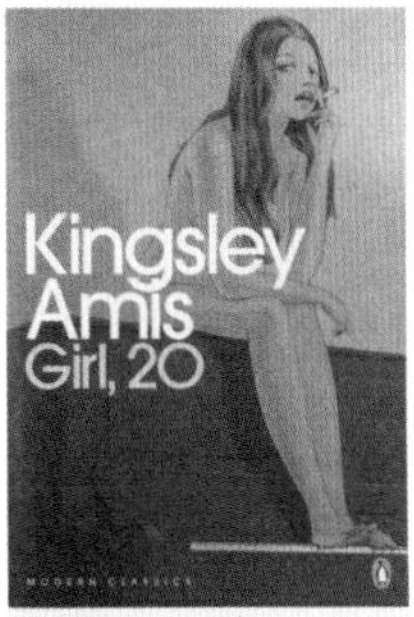

1980 Penguin Books
2011 Modern Classics
intro. Howard Jacobson, 2011

The Riverside Villas Murder
1973

Fourteen-year-old Peter Furneaux helps Colonel Manton to join the dots between a stolen mummy, a soaking wet corpse and the tennis-club social. 'At the nasty bits,' writes the critic John Carey, 'you feel like someone coming across a meat-cleaver in a cot.'

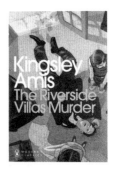

1984 Penguin Books
2012 Modern Classics
—

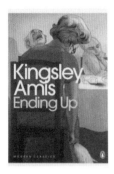

1987 Penguin Books
<u>2011</u> Modern Classics
intro. Helen Dunmore, 2011

Ending Up 1974

Five septuagenarians living together in Tuppenny-hapenny Cottage bicker as they slide into dotage, cope with their various ailments and dread the approach of Christmas.

Difficulties with Girls

1988

In this sequel to *Take a Girl Like You* (133), Jenny Bunn and Patrick Standish have settled in London, but their relationship is tested by seductive neighbours and the Hampstead literary set. 'While not wishing to hose down Kingsley Amis with embarrassing praise,' wrote the critic and biographer Roger Lewis, 'it does seem to me that what we have here is the greatest English novelist since Evelyn Waugh (67), and the only living writer who will be with Dickens and George Eliot at his death.'

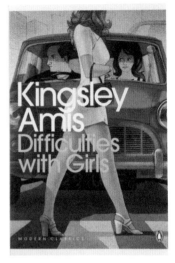

1989 Penguin Books
<u>2013</u> Modern Classics
—

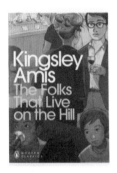

1991 Penguin Books
<u>2012</u> Modern Classics
intro. Henry Hitchings, 2012

The Folks That Live on the Hill

1990

Harry Caldecote is a retired librarian presented with a choice between responsibility and freedom. Should he continue to support his dysfunctional friends and family in Highgate, London, or accept a cushy position at the Institute of Cultural and Commercial History in America?

The King's English
A Guide to Modern Usage

1995, pub. 1997

'I would guess that for every acquaintance of mine who looks on me as some sort of authority on correct usage or pronunciation there is at least one who sees me as an officious neurotic who sets right venial blunderers uninvited.' This is Amis's guide to the proper use of the English language, in which he steers an opinionated course between illiteracy and pretension. The manuscript was discovered among his effects and published posthumously. It is 'a terrific book', writes the novelist Sebastian Faulks: 'learned, robust, aggressive, extremely funny [...] a marvellous and quite unexpected bonus from beyond the grave'.

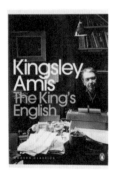

2011
intro. Martin Amis (160)
—

In his introduction, Amis's son Martin concludes that *The King's English* contains 'more concentrated artistic thrust' than any of his last five novels. 'The reason for this is, I think, clear enough. Love of life, like all human talents, weakens with age. But love of language, in his case, never did begin to fade.'

Angry Young Men

The Royal Court Theatre in London adopted the phrase 'angry young man' to publicize John Osborne's play *Look Back in Anger* (1956), in which the protagonist, Jimmy Porter, rails against suffocating middle-class values. The term was subsequently used to describe a number of irascible characters, as well as their authors, including Kingsley Amis (132), John Braine, Harold Pinter, Alan Sillitoe and John Wain (124). 'They have no manners, and are woefully unable to deal with any social predicament,' wrote Somerset Maugham (32) of these anti-heroes. 'Their idea of a celebration is to go to a public house and drink six beers. They are mean, malicious and envious. [...] They are scum.'

Nigel Dennis 1912–1989

Dennis was born in Surrey but grew up in Southern Rhodesia, now Zimbabwe. He moved as a teenager to Kitzbühel in the Austrian Tyrol, where he attended the same Foreign Office crammer as Ian Fleming (126). He then became a film and book reviewer in New York before returning to England and writing for *Time* magazine and the *Sunday Telegraph*. He spent his last years on Malta.

Cards of Identity 1955

In this dark social satire, the manor house has been rented for the annual conference of the 'Identity Club', a group of men claiming to be psychologists. Mr Paradise, his sister and other local townspeople are gradually admitted, brainwashed and forced to perform a Shakespearean pastiche called *The Prince of Antioch*. 'I have read no novel published during the last fifteen years with greater pleasure and admiration,' wrote W. H. Auden (95).

1960 Penguin Books
1966 Modern Classics
• —

John Christopher 1922–2012

Sam Youd was born in Knowsley, near Liverpool, during an unseasonable April snowstorm. After four and a half years of service in the Royal Corps of Signals, he began writing detective thrillers, light comedies and cricketing novels, as well as science fiction, which he published under the nom de plume 'John Christopher'. He lived in Rye, East Sussex, the only town in Britain that gives its name to a species of grass.

The Death of Grass 1956

A virus is wiping out the crops in China and it is mutating and spreading. Mass starvation and riots ensue, as wheat, barley and all 10,000 species of grass start to die. In Britain, society descends into barbarism, and John Custance must do whatever it takes to protect his family.

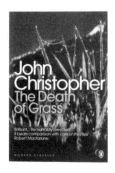

1958 Penguin Books
2009 Modern Classics
intro. Robert Macfarlane, 2009
—

'The novel, like so many narratives of eco-apocalypse,' writes Robert Macfarlane, 'is a vision of nature's revenge for its sustained mistreatment – a return of the repressed.'

Gerald Brenan 1894–1987

Edward FitzGerald Brenan, known as 'Gerald', was born on Malta and raised in South Africa, India and Northern Ireland. At seventeen, he ran away from home with a friend, planning to walk to China; his money ran out in Bosnia after 1,560 miles. Brenan then trained in Germany for the Indian police force, and fought in France during the First World War. Afterwards he visited Spain for the first time and decided to settle in the small village of Yegen in the Sierra Nevada. He married the American poet Gamel Woolsey and lived in Spain for the rest of his life.

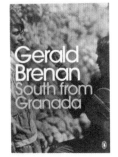

1963 Penguin Books
2008 Modern Classics
intro. Chris Stewart, 2008

—

The drummer Chris Stewart was a founding member of Genesis. He now lives on a farm in the Sierra Nevada with his wife and daughter. 'When I first read [*South from Granada*],' he writes, 'I was so intrigued by the descriptions of the Alpujarras that I was drawn to see the place for myself, and subsequently decided to settle and spend the rest of my days here, not fifteen miles as the crow flies from Yegen.'

South from Granada 1957

'When one looks south from Granada across the red towers of the Alhambra one sees a range of mountains known as the Sierra Nevada which have snow on them all the year round,' wrote Brenan. '[…] They are high enough to boast of having small glaciers, and if you cross them you will come to a broad, hollow country, very broken and separated from the sea by a coastal range. It is this country, which till quite recently could only be explored on foot or mule-back, that is the subject of this book.' Brenan evokes the way of life in rural Andalusia in the years before the Spanish Civil War and describes visits from his friends, including Lytton Strachey (64), Virginia Woolf (42) and the artist Dora Carrington, with whom he had an affair. *South from Granada* is 'the best of Brenan's books', wrote Cyril Connolly (107): 'he has a true and proper knowledge of the culture he describes'.

1958 Pelican Books
1984 Peregrine Books
1990 Penguin Books
<u>**2009**</u> Modern Classics
fwd. Simon Hoggart, 2009
intro. Lynsey Hanley, 2009
—
Richard Hoggart's son
Simon was a journalist and
the presenter of BBC Radio 4's
The News Quiz. In his foreword,
he recalled his father's
involvement in the *Lady
Chatterley* trial (56): 'Sir Allen
Lane (viii), the founder of
Penguin books, had liked *The
Uses of Literacy*, and published
the paperback. He thought
Dad would make an effective
witness, sharing parts of
D. H. Lawrence's background,
and – while an academic
– clearly not from an ivory
tower. [...] Penguin asked Dad
to write the introduction to the
first "legal" edition, and his
name is still preserved on the
Penguin tea mug of the title.'
Simon Hoggart predeceased
his father by three months.

Richard Hoggart

1918 – 2014

Hoggart was from a working-class family in Leeds. Both his parents died before he was nine, so he grew up with his grandmother and won a scholarship to grammar school. After serving in the Second World War, he taught literature at the universities of Hull, Leicester and Birmingham and went on to become Assistant Director-General of UNESCO, Chairman of the *New Statesman*, Vice-Chairman of the Arts Council and Warden of Goldsmiths, University of London. In 1957, Allen Lane (viii) offered Hoggart the chief editorship of Penguin Books; he declined.

The Uses of Literacy
Aspects of Working-Class Life 1957

In this landmark work of sociology, Hoggart celebrates the close-knit values of local communities, laments the loss of authentic working-class spirit and decries the arrival of homogenized, American mass culture. To avoid libel, Hoggart invented examples of deplorable pulp fiction, one of which he called *Death Cab for Cutie*. This title struck a chord: it became a 1967 song by the Bonzo Dog Doo-Dah Band and it is also the name of a cult American rock band.

Fred Hoyle

1915 – 2001

Fred Hoyle's father was a woollen-rag merchant and his mother was a teacher who moonlighted as a cinema pianist. Hoyle went on to become a prominent astronomer and broadcaster. He was the Plumian Professor of Astronomy and Experimental Philosophy at Cambridge University and founded the Cambridge Institute of Theoretical Astronomy. He also coined the term 'Big Bang', although he himself disputed the theory. He was knighted in 1972.

The Black Cloud

1957

A young astronomer spots a strange gaseous cloud approaching our solar system and threatening to block out the sun's rays. When a team of scientists assembles and investigates the nature of the cloud, it makes some shattering discoveries. In his afterword, Richard Dawkins calls *The Black Cloud* 'one of the greatest works of science fiction ever written, up there with the best of Isaac Asimov and Arthur C. Clarke'.

1960 Penguin Books
<u>**2010**</u> Modern Classics
aftwd. Richard Dawkins, 2010
—
Intriguingly, the archive of
Fred Hoyle's papers in the
library of St John's College,
Cambridge also contains a
pair of walking boots, five boxes
of photographs, two ice axes,
some dental X-rays, a telescope,
ten large film reels and an
unpublished opera called
*The Alchemy of Love, or, The
Daemon Servant's Retribution*.

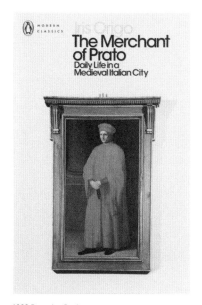

1963 Peregrine Books
1992 Penguin Books
2017 Modern Classics
—

Iris Origo
1902 – 1988

Iris Cutting was born in Gloucestershire, the daughter of a wealthy American diplomat father and a British aristocrat mother. The family travelled widely until her father died in 1910, after which Iris and her mother moved to Italy and settled in Fiesole, outside Florence. She married Antonio Origo in 1924 and they bought La Foce, an estate near Montepulciano in Tuscany. Origo remained at La Foce during the Second World War, sheltering refugee children, Italian partisans and escaped Allied prisoners of war in defiance of the fascist regime. She was made a dame in 1976.

The Merchant of Prato
Daily Life in a Medieval Italian City
1957

Drawing on a cache of more than a hundred thousand personal letters, ledgers, insurance policies and deeds of partnership, Origo meticulously reconstructs the life of the merchant Francesco di Marco Datini (c.1335–1410), who lived in Avignon and Prato. She presents an unparalleled portrait of a tough, enterprising man and the texture of life in 14th-century Italy. 'As a picture of the daily round in Tuscany before the dawn of the Renaissance,' wrote the *Sunday Times*, 'it is a complement to the *Decameron*.'

C. Northcote Parkinson
1909 – 1993

Cyril Northcote Parkinson was a painter, teacher, soldier, journalist, novelist and at one time the Raffles Professor of History at the University of Malaya. He was an authority on maritime history known, as his obituary put it, for 'his easy manner and witty turn of phrase'. In 1979, he published a biography of P. G. Wodehouse's fictional character Jeeves (48).

Parkinson's Law
or, The Pursuit of Progress
1957

'Work expands so as to fill the time available for its completion' is Parkinson's Law, and the first sentence of this entertaining, excruciating analysis of office life. Parkinson sets out nine further laws of the workplace, such as the fact that employees always tire three years before retirement; committees spend more time discussing small sums of money than large ones; and the best moment to arrive at a party is 45 minutes late.

C. Northcote Parkinson
Parkinson's Law

1965 Penguin Books
1986 Penguin Books
2002 Modern Classics
• intro. HRH The Duke of Edinburgh, 1986
ill. Osbert Lancaster, 1965
—

'*Parkinson's Law* has rightly become a classic,' wrote Prince Philip, who rather unexpectedly provided an introduction. 'Its relevance in this era of burgeoning bureaucracy is greater than ever. […] The Law should be compulsory reading at all business schools and for all management consultants.'

Michael Young 1915–2002

Lord Young of Dartington worked in the Labour Party research department and drafted the party's manifesto ahead of its decisive victory over Winston Churchill's Conservative government in the 1945 general election. He went on to help found more than 50 organizations, including the Institute of Community Studies, the Consumers' Association, the Open University, the Language Line and the School for Social Entrepreneurs; he was also the first Chairman of the Social Science Research Council. He wrote a dystopian alternative history, *The Rise of the Meritocracy, 1870–2033* (1958), which popularized the term 'meritocracy' and expressed concern for the losers in a meritocratic system.

Peter Willmott 1923–2000

Willmott was Young's colleague at the Labour Party and later at the Institute of Community Studies. They collaborated together on several books, including *Family and Class in a London Suburb* (1960) and *The Symmetrical Family* (1973). Willmott later became director of the Centre for Environmental Studies and head of the Greater London Council's central policy unit.

1962 Pelican Books
1986 Peregrine Books
2007 Modern Classics
intro. Kate Gavron &
Geoff Mulgan, 2007
—
Geoff Mulgan was the director of the Young Foundation, formed from the merger of the Institute of Community Studies and the Mutual Aid Centre. Kate Gavron was a trustee of the Young Foundation; she worked with Michael Young in the 1990s.

Family and Kinship in East London

1957

This pioneering work of modern sociology drew on extensive research in Bethnal Green in east London, documenting the conditions and interactions of established working-class communities and contrasting them with the experience of uprooted families on new housing estates in Essex. It records a vanishing world of children playing in the streets, neighbours bumping into friends, and families throwing parties in houses where they have lived for 50 years. It is 'observant, tactful, sympathetic, humorous', wrote Kingsley Amis (132). '[...] Nobody who wants to know how our society is changing can afford not to read Young and Willmott.' Today sociologists affectionately abbreviate the title to the acronym *Fakinel*, pronounced with a cockney accent.

D. W. Winnicott

1896–1971

Donald Woods Winnicott served as a medical officer on the destroyer HMS *Lucifer* during the First World War. He became Britain's first paediatrician to train as a psychoanalyst, conducting research into child development that drew on more than 40 years of clinical practice. During the Second World War, he was the consultant paediatrician to the children's evacuation programme and he was twice President of the British Psychoanalytical Society. 'Winnicott was the greatest British psychoanalyst who ever lived,' says Alain de Botton. 'He writes beautifully and simply about the problems of everyday life.'

The Child, the Family and the Outside World

1957, rev. 1964

This landmark text on child development continues to influence contemporary ideas on parenting. Winnicott discusses crying babies, toddler aggression, comfort blankets, shyness and sex education. His key recommendation is to ignore external pressures and for parents to trust their own instincts.

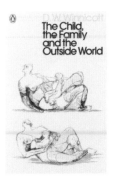

The 1964 Pelican edition collected two of Winnicott's previous books, *The Child and the Family* (1957) and *The Child and the Outside World* (1957), with some revisions. The 2021 reissue marks 50 years since Winnicott died.

1964 Pelican Books
2000 Penguin Books
2021 Modern Classics
—

John Mortimer 1923–2009

Mortimer worked under Laurie Lee (114) during the Second World War, making documentaries for the Ministry of Information, but his barrister father persuaded him to study law and he was called to the Bar in 1948, a year after he published his first novel. He married Penelope Dimont (146) and began developing a twin reputation as a criminal barrister and a playwright. The 'Writing Mortimers' eventually divorced in 1971; the next year, Mortimer married Penelope Gollop – 'Penny Two' as he called her – with whom he lived in Turville Heath Cottage, his childhood home in the Chiltern Hills. He was knighted in 1998.

A Voyage Round My Father
and The Dock Brief,
What Shall We Tell Caroline? 1957–70

This volume collects three plays. Mortimer's first, *The Dock Brief* (1957), is about an ageing hack barrister who defends a south London bird-fancier. It was subsequently staged at the Lyric Theatre, Hammersmith, in London, in 1958, along with *What Shall We Tell Caroline?*, which was inspired by Eugène Ionesco (324). His most famous script, however, is *A Voyage Round My Father* (1970). It is a nostalgic, autobiographical, comic drama that centres on the irascible Clifford Mortimer, enthusiastic gardener and former barrister, who has completely lost his eyesight, although the family dare not mention the fact.

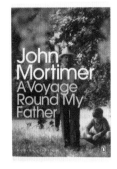

1982 Penguin Plays
2010 Modern Classics
• intro. Valerie Grove, 2010
—
Valerie Grove wrote a biography of Mortimer called *A Voyage Round John Mortimer* (2007). She has also published lives of Laurie Lee (114) and Kaye Webb (120).

Rumpole

1978–2002

Horace Rumpole, a dishevelled barrister-at-law at the Central Criminal Court in London – a.k.a. the Old Bailey – is an inveterate smoker of cigars, drinker of claret ('Château Fleet Street') and quoter of Wordsworth. He acquired his shabby wig 'from an ex-Attorney General of Tonga in 1932' and is married to the formidable Hilda, 'She Who Must Be Obeyed'. Mortimer's most famous creation first appeared in a BBC *Play for Today* in 1975, with Leo McKern in the lead role. This developed into a series for Thames Television that subsequently formed the basis for Mortimer's popular series of Rumpole books. 'Rumpole, on the page, is quite a cocktail,' writes the journalist Sam Leith; 'there's a very generous slosh of P. G. Wodehouse (48), a dash of Falstaff at his more benign, a tincture of Tony Hancock and a faint but discernible backnote of G. K. Chesterton's Father Brown (41).'

1978 Penguin Books
2019 Modern Classics
—

1979 Penguin Books
2021 Modern Classics
—

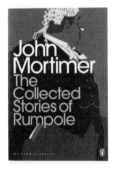

2013
ed. Chloe Campbell, 2012
intro. Sam Leith, 2012
—
The Collected Stories of Rumpole selects two or three of the best stories from *Rumpole of the Bailey* and each of the subsequent Rumpole books, from *The Trials of Rumpole* (1979) to *Rumpole and the Primrose Path* (2002). 'Rumpole, like Jeeves (49) and Sherlock Holmes,' wrote P. D. James, 'is immortal.'

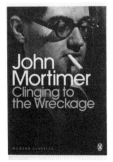

1983 Penguin Books
2010 Modern Classics
intro. Valerie Grove, 2010

Clinging to the Wreckage
A Part of Life
1982

In the first of five autobiographical volumes, Mortimer recounts his solitary childhood and adolescence. He describes his dreams of a tap-dancing career; his one-boy communist cell at Harrow School; his first marriage, to Penelope Dimont (146); his 'taking silk' as a Queen's Counsel in 1966; and his successful 1968 appeal against the conviction of Hubert Selby Jr.'s *Last Exit to Brooklyn* (510) for obscenity.

The Titmuss Trilogy

Paradise Postponed, Titmuss Regained,
The Sound of Trumpets 1985–98

Why has a socialist clergyman left his
fortune to the ruthlessly ambitious Tory
MP Leslie Titmuss? Set in Mortimer's native
Chiltern Hills, *Paradise Postponed* (1985) is
a political satire that became the first of a
trilogy. In *Titmuss Regained* (1990), the Right
Honourable Leslie Titmuss is Secretary of
State at the Ministry of Housing, Ecological
Affairs and Planning, but his
beautiful Rapstone Valley is under
threat from developers. A Tory
MP is found dead in a swimming
pool, wearing a leopard-skin
bikini in *The Sound of Trumpets*
(1998), so Lord Titmuss re-enters
the political arena.

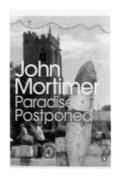 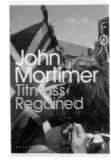 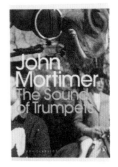

1986 Penguin Books
2010 Modern Classics
intro. Jeremy Paxman, 2010

1991 Penguin Books
2010 Modern Classics
• —

2010
• —
In 1992, Penguin published
an omnibus volume of
the trilogy with the title
The Rapstone Chronicles.

A. E. Ellis 1920–2000

Derek Lindsay was orphaned at the age of three and raised by an
aunt. He fought in the Second World War and attended Oxford
University, before being diagnosed with tuberculosis. He was confined
to a sanatorium in the French Alps, where he underwent an interminably
slow cure. He wrote one novel and two plays, under the pen name
'A. E. Ellis'. Cyril Connolly (107) called him 'a Proust (166), a Leopardi
of the sanatorium [...] an English Camus (181) steeped, Englishwise,
in Flaubert'.

1961 Penguin Books
1988 Modern Classics
• —

The Rack 1958

Paul Davenant is treated for tuberculosis in the
French Alps, enduring depression, claustrophobia,
bad food, uncaring doctors and excruciating
therapy. *The Rack* has been compared to Thomas
Mann's *The Magic Mountain* (246), which is also
set in an Alpine sanatorium. 'There are certain
books which we call great for want of a better
term,' wrote Graham Greene (88), 'that rise like
monuments above the
cemeteries of literature:
Clarissa Harlowe, Great
Expectations, Ulysses (10).
The Rack, to my mind,
is of this company.'

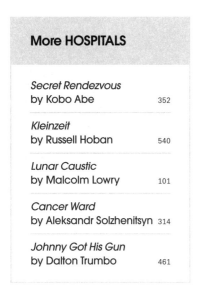

More HOSPITALS

Secret Rendezvous by Kobo Abe	352
Kleinzeit by Russell Hoban	540
Lunar Caustic by Malcolm Lowry	101
Cancer Ward by Aleksandr Solzhenitsyn	314
Johnny Got His Gun by Dalton Trumbo	461

R. D. Laing

1927–1989

Ronald David Laing was
a Scottish psychiatrist who
was fascinated by music and
existential philosophy (186).
He became a guru of the
1960s counterculture (526).

The Divided Self

An Existential Study in Sanity and Madness

1960

Laing's landmark text revolutionized the way
we perceive mental illness. It describes psychosis as
a result of the 'divided self', the tension between the
two personae within us: our authentic, private identity,
and the false, 'sane' self that we present to the world.

1965 Pelican Books
1990 Penguin Books
2010 Modern Classics
intro. Anthony David, 2010

Muriel Spark

1918 – 2006

Muriel Camberg was born in Edinburgh. She married Sydney Oswald Spark in 1937 and moved with him to Southern Rhodesia, now Zimbabwe. Sydney was depressive and abusive, and she eventually disowned both him and their son Robin, returning to England in 1944 to work in the Intelligence Service. She became editor of the *Poetry Review* in 1947 and published her first novel, *The Comforters*, in 1957. After living in a bedsit in Camberwell, south London, for more than ten years, she moved to New York and then Italy, where she lived with the sculptor Penelope Jardine. Muriel Spark was made a dame in 1993.

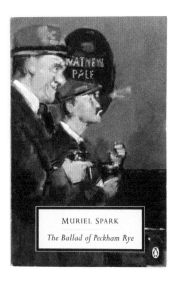

1963 Penguin Books
1999 Twentieth-Century Classics
intro. William Boyd, 1999

The Ballad of Peckham Rye 1960

Dougal Douglas, or perhaps Douglas Dougal, is a fiendishly charming Scotsman who arrives in Peckham, in south London, to wreak moral havoc as an employee of a local nylon-textiles manufacturer. 'In [*The Ballad of*] *Peckham Rye* we see clear evidence of a novelist in exhilarating command of her material and her tone of voice,' writes William Boyd – 'the Sparkian world in full-throated and exuberant splendour.'

The Prime of Miss Jean Brodie 1961

Miss Brodie is an enchanting and unconventional teacher at the Marcia Blaine Academy, a thinly disguised version of James Gillespie's School for Girls in Edinburgh, where Spark herself was taught by the charismatic Miss Christina Kay. Brodie prepares her pupils, her 'crème de la crème', for the adult world beyond the school gates, but disconcerting flashes forward reveal glimpses of their future careers.

1965 Penguin Books
2000 Modern Classics
intro. Candia McWilliam, 2000
—
'*The Prime of Miss Jean Brodie* is technically beyond praise,' writes the novelist Candia McWilliam. 'The pressure it exerts upon the mind is controlled by a guiding spirit that reveals to us the moral universe while affording the refreshment of laughter and revelation. I've read it more than twice a year since I was ten, when I received it in my Christmas stocking, I believe in Penguin paperback.'

The Driver's Seat 1970

Lise has worked for a dull accountancy firm in northern Europe for sixteen years, until she suddenly flies abroad in search of adventure. At the beginning of *The Driver's Seat*, which Spark considered her best book, she reveals that Lise is going to be murdered and the novel becomes what she calls a 'whydunnit'. 'Has any novelist ever been as consistently good at openings as Muriel Spark?' asks John Lanchester. It is 'an extraordinary tour de force,' writes David Lodge, 'a crime story turned inside out.' The 1974 Italian film adaptation starred Elizabeth Taylor and Andy Warhol (543).

1974 Penguin Books
2006 Modern Classics
intro. John Lanchester, 2006

Brian Aldiss 1925–2017

Aldiss was born above a Norfolk draper's shop, fought in the jungles of Burma during the Second World War and worked as a bookseller in Oxford. In 1964, he founded the first journal of science fiction criticism, *Science Fiction Horizons*, with Harry Harrison (530). He edited science fiction anthologies for Penguin and his 1969 short story 'Super-Toys Last All Summer Long' was developed by Stanley Kubrick for the film that was eventually directed by Steven Spielberg as *A.I.* (2001). He was 'the pre-eminent English science-fiction writer of his generation', says the author Neil Gaiman.

Hothouse 1961

The earth has stopped spinning: the world is now baking hot and dominated by carnivorous tropical vegetation, including enormous, spider-like monsters that spin interplanetary cobwebs. The few remaining humans, on the brink of extinction, shelter in the canopy of a banyan tree.

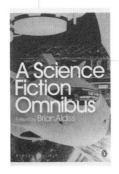

2008 intro. Neil Gaiman
aftwd. Brian Aldiss

A SCIENCE FICTION OMNIBUS 1941–2007

'Science fiction stories are the fables of a technological age,' wrote Brian Aldiss in the introduction to the most recent edition of his classic anthology. His omnibus spans six decades, from Isaac Asimov's 'Nightfall' to 'Friends in Need' by Eliza Blair, with contributions from John Steinbeck (440), Harry Harrison (530), J. G. Ballard, Ted Chiang, Aldiss himself and many others. The stories feature cosmic journeys, time travel, alien races, genetic engineering and mind-bending thought experiments.

1961–4 Penguin Books
Penguin Science Fiction anthologies
1973 Penguin Books
The Penguin Science Fiction Omnibus
2007 Modern Classics *revised and expanded*
ed. Brian Aldiss, 1961–2007

Caradog Prichard

1904–1980

Prichard was born in Bethesda in northwest Wales. He was five months old when his father died in a slate-quarry accident; his mother then suffered from mental illness, in 1923 entering an institution from which she never returned. Between 1927 and 1929, Prichard's poetry won the Crown of the National Eisteddfod a record three years running. He worked as a journalist for Welsh-language newspapers, then the *Daily Telegraph*.

1999
• trans. Philip Mitchell
intro. Menna Baines
—
This parallel-text edition presents the original Welsh opposite the English translation.

One Moonlit Night / Un Nos Ola Leuad 1961

Prichard's only novel, written in Welsh, is a dreamlike portrait of his native Bethesda. The narrator walks at night through the Ogwen Valley, recalling memories that draw on Prichard's own childhood, revealing a dark underworld of madness, sexual perversion and violence.

E. H. Carr 1892–1982

Edward Hallett Carr worked in the British Foreign Office until 1936, when he became Woodrow Wilson Professor of International Politics at the University College of Wales, Aberystwyth. He published a fourteen-volume *History of Soviet Russia* (1950–78).

What is History? 1961

'The facts are […] like fish on the fishmonger's slab,' wrote Carr. 'The historian collects them, takes them home and cooks and serves them in whatever style appeals to him.' This influential book is based on the lively and controversial lectures that Carr delivered at Cambridge University in 1961.

1964 Pelican Books
1987 Penguin Books *revised*
1990 Penguin Books
2018 Modern Classics
ed. R. W. Davies, 1987
intro. Richard J. Evans, 2001

John le Carré 1931–2020

David Cornwell's father was an associate of the notorious Kray twins; his mother disappeared when he was five years old. Cornwell went to Sherborne School in Dorset and the chaplain later became a model for Le Carré's most famous creation, the self-effacing intelligence officer George Smiley. Cornwell taught at Eton before becoming an MI5 officer in 1958 and transferring to MI6 in 1960, moving from security to intelligence. Lord Clanmorris, the novelist, MI5 spy and another model for Smiley, encouraged him to write, which he did under the pen name 'le Carré', French for 'square'. He left MI6 in 1964, after the double agent Kim Philby blew his cover, and became a full-time writer. He lived at St Buryan, at the tip of Cornwall, for more than 40 years. The Swedish crime writer Henning Mankell hailed him as 'the master'.

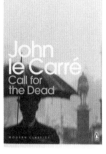

Call for the Dead 1961

Le Carré's first novel introduces George Smiley, the overweight, bespectacled, bureaucratic spy, a conscious antidote to James Bond (126). In this mystery story, Smiley investigates the apparent suicide of a suspected communist and comes under increasing pressure from his superiors at the 'Circus', a fictionalized version of MI6 headquarters.

1964 Penguin Books
2011 Modern Classics
—

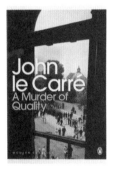

A Murder of Quality 1962

Smiley is called in to solve a murder at Carne, a boys' public school. Unusually he is cast as a detective, not a spy.

1964 Penguin Books
2011 Modern Classics
aftwd. John le Carré, 2011

The Spy Who Came in from the Cold 1963

'A worn-out middle-aged military kind of man in a stained raincoat slammed a handful of mixed foreign change onto the bar and in gritty Irish accents ordered himself as much Scotch as it would buy,' wrote le Carré, recalling a wordless encounter at Heathrow airport. 'In that moment, Alec Leamas was born.' Leamas is an alcoholic spy, the tragic hero of this instant bestseller. 'Superbly constructed,' wrote J. B. Priestley (87), 'with an atmosphere of chilly hell.' Graham Greene (88) called it 'the best spy story I have ever read'.

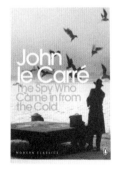

2010 Modern Classics
2014 Modern Classics
intro. William Boyd, 2010
aftwd. John le Carré, 2014

The 2014 edition includes archive material: letters, photographs, contemporary articles, book jackets, and pages of script from the 1965 film adaptation starring Richard Burton. 'I wrote The Spy Who Came in from the Cold at the age of thirty under intense, unshared, personal stress,' recalled le Carré in his afterword. 'As an intelligence officer in the guise of a junior diplomat at the British embassy in Bonn, I was a secret to my colleagues, and much of the time to myself.'

The Looking Glass War 1965

Deactivated agent Fred Leiser is sent to snow-muffled East Germany on an increasingly deadly and disorganized espionage mission.

2011
—

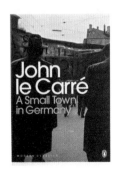

2011
intro. Hari Kunzru

A Small Town in Germany

1968

Alan Turner travels to Bonn in West Germany to investigate the disappearance of a British diplomat. 'The problem of the Cold War,' said le Carré, 'is that, as Auden (95) once wrote, we haunt a ruined century. Behind the little flags we wave, there are old faces weeping, and children mutilated by the fatuous conflicts of preachers.'

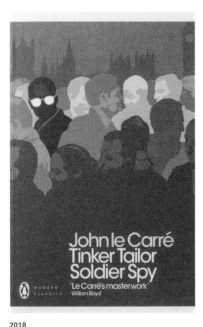

2018
—

The Naive and Sentimental Lover 1971

As his marriage collapses, wealthy Aldo Cassidy is drawn into the orbit of a bohemian couple, Shamus and Helen. Based on le Carré's own relationship with the writer James Kennaway and his wife Susan, this novel was published the same year he divorced his first wife. It is one of his few novels not to involve espionage.

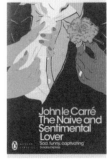

2018
—

Tinker Tailor Soldier Spy 1974

A Soviet mole has infiltrated the highest ranks of the British Intelligence Service and George Smiley is brought out of retirement to hunt him down. 'Le Carré's masterwork', as William Boyd describes it, draws on his memories of Kim Philby, one of the 'Cambridge Five' group of Soviet double agents active from the 1930s to the 1950s. This is the first instalment of the 'Karla' trilogy, named after Smiley's opposite number, the head of Soviet Foreign Intelligence.

2018
—

The Honourable Schoolboy 1977

In the second instalment of the 'Karla' trilogy, Smiley attempts to rebuild the Circus's damaged reputation by exposing a Russian money-laundering scheme in southeast Asia. He dispatches Jerry Westerby, a journalist and occasional spy, to Hong Kong.

Smiley's People 1979

Smiley investigates the assassination of a Soviet defector and ends up travelling to Cold War Berlin for a showdown with his nemesis, Karla. This is the concluding instalment of the 'Karla' trilogy, and the last time that George Smiley featured as a main character. Le Carré felt that, after the success of the BBC adaptation of *Tinker Tailor Soldier Spy* (1979), Smiley had become too well known to write about.

The Little Drummer Girl 1983

Charlie Ross is a young English actress and activist recruited by the Israeli secret service to entrap a Palestinian terrorist. She may have been inspired by the American journalist Janet Lee Stevens, nicknamed 'the little drummer girl' by the Palestinians. Stevens had given le Carré a tour of Lebanese refugee camps in 1982 and died in the Hezbollah bombing of the US embassy in Beirut in 1983.

2018
—
In his author's note, le Carré thanked Lieutenant-Colonel John Gaff, who 'acquainted me with the banal horrors of homemade bombs and made sure I was not inadvertently providing a recipe for their manufacture'.

A Perfect Spy
1986

Magnus Pym has disappeared. The hunt for the missing secret agent reveals details of his boyhood, his con-man father, his moral education and his diplomatic career, painting a picture of a man lost among the many roles he performs. It is le Carré's most autobiographical novel; Philip Roth called it 'the best English novel since the war'.

2018
—

The Russia House 1989

Barley Blair is a British publisher who meets a Soviet nuclear physicist during the Moscow Book Fair. When the physicist attempts to pass him sensitive information, however, British Intelligence's 'Russia House' becomes involved. 'You only get two shots to write with authority about a country, as every journalist knows,' said le Carré in 1987, recalling his first visit to the Soviet Union.

2011
aftwd. John le Carré

'The first is when you arrive there from the moon, and each impression hits you like an express train. The second is thirty years on when, just possibly, if you've been very diligent and very lucky, you know the place from the inside. Obliged to content myself with the first, I sat up half of every night recording my precious memories in a notebook while they were oven-fresh: the reek of Russian petrol that you cease to notice on the third day, the drab procession of anonymous grey buildings – are you a hospital, a ministry, a hotel? – the prison-like hostility of the breakfast queue in the hotel canteen, the crappy, rusting ironmongery of Communist insignia at every second street corner, recalling the first-floor Madonnas that overlook Italian street crossings.'

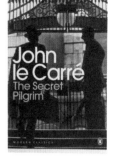

The Secret Pilgrim
1990

The Iron Curtain has fallen, and the director of the Sarratt spy academy invites his old mentor, George Smiley, to deliver a speech. Smiley's words trigger memories that span the director's career, making him question the purpose and personal consequences of a life in espionage. Le Carré dedicated his final Smiley novel to Alec Guinness, who portrayed George Smiley in the BBC adaptations of *Tinker Tailor Soldier Spy* (1979) and *Smiley's People* (1982), 'with affection and thanks'.

2011
aftwd. John le Carré

The Night Manager 1993

In le Carré's first novel set entirely after the Cold War, the former soldier Jonathan Pine is the night manager of a luxury hotel in Cairo who is drawn into the world of espionage and international drugs and arms smuggling.

2013
—

2015
—

Our Game 1995

Tim Cranmer has retired from the secret service, but when his old school friend Larry Pettifer, a former double agent, goes missing, he is forced to track him to the wilds of the Caucasus. 'Our Game' refers to Winchester College football, the peculiar sport played at the public school where Tim and Larry first met.

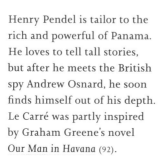

The Tailor of Panama 1996

Henry Pendel is tailor to the rich and powerful of Panama. He loves to tell tall stories, but after he meets the British spy Andrew Osnard, he soon finds himself out of his depth. Le Carré was partly inspired by Graham Greene's novel *Our Man in Havana* (92).

2017
—

2018
—

Single & Single
1999

'Tiger' Single is an unscrupulous financier with links to a Russian crime syndicate and an international money-laundering operation, but customs officer Nat Brock is on his trail.

2018
–

The Constant Gardener
2001

Justin Quayle is a reserved, garden-loving British diplomat in Kenya who sets out to investigate the murder of his young wife Tessa, only to uncover a global pharmaceutical conspiracy. The book is based on real events and dedicated to the activist Yvette Pierpaoli, 'who lived and died giving a damn'. 'By comparison with the reality,' wrote le Carré, 'my story was as tame as a holiday postcard.'

2018
–

Absolute Friends 2004

Ted Mundy is a washed-up English tour guide in Germany. In East Berlin he bumps into his old friend Sasha, a disillusioned member of the Stasi secret police, and he finds himself drawn into a perilous mission.

A Most Wanted Man
2008

An illegal Muslim immigrant is suspected of being a jihadist by the British, German and American Intelligence Services, but his case is taken up by an idealistic young human-rights lawyer. This post-9/11 novel draws parallels with the real-life story of Murat Kurnaz, a Turkish citizen who endured torture at the Guantánamo Bay detention camp.

2018
–

The Mission Song 2006

When Bruno Salvador, an interpreter of African languages, is recruited by British Intelligence to help stage a coup in the Eastern Congo, he is forced to get his hands dirty.

Penelope Mortimer 1918–1999

Penelope Fletcher was born in North Wales, the daughter of a sexually abusive clergyman. She had children by her first husband, Charles Dimont, her second husband, John Mortimer (139), and through two extramarital affairs. She wrote psychologically fraught novels about broken marriages, child-bearing and nightmarish domesticity.

The Pumpkin Eater 1962

'I have put into this novel practically everything I can say about men and women and their relationship to one another,' said Mortimer about this semi-autobiographical book, which opens with Mrs Armitage having a breakdown in the linen section of Harrods department store. It is a 'strange, fresh, gripping book', writes Nick Hornby (162): 'Mortimer peels several layers of skin off the subjects of motherhood, marriage, and monogamy, so that what we're asked to look at is frequently red-raw and painful without being remotely self-dramatizing.' The title comes from the old nursery rhyme:

> Peter, Peter, Pumpkin eater,
> Had a wife and couldn't keep her.
> He put her in a pumpkin shell
> And there he kept her very well.

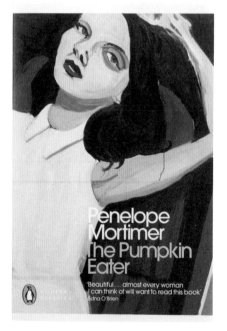

1964 Penguin Books
2015 Modern Classics
intro. Daphne Merkin, 2011

Len Deighton

b. 1929

2021
—

The IPCRESS File was adapted as a film in 1965, starring Michael Caine and produced by Harry Saltzman. Over lunch, Caine and Saltzman discussed the need to give the anonymous character a name. Sitting opposite Saltzman, Caine suggested 'Harry', and then 'Palmer' because it was the surname of the most boring boy at his school. Caine returned as Harry Palmer in the hit *Funeral in Berlin* (1966) and *Billion-Dollar Brain* (1967), which flopped, kyboshing the film adaptation of *Horse Under Water* scheduled for 1968. At one point in Deighton's *IPCRESS File*, a character addresses the narrator as 'Harry'. 'Now my name isn't Harry,' he clarifies, 'but in this business it's hard to remember whether it ever had been.'

Aged eleven, Leonard Cyril Deighton witnessed the arrest of his neighbour, a Nazi spy called Anna Wolkoff. He served in the RAF, then studied at the Royal College of Art in London, going on to design book jackets, including the first British edition of Jack Kerouac's *On the Road* (470). As well as hugely successful spy novels, he wrote works of historical fiction such as *Bomber* (1970) – the first novel to be composed on a word processor – alternative histories such as *SS-GB* (1978), and cookery books, including *Len Deighton's Action Cook Book* (1965). 'Fleming (126) made spy fiction globally popular,' wrote the *Daily Telegraph*, 'but it took Deighton in the Sixties to make it hip.'

The IPCRESS File 1962

The unnamed narrator of *The IPCRESS File* is a tough, Gauloises-smoking working-class spy. We read his filed report on the IPCRESS incident, a conspiracy surrounding a missing biochemist and Cold War brainwashing. 'The rattle of wit in the dialogue, the side-of-the-mouth comments, the evident pleasure in cocking a snook at the British spy story's upper-middle-class tradition – all these, together with the teasing convolutions of the plot, made it clear that a writer of remarkable talent in this field had appeared,' ran the *New York Times* review. The chapter headings are quotations from horoscopes.

Horse Under Water 1963, rev. 1965

The narrator of *The IPCRESS File* investigates the wreck of a giant Nazi U-boat off southern Portugal. Something is hidden inside its rusting hull and sinister figures are gathering on the Algarve. Each chapter heading is a crossword clue.

1966 Penguin Books
2021 Modern Classics
—

The 1966 Penguin publication of *Funeral in Berlin* was 'a turning point in Penguin's history', recalls Deighton, 'marking a change to competitive publishing in a market that was becoming ever more cut-throat'. There was a big-budget launch party in Berlin, to which journalists and booksellers were flown in a chartered aeroplane. The trip coincided with the shooting of the film adaptation, so Michael Caine gave the guests a guided tour of the city.

Funeral in Berlin 1964

In this instalment, Deighton's narrator is enlisted to help a top Soviet scientist defect to the West by crossing the Berlin Wall in an elaborate coffin. But there is more to this deadly game of cat and mouse than meets the eye. The chapter headings are rules of chess.

Billion-Dollar Brain 1966

The fourth 'Harry Palmer' novel sees a Texas billionaire trying to bring down the USSR with an all-powerful supercomputer known as 'the Brain', and he will go to any extreme to achieve his aim. The chapter headings are nursery rhymes.

Deighton in Penguin

Deighton provided cover illustrations for the 1958 Penguin editions of Maurice Walsh's *The Key Above the Door* (1926) and *The Small Dark Man* (1929). He also illustrated the cover for the 1960 edition of John Wain's *Hurry on Down* (124). His own first Penguin title was *Horse Under Water*, in September 1965, followed the next month by a new strip-cartoon French cookery book, *Où est le Garlic?* The four titles featured here joined Modern Classics in April 2021. By the time this book is published, however, 27 more Deighton titles will have been added to the list.

1965 Penguin Books
2021 Modern Classics
—

1967 Penguin Books
2021 Modern Classics
—

Anthony Burgess

1917–1993

John Burgess Wilson was born in
Manchester and took Anthony as
a middle name at his confirmation.
He spent six years in the Army
Education Corps before teaching
for the British colonial service
in Malaya and Brunei, where he
wrote the *Malayan Trilogy* (1956–9).
In 1959, he was diagnosed with
an inoperable brain tumour and
given less than a year; so he
became a full-time writer, and
went on to live for another 30 years,
producing novels and essays, and
translating T. S. Eliot's *The Waste
Land* (11) into Persian. He invented
a prehistoric language for his
screenplay, *Quest for Fire* (1981),
and he was a prolific composer,
writing several full-scale orchestral
works and a musical based on
Joyce's *Ulysses* (10).

1973 Penguin Books
2004 Modern Classics
intro. Gilbert Adair, 2004
—
On the title page, Burgess includes a musical stave
marked '*mf*' (mezzo forte), on which are two notes,
A and B: his initials.

A Clockwork Orange 1962

Burgess's pregnant wife was robbed and assaulted
by four American deserters during a Second World
War blackout in London, and she later miscarried.
This traumatic incident inspired Burgess's darkly
dystopian novel, in which teenage Alex and
his droogs tank up on moloko plus and wreak
their own brand of ultra-violence, before Alex
is arrested and subjected to a chilling form of
aversion therapy. Much of the book is written in
'nadsat talk', invented by Burgess. 'I do not know
of any other writer who has done as much with
language,' wrote his drinking partner, William
S. Burroughs (481), who considered *A Clockwork
Orange* 'a very funny book'. 'If you don't take
to it all,' said Kingsley Amis (132), 'then I can't
resist calling you a starry ptitsa who can't viddy
a horrorshow veshch when it's in front of your
glazzies. And yarbles to you.'

The Complete Enderby

*Inside Mr Enderby, Enderby Outside,
The Clockwork Testament,
Enderby's Dark Lady* 1963–84

In this quartet of comic novels, Burgess presents
the semi-autobiographical life of Francis Xavier
Enderby, an obstreperous poet and lapsed
Catholic, who composes verses while sitting on
the lavatory and uses his bathtub to file his papers.
He inadvertently marries the editor of a women's
magazine, changes his name to Piggy Hogg, becomes
implicated in the murder of a rock singer, writes
a film about Nazis and nuns and produces a musical
about the life of Shakespeare. 'The Enderby series
are even finer comedies than those by the so much
admired Evelyn Waugh (67),' wrote Gore Vidal.

M/F 1971

Student Miles Faber leaves New York for the
Caribbean, where he embarks on a disturbing and
dangerous artistic pilgrimage. 'The situation, as far
as I'm concerned, is what you might term an interesting one,' he explains.
'In two days in a strange country I've acquired a mother in the form
of a Welsh-speaking Bird Queen. […] I've spent some hours in prison,
I've discovered the works of an unknown superlative artist in a garden shed,
and I've been shot at by a riddling lionfaced expert on Bishop Berkeley.
[…] Most interesting of all, I'm due tonight to be married by a circus clown
to my own sister.' Burgess conceived the novel as 'a black Oedipus' story,
so the title could be read as 'motherfucker'.

1972 Penguin Books
1996 Twentieth-Century Classics
intro. Blake Morrison, 1996

2013 Modern Classics
Restored Edition
ed. Andrew Biswell, 2012
fwd. Martin Amis (160), 2012
—
A Clockwork Orange was
the basis for the famously
controversial 1971 film
adaptation directed by Stanley
Kubrick. 'The film made it
easy for readers of the book
to misunderstand what
it was about,' wrote Burgess,
'and the misunderstanding will
pursue me till I die.' Andrew
Biswell, biographer of Burgess
and director of the International
Anthony Burgess Foundation,
collated the 50th anniversary
'Restored Edition' of
A Clockwork Orange using
the original 1961 typescript.

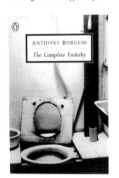

1966–78 Penguin Books
individual titles
1995 Twentieth-Century Classics
● —

Earthly Powers 1980

'It was the afternoon of my eighty-first birthday,' opens this epic novel, 'and I was in bed with my catamite when Ali announced that the archbishop had come to see me.' What follows is an outrageous panoramic sweep through the literary, social and moral history of the 20th century, as seen by an ageing pederastic novelist called Kenneth Toomey. It is 'a considerable achievement', writes Martin Amis (160), 'crowded, crammed, bursting with manic erudition, garlicky puns, omnilingual jokes'.

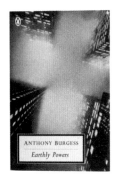

1981 Penguin Books
1997 Twentieth-Century Classics
• —

E. P. Thompson 1924–1993

Edward Palmer Thompson served in a tank unit in Italy during the Second World War before reading history at Cambridge. He was a Marxist social historian, and a leading member of the Communist Party of Great Britain and of the Campaign for Nuclear Disarmament. He married Dorothy Towers, a fellow left-wing historian, and wrote biographies of William Morris and William Blake, who provides an epigraph for *The Making of the English Working Class*: 'The Beast & the Whore rule without control.'

The Making of the English Working Class 1963, rev. 1968

Thompson portrays the customs, aspirations and experiences of British artisans and labourers during the Industrial Revolution, charting the creation of a working-class consciousness in England. 'I am seeking to rescue the poor stockinger, the Luddite cropper, the "obsolete" hand-loom weaver, the "utopian" artisan,' he wrote in his preface, '[…] from the enormous condescension of posterity.' This landmark work of 'history from below' had a profound influence on subsequent writers. 'Thompson's work combines passion and intellect,' said the historian Eric Hobsbawm, 'the gifts of the poet, the narrator and the analyst.'

1968 Pelican Books
2013 Modern Classics
intro. Michael Kenny, 2013
—
The 1968 first Pelican edition was number 1,000 in the Pelican series (xiii).

Charles Chaplin 1889–1977

Chaplin was born in Walworth, south London, the son of music-hall performers. His alcoholic father abandoned his mentally unstable mother, who raised Charles and his older half-brother Sydney in conditions of desperate poverty, enduring more than one stint in the Lambeth Workhouse in Kennington (now home to the Cinema Museum). At nine years old, Chaplin became a member of a clog-dancing troupe, and at 19 he joined the prestigious Fred Karno music-hall company, along with Stan Laurel. While touring the USA in 1913 he was signed by the fledgling Keystone Film Company, with whom he first developed his iconic 'Little Tramp' persona. His enormously popular films made him one of the most famous men in the world, and in 1919 he co-founded United Artists, after which he had complete control over his films, directing, producing, starring, editing and composing the music. In 1952, after a decade of paternity scandals and accusations of communist sympathies, he left America, and lived in Switzerland for the rest of his life. In 1972, he was given an honorary Academy Award and he was knighted in 1975.

My Autobiography
1964

Chaplin's affectingly honest memoir describes his childhood in the slums of south London, his music-hall career and his lucky break in America, as well as his string of failed marriages. It is 'the best autobiography ever written by an actor', wrote the *Chicago Tribune*. 'An astonishing work.'

1966 Penguin Books
2003 Modern Classics
intro. David Robinson, 2003

Daphne du Maurier 1907–1989

Du Maurier was the granddaughter of the author and illustrator George du Maurier, who invented the curate's egg, the trilby hat and the demonic hypnotist Svengali. She began writing short stories in 1928 and her first novel, *The Loving Spirit*, was published in 1931. *Rebecca* (1938) made her a household name, and was filmed by Alfred Hitchcock in 1940. Subsequent film adaptations of her suspenseful works include *The Birds* (Hitchcock, 1963) and *Don't Look Now* (Nicolas Roeg, 1973). After du Maurier's husband died in 1965, she moved to Kilmarth, near Fowey in Cornwall, where she became increasingly reclusive. She was made a dame in 1969.

Don't Look Now
and Other Stories 1964–71, pub. 1971

Originally published as *Not After Midnight* in the UK, this collection of five short stories demonstrates du Maurier's talent for the macabre. The earliest, 'The Breakthrough', is about a scientist attempting to isolate the human soul and was written in 1964 at the request of Kingsley Amis (132). In 'Don't Look Now', John and Laura travel to Venice to escape the memory of their young daughter's death, but they encounter two old women, one of whom has second sight, and get drawn into a series of unsettling and potentially deadly events.

1973 Penguin Books
<u>**2006**</u> Modern Classics
—

1968 Penguin Books
<u>**2011**</u> Modern Classics
pref. Alexander McCall Smith, 2011

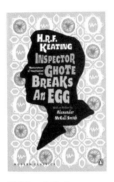

1974 Penguin Books
<u>**2011**</u> Modern Classics
pref. Alexander McCall Smith, 2011

1976 Penguin Books
<u>**2011**</u> Modern Classics
pref. Alexander McCallSmith, 2011

1987 Penguin Books
<u>**2011**</u> Modern Classics
pref. Alexander McCall Smith, 2011

Alexander McCall Smith, author of *The No. 1 Ladies' Detective Agency* books, calls Keating's novels 'beautiful little classics'. His preface is reproduced in all four Inspector Ghote mysteries published in Modern Classics.

H. R. F. Keating

1926–2011

Henry Reymond Fitzwalter Keating was born in St Leonards-on-Sea in Sussex. After a stint in the engineering department at the BBC and some 'totally undistinguished' years in the army, he began writing crime fiction. He is most famous for his 26 Inspector Ghote novels, set in Bombay, now Mumbai, although he first visited India ten years after he started writing about it.

The Perfect Murder 1964
The First Inspector Ghote Mystery

Inspector Ganesh Ghote of the Bombay CID is an affable officer. In his first adventure, he must solve the twin mysteries of a missing single rupee and a deadly attack on Mr Perfect. *The Perfect Murder* won the Crime Writers' Association's Gold Dagger award.

Inspector Ghote
Trusts the Heart 1972

Crooks have kidnapped the young son of a wealthy business tycoon – but they took the wrong boy. Only Inspector Ghote can untangle the mess.

Inspector Ghote
Breaks an Egg 1970

Fifteen years ago, a politician's wife died under suspicious circumstances in a provincial Indian town. Inspector Ghote is asked to investigate, but the chief suspect is a powerful figure, the whole district is against the detective and a holy man is fasting to death in protest at his prying.

Under a Monsoon Cloud
An Inspector Ghote Mystery 1986

Inspector Ghote has witnessed the accidental killing of a police sergeant by an infuriated deputy inspector-general. As the monsoon rain falls, he is unsure how to proceed.

Peter Shaffer 1926–2016

Shaffer was born in Liverpool, the twin brother of Anthony Shaffer, another playwright. He was conscripted as a 'Bevin Boy' to mine coal in the 1940s; then he worked in the acquisitions department of the New York Public Library, and for the London music publisher Boosey & Hawkes. After his talents as a playwright emerged, he wrote frequently for the National Theatre and won dozens of awards. He was knighted in 2001.

The Royal Hunt of the Sun
A Play Concerning the Conquest of Peru 1964

First staged at the Chichester Festival Theatre in Sussex, this spectacular drama presents the fatal clash of two worldviews, represented by the Inca ruler Atahuallpa – son of the Sun – and the Spanish conquistador Francisco Pizarro. The music for the original production, written by Marc Wilkinson, incorporated bird cries, plainchant and a fantasia for organ; the score has now become an integral part of the play. Shaffer said that the play was 'an attempt to define the concept of God'.

1981 Penguin Plays
2007 Modern Classics
—

Equus
1973

A child psychiatrist attempts to understand why a 17-year-old stable boy blinded six horses with a spike. The boy's sublimated sexuality is gradually revealed through a complex private belief system involving horses and a god named 'Equus'. It won the 1975 Tony Award for best play.

1977 Penguin Books
1984 Penguin Plays
2007 Modern Classics
—

Amadeus
1979

Shaffer's fictionalized portrait of the clown-genius Wolfgang Amadeus Mozart and his murderously jealous rival, Antonio Salieri, draws on an 1830 play by Alexander Pushkin. In 1979, it won the *Evening Standard* Drama Award in London and in 1981 the Tony Award in New York, where it ran for more than 1,000 performances on Broadway. The film adaptation won eight Academy Awards, including Best Picture.

1981 Penguin Plays
1985 Penguin Books
2007 Modern Classics
—

More OSCAR-WINNERS

1941 *How Green Was My Valley*
by Richard Llewellyn   110

1949 *All the King's Men*
by Robert Penn Warren   489

1953 *From Here to Eternity*
by James Jones   500

1958 *Gigi*
by Colette   172

1967 *In the Heat of the Night*
by John Ball   527

1967 *Closely Watched Trains*
by Bohumil Hrabal   285

1971 *The Garden of the Finzi-Continis*
by Giorgio Bassani   225

1975 *One Flew Over the Cuckoo's Nest*
by Ken Kesey   520

1981 *Mephisto*
by Klaus Mann   256

1985 *Out of Africa*
by Karen Blixen   240

1987 *'Babette's Feast'*
by Isak Dinesen   242

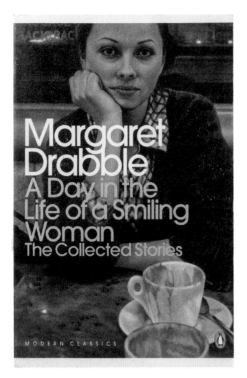

2012
ed. José Francisco
Fernández, 2011

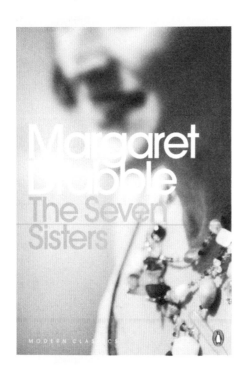

2003 Penguin Books
2011 Modern Classics
• —

Margaret Drabble b. 1939

Drabble was born in Sheffield, the younger sister of the novelist A.S.Byatt. She was briefly a member of the Royal Shakespeare Company, before dedicating herself to writing. She has written 20 novels and many works of non-fiction, and she edited the fifth and sixth editions of *The Oxford Companion to English Literature* in 1985 and 2000. She is married to the biographer Michael Holroyd and was made a dame in 2008.

A Day in the Life of a Smiling Woman
The Collected Stories 1964 – 2000

This volume collects the best of Drabble's stories, about cruel and loving relationships, joyful fantasies and grim realities, social change and personal obsessions. Her writings 'brim with sharply observed life and the author's seemingly infinite sympathy for "ordinary women"', says Joyce Carol Oates.

Jerusalem the Golden 1967

Clara Maugham comes from a stifling, emotionless home in the north of England and is dazzled when she moves to sixties London and falls in with the bohemian Clelia Denham and her family. The critic Lisa Allardice, in her introduction, calls *Jerusalem the Golden* 'a fairytale of its time'. It won the James Tait Black Memorial Prize in 1967.

1969 Penguin Books
2011 Modern Classics
intro. Lisa Allardice, 2011

The Needle's Eye 1972

The former heiress Rose Vassiliou has turned her back on family money and is now a single parent in a decaying house, trying to raise three children.

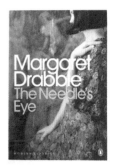

1973 Penguin Books
2011 Modern Classics
• —

The Seven Sisters 2002

Candida Wilton was ignored by her husband and children, even before her divorce. Now she lives quietly in London, until an unexpected windfall allows her to gather six female travelling companions and embark on a dream voyage around the Mediterranean.

Ian Nairn 1930–1983

After two 'false starts' – as a mathematician and as an RAF pilot – Nairn began writing for the *Architectural Review* in 1954. He became a correspondent for the *Observer* and made television films about buildings for the BBC. He particularly admired pubs, and eventually drank himself to death. He once said of his handsome second wife, Judy Perry, that she 'would certainly have been in *Nairn's London* had she only been made of brick or stucco'. He co-authored two of Nikolaus Pevsner's Buildings of England series: *Surrey* (1962) and *Sussex* (1965).

Nairn's London 1966

'This guide is simply my personal list of the best things in London,' explained Nairn: '[…] a record of what has moved me, between Uxbridge and Dagenham.' Nairn sketches the streets and buildings of London with unforgettable vigour. This, for example, is his description of St Mark's Church in Silvertown, in London's docklands, designed by S. S. Teulon and built in the early 1860s: 'A hard punch right in the guts […] glittering poetry, all knobbly with harsh polysyllables. Apse builds up and into stair turret, gabled clerestory builds up and over to gabled tower. Imploded, savage inward raids into the heart's essence, an architectural imagination the size of Blake's. It is the nearest thing to a mystic's revelation that London has.'

ORIGINAL 1966 EDITION

1966 Penguin Books
2014 Modern Classics
aftwd. Gavin Stamp, 2014

Adrian Henri 1932–2000

The grandson of a Mauritian sailor, Henri grew up in Wales and studied fine art before moving to Liverpool in 1957. He painted scenery at the Playhouse theatre, where he met Roger McGough and Brian Patten in 1961 and became interested in poetry performance. He led the poetry/rock group the Liverpool Scene and had a ten-year relationship with Carol Ann Duffy, who would later become Poet Laureate.

Roger McGough b. 1937

McGough was born in Liverpool, the son of a docker. He was one third of The Scaffold, whose comic song 'Lily the Pink' reached number one in the UK singles chart. He has published more than 50 books of poetry, helped write the script for the animated Beatles film *The Yellow Submarine* (1968) and now presents the BBC Radio 4 programme *Poetry Please*. Carol Ann Duffy has described him as 'the patron saint of poetry'.

Brian Patten b. 1946

Patten was born in Bootle, near the Liverpool docks, and left school at fifteen to work for the *Bootle Times*. He has written collections of verse for adults and children and he edited *The Puffin Book of Twentieth-Century Children's Verse* (1991). 'Poetry helps us understand what we've forgotten to remember,' writes Patten. 'It reminds us of things that are important to us when the world overtakes us emotionally.'

The Mersey Sound 1967

This landmark poetry anthology, the tenth in the Penguin Modern Poets series, captures the irreverent, experimental, freewheeling mood of the sixties, focusing on real lives, young love, petrol-pump attendants and bus conductors. The form and style of the poems are innovative, influenced in part by the Beat Generation (491), and the book became one of the bestselling English-language poetry anthologies of all time. The three authors took their title from the 'Mersey Sound' explosion of Liverpool pop culture, which centred on the Beatles.

1967 Penguin Modern Poets
1974 Penguin Modern Poets *revised*
1983 Penguin Books *revised*
2007 Modern Classics *restored*
—

Anna Kavan 1901–1968

Helen Woods was born in Cannes, the only child of wealthy British parents. She claimed that she was introduced to heroin as a young woman by her tennis coach. She soon became addicted, describing her syringe as her 'bazooka'. When her second marriage collapsed, she was hospitalized with depression and addiction, the first of many such confinements. Initially she published under her married name, Helen Ferguson, but in 1940 she dyed her hair blonde and changed her name to Anna Kavan, a character from her own novel *Let Me Alone* (1930). Brian Aldiss (142) described her as 'De Quincey's heir and Kafka's (280) sister'.

Ice 1967

In a post-nuclear world, ice is creeping across the earth, and our unnamed narrator is pursuing a mysterious, silver-haired girl as she flees her sinister 'warden'. This hallucinogenic science fiction novel is written in a dreamy, detached style that Kavan called her 'nocturnal language'.

2017
—

More ICE

Snow Country by Yasunari Kawabata	348
Northland Stories by Jack London	404
South by Ernest Shackleton	12
The Ice Palace by Tarjei Vesaas	238
Cat's Cradle by Kurt Vonnegut	523

John Berger 1926–2017

Berger served in the army in the Second World War before enrolling at the Chelsea School of Art in London. He subsequently painted, taught drawing, and worked as an art critic for the *New Statesman*. In 1972, he presented the landmark BBC television series *Ways of Seeing* and won the Booker Prize for his historical novel *G*. By this time, he had left Britain permanently, moving first to Geneva and then to a small village in the French Alps. 'He handles thoughts the way an artist handles paint,' writes the novelist Jeanette Winterson.

Understanding a Photograph

1967–2007

The author Geoff Dyer selects essays, articles and extracts that present the best of Berger's writing on photography, including several previously uncollected pieces. These include essays on Henri Cartier-Bresson and W. Eugene Smith, and one piece in response to Susan Sontag's *On Photography* (525).

Ways of Seeing 1972

This bestselling book accompanied Berger's acclaimed four-part television series for the BBC. It consists of seven chapters, three of which are made up of images only. The book and the series changed how we think about painting and art criticism, developing the ideas in Walter Benjamin's 'The Work of Art in the Age of Mechanical Reproduction' (251). Through depictions of the female nude and modern advertisements, Berger reveals the layers of objectification and commodification involved in the language of images. The text of the book starts on the front cover.

Confabulations 2016

Confabulations was one of Berger's final works. It is a collection of essays about language and how it relates to thought, art, song, storytelling and political discourse. 'A spoken language is a body, a living creature,' wrote Berger. '[…] And this creature's home is the inarticulate as well as the articulate.'

Understanding a Photograph
John Berger
Edited and introduced by Geoff Dyer

2013
ed. Geoff Dyer

Ways of Seeing
John Berger

1972 Pelican Books
2008 Design Classics
—

Ways of Seeing is set in the typeface Univers, designed by Adrian Frutiger in 1957. Univers is used throughout this volume for author biographies, pull-out boxes and side notes, like this one.

Confabulations
John Berger

2016
—

Peter Brook b. 1925

Brook was born in London to Latvian Jewish parents. His began directing plays in 1942, influenced by Antonin Artaud's 'Theatre of Cruelty' (xix) and the work of the director Joan Littlewood. His production of *A Midsummer Night's Dream* (1970) was set in a white box, with fairies on trapezes; the *Sunday Times* called it 'the sort of thing one sees only once in a generation, and then only from a man of genius'.

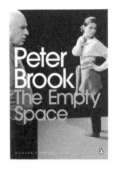

The Empty Space 1968

'I can take any empty space and call it a bare stage,' Brook writes. 'A man walks across this empty space while someone else is watching him, and this is all that is needed for an act of theatre to be engaged.' Brook's influential manifesto is based on lectures he delivered in 1965. He examines four approaches to drama: the 'Deadly Theatre', the 'Holy Theatre', the 'Rough Theatre' and the 'Immediate Theatre'. 'To play needs much work. But when we experience the work as play, then it is not work any more,' he concludes. 'A play is play.'

1972 Pelican Books
1990 Penguin Books
<u>**2008**</u> Modern Classics
—

Barry Hines 1939–2016

Hines was born in the village of Hoyland Common, near Barnsley in South Yorkshire, where his father worked in the local coal mine. He played in the England Grammar Schools' football team and then for the Barnsley reserves, while working as an apprentice mining surveyor at Rockingham Colliery and as a PE teacher. He went on to write nine novels and the screenplay for the BAFTA-winning *Threads* (1984), a terrifying television film about the nuclear apocalypse in Sheffield.

1969 Penguin Books
<u>**1999**</u> Twentieth-Century Classics
aftwd. Barry Hines, 1999

A Kestrel for a Knave 1968

Billy Casper is a teenager growing up in a mining town who adopts an injured kestrel. Hines was inspired by reading *The Goshawk* by T. H. White (106), and by his brother Richard, who tamed a hawk when they were boys. It is 'a slim book about a no-hoper and a hawk', Hines wrote in his afterword. 'But somehow the chemistry works, and over the years I have received many rewarding letters from readers, saying how much they enjoyed the novel and in some cases how it has actually changed their lives.' It was filmed by Ken Loach as *Kes* (1969).

Ronald Blythe b. 1922

Blythe was born in Suffolk, the descendant of generations of East Anglian farmers. After serving briefly in the Second World War, he worked as a librarian in Colchester, and forged friendships with the painter John Nash, the composer Benjamin Britten and the writer E. M. Forster (38).

Akenfield
Portrait of an English Village 1969

This fictionalized history of a Suffolk village is based on conversations Blythe recorded with his neighbours in the small villages of Debach and Charsfield: farmers and farmworkers, the local schoolteacher, doctor, blacksmith, saddler, district nurse and magistrate. It is a colourful, perceptive document of a vanished way of life. 'There are various ways to describe a time, a place, a condition,' explains Blythe in his preface. 'One can come to them from outside and say what one saw. Or one can emerge from within a community, as so many rural writers do, and be at a particular moment its indigenous voice.'

1972 Penguin Books
<u>**1999**</u> Twentieth-Century Classics
pref. Ronald Blythe, 1999

Akenfield was commissioned by Tony Godwin (ix) and first published by 'Allen Lane The Penguin Press', a hardback imprint established in 1967. *Akenfield* was number 100 in the series.

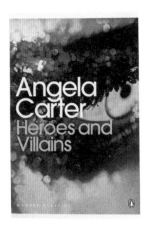

1981 King Penguin
1990 Penguin Books
2011 Modern Classics
intro. Robert Coover
(536), 2011
—
Carter borrowed her
title from the Beach
Boys song, which was
popular at the time.

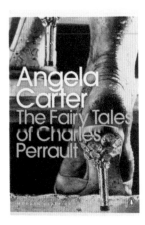

2008
intro. Jack Zipes

Angela Carter 1940–1992

Angela Olive Stalker was born in Eastbourne in Sussex, and was almost immediately evacuated to Yorkshire to live with her grandmother during the Second World War. She worked as a journalist for the *Croydon Advertiser* before studying English at Bristol and publishing her first novel in 1966. Her third novel, *Several Perceptions* (1968), won the Somerset Maugham (32) Award and she used the proceeds to escape her first marriage, to Paul Carter, moving to a remote Japanese fishing village and writing *The Infernal Desire Machines of Doctor Hoffman*. She produced several more novels, as well as stories, a radio drama about Ronald Firbank (64) and an opera adaptation of Virginia Woolf's *Orlando* (44). 'I see my business, the nature of my work,' she said, 'as taking apart mythologies, in order to find out what basic, human stuff they are made of in the first place.' When she died, Salman Rushdie said that 'English literature has lost its high sorceress, its benevolent witch queen'.

Heroes and Villains 1969

Marianne lives in a fortified white tower 'made of steel and concrete' and surrounded by thick woods and wild beasts. When her father is murdered, however, she makes the perilous journey beyond the wire fences to discover a dark, decaying paradise, populated by barbarians and magicians. Carter had been labelled a 'Gothic' writer, so with this book she decided that she would 'indeed write a Gothic novel, a truly Gothic novel full of dread and glamour and passion'.

The Infernal Desire Machines of Doctor Hoffman 1972 →

Desiderio is an employee of 'the city' and desperately in love with Albertina, the glassy daughter of the illusionist Doctor Hoffman. Hoffman's mysterious contraptions are attacking the very fabric of reality, populating Desiderio's world with cannibals, centaurs and acrobats, and stimulating madness, crime and sexual excess. The novel is Carter's 'real, still underrated, classic', writes Ali Smith. 'This imagistically cornucopic and virtuoso performance is a visionary book for a virtual age.'

The Fairy Tales of Charles Perrault 1977

In 1976, Carter was commissioned to translate the 17th-century fairy tales of Charles Perrault, including 'Little Red Riding Hood', 'Bluebeard' and 'Sleeping Beauty'. 'Perrault inspired Carter to delve more deeply into the origins and meanings of fairy tales,' writes the scholar Jack Zipes, 'but she had to misread him or reinterpret him to make his tales more palatable to her feminist and political sensitivity.' The twin results of Carter's commission were this witty retelling of Perrault's stories and *The Bloody Chamber* (1979), her famous feminist reworking of these and other fairy tales.

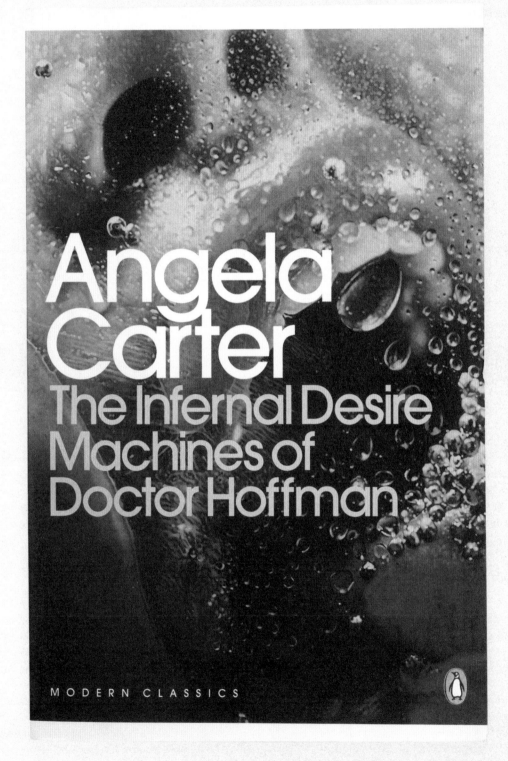

Angela Carter

The Infernal Desire Machines of Doctor Hoffman

MODERN CLASSICS

1982 King Penguin
1990 Penguin Books
2011 Modern Classics
intro. Ali Smith, 2011

The cover of the 2011 edition shows a detail
from *Pop Rocks* (2009) by Marilyn Minter.

Richard Adams 1920–2016

Adams was raised at Wash Common in Berkshire, and in later years lived in Whitchurch, ten miles away. After serving in the army in the Second World War, he worked in the civil service for 25 years, until the success of *Watership Down* allowed him to become a full-time writer. He once listed his enthusiasms as 'English literature, music, chess, beer and shove-ha'penny, bird-song, folk-song and country walking'.

Watership Down 1972

After a terrifying prophecy, a band of rabbits defy their chief and flee their warren. Led by Hazel, they embark on an epic journey, negotiating snares, dogs and the sadistic rabbit tyrant General Woundwort, before they can reach their new home on Watership Down, a real hillside in north Hampshire. The book draws on Homer's *Odyssey* and Virgil's *Aeneid*, creating a rabbit mythology and the rabbit language 'Lapine'. It won both the Carnegie Medal children's book award and the *Guardian* award for children's fiction.

1973 Puffin Books
1974 Penguin Books
2001 Modern Classics
● intro. Nicholas Lezard, 2001
—
In Nicholas Lezard's introduction, he recalls an apocryphal notice in a butcher's window: 'You've read the book, you've seen the film, now eat the cast.'

Emanuel Litvinoff 1915–2011

Litvinoff was born in Whitechapel, east London, to Russian Jewish immigrant parents. He left school at fourteen and cadged a living in Soho and Fitzrovia before enlisting in the army and serving in the Second World War, rising to the rank of acting major. He began writing poetry and novels, and dedicated the rest of his life to literature and campaigning against racism. In 1979, he edited the *Penguin Book of Jewish Short Stories*.

Journey Through a Small Planet 1972

'Until I was sixteen I lived in the east London borough of Bethnal Green, in a small street that is now just a name on the map,' wrote Litvinoff. 'Almost every house in it has gone and it exists, if at all, only in the pages of this book.'
In this 'dreamscape', Litvinoff recalls his working-class Jewish childhood, a vanished world of crowded tenements, Yiddish chatter and pickled herrings. He also tells the story of his parents, who emigrated from Odessa to Whitechapel in 1913. Soon after Litvinoff was born, his father was repatriated to Russia to fight in the First World War and he never returned.

1976 Penguin Books
2008 Modern Classics
intro. Patrick Wright, 2008
—
The 2008 edition appends a few prose pieces and poems, including 'To T. S. Eliot' (1953), in which Litvinoff accuses Eliot (11) of anti-Semitism.

Leonora Carrington 1917–2011

When Carrington was a 19-year-old English debutante, she eloped to France with the much older painter Max Ernst. She embraced Surrealism (176) and became an artist herself. She attended parties dressed in only a sheet, and would serve omelettes garnished with her guests' own hair. When the Second World War broke out Ernst was arrested by the Germans, while Carrington was hospitalized in Spain, where she endured spasm-inducing drugs until her nanny arrived by submarine to rescue her. She married a Mexican diplomat in order to cross the Atlantic, after which she divorced amicably and settled in Mexico City.

2005
intro. Ali Smith
—
Carrington wrote *The Hearing Trumpet* in English, but it first appeared in 1974 in her own French translation. The original English text was first published in 1976.

The Hearing Trumpet 1974

Ninety-two-year-old Marian Leatherby has a short grey beard 'which conventional people would find repulsive'. When her friend Carmella gives her an ornate hearing trumpet, she discovers that her family is plotting to commit her to a sinister retirement home: situated in a converted medieval Spanish castle, it is run by a religious organization called 'the Well of Light Brotherhood'. Once there, Marian learns the story of a mysterious abbess, turns into a geriatric anarchist and stages a revolution. 'Reading *The Hearing Trumpet* liberates us from the miserable reality of our days,' wrote Luis Buñuel.

J. L. Carr 1912–1994

Joseph Lloyd Carr preferred to call himself 'James'. He came from a Yorkshire Methodist family, and served with the RAF as an aerial photographer in Africa during the Second World War. For fifteen years, he was the eccentric head teacher of a Northamptonshire primary school, before running the small Quince Tree Press. He published pocket poetry books, historical county maps, and unusual reference works with names such as *Welbourn's Dictionary of Prelates, Parsons, Vergers, Wardens, Sidesmen and Preachers, Sunday-School Teachers, Hermits, Ecclesiastical Flower-Arrangers, Fifth Monarchy Men and False Prophets*. All his Quince Tree Press books had two prices: a lower one for children and a higher one for adults. In an interview for *Vogue* magazine, he was asked to provide a dictionary definition of himself: 'James Lloyd Carr, a back-bedroom publisher of large maps and small books who, in old age, unexpectedly wrote six novels which, although highly thought of by a small band of literary supporters and by himself, were properly disregarded by the Literary World.'

How Steeple Sinderby Wanderers Won the FA Cup

1975

In their buttercup-yellow strip, England's most obscure football team storms through the Fenland League and goes on to beat Glasgow Rangers at Wembley. Carr narrates the story through unreliable accounts, local newspaper articles and surreal committee minutes. 'Is this story believable?' he asks in his foreword. 'Ah, it all depends upon whether you *want* to believe it.'

2016
intro. D. J. Taylor

A Month in the Country 1980

Old Tom Birkin looks back on a vanished summer when, as a young, damaged veteran of the First World War, he was commissioned to remove layers of whitewash from the walls inside the village church of Oxgodby, revealing a huge medieval painting of the Last Judgement. In the peace and beauty of the countryside, Tom starts to feel a sense of renewal and a growing belief in the future.

1980 Penguin Books
2000 Modern Classics
intro. Penelope Fitzgerald, 2000

Olivia Manning 1908–1980

Manning was born in Portsmouth, the daughter of a naval officer. She married the lecturer Reggie Smith in 1939 – their bridesmaid was Stevie Smith (108) and the best man was Louis MacNeice – and she moved with him to Bucharest, where he was working for the British Council. When the Second World War broke out, the couple first fled to Athens, then were evacuated to Egypt, and finally moved to Jerusalem, where Reggie was put in charge of the Palestine Broadcasting Station. These peripatetic wartime experiences formed the basis of the series of novels for which Manning is best remembered. Olivia and Reggie returned to London in 1946, where she wrote books, articles, poetry and radio dramas.

The Levant Trilogy

The Danger Tree, The Battle Lost and Won, The Sum of Things 1977–80

The Balkan Trilogy (1960–65) and *The Levant Trilogy* form a single narrative known as *Fortunes of War*. The six novels follow Guy Pringle and his wife Harriet as they move through eastern Europe and the Middle East during the Second World War and their marriage becomes increasingly strained. *The Levant Trilogy* is set in Egypt, Jerusalem and Syria, and contrasts civilian life with scenes of desert warfare. Anthony Burgess (148) described the saga as 'the finest fictional record of the war produced by a British writer'. The trilogies were adapted for television in 1987, starring Emma Thompson and Kenneth Branagh.

1979–82 Penguin Books
individual titles
1982 Penguin Books
collected edition
1996 Twentieth-Century Classics
● —

Isabel Colegate b. 1931

At nineteen, Colegate worked as the assistant to the literary agent Anthony Blond. When Blond moved into publishing, he commissioned her first novel, *The Blackmailer* (1958). She went on to write a dozen more. Colegate used to live near Bath in Midford Castle, a Gothic folly shaped like a giant ace of clubs.

1982 Penguin Books
2007 Modern Classics
intro. Julian Fellowes, 2007
—
'As the screenwriter for *Gosford Park*, it is no secret that I owe much to Isabel Colegate,' confesses Julian Fellowes in his introduction. '[…] She looks behind the glamorous and ordered curtain of post-Edwardian luxury to find the private motives, the dreams and the frustrations of the individuals, from both sides of the social divide.'

The Shooting Party 1980

In the autumn before the outbreak of 'what used to be known as the Great War', a shooting party assembles at Nettleby Park, the Oxfordshire home of Sir Randolph Nettleby. The aristocratic, adulterous guests move between rituals of eating and slaughter, until the intrusion of real danger presages the end of their privileged era. The novel won the W. H. Smith Annual Literary Award and was adapted into a 1985 film starring James Mason, James Fox and John Gielgud.

2018
—

Richard Cobb 1917–1996

Cobb was a historian of France. During the Second World War, he served in the Air Ministry and then Belgium and France, where he remained until 1955, working on his doctoral thesis. He subsequently taught at the universities of Wales, Manchester, Leeds and Oxford. 'His idiosyncratic character, unrestrained opinions, strong likes and dislikes, and fondness for liberal, noisy entertainment,' reads his entry in the *Oxford Dictionary of National Biography*, 'gave him something of a legendary reputation among students and colleagues.'

French and Germans, Germans and French
A Personal Interpretation of France under Two Occupations 1914–1918 / 1940–1944 1983

This intimate, meditative essay is 'a very tentative approach to the elusive problems of the relations between soldiers and civilians, *occupants* and *occupés*'. It examines France under German occupation, twice in 30 years, and its strange mixture of compromise, betrayal, collaboration and resistance.

Martin Amis b. 1949

Martin Amis, son of Kingsley Amis (132), was educated in Britain, Spain and the USA. As a teenager, he played John Thornton in the film adaptation of *A High Wind in Jamaica* (86). His first novel, *The Rachel Papers* (1973), won the Somerset Maugham (32) Award and his memoir *Experience* (2000) won the James Tait Black Memorial Prize. Until 2011, Amis was Professor of Creative Writing at the University of Manchester.

Money
A Suicide Note 1984

'This is a suicide note. By the time you lay it aside (and you should always read these things slowly, on the lookout for clues or giveaways), John Self will no longer exist. Or at any rate that's the idea. You never can tell, though, with suicide notes, can you?' Self is a profligate hedonist slob, invited to New York to direct his first feature film, *Good Money*. As he sates his ravenous appetite for alcohol, tobacco, pills, pornography and junk food, the production careers towards disaster and he decides to rename it *Bad Money*. The novel was partly inspired by Amis's own experience working on the screenplay for *Saturn 3* (1980).

1985 Penguin Books
2000 Modern Classics
● —
Amis appears as a character in the plot of *Money*. Apparently Kingsley Amis (132), his father, threw the book away at this point, complaining that Martin was 'breaking the rules, buggering about with the reader, drawing attention to himself'.

Penelope Lively b. 1933

Penelope Low grew up in Egypt and settled in England after the Second World War. She married Jack Lively in 1957, who went on to be Professor of Politics at Warwick University. She began writing books for children and won the Carnegie Medal children's book award for *The Ghost of Thomas Kempe* (1973). Her first adult novel, *The Road to Lichfield* (1977), was shortlisted for the Booker Prize, as was *According to Mark*, and she won the prize in 1987 with *Moon Tiger*. She was made a dame in 2012.

According to Mark
1984

Mark Lamming is a literary biographer working on a life of the writer Gilbert Strong. His happily married life is shaken up when he falls unexpectedly in love with Strong's granddaughter.

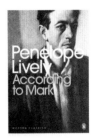

1985 Penguin Books
2011 Modern Classics

Moon Tiger 1987

1988 Penguin Books
2006 Modern Classics
intro. Anthony Thwaite, 2006

–

'Of all her many adult novels,' says the poet Anthony Thwaite in his introduction, '[…] it is *Moon Tiger* that most radically and most successfully exemplifies her astringent and powerful flavour.'

'I'm writing a history of the world,' declares the 76-year-old writer Claudia Hampton. '[…] The whole triumphant murderous unstoppable chute – from the mud to the stars, universal and particular, your story and mine. […] A history of the world, yes. And in the process, my own.' Lying on her hospital deathbed, she gradually pieces together a mosaic of memories and flashbacks. Lively's masterpiece 'leaves its traces in the air long after you've put it away', writes the novelist Anne Tyler.

Oleander, Jacaranda
A Childhood Perceived 1994

In this memoir of her colonial upbringing in Egypt, Lively recalls the heat, the sugar cane, the barefoot children, the snake charmers, the broad, brown Nile, and the flower-laden oleander and jacaranda trees.

1995 Penguin Books
2006 Modern Classics
–

Heat Wave 1996

Pauline is spending the summer at World's End in the English countryside, along with her daughter Teresa, her son-in-law Maurice and her baby grandson. As secrets emerge in the heat, growing tensions lead to a violent climax. *Heat Wave* is 'extraordinarily good', writes Susan Hill, 'intelligent and perceptive […] very moving'.

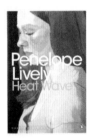

1997 Penguin Books
2011 Modern Classics
–

John Healy b. 1943

Healy was born in Kentish Town, northwest London, to poor Irish parents. He left school at fifteen and began a downward spiral into alcoholism. He joined the army, where he became a boxer, but was dishonourably discharged for drunkenness. He spent the next fifteen years in the 'grass arena': a terrifying world of dimly lit London parks, prowled by vagrant alcoholics, beggars and thieves armed with broken bottles and knives. During one stint in prison, Healy was taught to play chess by fellow inmate Harry 'the Fox', and he discovered a remarkable natural ability. He went on to become a tournament champion, who made press headlines and played against grandmasters, and this unexpected chess career helped him to overcome his addictions.

The Grass Arena
An Autobiography 1988

Healy's remarkable memoir won the J. R. Ackerley (99) Prize for autobiography. 'There is no perceptible distance between the words, which seem to have chosen themselves, and the experiences from which they blossomed like a garden of wild flowers,' writes the actor Daniel Day-Lewis. '[…] He is our jaunty, gleeful tour guide and messenger from hell.'

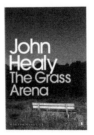

2008 Modern Classics
2012 Modern Classics
revised
pref. Daniel Day-Lewis, 2008
aftwd. Colin MacCabe, 2008

'Beside it, a book like Orwell's *Down and Out in Paris and London* (81) seems a rather inaccurate tourist guide,' says the film producer Colin MacCabe.

Lad Lit

In the 1990s, glossy 'lads' mags' such as *Arena*, *FHM*, *Loaded* and *GQ* became popular in Britain, and publishers invented the term 'lad lit' to promote books to the same audience. Charmingly inept male protagonists, devoted to football, beer, music and sex, suffer identity crises in the face of social pressures and an inability to communicate with women. Key texts of the genre include Nick Hornby's novels *High Fidelity* (1995) and *About a Boy* (1998), Tony Parsons's *Man and Boy* (1999) and *White City Blue* (1999) by Tim Lott. 'At the low end of the market,' writes the critic Elaine Showalter, 'Ladlit was the masculine equivalent of the Bridget Jones phenomenon; at the high end of the high street, it was a masterly examination of male identity in contemporary Britain.'

Nick Hornby b. 1957

Hornby's 'lad lit' novels include *High Fidelity* (1995) and *About a Boy* (1998), both of which have been turned into films. In 2010 he co-founded the Ministry of Stories, a non-profit organization in east London that helps young people develop their writing skills.

Fever Pitch 1992

Since he was a boy, Arsenal's football ground has been the crucible for Hornby's strongest emotions: joy, humiliation, heartbreak, frustration and hope. In this memoir, he describes his parents' separation, his early romances and his career as a teacher, all infused with his love of football. It won the William Hill Sports Book of the Year award in 1992.

Tim Lott b. 1956

Lott is a journalist who worked for the magazines *Sounds* and *Flexipop!* After two weeks as editor of *City Limits* in the late 1980s, however, he resigned, suffering from severe depression. His parents helped him to recover, but then his mother took her own life. He has since written novels for adults and children and a television documentary called *The New Middle Classes* (2007).

The Scent of Dried Roses 1996

Lott reconstructs his mother's suicide and then scrolls back through the lives of his parents, describing their pebble-dashed home and his own suburban childhood in Southall, west London, seeking to understand what brought her to that extreme. The book is a meditation on grief, loss and the power of memory, and a portrait of post-war England. It is a 'remarkable memoir', wrote Ruth Rendell; '[…] to read it is to be spellbound as by a gripping novel'.

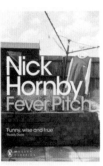

2000 Penguin Books
2012 Modern Classics
aftwd. Nick Hornby, 2012

1997 Penguin Books
2009 Modern Classics
intro. Blake Morrison, 2009

2013 Penguin Classics
2015 Modern Classics
—

In 2011, Morrissey revealed in a BBC interview that he had written a 660-page memoir, but he was yet to find a publisher. 'I'd like it to go to Penguin,' he mused, 'but only if they published it as a Classic.' Two years later, *Autobiography* was published in the Penguin Classics black livery to both widespread amusement and some consternation. The audiobook is read by the actor David Morrissey (no relation).

Morrissey b. 1959

The singer-songwriter Steven Patrick Morrissey grew up in Manchester. In 1982, he co-founded The Smiths with Johnny Marr, which gathered a global following before breaking up acrimoniously, five years – and nine top-ten albums – later. Known for his quiff, his angst-ridden lyrics and his anti-popstar lifestyle, Morrissey has since built a successful solo career, with three British number-one albums in three different decades.

Autobiography 2013

Morrissey reminisces about his tough childhood and career, with cantankerous revelations about his sexuality, The Smiths and his fraught relationship with Johnny Marr; the *Guardian* called the book a 'Mozery Memoir'. Morrissey compares himself to the poet A. E. Housman (31), who 'said more about human relationships than those who manage to feast on them'.

WESTERN EUROPE

André Gide Journals 1889-1949

André Gide Fruits of the Earth

André Gide · The Immoralist

André Gide Strait is the Gate and The Vatican Cellars

André Gide · La Symphonie Pastorale

André Gide If It Die

André Gide The Vatican Cellars

André Gide The Counterfeiters

MARCEL PROUST Against Sainte-Beuve and Other Essays

PMC

MARCEL
PROUST
JEAN
SANTEUIL

MARCEL PROUST Swann's Way

2685

14003178 2

1497

2315

1950

ISBN 0 14
00.1234 6

1404

2415

ISBN 0 14
01.8525 9

ISBN 0 14
00.7203 9

ISBN 0 14
11.8058 7

France

André Gide

1869 – 1951

André-Paul-Guillaume Gide's obituary in the *New York Times* hailed him as 'the greatest French writer of this century'. After a puritanical upbringing, he visited North Africa where he met Oscar Wilde (3) and discovered the pleasures of beautiful Arabic boys. He married his cousin Madeleine, but their marriage was never consummated. Gide wrote more than 50 books, including poetry, biography, fiction, drama, criticism, travelogues and translations of Joseph Conrad (28). In 1918, he met the author Dorothy Bussy (97), who became a lifelong friend and translated many of his works into English. In 1947, he was awarded the Nobel Prize for Literature (576). 'My writings are comparable to Achilles' spear,' he wrote, 'with which a second contact cured those it had first wounded. If one of my books disconcerts you, reread it. Under the obvious poison, I took care to hide the antidote.'

1967
● trans. Justin O'Brien, 1947–51

Journals

1889 – 1949, pub. 1939 – 50

Originally begun as a literary exercise, Gide's diary gradually became his 'obsession', as André Malraux (184) described it. Now regarded as one of his greatest achievements, Gide's journals cover 60 years and contain insights into his writing as well as contemporary events such as the Dreyfus Affair and both world wars.

1970
● trans. Dorothy Bussy (97), 1927

Fruits of the Earth
and **Later Fruits of the Earth** 1897 – 1935

This curious mixture of poetry, quotation, travelogue and memoir is addressed to an imaginary young man called Nathaniel. Inspired by Gide's sexual awakening in North Africa and his near death from tuberculosis, it is a hymn to pleasure and the importance of living in the moment. It was an inspiration for existentialists (186) such as Jean-Paul Sartre (185) and Albert Camus (181). 'Throw away my book,' Gide concluded; 'say to yourself that it is only *one* of the thousand possible postures in life. Look for your own. Do not do what someone else could do as well as you.' In 1935, during a brief spell as a communist, Gide wrote *Later Fruits of the Earth*, a reaffirmation of his earlier work.

The Immoralist

1902

In this shocking, semi-autobiographical book, Michel and Marceline travel to Tunisia on their honeymoon. While there, Michel is captivated by a beautiful Arab boy and renounces his moral values, deciding to live only according to his desires. But with this newfound freedom comes a sickening ennui: 'Knowing how to free oneself is nothing,' says Michel; 'the difficult thing is knowing how to live with that freedom.'

1960 Penguin Books
1964 Modern Classics
● trans. Dorothy Bussy (97), 1930
2000 Modern Classics
trans. David Watson, 2000
intro. Alan Sheridan, 2000
—
Gide described *The Immoralist* as 'a fruit filled with bitter ash, like those colocynths which sprout in the most arid deserts: rather than quench your thirst, they scorch your mouth even more, yet against their backdrop of golden sand they are not without a certain beauty'.

Penguin Modern Classics 3/6

André Gide
The Immoralist

1952 Penguin Books
1965 Modern Classics
with The Vatican Cellars
1969 Modern Classics
separate volume
trans. Dorothy Bussy (97),
1924

Strait is the Gate 1909

Young Jerome Palissier spends
his summers in Normandy,
where he falls in love with
his cousin Alissa. She returns
his love, but gradually comes
to believe that her soul is being
compromised, so she crushes
her feelings. Gide described
the novel as 'the twin' of
The Immoralist (164): 'the two
subjects grew up concurrently
in my mind, the excess of one
finding a secret permission
in the excess of the other and
together establishing a balance'.

The Vatican Cellars
1914

Set in late 19th-century
Rome, this picaresque romp
centres on Lafcadio Wluiki,
a charismatic boy who kills
a stranger in a liberating
acte gratuit. The plot involves
saints, adventurers, adultery,
bastardy and the alleged
abduction of the Pope.

1959 Penguin Books
1965 Modern Classics
with Strait is the Gate
1969 Modern Classics
separate volume
● trans. Dorothy Bussy (97),
1927

1963
● trans. Dorothy Bussy (97),
1931

La Symphonie Pastorale
and **Isabelle** 1911–19

In *La Symphonie Pastorale* (1919),
a Protestant country minister
adopts a mute blind girl and
gradually coaxes her into
speaking. In *Isabelle* (1911),
a young scholar falls in love
with a miniature portrait of
a young woman, with unhappy
consequences.

1957 Penguin Books
1977 Modern Classics
● trans. Dorothy Bussy
(97), 1950
—
This cover of the 1977
Penguin edition shows
a detail from *André Gide
and His Friends at
the Café Maure of the
Exposition Universelle
of 1900* by Jacques-Émile
Blanche, which is held
in the Musée des
Beaux-Arts in Rouen.

1966
trans. Dorothy
Bussy (97), 1931

If It Die 1920

This is Gide's memoir of his childhood, with uninhibited
details of his adolescent sexuality. It concludes with
his mother's death and his engagement to his cousin
Madeleine in 1895. The title is taken from John 12:24:
'Except a corn of wheat fall into the ground and die, it
abideth alone: but if it die, it bringeth forth much fruit.'

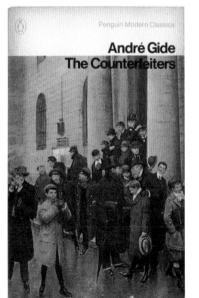

The Counterfeiters 1925

This encyclopaedic examination of human weakness and despair was the only
one of Gide's books that he described as a *roman* or 'novel'. The plot is loose
and complex. Among the many characters are an author, Édouard, who is
writing a novel called *The Counterfeiters*, a gang of schoolboys who are forging
gold coins, and several openly bisexual and gay figures. The character of the
Comte de Passavant is a portrait of Jean Cocteau (178).

Marcel Proust

1871–1922

Valentin-Louis-Georges-Eugène-Marcel Proust was born in Auteuil, on the rural outskirts of Paris. He was a sickly child with chronic asthma, but he devoted his twenties to hosting lavish dinner parties, attending fashionable Paris salons, enjoying male prostitutes and having a relationship with the composer Reynaldo Hahn. As his health deteriorated, however, and following the deaths of his beloved mother and father, Proust became increasingly reclusive. Eventually he retreated into a cork-lined room on the Boulevard Haussmann in the heart of Paris. Here he slept all day and dedicated his nights to writing his extraordinary multi-volume masterpiece, *À la Recherche du Temps Perdu* (168). Graham Greene (88) considered Proust the 'greatest novelist of the twentieth century'.

1988 Penguin Classics
1994 Twentieth-Century Classics
• trans. John Sturrock, 1988

Against Sainte-Beuve
and Other Essays

1891–1922, pub. 1954

This unfinished book of essays was discovered among Proust's papers and published posthumously. Three of the essays attack Charles-Augustin Sainte-Beuve, a 19th-century literary critic, who believed that knowledge of a writer's biography was essential to understanding his or her work.

1985
• trans. Gerard Hopkins, 1955
pref. André Maurois, 1955

Jean Santeuil

1896–1900, pub. 1952

Proust's unfinished first novel was also discovered after his death. It is a prototype for *In Search of Lost Time* (168): a young man, Jean Santeuil, recalls the impressions and emotions of his boyhood summers and his entry into Parisian high society. In *Jean Santeuil*, 'Proust was still living in the illusory world of Time, floating on the dead sea of the phenomenal world and trying in vain to drown,' wrote George Painter, Proust's biographer: 'he could not regain Time because he had not yet lost it...'

Proust in Penguin

The first English translation of *À la Recherche du Temps Perdu* was made by C. K. Scott Moncrieff, a reclusive homosexual like Proust, who corresponded with him and published translations of the first six volumes between 1922 and 1930, although he died before translating the seventh. Moncrieff took liberties with Proust's text, not least changing the title to *Remembrance of Things Past*, which he borrowed from a Shakespeare sonnet, but nonetheless his translation has become a classic in its own right. Penguin published Moncrieff's first volume, *Swann's Way*, in 1957. In 1981, Terence Kilmartin used the corrected French edition of 1954 to revise the Moncrieff translation; this was published by Penguin in three volumes in 1983, and then in Penguin Classics in 1985, in Twentieth-Century Classics in 1989 and they were bound in cloth in 2016. After the publication of the definitive French Pléiade edition of 1987–89, the Moncrieff–Kilmartin translation was revised for a second time, by D. J. Enright, and published in 1992 under the more accurate title *In Search of Lost Time* (168). Finally, in 1995, Penguin commissioned the first entirely new translation of the work, under the general editorship of the scholar Christopher Prendergast, who gathered seven translators, including the American writer Lydia Davis and the Australian novelist James Grieve. This new composite translation, in six volumes, was first published, in hardback, in 2002.

MARCEL PROUST

Swann's Way

1957 Penguin Books
<u>**1997**</u> Twentieth-Century Classics
● trans. C. K. Scott Moncrieff, 1922

The artwork on the cover of the 1997 edition is a detail
from *The Sheltered Path* (1873) by Claude Monet.

In Search of Lost Time

1909–22, pub. 1913–27

It is 'a treasure hunt where the treasure is time and the hiding place the past', wrote Vladimir Nabokov (304). 'The ebb and tide of memory, waves of emotions such as desire, jealousy, and artistic euphoria – this is the material of [this] enormous and yet singularly light and translucid work.' The narrator of this long novel, who is similar but not identical to Marcel Proust, attempts to recover the past through memory and render those memories into art. The novel is a reverie on the fleeting nature of experience and the challenges of the artistic process, but it is also a social comedy set in fin-de-siècle France (3). It is written in dreamy, ruminative prose that encompasses lyrical descriptions, witty repartee and meditations on love, jealousy, homosexuality and life's lack of meaning. 'A giant miniature,' Jean Cocteau (178) called it, 'full of images, of superimposed gardens, of games conducted between space and time.'

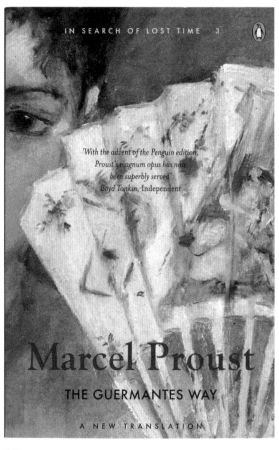

2003
trans. Lydia Davis, 2002

2003
trans. James Grieve, 2002

2003
trans. Mark Treharne, 2002

Proust's opening volume was initially refused publication by the *Nouvelle Revue Française* on André Gide's (164) advice. Gide later wrote to Proust to apologize, calling it 'the most serious mistake ever made by the N.R.F. – and (since to my shame I was largely responsible for it) one of the sorrows, one of the most bitter regrets of my life'. Proust initially envisaged a novel in three volumes, but when he realized he would not survive to write another book, he expanded his plan to seven.

At his death, Proust left the last three volumes complete but not fully revised; they were edited and published posthumously by his brother, Robert Proust. They do contain inconsistencies, however, as well as some fragmentary and unpolished passages.

2003
trans. John Sturrock, 2002

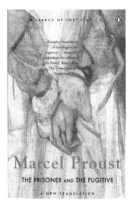

2003
trans. Carol Clark
& Peter Collier, 2002

2003
trans. Ian Patterson, 2002

The first volume, *The Way by Swann's* (1913), introduces the theme of involuntary memory. A *petite madeleine*, soaked in tea, transports the narrator back to his boyhood in the village of Combray, where he recalls his parents and neighbours, especially the fashionable dilettante Charles Swann, whose house lay along one of the family's favourite walking routes. This volume also includes the story within a story of Swann's tortuous affair with the beautiful courtesan Odette de Crécy.

In the Shadow of Young Girls in Flower (1919) was supposed to be published in 1914, but it was delayed by the First World War. The narrator recalls the seaside resort of Balbec in Normandy and meditates on the different forms of adolescent love. This volume introduces the hilariously dull M. de Norpois and two characters who become increasingly important in later volumes: the arrogant Baron de Charlus and the mercurial Albertine. It won the Prix Goncourt.

The Guermantes Way (1920–21) depicts the dazzling world of fashionable Paris in the late 19th century, a constellation of brilliant but shallow literary and aristocratic salons. One episode was inspired by Proust's year of military service in the Coligny Barracks at Orléans.

Sodom and Gomorrah (1921–2) is a portrait of homosexual love, male and female, and the destructive power of sexual jealousy. Albertine and the Baron de Charlus return as major characters.

The fifth and sixth volumes, *The Prisoner* (1923) and *The Fugitive* (1925), printed together in the Penguin edition, are known collectively as *Le Roman d'Albertine*. In *The Prisoner*, Albertine is living with the narrator; in the second, she has left him. *The Fugitive* includes a memorable description of Venice.

The final volume, *Finding Time Again* (1927), presents a striking panorama of Paris during the First World War. It shows the narrator facing his own mortality, resolved to preserve his life through a record of his memories: the novel you have just finished reading. 'My great adventure is really Proust,' said Virginia Woolf (42). 'Well – what remains to be written after that? [...] One has to put the book down and gasp. The pleasure becomes physical – like sun and wine and grapes and perfect serenity and intense vitality combined.'

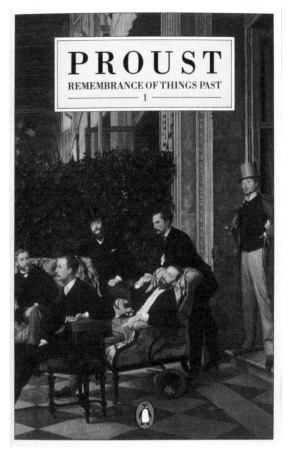

1983 Modern Classics
1985 Penguin Classics
1989 Twentieth-Century Classics
2016 Clothbound Classics
trans. C. K. Scott Moncrieff, 1922–4

1983 Modern Classics
1986 Penguin Classics
1989 Twentieth-Century Classics
2016 Clothbound Classics
trans. C. K. Scott Moncrieff, 1925–8

1983 Modern Classics
1986 Penguin Classics
1989 Twentieth-Century Classics
2016 Clothbound Classics
trans. C. K. Scott Moncrieff & Stephen Hudson, 1929–31

Colette

1873 – 1954

Sidonie-Gabrielle Colette moved to Paris at the age of 20 with her husband, the author and notorious womanizer Henri Gauthier-Villars, known by his pen name 'Willy'. He introduced her to Paris's literary salons, encouraged her to pursue lesbian affairs, and locked her in a room, forcing her to write the wildly successful *Claudine* novels, which he published under his own name. Their marriage collapsed in 1906, and Colette spent the next six years scraping a living in music halls, occasionally acting the part of Claudine in adaptations of her own books. She had a five-year relationship with a fellow actress and their onstage kiss in January 1907 caused an uproar. Colette's second husband was Henry de Jouvenel, editor of *Le Matin*; they had one daughter, but the marriage broke up after Colette began sleeping with Jouvenel's 16-year-old son. In 1951, Katherine Anne Porter (427) hailed her as 'the greatest living French writer of fiction', adding that she had been the greatest even 'while Gide (164) and Proust (166) still lived'.

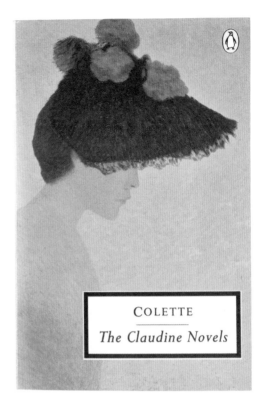

The Claudine Novels 1900 – 1903

Claudine at School, Claudine in Paris, Claudine Married, Claudine and Annie

'You ought to jot down on paper some memories of the Primary School,' suggested Colette's husband 'Willy'. 'Don't be afraid of racy details.' *Claudine at School* and its sequels were published under Willy's name and became a sensation, inspiring fashions, plays and beauty products. The books follow the 15-year-old Claudine from her Burgundian village school to the literary salons of turn-of-the-century Paris. She is unconventional and emancipated, a candid, beguiling narrator, with a *soupçon* of homoeroticism. Colette 'said what no man could have said', wrote André Maurois, 'and she spoke of sensations and feelings as nobody had spoken of them before'.

1963 Penguin Books *individual titles*
1987 Penguin Books
1990 Twentieth-Century Classics
● trans. Antonia White, 1956–62

1985 Penguin Books
1989 Twentieth-Century Classics
● ed. Robert Phelps, 1983
trans. Matthew Ward et al., 1957–83

The Collected Stories

1908 – 45

'I cannot interest myself in anything that is not life,' wrote Colette. The 100 short stories that make up this volume include her masterpieces 'Bella-Vista', 'The Tender Shoot' and 'Le Képi', moving from the theatres of Paris to the verdant French countryside and the Mediterranean coast. 'Look for a long time at what pleases you,' she advised a younger writer, 'and longer still at what pains you.'

The Innocent Libertine

1909

Minnie is delicate and sensuous, with wild dreams of idealized love and physical bliss. As she haunts the streets and salons of Paris, however, hope turns gradually to despair.

1972 Penguin Books
1987 Modern Classics
● trans. Antonia White, 1968

The Vagabond 1910

In this semi-autobiographical novel, Renée Néré escapes a failed marriage and takes refuge in the shabby world of the music hall.

1960 Penguin Books
1986 Modern Classics
• trans. Enid McLeod, 1954

The Captive 1913

The sequel to *The Vagabond* sees Renée living quietly on the French Riviera. Her looks and fame are fading, but she is as passionate as ever.

1970 Penguin Books
1986 Modern Classics
• trans. Antonia White, 1964

Chéri and The Last of Chéri 1920–26

Fred Peloux is 'Chéri', devilishly handsome, charming and capricious. Raised in the demi-monde of wealthy Parisian courtesans, he is 'lent' by his mother to her friend Léa de Lonval, so that he can be tutored in the art of love. After four years, Chéri breaks Léa's heart and destroys his own chances of a conventional life, leading to an emotional denouement. In *The Last of Chéri* (1926), Peloux is a minor war hero who cannot escape memories of his carefree, love-lavished youth.

My Mother's House and Sido 1922–9

These two fictionalized autobiographies describe Colette's magical childhood in Saint-Sauveur in Burgundy. The house overflows with dogs, cats and children, and is presided over by Colette's mother, Adèle-Eugénie-Sidonie, known as 'Sido', who has a deep understanding of nature and her family. She was 'the personage who little by little dominated the rest of my work', wrote Colette.

1966 Penguin Books
1986 Modern Classics
• trans. Roger Senhouse, 1953

1954 Penguin Books
1962 Modern Classics
• trans. Roger Senhouse, 1930–33
intro. Raymond Mortimer, 1951

More SEXUAL AWAKENINGS

Ripening Seed 1923

Philippe and Vinca are childhood friends, who meet every summer at a seaside resort in Brittany. This year, their incipient adolescence complicates their relationship, especially when the beautiful Madame Dalleray takes it upon herself to educate Philippe in the ways of love. Colette wrote *Le Blé en Herbe* in her house at Saint-Coulomb, on the coast near Saint-Malo.

1972 Penguin Books
1989 Twentieth-Century Classics
● trans. Elizabeth Tait & Roger Senhouse, 1960

The Other One
1929

Dark, voluptuous Fanny is married to the playwright Farou, infamous for his many mistresses. She smoulders fretfully in their summer villa, where she lives with her stepson Jean and her friend Jane, Farou's beautiful secretary. 'There is nothing to explain, nothing to criticize,' wrote Henry de Montherlant (198), 'one has only to admire.'

1959 Penguin Books
1961 Modern Classics
● trans. Roger Senhouse, 1955

Gigi and The Cat 1933 – 44

Fifteen-year-old Gilberte Alvar, known as 'Gigi', is preparing to be the perfect courtesan. She knows how to eat lobster and how to choose cigars for her wealthy admirers; but when she meets Gaston Lachaille, handsome, rich and bored, she breaks the rules by marrying him. In 1951, *Gigi* (1944) was adapted for the stage by Anita Loos (432), in a Broadway production starring the previously unknown Audrey Hepburn, who was selected personally by Colette. The play was turned into a musical film and won nine Academy Awards in 1959, including Best Picture. *The Cat* (1933) is about a strong-willed Russian Blue cat named Saha, who is not best pleased when the seductive Camille starts competing for her master's affections.

1958 Penguin Books
1986 Modern Classics
● trans. Roger Senhouse & Antonia White, 1953

The Pure and the Impure
1932

This 'curious volume', as Janet Flanner called it in her introduction, is a semi-fictional survey of female homosexuality: portraits of women and their love lives, including the coquette Charlotte, the poetess Renée, the actress Amalia X and the masculine femme fatale 'La Chevalière'.

1971 Penguin Books
1987 Modern Classics
● trans. Herma Briffault, 1968
intro. Janet Flanner, 1968
—
Colette originally called the book *Ces Plaisirs* (*These Pleasures*).

Chance Acquaintances and Julie de Carneilhan
1940 – 41

In *Chance Acquaintances* (1940), the narrator visits a health resort with her cat. She meets Gérard and Antoinette Haume and becomes increasingly embroiled in their mysterious relationship. *Julie de Carneilhan* (1941) is set in pre-war Paris and is a fictionalized account of Colette's second marriage.

1957 Penguin Books
1989 Twentieth-Century Classics
● trans. Patrick Leigh Fermor, 1952

Anatole France 1844–1924

Jacques-Anatole-François Thibault was the only son of a rare-book dealer on the Quai Malaquais in Paris. He worked for 20 years as a publisher's reader, contributing prefaces to classic editions of Racine and Molière and writing his own poetry, drama, novels and reviews. For fourteen years, he was assistant librarian of the French Senate, but he really made his reputation after he became literary editor of *Le Temps* and began an affair with Mme Arman de Caillavet, who ran an influential literary salon. In 1896, he was elected to the Académie Française, and in 1921 he won the Nobel Prize for Literature (576). He is thought to be the model for the author Bergotte in Proust's *In Search of Lost Time* (168).

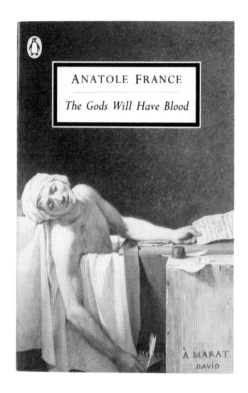

The Gods Will Have Blood 1912

Set in 1793, at the height of the Terror, *Les Dieux Ont Soif* is a portrait of idealism and a warning against the dangers of political fanaticism. Évariste Gamelin is a young artist appointed as a magistrate on the Revolutionary Tribunal, who is gradually corrupted by power.

1979 Penguin Classics
1990 Twentieth-Century Classics
2004 Penguin Classics
trans. Frederick Davies, 1979

Alain-Fournier 1886–1914

Henri-Alban Fournier was born in La Chapelle-d'Angillon, in central France, the son of a country schoolmaster. In 1905, while at school in Paris, Fournier met the beautiful Yvonne de Quiévrecourt for a few moments on the banks of the River Seine. He dreamt of her for years and immortalized her as Yvonne de Galais in his only novel, *Le Grand Meaulnes*. They met once again, after the novel was published, by which time Yvonne was married with two children. Fournier was killed in action on the River Meuse in September 1914.

Le Grand Meaulnes 1913

François Seurel, the son of the village schoolmaster, recalls the arrival at school of the charismatic Augustin Meaulnes. During a dreamlike escapade, Meaulnes stumbles across a fabulous engagement party at a mysterious chateau, and falls in love with the beautiful Yvonne de Galais. Afterwards François helps him in his restless search for her.

1966 Modern Classics
● trans. Frank Davison, 1959
2007 Penguin Classics
The Lost Estate
trans. Robin Buss, 2007
intro. Adam Gopnik, 2007
—
Alain-Fournier's title is said to have inspired F. Scott Fitzgerald's *The Great Gatsby* (424). The book's English translations have had various titles, such as *The Wanderer* and *The Lost Estate*, which is the title of the 2007 Penguin translation.

Henri Barbusse

1873–1935

Barbusse was a journalist and writer who volunteered to fight in the First World War at the age of 41. Cited twice for bravery, and invalided out of the front line after seventeen months, he became a pacifist and a communist. He travelled to Moscow in 1918, married a Russian wife and joined the Communist Party. He wrote a socialist, wartime novel, *Light* (1919), and died in Russia while working on a biography of Stalin.

Under Fire 1916

One of the first novels of the First World War, published while the fighting was still raging, *Le Feu* was criticized initially for its bleak descriptions of trench warfare: a world of mud, stench and monotony, where soldiers are plagued by a creeping black depression known as *le cafard*, 'the cockroach'. Barbusse presents episodic, anecdotal snapshots of a single French battalion.

2003
trans. Robin Buss
intro. Jay Winter

1971 Modern Classics
● trans. Robert Baldick, 1971
2011 Modern Classics
2019 Penguin Classics
trans. A. M. Sheridan Smith, 1968
intro. Fay Weldon, 2011
—
'*The Devil in the Flesh* deals out paradox after paradox,' writes Fay Weldon, 'like a cardsharper dealing from a trick pack of cards.' Weldon was born in Birmingham, but grew up in New Zealand. She has written more than 30 novels and is perhaps best known for *The Life and Loves of a She-Devil* (1983). She has adapted Radiguet's novel as an opera.

Raymond Radiguet

1903–1923

Radiguet, the son of a cartoonist, seduced a soldier's wife at the age of fifteen and then abandoned school. He inveigled his way into Parisian literary and artistic circles, where he became known as 'Monsieur Bébé', and Jean Cocteau (178) adopted him as his protégé. He died of typhoid fever in December 1923, at the age of 20, and Coco Chanel arranged his funeral, which was attended by Picasso, Modigliani and Brancusi.

The Devil in the Flesh 1923

Radiguet wrote *Le Diable au Corps* while on holiday with Jean Cocteau (178). Set in the last year of the First World War, 16-year-old François seduces Marthe, the 19-year-old wife of a soldier at the front. The controversial book was a bestseller. 'No adolescent before Radiguet has delivered to us the secret of that age,' wrote François Mauriac.

François Mauriac

1885–1970

Mauriac was born in Bordeaux and raised a strict Catholic. He held strong principles, opposing General Franco, joining the French Resistance, clashing with Albert Camus (181) over the treatment of Nazi collaborators, and challenging French rule in Vietnam. In 1933, he was elected a member of the Académie Française and in 1952 he won the Nobel Prize for Literature (576).

The Desert of Love

1925

Maria Cross is a proud, intelligent woman, desired equally by two men: a conscientious doctor and his impulsive teenaged son. 'He writes with an intense, almost tempestuous force about the life of the emotions,' said Olivia Manning (159).

1989
● trans. Gerard Hopkins, 1949

Thérèse Desqueyroux 1927

After attempting to poison her husband, Thérèse Desqueyroux walks free when family honour proves more powerful than the truth. Returning to her stifling marriage, however, she finds her punishment is only just beginning. Mauriac adopts devices from silent films, including a dramatic opening scene, flashbacks and jump cuts. *Thérèse Desqueyroux* has been adapted for the screen twice, most recently in 2012 starring Audrey Tautou.

It's 'a great novel', wrote Beryl Bainbridge. 'The brilliance of its structure and the elegance of its prose never fail to take my breath away.'

1959 Penguin Books
Thérèse
1975 Modern Classics
trans. Gerard Hopkins, 1947

2013 Modern Classics
Thérèse Desqueyroux
trans. Gerard Hopkins, 1947

The 'omnibus edition' of *Thérèse* comprises *Thérèse Desqueyroux* (1927), two short stories, 'Thérèse Chez le Docteur' and 'Thérèse à l'Hôtel', and another Thérèse novel, *La Fin de la Nuit* (1935). It is still in print in Modern Classics; the 2013 edition contains *Thérèse Desqueyroux* only.

1985
● trans. Gerard Hopkins, 1951
intro. David Lodge, 1985

The Knot of Vipers 1932

The old lawyer Louis is dying at his house amidst the vineyards of Bordeaux. He writes a long letter to his wife, cursing her and their children, denying them the wealth he has accumulated during his avaricious and mean-spirited life. But, as he writes, his letter becomes a confession, and then a desperate cry for spiritual absolution. *The Knot of Vipers* is 'Mauriac's last undisputed masterpiece', says David Lodge. 'If there was ever such a thing as the "Catholic novel", this is a classic example of the genre.'

1986
● trans. Gerard Hopkins, 1951

The Frontenac Mystery 1933

'Before beginning a novel,' wrote Mauriac, 'I recreate inside myself its places, its milieu, its colours and smells. I revive within myself the atmosphere of my childhood and youth – I *am* my characters and their world.' The Frontenacs are landed gentry in the Bordeaux, united by a smothering sense of family honour. The novel describes the enduring aftermath of a death.

The Unknown Sea 1939

When the wealthy Bordelais lawyer Oscar Revolou takes his own life, the shock waves reverberate in increasingly nasty ways through his mistress, his wife, his son, his daughter and his friends. 'Fidelity is [Mauriac's] enormous virtue as a novelist,' wrote V. S. Pritchett (110). 'Brilliant in its pattern, this novel discloses each character to the full.'

1962
● trans. Gerard Hopkins, 1948

A Woman of the Pharisees 1941

Brigitte Pian appears to be a devoted matriarch, devout Christian and benefactress of the poor, but gradually her outward piety is revealed as a mask for her terrible true nature.

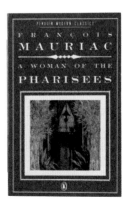

1988
● trans. Gerard Hopkins, 1946

André Breton 1896–1966

Breton was born in Normandy and attended medical school. He became fascinated by mental illness and worked in a neurological ward during the First World War. Afterwards he became involved in Dadaism (263), experimented with automatic writing, and founded the Surrealist movement in 1924, publishing two manifestos and a seminal treatise, *Surrealism and Painting* (1928). He wrote essays, criticism, poetry and memoirs, and married three times. After the Second World War, he became an anarchist. 'It was in the black mirror of anarchism that surrealism first recognized itself,' he wrote.

Nadja 1928

'Who am I?' begins this highly unusual love story. After a lengthy discussion of Surrealism, the text purports to be an autobiographical journal describing a ten-day affair with a mysterious and unpredictable woman. She calls herself Nadja, 'because in Russian it's the beginning of the word hope, and because it's only the beginning'. The text includes 44 illustrations and multiple references to other Surrealist writers. It ends with a rallying cry: 'Beauty will be CONVULSIVE or will not be at all.'

1999
trans. Richard Howard, 1960
intro. Mark Polizzotti, 1999
—
'The first thing is, this is not a novel,' writes the critic Mark Polizzotti in his introduction. 'The second: it's not strictly factual, either. [...] It is the artful mixture of almost painful confession and total disregard for the common ingredients of life that has made *Nadja* the quintessential Surrealist romance.'

Georges Bataille 1897–1962

Bataille, the son of a postmaster, became a librarian, a pornographer and a fervent Catholic, who considered the whorehouse to be his 'true church'. As well as erotica, Bataille was interested in Surrealism, mysticism, consumerism, numismatics and medieval manuscripts. In 1946, he founded the literary review *Critique*, which he edited until his death. His writing influenced post-structuralists (194) such as Jacques Derrida, Jean Baudrillard, Jacques Lacan and Michel Foucault (192), who called Bataille 'one of the most important writers of the twentieth century'.

Story of the Eye by Lord Auch 1928

Bataille published his first novel under the pseudonym 'Lord Auch', short for 'Aux chiottes!' – 'To the shithouse!' It is a pornographic fantasy, in which the teenage narrator embarks on a series of sexual adventures with his lover Simone, experimenting with sadism, torture, orgies and defilement. They shockingly exploit a mentally ill 16-year-old and titillate a voyeuristic English émigré. The *New Statesman* called it Bataille's 'black masterpiece' and a 'brilliant, exquisitely fetishistic tale of sexual agitation'.

1982
trans. Joachim Neugroschal, 1977

This edition includes Susan Sontag's study of pornography as art, 'The Pornographic Imagination' (524), and Roland Barthes's essay 'The Metaphor of the Eye', in which he considers the eye as a metaphor for an egg, the sun, the earth and a testicle.

SURREALISM

The term 'Surrealism' was coined in 1917 by the poet Guillaume Apollinaire, in his programme notes to the premiere of Erik Satie's ballet *Parade*, which included a sequence created by Jean Cocteau (178). The movement was formally initiated, however, in 1924 with the publication of André Breton's 'Surrealist Manifesto'. Evolving out of Dadaism (263) and strongly influenced by Freud's (265) work with dream analysis and free association, Surrealism embraced anti-rational forms of art, with unexpected juxtapositions, symbols and elements of psychic automatism. Breton stated its aim as to 'resolve the previously contradictory conditions of dream and reality into an absolute reality, a super-reality'. In visual art, its exponents included Giorgio de Chirico, Salvador Dalí, Max Ernst, René Magritte and Man Ray (521); in literature, Louis Aragon, Leonora Carrington (158), Paul Éluard, Raymond Queneau (196), Philippe Soupault and Breton himself. By the end of the 1930s, Surrealism had dissolved as a coherent movement, but its pervasive influence continued throughout the 20th century.

Blue of Noon 1935, pub. 1957

In this dark tale of depravity and violence, the narrator lurches through
a surreal sexual nightmare, in which squalor, sadism, incest and necrophilia
are reflected externally in street fighting and a political slide towards fascism.
In his introduction, the novelist Will Self suggests that readers approach
Blue of Noon as 'a vehicle – whether drunk-driven car, or runaway train –
that will transport them to regions of human experience where Bataille's
own view of lust as an annihilator of human difference becomes analogous
to the way the Nazis' lust for power threatened humanity with annihilation'.

2001
trans. Harry Mathews, 1979
intro. Will Self, 2001

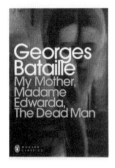

2012
trans. Austryn Wainhouse,
1969–89

—

This edition includes Yukio
Mishima's (350) essay
'Georges Bataille and Divinus
Deus' and Ken Hollings's
'In the Slaughterhouse of Love'.

My Mother
Madame Edwarda
The Dead Man 1941–56, pub. 1941–67

These three short works combine sex and spirituality.
In *My Mother* (1966), a young man is sexually initiated
by his own mother; *Madame Edwarda* (1941) is about
a prostitute who calls herself God. Yukio Mishima (350)
observes how these two stories, and their central
female protagonists, 'overlap'. *The Dead Man* (1967)
is a very short tale of desire and cruelty with unusual
textual formatting.

L'Abbé C 1950

Charles and Robert are brothers, but Charles dedicates
his life to vice and depravity, whereas Robert is a priest
so devout that he has earned the nickname of 'l'Abbé'.
In this dreamlike novel, set during the Second World
War, both brothers' lives are upturned by the arrival
of the sexually unpredictable Eponine.

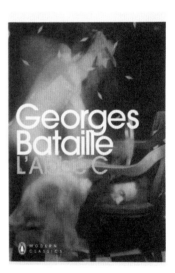

2012
trans. Philip A. Facey, 1983

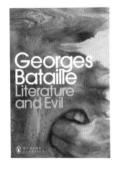

2012
trans. Alastair Hamilton, 1973

Literature and Evil 1957

'These studies are the result of my attempts to extract
the essence of literature,' wrote Bataille in his preface.
'Literature is either the essential or nothing. I believe
that the Evil – an acute form of Evil – which it expresses,
has a sovereign value for us. [...] Literature is not
innocent.' He goes on to analyse evil in the works
of Emily Brontë, William Blake, Marcel Proust (166),
Franz Kafka (280) and Jean Genet (190).

Eroticism 1957

In this anthropological work, Bataille proposes that sex is always
surrounded by taboos, and we are driven to transgress those
boundaries in order to overcome an ingrained sense of separation.
He traces this idea through incest, prostitution, marriage, murder,
sadism, sacrifice and religion.

2001
trans. Mary Dalwood, 1962
intro. Colin MacCabe, 2001

—

Bataille once founded
a secret society, Acéphale,
from the Greek word for
'headless', and is said to
have volunteered himself,
unsuccessfully, as a human
sacrifice at the inauguration.

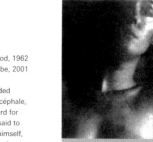

Jean Cocteau

Les Enfants Terribles

Translated by Rosamond Lehmann

PENGUIN MODERN CLASSICS 2/6

1962
● trans. Rosamond Lehmann
(77), 1955

Antoine de Saint-Exupéry

1900 – 1944

Antoine Marie Jean-Baptiste Roger, Comte de Saint-Exupéry – or 'Saint-Ex' to his friends – grew up in his family chateau near Lyon. He qualified as a pilot in 1922 and went on to become a pioneering commercial aviator for airmail services in North Africa and South America, flying primitive planes in extremely dangerous conditions. He failed his medical at the start of the Second World War, so he served in a reconnaissance squadron. He disappeared in July 1944; most likely he was shot down somewhere over the Mediterranean. Saint-Exupéry liked to write and read in his cockpit, and once circled an airfield for an hour while finishing a novel. 'A Conrad (28) of the air,' André Maurois called him. '[...] Like Conrad, Saint-Exupéry is a poet of action.' The airport at Lyon is named in his honour.

Jean Cocteau 1889–1963

Jean-Maurice-Eugène-Clément Cocteau published his first volume of poetry at the age of nineteen and quickly took up with fellow bohemian artists in Paris. Known as 'the Frivolous Prince' – the title of his second poetry book – he embarked on a highly varied career in which he created impishly imaginative novels, plays, murals, illustrations, glassware, pottery, music, ballet and films. He had a series of openly homosexual relationships and haunted a bar called Le Boeuf sur le Toit (The Ox on the Roof), with friends including Proust (166), Gide (164), Cendrars (263), Picasso, Modigliani, Diaghilev, Poulenc, Satie and Stravinsky. He was a man 'to whom every great line of poetry was a sunrise', wrote Edith Wharton (401), 'every sunset the foundations of the Heavenly City'. He was elected to the Académie Française in 1955, and it is said his heart failed on hearing the news of his friend Édith Piaf's death.

Les Enfants Terribles 1929

Two siblings, Elisabeth and Paul, share a bedroom and develop a sinister private psychodrama, which they call 'the Game'. They score points off each other with jibes and taunts, each attempting to annoy the other into a display of irritation. As they grow up and find love, they are irresistibly drawn back to their dangerous contest. Cocteau wrote the novel in three weeks while weaning himself off an opium addiction and suffering from withdrawal symptoms. It is illustrated with his own line drawings.

Southern Mail and Night Flight 1929–31

Saint-Exupéry wrote *Southern Mail* (1929) while working for the French airmail service as the manager of a tiny airfield in Morocco. The novel describes flying in heat and rain, and rescuing a stranded pilot from rebel tribesmen. *Night Flight* (1931) is a novel based on his posting in Buenos Aires, as the director of the Argentine airmail service, and on the pioneering overnight mail-delivery flights that he developed. It combines dramatic aerial action over the Andes with profound moral reflections on the source of happiness.

Penguin Modern Classics
Antoine de Saint-Exupéry
Southern Mail/Night Flight

1939 Penguin Books
Night Flight
1976 Modern Classics
trans. Curtis Cate & Stuart Gilbert, 1932–71
pref. André Gide, 1931
—
'What I like most in this stirring story,' wrote André Gide (164) about *Night Flight*, 'is, I think, its nobility. We are all too familiar with men's weaknesses, renunciations, and backslidings, and contemporary literature has been only too assiduous in denouncing them; but what we needed to have shown to us was above all this surpassing of oneself which can be obtained through sheer force of will.'

Wind, Sand and Stars

1939

In *Terre des Hommes* (*Land of Men*), Saint-Exupéry's memoir, he describes his awe-inspiring experiences flying over France, the Sahara and Patagonia. The narrative climaxes with a thrilling account of his near-fatal accident in January 1935: attempting to beat the Paris–Saigon record, Saint-Exupéry and his navigator crash-landed in the Libyan desert and almost died of thirst.

1966 Penguin Books
<u>**1969**</u> Modern Classics
• trans. Lewis Galantière, 1939
1995 Twentieth-Century
Classics
trans. William Rees, 1995

<u>**1961**</u> Modern Classics
• trans. Lewis Galantière, 1942
1995 Twentieth-Century Classics
trans. William Rees, 1995

Flight to Arras 1942

Saint-Exupéry condenses several months of wartime experience into the story of a single flight in late May 1940: a reconnaissance operation from Orly to Arras, as the Germans invaded France. It is a highly dangerous, probably pointless mission, which prompts a profound and passionate meditation on mortality and war. *Time* magazine called it 'a magic text, at times almost Biblical, of why men fight and how they feel in the presence of death'.

The Little Prince and
Letter to a Hostage 1943

Saint-Exupéry will for ever be immortalized as the author of the entrancing children's fable *Le Petit Prince*. It has been translated into more than 300 languages, and it is one of the bestselling books of all time. Illustrated with Saint-Exupéry's own watercolours, it tells the story of an aviator who crash-lands in the desert and meets a remarkable little boy, who comes from a planet not much bigger than himself. The poet Naomi Lewis called it 'an entirely original fable, brilliantly walking a tightrope over the whimsical'. *Le Petit Prince* is dedicated to Saint-Exupéry's friend Léon Werth, a Jewish intellectual who was in hiding during the Second World War. Two months before the book's publication, Saint-Exupéry published *Letter to a Hostage*, an open letter to Werth, which addresses many of the same themes as *Le Petit Prince*.

1962 Puffin Books
The Little Prince
• trans. Katherine Woods,
1943
<u>**1995**</u> Twentieth-Century
Classics
2021 Clothbound Classics
trans. T. V. F. Cuffe, 1995
—
The prince's home is Asteroid
B-612. In 1993, a newly
discovered asteroid was
named 46610 Bésixdouze;
in hexadecimal notation,
46610 becomes B612.

Louis-Ferdinand Céline 1894–1961

Dr Louis Ferdinand Destouches began studying medicine during the First World War, while convalescing after a severe injury. After qualifying as a doctor, he abandoned his wife and daughter and began travelling the world. He worked as a ship's surgeon, joined missions in Africa and visited Russia, before returning to run clinics in the slums of Paris. Céline published several anti-Semitic pamphlets, and he declared himself a fascist when the Nazis invaded France in 1940. He collaborated with the Vichy government and is said to have been Marshal Pétain's personal physician at one time. After the war, he was sentenced to a year's imprisonment and 'national degradation'. His writings influenced Samuel Beckett (20), Raymond Queneau (196) and Jean Genet (190), and American writers such as Charles Bukowski, William S. Burroughs (481), Edward Abbey (542) and Ken Kesey (520). The novelist Will Self praises his scorching 'invective, which – despite the reputation he would later earn as a rabid anti-Semite – is aimed against all classes and races of people with indiscriminate abandon'.

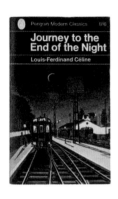

1966
● trans. John H. P. Marks, 1934

Journey to the End of the Night 1932

Céline's first novel follows the protagonist Ferdinand Bardamu on a nightmarish, violent odyssey through the First World War, African jungles, Parisian slums and the factories of Detroit as he continually bumps into a mysterious doppelgänger called Robinson. Written in working-class slang and bleakly pessimistic in tone, it presents a worldview in which humanity is adrift, doomed and fundamentally ignoble. 'It is not reality which Céline paints,' wrote André Gide (164), 'but the hallucination of reality.'

Simone Weil 1909–1943

Weil declared herself a Bolshevik at the age of ten, began learning Ancient Greek at twelve and taught herself Sanskrit. Known as 'the Martian', she studied philosophy at the École Normale Supérieure, coming top in one of the entrance exams. In the 1930s, she taught philosophy, worked in a car factory and joined an anarchist column during the Spanish Civil War, although her comrades kept a safe distance during rifle training because she was so short-sighted. After she had a spiritual revelation in 1938, reading George Herbert's poem 'Love (III)', her philosophy became increasingly mystical. In the Second World War she joined the French Resistance before fleeing to New York, ultimately serving with the Free French in London, where she developed tuberculosis and died at the age of 34. She completed her most famous book, *The Need for Roots* (1949) – for which T. S. Eliot (11) later wrote a preface – but most of her prolific writing was still in progress when she died. She was 'the only great spirit of our time', wrote Albert Camus (181), who oversaw most of her posthumous publications. Simone de Beauvoir (187), Weil's contemporary at the École Normale Supérieure, said she envied her 'for having a heart that could beat right across the world'.

2005
ed. Siân Miles, 1986, 2005
trans. Emma Crawford, Mary
McCarthy (507) et al., 1945–62
—
An edition of Weil's *The
Need for Roots* is scheduled
to join the Modern Classics
list in late 2021.

An Anthology 1932–43, pub. 1986

This anthology surveys the range of Weil's thought, with essays and extracts addressing the ways in which modern society fails the human soul, the misuse of language by those in power, and the rights and responsibilities of individuals. Weil insists on putting political and religious theories into practice and demands that individuals associate themselves with the oppressed, whoever they may be, as the only means of redressing social injustice. Every second extract is taken from *Gravity and Grace* (1947), a posthumously edited collection of Weil's notebooks. The Nobel Prize-winning poet Seamus Heaney drew on Weil when he wrote that the 'redressing effect of poetry comes from its being a glimpsed alternative, a revelation of potential that is denied or constantly threatened by circumstances'.

Albert Camus 1913–1960

The year after Camus was born in French Algeria, his father died in the First World War. As a teenager, Camus played football and organized the Théâtre du Travail (the 'Workers' Theatre'), an avant-garde dramatic group. He also developed tuberculosis, which dogged him throughout his life. He moved to Paris during the Second World War, where he worked on the newspaper *Paris-Soir* and befriended the existentialists Jean-Paul Sartre (185) and Simone de Beauvoir (187). He also joined the Resistance and edited its underground newspaper *Combat*. He was awarded the Nobel Prize for Literature (576) in 1957 and he was killed in a car accident at the age of 46 with his publisher Michel Gallimard behind the wheel. 'Camus could never cease to be one of the principal forces in our cultural domain,' wrote Sartre, 'nor to represent, in his own way, the history of France and of this century.'

1980 Penguin Books
1984 Modern Classics
• trans. Ellen Conroy Kennedy, 1976
intro. Paul Viallaneix, 1973

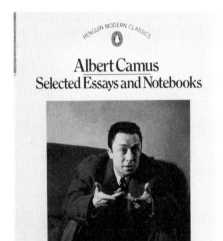

1970 Peregrine Books
1979 Penguin Books
1984 Modern Classics
• trans. Philip Thody, 1970

Youthful Writings
(Cahiers II) 1932–4, pub. 1973

This volume contains examples of Camus's early writings, including his 'Essay on Music', notes on reading Stendhal and Gide (164), a poem about the Mediterranean and three fairy tales.

Selected Essays and Notebooks 1935–55

This selection includes lyrically descriptive essays, such as 'Summer in Algiers' and 'The Sea Close By', as well as critical essays on Jean-Paul Sartre's *Nausea* (185), 'The Future of Tragedy', and pieces about his own novels *The Outsider* (182) and *The Plague* (183). It also includes selections from his notebooks, or *carnets*, which the editor Philip Thody presents as 'Sketches for a Self-Portrait'. 'The *Carnets* give us, in their scraps of thought and flights of thinking, their experimental mixings of colour on the palette, a sort of private view of one of the most candid minds of the age,' wrote Anthony Burgess (148).

1973 Penguin Books
1984 Modern Classics
trans. Richard Howard, 1972
aftwd. Jean Sarocchi, 1971

A Happy Death
1936–8, pub. 1971

This early novel, a preliminary sketch for *The Outsider* (182), was published posthumously. After committing a murder, Patrice Mersault, a young Algerian, experiments with more or less successful ways of achieving a death 'without anger, without hatred, without regret'.

Personal Writings 1937–54
The Wrong Side and the Right Side, Nuptials, Summer

The essays in *The Wrong Side and the Right Side* (1937), Camus's first published book, describe his childhood and youth in a working-class neighbourhood of Oran; the four essays in *Nuptials* (1939) mark his first exploration of absurdism (184); and *Summer* (1954) returns to Algiers to discuss questions of nature and identity.

2020
trans. Ellen Conroy Kennedy & Justin O'Brien, 1955–67
fwd. Alice Kaplan, 2020

1975 Modern Classics
2000 Modern Classics
trans. Justin O'Brien,
1955
intro. James Wood,
2000
—
This volume also
includes shorter
essays from *Nuptials*
and *Summer* (181).

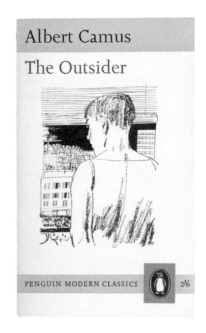

1961 Penguin Books
1962 Modern Classics
● trans. Stuart Gilbert,
1946
intro. Cyril Connolly
(107), 1946
1983 Modern Classics
● trans. Joseph Laredo,
1982
2013 Modern Classics
trans. Sandra Smith,
2012
—
To fine-tune the
nuances of her
translation, Sandra
Smith worked alongside
a recording of Camus
reading his novel for
French radio in 1954.

The Myth of Sisyphus 1942

Camus expounds his theory of the absurd (184) in
this famous essay, drawing on Kafka (280) and on the
mythological figure of Sisyphus, condemned repeatedly
to roll a rock up a hill. In a meaningless world, Camus
concludes, freedom and happiness can only be gained
through an awareness and acknowledgement of pure
existence. It is 'a tract aimed at evacuating God', writes
James Wood in his introduction, 'and a promise to live
by the rigour of that evacuation'.

The Outsider 1942

'My mother died today. Or maybe yesterday. I don't
know.' Unmoved by his mother's death and unfazed
by his own random act of violence on an Algerian
beach, Meursault's lack of contrition marks him out as
a stranger to society. He confronts the meaninglessness
of existence, refusing to play by society's rules, even if
it means his own death. *The Outsider* is 'so well written
and profoundly disturbing that it is in a class by itself',
declared John Betjeman (88). '[…] Seldom have I read
a work which says so much in so short a space.'

Committed Writings

1943 – 57

Letters to a German Friend,
Reflections on the Guillotine,
The Nobel Speeches

For Camus, commitment to
one's beliefs was paramount.
The essays and speeches
in this volume represent
various forms of commitment.
His *Letters to a German Friend*
(1943–5) were written during
the Nazi occupation; *Reflections*
on the Guillotine (1957) is an
impassioned polemic against
the death penalty; and his
Nobel Speeches (1957) demand that artists dare
to engage with the world and 'create dangerously'.

2020
trans. Justin O'Brien & Sandra
Smith, 1960–2019
fwd. Alice Kaplan, 2020

Caligula
and Other Plays 1944 – 59

Caligula, Cross Purpose,
The Just, The Possessed

Caligula is a monstrous,
nihilistic portrait of the
historical Roman emperor,
who destroys everything
around him. The other
plays in this volume touch
on the random cruelty
of the universe and the
theme of revolt in the name
of liberty. *The Possessed*
(1959) is an adaptation
of Fyodor Dostoyevsky's
novel *Demons* (1871–2).

1965 Penguin Plays
Cross Purpose & Caligula
1970 Penguin Plays
The Just & The Possessed
1984 Penguin Plays
1989 Twentieth-Century Classics
trans. Stuart Gilbert, Henry
Jones & Justin O'Brien, 1948–65
intro. John Cruickshank, 1984

The Plague 1947

It started with the rats, dying in the streets; now the Algerian coastal town of Oran is in the grip of a deadly plague. The quarantined townspeople react in various ways to the fear, isolation and claustrophobia: some are stoical, some seek revenge, but the best join forces to resist the terror. The novel is partly an allegory for the Nazi occupation of France, while also addressing the fundamental nature of human dignity.

Camus includes a character reading Kafka's *The Trial* (282).

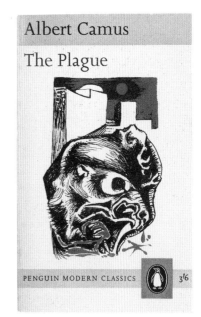

1960 Penguin Books
1962 Modern Classics
• trans. Stuart Gilbert, 1948

2002 Modern Classics
trans. Robin Buss, 2001
intro. Tony Judt, 2001

The Rebel 1951

'What is a rebel?' asks Camus. 'A man who says no: but whose refusal does not imply a renunciation.' In this essay, Camus attempts a radical assessment of the modern era, its 'crimes of logic' and the importance of resisting nihilism and terror. It is a humanist manifesto, and Camus's personal favourite among his works.

1962 Peregrine Books
1971 Modern Classics
• fwd. Herbert Read (103), 1953
2000 Modern Classics
trans. Anthony Bower, 1953
intro. Olivier Todd, 2000

1963 Penguin Books
1984 Modern Classics
2000 Modern Classics
• trans. Justin O'Brien, 1957
intro. Olivier Todd, 2000
2006 Modern Classics
trans. Robin Buss, 2006

The Fall 1956

Jean-Baptiste Clamence was once a handsome, successful lawyer, but in the face of meaningless existence he has fallen into a cycle of drunkenness, debauchery and self-loathing. Over a series of nights in Amsterdam, he regales a chance acquaintance with tales of his travels and sexual conquests. Sartre (185) considered it 'perhaps the most beautiful and least understood' of Camus's books.

Exile and the Kingdom
Stories 1957

These six lyrical short stories examine, in a variety of prose styles, what it means to rebel against the status quo. Camus takes us to the shimmering deserts of Algeria and the dense jungles of Brazil, with protagonists facing a variety of existential crises (186).

1962 Penguin Books
1984 Modern Classics
• trans. Justin O'Brien, 1958
2006 Modern Classics
trans. Carol Cosman, 2006

The First Man 1960, pub. 1994

The manuscript for Camus's unfinished novel was discovered in the mud and wreckage of his fatal car accident. It was later collated by his daughter and published three decades later. In this highly autobiographical narrative, Jacques Cormery returns to his native Algiers and recalls memories of his fatherless childhood, playing football as a boy, and a particular teacher who inspired his career as a writer.

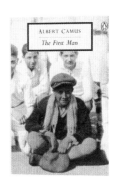

1996 Penguin Books
1997 Twentieth-Century Classics
trans. David Hapgood, 1995
ed. Catherine Camus, 1994

1961 Penguin Books
1975 Modern Classics
• trans. Alastair MacDonald, 1934
2009 Modern Classics *Man's Fate*
trans. Haakon M. Chevalier, 1961
intro. Philip Gourevitch, 2009

The title *La Condition Humaine*, literally *The Human Condition*, has been translated as both *Man's Estate* and *Man's Fate*.

André Malraux

1901–1976

After studying archaeology and investigating temple complexes in Angkor, Cambodia, Malraux became increasingly involved in politics. He visited China and became a prominent anti-fascist in the 1930s, helping to organize the air force of the Spanish republican government. During the Second World War, he was a member of the French Resistance. In 1945, he was appointed Minister of Information in Charles de Gaulle's first government, and later served for ten years as France's Minister of Cultural Affairs. He was a friend of François Mauriac (174) and Jean Cocteau (178). 'To those who actually met him,' ran his obituary in *The Times*, 'Malraux never seemed a very happy man. He chain-smoked incessantly, had a face ravaged by nervous tics and a ceaseless flow of brilliant conversation that was all the more terrifying because of his clear inability ever to stop being a genius.'

Man's Estate 1933

La Condition Humaine opens at midnight, with an assassin wielding a knife above his victim. Set in Shanghai, the novel describes the failed and bloody communist rebellion of 1927, interweaving the lives of an idealist leader, a ruthless killer, a French opium-dealer and a Russian revolutionary. J. B. Priestley (87) called it 'a genuine poetic creation'. It won the Prix Goncourt.

Days of Hope 1937

Often compared with George Orwell's Homage to Catalonia (83), *L'Espoir* is a novel of the Spanish Civil War, in which the adventurous Manuel and Magnin arrive in Madrid to assist the anti-fascists.

1970 Penguin Books
1982 Modern Classics
• trans. Stuart Gilbert & Alastair MacDonald, 1938

The Absurd

Jean-Paul Sartre (324) defined 'the absurd' as 'that which is meaningless'. The concept grew out of existentialism (186) and describes the conflict between our tendency to seek meaning and our inability to find meaning in an irrational universe. It was developed by Albert Camus (181), especially in *The Outsider* (182) and *The Myth of Sisyphus* (182), in which he wrote that 'man is always prey to his truths. Once he has admitted them, he cannot free himself from them.' Kafka's (280) works have been described as 'absurdist', and a 'Theatre of the Absurd' (324) emerged in the mid-20th century. Rather than fall into nihilism, Camus encourages his readers to embrace their absurd condition and find meaning in the search for it.

Jean-Paul Sartre 1905–1980

Sartre, the founder of French existentialism (184), was a philosopher, novelist, playwright, critic and Marxist. He studied at the École Normale Supérieure in Paris, where he met his lifelong partner, Simone de Beauvoir (187), then taught philosophy in Le Havre, Laon, Berlin and Paris. He was conscripted into the army in 1939, captured in June 1940 and imprisoned in Stalag XIID in Trier. He managed to get back to Paris, where he played an active role in the Resistance, contributing to Albert Camus's (181) clandestine newspaper *Combat*. 'The basic question of freedom was put before us,' he wrote; 'and we were brought to the point of the deepest knowledge a man can have of himself. The secret of a man is [...] the limit of his own freedom; his capacity for standing up to torture and death.' In 1944, he abandoned teaching and devoted the rest of his life to writing and political activism, travelling widely, meeting world leaders, reading Frantz Fanon (557), quarrelling with Camus and defending the Soviet Union. He refused the *Légion d'Honneur* in 1945 and the Nobel Prize for Literature (576) nineteen years later. When he died in 1980, 50,000 Parisians escorted his funeral cortège.

Altona
and Other Plays 1943–59
Altona, Men Without Shadows, The Flies

1962 Penguin Plays
1989 Twentieth-Century Classics
• trans. Sylvia & George Leeson et al., 1946–60

'You can't write a play without urgency in it,' said Sartre. 'And this urgency comes back to you because it is felt by the audience.' *The Flies* (1943) is a reworking of the Electra myth, first performed in occupied Paris, and *Men Without Shadows* (1946) is based on Sartre's experience of working for the Resistance. *Altona* (1959), one of his last plays, describes the German Franz, plagued by war-guilt, who creates a private world of self-judgement and punishment in a secret upstairs room.

Nausea 1938

In the fictional Bouville ('Mudtown'), Antoine Roquentin finds himself constrained by the rules of organized society, which restrict his intellectual and spiritual freedom and evoke a feeling of nausea. The novel draws on *Journey to the End of the Night* (180) by Louis-Ferdinand Céline, and Iris Murdoch considered it 'a young man's *tour de force*'. Sartre dedicated the book 'to the Beaver', his pet name for Simone de Beauvoir (187).

Modern Times
Selected Non-Fiction 1938–73

In 1945, Sartre founded a left-wing literary-political review called *Les Temps Modernes*, named after the Charlie Chaplin (149) film *Modern Times* (1936). It ran for 74 years and only ceased publishing in June 2019. It provides the title for this anthology of Sartre's non-fiction, which includes descriptions of New York, Venice and Havana, essays on Surrealism (176), Stalinism and masturbation, and pen portraits of Gide (164), Genet (190) and Camus (181).

Three Plays 1944–51
The Respectable Prostitute, Lucifer and the Lord, Huis Clos

In perhaps his most famous play, *Huis Clos* (1944), Sartre traps a coward, a lesbian and an infanticide in a purgatorial drawing room. It includes the famous line, 'L'enfer, c'est les autres' ('Hell is other people'). *The Respectable Prostitute* (1946) is set in the American Deep South, where the testimony of the titular prostitute will decide the fate of a black man on the run. *Lucifer and the Lord* (1951) is about a 16th-century German warlord, Goetz, partly modelled on Jean Genet (190).

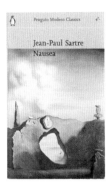

1965 Modern Classics
2000 Modern Classics
trans. Robert Baldick, 1965
intro. James Wood, 2000

2000
trans. Robin Buss
ed. Geoffrey Wall

1958 Penguin Plays *Three European Plays, including In Camera*
1965 Penguin Plays *Two Plays: The Respectable Prostitute & Lucifer and the Lord*
1988 Modern Classics *Three Plays*
1990 Twentieth-Century Classics *In Camera and Other Plays*
2000 Modern Classics *Huis Clos and Other Plays*
trans. Kitty Black & Stuart Gilbert, 1946–52

—

The title *Huis Clos* is the French equivalent of the legal term 'in camera', meaning 'in a private room'; the play has also been translated as *No Exit*.

Existentialism

In October 1945, Jean-Paul Sartre (185) adopted the term 'existentialism' to describe the strand of philosophy he had been developing with Simone de Beauvoir (187), based on the works of Søren Kierkegaard, Martin Heidegger and others. Existentialism, as expressed by Sartre, is an atheist philosophy that addresses human freedom in a meaningless universe. Its fundamental premise is that 'existence precedes essence'; in other words, humans must construct their own values and meaning. We are 'condemned to be free', the existentialists argued, and to be authentic we must embrace the anguish of this condition and its associated responsibilities. Existentialism is a way of approaching the absurd (184) and has influenced writers including Albert Camus (181), Franz Kafka (280), Hermann Hesse (247), Luigi Pirandello (215), Ralph Ellison (458) and Jack Kerouac (469).

1961 Penguin Books
1982 Modern Classics
1986 Modern Classics
trans. Eric Sutton, 1947
intro. David Caute, 1986

1963 Penguin Books
1982 Modern Classics
1986 Modern Classics
trans. Eric Sutton, 1947, rev. 1963
intro. David Caute, 1986

1963 Penguin Books
1982 Modern Classics
1985 Modern Classics
trans. Gerard Hopkins, 1950
intro. David Caute, 1985
—
The Roads to Freedom trilogy was originally conceived as a tetralogy, but Sartre never completed the fourth instalment, which was to have been called *The Last Chance*.

The Roads to Freedom Trilogy 1945–49

The Age of Reason, The Reprieve, Iron in the Soul

In *The Age of Reason* (1945), Mathieu Delarue, a philosophy teacher and bourgeois intellectual, is trying to raise 4,000 francs so that his mistress Marcelle can have a safe abortion. It is set over two days in August 1938. *The Reprieve* (1945) is set in September, with the whole of Europe anxiously awaiting the outcome of the Munich Conference and wondering whether Britain and France will go to war with Nazi Germany. It is a montage of private and public concerns, again featuring Mathieu Delarue. *Iron in the Soul* (1949) describes the fall of France to the Germans in the summer of 1940 and the psychological effects on both Delarue, as he attempts to defend a village, and his communist friend Brunet in a prisoner-of-war camp. Sartre draws graphic parallels between ideas of constrained personal freedom and the occupation of France.

Words 1964

Sartre's memoir of his childhood is divided into two sections: 'Reading' and 'Writing'. Through witty descriptions of provincial France, early literary influences and gradual disenchantment, Sartre conducts a revealing feat of self-analysis. 'Flawless,' summarized the critic George Steiner. '*Words* takes its place beside Proust (166) and Lévi-Strauss's *Tristes Tropiques* (194) amid the classics of memory'.

1967 Penguin Books
1992 Twentieth-Century Classics
trans. Irene Clephane, 1964

Simone de Beauvoir 1908–1986

Simone-Lucie-Ernestine-Marie Bertrand de Beauvoir was born above the Café de la Rotonde in Montparnasse, Paris. As a child she considered becoming a nun, but instead became an existential philosopher (186), political activist and pioneering feminist author. She met Jean-Paul Sartre (185) at the Sorbonne: in the École Normale Supérieure *agrégation* in philosophy he came top, she came a close second, and they subsequently became lifelong 'soul partners'. She described her relationship with Sartre as the 'one undoubted success in my life'. De Beauvoir qualified as a teacher alongside Claude Lévi-Strauss (194) and taught at *lycées* in Marseille, Rouen and eventually Paris, before dedicating herself to writing. Her first novel, *L'Invitée* (*She Came to Stay*, 1943), was inspired by a *ménage à trois* between her, Sartre and one of her female students; her novel *Les Mandarins* (1954) won the Prix Goncourt. Though de Beauvoir had many affairs with men and women, she never married and never had children. Betty Friedan (522) called her an 'authentic heroine in the history of womanhood'.

Memoirs of a Dutiful Daughter

1958

De Beauvoir describes her stiflingly respectable childhood, her revolt against bourgeois values at the Sorbonne, and her first meeting with Jean-Paul Sartre (185). 'Mlle de Beauvoir is clear, honest, an excellent psychologist,' wrote V. S. Pritchett (110), 'and the central part of her book, which carefully takes the years between thirteen and seventeen to pieces, is admirable.'

The Prime of Life 1960

Following the success of *Memoirs of a Dutiful Daughter*, de Beauvoir wrote a second volume of autobiography, describing her years of teaching in the 1930s, her war experiences and the liberation of Paris from the Germans in 1944.

The Blood of Others

1945

Jean Blomart, a patriotic leader of the French Resistance, sits at the bedside of his dying lover Hélène. Over the course of one seemingly endless night, Jean looks back over the course of their tortuous relationship. De Beauvoir wrote the novel during the German occupation of France, in the Café de Flore in Paris.

1964 Penguin Books
1986 Modern Classics
• trans. Yvonne Moyse & Roger Senhouse, 1948

The Second Sex 1949

'One is not born, but rather becomes, a woman.' In this landmark feminist work, a catalyst for second-wave feminism (522), de Beauvoir articulates for the first time the way in which gender is constructed. Through erudite, witty and devastating argument, she examines the biological, historical, sociological, literary, psychoanalytical and mythological status of women in the 20th century. 'There has not been so important a contribution to this subject since the publication of Virginia Woolf's *A Room of One's Own* (45),' wrote the *Times Literary Supplement* reviewer – de Beauvoir 'is not only a careful and scholarly writer: she is a novelist, and the value of her work owes a great deal to the penetrating power of her imagination'.

1963 Penguin Books
1986 Modern Classics
trans. James Kirkup, 1959

The cover image is a photograph of Simone de Beauvoir at the age of five.

1965 Penguin Books
1986 Modern Classics
• trans. Peter Green, 1962

PENGUIN MODERN CLASSICS

Simone de Beauvoir
The Second Sex

The first English
translation of
The Second Sex,
by Howard Parshley,
was rushed out in
America, because
Blanche Knopf,
wife of the publisher
Alfred A. Knopf,
was keen to promote
de Beauvoir's work.
But Parshley was
a zoologist with
a basic knowledge
of French and
his translation is
inaccurate and oddly
abridged. In 1985,
de Beauvoir herself
said she would
'very much like for
another translation
of *The Second Sex*
to be done'; but
it was not until
2009 that a more
accurate translation
was published,
by Constance
Borde and Sheila
Malovany-Chevallier.
The artwork on
the cover of the
1983 edition is one
of Henri Matisse's
Blue Nude cut-outs
from 1952.
—
1972 Penguin Books
1983 Modern
Classics
● trans.
H. M. Parshley, 1953

1968 Penguin Books
1987 Modern Classics
• trans. Richard Howard, 1965

Force of Circumstance

1963

In de Beauvoir's third volume of autobiography, which covers the years 1944 to 1952, she describes her friendships with Jean Genet (190) and Arthur Koestler (278), Sartre's famous quarrel with Albert Camus (181) and her own affair with the American author Nelson Algren, to whom she wrote letters addressed to 'my beloved husband'.

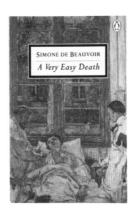

A Very Easy Death

1964

This slim but powerful book is an account of de Beauvoir's mother's death from cancer.

1969 Penguin Books
1990 Twentieth-Century Classics
• trans. Patrick O'Brian, 1966
—
Patrick O'Brian translated several of Simone de Beauvoir's works and wrote novels himself. He is best known for *Master and Commander* (1969) and its sequels.

Old Age 1970

'Are the old really human beings?' asks de Beauvoir. 'Judging by the way our society treats them, the question is open to doubt […] That is the very reason why I have written this book. I have tried to give a wholly truthful account of the state of these outcasts and of the way in which they experience this attitude in their daily lives; I have tried to make the reader hear their voices – and those who hear will be forced to acknowledge that these are the voices of human beings.'

1977 Penguin Books
1987 Modern Classics
• trans. Patrick O'Brian, 1974

All Said and Done

1972

De Beauvoir's fourth and final memoir covers the years from 1962 to 1972, and looks back over her whole life, considering her relationship with Sartre (185), the development of her writing, and her commitment to left-wing politics and feminism.

1977 Penguin Books
1985 Modern Classics
• trans. Patrick O'Brian, 1972

Adieux
A Farewell to Sartre 1981

This moving tribute, written a year after the death of de Beauvoir's friend, lover and collaborator, Jean-Paul Sartre (185), is an account of the last ten years of his life and a celebration of more than half a century of living, loving and working together. It is based partly on a series of taped conversations the couple made in 1974, on subjects ranging from women and politics to religion and food. 'When we were young and one of us gained a brilliant victory over the other in an impassioned argument, the winner used to say, "There you are in your little box!" ' recalled de Beauvoir. 'You are in your little box, you will not come out of it and I shall not join you there.'

1985 Penguin Books
1994 Twentieth-Century Classics
• trans. Patrick O'Brian, 1984

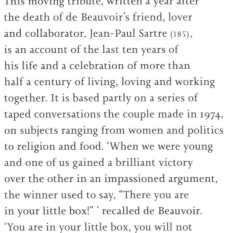

More OLD AGE

Jean Genet 1910–1986

Genet was the illegitimate child of a prostitute, abandoned as an infant and raised by foster families. As a teenager, he made an 'existentialist (186) choice' to become a thief and, as a result, was sent to the juvenile reformatory at Mettray for three years. He spent the 1930s wandering Europe in the company of vagabonds and prostitutes, with frequent spells in prison. In Paris, he met Jean Cocteau (178) and Jean-Paul Sartre (185), who led a successful public appeal when he was sentenced to life imprisonment in 1949. Genet began writing dark, sexually explicit novels and plays on brown paper stolen from the prison workshop where he was meant to be making paper bags. He became a political activist in later life. 'Not even the Marquis de Sade went further in exploring the potentialities and disappointments of evil,' ran his obituary in *The Times*.

Miracle of the Rose 1946, pub. 1951

This autobiographical novel is based on Genet's experiences in the Mettray juvenile reformatory. He describes the squalor of prison but imbues the chains and cells with sensual beauty and homoerotic passion. One condemned prisoner, Harcamone, has a miraculous rose in his heart.

The Thief's Journal 1949

Genet describes his experiences in the 1930s, travelling with con artists, pimps and male prostitutes, wearing rags and treating burglaries like religious rituals. He transmutes the grime and violence and glorifies his inverted trinity of virtues: homosexuality, theft and betrayal. The book is dedicated to Simone de Beauvoir (187) and Jean-Paul Sartre (185), who wrote that 'Genet's art is a mirage, a confidence trick, a pitfall. In order to make us eat shit, he has to show it to us from afar, as rose jam.'

1971
● trans. Bernard Frechtman, 1965
—
The Celtic punk band the Pogues wrote a song in 1990 called 'Hell's Ditch' which contains multiple references to *Miracle of the Rose*.

1967
● trans. Bernard Frechtman, 1965

Boris Vian 1920–1959

Vian worked as a civil servant and later for a pulp and paper trade organization. He also experimented with mescaline, played jazz trumpet with the Hot Club de France and befriended Jean-Paul Sartre (185), who had an affair with his wife. He wrote plays, poems and several novels, including tough crime thrillers, which he published under a pen name. He died of a heart attack while attending a screening of an unsatisfactory film adaptation of his book *I Will Spit on Your Graves* (1946).

Froth on the Daydream 1947

'Only two things really matter,' wrote Vian in his foreword – 'there's love, every kind of love, with every kind of pretty girl; and there's the music of Duke Ellington.' Colin lives in a luxurious flat, with an erudite manservant called Nicolas, but things become strange when he gives his friend Chick 25,000 doublezoons to get married. Chick squanders the money on manuscripts by the philosopher Jean-Pulse Heartre, Colin's wife Chloe develops a chronic disease, Nicolas ages years in a week and Colin's flat starts shrinking. Colin eventually becomes so depressed that his pet mouse kills himself. *L'Écume des Jours* has been filmed three times, most recently as *Mood Indigo* (2013) by Michel Gondry.

1970
● trans. Stanley Chapman, 1967
—
Vian signed his first poem 'Bison Ravi' ('Delighted Bison'), an anagram of his name. The cover of the Penguin edition is a detail from *Bison Ravi* by the Surrealist (176) painter Félix Labisse.

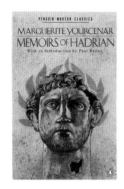

1959 Penguin Books
1986 Modern Classics
trans. Grace Frick, 1955
intro. Paul Bailey, 1986

—

Grace Frick translated *Memoirs of Hadrian* in collaboration with Yourcenar, her life partner. The couple are buried alongside each other in Maine. The Penguin edition appends Yourcenar's 'Reflections on the Composition of *Memoirs of Hadrian*'.

Marguerite Yourcenar 1903 – 1987

Marguerite-Antoinette-Jeanne-Marie-Ghislaine Cleenewerck de Crayencour was born in Brussels to a French father and a Belgian mother, who died a few days later. Raised in France by her father, Marguerite was reading Racine at the age of eight, Latin at ten, Greek at twelve and she published her first book of poetry at the age of eighteen, under the pseudonym 'Yourcenar', a near anagram of Crayencour. When her father died, Yourcenar travelled around Europe, writing novels, essays and stories, and translating *The Waves* (45) by Virginia Woolf. In 1939, she moved to America with her friend and lover, the academic Grace Frick, where she taught comparative literature in New York. In 1981, after she became the first woman elected to the Académie Française, her fellow academician Jean d'Ormesson quipped that the bathroom labels would need to be changed to 'Messieurs' and 'Marguerite Yourcenar'.

Memoirs of Hadrian 1951

'The melancholy of the antique world seems to me more profound than that of the moderns,' wrote Gustave Flaubert. 'Just when the gods had ceased to be, and the Christ had not yet come, there was a unique moment in history, between Cicero and Marcus Aurelius, when man stood alone.' This quotation inspired Yourcenar to recreate the lost memoirs of the Roman emperor Hadrian in the form of a letter to his successor and adoptive son, Marcus Aurelius. 'I begin to discern the profile of my death,' writes Hadrian, as he reflects on his childhood, his career, and his love for poetry, philosophy and the beautiful youth Antinous.

Henri-Pierre Roché 1879 – 1959

Roché was a journalist and an art dealer of the Parisian avant-garde. He knew Marcel Duchamp, Pablo Picasso and Gertrude Stein, who included a description of him in *The Autobiography of Alice B. Toklas* (410). 'He was a very earnest, very noble, devoted, very faithful and very enthusiastic man who was a general introducer,' Stein said. 'He knew everybody, he really knew them and he could introduce anybody to anybody.' In 1916, Roché travelled to New York and set up a Dadaist (263) magazine called *The Blind Man*. He published *Jules et Jim*, his first novel, at the age of 74.

Jules et Jim 1953

Jules and Jim are bohemian friends, living a carefree life in Paris and both in love with the same woman. In this semi-autobiographical novel, Jim is based on Roché himself and Jules is based on his friend Franz Hessel, who later translated Proust (166) into German with Walter Benjamin (251). François Truffaut's 1962 film adaptation became the seminal work of French New Wave cinema; Truffaut called Roché's book 'a perfect hymn to love and perhaps to life'.

2011
trans. Patrick Evans, 1963
aftwd. François Truffaut, 1980
intro. Agnès Catherine Poirier, 2011

—

Roché wrote one other novel, *Two English Girls* (1956), which was also adapted for the screen by François Truffaut.

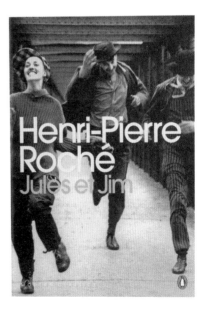

Françoise Sagan 1935–2004

Françoise 'Kiki' Quoirez was the daughter of wealthy
parents. After being expelled from two schools
and failing her second-year exams at the Sorbonne,
she decided, at the age of eighteen, to write a novel.
She took her pen name, 'Sagan', from the Princesse
de Sagan in Proust's *In Search of Lost Time* (168),
and her novel, *Bonjour Tristesse*, was an immediate
succès de scandale. Sagan became a celebrity
and proceeded to have multiple affairs and indulge
her passion for fast cars, cocaine, and gambling at
Monte Carlo. In 1957, she had a near-fatal accident
in her Aston Martin.

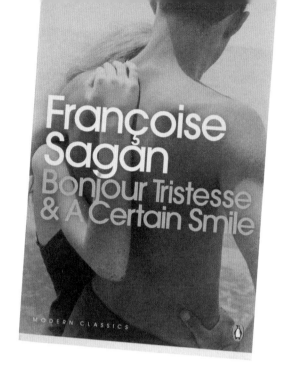

Bonjour Tristesse and A Certain Smile 1954–5

Bonjour Tristesse (1954) – or *Hello Sadness* – is a coming-of-
age novel about 17-year-old Cécile and the sexual politics
of a sultry holiday on the French Riviera with her playboy
father and his mistresses. In *A Certain Smile* (1955),
Sagan's second novel, Dominique is a bored 20-year-old
law student who tries an affair with an older man.

1958 Penguin Books
Bonjour Tristesse
1960 Penguin Books
A Certain Smile
2008 Modern Classics
• trans. Irene Ash, 1955–6
2013 Modern Classics
trans. Heather Lloyd, 2013
intro. Rachel Cusk, 2008

'These two novels,' writes Rachel Cusk,
'so spare and rigorous, so artistically
correct, so thorough in their psychological
realism, are the highest expression of the
triangular purity of their author's strange
and beautiful *esthétique*.' Heather Lloyd's
2013 translations restore explicitly sexual
scenes that were excised from Irene Ash's
earlier renditions.

Michel Foucault 1926–1984

Paul-Michel Doria Foucault was born in Poitiers, the son of a surgeon. Although he later described
himself as a 'juvenile delinquent', he went on to study at the École Normale Supérieure and became one
of the 20th century's most influential and radical thinkers. He was known for his turtleneck sweaters and
for investigating the relationship between knowledge and power and the systems by which they are used
to exert societal control. His landmark books are *Madness and Civilization* (1961), *Discipline and Punish* (193)
and *The History of Sexuality* (193), a four-volume analysis of insanity, punishment and sexual desire over
the course of history, employing a method he described as 'archaeology'. He died in Paris from AIDS, the
first French public figure to do so, and his partner Daniel Defert founded the AIDES charity in his memory.
'Foucault leaves no reader untouched
or unchanged,' wrote Edward Said (335).

Essential Works 1954–84

Ethics, Aesthetics, Power

'My objective,' wrote Foucault, 'has been
to create a history of the different modes
by which, in our culture, human beings
are made subjects.' This three-volume thematic
collection presents articles, interviews and
lectures that Foucault wrote alongside his
books. Foucault's biographer Didier Eribon
calls it 'a fabulous journey through thirty
years of political and intellectual ferment'.

2000 Penguin Books
2020 Modern Classics
ed. Paul Rabinow, 1997
trans. Robert Hurley et al.,
1981–97

2000 Penguin Books
2020 Modern Classics
ed. James Faubion, 1998
trans. Robert Hurley et al.,
1971–98

2000 Penguin Books
2020 Modern Classics
ed. James Faubion, 1998
trans. Robert Hurley et al.,
1971–98

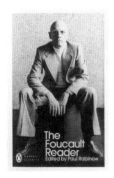

1986 Peregrine Books
1991 Penguin Books
2020 Modern Classics
ed. Paul Rabinow, 1984
trans. Donald F. Bouchard
et al., 1967–82

The Foucault Reader
1961–84

This single-volume reader is designed to introduce the range of Foucault's writing. It includes excerpts from all his major works, including *Madness and Civilization* (1961), as well as interviews, unpublished manuscripts and his essay 'What Is an Author?', which he wrote in response to Roland Barthes's seminal essay 'The Death of the Author'.

Discipline and Punish
The Birth of the Prison 1975

Foucault's revolutionary study of the history of punishment concludes that modern society is inherently disciplinary and that we are controlled by utilitarian institutions such as schools, factories and hospitals. The text is divided into four sections – 'Torture', 'Punishment', 'Discipline' and 'Prison' – and it includes Foucault's famous discussion of 'panopticism', the apprehension that we are under constant surveillance.

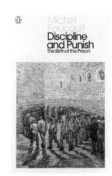

1979 Peregrine Books
1991 Penguin Books
2020 Modern Classics
trans. Alan Sheridan, 1977

2004 Penguin Books
2020 Modern Classics
ed. Mauro Bertani
& Alessandro
Fontana, 1997
trans. David Macey,
2003
intro. Arnold
I. Davison, 2003

Society Must be Defended
Lectures at the Collège de France, 1975–6 1997

In 1970, Foucault became Professor of the History of Systems of Thought at the Collège de France in Paris, a position he held until his death. These lectures 'mark a sort of pause', as the editors Bertani and Fontana put it, 'a momentary halt and no doubt a turning point in which he evaluates the road that he has travelled and outlines future lines of investigation'. Drawing on historical examples from the Trojan War to Nazi Germany, Foucault presents a critique of power systems and of the control that he saw as inherent to human civilization.

The History of Sexuality 1976–1984, pub. 1976–2018
The Will to Knowledge, The Use of Pleasure, The Care of the Self, Confessions of the Flesh

Foucault's four-volume history of sexuality analyses the changing nature of desire in western society. In *The Will to Knowledge* (1976), he overturns the 'repressive hypothesis' that sexuality was increasingly stifled between the 17th and mid-20th centuries; instead, he demonstrates how this period saw an explosion in discussions about sex and sexual 'perversions'. *The Use of Pleasure* (1984) looks at sex in classical Greek culture; *The Care of the Self* (1984) investigates how Ancient Rome made sexuality a moral issue; and *Confessions of the Flesh* (2018) brings the story full circle by examining early Christianity and the notion of the sinful body.

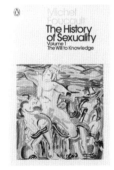

Confessions of the Flesh was left complete but unpublished when Foucault died. He explicitly forbade posthumous publications, so it lay for 30 years in a Paris bank vault. In 2013, however, it moved to the National Library of France as part of the Foucault archive; at which point, as it was now partially accessible, Foucault's family felt it could and should be more widely available, and it was finally published in France in 2018.

1981 Pelican Books
1986 Peregrine Books
1990 Penguin Books
2020 Modern Classics
trans. Robert Hurley, 1978

1987 Peregrine Books
1992 Penguin Books
2020 Modern Classics
trans. Robert Hurley, 1985

1990 Penguin Books
2020 Modern Classics
trans. Robert Hurley, 1986

2021 Hardback Classics
2022 Modern Classics
trans. Robert Hurley, 2021

Structuralism

Structuralism derived from the theories of the early 20th-century Swiss linguist Ferdinand de Saussure, who broke language down into constituent units and studied the way in which we combine those units to convey meaning. Half a century later, in his book *Structural Anthropology* (1958), Claude Lévi-Strauss applied the same idea to human culture, analysing the interrelationships between individuals and family units and looking for underlying patterns. He analysed myths in the same way, identifying common 'mythemes' across cultures and investigating how they combine to create narratives. In the 1960s, structuralist literary critics such as Roland Barthes began considering texts in terms of how they related to societal codes and conventions, independent of the reader and even the author: Barthes wrote his landmark essay 'The Death of the Author' in 1967, which opened the door to post-structuralism.

Post-structuralism

'Post-structuralism' or 'deconstructionism' are umbrella terms for a set of cultural theories that arose in France in the late 1960s in response to structuralism. They are a reaction against the scientific objectivity of structuralism and specifically an assertion that texts and language are indeterminate: there are no absolute meanings and readers should be liberated to interpret texts for themselves. The key figures associated with post-structuralism are the philosopher Jacques Derrida, who saw language as a series of infinitely nested signifiers; Michel Foucault (192), who saw all discourse as inherently connected to societal power structures; and the psychoanalyst Jacques Lacan, who believed that the human unconscious is structured like a language.

Claude Lévi-Strauss 1908–2009

Lévi-Strauss spent the First World War living with his grandfather, the rabbi of the Versailles synagogue, before studying law and philosophy at the Sorbonne. After training with Simone de Beauvoir (187) and teaching in *lycées*, he travelled to Brazil with his wife Dina to take up a role as visiting Professor of Sociology at the University of São Paulo, while she was visiting Professor of Ethnology. Together they studied the Guaycuru and Bororó communities, and made a year-long expedition to visit the Nambikwara, Tupi-Kawahib and previously unknown Mundé people. Lévi-Strauss spent most of the Second World War in New York before returning to France and publishing *Tristes Tropiques*, which made him a literary celebrity. He held several prestigious professorial positions and was elected to the Académie Française in 1973, taking over Henry de Montherlant's (198) seat. As the founder of structural anthropology, his impact on the field has been compared with that of James Frazer (27).

Tristes Tropiques 1955

'I hate travelling and explorers,' opens Lévi-Strauss. 'Yet here I am proposing to tell the story of my expeditions.' Lévi-Strauss recalls his experiences in Brazil in the 1930s, describing Amazonian communities and challenging notions of 'primitive' man. He concludes that human characteristics are universal: we all share the same structures of thought. As well as being a landmark work of anthropology, *Tristes Tropiques* (*Sad Tropics*) is also a masterpiece of travel writing and a witty, erudite and poignant autobiography. It is 'one of the great books of our century', wrote Susan Sontag (524). 'It is rigorous, subtle, and bold in thought. It is beautifully written. And, like all great books, it bears an absolutely personal stamp; it speaks with a human voice.'

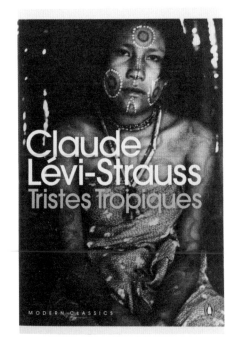

1976 Penguin Books
1984 Peregrine Books
1992 Penguin Books
2011 Modern Classics
trans. John & Doreen Weightman, 1974

Daniel Anselme 1927–1989

Daniel Rabinovitch was born in Paris, to a Dutch mother and Russian father. The family adopted the name Anselme when Daniel's father joined the Resistance during the Second World War. Daniel also fought for the Resistance as a 16-year-old; he then joined the Communist Party and worked as a journalist in Glasgow and Paris. He was extremely overweight and divided his time between campaigning for trade unionism and amusing his friends in Parisian Left Bank cafés.

On Leave 1957

Anselme's first novel is about the Algerian war for independence, written just as it was becoming increasingly savage. A sergeant, a corporal and an infantryman return to Paris for ten days' leave over Christmas; they attempt to reconnect with their families and friends, before catching the night train back to Algeria. The *Independent* called it 'a novel with a solar-plexus punch that was written from the dark heart of conflict'.

2015
trans. David Bellos, 2014
—
Bellos's edition includes an interview with Anselme as an appendix. 'I wrote journalism of the most polemical kind until I could no longer find an organ that matched my convictions,' he said. 'A book is the only place you can express opinions freely in France.'

'Urgent, slangy, raw-nerved ... a novel with a solar-plexus punch' Boyd Tonkin, Independent

Daniel
Anselme
On Leave

André Schwarz-Bart 1928–2006

Before Schwarz-Bart was born, his Jewish parents moved to France from Poland; his first language was Yiddish. In 1941, both his mother and father were deported to Auschwitz, and he joined the French Resistance as a teenager. He then worked in a factory and in Les Halles, Paris's vegetable market. He was awarded the Jerusalem Prize in 1967 and spent his last years in the homeland of his Guadeloupean wife, the author Simone Schwarz-Bart.

The Last of the Just 1959

In Jewish legend, at any one time there are 36 'Lamed-Vov', 'just men', who are born to take on the burden of the world's suffering. This novel follows a Jewish family over eight centuries, from the murder of Rabbi Yom Tov Levy in York in 1185 to his descendant Ernie Levy, a schoolboy, who dies in the gas chambers at Auschwitz. 'No one who reads *The Last of the Just* can ever be quite the same again,' wrote the American journalist William L. Shirer. 'Though it is stark tragedy on an epic scale, it is told with subtle and warm understanding for the foibles of mankind and for the irony and humor of man's way in this strange world.' It won the Prix Goncourt.

Penguin Modern Classics

André Schwarz-Bart
The Last of the Just

1977
• trans. Stephen Becker, 1961

Raymond Queneau 1903–1976

Queneau was a novelist, poet, essayist, lyricist, scriptwriter, translator, film director and amateur mathematician. He was briefly involved with the Surrealist movement (176), and he co-founded the ironically anti-scientific College of Pataphysics in 1948 with Eugène Ionesco (324) and Jean Genet (190), as well as its subcommittee, the Oulipo group (197). He worked for the publisher Gallimard, where he became director of the legendary *Encyclopédie de la Pléiade*.

Zazie in the Metro 1959

Impish, foul-mouthed Zazie arrives in Paris to stay with her transvestite Uncle Gabriel for 36 hours. She longs to travel on the Métro, but it is closed because of a strike, so she ranges around the city having wild, comical adventures with a variety of dubious characters. The book was filmed by Louis Malle in 1960, a key work of French New Wave cinema.

2000
trans. Barbara Wright, 1960
intro. Gilbert Adair, 2000
—
Zazie in the Metro is 'one of the last recorded examples', wrote the Scottish novelist and poet Gilbert Adair, 'of that terminally endangered species: an authentic popular classic'. In 1994, Adair translated Georges Perec's novel *La Disparition* (1969), in which the letter 'e' is never used, into English, also without using the letter 'e'; he called it *A Void*.

Georges Perec 1936–1982

George Peretz was the son of immigrant Polish Jews killed in the Second World War. After failing to complete a history degree at the Sorbonne, Perec became an archivist at the university's Neurophysiological Research Laboratory, a job he held for most of his working life. In 1967, he became a key member of the Oulipo group (197), and he wrote film scripts, radio plays, reviews and crossword puzzles. He is best known for his 300-page novel *La Disparition* (1969), a 'lipogram' written without using the letter 'e'; *Les Revenentes* (1972), a 'univocalic' piece that, of the vowels, *only* uses 'e'; and his masterpiece, *Life: A User's Manual* (1978), dedicated to Raymond Queneau, which describes a multistorey apartment block, moving around the building as if on a 'knight's tour' of a chessboard. Italo Calvino (218) called him 'one of the most significant literary personalities in the world'.

1997 Twentieth-Century
Classics
1999 Twentieth-Century
Classics *revised*
2008 Penguin Classics
trans. John Sturrock,
1997, 1999

Species of Spaces
and Other Pieces 1959–82, pub. 1974–93

This anthology comprises 'the brightest and/or most endearing' of Perec's non-fictional and occasional writings, selected by the translator and literary critic John Sturrock. The title piece, *Espèces d'Espaces* (1974), examines various urban and domestic spaces through wordplay and digression. Other titles include 'The Gnocchi of Autumn', 'Brief Notes on the Art and Manner of Arranging One's Books' and 'Attempt at an Inventory of the Liquid and Solid Foodstuffs Ingurgitated by Me in the Course of the Year Nineteen Hundred and Seventy-Four'.

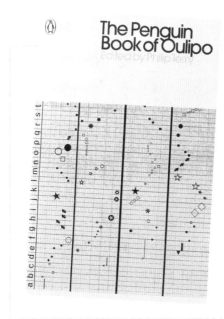

THE PENGUIN BOOK OF OULIPO 1960 – 2012
Queneau, Perec, Calvino and the Adventure of Form

The *Ouvroir de Littérature Potentielle*, or 'Oulipo' for short, is a writing collective that delights in constructing poems, stories and word games using various playful constraints, puzzles and mathematical devices. Founded in 1960 by Raymond Queneau (196), with Georges Perec (196) and Italo Calvino (218) as early members, the group is still active. This volume is the most comprehensive anthology of Oulipian writing in English: it features 100 pieces, including Queneau's *A Hundred Thousand Billion Poems* (1961) and extracts from Perec's *A Void* (1969) and Calvino's *The Castle of Crossed Destinies* (1973), as well as a number of 'anticipatory plagiarists', such as Rabelais, George Herbert, Jonathan Swift, Lewis Carroll and Jorge Luis Borges (572).

2020
ed. Philip Terry, 2019
trans. Stanley Chapman
et al., 2019

Romain Gary
1914 – 1980

Roman Kacew was born in Vilnius, in the Russian Empire, to Lithuanian Jewish parents, but his father abandoned the family so he moved with his mother to Nice. During the Second World War, he flew for the French air force and was awarded the *Croix de Guerre*. After the German occupation, he worked for the Resistance and flew for the Free French Air Force, at which point he changed his name to Gary. He wrote more than 30 novels and had a penchant for literary hoaxes. He is the only author to have won the prestigious Prix Goncourt twice, which is impossible according to the award's rubric: his second win was for *The Life Before Us* (1975), published under the pseudonym 'Émile Ajar'; it became the bestselling French novel of the 20th century. In 1956, he was appointed consul general in Los Angeles, and once challenged Clint Eastwood to a duel. Gary died of a self-inflicted gunshot wound in Paris, a few months after completing *The Kites*.

2018
trans. John Markham Beach, 1961
—
The cover of *Promise at Dawn* shows Gary in 1939.

Promise at Dawn
A Memoir 1960

'What a gold mine!' exclaimed Jean-Paul Sartre (185) on hearing Gary's life story in 1945. In his gripping, romantic autobiography, Gary describes his eccentric mother and her great ambitions for him. It tells the mostly true story of his journey from poverty in eastern Europe to his spectacular career as a pilot, diplomat, film-maker and author. He was married twice, to the British historian Lesley Blanch and the French film actress Jean Seberg, who starred in the 1958 adaptation of *Bonjour Tristesse* (192). Seberg also appeared in two films written and directed by Gary: *Birds in Peru* (1968) and *Kill! Kill! Kill! Kill!* (1971).

The Kites 1980

Young Ludo is living with his eccentric kite-making uncle Ambrose in a quiet French village, when he encounters Lila, a beautiful Polish girl, in a strawberry field. He knows he will never forget her, despite the onset of the Second World War and the German occupation. It is 'an extraordinary novel', writes D. J. Taylor, 'about lost love, memory, resistance to tyranny and individual lives caught up in the rush of history'.

2019
trans. Miranda Richmond Mouillot, 2017

Pierre Boulle 1912-1994

Pierre-François-Marie-Louis Boulle moved to Malaya in 1936 to work on a rubber plantation. During the Second World War, he joined the French army and worked in Indochina as a secret agent for the French Resistance, but he was captured by the Vichy French in 1943 and sentenced to life imprisonment with hard labour. After the war, his novel *The Bridge over the River Kwai* (1952) became an international bestseller, and David Lean's 1957 film adaptation won seven Academy Awards.

Planet of the Apes 1963

In the year 2500, a group of astronauts visits a planet orbiting the star Betelgeuse, where giant apes are the master race and humans are savages, caged in zoos and hunted for sport. When Ulysse Mérou, one of the astronauts, is captured, his struggle to survive leads to a climactic and horrifying revelation. The book was adapted into an Academy Award-winning film in 1968, which spawned four cult sequels, as well as several remakes, reboots and television series.

1966 Penguin Books
Monkey Planet
2001 Modern Classics
• trans. Xan Fielding,
1964
intro. Brian Aldiss (142),
2001

Pierre Boulle Planet of the Apes

Henry de Montherlant 1896-1972

Henry-Marie-Joseph-Millon de Montherlant was born into an aristocratic and eccentric French family. At the age of fifteen, he was sent to Spain, where he trained as a matador. He volunteered for the army in the First World War and afterwards became a novelist, playwright and essayist. Many of his works express closet pederasty, and his anti-feminist tendencies were analysed by Simone de Beauvoir in *The Second Sex* (187). He was elected a member of the Académie Française in 1960 and shot himself after swallowing cyanide in 1972. He is remembered for the aphorism, 'Happiness writes in white ink on white pages.'

Chaos and Night 1963

Montherlant's last novel describes Celestino, an old, exiled Spanish anarchist living in Paris in the 1960s, who torments his daughter and festers with anger towards General Franco. Possessed with memories of the Spanish Civil War and aware of his approaching death, he returns to Spain for a final confrontation.

1966
• trans. Terence
Kilmartin, 1964
intro. Peter
Quennell, 1964

J. M. G. Le Clézio b. 1940

Jean-Marie Gustave Le Clézio was born in Nice during the Second World War while his Mauritian father was serving in the British army in Nigeria. Le Clézio's first novel was shortlisted for the Prix Goncourt, and he has gone on to write more than 40 acclaimed books. In 2008, he won the Nobel Prize for Literature (576). He divides his time between Nice, Albuquerque and Mauritius.

Fever 1965

'These nine tales of little madness are fiction,' writes Le Clézio; 'and yet they are not invented. Their subject matter is drawn from familiar experience. […] Our skins, our eyes, our ears, our noses, our tongues, store up millions of sensations every day and not one of them is forgotten. That's the danger. We're absolute volcanoes.'

2008
trans. Daphne Woodward, 1967

The Flood 1966

François Besson drifts around a provincial city: he listens to a recording of a girl contemplating suicide, sets fire to his own apartment, scrutinizes a naked woman lying beside him. 'This terrifying vision of existence is conveyed with intense poetic power,' wrote the *Guardian*, 'and the sound of a living man wrestling with his winding-sheet demands to be heard.'

2008
trans. Peter Green, 1967

Terra Amata 1967

Chancelade chronicles his life in exquisite detail, from childhood impressions of playing on the beach, through adolescence and first love, to the death of his father and the end of his own life, describing minute sensory details as well as cosmic ruminations.

2008
trans. Barbara Bray, 1969

Michel Tournier 1924–2016

Tournier's parents met while studying German and he spent many of his childhood holidays in Germany. He studied philosophy at the Sorbonne and in Tübingen and then worked for French radio and television as a journalist and German translator. He wrote novels, stories, essays and several books for children.

The Ogre 1970

Abel Tiffauges is a sadist, fantasist and the manager of a French garage. This fictional journal describes the outbreak of the Second World War, Tiffauges's capture and imprisonment by the Germans, and how he came to work for Hermann Göring, recruiting young children to be Nazis. This jet-black tale of the 'ogre' Tiffauges is infused with mythical symbolism, surreal adventure and brutal savagery. It won the Prix Goncourt.

2000
• trans. Barbara Bray, 1972
intro. Michael Wood, 2000
—
Tournier dedicated
The Ogre to the 'slandered
memory' of Rasputin.

Patrick Modiano

b. 1945

Modiano was born in Paris to a Flemish mother and an Italian Jewish father. His parents soon separated and he was raised with Flemish as his first language. As a teenager, he was taught geometry by Raymond Queneau (196), who also encouraged him to write. Queneau and André Malraux (184) were ushers at his wedding. Modiano has since produced novels, plays and children's books, and in 2014 he won the Nobel Prize for Literature (576).

Missing Person 1978

'I am nothing. Nothing but a pale shape, silhouetted that evening against the café terrace, waiting for the rain to stop.' Guy Roland is a private detective, suffering from amnesia. He moves through shadowy streets, from Rome to Polynesia, searching for scraps of stories and piecing together his own past and lost identity. The French title is *Rue des Boutiques Obscures*, after a street in Rome – La Via delle Botteghe Oscure – where Modiano lived for a time. *Missing Person* won the Prix Goncourt.

2019
trans. Daniel Weissbort, 1980

More MEMORY LOSS

Julian Green

1900 – 1998

Green was born in Paris to American parents and lived in France throughout his life, writing more than 60 books in French, including Gothic novels, meditative essays and his diary, published in several volumes. During the First World War, he served in the American Red Cross and the French army; in the Second he worked for the US Office of War Information, broadcasting over the radio to France. In 1971, he became the first foreign member of the Académie Française, taking the chair previously held by François Mauriac (174).

Paris 1983

This lyrical love letter to the French capital takes the reader on an eccentric and imaginative journey through the hidden spaces of Paris: secret stairways, courtyards and alleys, obscure churches, vanished buildings, memories of certain trees. Green recommends getting lost and wasting time as the best ways of discovering a city. The *Observer* calls *Paris* 'the most bizarre and delicious of travel books'.

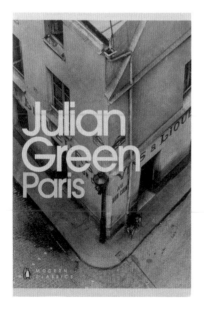

2012 Modern Classics
● trans. J. A. Underwood, 1991
intro. Lila Azam Zanganeh, 2012
2020 Modern Classics
trans. J. A. Underwood, 1991
—
This parallel text edition has photographs taken by Green himself.

Belgium

Willem Elsschot 1882–1960

Alfons Jozef de Ridder was born in the Flemish port of Antwerp, the son of a baker. He studied business and worked abroad before establishing an Antwerp advertising agency, which he ran until he died. He was celebrated for his novellas, written in Dutch and published under the pseudonym 'Willem Elsschot', with titles such as *Soft Soap* (1924), *Cheese* (1933) and *Will-o'-the-Wisp* (1946). 'The sole reason I write is to produce classic prose,' he said, 'which is beautiful and will stay beautiful.'

Villa des Roses 1910, pub. 1913

Elsschot's first novel is set in a small Parisian *pension* on the shabby Rue d'Armaillé. The advertisement outside promises a 'first-class family boarding-house', but inside we find blackly comic seductions, suicides and popping champagne corks.

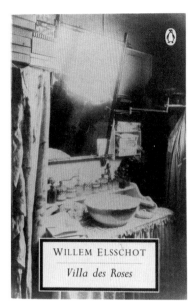

1992
● trans. Paul Vincent

Georges Simenon 1903–1989

Simenon left school at fifteen and took a job at the *Gazette de Liège*, where he accessed police investigations and attended lectures on criminology. He had his first novel published while still a teenager. He went on to write hundreds of novels, many of which feature the detective Jules Maigret (202), and even more short stories. Simenon moved to Paris in 1922, where he fell in with artists, anarchists and petty criminals. He loved canals and lived for a while on a boat called *Ostrogoth* with his wife Tigy, his Great Dane Olaf and his housekeeper, cook and mistress, Henriette Liberge. Simenon married twice and had many affairs: in 1977, he told Federico Fellini that he had slept with 10,000 women. In 1952, he was elected to the Académie Royale de Belgique. 'My motto, to the extent that I have one, has been noted often enough,' he wrote. 'It's the one I've given to old Maigret, who resembles me in certain points [...] "understand and judge not".' 'When [people] come to me to ask, "What should I read of his?"' said André Gide (164), 'I reply, "Everything."'

2014
trans. Anna Moschovakis, 2007

Mr Hire's Engagement 1933

When the body of a young prostitute is found murdered near his apartment block, suspicion conveniently falls on Mr Hire, an unsavoury and unpopular pornographer. *Mr Hire's Engagement* is one of Simenon's first *romans durs*, his gritty, psychological 'hard novels'. The '*romans durs* are extraordinary', writes the novelist John Banville: 'tough, bleak, offhandedly violent, suffused with guilt and bitterness, redolent of place [...] utterly unsentimental, frightening in the pitilessness of their gaze, yet wonderfully entertaining'.

Maigret in Penguin

In contrast to his *romans durs,* Georges Simenon wrote *romans populaires*, crime mysteries featuring the detective Jules Maigret. Between 1930 and 1972, Simenon wrote 75 Maigret novels and 28 Maigret short stories, many of which have appeared in translation under more than one title. The first Penguin edition appeared in January 1950: it was a green, tri-band double volume comprising *A Battle of Nerves* (203) and *At the 'Gai-Moulin'* (203). Over the next half-century, almost all the Maigret titles joined the Penguin list in a variety of designs, collections and omnibus editions. In 2003, fourteen

titles were published in Penguin Modern Classics to mark the 100th anniversary of Simenon's birth. Then, in November 2013, Penguin began a major project of republishing all the Maigret novels in new translations, bringing out one each month in chronological order. They form their own sub-series and the covers feature photographs by Harry Gruyaert, the Belgian travel photographer. The last, *Maigret and Monsieur Charles* (209), was published in January 2020, with an image commissioned to echo the cover of *Pietr the Latvian*. Gruyaert took the image on the Quai des Orfèvres, where Maigret's office is located.

1950 Penguin Books
◦ trans. Geoffrey Sainsbury, 1939–40

Pietr the Latvian 1930

Pietr-le-Letton was the novel that introduced Jules Maigret of the Paris Flying Squad. 'He shaved every day and looked after his hands,' wrote Simenon. 'But his frame was proletarian. He was a big, bony man. Iron muscles shaped his jacket sleeves and quickly wore through new trousers.' Maigret absorbs the details of a case, then looks for a 'crack in the wall' to solve it. In this first outing, he attempts to intercept a mysterious Latvian at the Gare du Nord. 'I love reading Simenon,' wrote William Faulkner (433). 'He makes me think of Chekhov.'

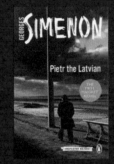

1963 Penguin Books
Maigret and the Enigmatic Lett
◦ trans. Daphne Woodward, 1963
2013 Inspector Maigret
trans. David Bellos, 2013
—
David Bellos is an award-winning translator and the author of *Is That a Fish in Your Ear?* (2011).

The Late Monsieur Gallet 1931

When Monsieur Gallet is found murdered, Maigret discovers there is more to his family than meets the eye.

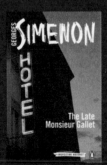

1963 Penguin Books
Maigret Stonewalled
◦ trans. Margaret Marshall, 1963
2013 Inspector Maigret
trans. Anthea Bell, 2013
—
Anthea Bell was a celebrated translator of Franz Kafka (280), Stefan Zweig (271), the Asterix comics and W. G. Sebald.

The Hanged Man of Saint-Pholien 1931

Maigret investigates an old secret society in Liège and a death at the church of Saint-Pholien.

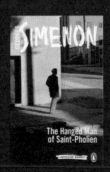

1963 Penguin Books *Maigret and the Hundred Gibbets*
◦ trans. Tony White, 1963
2014 Inspector Maigret
trans. Linda Coverdale, 2014

Lock 14 1931

A well-dressed woman has been strangled near Lock 14 on the Marne Canal, and suspicion falls on the crew of a barge, *La Providence*.

1963 Penguin Books
Maigret Meets a Milord
2003 Modern Classics
2006 Red Classics
◦ trans. Robert Baldick, 1963
2014 Inspector Maigret
The Carter of La Providence
trans. David Coward, 2014

The Yellow Dog 1931

In Concarneau, a windswept seaside town, shootings have taken place, while a strange yellow dog lurks in the shadows.

1952 Penguin Books
A Face for a Clue
◦ trans. Geoffrey Sainsbury, 1939
2003 Modern Classics
2006 Red Classics
◦ trans. Linda Asher, 1987
intro. Richard Vinen, 2003
2014 Inspector Maigret
trans. Linda Asher, 1987, 2014

Night at the Crossroads 1931

A Jewish diamond merchant is murdered outside Paris, at a place known as 'Three Widows Crossroads'.

1963 Penguin Books
Maigret at the Crossroads
◦ trans. Robert Baldick, 1963
2014 Inspector Maigret
trans. Linda Coverdale, 2014

A Crime in Holland 1931

Maigret attempts to solve a crime in the seemingly respectable Dutch town of Delfzijl.

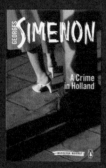

1952 Penguin Books
๏ trans. Geoffrey Sainsbury, 1940
2014 Inspector Maigret
trans. Siân Reynolds, 2014

The Grand Banks Café 1931

While on holiday, Maigret is asked to look into a disastrous fishing trip above the Grand Banks off Newfoundland.

1970 Penguin Books
The Sailors' Rendezvous
๏ trans. Margaret Ludwig, 1940
2014 Inspector Maigret
trans. David Coward, 2014

A Man's Head 1931

Maigret hopes to exonerate Joseph Heurtin, a young drifter accused of a double murder.

1950 Penguin Books
A Battle of Nerves
2003 Modern Classics
2006 Red Classics
๏ trans. Geoffrey Sainsbury, 1939
intro. Patrick Marnham, 2003
2014 Inspector Maigret
trans. David Coward, 2014

The Dancer at the Gai-Moulin 1931

Two teenage boys, Jean and René, are accused of killing a foreigner in a seedy Liège nightclub.

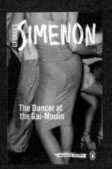

1950 Penguin Books
At the 'Gai-Moulin'
๏ trans. Geoffrey Sainsbury, 1940
2014 Inspector Maigret
trans. Siân Reynolds, 2014

The Bar on the Seine 1932

A hint dropped by a condemned man leads Maigret to a sleazy bar on the River Seine.

2003 Modern Classics
2006 Red Classics
๏ trans. David Watson, 2003
intro. Michael Dibdin, 2003
2014 Inspector Maigret
The Two-Penny Bar
trans. David Watson, 2003, 2014

The Shadow Puppet 1932

In the Place des Vosges, the owner of a pharmaceutical company has been shot dead at his desk.

1964 Penguin Books
Maigret Mystified
๏ trans. Jean Stewart, 1964
2014 Inspector Maigret
trans. Ros Schwartz, 2014

The Saint-Fiacre Affair 1932

An anonymous note predicts that a crime will occur in Maigret's home town, which he last visited for his father's funeral.

1967 Penguin Books
Maigret Goes Home
๏ trans. Robert Baldick, 1967
2014 Inspector Maigret
trans. Shaun Whiteside, 2014

The Flemish House 1932

A young woman summons Maigret to the border town of Givet, where the turbulent Meuse River is in flood.

2014
trans. Shaun Whiteside

The Madman of Bergerac 1932

When a distressed passenger leaps off a train, Maigret finds himself pursuing a lunatic through the streets of Bergerac.

1952 Penguin Books –
in *Maigret Travels South*
2003 Modern Classics
๏ trans. Geoffrey Sainsbury, 1940
intro. Richard Vinen, 2003
2015 Inspector Maigret
trans. Ros Schwartz, 2015

The Misty Harbour 1932

A man wanders the streets of Paris, with no memory of how he got there, leading Maigret to a harbour town in Normandy.

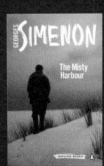

2015
trans. Linda Coverdale

Liberty Bar 1932

Maigret must look beyond the palm trees and yachts of the Côte d'Azur to uncover some dark secrets.

Lock No. 1 1933

How is a girl in a white nightdress connected to the man hauled out of a lock on the Marne Canal at Charenton?

Maigret 1934

Maigret's nephew is falsely implicated in a crime. After this book, Simenon stopped writing Maigret novels for eight years, focusing on his *romans durs*.

Cécile is Dead 1942

Simenon revived Maigret for this story about a dowdy spinster convinced that someone is breaking into her aunt's apartment.

The Hotel Majestic 1942

Below stairs at an opulent hotel, the wife of a wealthy American has been killed, and Maigret finds a gun in her purse.

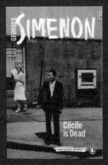

1952 Penguin Books –
in *Maigret Travels South*
⇒ trans. Geoffrey Sainsbury,
1940
2015 Inspector Maigret
trans. David Watson, 2015

1952 Penguin Books
The Lock at Charenton –
in *Maigret Sits It Out*
⇒ trans. Margaret Ludwig,
1941
2015 Inspector Maigret
trans. David Coward, 2015

1952 Penguin Books
Maigret Returns –
in *Maigret Sits It Out*
⇒ trans. Margaret Ludwig,
1941
2015 Inspector Maigret
trans. Ros Schwartz, 2015

1979 Penguin Books
Maigret and the Spinster –
in *The Fourteenth Simenon Omnibus*
⇒ trans. Eileen Ellenbogen,
1977
2015 Inspector Maigret
trans. Anthea Bell, 2015

1982 Penguin Books
Maigret and the Hotel Majestic
– in *Maigret and the Ghost*
2003 Modern Classics
⇒ trans. Caroline Hillier, 1977
2015 Inspector Maigret
The Cellars of the Majestic
trans. Howard Curtis, 2015

The Judge's House 1942

An old woman reports finding a dead body in the house of a judge in a little fishing village on the Normandy coast.

Signed, Picpus 1944

A mysterious note predicts the murder of a fortune teller.

Inspector Cadaver 1944

Maigret investigates the death of a young man in a provincial town, meeting again a pale-faced former policeman known as 'Inspector Cadaver'.

Félicie 1944

Investigating the death of a retired sailor, Maigret is intrigued by the man's vivacious young housekeeper, Félicie.

Maigret Gets Angry 1947

Maigret is summoned out of retirement by an 82-year-old woman whose teenage granddaughter has been found dead.

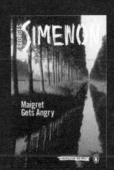

1983 Penguin Books
Maigret in Exile
⇒ trans. Eileen Ellenbogen,
1978
2015 Inspector Maigret
trans. Howard Curtis, 2015

1958 Penguin Books
To Any Lengths
⇒ trans. Geoffrey Sainsbury,
1950
2015 Inspector Maigret
trans. David Coward, 2015

1985 Penguin Books
Maigret's Rival
2003 Modern Classics
⇒ trans. Helen Thomson, 1979
intro. Paul Bailey, 2003
2015 Inspector Maigret
trans. William Hobson, 2015

1983 Penguin Books
Maigret and the Toy Village –
in *Maigret in Exile*
⇒ trans. Eileen Ellenbogen,
1978
2015 Inspector Maigret
trans. David Coward, 2015

1981 Penguin Books
Maigret in Retirement –
in *Maigret's Christmas*
⇒ trans. Jean Stewart, 1976
2015 Inspector Maigret
trans. Ros Schwartz, 2015

Maigret in New York 1947

Maigret is persuaded by a young law student to sail to New York, where he investigates a mysterious and wealthy businessman.

1985 Penguin Books –
in *Maigret's Rival*
◦ trans. Adrienne Foulke, 1955
2016 Inspector Maigret
trans. Linda Coverdale, 2016

Maigret's Holiday 1948

When Maigret's wife falls ill on their seaside holiday, a visit to the hospital leads to an unexpected quest for justice.

1970 Penguin Books
Maigret on Holiday
◦ trans. Jacqueline Baldick, 1970
2016 Inspector Maigret
trans. Ros Schwartz, 2016

Maigret's Dead Man 1948

Maigret receives a series of frightened phone calls – then a dead body turns up in the Place de la Concorde.

1966 Penguin Books
Maigret's Special Murder
◦ trans. Jean Stewart, 1964
2016 Inspector Maigret
trans. David Coward, 2016

A Maigret Christmas and Other Stories 1948–50

These stories are set in Paris at Christmas time – dark secrets lie beneath the sparkling lights.

1981 Penguin Books
Maigret's Christmas
◦ trans. Jean Stewart, 1976
2018 Modern Classics
trans. David Coward, 2017

Maigret's First Case 1949

Simenon tells the story of Maigret's first investigation when, as a police secretary, he unpicks the incredible testimony of a young musician.

1961 Penguin Books
◦ trans. Robert Brain, 1958
2016 Inspector Maigret
trans. Ros Schwartz, 2016

My Friend Maigret 1949

An officer from London is in Paris to study Maigret's methods, when they receive an urgent call from an island off the Côte d'Azur.

1959 Penguin Books
2003 Modern Classics
2006 Red Classics
◦ trans. Nigel Ryan, 1956
2016 Inspector Maigret
trans. Shaun Whiteside, 2016

Maigret at the Coroner's 1949

While Maigret tours the United States to observe American policing methods, a visit to a coroner's inquest in Arizona unravels a tragic tale.

2016
trans. Linda Coverdale

Maigret and the Old Lady 1950

When an elderly widow appeals for help, Maigret travels to the seaside town of Étretat in Normandy to recover a lost fortune.

1962 Penguin Books
◦ trans. Robert Brain, 1958
2016 Inspector Maigret
trans. Ros Schwartz, 2016

The Friend of Madame Maigret 1950

Maigret's wife follows a woman in a white hat and unearths a grisly tale involving a bookbinder's stove.

1967 Penguin Books
Madame Maigret's Friend
2003 Modern Classics
2006 Red Classics
◦ trans. Helen Sebba, 1959
2016 Inspector Maigret
Madame Maigret's Friend
trans. Howard Curtis, 2016

Maigret's Memoirs 1951

Maigret himself describes his childhood, his marriage and how he met his chronicler, 'Georges Sim'.

1966 Penguin Books
◦ trans. Jean Stewart, 1963
2016 Inspector Maigret
trans. Howard Curtis, 2016

Maigret at Picratt's 1951

A cabaret dancer at a Montmartre nightclub and a drug-addled countess have both been murdered.

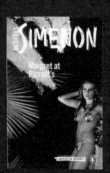

1958 Penguin Books
Maigret in Montmartre
• trans. Daphne Woodward, 1954
2016 Inspector Maigret
trans. William Hobson, 2016

Maigret Takes a Room 1951

When one of his best inspectors is shot, Maigret occupies lodgings in a nearby boarding house in order to find the murderer.

1965 Penguin Books
• trans. Robert Brain, 1960
2016 Inspector Maigret
trans. Shaun Whiteside, 2016

Maigret and the Tall Woman 1951

A woman, previously arrested by Maigret, visits him to report that her husband, a burglar, has found a body while on a job.

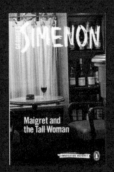

1959 Penguin Books
Maigret and the Burglar's Wife
• trans. Julian Maclaren-Ross (119), 1955
2016 Inspector Maigret
trans. David Watson, 2016

Maigret, Lognon and the Gangsters 1952

When Maigret's colleague Lognon is menaced by a group of mobsters, Maigret sets out to bring them to justice.

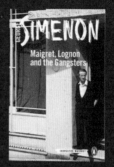

1977 Penguin Books
Maigret and the Gangsters – in
The Twelfth Simenon Omnibus
• trans. Louise Varèse, 1954
2017 Inspector Maigret
trans. William Hobson, 2017

Maigret's Revolver 1952

A troubled young man steals Maigret's gun, so he follows him as far as London and a denouement at the Savoy Hotel.

1959 Penguin Books
• trans. Nigel Ryan, 1956
2017 Inspector Maigret
trans. Siân Reynolds, 2017

The Man on the Boulevard 1953

When Maigret learns that a murder victim used to spend his days sitting on a nondescript boulevard bench, he wonders why.

1978 Penguin Books *Maigret and the Man on the Boulevard* – in *The Thirteenth Simenon Omnibus*
2003 Modern Classics
2006 Red Classics
• trans. Eileen Ellenbogen, 1975
2017 Inspector Maigret *Maigret and the Man on the Bench*
trans. David Watson, 2017

Maigret is Afraid 1953

Maigret visits an old college friend in a provincial town and is drawn into a triple-murder inquiry.

1965 Penguin Books
Maigret Afraid
• trans. Margaret Duff, 1961
2017 Inspector Maigret
trans. Ros Schwartz, 2017

Maigret's Mistake 1953

Maigret almost fails in his investigation of a mysterious young woman murdered in a luxury Paris apartment.

1958 Penguin Books
• trans. Alan Hodge, 1954
2017 Inspector Maigret
trans. Howard Curtis, 2017

Maigret Goes to School 1954

When a postmistress in a small coastal town is murdered, suspicion falls on the schoolteacher, who appeals to Maigret to prove his innocence.

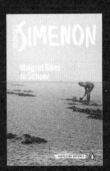

1992 Penguin Books
• trans. Daphne Woodward, 1957
2017 Inspector Maigret
trans. Linda Coverdale, 2017

Maigret and the Dead Girl 1954

Maigret and his colleague Inspector Lognon investigate the case of a young woman whose new start in Paris is cut tragically short.

2017
trans. Howard Curtis

Maigret and the Minister 1954

Maigret is summoned to a secret meeting with a government minister and enters a world of corruption and scandal.

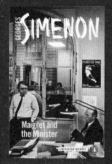

1971 Penguin Books –
in *The Third Simenon Omnibus*
• trans. Moura Budberg (300),
1969
2017 Inspector Maigret
trans. Ros Schwartz, 2017

Maigret and the Headless Corpse 1955

First a man's arm is fished out of the Canal Saint-Martin in Paris, then a leg, then the rest of him – apart from his head.

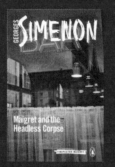

1971 Penguin Books – in
The Fourth Simenon Omnibus
• trans. Eileen Ellenbogen,
1967
2017 Inspector Maigret
trans. Howard Curtis, 2017

Maigret Sets a Trap 1955

Someone is killing women on the streets of Paris, so Maigret hatches a plan to entrap the murderer.

1968 Penguin Books
2004 Modern Classics
• trans. Daphne Woodward,
1965
2017 Inspector Maigret
trans. Siân Reynolds, 2016

Maigret's Failure 1956

A wealthy businessman and infamous bully asks Maigret for protection but, recalling an old grudge, the inspector does little to help him.

1965 Penguin Books
• trans. Daphne Woodward,
1962
2017 Inspector Maigret
trans. William Hobson, 2017

Maigret Enjoys Himself 1957

While Maigret is meant to be away on leave, he can't resist playing a few tricks on his trusted assistant Janvier.

2017
trans. David Watson

Maigret Travels 1957

When an English billionaire dies in a Paris hotel, Maigret travels to the French Riviera and then Switzerland in search of answers.

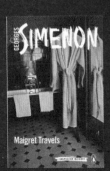

1976 Penguin Books *Maigret
and the Millionaires* – in *The
Eleventh Simenon Omnibus*
• trans. Jean Stewart, 1974
2018 Inspector Maigret
trans. Howard Curtis, 2018

Maigret's Doubts 1958

A toy salesman, who specializes in model railways, thinks his wife is poisoning him, but she approaches Maigret with a different story.

1962 Penguin Books
Maigret Has Scruples
• trans. Robert Eglesfield,
1959
2018 Inspector Maigret
trans. Shaun Whiteside, 2018

Maigret and the Reluctant Witnesses 1959

Maigret struggles to investigate the murder of Léonard Lachaume, a down-on-his-luck biscuit magnate, when the family closes ranks.

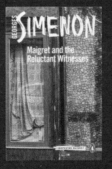

1962 Penguin Books
• trans. Daphne Woodward,
1959
2018 Inspector Maigret
trans. William Hobson, 2018

Maigret's Secret 1959

At a dinner party, Maigret recalls an old and painful case involving the execution of a man who may well have been innocent.

1971 Penguin Books
Maigret Has Doubts –
in *The Third Simenon Omnibus*
• trans. Lyn Moir, 1968
2018 Inspector Maigret
trans. David Watson, 2018

Maigret in Court 1960

Maigret testifies in court, expressing doubts about the case against a picture framer accused of murder.

1965 Penguin Books
2003 Modern Classics
2006 Red Classics
• trans. Robert Brain, 1961
2018 Inspector Maigret
trans. Ros Schwartz, 2018

Maigret and the Old People 1960

A bundle of intimate letters sheds light on the murder of a distinguished former ambassador.

Maigret and the Idle Burglar 1961

When the body of a likeable crook is found dumped in the Bois de Boulogne, Maigret defies orders to find out what really happened.

Maigret and the Good People of Montparnasse 1962

Maigret investigates the shooting of a seemingly decent family man.

Maigret and the Saturday Caller 1962

One evening, a man with a harelip follows Maigret home and confesses that he intends to kill his wife and her lover.

Maigret and the Tramp 1963

After a tramp known as 'Doc' is knocked unconscious and thrown into the Seine, Maigret wonders why someone would want to kill him.

1965 Penguin Books
Maigret in Society
• trans. Robert Eglesfield, 1962
2018 Inspector Maigret
trans. Shaun Whiteside, 2018

1966 Penguin Books
Maigret and the Lazy Burglar
2004 Modern Classics
2006 Red Classics
• trans. Daphne Woodward, 1963
2018 Inspector Maigret
Maigret and the Lazy Burglar
trans. Howard Curtis, 2018

1979 Penguin Books
Maigret and the Black Sheep
– in *The Fourteenth Simenon Omnibus*
• trans. Helen Thomson, 1975
2018 Inspector Maigret
trans. Ros Schwartz, 2018

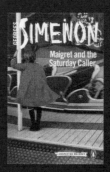

1968 Penguin Books
• trans. Tony White, 1964
2018 Inspector Maigret
trans. Siân Reynolds, 2018

1977 Penguin Books
Maigret and the Dosser – in
The Twelfth Simenon Omnibus
• trans. Jean Stewart, 1973
2018 Inspector Maigret
trans. Howard Curtis, 2018

Maigret's Anger 1963

While investigating the murder of a nightclub owner, Maigret uncovers another crime – one that threatens his own reputation.

Maigret and the Ghost 1964

After Maigret's colleague Inspector Lognon is shot, a key witness vanishes.

Maigret Defends Himself 1964

Accused of rape, Maigret must find the culprit to prove his own innocence.

Maigret's Patience 1965

Maigret investigates the murder of an elderly gangster whom he has been keeping under surveillance for years.

Maigret and the Nahour Case 1966

Félix Nahour, a Lebanese professional gambler, is shot dead in his elegant Parisian home.

1967 Penguin Books
Maigret Loses His Temper
• trans. Robert Eglesfield, 1965
2018 Inspector Maigret
trans. William Hobson, 2018

1982 Penguin Books – in
Maigret and the Ghost
2003 Modern Classics
• trans. Eileen Ellenbogen, 1976
2018 Inspector Maigret
trans. Ros Schwartz, 2018

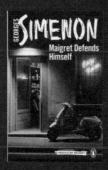

1968 Penguin Books
Maigret on the Defensive
• trans. Alastair Hamilton, 1966
2019 Inspector Maigret
trans. Howard Curtis, 2019

1970 Penguin Books
The Patience of Maigret – in
The Second Simenon Omnibus
• trans. Alastair Hamilton, 1966
2019 Inspector Maigret
trans. David Watson, 2019

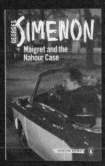

1970 Penguin Books –
in *The First Simenon Omnibus*
• trans. Alastair Hamilton, 1967
2019 Inspector Maigret
trans. William Hobson, 2019

Maigret's Pickpocket 1967

When Maigret has his pocket picked, the thief rings him up and asks for help to find his wife's killer.

Maigret Hesitates 1968

Maigret receives anonymous letters and attempts to solve a murder that is yet to be committed.

Maigret in Vichy 1968

While enjoying a rest cure in the spa town of Vichy, Maigret is drawn into a local murder investigation.

Maigret's Childhood Friend 1968

Maigret attempts to untangle the affairs of a long-lost schoolmate who has fallen on hard times.

Maigret and the Killer 1969

A young man is fatally stabbed while clutching a tape recorder. Could the cassette identify his killer?

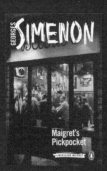

1970 Penguin Books – in
The Second Simenon Omnibus
• trans. Nigel Ryan, 1968
2019 Inspector Maigret
trans. Siân Reynolds, 2019

1975 Penguin Books – in
The Eighth Simenon Omnibus
• trans. Lyn Moir, 1969
2019 Inspector Maigret
trans. Howard Curtis, 2019

1974 Penguin Books
Maigret Takes the Waters – in
The Seventh Simenon Omnibus
• trans. Eileen Ellenbogen,
1969
2019 Inspector Maigret
trans. Ros Schwartz, 2019

1972 Penguin Books
Maigret's Boyhood Friend –
in *The Fifth Simenon Omnibus*
• trans. Eileen Ellenbogen,
1970
2019 Inspector Maigret
trans. Shaun Whiteside, 2019

1974 Penguin Books – in
The Seventh Simenon Omnibus
• trans. Lyn Moir, 1971
2019 Inspector Maigret
trans. Shaun Whiteside, 2019

Maigret and the Wine Merchant 1970

When a wealthy vintner is shot in the street, he turns out to have a long list of enemies.

Maigret's Madwoman 1970

A little old lady believes things are being moved about in her apartment. But perhaps she is not as dotty as she first seems.

Maigret and the Loner 1971

When a vagrant is shot dead in a condemned building, Maigret must unravel events from 20 years earlier.

Maigret and the Informer 1971

An anonymous tip-off involves Maigret in the machinations of a criminal gang and a small man known as 'the Flea'.

Maigret and Monsieur Charles 1972

The last Maigret novel sees him refusing a promotion and investigating the disappearance of a promiscuous lawyer.

1972 Penguin Books –
in *The Sixth Simenon Omnibus*
• trans. Eileen Ellenbogen,
1971
2019 Inspector Maigret
trans. Ros Schwartz, 2019

1976 Penguin Books
Maigret and the Madwoman
– in *The Tenth Simenon
Omnibus*
• trans. Eileen Ellenbogen, 1972
2019 Inspector Maigret
trans. Siân Reynolds, 2019

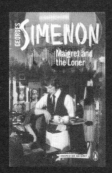

1978 Penguin Books –
in *The Thirteenth Simenon
Omnibus*
• trans. Eileen Ellenbogen, 1974
2019 Inspector Maigret
trans. Howard Curtis, 2019

1975 Penguin Books *Maigret
and the Flea* – in *The Eighth
Simenon Omnibus*
• trans. Lyn Moir, 1972
2019 Inspector Maigret
trans. William Hobson, 2019

1976 Penguin Books –
in *The Ninth Simenon Omnibus*
• trans. Marianne Alexandre
Sinclair, 1973
2020 Inspector Maigret
trans. Ros Schwartz, 2020

The Man from London

1934

Soon after the daily ferry from England arrives in Dieppe, a railway signalman witnesses a brutal murder. *Le Monde* described *The Man from London* as 'one of Simenon's darkest novels'; it was adapted as a film in 2007 by the Hungarian directors Béla Tarr and Ágnes Hranitzky.

2020
trans. Howard Curtis

The Pitards 1935

Captain Lannec has bought his own ship at last, with the help of his in-laws, the snobbish Pitards. When his wife Mathilde insists on joining the vessel's first voyage, however, conditions are stormy above and below deck.

The Pitards

'Read him at your peril, avoid him at your loss' *Sunday Times*

2019
trans. David Bellos, 2017

The Man Who Watched the Trains Go By 1938

Kees Popinga is a quiet Dutch clerk from Groningen who enjoys watching trains. When his boss bankrupts the shipping firm he works for, however, Popinga boards a random train and embarks on a new life of crime and reckless violence.

1964 Penguin Books
2004 Modern Classics
2006 Red Classics
● trans. Stuart Gilbert, 1942
rev. David Watson, 2004
intro. Anita Brookner, 2004
2016 Modern Classics
trans. Siân Reynolds, 2016

1967 Penguin Books *Stranger in the House*
● trans. Robert Baldick, 1967
2004 Modern Classics
● trans. Geoffrey Sainsbury, 1951
rev. David Watson, 2004
2021 Modern Classics
Strangers in the House
trans. Howard Curtis, 2021

The Strangers in the House 1940

Hector Loursat was once a lawyer in Moulins, but when his wife leaves him he becomes an alcoholic recluse, hiding from the world and his own daughter, Nicole. Eighteen years later, someone fires a gun in his house and he is dragged out of self-imposed isolation.

The Krull House 1939

The Krulls are a long-settled German immigrant family who live on the periphery of a rural French town. But when their relative Hans arrives, they become the target of hostility. This darkly prophetic novel was written on the eve of the Second World War. It is 'vintage Simenon', writes John Banville, 'a dark masterpiece. A calmly, almost diffidently narrated yet terrifying study of race hatred and mass hysteria.'

2020
trans. Howard Curtis, 2018

Monsieur Monde Vanishes

1945

On his 48th birthday, Norbert Monde, a prominent Parisian businessman, withdraws a huge sum of money from the bank and disappears.

1970 Penguin Books –
in *The First Simenon Omnibus*
2004 Modern Classics
● trans. Jean Stewart, 1967

The Mahé Circle 1946

While holidaying with his family on the sunny Mediterranean island of Porquerolles, Dr Mahé is called to attend a sick woman in a squalid disused barrack block, where he glimpses something that comes to obsess him.

2014
trans. Siân Reynolds

Three Bedrooms in Manhattan 1946

A divorced actor encounters a lonely woman in a New York diner and they drift between neon-lit streets and rented rooms. Based on the story of Simenon meeting his second wife, it was described as 'one of his most erotic and emotionally charged stories' by *The Times*.

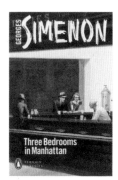

1982 Penguin Books
Three Beds in Manhattan
– in *Maigret and the Ghost*
● trans. Lawrence G. Blochman, 1976
2020 Modern Classics
trans. Marc Romano
& Lawrence G. Blochman, 1976–2003

The Snow Was Dirty 1948

Nineteen-year-old Frank is a thug and a thief, who decides to spend a bleak winter during the German occupation of France committing increasingly violent and sordid crimes. Simenon wrote this novel soon after his younger brother Christian had been killed fighting in French Indochina. The *New Yorker* ranks it 'among the best novels of the twentieth century' and the *Independent* calls it 'so noir it makes Raymond Chandler (461) look beige'.

1964 Penguin Books
The Stain on the Snow
● trans. John Petrie, 1953
2016 Modern Classics
trans. Howard Curtis, 2016

The Little Man from Archangel 1956

Jonas Milk, a bookseller in the little Breton town of Vieux-Marché, is the son of Russian Jewish parents, who fled Archangel during the revolution. When his promiscuous wife steals his valuable stamp collection and fails to come home one night, Milk's innocent attempt to protect her reputation raises neighbours' suspicions and eventually a police inquiry.

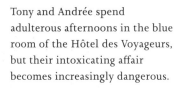

1964 Penguin Books
2004 Modern Classics
● trans. Nigel Ryan, 1957
2021 Modern Classics
trans. Siân Reynolds, 2021

When I Was Old

1960 – 62 , pub. 1970

'For personal reasons, or for reasons I don't know myself, I began feeling old, and I began keeping notebooks,' wrote Simenon. 'I was nearing the age of sixty.' The observations, anecdotes, anxieties and fears that Simenon recorded in his private notebooks form the basis of this candid self-portrait.

1973 Penguin Books
2016 Modern Classics
trans. Helen Eustis, 1972

The Hand 1968

Donald Dodd, a Connecticut lawyer, narrates this story about the disappearance of his friend, the adulterous advertising executive Ray Sanders, during a blizzard at Yellow Rock Farm. Simenon drew on memories of living at Shadow Rock Farm in Lakeville, Connecticut, in the early 1950s.

1976 Penguin Books –
in *The Tenth Simenon Omnibus*
● trans. Moura Budberg (300), 1970
2016 Modern Classics
trans. Linda Coverdale, 2016
—
In 2016, David Hare adapted this novel for the stage as *The Red Barn*; it was produced at the National Theatre in London and directed by Robert Icke.

The Blue Room 1964

Tony and Andrée spend adulterous afternoons in the blue room of the Hôtel des Voyageurs, but their intoxicating affair becomes increasingly dangerous.

1968 Penguin Books
● trans. Eileen Ellenbogen, 1964
2015 Modern Classics
trans. Linda Coverdale, 2015

1991 Penguin Books
1994 Twentieth-Century Classics
• trans. Arnold J. Pomerans, 1990

Hugo Claus 1929–2008

Claus was born in Bruges and attended a boarding school run by nuns. He was taught by Flemish nationalists and was drawn towards their fascist youth movement during the German occupation of Belgium, although in later life he became increasingly socialist. He wrote more than 100 works of fiction, poetry and drama, and was also a painter and film director. He died by euthanasia.

The Sorrow of Belgium 1983

This semi-autobiographical novel, written in Dutch, describes the devastating experiences of a young Flemish boy, Louis Seynaeve, during the Second World War and the German occupation of his country. The first half of the book is called 'The Sorrow' and is divided into 27 chapters; the second half, 'Of Belgium', has no chapter breaks. 'Impressive in size and ambition,' wrote the *Independent*: 'Bildungsroman and epic, it is as if *A Portrait of the Artist as a Young Man* (8) were written to the scale of *Ulysses* (10).' J. M. Coetzee calls it 'one of the great novels of post-war Europe'.

The Netherlands

THE PENGUIN BOOK OF DUTCH SHORT STORIES 1915–2014

The 36 stories in this anthology feature gruesome fridges, haunting commutes, monstrous diseases and mad artists. 'Dutch writers frequently explore the vague borderland between delusion and reality,' says the novelist Joost Zwagerman, 'often sketching the disturbing process of delusion eating away at those borders and ultimately conquering the entire territory.' Many of these innovative and subversive pieces have been translated into English for the first time.

2016
ed. Joost Zwagerman
trans. Paul Vincent et al., 1962–2016

Italy

Giovanni Verga 1840–1922

Verga was born in Catania on the east coast of Sicily. He used the money intended for his university education to publish his first stories, and wrote several novels before his epistolary *Storia di una Capinera* (*Story of a Black Cap*, 1871) found success. His writing falls into two periods: earlier sentimental novels, and his celebrated mature works, in the *verismo* style, in which he described the struggles of Sicilian peasants. He returned to live in Catania in 1894 and died in the house where he was born.

Little Novels of Sicily 1883

1973 Modern Classics
● trans. D.H. Lawrence (50), 1925
intro. Andrew Wilkin, 1973
1999 Penguin Classics
Cavalleria Rusticana and Other Stories
trans. G.H. McWilliam, 1999
–
McWilliam's 1999 translation comprises eight of the *Little Novels*, as well as 'Nedda', 'Springtime' and stories from *Vita dei Campi* (*Life of the Fields*, 1880), including 'Cavalleria Rusticana', the story of a young man's return from the army and the basis of Mascagni's opera.

The twelve stories that form the *Novelle Rusticane* are set in the 'solemn and changeless landscape' around Catania. They present psychological studies of individuals battling drought, heat and malaria, clambering up and down the social scale within their communities.

Mastro-Don Gesualdo 1889

Verga intended to write an epic cycle of five Sicilian novels, called 'I Vinti' ('The Defeated'), but he completed only the first two volumes: *The House by the Medlar Tree* (1881), about the downfall of a poor fishing community; and *Mastro-Don Gesualdo*, which describes the rise and fall of the wealthy peasant Gesualdo Motta, who marries an aristocrat but ends up resented by peasantry and gentry alike. 'The title, Mastro-Don Gesualdo, is an irony in itself,' explained D.H. Lawrence (50), who translated this edition. 'Mastro, *Maestro*, is the form of address used to a workman. A true peasant is *Compare* – *compère*. A workman, such as a carpenter, a mason, a barber, is *Mastro*. A gentleman is *Don*. *Mastro-don* is therefore *Workman-gentleman*. – But Don is applied, half ironically, to footmen, to the sexton, and to such as are in direct attendance on the gentry.'

1970 ● trans. D.H. Lawrence, 1925

Verismo

The *verismo* movement – the 'poetry of the real' – emerged in Italy in the 1870s, drawing inspiration from the French Naturalists and the Italian 'Macchiaioli' painters. Based in Milan, the author Luigi Capuana encouraged writers such as Grazia Deledda, Renato Fucini, Federico de Roberto, Matilde Serao and especially his friend Giovanni Verga, who became the greatest exponent of *verismo*. 'One day, I don't know how,' recalled Verga, 'there came into my hand a sort of broadside, a halfpenny sheet sufficiently ungrammatical and disconnected, in which a sea-captain succinctly related all the vicissitudes through which his sailing ship had passed. Seaman's language, short, without an unnecessary phrase. It struck me, and I read it again; it was what I was looking for, without definitely knowing it. Sometimes, you know, just a sign, an indication is enough. It was a revelation.'

Italo Svevo <small>1861 – 1928</small>

Ettore Schmitz was born and lived in Trieste: his Jewish parents were German and Italian, he grew up speaking the German-Venetian Triestine dialect, and his native city changed hands from Austria to Italy during his lifetime. He chose his pen name, 'Italo Svevo' ('Italian Swabian'), to express this mixed heritage. Schmitz spent 20 years working as a bank clerk and yearning to be an author. His first two novels, about bored clerks with cultural pretensions, were unsuccessful, so he gave up writing, married his cousin Livia Veneziani and worked for his father-in-law's ships' paint business. In 1906, however, he met a young James Joyce (8), who was tutoring English in Trieste and hoping to find a publisher for *Dubliners*. Joyce encouraged Svevo's writing, promoting *La Coscienza di Zeno* around Europe and transforming Svevo into a literary celebrity. Svevo's modernist (11) prose has been compared to Proust (166) and Kafka (280), as well as to Joyce himself. V. S. Pritchett (110) described him as 'one of the most original artists of an original generation'.

1982
• trans. Archibald Colquhoun, 1963

A Life <small>1892</small>

Alfonso Nitti is a bank clerk who wants to become a writer; but he stumbles into an insincere affair with his boss's daughter and drifts listlessly towards failure.

1965
• trans. Beryl de Zoete, 1932

As a Man Grows Older <small>1898</small>

Emilio Brentani is an insurance company clerk, the author of a single, unsuccessful novel. Now stagnating and unable to write, he becomes embroiled in an unsuitable love affair and slowly succumbs to inertia and premature old age. *Senilità* was Joyce's (8) favourite of Svevo's novels and it was Joyce who suggested the English title.

Confessions of Zeno <small>1923</small>

At the suggestion of his psychoanalyst, the fictional Zeno Cosini has written his memoirs – an elliptical, obsessive, hilarious account of his career, his marriage, his affairs, and above all his guilty passion for smoking and his constant attempt to make the next cigarette the 'ultima sigaretta!!' *Confessions of Zeno* was promoted by Joyce (8) and praised by Eugenio Montale (215); the author Paul Bailey calls it 'arguably the greatest comic novel of the 20th century'.

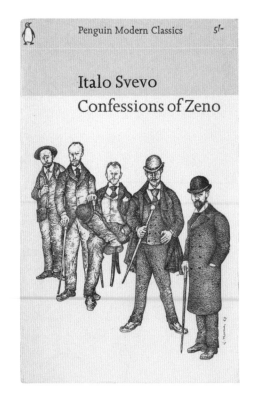

1964 Modern Classics
• trans. Beryl de Zoete, 1930
note Édouard Roditi, 1962
2002 Modern Classics *Zeno's Conscience*
trans. William Weaver, 2001

—

In 1928, Svevo had a road accident on the way to a spa holiday. When he was refused a cigarette in hospital, he said, 'That really would have been the last.' He died a few hours later.

Sibilla Aleramo 1876–1960

As a teenager, Marta Felicina Faccio was raped by a co-worker, ten years her senior, at the glass factory where her father was manager. She didn't speak out at the time, and when her rapist later proposed, she found herself forced by her family into an abusive and violent marriage. In 1901, she escaped to Rome and lived with Giovanni Cena, a writer and journalist, who persuaded her to write a novel based on her experience. She became a leading Italian feminist and suffragist.

A Woman 1906

A nameless narrator recalls her carefree childhood and brutal marriage. Her growing awareness of the plight of other women leads to a dramatic decision: she must leave her husband. *La Repubblica* called it 'the first Italian feminist novel'.

2020
trans. Erica Segre
& Simon Carnell

1962 Penguin Plays
Henry IV and *Right You Are!*
(If You Think So)
● ed. E. Martin Browne, 1962
trans. Robert Rietti & Frederick
May, 1962
1995 Twentieth-Century
Classics
trans. Mark Musa, 1995

Luigi Pirandello 1867–1936

Pirandello was born in Sicily to a wealthy family that owned sulphur mines. He studied in Palermo, Rome and Bonn, became a teacher, married, and began writing poetry and short stories. In 1903, however, the sulphur mines flooded and his family's wealth evaporated, which caused his wife to suffer an irrevocable nervous breakdown. Increasingly, Pirandello turned towards the 'unreal' and the absurd (184) in his writing. His celebrated modernist (11) novel *The Late Mattia Pascal* appeared in 1904, but his international reputation was secured by the plays he wrote from 1917 onwards. In 1925, he founded the Arts Theatre in Rome, with the help of Mussolini, and in 1934 he was awarded the Nobel Prize for Literature (576).

Six Characters in Search of an Author and Other Plays 1917–22
Six Characters in Search of an Author, Henry IV, So It Is (If You Think So)

'The mystery of artistic creation,' wrote Pirandello, 'is the same mystery as natural birth.' The first performance of *Sei Personaggi in Cerca d'Autore* (1921) ended in disaster, with the audience shouting 'Manicomio!' – 'Madhouse!' It soon became Pirandello's most popular play, however. In this piece of meta-theatre, actors are rehearsing a play by Luigi Pirandello when six strange 'characters' invade the stage and insist on being included. In *Enrico IV* (1922), a deluded man believes he is the notorious 11th-century Holy Roman Emperor. *Così È (Se Vi Pare)* (1917) involves a squabbling son and mother-in-law, one of whom may be telling the truth and one of whom may be mad.

Eugenio Montale
1896–1981

Montale was born in Genoa and worked as a journalist and critic, co-founding the Turin review *Primo Tempo* and later serving as literary editor of the Milanese daily *Corriere della Sera*, where he overlapped with Dino Buzzati (217). From 1925, he developed a reputation as a poet, and he was an early opponent of fascism. He was awarded the Nobel Prize for Literature (576) in 1975.

Poems 1925–77

In this unusual anthology, the editor Harry Thomas has assembled 100 of Montale's poems in a mixture of translations, adaptations and homages by more than 50 English, Scottish, American, Australian, Italian and Irish writers, including Samuel Beckett (20), Anthony Burgess (148), Geoffrey Hill, Robert Lowell and Michael Hofmann. With its range of approaches to poetic translation, the book presents a multifaceted overview of Montale's poetic achievement, from his major early collections, such as *Cuttlefish Bones* (1925), in which he describes his native Ligurian landscape, to his later work, in which he became increasingly disillusioned by Italian society after the Second World War.

1969 Penguin Poets
Selected Poems
● trans. George Kay, 1964
2002 Modern Classics
● ed. Harry Thomas, 2002

Futurism

In 1908, Filippo Tommaso Marinetti drove his motor car into a ditch to avoid two cyclists. The incident inspired the first 'Futurist Manifesto' (xix), which he printed on the front page of *Le Figaro*. 'We wish to glorify war,' runs the manifesto – 'the sole cleanser of the world. […] We wish to destroy museums, libraries, academies of any sort, and fight against moralism, feminism, and every kind of materialistic, self-serving cowardice.' Like Vorticism (62), the movement was an attempt to express the dynamism and speed of the machine age, but its aggressive, masculine cult of warfare was soon co-opted and absorbed into the rise of Italian fascism. In literary terms, the Futurists' main output was a series of manifestos, as well as some unusually formatted poems. Marinetti also organized 'Futurist Evenings', at which Futurists would declaim their manifestos and a crowd would gather to pelt them with vegetables.

Filippo Tommaso Marinetti 1876–1944

Marinetti grew up in Egypt, where he was nearly expelled from his Jesuit school for including Émile Zola in the school magazine. He is best known as the founder of Futurism and as a supporter of fascism; he wrote the 'Futurist Manifesto' (xix) in 1909 and co-wrote the 'Fascist Manifesto' in 1919. Contradictory, provocative and eccentric, Marinetti fought a duel once with a hostile critic, worked as a war correspondent, and served on the Eastern Front in the Second World War despite being 65. He immortalized his experience of the Battle of Adrianople, during the First Balkan War, in the typographically experimental sound poem 'Zang Tumb Tumb' (1912–14).

The Futurist Cookbook 1932

This document is part manifesto and part artistic joke. Marinetti argues that 'people think, dress and act in accordance with what they drink and eat'. In a nationalistic attempt to transform the Italian people, therefore, he suggests abolishing pasta and provides recipes for ice cream on the moon, candied atmospheric electricities, nocturnal love feasts and sculpted meats. 'The Futurist Cookbook is an extraordinary and unique book,' writes the journalist Lesley Chamberlain. 'It is funny, almost slapstick in its attacks on bourgeois habits, stuffy professors and the war between the sexes. At eating times it has the atmosphere of a children's party.'

2014
trans. Suzanne Brill, 1989
aftwd. Lesley Chamberlain, 1989

Daniele Varè 1880–1956

Varè was the son of an exiled Italian nationalist. He grew up in England and Scotland until the family moved to Italy when he was eleven. He eventually entered the diplomatic service, serving in Vienna, Geneva and Luxembourg, with two postings in Beijing, first as a junior diplomat in 1912 and later as the minister (ambassador) in 1927. Living in China with his wife, three daughters and a menagerie of pets, he witnessed the overthrow of the Qing dynasty, the civil war and the effects of the Russian Revolution and the First World War. In 1932, while serving as ambassador to Denmark, he was forced to resign by the Italian fascist regime, and he then began to write and publish in English.

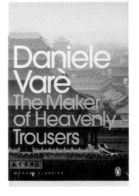

2012
● intro. Frances Wood
—
The Maker of Heavenly Trousers had two sequels, *The Gate of Happy Sparrows* (1937) and *The Temple of Costly Experience* (1939). Varè wrote the trilogy in English and only subsequently translated it into Italian.

The Maker of Heavenly Trousers 1935

Drawing on personal experience, Varè describes the delicate social structures, intricate names and turbulent history of old Peking. His narrator unexpectedly finds himself the guardian of a young half-Swedish, half-Italian girl, known as 'Kuniang', whose father works on the Chinese railway. She grows up among a motley cast of characters, including an enigmatic former mistress of Rasputin, a flamboyant American fashion designer and an English millionaire.

Carlo Emilio Gadda 1893–1973

Gadda was a Milanese electrical engineer who helped
to construct the Vatican power station for Pope Pius XI.
He became a full-time author in the 1940s, writing experimental
novels and short stories. His style has been described as
'baroque', observes the scholar G. M. Carsaniga, 'but it is in fact
more like a medieval writer's, for whom words are substances,
things endowed with magical creative and regenerative
powers, not mere substitutes for real objects or flimsy labels
for flimsier ideas.' The occasionally impenetrable effect has
been compared to that of James Joyce (8).

2017 Penguin Classics
2023 Modern Classics
trans. Richard Dixon,
2017
—
Gadda began writing
The Experience of Pain,
his first novel, after his
mother's death in April
1936, and he published
seven of the chapters
serially between 1938
and 1941. It was not
published in book form
until 1963, and it was not
printed with the final two
chapters until 1970.

The Experience of Pain 1936–41, pub. 1938–70

'With mother I was nasty and think I always will be, since we have too many differences on everything,' wrote
Gadda in his diary. This semi-autobiographical novel describes Don Gonzalo Pirobutirro d'Eltino, a young man
who lives with his mother in a fictional South American country. The state's repressive regime mirrors the fascist
government in Italy, and Gonzalo relieves his frustration by having increasingly ferocious arguments with his
ageing mother. *The Experience of Pain* won the Prix Formentor.

Dino Buzzati 1906–1972

Buzzati was born in his family's ancestral villa at Belluno, at the
foot of the Dolomites, and mountains feature in much of his writing.
His first story, written when he was fourteen, was called 'The Song
of the Mountains', and his first novel was *Barnabus of the Mountains*
(1933). At the age of 22, he started working for the Milanese
newspaper *Corriere della Sera* and would continue to do so until his
death. He wrote novels, short stories, a children's book and a graphic
novel. 'There are names that the coming generations will not resign
themselves to forget,' wrote Jorge Luis Borges (572). 'Surely one of
them is that of Dino Buzzati.'

Dino Buzzati The Tartar Steppe

2000
● trans. Stuart Hood, 1952
intro. Tim Parks, 2000

The Tartar Steppe 1938, pub. 1945

Giovanni Drogo is a young officer,
dispatched to a remote mountain
garrison overlooking the desolate
Tartar desert. As he yearns
for military glory and personal
fulfilment, he finds the months and
then the years slipping away, and he
realizes he may never have an opportunity to prove his gallantry among
the dark gorges and dazzling ice fields. Inspired by Buzzati's mind-numbing
night shifts at the *Corriere della Sera*, the novel has been compared to those
of Kafka (280) and Beckett (20). 'The Tartar Steppe is a nightmare,' writes
the man of letters Alberto Manguel, 'a comedy of errors, a beautiful and
anguished fable, a call to resistance against folly, the inspired assurance
that one last act may justify our lifelong struggle to remain human.'

Italo Calvino 1923–1985

Calvino was born in Santiago de las Vegas in Cuba to a pair of Italian botanists. He grew up on the Ligurian coast, between an experimental floriculture station and the hill farm where his parents grew avocados and grapefruit. During the Second World War, he studied agriculture at the University of Turin; in 1943, he refused national service, and in 1944 he joined the anti-fascist Resistance, hiding and fighting in the Alps until liberation the following year. After the war, he returned to university, wrote a thesis on Joseph Conrad (28), and embarked on a literary career. He worked as a journalist for the communist newspapers *L'Unità* and *Rinascita* and at Giulio Einaudi's publishing house. Having been an exponent of Italian neorealism, he increasingly embraced allegorical fantasy. He joined the Oulipo group (197), and today he is best known for his experimental masterpieces *Invisible Cities* (1972) and *If on a winter's night a traveller* (1979). He was a close friend of Cesare Pavese and Giorgio Bassani (224), and in 1964 he married the Argentinian translator Esther Judith Singer. 'Like Jorge Luis Borges (572) and Gabriel García Márquez (562), Italo Calvino dreams perfect dreams for us,' wrote John Updike (514). '[...] Of the three, Calvino is the sunniest, the most variously and benignly curious about human truth as it comes embedded in its animal, vegetable, historical and cosmic contexts.'

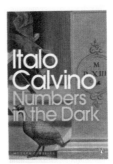

Numbers in the Dark
and Other Stories
1943–84, pub. 1993

2009
pref. Esther Calvino, 1993
trans. Tim Parks, 1995

This posthumously published collection of Calvino's stories opens with a selection of early fables, or *raccontini*. 'One writes fables in periods of oppression,' he said in 1943. 'When a man cannot give clear form to his thinking, he expresses it in fables.' These little stories correspond to a young man's political and social experiences during the death throes of Fascism.' This selection also features witty and sinister tales from the rest of his career.

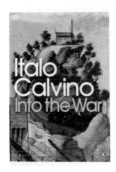

Into the War 1954

2011
trans. Martin McLaughlin

This trio of semi-autobiographical tales is set during the summer of 1940. The title story deals with 'a transition from adolescence into youth'. 'The Avanguardisti in Menton' is about an anti-climactic trip to the captured French town of Menton on the Riviera; and 'UNPA Nights' is a tale of friendship in a blackout (the UNPA was the Italian air-raid protection organization).

The Path to the Spiders' Nests 1947

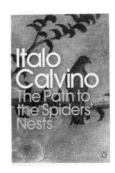

2009
trans. Archibald Colquhoun, 1956
rev. Martin McLaughlin, 1998

'This is the first novel I wrote,' recalled Calvino. 'I could almost say it was my very first piece of writing apart from a few short stories.' Pin, an adolescent cobbler's assistant, steals a German's pistol and hides it among the spiders' nests in the wood. The novel was based on Calvino's own wartime experiences and the *New York Times* described it as having 'the stark black-and-white quality of the classic Italian neo-realist films'.

Why Read the Classics? 1954–85, pub. 1991

2009
pref. Esther Calvino, 1991
trans. Martin McLaughlin, 1999

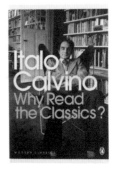

Calvino's widow Esther published several of his uncollected works after his death. 'In this volume,' she wrote, 'the reader will find most of the essays and articles by Calvino on "his" classics: the writers, poets and scientific authors who had meant most to him, at different stages of his life.' In 36 essays he discusses Balzac, Borges (572), Hemingway (428), Homer, Montale (215), Pasternak (302), Queneau (196) and many others.

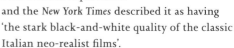

Why Read the Classics?

In his 1981 essay 'Why Read the Classics?' (218), Italo Calvino proposed fourteen definitions for what we might mean by 'classic' literature.

1. The classics are those books about which you usually hear people saying: 'I'm rereading…', never 'I'm reading…'

2. The classics are those books which constitute a treasured experience for those who have read and loved them; but they remain just as rich an experience for those who reserve the chance to read them for when they are in the best condition to enjoy them.

3. The classics are books which exercise a particular influence, both when they imprint themselves on our imagination as unforgettable, and when they hide in the layers of memory disguised as the individual's or the collective unconscious.

4. A classic is a book which with each rereading offers as much of a sense of discovery as the first reading.

5. A classic is a book which even when we read it for the first time gives the sense of rereading something we have read before.

6. A classic is a book which has never exhausted all it has to say to its readers.

7. The classics are those books which come to us bearing the aura of previous interpretations, and trailing behind them the traces they have left in the culture or cultures (or just in the languages and customs) through which they have passed.

8. A classic is a work which constantly generates a pulviscular cloud of critical discourse around it, but which always shakes the particles off.

9. Classics are books which, the more we think we know them through hearsay, the more original, unexpected, and innovative we find them when we actually read them.

10. A classic is the term given to any book which comes to represent the whole universe, a book on a par with ancient talismans.

11. 'Your' classic is a book to which you cannot remain indifferent, and which helps you define yourself in relation or even in opposition to it.

12. A classic is a work that comes before other classics; but those who have read other classics first immediately recognize its place in the genealogy of classic works.

13. A classic is a work which relegates the noise of the present to a background hum, which at the same time the classics cannot exist without.

14. A classic is a work which persists as background noise even when a present that is totally incompatible with it holds sway.

Italian Folktales 1956

1982 Penguin Books
2000 Modern Classics
trans. George Martin, 1980

In 1954, the publisher Giulio Einaudi commissioned Calvino to create the Italian equivalent of the folktales of the Brothers Grimm. He spent two years scouring dozens of folktale anthologies, gathering, translating and adapting some 200 stories, in order to create this treasury of Italian adventurers, tricksters, lovers, sorcerers and talking animals.

Hermit in Paris
Autobiographical Writings 1954–85, pub. 1994

This collection features elegant essays on Italy's anti-fascist Resistance, the end of the Second World War in Italy and the joys of living in Paris, as well as a previously unpublished diary of Calvino's trip to the USA in 1959–60.

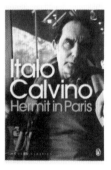

2011
pref. Esther Calvino, 1994
trans. Martin McLaughlin, 2003

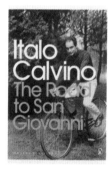

2009
fwd. Esther Calvino, 1990
trans. Tim Parks, 1993

The Road to San Giovanni 1962–77, pub. 1990

'One day in the spring of 1985, Calvino told me he was going to write twelve more books,' recalled his widow Esther. '[…] Of the works he was planning, one was to be made up of a series of "memory exercises". I have brought together five of these here, written between 1962 and 1977.' Calvino's autobiographical meditations recall awkward childhood walks with his father, a lifelong obsession with the cinema, and fighting in the Italian Resistance.

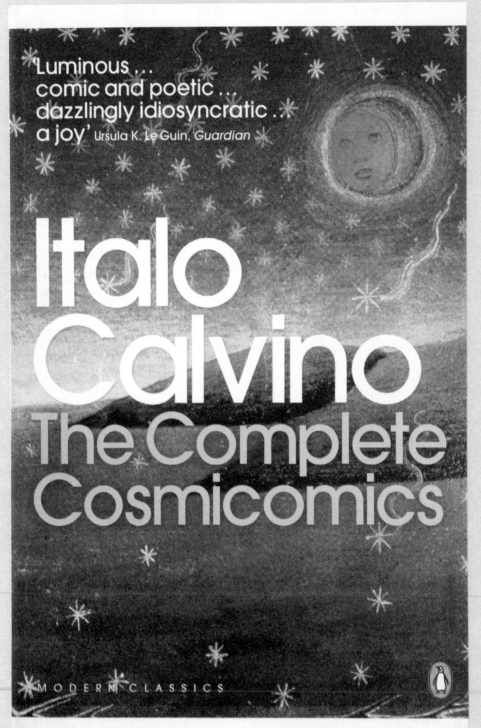

'Luminous ...
comic and poetic ...
dazzlingly idiosyncratic ...
a joy' Ursula K. Le Guin, *Guardian*

Italo
Calvino
The Complete
Cosmicomics

MODERN CLASSICS

2010
trans. Martin
McLaughlin,
Tim Parks & William
Weaver, 1968–2009
intro. Martin
McLaughlin, 2009
—
This volume collects,
for the first time in
English, the twelve
stories from the
original *Cosmicomics*
(1965), eleven stories
from *Time and the
Hunter* (1967), eight
stories from the
little-known private
publication *World
Memory and Other
Cosmicomic Stories*
(1968), as well as two
stories that Calvino
added to the 1984
collected edition.
The cover shows a
detail from *The Last
Judgement: The Stars
Fall and Everything
is Turned Upside
Down*, an anonymous
15th-century painting
in the Biblioteca
Reale in Turin.

← The Complete Cosmicomics
1965 84

Qfwfq is a morphing 'cosmic know-all' who
has observed the entire history of the universe.
Taking the shape of a dinosaur, a mollusc,
a steamship captain and a moon-milk gatherer,
he narrates whimsical stories that span galaxies
and millennia, blending scientific fact with
exuberant flights of fancy. Ursula K. Le Guin
called these stories 'dazzlingly idiosyncratic',
while Salman Rushdie says: 'If you have never
read *Cosmicomics*, you have before you […]
the most joyful reading experience of your life.'

Under the Jaguar Sun
1972–84, pub. 1986

When he died, Calvino was working on a series of five stories,
each based on one of the five senses, but he never completed
'sight' or 'touch'. The other three stories were published
posthumously: in 'Under the Jaguar
Sun', a couple making a gastronomic
journey across Mexico are drawn
to a special and sinister ingredient;
in 'A King Listens', a paranoid
monarch turns his palace into
an enormous earpiece; and in
'The Name, the Nose', three men
– a caveman, a count and a rock
musician – search for the scents
of lost women.

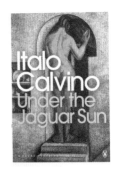

2009
trans. William Weaver, 1988

2013
trans. Martin McLaughlin

Collection of Sand
Essays 1974–84, pub. 1984

'Some traits of the author's physiognomy come through in these "occasional" pieces,' wrote
Calvino: 'an omnivorous, encyclopedic curiosity, and a desire to distance himself discreetly
from any form of specialism'. Arranged under the categories 'Exhibitions – Explorations',
'The Eye's Ray', 'Accounts of the Fantastic' and 'The Shape of Time', these disparate essays
touch on the imaginative pleasures of maps, the earliest forms of written language, Japanese
gardens and Mexican temples.

Six Memos for the Next Millennium
The Charles Eliot Norton Lectures 1985–86 1985, pub. 1988

'The millennium about to end has […] been the millennium of the book, in that it has
seen the object we call a book take on the form now familiar to us. […] My confidence in
the future of literature consists in the knowledge that there are things that only literature
can give us, by means specific to it. I would therefore like to devote these lectures to
certain values, qualities or peculiarities of literature that are very close to my heart, trying
to situate them within the perspective of the new millennium.' Calvino was invited to
give the six Charles Eliot Norton Lectures at Harvard University, but he died before he
could deliver them. His drafts were published posthumously, under the titles 'Lightness',
'Quickness', 'Exactitude', 'Visibility' and
'Multiplicity'; the sixth, unwritten lecture
was to have been called 'Constancy'.

2009 Modern Classics
• pref. Esther Calvino, 1988
trans. Patrick Creagh, 1988
2016 Modern Classics
trans. Geoffrey Brock, 2016

Letters 1941–85

For the first time in English, this collection presents Calvino's
extensive correspondence with Umberto Eco, Primo Levi (222), Pier
Paolo Pasolini, Gore Vidal and many other contemporaries. 'These
letters place Calvino in the larger frame of 20th-century Italy and
provide a showcase for his refined and civil voice,' wrote the *Guardian*.

2014
trans. Martin McLaughlin,
2013
ed. Michael Wood, 2013
—
Michael Wood made his
selection from *Lettere,
1940–1985* (2000), edited
by Luca Baranelli.

221

FANTASTIC TALES
Visionary and Everyday 1805–99, pub. 1983

Italo Calvino (218) edited and introduced this anthology of 19th-century horror, terror and fantasy, and his selection provides a fascinating insight into his own tastes and interests. The 26 authors include Jan Potocki, E. T. A. Hoffmann, Nikolai Gogol, Edgar Allan Poe, Charles Dickens, Guy de Maupassant, Henry James (397), Rudyard Kipling (22) and H. G. Wells (26).

2001
ed. Italo
Calvino, 1983
trans. Martin
McLaughlin
et al.,
1930–2001

1982 King Penguin
1990 Twentieth-Century
Classics
trans. Frances Frenaye, 1947

Carlo Levi 1902–1975

Levi trained as a doctor in Turin, but devoted most of his life to art, literature and political activism. In 1935, he was arrested for championing the anti-fascist movement Giustizia e Libertà and exiled to the hilltop village of Aliano in the region of Lucania, the 'instep' of the Italian boot. He spent a year there, painting and practising medicine. He was arrested again during the Second World War, and afterwards wrote and travelled; in 1963, he was elected to the Italian Senate. He is buried in Aliano.

Christ Stopped at Eboli 1945

Levi is chiefly remembered for this poetic account of his year of exile in Aliano, which he calls 'Gagliano', 1935–6. The title comes from a local expression that 'Christ stopped short of here, at Eboli', the town where the road and railway leave the coast and run into remote and barren Lucania – a region seemingly bypassed by Christianity, morality and even history. 'No message, human or divine, has reached this stubborn poverty,' wrote Levi. The book instigated a post-war trend towards social realism in Italian literature and was adapted for the cinema in 1979 by Francesco Rosi.

Primo Levi 1919–1987

Levi was born on the Corso Re Umberto in Turin, in the apartment where he lived almost his entire life. Before the Second World War, he trained as a chemist; but when the Germans invaded northern Italy, he escaped to the Alps to join the anti-fascist partisans. He was captured in December 1943, and as a Jew he was deported to Auschwitz. At the time, the life expectancy in the camp was three to four months, but Levi survived for a year, until he was liberated on 27 January 1945. Returning to Turin, he worked as a chemist in a paint factory for 30 years. In 1987, suffering from depression, he fell to his death from the third-floor landing of his apartment block. Elie Wiesel (325) commented: 'Primo Levi died at Auschwitz forty years later.' Italo Calvino (218) called Levi 'one of the most important and gifted writers of our time'.

If This is a Man
and The Truce 1947–63

If This is a Man (1947) is Levi's account of the year he spent at Auschwitz, smuggling soup rations, learning to speak German, synthesizing rubber in the camp factory, avoiding hard labour in freezing conditions. It is a chronicle of the triumph of human dignity in the face of human evil. He wrote the book in a flurry in 1946, between shifts while working at a paint factory: one chapter, 'The Canto of Ulysses', was almost entirely written during a single, half-hour lunch break. *If This is a Man* was initially published with little fanfare by a small press; the publisher Einaudi's 1958 edition was an international success, however, and prompted Levi to write a sequel, *The Truce* (1963), about his convoluted, eight-month journey home after the camp was liberated by Soviet troops in January 1945. 'In Levi's writing,' wrote Saul Bellow (477), 'nothing is superfluous and everything is essential.'

1979
• trans. Stuart Woolf, 1959–65
intro. Paul Bailey, 1971

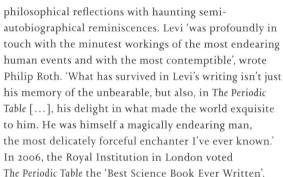

The Periodic Table 1975

2000
trans. Raymond
Rosenthal, 1984
essay by Philip
Roth, 1986

Each of these
21 stories is inspired
by one of the
chemical elements,
such as argon, zinc
or vanadium. The
collection combines
philosophical reflections with haunting semi-autobiographical reminiscences. Levi 'was profoundly in
touch with the minutest workings of the most endearing
human events and with the most contemptible', wrote
Philip Roth. 'What has survived in Levi's writing isn't just
his memory of the unbearable, but also, in *The Periodic
Table* [...], his delight in what made the world exquisite
to him. He was himself a magically endearing man,
the most delicately forceful enchanter I've ever known.'
In 2006, the Royal Institution in London voted
The Periodic Table the 'Best Science Book Ever Written'.

The Search for Roots
A Personal Anthology

6th century BCE – 1978, pub. 1981

'I accepted willingly and with curiosity the proposal to
compile a "personal anthology",' wrote Levi in his preface,
'not in the Borgesian (572) sense
of an auto-anthology but in that
of a harvesting, retrospectively
and in good faith, which would
bring to light the possible
traces of what has been read
on what has been written.'
He chooses and introduces
30 pieces of fiction, poetry and
philosophy, from the Book of
Job to the latest theory on black
holes, with authors including
Isaac Babel (321), Joseph Conrad
(28), Thomas Mann (245) and
Antoine de Saint-Exupéry (178).

2002
• trans. Peter Forbes, 2001
aftwd. Italo Calvino (218), 1981

A Tranquil Star
Unpublished
Stories 1949 – 86, pub. 2007

These seventeen short
stories were collected and
translated into English for
the first time in 2007. They
include tales about impossibly
beautiful poems, magical
paint and deadly weapons.
The title story, 'A Tranquil Star',
is a meditation on language,
imagination and infinity.

2008
ed. Ann Goldstein, 2007
trans. Ann Goldstein,
Alessandra Bastagli
& Jenny McPhee, 2007

1987 Penguin Books
1995 Twentieth-Century
Classics
2001 Modern Classics
trans. Ruth Feldman, 1979–86
intro. Michael Ignatieff, 2001

Moments of Reprieve:
A Memoir of Auschwitz 1981

Levi recalls fifteen individuals
he met at Auschwitz: 'the ones
in whom (if only for a moment)
I had recognized the will and
capacity to react, and hence a
rudiment of virtue'. Each story
describes one individual who
somehow, through a piece of
clowning, a slice of apple or
a simple letter, created 'bizarre,
marginal moments of reprieve'.

If Not Now, When? 1982

In this novel, Mendel
Nachmanovich Dajcher,
a former watch repairer, joins
the ranks of Russian, Polish
and Jewish partisans fighting
behind enemy lines during the
Second World War. He must
struggle to stay alive, sabotage
the Germany army and seek
a new home. Levi wrote a
partisan song with the refrain:

> If I'm not for myself,
>   who will be for me?
> If not this way, how?
>   And if not now, when?

1986 Penguin Books
2000 Modern Classics
trans. William Weaver, 1985
intro. Mark Mazower, 2000

Vitaliano Brancati 1907–1954

Brancati was born in Sicily and joined the Fascist Party in 1924, describing himself as 'fascist to the roots of my hair'. But he later repudiated the party and returned to work as a schoolteacher in Catania, writing novels, stories and plays.

Beautiful Antonio 1949

Antonio Magnano is the most handsome man in Catania: men envy him and women fall at his feet. He is the embodiment of *gallismo*, the southern Italian cocktail of sexual prowess and aggressive machismo. When he marries the beautiful Barbara Puglisi, however, rumours start to circulate that he can't perform in bed. Soon the whole town is in uproar and his family's honour is at stake.

2007
trans. Patrick Creagh, 1993
intro. Tim Parks, 2007
—
The photograph on the cover is from the 1960 film adaptation of *Il Bell'Antonio*, directed by Mauro Bolognini and starring Marcello Mastroianni and Claudia Cardinale.

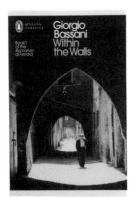

2016
trans. Jamie McKendrick
—
In 1974, Bassani collected *Within the Walls*, *The Gold-Rimmed Spectacles*, *The Garden of the Finzi-Continis*, *Behind the Door*, *The Heron* and *The Smell of Hay* in a single volume, which he called *The Novel of Ferrara*. In 2018, Penguin published *The Novel of Ferrara* as an 848-page hardback omnibus edition.

Giorgio Bassani 1916–2000

Bassani grew up in the north Italian city of Ferrara. In 1943, he was imprisoned for anti-fascist activities; on his release he married Valeria Sinigallia, and they moved to Florence and then to Rome. Bassani lived in the capital for the rest of his life, teaching, translating Hemingway (428), writing film scripts for Michelangelo Antonioni and Luchino Visconti, and working for the publisher Feltrinelli, for whom he 'discovered' and published posthumously *The Leopard* (1958) by Giuseppe Tomasi di Lampedusa. He wrote a sequence of interconnected novels and short stories set in his native city and is buried in its Jewish cemetery.

Within the Walls 1956, rev. 1980

The first instalment of *The Novel of Ferrara* is a book of five short stories that won the Strega Prize. It is a portrait of the walled city of Ferrara in the years before and after the Second World War, a city of broken relationships, faded photographs, tragic deaths and remarkable revenants.

The Gold-Rimmed Spectacles 1958

The second book in the *Novel of Ferrara* sequence is narrated by a Jewish student at Bologna University and tells the story of a homosexual doctor, Fadigati, who arrives in the close-knit community of Ferrara.

1963 Penguin Books
• trans. Isabel Quigly, 1960
2012 Modern Classics
trans. Jamie McKendrick, 2012

MODERN CLASSICS

Giorgio Bassani
The Garden of the Finzi-Continis

1969 Penguin
Books
● trans. Isabel
Quigly, 1965
<u>2007</u> Modern
Classics
trans. Jamie
McKendrick, 2007

The Garden of the Finzi-Continis 1962

The best-known instalment of Bassani's *Novel of Ferrara* centres on the aristocratic Finzi-Continis' beautiful garden and tennis courts, which become a refuge for the city's threatened Jewish community. The narrator, a young Jewish student, becomes increasingly attracted to Micòl Finzi-Contini. The book won the Viareggio Prize and was adapted into an Academy Award-winning film by Vittorio De Sica in 1970.

Behind the Door 1964

In this novel of teenage hierarchies and rivalries, Bassani drew on the experience of his own schooldays in Ferrara. Under the looming threat of fascism, darker prejudices start to emerge in both the classroom and playground.

2017
trans. Jamie McKendrick

The Heron 1968

Edgardo Limentani, 45 years old, joins a shooting party outside Ferrara one cold Sunday. Over the course of the day, he contemplates his life and its many disappointments.

2018
trans. Jamie McKendrick

The Smell of Hay 1972

The last instalment of *The Novel of Ferrara* is another volume of short stories about the city's Jewish community. It is a lost world of unrequited loves, faded grandeur and the smell of freshly mown hay within the walls of the Jewish cemetery. 'This towering work [*The Novel of Ferrara*] by one of the most uncompromising, most longsighted, most unflinching and most mercilessly precise of twentieth-century novelists, climaxes on this, the book in your hands,' writes Ali Smith in her introduction.

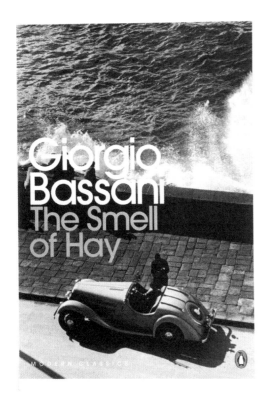

Giorgio Bassani
The Smell of Hay

MODERN CLASSICS

2014
trans. Jamie
McKendrick
intro. Ali Smith

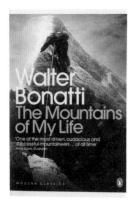

2010
trans. Robert Marshall, 2001
—
Robert Marshall is an Australian
doctor, skier and hiker, with
a passion for mountains and
mountaineering. In correspondence
with Bonatti, he selected and
translated these extracts from
Bonatti's many books.

Walter Bonatti 1930–2011

As a teenager, Bonatti dedicated himself to mountain-climbing, and for seventeen years he climbed a succession of increasingly difficult routes in the Alps, the Himalayas and the Andes. By the 1950s, he was regarded as the best climber in Italy, perhaps the world; but after a solo direct ascent of the north face of the Matterhorn in midwinter, he abandoned extreme mountaineering and spent the rest of his life writing and travelling to remote places as a photojournalist. He was awarded medals for bravery in Italy and France, and honoured in Germany and the USA. The climber Andy Cave calls him 'one of the most driven, audacious and successful mountaineers of all time'.

The Mountains of My Life 1961–96, pub. 1998

'For me, the value of a climb is the sum of three inseparable elements, all equally important: aesthetics, history, and ethics,' writes Bonatti. '[…] I don't deny that there can be an element of escapism in mountaineering, but this should never overshadow its real essence, which is not escape but victory over your own human frailty.' This collection of his classic writings covers all his toughest ascents as well as the controversy around the Italian ascent of K2 in 1954.

Bruno Munari 1907–1998

Munari was a Milanese designer and graphic artist, described by Picasso as 'the new Leonardo'. After a flirtation with Futurism (216), when he created a number of geometric abstract works and 'useless machines', he worked as a designer for the publisher Mondadori, co-founded the Movimento Arte Concreta ('Movement for Concrete Art'), and went on to design many household objects, including ash trays, televisions, espresso machines and children's toys; he also wrote and illustrated books for children, including *The Elephant's Wish* (1945) and *The Circus in the Mist* (1968). He twice won the prestigious Compasso d'Oro design award and has had major exhibitions of his work in Europe, the USA and Japan.

Design as Art 1966

'The artist has to regain the modesty he had when art was just a trade,' wrote Munari in his preface, 'and instead of despising the very public he is trying to interest he must discover its needs and make contact with it again. This is the reason why the traditional artist is being transformed into the designer, and as I myself have undergone this transformation in the course of my working career I can say that this book of mine is also a kind of diary in which I try to see the why and wherefore of this metamorphosis.'

1971 Pelican Books
2008 Design Classics
trans. Patrick Creagh, 1971

2014
trans. Anne Milano
Appel, 2013
pref. Angelo
Pellegrino, 1997, 2006

Goliarda Sapienza

1924 – 1996

Sapienza was born in Catania in Sicily, but moved to Rome to study at the Academy of Dramatic Arts. She worked as an actress in film and theatre until the late 1950s, after which she concentrated on writing. She published four novels in her lifetime, but her masterpiece, *The Art of Joy*, was considered too long and too shocking; it was published posthumously by her husband, the actor Angelo Pellegrino.

The Art of Joy 1967 – 76, pub. 1998

Modesta is born in Sicily on 1 January 1900, and grows up with the 20th century, experiencing violence, brutality, luxury, war, seduction, love and murder. This fictionalized memoir is also a sexual adventure, a family saga and a coming-of-age novel. The *Independent* called it 'a masterwork […] as irresistible as the woman at its heart'.

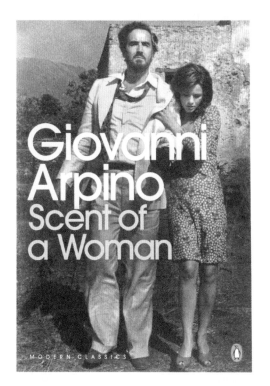

2011
trans. Anne Milano
Appel
—
Appel's translation
won the John Florio
Prize for Italian
translation in 2012.

Giovanni Arpino

1927 – 1987

Arpino lived in Turin and worked for most of his life as a sports journalist. He wrote his first novel at 25 and won the Strega Prize for *The Shadow of the Hills* in 1964. He also wrote poems, plays, epigrams, and stories for children.

Scent of a Woman

1969

Fausto, a one-armed blind soldier, is guided by the narrator, his younger comrade, through Genoa, Rome and Naples, returning to the scene of a stifled and tragic love affair. *Il Buio e il Miele* – literally *The Darkness and the Honey* – has been adapted for film twice, both titled *Scent of a Woman*: in 1974, starring Vittorio Gassman; and in 1992, starring Al Pacino, who won an Academy Award.

Elsa Morante 1912–1985

Morante published a children's book, *Someone Knocks on the Door*, in 1935–6. Five years later, she married the author Alberto Moravia, a staunch opponent of Mussolini; the couple were both half Jewish, and were forced to go into hiding in the countryside near Cassino in central Italy. During the war, Morante translated Katherine Mansfield (388); afterwards her first novel for adults, *House of Liars* (1948), won the Viareggio Prize. She went on to write several more novels, as well as poems and essays.

History
A Novel 1974

This epic novel tells the story of the 20th century, but focuses particularly on the years 1941 to 1947, and on the experience of Ida Mancuso, a Jewish widow in Rome. The book opens with a German soldier, who can speak only four words of Italian, propositioning her as she returns home laden with shopping. The title, *La Storia*, can mean either 'history' or 'the story' in Italian. *La Storia* is 'one of the few novels in any language', wrote the American author Alfred Kazin, 'that renders the full horror of Hitler's war'.

Elsa Morante History: A Novel

1980 Penguin Books
1985 King Penguin
2002 Modern Classics
• trans. William Weaver, 1977
intro. William Rivière, 2002

Patrizia Cavalli b. 1949

Cavalli was born in Umbria and now lives in Rome. She is a much-loved poet in Italy, regularly reading to packed audiences. The philosopher Giorgio Agamben describes her work as 'the most intensely "ethical" poetry in Italian literature of the twentieth century'. Cavalli has made Italian translations of Shakespeare and Molière.

My Poems Won't Change the World
Selected Poems 1974–2006

Cavalli's poems are thoughtful, intimate and comic, touching on love, pasta, cats and the city. This is the most substantial gathering of her verse in English, drawn from six collections, including *My Poems Won't Change the World* (1974), *The Sky* (1981) and *Lazy Gods, Lazy Fate* (2006). 'Reading Patrizia Cavalli is nothing short of ecstasy,' says the writer Jhumpa Lahiri.

2018
ed. Gini Alhadeff, 2013
trans. Gini Alhadeff et al., 1998–2013

Roberto Calasso 1941–2021

Calasso was born in Florence. He worked for the Milanese publishing house Adelphi for 40 years, from its foundation in 1962, introducing their influential classics editions, which he described as 'links in a single chain [...] fragments in a single book'. He lived in Milan, surrounded by 20,000 books, and was fluent in several languages, including Latin and Ancient Greek; and he was the author of a series of books that he saw as an ongoing investigation into the ways in which myths are interpreted. He won the Prix Formentor in 2016. 'If you want a dazzling, complex, erotic and utterly original European novel of ideas,' wrote William Dalrymple, 'Calasso is your man, and *Ka* is his masterpiece.'

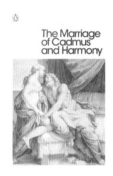

2019
trans. Tim Parks, 1993

The Marriage of Cadmus and Harmony

1988

Cadmus, the first king of Thebes, married Harmonia, goddess of concord, and the gods of Olympus shared the marriage feast with mortals. Calasso begins with this story and goes on to retell a panoply of Greek myths, exploring fundamental aspects of the human condition. It is 'the kind of book one comes across only once or twice in one's lifetime', wrote Joseph Brodsky (316).

Ka 1996

Calasso reimagines Hindu myths from ancient texts such as the *Rig Veda*, the *Upanishads* and the *Mahabharata*. He repeatedly asks the question, 'Ka?' – 'Who?' The Sanskrit scholar Wendy Doniger calls it 'the very best book about Hindu mythology that anyone has ever written'.

2019
trans. Tim Parks, 1998

2020
trans. Geoffrey Brock, 2005

K. 2002

This book-length essay unpacks the works of Franz Kafka (280), asking what the stories are about, how they relate to Kafka's life and who is the character K.? 'No one could bring more intelligence and cultural range to a fresh encounter with Kafka,' wrote the *New York Review of Books*.

Tiepolo Pink 2006

Inspired by references to the 18th-century artist Giambattista Tiepolo in Proust's *In Search of Lost Time* (168), Calasso sets out to assemble a fragmentary portrait of the Venetian painter, illustrating the text with numerous details from Tiepolo's expansive frescos and bizarre etchings.

2020
trans. Alastair McEwen, 2009

Spain

Federico García Lorca 1898–1936

Federico del Sagrado Corazón de Jesús García Lorca grew up in Andalusia, in the valleys outside Granada. As a student in Madrid, he met the poet Juan Ramón Jiménez, the film-maker Luis Buñuel and the artist Salvador Dalí, and became an influential member of the Generation of '27 (231). He grew increasingly estranged from Dalí and Buñuel, however, and interpreted their film *Un Chien Andalou* (1929) as a personal attack. The success of Lorca's *Gypsy Ballads* (1928) allowed him to travel the following year to New York, where he studied English at Columbia University. On his return to Spain in 1930, he was appointed co-director of La Barraca, a government-sponsored student theatre company that toured the country with a portable stage and minimal equipment. In the mid-1930s, Lorca's outspoken socialist opinions clashed with a growing right-wing nationalist movement, and soon after the outbreak of the Spanish Civil War he was murdered by nationalist partisans in Granada; his body has never been found. His early death and passionate poetry have made him an icon around the world: Seamus Heaney declared him 'the epitome of Romantic Spain'.

1960 Penguin Poets
● trans. J. L. Gili, 1960
1997 Twentieth-Century Classics
trans. Francisco Aragón et al., 1989–94
ed. Christopher Maurer, 1995
—
'The "essential" Lorca is an elusive, and perhaps imaginary, figure,' writes Christopher Maurer in his introduction, 'but this is the most complete anthology of his poems ever published in English.' The cover of the 1997 edition features an illustration by Lorca himself.

Selected Poems 1918–36

Lorca is often described as the greatest Spanish poet of the twentieth century. Christopher Maurer's parallel text anthology includes examples from every book of poems Lorca wrote, from the playful *Suites* (1920–23) to the stylized *Gypsy Ballads* (1928), the dark *Poet in New York* and his masterpiece, *Lament for Ignacio Sánchez Mejías* (1935), an elegy for a bullfighter. Lorca's poetry draws on music, drama, mythology, Arabic verse and Andalusian folk songs to recreate intense impressions of the natural world and human experience.

Five Plays
Comedies and Tragicomedies 1919–35

The Billy-Club Puppets, *The Shoemaker's Prodigious Wife*, *The Love of Don Perlimplín and Belisa in the Garden*, *Doña Rosita the Spinster*, *The Butterfly's Evil Spell*

These experimental plays draw on the folk culture of Spain and combine fantasy with reality. Lorca's first play, *The Butterfly's Evil Spell* (1919), is about the impossible love between a cockroach and a butterfly; it was laughed off stage. *The Shoemaker's Prodigious Wife* (1930) is a farce about the flirtatious wife of a henpecked cobbler, and Lorca described *The Love of Don Perlimplín and Belisa in the Garden* (1931) as 'an erotic lace-paper valentine'.

1970 Penguin Plays
1987 Modern Classics
● trans. James Graham-Lujan & Richard L. O'Connell, 1965
intro. Francisco García Lorca, 1965
—
Francisco García Lorca was Federico's brother, known as 'Paquito'.

Poet in New York 1929–30, pub. 1940

Published posthumously, this volume collects the poems that Lorca wrote during the year he spent in America. Through tortured images of crowds, skyscrapers, loneliness and despair, Lorca paints a picture of New York as a city of brutal materialism. He describes the Wall Street Crash of October 1929, which he witnessed first-hand. This edition includes letters that Lorca sent home and photographs from his trip.

1990
trans. Greg Simon & Steven F. White, 1988
ed. Christopher Maurer, 1988

Generation of '27

In 1927, a group of writers and intellectuals met in Seville to mark 300 years since the death of the great Spanish poet Luis de Góngora. This group and their contemporaries have come to be known as the 'Generation of '27', a constellation of figures rather than a formal literary movement, although many of the members did draw on contemporary artistic trends such as Futurism (216) and Surrealism (176). Generation of '27 writers include Rafael Alberti, Francisco Ayala (232), Miguel Hernández and Federico García Lorca (230).

Three Tragedies 1933–6

Blood Wedding, Yerma, The House of Bernarda Alba

Lorca wrote his three great rural tragedies while touring Spain with the student theatre company La Barraca. All of them are fierce protests against claustrophobic, bourgeois Spanish society, passionate hymns to freedom, and resounding calls for social equality. In *Blood Wedding* (1933), a bride yearns for her lover; in *Yerma* (1934), a childless woman desperately longs for motherhood; and in *The House of Bernarda Alba* (1936), a powerful matriarch rules over a stifling household of five daughters. 'The theatre is a school of weeping and of laughter,' wrote Lorca, 'a free forum, where men can question norms that are outmoded or mistaken and explain with living example the eternal norms of the human heart.'

1961 Penguin Plays
1987 Modern Classics
• trans. James Graham-Lujan & Richard L. O'Connell, 1941–6 intro. Francisco García Lorca, 1959
1992 Twentieth-Century Classics *Three Plays*
2001 Modern Classics *The House of Bernarda Alba and Other Plays* trans. Michael Dewell & Carmen Zapata, 1987 intro. Christopher Maurer, 1992

Felipe Alfau 1902–1999

Alfau was born in Barcelona but emigrated to the USA during the First World War. He wrote about music for *La Prensa*, a Spanish newspaper in New York, before taking a job as a translator in a bank, a position he held for the rest of his working life. He wrote *Locos* in English and also a book of children's stories called *Old Tales from Spain* (1929). The novelist Dawn Powell recalled his 'brilliant, dazzling mind' and remembered him as having 'a mental performance similar only to Cummings (427), but a scholar – erudite, fascinating, above all a romantic about his Spain, fiercely patriotic, a figure out of a medieval romance'.

Locos
A Comedy of Gestures 1928, pub. 1936

The author describes a number of strange characters in Toledo's Café de los Locos (Café of the Crazy). These characters then take over his book, crossing the line between fiction and reality: 'For them reality is what fiction is to real people,' the beleaguered author explains; 'they simply love it and make for it against my almost heroic opposition.' This unpredictable, shape-shifting, experimental book contains paradoxes and startling twists within its interlocking stories. 'From the outset it is clear that we are in the shadowlands between reality and fiction,' wrote the *Independent*, 'where anything could happen, and usually does.'

1991
• aftwd. Mary McCarthy, 1988
—
Alfau finished *Locos* in 1928 but took eight years to find a publisher. The first edition was mostly overlooked, although Mary McCarthy (507) wrote a favourable review in the *Nation*. The novel was rediscovered in 1987 by Steven Moore, an editor at the Dalkey Archive Press, who found an old copy at a barn sale in Massachusetts. He tracked down Alfau's phone number and republished the book with a new afterword by McCarthy. Alfau refused any payment, asking Moore to use the royalties to fund someone else's unpublished work. Alfau also revealed he had the manuscript of another novel, *Chromos*, which had lain in a drawer since 1948. It was published in 1990 and was nominated for the National Book Award.

THE PENGUIN BOOK OF SPANISH CIVIL WAR VERSE 1936–44

'The poet's war,' Stephen Spender (95) called it, because among the many
British volunteers who fought in the Spanish Civil War there were dozens
of writers from the thirties generation (95). Under chronological sections
with titles such as 'The Map of Pain', 'Junker Angels in the Sky' and 'Talking
Bronco', the scholar Valentine Cunningham arranges poems by Spender,
W. H. Auden (95), Laurie Lee (114), Louis MacNeice, Herbert Read (103) and
Sylvia Townsend Warner (75), as well as some Spanish poems in translation
and a smattering of 'supporting prose' – letters, diary entries,
essays and reviews. 'The Crime was in Granada' has poems
about the death of Federico García Lorca (230) and 'Prisoner'
has the stark concentration-camp poetry of Clive Branson.
It is 'a fascinating anthology', wrote the *Financial Times*,
'arranged so that you can follow the progress of the war'.

1980 Penguin Poets
1996 Twentieth-
Century Classics
● ed. Valentine
Cunningham, 1980
trans. Stephen
Spender et al.,
1936–9

*The Penguin Book of
Spanish Civil War Verse*

Francisco Ayala 1906–2009

Ayala was born in Granada but moved
to Berlin in 1929, where he met his first
wife and witnessed the rise of Nazism.
During the Spanish Civil War, he worked for
the republican government and afterwards
emigrated to Buenos Aires, where he lived
for ten years. He remained in the Americas,
teaching in Puerto Rico, Chicago and
New York, until General Franco died in 1975,
after which he returned to live permanently
in Spain. He was elected to the Real
Academia Española in 1983, and in 1991
he won the Cervantes Prize, the most
prestigious award for writers of Spanish.

Usurpers 1939–47, pub. 1949

Ayala wrote these seven stories in
Buenos Aires. They are set in medieval
and Golden Age Spain, but inspired by
the timeless idea that 'power exercised
by man over his fellow man is always
a usurpation'. They evoke dark worlds
of beauty, ambition, violence and
horror. 'The universes of Kafka (280)
and of Herman Melville are filled with
anguish,' wrote Jorge Luis Borges (572);
'in Ayala's we perceive, beneath the
vermicular stirring of its multitudes,
a calm and atrocious desperation.'

1996
● trans. Carolyn Richmond,
1987
—
The translator Carolyn
Richmond was Ayala's second
wife. The cover of the Penguin
edition shows a 1673 portrait
of Charles II of Spain by
Juan Carreño de Miranda.

Ana María Matute 1925–2014

Matute was a leading novelist of the period after the Spanish Civil War,
despite the heavy censorship of the Francoist regime which banned her
journalism and forced her to make changes to her books. She was elected
a member of the Real Academia Española in 1996 and won the prestigious
Cervantes Prize in 2010, the third woman to do so.

The Island 1959

Primera Memoria (First Memory) is narrated by Matia, an adolescent girl who finds
herself on the island of Mallorca during the Spanish Civil War, frustrated by her
domineering grandmother, fascinated by her mercurial cousin Borja and intrigued
by silent Manuel from the local Jewish community. It won the Nadal Prize in 1959.

2020
trans. Laura
Lonsdale

Javier Marías b. 1951

Marías grew up in Spain and the USA, where his father taught philosophy. At seventeen, he ran away to Paris and wrote his first novel. He has since produced more novels and translated English-language works into Spanish, including an award-winning edition of Laurence Sterne's *Tristram Shandy*, and works by Joseph Conrad (28), William Faulkner (433), Vladimir Nabokov (304) and John Updike (514). He has held academic posts in Spain, the USA and the UK, where he lectured at Oxford University for two years. In 2006, he was elected to the Real Academia Española, and in 2013 he won the Prix Formentor. 'I think it was Faulkner who once said that when you strike a match in a dark wilderness it is not in order to see anything better lighted, but just in order to see how much more darkness there is around,' says Marías. 'I think that literature does mainly that.'

The Man of Feeling 1986

An operatic tenor recalls a train journey he made in his youth, during which he shared a compartment with a middle-aged banker, his beautiful wife and their male travelling companion. It is 'a book that reflects on the torture of love', wrote the *Washington Times*, 'the way arias reflect heartbreak'.

2012
trans. Margaret Jull Costa, 2003

Marías considers this novel to be the first written in what has become his characteristic style. 'A Marías sentence is a place of infinite richness and surprises,' says the *Independent*, 'a place full of fascinating by-ways and glimpses of a distant landscape that hoves into view and then fades away.'

All Souls 1989

Like Marías, the Spanish narrator of *All Souls* was once a visiting lecturer at Oxford University. He recalls an affair with a pretty young tutor called Clare Bayes. 'All campus novels are, at a certain level, acts of revenge,' writes John Banville in his introduction – 'on institutions, on colleagues, on students, even on set texts – and *All Souls* is as stylishly vengeful as the most embittered and rancorous junior lecturer could wish for; it is also fond, profound, moving, delightfully strange and wonderfully funny.' The novel features a description and photographs of John Gawsworth, the real-life poet who inherited the kingdom of Redonda – a tiny, uninhabited Caribbean rock.

2012
trans. Margaret Jull Costa, 1992
intro. John Banville, 2012

When I Was Mortal 1991–6, pub. 1996

These chilling short stories feature doctors dispensing treatments for dissatisfied wives, mothers auditioning for porn films and voyeurs watching as people die. Marías 'discovers a lurid world of greed, lust and murder under every seemingly innocuous encounter', wrote the *Sunday Times*.

A Heart So White 1992

2013
trans. Margaret Jull Costa, 1999

'The wisp of a plot can be summarized in a few words,' writes Jonathan Coe – 'newlywed translator learns the deadly secret behind his father's three marriages.' This novel opens with the story of a young wife who goes to the bathroom in the middle of a family lunch and shoots herself in the heart. 'He uses language like an anatomist uses the scalpel,' wrote W. G. Sebald of Marías, 'to cut away the layers of flesh in order to lay bare the innermost secrets of that strangest of species, the human being.'

2012
trans. Margaret Jull Costa, 1995
intro. Jonathan Coe, 2012
—
Marías and Margaret Jull Costa were joint winners of the 1997 International IMPAC Dublin Literary Award for this English version. Marías took the title from Shakespeare's *Macbeth*.

2012
trans. Margaret Jull Costa,
1996
—
The title comes from
Shakespeare's *Richard III*.

2016
trans. Margaret Jull Costa, 2006

Tomorrow in the Battle Think on Me 1994

When Victor, a ghost-writer, is about to have an affair with a married woman, she dies in her bed, half-undressed. He panics and slips away, but Deán, the widowed husband, knows his wife was not alone. 'The narrative runs like a psychological thriller,' wrote the *Independent on Sunday*, 'with macabre and comic interludes.' It won the Venezuelan Rómulo Gallegos Prize.

Dark Back of Time 1998

This 'false novel', as Marías calls it, fictionalizes the success of Marías's previous novel *All Souls* (233). The narrator, called Javier Marías, describes how the reigning king of Redonda, Jon Wynne-Tyson, abdicated in 1997 and gave the throne to Marías, which he actually did. Playing with reality and fantasy, time and memory, the narrator reaches into the 'dark back of time' to recall the figures who shaped his past.

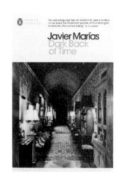

2013
trans. Esther Allen, 2001

Since inheriting the kingdom of Redonda, Javier Marías has set up a small publishing imprint called Reino de Redonda, which has published Spanish-language editions of *The Mirror of the Sea* (29) by Joseph Conrad, *Ehrengard* (242) by Isak Dinesen, *Alamein to Zem Zem* (116) by Keith Douglas and *The Celtic Twilight* (5) by W. B. Yeats, among many other titles. He confers ennoblements on his friends, such as William Boyd (Duke of Brazzaville), A. S. Byatt (Duchess of Morpho Eugenia), W. G. Sebald (Duke of Vértigo) and Jonathan Coe (Duke of Prunes) and he used to run a literary prize, the winner of which received a duchy.

Written Lives 2000

'The idea […] was to treat these well-known literary figures as if they were fictional characters,' explains Marías, 'which may well be how all writers, whether famous or obscure, would secretly like to be treated.' What follows is a series of 26 eccentric and irreverent portraits of great writers, including Joseph Conrad (28), Isak Dinesen (240), William Faulkner (433), Henry James (397), James Joyce (8), Rudyard Kipling (22), Malcolm Lowry (101), Thomas Mann (245), Yukio Mishima (350), Vladimir Nabokov (304), Rainer Maria Rilke (269) and Oscar Wilde (3). 'An artful antidote to the "exhaustive and futile erudition" of biography', wrote *The Times*. 'Marías sups from the marrow of their bones with a very long spoon.'

Your Face Tomorrow 2002–7

Fever and Spear, Dance and Dream, Poison, Shadow and Farewell

This trilogy of novels is considered by many to be Marías's greatest achievement to date. Together they form, as Ali Smith puts it, 'one of contemporary literature's major works'. In the first instalment, *Fever and Spear* (2002), the narrator, Jacques Deza, describes his uncanny ability to psychoanalyse a person by looking at their face, to the extent that he can predict what will become of them. At a dinner party hosted by retired Oxford professor Sir Peter Wheeler, Deza is recruited into a shady world of espionage and asked to observe an assortment of politicians, celebrities and seemingly ordinary citizens. In the second volume, *Dance and Dream* (2004), Deza is forced to witness a horrifying scene in a nightclub, and finds himself increasingly haunted by memories of the Spanish Civil War. Finally, in *Poison, Shadow and Farewell* (2007), Deza finds himself watching incriminating videos of public figures committing sordid acts. The novelist James Lasdun said that this 'triumphant finale […] may very well be the first authentic literary masterpiece of the twenty-first century.'

2018
trans. Margaret Jull Costa, 2005

2018
trans. Margaret Jull Costa, 2006

2018
trans. Margaret Jull Costa, 2009

Portugal

Fernando Pessoa 1888–1935

Born in Lisbon and raised in South Africa, Pessoa was an autodidact who made a living translating foreign correspondence for commercial firms. He wrote poetry and prose in English, Portuguese and French, under an array of 'heteronyms', including 'Charles Robert Anon', 'Diablo Azul', 'A. A. Crosse', 'Inspector Guedes', 'Adolph Moscow', 'the Chevalier de Pas', 'Efbeedee Pasha', 'Pip', 'Uncle Pork', 'Professor Trochee', 'Dr Gaudencio Turnips', 'Vadooisf' and 'the Reverend Walter Wyatt'. These were fully developed fictional characters, with distinctive writing styles, whom Pessoa inhabited. 'Pessoa was one of the great twentieth-century poets,' wrote John Ashbery, 'the equal of Yeats (4), Rilke (269), Valéry, Lorca (230), Pasternak (302), or Hart Crane.'

1974 Penguin Poets
1982 Penguin Books
1996 Twentieth-Century Classics
trans. Jonathan Griffin, 1974, 1982
2006 Penguin Classics
A Little Larger Than the Entire Universe
trans. Richard Zenith, 2006

Selected Poems 1902–35

Pessoa's three principal heteronyms were the uneducated genius Alberto Caeiro (1889–1915) and his disciples Ricardo Reis (b. 1887), a doctor, and Álvaro de Campos (b. 1890), a naval engineer. 'These individuals should be considered distinct from their author,' wrote Pessoa. 'Each one forms a kind of drama, and all of them together form another drama.' Both Jonathan Griffin's and Richard Zenith's editions feature all three heteronyms, as well as verses written by Pessoa as himself, including 'Ah! The Anguish', 'Ah, It Is' and 'I Know I'm a Sick Man'.

2002
trans. Richard Zenith, 2001
—
The Book of Disquiet was first published in 1982, 47 years after the death of Pessoa, who died at the age of 47.

The Book of Disquiet 1913–35, pub. 1982

'In these random impressions, and with no desire to be other than random, I indifferently narrate my factless autobiography, my lifeless history. These are my Confessions, and if in them I say nothing, it's because I have nothing to say.' This extraordinary, fragmentary manuscript was discovered in a domed, wooden trunk after Pessoa's death. It claims to be the work of 'Bernardo Soares', an assistant bookkeeper in Lisbon, and consists of random numbered entries from notebooks and odd scraps of paper. 'What is this *Livro do Desassossego?*' asked the critic George Steiner. 'Neither "commonplace book", nor "sketchbook", nor "florilegium" will do. Imagine a fusion of Coleridge's notebooks and marginalia, of Valéry's philosophic diary and of Robert Musil's (270) voluminous journal. Yet even such a hybrid does not correspond to the singularity of Pessoa's chronicle.'

More
UNCLASSIFIABLE BOOKS

NORTHERN EUROPE

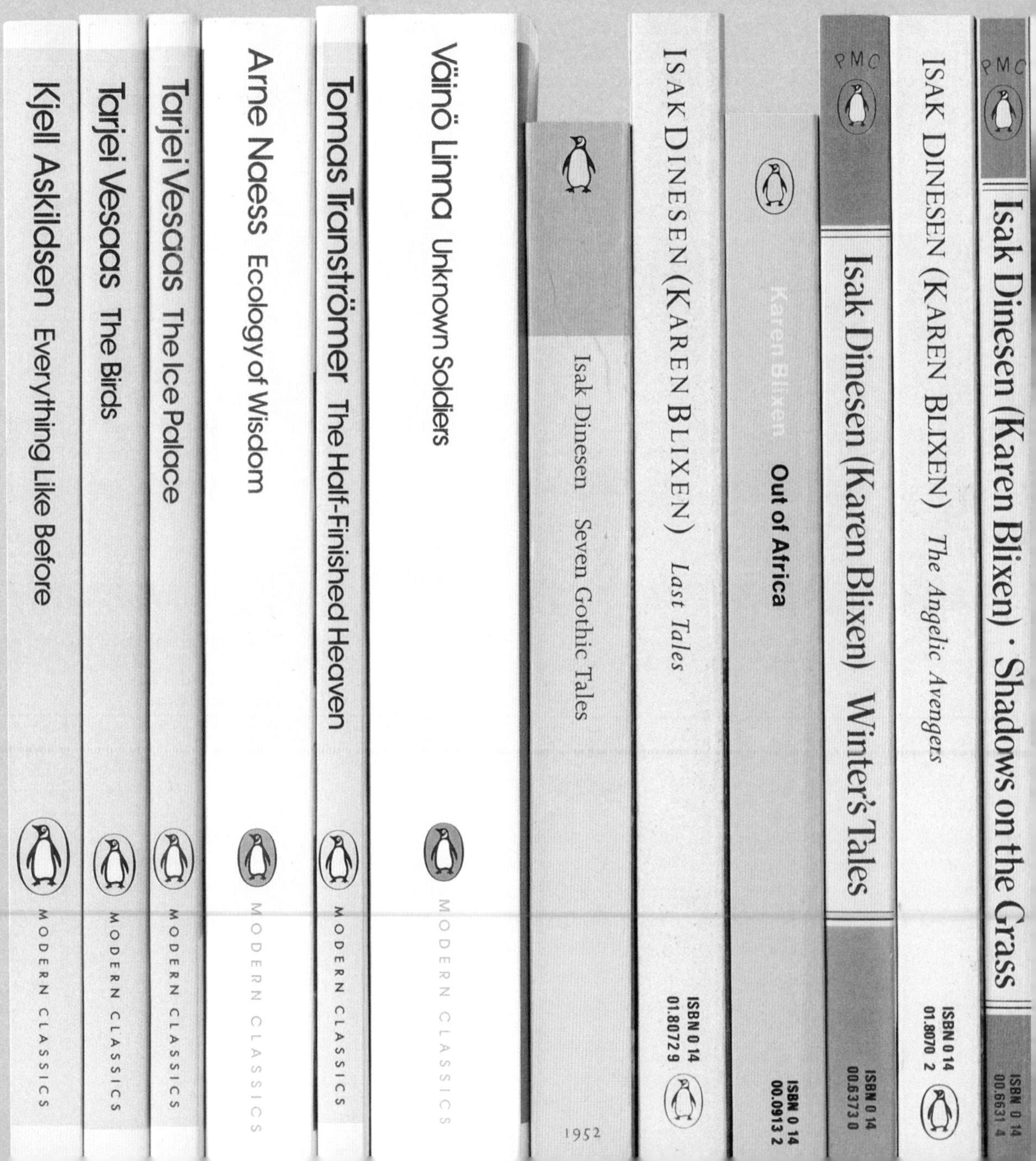

Kjell Askildsen Everything Like Before
MODERN CLASSICS
Tarjei Vesaas The Birds
MODERN CLASSICS
Tarjei Vesaas The Ice Palace
MODERN CLASSICS
Arne Naess Ecology of Wisdom
MODERN CLASSICS
Tomas Tranströmer The Half-Finished Heaven
MODERN CLASSICS
Väinö Linna Unknown Soldiers
MODERN CLASSICS
Isak Dinesen Seven Gothic Tales
1952
ISAK DINESEN (KAREN BLIXEN) Last Tales
ISBN 0 14 01.8072 9
Karen Blixen Out of Africa
ISBN 0 14 00.0913 2
PMC
Isak Dinesen (Karen Blixen) Winter's Tales
ISBN 0 14 00.6373 0
ISAK DINESEN (KAREN BLIXEN) The Angelic Avengers
ISBN 0 14 01.8070 2
PMC
Isak Dinesen (Karen Blixen) · Shadows on the Grass
ISBN 0 14 00.6631 4

Norway

Kjell Askildsen b. 1929

Askildsen was born in Mandal, on the southern coast of Norway. His father, a politician, was interned during the Nazi occupation of Norway. Askildsen's first collection of stories, *From Now On I'll Take You All the Way Home*, was published in 1953, and he has gone on to build a reputation as a master of bleak minimalism. 'Sincere, devastating and merciless,' writes *El Pais*; '[he] can be compared to Hemingway (428) and Carver stylistically, and Kafka (280), Beckett (20) and Camus (181) thematically.' Askildsen has received numerous awards, including the Norwegian Critics' Prize, the Brage Honorary Prize and the Swedish Academy's Nordic Prize.

Everything Like Before
Stories 1953–2015

This selection spans Askildsen's career; it describes unnerving encounters, lonely individuals and fractured families. 'Askildsen's dry, absurd humour is not unlike that of Beckett (20),' wrote the *Times Literary Supplement*. '[…] His short stories are packed with irony.'

2021
trans. Seán Kinsella, 2021

Tarjei Vesaas 1897–1970

Vesaas was born in Vinje, in the mountainous region of Telemark in southern Norway. He briefly attended a folk high school, and travelled the world before returning to run a farm in Vinje. He wrote 23 novels and four books of short stories in Nynorsk, one of the two standard forms of written Norwegian. In 1953, he was the only ever winner of the short-lived Venezia Prize, for his story collection *The Winds* (1952).

The Birds 1957

Mattis is a simple-minded adult who lives with his sister Hege on the shore of a remote lake. Finely attuned to the natural world, he senses that his life is about to be disrupted irrevocably. The Norwegian writer Karl Ove Knausgaard calls *The Birds* 'the best Norwegian novel ever'.

2019
trans. Torbjørn Støverud & Michael Barnes, 1968

Tarjei Vesaas
The Ice Palace

2018
trans. Elizabeth
Rokkan, 1966

The Ice Palace 1963

In the dead of winter, the local schoolchildren
are fascinated by the 'ice palace': a frozen
waterfall with spectacular translucent walls,
sparkling turrets and secret glassy chambers.
When her friend Unn disappears, Siss must
learn to escape her own internal ice palace.
'How simple this novel is. How subtle.
How strong. How unlike any other,' wrote
Doris Lessing. 'It is unique. It is unforgettable.
It is extraordinary.'

Arne Naess
Ecology
of Wisdom

2016
ed. Alan Drengson
& Bill Devall, 2008

Arne Naess 1912 – 2009

In 1939, Naess became Norway's only
Professor of Philosophy, and the youngest
ever professor at the University of Oslo.
He was also an intrepid mountaineer,
environmentalist and non-violent activist.
In 1938, he built an isolated wooden hut,
high up in the Hallingskarvet mountains,
where he spent a quarter of his life,
developing concepts such as 'ecosophy'
and 'deep ecology'. Inspired by Spinoza,
Gandhi (340) and Rachel Carson (504),
he campaigned for the Green Party and was
the first Chairman of Greenpeace Norway.

Ecology of Wisdom 1962 – 2006

This volume brings together the best of Naess's
writings on deep ecology, environmental
methodology, non-violence and the future.
He believed that all living things have value,
and he emphasizes the joy and wonder of nature
and the importance of 'beautiful actions'.

Sweden

Tomas Tranströmer 1931–2015

Tranströmer worked as a psychologist for juvenile offenders while writing twelve books of poetry and a memoir. He suffered a stroke in 1990, which left him partially paralysed and unable to speak, but he continued to compose and publish poetry and learned to play his beloved piano one-handed. His poems have won numerous awards and been translated into more than 50 languages. In 2011, he won the Nobel Prize for Literature (576).

The Half-Finished Heaven
Selected Poems 1954–2004

This selection of Tranströmer's luminous poems was translated and chosen by the American poet Robert Bly, Tranströmer's friend and collaborator. 'He was a genius,' writes Bly in his afterword – 'for things in human communication that are half-sensed, half-understood, only partially risen into consciousness, liable, like a fish, to disappear into the lake a moment later.'

1974 Penguin Poets
Selected Poems with Paavo Haavikko
● trans. Robin Fulton, 1974
2018 Modern Classics
trans. Robert Bly, 2001–17

Finland

2016
trans. Liesl
Yamaguchi, 2015

Väinö Linna 1920–1992

Väinö Linna was the son of a slaughterman. He worked as a tree-feller, a farmhand, and a factory worker in a textile mill, and he loved reading. In 1940, after Finland had allied itself with Germany, Linna was conscripted into the Finnish army and fought against the Soviet Union in the Continuation War, a protraction of the Winter War.

Unknown Soldiers 1954

Linna's gritty novel, based on his own wartime experiences, is an attempt to 'give the soldiers, who bore the weight of the calamity, all the appreciation and strip war of its glory'. It follows the motley troops of a Finnish machine-gun company as they fight the Russians on the Eastern Front. Doggedly tramping through swamps and pine forests, they argue, joke, swear and find ways to cope with the boredom, fear and horror.

Denmark

1963
—

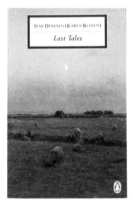

1986 Penguin Books
1990 Twentieth-Century Classics
• —

1983
—

Karen Blixen
(Isak Dinesen) 1885–1962

Karen Dinesen was born on her family's estate of Rungstedlund, north of Copenhagen. Her earliest stories were published under the pseudonym 'Osceola', the name of her father's dog. She studied art before marrying her cousin Baron Bror Blixen-Finecke in Kenya in 1914 and managing a coffee plantation with him at the foot of the Ngong Hills in the Great Rift Valley. They separated in 1919, but Baroness Blixen continued to run the plantation for more than ten years, until the collapse of the coffee market forced her to return to Rungstedlund. She lived there the rest of her life, writing books in English and then translating them into Danish. In 1959, she visited the USA, where she was feted by US celebrities, including John Steinbeck (440), e e cummings (427), Arthur Miller (486) and Marilyn Monroe. Today her homes in Denmark and Kenya are both museums.

Seven Gothic Tales

1934

Published under the pen name 'Isak Dinesen', these interwoven stories are set mostly in the 19th century and feature a cast of romantics, adventurers, melancholics and dreamers. They are 'luminous', wrote John Updike (514), '[…] rich, strange and free'.

Last Tales 1934–53, pub. 1957

This volume gathers stories from three separate projects. It includes episodes from *Albondocani*, an uncompleted novel, and two volumes of short stories, *New Gothic Tales* and *New Winter's Tales*. 'They have a vigor which persuades us that vigor perfectly solves the secret of delicacy,' wrote Eudora Welty (457), 'for her stories are the essence of delicacy.' *Anecdotes of Destiny* (242) was going to be a fourth section of *Last Tales*, but Blixen decided to publish it separately.

Out of Africa 1937 →

Blixen is most famous for this elegiac memoir, published under her own name, which recalls the seventeen years she spent on her beloved farm. She describes the Kenyan peoples, the landscape, the animals and her passionate infatuation with the British big-game hunter Denys Finch-Hatton.

Winter's Tales 1942, rev. 1958

These eleven stories, published during the Second World War, are mostly set in contemporary Europe. The best known is 'Sorrow-Acre', a modern rendition of a Danish folk story. 'I love her tales,' writes the biographer Hilary Spurling, '[…] for their sleek compact build, their buoyancy and precision, the way they ride like ships so easily and lightly on tides of powerful emotion and profound experience. Dinesen's stories, like the visions they contain, are grave, impersonal, intoxicating, at once minutely detailed and almost abstract in their phenomenal intensity.'

Penguin Modern Classics

Karen Blixen
Out of Africa

1954 Penguin Books
1979 Modern Classics

Out of Africa was adapted as a film in 1985, directed by Sydney Pollack and starring Meryl Streep and Robert Redford; it won seven Academy Awards, including Best Film, Best Director and Best Score, by John Barry. The cover of the 1979 edition shows Karen Blixen's own painting of a young Kikuyu girl.

1984
—
The cover shows Karen
Blixen's own portrait of
Abdullahi Ahamed, who
features in the stories.

More FEASTS

The Angelic Avengers 1946

Blixen's only full-length novel is the
story of Lucan and Zosine, two homeless
girls in 19th-century London, who
are taken in by the sinister Reverend
Pennhallow and his wife.

Shadows on the Grass

1950–60, pub. 1960

These four pieces return to Kenya and
characters familiar from Out of Africa
(240). The first three were written in the
1950s; the last, 'Echoes from the Hills',
was written in 1960 for this volume.

Anecdotes of Destiny
and Other Stories 1958

These five witty tales are among the last
to be written by Blixen. They are linked
thematically and formally, with the first
and last stories acting as prologue and
epilogue. The 'effect is the immensely
satisfying one of total inevitability',
wrote the Times Literary Supplement.
The collection includes 'Babette's Feast',
about a mysterious and talented Parisian
woman who is sheltered by a pair
of spinster sisters on the bleak coast
of Jutland in the 19th century. The film
adaptation won the 1987 Academy Award
for Best Film in a Foreign Language.

Ehrengard 1962, pub. 1963

'An old lady told this story,' is the
opening line of Blixen's last novella,
published posthumously. Set in the
Grand Duchy of Babenhausen in the
early 19th century, it is the tale of a
portrait painter besotted with Ehrengard,
maid-of-honour to Princess Ludmilla.
He attempts to seduce her by painting
a portrait of her as Venus bathing.
'Ehrengard is the lightest, the most purely
comic and pastoral story she ever wrote,'
said Robert Langbaum, Blixen's
biographer; '[…] it is unsurpassed
for sheer loveliness.'

1986 Penguin Books
1994 Twentieth-Century
Classics
—
The Angelic Avengers was first
published under the pen name
'Pierre Andrézel'.

1986 Penguin Books
1991 Twentieth-Century
Classics
2013 Modern Classics
*Babette's Feast and Other
Stories*
—

1986 Penguin Books
1998 Twentieth-Century
Classics
● —

2021
trans. Tiina Nunnally
& Michael Favala
Goldman, 1985–2020
—
The Danish title of
Dependency is *Gift*,
which means both
'married' and 'poison'.

Tove Ditlevsen

1917 – 1976

Ditlevsen was born in the working-class district of Vesterbro in Copenhagen. She began writing and publishing poetry at a young age and produced more than 30 celebrated books, including short stories, novels and memoirs. She struggled with alcoholism, however, and an addiction to painkillers. She married and divorced four times, was admitted to several psychiatric hospitals, and took her own life in 1976.

Childhood, Youth, Dependency
The Copenhagen Trilogy
1967 – 71

Ditlevsen wrote this lyrical autobiographical trilogy after a devastating period of depression. The books 'act as a manifesto for art', says John Self in the *New Statesman*, 'showing that literature is not the base metal: it is the process of alchemy, and the gold that results.' In *Childhood* (1967), Ditlevsen describes her claustrophobic upbringing, her intoxicating friend Ruth, her unstable mother, and the gnawing itch that drove her to write poetry. In *Youth* (1967), she is forced to leave school and take a series of menial jobs. As the Second World War breaks around her, she contends with unwelcome sexual advances and Nazi landladies, and finally a miracle occurs: her first book of poetry, *Pigesind* (A Girl's Mind), is published in 1939. In *Dependency* (1971), Ditlevsen is married, 20 years old and already famous for her poetry, but over the ensuing years her literary success is dogged by unequal love affairs, unwanted pregnancies and spiralling addiction.

The Faces 1968

Lise is a writer of children's books; she's a married mother of three; and she's teetering on the brink of madness. She sees cupboards as 'disturbing cavities' and her husband's features seem large and hairy, like an animal's. Ditlevsen wrote this haunting novel after the failure of her own third marriage.

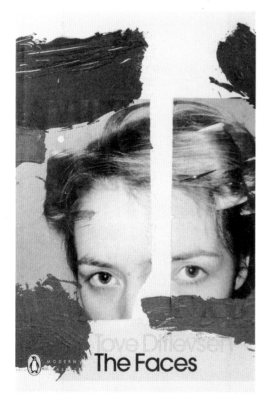

2021
trans.
Tiina Nunnally

CENTRAL EUROPE

Thomas Mann — Little Herr Friedemann and Other Stories

ISBN 0 14
00.3398 X

Thomas Mann — Mario and the Magician and Other Stories

ISBN 0 14
00.3902 3

Thomas Mann · Death in Venice Tristan Tonio Kröger

1082

Thomas Mann — Buddenbrooks

ISBN 0 14
00.1214 1

Thomas Mann — Royal Highness

ISBN 0 14
00.3771 3

Thomas Mann · The Magic Mountain

1475

Thomas Mann Joseph and His Brothers

ISBN 0 14
00.4545 7

Thomas Mann — Lotte in Weimar

2850

Germany

Thomas Mann 1875–1955

The Mann family of Lübeck, in northern Germany, was a dynasty
of prosperous Baltic merchants. Mann's father was the head of
the ancestral firm, but he died when Mann was still a teenager;
the firm was liquidated, and Mann's Brazilian mother moved
the family south to Munich. Mann found work in an insurance
office but, inspired by his older brother Heinrich (250), he tried
his hand at writing and went on to produce a series of masterful
novels, the 'fragments of a great confession'. He was awarded
the Nobel Prize for Literature (576) in 1929. In 1933, when Hitler
came to power, Mann moved his own family to Switzerland,
and then, after his German citizenship was revoked, to the
USA, where he recorded monthly anti-fascist dispatches which
were broadcast to Germany by the BBC. He is 'one of the great
German writers', wrote Malcolm Bradbury,
'the spokesman for a modern humanism'.

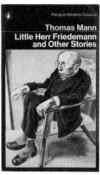

1972 Modern Classics
● trans. H. T. Lowe-Porter, 1961
1993 Twentieth-Century
Classics *Selected Stories*
● trans. David Luke, 1990

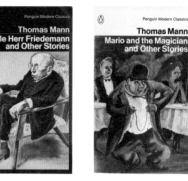

1975
● trans. H. T. Lowe-Porter, 1961
—
Little Herr Friedemann contains
a selection of Mann's earlier
stories, from the period
1896–1912, as does David
Luke's *Selected Stories*. Luke's
edition also includes *Tristan*,
Tonio Kröger and *Death in
Venice*. *Mario and the Magician*
covers Mann's later stories,
written between 1918 and 1953.

Buddenbrooks
The Decline of a Family 1901

Mann published his first novel at the age
of 26. It covers 40 years of the Buddenbrook
family, a Baltic trading dynasty. Drawing
heavily on his own experience, Mann charts
the weakening of the family's prosperity
as younger generations of Buddenbrooks
incline towards the arts rather than
commerce. Mann uses recurring motifs,
inspired by a similar technique in Wagner's
music: images of old houses and rotting
teeth recur throughout the novel. In the
1930s, it was banned and burned by the
Nazis. The *New York Times* called it 'perhaps
the first great
novel of the
20th century'.

1957 Penguin Books
1971 Modern Classics
● trans. H. T. Lowe-Porter, 1924
—
Blanche Knopf, the wife of
the New York publisher Alfred
A. Knopf, met Thomas Mann
and found the translator Helen
Tracy Lowe-Porter to translate
his work. In 1938, it was
Blanche who helped Mann
and his family move to the USA.

Stories 1896–1953

'Little Herr
Friedemann', Mann's
first short story, is
about a solitary, puritanical hunchback
convulsed by sexual passion. Other stories
include 'Gladius Dei', about the conflict
between intellect and beauty, the humorous
'A Man and His Dog', and 'Mario and the
Magician', an open attack on fascism, which
tells the disturbing story of a dangerously
autocratic Italian hypnotist.

Death in Venice
Tristan
Tonio Kröger 1903–12

These three novellas all examine aspects
of the life of the artist. In *Death in Venice*
(1912), the writer Gustave von Aschenbach
becomes tragically obsessed with a beautiful
14-year-old Polish boy called Tadzio, just as a cholera epidemic
sweeps through Venice. Mann developed periodic obsessions with
young boys, including his own son Klaus (256), and this story is based
on an actual trip he made to Venice in 1911, when he became infatuated
with a 10-year-old boy called Władysław 'Adzio' Moes. It was adapted
for the screen by Luchino Visconti in 1971, with Dirk Bogarde in
the starring role, and was the basis of Benjamin Britten's last opera.
Tristan (1903) is about two patients in a Swiss sanatorium, and is based
on the romance of Tristan and Isolde; and *Tonio Kröger* (1903) follows
a solitary writer as he makes a journey in search of his roots.

1955 Penguin Books
1962 Modern Classics
● trans. H. T. Lowe-Porter, 1928

H. T. Lowe-Porter's translation
of *Death in Venice* was
published separately by Penguin
in 1971, the same year that
Visconti's film adaptation was
released. The separate edition
joined Penguin Twentieth-
Century Classics in 1990.

1975
• trans. A. Cecil Curtis, 1916
rev. Constance McNab, 1962

Royal Highness 1909

When His Royal Highness Prince Klaus Heinrich meets the exotic and liberal-minded Miss Spoelmann, she offers him a life beyond his ducal duties.

The Magic Mountain 1924

In 1912, Mann visited a sanatorium in the Swiss Alps with his wife. The experience inspired his masterpiece, this 'dialectic novel', in which young Hans Castorp comes to a Swiss sanatorium for three weeks, to visit his ailing cousin, and stays for seven years. Removed from mundane affairs, the eccentric patients become a rarefied microcosm of Europe's intellectual malaise before the First World War. The enigmatic narrative incorporates myths, fairy tales and magic. It is 'a masterwork, unlike any other', writes A. S. Byatt, '[…] a delight, comic and profound, a new form of language, a new way of seeing'.

1960 Penguin Books
1962 Modern Classics
• trans. H. T. Lowe-Porter, 1928

—

Mann advised those who wished to understand *The Magic Mountain* to read it again.

1978
• trans. H. T. Lowe-Porter, 1934–44

Joseph and His Brothers

The Tales of Jacob, Young Joseph, Joseph in Egypt, Joseph the Provider
1933 – 43

Mann began work on this epic recasting of the biblical story just as he was preparing to go into voluntary exile in Switzerland. The tetralogy describes the exiled Joseph, shunned by his brothers, who achieves success in Egypt and is finally reunited with his family. Mann published the first instalment from Switzerland and the last from Pacific Palisades in Los Angeles.

More MOUNTAINS

The Mountains of My Life
by Walter Bonatti   226

'The Snows of Kilimanjaro'
by Ernest Hemingway   428

The Sound of the Mountain
by Yasunari Kawabata   348

At the Mountains of Madness
by H. P. Lovecraft   417

Solo Faces
by James Salter   508

Lotte in Weimar 1939

Charlotte Kestner, the woman who inspired Goethe's famous novel *The Sorrows of Young Werther* (1774), travels to Weimar to visit the celebrated author 44 years after their youthful romance. Mann recreates the provincial court of the grand duchy, with its theatres, its academies and its ageing polymathic genius.

1968
• trans. H. T. Lowe-Porter, 1940

Doctor Faustus
The Life of the German Composer Adrian Leverkühn as Told by a Friend 1947

The composer Adrian Leverkühn deliberately contracts syphilis so that the associated madness will enhance his artistic inspiration. In his delirium, he strikes a Mephistophelian contract, selling his soul to the Devil in exchange for 24 years of genius.

1968
• trans. H. T. Lowe-Porter, 1949

1961
• trans. H.T. Lowe-Porter, 1952

The Holy Sinner 1951

In this reimagining of the medieval epic poem *Gregorius*, Gregory is the incestuous offspring of a brother and sister, the son and daughter of the Duke of Flanders. Abandoned at sea, he survives and returns like Oedipus to marry his mother, before eventually becoming Pope.

Confessions of Felix Krull, Confidence Man
Memoirs Part I 1954

Felix Krull is a young, good-looking charlatan, the son of a Rhenish producer of poor-quality sparkling wine. He waits on Parisian tables by day, and becomes a man about town at night, seducing the wife of a rich manufacturer of lavatory fittings and wangling his way into an all-expenses-paid round-the-world trip. 'Here is that unheard of, that supposedly impossible thing,' wrote the *Listener*, 'a good German comic novel – a marvellously good one.' Mann intended to produce a second instalment, but he died before it was written.

Letters 1889–1955, pub. 1961–5

Writing an autobiography is 'an impossible task', Mann believed, 'from the point of view of literary tact', so his letters must stand for the memoir he never wrote. This selection evokes Mann's experiences in Germany, Switzerland and America, and includes many incidents and characters that he worked into his novels.

1958 Penguin Books
1962 Modern Classics
• trans. Denver Lindley, 1955

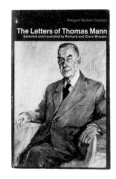

1975
• trans. Richard & Clara Winston, 1970
intro. Richard Winston, 1970

1973 Penguin Books
1982 Modern Classics
• trans. W. J. Strachan, 1961

Hermann Hesse 1877–1962

Hesse was born in the Black Forest, the grandson of missionaries to India. After running away from a strict seminary in Baden-Württemberg, he visited Sri Lanka and Indonesia and lived in Switzerland, where he worked as a bookseller and wrote poetry and novels. During the First World War he volunteered for the Red Cross, and when his frequent bouts of depression grew worse, he underwent psychoanalysis with Josef Lang, a disciple of Carl Jung (262). A committed anti-fascist, Hesse helped Thomas Mann (245) and Bertolt Brecht (255) flee Germany in 1933, and his own books were banned by the Nazis. He won the Nobel Prize for Literature (576) in 1946 and became a favourite of the 1960s counterculture (523).

Peter Camenzind 1904

Hesse's first novel tells the story of a young man, an artist and dreamer, who learns to marshal his abilities and develops a deep love of nature. It was greatly admired by Sigmund Freud (265).

The Prodigy 1905

This is the semi-autobiographical story of a brilliant young boy, Hans Giebenrath, whose spirit is systematically broken first by his parents and then by his strict seminary teachers. The German title is *Unterm Rad* (*Beneath the Wheel*).

1973 Penguin Books
1983 Modern Classics
● trans. W. J. Strachan, 1961

Strange News from Another Star
and Other Stories

1913–18, pub. 1919

These dreamlike stories were published in German under the title *Märchen* (*Fairy Tales*). They describe mystical cities, solitary poets and the nature of love.

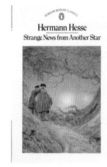

1976 Penguin Books
1983 Modern Classics
● trans. Denver Lindley, 1972

Siddhartha 1922

Set in India, in the 5th century BCE, this is the story of handsome Siddhartha and his spiritual quest for the meaning of life. Siddhartha is not Siddhartha Gautama, who became the Buddha, but he does seek a parallel path. Hesse lived as a semi-recluse while writing the book, immersed in Hindu and Buddhist scriptures and attempting to achieve enlightenment himself.

2008
trans. Hilda Rosner, 1954
intro. Paulo Coelho, 2008
—
'The first time I laid my hands on a copy of *Siddhartha* was back in 1967,' writes Paulo Coelho. 'I was twenty years old and had been committed to an asylum by my parents. [...] I was inside a cell, but my spirit was transported to the dusty paths of India and like Govinda, his best friend, I decided to follow the turmoil of a man eager to find enlightenment.'

Gertrude 1910

The narrator, a composer, recalls his hopeless obsession with the singer Gertrude Imthor and how he managed to draw artistic inspiration from the pain of watching her marry his friend. It has 'a rare flavour of truth and simplicity', wrote Stevie Smith (108).

1974 Penguin Books
1984 Modern Classics
● trans. Hilda Rosner, 1963

Demian 1919

Directly inspired by Hesse's Jungian (262) psychoanalysis, this novel describes Emil Sinclair's split personality. Emil struggles to bridge the gap between the safe, respectable world of his bourgeois parents and the dark world of sensual experience, servants' gossip and ghost stories. He is guided through adolescence by his mysterious friend Max Demian.

2017
trans. W. J. Strachan, 1958

Steppenwolf 1927

Steppe wolves are grey wolves native to central Asia. In this set of hallucinatory notebooks, Harry Haller, a seemingly respectable, educated man, reveals the wolfish side of his own nature: his savage instincts, his sense of alienation and his detestation of the modern world. Hesse wrote the book during a period of isolation, trauma, and estrangement from his second wife.

1965 Modern Classics
● trans. Basil Creighton, 1929
rev. Walter Sorrell, 1963
2012 Modern Classics
trans. David Horrocks, 2012

1972
● trans. Richard and Clara
Winston, 1960

Narziss and Goldmund 1930

In medieval Germany, two young novices become friends in a monastery. Narziss is older and more serious; Goldmund is sunny and childlike and soon realizes that he is not cut out for monastic life. He sets off around medieval Europe in search of the meaning of existence, experiencing sin, plague and war along the way. Many years later, he meets Narziss again. Thomas Mann (245) called this 'a poetic novel unique in its fascination'.

The Glass Bead Game 1943

Hesse's final masterpiece claims to be 'a tentative sketch of the life of Magister Ludi Joseph Knecht together with Knecht's posthumous writings'. Several centuries in the future, the province of Castalia in central Europe is devoted to the education of scholars and the perfection of the intellectual 'Glass Bead Game', an abstract board game that synthesizes all human knowledge and takes a lifetime to master. The novel describes how Knecht eventually becomes Master of the Glass Bead Game, the most exalted office in Castalia. *The Times* called it 'one of the truly important books of the century, in any language'.

1971 Modern Classics
● trans. Geoffrey Dunlop, 1932
2017 Modern Classics
Narcissus and Goldmund
trans. Leila Vennewitz, 1993

Jakob Wassermann

1873 – 1934

Wassermann was born in Fürth, near Nuremberg in Bavaria, the son of a Jewish shopkeeper. After an unhappy childhood, he contributed stories and poems to the satirical literary magazine *Simplicissimus*, before moving to Austria in 1898 and writing novels. He was a friend of Thomas Mann (245) and Rainer Maria Rilke (269), and he lived just long enough to see his books banned and burned by the Nazis.

Caspar Hauser
The Inertia of the Heart 1908

This dark psychological novel is based on the true story of Caspar Hauser, the 17-year-old who was found tottering across a medieval square in Nuremberg in 1828, having spent his whole life locked up by himself in a darkened cell. But was he really the innocent he appeared to be? Was he an unacknowledged prince of the royal house of Baden? Speculation increased after Hauser was stabbed to death by an unknown assassin in 1833, and his story has inspired many artists, including Rainer Maria Rilke (269), Paul Verlaine and Werner Herzog. 'The idea behind *Caspar Hauser* was to show how people of every quality [...] are all without exception utterly dull and utterly helpless when confronted with the phenomenon of innocence,' wrote Wassermann in 1921.

1992
● trans. Michael Hulse

My First Wife 1934

Wassermann married Julie Speyer in 1901; they divorced acrimoniously in 1915. This, his last novel, is a barely fictionalized account of their tempestuous marriage.

2013
trans. Michael Hofmann, 2012

1984
● trans. Ernest Boyd, 1921

Heinrich Mann 1871–1950

Mann was born in the northern city of Lübeck, the older brother of Thomas Mann (245). When the family moved to Munich, he began to write politically engaged, Expressionist (269) novels. He had early success with *Professor Unrat* (1905), later adapted into the film *The Blue Angel* (1930), starring Marlene Dietrich. Mann was an active anti-fascist and in 1933 he fled to France, where he worked on a two-volume historical novel about Henri IV. In 1940, he was captured briefly, but he managed to escape to the USA, where he lived for the rest of his life.

Man of Straw 1918

In *Der Untertan* – literally *The Subject* – Diederich Hessling is the German state's loyal *untertan*, who barges his brutish way through life, embodying the vanities and authoritarian menace of the regime under Kaiser Wilhelm II. The novel is a chilling and prophetic warning against state militarism.

Ernst Jünger

1895–1998

As a teenager who loved insects and adventure novels, Jünger ran away from school and enlisted in the French Foreign Legion. On the first day of the First World War, he volunteered to join the German army as a private. He fought throughout the war: he was promoted to lieutenant, survived several wounds and became the youngest ever recipient of the *Pour le Mérite*, the highest military decoration in the German Empire. He then studied zoology in Leipzig and Naples, with a particular interest in crustaceans, butterflies, weevils, gastropod molluscs and spiders. Frequently quoted by the Nazis, Jünger was nonetheless obliquely critical of the Third Reich. He spent most of the Second World War as a captain in the German army, stationed in Paris, drinking at Maxim's and chatting to Jean Cocteau (178) and Pablo Picasso. After the war, he wrote magical realist (563) novels and experimented with drugs, taking LSD with its inventor, Albert Hofmann. He died at the age of 102.

Storm of Steel 1920, rev. 1961

Based on Jünger's diaries, *In Stahlgewittern* was one of the earliest personal accounts of trench warfare. He describes arriving at the Champagne front, fighting on the Somme and at Arras and Ypres, and leading a company of assault troops in the 1918 Spring Offensive, when he earned the *Pour le Mérite*. He evokes not only the horrors of war but also its revelatory qualities and describes moments of ecstatic clarity. 'Without question the finest book on war that I know,' wrote André Gide (164) in his diary: 'utterly honest, truthful, in good faith.'

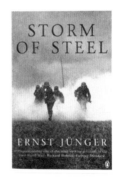

2004
trans. Michael Hofmann, 2003
—
Jünger printed the first edition of 2,000 copies himself: the apparent 'publisher', Robert Meier, was in fact his family gardener. Michael Hofmann's translation of the definitive 1961 edition won the 2004 Oxford-Weidenfeld Translation Prize.

1970
● trans. Stuart Hood, 1947
intro. George Steiner, 1970
—
'A "twentieth-century classic"?' asked the critic George Steiner. 'Perhaps so. And in an almost mathematical sense. *On the Marble Cliffs* is a theorem of limitation. It enacts the precise incommensurability between a certain cast of abstract humanism or high civilization and the realities of modern terror.'

On the Marble Cliffs 1939

In this prescient parable, an idyllic agricultural society of botanists and philosophers is gradually destroyed when the 'Foresters of the Campagne', led by the jovial Chief Ranger, establish a dictatorship based on violence, torture and death camps. 'When all buildings shall be destroyed, language will none the less persist,' wrote Jünger in 1943. 'It will be a magic castle with towers and battlements, with primeval vaults and passageways which none will ever search out. There, in deep galleries, *oubliettes* and mine-shafts it will be possible to find habitation and be lost to the world. Today that thought consoles me.'

Walter Benjamin 1892 – 1940

Born into an intellectual Jewish family in Berlin – his uncle William devised the IQ intelligence quotient – Benjamin feigned illness in order to avoid conscription during the First World War and continue working on his translation of Baudelaire. He then made a precarious living as a literary critic, translator and freelance essayist, with an interest in aesthetic theories and historical materialism. He befriended Rainer Maria Rilke (269) and Bertolt Brecht (255), and became associated with the philosopher Theodor Adorno and the 'Frankfurt School' of critical theory. When the Nazis came to power in 1933, however, Benjamin fled to Paris, where he met Hannah Arendt (258) and Hermann Hesse (247), became a prominent critic of Hitler's regime and worked on his magnum opus, *The Arcades Project*, an immense study of 19th-century Parisian life. When Germany invaded France in 1940, Benjamin gave the unfinished manuscript to Georges Bataille (176) and attempted to flee to the USA via Spain and Portugal. At the border town of Portbou, Spanish officials barred his entry, and he died after taking an overdose of morphine tablets. 'There has been no more original, no more serious critic and reader in our time,' wrote the philosopher George Steiner.

2008 Great Ideas *The Work of Art in the Age of Mechanical Reproduction*
2009 Modern Classics
trans. J. A. Underwood, 2008–9
intro. Amit Chaudhuri, 2009
—
Underwood's translations of 'The Work of Art in the Age of Mechanical Reproduction' and Benjamin's essays on Kafka and Proust originally appeared in the Penguin Great Ideas (xvii) edition, which was expanded for the Modern Classics selection.

One-Way Street and Other Writings 1921 – 35

These essays demonstrate Benjamin's inventive critical ability and his poetic use of language: 'One-Way Street' presents a series of aphoristic observations on urban life; 'Unpacking my Library' is a meditation on book-collecting; and the seminal 'The Work of Art in the Age of Mechanical Reproduction' argues that technology damages the 'aura' of an original work of art. Also included are essays on Proust (166), Kafka (280), violence, and Surrealism (176). 'His major essays seem to end just in time,' wrote Susan Sontag (524), 'before they self-destruct.'

Hans Fallada 1893 – 1947

As a child, Rudolf Ditzen was severely injured by a horse, an accident that initiated a life of depression and substance abuse. As a teenager, he attempted a double suicide with a fellow homosexual and was placed in a psychiatric institution. He worked on farms in order to fund an addiction to morphine and spent several years in prison for embezzling funds. When he began writing, he chose a pseudonym based on two Brothers Grimm fairy tales: 'Hans' is from 'Hans in Luck', and the magical talking horse in 'The Goose Girl' is called 'Falada'. Fallada remained in Germany during the Second World War and was committed to a Nazi insane asylum. This led to a relapse into drug and alcohol abuse and he died soon after the war from an overdose of morphine.

2013
trans. Michael Hofmann, 2012
fwd. Jenny Williams, 2012

2014
trans. Michael Hofmann, 2011–14
fwd. Jenny Williams, 2014

Tales from the Underworld
Selected Shorter Fiction
1925 – 46

This selection spans Fallada's career, from his first published story, 'The Wedding Ring', to one of his last, 'The Old Flame', published just three months before his death. They are stark, streetwise tales of desperation, addiction and love.

A Small Circus 1931

Between 1928 and 1930, Fallada worked for an ailing local newspaper in the small provincial town of Neumünster in Schleswig-Holstein, an experience that inspired his first successful novel. In *Bauern, Bonzen und Bomben* (literally *Peasants, Bosses and Bombs*), small-time journalists become embroiled in blackmail, as workers plot against bosses and communists fight Nazis in the streets. It is 'one of the best fictional representations of the forces that brought the Weimar Republic to its knees and paved the way for National Socialism', writes Fallada's biographer, Jenny Williams.

2019
trans. Michael Hofmann

Little Man, What Now? 1932

A young couple, Johannes 'Boy' Pinneberg and Emma 'Lämmchen' Mörschel, fall in love, marry and start a family. But this is the time of the Great Depression, and National Socialism is on the rise. They find themselves struggling against inflation, unemployment, unpaid bills and Nazi street fighters. Published just before Hitler came to power, this is the novel that made Fallada's reputation. 'Fallada deserves high praise,' wrote Hermann Hesse (247), 'for having reported so realistically, so truthfully, with such closeness to life.'

2012
trans. Eric Sutton, 1934
rev. Nicholas Jacobs, Gardis Cramer von Laue & Linden Lawson, 2012
aftwd. Jenny Williams, 2012

Once a Jailbird 1934

Willi Kufult is released from prison, but will he ever be truly free? He tries to make a new life for himself in Hamburg but he soon finds himself sucked back into a seedy underworld of drink, deceit and desperation.

Iron Gustav
A Berlin Family Chronicle 1938

Gustav Hackendahl runs a successful coach business, which he inherited from his father-in-law. Known as 'Iron Gustav', he dominates his family with unyielding discipline until the First World War, when his children start to slip from his grasp. Fallada wrote this poignant family chronicle with a film adaptation in mind. It is based on the life of Gustav Hartmann, a real Berlin cabman famous for driving from Berlin to Paris.

2014
trans. Philip Owens, 1940
rev. Nicholas Jacobs & Gardis Cramer von Laue, 2014
fwd. Jenny Williams, 2014

—

Before *Iron Gustav* was first published, Joseph Goebbels, the Reichsminister for Propaganda, intervened personally and insisted on a revised ending, in which Hackendahl becomes an ardent Nazi. Reluctantly, Fallada capitulated. In 1940, Putnam published an English translation of the German novel in London – a remarkable decision during the war – which used Fallada's original ending, though with several major cuts. In 1962, the editor Günter Caspar reconstructed Fallada's original text in German, and the 2014 Penguin edition reinstates excisions from the 1940 translation.

Alone in Berlin 1947

In 1940, an ordinary German couple, Otto and Anna Quangel, embark on a subversive act of resistance. They start to write thousands of anonymous postcards, attacking Hitler and his regime, and they drop them around Berlin, blanketing the city with anti-Nazi propaganda. Their campaign comes to the attention of the Gestapo's Inspector Escherich and a deadly game of cat-and-mouse ensues. Primo Levi (222) called it 'the greatest book ever written about the German resistance'. Fallada wrote *Jeder Stirbt für Sich Allein* (*Every Man Dies Alone*) in 24 days, while recuperating in a mental institution. It is based on the real case of Otto and Elise Hampel, whose Gestapo file was passed to Fallada by his friend, the poet Johannes R. Becher, who later became cultural minister in East Germany's post-war government. On completion, Fallada told his family he had finally written 'a great novel'; he died a few months later, only weeks before it was published.

2010
trans. Michael Hofmann, 2009
aftwd. Geoff Wilkes, 2009

—

The Penguin edition includes material from the Hampels' Gestapo file, including images of the actual postcards they left around Berlin.

More RESISTANCE

1986
• trans. Eric Sutton, 1928

Arnold Zweig 1887–1968

Zweig was a German Jewish intellectual who studied at the universities of Breslau, Munich, Berlin, Göttingen, Rostock and Tübingen. He volunteered for the army in the First World War, serving as a private soldier in France, Hungary and Serbia. He then became a pacifist and Zionist, editing the *Jüdische Rundschau* (*Jewish Review*) magazine in Berlin until 1933, when his manuscripts were confiscated and his books condemned. He spent time with Thomas Mann (245) in France before migrating to Palestine, where he befriended Max Brod (280). He returned to East Germany in 1948 and became a Member of Parliament, a delegate to the World Peace Council Congresses and President of the Academy of Arts. He was awarded the Lenin (299) Peace Prize in 1958.

The Case of Sergeant Grischa 1927

Sergeant Grischa Paprotkin is a Russian soldier in the First World War who escapes from a German prison camp. When he adopts the identity of a dead soldier, however, he discovers that he has taken the name of a Russian deserter and he is arrested again as a spy. It is 'the greatest novel on a war theme', wrote J. B. Priestley (87), '[…] from any country'.

Alfred Döblin 1878–1957

Bruno Alfred Döblin was born in the Baltic city of Stettin, now Szczecin in Poland. His father was a tailor who eloped with a seamstress when Döblin was ten years old. His mother then moved the family to Berlin, where he lived for the next 45 years, working as a doctor and a psychiatrist, contributing to the Expressionist (269) journal *Der Sturm* (*The Storm*) and writing novels, science fiction stories, essays, radio plays and philosophical treatises. He was a friend of Thomas Mann (245), Bertolt Brecht (255), Joseph Roth (273), Arthur Koestler (278) and Robert Musil (270). He fled Germany in 1933, moving first to France and then Los Angeles. 'He'll discomfort you,' wrote Günter Grass, 'give you bad dreams. If you're satisfied with yourself, beware of Döblin.'

Alfred Döblin
Berlin Alexanderplatz

1978 Penguin Books
1982 Modern Classics
• trans. Eugene Jolas, 1931
2019 Modern Classics
trans. Michael Hofmann, 2018

—

Eugene Jolas, who made the first English translation of *Berlin Alexanderplatz* in 1931, was a friend of James Joyce (8).

Berlin Alexanderplatz 1929

The murderer Franz Biberkopf is released from prison and back on to the streets of Berlin. Determined to go straight, he is ineluctably drawn back to the working-class district around the Alexanderplatz and to the murky underworld of pimps and thugs that he hoped to escape. Hailed by critics as 'Europe's *Moby-Dick*' and 'the counterpart to *Ulysses* (10)', this great Expressionist novel (269) is a dazzling literary montage that depicts the German capital through multiple points of view, sound effects, newspaper reports, Bible stories, drinking songs and urban slang. In 1980, it was adapted by Rainer Werner Fassbinder into a fourteen-part, fifteen-hour film. 'I learned more about the essence of the epic from Döblin than from anyone else,' wrote Brecht (255). 'His epic writing and even his theory about the epic strongly influenced my own dramatic art.'

Exilliteratur

When Hitler's Nazi Party won the parliamentary election in 1933, many German authors left the country. More German-language writers followed in 1938 when Austria was annexed during the *Anschluss* and freedom of the press was abolished in Germany. These émigré authors wrote anti-Nazi literature that has come to be known collectively as *Exilliteratur*. They include Hannah Arendt (258), Bertolt Brecht (255), Hermann Broch (272), Elias Canetti (328), Alfred Döblin, Hermann Hesse (247), Heinrich Mann (250), Klaus Mann (256), Thomas Mann (245), Robert Musil (270), Joseph Roth (273), Franz Werfel (273), Arnold Zweig and Stefan Zweig (271).

Irmgard Keun 1905–1982

'Irmgard Keun had a very special relationship with the facts of her life,' writes her long-suffering biographer, Hiltrud Häntzschel: 'sometimes she was straightforward, sometimes reckless, sometimes inventive because she longed for success, sometimes wilfully inventive, sometimes necessarily dishonest.' Keun seems to have grown up in Cologne, where she trained as an actress, but she gave up acting at sixteen and turned to writing, encouraged by Alfred Döblin (253). Her first two novels were instant bestsellers, but the Nazis blacklisted her in 1933. She attempted to sue the Gestapo for loss of earnings before leaving both Germany and her Nazi-supporting husband in 1936. She spent the next two years travelling around Europe with the writer Joseph Roth (273), who died in 1939. When her suicide was erroneously reported in 1940, Keun managed to smuggle herself back into Germany, spending the rest of the war living in Cologne under a false name. Afterwards she wrote satirical pieces for magazines and raised her daughter. She suffered increasingly from alcoholism and spent six years on a psychiatric ward before being 'rediscovered' by *Stern* magazine in 1977.

2019
trans. Geoff Wilkes, 2013

Gilgi, One of Us 1931

Keun's first novel was an instant success. Gilgi is a young, ambitious woman, who manages to negotiate the workplace and her male colleagues, but finds herself falling for the feckless Martin. 'Gilgi' entered the language of Weimar Germany as a term for a modern young woman, and a film adaptation was produced in 1932.

2019
trans. Kathie von Ankum, 2002

The Artificial Silk Girl 1932

Keun's second novel was an even greater success than her first. Doris moves to Berlin, dressed in dazzling rayon and determined to become a film star; but instead of fame she finds hunger, squalor and exploitative men.

Child of All Nations 1938

Kully is a child whose father has written the wrong things about Germany. As a result, the family is forced to move around Europe, chasing visas, staying in hotels, racking up bills and facing greater and greater hardship. Narrated from Kully's point of view and drawing heavily on Keun's own experiences with Joseph Roth (273), this is her bittersweet masterpiece. 'A truly great read,' writes Ali Smith – 'funny and deft, heartening and terrible.'

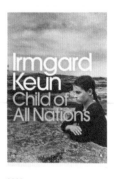

2009
trans. Michael Hofmann, 2008

After Midnight 1937

Frankfurt is in uproar on the day that Hitler comes to visit, but nineteen-year-old Sanna has her own problems: her best friend Gerti is in love with a Jewish boy, her brother's books have been blacklisted, and her own aunt may denounce her to the authorities at any moment.

2020
trans. Anthea Bell, 1985

Ferdinand, the Man with the Kind Heart 1950

Keun's last novel, the only one set in post-war Germany, is a portrait of bombed-out Cologne, where people steal eggcups from half-destroyed houses and the black-market trade in jam and corsets is brisk. Recently released from a prisoner-of-war camp, Ferdinand drifts around the city, avoiding his fiancée, drinking brandy and dispensing free advice.

2021
trans. Michael Hofmann

New Objectivity

In the 1920s and 1930s, a new movement emerged in German art and literature, known as the 'Neue Sachlichkeit'. The New Objectivity was a reaction against Expressionism (269) and a response to a highly turbulent political period. The movement aimed to produce works of emotionless reportage, with precise details and straightforward language. Examples include Hans Fallada's *Little Man, What Now?* (252), Irmgard Keun's *The Artificial Silk Girl* (254) and Bertolt Brecht's development of 'epic' theatre.

Bertolt Brecht 1898–1956

Eugen Berthold Friedrich Brecht studied natural science and philosophy in Munich and Berlin, before working as a medical orderly in a military sexual-health clinic during the First World War. He wrote his first play, *Baal*, in 1918 and went on to write 39 more. In the 1920s, he was the dramaturge at the Munich Kammerspiele and then the Deutsches Theater in Berlin. In 1928, he wrote and staged an adaptation of John Gay's 18th-century *Beggar's Opera*. *The Threepenny Opera*, with music by Kurt Weill, became the greatest theatrical success of the Weimar Republic. At about the same time, he converted to Marxism and developed his concept of 'epic' or 'dialectical' theatre, a key element of which is the *Verfremdungseffekt*, the technique of distancing the audience through alienation devices, reminding spectators that they are watching a play and forcing them to think about, react to and act on what they are seeing. When the Nazis came to power in 1933, Brecht fled first to Denmark and later to California. In 1949, he returned to East Germany and founded the Berliner Ensemble, which he managed for the rest of his life. He was a prolific poet and an enthusiastic guitarist.

Threepenny Novel 1934

Following the success of *The Threepenny Opera* on stage, Brecht turned it into a novel. Both versions tell the bitingly satirical story of Polly Peachum, Jenny and the deadly MacHeath – 'Mackie the Knife' – set in a sordid, early 20th-century London riven by crooked deals and ruinous capitalism. The novel is explicitly Marxist, in some places borrowing directly from *Das Kapital* (1867–94). '[Brecht] draws the epochs together and billets his gangster type in a London that has the rhythm and appearance of the age of Dickens,' wrote Brecht's friend Walter Benjamin in his seminal essay on the novel. '[…] These Londoners have no telephones but their police already have tanks.'

1961 Penguin Books
1965 Modern Classics
• trans. Desmond I. Vesey & Christopher Isherwood, 1937
—
Christopher Isherwood (103) translated the verse sections of *Threepenny Novel*.

Parables for the Theatre

The Good Woman of Setzuan,
The Caucasian Chalk Circle
1943–8

1966 Penguin Plays
1987 Modern Classics
2007 Modern Classics *as individual titles* trans. Eric Bentley, 1948, 1966

Brecht wrote these plays while exiled in California. Both demonstrate his principles of 'epic' theatre and both are about solitary women fighting to retain their humanity. In *The Good Woman of Setzuan* (1943), a young prostitute, Shen Te, struggles to remain honest and generous in pre-communist China. When the gods grant her a tobacco shop, she is forced to invent an intimidating male alter ego in order to protect herself. *The Caucasian Chalk Circle* (1948) is inspired by a 14th-century Chinese play: in the Georgian Caucasus, the peasant Grusha adopts her exiled employer's baby son and proves herself a better mother than the boy's natural parents.

Klaus Mann 1906–1949

Klaus Heinrich Thomas Mann, known as 'Eissi', was the second child of Thomas Mann (245). Klaus was always close to his older sister Erika, and in 1924 they performed in his first play, *Anja and Esther*, alongside Gustaf Gründgens and their childhood friend Pamela Wedekind, daughter of the playwright Frank Wedekind. Erika married Gustaf in 1926, despite his being gay; Mann, also gay, was briefly engaged to Pamela. He published his first novel in 1925 and became increasingly addicted to opium, morphine and later heroin. Deprived of German citizenship by the Nazis, he fled to Amsterdam and then Princeton, New Jersey, becoming a US citizen in 1943. He died in 1949 from an overdose of sleeping pills.

1983 Penguin Books
1995 Twentieth-Century Classics
trans. Robin Smyth, 1977

Mephisto 1936

Mann's best-known novel is a thinly disguised portrait of his former brother-in-law, Gustaf Gründgens, whom his older sister Erika divorced in 1929. Exactly like Gründgens, the protagonist renounces his communist past when the Nazis come to power and he impresses Field Marshal Hermann Göring with his uncanny performance as Mephistopheles in Goethe's *Faust*. He is appointed director of the State Theatre, lives in a castle-like villa and becomes the leader of theatrical life in the Third Reich; but eventually the moral consequences come to haunt him and turn his fantasy of fame into a nightmare. Mann wrote the novel in order to 'analyse the abject type of treacherous intellectual who prostitutes his talent for the sake of some tawdry fame and transitory wealth'.

Anne Frank 1929–1945

Annelies Marie Frank was born in Frankfurt to a middle-class German Jewish family. She was four years old when the Nazis came to power and the family fled first to Aachen on the Dutch border and then to Amsterdam. When Germany invaded the Netherlands in May 1940, the Jewish community found themselves increasingly persecuted through discriminatory laws and mandatory registration. In 1941, the Franks were stripped of their German citizenship, and in July 1942 Anne's sister Margot received a summons to a labour camp. At that point, Anne and her family went into hiding in the *Achterhuis*, a secret annexe behind a moveable bookcase in her father Otto's office building. They lived there for two years, sheltered by Otto Frank's employees, and sharing the small set of rooms with the van Pels family: an anxious and traumatic experience that Anne recorded in detail in her diary. On 4 August 1944, all eight inhabitants were arrested and put on the last transport to Auschwitz, where Anne was forced to haul rocks. In October, bald and emaciated, she was moved to Bergen-Belsen concentration camp with Margot, where they both died in a typhus epidemic, four months before Anne's sixteenth birthday and less than two months before the camp was liberated. In 1960, the Anne Frank House opened in Amsterdam, allowing visitors to see the offices and annexe rooms, which still display photographs of film stars that Anne pinned to the wall.

The Diary of a Young Girl →
The Definitive Edition
1942–4, pub. 1947, rev. 1995

'I hope I will be able to confide everything to you, as I have never been able to confide in anyone, and I hope you will be a great source of comfort and support,' wrote Frank on 12 June 1942: the first entry in her new diary, bound in red-and-white chequered cloth, which was a birthday present. Writing in Dutch, addressing a fictional friend 'Kitty', Anne describes her girlfriends, riding her bicycle and flirting with boys before the family goes into hiding, after which she records the anxious weeks, months and years, the family tensions, the horse chestnut tree outside the window and the BBC reports of Jews being sent to gas chambers. The last diary entry is dated 1 August 1944, three days before the family were arrested. Otto Frank's secretary rescued the manuscript and after the war she gave it to him; he was the only member of the family to survive. Anne Frank's diary has now been read by tens of millions of people. 'Of the multitude who throughout history have spoken for human dignity in times of great suffering and loss,' said President John F. Kennedy, 'no voice is more compelling than that of Anne Frank.'

ANNE FRANK

The Diary of a Young Girl

1997 Twentieth-
Century Classics
Definitive Edition
2019 Penguin Classics
ed. Otto H. Frank
& Mirjam Pressler,
1947, 1995
trans. Susan Massotty,
1995
intro. Elie Wiesel (325),
1997
—

There are three 'texts'
of Anne's diary:
her original entries;
edited entries that
she prepared in 1944
in the hopes of future
publication; and
Otto Frank's 1947
amalgamation of
the two, from which
he omitted material
relating to Anne's
emerging sexuality,
her feelings for young
Peter van Pels and her
difficult relationship
with her mother.
A Dutch 'critical
edition' of all three
texts was published in
1986, on which Susan
Massotty's 'definitive'
translation is based.
In May 2018, some
new pages were
discovered, previously
obscured with brown
paper, which record
some smutty jokes that
Anne had overheard.
The cover of the 1997
Penguin edition shows
a detail of what was
probably the last
photograph of Anne,
taken in 1942.

Rubble Literature and Gruppe 47

Trümmerliteratur is a loose term for literature that emerged in the immediate aftermath of the Second World War, when German homes and ideals lay in ruins. Representative authors include Heinz Rein, Heinrich Böll and Wolfgang Borchert, whose works tend to describe the destruction without attempting evaluation or judgement. At the same time, a group of German-language writers established Gruppe 47. This was an organization aimed at the renewal of German literature, promoting young writers and discussing literary criticism. In 1950, the group instigated the Gruppe 47 Prize, won at various times by Heinrich Böll, Günter Grass and Ingeborg Bachmann (275). Other writers involved with the group include Paul Celan (325) and Peter Handke (274). Their last conference was held in 1967.

Heinz Rein 1906–1991

Rein was a bank clerk who wrote novels and sports reports as a sideline. In 1934, the Nazis banned him from writing, because of his political views, and during the Second World War he was forced to work on the German National Railway. After the war, he became a leading writer of 'Rubble Literature' and an employee of the state's cultural advisory board for publishing in East Germany. In the 1950s, he moved to the West and lived in Baden-Baden until his death.

2019
trans. Shaun Whiteside

Berlin Finale 1947

In April 1945, in the chaotic last days of the Nazi regime, a small band of Resistance fighters gathers while Gestapo officers continue to hunt for traitors. This novel was one of the first German bestsellers after the war. The thriller writer Lee Child calls it 'a wonderful rediscovery […] human, suspenseful, shot through with hard-earned wisdom'.

Hannah Arendt 1906–1975

Johanna Arendt was raised in Königsberg, now Kaliningrad, the child of wealthy German Jews. At the University of Marburg, she was taught by the philosopher Martin Heidegger, with whom she had a brief affair. In 1929, she married Günther Stern, a fellow pupil of Heidegger and Walter Benjamin's (251) first cousin, and she began researching anti-Semitic propaganda for the Zionist Federation of Germany. In 1933, she was denounced, and arrested and briefly imprisoned by the Gestapo. She fled over the mountains to Czechoslovakia, and then to Switzerland, where she worked for the League of Nations, helping Jewish refugee children migrate to Palestine. In 1937, she was stripped of her German citizenship and she divorced Stern; three years later, she married the Marxist philosopher Heinrich Blücher. When Germany invaded France, Arendt was detained in a French internment camp as an 'enemy alien', but she escaped with Blücher to New York, via Portugal, and was made an American citizen in 1950. She became a close friend of Mary McCarthy (507) and worked as the research director of the Conference on Jewish Relations, executive director of Jewish Cultural Reconstruction in New York City, chief editor of Schocken Books and as a visiting professor of several universities.

The Origins of Totalitarianism 1951

Arendt's masterpiece is structured as three essays on 'Antisemitism', 'Imperialism' and 'Totalitarianism'. She discusses the root conditions that lay behind the Nazi and Soviet totalitarian regimes, examining their use of propaganda, scapegoats, terror and political isolation. She describes totalitarianism as a 'novel form of government' that 'differs essentially from other forms of political oppression'. The *New York Times* called *The Origins of Totalitarianism* 'a non-fiction bookend to *Nineteen Eighty-Four* (84)'.

2017
—

Eichmann in Jerusalem
A Report on the Banality of Evil 1963, rev. 1964

On 11 April 1961, SS-Obersturmbannführer Adolf Eichmann, one of the chief organizers of the Holocaust, was brought to trial in Jerusalem. Attending as a reporter for the *New Yorker* magazine, Arendt was struck by Eichmann's appearance as a balding bureaucrat. He was 'terribly and terrifyingly normal', she realized, and Eichmann's bland demeanour gave rise to her famous phrase, 'the banality of evil'. Her report was controversial, however, as it was seen by some to diminish the monstrosity of Nazi crimes. Others have seen it as an unflinching attempt to understand 'the greatest problem of our time', as the psychologist and concentration-camp survivor Bruno Bettelheim put it, '[…] the problem of the human being within a modern totalitarian system'.

1977 Penguin Books
1994 Twentieth-Century Classics
2006 Penguin Classics intro. Amos Elon, 2006

On Revolution 1963, rev. 1965

Arendt compares the 'failed' French Revolution with the 'successful' American Revolution in this classic analysis. She examines the principles that underlie all revolutions and prophesies changes to international relations that will make revolutions increasingly important.

1973 Pelican Books
1990 Twentieth-Century Classics
● —

Wolfgang Koeppen 1906–1996

Koeppen was born in Greifswald, on the Baltic coast, before working as a writer and journalist in Berlin and the Netherlands. He returned to Germany in 1939 to work as a scriptwriter and settled in Munich in 1943. He is best remembered for his loose trilogy of mordant post-war novels: *Pigeons on the Grass* (1951), *The Hothouse* (1953) and *Death in Rome*. He was a friend of Günter Grass and won the Georg Büchner Prize in 1962.

Death in Rome 1954

Four members of a German family meet by chance in Rome: Siegfried Pfaffrath, a composer; Siegfried's estranged father, an ex-Nazi administrator; Siegfried's uncle, a former SS general; and Siegfried's renegade cousin, who is preparing to enter the Catholic priesthood. Representing music, bureaucracy, murder and religion, each family member tells his story, in a collective examination of the Holocaust, German national guilt and the conflict between generations. The ending parodies Thomas Mann's *Death in Venice* (245).

1994
● trans. Michael Hofmann, 1992
—
Hofmann's translation was the joint winner of the 1993 Schlegel-Tieck Prize. He includes an acknowledgement to 'Joseph Brodsky (316), for the gift of a Mussolini T-shirt, in which I did as much of the work as was decently possible'.

Werner Heisenberg 1901–1976

Heisenberg studied physics at the University of Munich and wrote his doctoral dissertation on turbulence in fluid streams. He went on to study atomic physics under Niels Bohr in Copenhagen. Heisenberg was the pioneer of quantum mechanics: in 1925, he published a breakthrough paper on the 'quantum-theoretical reinterpretation of kinetic and mechanical relationships', and then a paper in 1927 on his famous 'uncertainty principle'. In 1932, he was awarded the Nobel Prize in Physics 'for the creation of quantum mechanics'. When the Second World War broke out, he was a professor at the University of Leipzig. Despite some attacks from Nazi propagandists, he was appointed director of the Kaiser Wilhelm Institute for Physics in Berlin in 1942. After the war, he became director of the Max Planck Institute for Physics and Astrophysics.

Physics and Philosophy
The Revolution in Modern Science
1955–6, pub. 1962

Heisenberg's Gifford Lectures at St Andrews University were later published under this title. They present his first-hand account of the quantum revolution, and pose profound philosophical questions about the nature of reality. It is 'a book which every scientist, every person interested in the history of ideas, will find profitable and enjoyable', wrote *Science* magazine.

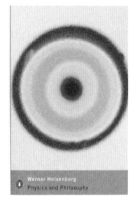

1989 Pelican Books
1990 Penguin Books
2000 Modern Classics
intro. Paul Davies, 1989
—
Physics and Philosophy 'carries the reader', writes the distinguished physicist Paul Davies, 'with remarkable clarity, from the esoteric world of atomic physics to the world of people, language and the conception of our shared reality'.

Sybille Bedford 1911–2006

Sybille von Schoenebeck was born in Charlottenburg, near Berlin. She was raised first by her aristocratic art-collector father in Schloss Feldkirch, in Baden-Württemberg, then by her Jewish mother in Italy and on the south coast of France, where she befriended Thomas Mann (245), Bertolt Brecht (255) and Aldous Huxley (65). After publishing an article in 1933 criticizing the Nazi regime, she married and divorced a gay Englishman, Walter Bedford, in order to obtain a British passport. She spent the Second World War in California with the Huxleys, and subsequently lived in France, Italy, Britain and Portugal, writing semi-autobiographical novels in English and pursuing a number of same-sex relationships. She settled in London in 1979. The travel writer Bruce Chatwin called her 'one of the most dazzling practitioners of modern English prose' and listed her 'three inseparable passions [...] writing, friendship and the finest claret'.

1964 Penguin Books
1999 Twentieth-Century Classics
intro. Sybille Bedford, 1999

A Legacy 1956

'I spent the first nine years of my life in Germany, bundled to and fro between two houses,' is the opening line of this novel. It describes the overlapping worlds and unlikely marriage of the eccentric aristocratic aesthete Julius von Felden and the urbane Jewish heiress Melanie Merz, told from their daughter's perspective. Nancy Mitford (117) called it 'one of the very best novels I've ever read'. 'New, cool, witty, elegant,' was Evelyn Waugh's (67) assessment. '[...] We salute a new artist.'

A Favourite of the Gods 1963

A lovely but unscrupulous American heiress marries a young and naïve Roman prince. V. S. Pritchett (110) called it 'a statement of what Henry James either did not or would not know about the darker side of the portrait of the lady (398). Bedford's mind is radiant. Her alarming economy of style burns.'

2000
• intro. Sybille Bedford

2000
• intro. Sybille Bedford

A Compass Error 1968

In this sequel to *A Favourite of the Gods*, the protagonists' granddaughter, Flavia, hopes to win a place at Oxford, write great novels and fall in love.

Jigsaw
An Unsentimental Education
A Biographical Novel 1989

Following on from the semi-autobiographical *A Legacy* (260), *Jigsaw* is inspired by Bedford's experiences living near Aldous Huxley (65) in southern France, with a mother who was becoming increasingly addicted to morphine. '*Jigsaw* is my fourth novel and, I very much fear, my last,' she wrote in 1999. 'I finished it over ten years ago – a long time that went quickly, in idleness, in pleasures, in much private grief. The decade before, a good chunk of it, went into gathering the strength of mind to shape, reshape and finally write this novel with two sub-titles'. John Fowles called it 'a deliciously evoked return to worlds, and a Europe, now almost vanished; it will ravish connoisseurs of the lost'.

1990 Penguin Books
1999 Twentieth-Century Classics
• intro. Sybille Bedford, 1999

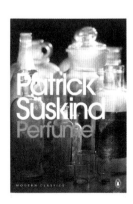

2005
trans. Leigh Hafrey, 1983
intro. Ian McEwan, 2005

Peter Schneider b. 1940

Schneider was born in Lübeck. In the 1960s, he became a spokesperson and organizer of the 68er-Bewegung, the student protest movement that hoped to found a new proletarian political party in West Germany. His novel *Lenz* (1973) is now a cult text for the German left and he has taught at Stanford, Princeton and Harvard universities.

The Wall Jumper 1982

Werner Herzog has called *The Wall Jumper* the 'ultimate depiction' of the Berlin Wall, which physically and ideologically divided the city from 1961 until 1989. 'Nothing more need be said.' The book portrays residents of the divided community, all of whom become 'wall jumpers' in different ways.

Patrick Süskind b. 1949

Süskind's father was a close friend of Klaus Mann (256). After studying medieval and modern history in Munich, Süskind moved to Paris and began writing. *The Pigeon* (1988), his second novel, is about a man trapped in his Paris apartment by a bird. Süskind now lives as a recluse; he refuses to grant interviews or have his photograph taken.

Perfume The Story of a Murderer 1985

Jean-Baptiste Grenouille is an orphan, abandoned in the foulest district of 18th-century Paris, who discovers that he has a superhuman sense of smell. He uses his talent to create the most sublime perfumes, but his olfactory ambitions become increasingly macabre. The book became an overnight international bestseller.

1987 King Penguin
2006 Red Classics
2007 Modern Classics
trans. John E. Woods, 1986

Switzerland

C.G. Jung 1875–1961

Carl Gustav Jung began his career as a research scientist at the Burghölzli psychiatric hospital in Zürich. He contacted Sigmund Freud (265) and the two began a lively correspondence and intellectual collaboration. When they first met in Vienna, they spoke without a break for thirteen hours. In 1910, Freud secured Jung's appointment as president of the new International Psychoanalytical Association, but they began to differ over

1991
• ed. William McGuire, 1974
trans. Ralph Manheim &
R.F.C. Hull, 1974
abridged Alan McGlashan,
1979

their interpretation of the libido (268), and Jung later regretted that his publication of *Psychology of the Unconscious* in 1912 'cost me my friendship with Freud'. Unable to reconcile their differences, they met for the last time in September 1913. During the First World War, Jung worked as the commandant of an internment camp for British soldiers. Afterwards he continued his private practice, travelling widely and writing books that set out his analytical psychology, a key concept of which is the 'collective unconscious', a pool of common stories and archetypes.

The Freud/Jung Letters 1906–14, pub. 1974
The Correspondence between Sigmund Freud and C.G. Jung

These 360 letters, spanning eight years, document the establishment of psychoanalysis in Vienna and Zürich and trace the intense growth and violent rupture of a personal and intellectual friendship between two very different men. 'There is only one word for this correspondence: overwhelming,' wrote Cyril Connolly (107). 'It is as if Voltaire and Rousseau, or Lenin (299) and Trotsky (322) had written to each other every day.'

Robert Walser 1878–1956

Walser grew up in Biel/Bienne, on the border between two German- and French-speaking cantons. He left school at fourteen and took a number of precarious jobs in offices, on stage, as a butler in a Silesian castle, as a copyist (under the false name 'Joseph Marti') and as an inventor's assistant. He wrote poems, essays, three novels and dozens of short stories, which were admired by Hermann Hesse (247), Stefan Zweig (271) and Franz Kafka (280). After a suicide attempt, Walser entered an asylum in Herisau, where he lived for the next 23 years, gluing paper bags and sorting beans. 'I'm not here to write,' he said, 'I'm here to be mad.' He died of a heart attack on Christmas Day and was found lying in a snowy field near the asylum.

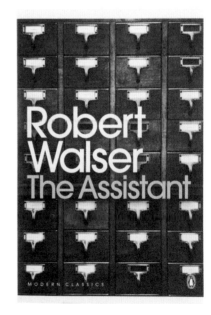

The Assistant 1908

Written in Swiss German, Walser's second novel is based on his experience as an employee of the hapless inventor Carl Dubler. In the novel, Joseph Marti comes to work for the inventor Carl Tobler, who has a large family and hopes to stave off his creditors by inventing a clock that displays a variety of advertisements.

2008
trans. Susan
Bernofsky,
2007

Dada

Jean Arp said that the word 'Dada' was invented by the poet Tristan Tzara at 6 p.m. on 6 February 1916, in the Café de la Terrasse in Zürich; others say that the writer Richard Hülsenbeck slid a paperknife into a dictionary and found the word 'dada', a colloquial French term for a hobby horse; still others say it was coined by the poet Hugo Ball at Zürich's Cabaret Voltaire. Whatever its origins, Dada emerged in Switzerland as a form of 'anti-art', an anarchist reaction against establishment values. Ball and Tzara wrote nihilistic manifestos (xix) expressing 'Dadaist disgust', and a Dada group began to assemble in Paris, including Marcel Duchamp, Man Ray (521), André Breton (176), Louis Aragon and Max Ernst. They created 'depthless' collage pictures, phonetic poems, photograms, cut-up texts (484) and 'readymades', including Duchamp's famous Fountain (1917). The movement was largely superseded by Surrealism (176), but remained influential for Andy Warhol (543) and pop art in the 1950s and 1960s.

Blaise Cendrars 1887–1961

Frédéric Sauser once claimed to have escaped his parents at the age of fifteen by swinging down from a fifth-floor balcony and running away to Moscow and Beijing. In truth, he was apprenticed to a Swiss watchmaker in St Petersburg and probably never visited China. After losing an arm in the First World War he became a naturalized French citizen, but continued to live a nomadic life, working as a businessman, film director, jeweller and journalist. Declared the pioneer of modernist poetry (11), he befriended Guillaume Apollinaire, Marc Chagall (319) and Ernest Hemingway (428) in Paris. He drove an Alfa Romeo refitted by Georges Braque, and his poems were translated into English by John Dos Passos (426). He took the pen name 'Blaise Cendrars' in 1912.

Moravagine 1926

This feverish, fantastical novel is narrated by a young French doctor, who meets a psychopathic murderer, Moravagine, in a Swiss lunatic asylum. The doctor helps Moravagine escape and together they embark on a worldwide bender, aiding the Russian Revolution, nearly being eaten by cannibals, and fighting in the First World War, when 'the whole world was doing a Moravagine'. 'How can I convince the sceptic that I was ravished by Cendrars's *Moravagine*?' asked Henry Miller (451). 'How does one know immediately that a thing is after one's own heart?'

1979
● trans. Alan Brown, 1968
—
'Moravagine' is a pun in French: it sounds like 'mort-a-vagin': 'death-has-vagina'.

Gruppe Olten

The Olten Group was a club of Swiss writers who broke away from the establishment Swiss Writers' Association (Schweizerischer Schriftstellerverein) in 1971 and began meeting in the railway-station restaurant in the city of Olten. They included Max Frisch, Adolf Muschg and Friedrich Dürrenmatt. The group had a specific political goal: to 'build a democratic-socialist society'. It disbanded in 2002.

Max Frisch 1911–1991

The son of an architect, Frisch worked as a journalist before retraining as an architect himself. As well as novels, he wrote plays, including *The Fire Raisers* (1953), and was the first non-German to win the Georg Büchner Prize. He was a lifelong friend of the dramatist Friedrich Dürrenmatt, and for five years had a passionate but fraught relationship with Ingeborg Bachmann (275).

I'm Not Stiller 1954

'I'm not Stiller!' opens this novel, which takes the form of notebooks written by a prisoner who claims to be an American called James Larkin White. He insists that he is not the Swiss sculptor Anatol Ludwig Stiller, who vanished ten years earlier, despite being positively identified by Stiller's wife, brother and mistress. 'Every word is false and true,' wrote Frisch, 'that is the nature of words.'

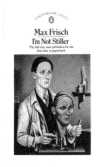

1961 Penguin Books
1983 Modern Classics
● trans. Michael Bullock, 1958, 1982

Homo Faber
A Report by Max Frisch 1957

Walter Faber is a middle-aged Swiss engineer, whose
worldview is based on faith in technology. When his plane
is forced to make an emergency landing in the Mexican
desert, however, a series of strange coincidences dredge
up repressed memories and change the course of his life.
The novel is, in part, a reflection on Switzerland's neutrality
during the Second World War.

1974 Penguin
Books
1983 Modern
Classics
trans. Michael
Bullock, 1959
—
The title is
a reference to
an enduring view
of humanity as
'man the maker',
discussed by
philosophers
including Henri
Bergson and
Hannah Arendt
(258). *Homo
Faber* was filmed
in 1991 as
Voyager, starring
Julie Delpy and
Sam Shepard.

1985
• trans. Geoffrey Skelton, 1983

Bluebeard 1982

In Frisch's last novel, Doktor
Felix Schaad's sixth wife has been
found strangled in his apartment.
He is acquitted of murder for
lack of evidence, but gradually
he sinks under the burden of
growing isolation and compulsive
self-examination. The title is
a reference to Charles Perrault's
murderous fairy tale (156).

Albert Cohen 1895–1981

Abraham Albert Coen was born on the island of Corfu,
to Greek Jewish parents who owned a soap factory. The family
emigrated to France and he studied law at the University of
Geneva, becoming a Swiss citizen in 1919, when he also added
an 'h' to his name. He edited *The Jewish Review* in Paris, with
contributions from Albert Einstein and Sigmund Freud (265),
before working for the League of Nations in Geneva. He moved
to London during the Second World War and served as the
legal advisor to the Intergovernmental Committee on Refugees.
In 1947, he returned to Geneva and led a division of the United
Nations International Refugee Organization.

More MIDLIFE CRISES

Belle du Seigneur 1968

Cohen wrote four novels about his handsome alter ego, 'Solal'. *Belle
du Seigneur*, the third in the sequence, is considered his masterpiece.
Solal, Under-Secretary-General of the League of Nations in Geneva,
is disillusioned by international affairs and decides to seduce
the beautiful Ariane Deume, wife of a dull-witted fellow employee.
What follows is a satire of middle-class ambitions and international
bureaucracy. It is 'one of the great novels of French literature', said
the writer André Brink, 'and a pillar of twentieth century fiction [...]
No wonder *Belle du Seigneur* has been acclaimed by many as "the greatest
love story ever written".'

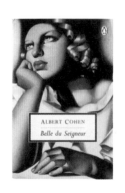

1997 Twentieth-
Century Classics
2005 Modern
Classics *Her Lover*
trans. David
Coward, 1995
—
Coward's
translation was
awarded the
Scott-Moncrieff
(166) Prize for
Translation in 1996.

Austria

Freud in Penguin

Freud's first English translator
was Abraham Brill, some of whose
translations were published as
Pelican Books (xiii). The 24-volume
Standard Edition (1953–74) was
translated into English by a team
overseen by James Strachey,
brother of Lytton Strachey (64)
and Dorothy Bussy (97), and these
editions formed the basis of the
Pelican Freud Library (1973–87),
which was edited by Angela
Richards and Albert Dickson.
Then, in 2002, Penguin launched
a new series of Freud translations,
edited by Adam Phillips, which
treated the books primarily
as works of literature. As John
Updike (514) observed, Freud
wrote 'narratives that have the
colour and force of fiction'.

MODERN CLASSICS

Sigmund Freud and Joseph Breuer
Studies in Hysteria

1974 Pelican Freud Library
Studies on Hysteria
● trans. James & Alix Strachey,
1955
ed. Angela Richards, 1974
2004 Modern Classics
trans. Nicola Luckhurst, 2004
intro. Rachel Bowlby, 2004

The 2004 edition
appends Freud's
1908 paper
'Hysterical
Phantasies and
their Relation
to Bisexuality'.

Sigmund Freud 1856–1939

Sigismund Schlomo Freud lived in Vienna for 78 years. He learned
to read German, English, French, Italian, Spanish, Hebrew, Latin
and Greek, and he studied philosophy, physiology and zoology,
comparing human brains with those of frogs and crayfish.
He began his medical career at the Vienna General Hospital, where
he met the psychiatrist Joseph Breuer, and in 1888 he set up his
own clinical practice, specializing in 'nervous disorders'. By 1896,
he had developed what he termed 'psychoanalysis', which began
as a talking cure and soon became a universal investigation into the
workings of the human mind. Above all, Freud explored his concept
of the unconscious and the ways in which it affects our dreams,
thoughts and actions. In 1906, he began corresponding with Carl Jung
(262), but their friendship ended acrimoniously. In 1938, when Hitler
annexed Austria, Freud fled Vienna on the Orient Express with his
wife Martha and daughter Anna (274). He took refuge in London,
where he met Salvador Dalí, Virginia Woolf (42), H. G. Wells (26)
and Stefan Zweig (271); Zweig spoke at Freud's funeral the following
year. Although Freud has been criticized by feminists such as Simone
de Beauvoir (187) and Betty Friedan (522) for his 'phallocentric' ideas,
he nonetheless had a seismic cultural influence on the 20th century.
'The Freudian theory is one of the most important foundation stones
for an edifice to be built by future generations, the dwelling of a freer
and wiser humanity,' wrote Thomas Mann (245).

Studies in Hysteria with Joseph Breuer 1893–5

This founding text of psychoanalysis was written by Freud and
his older colleague Joseph Breuer, a distinguished neurophysiologist
with a penchant for hypnosis therapy. 'Hysteria' was the prevalent
term for the physical manifestations of a troubled mind, but Freud
and Breuer proposed that it derived specifically from past trauma
in a patient's life. *Studies in Hysteria* comprises
individual case studies of hysterics, including
that of Breuer's famous patient 'Anna O.', as well
as a joint introductory essay.

Interpreting Dreams 1899

Freud's ground-breaking masterpiece argues
that dreams express the wish fulfilments
of the unconscious mind. The obscure
symbolism of dreams can be analysed to reveal
a patient's repressed desires. Freud maps out
his theoretical model of the mind, with its
unconscious, preconscious and conscious
realms, and describes the 'Oedipus complex'
for the first time. 'Insight such as this,' he
wrote, 'falls to one's lot but once in a lifetime.'

MODERN CLASSICS

Sigmund Freud

1976 Pelican Freud Library
The Interpretation of Dreams
● trans. James Strachey, 1953–8
ed. Angela Richards, 1976
2006 Modern Classics
trans. J. A. Underwood, 2006
intro. John Forrester, 2006

1963 Pelican Books *Leonardo*
• trans. Alan Tyson, 1957
intro. Brian Farrell
1985 Pelican Freud Library
Art and Literature
• trans. James Strachey et al,
1953–62
ed. Albert Dickson, 1985
2003 Modern Classics
trans. David McLintock, 2003
intro. Hugh Haughton, 2003

1976 Pelican Freud Library
*Jokes and Their Relation
to the Unconscious*
• trans. James Strachey, 1960
ed. Angela Richards, 1976
2002 Modern Classics
trans. Joyce Crick, 2002
intro. John Carey, 2002

The Uncanny 1899–1919

This selection of Freud's writings on
imagination and creativity includes the title
essay, 'The Uncanny', in which he analyses
the unheimlich feeling induced by *déjà vu*,
missing eyes and living dolls. 'The Creative
Writer and Daydreaming', an influential text
for modernism (11), describes how artists
access memories of childhood daydreams;
and 'Leonardo da Vinci and a Memory of his
Childhood' is a retrospective psychoanalysis
of the Renaissance polymath, based on
his paintings and his childhood memory
of being attacked by a vulture.

The Psychopathology of Everyday Life

1901

Freud analyses our trivial slips of the
tongue, and shows how they reveal our
secret ambitions and sexual fantasies. This entertaining and
accessible book made Freud's name: new patients – including
the 'Ratman' (267) – sought him out after reading it. It is the
origin of the proverbial 'Freudian slip'.

The Joke and Its Relation to the Unconscious 1905

Freud anatomizes the joke and concludes that the reason we laugh
is because jokes satisfy our unconscious desires. They release us
from inhibitions, allowing us to express sexual, aggressive or playful
instincts that we otherwise repress. His study doubles as a treasury
of puns, one-liners and anecdotes from early 20th-century Vienna.

The Psychology of Love 1905–31

'Fragment of an Analysis of Hysteria' is a controversial case study
of a sexually abused patient, 'Dora', who loses her voice. In *Three Essays
on Sexual Theory* (1905), Freud famously describes childhood sexuality
as 'polymorphously perverse' and demonstrates how it develops into
the adult libido. Other pieces in this selection include discussions
of masturbation, fetishism, paedophilia and bestiality.

Mass Psychology and Other Writings 1907–38

In these iconoclastic works, Freud systematically deconstructs religious
faith. In 'Mass Psychology and Analysis of the "I"', he looks at how
institutions such as the Church and the army command unswerving
loyalty; 'The Future of an Illusion' is a psychoanalysis of religion;
and 'Moses the Man and Monotheistic Religion', written just as Freud
was fleeing from Nazism, is a warning of the dangers of nationalism.

Sigmund Freud
The Psychopathology of Everyday Life

1938 Pelican Books
• trans. A. A. Brill, 1914
1975 Pelican Freud Library
• trans. Alan Tyson, 1960
ed. Angela Richards, 1975
2002 Modern Classics
trans. Anthea Bell, 2002
intro. Paul Keegan, 2002

1977 Pelican Freud
Library *On Sexuality*
• trans. James Strachey
et al, 1949–61
ed. Angela Richards, 1977
2006 Modern Classics
trans. Shaun Whiteside,
2006
intro. Jeri Johnson, 2006

1985 Pelican Freud
Library *The Origins
of Religion*
• trans. James Strachey
et al, 1953–64
ed. Albert Dickson, 1977
2004 Modern Classics
trans. J. A Underwood,
2004
intro. Jacqueline Rose,
2004

The 'Wolfman'
and Other Cases 1909–18

The 'Wolfman' was a young Russian man who was terrified of wolves. After four years of treatment, Freud successfully cured his neuroses, and it became his most celebrated case. This volume also includes his case studies of 'Little Hans', who was scared of horses, and the 'Ratman', who was afraid of rats gnawing through the anuses of his father and his lover.

1977 Pelican Freud Library *Case Histories I: 'Dora' and 'Little Hans'*
• trans. Alix & James Strachey, 1953–55
ed. Angela Richards, 1977
2002 Modern Classics
trans. Louise Adey Huish, 2002
intro. Gillian Beer, 2002

Wild Analysis 1910–37

This volume brings together Freud's writing on the techniques of psychoanalysis. 'On "Wild" Psychoanalysis' warns of the dangers of untrained practitioners dabbling in psychoanalysis, whereas 'The Question of Lay Analysis' encourages non-medics to take it up. 'Constructions in Analysis', some of his last writing on the subject, discusses the complex relationship between patient and analyst.

1962 Pelican Books *Two Short Accounts of Psycho-Analysis*
• trans. James Strachey, 1957–9
2002 Modern Classics
trans. Alan Bance, 2002
intro. Adam Phillips, 2002
—
In 'The Question of Lay Analysis', Freud infamously used the English phrase 'dark continent' to describe the sexual life of adult women.

The Schreber Case 1911

In 1903, Daniel Paul Schreber, a German judge, published *Memoirs of My Nervous Illness*, in which he described experiencing a special relationship with God and a passionate desire to become a woman. Eight years later, Freud attempted to psychoanalyse Schreber using the memoir.

1979 Pelican Freud Library *Case Histories II: 'Rat Man', Schreber, 'Wolf Man', Female Homosexuality*
• trans. Alix & James Strachey, 1955–58
ed. Angela Richards, 1979
2002 Modern Classics
trans. Andrew Webber, 2002
intro. Colin MacCabe, 2002

The Unconscious 1911–39

These works expand on Freud's central premise that unacceptable feelings are repressed into the unconscious, where they continue to exert an influence. Several of these pieces, including 'The Unconscious', are taken from Freud's *Introductory Lectures on Psychoanalysis* (1915–17), in which he set out his developing theories.

1973 Pelican Freud Library *Introductory Lectures on Psychoanalysis*
• trans. James Strachey, 1962–3
ed. Angela Richards, 1974
2005 Modern Classics
trans. Graham Frankland, 2005
intro. Mark Cousins, 2005

1938 Pelican Books *Totem and Taboo*
• trans. A. A. Brill, 1919
2005 Modern Classics
trans. Shaun Whiteside, 2005
intro. Maud Ellmann, 2005

On Murder, Mourning and Melancholia 1913–36

The centrepiece of this selection of anthropological works is *Totem and Taboo* (1913). Inspired by James Frazer's *The Golden Bough* (27), its comparison of tribal rites with obsessive neurotic behaviour was praised by Thomas Mann (245) and ridiculed by Simone de Beauvoir (187). 'Mourning and Melancholia' concerns the differences between grief and depression, and 'Why War?' is a letter to Albert Einstein that presents a grimly persuasive portrait of humankind's propensity for war.

Beyond the Pleasure Principle
and Other Writings 1914–26

Beyond the Pleasure Principle (1920) marked a turning point in Freud's theory of the mind: it introduced his concept of an innate 'death drive', locked in a struggle with the libido, which finds expression through compulsive repetition, aggression and neurotic guilt. Other pieces in this collection describe the psychodynamics of the id, ego and super-ego, Freud's conceptualization of the different levels of consciousness.

1985 Pelican Freud Library
Civilization, Society and Religion
• trans. James Strachey et al, 1955–64
ed. Albert Dickson, 1985
2002 Modern Classics
trans. David McLintock, 2002
intro. Leo Bersani, 2002
—
The 2002 edition also includes ' "Civilized" Sexual Morality and Modern Nervous Illness', an early paper on the repressive hypocrisy of 'civilized sexual morality'.

Civilization and Its Discontents

1930

Civilization and Its Discontents is an ambitious examination of the tension between civilized behaviour and the natural urges of an individual. In Freud's view, we each harbour immutable primitive instincts, sexual and violent, which are prohibited by civilized society, leading to feelings of resentment. Many people learn to curb these instincts; those who don't, become criminals or perverts, or else suffer from neuroses.

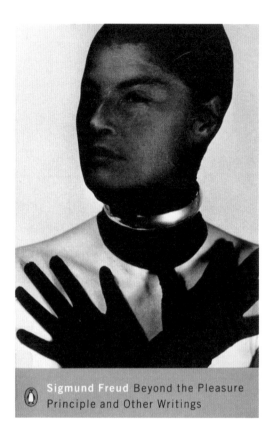

1979 Pelican Freud Library
On Psychopathology
• trans. James Strachey et al, 1953–62
ed. Angela Richards, 1979
1984 Pelican Freud Library
On Metapsychology
• trans. James Strachey et al, 1955–61
ed. Albert Dickson, 1984
2003 Modern Classics
trans. John Reddick, 2003
intro. Mark Edmundson, 2003

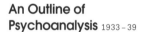

An Outline of Psychoanalysis 1933–39

These late works represent Freud's summation of his achievement. His *Introductory Lectures on Psychoanalysis: New Series* (1933) are an extension and refinement of his earlier Introductory Lectures (267), while An Outline of Psychoanalysis (1940), his last masterpiece, is an attempt to 'offer as it were a dogmatic conspectus of psychoanalysis by bringing together all its doctrines in the most concentrated and clear-cut form'. It was published posthumously.

1973 Pelican Freud Library
New Introductory Lectures on Psychoanalysis
• trans. James Strachey, 1964
ed. Angela Richards, 1973
1987 Pelican Freud Library
Historical and Expository Works on Psychoanalysis
• trans. James Strachey et al, 1955–61
ed. Albert Dickson, 1987
2003 Modern Classics
trans. Helena Ragg-Kirkby, 2003
intro. Malcolm Bowie, 2003

The Penguin Freud Reader 1899–1939

The aim of this volume is 'to enable the curious […] to discover what, if anything, is so haunting about Freud's writing'. Adam Phillips, general editor of the Penguin Freud translations, selects excerpts from Freud's most famous works and includes translations commissioned especially for this volume, such as 'Lapses' from the Introductory Lectures on Psychoanalysis (267) and a 'Note on the "Magic Notepad"'.

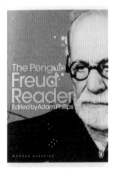

2006 Penguin Books
2008 Modern Classics
ed. Adam Phillips, 2006
trans. Alan Bance et al., 2002–6
—
Adam Phillips was formerly Principal Child Psychotherapist at Charing Cross Hospital in London. He is the author of several books, including *On Kissing, Tickling and Being Bored* (1993).

Adolf Loos 1870 – 1933

Loos was the son of a German stonemason. He became a pioneer of modernist architecture (11) and a major figure in Viennese art and design before the First World War, remembered today primarily for the interior of the Café Museum (1899), the American Bar (1908) and the Loos House (1910). He was a friend of Ludwig Wittgenstein, Arnold Schönberg and the writer Karl Kraus, and was married and divorced three times.

Ornament and Crime
Thoughts on Design and Materials
1897 – 1924

These lectures and essays compose an influential statement on modernist (11) aesthetics, touching on architecture, cities, glassware and underwear. In every case, Loos advocated stripped-down simplicity and well-chosen materials. 'The evolution of culture,' he wrote, 'comes to the same thing as the removal of ornament from functional objects.'

Ornament
and Crime
Adolf Loos

2019
trans. Shaun Whiteside

Rainer Maria Rilke 1875 – 1926

After an uncomfortable childhood, in which his father wanted him to become a soldier and his mother pretended he was a girl, René Maria Rilke dedicated his life to poetry. He travelled restlessly around Europe, meeting Tolstoy in Russia, working as Rodin's secretary in Paris, enjoying aristocratic patronage from Marie von Thurn und Taxis, and finally settling in a medieval Swiss tower not much larger than a hermit's cell. As well as poems he wrote an Expressionist (269) novel, *The Notebooks of Malte Laurids Brigge* (1910). He married once, briefly, and fell in love with a married woman, Lou Andreas-Salomé, who remained an important confidante throughout his life. She persuaded him to spell his name in the Germanic style, 'Rainer', and told him about her experiences of studying under Sigmund Freud (265). Rilke died of leukaemia, though one story says he expired after pricking his finger on a rose. His epitaph, which he wrote himself, reads: 'Rose, oh the pure contradiction, delight / of being no one's sleep under so many lids.'

Selected Poems 1899 – 1926

Rilke was one of the greatest lyrical poets in the German language and this anthology spans his whole career, from early Symbolist (303) works that plumbed the dark realms of love, death, sex and subconscious fear, to his *New Poems* of 1907–8, in which he examined objects intensely until they revealed their oracular, mystic qualities. Finally it includes the quasi-religious ecstasies of his late masterworks, *The Duino Elegies* (1923) and *The Sonnets to Orpheus* (1923).

RAINER MARIA RILKE
Selected Poems

1964 Penguin Poets
1991 Twentieth-Century Classics
trans. J. B. Leishman, 1960

Expressionism

Expressionism became the dominant artistic style in German-speaking Europe between 1910 and 1924. It began as a visual movement, exemplified by the *Blaue Reiter* ('Blue Rider') group, but it quickly came to influence German drama, poetry, novels, music and film. Like other modernist movements (11), it was primarily a reaction against realism, an attempt to express feelings and psychological states through distortion, dreams and the assertion of irrationality in a mechanized world. The leading Expressionist journal, *Der Sturm* (*The Storm*), was founded in Berlin in 1910, and had contributors such as Max Brod (280), Anatole France (173), Knut Hamsun, Adolf Loos (269) and Heinrich Mann (250). Playwrights such as Ernst Toller and Bertolt Brecht (255) introduced abstract characterization and structural discontinuity to the stage; the poets Gottfried Benn and Franz Werfel (273) used broken syntax and symbols; and the great Expressionist novels were written by Alfred Döblin (253), Rainer Maria Rilke (269) and, above all, Franz Kafka (280). The term is perhaps best known today through the influence of Expressionist films such as Robert Wiene's *The Cabinet of Dr Caligari* (1920), F. W. Murnau's *Nosferatu* (1922) and Fritz Lang's *Metropolis* (1927).

Arthur Schnitzler 1862–1931

Schnitzler, son of a Viennese throat specialist, trained as a doctor and worked at the Vienna General Hospital, where he took an interest in psychiatry and hypnosis at the same time as Freud (265). 'You have learned through intuition,' wrote Freud, '[...] everything that I have had to unearth by laborious work.' Schnitzler's plays, novellas and stories challenged the morality of *fin-de-siècle* (3) Vienna and unearth the subconscious drives of human sexuality. In his scandalous play *La Ronde* (1896–7), for example, Schnitzler presents a circular chain of ten characters connected by sexual intercourse.

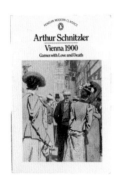

1973 Penguin Books
1985 Modern Classics
• trans. Agnes Jacques et al., 1914–29
1999 Twentieth-Century Classics *Beatrice and Her Son*
• trans. Shaun Whiteside, 1999
intro. Martin Swales, 1999

Vienna 1900
Games with Love and Death 1900–1917
Mother and Son, The Man of Honour, A Confirmed Bachelor, The Spring Sonata

These four novellas are studies in psychological eroticism. In *Mother and Son* (1913; also known as *Beatrice and Her Son*), a young widow succumbs to a sensuous but taboo liaison; in *The Man of Honour* (1910), a murderous lawyer chooses between his mistress and his fiancée; in *A Confirmed Bachelor* (1917), a former ship's doctor's life is thrown into disarray after his sister's suicide; and in *The Spring Sonata* (1900), the widow Bertha Garlan glimpses happiness when she meets her childhood sweetheart in Vienna.

Dream Story 1926

When Dr Fridolin's loving wife describes a sexual fantasy involving another man, he is drawn into a dreamlike, nocturnal adventure that takes him to seedy cafés, decadent villas, hospitals, orgies and the morgue. In the German title, *Traumnovelle*, *Traum* suggests both 'dream' and 'trauma'.

1999 Twentieth-Century Classics
2020 Penguin Classics
trans. J. M. Q. Davies, 1999
intro. Frederic Raphael, 1999
—
The novelist Frederic Raphael co-authored, with Stanley Kubrick, the screenplay for *Eyes Wide Shut* (1999), Kubrick's film adaptation of *Dream Story* starring Nicole Kidman and Tom Cruise.

Robert Musil 1880–1942

Musil trained as a mathematician, behavioural psychologist, engineer and philosopher. He met Franz Kafka (280) in Prague and was friends with Rainer Maria Rilke (269). Throughout his life, he turned down academic and military opportunities in order to pursue his writing. With the German annexation of Austria in 1938, he and his Jewish wife fled to Switzerland. He is best remembered for his unfinished novel, *The Man without Qualities* (1924–42), about a year in the life of an Austrian intellectual who struggles to commit to a career. It is considered one of the most influential modernist (11) novels of the 20th century.

1961 Penguin Books
• trans. Eithne Wilkins & Ernst Kaiser, 1955
2001 Modern Classics
trans. Shaun Whiteside, 2001
intro. J. M. Coetzee, 2001

The Confusions of Young Törless 1906

Musil's first novel draws on his experience at two military boarding schools. Young Törless finds himself participating in a cycle of sadistic and sexual bullying in an elite boys' academy. In hindsight, the book appears to prophesy in microcosm the rise of fascism amongst those who reached adulthood after the First World War.

Posthumous Papers of a Living Author 1920s, pub. 1936

These short stories, scenes, parables and vignettes were mostly written in the 1920s. They were collected and arranged by Musil in three sections – 'Pictures', 'Ill-Tempered Observations' and 'Unstorylike Stories' – and touch on monkeys, microscopes, a fly's tragic struggle, the Oedipus complex (265) and a laughing horse.

1995
• trans. Peter Wortsman, 1987

Alfred Kubin 1877–1959

Kubin was a strange child with a 'burning curiosity' for corpses. He once attempted suicide on his mother's grave. He was primarily an Expressionist artist (269), gripped by hysterical flashes of insight; he associated with the *Blaue Reiter* ('Blue Rider') group and illustrated the works of Edgar Allan Poe, E. T. A. Hoffmann and Fyodor Dostoyevsky. For the last 50 years of his life, he lived in the 12th-century manor house at Zwickledt, which is now a museum in his memory.

The Other Side 1908

Kubin wrote his only novel in twelve weeks. An artist and his wife are persuaded to relocate to a claustrophobic 'Dream Kingdom' in central Asia, a land of epidemics, shadowy characters and baffling absurdity. *The Other Side* was much admired by Kafka (280).

The Other Side

• trans. Denver Lindley, 1969
—
Kubin illustrated *The Other Side* himself.

Stefan Zweig 1881–1942

Zweig published his first book of poetry at nineteen. Between the wars he lived in Salzburg, travelled widely and became a world-renowned author of psychologically astute stories and literary biographies. He was a friend of Thomas Mann (245), Rainer Maria Rilke (269), Arthur Schnitzler (270) and Sigmund Freud (265), to whom he once wrote a letter saying that 'psychology is the great business of my life'. An Austrian Jew, he fled to England in 1934, America in 1940 and finally Brazil. On 21 February 1942, he completed his memoir, *The World of Yesterday*. The following day, he and his wife took an overdose of barbiturates; their bodies were found holding hands. Elie Wiesel (325) called Zweig 'one of the greatest masters to whom we are all indebted'.

The Royal Game and Other Stories 1913–42

'The Royal Game' (or 'Chess') was written in the last few months of Zweig's life. It takes place on a cruise ship, bound for Buenos Aires. When the passengers challenge a world chess champion, one of them turns out to have unexpected talents. Zweig's other stories feature obsession, guilt and adultery. Zweig is 'one of the masters of the short story and novella', wrote the critic Nicholas Lezard in the *Guardian*, 'and by "one of the masters" I mean that he's up there with Maupassant, Chekhov, James (397), Poe, or indeed anyone you care to name'.

Beware of Pity 1939

Zweig's greatest novel tells the story of Lieutenant Anton Hofmiller, who makes a misguided promise while visiting a Hungarian castle which leads inexorably to disaster. Ali Smith calls it a 'frighteningly gripping' novel. 'It's just a masterpiece,' writes the director Wes Anderson, whose film *The Grand Budapest Hotel* (2014) was partly inspired by Zweig's stories.

Young Vienna

A loose group of *fin-de-siècle* (3) writers would meet in Viennese *Kaffeehausen* such as the Café Griensteidl. They called themselves 'Jung-Wien' ('Young Vienna'), and discussed their experiments in modernism (11). Members included Hugo von Hofmannsthal, Karl Kraus, Arthur Schnitzler (270), Jakob Wassermann (249) and Stefan Zweig (271). The Café Griensteidl was a long-standing haunt of artists and writers on Michaelerplatz in Vienna; it closed permanently in 2017.

1984 Modern Classics
• trans. Jill Sutcliffe, 1981
intro. John Fowles, 1981
2006 Red Classics *Chess*
2017 Modern Classics
trans. Anthea Bell, 2006
—
The current edition, translated by Anthea Bell, contains 'Chess' only.

1985 Modern Classics
• trans. Phyllis & Trevor Blewitt, 1982
2016 Modern Classics
Impatience of the Heart
trans. Jonathan Katz, 2016
—
The novel's German title *Ungeduld des Herzens* translates literally as *Impatience of the Heart*, but the novel is also known as *Beware of Pity* because the first English translation in 1939 used that title, as did the 1946 English-language film adaptation.

Hermann Broch 1886–1951

'One thing at least I have in common with Kafka (280) and Musil (270),' wrote Broch: 'none of us has an actual biography; we lived and wrote, nothing more.' For the first 40 years of his life, Broch ran his father's Viennese textile firm, but then he decided to sell the business, study philosophy and mathematics and start writing. He made his debut with his trilogy, *The Sleepwalkers*, through which he met Stefan Zweig (271), Robert Musil and Elias Canetti (328). He was Jewish, and was briefly imprisoned by the Nazis in 1938, but James Joyce (8) helped him escape to Scotland, where his English-language translators, Willa and Edwin Muir, enabled him to emigrate to America. He lived in the USA for the rest of his life, writing a study of mass hysteria.

The Sleepwalkers 1930–32

The Romantic, The Anarchist, The Realist

Broch's panoramic, 'polyhistorical' trilogy spans the decades leading up to the First World War. The instalments are set at fifteen-year intervals and written in distinct literary styles: 19th-century realism, early Expressionism (269) and fragmented modernism (11). The trilogy was admired by Albert Einstein, Thornton Wilder (436), T. S. Eliot (11) and Stephen Spender (95), who called it 'one of the few really original and thoughtful novels of this century'.

In 1888, Joachim von Pasenow is the neurotic 'romantic', an aristocratic Prussian officer, torn between his love for a Czech prostitute and his duty to his upper-class fiancée. He is a 'sleepwalker' in the sense that he is living between two states of being, between one crumbling value system and another that is emerging.

In 1903, the lustful Luxembourger August Esch is the 'anarchist', who finds himself simultaneously promoting a bizarre female wrestling act and attempting to avenge his friend, a political activist. 'With unerring precision,' wrote W. G. Sebald, 'Broch finds the fault lines that run from the late nineteenth century into our calamitous age.'

2000
● trans. Willa & Edwin Muir, 1932
intro. John White, 2000
essay Milan Kundera, 1986

2000
● trans. Willa & Edwin Muir, 1932
aftwd. John White, 2000

2000
● trans. Willa & Edwin Muir, 1932
aftwd. John White, 2000
—
Milan Kundera's *The Art of the Novel* (1986) includes a chapter entitled 'Notes Inspired by *The Sleepwalkers*', in which he describes the 'radical difference between *The Sleepwalkers* and the other great twentieth-century "frescoes" (those of Proust (166), Musil (270), Thomas Mann (245), etc.)'. 'In Broch,' he writes, 'it is continuity neither of action nor of biography (a character's or a family's) that provides the unity of the whole. It is something else, something less apparent, less apprehensible, something hidden: the continuity of one theme (that of man facing the process of a disintegration of values).'

In 1918, the elderly Major von Pasenow is now the commandant of Kur-Trier, a small town on the River Moselle, where August Esch runs the local newspaper. In the last months of the First World War, the deserter Wilhelm Huguenau is the 'realist', who arrives in the town and sets about ruthlessly exploiting its inhabitants. 'We are haunted by the strange and disquieting feeling that we are at the very limits of the expressible,' wrote Aldous Huxley (65). 'Broch performs with an impeccable virtuosity.'

The Death of Virgil 1945

Broch's lyrical masterpiece covers the last eighteen hours in the life of Virgil. As the Roman poet lies dying in Brundisium (modern Brindisi, in southern Italy), he slips in and out of hallucinations, speaks with his patron the Emperor Augustus, and decides to burn the unfinished manuscript of the *Aeneid*. Broch asks whether even the greatest work of literature is worth as much as the simplest act of friendship. *The Death of Virgil* is 'one of the most extraordinary and profound experiments ever to have been undertaken', wrote Thomas Mann (245).

2000
● trans. Jean Starr Untermeyer, 1945
intro. Malcolm Bull, 2000
—
The German and English editions of *The Death of Virgil* were published simultaneously, and in fact Broch finished writing the novel in collaboration with his English translator, Jean Starr Untermeyer.

Joseph Roth 1894–1939

Roth never knew his father, who went mad before he was born and died in Russia. Raised in a Jewish community on the easternmost borders of the Austro-Hungarian Empire, Roth fought for Austria in the First World War before finding work as a journalist in Vienna, Berlin and Frankfurt. In 1933, he fled to France, where he became an outspoken opponent of Nazism. 'They have succeeded in establishing a reign of barbarity,' he wrote to his friend Stefan Zweig (271). 'Do not fool yourself. Hell reigns.' Roth penned thirteen novels, many about father–son relationships, the First World War and the fate of 20th-century 'wandering Jews'. He himself spent two years travelling around Europe with Irmgard Keun (254) before dying of alcoholism in Paris.

1984 Modern Classics
• trans. Geoffrey Dunlop, 1933
rev. Eva Tucker, 1974
1995 Twentieth-Century
Classics
trans. Joachim Neugroschel,
1995
intro. Nadine Gordimer, 1991
—
The novel is named after
the famous 1848 march by
Johann Strauss, Sr. written
to honour the Austrian Field
Marshal Joseph Radetzky von
Radetz. The music features
at several important moments
in the narrative.

The Radetzky March 1932

Roth's masterpiece is a saga that chronicles three generations of the grand Trotta dynasty in the decades before the First World War. With droll irony, the novel shows how well-intentioned actions lead to both the decline of the family and the fall of the Austro-Hungarian Empire. Roth wrote a sequel, *The Emperor's Tomb* (1938), which continued the story up to the *Anschluss* (the German annexation of Austria) in 1938.

Weights and Measures 1937

When Anselm Eibenschütz leaves the Austro-Hungarian army after the First World War to become the inspector of weights and measures in a provincial town near the Russian border, his self-respect falls apart in a welter of petty corruption and alcoholism.

2017
trans. David Le Vay, 1982

Franz Werfel 1890–1945

Werfel was born in Prague, a friend of Rainer Maria Rilke (269), Max Brod (280) and Franz Kafka (280). In the First World War, he worked as a telephone operator on the Russian front, and then for the Military Press Bureau in Vienna, alongside Rilke and Robert Musil (270). He became a well-known novelist, playwright and Expressionist (269) poet, and married Alma Mahler-Gropius, the widow of both Gustav Mahler and Walter Gropius. As a Jew, Werfel was forced to resign from the Prussian Academy of Arts in 1933, and in 1938 he fled with Alma to a French fishing village, near Bertolt Brecht (255) and Thomas Mann (245). When Germany invaded France, Werfel narrowly avoided capture by claiming sanctuary at Lourdes, an experience that inspired his novel *The Song of Bernadette* (1941). He and Alma escaped over the Pyrenees and eventually settled in Los Angeles.

2018
trans. Geoffrey Dunlop, 1934
rev. James Reidel, 2012
—
Werfel published his novel in
1933, in Nazi Germany, even as
his previous books were being
burned. In February 1934, all
unsold copies of *Forty Days*
were seized and destroyed.
'In the so-called "prime of life"
after working nonstop,' he
wrote, 'I stand in my own
ruins.' Geoffrey Dunlop's 1934
translation, however, became
a bestseller in the English-
speaking world. At Werfel's
suggestion, Dunlop abridged
the original by about 90 pages,
taking out scenes of violence
and rape. 'Restoring what
Dunlop omitted,' says James
Reidel, in his note to the
revised edition, 'allows readers
to see more of the book that
Germans read in the first year
of Hitler's regime.'

The Forty Days of Musa Dagh 1933

Werfel's masterpiece brought the horror of the Armenian genocide to the world's attention. During the First World War, the nationalist 'Young Turk' government instigated a programme of deportations, concentration camps and finally a massacre which destroyed the Armenian population in Turkey. Six villages, however, on the slopes of the Musa Dagh mountain in Turkey's south-west resisted for weeks, until being evacuated by French and British warships. Werfel's fictionalized account of the episode has become a talismanic story of resistance, written as the Nazi Party was coming to power and eerily foreshadowing the Holocaust.

Anna Freud 1895–1982

Anna, the youngest daughter of Sigmund Freud (265), qualified as a psychoanalyst with the Vienna Psychoanalytical Society in 1922 and was appointed director of the Vienna Psychoanalytical Training Institute in 1935. Among her first patients were the children of Dorothy Burlingham, heiress to the Tiffany fortune, who became her personal and professional partner for the rest of her life. In 1938, Anna Freud fled Austria with her father and settled in north London, where she opened the Hampstead Child Therapy Course and Clinic in 1952. It became the world's leading centre for the psychoanalytic study of children and still exists as the Anna Freud National Centre for Children and Families. When Anna died, her home in Hampstead was opened as the Freud Museum, in honour of her father.

Selected Writings
1936–76

This anthology presents a definitive overview of Anna Freud's career, from her early monograph *The Ego and the Mechanisms of Defence* (1936), which she presented to her father on his 80th birthday, to papers on adolescence, trauma, aggression and analytical technique.

1986 Pelican Books
1998 Penguin Books
2015 Modern Classics
ed. Richard Ekins & Ruth Freeman, 1986

S. Y. Agnon 1888–1970

Shmuel Yosef Halevi Tschatsky was born in Buczacz, Galicia, now in Ukraine. He was the son of an ordained rabbi and wrote poems and stories in Yiddish and Hebrew as a boy. He emigrated to Jaffa in 1908, and published a story under the pen name 'Agnon'. He then lived in Berlin for ten years, but returned to Palestine after a fire destroyed his library and he lived in Jerusalem for the rest of his life. He was a pre-eminent author of Hebrew literature and shared the Nobel Prize for Literature (576) in 1966 with the German-Swedish Jewish poet Nelly Sachs.

1971
• trans. Walter Lever, 1966
pref. Allen Mandelbaum, 1966

Two Tales
Betrothed, Edo and Enam
1943–50

Betrothed (1943) is a tale of passivity: Jacob Rechnitz, a marine biologist, moves to Jaffa in the years before the First World War and dallies idly with six different girls. *Edo and Enam* (1950), in contrast, is a story of restlessness: it follows the aimless wanderings of the married Greifenbachs and the scholars Gamzu and Ginath, the four of whom meet with unexpectedly tragic consequences.

Peter Handke b. 1942

Handke was born in Griffen, southern Austria, and raised by an alcoholic stepfather. He is a novelist, playwright, translator and film-maker: he has collaborated several times with the director Wim Wenders, most notably on *Wings of Desire* (1987) and their 1972 film adaptation of *The Goalkeeper's Anxiety at the Penalty Kick*. He has won many international literary awards, including the Nobel Prize for Literature (576) in 2019. 'Handke is a kind of nature poet,' wrote John Updike (514), 'a romantic whose exacerbated nerves cling like pained ivy to the landscape.'

The Goalkeeper's Anxiety at the Penalty Kick 1970

Joseph, a once-famous goalkeeper turned construction worker, commits a random murder and wanders the streets, experiencing a nervous breakdown. Handke's strange, alienating novella has been compared to both Kafka (280) and Camus (181).

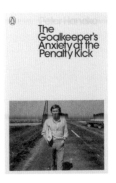

2020
trans. Michael Roloff, 1972

2020
trans. Ralph Manheim, 1978
—
The cover shows a still from the 1978 film adaptation of *The Left-Handed Woman*, which Handke wrote and directed himself. It was nominated for the Palme d'Or at the Cannes Film Festival.

The Left-Handed Woman 1976

Marianne is a suburban housewife who realizes her husband will leave her one day, so she pre-empts him by sending him away and fending for herself and her young son.

Repetition 1986

Filip is an Austrian teenager who goes looking for his missing older brother armed only with two books: his brother's school copybook and a dictionary in which certain words have been marked. '*Repetition* made a great and, as I have since learned, lasting impression on me,' wrote W. G. Sebald.

Repetition

2020
trans. Ralph Manheim, 1988

Ingeborg Bachmann 1926–1973

Bachmann was the daughter of a Nazi teacher. She studied the philosophy of Heidegger and became known as a poet, writing existential lyrics about the possibility of German poetry 'after Auschwitz'; her collection *Borrowed Time* (1953) won the Gruppe 47 Prize (258). She also wrote essays, stories and radio plays, and had affairs with Paul Celan (325), Max Frisch (263) and Henry Kissinger. In 1964, she won the Georg Büchner Prize. At the end of her life she was living in Rome, dependent on alcohol and barbiturates; she died in a bedroom fire caused by a lit cigarette.

Malina

Malina 1971

In Bachmann's only novel, a female writer in post-war Vienna is torn between two men: the young and beautiful Ivan and the fastidious, older civil servant Malina. Gradually her fragile identity starts to crack, as reality blurs with hallucinatory memories of war, rape, horror and gas chambers. It is an 'intense, courageous novel', wrote the *New York Times*, 'equal to the best of Virginia Woolf (42) and Samuel Beckett (20)'.

2019
trans. Philip Boehm, 1990, 2019
intro. Rachel Kushner, 2019
—
The novelist Rachel Kushner calls *Malina* 'a portrait, in language, of female consciousness, truer than anything written since Sappho'.

More IDENTITY CRISES

The Face of Another by Kobo Abe	352
Cards of Identity by Nigel Dennis	135
Demian by Hermann Hesse	248
The Bird's Nest by Shirley Jackson	469
Journey to the Border by Edward Upward	79

Walter Abish b. 1931

Abish was born in Vienna, but his Jewish family fled to Italy, France and finally Shanghai, where he lived throughout the 1940s. In 1949, he moved to Israel, where he served in the army, before relocating to the USA. He became an American citizen in 1960. He has taught at many universities and colleges, including Columbia, Brown and Yale, and he has written novels, stories and a book of poetry. He wears a black eyepatch.

How German Is It 1980

In this postmodern (505) thriller, the fictional community of Brumholdstein is built on the remains of a concentration camp. As mass graves are gradually unearthed, people start to disappear, and the Hargenau brothers, Ulrich and Helmuth, are forced to confront the unsettling cracks appearing in the new democratic West Germany. *How German Is It* won the inaugural PEN / Faulkner Award (433) in 1981; and John Updike (514) later called it a 'compelling, prize-winning, fully stocked novel'.

2005
• trans. Michael Hofmann

Thomas Bernhard

1931–1989

Nicolaas Thomas Bernhard was the son of an Austrian maid; he never met his father. He grew up in Vienna, then moved to Traunstein in Germany, where he was forced to join the Hitler Youth. Following a series of sadistically repressive schools run by Catholic priests and Nazis, his dream of becoming an actor and singer was crushed when he developed pleurisy and tuberculosis, which left him with lifelong respiratory problems. He wrote a series of blackly comic, pessimistic and frequently offensive novels and plays, setting out to assault what he called the 'mindless cultural sewer' of his native Austria. This has led some compatriots to label him a *Nestbeschmutzer*, 'one who dirties his own nest'. In 1989, he died in Gmunden by assisted suicide and left a will banning any future publication or staging of his work in Austria. He won the Georg Büchner Prize in 1970.

Old Masters
A Comedy 1985

For more than 30 years, Reger, an octogenarian music critic, has been coming to sit in front of Tintoretto's *Portrait of a White-Bearded Man* in the Kunsthistorisches Museum in Vienna. This novel describes the day he invites an elderly friend, Atzbacher, to join him. Through their conversation, we gradually learn about Reger's rancorous disgust for contemporary society, famous artists and public lavatories.

Extinction 1986

In Bernhard's last novel, Franz-Josef Murau has left the Austria he loathes for self-exile in Rome. When his parents and older brother die, however, he inherits the large Wolfsegg estate and returns, seeking both metaphysical and literal 'extinction'. The character of the poet Maria is modelled on Bernhard's friend Ingeborg Bachmann (275). This novel features what the author Geoff Dyer calls 'without doubt, the funniest passage in the whole of literature', when Murau attempts to explain his 'theory of exaggeration'. The Norwegian writer Karl Ove Knausgaard describes *Extinction* as 'a must-read for everybody'.

2010 Central European Classics
2020 Modern Classics
trans. Ewald Osers, 1989

1996
● trans. David McLintock, 1995

Gregor von Rezzori 1914–1998

Rezzori was born in Czernowitz, Bukovina, then part of the Austro-Hungarian Empire; it later became part of Romania before being annexed by the Soviet Union. Now it is in Ukraine. After several different nationalities and a period of statelessness, Rezzori eventually became an Austrian citizen. He was fluent in several languages and worked as an actor, artist and art critic, writing novels, memoirs, travel books and radio plays in German. Rezzori's ancestry was Italian and he spent his final years in Tuscany.

The Snows of Yesteryear
Portraits for an Autobiography 1989

Through vignettes of his boar-hunting father, his fragile mother, his beloved sister and his devoted governess, Rezzori evokes his multi-ethnic, multilingual childhood in the twilit years between the two World Wars. 'His voice echoes with the disturbing and wonderful magic of a true storyteller,' wrote Elie Wiesel (325).

2010 Central European Classics
2018 Modern Classics
trans. H. F. Broch de Rothermann, 1989

Hungary

Gyula Krúdy 1878 – 1933

Krúdy worked as a journalist before moving to Budapest at the age of eighteen, where he wrote bestselling short stories and novels, many of which featured his alter ego, 'Szindbad'. After the First World War, however, alcohol and gambling meant he lived in increasingly straitened circumstances with his second wife. He finally died in obscurity, in a crumbling hovel on the outskirts of Budapest. It was only with Sándor Márai's novel *Szindbad Goes Home* (1943), a fictionalized account of the last days of Krúdy's life, that his reputation revived.

Life Is a Dream 1925 – 30, pub. 1931

Krúdy self-published his 'most beloved book' of short stories in order to qualify for a Hungarian PEN award. His selection draws on his 'dearest and finest imaginings [...] about eating, digestion, wine, illness, life's real dreams'. They include his best-known tales, 'Last Cigar at the Grey Arabian' and 'The Journalist and Death', as well as the novella *The Green Ace* (1930). They provide dreamlike, ironic, wise observations on the human condition and the futility of life.

2010
trans. John Batki

Ödön von Horváth 1901 – 1938

According to the American writer Lydia Davis, Ödön von Horváth was once walking in the Bavarian Alps when he came across the skeleton of a long-dead hiker: the hiker's knapsack was still intact and inside was a postcard that read, 'Having a great time.' Horváth posted it for him. As the son of a Hungarian diplomat, Horváth was raised in Belgrade, Budapest, Munich, Bratislava and Vienna. He fled to Paris in 1938 and in June that year he was walking along the Champs-Élysées during a storm; the wind cracked the branch of a chestnut tree, which fell and killed him instantly. 'In Ödön von Horváth literature has lost a most gifted writer,' wrote Stefan Zweig (271). 'His two novels, *The Age of the Fish* and *Child of Our Time* [1938], present perhaps the most realistic picture of that generation which grew up during the despairing years after the First World War.'

The Age of the Fish 1937, pub. 1938

A schoolteacher comes to dread the glassy eyes of his students, whose ardent fascism develops from xenophobia into violence. The original German title was *Jugend ohne Gott* (Youth without God); it was published posthumously.

1985
• trans. R. Wills Thomas, 1939

Arthur Koestler 1905–1983

Koestler was born in Budapest and later lived in Vienna, where his mother was briefly a patient of Sigmund Freud (265). He became a foreign correspondent and travelled around the world, once flying over the Arctic in a zeppelin. In 1931, he joined the Communist Party of Germany and later fought in the Spanish Civil War, during which he met W. H. Auden (95) and was captured and imprisoned by Franco's troops. In 1938, he gave up communism and journalism, and he fought for the French Foreign Legion and the British army during the Second World War. Afterwards he settled in Britain, where he wrote novels, memoirs and political essays in English. 'He had lunch with Thomas Mann (245),' writes the historian Anne Applebaum, 'got drunk with Dylan Thomas (98), made friends with George Orwell (80), flirted with Mary McCarthy (507) and lived in Cyril Connolly's (107) London flat.' As Vice President of the Voluntary Euthanasia Society, Koestler wrote a pamphlet on suicide in 1982; the following year, he and his third wife took a fatal overdose of barbiturates at their London home. They left a bequest of almost £1 million to endow a chair of parapsychology at Edinburgh University.

1947 Penguin Books
1964 Modern Classics
• trans. Daphne Hardy, 1940
—
Daphne Hardy was a British sculptor living in Paris. She met Koestler in 1939 and they started living together. She translated *Darkness at Noon* and smuggled the manuscript into Britain, where she arranged its publication. Having arrived in Britain without an entry permit, Koestler was in prison himself when the book was first published. A 'restored' translation based on the rediscovered German original was published in 2019.

Darkness at Noon 1940

Rubashov is an indignant, imprisoned old revolutionary, a victim of a political purge, awaiting his show trial and execution. *Darkness at Noon* is a tense drama of prison psychology and a damning indictment of totalitarian government. 'Brilliant as this book is as a novel, and a piece of prison literature,' wrote George Orwell (80), 'it is probably most valuable as an interpretation of the Moscow "confessions" by someone with an inner knowledge of totalitarian methods.' Its attack on Stalinism was one of the inspirations for Orwell's *Animal Farm* (84) and *Nineteen Eighty-Four* (84).

1969 Penguin Books
1984 Modern Classics
• —
Stephen Spender (95) said of the country Neutralia that 'names like that should not be allowed in novels!'

Arrival and Departure 1943

The revolutionary Peter Slavek has escaped the dictatorship in his country, after withstanding interrogation by torture. But now he waits interminably in Neutralia – a fictional version of Portugal – a tense, non-aligned clearing-house for refugees. Koestler thought of this novel as the last in a trilogy, following *The Gladiators* (1939) and *Darkness at Noon*, on 'the conflict between morality and expediency'.

The Sleepwalkers
A History of Man's Changing Vision of the Universe
1959

This history of cosmology traces the story of how humankind grew to understand the universe. Through biographies of Copernicus, Kepler, Galileo and Newton, it suggests that pioneering scientists, like sleepwalkers, are not fully aware of what guides their research, or the implications of what they discover.

1964 Penguin Books
1968 Pelican Books
1986 Peregrine Books
2014 Modern Classics
intro. John Gray, 2014

2012
trans. Tibère Kremer, 1960
rev. Richard Seaver, 1993, 2011
intro. Richard J. Evans, 2012
aftwd. Bruno Bettelheim, 1960

Miklós Nyiszli
1901–1956

Nyiszli was a Hungarian Jewish doctor who worked as a forensic pathologist in Germany. In 1937, he returned to his home in Transylvania, before migrating to Hungary in 1940. In 1944, Nyiszli and his family were arrested and transported to Auschwitz, where he was forced to work as a pathologist in the Birkenau extermination camp under the notorious camp doctor, Josef Mengele.

Auschwitz
A Doctor's Eyewitness Account 1946

With a doctor's objectivity, Nyiszli describes the work he was forced to perform while imprisoned at Auschwitz in 1944. He recalls the huge crematoria, the 'nauseating odor of burning flesh and scorched hair', the medical experiments on dwarfs and twins, the autopsies of warm bodies, the tens of thousands of deaths. At one point, a young girl survived under a mound of bodies in a gas chamber: Nyiszli tried to hide her, but she was found and shot. When he heard that Women's Camp C, where his wife and daughter were imprisoned, was to be destroyed, he bribed an SS officer to transfer them to a women's work camp. All three survived the war, but Nyiszli never worked with a scalpel again.

2010
trans. Kathleen Szasz, 1962
—
Faludy wrote *My Happy Days in Hell* in England. It was first published in English translation, and did not appear in the original Hungarian until 1987.

György Faludy 1910–2006

The poet Faludy was born and died in Budapest. He fled Hungary in 1938, because of his Jewish ancestry, and served with the US army during the Second World War, but he returned to his native land afterwards. In 1949, the communist government sent him to the Recsk labour camp on trumped-up charges; he spent several years there and was one of the few survivors. After the failed revolution of 1956, Faludy left Hungary again, this time for London and then Toronto, where he worked as a translator and editor of Hungarian literary journals. He finally returned to Budapest after the fall of communism and was awarded the 1994 Kossuth Prize, Hungary's most prestigious literary award.

My Happy Days in Hell
1962

Faludy's lyrical memoir describes his flight to Paris, North Africa and America before the Second World War. It also includes a stark description of his torture and slow starvation in the communist labour camp, where he lectured the other prisoners on literature, history and philosophy.

Stephen Vizinczey b. 1933

Vizinczey was two when the Nazis killed his father; two decades later, the communists murdered his uncle. As a student in Budapest he wrote poems and plays, which were banned by the communist regime. He fought in the failed revolution of 1956 before fleeing to Toronto, arriving speaking fewer than 50 words of English. He learned the language by writing scripts for the National Film Board of Canada, but quit his job in 1965 and borrowed money to self-publish *In Praise of Older Women* distributing copies by car and through the post. The book became a surprise international bestseller. Vizinczey 'can teach the English how to write English', wrote Anthony Burgess (148).

In Praise of Older Women
The Amorous Recollections of András Vajda 1965

'This book is addressed to young men and dedicated to older women – and the connection between the two is my proposition,' writes the fictional philosopher András Vajda. 'I'm not an expert on sex, but I was a good student of the women I loved, and I'll try to recall those happy and unhappy experiences which, I believe, made a man out of me.' He describes encounters with women in Hungary, Italy and Canada. 'You cannot put it down,' writes Margaret Drabble (152): 'witty, moving and it's all about sex.'

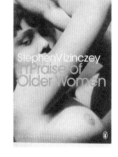

2010
• —

Czechoslovakia

Franz Kafka 1883–1924

Kafka was the son of wealthy German-speaking Czech Jewish parents. He studied law at Charles University, where he met his lifelong friend Max Brod. For most of his adult life, Kafka lived in Prague with his difficult father, spending the days as a clerk in the Workers' Accident Insurance Office and writing at night. He was engaged three times, but he never married. In 1917, he was diagnosed with laryngeal tuberculosis and spent his last years in a series of sanatoriums, slowly starving as his throat grew increasingly painful. Writing was for him a 'form of prayer', but only a handful of stories were published in his lifetime. The rest he destroyed or left to be burned by Brod. Thankfully, Brod declined this dying request and posthumously published Kafka's three novels – what Brod called his 'trilogy of loneliness' – as well as his diaries, letters and unpublished stories. 'Kafka's art consists in compelling the reader to re-read him,' wrote Albert Camus (181); W. H. Auden (95) called him 'the Dante of the twentieth century'.

Metamorphosis →
and Other Stories 1904–24, pub. 1908–24

Kafka considered very little of his work worthy of publication; this volume collects all the stories he published during his lifetime. One of the earliest, 'The Judgement', was written in a single night, a 'total opening of body and soul'. The collection *A Country Doctor* (1919) is dedicated to Kafka's father: when Kafka presented him with a copy, his father said, without looking at it, 'Lay it on my nightstand.' Kafka is perhaps best known for the story 'Metamorphosis', in which Gregor Samsa wakes up to find himself transformed into a monstrous insect. Elias Canetti (328) called it 'one of the few great and perfect works of poetic imagination written during the twentieth century'.

Kafka in Penguin

Kafka's first English-language translators were the Scottish couple Willa and Edwin Muir; they began with *The Castle* (283) in 1930, and their translations were all published by Penguin. In 1961, the scholar Malcolm Pasley acquired most of Kafka's original manuscripts for the Bodleian Library in Oxford and subsequently led a team that reconstructed critical editions in the original German (1982–90), which formed the basis for a new set of translations. Finally, the award-winning translator Michael Hofmann has produced new English editions for Modern Classics.

Description of a Struggle
and Other Stories

1904–24, pub. 1931–58

In 1931, Max Brod edited *The Great Wall of China*, the first selection of Kafka's unpublished stories, and more of his short fiction has been discovered and published since. His posthumously published tales includes 'Blumfeld, an Elderly Bachelor', in which a man is pursued by mysterious bouncing balls; 'Investigations of a Dog', in which a dog considers the limits of canine knowledge; and 'The Burrow', in which an unidentified animal becomes increasingly paranoid in its hole.

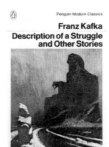

1979 Modern Classics
● trans. Willa & Edwin Muir, Malcolm Pasley, Tania & James Stern, 1933–73
1991 Twentieth-Century Classics *The Great Wall of China and Other Short Works*
● trans. Malcolm Pasley, 1973
2017 Modern Classics *The Burrow and Other Stories*
2019 Penguin Classics trans. Michael Hofmann, 2017

—

The 1979 edition includes the adolescent piece 'Description of a Struggle', excluded from later editions. Among Kafka's unpublished work it is the only manuscript to survive in a complete and fair copy. The 1991 edition also features 'The Complete Aphorisms', 109 pithy fragments that Kafka wrote while convalescing in Zürau with his favourite sister, Ottla.

—

1983 Penguin Books
1989 Modern Classics
● ed. Nahum N. Glatzer, 1971 trans. Willa & Edwin Muir, 1933–54

Franz Kafka

Metamorphosis and Other Stories

PENGUIN MODERN CLASSICS

3/6

1961 Modern Classics
• trans. Willa & Edwin Muir, 1933–49
1978 Modern Classics
Wedding Preparations in the Country and Other Stories
• trans. Willa & Edwin Muir, Ernst Kaiser & Eithne Wilkins, 1949–54

1992 Twentieth-Century Classics *The Transformation and Other Stories*
2000 Modern Classics
• trans. Malcolm Pasley, 1992
2007 Modern Classics
2019 Penguin Classics
trans. Michael Hofmann, 2007

The illustration on the cover of the 1961 edition is by the Austrian-born Israeli painter Yosl Bergner. The 1978 edition also includes 'Wedding Preparations in the Country', an unpublished, incomplete attempt at a novel, and 'Letter to His Father', a heart-rending missive that was never delivered.

The Diaries

1910–23, pub. 1948–9

Kafka kept a diary between the ages of 27 and 39, giving it up a year before his death. As well as recording ideas for stories and details of his daily life, he lays bare his isolation and frustration, writing about his sense of guilt, his relationship with his father and his feelings for the women he could never bring himself to marry.

1964 Peregrine Books
<u>1972</u> Modern Classics
• ed. Max Brod, 1948–9
trans. Joseph Kresch, Martin Greenberg & Hannah <u>Arendt</u>
(258), 1948–9

America
The Man Who Disappeared

1911–14, pub. 1927

Kafka's first novel was his last to be published. Sixteen-year-old Karl Rossmann is sent to the United States, where he encounters a baffling and surreal new world. The story was inspired by Yiddish theatre in Prague and based on the experiences of Kafka's relatives who had migrated to America. 'The innocence of [Kafka's] fantasy gives this book of adventure its peculiar colour,' wrote Max Brod.

1967 Penguin Books
<u>1974</u> Modern Classics
• trans. Willa & Edwin Muir, 1938
1997 Twentieth-Century Classics *The Man Who Disappeared*
2007 Modern Classics *Amerika*
2019 Penguin Classics
trans. Michael Hofmann, 1996
—
Kafka's working title for this novel was *Der Verschollene (The Missing Person)* but Brod called the first published edition *Amerika*.

Letters to Felice

1912–17, pub. 1967

In 1912, Kafka met Felice Bauer, a relative of Max Brod, and she became Kafka's muse for the next five years. Though they saw each other rarely, they corresponded by letter and were twice engaged. Kafka poured his tortured soul into his letters to Felice, which bear all the 'earmarks of his fiction', as the critic Michiko Kakutani puts it: 'the same nervous attention to minute particulars; the same paranoid awareness of shifting balances of power; the same atmosphere of emotional suffocation'. Felice's letters to Kafka have not survived.

1978
• ed. Erich Heller & Jürgen Born, 1967
trans. James Stern & Elizabeth Duckworth, 1973
—
This edition also includes *Kafka's Other Trial* (328), in which Elias Canetti draws parallels between Kafka's letters to Felice and certain episodes in *The Trial*.

The Trial

1914–15, pub. 1925

'Somebody must have made a false accusation against Josef K., for he was arrested one morning without having done anything wrong.' On his 30th birthday, Josef K., a chief cashier at a bank, is prosecuted and taunted by a mysterious, inaccessible authority. Kafka began writing *The Trial* soon after breaking his first engagement with Felice Bauer and it incorporates the short story 'Before the Law', which he originally published in his collection *A Country Doctor* (280). Although *The Trial* is unfinished and disordered, it does include a final chapter. 'It is the fate and perhaps the greatness of that work,' wrote Albert Camus (181), 'that it offers everything and confirms nothing.'

1953 Penguin Books
<u>1962</u> Modern Classics
• trans. Willa & Edwin Muir, 1937
1994 Twentieth-Century Classics
2019 Penguin Classics
trans. Idris Parry, 1994
—
The Trial was adapted for the screen in 1962 by Orson Welles, who played the Advocate. 'Say what you like,' he declared, 'but *The Trial* is the best film I have ever made.'

Letters to Milena 1920–20, pub. 1952

Milena Jesenská was a married journalist who asked Kafka's permission to translate his story 'The Stoker' – the first chapter of *America* – into Czech. They met in 1920 and became deeply attached for about two years. Kafka's passionate daily letters expressed bliss and despair, but Milena could not leave her husband and Kafka broke off the correspondence after a while. Milena died in Ravensbrück concentration camp in 1944.

1983
• trans. Willy Haas, Tanis & James Stern, 1952–3

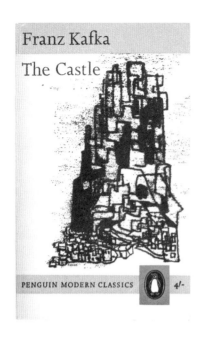

The Castle 1922, pub. 1926

K. is a land surveyor. He travels to take up a job at a castle, but finds himself in administrative limbo: unable to attain admittance to the castle, unable to find acceptance in the village below, and unable to leave. The unfinished novel ends mid-sentence, but Kafka once told Max Brod it would have concluded with K.'s death. The German title, *Das Schloss*, means both 'the castle' and 'the lock'.

1957 Penguin Books
1962 Modern Classics
• trans. Willa & Edwin Muir, 1930
1997 Twentieth-Century Classics
2019 Penguin Classics trans. J. A. Underwood, 1997
intro. Idris Parry, 1997

1983 Penguin Books
The Collected Novels of Franz Kafka
1990 Twentieth-Century Classics
• trans. Willa & Edwin Muir, 1930–38

More CASTLES

The Enchanted April
by Elizabeth von Arnim   380

We Have Always Lived in the Castle
by Shirley Jackson   68

Titus Groan
by Mervyn Peake   118

Brideshead Revisited
by Evelyn Waugh   69

Summer Lightning
by P. G. Wodehouse   49

Karel Čapek 1890 – 1938

Čapek studied philosophy in Prague, Berlin and Paris, before travelling around Europe as a journalist. He coined the word 'robot' in his 1920 play about sentient androids, *R.U.R. (Rossum's Universal Robots)*. As a left-leaning Czech journalist, he was identified by the Gestapo as a 'public enemy', but he died of double pneumonia on Christmas Day 1938, less than three months before the Nazi takeover of Czechoslovakia. 'There was no writer like him,' wrote Arthur Miller (486). 'Prophetic assurance mixed with surrealistic humour and hard-edged social satire: a unique combination.'

Apocryphal Stories 1920 – 38, pub. 1945

These subversive vignettes invent humorous episodes in the lives of famous historical, classical, biblical and literary figures such as Lazarus, Alexander the Great, St Francis of Assisi, Napoleon and Hamlet. They were published posthumously.

War with the Newts 1936

Captain van Toch discovers a colony of giant intelligent newts on a small island off Sumatra. The newts are capable of learning speech and using tools and soon they are exploited around the world, forced to perform menial tasks for humans and trained to fight wars. But the newts' growing intelligence has deadly consequences.

1975
• trans. Dora Round, 1949

1998 Twentieth-Century Classics
intro. Ivan Klíma, 1998
2010 Central European Classics
2018 Modern Classics
trans. M. & R. Weatherall, 1937
—
The 1998 edition included an introduction by Ivan Klíma, Čapek's biographer, who credits Čapek and Hašek (284) for reviving 20th-century literature in the Czech language.

Jaroslav Hašek 1883–1923

Hašek's father was a maths teacher who drank himself to death. Initially Hašek worked as a chemist and a bank clerk, but soon adopted an eccentric, bohemian life of haunting taverns, playing practical jokes and tramping around central Europe. He wrote stories, performed in cabarets, edited the anarchist magazine *Komuna* (*Commune*) and founded an anti-political 'Party of Moderate and Peaceful Progress within the Limits of the Law'. During the First World War, he enlisted with an infantry regiment and was taken prisoner by the Russians. He promptly deserted the Austrian army, joined the nationalist Czechoslovak Legion and then the Russian Communist Party, and finally became a Bolshevik commander, leading attacks on the Austrians. In 1920, he returned to independent Czechoslovakia and began writing *The Good Soldier Švejk*. He planned to write six volumes of *Švejk*, but his health declined sharply as he grew increasingly obese and alcoholic. He dictated chapters from his deathbed and died having completed only three volumes and the start of a fourth. 'Hašek was a humorist of the highest calibre,' wrote Max Brod (280). 'A later age will perhaps put him on a level with Cervantes and Rabelais.'

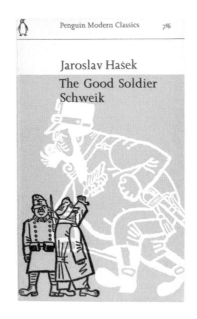

1939 Penguin Special *abridged*
1951 Penguin Books
1965 Modern Classics
● trans. Paul Selver, 1930
1974 Penguin Books
The Good Soldier Švejk
1983 Modern Classics
2005 Penguin Classics
trans. Cecil Parrott, 1973

A year after Hašek's death, his friend the cartoonist Josef Lada was commissioned to illustrate *Švejk*. He produced more than 900 illustrations; 156 are included in the current Penguin edition. Cecil Parrott's translation reinstates the vulgar expressions and cruder passages that Paul Selver had previously omitted. Parrott was British ambassador to Prague in the 1960s and the author of Hašek's biography, *The Bad Bohemian* (1978).

The Good Soldier Schweik
and His Fortunes in the World War 1921–3

Little Josef Švejk, a dealer in stolen dogs, attempts to enlist in the Austrian army, but his bumbling incompetence leads to a series of increasingly farcical scrapes with preposterous authority figures. The novel is both hilarious and darkly satirical. Written in the pubs of Prague, it has been translated into more languages than any other work of Czech literature and the verb 'to švejk' has entered the Czech language. It inspired Joseph Heller to write *Catch-22* (1961) and Bertolt Brecht (255) penned a sequel set in the Second World War. George Monbiot calls it 'perhaps the funniest novel ever written'.

1991 Penguin Books
2002 Modern Classics
● trans. Rita Klímová & Roslyn Schloss, 1989
pref. Philip Roth, 1989

Jiří Weil 1900–1959

Weil was a Jewish writer in Czechoslovakia and a militant communist, but he was expelled from the party after working for the Moscow-controlled Communist International (Comintern). He then found a job at the Jewish Museum in Prague until 1942, when he was ordered to a concentration camp. He managed to escape first, by staging his own death, and he spent the rest of the war in hiding.

Life with a Star 1949

In German-occupied Prague, the bank clerk Josef Roubicek is forced to wear the Star of David, which transforms the familiar city into an alien world of hunger, poverty and isolation. 'There are some great fictions about the Holocaust,' wrote Josef Škvorecký (285), 'but I know of no novel like *Life with a Star*.'

Josef Škvorecký 1924–2012

Škvorecký was the son of a bank clerk. He worked as a teacher and the editor of a monthly journal of world literature. In 1958, *The Cowards* was banned by the communist authorities and Škvorecký lost his job. He became a freelance writer and fled to Canada in 1968 after the Prague Spring, where he lived the rest of his life. With his wife, he founded 68 Publishers, dedicated to publishing banned Czech and Slovak authors such as Milan Kundera, Bohumil Hrabal and Václav Havel. 'Škvorecký means to Czech literature something akin to what the name Joseph Conrad (28) means to English literature, Günter Grass to contemporary German writing or J.D.Salinger (499) to American letters,' declared the novelist Arnošt Lustig when Škvorecký won the Neustadt International Prize in 1980. After Havel became president of post-communist Czechoslovakia, he awarded Škvorecký the Order of the White Lion in 1990.

The Cowards 1958

1972 Modern Classics
2010 Central European Classics
trans. Jeanne Němcová, 1970

Set in a small fictional town, this semi-autobiographical novel describes the single week in May 1945 that began with German occupation and ended with Soviet liberation. Danny Smiřický is a teenager, the son of a bank clerk and a passionate disciple of jazz. As prisoners of war stream through the town, Danny tries to play groovy music, impress girls and become a dashing partisan. The title refers to the town's yellow-livered middle-class authority figures.

Bohumil Hrabal 1914–1997

Hrabal was a railway labourer and dispatcher during the Second World War. He published his first book of poetry in 1948, but it was withdrawn by the communist regime, and he then worked as an insurance agent, travelling salesman, steel worker, paper-packer and scene-shifter. He decided to devote himself to writing in 1962, however, and soon became one of the most admired Czech writers of the 20th century. In 1997, he fell to his death from the fifth floor of a Prague hospital while attempting to feed the pigeons. At his request, he was buried in a coffin marked *Pivovar Polná*, 'Polná Brewery', where his mother had worked. 'His mode is a sort of dancing realism, somewhere between fairytale and satire,' writes Julian Barnes; 'the narrative likes to hop jauntily into the air and glide along for a page or two, returning to earth before you can tire of the trick. Hrabal is a most sophisticated novelist, with a gusting humour and a hushed tenderness of detail.'

1982 Penguin Books
2017 Modern Classics
trans. Edith Pargeter, 1968

Closely Watched Trains 1965

Miloš Hrma is the dopey but lovable apprentice at a provincial Czech railway station, who longs to lose his virginity but unexpectedly finds himself supporting the Czech Resistance during the Second World War. The film adaptation by Jiří Menzel is the apogee of Czechoslovak New Wave cinema and won the Academy Award for Best Foreign Language Film in 1968.

2017
trans. James
Naughton, 1993

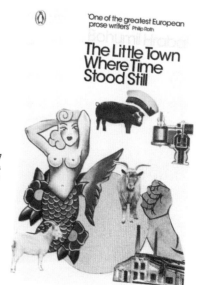

The Little Town Where Time Stood Still 1973

Originally self-published in a clandestine *samizdat* (317) edition, this is the elegiac story of a young boy growing up in an idyllic Czech backwater with his family and his raucous Uncle Pepin, against a backdrop of the German occupation during the Second World War and the new communist regime.

2017
trans. James Naughton, 1993

Cutting It Short 1976

Maryska, the brewer's wife with golden hair, scandalizes the neighbours by trimming her skirt short and riding her bicycle. She likes butchering pigs and devouring cream horns. Uncle Pepin (285) returns in this novel.

All My Cats 1986

In 1965, after the unexpected success of his first books, Hrabal bought a weekend cottage in the countryside outside Prague and found himself tending a community of adorable stray cats. In this confessional chronicle, Hrabal describes his intense and sometimes overwhelming relationship with the swiftly multiplying moggies.

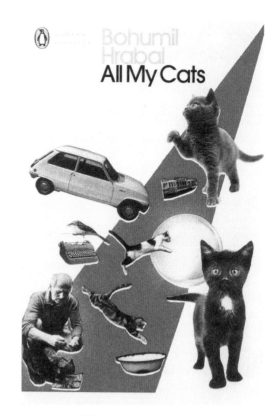

2020
trans. Paul Wilson, 2019

Ota Pavel

1930 – 1973

Otto Popper was the son of Jewish travelling salesman. His father and older brothers were sent to concentration camps in the Second World War, but survived. He was an enthusiastic ice-hockey player and a keen fisher. He found work as a broadcast sports journalist, changing his name to 'Ota Pavel'; but he became severely ill while covering the 1964 Winter Olympics in Innsbruck. Diagnosed with bipolar disorder, he spent the rest of his life in mental hospitals, during which time he wrote *How I Came to Know Fish.*

2010
trans. Jindriska Badal & Robert McDowell, 1990

How I Came to Know Fish

1968 – 73, pub. 1974

This moving memoir of Pavel's childhood evokes peacetime fishing trips with his father and his Uncle Prosek, the 'two finest fishermen in the world'. It also describes stealing back fish that were confiscated by the SS during the German occupation.

More CATS

The Cat Inside
by William S. Burroughs   485

The Cat
by Colette   172

The Lion of Boaz-Jachin and Jachin-Boaz
by Russell Hoban   540

Cat Country
by Lao She   346

A Tiger for Malgudi
by R. K. Narayan   344

Poland

Czesław Miłosz 1911–2004

Miłosz was born in the village of Szetejnie in the Russian Empire, in what is now Lithuania. He was the son of a Polish civil engineer and learned to speak Polish, Lithuanian, Russian, English, French and Hebrew. He began to write poetry in the 1930s, while working for radio stations in Vilnius and Warsaw. During the Second World War, he remained in Warsaw under the Nazi occupation, attending covert lectures, translating T. S. Eliot's *The Waste Land* (11) and hiding Polish Jews. After the war, he worked as a cultural attaché for the communist People's Republic of Poland, but he fell out of favour and defected in 1951, seeking asylum in France. He met Albert Camus (181) in Paris and published *The Captive Mind*, two poetry collections, two novels and a memoir, before emigrating to the USA, where he taught for many years at the University of California, Berkeley. In 1980, he won the Nobel Prize for Literature (576), after which his work was published in Poland for the first time in 30 years. When he died, he was given a state funeral in Kraków and thousands lined the streets. He was 'one of the great poets of our time', wrote Joseph Brodsky (316); 'perhaps the greatest'.

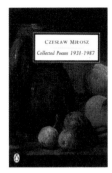

1997 Twentieth-Century Classics
• pref. Czesław Miłosz, 1988
2005 Modern Classics *New and Collected Poems*
intro. Czesław Miłosz, 2001

2014
ed. Robert Haas & Anthony Miłosz, 2011
fwd. Seamus Heaney, 2004
—
Collected Poems, 1931–1987 gathered all of Miłosz's poems that had been translated into English at the time. It was superseded by *New and Collected Poems, 1931–2001*, for which Miłosz translated more poems himself. *Selected and Last Poems, 1931–2004* presents a representative, posthumous anthology, with a number of late poems translated by Miłosz's son Anthony.

Poems 1931–2004

Miłosz's early 'catastrophist' poems reflect the politically turbulent 1930s through Surrealist (176) imagery and formal experimentation. 'Though he confronted the brutality of the modern age,' wrote Seamus Heaney, 'Miłosz believed in the joy-bringing potential of art and intellect.' The poems in the collection *Rescue* (1945) are among his best known, and *A Treatise on Poetry* (1957) is considered his magnum opus. It is 'so powerful', wrote the scholar Helen Vendler, 'that it bursts the bounds in which it was written – the bounds of language, geography, epoch'.

Proud to be a Mammal
Essays on War, Faith and Memory 1942–97

These diverse essays cover Miłosz's happy childhood, his passion for poetry and his love for the Polish language. 'Dictionary of Wilno Streets' is a celebratory verbal map of Vilnius, though he also writes about his native Poland as the 'Anus Mundi'.

2010
trans. Catherine Leach, Bogdana Carpenter & Madeline G. Levine, 1968–2001

1980 Penguin Books
1985 King Penguin
1997 Twentieth-Century Classics
trans. Jane Zielonko, 1953

The Captive Mind 1953

This influential work is a definitive denunciation of totalitarianism, condemning Stalinism and championing intellectual and psychological freedom. Miłosz examines the work of four Polish writers, including Tadeusz Borowski (293), and the ways in which they were affected by communism. *The Captive Mind* has been compared to both *Darkness at Noon* (278) by Arthur Koestler and Orwell's *Nineteen Eighty-Four* (84).

2001
• trans. Louis Iribarne, 1981

The Issa Valley 1955

'Thomas was born in the village of Gine at that time of year when a ripe apple thumps to the ground during an afternoon lull and when vats of freshly brewed ale stand in the hallway after the autumnal harvest.' Miłosz's semi-autobiographical novel evokes his own golden childhood on the Polish–Russian border. It is 'a masterpiece', wrote the critic John Bayley, '[…] an idyll of immense charm and poetic depth'. The *Observer* said that it 'reads like a Hanseatic *Cider with Rosie* (114)'.

Native Realm
A Search for Self-Definition 1959

Miłosz evokes his native Poland by describing his years away from it. Through vignettes, he portrays the destruction of his country during and after the Second World War and the ways in which the fate of his nation shaped him and his fellow émigrés.

1988 King Penguin
2014 Modern Classics
trans. Catherine S. Leach, 1968

Isaac Bashevis Singer 1902 – 1991

Singer grew up in the Jewish quarter of Warsaw. His father and grandfather were both rabbis and he embarked on rabbinical training himself. He abandoned his studies in 1921, however, and his older brother, Israel Joshua (291), found him work as a proofreader at a Yiddish literary magazine. Singer won the magazine's short-story competition and began to contribute his own pieces, using his mother's first name, 'Baszewis', a form of 'Bathsheba', as a pseudonym. In 1935, he followed his brother Israel to America, where he worked as a journalist, writing novels, children's books and *shtetl* tales of Jewish village life. He always wrote in Yiddish: 'Yiddish contains vitamins that other languages don't have,' he explained. But he supervised his English translations closely and thought of them as 'second originals'. 'Literature is the story of love and hate,' said Singer, 'a description of the mad hurricane of human passions and the struggle with them.' In 1978, he was awarded the Nobel Prize for Literature (576).

1981 Penguin Books
1993 Twentieth-Century
Classics
• trans. Jacob Sloan, 1958
—

'The atmosphere of this novel is medieval, the style classic, at times even archaic, the structure epic, the tone detached, the image remarkably concrete and evocative at one and the same time,' wrote the translator Jacob Sloan. 'Isaac Bashevis Singer's *Satan at Goray* is a masterpiece of the Yiddish language.'

Satan in Goray 1933

Singer's first novel is set in 1665–6, in the aftermath of the Chmelnicki massacres that annihilated the Polish Jews. Goray is a *shtetl* in southeast Poland, north of Bilgoray, where Singer himself spent the First World War. Driven to desperation by pogrom and famine, the villagers of Goray usurp their rabbi and establish a dark messianic cult. The book was originally serialized in the Polish Yiddish literary magazine *Globus*, co-founded by Singer.

1980 Penguin Books
1994 Twentieth-Century
Classics
● trans. A. H. Gross, 1950

—

Singer dedicated *The Family Moskat* to his brother I. J. Singer (291), who died in 1944. 'To me he was not only the older brother, but a spiritual father and master as well. I looked up to him always as to a model of high morality and literary honesty.'

The Family Moskat 1945–8

In New York, Singer began contributing to the *Jewish Daily Forward*, as his brother I. J. Singer (291) had done, and almost all his subsequent writing was first published in its pages. This epic novel, which describes Jewish life in Warsaw in the decades before the Nazi invasion, was serialized over several years. Abraham Cahan (318), editor of the *Forward*, almost dropped it after Singer set a double adultery during Yom Kippur, but it was allowed to continue at the insistence of readers. In 1950, it became Singer's first work to be translated into English, when reviewers compared it with *Buddenbrooks* (245) and the *Forsyte Saga* (47).

Stories 1945–88

The short story 'constitutes the utmost challenge to the creative writer', said Singer. 'Unlike the novel, which can absorb and even forgive lengthy digressions, flashbacks, and loose construction, the short story must aim directly at its climax. It must possess uninterrupted tension and suspense.' Singer's stories range from the traditional *shtetls* of central and eastern Europe to the streets of New York, and touch on passion and restraint, loyalty and treachery, religious fervour, sexual perversity, the power of memory and the permanence of loss. 'Yentl the Yeshiva Boy', about an Ashkenazi Jewish girl who dresses as a boy in order to study Talmudic Law, was the basis for the award-winning 1983 musical film *Yentl*, directed by and starring Barbra Streisand. 'No matter whether he writes about a prostitute, a thief, a murderer, an apostate or what,' said Henry Miller (451), 'Singer invests his characters with an aura of sanctity.'

1975 Penguin Books
1993 Twentieth-Century
Classics
● trans. Joseph Singer & Elaine Gottlieb, 1967

The Manor and The Estate 1952–5

These two works were initially serialized as a single novel and later translated in separate parts. They are set between the Polish insurrection of 1863 and the end of the 19th century, and form a prequel to *The Family Moskat*. They follow the tribulations of Calman Jacoby, a devout traditionalist from the village of Jampol. Plagued by his promiscuous ex-wife and troubled by his daughters' problematic marriages, he nevertheless discovers unforeseen opportunities in his newly industrializing country.

1975 Penguin Books
1993 Twentieth-Century
Classics
● trans. Joseph Singer, Elaine Gottlieb & Elizabeth Shub, 1969

—

The translator Joseph Singer was Isaac Bashevis Singer's nephew, the son of I. J. Singer (291).

The Magician of Lublin 1959

Yasha, the travelling magician, is a sword swallower, fire eater, acrobat and escapologist in late 19th-century Poland. Half Jewish, half Gentile, he has a jealous wife and a loyal assistant – and he has a woman in every town. Now he is sorely tempted to make one final escape: from his marriage, his country and his religion.

1974–9 Penguin Books
individual story collections
1984 Penguin Books
Collected Stories
1988 Modern Classics
trans. Evelyn Torton Beck et al., 1953–82

1989 Penguin Books
The Image and Other Stories
1993 Twentieth-Century Classics
● trans. Judy Beeber et al., 1965–86

1990 Penguin Books
The Death of Methuselah and Other Stories
1993 Twentieth-Century Classics
● trans. Ruth Schachmer Finkel et al., 1971–88

—

In 1953, 'Gimpel the Fool' became the first of Singer's short stories to appear in English, in a translation by Saul Bellow (477). Twenty years later, *A Crown of Feathers and Other Stories* (1973) shared the National Book Award for Fiction with Thomas Pynchon's *Gravity's Rainbow*. Singer chose 47 tales for his *Collected Stories*, which the *New York Times* called 'a cornucopia of invention'. More stories followed in *The Image and Other Stories* (1986) and *The Death of Methuselah and Other Stories* (1988).

1979 Penguin Books
1994 Twentieth-Century Classics
trans. Elaine Gottlieb & Joseph Singer, 1960

1974 Penguin Books
1996 Twentieth-Century
Classics
trans. Isaac Bashevis Singer
& Cecil Hemley, 1962
—
There is a prominent theme
of vegetarianism in *The Slave*.
Singer became an ardent
vegetarian in 1962.

1977 Penguin Books
1994 Twentieth-Century
Classics
trans. Aliza Shevrin & Elizabeth
Shub, 1972
—
'Although I did not have
the privilege of going through
the Hitler holocaust,' wrote
Singer in a prefatory note,
'I have lived for years in
New York with refugees
from this ordeal.'

The Slave
1960 – 61

Almost three decades after
writing *Satan in Goray* (288),
Singer returned to the aftermath
of the 17th-century Chmelnicki
pogroms in this story of Jacob,
a scholar sold as a slave to a
family of peasant farmers. He
was writing just as the horrific
extent of the Nazi Holocaust was
coming to light. It is 'a burningly
radiant, intensely beautiful
book', said Ted Hughes. 'Singer is
answering his age like a prophet.'

Enemies
A Love Story 1966

Herman Broder, Holocaust
survivor and refugee, is caught
between three women: Yadwiga,
the Polish peasant, who hid
him from the Nazis and who
has come with him to America
as his wife; Masha, his true love,
another Holocaust survivor,
with whom he is having an
affair; and Tamara, his first wife
from Poland, who has arrived
unexpectedly in New York.

Scum
1967

Buenos Aires, 1906.
Max Barabander is a sleazy
property developer who cares
more about his sapped virility
than the death of his son.
Abandoning his grieving wife,
he revisits his native Warsaw
to pose as a wealthy widower
and attempt to seduce women.

1992 Penguin Books
1995 Twentieth-Century Classics
● trans. Rosaline Dukalsky Schwartz, 1991
—
The English translation of *Scum* was first
published a few months before Singer died.

1979 Penguin Books
1994 Twentieth-Century
Classics
● trans. Channah Kleinerman-
Goldstein, Elaine Gottlieb &
Joseph Singer, 1966
—
The 1966 English translation
is dedicated to the memory of
Cecil Hemley, editor, translator
and a close friend of Singer,
who died that same year. 'His
wife Elaine Gottlieb translated a
part of this work,' writes Singer,
'and it was all done with Cecil's
advice. His love for literature
was as great as his taste.'

1994
● trans. Leonard Wolf, 1992

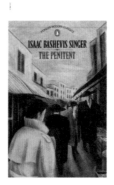

1986
trans. Joseph Singer, 1983

In My Father's Court
A Memoir 1963

In the days before the First
World War, Singer's father
convened a *Beth Din*, a rabbinical
court, at the family home on
Krochmalna Street in Warsaw.
It became 'a kind of blend of
a court of law, synagogue, house
of study, and […] psychoanalyst's
office', always full of people and
extraordinary events. This volume
collects Singer's memories of
his remarkable childhood.

The Certificate
1967

David Bendiger arrives in
Warsaw in 1922, eighteen years
old, penniless and determined to
become a writer. But he quickly
becomes entangled with three
different women and finds
himself emigrating to Palestine.
'It is impossible not to feel
the charm of this book,' wrote
Elie Wiesel (325), 'which may
be the most Jewish of all Singer's
works. The warmest and the
saddest too. A great tenderness
emerges from its pages.'

The Penitent 1973

Joseph Shapiro is disillusioned
and aimless. He flees Poland for
America, where his self-made
life of wealth proves unrewarding
and his marriage fails. He then
seeks spirituality in Israel. 'I often
discussed with my brother (291)
the lack of dignity and the
degradation of modern man,'
wrote Singer. '[…] The agonies
and the disenchantment of
Joseph Shapiro may to a degree
stir a self-evaluation in both
believers and sceptics.'

Shosha 1974

Aaron Greidinger is an aspiring young writer, the son of a rabbi, who is surprised to rediscover Shosha, his childhood sweetheart, who has hardly changed since he last saw her. The story is set in Warsaw in the 1930s.

1979 Penguin Books
1993 Twentieth-Century Classics
trans. Joseph Singer, 1978

Meshugah 1981–3, pub. 1994

This novel, discovered posthumously, is a sequel to *Shosha*. Aaron is working in New York in the early 1950s and meets up with his old friend Max, a 'glutton, guzzler, womanizer', and Max's smart-talking mistress, Miriam. *Meshugah* in Yiddish means 'crazy, senseless, insane'.

1996
• trans. Isaac Bashevis Singer & Nili Wachtel, 1994

Love and Exile 1974–8
An Autobiographical Trilogy

*A Little Boy in Search of God,
A Young Man in Search of Love,
Lost in America*

These volumes trace Singer's early years from his bookish boyhood in Warsaw to his first love affairs and emigration to America, and the loneliness and depression that threatened to overwhelm him there. 'The true story of a person's life can never be written,' warned Singer. 'It is beyond the power of literature. The full tale of any life would be both utterly boring and utterly unbelievable.'

The King of the Fields

1988

Singer's late novel imagines the ancient lands that would one day become Poland, as hunter-gatherers battle with farmers for control. It is in part a historical novel and in part a parable of modern civilization. 'It is as if he were not inventing, but taking heavenly dictation,' wrote the *Financial Times*.

2012
trans. Joseph Singer, 1976–81
intro. Isaac Bashevis Singer, 1984

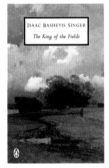

1990 Penguin Books
1994 Twentieth-Century Classics
trans. Isaac Bashevis Singer, 1989

I. J. Singer 1893–1944

Israel Joshua Singer, older brother of Isaac Bashevis Singer (288), wrote for Yiddish newspapers in Warsaw, Kiev and Moscow. In 1921, Abraham Cahan (318), editor of the *Jewish Daily Forward* in New York, spotted Singer's story 'Pearls' and hired him as a foreign correspondent. Singer worked for *The Forward* for the rest of his life, emigrating to New York in late 1933.

The Brothers Ashkenazi 1935–6

In this sweeping family saga, set in Łódź in central Poland, Max Ashkenazi is desperate to be more successful than his twin brother Jacob. He breaks from his bourgeois Jewish upbringing to embrace capitalism, but as the First World War approaches he starts to question his life choices. Saul Bellow (477) called it 'a wonderful novel'.

1993
• trans. Joseph Singer, 1980
intro. Irving Howe, 1980

—

The translator, Joshua Singer, was Israel's son. He also translated the works of his uncle, Isaac Bashevis Singer (288).

Witold Gombrowicz

1904–1969

The Second World War began
while Gombrowicz was sailing
from Poland to Argentina. He
had already published a book
of unsuccessful short stories,
a play that anticipated the
Theatre of the Absurd (184)
and a controversial first novel,
Ferdydurke. He decided to
weather the war in Buenos
Aires, but ended up staying
for 25 years, working as a bank
clerk and continuing to write.
He moved to France in 1964 and
won the Prix Formentor in 1969.
He kept a long, idiosyncratic
diary, which opens:

Monday	*Me.*
Tuesday	*Me.*
Wednesday	*Me.*
Thursday	*Me.*

1986 Penguin Books
1989 Twentieth-Century Classics
• trans. Eric Mosbacher, 1961
intro. Czesław Miłosz (287),
1982

Ferdydurke 1937

A 30-year-old man is transformed into an
adolescent boy and plunged into a world of teenage
cruelty, toilet humour and pubescent eroticism.
Gombrowicz anticipates Sartre (185) by unmasking
constructed identities. 'Think Kafka (280) translated
by Groucho Marx (432), with commentaries,'
suggests Kirkus Reviews.

Pornografia 1960

During the Second
World War, two ageing
intellectuals visit
a country estate and

1991
• trans. Alastair Hamilton, 1966

amuse themselves by imagining a love affair between
Henia, their hosts' daughter, and Karol, the local
administrator's son; but their little game becomes
increasingly bizarre and obscene. The novel is
a fusion of pastoral romance, melodramatic farce,
philosophical fiction, political thriller and murder
mystery. 'How disturbing his writings are,' wrote
Czesław Miłosz (287), 'how challenging and enigmatic.'

Jan Karski 1914–2000

Jan Kozielewski served apprenticeship
postings to Romania, Germany, Switzerland
and Britain before joining the Polish
diplomatic service in 1939, a few months
before Germany and Russia invaded his
country. He was captured by the Soviets
and narrowly avoided the Katyn Forest
massacre in 1940. He managed to escape
to German-occupied Warsaw, where he
adopted the *nom de guerre* 'Jan Karski'
and joined the Resistance, repeatedly
crossing enemy lines to courier messages
to the Polish government-in-exile in France
and in Britain. In 1943, he completed a final
mission to London, where he met Arthur
Koestler (278), before travelling to the USA,
where he personally briefed President
Roosevelt in the Oval Office. He became
an American citizen in 1954 and taught for
many years at Georgetown University in
Washington, DC, where the future president
Bill Clinton was among his students.

2012 Penguin Books
2019 Modern Classics
aftwd. Andrew Roberts, 2011

Story of a Secret State was
originally written in English.
In 1999, a Polish translation
was published with additional
material provided by Karski.
These additions have been
translated, by Sandra Smith,
and appear for the first time in
English in the Penguin edition.

Story of a Secret State
My Report to the World 1944

Karski smuggled information to
the Allied governments about the
conditions in the Warsaw Ghetto
and the extermination camps
operating on Polish soil; his 1942
report was one of the earliest
and most accurate accounts of
the Holocaust to reach the Allies.
He twice broke in to the Warsaw
Ghetto to observe conditions.
'My job was just to walk. And observe.
And remember,' he said. 'The odour.
The children. […] We were walking
the streets and my guide kept
repeating: "Look at it, remember,
remember." And I did remember.'
He published his 'report to the world'
in 1944; it had already sold 400,000
copies before the end of the war.

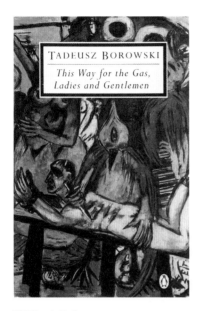

1976 Penguin Books
<u>**1992**</u> Twentieth-Century Classics
2008 Penguin Classics
trans. Barbara Vedder, 1967
intro. Jan Kott, 1976

Tadeusz Borowski 1922–1951

Borowski was born in Russian Zhytomyr, in what is now Ukraine. His father was a Polish bookseller who was sent to the Gulag in 1926 and his mother was deported to Siberia in 1930. Borowski lived with his aunt for two years until the family was finally reunited and expatriated to Poland. Under German occupation, Borowski was denied education, but he attended underground school and university classes nonetheless, and he published a *samizdat* (317) book of poems in 1942. Later that year, he was arrested because his fiancée Maria Rundo was a member of the Polish Resistance. They were both sent to Auschwitz; but, amazingly, they both survived the experience. After the war they married, and Borowski began writing about the experience of the death camps. He won Poland's National Literary Prize in 1950. The next year, a few days after the birth of his daughter, the 28-year-old Borowski opened the gas valve in his kitchen stove and took his own life.

This Way for the Gas, Ladies and Gentlemen
and Other Stories 1948

'All of us walk around naked. The delousing is finally over, and our striped suits are back from the tanks of Cyclone B solution, an efficient killer of lice in clothing and of men in gas chambers.' Borowski's appalling stories are told from the first-hand perspective of an Auschwitz inmate. He describes slave labour in freezing conditions, building the railway ramp for unloading human cargo and working in the hospital where medical experiments were conducted.

The stories in this edition are drawn from two collections, *Farewell to Maria* (1948) and *A World of Stone* (1948).

Gustav Herling 1919–2000

Gustaw Herling Grudziński was studying literature in Warsaw when Poland was invaded. He became an active member of the Polish Resistance, but was arrested by the Soviets in 1940 and sent to the Gulag at Yercevo, near Archangel on the White Sea. Freed in 1942, he left Russia with the Polish general Władysław Anders's army and fought in the Middle East and Italy, for which he was awarded the *Virtuti Militari*, Poland's highest military decoration. After the war, he moved to Italy and founded the Polish émigré journal *Kultura*, publishing the works of Czesław Miłosz (287), the future Nobel Laureate Wisława Szymborska and Witold Gombrowicz (292).

A World Apart
A Memoir of the Gulag 1951

Herling's account of his two horrific years in the Soviet Gulag was one of the first descriptions of communist crimes against humanity, published ten years before Solzhenitsyn's *One Day in the Life of Ivan Denisovich* (314). Herling describes the dehumanizing conditions, desperate hunger and hard labour in Arctic temperatures. 'This book should be published and read in every country,' wrote Albert Camus (181), 'as much for what it is as for what it says.'

1996 Penguin Books
<u>**2005**</u> Modern Classics
• trans. Andrzej Ciołkosz, 1951
pref. Bertrand Russell, 1951
intro. Anne Applebaum, 2005
—
Herling's title is taken from Fyodor Dostoyevsky's *The House of the Dead* (1862), which is based on the Russian writer's experiences of a Siberian prison camp in the early 1850s. 'Here there is a world apart,' Dostoyevsky wrote, 'unlike everything else, with laws of its own, its own manners and customs.'

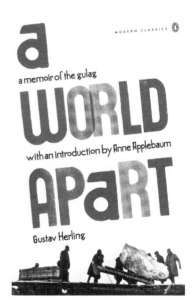

Stanisław Lem 1921–2006

'I was a monster,' wrote Lem about his childhood. He worked as a car mechanic during the Second World War, smuggling munitions to the Polish Resistance under Soviet, Nazi and again Soviet occupation. When eastern Poland was annexed by Ukraine in 1945, Lem and his family were forcibly relocated west and settled in Kraków, where he studied medicine and began writing. After 1956, once communist censorship became less stringent, he made his name as a writer of science fiction. His works have since been translated into dozens of languages and sold more than 45 million copies. His best-known novel, *Solaris* (1961), has been filmed three times. The *New York Times* called Lem 'a Jorge Luis Borges (572) for the Space Age, who plays in earnest with every concept of philosophy and physics, from free will to probability theory'.

The Star Diaries 1954–71

Ijon Tichy is an accident-prone astronaut who narrates his strange adventures around the cosmic wilderness. In these playful, satirical, thought-provoking voyages, Tichy encounters clones, mutinous robots, his future self, and an orbiting sirloin steak.

2015
trans. Michael Kandel, 1971
ill. Stanisław Lem, 1957–71
—
The numbered voyages that form *The Star Diaries* were written out of order, over a number of years, with new instalments added to each new edition. The order in which they were written is 22, 23, 25, 11, 12, 13, 14, 7, 8, 28, 20, 21. This translation is based on Lem's 1971 definitive edition and omits voyages 18, 24 and 26.

The Cyberiad
Fables for the Cybernetic Age 1965

Most of these fantastical short stories involve Trurl and Klapaucius, two 'constructors', who travel through a medieval-style universe of knights, princesses and dragons, offering their technical expertise. Their anarchic adventures involve UFOs, a crew of PhD pirates, and a king who oppresses his people with parlour games.

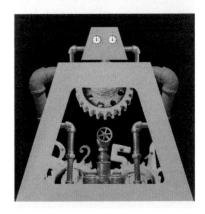

2014
trans. Michael Kandel, 1974
intro. Christopher Priest, 2014
ill. Daniel Mróz, 1972

Tales of Pirx the Pilot 1968

In the near future, space travel between earth, the moon and Mars has become routine and unremarkable. These stories follow the hapless everyman Pirx as he bumbles and blunders around the solar system, learning to fly a spaceship.

1982 King Penguin
2019 Modern Classics
trans. Louis Iribarne, 1979

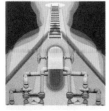

2017
trans. Michael Kandel, 1974

The Futurological Congress 1971

Ijon Tichy, narrator of *The Star Diaries*, is sent back to earth to attend the Eighth Futurological Congress in Costa Rica. A riot erupts in the Hilton Hotel, however, when the water is laced with hallucinogenic drugs. Tichy starts to lose touch with time and reality.

More EXTRATERRESTRIALS

Mortal Engines

1971–6

This selection of short stories ranges from surreal fables about monsters and paranoid kings to longer works, such as the chilling thriller 'The Hunt' and 'The Mask', a bizarre love story about a shape-shifting assassin.

2016
trans. Michael Kandel, 1977, 1992

Fiasco

1986

Lem wrote several stories about first contact with aliens. In this, his last novel, the spaceship *Hermes* arrives at the planet Quinta, but if there are aliens among the planet's strange mounds and webs, they are eerily quiet.

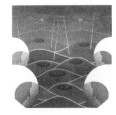

Fiasco

2018
trans. Michael Kandel, 1987

Leszek Kołakowski 1927–2009

Kołakowski studied philosophy as a student, and taught at Warsaw University until he was expelled in 1968 for criticizing communism. Banned from teaching and publishing in Poland, he moved to Canada, the USA and finally Oxford in 1970, where he was a Senior Fellow of All Souls College. As an internationally respected philosopher, he inspired the anti-communist 'Solidarity' movement in Poland in the 1980s. The historian Tony Judt has called him 'the last illustrious citizen of the Twentieth-Century Republic of Letters'.

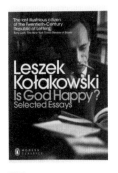

2012
trans. Agnieszka Kołakowska
—
The translator, Agnieszka Kołakowska, is Leszek Kołakowski's daughter and a philosopher in her own right.

Is God Happy? Selected Essays 1956–2006

These essays address eternal philosophical problems around the existence of God and the nature of truth as well as urgent issues of the modern age, such as the merits of being a snob and the importance of being late. They are organized thematically under three headings: 'Socialism, Ideology and the Left', 'Religion, God and the Problem of Evil' and 'Modernity, Truth, the Past and Some Other Things'.

Sławomir Mrożek 1930–2013

Mrożek was a political journalist, playwright and cartoonist, who became increasingly disenchanted with communism, defected to Italy in 1963 and then moved to France. His condemnation of the Polish involvement in the Soviet-led invasion of Czechoslovakia in 1968 led to his works being banned in Poland. He lived in Mexico for some years before returning to Kraków in 1996.

The Elephant 1957

These absurd micro-stories portray life in communist Poland through a cast of pedantic bureaucrats, rubber elephants, inhuman officials and drunken swans. 'Mrożek's brief fables are something like Kafka's (280) stories,' wrote the *Spectator*, 'but they're funnier.'

2010
trans. Konrad Syrop, 1962
ill. Daniel Mróz, 1957

Ryszard Kapuściński 1932–2007

Kapuściński was born in Pinsk, now part of Belarus. He attended Primary School Number Five before the war and later took up poetry and amateur boxing. He became a domestic reporter and then a foreign correspondent, working for PAP, the Polish Press Agency, until 1981. He visited Africa, Asia and Latin America, witnessed 27 revolutions and coups, was imprisoned 40 times and escaped four death sentences. He won numerous international literary awards and was named 'journalist of the century' in Poland. Kapuściński's writings have 'the narrative power of a Conrad (28) or Kipling (22) or Orwell (80)', says the poet Blake Morrison.

1988 Penguin Books
2001 Modern Classics
trans. William R. Brand
& Katarzyna Mroczkowska-
Brand, 1987
rev. Klara Glowczewska, 1987

Nobody Leaves
Impressions of Poland
1959–62, pub. 1962

When Kapuściński first worked for the Polish Press Agency, he contributed essays about the wildest regions of his native country,

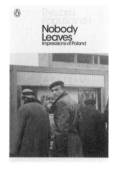

2019
trans. William R. Brand, 2017

what he called 'the Polish Bush'. These pieces describe remote villages, medieval ways of life, collective farms, and uneasy communities on the brink of modernity.

Another Day of Life 1976

'This is a very personal book,' wrote Kapuściński, 'about being alone and lost.' In 1975, he hitched a lift on one of the last Portuguese military aircraft flying to Angola and wrote this account of the country's civil war, which brought 400 years of colonial rule to an end. 'One Kapuściński is worth more than a thousand whimpering and fantasizing scribblers,' writes Salman Rushdie. 'His exceptional combination of journalism and art allows us to feel so close to what Kapuściński calls the inexpressible true image of war.'

2006
trans. William R. Brand
& Katarzyna Mroczkowska-
Brand, 1983
intro. Neal Ascherson, 2006

The Emperor
Downfall of an Autocrat 1978

Kapuściński's masterpiece is an account of the decline and fall in the 1970s of Haile Selassie, last Emperor of Ethiopia, descendant of the Queen of Sheba. Based on the testimony of Selassie's surviving courtiers, Kapuściński's book evokes the emperor's lavish world of opulence and corruption, depicting a reign of absolute power over an impoverished people. It can also be read as a veiled commentary on the communist government of Poland.

Shah of Shahs 1982

The last Shah of Persia, the tyrannical Mohammad Reza Pahlavi, was overthrown in 1979. Kapuściński's account of his final years is also a meditation on the nature of revolutions and the ironies and inequalities that produce them. Following The Emperor, this was the second in a projected trilogy on absolute power; the third volume was to have been about the notorious Ugandan dictator Idi Amin.

2006
trans. William
R. Brand
& Katarzyna
Mroczkowska-
Brand, 1985
intro. Christopher
de Bellaigue, 2006

Ryszard Kapuściński
Shah of Shahs

Kornel Filipowicz 1913–1990

Filipowicz worked for the Polish Resistance during the Second World War until he was arrested and imprisoned in the Gross-Rosen and Sachsenhausen concentration camps. In 1943, he published a clandestine book of poetry, in an edition of ten copies, which marked his arrival as a leading figure of the Polish avant-garde. He was a close friend of the poet and future Nobel Laureate Wisława Szymborska, with whom he established a daily correspondence.

The Memoir of an Anti-Hero 1961

An anonymous Polish narrator is on holiday in the beautiful countryside of his homeland when the Germans invade in 1939. Determined to avoid unnecessary heroics, he decides to survive the war whatever it takes, but he gradually becomes increasingly and chillingly alienated from the people around him.

2020
trans. Anna Zaranko, 2019

—

Anna Zaranko's translation won the Polish Book Institute's translation award.

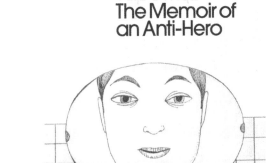

'Provocative, troubling, awkward … a proper classic'
Sunday Times

Kornel Filipowicz

The Memoir of an Anti-Hero

Louis Begley b. 1933

Ludwik Begleiter was born in Stryj, now part of Ukraine. The son of a Jewish doctor, he only survived the Second World War by pretending to be Catholic. The family moved to New York in 1947, where they changed their name. Begley studied at Harvard Law School and worked at the prestigious law firm Debevoise & Plimpton, where before his retirement he was senior partner and head of the firm's international practice. He is the author of several novels, including *About Schmidt* (1996).

Wartime Lies 1991

Begley's award-winning, semi-autobiographical novel is narrated by young Maciek, a Polish Jew who learns to lie in order to survive the Second World War. He travels with his beautiful, brave Aunt Tania, using forged identity papers and false names, never more than one step ahead of the Germans and the threat of the extermination camps.

2007
aftwd. Louis Begley, 2004

—

Stanley Kubrick, whose father had Polish Jewish heritage, wrote a screen adaptation of *Wartime Lies* called *Aryan Papers*. He got as far as casting Uma Thurman as Aunt Tania, but abandoned the project after Steven Spielberg's *Schindler's List* (1993) was announced.

MODERN CLASSICS

Louis Begley
Wartime Lies

EASTERN EUROPE

FYODOR SOLOGUB *The Little Demon*

V. I. LENIN *What is to be Done?*

V. I. LENIN *The State and Revolution*

MAXIM GORKY *The Life of a Useless Man*

MAXIM GORKY *My Childhood*

MAXIM GORKY *My Apprenticeship*

MAXIM GORKY *My Universities*

MAXIM GORKY *Fragments from My Diary*

OSIP MANDELSHTAM *Selected Poems*

ANNA AKHMATOVA *Selected Poems*

BORIS PASTERNAK *Selected Poems*

Boris Pasternak *The Last Summer*

Andrei Bely *Petersburg*

PMC

ISBN 0 14 01.8638 7

ISBN 0 14 01.8126 1

ISBN 0 14 01.8435 X

ISBN 0 14 01.8362 0

ISBN 0 14 01.8285 3

ISBN 0 14 01.8284 5

ISBN 0 14 01.8286 1

ISBN 0 14 01.8283 7

ISBN 0 14 01.8474 0

ISBN 0 14 01.8617 4

ISBN 0 14 01.8466 X

ISBN 0 14 00.6412 5

Russia

Fyodor Sologub 1863 – 1927

Fyodor Kuzmich Teternikov worked as a schoolteacher for 25 years, until the success of *The Little Demon* allowed him to devote himself to literature. He wrote under the pseudonym 'Sologub', and became a leading poet of the Russian Symbolist movement (303). 'His face was pale, long, without eyebrows,' wrote the humorist Teffi; 'by his nose was a large wart; a thin reddish beard seemed to pull away from his thin cheeks. [...] He was always tired, always bored.'

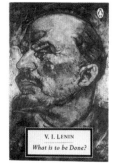

1994 Twentieth-Century Classics
• trans. Ronald Wilks, 1994
intro. Victor Erofeyev, 1994
2013 Penguin Classics
trans. Ronald Wilks, 1994
intro. Pamela Davidson, 2013
—
The character Peredonov's distinctive brand of deranged sadomasochism became known as 'Peredonovism'.

The Little Demon 1892 – 1902, pub. 1905 – 7

Ardalyon Borisych Peredonov is a provincial schoolteacher who descends through paranoia and sexual perversion into hallucinatory fantasy, arson, torture and eventually murder. He embodies the Russian concept of *poshlost* – the banality of evil (259) – which would become a favourite subject of Vladimir Nabokov (304). The Symbolist poet (303) Aleksandr Blok said that *The Little Demon* was a 'classic work' read by 'the whole of educated Russia'. When asked if the book was autobiographical, Sologub replied: 'No, my dear contemporaries, it is of you that I have written my novel about the little demon.'

V. I. Lenin 1870 – 1924

Vladimir Ilich Ulyanov was a brilliant law student. In the 1890s, he began to associate with clandestine Marxist groups until he was arrested and exiled to Siberia in 1895. After that, he lived as an émigré in western Europe, adopting the alias 'Lenin' and running the Marxist newspaper *Iskra* (*Spark*) in Munich and London, where he befriended Leon Trotsky (322). In exile, he became a prominent theorist within the Russian Social-Democratic Labour Party, leading the Bolshevik faction when the party split in 1903. Following the February Revolution of 1917 and the abdication of Tsar Nicholas II, Lenin travelled to Petrograd in a sealed train and swept the Bolsheviks to power in the October Revolution, becoming Chairman of the first Soviet government. He instigated wide-ranging social and economic reforms in Russia, while also operating a ruthless dictatorship and rolling out the Gulag system. When he died, Petrograd was renamed Leningrad in his honour and his body was embalmed; it is still on display in Moscow's Red Square.

What is to be Done?
Painful Questions of Our Movement 1902

This slim pamphlet outlines Lenin's radical proposals for overthrowing the Russian monarchy and establishing a centralized, national *soviet*, or 'council'. At the time, it led directly to the schism between the Bolshevik ('majority') and Menshevik ('minority') factions of the Russian Social-Democratic Labour Party; now, it is regarded as a key statement of Lenin's Marxist ideology.

1988 Penguin Classics
1989 Twentieth-Century Classics
• trans. Joe Fineberg & George Hanna, 1962
intro. Robert Service, 1988
—
Lenin borrowed his title from the pro-revolutionary novel *What is to be Done?* (1863) by Nikolai Chernyshevsky, his favourite author.

The State and Revolution 1917

Written between the February and October Revolutions of 1917, while Lenin was hiding in Finland, this impassioned polemic distils the rationale behind Lenin's subsequent regime. Addressing revolutionaries across Europe, he prophesies a proletariat uprising that would give birth to a socialist state and, ultimately, establish a perfect communist society.

1992 Twentieth-Century Classics
2009 Penguin Classics
trans. Robert Service, 1992

1975 Penguin Books
1989 Twentieth-Century
Classics
• trans. Moura Budberg, 1971
—

Baroness Moura Budberg
was a Russian aristocrat at
the court of Tsar Nicholas II.
Her husband was beaten
to death by peasants on
his Estonian estate, but she
was protected by Gorky, with
whom she subsequently lived
as his secretary and common-
law wife. She later settled
in England, had an affair
with H. G. Wells (26), and
was suspected of being an
undercover agent, working for
Russia or Britain, or perhaps
both. One MI5 informant
praised her ability to 'drink
an amazing quantity, mostly
gin'. She translated works
by writers including Georges
Simenon (201), Anton Chekhov
and Ivan Turgenev.

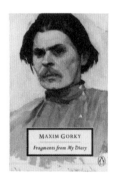

1940 Penguin Books
1975 Penguin Books *revised*
1986 Penguin Classics
1990 Twentieth-Century
Classics
• trans. Moura Budberg,
1940, 1972

Maxim Gorky 1868 – 1936

After an unsuccessful suicide attempt, Alexei Maximovich
Peshkov began writing for provincial newspapers under the
pseudonym 'Gorky', which means 'bitter'. His grim stories
proved unexpectedly popular, and his play *The Lower Depths*
(1902) was a success at the Moscow Art Theatre. He then
collaborated with Konstantin Stanislavski, became active in the
revolutionary movement and befriended Lenin (299). In 1917, he
founded *Novaya Zhizn* (*New Life*), a daily newspaper promoting
radical socialism, but he became increasingly critical of Lenin's
dictatorial methods, calling him at one stage a 'cold-blooded
trickster'. In 1921, Gorky left Russia for Italy. Ten years later,
however, at Stalin's personal invitation, he returned triumphantly
to Russia, was awarded the Order of Lenin and given a mansion
in Moscow. His home city of Nizhny Novgorod was renamed
Gorky, as were the Moscow Art Theatre and Moscow's main
park. He was made Chairman of the new Union of Soviet
Writers and promoted Socialist Realism (312). When he died
five years later, Stalin carried his funerary urn, although Gorky
was probably poisoned on Stalin's orders.

The Life of a Useless Man

1908

'You are plastic,' wrote Chekhov
to Gorky; 'that is, when you
describe a thing you see it and
touch it with your hands. That
is real art.' In this novel, Yevsey
Kimkov is manipulated into
working as an agent provocateur
for the tsarist regime during
the Revolution of 1905.

Fragments from My Diary

1924

These 'fragments' were edited
by Gorky into a mosaic portrait
of his years on the road, his time
spent among the urban poor,
his meetings with writers and
his clashes with revolutionaries.
'Leo Tolstoy once said to a lizard
in a low whisper: "Are you happy,
eh?"' he recounts. 'The lizard was warming itself on a
stone among the shrubs that grew on the road to Dulber,
while he stood watching it, his hands thrust inside his
leather belt. Then, cautiously looking round, the great
man confided to the lizard: "As for me – I'm not!"'

My Childhood
My Apprenticeship
My Universities 1913 – 23

In the first instalment of
Gorky's autobiographical trilogy,
My Childhood (1913), he describes
living with his mother and
grandparents: his brutal
grandfather, who regularly beat
him unconscious, and his tender,
mountainous grandmother,
who told him wonderful
bedtime stories. Gorky's mother
died when he was eleven, at
which point Gorky ran away.
In My *Apprenticeship* (1916), he
covers his bitter teenage years,
wandering around the Russian
Empire as a tramp, working as a baker's boy, a dish-washer
on a barge and an apprentice in an icon-painter's workshop.
The Russian title translates literally as *Among the People*.
My Universities (1923) portrays the dark cellars and
dead-end jobs where Gorky rubbed shoulders with
dreamers, drifters and revolutionaries. He recalls days of
drudgery and nights of reading books. In 1887, he bought
a revolver and attempted to shoot himself. 'I ask you to
blame the German poet Heine for my death,' he wrote
in his suicide note; 'he invented toothache in the heart.'

1966 Penguin Classics
1990 Twentieth-Century Classics
trans. Ronald Wilks, 1966

1974 Penguin Classics
1989 Twentieth-Century Classics
• trans. Ronald Wilks, 1974

1979 Penguin Classics
1991 Twentieth-Century Classics
• trans. Ronald Wilks, 1979

Osip Mandelshtam 1891–1938

Osip Emilevich Mandelshtam befriended the poet Nikolai Gumilev and became a leading member of the Acmeists in St Petersburg. In the 1930s, he began to criticize the communist regime, writing a poem about Stalin describing his 'fat fingers slimy as worms' and 'cockroach moustache'. A few months later, he was arrested and exiled to Cherdyn in the Ural region, where he attempted suicide. During the Stalinist purges, he was rearrested and died in Siberia on his way to the Gulag. 'Only in Russia is poetry respected,' he wrote – 'it gets people killed. Is there anywhere else where poetry is so common a motive for murder?'

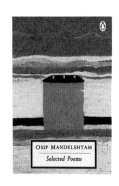

1977 Penguin Poets
Selected Poems
● trans. Clarence Brown
& W. S. Merwin, 1974
<u>1991</u> Twentieth-Century
Classics *Selected Poems*
trans. James Greene, 1977–91
fwd. Nadezhda Mandelshtam,
1976
fwd. Donald Davie, 1977
intro. Donald Rayfield, 1988
—
'Mandelshtam said that
the contents are squeezed
from the form as water from
a sponge,' wrote his wife
Nadezhda in her foreword.
'If the sponge is dry, there
would be no moisture at all.
So, to render the content
– which Mr Greene [the
translator] has succeeded
in doing – is to give, in a
way, the form or harmony.'

Selected Poems 1908–37

In *Stone* (1913), *Tristia* (1922) and *Poems* (1928), as well as in many verses published posthumously, Mandelshtam forged new forms of poetry to describe his ambivalent feelings towards St Petersburg, the pain and joy of human love, and the upheaval and horror following the events of 1917. Anna Akhmatova called his poetry a 'new, divine harmony'.

Anna Akhmatova 1889–1966

1969 Penguin Poets *Selected Poems*
● trans. Richard McKane, 1969
essay Andrei Sinavsky, 1964
1988 Penguin Poets *Selected Poems*
<u>1992</u> Twentieth-Century Classics
2006 Penguin Classics
● trans. D. M. Thomas, 1976–85

Anna Andreevna Gorenko grew up in Tsarskoe Selo, the imperial summer residence outside St Petersburg. She began writing poetry at the age of eleven and was first published in 1907, under the pen name 'Akhmatova', her Tatar grandmother's name. In 1910, she married the poet Nikolai Gumilev, leader of the Acmeist movement, and became famous for both her poetry and her glamorous personality. She became close friends with Boris Pasternak (302), had an affair with Osip Mandelshtam, and Amedeo Modigliani drew her portrait numerous times. After 1921 – when Gumilev was shot as an alleged counter-revolutionary – Akhmatova fell out of favour with the Soviet regime; she was reduced to writing *samizdat* (317) poems for her friends to read, memorize and burn. She was followed by police agents until Stalin's death in 1953, after which she regained some recognition in Russia.

Selected Poems 1909–64

Akhmatova's poetry falls into two periods. Her earlier verses are lucid and lyrical – touching on love, the Russian countryside and the experience of reading *Hamlet* – and are mostly apolitical. Her later poetry expresses the horror of the Stalinist regime. Her two masterpieces are the intricate cycle *Requiem* (1935–61), composed in secret, in which 'a hundred million' voices cry through her 'tormented mouth', and *Poem Without a Hero* (1940–62), which superimposes tsarist St Petersburg and Soviet Leningrad in a love poem to the city.

Acmeism

In 1910, the poet Mikhail Kuzmin condemned the 'incomprehensible, dark cosmic trappings' of Symbolism (303). His essay 'Concerning Beautiful Clarity' heralded a new poetic school, a movement towards concision, concrete imagery, and a desire to 'admire a rose because it is beautiful' not because of what it might symbolize. The group met at the Stray Dog Café in St Petersburg and called themselves the 'Guild of Poets', though they were ironically dubbed the 'Acmeists'. The greatest proponents of Acmeism were Nikolai Gumilev, Anna Akhmatova and Osip Mandelshtam, who described the movement as 'a neo-classical form of modernism (11)'. Acmeism was concurrent with, and in some ways similar to, Imagism (61).

1984 Penguin Poets
1991 Twentieth-Century
Classics
• trans. Jon Stallworthy
& Peter France, 1983
fwd. Y. B. Pasternak, 1983
—
The critic Yevgeny Borisovich
Pasternak was Pasternak's
eldest son.

Boris Pasternak 1890–1960

Boris Leonidovich Pasternak's father was a painter, his mother a pianist. Among their family friends they counted Rainer Maria Rilke (269), Leo Tolstoy – whose work Leo Pasternak illustrated – and the composer Sergei Rachmaninoff. Pasternak studied music, and initially hoped to become a composer, before turning to poetry. His first collection, *My Sister, Life* (1922), established him as one of Russia's leading poets. In the 1930s, he felt increasing pressure to conform to the principles of Socialist Realism (312), so he stopped writing original poetry. He completed *Doctor Zhivago* in 1957, but it was banned by the Soviet Union. Set between the Revolution of 1905 and the Second World War, it is an epic tale of romance, poetry, religion and philosophy shot through with criticism of the Stalinist regime. The manuscript was smuggled out of Russia and published in Italy. In 1958, Pasternak was awarded the Nobel Prize for Literature (576), but the enraged Communist Party banned him from accepting it. *Doctor Zhivago* was not published in the Soviet Union until 1988; the following year, Pasternak's son Yevgeny travelled to Stockholm to accept the Nobel medal on his late father's behalf.

Selected Poems 1912–59

Pasternak's early lyrics have a musical quality and convey an intense passion for nature. His supreme achievement, perhaps, is the final section of *Doctor Zhivago*, which consists entirely of poems. 'Pasternak is a poet of microcosm, of stereoscopic vision,' wrote Joseph Brodsky (316). 'The overall feeling is that you're handling a crystal, that you have been given the world in the multi-faceted eye of the honey-bee.'

The Last Summer 1934

This novella opens in the winter of 1915, in the Ural mountains. A young Muscovite half remembers and half dreams the love and laughter of the summer of 1914 – the last summer of peace.

1960 Penguin Books
1965 Modern Classics
• trans. George Reavey, 1959,
1960
intro. Lydia Slater, 1960
—
This cover shows a drawing
of Boris Pasternak by his
father Leo. Lydia Slater, who
provides an introduction, was
Pasternak's sister. A research
chemist and poet, she settled
in Oxford in the 1930s.

Andrei Bely 1880–1934

Boris Nikolayevich Bugayev studied mathematics, zoology and philosophy before becoming a leading writer of Russian Symbolism (303). He began using the pseudonym 'Andrei Bely' in 1902 to avoid embarrassing his father, an eminent professor of mathematics. Bely supported the Bolsheviks in the October Revolution in 1917, and served on the Union of Soviet Writers, but he became increasingly disillusioned by the communist regime. 'Mathematics, poetry, anthroposophy, fox-trot – these are some of the sharpest angles that make up the fantastic image of Andrei Bely,' said Yevgeny Zamyatin (303). '[He is] a writer's writer.'

Petersburg A Novel in Eight Chapters 1913–14

Nikolai Ableukhov is a university student who becomes involved with a revolutionary terror organization in 1905. When he is ordered to kill a government official with a time bomb, however, his target turns out to be his own father. *Petersburg* is the pinnacle of Symbolist prose (303), an impressionistic, synaesthetic, panoramic tour of Russia's imperial capital. Like Joyce's *Ulysses* (10), it incorporates wordplay, literary allusion and experimental modernist (11) techniques. Anthony Burgess (148) called *Petersburg* 'the one novel that sums up the whole of Russia'.

1983 Modern Classics
• trans. John E. Malmstead
& R. A. Maguire, 1978
1995 Twentieth-Century Classics
2011 Penguin Classics
trans. David McDuff, 1995
intro. Adam Thirlwell, 2011
—
Vladimir Nabokov (304)
considered *Petersburg* one of the
four greatest novels of the 20th
century, alongside *Ulysses* (10),
Kafka's 'Metamorphosis' (10)
and the first half of Proust's 'fairy
tale', *In Search of Lost Time* (168).

Yevgeny Zamyatin 1884–1937

'True literature can exist only when it is created, not by diligent and reliable officials, but by madmen, hermits, heretics, dreamers, rebels and sceptics,' wrote Yevgeny Ivanovich Zamyatin. The son of a priest, he was a naval engineer who was exiled twice for supporting the Bolsheviks and spent two years in England building Russian icebreakers in the shipyards of Newcastle. He returned to Russia in time for the October Revolution in 1917, but became increasingly critical of the communist regime. In 1931, he wrote to Stalin personally, asking permission to leave the country, a request that was only granted after Gorky (300) interceded. Zamyatin then moved to Paris, where he lived in poverty until he died.

More BANNED BOOKS

The Dragon and Other Stories 1913–35

These fifteen stories and vignettes are ribald, poetic and poignant. In 'The Dragon', a little man in uniform transforms into a monster when given a gun; 'A Story about the Most Important Thing' describes a city as a barren, prehistoric landscape; and 'The Flood' is the tale of a woman's rebellion against infertility.

1975
• trans. Mirra Ginsburg, 1966

We 1920–21, pub. 1924

In the 26th century, spacecraft engineer D-503 lives in the totalitarian One State, where the buildings are made of glass, secret police conduct mass surveillance and numbered citizens are ruled by an all-powerful 'Benefactor'. This archetypal modern dystopia anticipated and influenced Aldous Huxley's *Brave New World* (66), Vladimir Nabokov's *Invitation to a Beheading* (307), Ayn Rand's *Anthem* (450) and George Orwell's *Nineteen Eighty-Four* (84). Ursula K. Le Guin called it 'the best single work of science fiction yet written'.

1972 Modern Classics
• trans. Mirra Ginsburg, 1972
1993 Twentieth-Century Classics
2007 Penguin Classics trans. Clarence Brown, 1993
—
In 1921, *We* became the first book to be banned by the Soviet censorship board. Zamyatin smuggled the *tamizdat* (317) manuscript to New York, however, where it was published in English translation in 1924. The first Russian edition was printed in Prague in 1927 and smuggled back into the USSR. It was not published in the Soviet Union until 1988.

Symbolism

The Symbolist movement originated in late 19th-century France, with the poetry of Charles Baudelaire, Paul Verlaine, Arthur Rimbaud and Stephane Mallarmé. It was one of several reactions against realism, an attempt to depict effects rather than objects. The poet Jean Moréas published the 'Symbolist Manifesto' in 1886: 'scenes from nature, human activities, and all other real world phenomena will not be described for their own sake,' he wrote; 'here, they are perceptible surfaces created to represent their esoteric affinities with the primordial Ideals'. Symbolist verse was a poetry of suggestion, of subjective moods, of epiphany. It had affinities with *fin-de-siècle* aestheticism (3) and had a widespread influence in the visual arts, drama and music across Europe. In France, in the early 20th century, the movement passed into Surrealism (176) and it remained a major influence in Russia, particularly on poets and novelists such as Aleksandr Blok, Andrei Bely (302) and Marina Tsvetaeva.

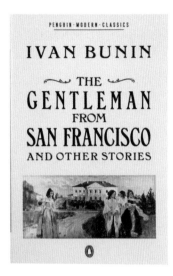

1987
trans. David Richards & Sophie
Lund, 1984

Ivan Bunin 1870–1953

Ivan Alekseevich Bunin achieved literary renown by the age of 30, having published two volumes of poetry and a selection of short stories about the lives of peasants. His language is so richly textured it has been described as 'Bunin brocade'. He was a close friend of Maxim Gorky (300), who called him 'the first poet of our times'. In 1920, however, the 50-year-old Bunin moved to France and was condemned as a traitor by the Soviet authorities. André Gide (164) welcomed him to Paris, and he won the Nobel Prize for Literature (576) in 1933 – the first Russian to do so.

The Gentleman from San Francisco
and Other Stories 1915–44

Bunin was inspired to write the title story after he heard about an American gentleman who died on the island of Capri while waiting to go into dinner at the Hotel Quisisana. Other stories in this volume include 'Late Hour', about an old man's return to the town of his youth; 'Mitya's Love', about the dangerous consequences of sexual insecurity; and 'Night', a lyrical prose poem about the sea.

Vladimir Nabokov 1899–1977

As a child in St Petersburg, Vladimir Vladimirovich Nabokov developed a lifelong passion for butterflies. His wealthy family was forced to flee Russia when the Bolsheviks came to power, living first in England, where Nabokov studied at Cambridge University, and then in Germany. Nabokov's father died in Berlin when he stepped in front of an assassin's bullet in 1922. Nabokov spent much of the twenties and thirties there, publishing poetry, stories and novels in Russian, and coaching tennis and boxing. His wife Véra, who was Jewish, lost her job in 1936 and the couple migrated to France the following year, and then to the USA when Germany invaded France in 1940. Nabokov volunteered as an entomologist at the American Museum of Natural History in New York until he found a teaching post in Massachusetts. He began publishing novels in English, and the success of *Pnin* (309) secured his literary reputation. He taught literature at Cornell University for ten years, where Thomas Pynchon was one of his students. In 1961, the Nabokovs moved into a suite at the Montreux Palace Hotel in Switzerland, where he lived for the last seventeen years of his life, translating Alexander Pushkin's *Eugene Onegin* (1825–32) into English and pursuing butterflies through the Alps. 'It is not improbable,' he admitted in 1967, 'that had there been no revolution in Russia, I would have devoted myself entirely to lepidopterology and never written any novels at all.'

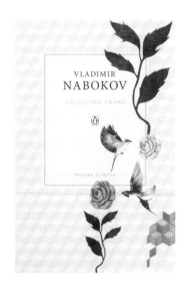

2013
trans. Dmitri Nabokov, 1984–2012
intro. Thomas Karshan, 2012
—
Dmitri Nabokov translated many
of his father's works, from and into
four different languages. He was
also a singer, who sang bass roles
in opera houses around the world.

Collected Poems 1514–74

This anthology is an expansion of *Poems and Problems*, a poetry collection that Nabokov assembled in 1969. The poems span 60 years, from his first, 'Music', to one of his last, 'To Véra', and they touch on butterflies, sport, love and exile. The autobiographical *University Poem* (1926), which recalls his experiences at Cambridge in 1919–22, is written in Onegin stanzas.

Stories 1921–52

Most of Nabokov's stories were written in Russian, while he was living in Berlin and Paris in the 1920s and 1930s and surrounded by émigrés dreaming of a lost world of silver samovars and *thé-dansants*. He evokes magic and melancholy, ambiguity, irony and loss in stories about fading society beauties, cocaine-snorting waiters, neurotic actors, eccentric lodgers and woodland elves. The autobiographical 'First Love' and 'Mademoiselle O' later became chapters in *Speak, Memory* (308). Nabokov selected four short-story volumes in his lifetime, all of which contained a Nabokovian baker's dozen of thirteen tales. When he died, he was working on a fifth. The Penguin edition of *Collected Stories* comprises every known short story he wrote, including thirteen never previously published in English.

Strong Opinions
Think, Write, Speak

1921–77, pub. 1973–2019

'I think like a genius, I write like a distinguished author, and I speak like a child,' wrote Nabokov in 1973, in his foreword to *Strong Opinions*, a miscellaneous collection of interview transcripts, letters to editors and newspaper articles. As he explains, he always insisted on receiving his interlocutors' questions in advance and composed careful responses, whether he was discussing his own literary celebrity, Stanley Kubrick's film adaptation of *Lolita* (309), or butterflies. *Think, Write, Speak* is a posthumous volume of previously uncollected material, ranging from precocious essays written as a university student to Nabokov's very final interviews.

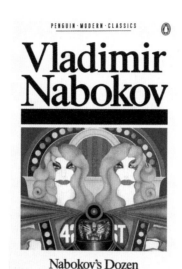

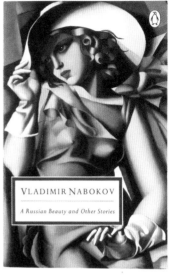

1960 Penguin Books
1987 Modern Classics
trans. Peter Pertzov & Vladimir Nabokov, 1958
fwd. Vladimir Nabokov, 1958

1975 Penguin Books
1989 Twentieth-Century Classics
• trans. Dmitri Nabokov, Simon Karlinsky & Vladimir Nabokov, 1973
fwd. Vladimir Nabokov, 1973

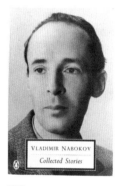

1981 Penguin Books
1990 Twentieth-Century Classics
• trans. Dmitri Nabokov & Vladimir Nabokov, 1975
fwd. Vladimir Nabokov, 1975

1994
• trans. Dmitri Nabokov & Vladimir Nabokov, 1976
fwd. Vladimir Nabokov, 1976

1997
trans. Dmitri Nabokov, 1995
—

2011
• fwd. Vladimir Nabokov, 1973

2020
ed. Brian Boyd & Anastasia Tolstoy, 2019
—
Brian Boyd wrote his MA thesis on Nabokov, which Nabokov himself described as 'brilliant'. Boyd is now a professor of English at the University of Auckland in New Zealand. He is the author of an award-winning two-volume biography, *Nabokov: The Russian Years* (1990) and *Nabokov: The American Years* (1991).

2016
trans. Olga Voronina & Brian
Boyd, 2014

1973 Penguin Books
1990 Twentieth-Century
Classics
trans. Michael Glenny
& Vladimir Nabokov, 1970
—
All of Nabokov's Russian novels
were published under the *nom
de plume* 'V. Sirin'. The *sirin*
is a creature in Russian folklore
similar to the sirens of Greek
mythology, with the head and
chest of a beautiful woman and
the body of an owl. Sirins sang
mellifluous songs that lured
men to their death.

1994
trans. Michael Scammell
& Vladimir Nabokov, 1964
fwd. Vladimir Nabokov, 1964

Letters to Véra 1923–76

In May 1923, Nabokov met the Russian Jewish Véra Evseyevna Slonim at a charity ball in Berlin. 'You are the only person I can talk with about the shade of a cloud,' he wrote, 'about the song of a thought.' They married in April 1925, and their son Dmitri was born in 1934. Véra was Nabokov's inspiration, editor and first reader; all of his works are dedicated to her. She drove him on butterfly-hunting excursions, and kept a handgun in the glove compartment to protect him. Several times she stopped him burning the manuscript of *Lolita* (309). Throughout half a century of marriage, Nabokov wrote countless letters to Véra, collected here for the first time.

The Tragedy of Mister Morn

1923–4, pub. 2008

In Nabokov's experimental, neo-Shakespearean blank verse drama, Morn is the restored king of an unnamed European country, recently rocked by revolution.

2012
trans. Anastasia Tolstoy
& Thomas Karshan
intro. Thomas Karshan

Mary 1926

Nabokov's first novel opens in a dark, broken elevator in a Berlin boarding house, where a Russian émigré, Lev Glebovich Ganin, meets the husband of his childhood sweetheart, Mary. The character of Mary was inspired by Nabokov's own first love, Valentina Evgenievna Shulgin, whom he described under the pseudonym 'Tamara' in the last chapter of *Speak, Memory* (308).

King, Queen, Knave 1928

The department-store sales assistant Franz Bubendorf embarks on a secret affair with Martha, the wife of his employer. 'Of all my novels this bright brute is the gayest,' wrote Nabokov. The names of two characters, Blavdak Vinomori and Vivian Badlook, are near anagrams of Vladimir Nabokov.

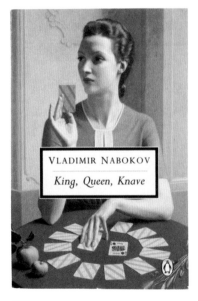

1993
trans. Dmitri Nabokov
& Vladimir Nabokov, 1968
fwd. Vladimir Nabokov, 1968

The Luzhin Defense 1930

Aleksandr Ivanovich Luzhin is a fictional chess grandmaster, destroyed by his own genius after he invents a brilliantly ingenious defence. In 1930, Nabokov was devising chess problems for the émigré press in Berlin, and he plotted this novel as a sequence of chess moves. 'Chess problems,' he wrote, 'demand from the composer the same virtues that characterize all worthwhile art: originality, invention, conciseness, harmony, complexity, and splendid insincerity.'

The Eye 1930

Smurov is a lovelorn Russian tutor in Berlin. When he attempts suicide, it is unclear whether he has succeeded or not; the narrator drifts around the city struggling to glean further information. 'It is unlikely that even the most credulous peruser of this twinkling tale will take long to realize who Smurov is,' wrote Nabokov in his foreword. 'I tried it on an old English lady, two graduate students, an ice-hockey coach, a doctor, and the twelve-year-old child of a neighbor. The child was the quickest, the neighbor, the slowest.'

1992
trans. Dmitri Nabokov
& Vladimir Nabokov, 1965
fwd. Vladimir Nabokov, 1965

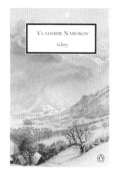

Glory 1932

Told through impressionistic vignettes, this tale of young Martin Edelweiss draws heavily on Nabokov's own experience of fleeing the Russian Revolution and studying in Cambridge. 'Nabokov writes prose the only way it should be written,' said John Updike (514), 'that is, ecstatically.'

1974 Penguin Books
1990 Twentieth-Century Classics
trans. Dmitri Nabokov
& Vladimir Nabokov, 1971
fwd. Vladimir Nabokov, 1971

Laughter in the Dark 1932

Albinus is a rich, married, middle-aged art critic who lusts after a coquettish young cinema usherette called Margot. Their mutually parasitic relationship eventually leads to duplicity and death.

Laughter in the Dark

1963 Penguin Books
1986 Modern Classics
1998 Twentieth-Century Classics
• trans. Vladimir Nabokov, 1938
aftwd. Craig Raine, 1998
2010 Modern Classics
trans. Vladimir Nabokov, 1938
—
The Russian title translates as Camera Obscura, which is better in some ways than Laughter in the Dark, but Nabokov detested the 1936 English translation by Winifred Roy, so he retranslated and retitled the novel himself.

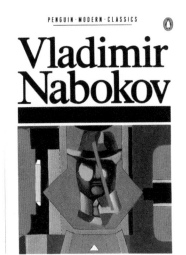

Despair

1981 Penguin Books
1987 Modern Classics
trans. Vladimir Nabokov, 1937, 1965
fwd. Vladimir Nabokov, 1965
—
Nabokov recalled the 1937 translation of Despair as his 'first serious attempt [...] to use English for what may be loosely termed an artistic purpose'.

Despair 1934

When Hermann Karlovich, the owner of a chocolate factory, meets a homeless man in Prague, he decides he is his doppelgänger and starts to concoct a magnificent crime involving swapped identities, betrayal and murder. 'To read [Nabokov] in full flight is to experience stimulation that is at once intellectual, imaginative and aesthetic,' writes Martin Amis (160), 'the nearest thing to pure sensual pleasure that prose can offer.'

Invitation to a Beheading 1935–6

Drafted in a fortnight 'of wonderful excitement and sustained inspiration', this is the nightmarish story of Cincinnatus C., sentenced to death for obscure metaphysical reasons. Elements of the novel have been compared to Lewis Carroll's Alice's Adventures in Wonderland (1865), Franz Kafka's The Trial (282) and James Joyce's Ulysses (10). Nabokov himself called it 'a violin in a void'.

'Incidentally,' wrote Nabokov in his foreword to Invitation to a Beheading, 'I could never understand why every book of mine invariably sends reviewers scurrying in search of more or less celebrated names for the purpose of passionate comparison. During the last three decades they have hurled at me (to list but a few of these harmless missiles) Gogol, Tolstoevski, Joyce (8), Voltaire, Sade, Stendhal, Balzac, Byron, Beerbohm (60), Proust (166), Kleist, Makar Marinski, Mary McCarthy (507), Meredith (!), Cervantes, Charlie Chaplin (149), Baroness Murasaki, Pushkin, Ruskin, and even Sebastian Knight (308).'
—
1963 Penguin Books
1990 Twentieth-Century Classics
trans. Dmitri Nabokov
& Vladimir Nabokov, 1959
fwd. Vladimir Nabokov, 1959

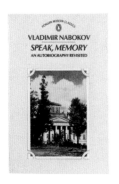

1969 Penguin Books
1987 Modern Classics
fwd. Vladimir Nabokov, 1967
—
The chapters of *Speak, Memory* initially appeared as magazine pieces and were first collected in 1951. Nabokov wanted to call the volume *Speak, Mnemosyne* – the muse of memory – but his publisher thought readers should be able to pronounce the title. In 1954, he translated the book into Russian, as *Drugie Berega (Other Shores)*, with considerable changes. He liked these amendments, so he 'revisited' the English version in 1966. The 2000 Penguin edition appends 'Chapter Sixteen', a pseudo-review written in 1950 by Nabokov himself: 'A unique freak as autobiographies go,' he summarized, 'Mr Nabokov's book is easier to define in terms of what it is not than in terms of what it is.'

Speak, Memory
An Autobiography Revisited 1936–1951, rev. 1954–66

'The cradle rocks above an abyss,' wrote Nabokov, 'and common sense tells us that our existence is but a brief crack of light between two eternities of darkness.' The first twelve chapters of *Speak, Memory* recall his idyllic childhood growing up in pre-revolutionary St Petersburg and on the family's country estate, where he discovered butterflies and fell in love for the first time. In the last three chapters, he describes his student years at Cambridge and the émigré community in Berlin and Paris in the 1920s and 1930s. Penelope Lively (161) calls *Speak, Memory* 'a celebration not just of language but also of an unquenchable vision'.

The Gift 1937–8

Fyodor Godunov-Cherdyntsev is an aspiring writer living in Berlin. Borrowing the styles of different Russian authors, he makes various literary attempts, while pursuing a relationship with the elusive Zina. 'Its heroine is not Zina,' reflected Nabokov in 1963, 'but Russian Literature.'

The Enchanter 1939, pub. 1986

This 'pre-Lolita (309) novella' is about a middle-aged man who is obsessed with young girls and marries an ailing mother in order to seduce her russet-haired, roller-skating daughter. It has the same black humour as *Lolita*, but the plot goes in a very different direction.

1981 Penguin Books
1992 Twentieth-Century Classics
2001 Modern Classics
trans. Martin Scammell, Dmitri Nabokov & Vladimir Nabokov, 1963
fwd. Vladimir Nabokov, 1963
—
The fourth chapter of *The Gift*, a pseudo-biography of Lenin's (299) favourite author, Nikolai Chernyshevsky, was initially censored in the serialized publication. The 2001 Penguin edition also reintroduces 'Father's Butterflies: Second Addendum to *The Gift*', written in 1939. It was translated by Dmitri Nabokov and published posthumously for the first time in *Nabokov's Butterflies* (2000), edited by Brian Boyd and Robert Michael Pyle.

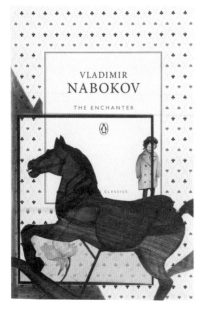

2009
trans. Dmitri Nabokov, 1986
—
The Enchanter was the last work of fiction Nabokov composed in Russian. He wrote it in Paris, but the manuscript was mislaid during his move to America in 1940. He rediscovered it in 1959, after he had written *Lolita*. It was published posthumously in translation in 1986, the same year that Nabokov was published in the Soviet Union for the first time.

The Real Life of Sebastian Knight

1939, pub. 1941

The first novel Nabokov wrote in the English language is a postmodern work (505) about language itself and its inability to convey meaning. The narrator, V., frustrated by a 'slapdash' biography of his half-brother, the novelist Sebastian Knight, attempts to write a 'real life' of him, but is repeatedly derailed by quotation, digression and the slipperiness of words. Nabokov 'did us all an honour by electing to use, and transform, our language', said Anthony Burgess (148).

1963 Penguin Books
1989 Twentieth-Century Classics
1995 Twentieth-Century Classics
● aftwd. John Lanchester, 1995
2011 Modern Classics
—
Nabokov wrote *Sebastian Knight* while living in Paris. He sat in the bathroom, with his briefcase across the bidet as a desk. As well as being the first novel he wrote in English, it was the first he published under his own name.

Nikolai Gogol 1944

Gogol was 'the oddest Russian in Russia': he wrote *Dead Souls* (1842), 'The Overcoat' (1842) and *The Government Inspector* (1836), and he died with medicinal leeches hanging from his nose. This eccentric critical biography is 'one of the most exhilarating, engaging, and original works ever written by one writer about another' in the opinion of the critic Elizabeth Hardwick. Nabokov analyses the Russian term *poshlost* – spelling it *poshlust* – which describes 'not only the obviously trashy but also the falsely important, the falsely beautiful, the falsely clever, the falsely attractive'.

2011
—

Bend Sinister 1947

The fictional European city of Padukgrad ('Toadtown') is ruled by the totalitarian Party of the Average Man, but a brilliant philosopher decides to fight for freedom of thought. Unfortunately, the head of the government is his old school enemy, whom he used to bully and call 'the Toad'. 'The term "bend sinister" means a heraldic bar or band drawn from the left side [...],' explains Nabokov. 'The choice of title was an attempt to suggest an outline broken by refraction, a distortion in the mirror of being, a wrong turn taken by life, a sinistral and sinister world.'

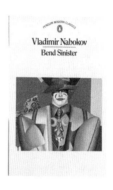

1974 Penguin Books
1986 Modern Classics
intro. Vladimir Nabokov, 1964
—
This dystopian fable was the first novel Nabokov wrote after he arrived in America. It was accepted by Allen Tate (459) at the publishing house Henry Holt.

1980 Penguin Books
1989 Twentieth-Century Classics
1995 Twentieth-Century Classics
aftwd. Craig Raine, 1995

Lolita 1955

'Lolita, light of my life, fire of my loins. My sin, my soul,' writes Humbert Humbert, the pseudonymous, unreliable narrator of Nabokov's infamous novel. 'Lo-lee-ta: the tip of the tongue taking a trip of three steps down the palate to tap, at three, on the teeth. Lo. Lee. Ta.' Humbert is a hebephile, attracted to pubescent children, who marries his landlady in order to seduce her gum-snapping 12-year-old 'nymphet' daughter Dolores. The novel has been interpreted in various ways: Gregor von Rezzori (276) called it 'the only convincing love story of our century'; Martin Amis (160) considered it 'a study in tyranny'; and Robertson Davies (395) described it as 'not the corruption of an innocent child by a cunning adult, but the exploitation of a weak adult by a corrupt child'. Others have seen real-life parallels with Charlie Chaplin (149), who met his second wife, Lillita Grey, when she was only eight. It has been adapted for the screen twice, by Stanley Kubrick in 1962, starring James Mason, and by Adrian Lyne in 1997, starring Jeremy Irons. '*Lolita* is a special favourite of mine,' said Nabokov. 'It was my most difficult book – the book that treated of a theme which was so distant, so remote, from my own emotional life that it gave me a special pleasure to use my combinational talent to make it real.'

Pnin 1957

Professor Timofey Pnin has fled Russia and found a teaching post in an American college, where he battles with life and language, takes wrong trains, delivers incomprehensible lectures and bumbles among the hazards of his absurd new world. This comic tour de force is based in part on Nabokov's own experiences teaching Russian at Wellesley College and Cornell University.

1960 Penguin Books
1986 Modern Classics
—
Pnin was the novel that established Nabokov's literary reputation in the USA. *Lolita* was not published in America until 1958, three years after its first publication in Paris.

 Vladimir Nabokov

The Annotated Lolita

1995 Penguin Books
2000 Modern Classics
ed. Alfred Appel, Jr. 1971,
1991

—

This annotated edition
of *Lolita* was prepared
by Nabokov's former
student Alfred Appel
in consultation with
Nabokov himself. It
features Nabokov's 1958
afterword, 'On a Book
Entitled *Lolita*', in which
he wrote that 'the first
little throb of *Lolita* went
through me late in 1939
or early in 1940, in Paris.
[...] The initial shiver of
inspiration was somehow
prompted by a newspaper
story about an ape in the
Jardin des Plantes, who,
after months of coaxing
by a scientist, produced
the first drawing ever
charcoaled by an animal:
this sketch showed
the bars of the poor
creature's cage.'
The image on the cover
is Nabokov's own drawing
of an imaginary butterfly,
Verina raduga Nab.,
dedicated to Véra Nabokov
in 1971.

1973 Penguin Books
1985 Modern Classics
2000 Modern Classics
• intro. Mary McCarthy, 2000
2011 Modern Classics
—

Pale Fire 1962

I was the shadow of
    the waxwing slain
By the false azure in
    the window pane

That is the opening couplet of the 999-line poem *Pale Fire* by the American poet John Shade (1898–1959). The book *Pale Fire* presents Shade's poem along with a foreword, commentary and notes by his neighbour and academic colleague, Charles Kinbote. As you read, however, Kinbote seems increasingly erratic, eccentric and perhaps even dangerous. '*Pale Fire* is a Jack-in-the-box,' wrote Mary McCarthy (507), 'a Fabergé gem, a clockwork toy, a chess problem, an infernal machine, a trap to catch reviewers, a cat-and-mouse game, a do-it-yourself novel.' Professor Pnin (309) appears as a minor character and 'Hurricane Lolita (309)' ravages the American coastline. It is 'full of plums', chuckled Nabokov, 'that I keep hoping somebody will find'. William Boyd has called *Pale Fire* 'one of the most brilliant and extraordinary novels ever written, let alone in the twentieth century'.

1971 Penguin Books
1991 Twentieth-Century Classics
—
'Ada' is pronounced with a long 'a', as a homophone of 'Ardour'. As well as a pun, the title may also be an oblique reference to one of Nabokov's favourite butterflies, the swallowtail, which has yellow wings and a black body, because Nabokov the synaesthete associated the letter 'a' with yellow and 'd' with black. *Ad* is also Russian for 'hell'.

Ada or Ardor
A Family Chronicle 1969

In his nineties, Van Veen remembers his first childhood meeting with Ada. He recalls their erotic, dreamlike relationship over 80 years and the truth about their singular relationship. Nabokov's longest work is set in a parallel but recognizable 'dream-bright' America. It is 'a great work of art, a necessary book', wrote the Nabokov scholar Alfred Appel, which 'provides further evidence that he is a peer of Kafka (280), Proust (166) and Joyce (8)'.

Transparent Things 1972

In this darkly comic novella, the American editor Hugh Person recalls four trips, made over four decades to a village in Switzerland, which involve murder, marriage, madness and prison. Martin Amis (160) called it 'mysterious, sinister and beautifully melancholic'.

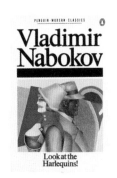

1980 Penguin Books
1987 Modern Classics
—

Look at the Harlequins! 1974

The last novel Nabokov published can be read as a fictional sequel to *Speak, Memory* (308). It is the unreliable memoir of Vadim Vadimovich N., a Russian-born writer who has some traits in common with Humbert Humbert (309), but whose biography and bibliography parallel Nabokov's own. Vadim recalls his extraordinary grand-aunt, Baroness Bredow, who told him to 'Look at the harlequins! […] Invent the world! Invent reality!'

The Original of Laura
(Dying is Fun) 1977, pub. 2009

Nabokov's dying wish was that this unfinished novel should be destroyed, but instead his wife Véra and son Dmitri placed it in a Swiss bank vault. Thirty years later, Dmitri decided to publish *The Original of Laura*. It is the story of Dr Wild and his flagrantly promiscuous wife Flora, and of how, when her infidelities are exposed, he begins a slow process of self-annihilation, starting by removing his own toes. The manuscript concludes with a list: 'efface, expunge, erase, delete, rub out, wipe out, obliterate'.

1975 Penguin Books
1987 Modern Classics
—

2012
ed. Dmitri Nabokov, 2009
—
Nabokov composed all his novels on index cards, which he shuffled, annotated and replaced as he worked. *The Original of Laura* exists as 125 handwritten cards, photographs of which are presented against a grey background in this edition, with a type transcript below each one. The 2009 hardback was published with perforations, so readers could punch out the cards and rearrange them.

1967
trans. Stephen Garry, 1934

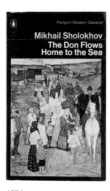

1974
● trans. Stephen Garry, 1940
—
The first three volumes of Sholokhov's epic masterpiece were published between 1928 and 1932, and translated together as *And Quiet Flows the Don*. The fourth and final volume appeared in 1940 and was translated separately as *The Don Flows Home to the Sea*.

Mikhail Sholokhov

1905 – 1984

Mikhail Aleksandrovich Sholokhov was born in the land of the Cossacks – the 'wild fields' of southern Russia, on the northern reaches of the River Don. Aged thirteen, he joined the Bolsheviks and fought in the Russian Civil War, before moving to Moscow and working as a dockhand, a stonemason, an accountant and a journalist. When the first volume of *And Quiet Flows the Don* was published in 1928, it caused a literary sensation. Sholokhov went on to become Vice-President of the Union of Soviet Writers. In 1937, he was elected to the Supreme Soviet of the Soviet Union, and in 1961 he became a member of the Communist Party's Central Committee under Nikita Khrushchev. In 1965, he was awarded the Nobel Prize for Literature (576), 'for the artistic power and integrity with which, in his epic of the Don, he has given expression to a historic phase in the life of the Russian people'.

And Quiet Flows the Don

1928 – 40

Sholokhov's epic is the greatest work of Socialist Realism. Spanning the decade from 1912 until 1922, it tracks the fortunes of the Don Cossacks in peacetime, war, revolution and then civil war, as they struggled for and against the tsarist and Bolshevik governments. The story centres on the tragic Gregor Melekhov, torn between loyalty to the Bolsheviks and to his Cossack people. Panoramic in scope, full of energy and steeped in local dialect, the novel won the Stalin Prize in 1941. Maxim Gorky (300) said that 'the work of Mikhail Sholokhov can only be compared with Tolstoy's *War and Peace*'. Sholokhov took his epigraph from an old Cossack song:

> Our gentle Don is adorned with youthful widows:
> Out gentle father Don is blossomed with orphans;
> The waves of the gentle Don are rich with fathers'
>   and mothers' tears.

Virgin Soil Upturned 1932 – 60

Sholokhov's other great work describes the collectivization of farming among the Cossacks of the Don. Full of colourful language, idealism and humour, it won the Lenin (299) Prize in 1960.

Socialist Realism

In 1934, Maxim Gorky (300) and the Union of Soviet Writers tried to homogenize Soviet literature into 'that unity which is guiding all the creative working energies of the country'. Gorky declared 'Socialist Realism' the only permissible form of literature in the Soviet Union, and it remained the officially endorsed literary style until 1989. Socialist Realism employed the techniques of late 19th-century realism to represent exemplary Soviet characters and a rosy future for socialism; it shunned the 'decadent' techniques of modernism (11) and Symbolism (303). Successful examples included Maxim Gorky's own novel *The Mother* (1907) and Mikhail Sholokhov's epic sagas, but in reality the doctrine acted chiefly to stifle creativity and became a serious obstacle to the development of Soviet literature. Many authors were forced to write in secret, circulating their works in *samizdat* editions (317).

Like *And Quiet Flows the Don*, the Penguin edition was split across two volumes.

1977
● trans. Stephen Garry, 1935

1978
● trans. H. C. Stevens, 1960

THE GOLDEN AGE OF SOVIET THEATRE 1929–44

Vladimir Mayakovsky, *The Bedbug*; Isaac Babel, *Marya*; Yevgeny Schwartz, *The Dragon*

Vladimir Vladimirovich Mayakovsky was a Futurist (216) poet and playwright, who championed Socialist Realism (312). In *The Bedbug* (1929), a bureaucrat is cryogenically frozen: he wakes up in 1979 to find himself an exhibit in a zoo, caged next door to a bedbug that was accidentally frozen at the same time. *Marya* (1933) by Isaac Babel (321) dramatizes Petrograd's underbelly during the Russian Civil War and draws on Babel's experience of working for Maxim Gorky's (300) newspaper *Novaya Zhizn* (*New Life*). In *The Dragon* (1944), Yevgeny Schwartz's most satirical drama, Sir Lancelot sets out to slay a three-headed, fire-breathing beast, only to discover that a totalitarian community is using the dragon to disguise their own abuse of power.

1966 Penguin Plays
Three Soviet Plays
1981 Penguin Plays
The Golden Age of Soviet Theatre
1990 Twentieth-Century Classics
• trans. Michael Glenny, Max Hayward & Harold Shukman, 1960–66
ed. Michael Glenny, 1966
—
The 1990 cover shows a photograph of Mayakovsky.

1999
• trans. Michael Henry Heim, 1984
intro. Will Self, 1999
—
'If an orthodox introduction to a conventional literary work is difficult enough to write,' says the novelist Will Self, 'how much more difficult is the introduction to a work of such murky provenance? It has to be a definitive statement on something entirely provisional.'

M. Ageyev 1898–1973?

Nothing is known for sure about the pseudonymous M. Ageyev. The Russian manuscript of his *Novel with Cocaine* was sent to Paris from Istanbul and first published in the émigré publication *Numbers*. Reviews compared Ageyev with Fyodor Dostoyevsky, Ivan Bunin (304) and 'V. Sirin', the *nom de plume* of Vladimir Nabokov (304). In 1983, Ageyev's novel was 'rediscovered' and translated into French and English. There was a widely held suspicion that the true author was Nabokov himself, but this was refuted by Nabokov's son Dmitri in his introduction to *The Enchanter* (308). A more likely candidate is Mark Lazarevich Levi, about whom little is known: he appears to have returned to the Soviet Union from Turkey during the Second World War and died in Armenia in 1973.

Novel with Cocaine 1934

Vadim Maslennikov is an adolescent schoolboy at the time of the 1917 Revolutions. Wracked with self-loathing and pursuing an affair with an older, married woman, he loses his 'nasal virginity' and spirals into a narcotic nightmare. 'When he comes to take cocaine, every detail [...] is rendered with a cool and edgy clarity,' wrote John Updike (514).

Victor Serge 1890–1947

Victor Lvovich Kibalchich was born in Brussels, the son of exiled Russian intellectuals. Raised in poverty, he left home at fifteen and joined a group of Parisian anarchists that included Henri Barbusse (174). After five years in prison, he adopted the pen name 'Victor Serge' and decided to aid the revolution in Russia. He eventually reached Petrograd in 1919, becoming a close associate of Leon Trotsky (322) and an outspoken critic of Stalin. He left Russia in 1936, lived in France until the German invasion in 1940, and then migrated to Mexico, arriving a few months after Trotsky's assassination. He died in a Mexican taxicab.

The Case of Comrade Tulayev

1940–42, pub. 1949

When apparatchik Comrade Tulayev is shot in the street, a culprit must be found. Written in French, this is a chilling portrait of the Stalinist purges. 'Serge never saw anybody as an anonymous agent of historical forces,' said John Berger (154). 'He identified himself imaginatively with everyone he encountered – workers, peasants, judges, crooks, rich lawyers, seamstresses, spies, traitors, heroes. It was methodologically impossible for a stereotype to occur in Serge's writing.'

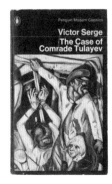

1968
• trans. Willard R. Trask, 1951

Varlam Shalamov 1907–1982

1990
trans. John Glad, 1980–81

—

John Glad was a professor in
the department of Slavic studies
at the University of Maryland.
'On 17 January 1982 I gave a
talk on Shalamov's life and work
for the Greater Washington, DC
chapter of the Russian Literary
Fund,' he recalled. 'It was the
coldest day in the city's history
– as if Kolyma had come to
Washington – and only a handful
of devoted admirers braved
the weather. We did not know
it at the time, but Shalamov had
died that very day.'

Varlam Tikhonovich Shalamov, a law student, was arrested in 1929 for attempting
to distribute Trotskyist pamphlets (322) and spent three years in a labour camp.
He was arrested again in 1937, and sentenced to five years in the Gulag in Kolyma.
His sentence was extended first to the end of the Second World War, and then again
after he described Ivan Bunin (304) as a 'classic Russian writer'. He spent seventeen
years in Kolyma, mining, logging and working as a hospital attendant. After his release,
he began publishing poetry, encouraged by Boris Pasternak (302). His short stories
began to appear in 1966, after he smuggled *tamizdat* (317) manuscripts out of Russia.
'Shalamov's experience in the camps was longer and more bitter than my own,' wrote
Solzhenitsyn, 'and I respectfully confess that to him and not me was it given to touch
depths of bestiality and despair toward which life in the camps dragged us all.'

Kolyma Tales 1954–73, pub. 1966–78

Kolyma is a region the size of France in the northeast of Siberia, bounded by the Arctic
Ocean, the Sea of Okhotsk and mountains. Between 1930 and the mid-1950s, it was gradually
covered with a network of forced labour camps where more than 3 million people died.
Solzhenitsyn called it a 'pole of cold and cruelty'. Shalamov's Chekhovian tales describe life
under these conditions. 'My First Tooth' recalls a beating in which his tooth was knocked
out and he was forced to stand naked in the cold; 'Cherry Brandy' narrates the death of
Osip Mandelshtam (301); and 'Condensed Milk' is the story of a fellow convict who tries
to lure Shalamov into an escape attempt in order to betray him to the camp authorities.

Aleksandr Solzhenitsyn 1918–2008

Aleksandr Isayevich Solzhenitsyn joined the Red Army in the Second World War: he signed up as a gunner,
was twice decorated and reached the rank of captain. He was arrested early in 1945, however, for making
derogatory comments about Stalin, and spent the next eight years in the Gulag. When he was released,
he taught maths at a provincial school and spent the nights writing in secret. The phenomenal success of
One Day in the Life of Ivan Denisovich encouraged him to become a full-time writer; in 1970, he was awarded
the Nobel Prize for Literature (576). He survived a KGB assassination attempt, but the *tamizdat* (317) publication
of *The Gulag Archipelago* (1973) led to his deportation. He lived in West Germany with Heinrich Böll and then
in the USA, before returning to Russia in 1994 after the fall of communism. 'Solzhenitsyn is a writer of genius,'
wrote the poet Julian Symons, 'able to illuminate reality through his fictions as no other living novelist can do.'

One Day in the Life of Ivan Denisovich 1962 →

Based on Solzhenitsyn's own experiences
in a labour camp in Kazakhstan, this novel
describes a day in the life of a prisoner
serving a ten-year sentence: a gruelling
regime of hard manual labour, freezing
conditions and brutal punishment.
'There were three thousand six hundred
and fifty-three days like that in his stretch,'
concludes the narrator. '[…] The three
extra days were for leap years.'

Cancer Ward 1964–6, pub. 1968

Solzhenitsyn describes the cancer
patients of Ward 13 in a hospital
in Uzbekistan. It is both a compassionate
account of inmates facing terminal illness
and an allegory of the cancerous Soviet
state. 'A man dies from a tumour,'
says the central character,
Oleg Kostoglotov, 'so how
can a country survive
with growths like labour
camps and exiles?'

1971 Penguin Books
1997 Twentieth-Century
Classics
• trans. Nicholas Bethell
& David Burg, 1968

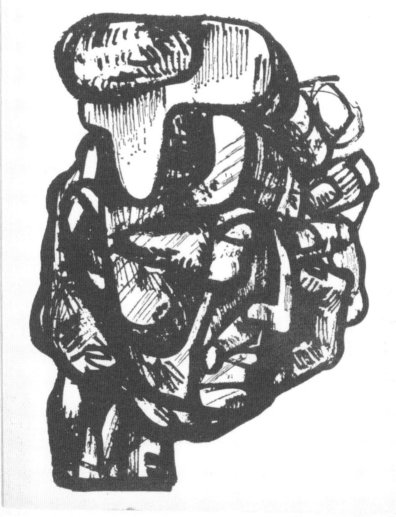

Nobel Prize Winner 1970
Alexander Solzhenitsyn
One Day in the Life of Ivan Denisovich

1963 Penguin Books
1968 Modern Classics
<u>1971</u> Modern Classics
with Nobel Prize
announcement
trans. Ralph Parker, 1963

One Day in the Life of Ivan Denisovich was the first account of the Gulag to be published within the USSR. The Soviet premier Nikita Khrushchev personally permitted the first instalment to be published in the November 1962 edition of *Novy Mir* (*New World*). It sold out immediately. The image on the 1968 and 1971 Penguin editions is by the Russian Expressionist (269) artist Ernst Neizvestny, whose works were described by Khrushchev as 'degenerate'.

Joseph Brodsky 1940–1996

Iosif Aleksandrovich Brodsky almost died as a small child during the German siege of Leningrad in the Second World War. He left school at fifteen to work in a factory, a morgue, a ship's boiler room and on geological expeditions, and he began writing poetry at eighteen, encouraged by Anna Akhmatova (301). His verses were denounced in 1963, however, as 'pornographic and anti-Soviet'. He was arrested for 'social parasitism' and sentenced to five years' internal exile in the Archangel region of northern Russia. 'Who enrolled you in the ranks of poets?' asked the judge. 'No one,' replied Brodsky. 'Who enrolled me in the ranks of the human race?' In 1972, he was expelled from the Soviet Union to Vienna, whence he travelled to London and then the USA with the help of W. H. Auden (95). He taught at the universities of Michigan, Yale, Cambridge and Columbia, had a brief affair with Susan Sontag (524), and won the Nobel Prize for Literature (576) in 1987.

1997 Twentieth-Century Classics
● ed. Joseph Brodsky, 1988
trans. Joseph Brodsky et al., 1965–85

Poems 1968–96

These selections of Brodsky's best poetry include memories of his childhood in Russia and his life as an émigré writer. *Gorbunov and Gorchakov* (1968), 1,400 lines long, is one of his greatest achievements: it consists of wandering conversations between two patients in a Russian mental asylum. 'Every encounter with Brodsky constituted a renewal of belief in the possibilities of poetry,' wrote Seamus Heaney. '[…] He was always putting the slughorn to his lips and blowing a note to call out the opposition – even the opposition with himself.'

1973 Penguin Poets
● trans. George L. Kline, 1973
fwd. W. H. Auden, 1973
2020 Modern Classics
ed. Ann Kjellberg, 2020
trans. Richard Wilbur et al.

—

Urania was the Greek muse of astronomy. 'Mr Brodsky is not an easy poet,' wrote W. H. Auden (95) in his foreword to the 1973 Penguin edition, 'but even a cursory reading will reveal that, like Van Gogh and Virginia Woolf (42), he has an extraordinary capacity to envision material objects as sacramental signs, messengers from the unseen.'

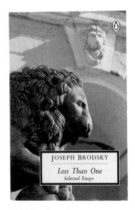
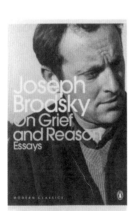

1987 King Penguin
1997 Twentieth-Century Classics
—

Essays

1977–95, pub. 1986–95

Brodsky's prize-winning collection *Less Than One* (1986) features autobiographical sketches, literary appreciations of W. H. Auden (95), Anna Akhmatova (301) and Osip Mandelshtam (301) and meditations on tyranny and evil. *On Grief and Reason* (1995) is a similarly diverse selection, including 'How to Read a Book', 'In Praise of Boredom' and Brodsky's Nobel lecture, 'Uncommon Visage'.

1997 Penguin Books
2011 Modern Classics

Brodsky includes an epigraph by Czesław Miłosz (287) in *Less Than One*: 'And the heart doesn't die when one thinks it should.'

Watermark
An Essay on Venice 1992

In later years, Brodsky spent his winters in Venice, and this is his elegant, emotional, literary paean to the Floating City. He describes the canals, the streets and palazzi, the food, the politics and the people. When Brodsky died, he was buried in Venice, on the cemetery island of San Michele, where he keeps company with Frederick Rolfe (40) and Ezra Pound (61).

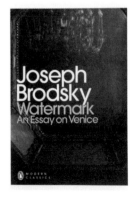

2013
—

Samizdat

Samizdat means 'self-published' in Russian. The term was coined in the 1940s by the poet Nikolai Glazkov and in the 1960s came to refer to a seam of clandestine publications across the communist bloc. Dissident writers circulated tatty, manually copied typescripts of works such as Aleksandr Solzhenitsyn's *One Day in the Life of Ivan Denisovich* (314), Mikhail Bulgakov's *The Master and Margarita* (302), Václav Havel's essay *The Power of the Powerless* (1978) and the poems of Anna Akhmatova (301) and Joseph Brodsky (316). The activist Vladimir Bukovsky defined the term thus: '*Samizdat*: I write it myself, edit it myself, censor it myself, publish it myself, distribute it myself, and spend time in prison for it myself.' In contrast, *tamizdat* is Russian for 'published there', and refers to clandestine works smuggled out of the Soviet Union, published in the West and filtered back in secret. One of the first full-length novels to be published in this way was *Doctor Zhivago* (302) by Boris Pasternak.

Ludmilla Petrushevskaya

b. 1938

Ludmilla Stefanovna Petrushevskaya was born in the Metropol Hotel in Moscow and evacuated from the city during the Second World War. She lived with an aunt and in an orphanage, 'stealing heads of herring from the neighbours' garbage bins'. She reunited with her mother when she was nine years old; they lived together under a desk in her grandfather's study. Her early writing was mostly banned by the Soviet government: her first collection of stories, *Immortal Love* (1987), was published when she was 49. She has gone on to publish several more volumes of stories, as well as novels and plays, and she is now a celebrated author in Russia. She speaks 'for all those who suffered domestic hell in silence', writes her translator Anna Summers, 'the way Solzhenitsyn (314) spoke for the countless nameless political prisoners'.

2011
trans. Keith Gessen & Anna
Summers, 2009

There Once Lived a Girl Who Seduced Her Sister's Husband, and He Hanged Himself
Love Stories 1972–2008

These dark 'love' stories are set in claustrophobic communal apartments. They feature insanity, infidelity and jet-black humour.

There Once Lived a Woman Who Tried to Kill Her Neighbour's Baby
Scary Fairy Tales 1987–2009

Petrushevskaya's mystical and fantastical tales are set in what she calls 'Orchards of Unusual Possibilities'. They include miracles and madness, disturbing deaths and midnight forests. This volume won the World Fantasy Award in 2010.

2013
trans. Anna Summers

There Once Lived a Mother Who Loved Her Children, Until They Moved Back In
Three Novellas About Family 1988–2002

In *Among Friends* (1988), Petrushevskaya's most controversial work, a devoted mother commits a terrible crime against her son in order to save him; in her masterpiece, *The Time Is Night* (1992), an ageing poet struggles for survival when her children return home; and *Chocolates with Liqueur* (2002) is the story of a young nurse terrified of her abusive husband. All three novellas feature unlikely heroines in horrific and haunting situations.

2014
trans. Anna Summers

Vladimir Sorokin

b. 1955

Vladimir Georgievich Sorokin was born in Moscow, where he still lives. After studying engineering at the Gubkin Institute of Oil and Gas, he became a *samizdat* (317) illustrator and author. Now his novels have been translated into 30 languages; he has won the Andrei Bely Prize (302), the Maxim Gorky Prize (300) and the Gregor von Rezzori Prize (276) and the *New York Times* has described him as 'Russia's most inventive contemporary author'.

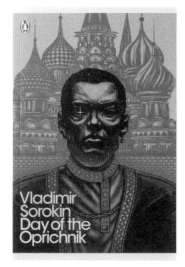

Day of the Oprichnik 2006

In this satirical vision of a dystopian future Moscow, we join Andrei Komiaga – an 'oprichnik', or henchman of the tsar – for a busy day of debauchery, drugs, orgies and exterminations.

2018
trans. Jamey Gambrell, 2011
—
The original *Oprichniki* were the brutal bodyguards of Tsar Ivan the Terrible in the 16th century.

The Blizzard

2010

2018
trans. Jamey Gambrell, 2015

In post-apocalyptic Russia, a doctor sets out into a blizzard: only he has the vaccine for a virus that has gripped the village of Dolgoye. But the journey is plagued by nightmarish apparitions and strange beasts, and it becomes a fantastical allegory for the human condition.

Lithuania

Abraham Cahan 1860–1951

Cahan was born in Paberžė, now part of Lithuania. Initially he studied to become a rabbi, but he secretly learned Russian and retrained as a teacher in Vilnius, where he mixed in revolutionary circles. When Tsar Alexander II was assassinated in 1881, all revolutionary sympathizers came under suspicion and Cahan fled to New York. In America he helped to organize the first Jewish trade unions and founded the *Jewish Daily Forward*, a Yiddish social-democratic newspaper, which he edited from 1902 until his death in 1951, publishing authors including Isaac Bashevis Singer (288), I. J. Singer (291) and Leon Trotsky (322).

The Rise of David Levinsky 1917

David Levinsky is an eastern European Jew who emigrates to America in the 1880s and undergoes a process of assimilation in turn-of-the-century New York. As he struggles out of poverty and builds a successful clothes business, he weighs the spiritual and emotional cost of becoming an American.

1993
● ed. Jules Chametzky

Belarus

Mary Antin 1881–1949

Maryashe Antin was born in Polotsk, in the Vitebsk region of the Russian Empire. At the time, Russian Jews were confined within the 'Pale of Settlement', which comprised modern Belarus and large parts of Ukraine, Poland and Lithuania. Following the repressive May Laws of 1882, many began to emigrate; Antin's father moved to Boston in 1891, and Maryashe followed three years later with her mother and three siblings. She wrote an account of the voyage in Yiddish, which was translated into English for the *American Hebrew*, and later appeared in book form in 1899. This was the basis for *The Promised Land*, which became a bestseller. Antin married a geologist and lived in New York, where she wrote stories and essays and lectured on the rights of migrants.

The Promised Land 1912

'I was born, I have lived, and I have been made over. Is it not time to write my life's story?' asked Antin at the start of her memoir. 'I am just as much out of the way as if I were dead, for I am absolutely other than the person whose story I have to tell. [...] My life I still have to live; her life ended when mine began.' She describes the process of uprooting and acclimatization, balancing amusing anecdotes with stark political commentary and painting a moving portrait of life in eastern Europe and as a Jewish immigrant in early 20th-century America.

1997 Twentieth-Century Classics
2012 Penguin Classics
ed. Werner Sollors, 1997
—
The 2012 'centennial' edition also includes two short stories by Antin: 'Malinke's Atonement' and 'The Lie'.

Marc Chagall 1887–1985

Moishe Shagall, the son of a herring monger, was born on the outskirts of Vitebsk and studied art in St Petersburg and Paris. He went on to become one of the greatest artists of the 20th century, creating whimsical, dreamlike paintings, stained-glass windows, stage sets, ceramics and tapestries, many of which depict scenes from his *shtetl* childhood populated with floating figures, transparent wombs, circus performers and fiddlers on roofs. He became Commissar of Arts in Vitebsk after the October Revolution in 1917, but returned to Paris six years later and lived there for the most of the rest of his life. 'When Matisse dies,' said Picasso in the 1950s, 'Chagall will be the only painter left who understands what colour really is.'

My Life 1922, pub. 1930

'I would climb up on to the roof. Why not? Grandfather used to climb up there too.' Chagall wrote this colourful, modernist (11) memoir in 1922, while waiting for the communist authorities to grant him an exit visa from Belarus. He describes his extended family and his beloved Vitebsk, and tells the story of how he learned to paint, first as a child and then in belle époque Paris. The text is peppered with Chagall's own illustrations.

2018
trans. Dorothy Williams, 1965
—
The cover image is Chagall's *Le Peintre de la Lune* (*The Painter of the Moon*, 1916–17).

Svetlana Alexievich b. 1948

Svetlana Alexandrovna Alexievich was born in Ukraine and raised in Belarus. She wrote for local newspapers in Naroulia before moving to Minsk and working as a correspondent for the literary magazine *Neman*, named after the river. She has developed her own genre of investigative non-fiction, depicting historical events through hundreds of first-hand testimonies. 'This is how I hear and see the world,' she says – 'as a chorus of individual voices and a collage of everyday details.' Most of her books were not published in Belarus before the country gained independence from the USSR in 1991, and she has spent long periods of exile in western Europe. In 2015, she became the first historian since Winston Churchill to win the Nobel Prize for Literature (576).

The Unwomanly Face of War 1985

In the 1970s, Alexievich read about a female accountant at a local car factory who had been a sniper during the Second World War and killed 75 people. She began interviewing other women who had fought in the war and gradually pieced together this elegiac tribute to feminine suffering and strength. Margaret Atwood calls it 'a must read'.

2018
trans. Richard Pevear & Larissa
Volokhonsky, 2017

Last Witnesses
Unchildlike Stories 1985

While working on The Unwomanly Face of War, Alexievich began interviewing the generation who had been children aged between three and fourteen during the Second World War. A hundred or so testimonies inform this child's-eye view of wartime horror and subsequent trauma.

2020
trans. Richard Pevear & Larissa
Volokhonsky, 2019

Boys in Zinc 1989

Between 1979 and 1989, a million Soviet troops were sent to fight in Afghanistan, and the corpses of young soldiers were returned in zinc coffins. Alexievich spent three years at home and in Kabul gathering first-hand accounts of the experience. 'I was trying to present a history of feelings, not the history of the war itself,' she writes. 'What were people thinking? What made them happy? What were their fears? What stayed in their memory?'

2017
trans. Andrew Bromfield

Chernobyl Prayer
A Chronicle of the Future 1997

On 26 April 1986, Reactor No. 4 at the Chernobyl power station blew apart and unleashed a nuclear disaster on an unprecedented scale. The effects were felt around the world, but 70 per cent of the impact was within Belarus, where the rate of cancer increased 74-fold. Living in Minsk, Alexievich spent ten years interviewing more than 500 eyewitnesses, including firefighters, first responders, politicians, doctors and physicists. She describes the explosion as 'the beginning of a new history' and felt at times as if she was 'recording the future'.

2016
trans. Anna Gunin & Arch Tait

Ukraine

Isaac Babel 1894-1940

Isaac Emmanuilovich Babel was a Jew, born in Odessa, who moved to Petrograd in 1915. He became a protégé of Maxim Gorky (300), who published his stories, employed him as a reporter and encouraged him to join a Red Army cavalry regiment. Babel fought in the 1920 war against Poland and his greatest stories were written in the following decade. He felt increasingly stifled in the 1930s, however. 'I am the master of a new literary genre,' he declared in 1934, 'the genre of silence.' In 1939, he was arrested by the NKVD, tortured and later executed and erased: his name was removed from dictionaries and his works were forbidden in schools and universities.

Collected Stories 1916-30

Babel's famous collection *Red Cavalry* (1926) is based on his experiences as a Red Army soldier in Poland. It contains vivid sketches of appalling cruelty and lurid landscapes. 'The music of its style contrasts with the almost ineffable brutality of certain scenes,' wrote Jorge Luis Borges (572). Babel's *Odessa Tales* (1923–4) describe the Jewish gangsters of his home city, led by the mob boss Benya Krik. 'No iron can enter the human heart as chillingly as a full stop placed at the right time,' wrote Babel.

1961 Penguin Books
1974 Modern Classics
● trans. Walter Morison et al., 1955
intro. Lionel Trilling (489), 1955
1994 Twentieth-Century Classics
2005 Penguin Classics *Red Cavalry and Other Stories*
trans. David McDuff, 1994
ed. Efraim Sicher, 1994

The cover of the 1974 edition shows a detail of a 1920 Soviet recruiting poster for the Red Cavalry.

Vaslav Nijinsky 1889-1950

The dancer Vaslav Fomich Nijinsky was a prodigy. He made his professional début at the age of seven, and was the first male to dance *en pointe*. He trained at the Imperial Theatrical School in St Petersburg and joined the Ballets Russes, a new company founded by the impresario Sergei Pavlovich Diaghilev, with whom he began a professional and sexual relationship. The Ballets Russes travelled to Paris, where Nijinsky embraced worldwide fame. He seemed able to defy gravity and his controversial choreography for *Afternoon of a Faun* (1912), with music by Claude Debussy, and *The Rite of Spring* (1913), by Igor Stravinsky, caused riots. When he married Romola de Pulszky, however, Diaghilev dismissed him from the company. His attempts to form his own ballet troupe were unsuccessful and his mental health began to deteriorate. In 1919, he was diagnosed with schizophrenia and he spent the rest of his life in institutions.

The Diary
Unexpurgated Edition
1919, pub. 1936

Nijinsky wrote his 'diary' over six weeks in early 1919, just as he was succumbing to psychosis. The two sections, 'On Life' and 'On Death', present his thoughts on bodily functions, homosexuality, materialism and war, as well as vivid recollections from his extraordinary, broken career. The original manuscript is filled with drawings of eyes and in some places Nijinsky writes as if he is God.

2000
● trans. Kyril Fitzlyon, 1995, 1999
ed. Joan Acocella, 1995

—

Nijinsky's wife Romola published an abridgement of three of his notebooks in 1936. This 'unexpurgated' edition restores the material she excised and includes a fourth notebook, as well as draft letters that gradually deteriorate into repetitive madness.

Mikhail Bulgakov 1891–1940

Mikhail Afanasevich Bulgakov trained as a doctor in Kiev. He volunteered for the Red Cross during the First World War, and he worked as an army medic for the short-lived Ukrainian People's Republic before it was subsumed into the Soviet Union in 1922. He moved to Moscow and made a living as a journalist, writing controversial plays and subversive novellas, including *A Dog's Heart* (1925). In 1929, the government censor banned the publication of his work. He devoted the last dozen years of his life to writing his secret masterpiece, *The Master and Margarita*, which was not published until a quarter of a century after his death. Anna Akhmatova (301) wrote a poem 'In Memory of Mikhail Bulgakov', in which she said:

> You died as unflinchingly as you lived,
> With magnificent defiance.

The Master and Margarita

1928–40, pub. 1966–7

The 'Master' has been detained by the secret police for writing a novel about Pontius Pilate. Excerpts from his naturalistic manuscript are interspersed within the fantastical story of his lover Margarita, who attempts to rescue him; meanwhile, the Devil stalks the streets of Moscow, calling himself Professor Woland and carrying a poodle-headed cane. Woland's henchmen include the giant gun-toting cat Behemoth, a fanged assassin and a female vampire. This frantic, fantastical, frightening satire of Stalinist Russia includes the famous line: 'manuscripts don't burn'.

1997 Twentieth-Century Classics
2007 Penguin Classics
trans. Richard Pevear & Larissa Volokhonsky, 1997
—
In 1930, Bulgakov burned the first draft of *The Master and Margarita* and began to rewrite it from memory. He worked on it until he died, and then his widow Yelena – whom he called 'Margarita' – had to wait 26 years before publishing a censored version in the magazine *Moskva*. The first uncensored edition in the USSR was published in 1973.

Leon Trotsky 1879–1940

Lev Davidovich Bronstein was born into a Ukrainian Jewish farming family. He soon became involved in revolutionary activities, and was imprisoned for helping to organize a workers' union. He escaped in a hay wagon and joined Lenin (299) in London in 1902, where he changed his name to 'Trotsky', the name of one of his jailers. During the 1905 Revolution, Trotsky returned to Russia and became president of the first St Petersburg Soviet, organizing much of the ensuing revolutionary activity. As a result, he was exiled to a penal colony, but he escaped en route and travelled to Vienna, where he edited *Pravda* (*Truth*), the clandestine newspaper for workers. He spent the First World War in New York, contributing to Abraham Cahan's (318) *Jewish Daily Forward*, before returning to Russia in May 1917. He was elected leader of the Bolsheviks, coordinating (under the exiled Lenin's direction) the insurrection that led to the October Revolution. As People's Commissar of War, he then created the Red Army, acting as its supreme commander during the Russian Civil War. Once the Soviet government was established in 1922, however, Trotsky increasingly opposed Stalin, and after Lenin's death he was expelled from the Soviet Union in 1929. Stalin proceeded to erase him from Soviet history books. Trotsky fled eventually to Mexico City, where he was assassinated – with an ice pick – at the age of 60.

2017
trans. Max Eastman, 1932
—
Max Eastman was an American radical writer. He edited *The Masses*, the leading socialist periodical in the US, with contributions from Sherwood Anderson (420), John Reed (420) and Upton Sinclair (409) among others. A dedicated Trotskyite, Eastman travelled to Russia in 1922 to study the Soviet regime and personally witnessed the power struggles between Trotsky and Stalin.

History of the Russian Revolution 1930

Trotsky's 'involvement in the struggle, far from blurring his sight, sharpens it', wrote Isaac Deutscher, the biographer of both Trotsky and Stalin. 'The *History* is his crowning work, both in scale and power and as the fullest expression of his ideas on revolution. As an account of a revolution, given by one of its chief actors, it stands unique in world literature.' Trotsky wrote this epic history of the events of 1917 while living on the Turkish island of Prinkipo, now Büyükada, after he was expelled from the USSR. It was originally published in three volumes: 'The Overthrow of Tsarism', about the February Revolution; 'The Attempted Counterrevolution', about the 'July Days'; and 'The Triumph of the Soviets', about the October Revolution.

Romania

Mihail Sebastian 1907–1945

Iosif Hechter grew up in the port of Brăila on the River Danube. He worked as a lawyer, and wrote plays, articles and novels under the pen name 'Mihail Sebastian'. He fell in with Emil Cioran and the influential Criterion Association; but Sebastian was Jewish, and as the fascist Iron Guard rose to power in Romania in the late 1920s, the Criterion shifted its allegiances and he found himself abandoned by his friends. Having survived the Holocaust, he was killed by a truck three weeks after the end of the Second World War as he crossed the street on his way to deliver a lecture on Balzac.

For Two Thousand Years 1934

A young Jewish student in Bucharest writes a journal, attempting to make sense of the anti-Semitism he experiences and accepting casual violence as a necessary cost of attending lectures. He rubs shoulders with revolutionaries, zealots, lovers and libertines. The character Ștefan D. Pârlea, a fascist sympathizer, is based on Emil Cioran. '[Sebastian's] prose is like something Chekhov might have written,' said Arthur Miller (486) – 'the same modesty, candour and subtleness of observation.'

2016
trans. Philip Ó Ceallaigh
—
Sebastian's mentor, the philosopher Nae Ionescu, provided a hurtfully anti-Semitic foreword for the first edition of *For Two Thousand Years*. Sebastian decided to include it nonetheless, which sparked intense controversy: some critics accused him of being 'Ionescu's lap dog'; others branded him a Zionist agent. Sebastian responded with *How I Became a Hooligan* (1935), a volume of essays defending the novel. The idealist professor Ghiță Blidaru in *For Two Thousand Years* is modelled on Ionescu.

E. M. Cioran 1911–1995

The Criterion Association

The Criterion Association was a salon of precocious young intellectuals in late 1920s Bucharest, including the cultural historian Mircea Eliade, Emil Cioran, Eugène Ionesco (324) and Mihail Sebastian. Eliade called it 'the most original and significant manifestation of the "young generation"'. Initially apolitical, the group was increasingly influenced by the philosophy of Nae Ionescu, which incorporated nationalism, existentialism (186), Christian mysticism and fascism. This shift coincided with the rise of the Legion of the Archangel Michael, an anti-Semitic paramilitary organization in Romania also known as 'the Iron Guard'.

Emil Mihai Cioran, the son of an Orthodox priest, was born in the Transylvanian village of Rășinari, which became part of Romania after the First World War. His mother once told him that if she'd known he would be so miserable, she would have had him aborted. He studied in Bucharest, where he met Eugène Ionesco (324), Mihail Sebastian and the cultural historian Mircea Eliade, and then in Berlin, where he was impressed by Hitler. In 1937, he moved to Paris and remained there for the rest of his life. He wrote works of pessimistic philosophy in French and lived in isolation with his partner Simone Boué. 'Bach's music,' he once said, 'is the only argument proving the creation of the Universe cannot be regarded as a complete failure.'

A Short History of Decay 1949

The first of Cioran's major philosophical works in French is a collection of witty and aphoristic essays expressing his deeply nihilistic views on mid-20th-century Europe and the utter pointlessness of human existence. It won the Rivarol Prize in 1950.

2010 Central European Classics
2018 Modern Classics
trans. Richard Howard, 1975

The Trouble with Being Born 1973

'Not to be born is best,' said Sophocles in *Oedipus at Colonus*. '[…] The next best thing, by far, is to go back where you came from, as quickly as you can.' 'Not to be born is undoubtedly the best plan of all,' agreed Cioran. 'Unfortunately it is within no one's reach.' Through pessimistic, nihilistic aphorisms, Cioran reflects on the 'laughable accident' of birth.

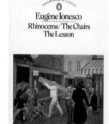

2020
trans. Richard Howard, 1976

Eugène Ionesco 1909–1994

Ionesco was born in Romania, to a Romanian father and French mother. He spent his childhood in Paris before returning to study French literature in Bucharest, where he befriended Emil Cioran (323), Mircea Eliade and Mihail Sebastian (323) and became involved with the Criterion Association (323). He married in 1936 and moved to France, where he wrote poetry, criticism, and eventually absurdist plays (184) inspired by the non sequiturs in his teach-yourself-English textbook. His plays placed him at the forefront of the French avant-garde, and in 1970 he was elected to the Académie Française. He was 'a serious artist dedicated to the arduous exploration of the realities of the human situation', wrote the critic Martin Esslin.

Rhinoceros
The Chairs
The Lesson 1951–59

These bleak 'anti-plays' express Ionesco's view of the absurd (184). 'Cut off from his religious, metaphysical and transcendental roots, man is lost,' he wrote; 'all his actions become senseless, absurd, useless.' In *Rhinocéros* (1959), the inhabitants of a small provincial town start to turn into horned pachyderms. The play has been interpreted as an allegory for ideological conformism, specifically the rise of the fascist Iron Guard in 1930s Romania. In *Les Chaises* (1952), an old man and old woman arrange dozens of empty seats in preparation for a speech that will reveal the meaning of life; and in *Le Leçon* (1951), a professor tutors a pupil using increasingly violent language.

1962 Penguin Plays
1985 Modern Classics
trans. Derek Prouse & Donald Watson, 1958–60

ABSURD DRAMA 1953–9

Eugène Ionesco, *Amédée, or, How to Get Rid of It*
Arthur Adamov, *Professor Taranne*
Fernando Arrabal, *The Two Executioners*
Edward Albee, *The Zoo Story*

'The Theatre of the Absurd' was a term coined in 1961 by the critic Martin Esslin to describe the plays of Samuel Beckett (20), Eugène Ionesco, Harold Pinter and others. He borrowed the concept of the absurd (184) from Albert Camus and his essay *The Myth of Sisyphus* (182), and his prime example was Beckett's *Waiting for Godot* (1953). 'The Theatre of the Absurd,' wrote Esslin, 'does not provoke tears of despair but the laughter of liberation.' The four plays in this anthology express various aspects of the absurd: *Amédée, or, How to Get Rid of It* (1954), Ionesco's first full-length drama, is about a playwright and his wife deciding how to get rid of a corpse; *Professor Taranne* (1953) is about an innocent man accused of escalating misdemeanours; a wife tortures her husband in *The Two Executioners* (1958) by Fernando Arrabal, who later founded the 'Panic Movement'; and in *The Zoo Story* (1959), two strangers meet on a bench in New York's Central Park with violent consequences.

1965 Penguin Plays
1990 Twentieth-Century Classics
• trans. Donald Watson, Peter Meyer & Barbara Wright, 1958–62
intro. Martin Esslin, 1965

Paul Celan 1920–1970

Paul Antschel grew up in a German-speaking Jewish family in Czernowitz, Bukovina. During the Second World War, both his parents were killed in the Holocaust; he survived in a ghetto, where he translated Shakespeare's sonnets. After the war, he travelled to Vienna, where he met Ingeborg Bachmann (275), and then to Paris, where he lived for the rest of his life, writing poetry and translating the works of Fernando Pessoa (235), Osip Mandelshtam (301) and Georges Simenon (201), among others. In 1952, he married the graphic artist Gisèle Lestrange, after a correspondence inspired by Franz Kafka's *Letters to Milena* (282). That same year, his first major book of poetry was published in Germany, under the pen name 'Celan'. He was soon acknowledged as one of the greatest German-language poets of the 20th century; he won the Georg Büchner Prize in 1960. At the age of 49, he drowned himself in the River Seine.

1972 Penguin Poets
1990 Twentieth-Century Classics *revised*
1996 Twentieth-Century Classics *revised*
trans. Michael Hamburger, 1972, 1988–95
—

'Celan's mysterious, spellbinding German poems have been transmuted into equally mysterious, equally euphonious, equally spellbinding English verse,' wrote the *Times Literary Supplement* of Michael Hamburger's parallel text edition. 'Through these exemplary translations the English reader can now enter the hermetic universe of a German-Jewish poet of our own day, a poet who made out of the anguish of his people, and his own representative sufferings, things of terror and beauty.'

Selected Poems 1952–76

Celan wrote poetry in order to 'outline reality' for himself. The Second World War and the loss of his parents are recurrent themes: he sought to express 'not only what the experience felt like, but also a sense of living, with comprehension, inside the experience'. He was influenced by both Surrealism (176) and Expressionism (269). The critic George Steiner called him 'almost certainly the major European poet of the period after 1945'.

Elie Wiesel 1928–2016

Wiesel was born in the Carpathian mountains, in northern Transylvania, into a Jewish family that spoke Yiddish, German, Hungarian and Romanian. In 1944, he was sent with his parents and younger sister to the concentration camps of Auschwitz and Buchenwald; he survived, and was later reunited with his older sisters in a French orphanage. He then lived in Paris, where he attended lectures by Jean-Paul Sartre (185) and worked as a journalist, before moving to New York in 1955 as a foreign correspondent for an Israeli newspaper. He remained in the USA for the rest of his life, teaching at Boston University and campaigning for victims of oppression around the world. He was awarded the US's Presidential Medal of Freedom and Congressional Gold Medal, and the Nobel Peace Prize.

Night 1958

Wiesel's autobiographical 'deposition' describes his experience of the Holocaust. At Auschwitz, his mother and sister were killed immediately; he and his father Shlomo were later deported to Buchenwald, where Elie cared for his father until he died after a beating. 'In *Night*,' he wrote, 'I wanted to show the end, the finality of the event. Everything came to an end – man, history, literature, religion, God. There was nothing left.'

1981 Penguin Books
• fwd. François Mauriac, 1958
trans. Stella Rodway, 1960
2006 Modern Classics
fwd. François Mauriac, 1958
trans. Marion Wiesel, 2006
—

François Mauriac (174), a close friend of Wiesel, saw in Wiesel 'the death of God in the soul of a child', and he was the first to encourage him to write about his experience of the Holocaust. The current Penguin edition was translated by Marion Wiesel, Elie's wife.

Aharon Appelfeld 1932–2018

Appelfeld was born in Jadova, Bukovina. In 1941, after a year of Soviet occupation, the fascist Romanian army recaptured the town: Appelfeld's mother was murdered and he was sent with his father to a forced labour camp in Transnistria. Aged nine he escaped, and he lived for three years in the forest, until he was picked up by the Soviet army and put to work in its field kitchens. After the war, he made his way to Italy and then migrated to Palestine in 1946, two years before Israeli independence. He learned Hebrew and began to write stories and novels in his newly adopted language. 'Among us, the writer survivors,' wrote Primo Levi (222), 'Aharon Appelfeld's voice has a unique, unmistakable tone, eloquent through reticence.'

Badenheim 1939 1978

In the spring of 1939, the Austrian resort town of Badenheim receives its annual stream of Jewish vacationers, but this year the holidaymakers struggle to ignore the town's new 'Sanitation Department' with its insidious rules, the sudden lack of outside communication, and the preparations for a mass trip to Poland. The *Guardian* called *Badenheim 1939* 'the greatest novel of the Holocaust'.

2005
● trans. Dalya Bilu, 1980
intro. Gabriel Josipovici, 2005
—
Philip Roth, Appelfeld's friend and champion, described him as 'a displaced writer of displaced fiction, who has made of displacement and disorientation a subject uniquely his own'. Appelfeld features as a character in Roth's novel *Operation Shylock* (1993).

Aharon Appelfeld
Badenheim 1939

Mircea Cărtărescu b. 1956

Cărtărescu spent the 1980s writing poetry in Bucharest, teaching the Romanian language and editing the magazine *Caiete Critice* (*Critical Papers*); since 1991, he has taught at the University of Bucharest. His novels and poetry are considered the best writing to emerge from post-communist Romania. They have been translated into fourteen languages and he has received many awards, including the Thomas Mann Prize (245) and the Prix Formentor.

Nostalgia 1989, rev. 1993

Cărtărescu's cult novel recreates the gritty, surreal atmosphere of Bucharest under communism. Blending dream and reality, he shows us games of Russian roulette, a child messiah working magic and a young man exploring the boundaries of gender.

2021
trans. Julian Semilian, 2005
intro. Andrei Codrescu, 2005
—
This novel was first published in 1989 in a censored form entitled *The Dream*. In 1993, it was republished in an uncensored edition with the title *Nostalgia*.

Yugoslavia

Milovan Djilas _{1911–1995}

Djilas, a Montenegrin Serb, joined the Yugoslav Communist Party in 1932, for which he was arrested, tortured, and imprisoned for three years. On his release, he was elected to the party's Central Committee, and in 1940 he became a member of its Politburo. During the German occupation in the Second World War, he helped Josip Broz Tito establish the partisan Resistance, commanding a guerrilla unit and running the propaganda newspaper *Borba* (*Struggle*). After the war he became Tito's vice-president, but increasingly found himself estranged from communist rule; eventually, in 1954, he was expelled from the Central Committee. He spent most of the next ten years in prison, translating *Paradise Lost* into Serbo-Croatian on rolls of toilet paper and publishing two devastating books outside the country: *The New Class* (1957), a direct and damaging attack on Tito, and *Conversations with Stalin*. After his release, he lived as a dissident in Belgrade for the rest of his life.

Conversations with Stalin ₁₉₆₂

In this damning eyewitness statement, Djilas describes several diplomatic missions he made as a representative of the Yugoslav communists to the Soviet Union, where he enjoyed all-night banquets with Stalin, Molotov, Khrushchev and Beria, among others. 'For the first time,' said the *Observer*, 'a man who was a senior Communist politician [...] writes of what he saw and heard as a human being writing about human beings.'

1963 Penguin Books
1969 Pelican Books
2014 Modern Classics
trans. Michael B. Petrovich, 1962
intro. Anne Applebaum, 2014

Anne Applebaum is the author of the Pulitzer Prize-winning *Gulag: A History* (2003).

Danilo Kiš _{1935–1989}

Kiš was the son of a Hungarian Jew and an Orthodox Christian from Montenegro – he described himself as an 'ethnographical rarity'. Kiš's father died in Auschwitz in 1944 and his mother died in 1950. He grew up under Marshal Tito's dictatorship, studying at Belgrade University, where he became Yugoslavia's first graduate in world literature. He wrote poems, plays and essays; his idea of literary perfection was 'a work that, after the first time round, can be read like an encyclopedia'. In 1979, he moved to Paris, where he lived for the rest of his life. His friend Susan Sontag (524) called him 'one of the handful of incontestably major writers of the second half of the century'.

The Encyclopedia of the Dead ₁₉₈₃

Kiš's last work of fiction is this anthology of nine 'pocket-sized novels' inspired by Jorge Luis Borges (572) and the Polish Jewish author Bruno Schulz. They combine fiction and history in uncanny tales about blasphemous miracles, beloved prostitutes, and magic mirrors. The title story is about an almighty Swedish biographical dictionary containing an entry for every ordinary person who has died since 1789. 'Danilo Kiš offers a vision that expands the domain of life at the expense of that of death,' wrote Joseph Brodsky (316). 'These stories present that vision with a journalist's precision, with a taxidermist's tactile knowledge of era and realm, with the tenacity of a true son of the century.'

1991 Penguin Books
2015 Modern Classics
trans. Michael Henry Heim, 1989
intro. Mark Thompson, 2015

Bulgaria

Elias Canetti 1905–1994

Canetti was born in Bulgaria, the son of Spanish Jewish parents. He was educated in Manchester, Lausanne, Zurich, Frankfurt and finally Vienna, where he lived as a young man. In 1927, he witnessed the July Revolt in Vienna and saw the Palace of Justice ablaze. He and his wife fled the *Anschluss* in 1938 and divided their time between London and Zurich. Canetti won the Georg Büchner Prize in 1972 and the Nobel Prize for Literature (576) in 1981.

1965
• trans. C. V. Wedgwood, 1946
—
Veronica Wedgwood was a historian of the 17th century. A revised edition of her classic work *The Thirty Years War* (1938) was published in Pelican Books in 1957.

Auto da Fé 1935

Die Blendung (*The Blinding*) is the story of Peter Kien, a reclusive Viennese sinologist who is gradually manipulated out of his book-lined apartment by his illiterate housekeeper and brutish concierge. He is inducted into the Viennese underworld by a chess-playing dwarf. It is 'a most remarkable book', wrote Iris Murdoch, 'one of the few great novels of the century; savage, subtle, beautiful, mysterious and very large'. 'The remorseless quality of the comedy builds one of the most terrifying literary worlds of the century,' says Salman Rushdie.

Crowds and Power 1960

After two decades of book research, Canetti produced this examination of the dynamics of crowds, from religious congregations to mob violence. As well as anthropological, biological and cultural evidence from many ages and every continent, it draws on his personal experiences in Vienna in the 1920s and 1930s. It is 'an immensely interesting, often profound reflection about the nature of society', wrote Susan Sontag (524), 'in particular the nature of violence.' It is poetic, passionate, and considered by many to be Canetti's masterpiece.

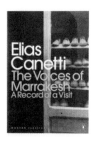

2012
trans. J. A. Underwood, 1978

The Voices of Marrakesh
A Record of a Visit 1968

These emotional essays, based on a brief trip to Marrakesh, capture the Moroccan city's smells and spices, crowds and cries. 'Canetti's sense of human societies and his gift – as in the Marrakesh book – for familiarising out-of-the-way places have something in common with the art of another and earlier Nobel Prize-winner, Rudyard Kipling (22),' wrote the critic John Bayley. 'But the timely comparison and contrast is with a more recent winner, the Polish poet Czesław Miłosz (287).'

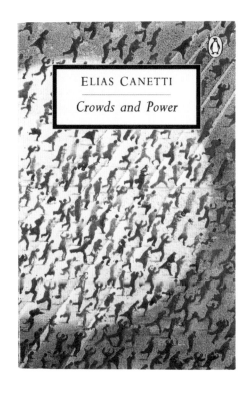

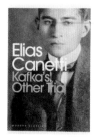

1978 Modern Classics
in Letters to Felice
1982 Penguin Books
2012 Modern Classics
trans. Christopher Middleton, 1974

Kafka's Other Trial
The Letters to Felice 1969

Canetti used Kafka's letters to his fiancee Felice (282) for this biographical reading of *The Trial* (282). The *Times Literary Supplement* called it 'perhaps the most revealing essay on Kafka ever published'.

1973 Penguin Books
1984 Peregrine Books
1992 Twentieth-Century Classics
• trans. Carol Stewart, 1962

Turkey

2017 Modern Classics
2021 Penguin Classics
trans. Maureen Freely & Alexander Dawe, 2016

Sabahattin Ali 1907–1948

Ali was born in Eğridere in the Ottoman Empire, now Ardino in southern Bulgaria. He trained as a teacher in Berlin and then taught German in Istanbul while writing poetry and editing a weekly newspaper. He was imprisoned twice for his political views, the first time for publishing a poem criticizing Atatürk, the first president of the Republic of Turkey. After his second release, Ali was killed in mysterious circumstances on the Bulgarian border while attempting to leave Turkey.

Madonna in a Fur Coat 1941–2

A Turkish man falls in love with an artist in 1920s Berlin, in this tale of young love and disenchantment. 'Moving and memorable,' said The Times – 'full of yearning and melancholy.'

2014
trans. Maureen Freely & Alexander Dawe, 2013
intro. Pankaj Mishra, 2013

Ahmet Hamdi Tanpinar

1901–1962

Tanpinar was born in Istanbul, the son of a judge. He initially studied to be a vet, but switched to literature at Istanbul University. He went on to write poems, novels and stories, as well as working as a teacher and briefly becoming a Member of the Turkish Parliament. The Nobel Laureate Orhan Pamuk calls him 'undoubtedly the most remarkable author in modern Turkish literature'.

The Time Regulation Institute 1961

Hayri İrdal narrates this memoir of his chaotic career at the fictional Time Regulation Institute, set up to change the time of Turkey's clocks to align with those in the rest of Europe. İrdal's absurdist (184) escapades satirize President Atatürk's westernizing policies. The New York Times called it a 'bittersweet sendup of Turkish culture'.

ASIA

WESTERN ASIA

G. I. Gurdjieff Meetings with Remarkable Men

Adonis Songs of Mihyar the Damascene

Kahlil Gibran The Prophet

Edward W. Said Orientalism

Azar Nafisi Reading Lolita in Tehran

MODERN CLASSICS

MODERN CLASSICS

PENGUIN CLASSICS

PENGUIN CLASSICS

MODERN CLASSICS

Armenia

G. I. Gurdjieff 1877–1949

The mystic philosopher George Ivanovitch Gurdjieff was born in Alexandropol in the Russian Empire, now Gyumri in Armenia. He trained as a doctor and a priest, before wandering for 20 years around the remote regions of central Asia and the Middle East, seeking ancient wisdom and accumulating a body of esoteric knowledge. He returned to Russia on New Year's Day 1912, gathering students in St Petersburg, teaching in various locations around the Black Sea and founding the Institute for the Harmonious Development of Man in Tiflis, now Tbilisi in Georgia. During the Russian Civil War, he moved to Istanbul, then to Berlin and London, and finally to the Château du Prieuré in Fontainebleau, where he reopened his institute and nursed Katherine Mansfield (388) on her deathbed. Gurdjieff believed that people live in a state of 'waking sleep' and used the techniques of monks, fakirs and yogis to help his students rouse themselves to full consciousness.

Meetings with Remarkable Men

1927–34, pub. 1960

In this spiritual adventure story, Gurdjieff recalls his wandering travels as a young man and all the remarkable figures – fellow 'Seekers of Truth' – who guided him on his spiritual quest. These include his father, a carpenter and poet, who could sing the epic of *Gilgamesh* from memory; an Armenian priest who gave him a map of 'pre-sand Egypt'; the Russian Prince Lubovedsky; a Persian dervish; 'Mr X'; a beautiful woman called Vitvitskaïa; and a faithful Kurdish sheepdog called Philos.

G. I. Gurdjieff
Meetings with Remarkable Men

More SPIRITUAL QUESTS

2015
trans. A. R. Orage, pub. 1963
intro. Gary Lachman, 2015
—
Alfred Orage worked with Gurdjieff in Paris and translated *Meetings with Remarkable Men* from Russian into English, although the book was never published in either of their lifetimes: it first appeared in French translation in 1960. T. S. Eliot (11) called Orage 'the finest critical intelligence of our days'. Gary Lachman was a founding member of the rock band Blondie; he is the author of several books on consciousness and the western esoteric tradition.

Syria

Adonis b. 1930

Ali Ahmad Said Esber was born into a farming family in the Syrian village of Al-Qassabin. At the age of fourteen, he recited one of his own poems to Shukri al-Quwatli, the first President of the Republic of Syria, who granted him a scholarship to the country's last French *lycée*. Adopting the pen name 'Adonis' at the age of seventeen, he went on to initiate 'a modernist (11) revolution in the second half of the twentieth century', as the critic Maya Jaggi puts it, 'exerting a seismic influence on Arabic poetry comparable to T. S. Eliot's (11) in the anglophone world'. In 1956, Adonis moved to Beirut, fleeing political persecution, but the Lebanese Civil War forced him to relocate to Paris in 1985, where he has lived ever since. He has received numerous honours, including the Ordre des Arts et des Lettres, the Goethe Prize and the PEN/Nabokov Award (304), and he is a perennial candidate for the Nobel Prize for Literature (576).

Songs of Mihyar the Damascene

1961

2021
trans. Kareem James Abu-Zeid & Iven Eubanks, 2019

Adonis's landmark poetry collection transformed the structures of Arabic verse and pioneered new ways of expressing modernity in the Middle East. Adonis relocates the 11th-century Persian poet Mihyar al-Daylami to 20th-century Damascus in these 141 short lyrics about Mediterranean myths, renegade Sufi mystics, wildernesses, mountains, palm trees and dust.

Lebanon

Khalil Gibran 1883–1931

Gibran Khalil Gibran was born in Bisharri in the mountains of Lebanon, which was then under Ottoman rule. He migrated to the USA in 1895, however, and lived there for most of his life. Supported by the photographer Fred Holland Day and then by Mary Haskell, the headmistress of a girls' school, Gibran began exhibiting drawings and writing poetry in Arabic. He gradually transitioned from an angry young man into a self-styled prophet, writing controversial and influential poetry, parables, fables and aphorisms. He was raised a Maronite Christian but was deeply influenced by Sufi mysticism and Jungian (262) psychology, as well as the poetry of William Blake and Walt Whitman. In 1920, he refounded the Pen League in New York, a society dedicated to raising the international profile of Arabic literature. When he died, he was buried in Bisharri, and he bequeathed his future royalties to his home town.

1992 Penguin Arkana
1998 Penguin Arkana *reissued*
2002 Modern Classics
intro. Robin Waterfield, 1998
—
Robin Waterfield wrote a biography of Gibran in 1998. He worked as a copy editor and a commissioning editor for Penguin and translated several Penguin Classics editions of Plato and other authors. He now lives on a small olive farm in southern Greece.

The Prophet 1923

In these 26 prose fables, the 'prophet' Almustafa pauses before departing the city of Orphalese to expound on the human condition, discussing joy and sorrow, reason and passion, good and evil, prayer and pleasure, religion and death, and the possibility of achieving divinity through love. 'Did I write it?' asked Gibran. 'It wrote me.' Together the fables present a guide to living that was particularly popular during the counterculture movement (526) of the 1960s. It became one of the bestselling books of all time and has been translated into more than 20 languages. It is illustrated by Gibran's own drawings.

Palestine

1985 Peregrine Books
2003 Modern Classics
aftwd. Edward Said, 1995
pref. Edward Said, 2003
—

'My idea in *Orientalism*,'
wrote Said in 2003, a few
months before he died, 'is to use
humanistic critique to open up
the fields of struggle, to introduce
a longer sequence of thought
and analysis to replace the short
bursts of polemical, thought-
stopping fury that so imprison
us in labels and antagonistic
debate whose goal is a belligerent
collective identity rather than
understanding and intellectual
exchange.' The cover of the 2003
edition shows the French artist
Jean-Léon Gérôme's painting
The Snake Charmer (1879).

Edward W. Said 1935–2003

Said was born to Palestinian parents. He grew
up in both Jerusalem and Cairo and studied the
western literary canon at British colonial schools.
After graduating from Princeton and Harvard
universities, he taught English and comparative
literature at Columbia for 40 years. He was
also the editor of *Arab Studies Quarterly*,
an executive board member of International PEN
and a member of the Palestinian National Council.
He was an accomplished pianist and co-founded
with Daniel Barenboim the West-Eastern Divan
Orchestra, which is made up of Israeli, Palestinian
and Arab musicians.

Orientalism 1978

Said's seminal critique of western literary
representations of 'the east' redefined our
understanding of imperialism and founded the
field of postcolonial studies. He demonstrates
how romanticized descriptions of exotic Arabic
and Islamic culture, which he traces from classical
antiquity to Conrad (28) and Kipling (22), have
served to affirm an ideology of European superiority
over the 'otherness' of eastern cultures and beliefs.

Postcolonial Literature

Postcolonial literature
is a broad term that covers
indigenous literature from
countries with a history
of European colonization,
especially works that deal
with issues of national and
ethnic identity, language,
race and imperialism. It draws
on the ideas introduced by
Edward Said in his foundational
text *Orientalism*, and other
key theorists such as Chinua
Achebe (359), Frantz Fanon (557)
and Ngũgĩ wa Thiong'o (365).
In practice, 'postcolonial
literature' tends to describe
writings from Africa (354),
the Indian subcontinent (336)
and the Caribbean (550), but
some critics have argued the
term should expand to embrace
texts from Australia, Canada,
Ireland, the USA and Wales.
Works of postcolonial literature
seek to unravel the complex
cultural conditions that
exist in relation to newfound
independence; examples
include Tayeb Salih's *Season
of Migration to the North* (357),
Jean Rhys's *Wide Sargasso Sea*
(552) and George Lamming's
In the Castle of My Skin (554).

Iran

Azar Nafisi b. 1948

Born and raised in Tehran, Nafisi
studied literature in England and the
USA before returning to her homeland
in 1979, during the Iranian Revolution.
She taught English literature at the
University of Tehran until she was
sacked in 1981 for refusing to wear
a veil. In 1997, she moved to America
with her family, following the 'green
light that Gatsby (424) once believed
in', and is now the director of the
Dialogue Project at the Foreign Policy
Institute of Johns Hopkins University.

Reading Lolita in Tehran
A Memoir in Books 2003

In 1995, Nafisi began a clandestine book club
with seven of her former students. They met
each Thursday morning and discussed forbidden
works of western literature, including Lolita (309),
The Great Gatsby (424), *Washington Square* (398) and
Pride and Prejudice. Nafisi interweaves biographical
passages with discussions of the books. *Lolita*,
in particular, becomes a metaphor for the Iranian
regime in the 1980s. 'I was enthralled and moved
by Azar Nafisi's account of how she defied, and
helped others to defy, radical Islam's war against
women,' wrote Susan Sontag (524).

2015
—

Nafisi uses a Czesław Miłosz
(287) quotation as an epigraph:
'To whom do we tell what
happened on the earth, for whom
do we place everywhere huge
mirrors in the hope that they will
be filled up and will stay so?'

SOUTH ASIA

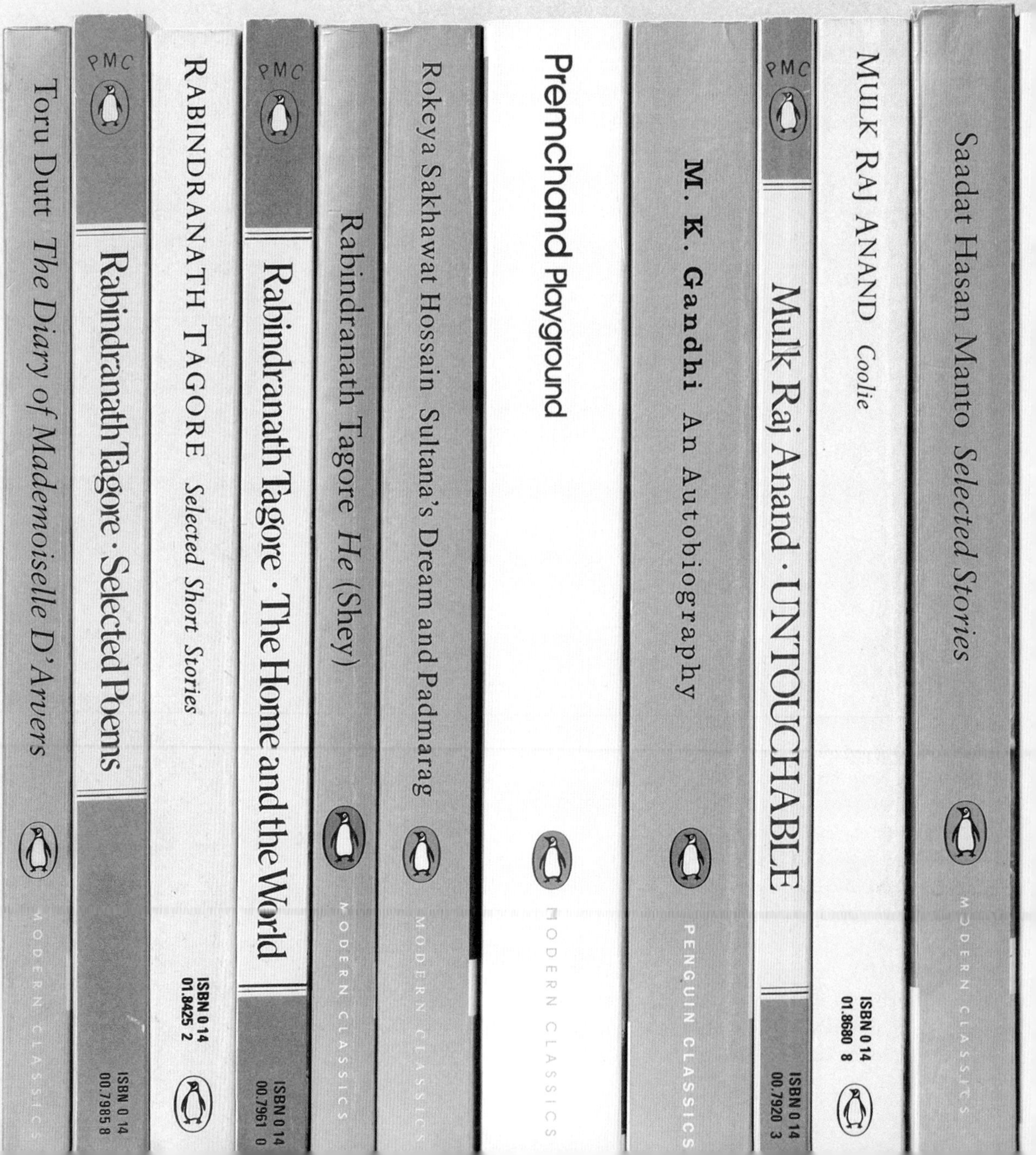

Toru Dutt The Diary of Mademoiselle D'Arvers
MODERN CLASSICS
PMC
Rabindranath Tagore · Selected Poems
ISBN 0 14 00.7985 8
RABINDRANATH TAGORE Selected Short Stories
ISBN 0 14 01.8425 2
PMC
Rabindranath Tagore · The Home and the World
ISBN 0 14 00.7961 0
Rabindranath Tagore He (Shey)
MODERN CLASSICS
Rokeya Sakhawat Hossain Sultana's Dream and Padmarag
MODERN CLASSICS
Premchand Playground
MODERN CLASSICS
M. K. Gandhi An Autobiography
PENGUIN CLASSICS
PMC
Mulk Raj Anand · UNTOUCHABLE
ISBN 0 14 00.7920 3
MULK RAJ ANAND Coolie
ISBN 0 14 01.8680 8
Saadat Hasan Manto Selected Stories
MODERN CLASSICS

India

2005
- trans. N. Kamala
intro. G. J. V. Prasad

Toru Dutt 1856–1877

Dutt was born into a Christian Bengali family in Calcutta, now Kolkata. She studied French and English as a child and learned Milton's *Paradise Lost* by heart. In 1869, the family made a trip to Europe; Toru and her sister Aru went to school in Nice and attended lectures at Cambridge University. The family returned to India in 1873, but Aru died of tuberculosis a year later, and Toru succumbed to the same disease in 1877, at the age of 21. Her English translations of French lyrics and Sanskrit ballads were admired by Edmund Gosse (49) and she left two novels: one in English, the unfinished *Bianca* (pub. 1878), and one in French, *Le Journal de Mademoiselle D'Arvers*. 'Toru Dutt remains one of the most astonishing women that ever lived,' wrote the translator Edward Thompson, 'a woman whose place is with Sappho and Emily Brontë, fiery and unconquerable of soul as they.'

The Diary of Mademoiselle D'Arvers

1875–7, pub. 1879

Marguerite D'Arvers is a 15-year-old Breton convent girl who writes a private journal about the experience of growing up and falling in love. It is the first novel written by an Indian in French.

Rabindranath Tagore 1861–1941

Rabindranath Thakur began writing poetry when he was eight and some of his earliest poems were mistaken for 17th-century Bengali classics. He studied law in London before moving to rural Shelidah in East Bengal, where he managed his wealthy family's estates and continued to write poetry, stories and songs. Following the partition of Bengal in 1905, he became involved in the *Swadeshi* campaign against the British Raj. 'Tagore has sung Bengal into a nation,' wrote Ezra Pound (61) in 1912. That year, under the anglicized name 'Tagore', his mystical lyrics, *Gitanjali*, were published in England, with an introduction by W. B. Yeats (4). They earned Tagore the Nobel Prize for Literature (576) in 1913. He received a knighthood in 1915, which he renounced following the Amritsar Massacre of 1919. A close friend of Mahatma Gandhi (340), Tagore made lecture tours of America, Europe and the Far East, donating the proceeds to Visva-Bharati University, an academy he established in Santiniketan, where pupils are still taught among groves of trees. At 60, he took up painting and staged exhibitions in Moscow, Berlin, Paris, London and New York; he also wrote hundreds of songs, two of which became the national anthems of India and Bangladesh. His complete works span 32 large volumes.

The Bengal Renaissance

In the late 19th century, a cultural and intellectual movement swept through Bengal. Related to growing demands for Indian independence, this flowering of the arts and sciences produced figures like Satyendra Nath Bose, a pioneer of quantum mechanics; Satyajit Ray, one of the 20th century's greatest film-makers; and the author Rabindranath Tagore, the first Asian and the only Indian to have won the Nobel Prize for Literature (576).

1985 Modern Classics
2005 Penguin Classics *revised*
trans. William Radice,
1985–2005

—

The poet William Radice is the son of Betty Radice, editor of the Penguin Classics series from 1964 until 1985. His translation of Tagore's poetry superseded a previous English translation by Edward Thompson, father of E. P. Thompson (149), to whom his edition is dedicated.

Selected Poems 1882–1941

Tagore's deceptively simple poetry captures the beauty of nature and the essence of emotions through formal experimentation, psychological insight and a mystic joy in the harmonies of the universe. He wrote more than 1,000 poems, of which this volume makes a representative selection.

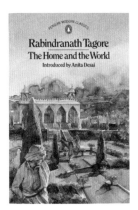

1991 Twentieth-Century Classics
2005 Penguin Classics
trans. William Radice

1985 Modern Classics
2005 Penguin Classics
trans. Surendranath Tagore, 1919
intro. Anita Desai, 1985
pref. William Radice, 2005

—

The Home and the World
was translated into English
by Rabindranath's nephew,
Surendranath, with contributions
from the author. It was adapted
as a film by Satyajit Ray in 1984.

2007
● trans. Aparna Chaudhuri
intro. Sankha Ghosh

—

Aparna Chaudhuri first read *Shey*
when she was ten years old, and she
began her translation soon afterwards.
It was published when she was 16
and in her final year at Calcutta Girls'
High School; she is now an Assistant
Professor of English at Ashoka
University in Sonipat. The text is
illustrated by Tagore's own sketches.

Selected Short Stories

1891–9

The 30 stories in this selection
were all written in the 1890s,
the decade Tagore spent on
the Padma River in East Bengal,
managing his family estates.
They evoke the changing
seasons and rural realities
of life in the Ganges Delta.

The Home and the World

1915–16

When Nikhil introduces his
wife Bimala to his old friend
Sandip, a radical leader of
the *Swadeshi* movement, Bimala becomes increasingly politicized, torn
between the traditions of home and the future of the revolution. Tagore
was similarly conflicted between a respect for western culture and a
belief in Indian independence, and the novel itself expresses this rift by
abandoning traditional literary language in favour of colloquial Bengali.

He (Shey) 1937

Tagore wrote and illustrated
these children's stories for his
nine-year-old granddaughter
Nandini. They are fantastical tales
of mythological heroes, strange
creatures and contemporary friends
of Tagore, narrated by the mysterious
'He' (*Shey*), a 'man constituted
entirely of words'.

Rokeya Sakhawat Hossain

1880–1932

Rokeya Khatun was born into a multilingual Muslim
family in East Bengal. At eighteen, she married the
38-year-old Khan Bahadur Sakhawat Hussain, who
encouraged her to write and learn languages. She became
a feminist author and a pioneer of women's liberation
in South Asia. Passionate about education, she founded
the Sakhawat Memorial School for Girls after her
husband's death, which continues to educate women
in Kolkata, formerly Calcutta. Begum Rokeya died on
what was probably her own birthday, 9 December, which
is celebrated annually as Rokeya Day in Bangladesh.

Sultana's Dream and Padmarag →

1905–24

'Sultana's Dream', written in English in 1905, is
a science fiction short story: in the feminist utopia
of Ladyland, men are in purdah and women rule
the household and the country, assisted by solar
ovens, flying cars and cloud condensers. The *Guardian*
called it a 'sort of gender based *Planet of the Apes* (199)'
Padmarag (1924), written in Bengali, imagines
a feminist community that provides a refuge for
women of all races, classes and religions. The title
translates as 'ruby', literally 'lotus-coloured'.

MODERN CLASSICS

Rokeya Sakhawat Hossain

Sultana's Dream and Padmarag

2005
• trans. Barnita Bagchi

The illustration on the cover is by Pinaki De.

Premchand 1880–1936

Dhanpat Rai Srivastava was born in a small village near Benares, now Varanasi, and grew up working for a book wholesaler. He wrote in Urdu under the name 'Nawab Rai' until his first collection of stories *Soz-e Watan* (*The Dirge of the Nation*, 1907) was seized for sedition, after which he changed his pseudonym to 'Premchand' and began writing in Hindi. He then worked as a teacher, but Gandhi's passive resistance movement inspired him to leave his job and he established a printing press and publishing house in Benares. He wrote more than a dozen novels and hundreds of short stories and articles, edited four different journals, and translated into Hindi works by Charles Dickens, George Eliot, John Galsworthy (47) and Leo Tolstoy. He is considered one of the greatest writers of Hindi fiction in the 20th century.

Playground
(Rangbhoomi) 1924

Rangbhoomi tells the story of the blind beggar Soordas as he struggles to retain ownership of his ancestral lands in the face of a cruel and corrupt colonial government.

2012
● trans. Manju Jain

M. K. Gandhi 1869–1948

'I have nothing new to teach the world,' said Mohandas Karamchand Gandhi. 'Truth and non-violence are as old as the hills.' Raised in western India, Gandhi studied in London and worked as a lawyer in South Africa for 21 years. He campaigned for the rights of the Indian community in South Africa by means of passive resistance, which he called *Satyagraha*, 'truth force'. In 1915, known already by the honorific title 'Mahatma' – 'great soul' – he returned to India. He campaigned tirelessly for *Swaraj*, 'self-rule', advocating hunger strikes and serving many terms in prison. In 1920, he became the leader of the Indian National Congress, promoting Hindu–Muslim unity, the abolition of untouchability (341) and the integrity of hand-spinning; he began wearing a homespun cotton dhoti and shawl. He was deeply dismayed by the religious hostility that followed the partition and independence of Pakistan and India in August 1947; and after a life spent promoting non-violence, he was assassinated on 30 January 1948. His birthday is now a national holiday in India. 'Generations to come,' said Albert Einstein, 'will scarce believe that such a one as this walked the earth in flesh and blood.'

An Autobiography 1925–9
or, The Story of My Experiments with Truth

'My writings should be cremated with my body,' wrote Gandhi. 'What I have done will endure, not what I have said or written.' Nonetheless, his autobiography has been acclaimed as one of the greatest spiritual works of the 20th century. Gandhi recounts the story of his life through an array of vignettes, in each of which he describes a different experiment in his search for Absolute Truth. 'His whole life was a sort of pilgrimage,' said George Orwell (80), 'in which every act was significant.'

1982 Penguin Books
2001 Modern Classics
2020 Penguin Classics
trans. Mahadev Desai
& Pyarelal Nayar, 1927–9
rev. Mahadev Desai
& Verrier Elwin, 1940
intro. Sunil Khilnani, 2001
—
Gandhi wrote his autobiography in his mother tongue, Gujarati, and the English translation was overseen by his personal secretary, Mahadev Desai. Desai has been variously described as Gandhi's Boswell, a Plato to Gandhi's Socrates and an Ananda to Gandhi's Buddha.

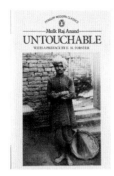

Mulk Raj Anand 1905–2004

Anand was educated at the universities of Punjab and London, where he studied the philosophy of Bertrand Russell. He lived in England for 20 years and befriended members of the Bloomsbury Group (44) as well as Eric Gill (96), D. H. Lawrence (50), George Orwell (80) and E. M. Forster (38), who was instrumental in seeing *Untouchable* to publication. In 1945, Anand returned to Bombay (now Mumbai) and founded the artistic journal *Marg* (*Pathway*).

1945 Penguin Books
<u>1993</u> Twentieth-Century Classics
—

1940 Penguin Books
<u>1986</u> Modern Classics
2014 Penguin Classics
pref. E. M. Forster, 1940
—
'Avoiding rhetoric and circumlocution,' wrote E. M. Forster (38) in his preface, '[*Untouchable*] has gone straight to the heart of its subject and purified it.' In 1955, India passed the Untouchability Act, prohibiting discrimination on the basis of caste.

Untouchable 1935

Bakha is an 'untouchable', a latrine cleaner. Untouchables were outcasts, born into an immutable caste system in which they were destined for ever to clear their neighbours' excrement. They 'polluted' others if they touched them, so they had a duty to call out and warn people of their approach. Over the course of a single day, Bakha accidentally brushes against a member of a higher caste, stops to hear Mahatma Gandhi (340) speaking and dreams of a world with flush toilets.

Coolie 1936

Fourteen-year-old Munoo leaves his hill village for a picaresque adventure in which he finds himself working as a servant, in a pickle factory and as a rickshaw-puller. 'Anand's picture is real, comprehensive and subtle,' wrote V. S. Pritchett (110), 'and his gifts in all moods from farce to comedy, from pathos to tragedy, from the realistic to the poetic, are remarkable.'

Saadat Hasan Manto 1912–1955

Manto was born in the Punjab and studied at Aligarh Muslim University. In his early twenties, he translated into Urdu works by Anton Chekhov, Maxim Gorky (300), Victor Hugo, Leo Tolstoy and Oscar Wilde (3), and in 1934 he travelled to Bombay, now Mumbai, where he wrote for magazines, newspapers, radio and films. He is best known for his short stories, of which he made 22 collections. He resisted the partition of India and Pakistan, but after independence, fearing anti-Muslim riots in India, he settled in Lahore with his wife and three daughters in 1948. He drank heavily in the last years of his life and died a few months before his 43rd birthday.

Selected Stories 1940–54

Manto was known for the frankness of his writing and he was prosecuted six times for obscenity. 'If you find my stories dirty, the society you are living in is dirty,' he explained. 'With my stories, I only expose the truth.' This collection includes 'The Wild Cactus', 'The Woman in the Red Raincoat' and 'The Price of Freedom'. 'Manto's irony and humanity raise him on a par with Gogol,' wrote the novelist Anita Desai.

2007 Modern Classics
2010 Modern Classics
Kingdom's End
● trans. Khalid Hassan, 2007

Stars from Another Sky
The Bombay Film World of the 1940s 1948–54

Manto wrote these nostalgic pieces after leaving Bombay, in order to recall the glamour, the scandal and the larger-than-life characters of the golden age of the Hindi film industry. They include witty pen portraits of the brilliant Ashok Kumar, the beautiful Nargis and the obsessive Sitara Devi, the 'dancing tigress from Nepal'.

1998 Penguin Books
<u>2010</u> Modern Classics
● trans. Khalid Hasan, 1998
intro. Jerry Pinto, 2010
—
In 2015, a Pakistani biopic of Manto's life was released in Urdu, directed by Sarmad Khoosat. Three years later, a Bollywood biopic by Nandita Das was released in Hindi.

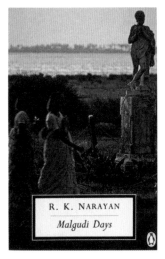

1984 King Penguin
1989 Penguin Books
1994 Twentieth-Century
Classics
2006 Penguin Classics
● intro. Jhumpa Lahiri, 2006
—
Narayan first published
Malgudi Days in 1943. The
revised 1982 edition includes
additional stories written in
the intervening four decades.

R. K. Narayan 1906–2001

Rasipuram Krishnaswami Narayan was raised in Madras (now Chennai) by his grandmother, who taught him maths, mythology, music and Sanskrit. His closest childhood friends were a peacock and a monkey. As a young man he became a journalist and began writing tales in English, rather than his native Tamil, set in the fictional South Indian city of Malgudi. 'The material available to a story writer in India is limitless,' he said. '[. . .] The writer has only to look out of the window to pick up a character.' Narayan has been compared to William Faulkner (433), who created the similarly semi-fictional setting of Yoknapatawpha County for his novels. Graham Greene (88) was instrumental in getting Narayan's first four novels published: 'Since the death of Evelyn Waugh (67),' he once wrote, 'Narayan is the novelist I admire most in the English language.'

Malgudi Days

1943, rev. 1982

'Few writers since Dickens can match the effect of colorful teeming that Narayan's fictional city of Malgudi conveys,' wrote John Updike (514); 'its population is as sharply chiseled as a temple frieze, and as endless, with always, one feels, more characters round the corner.' These stories feature an astrologer, a snake charmer, a postman, a chapatti wallah and a blind dog, among other denizens of Malgudi. Graham Greene (88) described Malgudi as 'that region of the imagination which seems to me now more familiar than Battersea or the Euston Road'.

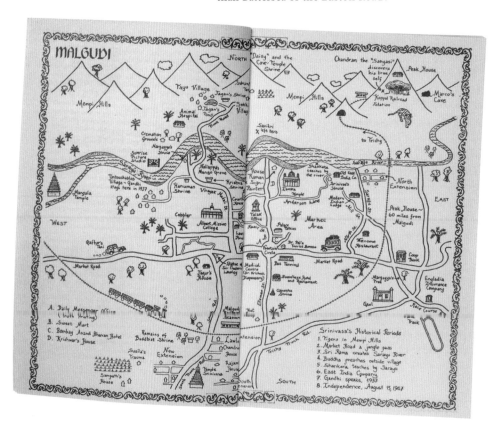

This map of Malgudi was compiled by the Narayan scholar Dr James Fennelly to illustrate his 1978 paper, 'The City of Malgudi as an Expression of the Ordered Hindu Cosmos'. Narayan asked to reproduce it in the 1982 edition of *Malgudi Days*.

1987 King Penguin
1989 Penguin Books
1993 Twentieth-Century
Classics
–

Under the Banyan Tree
and Other Stories 1947–84, pub. 1985

This collection presents more vignettes from Malgudi. The final story, 'Under the Banyan Tree', is about Nambi, a village storyteller, who holds his audiences spellbound until he takes a permanent vow of silence.

The Man-Eater of Malgudi 1961

Nataraj runs a small printing press in Malgudi and ill-advisedly rents his attic to the belligerent taxidermist Vasu, who fills the house with stuffed hyenas, pythons and tigers and sets his malevolent sights on the beloved temple elephant. This warm-hearted comedy is based on the Hindu myth of Bhasmasura the unconquerable, 'who scorched everything he touched and finally reduced himself to ashes by placing his fingers on his own head'.

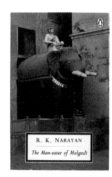

1983 King Penguin
1993 Twentieth-Century
Classics
–

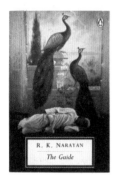

1988 King Penguin
1992 Twentieth-Century
Classics
2006 Penguin Classics
intro. Michael Gorra, 2006

The Guide 1956, pub. 1958

Railway Raju is a corrupt tourist guide, imprisoned for forgery. On his release from jail, however, he takes shelter in an abandoned temple by the Malgudi River, where he is mistaken for a spiritual guide, and he unwittingly becomes one of the greatest holy men in India. *The Guide* won the Sahitya Akademi Award, India's highest literary honour, and was adapted for the screen and the stage. Narayan wrote the novel in 1956, while visiting the USA on a Rockefeller Fellowship.

The Vendor of Sweets 1967

Jagan enjoys a peaceful life selling colourful sweetmeats and following the teachings of Mahatma Gandhi (340) and the *Bhagavad Gita* – until his wastrel son returns home from America with a plan to sell novel-writing machines.

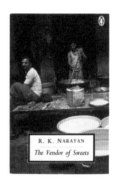

1983 King Penguin
1989 Penguin Books
1993 Twentieth-Century
Classics
–

1977 Penguin Books
1993 Twentieth-Century
Classics
2006 Penguin Classics
intro. Pankaj Mishra, 2006

The Ramayana
A Shortened Modern Prose Version of the Indian Epic 1972

In 1938, Narayan promised his dying uncle that he would translate the *Kamba Ramayanam*, an 11th-century Tamil version of the Sanskrit *Ramayana*, which dates from the 4th century BCE. Narayan condenses the sprawling tale of Prince Rama and the demon Ravana into the form of a novel, featuring vultures, monkey gods, love, loss and jealousy.

The Painter of Signs 1976

The earnest sign-painter Raman falls in love with the independent-minded Daisy, who works at the Family Planning Centre. 'Like Paul Theroux (543) and V. S. Naipaul (555),' wrote *The Times*, 'Mr Narayan has a faultless ear for the intricate eccentricities of Indian English, and the dialogue is a joy in itself.'

1982 King Penguin
1990 Penguin Books
1993 Twentieth-Century
Classics
–

2001
—
This edition includes
illustrations by R.K.Laxman,
Narayan's younger brother.

The Mahabharata
A Shortened Modern Prose Version of the Indian Epic
1978

'Although this epic is a treasure house of varied interests,' wrote Narayan, 'my own preference is the story.' In this slim volume, he distilled the longest poem in existence into a dramatic tale of a royal family at war. The *Mahabharata* is one of the founding epics of Indian culture and contains the *Bhagavad Gita*, a spiritual discussion between the god Krishna and the prince Arjuna, which is the cornerstone of Hinduism.

A Tiger for Malgudi
1983

An old, toothless tiger in the zoo at Malgudi narrates the story of his life, from his adventures as a wild cub in the jungle, through his ordeals as 'Raja the Magnificent' in a circus and his subsequent film career, to the friendship he forges with an ascetic holy man.

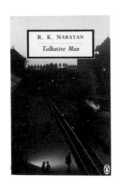

Talkative Man
1986

When a mysterious stranger arrives in Malgudi by train and takes up residence in the station waiting room, an aspiring local journalist wants to find out what's brought him there.

1987 Penguin Books
1994 Twentieth-Century Classics
• —

1984 King Penguin
1988 Penguin Books
1994 Twentieth-Century
Classics
• —

G. V. Desani 1909–2000

Govindas Vishnoodas Dasani was a British Indian novelist, born in Kenya and raised in India. As a child, he ran away from home three times and was expelled from school as 'unteachable'. He made his way to Britain in the 1920s, where he learned to speak English while working as a juvenile actor and by teaching himself to read the Bible in his spare time. He changed the spelling of his surname and spent the Second World War delivering lectures and broadcasting on the BBC. Following the stunned reception of his only novel – 'in all my experience', said T. S. Eliot (11), 'I have not met with anything quite like it' – he embarked on a fifteen-year spiritual journey, spending time with tantric yogis in India, Zen monks in Japan and Theravada Buddhists in Burma. He moved to the University of Texas in 1967, where he worked as the Professor of Philosophy, teaching holiday courses on Buddhism.

All About H. Hatterr 1948, rev. 1951–72

Herr Hatterr, the son of a European merchant seaman and a lady of Penang, narrates this poly-colloquial 'mosaic-organon' account of his quest for enlightenment. Taking advice from seven sages in seven Indian cities, he has adventures with pukka muggers, dubious swamis and alluring Rosie of the riding breeches. 'Milan Kundera once said that all modern literature descends from either Richardson's *Clarissa* or Sterne's *Tristram Shandy*,' wrote Salman Rushdie, 'and if Narayan (342) is India's Richardson then Desani is his Shandean other. *Hatterr*'s dazzling, puzzling, leaping prose is the first genuine effort to go beyond the Englishness of the English language.'

1972
• intro. Anthony Burgess, 1970
—

'It is the language that makes the book,' said Anthony Burgess (148) in his introduction, 'a sort of creative chaos that grumbles at the restraining banks. It is what may be termed Whole Language, in which philosophical terms, the colloquialisms of Calcutta and London, Shakespearian archaisms, bazaar whinings, quack spiels, references to the Hindu pantheon, the jargon of Indian litigation, and shrill babu irritability seethe together. It is not pure English; it is, like the English of Shakespeare, Joyce (8) and Kipling (22), gloriously impure.'

EAST ASIA

Lao She Mr Ma and Son

Lao She Cat Country

Eileen Chang Love in a Fallen City

Eileen Chang Lust, Caution

Eileen Chang Half a Lifelong Romance

Qian Zhongshu *Fortress Besieged*

The Beauty of Everyday Things Soetsu Yanagi

YASUNARI KAWABATA SNOW COUNTRY / THOUSAND CRANES

Yasunari Kawabata The Sound of the Mountain

YASUNARI KAWABATA THE MASTER OF GO

YASUNARI KAWABATA SNOW AND JADE(?)

PMC

MODERN CLASSICS

ISBN 0 14
00.8213 1

ISBN 0 14
00.8200
X

00.8201 8

China

Lao She 1899–1966

Shu Qingchun was born into a poor Manchu family in Beijing. His father, an imperial guardsman, was killed during the Boxer Rebellion when Shu was just two years old. He left China in his mid-twenties to teach Chinese at the University of London; he lived in Notting Hill for five years, reading the works of Dickens and Conrad (28) and starting

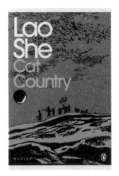

2014
• trans. William Dolby, 2003
intro. Julia Lovell, 2013

Mr Ma and Son 1929

Written and set in London, this Dickensian tragicomedy follows the misadventures of Mr Ma and his son Ma Wei after they inherit an old curiosity shop near St Paul's Cathedral. Suffering anti-Chinese racism from all sides, they navigate the alien social conventions of 1920s London, relying on the stern advice of the Reverend Ely and the kindness of their landlady, Mrs Wedderburn.

to write novels under the pen name 'Lao She'. He continued to teach when he returned to China, and he became a renowned novelist and playwright, perhaps most famous for his novel *Rickshaw Boy* (1945), about the tragic life of a Beijing rickshaw-puller. In 1966, during the Cultural Revolution, he was condemned as a counter-revolutionary and beaten by Red Guards on the steps of the temple of Confucius in Beijing; he was later found drowned in the city's Taiping Lake. Shu was posthumously 'rehabilitated' in 1978 and his former home is now a museum, where the persimmon trees he planted still grow in the courtyard.

Cat Country 1932–3

Lao She's only work of science fiction is a dark, satirical fable. A Chinese space traveller crash-lands on Mars and finds himself in the land of the Cat People, where he learns to speak Felinese, write cat-poetry and appreciate the narcotic effects of the reverie leaf. Soon, however, he discovers that the cats' government is corrupt, divided and vulnerable to attack from brutal invaders in a narrative that appears to draw parallels with Japan's 1931 invasion of China. *Cat Country* has been compared to Swift's *Gulliver's Travels* (1726) and *The First Men in the Moon* (1901) by H. G. Wells (26); the *Times Literary Supplement* called it 'an ideal companion piece to George Orwell's *Nineteen Eighty-Four* (84)'.

2014
• trans. William A. Lyell, 1970
intro. Ian Johnson, 2013

Eileen Chang 1920–1995

When Zhang Ying's parents divorced, her opium-addict father beat her and locked her in her room. Eventually she ran away and studied literature at the University of Hong Kong, but the Japanese attacked in December 1941 and she was forced to return to occupied Shanghai. There she began publishing stories and essays. 'Get your fame early in the game!' she wrote in 1944. 'Get it late, and the pleasure's lost its punch. [. . .] I have to hurry: faster, faster, or it'll be too late!' She married the writer Hu Lancheng, who was later condemned as a Japanese collaborator. With the rise of communism, Chang moved first to Hong Kong in 1952, and then to the USA three years later, where she worked at the Center for Chinese Studies at the University of California, Berkeley, researching the greatest work of Chinese literature, *The Story of the Stone*. Towards the end of her life she lived as a recluse in Los Angeles. The film director Ang Lee, who made an award-winning adaptation of *Lust, Caution* (347) in 2007, called her 'the fallen angel of Chinese literature'.

Love in a Fallen City and Other Stories 1943–4

These short fictions are set in the Hong Kong and Shanghai of the 1930s and

2007
trans. Karen S. Kingsbury
& Eileen Chang

1940s, a world of concubines, opium addicts and clandestine affairs. The title story is a novella about a beautiful divorcée, Bai Liusu, who finds love as bombs fall on Hong Kong.

Lust, Caution
and Other Stories 1944–79

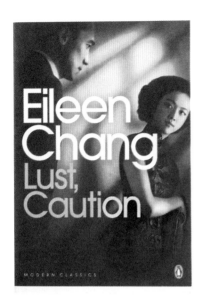

Set during the Japanese occupation of
Shanghai in the Second World War, the
title story is about the former actress
Wang Jiazhi, who is recruited by the Chinese
Resistance to seduce the enemy collaborator
Mr Yi in order to facilitate his assassination.
It may have been inspired by the true story
of the wartime spy Zheng Pingru. Other
tales include 'In the Waiting Room', 'Traces
of Love' and 'Steamed Osmanthus Flower'.

2014
trans. Karen S. Kingsbury
& Eileen Chang

2007
ed. Julia Lovell, 2007
trans. Julia Lovell et al., 1996–2007
—
In Chinese, the title is a pun: the
characters *Sè, Jiè* can be read as
'lust, caution' or as 'colourful ring',
a reference to an important object
in the story.

Half a Lifelong Romance

1950

Originally entitled *Eighteen Springs*, Chang's
first full-length novel spans eighteen years
and tells the story of a young Shanghai engineer
who falls in love with a beautiful factory worker.

Qian Zhongshu 1910–1998

Qian was the son of a Confucian scholar. He married the playwright Yang Jiang and
together they travelled to Europe in 1935, where they studied at the universities of
Oxford and Paris. Qian was a brilliant student, becoming fluent in English, Greek, Latin,
German, French, Italian and Spanish, as well as classical Chinese. In 1938, he returned
to China to teach at Tsinghua University, and during the Second World War Qian and
Yang lived in Shanghai under Japanese occupation. They barely survived the Cultural
Revolution under Chairman Mao, but in later
life Qian came to be regarded as the country's
leading scholar, the last in an unbroken chain
stretching back to Confucius.

Fortress Besieged 1947

Qian's novel opens on a ship to China in 1937,
on the eve of the Sino-Japanese War. The bumbling
Fang Hung-chien is returning from Europe with
a bogus degree from a fake college. When he finds
a teaching post at a newly established university in
Shanghai, we follow his misadventures as he falls
in and out of love, clashes with other pseudo-
intellectuals and attempts to evade calamity
as war breaks around him. The title of the novel
comes from a French proverb, which has now
become a Chinese proverb: 'Marriage is like
a fortress besieged; those who are outside want
to get in, and those who are inside want to get out.'

2006
trans. Jeanne Kelly
& Nathan K. Mao, 1979
fwd. Jonathan Spence, 2004

'*Fortress Besieged* is awash,
almost from the first page,
with images of bile, vomit
and phlegm,' writes the
historian Jonathan Spence
in his foreword. 'Human
bodies – and not just Fang's
– are continually revealing their
fallibility through their mouths
and their nostrils. There is
seasickness, airsickness,
carsickness, drunken vomiting,
babies' spittle and drool,
and snot.'

Japan

The Beauty of Everyday Things
Soetsu Yanagi

2019
trans. Michael Brase, 2017

The Beauty of Everyday Things
1920 – 59

Soetsu Yanagi 1889 – 1961

Yanagi coined the term *mingei* in 1924, along with the potters Shoji Hamada and Kanjiro Kawai. 'Literally, the word means "crafts of the people",' he wrote. 'It is meant to stand in contrast to aristocratic fine arts, and refers to objects used by ordinary people in their daily lives.' He became the first director of the Japan Folk Crafts Museum in 1936.

Yanagi believed everyday objects should be made with care, built to last and treated with respect, and that in this way they become beautiful. These essays, which span four decades, are 'radical and inspiring', writes the master potter Edmund de Waal. '[…] Yanagi's vision puts the connection between heart and hand before the transient and commercial.'

Yasunari Kawabata 1899 – 1972

Kawabata was orphaned at the age of two. His first stories were published as a schoolboy and he was commissioned to write for the literary journal *Bungei Shunju* (*Literary Chronicle*) while still a student at Tokyo Imperial University. He settled in Kamakura – a suburb of Tokyo home to many Japanese writers – where he became increasingly reclusive, writing lyrical novels, short stories and *haiku*. He won the Nobel Prize for Literature (576) in 1968, the first Japanese writer to do so, then never published anything again. He was haunted by nightmares following his friend Yukio Mishima's (350) suicide and he took his own life at the age of 73.

2011
trans. Edward G. Seidensticker, 1956
—
'*Snow Country* is perhaps Kawabata's masterpiece,' wrote the translator Edward Seidensticker. 'He has found in Shimamura's love affair the perfect symbol for a denial of love, and he has in the woman Komako and in the shadowy beauty of the snow country fit subjects for the *haiku*-like flashes that bring the denial forth.'

Snow Country 1935 – 48 →

Set in the hot-spring resort of Yuzawa, amidst the snowdrifts of Honshu island's western mountains, this delicate novel describes a love affair between Shimamura, a shallow businessman from Tokyo, and Komako, a beautiful geisha. Kawabata wrote much of the novel at Takahan Ryokan, a spa hotel in Yuzawa, and his room is now preserved as a museum.

Thousand Cranes →
1949 – 52

In contrast to the poetic simplicity of the Japanese tea ceremony, mortal love affairs appear sordid and crass. In post-war Japan, Kikuji falls first for his dead father's mistress and then for her daughter.

2011
trans. Edward G. Seidensticker, 1958

The Sound of the Mountain 1949 – 54

Ogata Shingo is growing old in Kamakura, near Tokyo. As his memories fade, he finds himself estranged from his wife and dangerously attracted to his daughter-in-law, while the rumble of a nearby mountain becomes the sound of his impending death.

1974 Penguin Books
2011 Modern Classics
trans. Edward G. Seidensticker, 1970

Shinkankakuha

In 1924, Riichi Yokomitsu and Yasunari Kawabata started the literary journal *Bungei Jidai* (*The Artistic Age*) to promote a new style of literature, *Shinkankakuha*, or 'new impressions'. In founding Japan's first modernist movement (11), they were reacting against naturalism.

PENGUIN MODERN CLASSICS

YASUNARI KAWABATA

SNOW COUNTRY AND THOUSAND CRANES

With an introduction by Kazuo Ishiguro

1971 Penguin Books
1986 Modern Classics
● intro. Kazuo Ishiguro, 1986
trans. Edward G. Seidensticker, 1956–8

The illustration on the cover of the
1986 edition is by Cathie Felstead.

The Master of Go 1951–4

In 1938, Kawabata reported on a six-month *go* match between Honinbo Shusai, the frail Meijin, or 'master', and Minoru Kitani, his young challenger. Kawabata later fictionalized the match in this 'chronicle-novel', which is an elegy both for a great player and for a lost tradition of respect. It was Kawabata's favourite among his works, and the only one he considered finished.

1976 Penguin Books
1985 Modern Classics
● trans. Edward
G. Seidensticker, 1972

This edition of *Dandelions* includes Kawabata's 1968 Nobel lecture, 'Japan, The Beautiful and Myself', in which he talks about Zen Buddhism and the beauty that emerges from isolation. 'The heart of the ink painting is in space, abbreviation, what is left undrawn,' he said.
—
2019
trans. Michael Emmerich, 2017

Beauty and Sadness 1964

Oki is a successful but unfulfilled writer, travelling by train to meet an old flame, Otoko, who is now a renowned and reclusive painter in Kyoto.

Dandelions 1964–8, pub. 1972

When Ineko makes love to her fiancé Hisano, she loses the ability to see him. In a psychiatric clinic, it is unclear whether Ineko's condition is a form of madness or an expression of her love. Kawabata's final novel was first published in its complete form after his death.

1979 Penguin Books
1986 Modern Classics
trans. Howard S. Hibbett, 1975

Yukio Mishima 1925–1970

As a child, Kimitake Hiraoka was banned from playing with other boys, or in direct sunlight. As a teenager, his father ripped up his stories and held him up to the side of speeding trains, but he continued to write secretly and began publishing under the pseudonym 'Yukio Mishima'. In 1944, he left school with a commendation from the emperor, and in 1946 he visited Yasunari Kawabata (348), who became his mentor. Inspired by Georges Bataille (176) and Witold Gombrowicz (292), Mishima wrote novels that broke social taboos, in a Japan that was changing rapidly. His interests included modelling, acting, bodybuilding, karate, kendo and training as a samurai. He founded a civilian militia, the Tatenokai ('Shield Society'), which was dedicated to restoring power to the emperor of Japan and overturning the parliamentary constitution of 1947. In 1970, he and four members attempted a military coup, which failed. After a rousing speech from a balcony, which was greeted by jeers, Mishima stepped inside and performed *seppuku*, ritual disembowelment and suicide. 'Mishima is lucid in the midst of emotional confusion,' wrote Christopher Isherwood (103), 'funny in the midst of despair.'

2017
trans. Meredith Weatherby, 1958
—
Mishima himself was conflicted in his sexuality. He had male lovers and visited gay bars, but in 1958 he married Yoko Sugiyama, with whom he had two children. After his death, she denied his homosexuality.

Confessions of a Mask 1949

Mishima's second novel made him a literary celebrity. The teenage Kochan loves his male classmate and masturbates over images of Saint Sebastian, naked and pierced with arrows; but he cannot reveal his true desires and hides behind a mask of conformity.

Thirst for Love 1950

Mishima's third novel centres on a female protagonist, the young widow Etsuko, who tolerates the molestations of her father-in-law while nursing a passion for the strapping farmhand Saburo.

1978 Penguin Books
1986 Modern Classics
● trans. Alfred H. Marks, 1969

1971 Penguin Books
1987 Modern Classics
trans. Alfred H. Marks,
1968

Forbidden Colours 1951

Shunsuké is a twisted, ageing author who has developed a festering hatred for women. So when he meets a beautiful young boy, Yuichi, he uses him to wreak revenge on the female sex. *Time* magazine described the novel as 'a leisurely lover's lesson on the giving and receiving of pain that makes John Updike's *Couples* (515) read like a children's story'.

The Frolic of the Beasts 1961

This novel parodies a 14th-century Nō drama. It is the horrifying story of a love triangle between three 'beasts': the young student Kōji, the beautiful Yūko Kusakado and her husband, the literary critic Ippei.

The Sea of Fertility

Spring Snow, Runaway Horses, The Temple of Dawn, The Decay of the Angel 1964–70, pub. 1965–71

Mishima wrote his last great work over several years. The tetralogy spans six decades in the life of Shigekuni Honda, starting as a law student in 1912, eventually becoming a judge.

1976–7 Penguin Books
individual titles
1985 Modern Classics
• trans. Michael Gallagher et al., 1972–5

In each instalment, he encounters a successive reincarnation of his school friend Kiyoaki Matsuagae, who returns as a terrorist, an indolent Thai princess and a manipulative, sadistic orphan. 'Finishing [*The Sea of Fertility*] makes me feel as if it is the end of the world,' wrote Mishima in October 1970. He finalized the last page on 24 November, the day before he performed *seppuku*. 'These four remarkable novels are the most complete vision we have of Japan in the twentieth century,' says Paul Theroux (543).

Death in Midsummer
and Other Stories 1952–63

These stories combine suicide, homosexuality and post-war nihilism. In the title story, a middle-class beach holiday ends with corpses; other pieces feature husbands planning *seppuku*, aristocratic voyeurs, affairs in San Francisco, and an ascetic monk who falls in love with a concubine. The selection also includes Mishima's play *Dojoji* (1957), based on an anonymous Nō drama.

1987
• trans. Ivan Morris, 1959
intro. Nancy Wilson Ross, 1959

The Temple of the Golden Pavilion 1956

In 1950, an unhappy and unbalanced student of Zen Buddhism, Hayashi Yoken, set fire to the famous 14th-century Golden Pavilion of Kinkakuji, one of Japan's national monuments. Mishima wrote this novelization of the event, told from the tormented arsonist's point of view, basing it on genuine newspaper reports and interviews with Hayashi in prison.

The Sailor Who Fell from Grace with the Sea 1963

When Fusako, an elegant widow, makes love to Ryuji, a naval officer, they are observed by her emotionless 13-year-old son Noboru, who conspires with his sinister group of schoolmates to teach Ryuji a lesson.

Life for Sale 1968

Hanio Yamada is an advertising copywriter. After a failed suicide attempt, he places an advert in a Tokyo newspaper: 'Life for sale. Use me as you wish. I am a twenty-seven-year-old male. Discretion guaranteed.' What ensues is a series of bizarre adventures, involving hidden cameras, home-made explosives, poisonous carrots and a vampire. Originally serialized in *Playboy Japan*, *Life for Sale* 'yields a rare glimpse of the pulp-fiction flipside that partnered the rhapsodic and mystical Mishima,' said *The Times*; it is 'grotesque, melodramatic, spectacular, utterly silly'.

2019
trans. Andrew Clare, 2018

1971 Penguin Books
1986 Modern Classics
• trans. Donald Keene et al., 1966

1970 Penguin Books
1990 Twentieth-Century Classics
• trans. John Nathan, 1966

2021
trans. Stephen Dodd, 2019

2006
trans. E. Dale Saunders, 1964
intro. David Mitchell, 2006
—
The Woman in the Dunes
is illustrated by Kobo's wife,
Machi Abe.

Kobo Abe 1924–1993

Kimifusa Abe was born in Tokyo but grew up in Manchuria on the edge of a swamp, where he collected insects and read <u>Franz Kafka</u> (280). In 1945, he married the artist Machi Yamada, and he sold home-made pickles to fund his medical degree at Tokyo Imperial University. He never practised medicine but became a writer instead, publishing novels under the pseudonym 'Kobo'. He was also a playwright, a theatre director, a musician and a photographer; in 1986, he patented a brand of snow chains for car tyres.

The Woman in the Dunes 1962

When an amateur entomologist misses the last bus home after a beetle-hunting trip, he seeks shelter for the night in a strange village where the houses are half buried by mountainous sand dunes and only accessible by rope ladder. In the morning, his ladder has gone and he finds himself imprisoned with his anonymous hostess.

The Face of Another 1964

Horribly disfigured in a laboratory accident, a scientist creates a prosthetic mask to cover his scars. But he finds himself behaving increasingly strangely, seducing his own estranged wife and losing touch with his old identity.

1972 Penguin Books
2006 Modern Classics
trans. E. Dale Saunders, 1966
intro. Kaori Nagai, 2006

The Ruined Map 1967

'The city – a bounded infinity. A labyrinth where you are never lost. Your private map where every block bears exactly the same number.' As a private detective investigates a missing person, he begins to suspect that perhaps it is he who is lost.

2020
trans. E. Dale Saunders, 1969
—
In 2020, the covers of the Penguin editions of Abe were all given images by Shuzo Takiguchi, an avant-garde poet, artist and friend of Abe.

2020
trans. E. Dale Saunders, 1974

The Box Man 1973

This 'record of a box man' describes the strange phenomenon of people abandoning society and living in cardboard boxes on the Tokyo streets. Initially unsettled, the narrator is gradually seduced by the anonymity and voyeurism of the box lifestyle. 'Abe's book is a stunning addition to the literature of eccentricity, those bitter, crying voices of Melville's Bartleby the scrivener and Dostoevsky's underground man,' said the *New York Times*. 'It gnaws at the reader, forces him to question his values, his Shibboleths and his ritualistic props, and shoots an energetic poison into his ear.'

Secret Rendezvous 1977

An ambulance takes a man's wife away, but there is nothing wrong with her; he searches for her in a vast underground hospital that appears increasingly sinister and surreal. Abe's novel 'reads as if it were the collaborative effort of Hieronymus Bosch, Franz Kafka (280) and Mel Brooks', writes the *Chicago Sun Times*.

2020
trans. Juliet
Winters
Carpenter,
1979

2018
trans. Geraldine Harcourt,
1983
—
Tsushima's epigraph is
taken from Rilke's *Sonnets
to Orpheus* (269):

Hark, my distant, quiet friend,
    and feel
Your breath still enriching this
    emptiness.

Yuko Tsushima 1947–2016

Satoko Tsushima was the daughter of the novelist Osamu Dazai, who took his own life when she was one year old. Raised by a single mother, and a single mother herself, Tsushima returned repeatedly to mother–daughter relationships in her novels and short stories, which won all of Japan's major literary prizes. 'It takes extraordinary courage, particularly in a very traditional society like Japan, to write about these things at all,' said Margaret Drabble (152) in 1991. 'And she writes about them with extraordinary freshness.'

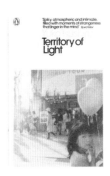

Child of Fortune 1978

Kōko Mizuno defies her family and friends by bringing up her daughter Kayako alone. When she becomes unexpectedly pregnant, however, her relationship with the 11-year-old is strained to breaking point, as is her own grip on reality. Angela Carter (156) considered this 'a terrific novel'.

Territory of Light 1978–9

A young woman, abandoned by her feckless husband, moves into a new Tokyo apartment with their two-year-old daughter. The seasons revolve through twelve chapters as we follow her first year as a single mother, illuminated by dappled sunlight, blinding reflections off floodwater, neon streetlamps and ominous explosions.

2019
trans. Geraldine Harcourt,
2018
—
Geraldine Harcourt was
a New Zealand translator
of Japanese literature who
was a friend of Tsushima.
'My conversations with
Tsushima helped me to
be sparing with the English
wording,' said Harcourt, 'to
try to capture the uncertainty
without putting a lot of
paraphrasing around it.'

Shusaku Endo 1923–1996

Endo was received into the Catholic Church at the age of eleven and his faith is the defining feature of his writing. His most famous novel is *Silence* (1966), about Catholic missionary priests in early 17th-century Japan. He won several major prizes and edited the literary journal *Mita Bungaku* (*Mita Literature*). 'Endo to my mind is one of the finest living novelists,' wrote Graham Greene (88).

The Samurai 1980

This historical novel is based on the true story of a group of samurai, led by Hasekura Rokuemon, who sailed in 1613 across the Pacific Ocean to Mexico, continued their journey overland and travelled to Europe, where they met the Pope. They were accompanied by an ambitious Spanish priest, Father Pedro Velasco, who hoped to become the first Bishop of Japan.

1983 King Penguin
1990 Penguin Books
2017 Modern Classics
trans. Van C. Gessel, 1982

More PRIESTS

Arrow of God
by Chinua Achebe   361

Death Comes to the Archbishop
by Willa Cather   414

The Power and the Glory
by Graham Greene   91

A Month of Sundays
by John Updike   516

The Bridge of San Luis Rey
by Thornton Wilder   436

AFRICA

NORTH AFRICA

Tayeb Salih Season of Migration to the North

PENGUIN CLASSICS

Sudan

Tayeb Salih

1929 – 2009

Salih was born in the small village of Al Dabbah in northern Sudan, when the country was still governed jointly by Britain and Egypt. He studied in Khartoum and then London, where he found work with the BBC Arabic Service and wrote a weekly literary column for the Arabic-language newspaper *Al Majalla* (*The Magazine*). He later worked as the Director-General of Qatar's Ministry of Information and for UNESCO in Paris.

Season of Migration to the North

1966

An unnamed narrator returns to independent Sudan in the 1960s, after spending seven years in Europe. In his home village he meets Mustafa Sa'eed, another 'travelled man', who tells the disturbing story of his journey to London shortly after the First World War, the tragic legacy of which is still unravelling. The novel is a counter-narrative to Conrad's *Heart of Darkness* (29), 'an *Arabian Nights* in reverse', as the *Observer* put it. In 2001, it was named the most important Arab novel of the 20th century by the Arab Literary Academy in Damascus.

Tayeb Salih
Season of Migration to the North

2003
trans. Denys Johnson-Davies, 1969
intro. Tayeb Salih, 2003
—
Mawsim al-Hijrah ila al-Shamal was first published in the Beirut journal *Hiwar* (*Dialogue*). It was initially banned in Sudan for its explicit descriptions of sex. Denys Johnson-Davies's English translation first appeared in the African Writers Series (362).

WEST AFRICA

The Penguin Book of Modern African Poetry

Chinua Achebe Things Fall Apart

Chinua Achebe No Longer at Ease

Chinua Achebe Arrow of God

Chinua Achebe A Man of the People

Chinua Achebe Anthills of the Savannah

Chinua Achebe The Education of a British-Protected Child

Cyprian Ekwensi Jagua Nana

Kole Omotoso The Combat

Kojo Laing Search Sweet Country

PENGUIN CLASSICS

MODERN CLASSICS

MODERN CLASSICS

PENGUIN CLASSICS

PENGUIN CLASSICS

PENGUIN CLASSICS

MODERN CLASSICS

MODERN CLASSICS

MODERN CLASSICS

MODERN CLASSICS

ISBN 0 14
11.8100 1

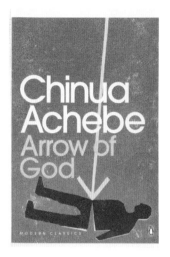

2010
—
Arrow of God was first published
in the African Writers Series (362).

2001
intro. Maya Jaggi

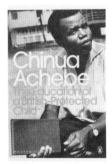

2011
—

No Longer at Ease 1960

Obi Okonkwo, the grandson of Okonkwo from *Things
Fall Apart* (359), is a civil servant in contemporary Lagos,
struggling to navigate corrupt government officials
and the constant temptation of bribes, especially when
he falls in love. The book is dedicated to Christie Okoli,
whom Achebe married in 1961. The title comes from
T. S. Eliot's (11) poem 'The Journey of the Magi'.

Arrow of God 1964

Ezeulu is the chief priest of the god Ulu, revered by
the six villages of Umuaro, but his authority begins to
slip under the influence of colonialism and Christianity.
He still believes he is an arrow in Ulu's bow, however
– and he is determined to lead his people even if it
means annihilation.

A Man of the People 1966

The idealistic Odili comes to work for his former teacher,
Chief the Honourable M. A. Nanga, MP, who is now
Minister for Culture in an unnamed, newly independent
African state. Nanga is a self-declared 'man of the people'
but he is also a ruthless opportunist. An increasingly
personal conflict spirals out of control and the novel
ends with a military coup. It is 'a bitter yet funny satire',
wrote Anthony Burgess (148), '[…] probably the best
book to come out of West Africa'.

Anthills of the Savannah 1987

Achebe's last novel was published after a gap of 21 years.
It follows three friends in the fictional African country
of Kangan: Chris Oriko, the government's Commissioner
of Information; Beatrice Okoh, an official in the Ministry
of Finance; and Ikem Osodi, a newspaper editor. His
Excellency, the Sandhurst-educated president, oversees a brutal military
regime of betrayal and corruption. The novel was shortlisted for the
Booker Prize, but was pipped by Penelope Lively's *Moon Tiger* (161).

The Education of a British-Protected Child
Essays 1988 – 2009, pub. 2009

In this selection of autobiographical essays, which Achebe gathered
in his late seventies, he 'wanted very much to shine the torch of variety
and of difference' on his diverse life experiences. He describes his
love of reading, growing up in colonial Nigeria and the fortunes of
his nation post-independence. He is 'a magical writer', says Margaret
Atwood – 'one of the greatest of the twentieth century'.

2010
—

2001
intro. Karl Maier
—

Coincidentally, *A Man of the
People* was published just days
before the first actual coup
was attempted in Nigeria.
Achebe came under suspicion,
because the government
thought he must have known
about it in advance.

Cyprian Ekwensi 1921–2007

Cyprian Odiatu Duaka Ekwensi was born in Nigeria, the son of an Ibo storyteller and elephant hunter. He worked as a forestry officer in Nigeria and then as a pharmacist in Romford, Essex. When he returned to Nigeria, he published *People of the City* (1954), one of the first modern African novels to be published internationally. He went on to write more than 40 books for adults and children. In 1968, he won the Dag Hammarskjöld International Prize.

2018
—

Jagua Nana was initially banned in schools and attacked by the Catholic and Anglican Churches. It was republished in 1975 in the African Writers Series.

Jagua Nana 1961

Jagua Nana is a brassy, big-hearted, chain-smoking sex worker in 1950s Lagos, who enjoys parties, scandals and wild nights at the Tropicana club. When she falls for young Freddie, however, she must use all her ageing charms to fund his teacher training in England. 'His glorious imagination captured ours,' writes Chimamanda Ngozi Adichie. '[…] *Jagua Nana* is my favourite of his novels.'

Kole Omotoso b. 1943

Bankole Ajibabi Omotoso was born into a Yoruba-speaking family in Nigeria. He studied in Lagos, Idaban and Edinburgh, and he became one of the leading English-language writers of post-independence Nigeria, until his controversial novel *Just Before Dawn* (1988) forced him to leave the country. He settled in South Africa, where he has become famous as a public intellectual and for appearing in Vodacom mobile phone commercials as the 'Yebo Gogo' ('Yes, Grandma') man.

The Combat 1972

In this poignant memorial to the Nigerian Civil War, two friends clash over the paternity rights of the child of a market girl, now a sophisticated businesswoman. 'It gradually changes from comedy through satire to a doom-laden atmosphere of inescapable tragedy,' wrote the South African *Sunday Times*. *The Combat* was later published in the African Writers Series.

2008
• —

The African Writers Series

In 1962, Heinemann republished Chinua Achebe's *Things Fall Apart* (359) as the first title in a new 'African Writers Series', which gave an international voice to post-independence African writing. Achebe served as the general editor of the series, selecting the first hundred titles and showcasing authors such as Cyprian Ekwensi, Nuruddin Farah (362), Bessie Head (377), Thomas Mofolo (368), Kole Omotoso, Tayeb Salih (357), Can Themba (373) and Ngũgĩ wa Thiong'o (365). The paperback books were designed for classroom use and published in London as well as cities across Africa. James Currey took over as general editor in 1972, incorporating writers such as Nelson Mandela (372), Dambudzo Marechera (377) and the Nobel Laureates Doris Lessing, Wole Soyinka, Naguib Mahfouz and Nadine Gordimer. The series ran on into the 1980s, but gradually petered out as Heinemann was bought by a succession of publishing conglomerates. In 2005, Penguin USA launched a 'Penguin African Writers Series' with a series introduction by Chinua Achebe and titles by Ngũgĩ wa Thiong'o.

Ghana

Kojo Laing 1946–2017

Bernard Kojo Laing was born in Ghana and educated in Scotland, graduating from Glasgow University in 1968. He returned to Ghana with his Scottish wife Josephine and worked for the civil service for ten years, before becoming the headmaster of the school that his mother had established in Accra. He began writing poetry in the 1970s, and his first novel, *Search Sweet Country*, appeared in 1986. When he died, he was survived by two wives and twelve children. The *Johannesburg Review of Books* described him as 'one of the unsung heroes of African fiction'.

Search Sweet Country 1986

This sprawling novel recreates Accra in the 1970s, its streets, marketplaces and crowded houses, its idealistic professors, corrupt politicians, witches, students, healers and other inhabitants, all of whom speak in Ghanaian Pidgin English. The author Binyavanga Wainaina calls it 'the finest novel written in English ever to come out of the African continent'.

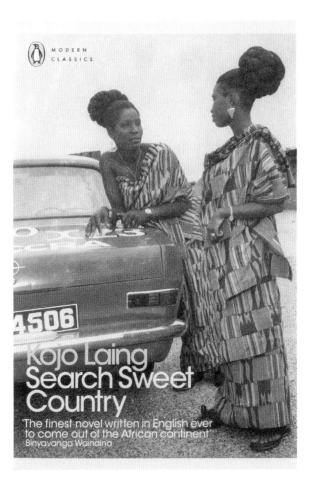

2019
—
This edition includes a glossary of Ghanaian words and some invented by Laing himself, including *fikifiki*, 'sexual intercourse'; *logologo*, 'genital'; and *zagazogo*, 'wild man'.

More INVENTIVE LANGUAGE

A Clockwork Orange by Anthony Burgess	148
Nova Express by William S. Burroughs	484
Riddley Walker by Russell Hoban	541
Finnegans Wake by James Joyce	11
On the Road by Jack Kerouac	470

EAST AFRICA

ELSPETH HUXLEY *Red Strangers*

Ngũgĩ wa Thiong'o The River Between

Ngũgĩ wa Thiong'o A Grain of Wheat

Ngũgĩ wa Thiong'o Petals of Blood

Nuruddin Farah From a Crooked Rib

PENGUIN CLASSICS

PENGUIN CLASSICS

PENGUIN CLASSICS

PENGUIN CLASSICS

Kenya

Elspeth Huxley 1907–1997

Elspeth Grant grew up on a Kenyan coffee farm. She
married Gervas Huxley, a cousin of Aldous Huxley (65),
and worked for the BBC during the Second World War
and on the BBC General Advisory Council in the 1950s.
She joined the Monckton Commission in 1959 and
advised on the futures of the colonies that would
become Malawi, Zambia and Zimbabwe. Alongside
her public career she wrote novels, detective stories,
biographies and travel books. 'She was not only
a talented writer,' ran her obituary in *The Times*,
'but an outstanding personality.'

Red Strangers 1939

This epic novel describes four generations of the Kikuyu
people in Kenya. It starts with the first arrival of European
settlers, nicknamed 'red' strangers because of their sunburn,
and ends with the birth of a baby girl, Aeroplane. It includes
a graphic description of female circumcision, which led to the
manuscript being turned down by Harold Macmillan, who was
working as a reader for the family publishing firm. As Huxley
put it, 'our future Prime Minister couldn't take clitoridectomy'.

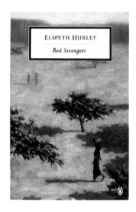

1999
intro. Richard Dawkins
—
In 1998, the atheist and
geneticist Richard Dawkins,
also born in Kenya, wrote an
article about *Red Strangers*
in the *Financial Times*,
challenging 'any reputable
publisher [...] to look at
Red Strangers with a view
to bringing out a new edition'.
Penguin took up the
suggestion and the title joined
the Twentieth-Century Classics
series the following year,
with Dawkins's article as
an introduction.

Ngũgĩ wa Thiong'o b. 1938

James Thiong'o Ngugi was born in Kamirithu, Kenya, and was a teenager
during the Mau Mau Rebellion, in which his mother was tortured. He studied
Joseph Conrad (28) at Kampala University and then George Lamming (554)
at Leeds, where he became heavily influenced by Marxism and especially
the writings of Frantz Fanon (557). He returned to independent Kenya to
teach at the University of Nairobi, changing his name to Ngũgĩ wa Thiong'o.
He advocated a new form of participative theatre, but in 1977 his incendiary
play *Ngaahika Ndeenda* (*I Will Marry When I Want*) was shut down by the
government and he was arrested and detained without trial in a maximum
security prison. During his year-long imprisonment, Ngũgĩ wrote the first
novel in the Gĩkùyũ language – *Caitaani Mũtharaba-Inĩ* (*Devil on the Cross*,
1980) – on prison toilet paper. On his release, he went into voluntary exile
in the USA, where he has taught at the universities of Yale, New York and
California and founded the Gĩkùyũ literary journal *Mũtĩiri* (*Mentor*).

The River Between 1965

Between two isolated mountain ridges runs the 'valley of life', home to the Gĩkùyũ
people; but now white settlers are arriving with a new religion. The Gĩkùyũ tribes
react in different ways: some embrace Christianity, others reject it. In the middle,
the visionary young leader Waiyaki attempts to bridge the two positions.

2002
intro. Jack Mapanje
—
Ngũgĩ's first novels were published
in the African Writers Series (362)
after he met Chinua Achebe (359)
at the 1962 African Writers
Conference in Kampala.

2002
intro. Abdulrazak Gurnah

A Grain of Wheat 1967, rev. 1986

In 1963, Kenya is on the verge of independence from the British and we follow the tangled stories of Kihika, a rebel leader who was betrayed, his sister Mumbi, torn between loyalty to her husband and the harsh realities of the Mau Mau Rebellion, and the quiet Mugo, a brave concentration-camp survivor with a dreadful secret.

Petals of Blood 1977

A triple murder takes place soon after Kenyan independence, and four suspects are detained in the small town of Ilmorog: the headmaster Munira, the teacher and activist Karega, the barmaid Wanja and the shopkeeper Abdulla. This was the last novel that Ngũgĩ wrote in English. 'Reading Ngũgĩ,' says the writer Moses Isegawa, 'is like feeling a fire scorching your psyche, your heart, your being.'

2002
• intro. Moses Isegawa

Somalia

Nuruddin Farah b. 1945

Farah was born in Baidoa in Italian Somaliland, now Somalia. He spoke Somali at home, but attended schools in neighbouring Ethiopia, where he also learned Amharic, Italian, Arabic and English. He worked for the Ministry of Education in the newly independent Somalia, before studying philosophy and literature in India and theatre at Essex University. After he published the controversial *A Naked Needle* (1976), an arrest warrant was issued in Somalia, so he went into self-imposed exile, teaching in the USA, Germany, Italy, Sweden, Sudan, India and Nigeria, and attempting 'to keep my country alive by writing about it'. Nadine Gordimer described him as one of the continent's 'true interpreters'. In 1998, he won the Neustadt International Prize.

2003
• intro. Richard Dowden
—
From a Crooked Rib was first published in the African Writers Series (362). Farah was influenced by reading Ibsen: 'I could not have written *From a Crooked Rib* if I had not read *A Doll's House*,' he says.

From a Crooked Rib 1970

Farah's first novel tells the story of Ebla, an illiterate, orphaned 18-year-old woman, who runs away from a forced marriage and her nomadic way of life in rural Somalia. She finds herself in Mogadishu, dependent on male relatives and slipping into a spiral of perfunctory marriages, poverty and violence. The novel is a cry against the powerlessness of women in traditional Somali society. The title comes from a Somali proverb: 'God created Woman from a crooked rib; and any one who trieth to straighten it, breaketh it.'

SOUTHERN AFRICA

Olive Schreiner **The Story of an African Farm**

Thomas Mofolo *Traveller to the East*

A S Mopeli-Paulus *The World and the Cattle*

J Percy FitzPatrick *Jock of the Bushveld*

W C Scully *Unconventional Reminiscences*

Frank Brownlee *Cattle Thief*

James Stevenson-Hamilton South African Eden

Cry, The Beloved Country

Es'kia Mphahlele *In Corner B*

DAPHNE ROOKE *Mittee*

14 000197 2

MODERN CLASSICS

MODERN CLASSICS

MODERN CLASSICS

MODERN CLASSICS

MODERN CLASSICS

MODERN CLASSICS

MODERN CLASSICS

ISBN 0 14
00.6448 6

ISBN 0 14
01.8431 7

MODERN CLASSICS

Lesotho

Olive Schreiner 1855–1920

Olive Emilie Albertina Schreiner was born in Cape Colony, on the border of what is now Lesotho, and named after three brothers who all died before she was born: Oliver, Albert and Emile. She was the daughter of an impractical missionary, and much of her unhappy childhood was spent in poverty before she left to work as a governess on remote farms. In 1881, she travelled to England with the manuscript of *The Story of an African Farm*, which was published in 1883, and she began to develop a reputation as a freethinking feminist campaigner. In 1889, she returned to South Africa, where she clashed with the Prime Minister of Cape Colony, Cecil Rhodes, and married the politician and farmer Samuel Cron Cronwright. She is buried under a cairn on top of Buffelskop mountain in the Eastern Cape with her husband, their baby and her favourite dog.

1939 Penguin Books
1971 Modern Classics
1982 Penguin English Library
1986 Penguin Classics
intro. Dan Jacobson, 1971

—

Schreiner first published
The Story of an African Farm
under the male pseudonym
'Ralph Iron'.

The Story of an African Farm 1883

Two orphaned girls, Em and Lyndall, live on a lonely ostrich farm in the South African veld with their sadistic, superstitious stepmother. Their lives are disrupted first by the arrival of Bonaparte Blenkins, a charismatic vagrant, and later by Gregory Rose, an Englishman who leases part of the farm. Through humour and uninhibited passion, this revolutionary novel cries for the emancipation of women, and the unconventional Lyndall, in particular, was greeted enthusiastically as one of the first 'New Women'. 'I read the novel when I was fourteen or so,' wrote Doris Lessing; 'understanding very well the isolation described in it; responding to her sense of Africa the magnificent – mine, and everyone's who knows Africa; realising that this was one of the few rare books. For it is in that small number of novels, with *Moby Dick*, *Jude the Obscure*, *Wuthering Heights*, perhaps one or two others, which is on a frontier of the human mind.'

Thomas Mofolo 1876–1948

Mofolo was born in a remote village in what was then the Basutoland Protectorate. He was a student and teacher at a Paris Evangelical Missionary Society school in Morija, where the missionaries encouraged him to write *Traveller to the East*. He later became the estate manager of the Basutoland gold mines. He wrote *Chaka* (1925), an epic historical novel about the legendary Zulu emperor-king, and today he is remembered as one of the first African novelists and the pioneer of Sesotho as a literary language. The library at the National University of Lesotho is named in his honour.

Traveller to the East 1906

Moeti oa Bochabela tells the story of a young chieftain's conversion to Christianity, interweaving traditional Sesotho myths and praise poems. 'Moeti is, of course, a Christian tract,' wrote the scholar Albert S. Gérard, 'but Mofolo is by no means insensitive to the more subtle relations between Christianity and African culture. His hero's conversion to a new faith is also a return to beliefs and manners that antedated Christianity.'

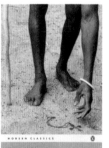

2007
● trans. Hugh Ashton, 1934
ed. Stephen Gray, 2007

—

Traveller to the East was
first serialized in 1906 in
the local Sesotho-language
newspaper *Leselinyana*
(*The Little Light*), under the
initials 'T.M.'; it was published
as a book a year later.

A. S. Mopeli-Paulus 1913–1994

2008
● –
Excerpts from *The World and the Cattle* were published in the mid-1950s, but the 2008 Penguin edition was the first publication of the complete text.

Attwell Sidwell Mopeli-Paulus was born in a village in Witzieshoek, a native reserve of the Basotho people; he was a descendant of a half-brother of King Moshoeshoe I of Basutoland. After training as a teacher, he served in the British army in North Africa during the Second World War and then became a leading figure in the Witzieshoek Rebellion, a Basotho uprising against the South African government. He wrote books in both Sesotho and English and translated three of Shakespeare's plays into Sesotho (*As You Like It*, *Julius Caesar* and *Macbeth*). When Witzieshoek gained independence as QwaQwa in 1975, he served as the deputy speaker of its legislative assembly.

The World and the Cattle 1954–5

'Peete was eaten by cannibals on the trek from Menkhoaneng to Thaba Bosiu.' Mopeli-Paulus's autobiography traces his ancestry, describes serving in the 'Grave Unit' during the Battle of El Alamein (116), and discusses the Witzieshoek Rebellion, the ensuing trial and his imprisonment under the new apartheid government. The South African *Observer* called it 'a true, more searingly honest book than Cry, the Beloved Country (371)'.

South Africa

J. Percy FitzPatrick 1862–1931

James Peter FitzPatrick was born in King William's Town, Cape Colony. He worked as a clerk in Cape Town's Standard Bank until 1884, at which point he resigned, changed his name to Percy and embarked on an adventurous life amidst the Transvaal gold rush. He helped to explore the unmapped region that became Southern Rhodesia (now Zimbabwe), took part in the infamous Jameson Raid (for which he was tried for high treason) and defended British imperial interests during the Second Boer War. He was knighted in 1902, established citrus farming in South Africa, and kept a menagerie of wild animals that he donated to form the Johannesburg Zoo. FitzPatrick's eldest son was killed during the First World War and in 1919 he suggested the two-minute silence that is now observed annually on Armistice Day.

1976 Puffin Books
2007 Modern Classics
● ed. Stephen Gray, 2007
–
The 2007 edition includes FitzPatrick's 'Postscript to *Jock*' and 'The Creed of *Jock*'.

Jock of the Bushveld 1907

FitzPatrick would tell his children stories about his adventures on the Bushveld with his plucky Staffordshire bull terrier Jock, and it was Rudyard Kipling (22) who encouraged him to collect them as a book along the lines of Jack London's *The Call of the Wild* (405). The stories were illustrated by Edmund Caldwell, the brother of Mary Tourtel (who created Rupert Bear), and they were quickly translated into Afrikaans, Dutch, French, Xhosa and Zulu. 'Like many a modern-day explorer,' wrote Wilfred Thesiger, 'as a boy my favourite reading was *Jock*.' The *Bookman* called it 'a remarkable companion picture to Olive Schreiner's masterpiece (368)'.

William Scully 1855–1943

William Charles Scully was born in Dublin and emigrated to South Africa with his parents in 1867. At the age of fourteen, he set off for the diamond fields of the Orange River and lived for many years as a prospector, panning for diamonds and gold. He then worked as a magistrate in the remote territories of Namaqualand and the Transkei.

Unconventional Reminiscences 1913

This volume collects Scully's *Reminiscences of a South African Pioneer* (1913) and *Further Reminiscences of a South African Pioneer* (1913), tracing his wanderings and adventures in the gold and diamond fields as 'one of that band of light-hearted, haphazard pioneers who, rejoicing in youthful energy and careless of their own interests, unwittingly laid the foundation upon which so many great fortunes have been built'. They are 'written with broad sympathy, geniality and remarkable freshness of outlook', said the South African *Sunday Times*.

2007
• –

2007
• ed. Stephen Gray
–

The 2007 edition also includes 'Chats with Christina', a previously unpublished oral testimony recorded by Brownlee. 'Yes, it's only an old Griqua woman what's talking to you,' says Christina. 'But we has our inside feelings.'

Frank Brownlee 1875–1952

Brownlee was the seventh son of Scottish missionaries in the Transkei territories. His grandfather, the Xhosa linguist John Brownlee, arrived in South Africa in 1816 and established the mission station that became King William's Town. While living in Butterworth in the Eastern Cape, and working as a magistrate, Brownlee began collecting oral histories of reavers and rustlers and other unruly figures.

Cattle Thief The Story of Ntsukumbini 1929

This novel combines dozens of oral histories into the story of a single fictional cattle rustler, Ntsukumbini, 'who lived on the banks of the Umzintlanga River at the foot of a high rocky koppie'. It is 'a picaresque novel', wrote the South African *Sunday Times*, 'its hero having a well developed inherited appetite for other people's property, notably their cattle and horses'.

James Stevenson-Hamilton 1867–1957

Stevenson-Hamilton was born in Dublin and grew up on his family estate in Scotland. He was educated at Rugby School and the Royal Military College, Sandhurst, and fought in the Second Boer War, after which he was appointed warden of the Sabi Game Reserve in the Lowveld, along the Eastern Transvaal border with Mozambique. Over the next two decades, he transformed the reserve, banning hunting, relocating kraals, training rangers, declaring war on poachers, and expanding the territory until he succeeded in founding the Kruger National Park in 1920. The Tsonga people nicknamed him 'Skukuza' – 'he who sweeps clean'. A dedicated ecologist and conservationist, Stevenson-Hamilton wrote books and articles on wildlife, landscape and the environment. He is commemorated by a species of South African dwarf gecko, *Lygodactylus stevensoni*.

South African Eden
From Sabi Game Reserve to Kruger National Park
1937, rev. 1956

Stevenson-Hamilton's memoir describes the creation and management of the Kruger National Park, setting out his passionate views on the preservation of indigenous animals. 'The writing is elegant and colourful,' praised the South African *Weekend Post*, 'and the anecdotes conjure up exciting, rewarding and often humorous times in the formative days of the world's most famous wildlife park.'

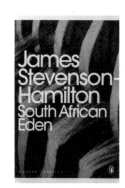

2008
• –

Alan Paton 1903–1988

Paton was born in the Colony of Natal, now a province of South Africa. He taught in Ixopo until 1935, when he became the principal of the Diepkloof Reformatory in Johannesburg, for delinquent young African offenders. He instigated a number of radical changes, transforming the institution from a prison into a school, and he began writing about South African social issues. He co-founded the Liberal Party in 1953 and later served as its president, dedicating the rest of his life to campaigning against the apartheid laws introduced by the National Party in 1948.

Cry, The Beloved Country
A Story of Comfort in Desolation 1948

Stephen Kumalo, a simple Zulu parson from rural Ixopo, travels to Johannesburg to find his sister Gertrude and his delinquent son Absalom. This passionate, polemical novel charts Stephen's odyssey through chaotic Johannesburg and the impenetrable convolutions of the South African legal system.

1958 Penguin Books
1966 Modern Classics
● —

Drum Magazine

Drum was co-founded in 1951 by the test cricketer Bob Crisp and by Jim Bailey, a former RAF pilot. It was immediately associated with the jazz, gangsters, dancing and defiance of Johannesburg's Sophiatown and the period of optimism and creativity in the early 1950s known as the 'Sophiatown Renaissance'. Contributors were known as the 'Drum Boys' and included Es'kia Mphahlele, Can Themba (373) and Bloke Modisane (374) as well as Bessie Head (378); their motto was 'live fast, die young and have a good-looking corpse'. The magazine combined inventive photography with fiction and investigative journalism, aiming to expose the realities and inequalities of apartheid. Following a programme of forced rehousing in 1955, however, Sophiatown was bulldozed to the ground and the community of writers largely dispersed overseas. The magazine fell into abeyance, but it has since been revived and is still published today in South Africa.

Es'kia Mphahlele 1919–2008

Ezekiel Mphahlele was born in Pretoria and raised in the Marabastad township. He was the fiction editor of *Drum* magazine, and he also worked as a teacher until he protested against the introduction of segregated 'Bantu' education and was consequently banned from teaching anywhere in South Africa. He went into exile, moving between Nigeria, France, Kenya and the USA. His autobiography *Down Second Avenue* (1959) recounts the black experience under apartheid and made his literary reputation. He went on to write novels and short stories and he edited the Penguin anthology *African Writing Today* (1967). When he returned to South Africa in 1977, he changed his name to Es'kia and became a national literary icon. 'He is the most important black South African writer of the present age,' said the critic George Moore in 1980, 'by virtue of his all-round achievement and his lifelong commitment to literature.'
In 1998, Mphahlele was awarded the Order of the Southern Cross by President Nelson Mandela (372).

In Corner B 1946–61, pub. 1967

Mphahlele selected the best stories from his two collections *Man Must Live* (1946) and *The Living and the Dead* (1961) and published them as *In Corner B*. They are stories about Sophiatown – the centre of black culture in Johannesburg – and life in the South African townships. 'It is only in Mphahlele's vision that the other side of the picture of everyday life in South Africa emerges,' wrote the *Times Literary Supplement*. '[...] For Mphahlele, it is the whites who are peripheral, even if they do have all the power.' The collection was banned in South Africa until 1978.

2006
● —
In Corner B has been published under various titles, including *The Unbroken Song* (1981) and *Renewal Time* (1988). The 2006 edition reprints the original collection along with more recent stories by Mphahlele.

Nelson Mandela

1918 – 2013

Nelson Mandela was born in
British South Africa, in Mvezo
in the Eastern Cape, the eldest son of a Thembu chief. His middle name,
Rolihlahla, is the Xhosa word for 'troublemaker'. He was expelled from
the University of the Witwatersrand in Johannesburg for participating
in a student demonstration and joined the African National Congress,
protesting against the apartheid laws introduced by the National Party
in 1948. He was charged with treason in 1956 but acquitted after
a lengthy trial. He then implemented a campaign of sabotage against
the government, which led to a second arrest in 1962. He spent the next
27 years in maximum-security prison, initially on Robben Island off Cape
Town. Finally, following increasing domestic and international pressure,
he was freed in February 1990. He was awarded the Nobel Peace Prize
in 1993 and became President of South Africa in 1994, the country's
first black head of state and the first president to be elected in
a fully representative democratic election. He became a global icon,
revered as 'Madiba', his Thembu clan name, and has been compared
to Mahatma Gandhi (340) and Martin Luther King, Jr. (502) as one
of the greatest anti-racist, anti-colonial leaders of the 20th century.

No Easy Walk to Freedom
Speeches, Letters and Other Writings 1953 – 63, pub. 1965

'There is no easy walk to freedom anywhere,' declared Mandela in 1953,
quoting the Indian Prime Minister Jawaharlal Nehru, 'and many of us will have
to pass through the valley of the shadow of death again and again before we
reach the mountain tops of our desires.' This anthology of articles, speeches
and letters spans the revolutionary years before Madiba's life imprisonment.
It includes the dignified statement he delivered during his trial in 1963.

Daphne Rooke 1914 – 2009

Daphne Pizzey was born in the Transvaal Colony,
later a province of South Africa, to an English
father who died in the First World War and an
Afrikaans mother, Maria 'Mittee' Maré, who was
a writer and teacher. Daphne became a writer
too and moved to Australia with her husband
Irvin 'Bertie' Rooke. When her second novel,
Mittee, became an international bestseller,
the couple returned briefly to South Africa, but
they found the politics disturbing. Rooke lived
in Australia until Bertie's death in 1989, after
which she moved to Cambridge in England.

Mittee 1951

'Sometimes she forgets I am a coloured girl and
calls me Sister. I love her and I hate her.' Selina
and Mittee have grown up as childhood playmates
in late 19th-century Transvaal, but Mittee is white,
Selina is her servant, and now they are rivals for
the attentions of the same man.

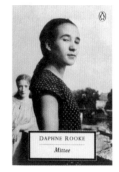

1991
● aftwd. J. M. Coetzee
—
'The family in Rooke's
imagination is the site of
a war of all against all,' writes
J. M. Coetzee in his afterword.
'It includes siblings locked
in murderous rivalries, revered
but treacherous fathers,
engulfing, devouring mothers.'

2002
fwd. Oliver Tambo, 1965
intro. Ato Quayson, 2002
—
No Easy Walk to Freedom was published in
the African Writers Series (362) in 1973, with
a foreword by Ruth First (375): 'Mandela, it
is whispered through prison walls, is as magnetic
a political prisoner as he was once mass
orator and underground political commander,'
she wrote, 'and he continues to radiate the
confidence, the strength and the moral authority
that has sustained the African freedom struggle
in its most difficult days; and that will, in time,
bring the apartheid system toppling down.'

2006
● ed. Stephen Gray

Can Themba 1924–1967

Daniel Canadoise 'Can' D'Orsay was born in the Marabastad township in Pretoria, but he moved to Johannesburg and won a *Drum* magazine (371) short-story competition in 1953. He became one of the magazine's leading writers and a key figure of the Sophiatown Renaissance. Later he edited *Africa!*, *Drum*'s sister magazine, and became the assistant editor of *The Golden City Post*, but growing frustrations with apartheid eventually forced him to move to Swaziland. In 1966, he was declared a 'statutory communist' in South Africa and his works were banned. He became increasingly alcoholic and died of a heart attack while reading a newspaper in bed at the age of 43. 'The poet laureate of the urban townships,' the novelist and fellow *Drum* contributor Lewis Nkosi called him. 'The supreme intellectual tsotsi of them all.'

Requiem for Sophiatown 1953–65

'No artist will ever be content to substitute the noise of war for the music of the soul,' wrote Themba. These 25 stories and sketches evoke the verve and optimism of the Sophiatown district of Johannesburg in the early 1950s. Titles include 'Forbidden Love', 'The Bottom of the Bottle' and 'The Dube Train'. 'The Suit', Themba's most famous story, is about Philemon, a middle-class lawyer, who discovers that his wife is having an affair and punishes her by forcing her to treat her lover's suit as an honoured guest, feeding it, entertaining it and taking it for walks.

2006
● aftwd. Es'kia Mphahlele
—
Es'kia Mphahlele (371) and Hutchinson were both teachers; they became friends after they lost their jobs in 1952.

Alfred Hutchinson 1924–1972

Hutchinson trained as a teacher at the University of Fort Hare in South Africa, but was subsequently dismissed from his teaching post for participating in an anti-apartheid campaign. After joining the executive committee of the African National Congress in 1954, he was arrested two years later and tried for treason alongside Nelson Mandela (372). He was held until October 1958, at which point he was granted temporary bail and fled the country, seeking political asylum in independent Ghana. He attended the first All-African People's Conference in Accra and then moved to Britain, where he worked as a teacher in Brighton. After ten years, he returned to Africa and died in Kano, Nigeria.

Road to Ghana 1960

Hutchinson describes his nail-biting escape from his treason trial in South Africa to freedom in Ghana. 'I had to stop reading it because I was crying,' wrote Doris Lessing, 'and I don't cry very easily. [...] It is the best work to come out of South Africa for years.' Alan Paton (371) called it 'a remarkable document'.

Penguin Modern Classics

The Sestigers

The 'Sixtiers' were an influential group of Afrikaans-language writers in the 1960s who opposed the South African National Party. They wrote literature inspired by European existentialism (186) which aimed to address the political, social and sexual problems they perceived in South Africa. The group was founded by André Brink, Breyten Breytenbach and Etienne Leroux, among others. The critic Judy H. Gardner has described their work as 'literature in exile in its own country'.

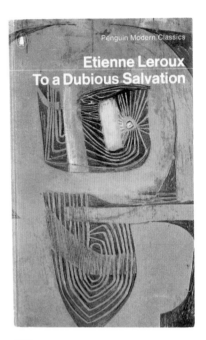

Etienne Leroux
To a Dubious Salvation

1972
● trans. Charles Eglington
& Amy Starke, 1964–8

Etienne Leroux 1922 – 1989

Leroux studied law at the University of Stellenbosch. After working briefly as a solicitor, he abandoned the law and took over a 42,000-acre sheep ranch in Koffiefontein, which he ran with his wife and three children. After a formative period in Paris, he helped to found the avant-garde Sestigers literary group and began writing psychosexual novels in Afrikaans.

To a Dubious Salvation
A Trilogy of Fantastical Novels 1962 – 8
Seven Days at the Silbersteins, The Third Eye, One for the Devil

'Mr Leroux will not find an instant audience; his novels are too original for that,' wrote Graham Greene (88). 'They tease, they trouble, they elude. His audience will be the audience that only a good writer can merit, an audience which assembles slowly from far away in ones and twos.' *Seven Days at the Silbersteins* (1962) is set in Welgevonden, a vast South African estate. It is the story of a prospective bridegroom, Henry van Eeden, engaged to the daughter of the Silbersteins, who is subjected to a week of bizarre trials. *The Third Eye* (1966) is a metaphysical thriller in which the detective Demosthenes de Goede tangles with nymphomaniacs and 'sex queens', and De Goede returns in *One for the Devil* (1968), investigating the murder of an 18-year-old Silberstein girl on the Welgevonden estate.

Bloke Modisane 1923 – 1986

BLOKE MODISANE
Blame Me On History

1990
● intro. Lewis Nkosi
—
Blame Me On History was banned in South Africa when it was first published.

William 'Bloke' Modisane was born in Sophiatown, a suburb of Johannesburg and the centre of black cultural life in the city. Conditions were precarious: his father was murdered, his sister died of malnutrition and his mother ran an illegal shebeen. He joined the team behind *Drum* magazine (371), working as a reporter, feature writer and theatre and music critic until Sophiatown was bulldozed to the ground in the 1950s. Distraught, Modisane left the country, first to work as an actor in London and then to lecture in the USA on African music and literature; he finally settled in West Germany.

Blame Me On History 1963

'Something in me died, a piece of me died, with the dying of Sophiatown,' opens Modisane's book, which attempts to raise the vibrant suburb from the rubble and rebuild its noise, music, violence and distinctive atmosphere in the reader's imagination. With pathos, humour and anger, he describes the political conditions that drove him into self-exile from his homeland.

Dugmore Boetie

1924?–1966

Douglas Mahonga Boetie was a one-legged, unemployed ex-convict – 'homeless, passless and legless', as he put it – whose first appearance in print was in 1963, when he published a story called 'The Last Leg'. He was a roguish, resilient scam artist, who died of lung cancer in his early forties.

Familiarity is the Kingdom of the Lost

1963–6, pub. 1969

'All it needed was guts and brains. And I think I had them both.' Boetie describes his eventful career in the Sophiatown district of Johannesburg, as an infantile delinquent, juvenile gangster and adult drug dealer, with wild flights of fancy and comic exaggeration. 'Nothing like this bullet-like prose has shot out – or been provoked out – of anywhere before,' wrote the *Guardian*. '[...] For it is a book with all of life and death in it.'

2008
● ed. Barney Simon, 1969
—
Boetie produced his text 'during years of snarled-up snooty hopping' – as the *Guardian* review put it – in collaboration with Barney Simon, the white South African editor of *The Classic* magazine. There was nowhere the two could meet under apartheid, so they exchanged manuscripts on Johannesburg street corners. Simon's original epilogue is included in this edition.

1965 Penguin Special
2006 Modern Classics
● aftwd. Albie Sachs, 1989
—
The 1965 first edition was published in the Penguin Special series (xiii). The photograph of First on the cover of the 2006 edition was taken on Human Rights Day, 10 December 1952.

Ruth First 1925–1982

First's parents were among the founding members of the Communist Party of South Africa. After studying at the University of the Witwatersrand in Johannesburg, where she met fellow student Nelson Mandela (372), First became a radical journalist, an anti-apartheid activist and a member of both the Communist Party and the African National Congress. She edited the political journal *Fighting Talk*, and both she and her activist husband Joe Slovo were defendants in Mandela's prolonged treason trial in the late 1950s. In 1960, they were 'listed' as banned persons, no longer able to publish or attend meetings in South Africa, and in 1963 First was arrested and held in isolation for 117 days. The following year, she went into exile in Britain, where she edited works by Nelson Mandela and co-authored a biography of Olive Schreiner (368). She was assassinated in Maputo, Mozambique, with a parcel bomb sent to her by South African security police.

117 Days An Account of Confinement and Interrogation under the South African Ninety-Day Detention Law 1965

When First was arrested in 1963, she withstood sensory deprivation and refused to provide information to the Special Branch. 'In prison you see only the moves of the enemy,' she wrote. 'Prison is the hardest place to fight a battle.' She published this account of her experience to 'focus world attention on the plight of the growing number of victims of the regime's physical and mental torture chamber', as her husband Joe Slovo put it. The BBC dramatized her account for television in 1966 with First playing herself.

Rose Rappoport Moss

b. 1937

Moss studied at the University of the Witwatersrand in Johannesburg, where she won the Arts Festival prize judged by Nadine Gordimer. She emigrated to the USA in 1964 and has written novels, short stories and reviews of South African literature, as well as teaching creative writing at Harvard University.

In Court and Other Stories 1970–2004

'South Africa is the soil of my imagination,' writes Moss. 'It appears in my work continually as the original world where things are as they must be.' These sixteen stories are set in South Africa; 'Exile' won the Quill Prize in 1970, and 'In Court' was nominated for the Pushcart Prize in 1991. Other titles include 'Light/Dark', 'A Gem Squash' and 'The House is Full of Cars This Morning'.

2007
● —

Michael Power b. 1933

Power was born in Pietermaritzburg and studied law at St Aidan's College, Grahamstown. In 1964, he co-founded Blue Crane Books in order to publish the works of the Zulu author Credo Mutwa. His own first novel was *Holiday* (1962).

Shadow Game 1972

2008
● —

'A web of laws had been spun to keep us apart.' This ground-breaking novel about an interracial gay romance is set in Johannesburg in the 1960s. Ray, a public-relations man, finds himself falling in love with Victor, a popular DJ on Radio Bantu. It is a love story and an exposure of police-state brutality, and it was originally published under the pseudonym 'Laurence Eben'.

Yvonne Burgess
b. 1936

2006
● —

Burgess was born in Pretoria and wrote for the *Eastern Province Herald* in Port Elizabeth during the 1960s. She has published several novels about South African women, including *A Life to Live* (1973), *The Strike* (1975) and *A Larger Silence* (2000), which won the Sanlam Literary Award.

Say a Little Mantra for Me 1979

Gran is confined to the flat she shares with her daughter Iris and her granddaughter Girlie. 'There was something going on with Iris and Girlie,' she thinks. 'Something fishy that I didn't know about.' The critic Cherry Clayton described Burgess's wickedly comic novel as 'a book about women written by a woman for women who dislike other women, particularly their mothers, grandmothers and daughters, but dislike men more'.

Dalene Matthee
1938 – 2005

After studying and teaching music, Matthee wrote stories and novels in Afrikaans; she was a four-time recipient of the Afrikaans Language and Cultural Association's literary award and twice won the Southern African Institute of Forestry Award. Many of her stories are set in and around the Cape's Knysna Forest, which she loved. her ashes were scattered at Krisjan-se-Nek, where an 800-year-old yellowwood has been renamed 'the Dalene Matthee Big Tree'.

Circles in a Forest 1984

'Hardy and D. H. Lawrence (50) have been brought to one American critic's mind by *Circles in a Forest*,' wrote the *Guardian* reviewer in 1984; '[…] I find myself thinking of Kipling (22) and Hemingway (428).' In the late 19th century, the Knysna Forest was home to wild elephants and bands of woodcutters. As a child, Saul Barnard develops a bond with a bull elephant called Old Foot; when a gold rush threatens the forest, he returns to help his old friend. 'A lot has been written in English about Knysna,' said Matthee, 'but hardly a word from the Afrikaaner's point of view. A lot of truth has been covered up very cleverly over the years. For instance, in 1886 there were between four and five hundred elephants (the most beautiful in the world) in this Forest. In 1972 there were twelve left. The truth behind this has never really been faced honestly. […] In *Circles in a Forest* I try to get to these truths as blatantly as possible.'

1985 Penguin Books
2005 Modern Classics
—
● trans. Dalene Matthee, 1984
—

Kringe in 'n Bos was Matthee's first novel to appear in English, in her own translation. It has since been translated into fourteen languages and was adapted as a feature film in 1989. The hiking trail from Krisjan-se-Nek is known as the 'Circles in a Forest Trail'.

Botswana

Bessie Head 1937–1986

Bessie Emery was born in a South African mental hospital, the illegitimate daughter of a wealthy white woman – also called Bessie Emery – and a black stable-hand. Interracial relationships were illegal at the time and Bessie was raised in a foster home until she was thirteen. She was sent to a mission school for five years and then worked as a journalist for *Drum* magazine (371) before marrying another journalist, Harold Head. Bessie Head joined the Pan-Africanist Congress in Johannesburg and in 1960 was arrested briefly in the aftermath of the Sharpeville Massacre, a brutal suppression of a demonstration against apartheid. This experience led to depression, attempted suicide, hospitalization, and lasting symptoms of bipolar disorder and schizophrenia. She also began to drink and smoke heavily. In 1964, she divorced Harold and emigrated to the Bechuanaland Protectorate, now Botswana, where she lived as a refugee for the next fifteen years, teaching in a primary school and writing novels. In 1979, she was granted citizenship, and she is now considered Botswana's most influential author. She died at the age of 48.

2002
● intro. Margaret Busby
—
'*A Question of Power* is by no means an easy book,' writes the Ghanaian-born publisher Margaret Busby, 'thronged as it is with imagery as hauntingly disquieting as a Hieronymus Bosch painting – but it is ultimately uplifting.' *A Question of Power* was later published as part of the African Writers Series (362); the cover of the 2002 edition shows a photograph of Head.

A Question of Power 1973

Elizabeth flees South Africa to start a new life in Botswana, in the village of Motabeng, 'the place of sand'. But her troubles are only just beginning: she is tormented by two men, Sello and Dan, and finds herself spiralling towards insanity. The novel was written after Head experienced a major psychotic episode in 1969. 'Her novels have a way of soaring up from rock bottom to the stars,' says Ronald Blythe (155).

Zimbabwe

Dambudzo Marechera

1952–1987

Marechera was born in a small farming township in Southern Rhodesia, now Zimbabwe. He emerged as a brilliant student at his mission boarding school, where he clashed with his teachers over the colonial syllabus. He was expelled from the University of Rhodesia for taking part in a demonstration, but won a scholarship to New College, Oxford, where he was sent down for antisocial behaviour. He then slept rough in England and Wales, becoming increasingly anarchic and self-destructive; his brother believed he had inherited a curse from their mother. Marechera returned to newly independent Zimbabwe in 1982 and lived a penniless existence until he died of AIDS in 1987, at the age of 35. 'My whole life,' he wrote, 'has been an attempt to make myself the skeleton in my own cupboard.'

The House of Hunger
Short Stories
1978

2002
● intro. Peter Godwin
—
In his introduction, the Zimbabwean author Peter Godwin calls Marechera 'African literature's permanent *enfant terrible*'. *House of Hunger* was first published in the African Writers Series (362) and is due to rejoin the Penguin Modern Classics series in 2022.

House of Hunger is a stylistically spectacular, semi-autobiographical novella, in which the narrator describes his troubled youth in colonial Rhodesia and his sense of alienation from his family, his country and eventually the whole world. The other explosive stories in this collection portray a world of madness, violence and chaos. It won the Guardian Fiction Prize in 1979. 'This man is a marvellous writer,' said Doris Lessing. 'From the first page you have to salute a formidable talent. A black man who has suffered all the stupid brutalities of the white oppression in Rhodesia – now Zimbabwe – his rage explodes, not in political rhetoric, but in a fusion of lyricism, wit, obscenity. Incredible that such a powerful indictment should also be so funny.'

AUSTRALASIA

Australia

Henry Handel Richardson

1870 – 1946

Ethel Florence Lindesay Richardson was born in Melbourne, the daughter of an Irish father and English mother. Her father had migrated to Australia in the early 1850s and was a successful doctor and businessman, but Richardson's childhood was increasingly overshadowed by the breakdown of his finances and mental health. After her father's death, she moved to Leipzig in 1888 to study the piano, and while there married J. G. Robertson, the Scottish scholar of German literature. The couple moved to London in 1903, where Richardson published a novel set in Leipzig, *Maurice Guest* (1908), under the pen name 'Henry Handel'. She went on to write several more novels, the research for which involved visiting boxing booths and opium dens. After her husband died in 1933 she maintained daily contact with him through séances.

The Fortunes of Richard Mahony

Australia Felix, The Way Home, Ultima Thule
1917 – 29

This complex trilogy is a semi-fictionalized portrait of Richardson's own father. In *Australia Felix* (1917), Mahony travels to Australia to join the Ballarat gold rush, and his personal story is interwoven with the dramatic development of the colony of Victoria. In *The Way Home* (1925), he returns to England to purchase a medical practice, but he discovers that he is now estranged from English society. *Ultima Thule* (1929), which won the Australian Literature Society Gold Medal, describes his financial failure and final mental disintegration.

1971 Penguin Books
1977 Modern Classics
• intro. Leonie Kramer, 1971

1971 Penguin Books
1977 Modern Classics
• intro. Leonie Kramer, 1971

1971 Penguin Books
1977 Modern Classics
• intro. Leonie Kramer, 1971
—
All three volumes include an introduction by Leonie Kramer, the first female professor of English in Australia and later the first female chancellor of the University of Sydney.

Elizabeth von Arnim 1866 – 1941

Mary Annette Beauchamp, a cousin of Katherine Mansfield (388), was born in Sydney but moved to Europe when she was a young girl and grew up in London and Switzerland. She married unhappily twice, both times becoming a countess. Her first husband, Count Henning August von Arnim-Schlagenthin, was the basis for the 'Man of Wrath' in *Elizabeth and Her German Garden* (1898). They lived together in Pomerania, where their children were tutored briefly by E. M. Forster (38). After the count's death, von Arnim had an affair with H. G. Wells (26), before marrying Francis, the second Earl Russell, Bertrand Russell's older brother. She left him in 1919 and moved between Switzerland, France and England, where her ashes are buried. Her gravestone reads *parva sed apta*, 'small but sufficient'.

The Enchanted April 1922

'To Those who Appreciate Wistaria and Sunshine,' reads an advert in *The Times*. 'Small mediaeval Italian Castle on the shores of the Mediterranean to be let Furnished for the month of April.' Four very different English ladies respond to this advertisement and find themselves sharing idyllic quarters overlooking the sea. The novel was based on a month-long stay von Arnim made to Castello Brown in Portofino, just as her second marriage was breaking down. 'The novel has a fairy-tale ending,' writes the novelist Salley Vickers. 'But fairy tales are more realistic than is often believed.'

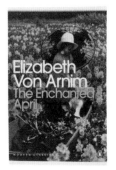

2012
intro. Salley Vickers

Frederic Manning 1882–1935

Manning was born in Sydney, the son of a politician. He befriended an English vicar in Australia, the Reverend Arthur Galton, and accompanied him when he returned to Britain in 1898. Manning then lived with Galton in Lincolnshire, studying philosophy and writing poetry. In 1915, despite persistent asthma, he enlisted as a private and fought at the Battle of the Somme. Afterwards he befriended Max Beerbohm (60), T. E. Lawrence (74) and Ezra Pound (61), who considered Manning his literary mentor.

The Middle Parts of Fortune
Somme and Ancre, 1916 1929

Inspired by the success of R. C. Sherriff's *Journey's End* (87), Manning wrote this stark novel about an ordinary British soldier, Private Bourne, who fights in the trenches, swears blue murder and succumbs to alcoholism, boredom and bloodlust. 'War is waged by men; not by beasts, or by gods,' Manning wrote. 'It is a peculiarly human activity. To call it a crime against mankind is to miss at least half its significance; it is also the punishment of a crime.' 'It is the finest and noblest book of men in war that I have ever read,' said Ernest Hemingway (428). 'I read it over once each year to remember how things really were so that I will never lie to myself nor to anyone else about them.'

1990 Twentieth-Century Classics
● ed. Paul Fussell, 1990
2000 Modern Classics
intro. Niall Ferguson, 2000
—
The Middle Parts of Fortune was originally published anonymously in a limited edition in 1929. The following year, an abridged version was published under Manning's service number, 'Private 19022', with the title *Her Privates We*. The unexpurgated text was first published publicly in 1977. Both titles come from the book's epigraph, a quotation from Shakespeare's *Hamlet*: 'On fortune's cap we are not the very button. [...] Then you live about her waist, or in the middle of her favours? [...] 'Faith, her privates we.'

Christina Stead 1902–1983

Stead was the daughter of a Sydney marine biologist. She left Australia in 1928 and worked in a Parisian bank before moving to the USA in 1935, where she taught creative writing at New York University and worked as a screenwriter in Hollywood. She lived for many years in Europe with her husband, the novelist William J. Blake, but after he died in 1968 she returned to Australia and became a fellow in creative arts at the Australian National University, Canberra. She won the Patrick White Award (382) in 1974. She was 'the Cassandra of the modern novel in English', wrote Angela Carter (156). 'Reading her seems like plunging into the mess of life itself.'

1989
● ed. R. G. Geering, 1986
—
Ron Geering, Stead's literary executor, assembled this manuscript for publication. 'What I inherited,' he wrote, '[...] was a huge mass of typescript ranging in finish from rough to polished and in length from page bits to different versions of whole chapters, along with piles of basic and supplementary material.'

I'm Dying Laughing
The Humourist 1962–83, pub. 1986

Stead's posthumously published novel follows the fat, freckled Emily Wilkes and her communist husband as they flee McCarthyism in Hollywood and their relationship teeters on the edge of collapse.

The Man Who Loved Children 1940, rev. 1965

Sam Pollit is good with children, but otherwise he is hopelessly impractical and selfish. As his growing family descends into squalor, Sam drives his wife to extremes of contempt and his adolescent daughter to violence. The character of Pollit was modelled on Stead's own father. 'The book intrudes on our better-regulated world like a bad dream from the grandparental past,' writes Jonathan Franzen. 'Its idea of a happy ending is like no other novel's, and probably not at all like yours.'

1970
● intro. Randall Jarroll, 1965
—
The Man Who Loved Children was originally set in Sydney but Stead changed the location to Washington, DC, for the 1965 reprint edition. 'When you have read it,' wrote the American poet Randall Jarrell, 'you have been, for a few hours, a Pollit; it will take you many years to get the sound of the Pollits out of your ears, the sight of the Pollits out of your eyes, the smell of the Pollits out of your nostrils.'

Patrick White 1912–1990

At the age of thirteen, White was sent to school in England, a 'four-year prison sentence' as he called it, before working for two years as a jackeroo below the Snowy Mountains, in New South Wales, and then returning to England to study languages at Cambridge University. During the Second World War, he served as an RAF intelligence officer in the Middle East, where he fell in love with a Greek army officer, Manoly Lascaris. White and Lascaris lived together in Cairo for six years and then moved to a small farm outside Sydney, where they sold flowers, vegetables, milk and cream, and bred schnauzers. In 1973, White won the Nobel Prize for Literature (576), the first and only Australian-born writer to have done so. He used the prize money to establish the annual Patrick White Award, the first recipient of which was Christina Stead (381). 'Patrick White did more than any other writer to put Australian literature on the international map,' read his obituary in *The Times*. '[. . .] His tormented *oeuvre* is that of a great and essentially modern writer.'

The Tree of Man 1955

Stan and Amy Parker set up a farmstead in the Australian wilderness and this epic novel follows their mixed fortunes over several decades. White began writing it soon after moving to a farm with his life partner, Manoly Lascaris. 'I felt the life was, on the surface, so dreary, ugly, monotonous, there must be a poetry hidden in it to give it a purpose,' he said, 'and so I set out to discover that secret core, and *The Tree of Man* emerged.'

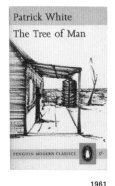

1961
• —

The Living and the Dead 1941

In 1930s London, Mrs Standish is ageing but amorous, her daughter has shameful secrets and her scholarly son is emotionally numb. In the years between the First World War and the Spanish Civil War, this alienated family starts to break apart.

The Aunt's Story 1948

When lonely Theodora Goodman's mother dies, she travels from Australia to Europe and experiences what is either a mental breakdown or an epiphany. Of all White's novels, *The Aunt's Story* is 'the one I have most affection for', he wrote, 'and I always find it irritating that only six Australians seem to have liked it'.

Voss 1957

Inspired by the historical German naturalist Ludwig Leichhardt, who disappeared in the Australian desert in 1848, White created this story of Johann Ulrich Voss, who sets out with a small band of settlers and Aborigines to cross the continent in the 1840s. It is a hellish journey in which Voss appears as both a godlike figure and a devil. 'In size, intention and achievement,' wrote Penelope Mortimer (146), 'Voss is the work of a man for whom Tolstoy is the only fitting rival.' *Voss* was the first winner of the Miles Franklin Award, Australia's most prestigious literary prize.

1967 Penguin Books
1992 Twentieth-Century Classics
• —

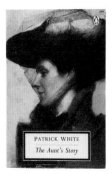

1963 Penguin Books
1993 Twentieth-Century Classics
• —

1960 Penguin Books
1962 Modern Classics
• —

The Jindyworobak Movement

The poet Rex Ingamells founded the Jindyworobak group in Adelaide in 1938. Inspired by bush ballads and the success of D. H. Lawrence's *Kangaroo* (54), they set out to 'free Australian art from whatever alien influences trammel it', looking for subjects in the Australian landscape and Indigenous mythology; the word 'Jindyworobak' means 'to join' in Woiwurrung, the language formerly spoken around Melbourne. They published a *Jindyworobak Anthology* every year from 1938 to 1953, and although they have been criticized for being culturally insular, they had a lasting influence on Australian literature. Patrick White's *Voss* has been described as a 'Jindy' novel and the great Australian poet Les Murray called himself 'the last of the Jindyworobaks'.

Riders in the Chariot

1961

Four strange figures all have the same vision of the fiery chariot from the Book of Ezekiel: mad Miss Hare, who haunts a crumbling mansion; an Aboriginal alcoholic artist, Alf Dubbo; Mordecai Himmelfarb, a Jewish professor and Holocaust refugee; and Ruth Godbold, a kindly washerwoman. Their stories coincide in the fictional Sydney suburb of Sarsaparilla. 'I well remember the look on J. G. Farrell's face when I sketched for him the plot of *Riders in the Chariot*,' recalled Paul Theroux (543) in 1976.

1964 Penguin Books
1974 Modern Classics
● —

The Cockatoos
Shorter Novels and Stories

1966–74, pub. 1974

This volume of shorter works was White's first publication after winning the Nobel Prize for Literature (576). Titles include 'The Night of the Prowler' and 'Sicilian Vespers'.

The Eye of the Storm

1973

Elizabeth Hunter is an aged, wealthy, former society beauty on her deathbed in Sydney. Her son and daughter are present, as are three nurses, her house-keeper and her solicitor. Even in her dying moments, she continues to manipulate and hurt those around her with callous determination. '*The Eye of the Storm* is as clever, imaginative, and true a novel as any you are likely to encounter this year, or even next,' wrote William Trevor (21) in 1973. '[…] *The Eye of the Storm* is timeless and universal.'

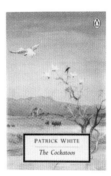

1978 Penguin Books
1993 Twentieth-Century Classics
● —

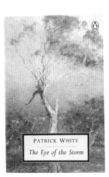

1975 Penguin Books
1992 Twentieth-Century Classics
● —

The Solid Mandala 1966

The Brown brothers are twins: Waldo is a blinkered man of reason; Arthur is an enlightened half-wit. White traces their mutually dependent and antagonistic relationship over half a century.

The Vivisector 1970

This portrait of an artist depicts Hurtle Duffield, who becomes a painter and exploits the people around him, dissecting their characters and emotions for his art. These living victims include his hunchback stepsister Rhoda; the prostitute Nance Lightfoot; the sugar heiress Boo Davenport; his Greek mistress, Hero Pavloussi; and the child prodigy Kathy Volkov. The novel is dedicated to the painter Sidney Nolan and his wife Cynthia.

A Fringe of Leaves 1976

When Ellen Roxburgh, a young Cornish woman, is shipwrecked off the coast of Australia in 1836, she is captured by Aborigines. In finding the inner strength to survive, she rediscovers her native sensuality. 'It is moving, thoughtful, vividly imagined and at times much more frightening than a thunderstorm 39,000 feet over the Yucatan, and I know because I was flying into Mérida as the lightning flashed,' writes Paul Theroux (543). '[White] uses cruelty and savagery to write of tenderness and beauty; this is one of his best novels.'

1969 Penguin Books
1993 Twentieth-Century Classics
● —

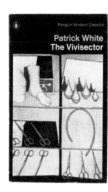

1973
● —

Duffield's paintings in *The Vivisector* recall the work of Francis Bacon, who was a close friend of White's in the late 1930s in London. Bacon designed a writing desk for White with a red linoleum top, which White used until his return to Australia in 1947.

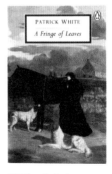

1978 Penguin Books
1993 Twentieth-Century Classics
● —

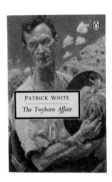

1981 Penguin Books
1992 Twentieth-Century
Classics
● —

The Twyborn Affair
1979

The soul of Eudoxia Vatatzes, the enchanting mistress of a Greek shipping merchant, transmigrates into Eddie Twyborn, a jackeroo in the Australian outback, and finally to Eadith Trist, the flamboyant madam of an elegant London brothel.

Flaws in the Glass
A Self-Portrait 1981

In this autobiography, White examines his own face in a cracked looking-glass. 'As an artist, my face is many-faceted,' he wrote, 'my body protean, according to time, climate and the demands of fiction.' In the second section, 'Journeys', he describes travelling around Greece with his life partner Manoly Lascaris, and the book is dedicated 'to Manoly, again'. It is 'a singularly penetrating act of self-scrutiny', writes David Lodge, 'a cold, calculating stare into the mirror of the artist's life'.

1983 Penguin Books
1992 Twentieth-Century
Classics
● —

Martin Boyd
1893 – 1972

Boyd was born in Switzerland to two wealthy Anglo-Australian painters, the à Beckett-Boyds, who divided their time between Australia and England. Boyd's training as an architect was interrupted by the First World War. He served in a British battalion and was the only officer not to be killed or wounded in the twelve months he spent with it on the Western Front. After the war, he lived in England as a journalist and became a member of an Anglican Franciscan community. He returned to Australia for three years before settling in Rome in 1957, where he lived for the rest of his life.

The Langton Quartet

The Cardboard Crown, A Difficult Young Man,
Outbreak of Love, When Blackbirds Sing
1952 – 62

Each instalment of Boyd's *Langton Quartet* focuses on a member of the upper middle-class Langton family, whose roots are in Somerset but who drift between Australia and England. In *The Cardboard Crown* (1952), Guy Langton pieces together the story of his unhappy grandmother Alice, who married Austin Langton and saved the family fortunes. *A Difficult Young Man* (1955) is about Dominic, Guy's older brother, who rebels against the vulgarity of his socially ambitious relatives. *Outbreak of Love* (1957) focuses on Guy's aunt Diana and her marriage to the unfaithful musician Wolfgang von Flugel; and *When Blackbirds Sing* (1962) follows Dominic during the First World War.

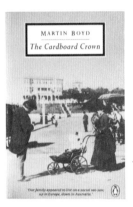

1993
● intro. Dorothy Green

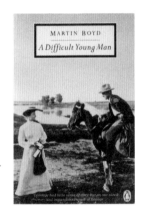

1993
● intro. Dorothy Green

1993
● intro. Dorothy Green

1993
● intro. Dorothy Green

D'Arcy Niland · The Shiralee

More PICARESQUE ADVENTURES

D'Arcy Niland 1917–1967

Darcy Niland was born in rural New South Wales and named after the Australian boxer Les Darcy. He later changed his name to 'D'Arcy'; but he was nonetheless obsessed with his pugilist namesake, working on a monumental biography of Darcy and collecting books, photographs, newspaper clippings, letters and taped interviews. Niland spent his childhood travelling with his father and then took a variety of odd jobs, including newspaper copy-boy, opal-gouger, circus hand, fruit picker, railway porter, woolshed rouseabout and a member of a travelling boxing troupe. In 1942, he married the New Zealand writer Ruth Park (391); they settled in Sydney, where they both wrote and raised five children.

Niland died suddenly of a heart attack at the age of 49, two days after finishing his last novel. Park completed his biography of Les Darcy, which she published as *Home Before Dark* (1995).

1978 Penguin Books
2001 Modern Classics
● intro. Les Murray, 2001
—
Les Murray was 'widely acknowledged to be the leading Australian poet of his generation', wrote J. M. Coetzee. Murray praises 'the desolate inner weakness of Macauley, the book's protagonist, and the book's real sense of poverty and exhaustion'.

The Shiralee 1955

A 'shiralee' is a swagman's burden, and for gruff Jim Macauley his shiralee is his own four-year-old daughter, Buster. But as they travel around rural Australia together, sleeping rough and relying on itinerant work, Macauley's griping resentment turns to something more affectionate.

Donald Horne 1921–2005

Horne was a journalist and editor of the Australian *Observer*, *The Bulletin* and *Quadrant* magazine. He became one of Australia's best-known public intellectuals following the sensation caused by *The Lucky Country*. Later he taught political science at the University of New South Wales, and campaigned for constitutional reform. He was made an Officer of the Order of Australia for his services to literature.

The Lucky Country
Australia in the Sixties 1964

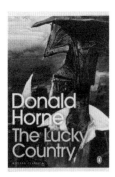

1964 Penguin Books
2009 Modern Classics
● intro. Hugh Mackay, 2009
—
The Lucky Country was first published by Australian Penguin Books (xv), which had recently launched in 1963.

'Australia is a lucky country, run mainly by second-rate people who share its luck.' This landmark indictment of Australian society criticizes the country's provincialism, philistinism and general lack of innovation and ambition, dismissing Australian prosperity as the 'lucky' combination of natural resources, reliable climate and inherited British systems. A contemporary review described the book as 'a bucket of cold saltwater emptied onto the belly of a dreaming sunbather'. Despite the negative connotations Horne intended, the title has since become a popular and usually positive nickname for Australia.

Randolph Stow 1935 – 2010

Julian Randolph Stow was born in Geraldton, Western Australia. He taught English at the universities of Adelaide, Western Australia and Leeds, and worked as an anthropologist and trainee patrol officer in New Guinea before settling in England for the last 50 years of his life. He wrote novels, poetry and opera libretti (to accompany music by Peter Maxwell Davies); he won the Miles Franklin Award in 1958 and the Patrick White Award (382) in 1979. 'He is a writer who commands our attention and respect,' said the *Times Literary Supplement*, a publication with which Stow had a long association, as both a reviewer and a letter writer.

The Merry-Go-Round in the Sea 1965

In this semi-autobiographical novel, Rob Coram is a boy growing up among the sheep stations inland from the west-coast port of Geraldton; he has heard of 'Australia', but doesn't know he lives there. In 1941, his older cousin Rick leaves to join the war; when he returns, disillusioned and restless, everything starts to change.

1968 Penguin Books
2008 Modern Classics
● —

Grunge Lit

The term 'grunge lit' was coined in the mid 1990s to describe Andrew McGahan's novel *Praise* (1991), a story of a doomed relationship fuelled by drugs. It came to encompass a subgenre of Australian semi-autobiographical fiction that featured urban experiences of casual sex, recreational drugs and alcohol. 'These stories are about the disintegration of love,' writes the critic Jean-François Vernay. 'The male characters in these novels are individualistic and detached from everything. [...] This separation breeds a disquiet which they try to assuage with violent erotic behaviour.' *Monkey Grip* has retrospectively been classed as grunge lit. Other titles include Edward Berridge's *The Lives of the Saints* (1995), John Birmingham's *He Died with a Felafel in His Hand* (1994) and Justine Ettler's *The River Ophelia* (1995).

Helen Garner b. 1942

Helen Ford was born in Geelong, Victoria. She married the actor and philosopher Bill Garner and taught in various high schools until she was fired for giving an unscheduled sex education lesson to 13-year-olds, inspired by graffiti in her students' ancient-history textbooks. She then began writing novels and works of non-fiction, for which she has won many awards, including the Melbourne Prize for Literature. The *Guardian* calls her 'one of Australia's greatest living writers'.

Monkey Grip 1977

Nora is a single mother in 1970s Melbourne, raising her daughter in shared homes and clinging to a relationship with an unreliable junkie called Javo. Based on Garner's own experiences, it is a gritty portrait of fluid relationships, fledgling artists, welfare, addiction and public baths. It won the National Book Council Award in 1978 and was adapted as a film in 1982. Writing a novel is like 'trying to make a patchwork quilt look seamless', says Garner. 'A novel is made up of scraps of our own lives and bits of other people's, and things we think of in the middle of the night and whole notebooks full of randomly collected details.'

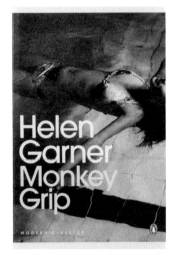

1978 Penguin Books
2008 Modern Classics
● —
In 2018, the BBC invited 108 critics, scholars and journalists to propose stories that had changed the world, 'stories they felt had shaped mindsets or influenced history'. The only Australian novel in the final list of 100 was *Monkey Grip*.

Honour and
Other People's Children 1980

Garner's second book comprises two novellas: *Honour* is about a divorced couple whose marriage nevertheless persists in spirit until the ex-husband takes a new lover; and *Other People's Children* is about the breakdown of a friendship between two women, Ruth and Scotty, one of whom loves the other's daughter 'as only the childless can love other people's children'. 'Helen Garner's Australia is a land both bucolic and exotic,' wrote the *New York Times*, 'a land of junkies and wallabies, of women's rights and outdoor plumbing, of homeless children in a beneficent atmosphere, of people looking up at night to see a thousand stars.'

1982 Penguin Books
2008 Modern Classics
● —

Robert Drewe b. 1943

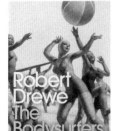

2001 Penguin Books
2009 Modern Classics
● —

Drewe was born in Melbourne, but grew up on the beaches of West Australia. After a career in journalism, he began writing novels and short stories in the 1970s. He has been married four times and has seven children.

The Bodysurfers 1986

These twelve sensuous, interconnected stories are set between the surf and the dunes of the Australian beach and trace three generations of the Long family. Titles include 'Shark Logic', 'Baby Oil' and 'Eighty Per Cent Humidity'. 'Taut yet teeming with life,' wrote the *Sydney Morning Herald*, 'they are shot through with gritty phrases that catch at one's throat.'

Elizabeth Jolley 1923–2007

Monica Elizabeth Knight was born in England and educated privately in her German-speaking home and at a Quaker boarding school near Banbury, Oxfordshire. She trained as an orthopaedic nurse and had an affair with a married patient, the librarian Leonard Jolley. The couple moved to Western Australia in 1959, where Jolley raised three children and worked as a nurse, a cleaner, a door-to-door saleswoman and ran a poultry farm. She published her first book at the age of 53 and went on to write fifteen novels, four short story collections and three works of non-fiction. She was made an Officer of the Order of Australia for services to literature in 1988. 'Jolley is one of our most daring writers,' says Helen Garner (386).

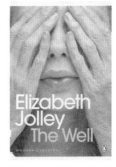

1987 King Penguin
2007 Modern Classics
● —

More FRIENDSHIPS

The Well 1986

Eccentric, middle-aged Miss Hester Harper brings Katherine home one day to be her young companion. The two women sew together, cook meals, make music and run their little farm until, driving down the track one night, they hit something. They heave the body off the 'roo bar' and drop it down the well shaft. But Katherine is drawn increasingly to the well's edge – and Miss Harper is driven to extreme measures to protect their special friendship. *The Well* won the Miles Franklin Award in 1986.

New Zealand

Katherine Mansfield 1888–1923

'All that I write – all that I am – is on the borders of the sea,'
wrote Kathleen Mansfield Beauchamp. 'It is a kind of playing.'
She was born in Wellington, a cousin of Elizabeth von Arnim (380),
and travelled to school in England at the age of fourteen, where
she met her lifelong companion, Ida Baker. Back in New Zealand
she had an intense relationship with Maata Mahupuku, a wealthy
young Māori woman, before returning to bohemian London in
1908 and falling in with D. H. Lawrence (50) and Virginia Woolf
(42). Pregnant by one man and disastrously married to another,
she fled briefly to the Bavarian spa town of Bad Wörishofen in
1909, where she read Chekhov's short stories for the first time.
She began publishing stories under the name 'K. Mansfield' and
became a contributor to the avant-garde literary review *Rhythm*,
edited by her lodger John Middleton Murry, whom she later
married. She lived alternately with her second husband, Murry,
and her 'wife', Ida Baker, until December 1917, when she was
diagnosed with extra-pulmonary tuberculosis. She then wandered
between European health resorts, attempting to shake off what
she called her 'horrid stray dog'. Her last days were spent at
G. I. Gurdjieff's (333) Institute for the Harmonious Development
of Man, where she died in January 1923, after running up a flight
of stairs. There is 'no point in writing', said Virginia Woolf on
hearing the news. 'Katherine won't read it.'

In a German Pension 1909–11, pub. 1911

Mansfield's first book collects stories inspired by her visit to Bad
Wörishofen in 1909. It describes the boisterous, snobbish inhabitants
of a German boarding house, including the Frau Oberregierungsrat,
the Herr Rat and the Frau Doktor. The book sold well, until the
publisher absconded and his firm was liquidated; Mansfield, though,
later disowned these stories as juvenilia.

Bliss
and Other Stories 1915–20, pub. 1920

Mansfield's younger brother, 'Chummie' Beauchamp,
was killed in the First World War in 1915, and
increasingly she began to write about her childhood
in New Zealand. She perfected her distinctive,
lyrical, impressionistic style in these fourteen
sparkling stories, which dispense almost entirely
with plot. 'Her voice,' writes Claire Tomalin,
her biographer, 'was the voice of modernity.'

1964 Penguin Books
1968 Modern Classics
● intro. John Middleton Murry,
1926
—
Murry tried to persuade Mansfield
to reissue *In a German Pension*.
'I must write an introduction
saying it is early, early work,' she
equivocated, 'or just that it was
written between certain years,
because you know [...] it's nothing
to be proud of.' The book remained
out of print until Murry released
a posthumous edition in 1926.

1962
● —
In 1918, Virginia and Leonard
Woolf (42) commissioned
Mansfield to write 'Prelude',
which became their second
publication at the Hogarth Press
and the opening piece in *Bliss
and Other Stories*. The story
describes a family moving house
to Karori, a suburb of Wellington.

Katherine Mansfield

The Garden Party

PENGUIN MODERN CLASSICS   2/6

1951 Penguin Books
1961 Modern Classics
● intro. W. E. Williams, 1951
1997 Twentieth-Century Classics
2007 Penguin Classics
● intro. Lorna Sage, 1997

The illustration on the
cover of the 1961 edition
is by Heather Standring.

The Garden Party
and Other Stories
1920–22, pub. 1922

1981 Modern Classics
2007 Penguin Classics
intro. Ali Smith, 2007

'The singular beauty of [Mansfield's] language consists, partly, in its hardly seeming to be language at all, so glass-transparent is it to her meaning,' wrote Elizabeth Bowen (13). This collection, published less than a year before Mansfield's death, is her masterpiece. The fifteen stories, many of which are set in New Zealand, present ordinary situations with vivid sensitivity and haunting detail.

The Collected Short Stories
1908–23

'All manuscripts note books papers letters I leave to John M. Murry,' wrote Mansfield in her will. 'I should like him to publish as little as possible and to tear up and burn as much as possible.' Murry released two posthumous volumes of her stories: *The Doves' Nest* (1923), six stories and fifteen fragments, and *Something Childish* (1924), 25 stories, including Mansfield's earliest, 'The Tiredness of Rosabel'. Five days before she died, Mansfield wrote to Elizabeth von Arnim (380), saying that she was 'tired' of her 'little stories like birds bred in cages'. *The Collected Stories* gathers all five of her story collections.

1996
● intro. Suzanne Raitt

Penguin Modern Classics
Katherine Mansfield
The Collected Short Stories

Letters and Journals
A Selection
1907–23, pub. 1927–8, rev. 1951–4

Murry published Mansfield's journal in 1927 and a two-volume selection of her letters in 1928. Their friend Sylvia Lynd described these posthumous publications as 'boiling Katherine's bones to make soup'. Nonetheless, this selection by the New Zealand novelist C. K. Stead presents a fascinating insight into Mansfield's life and early death. Dorothy Parker (419) said that 'The Journal of Katherine Mansfield is the saddest book I have ever read.'

1977
● ed. C. K. Stead
—
The portrait on the cover of the Penguin edition was painted by Anne Estelle Rice in 1918, at a hotel in Looe in Cornwall. 'A. came early and began the great painting,' Mansfield wrote in a letter – 'me in that red, brick red frock with flowers everywhere. It's awfully interesting, even now. I painted her in my fashion as she painted me in hers: her eyes… "little blue flowers plucked this morning…".'

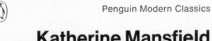

Penguin Modern Classics
Katherine Mansfield
Letters and Journals

1951 Penguin Books
2001 Modern Classics
• intro. Jill Greaves, 2001

2009
• —

Ruth Park 1917–2010

Park struggled to afford an education, but eventually graduated from Auckland University and found a job writing for the *Auckland Star* newspaper. In 1942, she left New Zealand for Australia. She married her long-time penfriend D'Arcy Niland (385) and the two young writers wandered around the Australian outback, taking odd jobs and attempting to make a living through writing. They settled briefly in Surry Hills, then an inner-city Sydney slum, and had five children together. Park wrote more than 50 books and the long-running radio serial *The Muddle-Headed Wombat* (1951–70). After Niland died unexpectedly in 1967, however, she moved to Europe, and then to Norfolk Island in the South Pacific, where she ran a bookshop. She won the Miles Franklin Award in 1977.

The Harp in the South Novels

The Harp in the South,
Poor Man's Orange,
Missus 1947–85

Park's first and most celebrated novel, *The Harp in the South* (1947), is set amidst the Catholic Irish community of Sydney's Surry Hills slum. The Darcy family live at 12½ Plymouth Street, in a cranky brown house where Grandma smokes a pipe, Hughie drinks, and Margaret struggles to look after their two daughters, Roie and Dolour. It is a bleak account of bedbugs, poverty and abortion. Park wrote a sequel called *Poor Man's Orange* (1949) that focuses on Dolour, and a prequel, *Missus* (1985), about Hughie and Margaret's courtship.

Ian Cross 1925–2019

Cross was raised in Whanganui, and worked as a reporter. He studied journalism at Harvard University in 1954, and later edited the *New Zealand Listener* and served as Chairman of the New Zealand Broadcasting Corporation.

The God Boy 1957

Cross's first novel is narrated by a delinquent 13-year-old boy at a convent school. Jimmy Sullivan tells the story of his parents' unhappy marriage and his own violent loss of faith.

1962 Penguin Books
2003 Modern Classics
• intro. Roger Robinson, 2003

Patricia Grace

b. 1937

Patricia Grace is a Māori writer of Ngāti Toa, Ngāti Raukawa and Te Āti Awa descent. She lives in Plimmerton on ancestral lands, close to the *marae* at Hongoeka Bay. She has written five novels, four short-story collections and several children's books: her award-winning book *Waiariki* (1975) was the first published collection of short stories by a Māori woman writer. In 2008, she won the Neustadt International Prize.

Potiki 1986

A small Māori fishing community lives and works around its beautifully carved *marae* meeting house, until 'the Dollarman' and his band of developers arrive and start to threaten their ancestral lands. Through Māori myth, memory and language, Grace paints a picture of a defiant community determined to protect its ancient way of life.

2020
—

THE AMERICAS

NORTH AMERICA

Robertson Davies *Tempest-Tost*

Robertson Davies *Leaven of Malice*

Robertson Davies *A Mixture of Frailties*

Robertson Davies Fifth Business

Robertson Davies *The Manticore*

Robertson Davies *World of Wonders*

Mordecai Richler *The Apprenticeship of Duddy Kravitz*

The Medium is the Massage. McLuhan/Fiore

Henry James Selected Short Stories

Henry James The Turn of the Screw and Other Stories

Henry James In the Cage and Other Stories

Henry James The Aspern Papers

Henry James The Europeans

MODERN CLASSICS

MODERN CLASSICS

MODERN CLASSICS

PENGUIN CLASSICS

MODERN CLASSICS

MODERN CLASSICS

MODERN CLASSICS

1919

3026
ISBN 014
00.3026 3

3500
ISBN 014
00.3500 1

ISBN 014
00.4101 X

2070

Canada

Robertson Davies

1913–1995

Davies was born in Thamesville, Ontario, the son of a journalist. He read voraciously as a child and worked variously as an actor with the Old Vic Company in England, the publisher of the *Peterborough Examiner* in Ontario, a professor at the University of Toronto, where he became the first Master of Massey College, and a writer of plays, essays and eleven novels, including *The Salterton Trilogy*, *The Deptford Trilogy* and *The Cornish Trilogy* (1981–8). He was instrumental in launching the Stratford Shakespearean Festival of Canada and he began a tradition at Massey College of writing and telling ghost stories at Christmas, in the manner of M. R. James (40). 'His books will be recognized with the very best works of this century,' said the *New York Times Book Review*.

The Deptford Trilogy 1970–75

Fifth Business, The Manticore, World of Wonders

Dunstan Ramsay and Percy Boyd Staunton are ten years old, playing in the snow, when Percy throws a snowball with a stone inside it. He accidentally hits the Baptist minister's pregnant wife, who goes into premature labour and gives birth to the sickly Paul Dempster. From that moment, the lives of the three boys are inextricably linked. Narrated by Dunstan Ramsay, whose initials are the reverse of Davies's own, *Fifth Business* (1970) is his most autobiographical novel. *The Manticore* (1972) presents a series of conversations between 'Boy' Staunton's son David and his Jungian (262) psychoanalyst; and *World of Wonders* (1975) is about Paul Dempster's career as a stage magician.

1980 Penguin Books
2006 Modern Classics
● intro. Margaret MacMillan, 2006

1980 Penguin Books
2006 Modern Classics
● intro. Margaret MacMillan, 2006

1980 Penguin Books
2006 Modern Classics
● intro. Margaret MacMillan, 2006

Margaret MacMillan is a distinguished Canadian historian, the former provost of Trinity College, Toronto.

The Salterton Trilogy 1951–8

Tempest-Tost, Leaven of Malice, A Mixture of Frailties

These interconnected novels are set in the fictional town of Salterton, Ontario. In *Tempest-Tost* (1951) love and jealousy rock an amateur production of *The Tempest*; *Leaven of Malice* (1954) opens with a false engagement announcement in the *Salterton Evening Bellman*; and *A Mixture of Frailties* (1958) follows a young girl with a beautiful singing voice when she moves to England. One of the characters in *A Mixture of Frailties* writes an operatic version of *The Golden Ass* by Apuleius, which Davies himself had done. 'Every novel from Robertson Davies is a cerebral adventure spliced with fantasy, sex and verbal gymnastics,' wrote Alan Sillitoe. 'He tantalizes you, but by God, it's more than your peace of mind is worth not to read it to the end.'

1977 Penguin Books
2002 Modern Classics
● intro. Timothy Findley, 2002
2005 Modern Classics
● intro. M. G. Vassanji, 2005

1977 Penguin Books
2005 Modern Classics
● intro. M. G. Vassanji, 2005

1977 Penguin Books
2005 Modern Classics
● intro. M. G. Vassanji, 2005

Mordecai Richler

1931–2001

Richler was born and raised on St Urbain Street, in the Jewish quarter of Montreal. 'Reading Fitzgerald (422) and Hemingway (428) made me feel inadequate,' he recalled. 'Then I came across an essay on the literary life by James Thurber (446). Writers, it seemed, got to sleep late and drink too much. Obviously there was going to be a place for me.' He moved to Paris at nineteen and spent many years in France, Germany and London, before returning to Montreal in 1972. He wrote novels, essays, children's books and works of non-fiction. He was twice awarded the Governor General's Award and in 1990 he won the Commonwealth Writers' Prize.

The Apprenticeship of Duddy Kravitz 1959

'A man without land is nobody,' said Duddy Kravitz's grandfather, and Duddy takes this maxim to heart. He sets out to acquire property ruthlessly and to beat society at its own materialistic game. This tragicomic coming-of-age satire is set around Montreal's St Urbain Street and told with colloquial gusto. 'The total effect is brash and blatant as a sports car rally – and as suggestive of power,' said the *New York Times Book Review*. Richler wrote the screenplay for a 1974 film adaptation starring Richard Dreyfuss, which received an Academy Award nomination for Best Adapted Screenplay.

1964 Penguin Books
2005 Modern Classics
● intro. Ann-Marie MacDonald, 2005

Marshall McLuhan 1911–1980

Herbert Marshall McLuhan was born in Edmonton, Alberta, and worked at the University of Toronto for most of his career. He was a media theorist and philosopher who popularized the term 'global village' and is regarded as having predicted the World Wide Web more than 25 years before it was invented; the *New York Times* called him 'the media prophet of the 1960s'. In Woody Allen's film *Annie Hall* (1977), McLuhan has a memorable cameo appearance as himself.

Quentin Fiore 1920–2019

Fiore was a self-taught New York graphic designer, who worked as an art director for Christian Dior and the Ford Foundation. He approached McLuhan and suggested collaborating on a design-led book adaption of McLuhan's key messages. The result was *The Medium is the Massage*.

1967 Penguin Books
2008 Design Classics
coordinated by Jerome Agel, 1967
—
The title *The Medium is the Massage* was a typesetter's error: it should have been *The Medium is the Message*. But McLuhan embraced it. 'Leave it alone!' he said. 'It's great, and right on target!' The new title puns on his key concept but suggests also that consumers might enjoy being 'massaged' by the media.

The Medium is the Massage
An Inventory of Effects 1967

This explosive collaboration blends text, image and photography in a visually startling manifesto for the modern age. McLuhan's underlying argument is that the means by which we communicate, the 'medium', affects us more than the content of the message. Fiore illustrates this concept by creating an anarchic, dissonant medium for McLuhan's argument. The book was a bestseller, praised by some as an icon of 1960s design, while others complained that 'it promoted illiteracy, encouraged drug use [and] corrupted the morals of the American youth'.

More UNUSUAL TYPESETTING

The USA

Henry James 1843–1916

James was born in New York, the second of five children and the younger brother of the philosopher and psychologist William James. As children, he and his siblings were given a 'sensuous education' around Europe. In 1869, he returned to Europe and moved between England, France and Italy, meeting John Ruskin, Charles Dickens, Matthew Arnold, William Morris, George Eliot, Émile Zola, Guy de Maupassant, Ivan Turgenev and many others. From Rome, he wrote to his brother William: 'At last – for the first time – I live!' He settled in London in 1877 and mostly remained in England for the rest of his life, moving in 1898 to Rye in East Sussex. He wrote novels, stories, plays and essays; Willa Cather (414) called him a 'mighty master of language and keen student of human actions and motives'. He became a British subject in 1915, a few months before his death. Edith Wharton (401) recalled sitting next to Henry James in Sussex. 'For a long time no one spoke,' she remembered; 'then James turned to me and said solemnly: "Summer afternoon – summer afternoon; to me those have always been the two most beautiful words in the English language."'

1947 Penguin Books
The Turn of the Screw
1973 Modern Classics
*The Turn of the Screw
and Other Stories*
• ed. S. Gorley Putt, 1973
2011 Penguin Classics
The Turn of the Screw
ed. David Bromwich, 2011
2017 Penguin Classics
*The Turn of the Screw
and Other Ghost Stories*
ed. Susie Boyt, 2017

The Turn of the Screw has been adapted for the screen many times. One of the most successful adaptations is *The Innocents* (1961), directed by Jack Clayton with a screenplay by Truman Capote (463) and John Mortimer (139).

1963 Modern Classics
Selected Short Stories
1983 Modern Classics
Daisy Miller and Other Stories
• ed. Michael Swan, 1963
2016 Penguin Classics
Daisy Miller and Other Stories
ed. Stephen Fender, 2016

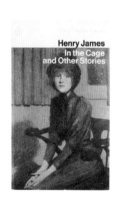

1973 Modern Classics
In the Cage and Other Stories
• ed. S. Gorley Putt, 1973
2001 Penguin Classics
Selected Tales
• ed. John Lyon, 2001

1976 Modern Classics
*The Aspern Papers
and Other Stories*
• ed. S. Gorley Putt, 1976
1986 Penguin Classics
*The Figure in the Carpet
and Other Stories*
• ed. Frank Kermode, 1986
2014 Penguin Classics
*The Aspern Papers
and Other Stories*
ed. Michael Gorra, 2014

Stories 1865–1908

James wrote stories and novellas throughout his career. *Daisy Miller* (1878) was probably his most popular single work in his lifetime: it tells the story of a beautiful, eccentric American travelling around Europe. In 'The Aspern Papers', a fanatical critic becomes obsessed with a dead poet's memorabilia; 'The Figure in the Carpet' is about an author who claims he has written a literary riddle, like a 'complex figure in a Persian carpet'; 'In the Cage' is the story of a telegraphist who deciphers cryptic telegrams; and *The Turn of the Screw* (1898), James's most famous ghost story, is the tale of an inexperienced governess in a haunted house. Oscar Wilde (3) called it 'a most wonderful, lurid, poisonous little tale'.

1969 Modern Classics
● ed. S. Gorley Putt, 1969
1986 Penguin Classics
ed. Geoffrey Moore, 1986
notes Patricia Crick, 1986

Roderick Hudson 1875

In James's 'first phase', he wrote stories that contrast Europe with America. His first published novel tells the story of Roderick Hudson, a talented American sculptor who is brought to Rome by a wealthy patron. Hudson falls in love with Christina Light but fails to live up to his early promise.

Washington Square 1880

Wealthy, sheltered Catherine Sloper of Washington Square, New York, is flattered when Morris Townsend proposes marriage and correspondingly distraught when her father forbids the match. 'The delicate, feline *Washington Square*,' wrote Graham Greene (88), '[is] perhaps the only novel in which a man has successfully invaded the feminine field and produced a work comparable to Jane Austen's.'

1966 Modern Classics
1984 Penguin English Library
● ed. Charles R. Anderson, 1984
2000 Penguin Classics
ed. Richard Lansdown, 2000

The Portrait of a Lady

1880 – 81

Isabel Archer is a wealthy American heiress travelling in Europe, who falls for the irresistible charms of an American expatriate. This early masterpiece is considered the culmination of James's 'first phase' and a bold experiment in portraying a complex and evolving psychology. The critic F. R. Leavis said that *The Portrait of a Lady* and *The Bostonians* were 'the two most brilliant novels in the language'.

The Bostonians 1885 – 6

In this comic novel, Basil Ransom is a conservative young lawyer from Mississippi who visits his feminist cousin Olive in Boston. After a meeting on the subject of women's emancipation, Basil and Olive both attempt to influence Olive's young protégée Verena Tarrant.

The Europeans
A Sketch 1878

Two raffish European siblings, Eugenia Münster and Felix Young, travel to Boston in the mid-19th century and disconcert their American cousins.

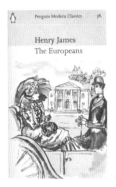

1964 Modern Classics
2008 Penguin Classics
ed. Andrew Taylor, 2008

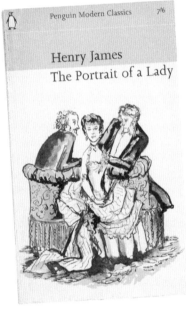

1963 Modern Classics
1984 Penguin English Library
● ed. Brian Lee, 1984
2007 Penguin Classics
ed. Martha Banta, 2007

1963 Modern Classics
1984 Penguin English Library
● ed. Geoffrey Moore, 1984
2011 Penguin Classics
ed. Philip Horne, 2011

The Princess Casamassima

1885 – 6

James's 'second phase' focused primarily on English subjects. This dramatic novel is set in London and contrasts Hyacinth Robinson, an impoverished bookbinder turned terrorist assassin, with the aristocratic Princess Casamassima, formerly Christina Light from *Roderick Hudson*.

1977 Modern Classics
1987 Penguin Classics
ed. Derek Brewer, 1987
notes Patricia Crick, 1987

The Tragic Muse

1889–90

Nick Dormer gives up his political career in order to paint, and creates a dramatic portrait of the ambitious actress Miriam Rooth posing as the muse of tragedy.

1978 Modern Classics
1995 Penguin Classics
ed. Philip Horne, 1995
—
James became increasingly interested in writing plays in the early 1890s, until the disastrous opening night of *Guy Domville* at the St James's Theatre in London in 1895: he came on stage to take a bow and was jeered by the audience. He subsequently decided to return to fiction. Incidentally, when *Guy Domville* folded, it was replaced at the St James's by the premiere of *The Importance of Being Earnest* by Oscar Wilde (3).

What Maisie Knew

1897

Maisie Farange travels between her divorced, narcissistic parents, as each remarries and takes lovers, and she feels increasingly abandoned and anxious. Her psychology has been compared with that in Freud's case study of 'Dora' (266). 'If it were not for Henry James's art – his subtlety, his grace, his handy euphemisms,' writes Paul Theroux (543) – 'this very modern story about aimless lives and messy marriages would be practically untellable.'

The Awkward Age 1898–9

When Nanda Brookenham comes of age and makes her debut in decadent London society, she finds herself competing with her own mother for the affections of the man she admires. Unusual among James's novels, *The Awkward Age* is written almost entirely in dialogue. 'One must make an effort to see and hear beyond the quicksilver talk and very slow movement of *The Awkward Age*,' writes Ronald Blythe (155). 'It is the surface alone which leads one to the story's depths, this shimmering surface which rises without warning to glitteringly dangerous points or lurches into blackness and vulgarity.'

1966 Modern Classics
1987 Penguin Classics
ed. Ronald Blythe, 1987
notes Patricia Crick, 1987

The Wings of the Dove 1902

James's last three masterpieces are seen as the apex of his 'third phase' of writing. In *The Wings of the Dove*, ruthless Kate Croy plans to exploit her extremely wealthy and gravely ill friend Milly Theale. Milly was based on James's own cousin Minny Temple, who died of tuberculosis: he set out to wrap her memory in the 'beauty and dignity of art'.

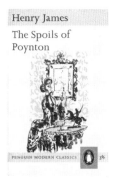

1963 Modern Classics
1987 Penguin Classics
intro. David Lodge, 1987
notes Patricia Crick, 1987

The Spoils of Poynton 1896

Mrs Gereth of Poynton Park has spent her life amassing a spectacular art collection. She would like her son to marry sensitive Fleda Vetch, who shares her taste for beautiful things, but Owen has inconveniently proposed to the athletic Mona Brigstock.

1966 Modern Classics
1985 Penguin Classics
● ed. Paul Theroux, 1985
2010 Penguin Classics
ed. Christopher Ricks, 2010
—
While composing *What Maisie Knew*, James began dictating to a typist, a method he used for the rest of his career. His style shifts noticeably in favour of long sentences with multiple clauses and single paragraphs that run for page after page.

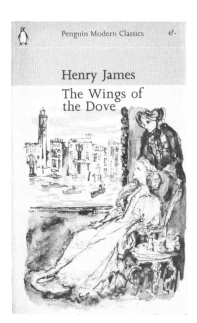

'To read (say) *The Golden Bowl* (400) or *The Wings of the Dove* is like taking a long walk uphill, panting and perspiring and almost of a mind to turn back,' wrote Max Beerbohm (60), 'until, when you look back and down, the country is magically expanded beneath your gaze, as you never saw it yet; so that you toil gladly up the heights for the larger prospects that will be waiting for you. I admit, you must be in good training.'
—
1965 Modern Classics
1986 Penguin Classics
● ed. Patricia Crick, 1986
intro. John Bayley, 1986
2008 Penguin Classics
ed. Millicent Bell, 2008

The Ambassadors

1903

Mrs Newsome of Woollett, Massachusetts, sends her fiancé Lambert Strether as an 'ambassador' to extricate her son Chad from the temptations of Paris. Strether finds the previously ungraceful Chad much improved, however, especially by his charming companion Madame de Vionnet – so Mrs Newsome is forced to send her daughter as a second 'ambassador' to retrieve her menfolk. 'Paris irradiates the book from end to end,' wrote E. M. Forster (38), '[…] and when we have finished the novel and allow its incidents to blur that we may see the pattern plainer, it is Paris that gleams at the centre.'

1973 Modern Classics
1986 Penguin Classics
● ed. Harry Levin, 1986
2008 Penguin Classics
ed. Adrian Poole, 2008

The Golden Bowl

1904

1966 Modern Classics
1985 Penguin Classics
● ed. Patricia Crick, 1985
intro. Gore Vidal, 1985
2009 Penguin Classics
ed. Ruth Bernard Yeazell, 2009

The American heiress Maggie Verver is engaged to be married, as is her widowed father. Maggie is to marry Prince Amerigo, a penniless Italian aristocrat; her father has proposed to Maggie's impoverished friend Charlotte Stant. Little do father or daughter know, however, that Amerigo and Charlotte share a secret past. James wrote the four characters' trains of thought as 'a system of clauses, sub-clauses, modifications, qualifications and in some cases ruminations', observes Colm Tóibín, thereby anticipating the modernist (11) techniques of Joyce (8) and Woolf (42).

The Outcry

1911

In 1908, Hans Holbein's portrait of *Christina of Denmark* (1538) was on display at the National Gallery in London, on loan from the Duke of Norfolk. The Duke was offered £40,000 for the portrait, by an American private collector; he decided to sell it, but he gave the gallery a month to match the offer. Following a public outcry, funds were raised to purchase the painting for the nation and James wrote a comic play about the incident in 1909. Two years later, he reworked the unproduced play as his last completed novel.

2001
● intro. Toby Litt
—
The 2001 Penguin edition was the first new publication of *The Outcry* since 1911; the cover reproduces Holbein's *Christina of Denmark*, which still hangs in London's National Gallery.

Edith Wharton 1862–1937

Edith Newbold Jones liked to turn the pages of books as an infant, making up stories; she attempted her first novel at the age of eleven. She was raised in Gilded Age New York, in the ostentatiously wealthy family sometimes said to have inspired the phrase 'keeping up with the Joneses'. She travelled frequently to Europe and spoke several European languages, crossing the Atlantic 60 times in the course of her life. She moved permanently to France in 1910, divorcing her husband Teddy Wharton three years later. She wrote dozens of novels and volumes of stories, poems, essays and memoirs, and was a close friend of Henry James (397), Sinclair Lewis (421), Jean Cocteau (178) and André Gide (164). 'Why, before long I shall become a classic!' exclaims the authoress Mrs Dale in Wharton's 1901 short story 'Copy'. 'Bound in sets and kept on the top book-shelf – brr, doesn't that sound freezing?' In 1926, Wharton was elected to the American National Institute of Arts and Letters.

The Muse's Tragedy
and Other Stories 1893–1916

These stories were mostly written before the First World War. They range from the earliest, 'The Fullness of Life', about a wife who dies and wakes up in a fabulous artistic afterlife, to the last, 'Xingu',

1992
• ed. Candace Waid, 1990

about the pretentious members of a literary lunch club. They include tales of love, marriage, divorce, death and ghosts – one of Wharton's favourite subjects. Wharton had a reputation as a short-story writer long before she turned to novels. In 1907, she confessed: 'I have always obscurely felt that I didn't know how to write a novel. I feel it more clearly after each attempt, because it is in sharp contrast to the sense of authority with which I take hold of a short story.'

The House of Mirth 1905

When Wharton began publishing fiction in 1899, she said it 'broke the chains which had held me so long in a kind of torpor'. *The House of Mirth* was an immediate success. Beautiful but shallow Lily Bart sails effortlessly through the drawing rooms of the privileged New York elite, hunting for a husband, until an unexpected hint of scandal threatens to capsize her charmed life. The title is taken from Ecclesiastes 7:4: 'The heart of the wise is in the house of mourning; but the heart of fools is in the house of mirth.'

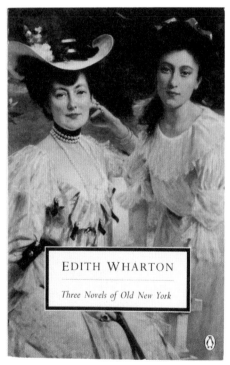

Ethan Frome 1911

Ethan Frome is a farmer, living with his hypochondriac wife Zeena in the harsh, wintry landscape of western Massachusetts. When Mattie, Zeena's cousin, comes to live with them, Ethan finds himself irresistibly drawn to her. Wharton wrote *Ethan Frome* after abandoning her own extramarital affair with the journalist Morton Fullerton. 'Before I knew you I had grown so impersonal, so accustomed to being my own only comrade [...],' she wrote to Fullerton. 'When one is a lonely-hearted and remembering creature as I am, it is a misfortune to love too late, and as completely as I have loved you.'

1988 Penguin Classics
1994 Twentieth-Century Classics
• ed. Sarah Higginson Begley, 1988
intro. Doris Grumbach, 1988
2005 Penguin Classics
ed. Elizabeth Ammons, 2005

1996 Twentieth-Century Classics
2012 Deluxe Classics
intro. Jonathan Franzen, 2012

Three Novels of Old New York comprises Wharton's greatest novels set in that glittering city: *The House of Mirth*, *The Custom of the Country* (403) and *The Age of Innocence* (403).

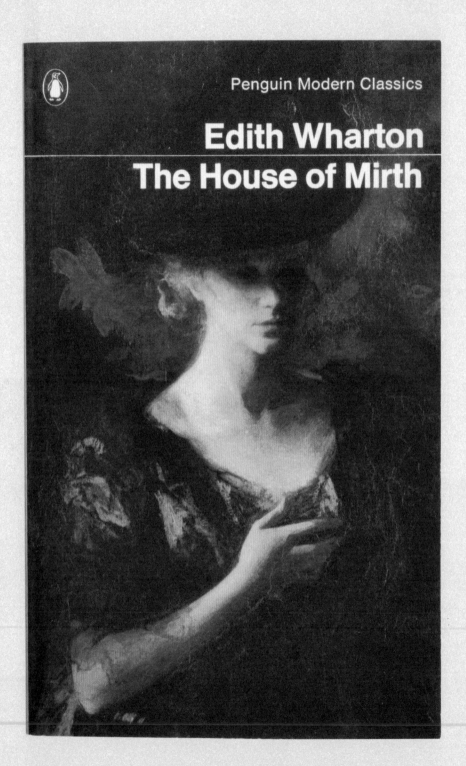

Penguin Modern Classics

Edith Wharton
The House of Mirth

1979 Modern Classics
1986 Penguin Classics
1993 Twentieth-Century Classics
2008 Penguin Classics
ed. Cynthia Griffin Wolff, 1986

The artwork on the cover of the 1979 edition
is a detail from *Portrait of a Lady* (1901)
by the American artist Frank Weston Benson.

The Reef 1912

'The Reef is arguably the most rigorous and the most finely wrought of Edith Wharton's creations,' wrote Anita Brookner in her introduction. '[…] It marks the peak of her most brilliant period of creativity.' Anna Leath is a straitlaced young American widow living in France, who intends to marry the diplomat George Darrow. Darrow's previous acquaintance with the vivacious governess Sophy Viner, however, threatens to become a reef on which Anna's hopes of happiness could founder. Henry James (397) admired the taut, tragic narrative: he wrote to Wharton comparing The Reef to Racine and George Eliot, saying, 'dearest Edith, you are stronger and firmer and finer than all of them put together'.

1994
● intro. Anita Brookner

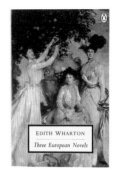

1996
● –
Three European Novels comprises *The Reef*, *The Buccaneers* and *Madame de Treymes* (1907), in which New Yorker Fanny Frisbee is unhappily married to a dissipated French marquis. The Madame de Treymes of the title is the marquis's enigmatic sister, who proposes an unusual arrangement.

The Custom of the Country 1913

1984 Modern Classics
1987 Modern Classics
● intro. Anita Brookner, 1987
2006 Penguin Classics
ed. Linda Wagner-Martin, 2006

In the year she divorced her husband, Wharton published *The Custom of the Country*, her most humorous novel. It follows the exploits of the ambitious parvenue Undine Spragg as she arrives in New York and marries and divorces her way through high society. 'As long as men and women seek to use each other – and to use each other badly,' wrote Anita Brookner – 'Edith Wharton can be counted upon to provide the ideal commentary.'

The Age of Innocence 1920

1974 Modern Classics
1996 Twentieth-Century Classics
2008 Penguin Classics
ed. Cynthia Griffin Wolff, 1996
notes Laura Dluzynski Quinn, 1996

Newland Archer is preparing to marry the beautiful but vapid May Welland when Ellen Olenska, May's exotic cousin, returns from Europe – a breath of fresh air in the stifling atmosphere of 1870s New York. With *The Age of Innocence*, Edith Wharton became the third recipient of the Pulitzer Prize for Fiction, in 1921. 'The novel glitters with epigrammatic moments, sequins of comedy […] and jewels of hard wisdom,' wrote John Updike (514). '[…] The Age of Innocence, beneath its fine surface, holds an abyss – the abyss of time, and the tragedy of human transience.'

Summer 1917

Summer, like *Ethan Frome* (401), is set in the Berkshire Hills of Massachusetts. When a handsome architect arrives for the summer, the neglected librarian Charity Royall dreams of escape. Wharton wrote *Summer* in six weeks, the only novel she published during the First World War. She spent the rest of the time working in Paris supporting unemployed women, orphaned children and Belgian refugees.

The Buccaneers

1937, pub. 1938

'This novel deals with the adventures of three American families with beautiful daughters who attempt the London social adventure in the 'seventies,' Wharton explained. The book follows the fortunes of five nouveau riche New York girls, including Nan St George, who unexpectedly marries the young Duke of Tintagel. Wharton's last novel was unfinished when she died, but she wrote a full synopsis so we know how it would have ended. 'Finished or unfinished,' wrote Sean O'Faolain (17), 'The Buccaneers is, nevertheless, so real and sincere as to be worth an indeterminable number of completed novels from the generations which ousted Mrs. Wharton from public adoration.'

1993 Twentieth-Century Classics
2008 Penguin Classics
ed. Elizabeth Ammons, 1993

1994 ● –

Edwin Arlington Robinson 1869–1935

Robinson described his life as 'a tragedy from the beginning'. His parents wanted a girl and put off naming him for six months. He attended Harvard University until his father's health failed, along with the family's finances. Then his mother died suddenly of black diphtheria and his brother Herman married the woman Edwin loved. Nearly destitute, Robinson found work as an inspector during the construction of the New York subway and self-published his first poetry collection in 1896. He went on to write eighteen books of lyric and narrative poetry and won the Pulitzer Prize for Poetry three times. 'His theme was unhappiness itself, but his skill was as happy as it was playful,' wrote Robert Frost (415). '[...] His life was a revel in the felicities of language.' In 1908, Robinson was elected to the National Institute of Arts and Letters.

Selected Poems
1896–1928

Robinson wrote poems about the loneliness and despair of life in small-town America, but with a wit and intelligence that rejuvenated *fin-de-siècle* poetry (3) in the USA and inspired the poets of the next generation, including T. S. Eliot (11), Ezra Pound (61) and Robert Frost (415). His most famous poem is 'Richard Cory', about a wealthy, well-respected man who shoots himself; it was the basis for the Simon and Garfunkel song of the same name.

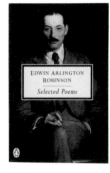

1997
● ed. Robert Faggen

Thorstein Veblen 1857–1929

Veblen was born in Wisconsin to Norwegian parents. He studied philosophy at Johns Hopkins and Yale universities, before teaching economics at Chicago and Stanford. He also co-founded the New School in New York, a private research institution. He is mentioned in *Nineteen Nineteen* (426) by John Dos Passos, *The Heart is a Lonely Hunter* (453) by Carson McCullers and *Main Street* (421) by Sinclair Lewis.

The Theory of the Leisure Class
An Economic Study of Institutions
1899

This witty analysis of American society coined the term 'conspicuous consumption' to describe the ostentatious display of wealth as a demonstration of social status. The sociologist Lewis Mumford called Veblen's book 'a stick of dynamite wrapped up to look like a stick of candy'.

1994 Twentieth-Century Classics
2007 Penguin Classics
intro. Robert Lekachman, 1967

Jack London 1876–1916

John Griffith Chaney grew up as a vagrant dockhand on the San Francisco waterfront, where he worked as an oyster pirate in a sloop called *Razzle Dazzle* before joining the San Francisco Bay fish patrol. In 1893, he sailed as far as Japan on a sealing schooner, and in 1897 he joined the gold rush to the Klondike. He took Darwin's *Origin of Species* and Milton's *Paradise Lost* and returned with less than $5 of gold dust and scurvy. 'It was in the Yukon that I found myself,' he wrote. 'There nobody talks. Everybody thinks. You get your true perspective.' He spent the rest of his life writing and sailing around the Pacific. He died on his ranch, Wolf House, in California. 'The greatest story he ever wrote,' said the critic Alfred Kazin, 'was the story he lived.'

Northland Stories
1899–1910

These tales draw on London's experience of the Klondike gold rush. They describe the hardships of the northern wilderness, its inhospitable weather, dangerous beasts and rugged codes of behaviour. Many of the tales describe uneasy and destructive interactions with Native Americans. According to George Orwell (80), 'Love of Life' was the last story that Lenin's wife read to Lenin (299) on his deathbed; it 'greatly pleased' him.

1997
● ed. Jonathan Auerbach

More DOGS

The Call of the Wild
White Fang
and Other Stories 1903–7

The Call of the Wild (1903) tells the story of a pampered pet dog who is kidnapped and enslaved as a sled-husky until he is tempted away from human companionship and becomes the leader of a Yukon wolf pack. E. L. Doctorow (538) considered it London's masterpiece. Following its success, London decided to 'reverse the process': *White Fang* (1906) tells the story of a wild Yukon wolf-dog, who slowly becomes devoted to a young gold prospector.

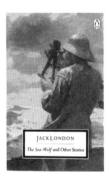

1981 Penguin American Library
1986 Penguin Classics
1993 Twentieth-Century Classics
2008 Penguin Classics
● ed. Andrew Sinclair, 1981
intro. James Dickey, 1981
2019 Penguin Classics
ed. Kenneth K. Brandt, 2019
intro. Earle Labor, 2019

—

The Call of the Wild was the first title in the Puffin Classics series, which began in 1982.

The Sea-Wolf
and Other Stories 1904–14

Humphrey Van Weyden, a shipwrecked literary critic, is rescued by the sealing schooner *Ghost* and comes under the influence of megalomaniac Captain Wolf Larsen, who has been compared to Melville's Captain Ahab and Milton's Lucifer. Ambrose Bierce (411) called Wolf Larsen a 'tremendous creation […]. The hewing out and setting up of such a figure is enough for a man to do in one life-time.'

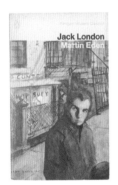

1967 Modern Classics
1984 Penguin American Library
1993 Twentieth-Century Classics
2008 Penguin Classics
ed. Andrew Sinclair, 1984

Martin Eden 1909

Martin Eden is an impoverished San Francisco seaman who dreams of writing fiction. London drew on his own struggle to make a living through his writing, portraying Eden's financial success as a betrayal of youthful idealism. 'One of my motifs, in this book, was an attack on individualism […],' London wrote inside the copy he sent to Upton Sinclair (409). 'I must have bungled it, for not a single reviewer has discovered it.'

1989
● ed. Andrew Sinclair

—

London, known as 'Wolf' to his friends, used a picture of a wolf as his bookplate.

Tales of the
Pacific 1909–16

These twelve stories are all set in the South Seas. They feature sailing ships, colonial oppressors and Hawaiian myths. Titles include 'The Whale Tooth', 'Koolau the Leper' and 'Shin-Bones'.

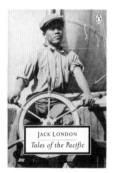

1989
ed. Andrew Sinclair

The Assassination Bureau, Ltd.

with Robert L. Fish 1916, pub. 1963

Ivan Dragomiloff is the founder of the Assassination Bureau, a secret syndicate of ruthless killers – but he finds himself pursued by the very organization he masterminded. London bought the idea for the plot of this suspense thriller from Sinclair Lewis (421) but he left the manuscript unfinished. It was later completed by the crime writer Robert L. Fish.

1978 Penguin Books
1994 Twentieth-Century Classics
● intro. Donald E. Pease, 1994

American Naturalism

Naturalism originated in France in the late 19th century. For Émile Zola, Naturalism was a post-Darwinian development of Realism, an almost scientific attempt to analyse social conditions and provide an environmental and evolutionary explanation of a character's actions. Frank Norris, one of the first exponents of American Naturalism, took a different approach: he saw Realism and Romanticism as opposing trends, and Naturalism as the combination of the two. Other American Naturalists included Sherwood Anderson (420), Stephen Crane, James T. Farrell (447), Hamlin Garland (416), Jack London (404) and Theodore Dreiser, whose *Sister Carrie* (407) is considered the quintessential expression of the movement.

Frank Norris 1870–1902

Benjamin Franklin Norris was born in Chicago, the son of a wholesale jeweller and a Shakespearean actress. The family moved to California in 1884 and Norris grew up in San Francisco, before studying art in Paris and deciding to write naturalistic novels in the style of Émile Zola. He wrote eight novels, as well as hundreds of poems, stories and essays, and died at the age of 32.

McTeague
A Story of San Francisco 1899

When a slow-witted dentist marries his beautiful patient, their sadomasochistic marriage spirals into poverty and violence. Contemporary readers were shocked by descriptions of rape fantasies, clothing fetishes, pants-wetting and chewed fingers. In 1924, Erich von Stroheim released an epic film adaptation called *Greed*, the original cut of which was nearly ten hours long.

1982 Penguin American Library
1985 Penguin Classics
1994 Twentieth-Century Classics
● intro. Kevin Starr, 1982

The Octopus
A Story of California 1901

The self-reliant wheat farmers of the San Joaquin Valley clash with the tentacular, monopolistic Pacific and Southwestern Railroad company, in a conflict that culminates in bloody violence, inspired by the historical 'Mussel Slough Tragedy' of 1880.

The Pit
A Story of Chicago 1902, pub. 1903

Norris's bestselling novel is set in the trading pit of the Chicago Board of Trade building, where Curtis Jadwin battles to corner the wheat market. His abused wife Laura has been compared to both Emma Bovary and Edna Pontellier in Kate Chopin's *The Awakening*.

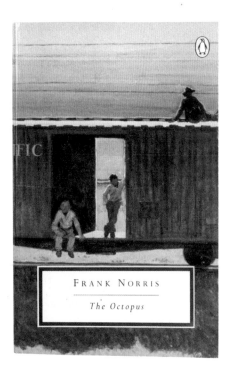

'My idea is to write three novels around the one subject of *Wheat*,' explained Norris. 'First, a story of California (the producer), second, a story of Chicago (the distributor), third, a story of Europe (the consumer) and in each to keep to the idea of this huge Niagara of wheat rolling from West to East.'

1986 Penguin Classics
1994 Twentieth-Century Classics
● intro. Kevin Starr, 1986

Norris died before completing his *Epic of the Wheat* trilogy; the third instalment would have been *The Wolf: A Story of Europe*. Incidentally, *The Pit* inspired a 1904 card game called *Pit: Exciting Fun for Everyone*. Players out-yell each other, attempting to corner the markets in corn, barley, wheat, rye, flax, hay and oats.

—
1994
● intro. Joseph R. McElrath, Jr. & Gwendolyn Jones

Charles W. Chesnutt 1858–1932

Charles Waddell Chesnutt was 'seven-eighths white' but chose to identify as African American. He grew up in Fayetteville, North Carolina, where he taught in black public schools. In 1887, he moved to Cleveland, Ohio, with his wife, where he established a legal-stenography business. He worked with W. E. B. Du Bois (408), Booker T. Washington and the National Association for the Advancement of Colored People, winning the NAACP's Spingarn Medal in 1928. He wrote two collections of short stories, three novels and a biography of the abolitionist Frederick Douglass.

The House Behind the Cedars 1900

Rena Walden joins her brother John in South Carolina, a few years after the Civil War, where he 'passes' for white and works as a lawyer. When she becomes engaged to a white friend of John's, however, she reveals her mixed-race heritage.

1993
• intro. Donald B. Gibson

The Marrow of Tradition 1901

Chesnutt dramatizes the Wilmington Massacre, when white supremacists took over Wilmington, North Carolina, in 1898 and ousted the elected biracial government in the only successful *coup d'état* in US history. Some of Chesnutt's own relatives had lived through the violence.

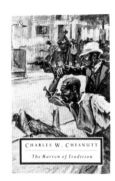

1993
• intro. Eric J. Sundquist

Theodore Dreiser 1871–1945

Theodore Herman Albert Dreiser was born in Indiana, the twelfth child of a German immigrant. He found work at the Chicago *Globe* before writing for New York magazines in the 1890s. He wrote controversial novels and campaigned for victims of social injustice, such as Nicola Sacco and Bartolomeo Vanzetti (425). 'The fellows of the ink-pots,' wrote Sherwood Anderson (420), 'the prose writers in America who follow Dreiser, [...] will never have to face the road through the wilderness of Puritan denial, the road that Dreiser faced alone.'

Sister Carrie 1900

Caroline Meeber is 'Sister Carrie', a country girl who becomes a successful actress in Chicago by sleeping with a series of influential men. Frank Norris (406) persuaded Frank Nelson Doubleday to publish the novel, but as it offended Doubleday's wife he refused to publicize the publication. It is now considered a landmark work of American Naturalism (406). Dreiser 'sought to grasp and to represent what to him was an American chaos',

1981 Penguin American Library
1994 Twentieth-Century Classics
2004 Penguin Classics
ed. James L. W. West III, 1981
intro. Alfred Kazin, 1981

said James T. Farrell (447), 'and he reflects this in his style as well as his content. Beauty, tragedy, pathos, rawness, sentimentality, clichés – all are smelted together [...] he wrote his novel as if he were "forging" images of American life.'

Jennie Gerhardt

1901, pub. 1911

Dreiser began writing *Jennie Gerhardt* in 1901, but the quiet reception of *Sister Carrie* meant he had to wait ten years before it was published. Jennie works at a hotel in Columbus, Ohio, when she catches the eye of George Brander, a US senator. '*Jennie Gerhardt* is the best American novel I have ever read,' said the critic H. L. Mencken in 1911. '[...] Am I forgetting *McTeague* (406) and *The Pit* (406) [...] or Mr. Dreiser's own *Sister Carrie*? No. [...] Taking it as it stands, grim, gaunt, mirthless,

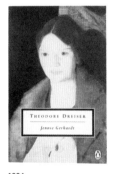

1994
• ed. James L. W. West III, 1992
—
The 1911 edition of *Jennie Gerhardt* was censored by the publishers; this edition reprints the unexpurgated version, which restores passages of social criticism and ultimately presents a stronger heroine.

shapeless, it remains, and by a long odds, the most impressive work of art that we have yet to show in prose fiction'.

1982 Puffin Books *The Wonderful Wizard of Oz*
1985 Puffin Books *The Emerald City of Oz*
<u>1998</u> Twentieth-Century Classics
2012 Penguin Threads
ed. Jack Zipes, 1998

L. Frank Baum 1856–1919

Lyman Frank Baum was born in Chittenango, New York State. He worked as a journalist, horticulturalist, chicken breeder, fireworks salesman, theatre manager, producer, actor, playwright and owner of a general store, as well as writing fourteen Oz novels and many other books. His last words to his wife were 'Now we can cross the shifting sands', a reference to the Deadly Desert that surrounds the Land of Oz.

The Wonderful World of Oz

The Wonderful Wizard of Oz, The Emerald City of Oz, Glinda of Oz
1900–1920

Oz was Baum's pacifist paradise land, a dream of rural America occasionally threatened by malevolent villains. In *The Wonderful Wizard of Oz* (1900), Dorothy Gale is blown in from Kansas and teams up with the Scarecrow, the Tin Woodman, the Cowardly Lion and a disappointing wizard to tackle the Wicked Witch of the West; in *The Emerald City of Oz* (1910), Dorothy returns to Oz with Aunt Em and Uncle Henry and saves the population from the Nome King; and in the last Oz novel, *Glinda of Oz* (pub. 1920), Dorothy and Princess Ozma struggle to prevent a battle between the Skeezers and the Flatheads.

W. E. B. Du Bois 1868–1963

William Edward Burghardt Du Bois was born in Massachusetts and became the first African American to earn a doctorate from Harvard University. He taught history at Atlanta University until 1910, when he resigned in order to help found the National Association for the Advancement of Colored People (NAACP). He spent his life campaigning against racial injustice, demanding immediate equality and full citizenship for African Americans. In 1944, he was elected to the National Institute of Arts and Letters. At the age of 93, in 1961, he moved to Ghana as director of the *Encyclopedia Africana*; he took Ghanaian citizenship in the year of his death.

The Souls of Black Folk 1903

'The problem of the Twentieth Century is the problem of the color-line,' wrote Du Bois in the introduction to this landmark collection of essays, borrowing a phrase from the abolitionist Frederick Douglass. He explores the dual identity of African Americans as both American and black, a state he calls 'double consciousness'.

1989 Penguin Classics
<u>1996</u> Twentieth-Century Classics
2001 Penguin Classics
● intro. Donald B. Gibson, 1989
2018 Penguin Classics
ed. Monica M. Elbert, 1989
intro. Ibram X. Kendi, 2018

O. Henry 1862 – 1910

William Sydney Porter served in his uncle's drugstore in North
Carolina, before moving to Texas to work on a ranch, in a cigar store,
as a pharmacist and as a bank teller. In 1896, he was charged with
embezzlement and fled to Honduras. When he returned to the USA
to visit his dying wife, he was arrested, and he served three years in
the Ohio state prison, where he spent his time writing short stories.
He then moved to New York and became a successful and prolific
comic writer, penning a story a week for *World* magazine under
the pseudonym 'O. Henry'. William Trevor (21) believed that Porter
took his pen name from a prison guard called Orrin Henry; the critic
Guy Davenport thought it was a contraction of 'Ohio Penitentiary'.

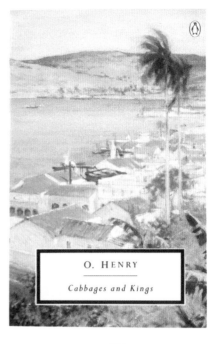

Cabbages and Kings 1904

O. Henry's first collection of eighteen stories
is also an episodic novel, set in the fictional
republic of Anchuria; he began writing it while
avoiding embezzlement charges in Honduras
in 1896–7. The episodic plot includes the first
use of the term 'banana republic'.

Selected Stories 1906 – 10, pub. 1906 – 17

O. Henry loitered in hotel lobbies, picking up stories from snippets
of overheard conversation. He wrote almost 300 short stories
about New York, the cattle ranches of the West and the sleepy
towns of Latin America. He was known for his vivid humour and
twist endings. This volume gathers 68 of his best tales.

1993 Twentieth-Century
Classics
2007 Penguin Classics
intro. Guy Davenport, 1993

1993
• intro. Guy Davenport
—
O. Henry's title is taken from
the poem 'The Walrus and the
Carpenter' in Lewis Carroll's
Through the Looking-Glass
(1871). The book contains
other objects mentioned in
the poem, including shoes,
ships and sealing wax.

Upton Sinclair 1878 – 1968

Sinclair was born in Baltimore, Maryland, and wrote dime novels as a teenager to fund
his schooling in New York. He made his name with *The Jungle* and used the proceeds
to found a utopian community in New Jersey called Helicon Hall; but the short-lived
experimental cooperative ended with a disastrous fire. In 1915, he moved to California
and ran repeatedly for public office, narrowly missing the governorship in 1934.
He wrote more than 100 books, including *Oil!* (1927), adapted by Paul Thomas Anderson
as *There Will be Blood* (2007), and *Boston* (1928), about the trial of Nicola Sacco and
Bartolomeo Vanzetti (425). He won the Pulitzer Prize for Fiction in 1943.

The Jungle 1905

Sinclair spent seven weeks observing the meat-packing industry in Chicago in order to write
this nightmarish novel. Jurgis Rudkus is a Lithuanian immigrant attempting to support his
teenage wife even as his soul is crushed by his unscrupulous employers. 'I aimed at the public's
heart,' wrote Sinclair, 'and by accident I hit it in the stomach.' Jack London (404) called it
'the *Uncle Tom's Cabin* of wage slavery'. The public outcry that accompanied the publication
of *The Jungle* led to the passage of the Pure Food and Drug Act and the Meat Inspection Act 1906.

1936 Penguin Books
1965 Modern Classics
1985 Penguin American
Library
1986 Penguin Classics
intro. Ronald Gottesman, 1985

Gertrude Stein 1874–1946

'Twentieth-century literature *is* Gertrude Stein,' said Gertrude Stein.
'[…] There are the big four: Poe, Whitman, James (397), myself.'
She studied psychology under William James, Henry James's brother,
and then settled in Paris, where she collected paintings by Matisse
and Cézanne, wrote avant-garde prose, and hosted an influential literary
and artistic salon on Saturday evenings. 'Matisse brought people,'
she recalled, 'everybody brought somebody, and they came at any
time and it began to be a nuisance, and it was in this way that Saturday
evenings began.' She befriended Pablo Picasso, F. Scott Fitzgerald (422),
Ernest Hemingway (428) and other writers of the Lost Generation (425).
The Polish American Alice B. Toklas joined her circle in 1907 and became
her devoted life partner. The couple remained in Paris throughout both
world wars and the occupation of Paris, despite their Jewish heritage,
and they doted on a beloved poodle called 'Basket'.

Three Lives 1905–6, pub. 1909

These three stories are all set in Bridgepoint, a fictional version of Baltimore,
where Stein had attended Johns Hopkins University. She attempts to recreate verbally the
techniques of three modernist (11) painters. 'The Good Anna' has a non-linear narrative
inspired by Cézanne; 'Melanctha' has the repeating angles of Picasso; and 'The Gentle Lena'
dispenses with plot or setting, in emulation of Matisse. The philosopher and psychologist
William James called it 'a fine new kind of realism'.

1979 Modern Classics
1990 Twentieth-Century Classics
2008 Penguin Classics
intro. Ann Charters, 1990
—
The cover of the 1979
Penguin edition shows one of
Cézanne's portraits of his wife,
Madame Cézanne (1878–88),
which hung above Stein's desk
as she was writing *Three Lives*.
This edition also includes
Q.E.D. (1903), a novella based
on Stein's same-sex affairs
at Johns Hopkins University.

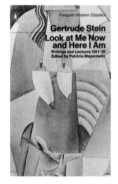

1971
● ed. Patricia Meyerowitz,
1967
intro. Elizabeth Sprigge, 1967

Look at Me Now and Here I Am
Writings and Lectures 1911–45

This anthology collects the best of Gertrude Stein's writing.
There are lectures such as 'What Is English Literature'
and 'What Are Masterpieces and Why Are There So Few
of Them', pen portraits of Henry James (397), Picasso
and Matisse, stories, plays and the long poem 'Before
the Flowers of Friendship Faded Friendship Faded'.
The centrepiece is *Tender Buttons* (1914), her experiment
in 'verbal Cubism', which comprises multiple miniature
prose poems about everyday objects, items of food and
'rooms'. Stein's poems were 'like whisky to me', wrote
Patrick Kavanagh in *The Green Fool* (15); 'her strange
rhythms broke up the cliché formation of my thought'.

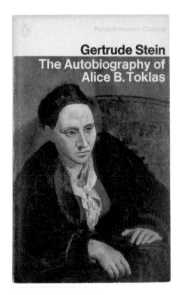

1966
—
The cover of the first Penguin
edition shows Picasso's portrait
of Stein, which he painted while
she was working on *Three Lives*.
Picasso intentionally echoed
Cézanne's portraits of his wife.

The Autobiography of Alice B. Toklas 1933

Stein's most popular work is written from the point of view of her partner,
Alice B. Toklas, describing their life in Paris at 27 Rue de Fleurus as 'a kaleidoscope
slowly turning', with visits from Ernest Hemingway (428), F. Scott Fitzgerald (422),
Sherwood Anderson (420), Sinclair Lewis (421), Ezra Pound (61) and Thornton
Wilder (436). 'The geniuses came and talked to Gertrude Stein,' wrote Stein,
as Toklas, 'and the wives sat with me.' Stein wrote the book in six weeks. She
describes Picasso's 'high whinnying Spanish giggle' and offended Hemingway
by calling him 'yellow'. He thought it 'a damned pitiful book'.

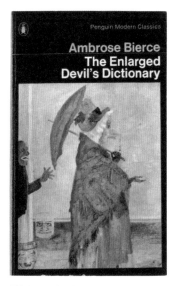

1971 Modern Classics
1983 Penguin American Library
1985 Penguin Classics
1989 Twentieth-Century Classics
ed. Ernest Jerome Hopkins, 1967
pref. John Myers Myers, 1967
—
The 1967 'enlarged' edition
added 851 newly discovered
words and definitions, including
some by Harry Ellington Brook,
a subsequent editor of the *Wasp*.

Ambrose Bierce 1842–1914?

Bierce was born in a log cabin in Ohio, the tenth of thirteen children whose names were Abigail, Amelia, Ann, Addison, Aurelius, Augustus, Almeda, Andrew, Albert, Ambrose, Arthur, Adelia and Aurelia. He left home at fifteen to become a printer's devil for the abolitionist newspaper the *Northern Indiana*. He fought in the American Civil War and then found work writing acidly humorous columns for newspapers such as *Fun*, the *Argonaut* and finally William Randolph Hearst's *Examiner*. H. P. Lovecraft (417) described his style as 'grim and savage'. Bierce wrote his *Devil's Dictionary* definitions during his editorship of the *Wasp*, between 1881 and 1886. In 1913, he set off for Chihuahua to witness the Mexican Revolution and disappeared.

The Enlarged Devil's Dictionary

1911, rev. 1967

Devil, n. The author of all our woes and proprietor of all the good things of this world.

Dictionary, n. A malevolent literary device for cramping the growth of a language and making it hard and inelastic. The present dictionary, however, is one of the most useful works that its author, Dr John Satan, has ever produced.

Zane Grey 1872–1939

After flirting with professional baseball, Pearl Zane Grey worked as a dentist in New York and wrote stories. When *Riders of the Purple Sage* became a spectacular success, however, he gave up dentistry and wrote novels about the Old West and travelled the world. He was also a record-breaking deep-sea fisherman. Ken Kesey (520) named his son Zane after Grey.

1990
• intro. Jane Tompkins

Riders of the Purple Sage

1912

Riders of the Purple Sage is the archetypal American Western novel. It is an adventure story, a desert romance and a book about Mormons, which traces a mythic narrative across locations with names such as Surprise Valley, Deception Pass and Balancing Rock. 'That wild, lonely, purple land of sage and rock took possession of me,' wrote Grey. 'The lure of the silent waste places of the earth, how inexplicable and tremendous!'

More DESERTS

The Sheltering Sky
by Paul Bowles   480

The Tartar Steppe
by Dino Buzzati   217

Alamein to Zem Zem
by Keith Douglas   116

Seven Pillars of Wisdom
by T. E. Lawrence   74

Voss
by Patrick White   382

1998
● ed. Holly Peppe

Edna St Vincent Millay

1892 – 1950

After graduating from Vassar College, the beautiful, red-haired Millay, known as 'Vincent', moved to Greenwich Village in New York, where she wrote poetry and plays and had bisexual affairs. In 1923, she won the Pulitzer Prize for Poetry for her collection *The Ballad of the Harp-Weaver* and the following year she co-founded the Cherry Lane Theatre, which continues to stage experimental drama. She also wrote short prose fiction under the pseudonym 'Nancy Boyd'. A road accident in 1936 left her in constant pain and dependent on morphine for the rest of her life. In 1943 she was awarded the Frost (415) Medal for her contribution to American poetry.

Early Poems

1912 – 21

This volume comprises Millay's first three poetry collections: *Renascence and Other Poems* (1917), *A Few Figs from Thistles* (1920, rev. 1922) and *Second April* (1921). Her lyrics and sonnets range from meditations on nature, love, life and loss to political commentaries and witty celebrations of feminism and female sexuality.

James Weldon Johnson

1871 – 1938

Johnson was born in Jacksonville, Florida, the son of the head waiter at the St James Hotel. He wrote hit Broadway songs with his brother John Rosamond Johnson, including 'Under the Bamboo Tree' and 'Nobody's Lookin' but de Owl and de Moon', and embarked on an extraordinary public career. In 1897, he became the first black lawyer admitted to the Florida Bar; in 1906, he was appointed American consul to Venezuela; in 1917, he organized a 10,000-strong march along Fifth Avenue in New York, protesting against race riots and lynch mobs; in 1920, he became the first black leader of the National Association for the Advancement of Coloured People (NAACP), a position he held for ten years; and in 1934, he became the first black professor at New York University. He was a leading voice in the Harlem Renaissance (413) and edited influential anthologies of African American poetry. 'James Weldon Johnson aptly, deeply, with love and humor and a powerful rhyming tongue, has told our story and sung our song,' said Maya Angelou.

JAMES WELDON JOHNSON
The Autobiography of an Ex-Colored Man

1990
● ed. William L. Andrews

The Autobiography of an Ex-Colored Man 1912

'In writing the following pages I am divulging the great secret of my life, the secret which for some years I have guarded far more carefully than any of my earthly possessions.' This novel purports to be the confessions of an unnamed, illegitimate son of a black mother and a white father. The narrator starts out as a ragtime pianist in New York with dreams of becoming 'a great man, a great colored man, to reflect credit on the race', but when he witnesses the lynching of a black man and decides to 'pass' as white.

The Harlem Renaissance

In the 1920s, an explosion of black cultural and intellectual activity reached its peak in Harlem, New York. This 'New Negro' movement focused on all aspects of the black cultural and political experience in America. James Weldon Johnson (412) was an active supporter, publishing *The Book of American Negro Poetry* in 1922. In the preface to that anthology, he pointed out that black literature and music were 'the only things artistic that have yet sprung from American soil and been universally acknowledged as distinctive American products'. Key writers associated with the Harlem Renaissance include Langston Hughes, Zora Neale Hurston, Nella Larsen (437), Claude McKay and Jean Toomer.

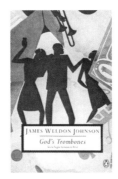

1976 Penguin Poets
1989 Modern Classics
● —

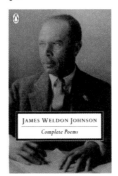

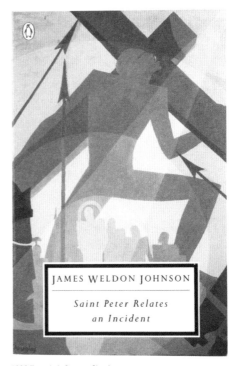

Poems 1917–35

Johnson is probably best remembered for *God's Trombones* (1927), his collection of experimental 'sermons in verse' which draw on the vocabulary and rhetoric of Southern black preachers. 'There are few persons who can afford not to have this book in their library,' said W. E. B. Du Bois (408). *Saint Peter Relates an Incident* (1935) is a selection of poems celebrating black life and indicting racial injustice. In the title poem, Saint Peter tells a story about Judgement Day, in which the Unknown Soldier emerges from Arlington National Cemetery as a 'black soldier-angel' to the horror of the Ku Klux Klan.

2000
● ed. Sondra Kathryn Wilson
—
God's Trombones is illustrated with a series of striking images by the painter Aaron Douglas, another major figure of the Harlem Renaissance. These have been used for the covers of several of the Penguin editions.

1993 Twentieth-Century Classics
2000 Twentieth-Century Classics
Lift Every Voice and Sing
● pref. Sondra Kathryn Wilson, 1993

Along This Way 1933, rev. 1937
The Autobiography of James Weldon Johnson

'It is difficult to imagine the Harlem Renaissance without James Weldon Johnson,' wrote the historian John Hope Franklin. 'It is impossible to understand the place of African-Americans in the life of this country without *Along This Way*.' In Johnson's candid autobiography, he sets out the philosophy by which he lived his life. 'I will not allow one prejudiced person or one million or one hundred million to blight my life,' he wrote. 'I will not let prejudice or any of its attendant humiliations and injustices bear me down to spiritual defeat. My inner life is mine, and I shall defend and maintain its integrity against all the powers of hell.'

1941 Penguin Books
1990 Twentieth-Century Classics
● intro. Sondra Kathryn Wilson, 1990

Willa Cather 1873 – 1947

When Wilella Sibert Cather was nine years old, her family headed west and joined the pioneer farmers in Nebraska, and she became deeply influenced by the wide-open prairies and the weather-beaten lifestyle. She taught English and worked as a journalist in Pittsburgh, Pennsylvania, for ten years, then moved to New York at the age of 33 to work as an editor for *McClure's Magazine*. She had several close relationships with women and lived with the editor Edith Lewis for the last 39 years of her life. In 1943, she was elected to the American Academy of Arts and Sciences, and in 1974 a tract of native prairieland was preserved near her childhood home in Nebraska as the Willa Cather Memorial Prairie.

O Pioneers! 1913

When Alexandra Bergson inherits her family farm, she struggles to squeeze a living from the wild, windswept Nebraskan plains. 'I decided not to "write" at all,' recalled Cather – 'simply to give myself up to the pleasure of recapturing in memory people and places I'd forgotten.' This is the first of Cather's three 'Great Plains' novels.

1989 Penguin Classics
1994 Twentieth-Century Classics
● intro. Blanche H. Gelfant, 1989
2018 Modern Classics
—
O Pioneers! is dedicated to the writer Sarah Orne Jewett, Cather's friend and mentor. The title is taken from the Walt Whitman poem 'Pioneers! O Pioneers!'

2018
—
Cather took her title from a painting of the same name by the French painter Jules Breton. *The Song of the Lark* (1884) is on display at the Art Institute of Chicago.

The Song of the Lark 1915

Thea Kronborg is a young girl from the small town of Moonstone, Colorado, who travels to Chicago to learn the piano and discovers she has a talent for singing. In this semi-autobiographical novel of an artist discovering her own talent, Thea travels the world singing opera, but she remains rooted in the prairies where she grew up. Cather's 'voice, laconical and richly sensuous, sings out with a note of unequivocal love for the people she is setting down on the page', says the writer Marina Warner. This is the second of Cather's 'Great Plains' novels.

My Ántonia 1918

The last of Cather's 'Great Plains' novels was inspired by her childhood friend Annie Sadilek Pavelka. It is narrated by Jim Burden, who moves to Nebraska at the age of ten and befriends Ántonia Shimerda, the daughter of Bohemian immigrants. Jim leaves for college and becomes a lawyer, but he is haunted by the memory of Ántonia, who remains and works the family farm. 'I felt that the grass was the country,' recalls Jim, 'as the water is the sea. The red of the grass made all the great prairie the colour of wine-stains, or of certain seaweeds when they are first washed up. And there was so much motion in it; the whole country seemed, somehow, to be running.'

1994 Twentieth-Century Classics
● intro. Joseph Murphy, 1994
2018 Modern Classics
—

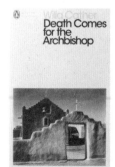

2018
—

Death Comes for the Archbishop 1927

Cather describes the lives of a French Catholic bishop and priest, dispatched to New Mexico in the late 19th century. Over the years, they are sustained by their faith and friendship in the face of dangers, loneliness and an unforgiving landscape. It is 'quite simply a masterpiece', writes the critic A. N. Wilson. 'I am completely bowled over by it: by the power of its writing, by the vividness of its scene painting and by the stories it tells.'

Robert Frost 1874–1963

Frost was born in California and grew up in Massachusetts.
For nine years, he worked as a farmer in New Hampshire, writing
poetry in the early mornings. After living in England for three years,
where his first volumes of poetry were published, he returned
to America in early 1915 and developed a reputation as a gruff
New England farmer-poet. He won four Pulitzer Prizes for Poetry and
was generally acknowledged as America's unofficial Poet Laureate.
He read his poem 'The Gift Outright' at President John F. Kennedy's
inauguration in 1961.

Selected Poems 1913–62

Frost had a gift for capturing colloquial vocabulary in traditional verse
forms, creating poems that seem to have grown out of the soil. 'He uses
what is rural and ordinary to provide a brief but adequate hint of spiritual
realities,' wrote Jorge Luis Borges (572). 'He is at the same time tranquil and
puzzling.' The two Penguin selections draw on all his major publications,
including *A Boy's Will* (1913), *New Hampshire* (1923) and *A Witness Tree* (1942).

ROBERT FROST
Selected Poems

1955 Penguin Poets
● intro. C. Day Lewis, 1955
1973 Penguin Poets
1990 Twentieth-Century
Classics
● ed. Ian Hamilton, 1973

Eugene O'Neill 1888–1953

O'Neill was born in a hotel room on New York's Broadway, the
son of two Irish actors. After two semesters at Princeton University,
he became a merchant seaman, working on ships and suffering from
depression and alcoholism. Diagnosed with tuberculosis, he entered
a sanatorium on Christmas Eve 1912 and spent the next six months
reading Chekhov, Ibsen, Strindberg, Shaw (4) and Synge (7).
He began writing his own plays in 1913, drawing on German
Expressionism (269) and Sigmund Freud (265) and forging for the
first time a distinctively American style of theatre. After winning
the Nobel Prize for Literature (576) in 1936, he didn't have a Broadway
production for ten years until he returned with his masterpieces
The Iceman Cometh (1946), *A Moon for the Misbegotten* (1947) and
his posthumously produced *Long Day's Journey into Night* (1956),
which won his fourth Pulitzer Prize for Drama and is frequently cited
as one of the greatest American plays of the 20th century. In his last
years, O'Neill suffered from Parkinson's disease and alcoholism, and
he died in a hotel in Boston. 'I knew it! I knew it!' were his last reported
words. 'Born in a goddam hotel room and dying in a hotel room.'

Early Plays 1916–22

This collection covers the first phase of O'Neill's work, with seven one-act
and five full-length plays: *Beyond the Horizon* (1918) and *Anna Christie* (1920),
both of which won the Pulitzer Prize for Drama; the autobiographical
The Straw (1919); *The Emperor Jones* (1920), a monologue by the dictator of
a West Indian state; and *The Hairy Ape* (1922), about a bestial ship's stoker
who has an existential crisis and is crushed to death by a gorilla.

EUGENE O'NEILL
Early Plays

1960 Penguin Plays
various collections
● ed. E. Martin Browne, 1960
2001 Twentieth-Century
Classics
● intro. Jeffrey H. Richards,
2001

Ring Lardner 1885 – 1933

Ringgold Wilmer Lardner was a sports reporter from Niles, Michigan. In 1914, he published a story narrated by a semi-literate baseball player called Jack Keefe, which was a success, and his volume of Keefe stories, *You Know Me Al* (1916), made him an international celebrity. Lardner moved to New York with his family and bought a house on Long Island, where he wrote short stories and drank heavily until he died at the age of 48. Virginia Woolf (42) admired his writing, and his friend F. Scott Fitzgerald (422) spoke at his funeral. Lardner found a way to transcribe colloquial American English, inspiring a generation of writers, from Sherwood Anderson (420) and Nathanael West (446) to Ernest Hemingway (428) and Eudora Welty (457).

Selected Stories

1916 – 24

'In his grotesque but searching tales of baseball-players, pugilists, movie queens, song-writers and other such dismal persons,' wrote the critic H. L. Mencken in his study of the American language, '[Lardner] set down common American with the utmost precision, and yet with enough imagination to make his work a contribution of genuine and permanent value to the national literature.' This selection of Lardner's best tales includes the full texts of his two story-cycle 'novels', *You Know Me Al* (1916) and *The Big Town* (1921).

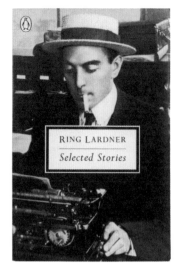

1997
● ed. Jonathan Yardley

Hamlin Garland 1860 – 1940

Hannibal Hamlin Garland worked on farms across the American Midwest, in Wisconsin, Iowa and South Dakota, before moving east to Boston in 1884 to become a writer. He is best remembered for his short stories in *Main-Travelled Roads* (1891) and for his memoir *A Son of the Middle Border*, but he wrote almost 50 other works of fiction, poetry, drama and non-fiction. He campaigned for tax reform, women's rights and fairer treatment of Native Americans, and he was also a believer in psychic phenomena.

Veritism

Hamlin Garland first set out a manifesto for a form of impressionism which he called 'veritism' in his 1894 work, *Crumbling Idols*. A veritist work is based on the personal experiences and memories of an individual writer, tempered in hindsight by verifiable facts. 'I sought to verify my impressions by comparing impressions separated [by] an interval of time,' wrote Garland in 1939. 'I sought to get away from the use of the word realism which implied predominant use of sexual vice and crime in the manner of Zola and certain of the German novelists. [...] As a veritist I recorded my perceptions.'

A Son of the Middle Border 1917

'All of this universe known to me in the year 1864 was bounded by the wooded hills of a little Wisconsin coulee, and its center was the cottage in which my mother was living alone – my father was in the war. As I project myself back into that mystical age, half lights cover most of the valley. The road before our doorstone begins and ends in vague obscurity – and Granma Green's house at the fork of the trail stands on the very edge of the world in a sinister region peopled with bears and other menacing creatures. Beyond this point all is darkness and terror.' Garland's story captures the pioneering spirit of thousands of other farmers along the Midwest frontier. The novelist William Dean Howells called it 'one of the truest and greatest books in the world'.

1995
● ed. Joseph B. McCullough

2002
ed. S. T. Joshi,
1999

2002
ed. S. T. Joshi,
2001

2005
ed. S. T. Joshi

H. P. Lovecraft 1890–1937

Howard Phillips Lovecraft was born in Providence, Rhode Island, where he lived for most of his life. His father was committed to an asylum and died when Lovecraft was eight, after which he was raised mainly by his maternal grandfather, Whipple Van Buren Phillips, who told him tales involving 'winged horrors' and 'deep, low, moaning sounds'. Lovecraft began writing horror stories and 'weird fiction', which he first published in the pulp magazine *Weird Tales*. He remained almost unknown in his lifetime and died in poverty at the age of 46. He wrote only three short novels and about 60 short stories, but he is credited with reinventing the horror genre and has inspired a posthumous cult following. Stephen King calls him 'the twentieth century horror story's dark and baroque prince'.

The Call of Cthulhu
and Other Weird Stories 1917–35, pub. 1919–36

Lovecraft saw humanity as an unimportant element of an uncaring cosmos. 'The Call of Cthulhu' is a tale of extraterrestrial terror, about a monstrous entity with 'a pulpy, tentacle head' on a 'grotesque and scaly body with rudimentary wings'. The story has spawned the 'Cthulhu Mythos', a shared fictional universe that continues to inspire artists, writers, musicians and video-game creators. Other stories in this selection include 'The Rats in the Walls', 'The Whisperer in Darkness' and 'The Shadow Over Innsmouth'.

The Thing on the Doorstep
and Other Weird Stories 1917–33, pub. 1919–41

This selection of nightmarish dreamscapes and supernatural horrors includes two novellas: Lovecraft's masterpiece, *At the Mountains of Madness* (1936), and *The Case of Charles Dexter Ward* (pub. 1941), which Anthony Powell described as a 'chronicle of reincarnation and unspeakable wickednesses'. Also featured are 'The Dunwich Horror', set in the backwoods of Lovecraft's native New England; 'The Music of Erich Zann', one of Lovecraft's personal favourites; and 'Under the Pyramids', which was ghost-written for Harry Houdini.

The Dreams in the Witch House
and Other Weird Stories 1918–35, pub. 1920–43

Several of these tales recall the witch-hunts of 17th-century New England, including 'The Shunned House' and 'The Dreams in the Witch House'. Other titles include 'The Shadow out of Time', 'The Terrible Old Man', 'The Lurking Fear' and the novella *The Dream-Quest of Unknown Kadath* (pub. 1943).

William Carlos Williams 1883–1963

Williams lived almost his whole life in Rutherford, New Jersey. By day, he was a paediatrician and ran a general medical practice; at night, he wrote modernist (11) poetry. Initially influenced by Imagism (61), he struggled all his life to create 'a new – an American – poetic language'. As well as poems, he wrote essays, plays, stories, novels and memoirs. He was a mentor to Allen Ginsberg and wrote the introduction to *Howl and Other Poems* (490). In 1959, he was elected to the American Academy of Arts, and he won a Pulitzer Prize for Poetry for his collection *Pictures from Brueghel* (1962).

Selected Poems 1917–62

'I'll write whatever I damn please,' said Williams in 1919, 'whenever I damn please, and as I damn please.' He was a master of observation and American vernacular rhythms who focused on 'the particular to discover the universal'. This anthology selects extracts from *Paterson* and poems from all Williams's major collections, including *Spring and All* (1923), his manifesto of the modernist (11) imagination, which features the famous 16-word poem 'The Red Wheelbarrow'. 'The greatness of a poet is not be measured by the scale but by the intensity and the perfection of his works,' wrote Octavio Paz (561). 'Also by his vivacity. Williams is the author of the most vivid poems of modern American poetry.'

1976 Penguin Poets
1990 Twentieth-Century Classics
ed. Charles Tomlinson, 1976

Objectivism

Objectivism was a short-lived American poetic movement in the early 1930s, led by William Carlos Williams and Louis Zukofsky, who edited *An 'Objectivists' Anthology* (1932). 'Objectivism looks at the poem with a special eye to its structural aspect, how it has been constructed,' wrote Williams. '[…] It arose as an aftermath of Imagism (61), which the Objectivists felt was not specific enough, and applied to any image that might be conceived.' Other poets associated with Objectivism included George Oppen, who founded the Objectivist Press, Carl Rakosi and Charles Reznikoff. It should not be confused with Ayn Rand's (450) philosophy of objectivism.

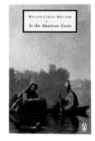

1971 Peregrine Books
1989 Twentieth-Century Classics
• intro. Horace Gregory, 1956

In the American Grain
1925

'History, history!' wrote Williams. 'We fools, what do we know or care? History begins for us with murder and enslavement, not with discovery.' In this lyrical history of America, from 'Red Eric' and Christopher Columbus to Edgar Allan Poe and Abraham Lincoln, Williams analysed the 'strange phosphorus' of what it means to be American.

White Mule
1937

In this novel, Joe and Gurlie Stecher are Norwegian immigrants struggling to raise their baby daughter in New York.

1970
• —

1972
• —

In the Money 1940

In the sequel to *White Mule*, Joe bids for a government printing contract and Gurlie becomes increasingly avaricious. Williams wrote a third novel, *The Build-Up* (1952), which completed the 'Stecher' trilogy.

1983 Penguin Poets
1990 Twentieth-Century Classics
• —
The cover of the 1990 edition shows the Passaic Falls. The Passaic River runs through the city of Paterson and the falls are a central image in the poem.

Paterson
1946–58

Williams's masterpiece was inspired by reading James Joyce's *Ulysses* (10). It is an epic poem, originally published in five volumes, which is both the biography of the city of Paterson in New Jersey and the life of a man named Paterson. Williams includes the mantra 'no ideas but in things', the crystallization of his poetic method. It is 'the best thing William Carlos Williams has ever written', said the poet Randall Jarrell. '[…] The organization of *Paterson* is musical to an almost unprecedented degree.'

Dorothy Parker 1893–1967

Dottie Rothschild's mother died when she was four years old, and she found she disliked her father and hated her new stepmother. She was educated at a Catholic convent school in Manhattan and then a school in New Jersey. When her father died in 1913, she played piano at a dance academy and began writing poetry. She found editorial work at *Vogue* and *Vanity Fair*, where she replaced P. G. Wodehouse (48) as the theatre critic, and began developing a reputation as the hard-drinking queen of stinging repartee. She was an early member of the Algonquin Round Table and in 1925 began writing for a nascent magazine, the *New Yorker*, to which she contributed stories for 30 years. She was briefly married to the stockbroker Edwin Pond Parker II, but later married, divorced and remarried the writer Alan Campbell, with whom she collaborated on Hollywood scripts. She wrote bitingly witty poems and short stories – as well as acerbic theatre and book reviews – which captured the cynical spirit of Jazz Age New York. She was arrested for protesting against the executions of Nicola Sacco and Bartolomeo Vanzetti (425) and she left her estate to the National Association for the Advancement of Colored People. She suggested her own epitaph: 'Excuse my dust'.

1977 Penguin Books *The Penguin Dorothy Parker*
1989 Twentieth-Century Classics
intro. Brendan Gill, 1973
aftwd. W. Somerset Maugham (32), 1944

The Collected Dorothy Parker 1918–62

Parker compiled *The Portable Dorothy Parker* in 1944 from the best stories and poems in *Enough Rope* (1926), *Death and Taxes* (1931) and her other collections. This expanded edition includes later stories, articles and book reviews. As the 'Constant Reader', Parker reviewed Vladimir Nabokov's *Lolita* (309), Shirley Jackson's *We Have Always Lived in the Castle* (468), Truman Capote's *Breakfast at Tiffany's* (464) and also A. A. Milne's *The House at Pooh Corner* (1928), to which her reaction was 'Tonstant Weader Fwowed up'. 'She managed to express her real feelings in stanzas which snap and glitter like a Chanel handbag,' wrote Peter Ackroyd.

Complete Stories 1922–58

This volume contains all Parker's short stories, including thirteen that were previously uncollected. It also has a selection of 'sketches', such as 'A Dinner Party Anthology' and 'Men I'm Not Married To'. 'To say that Mrs. Parker writes well is as fatuous, I'm afraid, as proclaiming that Cellini was clever with his hands,' said the poet Ogden Nash. 'The trick about her writing is the trick about Ring Lardner's (416) writing or Ernest Hemingway's (428) writing. There is no trick.'

1995
● ed. Colleen Breese
intro. Regina Barreca

Algonquin Round Table

The Algonquin Hotel is located at 59 West 44th Street in midtown Manhattan. From the summer of 1919, a group of wisecracking wordsmiths began to meet at the Algonquin every day for lunch. The central figure of this 'Vicious Circle' was Dorothy Parker; others included the journalist Alexander Woollcott, composer Irving Berlin, theatre director George S. Kaufman, playwright Noël Coward and comedian Harpo Marx. 'The price of admission,' quipped Groucho (432), 'is a serpent's tongue and half-concealed stiletto.' They loved games, from poker and croquet to charades and wink murder. The group disbanded in the early 1930s. 'These were not giants,' Parker recalled. 'Think who was writing in those days – Lardner (416), Fitzgerald (422), Faulkner (433) and Hemingway (428). Those were the real giants. The Round Table was just a lot of people telling jokes and telling each other how good they were.'

John Reed 1887–1920

Reed was a committed left-wing activist, supporting a silk-workers' strike in Paterson, New Jersey, chairing the meeting that founded the Communist Labor Party in America, and editing the radical magazine *Masses*, which published contributions from Upton Sinclair (409) and William Carlos Williams (418). He reported on the Mexican Revolution and the First World War, which led him to Russia in 1917 where he witnessed the October Revolution at first hand. He returned to Soviet Russia in 1920, where he died of typhus, and is buried on Moscow's Red Square, with a plaque on the wall of the Kremlin.

Ten Days That Shook the World 1919

'This book is a slice of intensified history,' wrote Reed – 'history as I saw it. [...] My sympathies were not neutral. But in telling the story of those great days I have tried to see events with the eye of a conscientious reporter, interested in setting down the truth.' His gripping account of the events of October 1917 describes the dramatic arrival of Lenin (299) in Petrograd, the fall of the provisional government and the triumph of the Bolsheviks.

1966 Penguin Books
1977 Penguin Books
1979 Modern Classics
2007 Penguin Classics
intro. V. I. Lenin, 1919
intro. A. J. P. Taylor, 1977
—
'With the greatest interest and with never-slackening attention I read John Reed's book, *Ten Days That Shook the World*,' wrote Lenin (299) in his introduction. 'Unreservedly do I recommend it to the workers of the world.'

Sherwood Anderson 1876–1941

Anderson was an Ohio businessman who sold preservative roof paint by mail order from a warehouse in Elyria. On 28 November 1912, he suffered a breakdown: he was dictating a letter to his secretary when he suddenly stopped, turned pale, laughed strangely and said, 'I have been wading in a long river and my feet are wet.' Then he walked out of his office, abandoning his job and his family, and set off along the railway track to Cleveland, with $6 in his pocket. This moment, to which he returned repeatedly in his writing, was for him the turning point in his career. He moved to Chicago, where he became a professional writer and a close friend of William Faulkner (433) and Thomas Wolfe (438), who called him 'the only man in America who ever taught me anything'. In 1937, he was elected to the American Academy of Arts.

Winesburg, Ohio 1919

Anderson was living alone on the Near North Side of Chicago in 1915. 'It was a late fall night and raining,' he recalled. '[...] I was there naked in the bed and I sprang up. I went to my typewriter and began to write. It was there, under those circumstances, myself sitting near an open window, the rain occasionally blowing in and wetting my bare back, that I did my first writing.' Each of the stories in *Winesburg, Ohio* arrived in a rush, as 'an idea grasped whole as one would pick an apple in an orchard'. Together they form Anderson's masterpiece: they are set in a small Ohio town, based on Anderson's childhood home of Clyde. The protagonist George Millard encounters a variety of Winesburg 'grotesques' who confide the secrets of their small-town lives.

1948 Penguin Books
1987 Penguin Classics
1992 Twentieth-Century Classics
2004 Penguin Classics
intro. Malcolm Cowley, 1960
—
Winesburg, Ohio is introduced by Malcolm Cowley (448). He calls Anderson 'the only story teller of his generation who left his mark on the style and vision of the generation that followed. Hemingway (428), Faulkner (433), Wolfe (438), Steinbeck (440), Caldwell, Saroyan, Henry Miller (451) ... each of these owes an unmistakable debt to Anderson, and their names might stand for dozens of others.'

The Egg
and Other Stories 1919–41

This selection of the best of Anderson's later stories includes five previously unpublished tales, discovered among Anderson's papers. Titles include 'Death in the Woods', 'An Ohio Pagan', 'Nobody Laughed' and 'There She Is – She Is Taking Her Bath'. 'The Egg' is about childhood on a chicken farm and a father obsessed with eggs.

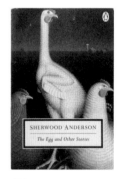

1998
• ed. Charles E. Modlin, 1992

Anzia Yezierska 1880?–1970

Yezierska was born in a Jewish *shtetl* in Russian Poland but migrated to the USA before she was ten years old. Her family settled in New York's Lower East Side, where by 1910 half a million other Jews would also be living. Yezierska described the immigrant experience in *Hungry Hearts* and the novel *Bread Givers* (1925), and she went on to write more novels, a book of essays and a memoir, *Red Ribbon on a White Horse* (1950).

Hungry Hearts 1920

These semi-autobiographical stories describe the clamorous streets of Manhattan's Lower East Side at the turn of the 20th century, with its noisy sweatshops, crowded tenements and families trapped by poverty. Titles include 'Hunger', 'The Fat of the Land' and 'How I Found America'.

1997
● intro. Blanche H. Gelfant
—
The cover shows a still from the MGM silent film adaptation of *Hungry Hearts* (1922).

Sinclair Lewis 1885–1951

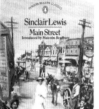

1950 Penguin Books
1985 Modern Classics
● intro. Malcolm Bradbury, 1985

Harry Sinclair Lewis interrupted his studies at Yale University to be a janitor at Upton Sinclair's (409) utopian Helicon Hall community in New Jersey, before working as a freelance journalist and selling plot ideas to Jack London (404). The sensational success of *Main Street* made Lewis's reputation, and in 1930 he became the first American to win the Nobel Prize for Literature (576). He struggled with alcoholism, however, and his last novels displayed a progressive decline. He died in Rome and his ashes were buried in his native Minnesota. 'He is the satirical realist who cannot but be drawn towards romanticism,' wrote Malcolm Bradbury, 'the hard critic of American life who still believes in its remote promise.'

Main Street
The Story of Carol Kennicott 1920

Carol Milford is an energetic, progressive university graduate who marries Dr Will Kennicott and moves to the small Minnesotan town of Gopher Prairie, where her attempts to modernize the main street are met with derision and disappointment. It is 'a fascinating book', wrote the *Daily News*. 'A novel which is as remarkable an achievement in town painting as Arnold Bennett's (36) early renderings of the Five Towns.'

Babbitt 1922

George Follansbee Babbitt is a 'god-fearing, hustling, successful, two-fisted Regular Guy' in the fictional Midwestern town of Zenith, who comes to resent the social pressure to conform to a small-town mentality. Babbitt 'is all of us Americans at forty-six', wrote Lewis, 'prosperous, but worried, wanting – passionately – to seize something more than motor cars and a house *before it's too late*'. H. G. Wells (26) called it 'one of the greatest novels I have read for a long time'.

1985
● —
Lewis dedicated *Babbitt* to Edith Wharton (401).

It Can't Happen Here
1935

2017
—
The Penguin edition of *It Can't Happen Here* was published on 20 January 2017, the same day as the inauguration of President Donald Trump.

Written soon after Hitler came to power in Germany, this dystopian novel imagines what would happen if a vain, outlandish, anti-immigrant demagogue were to run for the presidency of the USA and win. Berzelius 'Buzz' Windrip is the 'Professional Common Man', who promises poor, angry voters that he will make America proud and prosperous once more: as president, however, he institutes a totalitarian regime, policed by a ruthless paramilitary force. 'It is so crucial, so passionate, so honest, so vital,' declared the *New Yorker*, 'that only dogmatists, schismatics, and reactionaries will care to pick flaws in it.'

F. Scott Fitzgerald 1896 – 1940

In both his writing and his lifestyle, Francis Scott Fitzgerald defined the Jazz Age – a term he adopted for the glittering, irresponsible post-First World War wave of extravagance, in which he foresaw the inevitable crash and depression that were to follow. In 1917, he dropped out of Princeton University to join the army, and while stationed in Alabama he met the rich socialite Zelda Sayre (447). The phenomenal success of Fitzgerald's first two novels made him rich: he married Zelda and 'the prince and princess of their generation' – as Ring Lardner (416) described them – embarked on a non-stop spree of parties and hotels in America and Europe. 'There seemed to be some heavenly support beneath his shoulder blades,' Zelda later wrote in *Save Me the Waltz* (447), 'that lifted his feet from the ground in ecstatic suspension.' The couple had one daughter, Frances Scott 'Scottie' Fitzgerald, but their traumatic marriage was increasingly marred by pathological alcoholism, suspected affairs and Zelda's struggle with schizophrenia. The critics turned against Fitzgerald, and he resorted to hack writing to support their indulgent tastes and Zelda's medical bills. He drank heavily and scrounged work in Hollywood revising scripts, like 'a great sculptor who is hired to do a plumbing job', as Billy Wilder put it. Fitzgerald died of a heart attack at the age of 44, thinking his work had been forgotten. 'Poor son-of-a-bitch,' Dorothy Parker (419) is said to have muttered at his funeral, quoting *The Great Gatsby* (424). The last sentence of that novel is also inscribed on the gravestone that Fitzgerald shares with Zelda in Maryland: 'So we beat on, boats against the current, borne back ceaselessly into the past.'

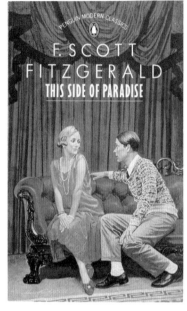

1963 Penguin Books
1986 Modern Classics
1996 Twentieth-Century Classics
ed. Patrick O'Donnell, 1996

This Side of Paradise 1920

With the end of the First World War, Fitzgerald found 'all Gods dead, all wars fought, all faiths in man shaken'. *This Side of Paradise* describes Amory Blaine, a Princeton student with literary aspirations, who faces moral disillusionment and falls in love. It combines conventional prose with free verse, streams of consciousness, and letters and poems. Fitzgerald used extracts from Zelda Sayre's (447) diaries for inspiration, and the book was such a commercial success it allowed the couple to marry.

Stories 1920 – 40

'It was an age of miracles, it was an age of art, it was an age of excess, and it was an age of satire.' Fitzgerald's first two story collections, *Flappers and Philosophers* (1920) and *Tales of the Jazz Age* (1922), defined and distilled the essence of 1920s New York. He published two further collections and dozens more tales in magazines. His stories include 'The Diamond as Big as the Ritz', a fairy tale of unlimited wealth; 'Bernice Bobs her Hair', about a fateful haircut; 'The Curious Case of Benjamin Button', about a man who lives his life backwards; and the experiences of Pat Hobby, a Hollywood hack writer. 'The Crack-Up' is an autobiographical piece that describes Fitzgerald's own nervous breakdown in 1936 and includes the famous line: 'in a real dark night of the soul it is always three o'clock in the morning'.

More JAZZ

Another Country by James Baldwin	493
Liveforever by Andrés Caicedo	563
The Mambo Kings Play Songs of Love by Oscar Hijuelos	548
Lady Sings the Blues by Billie Holiday	506
The Cowards by Josef Škvorecký	284

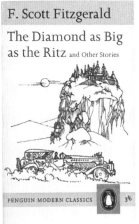

1962 Modern Classics
2001 Modern Classics
● —

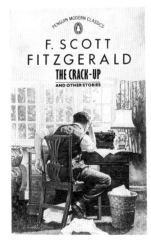

1965 Penguin Books
1986 Modern Classics
● —

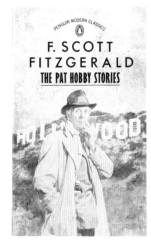

1967 Penguin Books
1986 Modern Classics
● intro. Arnold Gingrich, 1962

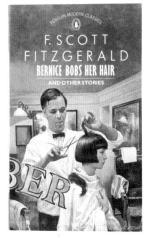

1968 Penguin Books
1986 Modern Classics
● —

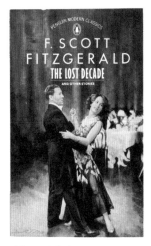

1968 Penguin Books
1986 Modern Classics
● —

1976 Penguin Books
1986 Modern Classics
● fwd. Scottie Fitzgerald Smith, 1973
pref. Matthew J. Bruccoli, 1973

Bits of Paradise comprises eleven stories by Scott Fitzgerald and ten by Zelda (447) that had originally been published under their joint signatures. *The Collected Short Stories* features the best of the previous Penguin story collections; it was expanded in 2010 under the title *Flappers and Philosophers*. *Jazz Age Stories* contains all the pieces in Fitzgerald's first two short-story collections.

1986 Penguin Books
1990 Twentieth-Century Classics
2010 Modern Classics
Flappers and Philosophers
intro. Sarah Churchwell, 2010

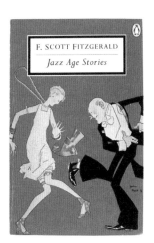

1999 Twentieth-Century Classics
● intro. Patrick O'Donnell, 1998

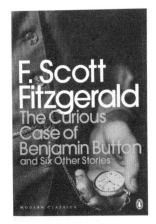

2008
—

The Beautiful and Damned 1922

Anthony Patch and his beautiful wife Gloria Gilbert drink heavily and dazzle the New York partygoers, but anxieties about money increasingly pave the way to their destruction. This quasi-autobiographical novel about the dark side of their hedonistic lifestyle made Scott and Zelda New York celebrities. 'Everyone must buy this book for the following aesthetic reasons,' wrote Zelda in a *New York Tribune* review: 'first, because I know where there is the cutest cloth-of-gold dress for only three hundred dollars in a store on Forty-second Street, and also, if enough people buy it, where there is a platinum ring with a complete circlet, and also, if loads of people buy it, my husband needs a new winter overcoat.'

1966 Penguin Books
<u>**1986**</u> Modern Classics
2004 Modern Classics
intro. Geoff Dyer, 2004

1950 Penguin Books
<u>**1961**</u> Modern Classics
1990 Twentieth-Century Classics
intro. Tony Tanner, 1990
—
Fitzgerald considered various working titles, including *Among Ash-Heaps and Millionaires*, *The Gold-Hatted Gatsby*, *The High-Bouncing Lover* and *Trimalchio in West Egg*. His final choice, *The Great Gatsby*, may have been inspired by Alain-Fournier's *Le Grand Meaulnes* (173).

The Great Gatsby 1925

Fitzgerald wanted 'to write something *new* – something extraordinary and beautiful and simple and intricately patterned'. The result was this novel about the nouveau riche bootlegger Jay Gatsby, who throws lavish Long Island parties that he doesn't attend. Gatsby obsesses about his former lover, the beautiful Daisy Buchanan, who lives across the bay in East Egg. The story takes place in the summer of 1922 and doubles as both a dazzling portrait of the Prohibition era and a cautionary tale about the corruptibility of the American Dream. Despite early praise from Edith Wharton (401), Willa Cather (414) and T. S. Eliot (11), who called the novel 'the first step American fiction has taken since Henry James (397)', it was widely snubbed by critics and sold poorly. Its reputation began to rise after Fitzgerald's death, when it was included as part of the US Armed Services Editions that circulated during the Second World War. In 1960, the *New York Times* said it was 'probably safe now to say that it is a classic of twentieth-century American fiction', and in 2000 the *Sunday Times* declared it 'perhaps the supreme American novel'.

Tender is the Night
A Romance 1934

'I want to give a really *bad* party. I mean it. I want to give a party where there's a brawl and seductions and people going home with their feelings hurt and women passed out in the cabinet de toilette. You wait and see.' Dick Diver is an alcoholic psychiatrist who falls in love with Nicole Warren, one of his patients. Their fragile relationship buckles, however, when Diver meets the film star Rosemary Hoyt. Fitzgerald completed *Tender is the Night* while Zelda was committed to a mental institution in Baltimore, Maryland, after he himself had had an affair with the Hollywood actress Lois Moran. He considered the book his greatest work. The narrative is told through flashbacks that are out of chronological order; the philosopher Slavoj Žižek has used the novel to illustrate the non-linear nature of experience.

1955 Penguin Books
<u>**1963**</u> Modern Classics
● ed. Malcolm Cowley (448), 1951
1998 Twentieth-Century Classics
ed. Arnold Goldman, 1982–6
intro. Richard Godden, 1998

Fitzgerald took his title from John Keats's 'Ode to a Nightingale'.

The Lost Generation

'You are all a lost generation,' said Gertrude Stein (410) to Ernest Hemingway (428), who used the line as an epigraph to his novel *The Sun Also Rises* (1926). Stein had apparently heard a French mechanic using the phrase *génération perdue* while her car was being serviced. The term came to apply to a group of young American writers, disillusioned by the First World War, adrift without moral bearings in bohemian Paris. As well as Hemingway and Stein, Lost Generation writers included F. Scott Fitzgerald (422), John Dos Passos (426), Ezra Pound (61), William Faulkner (433) and Hart Crane. Malcolm Cowley, a member of the Lost Generation himself, wrote a definitive account of the group in *Exile's Return* (448).

The Last Tycoon pub. 1941

Monroe Stahr is the last Hollywood producer with a sense of the romance of cinema; for him, the studio lot is 'thirty acres of fairyland' rather than a factory floor. Fitzgerald modelled Stahr on the legendary producer Irving Thalberg at MGM. Fitzgerald left the manuscript unfinished; it was edited by his friend, the literary critic Edmund Wilson, and published the year after his death. The 1976 film adaptation was scripted by Harold Pinter and Robert De Niro starred as Stahr.

1960 Penguin Books
1965 Penguin Books
1986 Modern Classics
ed. Edmund Wilson, 1941

A Life in Letters 1907–40

These letters chronicle Fitzgerald's artistic and emotional development as he transformed from hard-drinking playboy to frustrated writer and desperate husband. In the last year of his life, he wrote to his daughter: 'I wish now I'd never relaxed or looked back – but said at the end of *The Great Gatsby* (424): "I've found my line – from now on this comes first. This is my immediate duty – without this I am nothing."' 'He was better than he knew,' wrote the *New York Times* after his death, 'for in fact and in the literary sense he invented a "generation".'

1998
● ed. Matthew J. Bruccoli & Judith S. Baughman, 1995

Nicola Sacco 1891–1927

Sacco was born in southern Italy and worked in his father's vineyard before emigrating to the USA. He worked in a shoe factory in Milford, Massachusetts, and became a dedicated anarchist. In 1920, he was charged with murdering a paymaster and his guard in Braintree, Massachusetts. He was found guilty, and seven years later he was electrocuted in Boston's Charlestown State Prison.

Bartolomeo Vanzetti 1888–1927

Vanzetti was born in northern Italy and emigrated to the USA after the death of his mother. He lived in New York and then worked as a labourer in various cities in eastern Massachusetts. He became an anarchist in 1912 and was arrested along with Sacco; he was charged with the Braintree murders and also an attempted holdup in Bridgewater. He was electrocuted a few moments after his friend.

The Letters of Sacco and Vanzetti

1921–7, pub. 1928

The inquiry into the Sacco and Vanzetti case became a worldwide *cause célèbre*. Ambiguous testimonies, conflicting ballistics evidence and prejudicial pre-trial statements raised suspicions of anti-immigrant and anti-anarchist bias. A privately funded 'Sacco and Vanzetti Defense Committee' was established and protests held in cities across the USA, Europe and the rest of the world, with support from writers including Theodore Dreiser (407), Katherine Anne Porter (427) and Upton Sinclair (409). This collection of Sacco's and Vanzetti's letters sheds light on the most famous and controversial criminal case in American judicial history. 'Never in our full life could we hope to do such work for tolerance, for joostice, for man's onderstanding of man as now we do by accident,' said Vanzetti. 'Our words – our lives – our pains – nothing! The taking of our lives – lives of a good shoemaker and a poor fish-peddler – all! That last moment belongs to us – that agony is our triumph.'

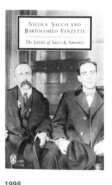

1998
● ed. Marion Denman Frankfurter & Gardner Jackson, 1928
intro. Richard Polenberg, 1997
—
On 23 August 1977, 50 years after the executions of Sacco and Vanzetti, Massachusetts Governor Michael Dukakis issued a proclamation that they had been unfairly tried and convicted and that 'any stigma and disgrace should be forever removed from the names of Nicola Sacco and Bartolomeo Vanzetti'.

John Dos Passos 1896–1970

John Roderigo Dos Passos was born in Chicago, the son of a half-Portuguese lawyer. He travelled around Europe as a child before studying at Harvard University, where he met e e cummings (427). In the First World War he served as a volunteer ambulance driver and he then became a freelance correspondent in Europe and the Middle East before devoting himself to writing experimental epics about American life. 'Dos Passos has invented only one thing,' wrote Jean-Paul Sartre (185), 'an art of storytelling. But that is enough to create a universe.' He was elected to the American Academy of Arts and Letters in 1947, succeeding to Willa Cather's (414) chair, and spent his last years on his farm in Virginia, writing historical works about the US Founding Fathers.

1987
intro. Jay McInerney, 1986

Three Soldiers 1921

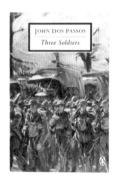

1990
•—

Dos Passos set out to write this novel like a 'doctor who comes in with his sharp and sterile instruments to lance the focuses of dead matter'. It follows three First World War soldiers – Andrews, a young composer; Chrisfield, a farm-boy from Indiana; and Fuselli, a city clerk – as they are inevitably crushed by the mechanization and regimentation of war. 'No war story can be written in the United States without challenging comparison with it,' said the critic H. L. Mencken. '[…] It changed the whole tone of American opinion about the war.'

Manhattan Transfer 1925

Published the same year as The Great Gatsby (424), this novel is a modernist (11) meditation on New York City in the early 1920s told through an experimental montage of fact and fiction. The multiple overlapping characters and stories present the city as a merciless machine filled with motion, bright lights and tragedy. 'It is the best modern book about New York,' said D. H. Lawrence (50). 'Just to rub it in,' said Sinclair Lewis (421), 'I regard Manhattan Transfer as more important in every way than anything by Gertrude Stein (410) or Marcel Proust (166) or even the great white boar, Mr. Joyce's Ulysses (10).'

U.S.A.

The 42nd Parallel, Nineteen Nineteen, The Big Money
1930–36

1966
—
U.S.A. was first published in a single volume in 1938.

Dos Passos' masterpiece presents a sweeping portrait of America in the first three decades of the 20th century, culminating with the execution of Nicola Sacco and Bartolomeo Vanzetti (425) in 1927 and the onset of the Great Depression in 1929. The three volumes in the trilogy are collages of different narrative modes: conventional stories following twelve overlapping fictional characters; 'newsreel' montages of clippings, articles and song lyrics; 'camera eye' fragments of poetic stream-of-consciousness autobiography; and miniature biographies of historical figures such as Woodrow Wilson, Thomas Edison, Henry Ford, Frank Lloyd Wright and William Randolph Hearst. Gradually these numerous elements cohere into a bleak anti-epic of American society and the country's political and economic prospects. 'Those three volumes of U.S.A. make up the idea of a "Great American Novel",' said Norman Mailer (496).

1971
● intro. e e cummings, 1922
—
While in prison, Cummings
wrote a letter to President
Woodrow Wilson, who
eventually secured his release.
He printed their exchange as
an introduction to his novel.

e e cummings 1894 – 1962

Edward Estlin Cummings, the avant-garde poet and painter, wrote thousands of poems in his lifetime using distinctive songlike rhythms, idiosyncratic grammar and unusual visual patterning. He preferred to write his own name with lower-case initials and no full stops. 'He established the poem as a visual object,' wrote the critic Jenny Penberthy. 'He revealed, by his x-ray probings, the faceted possibilities of the single word; and like such prose writers as Vladimir Nabokov (304) and Tom Stoppard, he promoted sheer playfulness with language.'

The Enormous Room 1922

In 1917, Cummings travelled to France as a volunteer ambulance driver. When he arrived, however, there was a miscommunication which led to his confinement for several months in a French concentration camp at La Ferté. He was 'entombed within the drooling, greenish walls' of a single enormous room, which he shared with 30 other detainees. This exuberant modernist (11) novel, his first book, describes their abject chores, the vile food, the brutal guards and his eccentric fellow prisoners. 'The reading is as sharp as being in prison,' said T. E. Lawrence (74). '[…] He uses some new alloys of words, and has rare passages as iridescent as decay in meat. The book is modern in feeling and new-world in pedigree, and all the more exciting on this side in consequence. It seems to me so much the best American war-period book.'

Katherine Anne Porter 1890 – 1980

Callie Russell Porter was born in Texas, and claimed to be a distant relation of O. Henry (409). Porter was two years old when her mother died and she was raised by her paternal grandmother, Catherine Anne Porter, whose name she adopted. She worked as an actress, a singer and a journalist before almost dying in the 1918 flu pandemic; her hair remained white for the rest of her life. She then lived in Mexico, Europe and New York, teaching at a number of universities and divorcing four husbands. She wrote fewer than 30 stories and only one novel, *Ship of Fools* (1962), which she published at the age of 72. Robert Penn Warren (489), however, said that 'she belongs to the relatively small group of writers […] who have done serious, consistent, original, and vital work in the form of short fiction – the group which would include James Joyce (8), Katherine Mansfield (388), Sherwood Anderson (420), and Ernest Hemingway (428).' Her *Collected Stories* won both a Pulitzer Prize for Fiction and the National Book Award in 1966, and she was awarded the Academy of Arts and Letters Gold Medal in 1967.

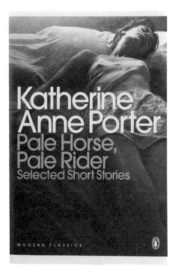

2011
ed. Sarah Churchwell

Pale Horse, Pale Rider Selected Short Stories 1922 – 39

This selection of Porter's best and most haunting stories ranges from revolutionary Mexico to rural Ireland, but most are set in the Deep South of her childhood and many feature her semi-autobiographical protagonist Miranda Gay. The title story takes place inside the fevered mind of Miranda during the 1918 flu pandemic, her childhood memories mingling with fears for her fiancé on his way to war. Porter 'solves the essential problem', wrote V. S. Pritchett (110): 'how to satisfy exhaustively in writing briefly'.

Ernest Hemingway 1899–1961

Ernest Miller Hemingway was born in Oak Park, a suburb of Chicago. In 1917, he worked as a junior reporter for the *Kansas City Star*, where the style guide specified: 'Use short sentences. Use short first paragraphs. Use vigorous English. Be positive, not negative.' Keen to join the First World War, he volunteered aged eighteen as an ambulance driver in Italy and was severely wounded, an experience he later recalled as the moment he 'ceased to be hard-boiled'. In the 1920s, he lived in Paris as a correspondent for the *Toronto Star*, where he met fellow expatriates Ford Madox Ford (46), John Dos Passos (426), Ezra Pound (61), James Joyce (8) and Gertrude Stein (410), who became godmother to his son Jack. Along with F. Scott Fitzgerald (422), Hemingway emerged as the leading writer of the Lost Generation (425). He had a compulsion for seeking out violence and confronting death, whether it was watching bullfights, hunting big game, deep-sea fishing or war reporting. In his later years, he divided his time between Key West in Florida and Cuba, where he wrote *The Old Man and the Sea* (1952), the novel that secured him the Nobel Prize for Literature (576) in 1954. He had four wives and three sons; and in 1961 he took his own life with a shotgun, as his father had done three decades earlier. 'Though there were many imitators,' wrote John Wain (124), 'there was never truly a "School of Hemingway", because the standard he set was too severe.'

1935 Penguin Books
1961 Modern Classics
• —
Hemingway gave a copy of *A Farewell to Arms* to James Joyce (8), in which he amended the text by hand, reinstating swear words that had been censored from the published edition. The Penguin edition of *A Farewell to Arms* was one of the very first batch of ten Penguin titles published in July 1935: it was number two after *Ariel* by André Maurois.

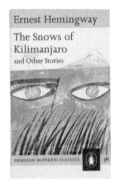

1963
• —
Hemingway's Modern Classics covers were designed by the artist and illustrator Paul Hogarth, who also illustrated covers for the New Penguin Shakespeare series and the novels of Graham Greene (88). His illustration for the 1962 Penguin edition of George Orwell's *Homage to Catalonia* (83) featured a self-portrait as a republican volunteer.

The Snows of Kilimanjaro
and Other Stories 1923–36

'A few things I have found to be true,' said Hemingway. 'If you leave out important things or events that you know about, the story is strengthened. If you leave or skip something because you do not know it, the story will be worthless.' In these early stories, Hemingway developed his terse, tough style, stripping narrative to the bone and expressing only 'the real thing, the sequence of motion and fact'. The title story is based on an East African safari he made in 1933. Most of the other stories in this volume were collected as *In Our Time* in 1925; several feature Nick Adams, a near self-portrait of a young man shaped by the First World War.

A Farewell to Arms 1929

'Hard, almost metallic,' was Arnold Bennett's (36) view of Hemingway's trademark style, 'glittering, blinding by the reflections of its hard surface, utterly free of sentimentality.' Hemingway applies his spare prose to this story of a wartime love affair, based on his own experiences in Italy. It followed the success of his first novel, *The Sun Also Rises* (1926), a disillusioned roman-à-clef set during fiesta time in Pamplona. Hemingway wrote at least 39 different endings to *A Farewell to Arms* before he was satisfied.

The Short Happy Life of Francis Macomber
and Other Stories 1930–36

The title story is about a rich American and his wife on safari in East Africa. Most of the other stories in this volume were collected in *Winner Takes Nothing* (1933), including 'The Light of the World', one of Hemingway's favourites, and 'A Clean, Well-Lighted Place', which James Joyce (8) described as 'one of the best short stories ever written'. 'A Natural History of the Dead' was first published as part of *Death in the Afternoon* (1932), Hemingway's lyrical treatise on the art of bullfighting.

1963
• —

1955 Penguin Books
1963 Modern Classics
● —

To Have and Have Not 1937

Hemingway wrote this novella while sailing around the Caribbean on his boat *Pilar*. It is the story of a poor fishing captain from Key West, Florida, who turns to smuggling during the Depression era. 'For Mr. Hemingway, toughness is all,' wrote the *Times Literary Supplement*, 'and his new novel is further proof of his ability to give us the anatomy of toughness.'

For Whom the Bell Tolls 1940

Hemingway's most famous novel is based on his experiences as a reporter during the Spanish Civil War. It is the story of Robert Jordan, an American volunteer in a guerrilla unit, who falls in love with a young Spanish woman called María. After sex, Jordan famously asks, 'Did thee feel the earth move?' The novel's 'contrapuntal structure' was apparently inspired by Hemingway's mother's cello lessons. 'This is the best book Ernest Hemingway has written, the fullest, the deepest, the truest,' said the *New York Times* reviewer. 'It will, I think, be one of the major novels in American literature.'

1955 Penguin Books
1961 Modern Classics
● —

Stephen Vincent Benét 1898 – 1943

Benét was born in Bethlehem, Pennsylvania, the son of an army officer. He studied at Yale University, where he met Thornton Wilder (436) and published three volumes of poetry, submitting the third in lieu of a thesis. He wrote poems, novels and short stories. He won the O. Henry (409) Award three times, and twice won the Pulitzer Prize for Poetry: for his American Civil War epic *John Brown's Body* (1928) – described by the *New York Times* as 'an American *Iliad*' – and posthumously for his unfinished *Western Star* (pub. 1943), about the settlement of the American West. When Benét died, President Franklin D. Roosevelt said that 'the world of letters has lost one of its most commanding figures'.

The Devil and Daniel Webster
and Other Writings 1923 – 43

This collection gathers together stories, poems and essays. The title story is a comic folktale, in which the famous 19th-century statesman defends a New Hampshire farmer who sells his soul to the Devil; it was adapted as a play, an opera and an Academy Award-winning film. Also included is the post-apocalyptic story 'By the Waters of Babylon' and selections from *John Brown's Body* and *Western Star*.

1999
● ed. Townsend Ludington

Anaïs Nin 1903–1977

Angela Anaïs Juana Antolina Rosa Edelmira Nin y Culmell was born in Paris to Cuban parents, both musicians, who separated when she was two years old. She lived with her mother in Paris and then Barcelona, moving to New York at the age of eleven. She worked as an artist's model before marrying her first husband, the banker Hugh Guiler, in Havana in 1923. The next year they moved to Paris, where they lived for fifteen years. Nin began writing, trained as a flamenco dancer and studied psychoanalysis under Otto Rank, with whom she had an affair. At the outbreak of the Second World War, Nin and Guiler returned to New York, where Nin briefly became a psychoanalyst, occasionally having sex with her patients on the couch. In 1947, she met the actor Rupert Pole in an elevator; he was sixteen years her junior. They married at Quartzsite, Arizona, in 1955, while Nin was still married to Guiler. Nin then established what she called a 'bicoastal trapeze', with husbands in both New York and Los Angeles. 'I tell so many lies I have to write them down and keep them in the lie box so I can keep them straight,' she explained. Through her diaries, short stories and novels, Nin attempted 'the quest of the self through the intricate maze of modern confusion'.

1978 Penguin Books
1983 King Penguin
1986 Modern Classics
● ill. Ian Hugo "[Hugh Guiler]", 1944
— i.e., her first husband

Journal of a Wife
The Early Diary, 1923–1927 pub. 1983

Nin kept diaries obsessively, for 60 years, starting at the age of eleven. They were her crucible and her confidante, where she experimented with language, shared her most intimate thoughts and analysed private emotions. Later they acted as a sourcebook for her fiction. In the sixties and seventies, Nin edited and published most of her diaries (1931–74) in seven large volumes. Her early diary (1914–31) was subsequently published in four volumes; this edition reprints the third volume, covering Nin's marriage to Hugh Guiler and their life in New York and Paris.

The Early Diary, 1927–1931 pub. 1986

This is the fourth and final instalment of Nin's early diary, describing life in Paris in her mid-twenties, reading Proust (166) and Colette (170), flirting with friends, and obsessing over the American writer John Erskine. She describes the moment she decided to turn to her diary for inspiration. 'Why not put my Journal into a book?' she asks. 'I am tired of writing just for myself. […] I know I could make others cry and make them infinitely, desperately, divinely alive.'

Henry and June
from the Unexpurgated Diary
1931–2, pub. 1986

Nin appointed her second husband Rupert Pole her literary executor, and after her death he began publishing a series of her 'unexpurgated' diaries. This volume describes Nin's intense relationship with Henry Miller (451) and his magnetic wife June. Nin is mesmerized by Miller's literary prowess and June's physical attractions, and embarks on intense friendships with both. The novelist Alice Walker calls it 'a very erotic book and profoundly liberating'.

Under a Glass Bell 1938–48, pub. 1948, rev. 1957

This volume of short stories was the publication that established Nin's literary reputation, especially after the critic Edmund Wilson reviewed it in the New Yorker. 'The pieces in this collection belong to a peculiar genre sometimes cultivated by the late Virginia Woolf (42),' he wrote. 'They are half short stories, half dreams, and they mix a sometimes exquisite poetry with a homely realistic observation. They take place in a special world, a world of feminine perception and fancy.'

1993
● ed. Rupert Pole, 1983
pref. Joaquín Nin-Culmell, 1983
—
Joaquín Nin-Culmell, Nin's brother, provided a preface for this volume. He described Hugh Guiler as 'a loving husband and an unswerving supporter'.

1995
● ed. Rupert Pole, 1986
pref. Joaquín Nin-Culmell, 1986

1990 Penguin Books
1992 Twentieth-Century Classics
ed. Rupert Pole, 1986

Delta of Venus 1940s, pub. 1977

In the 1940s, Nin was commissioned to write erotica for an anonymous American client known simply as 'the collector'. She was paid $1 a page and instructed to leave out poetic language and to concentrate on graphic, sexually explicit scenarios. Instead, Nin produced exquisite, literary stories that distil the essence of feminine sexuality. 'I had a feeling,' she wrote in her diary, 'that Pandora's box contained the mysteries of woman's sensuality, so different from man's and for which man's language was inadequate.' She later collected these stories in the bestselling *Delta of Venus* and *Little Birds*.

1990 Penguin Books
1992 Twentieth-Century Classics
—

Little Birds

1940s, pub. 1979

The thirteen short stories in this volume capture poignant moments of sexual awakening and fulfilment, and present lust and obsession as fundamental facets of the human condition. The 'little birds' of the title story are used by an exhibitionist to attract young schoolgirls to his attic.

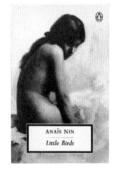

1990 Penguin Books
1992 Twentieth-Century Classics
—

A Spy in the House of Love 1954

In 1950s New York, Sabina pursues pleasure for pleasure's sake. She wears extravagant clothes and conducts affairs with four men simultaneously, playing a dangerous game involving desire and deception.

1973 Penguin Books
1982 King Penguin
1985 Modern Classics
—

Children of the Albatross

1959

When dreamy, 16-year-old Djuna wins a scholarship to a ballet school in Paris, she falls in with the artists and musicians of Montmartre and discovers love for the first time. 'She is a writer of real force,' said Lawrence Durrell. '[…] I have always thought of her as belonging to the great subjective-feminine tradition (Virginia Woolf (42), Djuna Barnes, Anna Kavan (154)) which has tried to give us a poetic notation of the female artist's world.'

1993
• —

Seduction of the Minotaur 1961

Lillian, a jazz pianist at the Black Pearl club in Mexico, recalls former lovers in Paris, her marriage in New York and the children she has left behind. The novel is based on a trip Nin made to Acapulco in 1947, recorded in her diary.

1993
• —

In Favour of the Sensitive Man and Other Essays

1965–76, pub. 1976

This collection of essays ranges from subjects such as the 'New Woman' and feminism to thoughts on the writing process, literary and film criticism and descriptions of Nin's exotic travels.

1992
• —

A Woman Speaks
The Lectures, Seminars and Interviews of Anaïs Nin

1966–73, pub. 1975

This volume presents the edited transcripts of public talks and interviews delivered by Nin. She speaks on subjects such as femininity and feminism, dreams and the psyche, art and alienation, and describes keeping a diary as 'a moment of stopping life in order to become aware of it'.

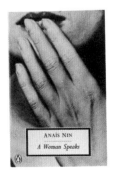

1992
• ed. Evelyn J. Hinz, 1975

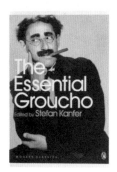

2000 Penguin Books
2008 Modern Classics
ed. Stefan Kanfer, 2000

Groucho Marx 1890–1977

'No, Groucho is not my real name,' explained Groucho, 'I'm just breaking it in for a friend.' Julius Henry Marx was born above a butcher's shop in New York City, the son of German Jewish immigrants. Encouraged by their mother, Julius and three of his brothers formed an irreverent act that took the vaudeville circuit and then Hollywood by storm. Each brother adopted a distinctive persona: Harpo wore a red wig and never spoke; Chico became an Italian immigrant; Zeppo played the juvenile lead; and Groucho wore a grease-paint moustache, champed a fat cigar and did most of the talking. Groucho also had a successful solo career, appearing in other films and hosting the quiz show *You Bet Your Life* in the fifties.

The Essential Groucho
Writings by, for and about Groucho Marx 1924–65

This wisecracking anthology includes excerpts from the brothers' first Broadway musical, *I'll Say She Is!* (1924), and from the films *Monkey Business* (1931), *Duck Soup* (1933), *A Night at the Opera* (1935) and *A Day at the Races* (1937). It also features a selection of Groucho's articles and letters, and an array of one-liners, such as: 'If you want to see a comic strip, you should see me in the shower.'

Anita Loos 1888–1981

Corinne Anita Loos was born in California. She began writing movie scripts when she was twelve, and became the first female staff scriptwriter in Hollywood at the age of 24. As well as dozens of screenplays, she produced novels, plays, stage adaptations of Colette's novellas *Gigi* (172) and *Chéri* (171), and two volumes of memoirs: *A Girl Like I* (1966) and *Kiss Hollywood Good-by* (1974).

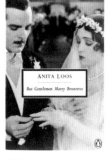

1989 Penguin Books
1992 Twentieth-Century Classics
1998 Twentieth-Century Classics *combined volume*
● ill. Ralph Barton, 1925–7
intro. Anita Loos, 1963
intro. Regina Barreca, 1998

Gentlemen Prefer Blondes
But Gentlemen Marry Brunettes 1925–7

In *Gentlemen Prefer Blondes* (1925), the 'illuminating diary of a professional lady', the flapper Lorelei Lee describes her outrageous adventures as she hunts for a millionaire husband. Her diary is riddled with spelling and grammatical mistakes: 'kissing your hand may make you feel very very good but a diamond and safire bracelet lasts forever,' she explains. Edith Wharton (401) described Loos's satire of the Jazz Age as 'the great American novel'. In the sequel, But *Gentlemen Marry Brunettes* (1927), Lorelei tells the life story of her friend Dorothy.

1985
● pref. Thomas Mann, 1931

Ludwig Lewisohn 1883–1955

Lewisohn was born into a German Jewish family in Berlin, but moved to the USA as a child; he grew up in Charleston, South Carolina. As well as teaching literature at Wisconsin, Ohio State and Brandeis universities, he worked as an editor for the *Nation* and *New Palestine* and wrote more than 30 books, including novels, memoirs, literary criticism, and translations of Jakob Wassermann (249) and Franz Werfel (273). He was married three times; his first marriage, to Mary Arnold, inspired *The Case of Mr Crump*.

The Case of Mr Crump 1926

'We have here, then, a novelistic document of life, of the *inferno* of a marriage,' wrote Thomas Mann (245) in his preface. 'That word exhausts the book's horrifying and infuriating subject matter – a marriage that should never have been contracted.' Herbert Crump finds himself crushed by his marriage to the hostile and domineering Anne. Lewisohn was unable to publish the book in the USA for fear of a libel suit until 1947.

William Faulkner 1897–1962

William Cuthbert Faulkner was raised in Oxford, Mississippi, where he lived
for most of his life. In 1925, he met Sherwood Anderson (420), who encouraged
him to write about his home town. Faulkner then embarked on a sequence of
stories set in the 'apocryphal county' of Yoknapatawpha in northern Mississippi.
Yoknapatawpha is based closely on his own native Lafayette County, with a
recognizable landscape of cabins, farms, decaying mansions and brush country:
a parallel universe with characters and locations that recur in his books. As well
as novels, he wrote Hollywood screenplays, including the 1946 adaptation of
The Big Sleep (461). When he won the Nobel Prize for Literature (576) in 1949,
he donated the prize money 'to establish a fund to support and encourage
new fiction writers'. This led to the PEN/Faulkner Award for Fiction, which
has been won by Walter Abish (275), Don DeLillo (537), E. L. Doctorow (538) and
John Updike (514). Faulkner fell from a horse in 1962 and died a month later.

1938 Penguin Books
1970 Modern Classics
● —
Faulkner wrote *Soldiers' Pay*
in New Orleans, where he lived
on the ground floor of a house
on Pirate's Alley. His rooms
are now the site of Faulkner
House Books – 'America's
most charming book store'
– and the headquarters of the
Pirate's Alley Faulkner Society.

Southern Gothic

The term 'Southern Gothic'
was first used by the critic
Ellen Glasgow in 1935 to
describe the works of Erskine
Caldwell and William Faulkner.
Gothic fiction employs
terror, suspense and haunting
locations, and the subgenre
of Southern Gothic sets these
techniques among the derelict
buildings, rotting plantations
and grotesque characters
of the Deep South. After the
American Civil War and the
collapse of the Confederacy
in 1865, the South experienced
widespread poverty and
enduring bitterness over
the issue of slavery. These
problems were expressed
by writers through stories
of warped communities,
sinister situations and violent
behaviour. Authors associated
with Southern Gothic writing
include Dorothy Allison (549),
Truman Capote (463), Thomas
Cullinan (528), William
Faulkner, Carson McCullers
(453), Flannery O'Connor
and Tennessee Williams (455).
When Eudora Welty (457)
heard the term, she exclaimed,
'They better not call me that!'

Soldiers' Pay 1926

Faulkner's first published novel describes a wounded
First World War soldier returning to his home in
the South. Sherwood Anderson (420) helped to see it
published. 'Faulkner is the coming man,' wrote Arnold Bennett (36) at the
time. 'He has an inexhaustible invention, powerful imagination, a wondrous
gift of characterization, a finished skill in dialogue; and he writes, generally,
like an angel. […] He has in him the elements of real greatness.'

The Sound and the Fury

1929

The Sound and the Fury is narrated by
different members of the disintegrating
Compson family of former Southern
aristocrats. The first section is a stream
of consciousness inside the head of
Benjy Compson, a 33-year-old with
learning difficulties. His account
jumps in time and makes unexplained
connections which are only gradually
and partially clarified in the subsequent
sections narrated by his brothers
Quentin and Jason. The title of this
experimental, modernist (11) novel
is taken from Macbeth's description
of life as 'a tale / Told by an idiot,
full of sound and fury, / Signifying
nothing'. 'Proust's (166) fictional technique *should
have been* Faulkner's,' wrote Jean-Paul Sartre (185).
'But Faulkner is a lost man, and it is because he
feels lost that he takes risks and pursues his thought
to its uttermost consequences.'

1964
● intro. Richard Hughes (86),
1954
—
The Sound and the Fury is
set in Jefferson, the county
town of Yoknapatawpha,
which resembles Faulkner's
native Oxford, Mississippi.

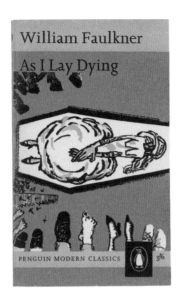

1963
• —

As I Lay Dying 1930

In 1929, the year of his marriage, Faulkner took a job as a coal-heaver on night work at the local power station and wrote *As I Lay Dying* over the course of six summer weeks, between the hours of midnight and 4 a.m. This grotesquely humorous Southern Gothic (433) novel tells the story of the death of old Addie Bundren and her dying wish to be buried in her native town of Jefferson. Her family's eventful journey with the coffin is narrated by fifteen different characters over 59 chapters, including Addie herself after she has died.

Collected Stories

1930–48, pub. 1951

1985 Penguin Books
1989 Twentieth-Century Classics
• —

Faulkner selected and assembled this collection of 42 stories which won the National Book Award in 1951. He arranged the tales under six themed headings: 'The Country', 'The Village', 'The Wilderness', 'The Wasteland', 'The Middle Ground' and 'Beyond'. 'If you imagine Huckleberry Finn living in the House of Usher and telling stories while the walls crumble about him,' wrote Malcolm Cowley (448), 'that will give you the double quality of Faulkner's work at its best.'

Light in August 1932

1960 Penguin Books
1973 Modern Classics
• —

Faulkner interweaves the stories of Joe Christmas, a victim of racial prejudice, and the pregnant Lena Grove, using flashbacks to reveal the connections between their lives. The narrative contains biblical parallels and revolves around a house fire, the flames of which are visible for miles around. 'Unquestionably *Light in August* is a good book,' wrote Compton Mackenzie (61); 'possibly it is a great book.'

Sanctuary 1931

1953 Penguin Books
1962 Modern Classics
• —

Faulkner claimed to have written this sensationalist novel purely in order to make money. It tells the horrifying story of the rape and abduction of Temple Drake, a Mississippi college girl, during the Prohibition era. André Malraux (184) called *Sanctuary* 'the intrusion of Greek tragedy into the detective story', in an article that was credited – in Malraux's obituary in *The Times* – with propelling Faulkner 'from the obscurity of the Deep South to the Nobel Prize for Literature (576)'.

The Unvanquished

1934–8, pub. 1938

1955 Penguin Books
1970 Modern Classics
• —

Originally published as a sequence of seven short stories, *The Unvanquished* is a prequel to Faulkner's first Yoknapatawpha novel, *Sartoris* (1929). Set during the American Civil War, it returns to the Sartoris family: its central character, Colonel Sartoris, is modelled on Faulkner's namesake, his great-grandfather Colonel William Falkner, a Confederate hero. 'William Faulkner has been compared with Dostoevsky,' wrote Jorge Luis Borges (572). 'The comparison is not unjust, but the world of Faulkner is so physical, so carnal, that next to Colonel Bayard Sartoris or Temple Drake that explanatory homicide Raskolnikov is as flimsy, as delicate, as one of Racine's princes.'

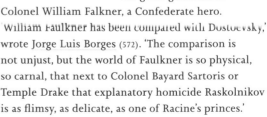

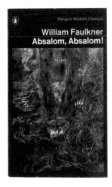

1971

● —

The 1983 *Guinness Book of World Records* cited *Absalom, Absalom!* as having the 'longest sentence in literature'. The sentence is in the sixth chapter: it has 1,288 words and goes on for three pages in the 1971 Penguin edition. Purists might argue, however, that *Guinness World Records* overlooked Molly Bloom's soliloquy in *Ulysses* (10), which has a 3,687-word sentence.

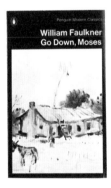

1960 Penguin Books
1970 Modern Classics
● —

1960 Penguin Books
1970 Modern Classics
● —

Absalom, Absalom!

1936

Quentin Compson from *The Sound and the Fury* (433) discusses with his Harvard room-mate the story of Thomas Sutpen, a 19th-century plantation owner. Gradually the details of Sutpen's life emerge: he dreamt of founding a dynasty, but his bigoted values led to ruin. The critic Walter Allen called *Absalom, Absalom!* 'the novel in which Faulkner most profoundly and completely says what he has to say about the South and the human condition'. James Baldwin (492) criticized Faulkner's racial politics in *Nobody Knows My Name* (493).

Go Down, Moses
and Other Stories

1940 – 42, pub. 1942

These seven interrelated stories are set in Yoknapatawpha County in the mid-19th century, and they examine both the curse of slavery in the South and the universal human urge to exploit others. The centrepiece is 'The Bear', which features a hunter called Boon Hogganbeck and a monstrously large bear known as Old Ben. 'He has been more willing perhaps than any other artist,' wrote Ralph Ellison (458) 'to start with the stereotype, accept it as true, and then seek out the human truth which it hides.'

Requiem for a Nun

1951

This sequel to *Sanctuary* (434) is set eight years later. Now married with a child, Temple Drake is still dealing with her traumatic past. The narrative is presented as a play script alternating with passages about the history of Yoknapatawpha County. It includes the famous line: 'The past is never dead. It's not even past.'

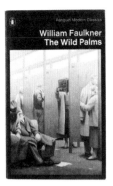

1961 Penguin Books
1975 Modern Classics
● —

The Wild Palms 1939

The novel contains two entirely distinct stories. *The Wild Palms* is about a man and a woman and a botched abortion; *Old Man* is about a man and woman and a dramatic birth. Faulkner compares and contrasts the narratives by alternating chapters between the stories. He wanted to call the combined book *If I Forget Thee, Jerusalem.*

1960 Penguin Books
1970 Modern Classics
● —

Intruder in the Dust 1948

The African American farmer Lucas Beauchamp – the protagonist of one of the stories in *Go Down, Moses* – is accused of murdering a white man. He defends his innocence with the help of a group of black and white teenagers and a spinster from a long-established Southern family. 'Intruder is marvelously funny,' wrote Eudora Welty (457). 'Faulkner's veracity and accuracy about the world around keeps the comic thread from ever being lost or fouled [...] His stories aren't decked out in humor, but the humor is born in them, as much their blood and bones as the passion and poetry.'

1970 Penguin Books
1976 Modern Classics
● —

The Reivers
A Reminiscence 1962

Faulkner finished his career with this picaresque novel about Boon Hogganbeck's road trip to Memphis to woo Miss Corrie, a prostitute. 'It easily surpasses Somerville and Ross or Surtees,' wrote V. S. Pritchett (110): 'it matches Mark Twain.' *The Reivers* was posthumously awarded the Pulitzer Prize for Fiction in 1963.

Thornton Wilder 1897–1975

Thornton Niven Wilder was born in Wisconsin and raised in Hong Kong, where his father was consul general. He taught at the University of Chicago for six years and later at Harvard; during the Second World War he worked in the Intelligence branch of the US Army Air Forces, stationed in North Africa and Italy. He wrote numerous plays, novels and the script for Alfred Hitchcock's film *Shadow of a Doubt* (1943). 'That an American of the present day can create with such delicacy and detachment touches the soul like a miracle,' said Albert Einstein. 'Here is quiet originality that comes from within.'

The Bridge of San Luis Rey 1927

'On Friday noon, July the twentieth, 1714, the finest bridge in all Peru broke and precipitated five travellers into the gulf below.' Brother Juniper, a Franciscan friar, witnesses this accident and decides to investigate the lives of the five travellers, hoping to explain why God allowed them to die. 'The book as a whole is like some faultless temple erected to a minor deity,' said Malcolm Cowley (448). This haunting novel won the Pulitzer Prize for Fiction.

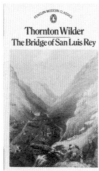

1941 Penguin Books
1982 Modern Classics
—

The Ides of March 1948

This historical novel is made up of numbered journal entries, love letters, dinner invitations, hate mail, anonymous notes, and snippets of gossip which form a mosaic portrait of the intrigues and scandals of Ancient

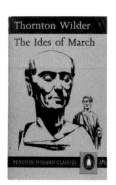

1961
• —

The Ides of March was one of the first new Penguin Modern Classics titles to be published in April 1961.

Rome in 45–44 BCE, culminating in the assassination of Julius Caesar. Everything is invented by Wilder except for poems by Catullus and the final entry, an excerpt from *The Twelve Caesars* by Suetonius. Wilder called the book both a 'fantasia' and 'a kind of crossword puzzle'. 'I adored Thornton's book, and what a huge success it is,' wrote the actor John Gielgud to Wilder's wife, 'only wish he could find it in his heart to adapt it as a play for me! I really could look very like Julius – baldness, big nose and all!'

Our Town
The Skin of Our Teeth
The Matchmaker

1938–54

Wilder felt that 'something had gone wrong' with theatre, so he responded by breaking all the established rules. *Our Town* (1938) is set in the theatre in which it is being performed: there is no set and the 'stage manager' speaks directly to the audience, reconstructing the everyday life of Grover's Corners, a small town in New Hampshire. 'It is an attempt to the smallest events in our daily life,' wrote Wilder. *The Skin of Our Teeth* (1942) is indebted to Joyce's *Finnegans Wake* (11). It is the circular story of the archetypal Antrobus family, set in a range of anachronistic eras, including an Ice Age, the Roaring Twenties, the Second World War and the end of the world. *The Matchmaker* (1954), a rewrite of Wilder's *The Merchant of Yonkers* (1938), is a farce about a determined Jewish widow in turn-of-the-century New York.

1962 Penguin Plays
1987 Modern Classics
2017 Modern Classics
Our Town and Other Plays
intro. John Lahr, 2017
—

Both *Our Town* and *The Skin of Our Teeth* won the Pulitzer Prize for Drama.

The Eighth Day

1967

Breckenridge Lansing, the director of a coal mine in the Midwest, is shot dead in 1902, and his best friend John Ashley is found guilty of his murder. Wilder traces the fortunes of both the Ashley and Lansing families before and after the killing. This was his first novel in almost 20 years; it won the National Book Award.

1969 Penguin Books
1987 Modern Classics
• —

Nella Larsen 1891–1964

Nellie Walker was the daughter of a Danish immigrant mother and a mixed-race father from the Danish West Indies; when her mother remarried, Nella took her stepfather Peter Larsen's surname. She grew up in Chicago; studied at Fisk University in Nashville, Tennessee; and lived in Denmark and New York, where she worked as a nurse and a librarian. She married the African American physicist Elmer Imes in 1919, through whom she came to know W. E. B. Du Bois (408) and James Weldon Johnson (412), and she became one of the leading novelists of the Harlem Renaissance (413).

Quicksand 1928

Larsen's first novel is the semi-autobiographical story of Helga Crane, the daughter of a white mother and an absent black father. She teaches at an all-black school in the South, before moving to Harlem, New York, and then Denmark in search of a stable life beyond the shifting sands of racial prejudice.

1999
● ed. Thadious M. Davis
—
Larsen's only other novel, *Passing* (1929), is currently available as a Penguin Classic. It tells the story of two mixed-race childhood friends reunited after making different life choices: one identifies as black, while the other has been 'passing' as white.

Robert E. Howard

1906–1936

Robert Ervin Howard was born and raised in Texas and lived most of his life in the town of Cross Plains. As a child, he liked amateur boxing and reading Jack London (404) and pulp magazines. In 1924, he began to write for the magazine *Weird Tales*, producing more than 100 stories that exemplify 'sword and sorcery', a subgenre incorporating fantasy, horror, romance and weapon-wielding heroics. He had a lively correspondence with H. P. Lovecraft (417), but his career lasted just twelve years. At the age of 30, when his mother was terminally ill, he shot himself outside the family home; his mother died the following day.

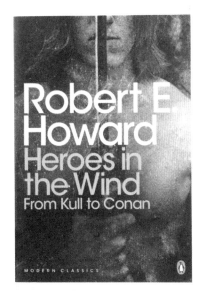

Heroes in the Wind
From Kull to Conan 1929–36

This selection of Howard's best stories includes iconic characters such as Kull of Atlantis, the Pict Bran Mak Morn, the 11th-century Irish warrior Turlogh Dubh O'Brien, the Tudor adventurer Solomon Kane, Detective Steve Harrison and Conan the barbarian Cimmerian. Conan 'is the most realistic character I ever evolved,' claimed Howard. 'He is simply a combination of a number of men I have known [...] some mechanism in my subconscious took the dominant characteristics of various prizefighters, gunmen, bootleggers, oil field bullies, gamblers, and honest workmen I had come in contact with'. This edition also features the Southern Gothic (433) 'Pigeons from Hell', and 'Vultures of Wahpeton' set in the 'Weird West'. There are lots of flexing muscles, flashing swords, serpent gods, deadly plots and epic conflicts. 'The force and fury of his writing [...] was powerful beyond the hero Conan's wildest dreams,' writes Stephen King.

2009
● ed. John Clute

Thomas Wolfe 1900–1938

'Tom's genius is gigantic, tremendous,' wrote F. Scott Fitzgerald (422).
Thomas Clayton Wolfe was born in Asheville, North Carolina, where his
mother ran a boarding house and his father a gravestone business, with an
angel in the window to attract customers. Wolfe taught English in New York
and spent years living between the USA and Europe. In 1925, he began a
relationship with Aline Bernstein, a married costume designer 20 years his
senior; the following year, he began writing the sprawling autobiographical
project that would consume the rest of his life. In 1938, he caught pneumonia,
which developed quickly into tuberculosis, and he died within two months,
at the age of 37. 'The stamp of genius was upon him,' wrote the *New York
Times*, 'though it was an undisciplined and unpredictable genius. [...]
There was within him an unspent energy, an untiring force, an unappeasable
hunger for life and for expression which might have carried him to the
heights and might equally have torn him down.'

1984 Modern Classics
2016 Modern Classics
intro. Elizabeth Kostova, 2016
—
The restored text of
Wolfe's original manuscript,
entitled *O Lost*, was compiled
by the scholars Arlyn
and Matthew J. Bruccoli
and published in 2000.
The Bruccolis described
it as 'nothing less than the
restoration of a masterpiece
to the literary canon'.

Look Homeward, Angel
A Story of the Buried Life 1929

Maxwell Perkins, the editor at Scribner's who 'discovered' Fitzgerald (422) and Hemingway (428),
worked with Wolfe to wrangle his sprawling first manuscript into *Look Homeward, Angel*.
Eugene Grant grows up in the fictional small town of Altamont, the son of a stonecutter father
and an entrepreneurial mother. This highly autobiographical novel is a wild chronicle of
family, identity and small-town American life told in gushing, poetic, impressionist prose.
Richard Aldington called it 'the product of an immense exuberance, organic in its form,
kinetic, and drenched with the love of life'.

Of Time and the River
A Legend of Man's Hunger in His Youth 1935

This voluminous sequel
to *Look Homeward, Angel*
took Maxwell Perkins
two years to edit. Eugene
Gant is still isolated and
over-sensitive, but he is
nonetheless filled with a
'quenchless hunger' for life.
He leaves his home town
and travels first to Harvard
University, then New York
and on to Europe, and finally
discovers his vocation as a
writer. *Of Time and the River* is
a majestic, lyrical expression
of America and American life.
It was a bestseller and made Wolfe's name famous,
although William Faulkner (433) said that Wolfe wrote
'like an elephant trying to do the hoochie-coochie'.

1971 Modern Classics
2016 Modern Classics
intro. Elizabeth Kostova, 2016
—
The working relationship
between Wolfe and Perkins
was dramatized in the 2016
film *Genius*, in which Jude Law
plays Wolfe and Colin Firth
plays Perkins.

The Web and the Rock

1935–8, pub. 1939

After the painful experience
of editing *Of Time and the River*,
Wolfe broke with Perkins and
found a new publisher. In 1938, he
delivered a 5,000-page manuscript
to Edward C. Aswell comprising
a novel in several volumes,
comparable in length to Proust's
In Search of Lost Time (168). Wolfe
died before it could be published,
but Aswell edited and divided the
manuscript and presented the bulk
of it posthumously in two volumes.
The first, *The Web and the Rock*, is
about a struggling writer called
George 'Monk' Webber and his love
affair with a sophisticated older
woman in New York. It includes the
phrase 'fear and loathing', later used
by Hunter S. Thompson (531).

1972
● intro. J. B. Priestley, 1947
—
'Wolfe is one of the small
and invaluable company of
essentially American creators,'
wrote J. B. Priestley (87),
'one of its huge, wild, shaggy
poets whose creations
which have nothing of Europe
in them, release in us the
wonder, fear and affection
we have felt so often as visitors
to the American scene.'

You Can't Go Home Again

1935 – 8, pub. 1940

In this continuation of *The Web and the Rock* (438), George Webber is now a published novelist, but he is lonely and nostalgic for his home town. He realizes, however, that 'You can't go back home to your family, back home to your childhood […] back home to a young man's dreams of glory and of fame […] back home to the old forms and systems of things which once seemed everlasting but which are changing all the time – back home to the escapes of Time and Memory.' 'When all is said and done, he will stand with Melville,' wrote Stephen Vincent Benét (429) in his review.

1970
• —

Damon Runyon 1880 – 1946

Alfred Damon Runyan wrote for newspapers in Colorado Springs, Denver and San Francisco before finding work with the *New York American* as a baseball columnist, publishing from the start under the misprinted name 'Runyon'. He became famous for his short stories about amiable New York low life and the sporting scene, which he wrote in 'Runyonese': a distinctive mixture of slang and formal language, in the present tense. He was a devoted gambler and a friend of the mobster accountant Otto Berman. When Runyon died, his ashes were scattered from a plane flying over New York's Broadway.

Guys and Dolls
and Other Stories 1929 – 37

Runyon's Prohibition-era tales teem with guys, gangsters, hustlers and bootleggers – such as Harry the Horse, Dave the Dude, Philly the Weeper and Big Jule – as well as a fast-talking array of dolls, Judies, pancakes, tomatoes, beautifuls and broads. Two of these stories – 'The Idyll of Miss Sarah Brown' and 'Blood Pressure' – were adapted by Frank Loesser as the hit 1950 musical *Guys and Dolls*, in which Sky Masterson falls in love, Nathan Detroit runs a floating crap game, and Nicely-Nicely Johnson sits down.

1956 Penguin Books
2005 Modern Classics
—
Runyon's first story collection was published in 1932 as *Guys and Dolls*. This posthumous anthology uses the same title, but selects the 20 best stories from *On Broadway* and *From First to Last*.

On Broadway

1929 – 38, pub. 1950

On Broadway comprises three of Runyon's story collections, *More Than Somewhat* (1937), *Furthermore* (1938) and *Take It Easy* (1938). All set on Broadway, the 'hardened artery of New York', they have titles that include 'Butch Minds the Baby', 'Madame La Gimp' and 'All Horse Players Die Broke'.

1990
intro. E. C. Bentley, 1937–8

From First to Last

1907 – 46, pub. 1954

This volume contains 'all the stories not included in *On Broadway*', including several early tales, a novella called *Money from Home* (1935) and eight short sketches written during Runyon's final illness, such as 'Why Me?', 'The Doctor Knows Best' and 'Death Pays a Social Call'.

1990
• —

John Steinbeck 1902–1968

Steinbeck was born in California, in the fertile Salinas Valley about 25 miles from the Pacific coast, known as 'the Salad Bowl of the Nation'; as a teenager, he would spend summers jobbing alongside migrant workers on sugar-beet farms. He left Stanford University without a degree in 1925 and spent the next few years as a labourer, a tour guide and a manufacturer of plaster mannequins. Eventually he moved near Monterey on the coast and his family lent him enough money to try his hand at writing. His first commercial success was *Tortilla Flat* (441), and he became known for his stories about working-class subjects, mostly set in and around the Salinas Valley. In 1948, he was elected to the American Academy of Arts and Letters, and in 1962 he won the Nobel Prize for Literature (576), a somewhat controversial decision described by a Swedish newspaper as 'one of the Academy's biggest mistakes'. (When Steinbeck was asked if he deserved the prize, he replied, 'Frankly, no.') Today, however, he is considered one of the greatest American writers of the 20th century, combining meticulous observation with deep romanticism, seeking common values in the face of a dehumanizing society.

1982 Penguin Books
1995 Twentieth-Century Classics intro. James Nagel, 1995

Cup of Gold

A Life of Sir Henry Morgan, Buccaneer, with Occasional Reference to History 1929

Steinbeck's first novel is a swashbuckling work of historical fiction about the infamous 17th-century Welsh pirate Henry Morgan, who longs to conquer the city of Panama, known as the 'Cup of Gold', and possess a mysterious and beautiful woman called 'La Santa Roja', 'the Red Saint'.

1976 Penguin Books
1995 Twentieth-Century Classics
—

The Pastures of Heaven 1932

These twelve interrelated stories are set in the lush Californian valley known, since its discovery by the Spanish around 1776, as 'Las Pasturas del Cielo'. Each story focuses on a different hard-working family as their small community starts to break apart.

To a God Unknown 1933

Joseph Wayne settles in California and develops a primal affinity with the land, coming to believe that an ancient oak tree embodies the benevolent spirit of his father and that its well-being determines that of the rest of the farm.

1976 Penguin Books
1995 Twentieth-Century Classics
intro. Robert DeMott, 1995

1976 Penguin Books *with The Pearl* (442)
1994 Twentieth-Century Classics intro. John Seelye, 1994

The Red Pony 1933–6, pub. 1937

These four short stories are about Jody Tiflin, a young boy who is given a pony by his father. Jody comes to learn harsh lessons about responsibility, mortality and the fallibility of adults. Steinbeck was inspired by memories of his own childhood friend, Max Wagner.

The Long Valley 1933–6, pub. 1938

These stories are all set in the Salinas Valley, a land of farms, ranches and distant mountains. Titles include 'The Vigilante', a tale of mob violence; 'The Chrysanthemums', perhaps Steinbeck's greatest short story; and the four instalments of *The Red Pony* (440). 'This collection of fifteen short stories is one of the most brilliant, as it is one of the most distressing, published in a long while,' said the *Times Literary Supplement*. 'Its author is pitiless. Seeing life as made up far more of despair and frustration than of beauty or even courage, he spares his reader nothing, refusing to blink an eyelid at that climax of horror, or to soften in the least degree that fine clarity of vision which gives the slightest of his pieces their distinction and their fascination.'

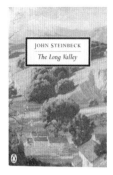

1986 Penguin Books
1995 Twentieth-Century Classics
intro. John H. Timmerman, 1995

1950 Penguin Books
1973 Modern Classics
1997 Twentieth-Century Classics
intro. Thomas French, 1997

Tortilla Flat 1935

Steinbeck's first commercial success was this comic novella about the *paisanos* of Monterey in California, a happy-go-lucky gang of lovable wastrels. When Danny unexpectedly inherits two houses in the shabby district of Tortilla Flat, the 'boys' move in and continue their uproarious adventures. Steinbeck draws parallels with King Arthur and the Knights of the Round Table.

In Dubious Battle 1936

A strike of migrant fruit-pickers spirals out of control in this novel, President Barack Obama's favourite book by Steinbeck. 'I have used a small strike in an orchard valley as the symbol of man's eternal, bitter warfare with himself,' explained Steinbeck. It is the first of three novels in which he focused on the Californian labouring class, and which are sometimes known collectively as the 'Dust Bowl' trilogy.

1979 Penguin Books
1992 Twentieth-Century Classics
intro. Warren French, 1992

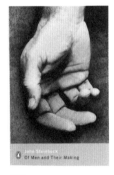

2003
● ed. Susan Shillinglaw & Jackson J. Benson, 2002

Of Men and Their Making
Selected Non-Fiction 1936–66

This anthology is organized thematically and spans Steinbeck's whole career, with pieces about his writing, his country, his travels and his friends, including the photojournalist Robert Capa, Woody Guthrie (474), Arthur Miller (486) and the marine biologist Ed Ricketts. It features 'The Harvest Gypsies', a series of articles Steinbeck wrote for the *San Francisco News* in 1936, which later formed the basis for *The Grapes of Wrath* (442).

Of Mice and Men 1937

George and Lennie are migrant workers during the Great Depression who find jobs on a ranch near Soledad in California. Kind-hearted, simple-minded Lennie has the strength of two men and a penchant for soft things. Despite George's best efforts, their dreams of an independent future are dramatically dashed. Steinbeck's first manuscript was ripped to shreds by his setter puppy Toby. 'I was pretty mad,' he said, 'but the poor little fellow may have been acting critically.'

1949 Penguin Books *with Cannery Row* (442)
1973 Modern Classics
1994 Twentieth-Century Classics *separately*
intro. Susan Shillinglaw, 1994

—

Of Mice and Men reads like a play because Steinbeck wrote it with a view to a stage adaptation. He experimented with two other 'play-novelettes': *The Moon is Down* (442) and *Burning Bright* (444).

The Grapes of Wrath 1939 →

The 'Dust Bowl' describes the Midwestern plains of America during the 1930s, when agriculture was destroyed by sustained dust storms, prompting a mass migration. Steinbeck's epic masterpiece follows the Joad family of Oklahoma sharecroppers, who are forced to pack up their home and set out for the promised land of California. He intersperses narrative chapters with commentary as the Joads' hopes, desires and dreams are raised, tested and then crushed. 'I've done my damndest [sic] to rip a reader's nerves to rags,' he wrote. Laden with biblical parallels and devastating imagery, this tale of human suffering won the National Book Award and the Pulitzer Prize for Fiction. Woody Guthrie's (474) album *Dust Bowl Ballads* (1940) evokes the story and spirit of *The Grapes of Wrath*.

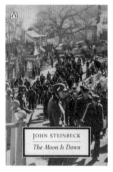

1982 Penguin Books
1995 Twentieth-Century Classics
intro. Donald V. Coers, 1995

The Moon is Down 1942

When a northern European town is invaded by fascist troops, a defiant Resistance organization emerges. Based on the Nazi invasion of Norway, this 'play-novelette' was translated into multiple languages and distributed by underground forces throughout Europe during the Second World War; merely owning a copy in fascist Italy was punishable by death. In 1945, Steinbeck was awarded the Norwegian King Haakon VII Freedom Cross.

Cannery Row 1945

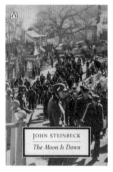

1949 Penguin Books
with *Of Mice and Men* (441)
1973 Modern Classics
1994 Twentieth Century Classics *separately*
intro. Susan Shillinglaw, 1994

Among the stinking sardine canneries and boiler pipes of Monterey, California, Mack and his ragtag group of good-natured misfits drift between the flophouse, the brothel, the grocery store and Doc's marine laboratory. Steinbeck based Cannery Row on Ocean View Avenue, where Ed Ricketts – the model for Doc – ran his laboratory. He laid 'open the page and let the stories crawl in by themselves'. In 1957, Ocean View Avenue was renamed Cannery Row.

The Log from the Sea of Cortez 1941, rev. 1951

In 1930, Steinbeck met the marine biologist Ed Ricketts and they became close friends. In 1940, they made a six-week, 4,000-mile specimen-collecting expedition around the Sea of Cortez, the gulf between the Baja California peninsula and mainland Mexico, and published a joint account. After Ricketts's death in 1948, Steinbeck reprinted his narrative portion as *The Log from the Sea of Cortez*, replacing Ricketts's species catalogue with a eulogy to his friend. 'There is more of the whole man, John Steinbeck, in *Sea of Cortez* than in any of his novels,' wrote the *New York Herald Tribune*.

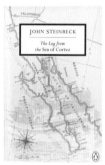

1977 Penguin Books
1995 Twentieth-Century Classics
intro. Richard Astro, 1995

Once There Was a War

1943, pub. 1958

'Do you know it, do you remember it, the drives, the attitudes, the terrors, and, yes, the joys?' asks Steinbeck, at the start of this collection of dispatches he filed as a war correspondent for the *New York Herald Tribune*. He starts in England in June 1943, before being posted to North Africa and joining a commando unit off the coast of Italy.

1977 Penguin Books
1994 Twentieth-Century Classics
—
After his stint as a war correspondent, Steinbeck wrote the script for Alfred Hitchcock's film *Lifeboat* (1944), a wartime survival film set entirely on a ship's boat, for which Steinbeck received an Academy Award nomination.

The Pearl

1947

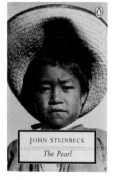

1976 Penguin Books with *The Red Pony* (440)
1994 Twentieth-Century Classics
intro. Linda Wagner-Martin, 1994
ill. José Clemente Orozco, 1947

In La Paz, on his 1940 expedition around the Sea of Cortez, Steinbeck heard a local legend that was 'so much like a parable that it almost can't be'. He later expanded the story into this lyrical novella, in which Kino, a Mexican pearl diver, discovers an enormously valuable pearl. The text is illustrated by the Mexican artist José Clemente Orozco.

John Steinbeck

The Grapes of Wrath

PENGUIN MODERN CLASSICS  5/-

1951 Penguin Books
1962 Modern Classics
1992 Twentieth-Century Classics
intro. Robert DeMott, 1992

The Grapes of Wrath was adapted for the screen by John Ford, starring Henry Fonda. It was in production at the same time as Lewis Milestone's film adaptation of *Of Mice and Men* (441), and Steinbeck was able to visit both productions on consecutive days. The illustration on the cover of the 1962 edition is by Brian Keogh.

Zapata 1949–52, pub. 1975

Emiliano Zapata, the 'Little Tiger', was an iconic leader of the early 20th-century Mexican Revolution. In 1949, Steinbeck wrote a 'narrative in dramatic form' depicting Zapata's life for the director Elia Kazan; he later revised it as a screenplay for the film *Viva Zapata!*, released in 1952. The film starred Marlon Brando and Anthony Quinn and won Steinbeck his third Academy Award nomination. This edition prints both versions of Steinbeck's narrative.

1993 Penguin Books
2001 Modern Classics
ed. Robert E. Morsberger, 1991

Burning Bright
A Play in Story Form 1950

Joe Saul longs for a child but may be sterile, so his adoring wife Mordeen conceives a child by his brash younger associate Victor instead. This intense 'play-novelette' is written in four scenes, each of which features the same archetypal characters but in a surreal range of settings: a circus, a farm, a ship and a hospital.

1983 Penguin Books
1994 Twentieth-Century Classics
–

Journal of a Novel
The *East of Eden* Letters

1951, pub. 1969

Each morning before work, Steinbeck would write a letter to his editor Pascal Covici in order to get his 'mental arm in shape to pitch a good game'. He drafted these letters on the left-hand pages of a notebook and filled the right-hand pages with the text of *East of Eden*. They provide a fascinating insight into Steinbeck's creative process as well as his views on family, politics and writing.

1991 Penguin Books
2001 Modern Classics
–

The Wayward Bus
1947

Juan Chicoy drives his bus 'Sweetheart' between Rebel Corners and San Juan de la Cruz, through the back roads of the Californian countryside. Over the course of his route, various passengers reveal the secrets of their past lives and future dreams.

1979 Penguin Books
1995 Twentieth-Century Classics
–

A Russian Journal
1948

In 1947, Steinbeck visited the USSR with the photojournalist Robert Capa in order to collaborate on this work of reportage: a rare glimpse behind the Iron Curtain just as it was being lowered. They travelled to Moscow, Kiev, Tbilisi and Stalingrad with the aim of 'honest reporting', portraying with compassion and humour the post-war reality of life in the Soviet Union in words and images.

2000
intro. Susan Shillinglaw, 1999

East of Eden 1952

Steinbeck's late masterpiece – described by the *New York Times* as 'a fantasia of history and myth' – is an ambitious saga tracing several generations of two families in the Salinas Valley. The Hamiltons were Steinbeck's own maternal family and he himself appears briefly in the novel as a small boy; the Trasks are a fictional clan helplessly

1980 Penguin Books
1992 Twentieth-Century Classics
intro. David Wyatt, 1992

replaying the fall of man and the rivalry of Cain and Abel, incited by the femme fatale Cathy Ames. 'It has everything in it I have been able to learn about my craft or profession in all these years,' wrote Steinbeck. 'I think everything else I have written has been, in a sense, practice for this.' He collaborated with the director Elia Kazan on the 1955 screen adaptation, James Dean's film debut.

Sweet Thursday 1954

'It was a Thursday, and it was one of those days in Monterey when the air is washed and polished like a lens.' This sequel to *Cannery Row* (442) revisits Mack and Doc after the Second World War and introduces new characters, including Suzy, a hustler who might just bring Doc happiness. 'Mr. Steinbeck's handling, deft and casual, gives the book very often a quality of inspired idiocy,' said the *Times Literary Supplement* review, 'a genuine harebrained charm.'

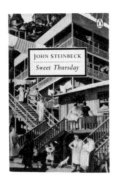

1979 Penguin Books
1996 Twentieth-Century Classics
—

The Winter of Our Discontent

1961

Steinbeck's last novel is set on Long Island, New York. Ethan Allen Hawley comes from a line of New England sea captains, but he now works as a clerk in a grocery store his family once owned. 'Steinbeck returns to the high standards of *The Grapes of Wrath* (442),' wrote Saul Bellow (477), 'and to the social themes that made his early work […] so powerful.'

1982 Penguin Books
1996 Twentieth-Century Classics
—

Travels with Charley
In Search of America

1962

In 1960, Steinbeck made a 10,000-mile road trip with his 'blue' standard French poodle, Charley. He refitted a pickup truck with a custom-built camper top, named it 'Rocinante' after Don Quixote's steed, and drove from Maine to California, and then back through Texas and Louisiana, observing the people he met and asking: 'What are Americans like today?' The *New York Times* described the travelogue as a 'pure delight, a pungent potpourri of places and people'.

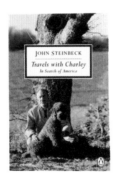

1980 Penguin Books
1997 Twentieth-Century Classics
intro. Jay Parini, 1997

In *The Pastures of Heaven* (440), Junius Maltby describes Robert Louis Stevenson's essays as 'nearly the finest things in English' and has read *Travels with a Donkey in the Cévennes* (1879) 'many times'. Steinbeck took inspiration from Stevenson when choosing his own title for *Travels with Charley*.

The Acts of King Arthur and His Noble Knights

1956 – 65, pub. 1976

Steinbeck retells the Arthurian legends, reworking Sir Thomas Malory's 15th-century *Morte D'Arthur* in his own distinctive style. He never finished this project and it was published posthumously.

2001
ed. Chase Horton, 1976

The Short Reign of Pippin IV
A Fabrication 1957

In this light-hearted political satire, Pippin Héristal is an amateur astronomer who is unexpectedly made king of France in the 1950s; it turns out he has been raised to the throne by communists so that they have a monarchy to fight against.

1977 Penguin Books
1994 Twentieth-Century Classics
ill. William Pène du Bois, 1957

A Life in Letters

1923 – 68

'I write as usual because I have never been able to trust speech as communication of anything except love and desire or hustling.' Steinbeck hated using the telephone, preferring to write letters instead. This selection forms an autobiographical account of his three marriages, his seventeen novels and his many travels. He stamped his letters with a 'Pigasus': a personal stamp of a pig with wings and the Latin phrase *Ad astra per alia porci*, 'to the stars on the wings of a pig'. He saw it as a symbol of himself, 'a lumbering soul but trying to fly'.

1976 Penguin Books
2001 Modern Classics
pref. Elaine A. Steinbeck & Robert Wallstein, 1975

Nathanael West 1903–1940

Nathan Wallenstein Weinstein was born in New York, the son of Russian Jewish immigrants. He attended Brown University and then lived in Paris briefly, where he changed his name to Nathanael West. He worked as the night manager of two residential hotels in Manhattan and edited the literary magazine *Contact* with William Carlos Williams (418) before spending the last five years of his life writing scripts for Hollywood. He died with his wife in a car accident at the age of 37, the day after the death of his friend F. Scott Fitzgerald (422). West wrote four short dark comic novels that reframe the American Dream as a grotesque nightmare; W. H. Auden (95) called them 'parables about a Kingdom of Hell'.

1963 Penguin Books *The Day of the Locust*
1991 Twentieth-Century Classics
—

The Day of the Locust and **The Dream Life of Balso Snell** 1931–9

West's last novel, *The Day of the Locust* (1939), is a satire in which the shiny façade of Tinseltown explodes into mob violence. It is 'the best of the Hollywood novels', wrote J. G. Ballard, 'a nightmare vision of humanity destroyed by its obsession with film'. West's first novel, *The Dream Life of Balso Snell* (1931), is a bizarre account of a Jewish poet crawling through the anus of the Trojan Horse, inside which his personality disintegrates. He described it as a book that is 'a protest against writing books'.

Miss Lonelyhearts and **A Cool Million** 1933–4

Miss Lonelyhearts is a male New York reporter who writes an agony column; during the Great Depression, the weight of real suffering in the letters he receives gradually overwhelms him. *A Cool Million* (1934), subtitled *The Dismantling of Lemuel Pitkin*, is a satire on the rags-to-riches myth. Pitkin remains gullibly optimistic as he loses his teeth, eyes, thumb, leg and scalp and ends up the heroic martyr of an American fascist organization that wears Davy Crockett hats. West dedicated the novel to the comedy writer S. J. Perelman, his brother-in-law.

1961
• —

James Thurber 1894–1961

'James Thurber was born on a night of wild portent and high wind in the year 1894, at 147 Parsons Avenue, Columbus, Ohio,' wrote the author himself. '[...] Thurber's life baffles and irritates the biographer because of its lack of design.' When he was seven, he was blinded in one eye while playing a game of William Tell with his brothers. In 1927, he became a staff writer for the *New Yorker*, in which he published most of his humorous stories, fables and cartoons. His sight deteriorated badly in the last 20 years of his life, but he continued to write and draw using enormous sheets of paper and a thick black crayon.

1953 Penguin Books
The Thurber Carnival
2000 Modern Classics
2014 Modern Classics
The Thurber Carnival

2013 Penguin Books
2016 Modern Classics
—
Thurber's 1945 collection was originally published as *The Thurber Carnival*, the title under which it first appeared in Penguin and which it now bears in Modern Classics. In 2013, a slimmer selection was published to coincide with the film adaptation of *The Secret Life of Walter Mitty* directed by and starring Ben Stiller.

The Secret Life of Walter Mitty
and Other Pieces 1931–45, pub. 1945

Thurber assembled this collection in 1945, comprising the best of his humorous, eccentric stories as well as his whimsical cartoons, which Dorothy Parker (419) described as having the 'outer semblance of unbaked cookies'. Titles include 'A Couple of Hamburgers', 'There's an Owl in My Room' and 'The Dog That Bit People'. His most famous tale, 'The Secret Life of Walter Mitty', is the story of a shy man whose daydreams are far more attractive than disappointing reality.

Zelda Fitzgerald 1900–1948

Zelda Sayre was born in Alabama, the daughter of a justice of the state's Supreme Court. As a teenager, she enjoyed drinking, smoking, hanging out with boys, high diving and ballet dancing. She met F. Scott Fitzgerald (422) when she was seventeen. They married in 1920 and moved to New York and 'all the iridescence of the beginning of the world'. Their daughter Frances Scott ('Scottie') was born in 1921 and they spent the next decade living riotously in America and France. Scott called Zelda 'the first American flapper'. She took up painting and writing and returned to ballet, but the marriage began to fall apart. Scott's drinking developed into alcoholism and Zelda became schizophrenic. 'I don't want you to see me growing old and ugly,' she wrote to him as a teenager. '[...] We will just *have* to die when we're thirty.' Zelda spent her last years in a series of sanatoriums, increasingly violent and reclusive, until she died in a hospital fire.

Save Me the Waltz 1932

Zelda wrote her only novel in six weeks, while recovering from a second bout of serious mental illness. It is the autobiographical story of a Southern belle, Alabama Beggs, who marries a promising young artist, David Knight. The couple honeymoon in Prohibition New York and spend years living at a 'broken and strident' tempo as expatriates in Paris and on the French Riviera. 'It moves me a lot,' wrote Malcolm Cowley (448): 'she has something there that nobody got into words before.' 'They sat in the pleasant gloom of late afternoon,' runs the final sentence, 'staring at each other through the remains of the party; the silver glasses, the silver tray, the traces of many perfumes; they sat together watching the twilight flow through the calm living-room that they were leaving like the clear cold current of a trout stream.'

1988
● pref. Harry T. Moore, 1967
notes Matthew J. Bruccoli, 1967
—
In Zelda's first draft, David Knight was called Amory Blaine, the name of Scott's alter ego in *This Side of Paradise* (422).

James T. Farrell

1904–1979

James Thomas Farrell grew up on Chicago's South Side, in a large, poor Irish American family. He took jobs in advertising and undertaking before moving to New York to write novels and short stories. He is best remembered for his *Studs Lonigan* trilogy, 'Danny O'Neill' pentalogy and 'Bernard Carr' trilogy. Inspired by Sherwood Anderson (420) and Theodore Dreiser (407), he wrote in a naturalistic (406) style, attempting to create 'as complete a story of America as I knew it, of the hopes, the shames, the aspirations'.

Studs Lonigan

Young Lonigan, The Young Manhood of Studs Lonigan, Judgement Day 1932–5

Written at the height of the Great Depression, Farrell's trilogy charts the short and unhappy life of William 'Studs' Lonigan: in *Young Lonigan* (1932), he is a teenager growing up in Chicago's working-class Catholic Irish community, full of energy and ambition; in *The Young Manhood of Studs Lonigan* (1934), his potential is relentlessly crushed by social and economic circumstances; and in *Judgement Day* (1935), he dies of pneumonia at the age of 29. 'I read *Studs Lonigan* in my freshman year at Harvard,' Norman Mailer (496) recalled, 'and it changed my life. [...] I realized you could write books about people who were something like the people you had grown up with. I couldn't get over the discovery.' The trilogy was adapted as a film in 1960 and a television series in 1979.

2001
● intro. Ann Douglas
—
The Chicago-based historian 'Studs' Terkel took his name from Farrell's character.

The Viking Press

For much of his career,
Malcolm Cowley was an
influential editor and talent
scout for the Viking Press.
He joined the New York
publishing house in 1944 to
work on their Portable Library
series: that year, he published
The Portable Hemingway
(428), and in 1946 *The Portable
Faulkner* (433), an event that
Robert Penn Warren (489)
described as the 'great
watershed' for Faulkner's
reputation. 'I owe Malcolm
Cowley the kind of debt no
man could ever repay,' said
Faulkner after winning the
Nobel Prize for Literature (576)
in 1949. Cowley encouraged
Viking to publish Jack
Kerouac's *On the Road* (470)
and *One Flew Over the
Cuckoo's Nest* by Ken Kesey
(520), his old student. He also
revitalized the reputations of
F. Scott Fitzgerald (422) and
Sherwood Anderson (420)
by publishing a restructured
edition of *Tender is the Night*
(424) and a new introduction
to *Winesburg, Ohio* (420).
Penguin Books acquired
the Viking Press in 1975 and
several of the Portable Library
editions are currently in print
as Penguin paperbacks. In
1990, the year after Cowley's
death, *The Portable Malcolm
Cowley* was published.
The Viking Press has published
many Modern Classics authors,
including Saul Bellow (477),
William S. Burroughs (481),
Ian Fleming (126), James
Weldon Johnson (412), Arthur
Miller (486), R. K. Narayan (342),
Octavio Paz (561), Upton
Sinclair (409), Wallace Stegner
(459), John Steinbeck (440)
and Patrick White (382).

Malcolm Cowley 1898–1989

Cowley spent the early 1920s writing poetry in Paris as a member
of the Lost Generation (425). Back in America, he worked as an editor
at the Viking Press and as a literary critic, he taught creative writing
to students including Larry McMurtry (530), Ken Kesey (520) and Wendell
Berry, and he twice served as President of the National Institute of Arts
and Letters. Wallace Stegner (459) called him 'our best and wisest student
of American writing'. Hemingway was less generous in *The Snows of
Kilimanjaro* (428), in which he described him as 'that American poet with
a pile of saucers in front of him and a stupid look on his potato face'.

Exile's Return
A Literary Odyssey of the 1920s 1934, rev. 1951

Cowley's anecdotal account of the Lost Generation (425)
is a fascinating first-hand record of the expatriate
adventures of American writers in 1920s Paris. Through
intimate portraits of e e cummings (427), John Dos
Passos (426), F. Scott Fitzgerald (422), Ernest Hemingway
(428), Gertrude Stein (410) and Thornton Wilder (436),
he shows how writers after the First World War
expanded the boundaries of art by detaching themselves
from earlier traditions. It is 'far and away the best book
about this generation', wrote the *New York Times*.

1976 Penguin Books
1994 Twentieth-Century
Classics
● ed. Donald W. Faulkner,
1994

Dashiell Hammett 1894–1961

Samuel Dashiell Hammett left school at fourteen to work as a
newsboy, and then as an operative for Pinkerton's Detective Agency
in Baltimore. He worked for Pinkerton's for five years, with a break
to volunteer as an ambulance driver in the First World War. After the
war he began writing stories about a nameless private investigator
called 'the Continental Op' and noir classics such as *The Maltese
Falcon* (1930), featuring Sam Spade, which was a major influence
for Raymond Chandler (461). Hammett was 'the ace performer', said
Chandler. 'He did over and over again what only the best writers can
ever do at all. He wrote scenes that seemed
never to have been written before.'

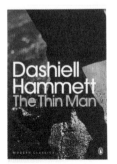

1935 Penguin Books
2011 Modern Classics
—

The Thin Man 1934

The 'thin man' is ex-detective Nick Charles, who is
married to the smart-talking socialite Nora. They plan
to spend Christmas in their Manhattan hotel suite with
their pet schnauzer and a case of Scotch, but instead
Charles finds himself investigating a bullet-riddled
corpse and a missing inventor. Nora was modelled on
Hammett's partner of 30 years, the fiery playwright
Lillian Hellman, to whom this book is dedicated.

John O'Hara 1905–1970

John Henry O'Hara was born in Pottsville, Pennsylvania, the eldest son of a doctor. He was expelled from school three times and took jobs as a ship's steward, gas-meter reader, soda jerk and press agent before becoming a journalist. He was film critic of the *Morning Telegraph*, football editor for the *New Yorker* and he also wrote for *Time* magazine. 'I have done everything,' he wrote, '[...] from covering girls' field hockey to a Congressional investigation.' He also penned realist novels and hundreds of short stories. 'I want the Nobel prize (576),' he wrote to his daughter, '[...] so bad I can taste it.' When Steinbeck (440) won the prize in 1962, O'Hara wired: 'I can think of only one other author I'd rather see get it.' O'Hara drafted his own epitaph: 'Better than anyone else, he told the truth about his time. He was a professional. He wrote honestly and well.'

Appointment in Samarra 1934

'I want to get it all down on paper while I can,' wrote O'Hara. '[...] I want to record the way people talked and thought and felt, and to do it with complete honesty and variety.' In this, his first novel, Julian and Caroline English are popular residents in the small town of Gibbsville, Pennsylvania; but when Julian commits three impulsive acts in three days, their carefully constructed social life starts to fall apart. 'If you want to read a book by a man who knows exactly what he is writing about and has written it marvellously well, read *Appointment in Samarra*,' said Ernest Hemingway (428). O'Hara went on to set many more novels and stories in Gibbsville, a thinly fictionalized version of his home town, Pottsville.

1944 Penguin Books
1997 Twentieth-Century Classics
● intro. Allan Massie, 1997
—
The title *Appointment in Samarra* is a reference to an ancient tale about a fruitless flight from death. O'Hara chose the title after Dorothy Parker (419) introduced him to W. Somerset Maugham's (32) retelling of the story.

Henry Roth 1906–1995

Roth was born in the Austro-Hungarian province of Galicia, but landed on Ellis Island at the age of two and grew up in the slums of Lower East Side New York. During the Second World War, he worked as a tool and gauge maker, afterwards moving to Maine where he took jobs as a waterfowl farmer, a maths teacher and an attendant in a state mental hospital.

Call It Sleep 1934

Roth's modernist (11) novel tells the autobiographical story of David Schearl, who arrives in New York as an infant and grows up on the Lower East Side with a violent, frustrated father and fiercely protective, Yiddish-speaking mother. Roth's innovative, multilingual style was compared favourably to James Joyce (8), but the novel was nonetheless neglected for 30 years. In the early 1960s, it was 'rediscovered' as an overlooked Depression-era masterpiece. 'One of the few genuinely distinguished novels written by a twentieth-century American,' declared the front page of the *New York Times Book Review*.

1977 Modern Classics
● aftwd. Walter Allen, 1964
2006 Modern Classics
intro. Alfred Kazin, 1991

Ayn Rand 1905–1982

Alisa Zinovyevna Rosenbaum was born in St Petersburg. She was one of the first Russian women to attend university, where she adopted the pen name 'Ayn Rand'. Visiting America in 1926, she was moved to tears by the Manhattan skyline. She settled in Hollywood, where a chance meeting with the director Cecil B. DeMille led to work as a screenwriter. The success of her novel *The Fountainhead* brought a coterie of followers she called 'the Class of '43', including the philosopher Leonard Peikoff and the future Chair of the Federal Reserve, Alan Greenspan. With this group she developed her philosophy of objectivism, which she summarized as 'the concept of man as a heroic being, with his own happiness as the moral purpose of his life'. She championed the 'virtue of selfishness', a view that she promoted through her polemical novels.

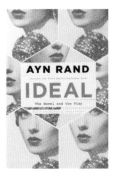

2015
intro. Leonard Peikoff
—
Rand wrote *Ideal* as a novel in 1934 and then reworked it as a play in 1936. Both versions are included in this volume, which is introduced by the philosopher Leonard Peikoff. Peikoff worked with Ayn Rand for 30 years and is also her heir and literary executor.

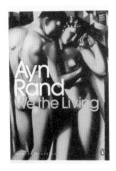

2010
fwd. Ayn Rand, 1959
intro. Leonard Peikoff, 2009
—
Sales of *We the Living* were slow in 1936, but following the spectacular success of *The Fountainhead* and *Atlas Shrugged*, Rand was prompted to release a revised edition in 1959, which has since sold several million copies.

Ideal 1934–6, pub. 1984–2015

When actress Kay Gonda is accused of murdering a millionaire, she goes on the run in Los Angeles, seeking help from six unknown men who had all written her fan letters calling her their ideal woman.

We the Living 1936, rev. 1959

In Soviet Russia, Kira Argounova is the daughter of a bourgeois family, determined to retain her independence and oppose the tyranny of dictatorship. Rand called her first novel 'as near to an autobiography as I will ever write. It is not an autobiography in the literal, but only in the intellectual, sense. The plot is invented, the background is not.'

Anthem 1938

In this dystopian novella, Equality 7-2521 is living in a totalitarian collectivist society where the word 'I' has been replaced by 'we'. Since the Great Rebirth, it has become a crime to think or act as an individual; but when Equality 7-2521 stumbles on a remnant of the 'Unmentionable Times', he is inspired to rebel and fall in love.

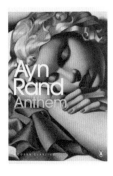

2008
intro. Leonard Peikoff, 1995
—
Rand wrote *Anthem* during a break from working on *The Fountainhead*. She approached Walt Disney, unsuccessfully, to discuss an animated adaptation.

The Fountainhead 1943

Young architect Howard Roark builds modernist (11) skyscrapers out of granite, scorning the double-dealing 'second-handers' who value weak conformity. Rand wrote this objectivist novel over seven years, fuelled by prescription amphetamines. A glorification of capitalist self-interest, the novel remains a bestseller, especially among architects and US Republicans. President Donald Trump has said that he identifies with Roark: *The Fountainhead* 'relates to business, beauty, life and inner emotions,' he says. 'That book relates to … everything.'

2007
intro. Ayn Rand, 1968

Atlas Shrugged 1957

'Who is John Galt?' Rand's magnum opus opens with this question. In a dystopian version of the USA, Galt is a mysterious visionary who persuades all the 'men of talent' – innovators, creators and businessmen – to shake off bureaucratic shackles and retreat to a mountainous hideaway to build an independent free economy while the rest of the nation collapses. It is a 'mystery story', explained Rand, 'not about the murder of man's body, but about the murder – and rebirth – of man's spirit'.

2007
—

Henry Miller 1891–1980

Henry Valentine Miller underwent a 'rosy crucifixion' (452) at the age of 33: he fell into a *ménage à trois* with his wife June and her lover Jean Kronski, began writing autobiographical novels and moved to Paris. Miller lived in Paris for ten years, supported financially by Anaïs Nin (430), with whom he had an affair, and mixing with the Surrealists (176). Most of his sexually explicit, obscenity-riddled books were published in Paris and banned in the USA, although smuggled copies were an influence on the Beat Generation (491), especially Jack Kerouac (469). Miller returned to America in 1940 and lived in California for the rest of his life, writing and painting watercolours. 'Read him for five pages, ten pages, and you feel the peculiar relief that comes not so much from understanding as from *being understood*,' said George Orwell (80). Bob Dylan has called him 'the greatest American writer'.

Tropic of Cancer 1934

'A momentous event in the history of modern writing,' declared Samuel Beckett (20); T. S. Eliot (11) called it 'very remarkable' and 'rather magnificent'; but Pennsylvania Supreme Court Justice Michael Musmanno described *Tropic of Cancer* as 'a cesspool, an open sewer, a pit of putrefaction, a slimy gathering of all that is rotten in the debris of human depravity'. Part novel, part autobiography, the book is a scandalous blend of philosophy, obscenity and mysticism: a nameless American writer has a series of encounters in 1930s Paris with artists, pimps, prostitutes, princesses, drunks and hustlers. 'The Paris book', Miller called it: 'first person, uncensored, formless – fuck everything!' Anaïs Nin (430) helped him edit the text and financed its first printing. 'His writing is flamboyant,' she wrote, 'torrential, chaotic, treacherous and dangerous.'

2015
—
The covers of the Penguin editions of *Tropic of Cancer* and *Tropic of Capricorn* are gouache paintings by Tracey Emin.

Aller Retour New York 1935

Miller left Paris to visit New York in 1935 and he wrote this account on his return journey, in the form of a long letter to the writer Alfred Perlès, his room-mate in Paris. 'New York is an aquarium,' Miller says, '[…] where there are nothing but hellbenders and lungfish and slimy, snag-toothed groupers and sharks.' This edition also includes *Via Dieppe–Newhaven* (1939), a short account of a failed attempt to visit England.

2016
—

Tropic of Capricorn 1939

This companion piece to *Tropic of Cancer* is a prequel, set in 1920s Brooklyn. Miller called it 'the June book', because it centres on his erotic exploits with the 'taxi dancer' June Smith – who became the second of his five wives – while he was working as the personnel manager of the Western Union Telegraph Company and attempting to compose the most important work of literature ever written. The book incorporates sections from two of Miller's early, unpublished novels: *Clipped Wings* and *Lucky Lesbians*. Norman Mailer (496) called it 'a tidal wave of prose'.

2015
—

2016
—

Quiet Days in Clichy

1940, pub. 1956

'We used to go to Paris,' recalled John Lennon, 'and everybody would buy Henry Miller books because they were banned.' This slim novel recalls Miller's bohemian existence in 1930s Paris, when he lived in an apartment with the writer Alfred Perlès in the suburban district of Clichy. Joey and Carl share sex lives and love affairs and the narrative climaxes in an impromptu orgy.

The Colossus of Maroussi 1941

In 1939, as the Second World War broke out, Miller travelled to Greece to visit his friend Lawrence Durrell. He spent nine months exploring Athens, Crete, Corfu, Poros and Delphi and visiting the flamboyant Greek poet George Katsimbalis (the eponymous 'Colossus'). The result was this lyrical, impressionistic travelogue, which the essayist Pico Iyer calls 'one of the five greatest travel books of all time'. It was Miller's favourite among his own books. 'American literature begins and ends with the meaning of what Miller has done,' wrote Durrell, who edited The Henry Miller Reader in 1959.

1950 Penguin Books
2016 Modern Classics
—

Henry Miller wrote to Penguin Books in December 1951: 'I suppose by this time the first edition (of 35,000) of the Colossus has been sold out. I'm wondering if you intend to reprint it, keep it in circulation. I do hope so! No book of mine has brought such welcome letters, such good friends. I hear about the sale of the Penguin edition from remote parts of the globe. (One fellow in Mombasa, Africa, wrote that it was "selling like hot cakes" there – which sounds incredible.)'

The 'Rosy Crucifixion' Trilogy

Sexus, Plexus, Nexus 1949–60

'I was approaching my thirty-third year, the age Christ was crucified. A wholly new life lay before me.' Conceived as early as 1927, this semi-autobiographical trilogy bridges the six years between the end of Tropic of Capricorn (451) and the start of Tropic of Cancer (451). Sexus (1949) describes the break-up of Miller's first marriage and his infatuation with Mona, a fictionalized version of June; Plexus (1953) charts his second marriage to the volatile Mona and his first steps towards becoming a writer; and Nexus (1960) is about his last months in New York, his ménage à trois with Mona and her lover Anastasia and his decision to leave for Paris. 'There is nothing like Henry Miller when he gets rolling,' said Norman Mailer (496), who described The Rosy Crucifixion as 'a literary cake large as the Himalayas […] across half at least of its sixteen hundred pages are peaks and avenues and haunches and battlements and arêtes and basins and summits and valleys of writing so good one shakes one's head. Pity the poor aspiring mediocrity of a writer who reads Miller without protection – he will never write another word if he has any decency left.'

The trilogy's title comes from a sentence near the end of Tropic of Capricorn (451): 'All my Calvaries were rosy crucifixions, pseudo-tragedies to keep the fires of hell burning brightly for the real sinners who are in danger of being forgotten.'

2015
—

2015
—

2015
—

1975 Penguin Books
1985 Modern Classics
ed. Margarita G. Smith,
1971

1961 Modern Classics
2008 Modern Classics
intro. Kasia Boddy, 2008

Carson McCullers 1917–1967

'A tall slender wand of a girl, slightly stooped,' wrote Truman Capote (463), recalling his first sight of Carson McCullers, 'with a fascinating face that was simultaneously merry and melancholy.' Lula Carson Smith left Georgia at the age of seventeen and took a steamship to New York ostensibly to study the piano; instead, she pursued a literary career. After a marriage to Reeves McCullers, she became infatuated with Katherine Anne Porter (427) and had a long-term friendship with the striptease artiste Gypsy Rose Lee, with whom she moved into February House on Brooklyn Heights, an artistic commune that included W. H. Auden (95), Benjamin Britten, Klaus Mann (256), Richard Wright (462), Paul Bowles (480) and Jane Bowles (474). McCullers was plagued by ill health throughout her life: she suffered three strokes before she was 31, which left her paralysed on one side, and she drank continually. She wrote novels, stories, essays, poems and a book of children's verse called *Sweet as a Pickle and Clean as a Pig* (1964). She spent the last 23 years of her life in Nyack, New York, where she once introduced Marilyn Monroe to Karen Blixen (240) over lunch. 'She has examined the heart of man with an understanding [...] that no other writer can hope to surpass,' said Tennessee Williams (455).

The Mortgaged Heart 1935–67, pub. 1971

McCullers's Southern Gothic (433) stories are infused with violence, deformity, frustration and pain. This collection, assembled posthumously by her younger sister Rita, brings together her earliest stories, including 'Sucker', the first she wrote, and 'Wunderkind', the first she published, as well as essays, articles and poems. It forms 'a kind of literary biography', wrote Paul Theroux (543). '[...] One sees the style and perception developing and expressing a unique sensibility.'

The Heart is a Lonely Hunter 1940

McCullers published her first novel at the age of 23 to instant acclaim. It tells the story of the lonely, deaf-mute John Singer, in a small town in the Deep South, who becomes the silent confidant of four unlikely and equally troubled characters, including 'Mick' Kelly, a tomboyish young girl who dreams of buying a piano, and Dr Benedict Copeland, an idealistic African American doctor. 'To me the most impressive aspect of *The Heart is a Lonely Hunter*,' wrote Richard Wright (462), 'is the astonishing humanity that enables a white writer, for the first time in Southern fiction, to handle Negro characters with as much ease and justice as those of her own race.'

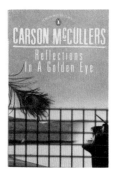

1967 Penguin Books
1987 Modern Classics
—

Reflections in a Golden Eye was filmed by John Huston in 1967, starring Elizabeth Taylor and Marlon Brando.

Reflections in a Golden Eye 1941

Secret desires simmer below the surface of a stifling army camp in the Deep South: Private Williams spies on Mrs Penderton; she is having an affair with Major Morris; and Captain Penderton is physically attracted to Private Williams. Written in a feverish two months, the book is full of violence and perversity; at one point a character cuts off 'the tender nipples of her breasts with the garden shears'. McCullers's speciality, as *The Times* put it, was 'dark-eyed Gothic novels of repressed Southern passions, the inexpressible heat under the skin'.

The Ballad of the Sad Café 1943

Miss Amelia Evans, strong and independent, falls in love with her hunchbacked relative Lymon and transforms her small-town store into a lively café, but she soon comes to regret relaxing her tough exterior. Originally serialized in *Harper's Bazaar*, the novella first appeared in book form in 1951, along with six short stories that are also reprinted in this edition. The playwright Edward Albee (324) adapted *The Ballad of the Sad Café* for the stage in 1963. After reading the novella, V. S. Pritchett (110) described McCullers as 'the most remarkable novelist, I think, to come out of America for a generation [...] What she has, before anything else, is a courageous imagination; that is to say that she is bold enough to consider the terrible in human nature without loss of nerve, calm, dignity or love.'

The Member of the Wedding 1946

Frankie Addams is a 12-year-old motherless tomboy who becomes obsessed with her older brother's wedding: she fantasizes about her role and plans to join the honeymoon as well. Ali Smith calls it a 'very funny, very dark novel'. McCullers's own 1950 stage adaptation won the New York Drama Critics Award.

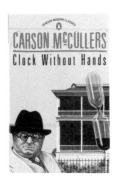

1965 Penguin Books
1986 Modern Classics
—

Clock Without Hands 1961

McCullers's last novel is about four seemingly very different men in a small town in the Deep South, whose lives turn out to be inextricably linked. It deals with prejudice, loneliness and human mortality. 'I become the characters I write about,' McCullers once said, 'and I bless the Latin poet Terence who said "Nothing human is alien to me".'

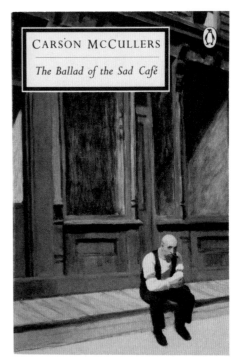

1963 Penguin Books
1990 Twentieth-Century Classics
—

1962 Modern Classics
2008 Modern Classics
intro. Ali Smith, 2008

Tennessee Williams 1911–1983

When Thomas Lanier Williams III was diagnosed with diphtheria at the age of seven, his violent, alcoholic father beat him for being weak. Williams dropped out of college during the Depression and worked in a shoe factory during the day, writing stories and plays at night. He changed his name to 'Tennessee', his father's home state, and completed a degree at the University of Iowa. In 1943, Williams's older sister Rose, having developed schizophrenia, underwent a botched lobotomy that left her incapacitated; the following year, his semi-autobiographical play *The Glass Menagerie* made him a celebrity. He went on to write many award-winning Broadway plays and film scripts, but after two decades of success, the 1960s and 1970s were overshadowed by bouts of depression, increasing dependence on alcohol and drugs, the death of his life partner Frank Merlo in 1963, and a series of theatrical failures. Today, however, Williams is considered one of the greatest American playwrights of the 20th century, alongside Eugene O'Neill (415) and Arthur Miller (486). 'He was a born dramatist as few are ever born,' wrote Peter Shaffer (151). 'Whatever he put on paper, superb or superfluous, glorious or gaudy, could not fail to be electrifyingly actable. [...] Tennessee Williams will live as long as drama itself.'

Mister Paradise
and Other
One-Act Plays

1935–66, pub. 2001–5

Williams wrote brief plays throughout his life. These thirteen one-act dramas were never published in his lifetime: they present poignant and hilarious characters, from disheartened poets to indefatigable drag queens. Titles include *Why Do You Smoke So Much, Lily?*, *The Fat Man's Wife* and *Adam and Eve on a Ferry*.

2006
ed. Nicholas Moschovakis & David Roessel, 2001–5
fwd. Eli Wallach & Anne Jackson, 2001–5

Period of Adjustment
and Other Plays 1948–72
Period of Adjustment, Summer and Smoke, Small Craft Warnings

Summer and Smoke (1948) is a two-act love story set in Mississippi; Williams granted half the royalties to his sister Rose to pay for her ongoing healthcare. *Period of Adjustment* (1960) is now published in *Sweet Bird of Youth and Other Plays* (457) and *Small Craft Warnings* (1972) is in *Suddenly Last Summer and Other Plays* (456).

1982 Penguin Plays
1989 Twentieth-Century Classics
• —

A Streetcar Named Desire
and Other Plays 1944–59
A Streetcar Named Desire, Sweet Bird of Youth, The Glass Menagerie

Williams coined the term 'memory play' to describe *The Glass Menagerie* (1944), which dramatizes Tom Wingfield's recollections of his fraught childhood, his suffocating mother Amanda and his shy, handicapped sister Laura, who has a 'menagerie' of glass figurines. This highly autobiographical play, first directed by Elia Kazan, won the New York Drama Critics' Circle Award. 'Everything in his life is in his plays,' said Kazan, 'and everything in his plays is in his life.' Williams's next play was his masterpiece, *A Streetcar Named Desire* (1947), which won the first of his two Pulitzer Prizes for Drama. It tells the story of a fading Southern belle, Blanche DuBois, who relies on the kindness of strangers and arrives in crowded New Orleans to stay with her sister Stella. 'They told me to take a streetcar named Desire,' says Blanche, 'and then transfer to one called Cemeteries and ride six blocks and get off at – Elysian Fields!' Elia Kazan filmed an adaptation in 1951, starring Vivien Leigh and Marlon Brando. *Sweet Bird of Youth* (1959) is now published in another Modern Classics volume (457).

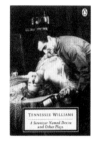

1959 Penguin Plays
A Streetcar Named Desire & The Glass Menagerie
1962 Penguin Plays
A Streetcar Named Desire and Other Plays
1989 Twentieth-Century Classics
• —

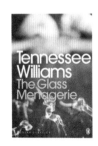

1988 Penguin Books
The Glass Menagerie
2009 Modern Classics
intro. Robert Bray, 1999

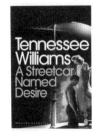

2009
intro. Arthur Miller (486), 2004

The Rose Tattoo and Other Plays 1951–7

The Rose Tattoo, Camino Real, Orpheus Descending

In *The Rose Tattoo* (1951), a Sicilian American widow discovers the truth about her dead husband and reawakens her own fiery sensuality. The *Sunday Times* called it 'a wild, poetic, earthy and hilarious story'. *Camino Real* (1953) is an Expressionist (269) experiment, set in a dead-end town surrounded by the desert, which Williams described as 'my conception of the time and world I live in'. Dream sequences involve characters such as Don Quixote, Casanova and Lord Byron. *Orpheus Descending* (1957) is a Southern Gothic (433) retelling of the Orpheus and Eurydice story in the hellish depths of the South. 'It was and still is the tale of a wild-spirited boy who wanders into a conventional community of the South and creates the commotion of a fox in a chicken coop,' wrote Williams.

1958 Penguin Plays
*The Rose Tattoo
& Camino Real*
1968 Penguin Plays
*The Night of the Iguana
& Orpheus Descending*
1976 Penguin Plays
*The Rose Tattoo and
Other Plays*
1990 Twentieth-Century
Classics
—

1957 Penguin Books
Baby Doll
1961 Penguin Plays
*Something Unspoken
and Other Plays*
1976 Penguin Plays
Baby Doll and Other Plays
1991 Twentieth-Century
Classics
2009 Modern Classics
revised
—
The 1961 Penguin Plays
(xiv) edition comprised
*Something Unspoken,
Suddenly Last Summer*
and *Orpheus Descending*.
In 2009, the current
Modern Classics edition
replaced *Suddenly Last
Summer* with *Summer
and Smoke* (455).

Baby Doll

and Other Plays 1953–8

Baby Doll, Something Unspoken, Suddenly Last Summer

Williams wrote the script for Elia Kazan's film *Baby Doll* (1956), the story of two rival cotton ginners and flirtatious 'Baby Doll' Meighan, played by Carroll Baker. 'Make no mistake about it,' wrote the playwright John Osborne (134) – 'this Baby Doll kid is a killer.' *Something Unspoken* (1953) is a one-act play about a wealthy and manipulative Southern spinster; it is sometimes played as a double bill with *Suddenly Last Summer* under the collective title *Garden District*.

Cat on a Hot Tin Roof

and Other Plays

*Cat on a Hot Tin Roof, The Milk Train Doesn't Stop Here Anymore,
The Night of the Iguana* 1955–63

The *Guardian* called it 'one of the hottest, sultriest plays ever written'. In *Cat on a Hot Tin Roof* (1955), 'Big Daddy' Pollitt, the wealthiest cotton planter in the Mississippi Delta, is celebrating his 65th birthday. His two sons have returned home: Gooper and Brick, an alcoholic former football hero, who arrives with his sultry wife 'Maggie the Cat'. This was Williams's favourite of his own plays; it won the Pulitzer Prize for Drama, and was made into a 1958 film starring Elizabeth Taylor and Paul Newman. *The Milk Train Doesn't Stop Here Anymore* (1963) is now published in *Suddenly Last Summer and Other Plays* and *The Night of the Iguana* (1961) is in *Sweet Bird of Youth and Other Plays* (457).

1957 Penguin Plays
Cat on a Hot Tin Roof
1969 Penguin Plays
*Cat on a Hot Tin Roof
and Other Plays*
1990 Twentieth-Century
Classics
• —

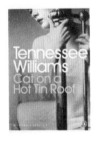

2009
—

2009
—

Suddenly Last Summer

and Other Plays 1958–72

Suddenly Last Summer, The Milk Train Doesn't Stop Here Anymore, Small Craft Warnings

Suddenly Last Summer (1958) is a Southern Gothic (433) one-act play about a family that tries to convince a doctor to perform a lobotomy on a young woman. Williams considered it 'perhaps the most poetic' of his plays. *The Milk Train Doesn't Stop Here Anymore* (1963) is set in Italy; it features a dying woman who exalts eroticism and mysticism. *Small Craft Warnings* (1972), the best of Williams's later plays, takes place in a seedy bar on the Californian coast, with a motley cast including a lusty, ageing beautician, a discredited alcoholic doctor, a vulnerable waif and two gay men.

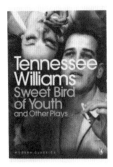

2009
—

Sweet Bird of Youth and Other Plays 1959–61
Sweet Bird of Youth, Period of Adjustment, The Night of the Iguana

In *Sweet Bird of Youth* (1959), a gigolo and drifter, Chance Wayne, returns to his home town to look for Heavenly Finley, the childhood sweetheart he left behind; what he finds is violent resentment and a lust for revenge. *Period of Adjustment* (1960) was written in a drug-induced frenzy. It tells the story of a pair of newlyweds who visit the husband's old army friend on Christmas Eve and experience an emotional and sexual crisis. *The Night of the Iguana* (1961) is the story of one sweltering night in an isolated Mexican hotel: the Reverend T. Lawrence Shannon, a disgraced ex-minister now working as a tour guide, is accused of having assaulted a 16-year-old girl in his group. It was made into a film in 1964, directed by John Huston and starring Richard Burton and Ava Gardner.

Memoirs 1975

Through witty vignettes and gossipy anecdotes, Williams narrates the story of his life from his days as an impoverished writer through the phenomenal success that greeted *The Glass Menagerie* (455) to the years of decline that followed. He describes life as a gay man, his experiences of depression, and his friendships with Carson McCullers (453), Truman Capote (463) and Ernest Hemingway (428).

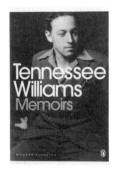

2007
intro. John Waters, 2006
aftwd. Allean Hale, 2006
—
The film-maker John Waters has directed transgressive films such as *Pink Flamingos* (1972) and *Female Trouble* (1974). 'Tennessee Williams saved my life,' he writes. '[…] I yearned for a bad influence and boy, was Tennessee one in the best sense of the word: joyous, alarming, sexually consuming and dangerously funny.' He compares the *Memoirs* to 'having a few stiff drinks with Tennessee on one of his good nights as he tells you juicy stories'.

Eudora Welty 1909–2001

Welty was born in Jackson, Mississippi, and lived there for most of her life. After college, she got a job with the Works Progress Administration under Roosevelt's New Deal, travelling around Mississippi taking photographs, conducting interviews and documenting daily life in the state. This experience led her to start writing short stories, the first of which was published in 1936 and was praised by Katherine Anne Porter (427), who provided the foreword to her first collection, *A Curtain of Green* (1941). Welty went on to write more story collections and novels, including the fairy tale *The Robber Bridegroom* (1942), *Delta Wedding* (1946) and *The Optimist's Daughter* (1972), which won the Pulitzer Prize for Fiction. She conducted a lengthy correspondence with Ross Macdonald (498). Her gravestone is inscribed with a line from *The Optimist's Daughter*: 'For her life, any life, she had to believe, was nothing but the continuity of its love.'

Stories 1936–68

'What I do in writing of any character is to try to enter into the mind, heart, and skin of a human being who is not myself,' wrote Welty. 'Whether this happens to be a man or a woman, old or young, with skin black or white, the primary challenge lies in making the jump itself.' Her *Collected Stories* (1980) finally brought Welty wide national acclaim: it comprises 41 stories drawn from all her major collections, as well as a couple that were not collected, such as 'Where Is the Voice Coming From?', which is written from the point of view of a racist assassin. The centrepiece is *The Golden Apples* (1949), perhaps Welty's greatest collection, a cycle of seven interrelated stories set in the fictional small town of Morgana, Mississippi. 'I doubt that a better book about "the South" […] has ever been written,' ran the *New Yorker* review. Katherine Anne Porter (427) said that Welty had 'an eye and an ear sharp, shrewd, and true as a tuning fork'.

1983 Penguin Books
1989 Twentieth-Century Classics
• pref. Eudora Welty, 1980

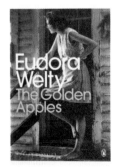

2011
intro. Paul Binding

Ralph Ellison 1913–1994

Ralph Waldo Ellison was born in Oklahoma and named after Ralph Waldo Emerson. His father died in a workplace accident when Ralph was just three, and he was forced to find work as a busboy, shoeshine boy, hotel waiter and dentist's assistant. He also learned to play jazz trumpet. In 1936, he settled in Harlem, New York City; he met Langston Hughes and Richard Wright (462) and began writing stories and articles. He went on to teach at a number of universities and lived for a time in Rome, where he befriended Robert Penn Warren (489). In 1975, he was elected to the American Academy of Arts and Letters, and the *New York Times* has since placed him 'among the gods of America's literary Parnassus'.

Flying Home
and Other Stories
1937–54, pub. 1940–96

Several of these early stories were unpublished in Ellison's lifetime. They describe Jim Crow laws in the South and the bingo parlours of New York's Harlem, capturing aspects of African American life with 'the simple elegance of Chekhov', as the *Washington Post* put it.

1998 Twentieth-Century Classics
2016 Modern Classics *revised*
intro. John F. Callahan, 1996

Invisible Man
1952

1965 Modern Classics
2001 Modern Classics
intro. John F. Callahan, 2001

From an underground room, a nameless African American man tells the story of his search for meaning in an incomprehensible world. He is invisible, he explains, 'simply because people refuse to see me'. Ellison's first novel won the National Book Award and became an instant landmark of 20th-century American literature. Saul Bellow (477) called it 'a book of the very first order', and it inspired Barack Obama's 1995 memoir *Dreams from My Father*. It is both an impassioned book about black identity and Marxism (546) and an archetypal myth about isolation.

Juneteenth
1954–94, pub. 1999

'Juneteenth' has been called America's 'second Independence Day'. It commemorates the announcement of emancipation from slavery in Texas on 19 June 1865. Ellison spent 40 years writing this novel and never completed it. He left behind 2,000 manuscript pages, which his friend, biographer and literary executor, John F. Callahan, condensed to 300. The book takes the form of a conversation between the racist Senator Adam Sunraider and a black Baptist minister, Daddy Hickman, a former jazz trombonist who raised the orphaned Sunraider. These two men confront their shared past and the events surrounding one particular Juneteenth celebration. Toni Morrison called it 'a majestic narrative concept'.

2000
ed. John F. Callahan, 1999
—
In 2010, Callahan published the complete manuscript of Ellison's last novel under the title *Three Days Before the Shooting...*

Sherwood King 1904–1981

Raymond Sherwood King wrote detective novels with titles such as *Between Murders* (1935) and *A Price for Murder* (1957). He is best remembered for *If I Die Before I Wake*, which was adapted for the screen by Orson Welles as *The Lady from Shanghai* (1947), starring both Welles and Rita Hayworth, whose real-life marriage was breaking up as they were filming. The movie is famous for its climactic shoot-out in a hall of mirrors.

If I Die Before I Wake
1938

Laurence Planter is a handsome ex-sailor working as a chauffeur. After his boss's business partner Grisby offers him money to help fake his own death, Planter becomes entangled with his boss's beautiful wife Elsa.

2010
—

The Fugitives, the Southern Agrarians and the New Criticism

In 1922, a group of poets associated with Vanderbilt University in Tennessee started a poetry magazine called *The Fugitive*. Their aim, according to the critic J. A. Bryant, was 'to demonstrate that a group of southerners could produce important work in the medium, devoid of sentimentality and carefully crafted'. The group included Allen Tate, Robert Penn Warren (489), John Crowe Ransom and Donald Davidson, all of whom also became members of the Southern Agrarians, a literary group that defended the South's rural outlook and traditional conservative and religious values. They published a manifesto collection of essays, *I'll Take My Stand* (1930), and their aesthetics influenced the New Criticism, a trend in mid-20th-century America towards objective close reading of texts, liberated from biographical and literary context. The movement was formalized by John Crowe Ransom in his book *The New Criticism* (1941), in which he synthesized theories developed by T. S. Eliot (11), William Empson (86) and I. A. Richards.

Allen Tate 1899–1979

The poet John Orley Allen Tate fell in with the 'Fugitives' group while studying at Vanderbilt University in Nashville, Tennessee, in 1921. He worked as a freelance poet and critic, editing literary journals, commissioning 'belles-lettres' for the publisher Henry Holt and teaching at various universities. In 1964, he was elected a member of the American Academy of Arts and Letters.

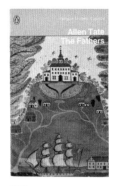

1969
● intro. Arthur Mizener, 1947, rev. 1959

The Fathers 1938

Tate's only novel is narrated by Lacy Buchan, an old man recalling the events of his boyhood during the American Civil War. He describes the collapse of two families related by marriage: the Buchans, Virginian gentleman landowners with outmoded feudal principles, and the Poseys, impulsive and violent, who use the war to their own advantage. The *Times Literary Supplement* called it 'one of the great novels of our time' and the critic Arthur Mizener said it was 'the novel *Gone with the Wind* ought to have been'.

Wallace Stegner 1909–1993

Wallace Earle Stegner was born in Lake Mills, Iowa, the son of Scandinavian immigrants. As a child, he travelled with his family all over the West and Canada, through North Dakota, Washington, Saskatchewan, Montana and Wyoming, before finally settling in Salt Lake City in 1921. He taught at the universities of Wisconsin, Harvard and Stanford, where he founded the famous Creative Writing Program, alumni of which include Edward Abbey (542), Wendell Berry, Ken Kesey (520) and Larry McMurtry (530). The novelist C. P. Snow called Stegner 'one of the deepest, truest, and most likeable writers in America'.

Collected Stories

1938–62, pub. 1990

'The thirty-one stories in this volume […] make a sort of personal record,' wrote Stegner in his foreword. 'I lived them, either as participant or spectator or auditor, before I made fictions of them.' Set in the American West, they are tales of 'young love and older wisdom', three of which won the O. Henry (409) Award. 'This is an age of the short story,' wrote the *Washington Post Book World*. 'None will be better or more worthy of admiration than Wallace Stegner's *Collected Stories*.'

2013
fwd. Wallace Stegner, 1990

The Big Rock Candy Mountain

1943

Over the course of 30 years, Bo Mason, his wife Elsa and their two sons, Chester and Bruce, drift around the West from town to town, living a life of transient poverty.

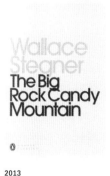

2013
—

A Shooting Star 1961

Sabrina Castro moves from
New England to marry
a wealthy Californian
doctor, and a brief dalliance
leads to a spiral of moral
disintegration.

All the Little Live Things
1967

Joe Allston, an east-coast
literary agent, moves to
California with his wife Ruth,
as they mourn the death
of their son. 'The Great Gatsby
(424) captures the twenties
and yet transcends them,'
wrote the Virginia Quarterly
Review. 'All the Little Live
Things is a comparable
achievement for the sixties
[…] Stegner's craft is
here at an apex.' It won
the Commonwealth Gold
Cup Medal.

Recapitulation
1979

Bruce Mason is a successful
statesman and diplomat who
returns to Salt Lake City in
Utah, ostensibly to arrange
his aunt's funeral, but really
to revisit the site of his
painful adolescence, which
he has managed to suppress
throughout his career.
'This is Stegner's The Sound
and the Fury (433),' wrote
the critic Jackson Benson.
'Like the Faulkner novel,
Recapitulation is a book about
time and its multiplicity
of meanings in human
experience, about the history
of a family and its decline.'

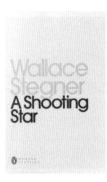

2013
—

2013
—

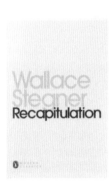

2013
—

2006
intro. Jane Smiley

Wolf Willow
A History, a Story, and a Memory of the Last Plains Frontier 1962

Stegner recalls his upbringing
in the remote and beautiful
expanses of southern
Saskatchewan. He combines
childhood remembrances
with adult reflections on
the history of the region.
Vladimir Nabokov (304) called
it 'enchanting, heartrending
and eminently enviable'.

Angle of Repose
1971

Lyman Ward is the ageing
author of several books
about the Western frontier.
Wheelchair-bound, he returns
to his ancestral home of
Grass Valley, in California's
Sierra Nevada, to retrace
his grandmother's life story
a hundred years earlier. Stegner
based much of the novel on the
unpublished frontier letters of
Mary Hallock Foote; it won the
Pulitzer Prize for Fiction in 1972.

The Spectator Bird
1976

When Joe Allston, from
All the Little Live Things, receives
a postcard from an old friend,
a Danish countess named Astrid,
he digs out the journal of a trip
he and his wife made to visit his mother's birthplace in
Denmark. The Spectator Bird won the National Book Award.

Crossing to Safety 1987

This semi-autobiographical novel is about two
couples: they first become friends in the 1930s, when
they have much in common; but over the years, and
after different life choices, their relationships become
increasingly complex.

2000
intro. Page Stegner

The novelist Page Stegner was
Wallace Stegner's son

2000 Penguin Books
intro. Jackson J. Benson

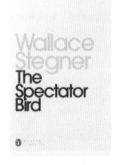

2013
—

Dalton Trumbo 1905–1976

James Dalton Trumbo worked night shifts for eight years, wrapping bread in an industrial Los Angeles bakery, before he became a writer. In 1934, he got a job with Warner Brothers in their story department and eventually became one of Hollywood's highest-paid screenwriters. In 1947, however, he was one of the 'Hollywood Ten' who refused to testify about their alleged communist affiliations before the House of Un-American Activities Committee. He was convicted for contempt of Congress and blacklisted in Hollywood, so he moved to Mexico and continued to write under pseudonyms. His screenplays for *Roman Holiday* (1953) and *The Brave One* (1956) both won Academy Awards that he couldn't claim at the time. He was not credited under his own name again until 1960, when he wrote the script for Stanley Kubrick's *Spartacus*.

Johnny Got His Gun 1939

Joe Bonham, a soldier in the First World War, wakes up in hospital to discover that he has been catastrophically wounded: he has lost both his arms, both his legs and all of his face, including his eyes, ears, teeth and tongue. Imprisoned inside his own body, he pursues memories, daydreams and fantasies, reflecting on the nature of war and struggling to remain sane. *Time* called it 'as sharp as bloodied barbed wire, retchsome as the smell of gas gangrene', and it won the National Book Award. Trumbo wrote the novel as a protest against potential US involvement in the Second World War; the 1959 reprint was released in protest against the Vietnam War.

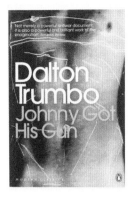

2009
intro. Dalton Trumbo, 1959
intro. E. L. Doctorow (538), 2009
—
Trumbo directed the 1971 film adaptation and co-wrote the script with Luis Buñuel; it stars Timothy Bottoms as Bonham and Donald Sutherland as Jesus Christ.

Raymond Chandler 1888–1959

Raymond Thornton Chandler was born in Chicago but his family moved to England when he was twelve. He went to school in London before joining the British civil service and working as a journalist. He returned to the USA in 1912 and lived in California, stringing tennis rackets and picking fruit for a living. He served in the Canadian army in the First World War, then worked for various oil companies, losing his job in the Great Depression and turning to writing fiction at the age of 44. His first novel, *The Big Sleep*, was a huge success and made his name as one of the great writers of detective fiction. He wrote screenplays for a number of films, including *Double Indemnity* (1944), *The Blue Dahlia* (1946) and *Strangers on a Train* (1951). In his later years, he suffered increasingly from depression, alcoholism and general ill health. 'His books should be read and judged, not as escape literature, but as works of art,' wrote W. H. Auden (95).

Three Novels 1939–53

The Big Sleep, Farewell My Lovely, The Long Goodbye

Hard-boiled Philip Marlowe is a fast-talking, trouble-seeking private investigator, a 'shop-soiled Galahad' in the neon wilderness of Los Angeles. In *The Big Sleep* (1939), Marlowe's first outing, he tangles with the wealthy Sternwood family and an array of double-crossing underworld figures, including Moose Malloy – 'about as inconspicuous as a tarantula on a slice of angel food' – and 'a blonde to make a bishop kick a hole in a stained glass window'. The book was filmed in 1946 by Howard Hawks, with Humphrey Bogart as Philip Marlowe and a screenplay by William Faulkner (433). There have been three film adaptations of *Farewell My Lovely* (1940), the second Marlowe novel; and Chandler considered *The Long Goodbye* (1953) his 'best book'. It was adapted for film in 1973.

1948–59
Penguin Books
individual titles
1993 Twentieth-Century Classics
2000 Modern Classics *The Big Sleep and Other Novels*
—

The Lady in the Lake
and Other Novels
The Lady in the Lake, The High Window, The Little Sister
1942–9

'Murder-a-day' Marlowe hunts for a jinxed gold doubloon in *The High Window* (1942) and a missing wife in *The Lady in the Lake* (1943). *The Little Sister* (1949) is about a prim young woman who may not be as innocent as she looks. 'Raymond Chandler was and remains a hard man to follow,' said Ross Macdonald (498). 'He wrote like a slumming angel, and invested the sun-blinded streets of Los Angeles with a romantic presence.'

1951–5 Penguin Books
individual titles
2001 Modern Classics
—

Raymond Chandler
The Lady in the Lake and Other Novels

Richard Wright 1908–1960

Wright grew up with his maternal grandparents, strict Seventh-Day Adventists who beat him frequently after he accidentally set the house on fire. In 1927, he moved to Chicago, joined the John Reed (420) Club and the Communist Party and began writing poetry and short stories. He then became the Harlem editor of the *Daily Worker*, a communist magazine in New York. His volume of four short stories, *Uncle Tom's Children* (1938), earned him a Guggenheim Fellowship that allowed him to complete his first novel, *Native Son*. After publishing an autobiography, *Black Boy* (1945), he moved with his wife and daughters to Paris, where he lived for the rest of his life. In Paris, he befriended fellow expatriates Chester Himes (509) and James Baldwin (492) and the existentialists (186) Jean-Paul Sartre (185), Simone de Beauvoir (187) and Albert Camus (181).

Penguin Modern Classics

Richard Wright
Native Son

1972
● —
The Penguin edition
is prefaced by Wright's
1940 article 'How
"Bigger" Was Born'.

Native Son 1940

'The day *Native Son* appeared, American culture was changed forever,' wrote the critic Irving Howe. 'No matter how much qualifying the book might later need, it made impossible a repetition of the old lies.' Twenty-year-old Bigger Thomas grew up in the slums of Chicago's South Side. He is the violent product of a racist world, forced to seize agency and seek self-knowledge by murdering those he loves. 'No American Negro exists,' wrote James Baldwin (492), 'who does not have his private Bigger Thomas living in his skull.' Baldwin called Wright 'the greatest black writer in the world'. Wright co-wrote a play adaptation of *Native Son* in 1941, which was directed on Broadway by Orson Welles; he also starred in a 1951 Argentinian film version, despite being 42 at the time.

Truman Capote 1924–1984

Truman Streckfus Persons's parents divorced when he was six and he was raised by his mother's relatives in Monroeville, Alabama. He became childhood friends with Harper Lee, who later used him as the model for Dill in *To Kill a Mockingbird* (1960). In 1932, he moved to New York City to live with his mother and her new Cuban husband, Joseph Garcia Capote, who adopted him and renamed him Truman Garcia Capote. After a brief job in the art department of the *New Yorker*, from which he was fired for upsetting Robert Frost (415), Capote devoted the rest of his life to writing. He became one of America's most notorious authors, producing stories, novels, screenplays and non-fiction works of New Journalism (464). Norman Mailer (496) called him 'the most perfect writer of my generation'. He cultivated a lifelong rivalry with Gore Vidal and became a familiar face on television talk shows, but his last years were dominated by drugs, alcohol and cosmetic procedures. When Capote died, Vidal described it as 'a wise career move'.

Stories 1940–83

Capote's first literary success came in 1945 with the publication of 'Miriam' in *Mademoiselle* magazine. This story of a widow plagued by an eerie young girl won him the contract to write *Other Voices, Other Rooms*, and he went on to publish about 20 more short stories, including the Gothic 'Shut a Final Door', which won an O. Henry (409) Award, and the tenderly autobiographical 'A Christmas Memory', which recalls his upbringing in Alabama and his loving friendship with his elderly cousin 'Sook'.

2005
intro. Reynolds Price, 2004

2017
fwd. Hilton Als, 2015

2020 Hardback Classics
2021 Modern Classics

—

In 2013, the Swiss publisher Peter Haag discovered fourteen unpublished stories in the New York Public Library archives, written when Capote was a teenager. They were published in 2015 as *The Early Stories*, to complement the 2004 volume of *The Complete Stories* which gathered all those that had been published at that point. *A Christmas Memory* features the title story, two sequels – 'The Thanksgiving Visitor' and 'One Christmas' – and two other Christmas stories.

Summer Crossing 1943–9, pub. 2005

The first novel Capote wrote is about a flame-haired New York socialite who becomes involved with a Jewish parking attendant. He abandoned it in 1950 and threw away the manuscript, and for 50 years it was believed lost. In 2004, however, it was revealed that a house-sitter had retrieved the text from the bin: the manuscript was auctioned at Sotheby's and subsequently purchased by the New York Public Library. It was published in 2005 and the *New York Times* hailed it as 'the lost novel that inspired *Breakfast at Tiffany's* (464)'.

2006
aftwd. Alan U. Schwartz, 2005

Other Voices, Other Rooms 1948

Capote's first published novel is set in a decaying Alabama mansion. Thirteen-year-old Joel Knox travels to live with a father he has never met, but instead meets his prim stepmother, her transvestite cousin Randolph and the local tomboy, Idabel, modelled on Capote's childhood friend Harper Lee. Gradually Joel comes to acknowledge his own identity amidst the secrets of this Southern Gothic (433) setting. 'Joel accepts his destiny, which is to be homosexual, to always hear other voices and live in other rooms,' writes Capote's biographer Gerald Clarke. 'Yet acceptance is not a surrender; it is a liberation.'

1964 Penguin Books
2004 Modern Classics
intro. John Berendt, 2004

The dust jacket of the 1948 first edition carried a provocative, erotically posed photograph of Capote taken by Harold Halma, which helped to fuel the book's reputation. A young Andy Warhol (543) was mesmerized by the image.

1961 Penguin Books
1993 Twentieth-Century
Classics
—
As in the 1958 first edition,
Breakfast at Tiffany's is printed
alongside three short stories:
'A Diamond Guitar', 'House
of Flowers' and 'A Christmas
Memory' (463).

Breakfast at Tiffany's 1958

A writer recalls 1940s New York and his friendship with
his fascinating neighbour Holly Golightly, 'top banana
in the shock department'. Holly is an 'authentic American
geisha', a café-society girl who survives by courting the
attentions of mafia gangsters and playboy millionaires,
and who sips martinis from cocktail hour until breakfast.
She is 'an extravagantly unconventional young lady',
wrote Dorothy Parker (419), 'entertaining to read about,
certainly, but the reader, though the author and the
characters in the tale in which he places her admire
her vastly, has always the feeling that to know the young
woman would be to find her a truly awful pest. But that,
of course, is no sort of criticism; it is doubtful if Hamlet
would have been fun to be with day on day.' The novella
was made into an iconic film in 1961, directed by Blake
Edwards and starring Audrey Hepburn.

In Cold Blood A True Account of a
Multiple Murder and Its Consequences 1965

Capote read a short article about the unexplained murder
of a farmer and his family in Holcomb, Kansas, in November
1959. He travelled to Holcomb with Harper Lee and spent
the next six years becoming acquainted with everyone
involved in the investigation, including the two murderers,
Perry Smith and Dick Hickock, who were eventually
executed in April 1965. That September, Capote published
this controversial 'non-fiction novel' about the event
and its aftermath, a landmark work of New Journalism.
'Mr. Capote is often not taken as seriously as he should
be,' said the author Rebecca West, 'and it is possible
that his new book, *In Cold Blood*,
may be regarded simply as a
literary *tour de force* instead of
the formidable statement about
reality which it is.'

1967 Penguin Books
1993 Twentieth-Century
Classics
—
The 2005 film *Capote*
dramatizes the writing of
In Cold Blood and stars Philip
Seymour Hoffman, who won
an Academy Award for his
portrayal of the author.

1993
—
Capote included 'Mojave'
as a story in his collection
Music for Chameleons (465);
this volume reprints the
other three extant chapters:
'Unspoiled Monsters',
'Kate McCloud' and
'La Côte Basque'.

Answered Prayers
The Unfinished Novel 1966–84?, pub. 1975–6

In 1966, Capote signed a contract for a new novel, which
he intended to be the American equivalent of Proust's
In Search of Lost Time (168). It was to be a thinly veiled, tell-all exposé of his jet-set contemporaries
and his coterie of wealthy female upper-class 'swans', as he called them. He was distracted,
however, by parties and his increasingly addictive lifestyle, and he repeatedly postponed his
delivery date. Eventually he published four standalone chapters in the mid-1970s, which were
indiscreet enough to cause uproar among his society friends and to strain friendships with
Tennessee Williams (455) and Katherine Anne Porter (427). He once said that *Answered Prayers*
would be his 'posthumous novel' – 'either I'm going to kill it, or it's going to kill me'. He claimed
to be working on it right up to his death, but the rest of the book has never been found.

New Journalism

In 1973, the author Tom
Wolfe published a manifesto
anthology called *The New
Journalism*, with articles
by himself, Truman Capote
(463), Joan Didion,
Norman Mailer (496),
Hunter S. Thompson (531)
and Gay Talese (519), among
others. New Journalism
emerged after the Second
World War, drawing on the
storytelling techniques of
fiction and immersing the
reporter within the narrative.
Classic examples include
John Hersey's *Hiroshima*
(488), Norman Mailer's
Armies of the Night (497),
Hunter S. Thompson's *Hell's
Angels* (531) and Truman
Capote's *In Cold Blood*. New
Journalism 'is a form that
is not merely *like a novel*,'
wrote Wolfe. 'It consumes
devices that happen to have
originated with the novel
and mixes them with every
other device known to prose.
And all the while, quite
beyond matters of technique,
it enjoys an advantage so
obvious, so built-in, one
almost forgets what power it
has: the simple fact that the
reader knows *all this actually
happened*. The disclaimers
have been erased. The screen
is gone. The writer is one
step closer to the absolute
involvement of the reader
that Henry James (397) and
James Joyce (8) dreamed
of but never achieved.'

Music for Chameleons
New Writing
1975–80, pub. 1980

The centrepiece of Capote's last book is *Handcarved Coffins* (1979), a 'non-fiction novel' about the apparently true crimes of a killer in a small Midwestern town, involving miniature coffins, a rattlesnake murder and a decapitation. Capote also gathered six short stories, including 'Music for Chameleons' and 'Mojave', and seven 'conversational portraits', which he originally wrote for Andy Warhol's (543) magazine *Interview*, in exchange for a portrait. These are affectionate pen portraits of Capote's contemporaries, including Marilyn Monroe and Willa Cather (414). *Music for Chameleons* is dedicated to Tennessee Williams (455).

1993
–

A Capote Reader
1945–83

This representative anthology gathers the best of Capote's short stories, novellas, travel sketches, conversational portraits, essays and longer works of reportage. It includes *Breakfast at Tiffany's* (464), *Handcarved Coffins* and *The Grass Harp* (1951), a novella about an orphaned boy and two elderly ladies in a tree house. *The Muses Are Heard* (1956) is Capote's brilliant account of a US state-sponsored production of George Gershwin's opera *Porgy and Bess* (1935) that toured Soviet Russia in the mid-1950s.

1993
–

James Agee 1909–1955

James Rufus Agee worked for *Fortune*, *Time* and the *Nation* magazines. He was best known in his lifetime for his film reviews and screenplays, including those for *The African Queen* (1951) and *The Night of the Hunter* (1955). He became increasingly dependent on alcohol and died of a heart attack at the age of 45.

A Death in the Family
1948–55, pub. 1957

This autobiographical novel reworks the demise of Agee's father in a car crash while driving home to Knoxville, Tennessee, after visiting his own ageing father in 1916. Agee's novel moves from one family member to another in a lyrical and insightful portrait of the pain and bewilderment of loss. Agee finished writing the book, but he had not completed its editing when he died; it was published posthumously, and won the Pulitzer Prize for Fiction in 1958.

2006
intro. Blake Morrison

Let Us Now Praise Famous Men
with Walker Evans 1941

In 1936, *Fortune* magazine commissioned James Agee and the photographer Walker Evans to spend eight weeks reporting on the conditions among sharecropper families in the South during the Dust Bowl years. The pair set out to produce a simple 'photographic and verbal record', but the project became increasingly ambitious. 'This is a *book* only by necessity,' wrote Agee. 'More seriously, it is an effort in human actuality, in which the reader is no less centrally involved than the authors and those of whom they tell.' Agee's lyrical, experimental, modernist (11) text describes the lives of three impoverished families, accompanied by Evans's stark photographs of haggard faces and desolate locations. 'I can understand why Southerners are haunted by their own landscape,' said Evans, 'and in love with it.' The resulting collaboration was hailed by Lionel Trilling (489) as 'the most realistic and important moral effort of our generation'.

2006
intro. Blake Morrison
–
Let Us Now Praise Famous Men inspired Aaron Copland's 1954 opera *The Tender Land*.

Shirley Jackson

1916–1965

Jackson was born in San Francisco and studied English literature in New York, where she met her husband, the future literary critic Stanley Edgar Hyman. They married in 1940 and both began contributing to the *New Yorker*, moving to Vermont when Hyman joined the faculty at Bennington College. In 1948, Jackson's award-winning short story 'The Lottery' brought her acclaim and notoriety. It established her as an author of disquieting, sinister and often shocking fiction: Dorothy Parker (419) called her the 'leader in the field of beautifully written, quiet, cumulative shudders'. A decade later, however, Jackson began to develop severe anxiety, which sometimes kept her housebound. In the early 1960s, she gained weight, smoked heavily and was prescribed an addictive combination of barbiturates and amphetamines, which led to her death at 48.

The Road Through the Wall 1948

Jackson's first novel was inspired by her childhood in San Francisco and written to 'get back' at her parents. It is the story of Pepper Street, a seemingly idyllic suburban neighbourhood separated from the rest of the city by a high wall; its affluent inhabitants are shallow, selfish and increasingly vicious.

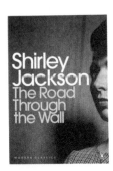

2013
fwd. Ruth Franklin
—
Ruth Franklin is a journalist and the author of the award-winning biography *Shirley Jackson: A Rather Haunted Life* (2016).

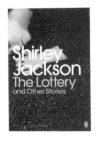

2009
—

2017
ed. Laurence Jackson Hyman & Sarah Hyman DeWitt, 1997

2017
—
Dark Tales is a ghoulish anthology of the most sinister stories from *Just an Ordinary Day* and *Let Me Tell You*.

Stories 1941–65

On 26 June 1948, the *New Yorker* published 'The Lottery': it sparked a torrent of readers' letters, more mail than the magazine had ever received in response to a work of fiction. It tells the story of a modern village in Vermont that practises an ancient and deadly harvest ritual. 'I hoped […] to shock the readers with a graphic dramatization of the pointless violence and general inhumanity of their own lives,' wrote Jackson; she was always proud that the story had been banned in South Africa. 'The Lottery' won the O. Henry (409) Award, and Donna Tartt calls it 'one of the most famous short stories of the twentieth century, and surely one of the most wicked'. In 1949, Jackson published *The Lottery and Other Stories*, the only story collection that appeared in her lifetime. In 1996, a crate of unpublished stories was discovered in a barn behind her house and the posthumous collections *Just an Ordinary Day* (1997) and *Let Me Tell You* (2015) were published, edited by her children Laurence Jackson Hyman and Sarah Hyman DeWitt. Jackson's unsettling tales are characterized by mutinous guests, vanished bridegrooms, creepy children, nightmarish games and murderous thoughts. 'Her fierce visions of dissociation and madness, of alienation and withdrawal, of cruelty and terror have been taken to be personal, even neurotic, fantasies,' wrote her husband Stanley Edgar Hyman. 'Quite the reverse: they are a sensitive and faithful anatomy of our times, fitting symbols for our distressing world of the concentration camp and the Bomb.'

Life Among the Savages

1948–53, pub. 1953

As well as macabre stories, Shirley Jackson also wrote humorous vignettes about family life, which she published in the *Ladies' Home Journal*, *Good Housekeeping* and *Woman's Day*. In 1953, she assembled the best of these as a memoir of her Vermont house, dealing with new children, their misbehaving imaginary friends, an oblivious husband and mounting domestic chaos. Betty Friedan (522) criticized Jackson for writing these tales of a 'happy housewife', but the *New York Times Book Review* called them 'genuinely subversive'.

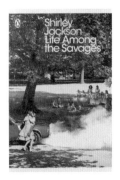

2019
—

2016
ed. Laurence Jackson Hyman
& Sarah Hyman DeWitt, 2015
fwd. Ruth Franklin, 2015

Let Me Tell You also includes a selection of essays,
reviews, articles, lectures and line drawings by Jackson.

2013
fwd. Francine Prose
—
Susan Scarf Merrell's novel
Shirley (2014) is a fictionalized
account of Jackson's writing
of *Hangsaman*; it was the basis
for the 2020 film *Shirley*,
starring Elisabeth Moss.

2021
—

Hangsaman 1951

Natalie Waite is a lonely college
student whose sense of identity falls
apart as she experiences nightmarish
parties, manipulative lecturers
and spiteful student cliques. She
increasingly withdraws into her own
elaborate and paranoid fantasies.

Raising Demons

1954–7, pub. 1957

In this sequel to *Life Among the
Savages* (466), the family moves to
a larger house where they deal with
thousands of books, numerous pets,
absent furniture and recalcitrant
former owners. 'A housewife-mother's
frustrations are transformed by
a deft twist of the wrist into, not
a grim account of disintegration and
madness, still less the poisoning of
her family, but light-hearted comedy,'
writes Joyce Carol Oates.

The Haunting of Hill House 1959

'Stepping into Hill House is like stepping
into the mind of a madman,' writes Stephen
King. Jackson's best-known novel follows
a mixed group of psychic investigators
who converge on a forbidding, apparently
sentient mansion and gradually descend
into a deadly psychological
nightmare. The *New York Times*
described it as 'caviar for the
connoisseurs of the cryptic,
the bizarre, the eerie'. It has
been filmed twice as *The
Haunting*, in 1963 and 1999.

1984 Penguin Books
2009 Modern Classics
—
'The books that have profoundly scared
me when I read them – made me want
to sleep with the light on, made the
neck hairs prickle and the goose bumps
march, are few,' says the novelist Neil
Gaiman. '[…] But Shirley Jackson's
The Haunting of Hill House beats them
all […]. It scared me as a teenager
and it haunts me still.'

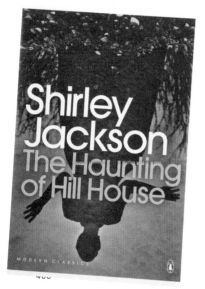

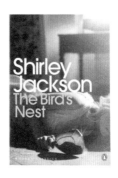

2014
fwd. Kevin Wilson

The Bird's Nest 1954

Elizabeth Richmond has
no friends and no parents.
When she starts to suffer
from unexplained
insomnia and backaches,
her identity suddenly
splinters into multiple
disturbing and wicked
personalities.

The Sundial 1958

A family of mean-spirited
eccentrics believe they have
been chosen to survive
the end of the world,
holed up in Halloran
House, a Gothic mansion
which has 'geometrically
flawless' grounds
except for a jarringly
asymmetrical sundial.

1986 Penguin Books
2014 Modern Classics
fwd. Victor LaValle, 2014

We Have Always Lived in the Castle

1962

'My name is Mary Katherine Blackwood. I am
eighteen years old, and I live with my sister
Constance. I have often thought that with any
luck at all I could have been born a werewolf,
because the two middle fingers on both my
hands are the same length.' Jackson's last
novel is narrated by the childlike 'Merricat'
Blackwood, whose family died six years ago,
poisoned by arsenic
in the sugar they
sprinkled over
their blackberries.
Joyce Carol Oates
calls it 'Jackson's
masterpiece of
gothic suspense'.

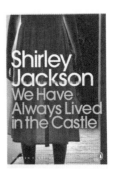

1984 Penguin Books
2009 Modern Classics
aftwd. Joyce Carol Oates,
2009

Jack Kerouac 1922–1969

'A very unique cat,' Allen Ginsberg (490) called him – 'a French Canadian Hinayana Buddhist Beat Catholic savant.' Jean-Louis Lebris de Kérouac was born in Lowell, Massachusetts, and grew up speaking *joual*, a French dialect; he became fluent in English only in his late teens. As a child, he recalled in *Lonesome Traveler* (472), he 'roamed fields and riverbanks day and night, wrote little novels in my room [...] also kept extensive diaries and "newspapers" covering my own-invented horseracing and baseball and football worlds'. He moved to New York in the 1940s, where he met William S. Burroughs (481), Allen Ginsberg and John Clellon Holmes (501), and he became, as the *New York Times* put it, the 'King of the Beats (491)'. *On the Road* (470), the second novel Kerouac published, made him an icon; it is the centrepiece of an autobiographical body of work which he called *The Duluoz Legend* (473). After a lifetime of heavy drinking, Kerouac died at the age of 47, while working on an unfinished book about his father's print shop.

2012
ed. Dawn M. Ward, 2011

The Sea is My Brother
The Lost Novel 1942–3, pub. 2011

During the Second World War, Kerouac served as a seaman on board a troopship for four months in 1942. The experience inspired his first novel, about two friends who take to the sea and play cards as they dodge torpedoes in the mid-Atlantic. *The Times* called it 'a revelation' when it was published posthumously. The Penguin edition also includes fragments of other early stories.

2015
ed. Todd Tietchen, 2014

The Haunted Life
and Other Writings 1942–63, pub. 2014

The Haunted Life (1942–4), Kerouac's 'lost novella', is a coming-of-age tale about Peter Martin, who grows up in the small fictional town of Galloway, Massachusetts, haunted by the knowledge that he is destined for bigger things. Kerouac lost the manuscript in 1944, but it was subsequently found in his Columbia University dorm room and sold at auction in 2002. This volume also includes a selection of letters, diary entries and literary fragments.

The Town and the City 1946–9, pub. 1950

Kerouac's first published novel follows Peter Martin as he moves from his provincial home town of Galloway to the heaving, multifaceted city of New York. Companions of Kerouac such as Allen Ginsberg (490) and William S. Burroughs (481) appear under pseudonyms; and he even includes an account of his friend Lucien Carr's murder of David Kammerer, a would-be lover, which he and Burroughs had previously described in *And the Hippos Were Boiled in Their Tanks* (491). *The Town and the City* was inspired by Thomas Wolfe's (438) novels and the death of Kerouac's own father in 1946. 'It is the sum of myself,' he wrote, 'as far as the written word can go.'

2000
intro. Douglas Brinkley

On the Road 1947–56, pub. 1957

'With his barbaric yawp of a book,' wrote *Time* magazine, 'Kerouac commands attention as a kind of literary James Dean.' After gathering material over several years, Kerouac sat down in April 1951 and typed uninterruptedly for three weeks. He taped together strips of drawing paper to form a continuous, 120-foot sheet which scrolled through his typewriter as he produced a single, spontaneous text, with no chapter or paragraph breaks, while his wife Joan stoked him with Benzedrine, cigarettes, bowls of pea soup and mugs of coffee. It describes Kerouac's cross-country American adventures with his friend Neal Cassady between 1947 and 1950. Using the names 'Sal Paradise' and 'Dean Moriarty', Kerouac recalls their fragmented odyssey of bebop and drugs, filling stations and pool halls, sinful cities and the great open road. '[We] embarked on a tremendous

1972 Modern Classics
1991 Twentieth-Century Classics
intro. Ann Charters, 1991

journey through post-Whitman America to FIND that America,' he later wrote. '[…] It was really a story about 2 Catholic buddies roaming the country in search of God. And we found him.' The text is written in what Kerouac called 'spontaneous prose', his distinctive blend of jazz improvisation punctuated with long dashes that replicate the 'breaths' of Buddhist meditation. Truman Capote (463) famously said, 'That's not writing, it's typing'; nonetheless *On the Road* transformed American literature and came to represent the Beat Generation (491) around the world. It is 'the most beautifully executed, the clearest, and most important utterance yet made by the generation Kerouac himself named years ago', wrote the *New York Times*. 'It changed my life,' said Bob Dylan, 'like it changed everyone else's.'

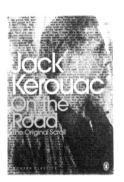

2008
ed. Howard Cunnell, 2007
intro. Howard Cunnell et al., 2007
—
Kerouac struggled to find a publisher for *On the Road* because of its experimental style and frank descriptions of sex and drugs. The text that appeared in print in 1957 was abridged and all the names were changed. In 2007, 50 years later, the complete text of the original scroll was published, with the real names and places restored. That same year, the scroll went on an exhibition tour around the world and was on display temporarily at the British Library in London.

2012
intro. Allen Ginsberg, 1972
—
Since its first publication, *Visions of Cody* has included an introductory essay by Allen Ginsberg (490), 'The Visions of the Great Rememberer'.

Visions of Cody 1951–2, pub. 1972

Kerouac compiled this text for inclusion in *On the Road*, but then decided to publish it separately. It is 'a 600-page character study of the hero of *On the Road*, "Dean Moriarty," whose name is now "Cody Pomeray"', he explained in his prefatory note. '[…] Instead of just a horizontal account of travels on the road, I wanted a vertical, metaphysical study of Cody's character and its relationship to the general America.' The book recapitulates the events of *On the Road*, interspersed with intense sensory 'sketches' of New York, and transcriptions of tape recordings made while Kerouac and Cassady talked, drank, and smoked marijuana.

Pic 1951–69, pub. 1971

This novella tells the story of Pictorial Review Jackson, a ten-year-old black boy from North Carolina who hitchhikes to New York with his older brother Slim.

Pic

2001 Modern Classics
with The Subterraneans (471)
2019 Modern Classics
—
The current Penguin editions of Jack Kerouac have Robert Frank photographs on their covers. Frank was a Swiss photographer who lived and worked in America; Kerouac wrote the introduction to his most famous book of photographs, *The Americans* (1958), which is often described as the most influential photography book of the 20th century.

More ROAD TRIPS

Americana
by Don DeLillo   537

The Reivers
by William Faulkner   435

As I Walked Out One Midsummer Morning
by Laurie Lee   114

The Road to Wigan Pier
by George Orwell   82

The Wayward Bus
by John Steinbeck   444

2012
—

2001 Modern Classics
with Pic (470)
intro. Ann Douglas, 2001
2020 Modern Classics
—

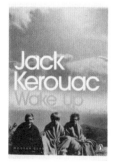

2008
intro. Robert A. F. Thurman

Doctor Sax Faust Part Three 1952, pub. 1959

When Kerouac was a child, he had an imaginary friend called 'Doctor Sax': 'my ghost, personal angel, private shadow, secret lover'. High on marijuana, Kerouac recalls his childhood games in Lowell, Massachusetts, and his spooky fantasies about the 'Great World Snake' and its attendant vampires, gnomes, spiders, black-mass ecclesiastics and werewolves of the soul. This was Kerouac's favourite of all his books.

Maggie Cassidy

1953, pub. 1959

Following on from *Doctor Sax*, this is an affectionate portrait of Kerouac's real-life relationship with his teenage sweetheart, Mary Carney.

The Subterraneans

1953, pub. 1958

Kerouac wrote this short novel over three nights, fictionalizing his brief but intense love affair with the hard-drinking Alene Lee: he calls himself 'Leo Percepied' and Lee is 'Mardou Fox'. They start to fall in love amidst the drunken, 'subterranean' intellectuals of San Francisco, until Leo destroys their relationship. The character of the young novelist Harold Sand is based on William Gaddis (505).

Wake Up
A Life of the Buddha

1954–5, pub. 1993–5

In 1954, Kerouac discovered Dwight Goddard's *A Buddhist Bible* (1938) in the library in San Jose, California. Encouraged by his friend, the poet Gary Snyder, he became increasingly fascinated by Buddhism, and over the following year he wrote this biography of Siddhartha Gautama, although it was never published in Kerouac's lifetime.

1993 Penguin Books
2000 Modern Classics
—

2019
—

Mexico City Blues 1955–7, pub. 1959

'I want to be considered a jazz poet blowing a long blues in an afternoon jam session on Sunday,' said Kerouac. He wrote this book of poetry under the influence of marijuana and morphine, while living in Mexico City with the heroin addict Bill Garver, a friend of William S. Burroughs (481). It comprises 242 spontaneous 'choruses', the arbitrary breaks between which replicate the page divisions in Kerouac's notebook. Some transcribe Garver's speech, others attempt to recreate sounds, others touch variously on life, death, memory, dreams and spirituality. Allen Ginsberg (490) described the collection as 'spontaneous bop prosody and original classic literature'; Gary Snyder has called it 'the greatest piece of religious poetry I've ever seen'.

Tristessa

1955–6, pub. 1960

Kerouac fictionalizes his love affair with a Mexican prostitute; Allen Ginsberg (490) called it 'a narrative meditation studying a hen, a rooster, a dove, a cat, a chihuahua dog, family meat, and a ravishing, ravished junky lady'.

1992 Penguin Books
2019 Modern Classics
—

Desolation Angels

1956–61, pub. 1965

The first section of this book, 'Desolation Angels', describes Kerouac's experience of three months living on his own in the wilds of Washington state as a fire lookout on Desolation Peak, hoping to 'come face to face with God or Tathagata and find out once and for all what is the meaning of all this existence and suffering'. The second section, 'Passing Through', traces 'one of the most true, comic and grizzly journeys in American literature', as Time magazine put it: a trip through Mexico, the USA, Morocco, France and England in the company of Allen Ginsberg (490) and William S. Burroughs (481).

2012
—

Visions of Gerard

1956, pub. 1963

When Kerouac was four, his nine-year-old brother Gerard died of rheumatic fever. He wrote this 'pain-tale' recalling his saintly sibling in two weeks, while staying with his sister. Kerouac called it his 'most serious, sad and true book'; it forms the first instalment in his projected memoir cycle, The Duluoz Legend (473).

1991 Penguin Books
2020 Modern Classics
—

1977 Penguin Books
2000 Modern Classics
2007 Modern Classics
intro. Ann Douglas, 2007

The Dharma Bums

1957, pub. 1958

Published the year after On the Road (470), this is Kerouac's fictionalized account of his spiritual quest for Dharma, or 'Truth', in the company of his friend, the poet Gary Snyder. They spend time in the solitude of California's High Sierras and among the jazz clubs and poetry jams of San Francisco, contrasting the wild outdoors with bohemian city life. The Dharma Bums was an influential text for the 1960s counterculture movement (526).

Lonesome Traveler

1960

These non-fiction travel pieces 'cover the United States from the south to the east coast to the west coast to the far northwest, cover Mexico, Morocco Africa, Paris, London, both the Atlantic and Pacific oceans at sea in ships, and various interesting people and cities therein included,' Kerouac explains. '[…] Its scope and purpose is simply poetry, or, natural description.'

2000
—

Big Sur 1961, pub. 1962

Kerouac struggled with the press attention that followed the success of On the Road (470) and in 1960 he felt he had to 'get away to solitude again or die'. He made three trips to the poet Lawrence Ferlinghetti's remote cabin at Bixby Canyon on the Californian coast, on one of which he wrote this novel in ten days. An account of Kerouac's downward spiral into self-doubt and alcoholism, it ends with the free-verse poem 'Sea', written from the perspective of the Pacific Ocean.

1991 Penguin Books
2012 Modern Classics
—

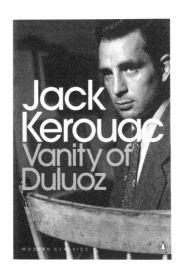

1994 Penguin Books
2012 Modern Classics
—

Satori in Paris 1965, pub. 1966

'I'll use my real name here,' wrote Kerouac, 'full name in this case, Jean-Louis Lebris de Kérouac, because this story is about my search for this name in France.' Although he keeps hitting genealogical dead ends, he does experience, in a Parisian taxi, a moment of *satori*, the Buddhist concept of sudden spiritual awakening.

Vanity of Duluoz 1967, pub. 1968
An Adventurous Education, 1935–1946

Kerouac's last published work is addressed to 'wifey': his third wife, Stella Sampas. As well as describing a formative decade in his youth – his transition from sporting jock to Beat (491) icon – Kerouac also comments on more recent events. 'People have changed so much […] in the past thirty years,' he wrote, 'to such an extent that I don't recognize them as people any more or recognize myself as a real member of something called the human race.'

2012
—

The Duluoz Legend

'My work comprises one vast book like Proust's *Remembrances of Things Past* (168),' wrote Kerouac at the start of *Visions of Cody* (470), 'except that my remembrances are written on the run instead of afterwards in a sick bed. Because of the objections of my early publishers I was not allowed to use the same personae names in each work. *On the Road* (470), *The Subterraneans* (471), *The Dharma Bums* (472), *Doctor Sax* (472), *Maggie Cassidy* (471), *Tristessa* (472), *Desolation Angels* (472) and the others are just chapters in the whole work which I call *The Duluoz Legend*. In my old age I intend to collect all my work and re-insert my pantheon of uniform names, leave the long shelf full of books there, and die happy. The whole thing forms one enormous comedy, seen through the eyes of poor Ti Jean (me), otherwise known as Jack Duluoz, the world of raging action and folly and also of gentle sweetness seen through the keyhole of his eye.' Kerouac never lived to old age, but there have been various posthumous attempts to reconstruct *The Duluoz Legend*, arranging his works of autobiographical fiction as a roughly continuous narrative. Here is a version of his chronological 'shelf full of books', with some of the changeable 'personae names' he used for himself and his friends.

	Jack Kerouac	**Neal Cassady**	**Allen Ginsberg** (490)	**William S. Burroughs** (481)
Visions of Gerard	Jack Duluoz			
Doctor Sax	Jack Duluoz			
Maggie Cassidy	Jack Duluoz			
The Town and the City	Peter Martin		Leon Levinsky	Will Dennison
Vanity of Duluoz	Jack Duluoz	Cody Pomeray	Irwin Garden	Will Hubbard
On the Road	Sal Paradise	Dean Moriarty	Carlo Marx	Old Bull Lee
Visions of Cody	Jack Duluoz	Cody Pomeray	Irwin Garden	Bull Hubbard
The Subterraneans	Leo Percepied	Leroy	Adam Moorad	Frank Carmody
Tristessa	Jack Duluoz			
The Dharma Bums	Ray Smith	Cody Pomeray	Alvah Goldbook	
Desolation Angels	Jack Duluoz	Cody Pomeray	Irwin Garden	Bull Hubbard
Big Sur	Jack Duluoz	Cody Pomeray	Irwin Garden	
Satori in Paris	Jean-Louis Lebris de Kérouac			

Woody Guthrie 1912–1967

Woodrow Wilson Guthrie grew up in Okemah, Oklahoma. At the onset of the Great Depression, he left his wife and three children and joined the thousands of 'Okies' migrating to California during the Dust Bowl years. He travelled around America by foot and freight train, writing songs and singing for dimes. He became one of America's greatest folk singers, famous for 'This Land Is Your Land' and particularly for his first album, *Dust Bowl Ballads* (1940), which drew inspiration from Steinbeck's *The Grapes of Wrath* (442). Considered by many to be the 'father of American folk music', Guthrie inspired musicians from Ramblin' Jack Elliott, Bob Dylan and Joan Baez to Bruce Springsteen, Joe Strummer and Billy Bragg. He frequently performed with the slogan 'THIS MACHINE KILLS FASCISTS' written on his guitar. 'Woody Guthrie and the ten thousand songs that leap and tumble off the strings of his music box are a national possession, like Yellowstone and Yosemite', wrote the *New Yorker*.

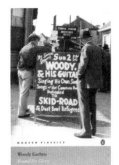

2004
intro. Joe Klein
—
Joe Klein is a political columnist and staff writer for the *New Yorker*. He is the author of *Woody Guthrie: A Life* (1980).

Bound for Glory

1943

'Now I been here an' I been there,' sang Guthrie. 'Rambled aroun' most everywhere.' This funny, cynical and unreliable autobiography describes his childhood in an Oklahoma oil-boom town and his life on the lonesome road, hopping freight trains and singing his way across the Dust Bowl. Nobel Laureate Bob Dylan loved the book: 'I went through it from cover to cover like a hurricane,' he wrote, 'totally focused on every word, and the book sang out to me like the radio. Guthrie writes like the whirlwind and you get tripped out on the sound of the words alone.' Guthrie illustrated the text himself.

Jane Bowles 1917–1973

Jane Stajer Auer was born in New York. She suffered physical and mental ill health throughout her life and developed extreme phobias of fire, water, mountains, elevators, dogs, sharks and jungles. She married the writer and composer Paul Bowles (480) in 1938, and their honeymoon in Latin America inspired her only novel, *Two Serious Ladies*. The Bowleses lived abroad after 1948, mostly in Morocco, and were both involved in homosexual affairs, but they remained married until Jane's death in 1973. As well as her novel, she wrote a few short stories and one play. Despite her small output, Truman Capote (463) considered her a 'modern legend', Sybille Bedford (260) praised her 'rare originality', and the poet John Ashbery called her 'one of the finest modern writers in any language'.

2000
• intro. Lorna Sage

Two Serious Ladies 1943

Christina Goering and Frieda Copperfield meet twice: first at a party, where they inspire each other to travel, seeking pleasure and perhaps salvation; then again, after separate careers in debauchery when they compare notes. This occasionally mystifying modernist (11) novel is both profound and poetic. Tennessee Williams (455) called it his 'favourite book'.

Plain Pleasures 1944–51, pub. 1966

'Your curious, slanted and witty style has always given me boundless delight,' wrote Carson McCullers (453) to Bowles. These six stories and one puppet play are unsettling and bizarre, exploring inner worlds and hidden lives.

2000
• intro Elizabeth Young

Bernard Malamud 1914–1986

Malamud, the son of Russian Jewish immigrants, taught night classes in New York until 1949, when he joined the staff of Oregon State University. He later joined the faculty at Bennington College in Vermont. 'He was a myth maker, a fabulist, a writer of exquisite parables,' wrote Saul Bellow (477). 'The accent of hard-won and individual emotional truth is always heard in Malamud's words. He is a rich original of the first rank.' In 1967, he was elected a member of the American Academy of Arts and Letters, and he left a bequest to establish the PEN/Malamud Award for 'excellence in the art of the short story'; among the winners of which are John Updike (514), Saul Bellow, Eudora Welty (457), James Salter (508) and Lydia Davis.

1985 Penguin Books
1993 Twentieth-Century
Classics
● —
Malamud chose the 25 tales
in *Selected Stories* (1983),
the best of his previous three
collections.

1992
● ed. Robert Giroux, 1989
—
This posthumous volume
includes sixteen previously
uncollected stories as well as
Malamud's unfinished novel,
The People, about an itinerant
Jewish pedlar who accidentally
becomes a Native American chief.

Stories 1943–85

'My short stories acknowledge indebtedness specifically to Chekhov, James Joyce (8), Hemingway (428), Sherwood Anderson (420),' wrote Malamud, 'and a touch perhaps of Sholem Aleichem and the films of Charlie Chaplin (149).' He wrote tales about the Jewish experience in America, about the desire to adapt and the need to remember. 'Man in the Drawer' won the O. Henry (409) Award in 1969. He is 'a short-story writer who is better than any of them', said Flannery O'Connor, 'including myself'.

The Natural 1952

Roy Hobbs is a baseball prodigy, a natural, until his career is brought to a sudden and violent halt. Years later, at the age when most first-class players retire, he tries again to realize his life's ambition. Malamud combines the mythology of American baseball with the legend of the Holy Grail. The novel is 'the best since the great Ring Lardner (416)', said *Time* magazine, '[…] a preposterously readable story about life'. The 1984 film starred Robert Redford as Hobbs.

1967 Penguin Books
1992 Twentieth-Century
Classics
● —

The Assistant

1957

Malamud's second
novel is set in
the working-class
Brooklyn of his
youth. Morris Bober
is an ageing Jewish
refugee who runs
a grocery store.
When he takes on
an Italian American
drifter as his assistant,
he is horrified when

1967 Penguin Books
1992 Twentieth-Century
Classics
● —

his daughter starts to fall in love. *The Assistant* won the Rosenthal Award and the Daroff Memorial Award and brought Malamud international acclaim. 'Malamud's most memorable fictions are set in an outer borough of Stygian darkness where the inner light of the soul is in constant danger of winking out,' said the writer Jonathan Rosen. 'When the psalmist cries, "O Lord, do not let me go down into the pit," he may have in mind something like Morris Bober's grocery store.'

A New Life 1961

Based on Malamud's own experience of moving to Oregon State University, this is the story of Sy Levin, who leaves New York to make a new start teaching English at Cascadia College in the Midwest. The epigraph is taken from James Joyce's *Ulysses* (10): 'Lo, levin leaping lightens in eyeblink Ireland's westward welkin!'

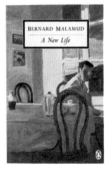

1968 Penguin Books
1995 Twentieth-Century
Classics
● —

1967 Penguin Books
1993 Twentieth-Century
Classics
● —

The Fixer 1966

Kiev in 1911 is seething with anti-Semitism.
When a 12-year-old Russian boy is found
stabbed to death and his body drained
of blood, Jews are accused of ritual child-
murder and Yakov Bok, a handyman or 'fixer',
is blamed, arrested, and imprisoned without
a trial. Malamud fictionalizes the notorious
real-life case of Mendel Beiliess in this novel
which won the National Book Award and
the Pulitzer Prize for Fiction. 'While *The Fixer*
isn't a book *about* morality, it is a *moral* book,'
writes the novelist Jonathan Safran Foer.
'That is, rather than offering a flimsy directive, it presents the reader
with a forceful question: Why aren't you doing anything?' The 1968
film adaptation was scripted by Dalton Trumbo (461).

The Tenants 1971

In a condemned New York tenement block, Harry Lesser struggles
to complete a novel while bickering with the building's only other
tenant: Willie Spearmint, a touchy anti-Semitic African American
who is also trying to write. 'Like Saul Bellow in *Mr. Sammler's Planet*
(478), like Ralph Ellison in *Invisible Man* (458),' said the *New York Times*,
'Malamud goes beyond the rhetoric of the revolutionaries to the
very root of the matter, to man's inhumanity not only to man, but
to himself.'

Dubin's Lives 1979

William Dubin is a middle-aged biographer working on a life of
D. H. Lawrence (50). He lives in Vermont, and he is happily married
to his wife Kitty – until he meets 23-year-old Fanny. 'I can't recall
a more tender portrait of a marriage,' ran the *Observer*'s review,
'or a more beautifully incisive, exact and well-judged chronicle
of the longings – not just, but chiefly, erotic
– that can worry away at such a bond.'

God's Grace 1982

Malamud's last completed novel is a fable
about a Jewish palaeologist who accidentally
survives a worldwide nuclear holocaust
through a 'minuscule error' on the part of
God. The palaeologist washes up on a desert
island with a speaking chimpanzee, and
together they attempt to build a new society.
'A fable it may be, *à la Lord of the Flies* (131),'
wrote the *New Statesman*, 'but its pleasures
lie in the absurdity of the treatment.'

1972 Penguin Books
1993 Twentieth-Century
Classics
● —

1979 Penguin Books
1994 Twentieth-Century
Classics
● —

1983 Penguin Books
1992 Twentieth-Century
Classics
● —

Saul Bellow 1915–2005

'The backbone of twentieth-century American literature has been provided by two novelists,' wrote Philip Roth in 2005 – 'William Faulkner (433) and Saul Bellow. Together they are the Melville, Hawthorne, and Twain of the twentieth century.' Solomon Bellows was born in Quebec to Lithuanian Jewish émigré parents. The family moved to the Humboldt Park neighbourhood of Chicago when he was nine years old, where his father worked as an onion importer and a bootlegger. Bellow became a naturalized US citizen in 1941, after which he joined the merchant marine; he wrote his first novel, *Dangling Man*, during the Second World War and published it under the name 'Saul Bellow'. He was married five times and lived most of his adult life in Chicago. The *Sunday Times* called him 'the most important writer in English in the second half of the 20th century'. He won the Nobel Prize for Literature (576) in 1976.

It All Adds Up
From the Dim Past to the Uncertain Future
A Nonfiction Collection
1948–94, pub. 1994

1995 Penguin Books
2007 Modern Classics
—

'If I were to write these pieces today, I think that I should say less about distraction and emphasize instead the importance of attention,' mused Bellow in his preface. This anthology collects the best of his articles, lectures, essays and travel pieces, including his Nobel lecture and 'An Interview with Myself'. 'There's hardly a sentence that doesn't have a distinctive twist,' said Malcolm Bradbury: 'an edge of unusual observation, the thrust of a wiry, hard-argued opinion.'

Stories 1951–90

'What Henry James (397) did for the geographically disoriented, Bellow does for the culturally traumatized in the six stories gathered in this collection,' wrote the *Los Angeles Times* about *Mosby's Memoirs* (1968). 'Truly, Bellow is one of God's spies.' The *Collected Stories* (2001), gathered by the author, spans four decades and incorporates the best of his three previous story anthologies, *Mosby's Memoirs*, *Him with His Foot in His Mouth* (1984) and *Something to Remember Me By* (1990).

Dangling Man 1944

Joseph wants to join the army during the Second World War, but his draft is delayed and he spends an idle year 'dangling' in Chicago. We read his diary as he grapples with existential questions. 'Behind the figure of Joseph,' writes J. M. Coetzee, 'can be discerned the lonely, humiliated clerks of Gogol and Dostoevsky, brooding upon revenge; the Roquentin of Sartre's *Nausea* (185), the scholar who undergoes a strange metaphysical experience that estranges him from the world; and the lonely young poet of Rilke's (269) *Notebooks of Malte Laurids Brigge*.'

1963 Penguin Books
1996 Twentieth-Century Classics
2007 Modern Classics
intro. J. M. Coetzee, 2007

The Victim 1947

Haunted by an old acquaintance who claims he ruined his life, Asa Leventhal descends into a spiral of self-doubt and paranoia. V. S. Pritchett (110) called it 'the best novel to come out of America – or England – for a generation'.

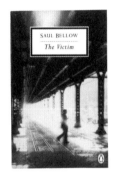

1966 Penguin Books
1998 Twentieth-Century Classics
—

1971 Penguin Books
1996 Twentieth-Century Classics
● —

1986 Penguin Books
1998 Twentieth-Century Classics
● —

2002 Penguin Books
2007 Modern Classics
pref. Janis Bellow, 2001
intro. James Wood, 2001
—
Janis Bellow is the author's widow. James Wood was a friend of Saul Bellow; they taught a literature class together at Boston University.

1966 Penguin Books
1996 Twentieth-Century
Classics
2001 Modern Classics
intro. Christopher Hitchens,
2001

1965 Penguin Books
2001 Modern Classics
● intro. Malcolm Bradbury,
2001
2019 Modern Classics
—

The Adventures of Augie March 1953

'*The Adventures of Augie March* is the Great American Novel,' writes Martin Amis (160). 'Search no further.' Bellow's picaresque masterpiece follows the life and adventures of a young Chicago immigrant drifting through the Great Depression and finding work as a butler, a thief, a dog-washer and a sailor. As a quest for identity, it has been compared with *Don Quixote*, *Moby-Dick* and *The Catcher in the Rye* (499). The opening words are a statement of self-definition for both March and Bellow himself: 'I am an American.'

Seize the Day 1956

Tommy Wilhelm is a washed-up actor in his forties, pigeonholed as 'the type that loses the girl'. Over the course of a single day, a mysterious con man inspires Tommy to shake off his spiritual malaise.

Henderson the Rain King 1959

When a disillusioned, middle-aged millionaire moves to Africa, he is unexpectedly hailed by the Wariri people as the 'Sungo', or 'rain king'. This colourful comic romp established Bellow's international reputation. Of all his characters, he felt that Eugene Henderson – an 'absurd seeker of higher qualities' – was most like himself. Philip Roth called the novel 'a screwball book, but not without great screwball authority'.

Herzog 1964

Moses E. Herzog is a failed writer, teacher, father, husband and friend. Navigating a second divorce, he analyses his suffering through endless letters to friends, enemies, colleagues and celebrities, none of which he sends. The *New Yorker* called it 'a well-nigh faultless novel'; the *Chicago Tribune* described Moses Herzog as being 'as natural an American phenomenon as the faces carved on Mount Rushmore'.

Mr. Sammler's Planet

1970

Artur Sammler, a one-eyed Auschwitz survivor, is the self-appointed 'registrar of madness', who records the absurdities of 20th-century New York, its utopian visions and doomsday prophecies, as the world anticipates the first lunar landing. The novel's conclusion is 'so powerful', writes Joyce Carol Oates, 'that it forces us to immediately reread the entire novel, because we have been *altered in the process of reading it*'.

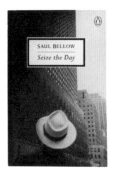

1966 Penguin Books
1996 Twentieth-Century
Classics
intro. Cynthia Ozick, 1996

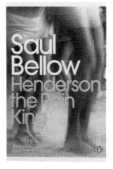

1965 Penguin Books
2007 Modern Classics
—

1971 Penguin Books
1996 Twentieth-Century
Classics
intro. Stanley Crouch, 1995

—

With *Mr. Sammler's Planet*,
Bellow became the first
author to win three National
Book Awards. He had
previously won for *The
Adventures of Augie March*
and *Herzog*.

Humboldt's Gift 1975

Bellow fictionalized his friendship with the poet Delmore Schwartz in this story of Charlie Citrine, a commercially successful writer who reflects on the death of his friend Humboldt Fleisher. Citrine's life is falling apart and Humboldt has left him an unexpected legacy. 'I think it A Work of Genius,' said John Cheever (544), 'I think it The Work of A Genius, I think it brilliant, splendid, etc. If there is literature (and this proves there is) this is where it's at.'

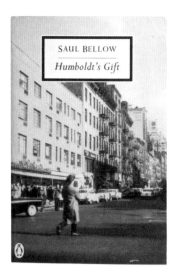

1976 Penguin Books
1996 Twentieth-Century Classics
—
Humboldt's Gift won the 1975 Pulitzer Prize for Fiction, a prize that Bellow described in the novel as 'just a dummy newspaper publicity award given by crooks and illiterates'.

To Jerusalem and Back
A Personal Account
1976

Bellow visited Israel in the mid-1970s, and this is his sensitive, meditative account of the trip, describing the history, the landscape, the culture, and the people he met. It is 'a plea for greater understanding of the state of Israel', wrote The Times, 'by one of its most articulate admirers'.

1978 Penguin Books
1998 Twentieth-Century Classics
—

The Dean's December
1982

When Albert Corde, the dean of a Chicago college, is accused of racism, he travels to Bucharest with his Romanian astrophysicist wife to visit her dying mother. He compares the corrupt communist city to the decay of Chicago and grapples with 'the big-scale insanities of the twentieth century'.

1983 Penguin Books
1998 Twentieth-Century Classics
—

More Die of Heartbreak 1987

Kenneth Trachtenberg travels to the Midwest to meet his uncle, the world-renowned botanist Benn Crader, and both men find themselves 'knee-deep in the garbage of a personal life'.

1989 Penguin Books
1996 Twentieth-Century Classics
2007 Modern Classics intro. Martin Amis, 1987
—
Amis's (160) introduction is the transcript of an early review he delivered at a Saul Bellow Conference in Haifa, Israel, in the presence of Bellow himself. 'I know that *More Die of Heartbreak* is a work of inspiration, another great efflorescence,' said Amis. 'How? Because it changes the way you see everything. It harrows and it enhances.'

The Actual 1997

The billionaire Sigmund Adletsky encourages Harry Trellman, an ageing Chicago businessman, to pursue the woman he has always loved. The novelist A. L. Kennedy called The Actual 'a taut, elegant, subtle and eloquent novella'.

Ravelstein 2000

Bellow's final novel, published when he was 85, is an affectionate fictional portrait of his friend, the philosopher Allan Bloom. The scholar Abe Ravelstein is dying and he asks his old friend Chick to write an account of his life. The book describes their last conversations as they wander the streets of Paris, and it becomes the memoir that Ravelstein requested. 'The world has never heard this prose before,' writes Martin Amis (160): 'prose of such tremulous and crystallized beauty.'

1998 Penguin Books
2008 Modern Classics
—

2001 Penguin Books
2008 Modern Classics
—

Paul Bowles 1910–1999

Paul Frederic Bowles was born in Jamaica, New York City. He began writing stories at the age of four and composing music at eight. He went to the University of Virginia because Edgar Allan Poe had studied there, but escaped to Paris where his poetry was starting to be published in the literary magazine *transition*. On a brief return visit to New York, he became the student and lover of the composer Aaron Copland; together they moved to Paris and, on Gertrude Stein's (410) advice, visited Tangier for the first time. Bowles travelled widely in North Africa and met Stephen Spender (95) and Christopher Isherwood (103) in Berlin. He returned to New York in 1937, married Jane Auer (474) in 1938, and lived in the city for a decade, working as the music critic for the *Herald Tribune*, writing an opera based on a poem by Lorca (230), and composing music for the stage productions of Tennessee Williams (455), Orson Welles and Elia Kazan. Inspired by Jane's novel *Two Serious Ladies* (474), he began writing short stories in 1945 and used the advance for *The Sheltering Sky* to move to Morocco in 1947. Jane joined him in 1948 and they lived in Tangier for the rest of their lives, apart from winters spent on their private island off Sri Lanka. The Bowleses received many visitors, including Truman Capote (463), Allen Ginsberg (490) and William S. Burroughs (481). 'Bowles was a mystic,' ran his obituary in the *Independent*. '[...] He will be seen as a major twentieth-century writer.' In 1981, he was elected to the American Academy of Arts and Letters.

2000 Modern Classics
2009 Modern Classics
aftwd. Barnaby Rogerson,
2009
—
The title *Let It Come Down* is a quotation from Shakespeare's *Macbeth*: it is the First Murderer's response to Banquo's greeting – 'It will be rain tonight' – just before attacking him. Bowles called it an 'admirable four-word sentence, succinct and brutal'.

Stories 1945–93

'Paul Bowles is *sui generis*,' writes Joyce Carol Oates. These dark and haunting stories feature strange caves, moments of violence, warped memories, the absence of God, and drug-induced transformations. Some are based on tape recordings of Moroccan folk tales; all of them present the reader with extreme situations and frequently disturbing conclusions. The *Sunday Times* called them 'eerie and alluring, like night in the desert'.

2000 Modern Classics
2009 Modern Classics
Collected Stories
intro. James Lasdun, 2000
—
There are 23 stories in the 2000 edition; the current edition of *Collected Stories* adds 39, a total of 62 stories.

The Sheltering Sky
1949

Bowles's semi-autobiographical first novel describes an American couple, Kit and Port Moresby. After ten years of marriage, they are sexually estranged, travelling through the remote Algerian desert, searching for meaning in the face of a hostile environment and mounting existential panic. Bowles wrote the book 'in bed in hotels in the desert'. Tennessee Williams (455) compared it to a summer thunderstorm, 'pulsing with interior flashes of fire'.

1969 Penguin Books
2000 Modern Classics
2009 Modern Classics
intro. Paul Theroux, 2009
—
Paul Theroux (543) met Bowles in 1994, an encounter he describes in the last chapter of *The Pillars of Hercules* (1995).

Let It Come Down 1952

Set in Tangier, *Let It Come Down* traces the disintegration of Nelson Dyar, an American who travels to Morocco to work for a travel agency only to be drawn into the city's dark underworld of brothels, corruption and hashish. 'Paul Bowles opened the world of Hip,' wrote Norman Mailer in *Advertisements for Myself* (496). 'He let in the murder, the drugs, the incest, [...] the call of the orgy, the end of civilization'.

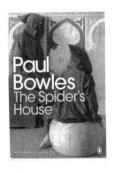

2009
intro. Francine Prose, 2003

The Spider's House

1955

Set in Fez in 1954, in the
run-up to Morocco gaining
independence, this politically
conscious novel revolves
around Stenham, an American
expatriate who reluctantly
witnesses the transformation
of the North African country.

Up Above the World

1966

An American couple, the
Slades, are holidaying in
Central America. When their
hotel burns down, they find
themselves dependent on their
new acquaintance, the charming
Grove Soto, with increasingly
sinister consequences.

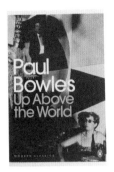

1970 Penguin Books
2009 Modern Classics
intro. Ange Mlinko, 2009

William S. Burroughs 1914–1997

J. G. Ballard called him 'the most important writer in the English language since the Second World War';
Angela Carter (156) said he was 'the most radical innovator in fiction since Joyce (8)'; and Norman Mailer
(496) described him as 'the only American novelist writing today who may conceivably be possessed of
genius'. In 1943, William Seward Burroughs met Allen Ginsberg (490) and Jack Kerouac (469) in New York,
and together they would go on to form the Beat Generation (491). Burroughs was a heroin junky, living with
fellow addict Joan Vollmer. The couple moved to Mexico, where Burroughs accidentally shot Vollmer dead
in 1951 before fleeing the country. Inspired by reading Paul Bowles (480), he relocated to Tangier in Morocco
and spent four years taking opiates and edible cannabis and producing a vast fragmentary manuscript:
he wrote obsessively to ward off what he called 'the Ugly Spirit'. In 1958, he moved to a shabby hotel in Paris
with Allen Ginsberg, the poet Gregory Corso and other Beats, where he experimented with occult mirrors
and mind-altering drugs. Burroughs met the artist Brion Gysin at the 'Beat Hotel' and together they began
developing their cut-up and fold-in literary techniques (484). After twelve years in London attempting to kick
his heroin addiction and dabbling in Scientology, Burroughs returned to the USA, met Andy Warhol (543)
and Susan Sontag (524) and embarked on a series of reading tours. He spent his last years in Kansas, collecting
firearms, making artworks by shooting cans of spray paint and performing 'chaos magic'. He featured on
the Beatles' *Sgt. Pepper's Lonely Hearts Club Band* album cover in 1967, and in 1983 he was elected to
the American Academy of Arts and Letters.

And the Hippos
Were Boiled in Their Tanks

with Jack Kerouac 1945, pub. 2008

In 1944, Burroughs and Kerouac (469) were both
arrested. Their friend Lucien Carr told them
that he had murdered his would-be lover David
Kammerer, which made them accessories after
the fact. The following year, the pair collaborated
on a hard-boiled fictional account of the incident,
writing alternate chapters under the names
'Will Dennison' and 'Mike Ryko'. The manuscript
became legendary in their lifetimes, but remained
unpublished until 2008. 'An insight into Kerouac
before he went on the road and Burroughs
before his drug use spiralled out of control,'
wrote GQ magazine, 'this is a major literary event.'

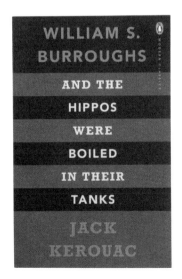

2009
aftwd. James Grauerholz, 2008
—
The unusual title came
from Burroughs's memory
of a newsreader on the
radio enjoying the report
of circus fire: 'And the hippos
were boiled in their tanks!'
James Grauerholz was
William S. Burroughs's
long-time manager and editor
and the executor of his estate.
When he found the manuscript,
Grauerholz promised Lucien
Carr he would not publish it
in Carr's lifetime. It appeared
in 2008, three years after
Carr died in 2005.

481

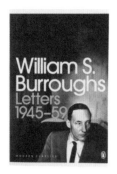

1994 Penguin Books
2009 Modern Classics
ed. Oliver Harris, 1993

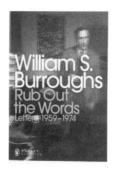

2013
ed. Bill Morgan, 2012

1977 Penguin Books
2002 Modern Classics
2008 Modern Classics *Definitive Text*
intro. Allen Ginsberg, 1977
ed. Oliver Harris, 2003

—

Written as *Junk*, *Junky* was first
published by Ace Books as *Junkie*.
The 1977 edition reinstated passages
relating to Burroughs's homosexuality
and the 2003 'definitive text' – edited
by Professor Oliver Harris, President
of the European Beat Studies Network
– integrated new material discovered
in the Ginsberg (490) literary archive.

Letters 1945–74

Burroughs wrote letters
throughout his itinerant
career in Mexico, Morocco,
France, England and the USA.
These volumes document his
friendships with Kerouac (469),
Ginsberg (490), the artist Brion
Gysin and others. 'These funny,
filthy and terrifically smart
letters reveal him in a way
that no biographer can,'
wrote *New York Newsday*.

Junky 1951–3, pub. 1953

Burroughs's first novel is the
semi-autobiographical account of
William Lee's life as a heroin addict.
Burroughs was a Harvard University
graduate in anthropology and this
is his first-hand field report from
the 'junk neighborhoods' of post-war
New York, New Orleans and Mexico City.
After the success of *Naked Lunch* (483),
Junky became a cult classic. It 'reads
today as fresh and unvarnished as
it ever has', says the novelist Will Self.

More ADDICTION

Novel with Cocaine
by M. Ageyev   313

Dependency
by Tove Ditlevsen   243

Bad Behavior
by Mary Gaitskill   548

Monkey Grip
by Helen Garner   386

Requiem for a Dream
by Hubert Selby Jr.   511

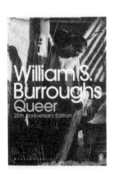

1987 Penguin Books
2010 Modern Classics
ed. Oliver Harris, 2010
—
The 2010 '25th anniversary'
edition was published with
a revised text and information
about Burroughs's infatuation
with Lewis Marker, a 21-year-
old student at Mexico City
College, who was the model
for Eugene Allerton.

Queer 1951–3, pub. 1985

Burroughs wrote *Queer* at the same time as Junky.
It is a companion piece, describing an addict's
withdrawal and the way that 'everything that has
been held in check by junk spills out'. With his
libido raging, William Lee stumbles through Mexico
City, pursuing Eugene Allerton from bar to bar as his
mind falls apart. It includes a quest to South America
in search of *yage*. 'Queer is a major work,' said
Allen Ginsberg (490). 'Burroughs's heart laid bare.'

The Yage Letters

with Allen Ginsberg 1953–63, pub. 1963

At the end of Junky, Burroughs stated his ambition to travel
in quest of *yage*, a legendary drug with hallucinogenic – and
perhaps even telepathic – properties. Burroughs wrote to Allen
Ginsberg (490), describing his journey through the Amazonian
rainforest in 1953 and the psychedelic adventures he experienced
by taking yagé, or ayahuasca. *The Yage Letters* also includes
an exchange some years later, when Ginsberg experimented
with yagé himself and wrote to Burroughs about the sensation.

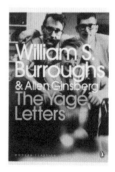

2008
ed. Oliver Harris, 2006

—

Oliver Harris's 2006 edition
demonstrates that most
of these letters are heavily
fictionalized; he recommends
thinking of the book as
an epistolary novel.

Interzone 1954–8, pub. 1989

While living in the Tangier International Zone
in the 1950s – a jointly controlled protectorate
in pre-independence Morocco – Burroughs produced
a huge quantity of writing he called the 'word hoard'.
He later repurposed this material in his subsequent
novels and in these short stories, which bridge the
gap between the fierce, confessional style of Junky (482)
and the wild fantasia of *Naked Lunch*. The Bloomsbury
Review called *Interzone* 'the statement of a man writing
for his life, a venting, a bloodletting'. In one gruesome
story – 'The Finger' – the narrator describes severing
his left little finger at the knuckle to impress a lover,
something that Burroughs actually did in 1939.
The climax of the collection is the frenzied, obscene,
novella-length WORD.

1990 Penguin Books
2009 Modern Classics
ed. James Grauerholz, 1989
–
Interzone also includes
Burroughs's very first
short story, 'Twilight's Last
Gleamings', which he wrote
in 1938 in collaboration with
his childhood friend Kells
Elvins. The villain of the story,
Doctor Benway, reappears
in *Naked Lunch*.

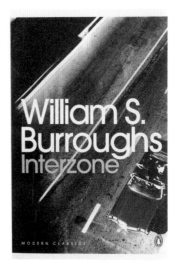

Naked Lunch 1959

Burroughs's masterpiece is a collection of vignettes,
or 'routines' as he called them, submitted to the
printer at random and intended to be approached
in any order. The reader is assailed by the experiences
of the junky William Lee as he wanders the
nightmarish 'Interzone' of Tangier, an orgiastic
wasteland of drugs, depravity, political corruption,
sadism and addiction. *Newsweek* called it 'a cry from
hell, a brutal, Priapic, terrifying, paranoiac, and
savagely funny book that swings giddily between
uncontrolled hallucination and fierce, exact satire'.
This cult cultural landmark is both shocking and
prophetic, seemingly forecasting the AIDS and crack
epidemics. It was the subject of the last obscenity trial
against a work of literature in the USA. As J. G. Ballard
put it, '*Naked Lunch* is a banquet you will never forget.'

2015
ed. James Grauerholz
& Barry Miles, 2001
–
In 1957, Ginsberg (490)
and Kerouac (469) travelled
to Tangier to help Burroughs
type, edit and arrange the
episodes that would become
Naked Lunch. After the first
edition appeared in Paris,
Burroughs received a $3,000
advance for the US publication,
which he used to buy drugs.
The 2001 'restored text'
includes Burroughs's notes
and various alternative drafts
and out-takes.

My Education
A Book of Dreams 1959–95, pub. 1995

This strange volume collates the scraps of paper and index cards on which
Burroughs charted, for more than three decades, his intense and deeply
singular dream life. The title comes from the first dream in the book:
Burroughs tries to board an aeroplane when a woman 'with the cold waxen
face of an intergalactic bureaucrat' bars his way, explaining: 'You haven't
had your education yet.' This was the last book Burroughs published before
he died. 'It is amusing to read reviews of Burroughs that try to classify his
books as nonbooks or as failed science fiction,' wrote Marshall McLuhan (396).
'It is a little like trying to criticize the sartorial and verbal manifestations
of a man who is knocking on the door to explain that flames are leaping
from the roof of our home.'

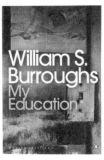

1996 Penguin
Books
2009 Modern
Classics
ed. James
Grauerholz, 1995

Technique | Cut-Up

the artist Brion

Gysin and the writer William
S. Burroughs (481) popularized the
'cut-up' technique in the early 1960s.

The cut-up technique of revealing hidden

meanings.   to create new

Drawing on Dada (263) methods, and

thereby challenging the traditional role
of the writer as creator and elevating
the creative act of editing. Burroughs

also believed the process had

occult purpose   word combinations,

inspired by modernist (11) writers

They took existing texts, sliced them

such as James Joyce (8), T. S. Eliot
(11), Gertrude Stein (410) and John
Dos Passos (426),

up and randomly shuffled the sections

Burroughs   personally preferred the

'fold-in' method: he would take
two sheets of text with the same
line-spacing, fold each sheet in half
vertically, and then place them
together to create a new page.

The Job
Interviews with William S. Burroughs
with Daniel Odier 1969

This collaboration with the Swiss poet
and screenwriter Daniel Odier 'was originally
conceived as a series of impromptu
interviews', explained Burroughs. 'However,
as Monsieur Odier asked questions I found
that I had in many cases already answered
these questions in various books, articles
and short pieces. So instead of paraphrasing
or summarizing I inserted the indicated
material. The result is interview form
presented as a film with fade-outs and
flash-back illustrating the answers.'
Burroughs expounds on literary techniques,
the Beat movement (491), Scientology,
capital punishment and drugs. 'In a quite
literal sense with Burroughs, the medium
is the message,' writes Joan Didion: 'the point is not what the voice
says but the voice itself, a voice so direct and original and versatile as
to disarm close scrutiny of what it is saying. Burroughs is less a writer
than a "sound", and to listen to the lyric may be to miss the beat.'

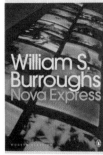
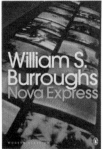

2014
ed. Oliver Harris

2010 Modern Classics
2014 Modern Classics
ed. Oliver Harris, 2014

2014
ed. Oliver Harris
—
In 1963, Burroughs published
Dead Fingers Talk, a novel
that reworks and recombines
sections from *Naked Lunch*,
The Soft Machine and *The Ticket
That Exploded* to create a new,
remixed narrative. A 'restored
edition' of *Dead Fingers Talk*
was published in 2020.

The Cut-Up Trilogy
*The Soft Machine, Nova Express,
The Ticket That Exploded* 1961–4

Burroughs saw these three experimental
novels as a 'mathematical extension'
of the themes and techniques he used in
Naked Lunch (483). He combines conventional narrative passages
with cut-up sections to create 'a new mythology for the space age'.
In *The Soft Machine* (1961, rev. 1966 and 1968), secret agent Lee can
switch bodies with anyone he chooses and uses this skill to defeat
a band of slave-driving mind-controlling Mayan priests. The
non-linear text involves dead soldiers, evil doctors, corrupt judges,
mythical monsters, time travel and media bombardment. *Nova Express*
(1961–4, pub. 1964) pits Inspector Lee and the Nova Police against
the Nova Mob, which includes such nightmarish characters as
'Sammy the Butcher', 'Izzy the Push', 'Jacky Blue Note', 'Limestone
John', 'Hamburger Mary' and 'Paddy the Sting'. On one level, the Mob
represents the viral grip of cultural control, which Burroughs seeks
to demolish; on another, it represents heroin – while the Nova Police
is 'apomorphine', the drug used to combat addiction. *The Ticket That
Exploded* (1962, rev. 1967), the final instalment of this loose trilogy,
stages one last battle between the Nova Police and the Nova Mob.
It features parasitical advertising language, Johnny Yen's chicken-
hypnotizing (beloved by Iggy Pop), and homoerotic escapades
on the planet Venus. 'Burroughs seems to revel in a new medium,'
wrote Anthony Burgess (118), '[…]
a medium totally fantastic, spaceless,
timeless, in which the normal sentence
is fractured, the cosmic tries to push its way
through the bawdry, and the author shakes
the reader as a dog shakes a rat.'

1989 Penguin Books
2008 Modern
Classics
ed. Daniel Odier,
1969

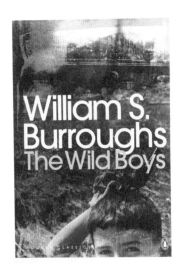

2008
—

The Wild Boys inspired David Bowie's Ziggy Stardust outfit. 'It was a cross between that and *Clockwork Orange* (148) that really started to put together the shape and the look of what Ziggy and the Spiders were going to become,' said Bowie. 'They were both powerful pieces of work, especially the marauding boy gangs of Burroughs's *Wild Boys* with their bowie knives. I got straight on to that.'

The Wild Boys
A Book of the Dead
1969, pub. 1971

This nightmarish novel follows a band of young homosexual boys in Africa, who take drugs, engage in ritualistic sex and enjoy guerrilla warfare, in an apocalyptic version of the late 20th century. Jack Kerouac (469) once said that Burroughs was 'the greatest satirical writer since Jonathan Swift'. In 1972, Burroughs wrote the screenplay for a low-budget hardcore pornographic film adaptation of the novel.

Exterminator! 1973

This hallucinatory book of short stories contains stolen faces, a doppelgänger virus, terrorist attacks and a 'purple-assed' mandrill who successfully runs for the US presidency. The title story is based on Burroughs's experience working as an insect exterminator in Chicago in 1942; it was incorporated into David Cronenberg's 1991 film adaption of *Naked Lunch* (483).

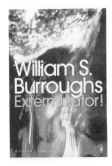

1979 Penguin Books
2008 Modern Classics
—

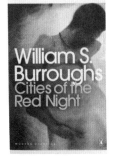

2010
—

The Red Night Trilogy
Cities of the Red Night, The Place of Dead Roads, The Western Lands 1981–7

In this loose trilogy of time-travelling, history-distorting adventures, Burroughs shapes a new literary 'mythography', as J. G. Ballard put it. *Cities of the Red Night* (1981) tells the twin stories of a handsome 18th-century pirate facing execution and a 20th-century opium addict lost in a jungle; Ken Kesey (520) thought it 'Burroughs's best work'. *The Place of Dead Roads* (1983) is about a gay gunfighter in America's Old West and his band of marauding outlaws, the Wild Fruits. Allen Ginsberg (490) called it 'a comedy and a nightmare of Bosch-like visions'. Burroughs's last novel, *The Western Lands* (1987), is set in Ancient Egypt on the western bank of the Nile, the Egyptian land of the dead. It blends Egyptian theology with Franz Kafka (280), war films and pornography.

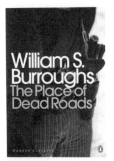

2015
—

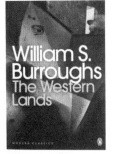

1989
Penguin
Books
2010
Modern
Classics
—

The Cat Inside 1986

Rather unexpectedly, Burroughs loved cats. In this slim book he reminiscences about the various cats in his life and muses on our mysterious relationship with felines. 'My relationship with my cats has saved me from a deadly, pervasive ignorance,' he wrote.

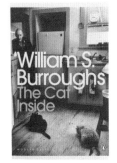

2002 Penguin Books
2009 Modern Classics
—

Arthur Miller 1915–2005

Miller was born in Manhattan, the son of wealthy Polish Jewish parents who lost everything in the 1929 Wall Street Crash and moved to Brooklyn. He began writing plays and radio scripts while at the University of Michigan and during the Second World War he worked in the Brooklyn naval shipyard. His first success came with *All My Sons*, directed by his friend Elia Kazan, and he went on to write a string of award-winning plays about principled men driven to actual or virtual suicide by the pressures of society. In 1956, he divorced his first wife, Mary, and married the film star Marilyn Monroe. Monroe converted to Judaism and considered

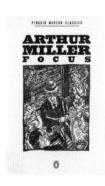

leaving Hollywood, but took a last leading role in the film *Misfits* (1961), directed by John Huston and written by Miller. The marriage disintegrated during filming and Monroe became increasingly dependent on sleeping pills. They divorced soon after the premiere; nineteen months later, Monroe died of an overdose. Miller then married the photographer Inge Morath, with whom he collaborated on travel books. In 1965, he became the President of International PEN, and in 2003 he was awarded the Jerusalem Prize. When he died, the theatres on Broadway dimmed their lights.

Focus 1945

1978 Penguin Books
1986 Modern Classics
intro. Arthur Miller, 1984

Miller's only novel is a story of anti-Semitism in New York. Mr Newman lives with his mother and shares the prejudices of his neighbours, so he is flabbergasted when he buys a new pair of spectacles and people start to mistake him for a Jew. He experiences increasing ostracism and persecution as the city's prejudices turn horrifically violent.

All My Sons
A Drama in Three Acts 1947

Joe Keller used to run a factory that supplied aeroplane engine parts during the Second World War; gradually, over the course of three acts, dark secrets start to emerge. *All My Sons* won the New York Drama Critics' Circle Award. 'The success of a play, especially one's first success, is somewhat like pushing against a door which is suddenly opened from the other side,' wrote Miller. 'One may fall on one's face or not, but certainly a new room is opened that was always securely shut until then.'

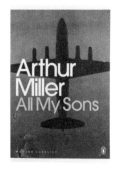

1961 Penguin Plays *with A View from the Bridge* (487)
1986 Modern Classics
2009 Modern Classics
intro. Christopher Bigsby, 2000
—
Christopher Bigsby is the author of *Arthur Miller: The Definitive Biography* (2008). In 2015, to celebrate what would have been Miller's 100th birthday, the Penguin editions of *All My Sons*, *Death of a Salesman*, *The Crucible* (487) and *A View from the Bridge* (487) were all expanded to include a selection of production photographs.

1961 Penguin Plays
1985 Modern Classics
—
'I remember walking and running and jumping out of the theater after seeing *Death of a Salesman*, like a child in the morning,' wrote the actor Philip Seymour Hoffman, who played Willy Loman in 2012, 'because Miller awakened in me the taste for all that must be – the empathy and love for the least of us, out of which bursts a gratitude for the poetry of these characters and the greatness of their creator.'

Death of a Salesman
Certain Private Conversations in Two Acts and a Requiem 1949

'Willy!' 'It's all right. I came back.' Miller retreated to a cabin in Connecticut with those opening lines in his mind; six weeks later he had written his masterpiece, which the *New York Times* calls 'one of the finest dramas in the whole of American theatre'. Travelling salesman Willy Loman becomes increasingly bewildered by his own failures, and his sons' loss of respect for him, as he spirals towards his death. The play won the New York Drama Critics' Circle Award and the Pulitzer Prize for Drama.

An Enemy of the People
An Adaptation of the Play by Henrik Ibsen 1950

Henrik Ibsen wrote *An Enemy of the People* in 1882, in response to the public outcry that greeted his previous play *Ghosts*. It is the story of a small Norwegian spa town, where a doctor discovers that the water is contaminated and so informs the authorities; but the townsfolk then brand him an 'enemy of the people', because they fear the news will damage the spa's reputation. Miller translates and updates the play; his version was filmed in 1978 starring Steve McQueen.

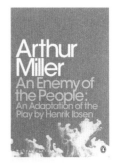

2015
—

1968 Penguin Books
1986 Modern Classics

The 1996 film adaptation of *The Crucible*, with a screenplay by Miller, starred Winona Ryder and Daniel Day-Lewis, who became Miller's son-in-law.

The Crucible
A Play in Four Acts 1953

In 1952, Miller was working with the director Elia Kazan on a film script set in the docks of Brooklyn when Kazan was called to appear before the House Un-American Activities Committee. To Miller's outrage, Kazan named eight members of the Communist Party. Miller then began writing *The Crucible*, set during the 1692 witch-hunts in Salem, Massachusetts, but equally applicable to the anti-communist McCarthyism of the 1950s. The play is a parable of mass hysteria, paranoia, and stubborn integrity in the face of false accusations. *The Sunday Times* called it 'one of a handful of great plays that will both survive the [20th] century and bear witness to it'.

A View from the Bridge
A Play in Two Acts 1955, rev. 1956

Elia Kazan directed *On the Waterfront* (1954), a film about a Brooklyn dockworker who heroically testifies against his corrupt union boss; Miller responded in 1955 with *A View from the Bridge*, a one-act play about a cowardly longshoreman who squeals on his co-workers. In 1956, he expanded the play to two acts. It is the story of Eddie Carbone, an illiterate Sicilian American who develops an unhealthy obsession with his wife's 17-year-old orphaned niece. The director Nicholas Hytner believes it 'will always stand with the masterpieces of Ibsen, Shakespeare and Sophocles'. Miller refused to betray his left-wing friends to the House Un-American Activities Committee, and was convicted of contempt of Congress in 1957.

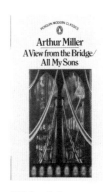

1961 Penguin Plays
with All My Sons (486)
1986 Modern Classics
with All My Sons
2010 Modern Classics
fwd. Philip Seymour Hoffman, 2009

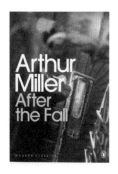

1968 Penguin Plays
2009 Modern Classics
—

After the Fall
A Play in Two Acts 1964

This deeply personal play takes place inside the mind of a successful New York Jewish intellectual. Through dreamlike episodes and flashbacks, Quentin reflects on his marriage to the beautiful but self-destructive singer Maggie and considers whether or not to marry Holga. Maggie is clearly a cipher for Marilyn Monroe, something for which Miller was criticized: the *New Republic* called the play 'a three and one half hour breach of taste'. Miller dedicated it to his third wife, Inge Morath.

Incident at Vichy
A Play 1964

In Vichy France in 1942, a group of Jews wait to be interviewed by German officials. As they wait, they discuss the rumours of trains locked from the outside and furnaces in Poland. 'The good and the evil are not compartments,' wrote Miller, 'but two elements of a transaction.' The *New York Times* called it 'one of the most important plays of our time'.

1966 Penguin Plays
in New American Drama
1985 Penguin Plays *separately*
1997 Twentieth-Century Classics
—

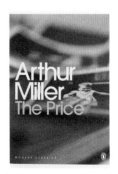

The Price
A Play 1968

In their dead father's over-crowded attic, two brothers haggle with a furniture-dealer. But Victor increasingly dwells on the price he paid 30 years earlier, when their father lost his fortune.

1970 Penguin Plays
2009 Modern Classics
—

The Ride Down Mt Morgan 1991

Lyman Felt is a business tycoon, a renowned poet and the father of loving children; he is also a bigamist. When he is taken to hospital following a car accident on an icy mountain road, his two wives meet in the waiting room for the first time.

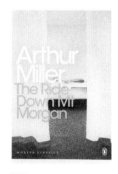

2015
—

Resurrection Blues
A Prologue and Two Acts 2002

Miller's penultimate play is set in an unnamed Latin American country, where a charismatic revolutionary has been captured who may, or may not, be the new messiah. In any event, General Felix Barriaux sees an opportunity to stage a live TV broadcast of his crucifixion.

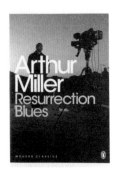

2015
—

John Hersey 1914 – 1993

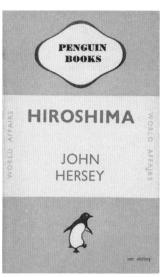

Hersey was born in Tientsin, China, the son of Protestant missionaries; his family returned to the USA when he was ten. After working as a secretary for Sinclair Lewis (421), he became a reporter for *Time* magazine and was one of the earliest exponents of New Journalism (464). During the Second World War, he worked as a correspondent for *Time*, *Life* and the *New Yorker*, which published his phenomenally successful *Hiroshima* in 1946. He also wrote novels, including the Pulitzer Prize-winning *A Bell for Adano* (1945), and an article about the dullness of school grammar textbooks that inspired Dr Seuss to create *The Cat in the Hat* (1957). From 1965 to 1970, Hersey was Master of Pierson College at Yale University, and his bulldog Oliver served as mascot of the Yale football team.

The 1946 Penguin edition was colour-coded grey for world affairs, with an unusual red title and author's name. It included the following publisher's note: 'Many accounts have been published telling – so far as security considerations allow – how the atom bomb works. But here, for the first time, is not a description of scientific triumphs, of intricate machines, new elements, and mathematical formulas, but an account of what the bomb does – seen through the eyes of some of those to whom it did it: of those who endured one of the world's most catastrophic experiences, and lived.' The current edition includes the chapter Hersey wrote in 1985 after returning to Hiroshima and following up the stories of the six men and women he had interviewed 40 years earlier.

Hiroshima 1946, rev. 1985

1946 Penguin Books
1958 Penguin Special
1972 Modern Classics
1986 Modern Classics *revised*
—

'At exactly fifteen minutes past eight in the morning, on August 6, 1945, Japanese time, at the moment when the atomic bomb flashed above Hiroshima, Miss Toshiko Sasaki, a clerk in the personnel department of the East Asia Tin Works, had just sat down at her place in the plant office and was turning her head to speak to the girl at the next desk.' Hersey's account of the explosion and horrifying aftermath of the world's first atomic bomb attack filled the entire issue of the *New Yorker* magazine on 31 August 1946. Through interviews with six survivors, he describes eyeballs melting and people vaporized, leaving only shadows etched on to walls. 'It is a vision of hell,' writes *The Times*, 'and its terrible images are […] reminiscent of Dante's *Inferno*.'

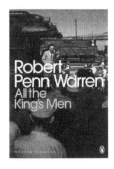

2007
–

Robert Penn Warren 1905–1989

Warren won the Pulitzer Prize for Poetry in 1958 and 1979, and is the only writer to have won Pulitzer Prizes for both poetry and fiction. He studied at Vanderbilt University in Tennessee, where he contributed to *The Fugitive* magazine (459). In 1965, he published a collection of interviews with civil rights leaders, including Malcolm X (528), Martin Luther King, Jr. (502) and James Baldwin (492). In 1986, he was named the USA's first Poet Laureate.

All the King's Men 1946

While teaching at Louisiana State University in the 1930s, Warren would have been aware of Huey Pierce Long, the recent governor of Louisiana, who may have inspired Warren to write this novel about the rise and fall of the radical populist Willie Stark, a man of the people willing to do whatever it takes to succeed in politics. It won the Pulitzer Prize for Fiction and the *New York Times* has called it 'the definitive novel about American politics'. The 1949 film adaptation won three Academy Awards, including Best Picture.

Dorothy B. Hughes 1904–1993

Dorothy Belle Flanagan was born in Kansas City, Missouri. She lived most of her life in New Mexico, working as a journalist and poet before she began to publish mystery novels in 1940. Influenced by Eric Ambler (108), Graham Greene (88) and William Faulkner (433), she wrote more than a dozen hard-boiled detective novels, three of which were made into successful films. In 1951, she won an Edgar Allan Poe Award from the Mystery Writers of America and then she largely gave up fiction in order to take care of an ailing mother and several grandchildren.

In a Lonely Place 1947

Cynical war veteran Dix Steele moves to Los Angeles, where a strangler is preying on young women. Steele follows the progress of the investigation as he befriends his new neighbour, the actress Laurel Gray. The classic 1950 film noir adaptation starred Humphrey Bogart and Gloria Grahame.

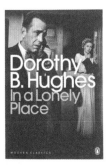

2010

Lionel Trilling 1905–1975

Lionel Mordecai Trilling was born in New York. He was educated at Columbia University, where he began teaching English in 1932; he became a professor of English in 1939, a post he held for the rest of his career. He was the leading US literary critic of his generation, writing about Matthew Arnold, E. M. Forster (38), Sigmund Freud (265), John Keats and George Orwell (80), and he was a member of the New York Intellectuals along with his wife and fellow critic Diana. Among Trilling's students at Columbia were Allen Ginsberg (490) and Jack Kerouac (469).

1963 Penguin Books
1977 Modern Classics
• intro. Lionel Trilling, 1975

The Middle of the Journey 1947

While recovering from a serious illness, John Laskell stays with some communist-intellectual friends, the Crooms. The ideological conflict that emerges between Laskell and his hosts mirrors the development of American liberal thinking in the 1930s and 1940s. The novel has 'a depth that recalls Dostoevsky and a subtlety worthy of Henry James (397)', wrote the *Listener*. '[It is] the most important novel by a non-genius since *Passage to India* (39).'

The New York Intellectuals

This loose group of mid-20th-century New York university literati included Lionel and Diana Trilling, Hannah Arendt (258), Saul Bellow (477), Mary McCarthy (507) and Susan Sontag (524). The group was characterized by its left-wing views, mostly Jewish heritage, and a conscious opposition to the New Criticism (459). 'As a group, it is busy and vivacious about ideas, and, even more, about attitudes,' wrote Trilling in the preface to his book of essays *Beyond Culture* (1965). 'Its assiduity constitutes an authority.'

Allen Ginsberg 1926–1997

Allen Ginsberg was 'probably the single greatest influence on the American poetical voice since Whitman,' said Bob Dylan. Ginsberg's father was a schoolteacher and a poet and his mother was a schizophrenic Russian Marxist. He grew up in Paterson, New Jersey, reading Walt Whitman and William Blake and corresponding with his hero and mentor, William Carlos Williams (418). At Columbia University, Lucien Carr introduced him to Jack Kerouac (469) and William S. Burroughs (481), and together they formed the core of the Beat Generation (491). He was taught by Lionel Trilling (489) and met several other important friends at Columbia, including John Clellon Holmes (501), the poet Gregory Corso and Neal Cassady. In San Francisco, he fell in with other poets and met his life partner Peter Orlovsky. Ginsberg wrote openly about his sexuality at a time when homosexual acts were illegal in every US state. When Lawrence Ferlinghetti, founder of the City Lights bookstore in San Francisco, published Ginsberg's first collection *Howl and Other Poems* (1956), copies were seized and Ferlinghetti was arrested, boosting Ginsberg's popularity. He emerged as a gay-rights activist, an anti-war campaigner and an icon of the 1960s counterculture movement (526). He studied eastern religions in Asia and took lessons from the Tibetan Buddhist Chögyam Trungpa, founder of the Naropa Institute in Colorado, where Ginsberg instituted the Jack Kerouac School of Disembodied Poetics in 1974. In 1979, Ginsberg was elected a member of the American Academy of Arts and Letters. 'He was a pioneer of openness and lifelong model of candor,' said Burroughs. 'He stood for freedom of expression and for coming out of all the closets long before others did.'

Poems 1947–97

'I saw the best minds of my generation destroyed by madness, starving hysterical naked, / dragging themselves through the negro streets at dawn looking for an angry fix.' 'Howl' is a scream for the sickness of urban America, an autobiography, a paean to Ginsberg's friend Carl Solomon, who demanded his own lobotomy, and a history of the Beats (491). Ginsberg's early verse encompasses both dark, rhapsodic celebrations of ecstasy and short, humorous, candid lyrics. He was inspired by modernism (11), jazz, William Blake, Tibetan Buddhism, Kerouac's 'spontaneous prose' (470) and his own Jewish background. 'Kaddish', for example, written after his mother's death in 1956, is a version of the Judaic mourning prayer. The title of his 1963 collection, *Reality Sandwiches*, was inspired by William S. Burroughs (481): 'a naked lunch is natural to us,' Ginsberg wrote, 'we eat reality sandwiches.' His later poetry incorporates musical scores and explicit social criticism and was frequently based on transcriptions of tape recordings he made while travelling.

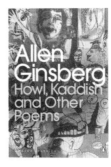

2009
intro. William Carlos Williams (418), 1956

—

This edition reprints Ginsberg's first two poetry collections, *Howl and Other Poems* (1956) and *Kaddish and Other Poems* (1961).

1987 King Penguin *Collected Poems, 1947–1980*
1988 Penguin Poets
1995 Twentieth-Century Classics *Collected Poems, 1947–1985*
2009 Modern Classics *Collected Poems, 1947–1997*
ed. Allen Ginsberg, 1984, 1995
ed. Eliot Katz & Danny Mulligan, 2006

Ginsberg in Penguin

Ginsberg was first published by Penguin Books in 1963, in the Penguin Modern Poets series alongside Lawrence Ferlinghetti and Gregory Corso. He gathered his *Collected Poems* in 1984, reprinting material from existing collections and rearranging the poems into the order in which they were composed. The edition gradually expanded: the final iteration comprises *Collected Poems, 1947–1980* (1984), *White Shroud: Poems, 1980–1985* (1986), *Cosmopolitan Greetings: Poems, 1986–1992* (1994) and *Death & Fame: Poems, 1993–1997* (1999). It also contains photographs, illustrations by Ginsberg's artist friends, and original prefaces. Three years before he died, Ginsberg assembled *Selected Poems*, presenting 'what I deem most honest, most penetrant of my writing'. *Wait Till I'm Dead* (2016) gathers more than 100 uncollected 'stray poems'. 'Want more poems?' Ginsberg wrote. 'Wait till I'm dead.'

1997
ed. Allen Ginsberg, 1996

2016
ed. Bill Morgan
fwd. Rachel Zucker

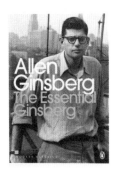

2015
ed. Michael
Schumacher

The Essential Ginsberg 1947–97

This anthology of poetry, letters, essays, interviews
and photographs was assembled by Michael Schumacher,
Ginsberg's biographer, to provide a representative
'sampling of the range and topography of Ginsberg's
mental landscapes'; it includes several previously
unpublished pieces. Lawrence Ferlinghetti called it
'an intellectually impeccable selection, distilling
Ginsberg as visionary mystic and dark prophet'.

Deliberate Prose
Selected Essays 1952–95

These essays, autobiographical
fragments, letters and magazine
articles are organized thematically
under headings including 'Politics
and Prophecies', 'Mindfulness and
Spirituality' and 'Drug Culture'.
Some of the most revealing pieces are
about other writers, such as William
Blake, Walt Whitman, William Carlos
Williams (418), Jack Kerouac (469)
and William S. Burroughs (481).

2001
● ed. David Carter
pref. Václav Havel
intro. Edmund White

Spontaneous Mind
Selected Interviews
1958–96

'A long time ago I figured out that
the interview and the media was a way
of teaching,' said Ginsberg. He saw
interviews as an art form and a platform
for his radical ideas about meditation,
jazz, ecology, drugs, sex and poetry.

2000
● ed. Bill Morgan
fwd. Edward Sanders
—
Ed Sanders is an American poet,
singer and activist, associated with
both the Beat Generation and the
counterculture movement (526).

The Best Minds of My Generation
A Literary History of the Beats 1977, pub. 2017

'I don't remember very much anymore,' said Ginsberg. 'I can't remember
who fucked who, when, or who wrote what.' In 1977, Ginsberg decided to teach
a course on the literary history of the Beat Generation at Naropa University
and this volume presents the best of these candid, illuminating lectures. With
discussions about Jack Kerouac (469), William S. Burroughs (481), John Clellon
Holmes (501), Gregory Corso and Neal Cassady, this is an intimate and gossipy
history of Ginsberg's contemporaries.

The Beat Generation

'Nobody knows whether we were catalysts or invented something, or just the froth
riding on a wave of its own,' said Allen Ginsberg (490). 'We were all three, I suppose.'
Jack Kerouac (469) first suggested the term 'Beat Generation' while discussing
the Lost Generation (425) with John Clellon Holmes (501) in 1948. 'More than mere
weariness, it implies the feeling of having been used, of being raw,' wrote Holmes in
1952, in his article 'This Is the Beat Generation'. 'It involves a sort of nakedness of mind,
and, ultimately, of soul: a feeling of being reduced to the bedrock of consciousness.'
Kerouac later associated the term with the 'beatific' ecstasy achieved through
drugs, sex or Zen Buddhism. A defining event for the Beats – described in Kerouac's
The Dharma Bums (472) – was a poetry reading in October 1955, held at the Six Gallery
in San Francisco, where Ginsberg read his poem 'Howl' (490). Other key works of the
movement are Kerouac's *On the Road* (470) and William S. Burroughs's *Naked Lunch*
(483). 'Beatnik' became a derogatory term for the Beats' imitators and hangers-on.

2018
ed. Bill Morgan, 2017
fwd. Anne Waldman, 2017

James Baldwin 1924–1987

Baldwin was born and raised in Harlem, New York City. He never knew his biological father, but his childhood and teenage years were dominated by his overbearing stepfather David Baldwin, a Baptist preacher. At 24, Baldwin bought a one-way plane ticket to Europe, and he spent most of the rest of his life in Paris and in Saint-Paul-de-Vence, in the south of France. In the 1960s, however, he became an influential figure in the American civil rights movement (502), appearing regularly on US television debates, taking the middle ground between the 'muscular approach' of Malcolm X (528) and the non-violence of Martin Luther King, Jr. (502). In 1963, he joined the March on Washington alongside his film-star friends Marlon Brando and Sidney Poitier. In France, he received visits from Josephine Baker, Miles Davis, Ray Charles, Nina Simone and Marguerite Yourcenar (191). 'You knew, didn't you, how I needed your language and the mind that formed it?' wrote Toni Morrison when he died. 'How I relied on your fierce courage to tame wildernesses for me?'

Notes of a Native Son 1948–55, pub. 1955

Baldwin's first collection of essays established him as the voice of a generation. 'The story of the negro in America is the story of America,' he wrote. '[…] It is not a very pretty story.' In the first two essays, he describes Richard Wright's *Native Son* (462) as a 'protest novel' and calls Wright 'the greatest black writer in the world'. In the title essay, he recalls the Harlem Riot of 1943, also the day of his stepfather's funeral and his own nineteenth birthday. He discusses movies, novels, life in Paris, and the complexities of racial, sexual and class distinctions at the dawn of the civil rights movement (502). 'As an essayist he is thought-provoking, tantalizing, irritating, abusing and amusing,' wrote Langston Hughes in the *New York Times*. 'And he uses words as the sea uses waves, to flow and beat, advance and retreat, rise and take a bow in disappearing.'

1995
—

Going to Meet the Man 1948–65, pub. 1965

Each of these eight stories illustrates the ways in which our earliest experiences can shape our lives. 'The Rockpile' is about an illegitimate child resented by his God-fearing father; 'Sonny's Blues' is about a black algebra teacher and his brother's drug addiction; and 'Going to Meet the Man' is about the initiation of a racist, taken as a child to watch the lynching of a black man.

Go Tell It on the Mountain 1953

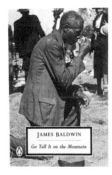

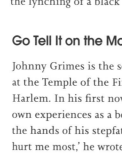

1991 Twentieth-Century Classics
2001 Modern Classics
intro. Andrew O'Hagan, 2001
—
Baldwin wrote *Go Tell It On the Mountain* in the Café de Flore in Paris, where Simone de Beauvoir had written *The Blood of Others* (187).

Johnny Grimes is the son of Gabriel, a preacher at the Temple of the Fire Baptized church in 1930s Harlem. In his first novel, Baldwin fictionalizes his own experiences as a boy preacher and his abuse at the hands of his stepfather. 'I had to deal with what hurt me most,' he wrote. 'I had to deal with my father.' In his introduction, the novelist Andrew O'Hagan suggests that *Go Tell It on the Mountain* shares a 'liturgical energy' with novels such as *A Portrait of the Artist as a Young Man* (8), *The Sound and the Fury* (433) and Toni Morrison's *Beloved* (1987).

1991
—

1991
● —
Baldwin later said that Marlon Brando lent him $75 so he could write this play; it was first performed in Los Angeles in 1965 and there was a short-lived musical adaptation in 1983.

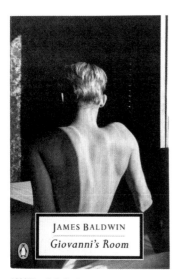

1990 Twentieth-Century Classics
2001 Modern Classics
intro. Caryl Phillips, 2001

More ROOMS

The Amen Corner

1954

This three-act play is set between a gospel-singing street-corner 'church' in Harlem and the apartment where Sister Margaret, the pastor, lives with her son and sister. One day, Margaret's husband Luke, a burned-out jazz musician, returns unexpectedly.

Nobody Knows My Name
More Notes of a Native Son

1954–61, pub. 1961

'These essays – lucid dissertations not only on the condition of the black man, but on the human condition – live and grow in the mind,' wrote the *Independent*. Baldwin's second essay collection includes polemical pieces, personal reflections, and thoughts on writers such as William Faulkner (433), André Gide (164), Norman Mailer (496) and Richard Wright (462). 'James Baldwin is a skillful writer,' wrote the critic Irving Howe in the *New York Times*, 'a man of fine intelligence and a true companion in the desire to make life human. To take a cue from his title, we had better learn his name.'

1991
● —

Giovanni's Room 1956

In 1949, Baldwin fell in love with Lucien Happersberger and was heartbroken when Happersberger married a woman three years later. Baldwin's second novel is about David, a young white American in Paris, who falls in love with Giovanni, an Italian barman. Told through flashbacks over the course of a single tortuous night, the narrative becomes increasingly claustrophobic, cramped within the peeling walls of Giovanni's bedsit. The critic James Wood called it 'not only one of the most exquisite novels of the last 30 years, but a feat of fire-breathing, imaginative daring'.

Another Country 1962

'Let our novelists (and our moralists) read Mr Baldwin and tremble,' wrote the *Sunday Times*. 'There is a whirlwind loose in the land.' *Another Country* is the story of Rufus Scott, a self-destructive Harlem drummer, and the effects of his death on his friends. It features bisexuality, interracial relationships, extramarital affairs, jazz and suicide. 'Baldwin created the essential American drama of the [20th] century,' writes Colm Tóibín, 'in which characters desperately seek to escape from the parody of themselves which has been constructed for them.' Baldwin described Rufus Scott as 'the black corpse floating in the national psyche'.

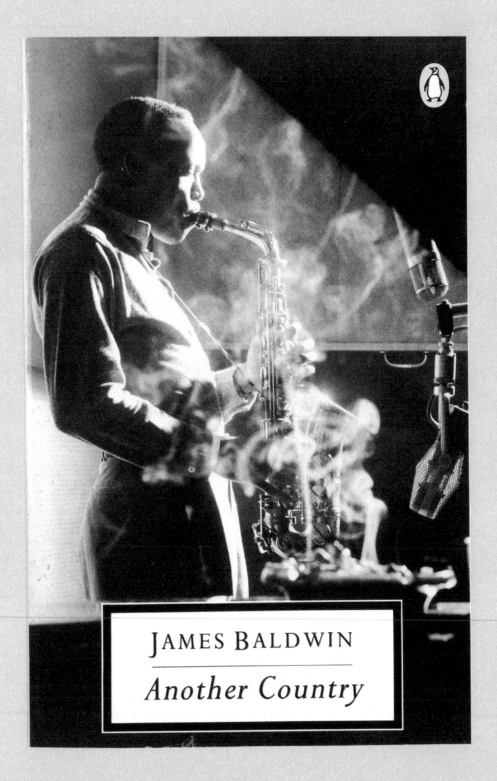

JAMES BALDWIN

Another Country

1990 Twentieth-Century Classics
2001 Modern Classics
intro. Colm Tóibín, 2001

The photograph on the cover of the
1990 edition is by Herman Leonard;
the saxophonist is Sonny Stitt.

The Fire Next Time 1962, pub. 1963

This bestselling, hugely influential volume galvanized America and propelled the civil rights movement (502). It is made up of two short 'letters': the first, 'My Dungeon Shook', is addressed to Baldwin's 14-year-old nephew on the 100th anniversary of emancipation; the second, 'Down at the Cross', is an indictment of racial tyranny, expressing all the seething discontent of the 1960s. Baldwin was featured on the cover of *Time* magazine in 1963 and the *New York Times Book Review* described this book as having 'elements of sermon, ultimatum, confession, deposition, testament, and chronicle. All are presented in the searing, brilliant prose that James Baldwin gives us no matter what form he is working in.'

1964 Penguin Books
1990 Twentieth-Century Classics
—

Tell Me How Long the Train's Been Gone 1968

In this novel, the black actor Leo Proudhammer suffers a heart attack on stage at the height of his career. He hovers between life and death and recalls fragmented episodes: his relationship with Barbara, a white woman, his childhood on the streets of Harlem and his convoluted journey into the world of theatre.

If Beale Street Could Talk 1974

Tish is nineteen and pregnant, and Fonny, the father of her child, is in prison. Tish hopes to win justice for Fonny and secure his release before the baby is born. Baldwin's novel 'affirms not only love between a man and a woman', writes Joyce Carol Oates, 'but love of a type that is dealt with only rarely in contemporary fiction – that between members of a family, which may involve extremes of sacrifice'. Baldwin took his title from W. C. Handy's 1917 song 'Beale Street Blues'.

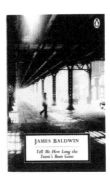

1994
—

1994
—

Just Above My Head 1979

'I model myself on jazz musicians and try to write the way they sound,' wrote Baldwin. 'I am not an intellectual, not in the dreary sense that word is used today, and do not want to be: I am aiming at what Henry James (397) called "perception at the pitch of passion".' Baldwin's last novel opens with the death of the singer Arthur Montana, the world-renowned 'Soul Emperor'. Montana's brother and manager Hall looks back at their lives and that of their many friends, from their childhoods in Harlem to careers spanning four continents and encounters with racism, incest, homophobia, war and the struggle for civil rights (502).

1994
—

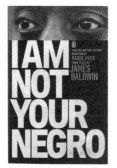

2017
intro. Raoul Peck

I Am Not Your Negro
compiled and edited by Raoul Peck 1979–87

When Baldwin died, he had been working on a project called *Remember This House*, a personal memoir of three friends and civil rights leaders, all of whom were murdered: Medgar Evers, Malcolm X (528) and Martin Luther King, Jr. (502). Thirty years later, the film-maker Raoul Peck took Baldwin's notes and combined them with extracts from his letters, manuscripts, speeches and books to create a 'libretto' for a 2016 documentary film narrated by Samuel L. Jackson. The *Guardian* called it 'a cinematic séance, and one of the best movies about the civil rights era (502) ever made'. It was nominated for an Academy Award and won the BAFTA for Best Documentary.

Norman Mailer 1923–2007

Norman Kingsley Mailer went to Harvard University at the age of sixteen. He published his first short story two years later and his first novel at 25: *The Naked and the Dead* was based on the hundreds of letters he wrote home while serving in the US army during the Second World War. He later described the war as 'the worst experience of my life, and also the most important'. Mailer co-founded *Village Voice* magazine in 1955; stabbed his second wife with a penknife in 1960; did jail time for demonstrating against the Vietnam War in 1967; and campaigned unsuccessfully to be mayor of New York in 1969. In a career that spanned 60 years, he wrote many bestselling novels and pioneering works of New Journalism (464), and he was also a poet, essayist, playwright and film-maker. He even acted occasionally, appearing as Stanford White in Miloš Forman's 1981 adaptation of E. L. Doctorow's *Ragtime* (538). Mailer married six times and had nine children.

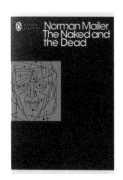

2018
intro. Norman Mailer, 1998

The Naked and the Dead 1948

'The best novel to come out of the war,' declared the *San Francisco Chronicle*, 'perhaps the best book to come out of any war.' Mailer's first novel follows a platoon of fourteen American soldiers on a reconnaissance mission through the jungle on a South Pacific island. Mailer drew on his wartime experience in the Philippines and the collage structure of John Dos Passos's *U.S.A.* (426), incorporating 'chorus' sections written as dramatic dialogue and 'Time Machine' capsule biographies of the characters. It was an instant bestseller that catapulted Mailer to fame. 'Part of me thought it was possibly the greatest book written since *War and Peace*,' he recalled.

More JUNGLES

The Lost Steps
by Alejo Carpentier 559

Almayer's Folly
by Joseph Conrad 28

The Jungle Books
by Rudyard Kipling 23

Brazil
by John Updike 517

Ninety-Two Days
by Evelyn Waugh 68

2018
—

Advertisements for Myself

1948–59, pub. 1959

This unusual book is a ragbag of repurposed 'pieces and parts, of advertisements, short stories, articles, short novels, fragments of novels, poems and part of a play'. Over its contents, Mailer then lays a swaggeringly self-confident commentary.

On the first page, for example, he asserts that his writing 'will have the deepest influence of any work being done by an American novelist in these years'. And he lists what he believes are the best pieces in the book: 'The Man Who Studied Yoga', a novella about a writer who fails to write; his seminal essay, 'The White Negro'; 'The Time of Her Time', a story he called 'the godfather of *Lolita* (309)'; 'Dead Ends', a poem; the self-mocking 'Advertisements for Myself on the Way Out'; and 'some of the writing in italics'. He later said that this *sui generis* work of self-exposure was 'the first work I wrote with a style I could call my own'.

Mind of an Outlaw
Selected Essays 1948–2006

Mailer's essays touch on boxing, Hemingway (428), politics, sex, and Marilyn Monroe. The selection includes his influential but controversial 1957 article 'The White Negro', which compares white American dropouts to marginalized African Americans; Mailer wrote the piece after meeting James Baldwin (492), who found it 'impenetrable'. Also featured is 'Superman Comes to the Supermarket', about the emergence of John F. Kennedy at the 1960 Democratic Party convention. This was the first time that Mailer gave himself an active role within a non-fiction narrative, a key characteristic of New Journalism (464).

2014
ed. Phillip Sipiora, 2013
intro. Jonathan Lethem, 2013

An American Dream 1964, pub. 1965

This surreal novel charts 32 hours in the life of Stephen Rojack, who appears to be living the American Dream: he is a TV celebrity, a war hero and the husband of a beautiful heiress. Things start to become more nightmarish, however, when Rojack murders his wife and descends into a smoky, depraved world of jazz clubs and Manhattan mobsters. Joan Didion calls it 'perhaps the only serious New York novel since *The Great Gatsby* (424)'.

The Armies of the Night
History as a Novel/The Novel as History 1968

On 21 October 1967, Mailer joined tens of thousands of people on a march to the Pentagon to protest against the Vietnam War. He subsequently described the events in this self-consciously 'non-fiction novel', a landmark work of New Journalism (464) that

won the National Book Award and a Pulitzer Prize for General Non-Fiction. 'Mailer's intuition is that the times demand a new form,' said the *New York Times Book Review*. 'He has found it.'

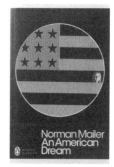

2018
—
Mailer first published *An American Dream* in eight monthly instalments in *Esquire* magazine, intentionally imitating the serial publication of Charles Dickens's novels.

Miami and the Siege of Chicago
An Informal History of the Republican and Democratic Conventions of 1968 1968

In the summer of 1968, the Vietnam War was raging and Martin Luther King, Jr. (502) had recently been assassinated. Mailer presents contrasting accounts of the Republican and Democratic conventions to elect their presidential candidates: in Miami, the Republican Richard Nixon arrives by helicopter to be greeted by dancers, a marching band and a small elephant; in Chicago, the Democrats back the ineffectual Hubert Humphrey, and the city erupts into violence.

1970 Penguin Books
2018 Modern Classics
—

1969 Penguin Books
2018 Modern Classics
—

A Fire on the Moon 1969, pub. 1970

As the world watched three men travel a quarter of a million miles to land on the moon, Mailer wrote an account of the events as they unfolded, considering the psychology of the astronauts, the feelings of their families and his own existential and social anxieties. 'I've worked as assiduously as any writer I know,' he wrote to Neil Armstrong, 'to portray the space program in its largest, not its smallest, dimension.'

2014
intro. Geoff Dyer

The Fight 1975

In 1974, the World Heavyweight Boxing Championship was held in Kinshasa, Zaire, an event that became known as the 'Rumble in the Jungle'. The silent genius of the ring, George Foreman, had never been defeated. He kept his hands 'in his pockets the way a hunter lays his rifle back into its velvet case'. But he was up against a new contender, Muhammad Ali, and 'if ever a fighter had been able to demonstrate that boxing was a twentieth-century art', wrote Mailer, 'it must be Ali'. 'This masterly book is of a similar order,' says the author Geoff Dyer, 'demonstrating that writing about sport can also be a twentieth-century art.'

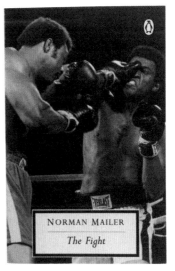

1991
—

Alfred Hayes 1911–1985

Hayes was born in London, but his family moved to the USA when he was three. He grew up in New York, where he wrote the poem 'I Dreamed I Saw Joe Hill Again', which was set to music and later performed by Joan Baez. He joined the US army during the Second World War and afterwards stayed in Rome, where he became involved in the neorealist film movement, writing for the directors Roberto Rossellini and Vittorio De Sica. In the late 1940s, he moved to Hollywood and worked as a screenwriter on films such as *The Lusty Men* (1952), *A Hatful of Rain* (1957) and *Lost in the Stars* (1974).

In Love 1953

In a New York bar, a middle-aged man recalls falling in love with a lonely young woman, and the stages by which their love turned sour. This noir novella was praised by Stevie Smith (62), Julian Maclaren-Ross (119) and Elizabeth Bowen (13), who called it 'a little masterpiece'.

1957 Penguin Books
2018 Modern Classics
—

1961 Penguin Books
2017 Modern Classics
—

2018
—

The Girl on the Via Flaminia 1949

Robert is a lonely American soldier in Rome who visits a brothel on the Via Flaminia and meets Lisa. What should have been a simple transaction turns into a prolonged involvement.

My Face for the World to See 1958

At a Hollywood beach party, a screenwriter rescues a young actress from a suicide attempt and they start a doomed relationship together.

More HOLLYWOOD

My Autobiography
by Charles Chaplin   149

The Last Tycoon
by F. Scott Fitzgerald   425

The Essential Groucho
by Groucho Marx   432

I'm Dying Laughing
by Christina Stead   381

The Day of the Locust
by Nathanael West   446

Ross Macdonald 1915–1983

Kenneth Millar attended the University of Michigan, where W. H. Auden (95) encouraged him to write. He began contributing stories to pulp magazines and eventually settled in Santa Barbara, California, the setting for his series of hard-boiled crime novels about a world-weary private investigator called Lew Archer, published under the pen name 'Ross Macdonald'. He conducted a long correspondence with Eudora Welty (457), who thought him 'a more serious and complex writer than Chandler (461) and Hammett (448) ever were'.

2012
intro. John Banville

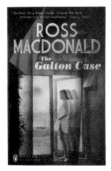

2012
—

The Drowning Pool 1950

Beautiful Maude Slocum hires Lew Archer to protect her family, but things become complicated when Maude's mother-in-law dies in the swimming pool. 'If you like them hard, hot and heavily seasoned,' ran the *New York Times*, 'this is your dish.' The 1975 film starred Paul Newman.

The Galton Case 1959

Lew Archer attempts to solve the mystery of Anthony Galton, a young wealthy heir who disappeared 20 years ago. He soon comes across a headless skeleton, a clever swindle and a terrified blonde.

The Chill 1964

Alex Kincaid's new bride Dolly has vanished
on the day of their wedding. As Lew Archer
investigates, he uncovers a sequence of brutal
murders. The screenwriter William Goldman,
who adapted two of Macdonald's Archer
novels, including *The Chill*, called them
'the finest series of detective novels ever
written by an American'.

  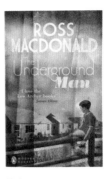

2012
—
 2012
—
 2012
—

The Goodbye Look 1969

Larry and Irene Chalmers ask Lew Archer to investigate
their son Nick, whom they suspect is involved in the
recent burglary of their mansion.

The Underground Man 1971

Archer pursues a kidnapped child while forest fires
rage in the hills above Los Angeles.

J. D. Salinger 1919–2010

Jerome David Salinger was born in New York, the son of a kosher cheesemonger. He dropped out of New York
University to study the meat industry in Austria, leaving just before the country was annexed by Germany
in 1938. He served in the US army during the Second World War, fighting on the beaches on D-Day, in the
Battle of Hürtgen Forest and in the Battle of the Bulge. He met Ernest Hemingway (428) in wartime Paris, who
said: 'Jesus, he has a helluva talent.' Following the phenomenal success of *The Catcher in the Rye*, Salinger
published a sequence of stories and novellas, all of which relate to the fictional Glass siblings: Seymour,
Buddy, Boo Boo, Walt, Waker, Zooey and Franny. He became increasingly reclusive, however, moving from
New York to a remote compound in New Hampshire and becoming fascinated variously with Zen Buddhism,
Vedanta Hinduism, Kriya yoga, Dianetics, Christian Science, homeopathy, acupuncture and macrobiotics.
The last story he published was in 1965. 'Not even a fire that consumed at least half his home on Tuesday
could smoke out the reclusive J. D. Salinger,' reported the *New York
Times* in 1992. '[He is] famous for having elevated privacy to an art
form.' Salinger continued writing until he died, colour-coding his
manuscripts red for posthumous publication 'as is' and blue for
'edit first'; his executors are still preparing the material for publication.

The Catcher in the Rye 1951

Seventeen-year-old Holden Caulfield recalls the weekend
after he was expelled from Pencey Preparatory Academy.
He wandered around New York City at Christmas time,
exploring his sexuality, buying records, getting drunk and
worrying about the ducks in Central Park. At one point he
fantasizes about protecting children in a rye field, catching
them before they fall off the edge of a cliff. The novel
is a portrait of adolescent alienation and a revolt against
a grown-up world of hypocrisy and 'phoniness'. John
Lennon's assassin Mark David Chapman bought a copy on
the day of the shooting in 1980 and inscribed it, 'To Holden
Caulfield, From Holden Caulfield'. He remained at the
scene of the murder reading the book until he was arrested.

1958 Penguin Books
1965 Modern Classics
● —
In 1959, after Salinger
was presented with
an upsettingly crude
cover design for
*For Esmé – with Love
and Squalor* (1953),
he had a clause
inserted in all his book
contracts insisting on
purely typographical
covers with no images.
The 1965 Modern
Classics edition was
therefore plain silver
and unillustrated.

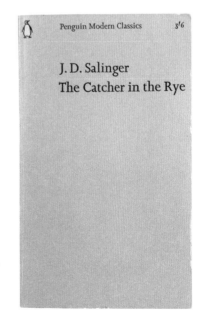

A. J. Liebling 1904–1963

Abbott Joseph Liebling tried to land a job at the *New York World* by hiring an out-of-work Norwegian sailor to walk up and down outside the Pulitzer Building for three days wearing a sandwich board that read 'Hire Joe Liebling'. When that failed, he joined the staff of the *New Yorker* in 1935, and contributed to that magazine for the rest of his life. He wrote about food, horse racing and other New York newspapers, and during the Second World War he reported on the London Blitz, the Normandy landings and the liberation of Paris. In later life, he married the novelist Jean Stafford.

The Sweet Science
Boxing and Boxiana: A Ringside View
1951–6, pub. 1956

The term 'sweet science' was coined in 1824 to describe the delicate balance of power between a boxer and his opponent; the three-time world heavyweight champion Lennox Lewis compares the level of strategy in a boxing match to that of chess. Liebling's book, which popularized the term, recreates America's golden age of boxing. He was 'a rollicking god among boxing writers', wrote the *Los Angeles Times*. '[…] Before Thomas Wolfe and Hunter S. Thompson (531) were out of diapers, Liebling was taking his readers on excursions through the hidden and often hilarious levels of this bruised subculture.' In 2002, *Sports Illustrated* named *The Sweet Science* 'the best American sports book of all time'.

2018
—

James Jones 1921–1977

James Ramon Jones enlisted in the US army at the age of seventeen. He served first in Hawaii, where he witnessed the Japanese attack on Pearl Harbor in 1941, and then on the South Pacific island of Guadalcanal, where he fought in the unusually named Battle of Mount Austen, the Galloping Horse and the Sea Horse. He was wounded in action, discharged in 1944 and spent the rest of his life writing novels and stories, many of which were inspired by his wartime experiences.

From Here to Eternity 1951

Jones's first novel is a study of the human condition within Company G, stationed on Hawaii in the months leading up to the Japanese attack on Pearl Harbor in December 1941. Private Robert E. Lee Prewitt, a former boxer, refuses to box for the company and receives a relentless campaign of physical and mental abuse, while

2013
aftwd. George Hendrick, 2011

Sergeant Milt Warden seduces the disenchanted wife of the company's commanding officer. *From Here to Eternity* was a bestseller and won the National Book Award; Norman Mailer (496) called it 'the best American novel since the war'. It was adapted as a film in 1953, starring Burt Lancaster, Montgomery Clift, Frank Sinatra and Deborah Kerr, which won eight Academy Awards, including Best Picture.

The Thin Red Line
1962

It is November 1942, and the infantrymen of C Company are about to enter combat on the island of Guadalcanal in the South Pacific. Jones orchestrates a wide range of characters, all of whom tread the line between heroism and cowardice, madness and sanity, life and death. It has been filmed twice, most recently by Terrence Malick in 1998; his adaptation was nominated for seven Academy Awards but failed to win any. Like *From Here to Eternity*, the title comes from Rudyard Kipling's *Barrack-Room Ballads* (22).

2014
—

When James Jones died, he was still working on *Whistle*, the third part of what he referred to as his war trilogy. *Whistle* is based on his experiences in hospital after being wounded in action and psychologically scarred in 1943. Its last few chapters were completed using Jones's notes by the writer Willie Morris and published posthumously in 1978. Jones said that these three books would 'say just about everything I have ever had to say, or will ever have to say, on the human condition of war and what it means to us'.

MODERN CLASSICS

John Clellon Holmes
Go

2006
intro. John
Clellon Holmes,
1976
aftwd. Seymour
Krim, 1988
aftwd. Ann
Charters, 2002
fwd. James
Atlas, 2006

John Clellon Holmes

1926–1988

Holmes was one of Jack Kerouac's (469) closest friends and responsible for popularizing the term 'Beat Generation' (491). Sometimes known as the 'quiet Beat', Holmes wrote *Go*, the first Beat novel; *The Horn* (1958), a jazz novel; and *Nothing More to Declare* (1967), a personal account of the Beats. Later he taught at Arkansas and Brown universities.

Go 1952

In *Go*, Holmes wrote about the bohemian lives of his friends Jack Kerouac (469), Allen Ginsberg (490), Neal Cassady and William S. Burroughs (481). 'The book is a *roman a clef* in the strictest sense of that term,' Holmes said, 'for very little in it is fictionalized. [...] Even whole conversations are verbatim.' The narrator is drawn to the riotous New York underworld of drugs, jazz and free love, while at the same time struggling to save his troubled marriage.

Penguin Modern Classics

David Karp

One

1960 Penguin
Books
1972 Modern
Classics
● —

David Karp 1922–1999

Karp enlisted in the US army in 1942 and served in the Signal Corps in the Philippines and Japan. After the Second World War, he returned to New York and completed his education at City College, which he funded by selling shirts, theatre-ushering and washing dishes. He then became a continuity writer for a New York radio station and made a career writing for radio and television, scripting episodes of *The Untouchables*, *The Defenders* and *Archer*, a series based on the novels of Ross Macdonald (498). He published his first novel in 1952.

One 1953

Professor Burden believes himself to be a loyal citizen of the 'benevolent state', until a routine check-up detects a trace of pride, which must be brainwashed out of him. 'The publishers have bracketed this novel with *Darkness at Noon* (278), *Nineteen Eighty-Four* (84), and *Brave New World* (66), which I at first thought presumptuous,' said Cyril Connolly (107); 'but now, after reading it, I am inclined to agree.' Karp wrote a television adaptation of *One*, which was produced twice in the 1950s.

Martin Luther King, Jr. 1929–1968

Michael King, Jr. was born in Atlanta, Georgia, the son of a Baptist minister. In 1934, his father made a pilgrimage to visit German sites associated with Martin Luther and on his return he changed both his and his son's name. As a teenager, King won a public-speaking prize on the subject of integration, but on the bus home he was forced to give up his seat for a white passenger. 'That night will never leave my memory,' he recalled. 'It was the angriest I have ever been in my life.' He became a Baptist minister, a key leader of the civil rights movement and one of the greatest activists in history, inspired by Gandhi (340) to lead a campaign of non-violence and civil disobedience. Through his leadership of the Southern Christian Leadership Conference (SCLC), and initiatives such as the 1955 Montgomery bus boycott, and the 1963 Birmingham campaign and March on Washington – which culminated in his famous 'I Have a Dream' speech – he struggled for desegregation in the USA. These efforts eventually culminated in the 1964 Civil Rights Act. That same year, he became the youngest person to have been awarded the Nobel Peace Prize. He was assassinated in 1968, and today his birthday is a national public holiday in the USA. As President Barack Obama said, Martin Luther King, Jr. 'changed the course of history'.

A Gift of Love
Sermons from *Strength to Love* and Other Preachings 1953–68, pub. 1963, rev. 1981

As both a Baptist minister and as a civil rights activist, King was an extraordinary orator. This collection of his most inspiring sermons is based on the volume he published in his lifetime, *Strength to Love* (1963). They promote his message of non-violence and demand that deep *agape*, or love for humanity, is harnessed in order to fight the evils of racism, poverty and war.

2017
fwd. Coretta Scott King, 1981
fwd. Raphael G. Warnock, 2012

Why We Can't Wait 1964

'Just as lightning makes no sound until it strikes,' wrote King, 'the Negro Revolution generated quietly. But when it struck, the revealing flash of its power and the impact of its sincerity and fervor displayed a force of frightening intensity.' This is King's account of the civil rights movement and his pivotal 1963 campaign in Birmingham, Alabama, 'the most segregated city in America'. King was arrested and jailed early in the campaign, and the centrepiece of the book is his influential 'Letter from Birmingham Jail'. The book is dedicated to King's children, 'Yolanda – Martin III – Dexter – Bernice, for whom I dream that one day soon they will no longer be judged by the color of their skin but by the content of their character'.

2018
–

The Civil Rights Movement

In the mid-1950s, the campaign for the rights of African Americans under the US constitution became known as 'the civil rights movement'. Previous groups, such as the National Association for the Advancement of Colored People (NAACP), were seen as too gradualist to combat the Jim Crow laws and increasing segregation of the South, so a coalition of organizations, including the Southern Christian Leadership Conference, the Student Non-Violent Coordinating Committee and the Congress on Racial Equality, began staging a variety of non-violent demonstrations in the form of boycotts, sit-ins and marches. These eventually led to the Civil Rights Act of 1964 and the Voting Rights Act of 1965, which banned discrimination on the basis of race, colour, religion, sex or national origin, prohibited racial segregation in schools, workplaces and public spaces, and secured the right of racial minorities to vote. Key figures in the movement were Martin Luther King, Jr., who preached non-violence and was awarded the Nobel Peace Prize in 1964; Malcolm X (528), who advocated violent action and inspired the Black Power movement; and James Baldwin (492), who took an intermediary position.

2010
aftwd. Matteo Codignola, 2009
—
The Italian publisher Adelphi
(229) re-released *Zia Mame*
in 2009 and it topped the Italian
bestseller charts for many weeks.
The Adelphi edition carried
an afterword by the translator
Matteo Codignola, which is
reproduced in the Penguin edition
in an English translation by Anne
Milano Appel. Codignola has
also translated Mordecai Richler
(396) and edited Adelphi's Italian
translations of Ian Fleming (126).

Patrick Dennis 1921–1976

Edward Everett Tanner III was nicknamed 'Pat' after the Irish heavyweight boxer Pat Sweeney, 'a dirty fighter known for kicking his opponents' (as Eric Myers, Dennis's biographer, put it). Tanner worked for a literary agency in New York and wrote sixteen novels, many of which were bestsellers and appeared under pseudonyms. He led a double life as both a conventional family man and a participant in Greenwich Village's gay scene. In the 1970s, his books fell out of fashion and he found work as a butler in Palm Beach, Florida, and then Chicago.

Auntie Mame
An Irreverent Escapade
1955

'As hilarious as a Marx Brothers comedy (432),' wrote *Vanity Fair*. 'As elegant as a Schiaparelli *eau de toilette*. As exhilarating as laughing gas.' Shy young Patrick is orphaned at the age of ten and adopted by his eccentric and extravagant New York socialite aunt. He describes his uproarious upbringing in a series of witty, whimsical vignettes. *Auntie Mame* was one of the bestselling American novels of the 20th century, adapted as a play, a film, a stage musical and a film musical.

More ORPHANS

The Secret Garden
by Frances
Hodgson Burnett   60

The Grass Harp
by Truman Capote   465

Kim
by Rudyard Kipling   24

The Decay of the Angel
by Yukio Mishima   351

Perfume
by Patrick Süskind   261

Sloan Wilson 1920–2003

Wilson sailed a schooner from Boston to Havana while studying at Harvard University. During the Second World War, he commanded a trawler for the US coast guard's Greenland Patrol. He worked as a researcher for *Time* magazine, as assistant director of the National Citizens Commission for Public Schools and as a professor at the University of Buffalo. He was the author of more than fifteen books, 'a novelist', wrote the *Guardian*, 'who documented the angst of post-war suburban America'.

The Man in the Gray Flannel Suit 1955

Tom Rath is the man in grey flannel. He has everything a middle-class American could want: a fine house, three children, a loving wife, a steady income; but he is trapped in the mind-numbing conformity of corporate life and haunted by memories of fighting in the Second World War. Increasingly desperate, he decides to escape the rat race. 'If you believe in love and loyalty and truth and justice,' writes Jonathan Franzen, 'you may finish reading *The Man in the Gray Flannel Suit*, as I did, with tears in your eyes.' It was made into a film in 1956, starring Gregory Peck, who is pictured on the Penguin cover.

2005
aftwd. Sloan Wilson, 1983
intro. Jonathan Franzen, 2002

Rachel Carson 1907–1964

'The revolution in our attitude towards pollution and the extravagant use of chemicals to control pests in the countryside is largely due to just one individual,' said the *Sunday Times* in 1998 – 'Rachel Carson.' Carson studied biology and marine zoology and worked for fifteen years as an aquatic biologist for the US Fish and Wildlife Service. After the success of her book *The Sea Around Us* (1951), she dedicated the rest of her life to raising awareness about ecology and the importance of conservation. In 1953, she met Dorothy Freeman, with whom she had an intense friendship mostly conducted through letters. She was made a Fellow of the Royal Society of Literature, elected into the American Academy of Arts and Letters and posthumously awarded the Presidential Medal of Freedom by President Jimmy Carter.

The Edge of the Sea 1955

'The shore is an ancient world,' wrote Carson, 'for as long as there has been an earth and sea there has been this place of the meeting of land and water.' This is the concluding volume of Carson's 'sea trilogy', formed by her first book, *Under the Sea Wind* (1941), and her bestseller *The Sea Around Us* (1951), which won a National Book Award and the John Burroughs Medal. 'Again,' said *Time* magazine, 'Rachel Carson has shown her remarkable talent for catching the life breath of science on the still glass of poetry.'

1999
● pref. Linda Lear, 1999
ill. Bob Hines, 1955
—
Linda Lear is the author of the biography *Rachel Carson: Witness for Nature* (1997). Bob Hines was a colleague of Carson's at the US Fish and Wildlife Service and the author and illustrator of *Ducks at a Distance* (1963).

Silent Spring 1962

Carson is best remembered for this searing prophetic warning about the danger to wildlife and damage to the food chain caused by the misuse of pesticides. 'What we have to face is not an occasional dose of poison which has accidentally got into some article of food,' she wrote, 'but a persistent and continuous poisoning of the whole human environment.' Despite the chemical industry, which tried to ban it, this book inspired a new pesticide policy in the USA and eventually a nationwide ban on DDT and other pesticides. It spurred a grassroots environmental movement that led to the creation of the US Environmental Protection Agency. In 2012, it was designated a 'National Historic Chemical Landmark' by the American Chemical Society.

1966 Penguin Books
1982 Pelican Books
1991 Penguin Books
1999 Twentieth-Century Classics
intro. Lord Shackleton, 1963
pref. Julian Huxley, 1963
aftwd. Linda Lear, 1999
—
Julian Huxley, the brother of Aldous Huxley (65), co-founded the World Wildlife Fund in 1961. Lord Shackleton, the son of Ernest Shackleton (12), was a geographer and Labour minister.

William Gaddis 1922 – 1998

Gaddis was expelled from Harvard University and worked as a fact checker for the *New Yorker* before spending five years travelling the world. In 1951, he returned to America and published his first novel, *The Recognitions*, to the critics' stupefaction. He then worked in public relations and documentary films for 20 years. The publication of Gaddis's second novel, *J R*, in 1975 established his reputation as a revolutionary postmodern novelist. He has influenced Don DeLillo (537), Jonathan Franzen, William H. Gass (529), Thomas Pynchon and David Foster Wallace, and in 1989 he was elected to the American Academy of Arts and Letters.

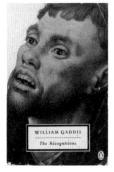

1985 Penguin Books
1993 Twentieth-Century Classics
● intro. William H. Gass (529), 1993
—
In his *New Yorker* article about *The Recognitions*, Jonathan Franzen makes a point of mentioning that he read it 'back in the early nineties [...] in a beautiful, newly issued Penguin edition'.

The Recognitions 1955

Wyatt Gwyon, the son of a Calvinist pastor, devotes himself to painting copies of old masters. He is content until he meets the ruthless collector Recktall Brown, who strikes a Faustian deal with Gwyon and starts passing off his copies as the real thing. Jonathan Franzen describes it as, 'by a comfortable margin, the most difficult book I ever voluntarily read in its entirety'. It has been compared to both Laurence Sterne's *Tristram Shandy* and the paintings of Hieronymus Bosch; the plot is based on a palindrome: 'trade ye no mere moneyed art'.

J R 1975

J. R. Vansant is an 11-year-old schoolboy who learns about the stock market on a class field-trip. Armed with a basic knowledge of capitalism and oodles of chutzpah, he manages to use a payphone to parlay a shipment of navy-surplus picnic forks and a single share of common stock into a vast financial empire incorporating timber, mineral and natural gas rights, a publishing business and a brewery. 'Gaddis has written the long-awaited great American novel,' wrote the *San Francisco Review of Books*. '[...] A beautiful book and a brilliant author.' Louis Auchincloss (519) praised it as 'worthy of Swift [...] Reading J R, I feel at times as if I were lying alone on a desolate plain under a dark cloudy sky from which come the mumbles and throbs of human speech in every sort of dialect and slang, replete with self-pity, smugness, officiousness, swagger – in short, every banality the brain of man can devise to evade thought.' It won the National Book Award.

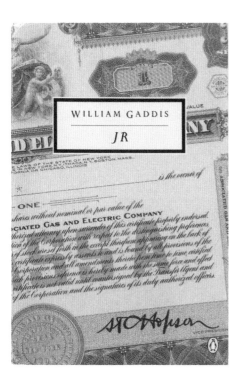

1985 Penguin Books
1993 Twentieth-Century Classics
● intro. Frederick R. Karl, 1993

Postmodernism

'Postmodernism' is an ambiguous term that generally describes a phase of late 20th-century western culture. Postmodernism retains the disorientating techniques and alienated mood of modernism (11) but abandons any quest for meaning in a fragmented world: whereas a modernist might use myth, symbol and formal complexity to 'make sense' of the confusion, a postmodernist accepts that meaning and authenticity have disappeared in an onslaught of disconnected television clips, adverts and media bombardment. A typically postmodern work might feature eclectic cultural references, elements of self-reflexivity and an apparent attitude of flippant indifference. The postmodern writer John Barth calls it 'the literature of exhaustion'; other exponents include William S. Burroughs (481), Italo Calvino (218), Angela Carter (156), William Gaddis, William H. Gass (529), Vladimir Nabokov (304), Thomas Pynchon and Kurt Vonnegut (523).

1984 Penguin Books
2018 Modern Classics
—

Lady Sings the Blues was ghost-written by William Dufty, a *New York Post* reporter and a musician himself, who based the book on a series of interviews with Holiday. She was a close friend of Dufty's wife Maely and godmother to their son Bevan.

Billie Holiday 1915–1959

Eleanora Fagan grew up in Baltimore, Maryland, scrubbing floors, running errands in a brothel and listening to the records of Louis Armstrong and Bessie Smith. After a period of teenage prostitution and a stint in prison, she began singing in Harlem speakeasies under the stage name 'Billie Holiday'. She was spotted by the producer John Hammond when she was seventeen: 'She was the first girl singer I'd come across who actually sang like an improvising jazz genius,' he recalled. Holiday never had any technical training or learned to read music, but she had huge commercial success in the 1930s and 1940s, performing with Teddy Wilson, Count Basie and Artie Shaw, recording with labels like Columbia and Decca, and singing songs such as 'Summertime' and 'Strange Fruit'. In the late forties, she was imprisoned briefly for the possession of narcotics, after which she was banned from working anywhere that sold alcohol, so she spent the fifties giving concert performances. She sold out New York's Carnegie Hall three times before she died at the age of 44, and she is still considered one of the greatest jazz singers of all time.

Lady Sings the Blues
with William Dufty 1956

Holiday's memoir 'captures the tart voice and unflinching eye of one of the most affecting and mythicized artists of the last century,' wrote the *San Francisco Chronicle*. '[…] It gets at jazz's great core.' She describes her rise to stardom and struggles with both addiction and racism with candour and humour. She released a new LP at the same time as this book, also called *Lady Sings the Blues*, with four new tracks and re-recordings of eight of her favourites. Her memoir was the basis for a 1972 biographical film, which also had the same title, starring Diana Ross.

Gladys Huntington

1887–1959

Gladys Theodora Parrish was the daughter of a wealthy Quaker businessman from Philadelphia. As a young woman, she travelled the world with her mother and sister and lived for a time in Italy, on Lake Como. In 1916, she married the publisher Constant Huntington and they moved to London, where Constant set up the London office of Putnam's. Gladys began writing *Madame Solario* early in their marriage, but it remained unpublished for 40 years; it finally appeared anonymously in 1956. Three years later, Gladys took her own life at her country home in Sussex.

Madame Solario 1956

In belle époque Italy, before the First World War, the mysterious Madame Solario arrives at the resort of Cadenabbia on the shore of Lake Como and scandalous whispers start to circulate. Paul Bowles (480) said the story was 'beautifully imagined and written', and Mary Renault compared it to Henry James (397) but 'achieved with more economy'.

1978 Penguin Books
1986 Modern Classics
● intro Alison Adburgham, 1986
—
The cover of the first Penguin edition called *Madame Solario* 'the famous anonymous novel', although *Life* magazine had in fact revealed Huntington's identity in 1957.

Mary McCarthy 1912 – 1989

McCarthy was orphaned at the age of six by the 1918 flu pandemic and raised in Minnesota by relations with Catholic, Protestant and Jewish backgrounds. She graduated from Vassar College in 1933, where she had been politically 'radicalized' by reading John Dos Passos (426), and began contributing to the *Partisan Review*, the *New Yorker*, *Harper's* and the *New York Review of Books*. She published her first novel, *The Company She Keeps*, in 1942 and was soon established as a leading New York Intellectual (489). She was elected a Fellow of the American Academy of Arts and Sciences in 1973 and received the National Medal for Literature in 1984. She married four times – her second husband was the influential critic Edmund Wilson – and she was a close friend of Hannah Arendt (258). 'Mary McCarthy's achievement was to invent herself as a totally new sort of woman who combined sense and sensibility; who was both coolly intellectual and boldly passionate,' wrote the *Observer*. 'Moreover, she managed to combine a lively and varied intellectual and erotic life with marriage and motherhood.'

1972 Penguin Books
2000 Penguin Travel Library
2006 Modern Classics
—

The Stones of Florence and Venice Observed 1956 – 9

These personal and perceptive travel books evoke two great Italian cities through their history and art. *Venice Observed* (1956) reveals a 'gold idol with clay feet', a city of illusion and spectacle, carnival and commerce. *The Stones of Florence* (1959) weaves the tempestuous history of the city from the time of the Medici to Savonarola's Bonfire of the Vanities – with a 20th-century appreciation of Renaissance splendour.

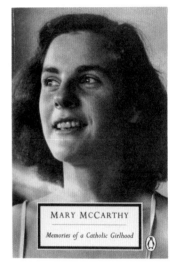

Memories of a Catholic Girlhood 1957

'Many a time, in the course of doing these memoirs,' wrote McCarthy, 'I have wished that I were writing fiction.' She describes her highly eccentric Minnesotan upbringing with wicked Uncle Myers, who beat her for her own good; Aunt Margaret, who laced her orange juice with castor oil and taped her lips at night to prevent unhealthy 'mouth-breathing'; her blood-curdling Catholic grandmother McCarthy; and her Jewish grandmother Morganstern, who wore a veil to hide a disastrous facelift. McCarthy wrote two more autobiographical works: *How I Grew* (1987) and *Intellectual Memoirs*, which was published posthumously in 1992.

1963 Penguin Books
1991 Twentieth-Century Classics
• —

The Group 1963

A group of eight friends graduate from Vassar College (McCarthy's own alma mater) in 1933 and McCarthy describes the next seven years as they each make choices between marriage and careers, sexual and social freedom. The novel was a runaway success and remained on the *New York Times* bestseller list for two years. 'Scalpel-keen prose, honed on ruthless wit and insight,' wrote the *Observer*. '[...] The best piece of comic writing about sex since the Greeks.'

1964 Penguin Books
1992 Twentieth-Century Classics
• —

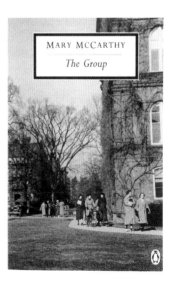

2007
pref. James Salter, 1997

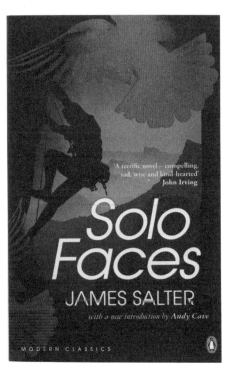

2008
intro. Andy Cave

James Salter

1925 – 2015

James Arnold Horowitz was a fighter pilot in the US Air Force and saw combat in the Korean War in 1952. Inspired by reading *Under Milk Wood* (98) by Dylan Thomas, he wrote his first novel, *The Hunters*, which he published under the pen name 'James Salter'. It was a success; he resigned his commission after selling the film rights, and changed his legal name to Salter. He had a brief career in film writing and directing: his last script, commissioned by Robert Redford, became his novel *Solo Faces*. In 2000, he was elected to the American Academy of Arts and Letters.

The Hunters

1956

Based on Salter's experiences as an F-86 Sabre pilot in Korea, this is the story of Captain Cleve Connell, an elite jet pilot who fails to live up to his potential and enters a tailspin of self-doubt. 'As other books of its era have fallen away,' wrote the *Times Literary Supplement* in 1998, 'this one turns out to be a classic.' It was made into a film in 1958, starring Robert Mitchum.

Light Years

1975

Nedra and Viri Berland seem to have everything: friends, children and a solid marriage. But gradually their perfect life starts to fall apart. 'Remarkable,' said *Esquire*, '[…] a moving ode to beautiful lives frayed by time.'

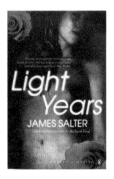

2007
intro. Richard Ford

—

Richard Ford is a Pulitzer Prize-winning novelist and was a friend of Salter. 'It is an article of faith among readers of fiction,' he says in his introduction, 'that James Salter writes American sentences better than anybody writing today.'

Solo Faces

1979

Verne Rand is a mountaineer who finds peace in the solitude of vertical rock faces. But then he becomes unexpectedly famous following a daring Alpine rescue. 'A terrific novel,' writes the author John Irving – 'compelling, sad, wise and kind-hearted.' The *Washington Post* called it 'a beautifully composed book that will remind readers of Camus (181) and Saint-Exupéry (178)'.

Chester Himes 1909 – 1984

Chester Bomar Himes was expelled from Ohio State University, convicted of armed robbery at the age of nineteen and sentenced to 20 to 25 years' hard labour. While in jail, he started to write and to publish stories in *Esquire* magazine. He was eventually released on parole at the age of 26 and met Langston Hughes, who encouraged his writing. He tried screenwriting in Hollywood but was fired on racial grounds; he later said that it was 'under the mental corrosion of race prejudice in Los Angeles I became bitter and saturated with hate'.

2011
intro. Luc Sante
—
The 2011 Penguin editions had covers by the award-winning illustrator Aaron Robinson. In 2021, they were rejacketed with collages by Romare Bearden, an artist associated with the Harlem Renaissance (413).

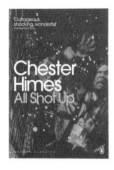

1978 Penguin Books
2011 Modern Classics
—
All Shot Up first appeared in French translation as *Imbroglio Negro*.

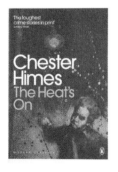

A Rage in Harlem 1957

This is the first outing for hard-boiled Harlem detectives Coffin Ed Johnson and Grave Digger Jones. It involves a failed money-making scheme, a hearse full of gold and a con man dressed as a Sister of Mercy.

All Shot Up

1959 (in French translation), 1960

Himes 'taught me the difference between a black detective and Sherlock Holmes', wrote Ishmael Reed (539). In *All Shot Up*, Grave Digger Jones and Coffin Ed Johnson are faced with a golden Cadillac, a hit-and-run victim and an unconscious politician.

The Heat's On

1961 (in French translation), 1966

A giant albino on the run, a dead drug-dealing dwarf, a lion-sized dog with an open head wound and an African with a slit throat: the heat is on for detectives Grave Digger Jones and Coffin Ed Johnson.

2011
intro. Noel 'Razor' Smith
—
'Razor' Smith has 58 criminal convictions and has spent most of his adult life in prison. While inside, he received an honours diploma from the London School of Journalism, took an AS level in law and won several Koestler (278) Awards for his writing. He first read *The Heat's On* in prison, he recalls: 'just the kind of novel that the authorities didn't want us getting hold of'. The novel first appeared in French translation as *Ne Nous Énervons Pas* (*Don't Get Upset*).

His first novel, *If He Hollers Let Him Go* (1945), like Richard Wright's *Native Son* (462), is about a black man struggling with both racism and his own violent reactions. In 1953, Himes moved to Paris, where he met James Baldwin (492), Malcolm X (528), Ishmael Reed (539) and his second wife, Lesley Packard. He lived in France and Spain for the rest of his life. The editor of Gallimard's crime list, Série Noire, commissioned Himes to write *A Rage in Harlem*, which first appeared in French translation in 1957 as *La Reine des Pommes* (*The Queen of Fools*) and won the Grand Prix de Littérature Policière.

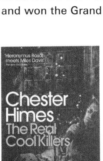

2011
—
The Real Cool Killers first appeared in French translation as *Il Pleut des Coups Durs* (*It's Raining Hard*).

1974 Penguin Books
2011 Modern Classics
intro. Will Self, 2011
—
Cotton Comes to Harlem first appeared in French translation as *Retour en Afrique* (*Back to Africa*).

The Real Cool Killers

1958 (in French translation), 1959

Ulysses Galen has been gunned down in Harlem. Grave Digger Jones and Coffin Ed Johnson find a smoking toy pistol and a gang called 'the Real Cool Moslems'. The *New York Times* described this instalment of Himes's Harlem series as 'Hieronymus Bosch meets Miles Davis'.

Cotton Comes to Harlem

1964 (in French translation), 1965

'A bawdy, brazen rollercoaster of a novel,' wrote the *New York Times*, '[…] the wildest.' The preacher Deke O'Malley has been conning the good people of Harlem and now thieves with machine guns have stolen his $87,000. It's up to Grave Digger Jones and Coffin Ed Johnson to find it. *Cotton Comes to Harlem* was adapted as a film in 1970.

Hubert Selby Jr. 1928–2004

Cubby Selby was born in Brooklyn, dropped out of school at fifteen and worked in the New York docks. When he joined the merchant marine he contracted tuberculosis from a shipment of infected cows and was given less than a year to live. He spent three years in and out of hospital, had several ribs and part of a lung removed and became addicted to morphine. Bedridden for almost ten years, he turned to writing. I knew the alphabet, he said. Maybe I could be a writer. He began composing stories in a strippedback style that ignored grammar and presented a stream of consciousness similar to Jack Kerouacs spontaneous prose (470). He didn/t like to use apostrophes, because the typewriter key was too far away. Instead he used a forward slash for contractions and nothing for possessives or quotations. I write, in part, by ear, he said. I hear, as well as feel and see, what I am writing. I have always been enamoured with the music of the speech in New York. Last Exit to Brooklyn, his first novel, appeared in 1964. Three years later he was arrested for possession of heroin and spent two months in the Los Angeles county jail. Thereafter he divided his time between Los Angeles and New York and taught creative writing at the University of Southern California. One of the great American novelists, the Guardian called him, and one who has helped us to understand the nature of addiction and the human condition better, perhaps, than any other.

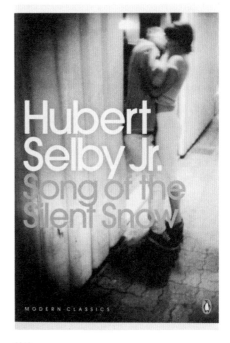

2012
—

Song of the Silent Snow 1957–81, pub. 1986

These fifteen short stories describe Fat Phil who can/t lose at dice, Harry whose life is ruled by fortune cookie mottoes and a nameless commuter who obsesses about a young woman on his subway train. The stories are spare and direct, said the New York Times, as subtle as a punch in the gut from a heavyweight boxer.

Last Exit to Brooklyn 1958–64, pub. 1964

Last Exit to Brooklyn will explode like a rusty hellish bombshell over America, said Allen Ginsberg (490), and still be eagerly read in 100 years. Selbys notorious masterpiece consists of six loosely connected stories, some of which he had already published as standalone pieces. The violent vignettes describe transvestites, prostitutes, gang rape, drug addiction, homosexuality, homelessness and poverty in Brooklyn. His books fill you up with a mixture of bile and beatification, wrote the Independent. It/s like reading the Bible without all the religious redemptive stuff. Last Exit to Brooklyn was made into a film in 1989, in which Selby had a cameo role as a taxi driver.

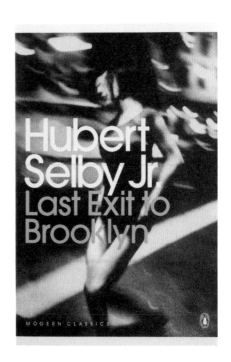

2011
intro. Irvine Welsh

Last Exit to Brooklyn was the subject of a 1967 obscenity trial in the UK and despite support from the poet Al Alvarez and the critic Frank Kermode it was banned by the English courts. The following year John Mortimer (139) defended an appeal and with support from Anthony Burgess (148) the court/s decision was overturned.

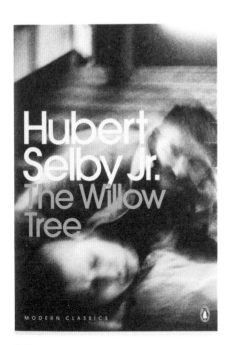

2011
—

2012
—

The Room 1971

Selby takes us into the unhinged mind of an insane criminal, locked in a remand cell, recalling his violent childhood and fantasizing about the horrible revenge he will wreak on those who have imprisoned him. Selby called it the most disturbing book ever written and said he could not reread it himself for 20 years.

The Demon 1976

Harry White is talented, rich and desirable, with a beautiful wife and family. But he has a demon inside him that lusts for adulterous sex, transgressive crime and eventually murder. The comedian Andy Kaufman called it his favourite book: that/s my mind in a nutshell, he said. William S. Burroughs (481) described it as a freight train of a novel with a climax like a kick in the stomach.

Requiem for a Dream 1978

While Harry, his girlfriend Marion and best friend Tyrone become increasingly addicted to heroin, hash and poppers, Harrys mother Sara dreams of appearing on television and can/t stop taking diet pills. If you read this, said The Velvet Undergrounds frontman Lou Reed, be careful…

The Willow Tree 1998

Bobby is a young African American boy who lives in a cramped Bronx apartment with his family. When he and his Hispanic girlfriend Maria are brutally attacked and Maria is disfigured with lye, Bobby turns to a reclusive doctor called Moishe, a Holocaust survivor, and starts to plan his revenge. The Willow Tree was Selbys first new novel in 20 years.

Waiting Period 2002

In Selbys last novel, a suicidal narrator tries to buy a gun to end his own life, but due to a computer malfunction he is forced to wait for a licence. As he hangs around he questions why he should die when there are so many others who deserve to go first. When Selby decides to attack, wrote the Los Angeles Times, it is with the shock of a practised mugger and with the speed and economy of a poet.

2011
—

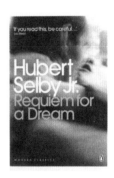

2012

Requiem for a Dream was adapted as a film in 2000, in which Selby had a cameo as an abusive prison guard.

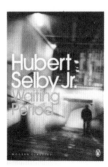

2012
—

Rona Jaffe 1931–2005

Born and raised in New York, Jaffe was working as an associate editor for Fawcett Publications when her first novel, *The Best of Everything*, was published. She then became a full-time writer, penning articles for *Cosmopolitan* and fifteen further novels.
In 1995, she founded the Rona Jaffe Foundation, which presents an annual award to promising women writers of literary fiction, poetry and creative non-fiction.

The Best of Everything 1958

Four young women have come to New York to find love and build careers. They compare notes as they negotiate workplace politics, broken engagements and tiny apartments. Jaffe's novel was a bestseller, and it was immediately adapted as a film starring Joan Crawford. 'This is a story that should be read by girls with dramatic ideas about New York,' said the *Cleveland Press*, 'parents with qualms about their daughters' ideas, and men with baffling questions about girls' minds.' The title comes from an actual advertisement in the *New York Times*:

> *you deserve the best of everything:*
> THE BEST JOB, THE BEST SURROUNDINGS,
> THE BEST PAY, THE BEST CONTACTS.

2011
fwd. Rona Jaffe, 2005

2012
aftwd.
Joshua
Ferris

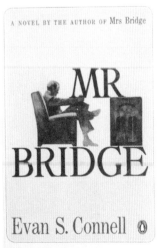

2013
aftwd.
Lionel
Shriver

Evan S. Connell 1924–2013

Evan Shelby Connell was born in Kansas City, Missouri, the son of a doctor. In the Second World War he served as a pilot in the US navy. He lived much of his life in Sausalito on the Californian coast, writing an eclectic series of books including essays, stories, novels, a biography of General Custer, and a poetic, philosophical miscellany called *Notes from a Bottle Found on the Beach at Carmel* (1962). In 2009, he was nominated for the Man Booker International Prize for lifetime achievement. Dorothy Parker (419) called him 'a writer of fine style and amazing variety'.

Mrs Bridge 1959

India Bridge is a housewife and mother in Kansas City, Missouri. Over the course of 117 vignettes, we observe her raising children between the wars, making a home for her husband Walter, shopping, playing bridge and visiting the country club. But times are changing and Mrs Bridge struggles to adapt to a new world of gender equality and civil rights (502). Connell modelled Mrs Bridge on his own mother and dedicated the book to his sister Barbara. The *New York Times* calls it 'a perfect novel […] economical, piquant, beautiful, true'.

Mr Bridge 1969

Connell's companion novel deals with the same key moments as *Mrs Bridge*, but from the perspective of Walter Bridge, India's husband. Walter is a successful suburban lawyer who, like his wife, has a poignantly narrow view of the world. Together the books form 'a curious double exposure', as the writer Gerald Shapiro put it, 'like a photograph taken once in shadow, once in light'. In 1990, they were made into a Merchant Ivory film, *Mr and Mrs Bridge*, starring Paul Newman and Joanne Woodward.

Walter Tevis 1928–1984

Tevis was born in San Francisco. As a child, he developed a rheumatic heart condition and was placed in a convalescent home for a year, where he was given heavy doses of phenobarbital. On his release, aged eleven, he travelled on his own to rejoin his family in Kentucky. During the Second World War, he served as a carpenter's mate aboard a naval destroyer; afterwards he studied English at the University of Kentucky while working in a pool hall. As well as writing novels and short stories, he taught in high schools across Kentucky and later at university level.

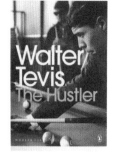

2009
● intro. Al Alvarez

The Hustler 1959

'I learned about gambling after enlisting in the Navy on my 17th birthday,' recalled Tevis. 'I played poker for 17 months on Okinawa.' No one can touch 'Fast Eddie' Felson the pool hustler, until he meets the legendary Minnesota Fats, an enormous yet graceful player with a facial tic. 'If Hemingway (428) had the passion for pool that he had for bullfighting,' wrote *Time* magazine, 'his hero might have been Eddie Felson.' *The Hustler* was made into an award-winning film in 1961 starring Paul Newman.

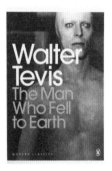

2009
● –

The Man Who Fell to Earth 1963

Thomas J. Newton travels from a distant drought-ridden planet and lands in rural Kentucky. He is a tall, frail and strange figure, who makes a fortune through licensing unimaginably advanced technologies. It is 'one of the most heart-breaking books I know', writes the *Boston Globe*, 'a threnody on great ambition and terrible failure'. Tevis described it as 'a very disguised autobiography', a version of his own arrival in Kentucky from San Francisco as a frail and solitary boy who would later fall prey to alcoholism. Nicholas Roeg made a cult 1976 film adaptation starring David Bowie.

The Queen's Gambit 1983

'*The Queen's Gambit* is sheer entertainment,' writes the novelist Michael Ondaatje. 'It is a book I reread every few years – for the pure pleasure and skill of it.' Young Beth Harmon plays her first game of chess at the age of eight and discovers that she is a prodigy. Growing up in a Kentucky orphanage, equally addicted to chess tournaments and tranquillizers, she must find a way to live alongside her all-consuming talent. It was adapted in 2020 as a Netflix miniseries starring Anya Taylor-Joy.

More BOARD GAMES

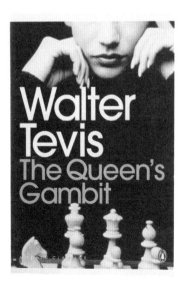

2009
● intro. Lionel Shriver
—
The 'Queen's Gambit' is a set of opening moves in chess, illustrated on the title page of Tevis's book. It is one of the oldest recorded chess openings, described in the Göttingen Manuscript of 1490, the earliest known book about chess as it is now played.

John Updike

1932 – 2009

John Hoyer Updike was born and raised in small-town Pennsylvania. After studying at Harvard University and the Ruskin School of Drawing and Fine Art in Oxford, he began contributing regularly to the *New Yorker*. In 1957, he moved to Ipswich, Massachusetts, where he wrote prolifically: 22 novels, as well as numerous collections of short stories and poems and critical essays. Although some feminist critics (522) have accused Updike of misogyny – the novelist David Foster Wallace famously described him as 'just a penis with a thesaurus' – most readers have agreed with Martin Amis (160), who considers him 'one of the great American novelists of the 20th century'. He is 'a master', writes Joyce Carol Oates, 'like Flaubert, of mesmerizing us with his narrative voice even as he might repel us with the vanities of human desire his scalpel exposes'.

The Poorhouse Fair

1959

Updike's first novel is about a geriatric rebellion in the Diamond County Home for the Aged, after their annual produce sale is a disappointment. It is set in the future, in 1977, and was written 'as a deliberate anti-*Nineteen Eighty-Four* (84)'. The *New Yorker* described it as 'a work of the macabre, far more littered with decay and disorder than any of the brooding mountains or melancholy Venice of Thomas Mann (245)'.

1968 Penguin Books
2006 Modern Classics
intro. John Updike, 1977

The Rabbit Series

Rabbit, Run, Rabbit Redux, Rabbit is Rich, Rabbit at Rest

1960 – 90

Updike is best known for his four 'Rabbit' novels, which chronicle the life of a middle-class everyman, Harry 'Rabbit' Angstrom. They were 'a ticket to the America all around me', he wrote. 'What I saw through Rabbit's eyes was more worth telling than what I saw through my own.' *Rabbit, Run* (1960) introduces Rabbit, a one-time high-school basketball superstar, now a disaffected salesman with an alcoholic wife and a young son. Rabbit runs away from his home and his family in a desperate thousand-mile bid to escape mediocrity. It was Updike's response to Kerouac's *On the Road* (470), demonstrating 'what happens when a young American family man goes on the road – the people left behind get hurt'. Set ten years later, *Rabbit Redux* (1971) is an evocation of the sixties and the summer of love. Rabbit's wife and teenage son have left him and he starts an impromptu commune with the 18-year-old Jill and her young black friend Skeeter. Another decade on, Rabbit has inherited his father's Toyota dealership in *Rabbit is Rich* (1981). He's getting fat, he wears good suits and he has his eye on the wife of a country-club friend, but still he's haunted by regrets. The third Rabbit novel won the Pulitzer Prize for Fiction, the National Book Award and a National Book Critics Circle Award. In *Rabbit at Rest* (1990), the final instalment, Rabbit is 56 and overweight, with a struggling business, a dysfunctional family and a dicky heart. It also won the Pulitzer Prize for Fiction and a National Book Critics Circle Award. 'The Rabbit novels, for all their grittiness, constitute John Updike's surpassingly eloquent valentine to his country,' writes Joyce Carol Oates. They are his 'masterpiece', says Ian McEwan, 'and will surely be his monument'.

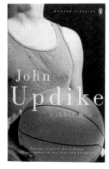

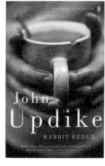

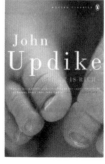

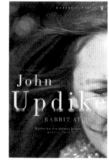

Updike's afterword, replicated in the first three volumes, was originally the introduction to the Everyman's Library omnibus edition in 1995.

1964 Penguin Books
2006 Modern Classics
aftwd. John Updike, 1995

1973 Penguin Books
2006 Modern Classics
aftwd. John Updike, 1995

1982 Penguin Books
2006 Modern Classics
aftwd. John Updike, 1995

1991 Penguin Books
2006 Modern Classics
aftwd. Justin Cartwright, 2006

The Centaur 1963

Updike takes the legend of Chiron, the noble centaur who taught the heroes of Greek mythology, and transplants it to small-town Pennsylvania, where a schoolteacher and his 15-year-old son are snowed in by a three-day blizzard. The novel won the National Book Award. '*Pale Fire* (311) was fully as drastic a formal innovation as *The Centaur*,' wrote the critic Renata Adler, 'with the difference that [...] Mr. Updike does not take cover in irony, and his novel is delivered to the critics in all the vulnerability of its seriousness.'

1968 Penguin Books
2007 Modern Classics
—

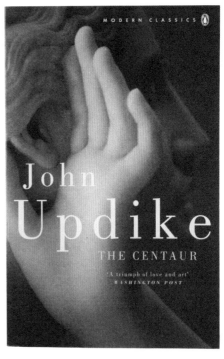

1966 Penguin Books
2007 Modern Classics
—

Of the Farm 1965

Joey Robinson is a divorced New York advertising consultant who makes an eventful trip with his new wife and 11-year-old stepson to visit his mother on the neglected family farm. 'This novel is, very clearly and very completely, a small masterpiece,' wrote the *New York Times*.

The Complete Henry Bech

Bech: A Book, *Bech is Back*, *Bech in Czech*
1965 – 98

Henry Bech is Updike's comical antithesis: a reclusive, unprolific Jewish novelist. He first appeared in *New Yorker* short stories and Updike collected three short-story cycles: *Bech: A Book* (1970), *Bech is Back* (1982) and *Bech at Bay* (1998). Bech is initially celebrated for his novel *Travel Light* and he goes on to produce one more blockbuster, *Think Big*, and win the Nobel Prize for Literature (576). 'Bech is one of the most entertaining comic creations in recent modern fiction,' wrote the *Financial Times*.

1972 Penguin Books
Bech: A Book
1983 Penguin Books
Bech is Back
1992 Penguin Books
The Complete Henry Bech
2006 Modern Classics
—
The third collection is listed on the Penguin title page as *Bech in Czech*, but this is properly the title of the first story in the collection *Bech at Bay* (1998).

Couples 1968

This notorious novel is about middle-class partner-swapping in the small town of Tarbox, Massachusetts, 'a cat's cradle of vigorous adultery', as Martin Amis (160) put it, 'as filtered through the sensibility of a modern James (397) – or a modern Joyce (8)'. It earned Updike the cover of *Time* magazine. 'The book is, of course, not about sex as such,' Updike clarified: 'it's about sex as the emergent religion, as the only thing left.'

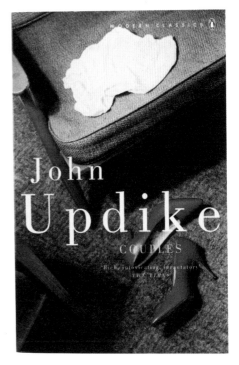

1970 Penguin Books
2007 Modern Classics
—
Tarbox is a thinly fictionalized version of Updike's home town of Ipswich, Massachusetts.

The 'Scarlet Letter' Trilogy
A Month of Sundays, Roger's Version, S.
1975 – 88

'John Updike is our time's greatest man of letters,' wrote Philip Roth, 'as brilliant a literary critic and essayist as he was a novelist and short-story writer. He is and always will be no less a national treasure than his nineteenth-century precursor, Nathaniel Hawthorne.' These three novels all draw inspiration from Hawthorne's *The Scarlet Letter* (1850) in order to explore the combination of religion and sexuality.
A Month of Sundays (1975) is the confession of the randy Reverend Marshfield, who has been prescribed a course of writing as occupational therapy in a desert retreat for errant clerics; *Roger's Version* (1986) is about Roger Lambert, a professor of divinity, whose life is upturned by a computer programme that claims to be able to prove the existence of God; and S. (1988) is an epistolary novel made up of letters from Sarah Worth ('S.'), who walks out on her doctor husband and joins an ashram in the Arizona desert.

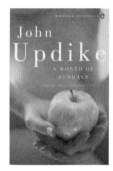
1976 Penguin Books
2007 Modern Classics
—

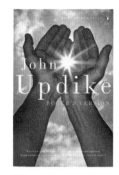
1987 Penguin Books
2006 Modern Classics
aftwd. John Banville

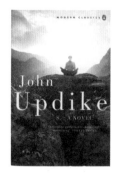
1989 Penguin Books
2006 Modern Classics
—

Marry Me
A Romance 1976

Jerry and Ruth Conant meet Sally and Richard Mathias in Connecticut one summer. Jerry and Sally start a passionate affair, but the rules of engagement keep shifting. Paul Theroux (543) said that 'Updike has never written better of the woe that is in marriage or (as Melville put it in a poem) "the sexual feud that clogs the aspiring life".'

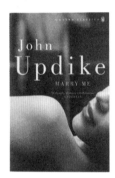
1977 Penguin Books
2006 Red Classics
2008 Modern Classics
—

The Coup 1978

Colonel Hakim Félix Ellelloû is the former dictator of Kush, a fictionalized desert land in sub-Saharan Africa. In his outrageous memoir, he describes his life and times, his rise to power and his ultimate downfall.

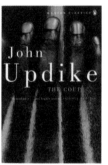
1980 Penguin Books
2006 Modern Classics
—

The Witches of Eastwick 1984

When their husbands leave them, Alexandra Spofford, Jane Smart and Sukie Rougemont discover they have extraordinary powers. Their newfound witchcraft wreaks havoc in the small Rhode Island community of Eastwick, especially when the devilish Darryl Van Horne arrives in town. The book is 'about female power, a power that patriarchal societies have denied', claimed Updike, who wrote it to 'make things right with my, what shall we call them, feminist detractors'. In 1987, George Miller directed a film adaptation starring Cher, Susan Sarandon, Michelle Pfeiffer and Jack Nicholson, and in 2008 Updike published a sequel, *The Widows of Eastwick*, which revisits the witches in their old age.

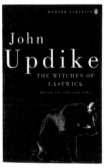
1985 Penguin Books
2007 Modern Classics
—

More WITCHES

The Wonderful Wizard of Oz
by L. Frank Baum   408

Armed with Madness
by Mary Butts   78

The Dreams in the Witch House and Other Weird Stories
by H. P. Lovecraft   417

The Crucible
by Arthur Miller   487

Lolly Willowes
by Sylvia Townsend Warner   75

Memories of the Ford Administration 1992

History professor Alf Clayton is completing a questionnaire from the Northern New England Association of American Historians (NNEAAH), which asks for his memories and impressions of Gerald Ford's term as president in the 1970s. But Clayton soon strays way off topic, recalling adulterous affairs and discussing his own biography of James Buchanan, the president before the American Civil War.

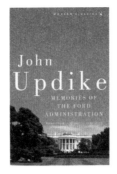

1993 Penguin Books
2007 Modern Classics
—

Brazil 1994

Updike updates the legend of Tristan and Isolde in a modern-day magical realist (563) version of Brazil. Tristão Raposo is a black teenager from the slums of Rio de Janeiro who meets wealthy white Isabel Leme on Copacabana beach. He presents her with a ring and they elope to the jungles of Brazil's wild west. Tristão and Isabel 'never quite realize the epic valor of their namesakes of medieval legend and Wagnerian drama,' comments Barbara Kingsolver drily. 'They mean well, but they just can't seem to resist silk shirts and kinky sex.'

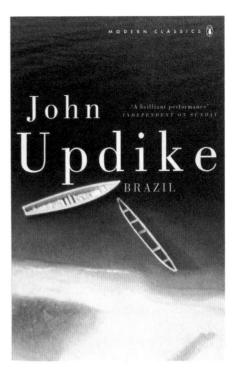

1995 Penguin Books
2006 Modern Classics
—

In the Beauty of the Lilies 1996

This saga follows four generations of the Wilmot family over the course of the 20th century, from Clarence, a Presbyterian clergyman, to Alma DeMott, goddess of the silver screen. It traces the decline of religion and the rise of cinema in American culture. Gore Vidal called it 'easily the most intensely political American novel of the last quarter-century'.

Toward the End of Time 1997

In the year 2020, America and China have just fought a thermonuclear war and society has descended into chaos. Ben Turnbull reads about the 'many-worlds' hypothesis and accidentally finds his identity branching into variants extending back through history and forward to the end of time. 'As *memento mori* and its obverse, *carpe diem*,' writes Margaret Atwood, '*Toward the End of Time* could scarcely be bettered.'

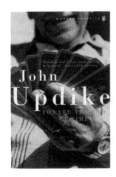

1998 Penguin Books
2006 Modern Classics
—

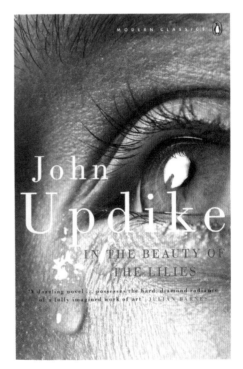

1997 Penguin Books
2006 Modern Classics
—

The writer Adam Gopnik predicts that in the future *In the Beauty of the Lilies* will be seen as a 'late masterpiece overlooked or praised by rote in its day, only to be rediscovered by another generation'.

Anne Sexton 1928–1974

Anne Gray Harvey married Alfred Sexton in 1948 and worked as a fashion model. She had her first mental breakdown following the birth of their first daughter Linda, in 1953, which led to repeated hospitalizations throughout her life and a diagnosis of what is now termed bipolar disorder. Her therapist encouraged her to write, and so she joined poetry workshops in Boston taught by Robert Lowell, through which she met Sylvia Plath. She won the Pulitzer Prize for Poetry in 1967. In 1973, she divorced Alfred, and, in the following year, she took her own life at the age of 45. She was 'one of the most important American poets of her generation', says Margaret Atwood.

Mercies Selected Poems 1960–74

Sexton's confessional poetry broke social and literary taboos, describing depression, suicidal tendencies, menstruation, adultery and personal family relationships. This new selection draws poems from all her major collections, including *To Bedlam and Part Way Back* (1960), *All My Pretty Ones* (1962), the Pulitzer Prize-winning *Live or Die* (1966) and *The Death Notebooks* (1974). 'She domesticates my terror, examines it and describes it, teaches it some tricks which will amuse me, then lets it gallop wild in my forest once more,' said Kurt Vonnegut (523). '[…] Good for her.'

2020
ed. Linda Gray Sexton
—
Linda Sexton is Anne Sexton's daughter and literary executor. She has edited several posthumous books of her mother's poetry and has written a memoir, *Searching for Mercy Street: My Journey Back to My Mother, Anne Sexton* (1994), in which she describes her own struggles with depression.

1964 Modern Classics
1983 Peregrine Books
● —
'*The Children of Sánchez* goes at once into Penguin Modern Classics,' reads the back cover of the 1964 edition, 'because this rare work stands like a monument at the point where literature meets life.'

Oscar Lewis 1914–1970

Oscar Lefkowitz was born in New York, the son of a synagogue sexton. He studied anthropology at Columbia University and changed his name to Lewis. He became a leading American anthropologist at the University of Illinois, where he founded the anthropology department in 1960. He first wrote about the Mexican Sánchez family in *Five Families* (1959), and he won a National Book Award for *La Vida* (1966), a controversial portrait of a Puerto Rican prostitute.

The Children of Sánchez Autobiography of a Mexican Family 1961

Lewis pioneered the concept of a 'culture of poverty' and was researching the idea in the Tepito slums of Mexico City when he first met Jesús Sánchez and his children, Manuel, Roberto, Consuelo and Marta. His literary masterpiece is based on interviews with the four children, which he weaves into a portrait of poverty full of brawling, thieving, drinking, swearing, whoring and gambling. It 'has the quality of a great novel', wrote the *Times Literary Supplement*.

Pedro Martínez A Mexican Peasant and His Family 1964

Lewis records the life story of Pedro Martínez: he was born in 1889, fought for Emiliano Zapata (444), held office three times in his village and lived a harsh life working the land with primitive tools. 'Dr Lewis has brought the Mexican village to life with an intimacy, a reality and a compassion which no one else has approached,' said V. S. Pritchett (110).

1980
● —

A Death in the Sánchez Family 1969

Aunt Guadalupe is a minor character in *The Children of Sánchez*, but when she dies of cancer her death is a major event and a crippling economic pressure for the Sánchez family. This slim volume is again made up of interviews with the Sánchez children. 'For the poor, death is almost as great a hardship as life itself,' wrote Lewis.

1972
● —

1996
• pref. Robert Coover (536)
intro. Patrick McGrath

John Hawkes
1925–1998

John Clendennin Talbot Burne Hawkes, Jr. was an asthmatic only child. He studied intermittently at Harvard University for six years, writing poetry with his friends John Ashbery and Frank O'Hara and taking time off to volunteer as an ambulance driver in the Second World War. He spent most of his life teaching creative writing at Brown University and penning surreal, often nightmarish works of postmodern (505) fiction which take place in the 'landscapes of the imagination'.'

The Lime Twig, Second Skin, Travesty
1961–76

The Lime Twig (1961) is set in the violent post-Second World War underworld of London, despite the fact that Hawkes had never been to England: he was inspired by the novels of Graham Greene (88) and the British troops he had met during the war. 'You suffer The Lime Twig like a dream,' wrote Flannery O'Connor. 'It seems to be something that is happening to you, that you want to escape from but can't.' Hawkes wrote Second Skin (1964) in the West Indies: it's a surreal, fragmented, mythical novella loosely based on Shakespeare's The Tempest. 'He is the master of an immensely artful, corrugated surface of language,' said Susan Sontag (524), reviewing Second Skin – 'a looped, virile, restless style.' Travesty (1976) is a terrifying, eroticized monologue, a portrait of the artist on a night drive in southern France.

Gay Talese b. 1932

Talese was born in New Jersey, the son of Italian immigrants. He began contributing to the New York Times in 1953 and found work with the New Yorker, Harper's and Esquire, becoming a pioneer of the New Journalism (464). He 'raises the magazine article to the level of an art form', wrote the Los Angeles Times. Mario Puzo called him 'the best non-fiction writer in America'. In 2011, Talese won the Norman Mailer (496) Prize for Distinguished Journalism.

Frank Sinatra Has a Cold
and Other Essays 1961–97

Talese learned his interview technique from his mother, who taught him to listen patiently and 'never to interrupt when people were having great difficulty in explaining themselves, for during such halting and imprecise moments [...] people are often very revealing'. In the title piece of this collection, Sinatra nurses a glass of bourbon, struck down with a cold and unable to sing, like 'Picasso without paint, Ferrari without fuel – only worse'. Other essay titles include 'Peter O'Toole on the Ould Sod', 'Mr. Bad News' and 'Origins of a Nonfiction Writer'.

2011
–

1972
• –

Louis Auchincloss 1917–2010

Auchincloss was a New York lawyer who also wrote novels and stories reflecting his legal experience and the New York high society circles in which he mixed. His novels have been compared to both Edith Wharton (401) and Henry James (397). 'Not since Dreiser (407),' said Gore Vidal, 'has an American writer had so much to tell us about the role of money in our lives.'

Portrait in Brownstone 1962

This multi-generational saga opens with a suicide at the turn of the 20th century and follows the extended family of Trasks, Denisons and Hartleys over 50 years as the men build financial empires and the women pull the strings. 'He writes drily and agreeably,' said Cyril Connolly (107), ' he has a Jamesian (397) feeling for right action and delicacy of speech.'

Philip K. Dick 1928–1982

Philip Kindred Dick was born in Chicago but lived most of his life in California. The critic Fredric Jameson calls him the 'Shakespeare of Science Fiction'. He wrote 44 novels and more than 100 short stories, blending philosophical speculation with androids, alternate realities, authoritarian governments, drug use and hallucination. Dick used amphetamines to keep to his punishing writing schedule and occasionally received epiphanies through a mysterious pink beam of light. His most famous books are *Do Androids Dream of Electric Sheep?* (1968), *Ubik* (1969) and *A Scanner Darkly* (1977) and many of his works have been adapted into cult films such as *Blade Runner* (1982), *Total Recall* (1990) and *Minority Report* (2002). He was married five times and died a few months before the release of *Blade Runner*. *Rolling Stone* called him 'the most brilliant science fiction mind on any planet'.

1967 Penguin Books
1987 Penguin Science Fiction
2001 Modern Classics
intro. Eric Brown, 2001
—
A fictional Axis victory has
also been explored in *SS-GB*
(1978) by Len Deighton (147)
and *Fatherland* (1992) by
Robert Harris.

The Man in the High Castle 1962

This alternative history made Dick's reputation. Set in 1962, it imagines that the Axis powers defeated the Allies in the Second World War and that the world is now divided between imperial Japan and Nazi Germany. The Nazis have destroyed Africa, drained the Mediterranean and colonized the moon. The former USA is split between Japan, which controls the Pacific coast states, and Germany, which controls New York and the east coast; in between is a Midwestern neutral buffer zone. Within the novel is another novel, an alternative history within the alternative history, which imagines a world where the Allies did defeat the Axis. Harry Harrison (530) called it 'a seminal work in science fiction – Philip K. Dick's best novel'. *The Man in the High Castle* won a Hugo Award and was adapted as a four-season television series by Amazon (2015–19), with Dick's daughter Isa Dick Hackett as an executive producer.

Ken Kesey 1935–2001

Kesey was a champion wrestler and TV magician in the timber country of Oregon. He took writing classes at Stanford University, taught by Wallace Stegner (459), Malcolm Cowley (448) and Frank O'Connor (16). At the same time, he participated in a government study into hallucinogenic drugs and worked graveyard shifts at a local mental hospital, experiences which inspired his first novel, *One Flew Over the Cuckoo's Nest*. He became a leading figure of the 1960s counterculture (526), establishing a base at La Honda, California, with an entourage known as the 'Merry Pranksters'. They staged LSD parties called 'Acid Tests', as described in Allen Ginsberg's (490) poems and works of New Journalism (464) such as Hunter S. Thompson's *Hell's Angels* (531) and Tom Wolfe's *The Electric Kool-Aid Acid Test* (1968). *Sometimes a Great Notion* (1964), Kesey's second novel, is an epic set in Oregon and written in the mould of Thomas Wolfe (438) and William Faulkner (433). In 1965, Kesey was arrested for possessing marijuana, faked his own suicide, fled to Mexico, was rearrested and imprisoned for six months. Thereafter he settled in his native state, where he raised cattle, coached high-school wrestling and taught at the University of Oregon.

One Flew Over the Cuckoo's Nest
1962

Nurse Ratched tyrannizes her ward in an Oregon state mental hospital, subduing her patients with mind-numbing medications and the threat of electric-shock therapy. But her regime is disrupted by the arrival of the maverick McMurphy, who resolves to oppose every rule on behalf of his fellow inmates. The story is told from the point of view of the seemingly mute Chief Bromden, a half Native American. Miloš Forman's 1975 film adaptation won five Academy Awards: Best Picture, Best Actor, Best Actress, Best Director and Best Adapted Screenplay; Kesey claimed never to have watched it.

1976 Penguin Books
2003 Modern Classics
intro. Robert Faggen, 2002

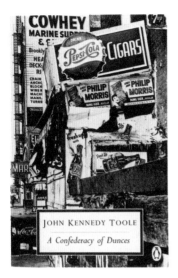

1981 King Penguin
1989 Penguin Books
1995 Twentieth-Century
Classics
fwd. Walker Percy, 1980
—
Toole's title comes from
an essay by Jonathan Swift:
'When a true genius appears in
the world, you may know him
by this sign, that the dunces are
all in confederacy against him.'

John Kennedy Toole 1937–1969

'Ken' Toole grew up in New Orleans with a flamboyant, controlling mother and a car-salesman father. In 1961, he was drafted into the US army and spent two years teaching English to Spanish-speaking recruits in Puerto Rico. During that time, he began writing *A Confederacy of Dunces* and completed it on his return to New Orleans in 1963. His repeated failure to find a publisher, however, led to increasing paranoia and depression and eventually he took his own life at the age of 31. Thelma Toole, his mother, continued resolutely to pitch his novel again and again, until eventually it was published by the Louisiana State University Press in 1980. In 1981, it won the Pulitzer Prize for Fiction.

A Confederacy of Dunces 1962–4, pub. 1980

Ignatius J. Reilly of New Orleans is the extraordinary central character of Toole's hilarious novel. He is a self-styled scholar who lives with his alcoholic mother – '[a] slob extraordinary, a mad Oliver Hardy, a fat Don Quixote, a perverse Thomas Aquinas rolled into one', marvelled Walker Percy, who helped the book into print, '[an] intellectual, ideologue, deadbeat, goof-off, glutton, who should repel the reader with his gargantuan bloats, his thunderous contempt and one-man war against everybody – Freud (265), homosexuals, heterosexuals, Protestants, and the assorted excesses of modern times.' Reilly's picaresque escapades with hot-dog stands and his beatnik (491) girlfriend Myrna Minkoff are patterned on the structure of Boethius' *Consolation of Philosophy*, while the dialogue hums with the dialects of New Orleans. It is 'my favourite book of all time,' says Billy Connolly. '[…] It stays with you long after you have read it – for your whole life, in fact.'

Man Ray 1890–1976

Emmanuel Radnitzky was born in Philadelphia, Pennsylvania, the eldest child of Russian Jewish parents; as a boy, he helped his father to tailor clothes. The family changed its surname to Ray and moved to New York, where Ray took drawing classes at his Brooklyn high school, visited museums and decided to become an artist. He befriended Marcel Duchamp and together they embraced Dada (263), publishing one issue of the magazine *New York Dada* in 1921. But 'dada cannot live in New York,' they decided. 'All New York is dada, and will not tolerate a rival.' That year Ray moved to Paris, where he lived for much of the rest of his life. He embraced Surrealism (176) and was part of the first Surrealist exhibition in 1925. He is buried in Paris's Montparnasse cemetery, where his epitaph reads 'unconcerned, but not indifferent'.

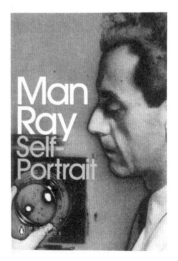

2012
—
Marcel Duchamp provided a
dictionary definition of Man Ray:
'n. m. synon. de joie jouer jouir'
– 'noun, masculine, synonymous
with joy, to play, to enjoy'.

Self-Portrait 1963

Ray's remarkable memoir charts his career as a painter, photographer, sculptor, film-maker, inventor and writer and evokes his glamorous life among the Parisian Surrealists (176). It contains portraits of Henri Matisse, Pablo Picasso, Salvador Dalí, Max Ernst, Ernest Hemingway (428), James Joyce (8), Gertrude Stein (410) and Jean Cocteau (178).

Feminist Literary Criticism

The founding texts of feminist literary criticism are often cited as Virginia Woolf's *A Room of One's Own* (45) and Simone de Beauvoir's *The Second Sex* (187); but the modern discipline really grew out of second-wave feminism, the phase inspired by Betty Friedan's *The Feminine Mystique*, activists such as Gloria Steinem and Angela Y. Davis (545), and the various protest movements of the 1960s. Initially second-wave feminist critics redressed misogyny in male writing – through works such as Mary Ellmann's *Thinking about Women* (1968) and Kate Millett's *Sexual Politics* (1970), which criticizes Sigmund Freud (265), D. H. Lawrence (50), Norman Mailer (496) and Henry Miller (451) – but gradually the focus moved towards celebrating the virtues of women's writing, re-evaluating neglected authors and rediscovering forgotten titles. Feminist publishing houses appeared around the world, such as Virago in the UK, The Women's Press in the USA and Éditions des Femmes in France, and key texts of this period include Ellen Moers's *Literary Women* (1976) and Elaine Showalter's *A Literature of Their Own* (1977). More recently feminist literary criticism has become increasingly variegated, in line with subsequent 'waves' of feminism.

Betty Friedan 1921–2006

Bettye Naomi Goldstein was born into a Jewish family in Illinois and married the theatre producer Carl Friedan. In 1957, she wrote a questionnaire for her former classmates at a college reunion and discovered that many women shared her frustration with the perceived roles of housewife and mother. This insight led to her writing *The Feminine Mystique*, the book that is often said to have initiated second-wave feminism. Friedan went on to co-found the National Organization for Women (NOW) in 1966, organize the nationwide Women's Strike for Equality in 1970 and co-convene the National Women's Political Caucus in 1971. 'Friedan succeeded where no other feminist writer had,' said the *New Yorker*. 'She touched the lives of ordinary readers.' 'The truth is I've always been a bad-tempered bitch,' Friedan wrote in her memoir *Life So Far* (2000). 'Some people say that I have mellowed some. I don't know.'

The Feminine Mystique 1963

1965 Penguin Books
1982 Pelican Books
2010 Modern Classics
intro. Lionel Shriver, 2010

'Each suburban wife struggled with it alone,' wrote Friedan. 'As she made the beds, shopped for groceries, matched slip-cover material, ate peanut butter sandwiches with her children, chauffeured Cub Scouts and Brownies, lay beside her husband at night, she was afraid to ask even of herself the silent question: "Is this all?"' Friedan's clear-eyed analysis of western women's lives in the mid-20th century established her as one of the chief architects of the women's liberation movement. It sold more than 3 million copies and the *New York Times* has called it 'one of the most influential non-fiction books of the twentieth century'.

THE PENGUIN BOOK OF FEMINIST WRITING 1405–2020

'The history of feminism is as big and complex as the history of patriarchy,' writes the historian Hannah Dawson, 'which is to say that it is the history of the world.' Dawson's global anthology gathers a remarkable array of feminist voices, from Christine de Pizan in the early 15th century to Lola Olufemi in 2020. She includes polemics, poems, novels, memoirs and manifestos – the diverse 'flares that writers have sent up into the sky' – with contributions from Mary Wollstonecraft, John Stuart Mill, Emmeline Pankhurst, Anna Akhmatova (301), Virginia Woolf (42), Simone de Beauvoir (187), Susan Sontag (524), Betty Friedan, Audre Lorde (534), Angela Carter (156) and Angela Y. Davis (545), as well as less familiar names such as Olympe de Gouges, Kishida Toshiko, Pandita Ramabai Sarasvati, Ding Ling and Jahan Ara Shahnawaz.

2021 Hardback Classics
2022 Modern Classics
ed. Hannah Dawson, 2021

Kurt Vonnegut 1922–2007

Vonnegut served in the US army in the Second World War and was captured during the Battle of the Bulge in December 1944. He survived the Allied firebombing of Dresden in February 1945 by taking refuge in a meat locker three storeys underground, in the slaughterhouse where he was imprisoned, an experience which inspired his most famous work, *Slaughterhouse-Five* (1969). After the war, he began writing short stories for magazines, and his first novel, *Player Piano*, appeared in 1952. 'Vonnegut will rightly be remembered,' wrote the *Los Angeles Times*, 'as a darkly humorous social critic and the premier novelist of the counterculture (526).'

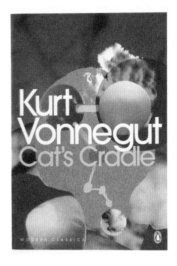

1965 Penguin Books
2008 Modern Classics
intro. Benjamin Kunkel, 2008

More TROPICAL ISLANDS

Cat's Cradle 1963

Through flashbacks, Jonah describes his quest to track down Dr Hoenikker – one of the creators of the atomic bomb – and his even deadlier invention, a lethal chemical called ice-nine. Along the way, he meets Newt the Dwarf, travels to the Caribbean island of San Lorenzo and joins a religious cult called Bokononism. This deadpan postmodern (505) science fiction novel satirizes science, religion and humanity's drive towards self-destruction. 'Vonnegut looked the world straight in the eye and never flinched,' said J. G. Ballard.

Charles Webb 1939–2020

Webb graduated from Williams College, Massachusetts, in 1961. The next year he married Eve Rudd, who later shaved her head and called herself 'Fred'. Leading figures of the 1960s counterculture (526), they lived a non-materialist lifestyle: Webb sold the film rights to *The Graduate* for a one-off payment of $20,000, declined an inheritance from his father and gave away artworks by Andy Warhol (543). The couple worked menial jobs, home-schooling their two sons in a VW camper van, and in 1981 they divorced but stayed together as a protest against the institution of marriage. They managed a nudist camp in New Jersey for a while and from 2000 they lived on the south coast of England. Their son David is a performance artist who once cooked and ate a copy of *The Graduate* with cranberry sauce.

The Graduate 1963

When Benjamin Braddock graduates from college, the rest of his suburban life stretches ahead of him. Until, that is, Mrs Robinson undresses and seduces him. Benjamin feels he may have found an escape, but things get complicated when Mrs Robinson's daughter Elaine comes home. 'The *Graduate* caught the spirit of the Sixties,' wrote the *Independent*. '[…] It captured a mood, a time, a rebellion.'

1968 Penguin Books
2010 Modern Classics
intro. Hanif Kureishi, 2010

—

Mike Nichols directed the hugely successful film adaptation of *The Graduate* in 1967, starring Anne Bancroft and Dustin Hoffman, with music by Simon and Garfunkel.

Susan Sontag 1933–2004

Susan Rosenblatt's father died in China when she was five years old; she later took her stepfather's surname, Sontag. She studied at the universities of California, Chicago, Harvard, Oxford and Paris before returning to the USA in 1959 and teaching philosophy of religion at Columbia in New York and writing for the *Partisan Review* and *New York Review of Books*. She established herself as a cultural critic and social campaigner, producing novels, stories, plays and films. In 1989, she met the photographer Annie Leibovitz, with whom she had a close relationship for the rest of her life. 'If literature has engaged me as a project, first as a reader, then as a writer,' said Sontag when she was awarded the Jerusalem Prize in 2001, 'it is an extension of my sympathies to other selves, other domains, other dreams, other worlds, other territories.' 'She regroups the familiar and makes the eye fresh,' says Hilary Mantel. '[...] She stands for what is articulate, independent, exploratory: for self as work in progress.'

2009
aftwd. Susan
Sontag, 1996

The Benefactor 1963

Sontag's first novel is the memoir of Hippolyte, a wealthy bohemian with a violently imaginative dream life who analyses his own consciousness until the boundary between reality and fantasy dissolves. 'She can make a real story out of dreams and thoughts,' said Hannah Arendt (258).

2009
–

Against Interpretation
and Other Essays 1963–5, pub. 1966

Sontag's first essay collection includes 'Notes on "Camp"', comprising 58 attempts to 'snare a sensibility in words' – a sensibility exemplified by Tiffany lamps, old Flash Gordon comics and the novels of Ronald Firbank (64) and Ivy Compton-Burnett (104) – and 'Against Interpretation', a fierce defence of style over content. Sontag writes about both 'high' and 'low' culture and engages with authors such as Samuel Beckett (20), Albert Camus (181), Eugène Ionesco (324), Claude Lévi-Strauss (194), Jean-Paul Sartre (185) and Simone Weil (180). The collection is 'a vivid bit of living history here and now', wrote the *New York Times*, 'and at the end of the sixties it may well rank among the invaluable cultural chronicles of these years'.

Styles of Radical Will
1966–8, pub. 1969

Sontag's second essay collection includes 'The Aesthetics of Silence' – a brilliant account of language, thought and consciousness – 'Trip to Hanoi', which was written during the Vietnam War, and 'The Pornographic Imagination', a taxonomy of pornography. Other pieces cover film, literature and politics.

2009
–

Death Kit 1967

Dalton 'Diddy' Harron works for a microscope manufacturer. When both his marriage and his attempt at suicide fail, he spirals into an increasingly nightmarish world of madness and murder. *Vogue* called Sontag's second novel 'a strange and wonderful book, a ritual exorcizing of modern terrors, a dream book of love and death'.

1970 Penguin Books
2009 Modern Classics
–

Under the Sign of Saturn Essays 1972–80, pub. 1980

'Susan Sontag's third book of essays has meditations on Antonin Artaud (xix), Elias Canetti (328), Leni Riefenstahl, Walter Benjamin (251) and Hans-Jürgen Syberberg's film about Hitler,' wrote the *New York Times*. She 'has long been an effective publicist for the more imposing European offshoots of high modernism (11)'. The volume is dedicated to Joseph Brodsky (316), with whom Sontag had a short affair.

2009
–

On Photography 1973–7, pub. 1977

Sontag's landmark critique of photography raises moral and aesthetic questions about the ubiquity of photographs and their power to shock, seduce, incriminate and memorialize. She worries about the 'chronic voyeuristic relation to the world' which they promulgate. These seven essays are 'a brilliant analysis of the profound changes photographic images have made in our way of looking at the world, and at ourselves', wrote the *Washington Post*. The book won a National Book Critics Circle Award.

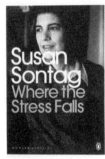

1979 Penguin Books
2002 Modern Classics
2008 Design Classics
—

Illness as Metaphor and AIDS and Its Metaphors 1978–89

Sontag wrote *Illness as Metaphor* (1978) while undergoing treatment for breast cancer. She examines the language around cancer in the 20th century and tuberculosis in the 19th, revealing a complex of victim-blaming metaphors that she encourages us to abandon. *Newsweek* called the study 'one of the most liberating books of our time'. A decade later, following the AIDS epidemic of the 1980s, she extended and re-examined her arguments in *AIDS and Its Metaphors* (1989).

1983 Penguin Books
Illness as Metaphor
1990 Penguin Books
AIDS and Its Metaphors
1991 Penguin Books
combined volume
2002 Modern Classics
—

In 1986, Sontag published the short story 'The Way We Live Now', an influential work of fiction that describes the beginning of the AIDS crisis in America.

Where the Stress Falls 1982–2001, pub. 2001

Sontag's last essay collection is divided into three thematic sections. 'Reading' has essays on Machado de Assis (564), W. G. Sebald, Roland Barthes, Robert Walser (262), Danilo Kiš (327), Witold Gombrowicz (292) and Jorge Luis Borges (572); 'Seeing' has pieces on film, dance, photography, painting, opera and theatre; and 'There and Here' covers her political writing and activism, including an account of the production of Samuel Beckett's (20) *Waiting for Godot*, which she directed in a candle-lit theatre in Sarajevo, during the siege of the Bosnian capital in the Yugoslavian civil war.

2009
—

The Volcano Lover
A Romance 1992

Sontag's bestselling historical novel is the story of Sir William Hamilton, the British ambassador at the court of Naples, his wife Emma and her love affair with Lord Nelson. Hamilton is the 'volcano lover' of the title, obsessed with Mount Vesuvius, but the scandal that erupts around his wife's liaison proves equally explosive. 'Impressive, at times enchanting, always interesting, always entertaining,' writes the novelist John Banville, '[…] a big, old-fashioned broth of a book. […] It operates in that broad but nebulous area between fiction and essay, in which Hermann Broch's *Death of Virgil* (272) is the supreme exemplar, and which in our time is occupied by writers such as Milan Kundera and V. S. Naipaul (555).'

2009
—

In America 2000

'The story of *In America* is inspired by the emigration to America in 1876 of Helena Modrzejewska, Poland's most celebrated actress,' wrote Sontag of her final work of fiction. The actress arrives with her entourage and attempts to found a utopian commune in California, before returning to the stage and becoming an American theatrical phenomenon. Christopher Hitchens called it 'a counter-romance, alternately hilarious and tragic'. It won the National Book Award.

2009
—

Timothy Leary 1920–1996

Leary studied psychology at the University of California, Berkeley, and taught clinical psychology at Berkeley and at Harvard University. In 1960, he was given psilocybin in Mexico, the chemical derivative of a sacred mushroom, and had a 'profound transcendent experience'. He then became a lifelong advocate of psychedelics, founding the Harvard Psilocybin Project, which involved 'tripping' parties with students. He was dismissed from Harvard in 1963, but continued his research with private funding. He became an icon of the counterculture and was invited to speak at the San Francisco 'Human Be-In' in 1967, where he popularized the phrase 'turn on, tune in, drop out'. Allen Ginsberg (490) called him 'a hero of American consciousness'; President Richard Nixon called him 'the most dangerous man in America'. The year after he died, 2.5 ounces of his ashes were launched into space aboard a Pegasus rocket.

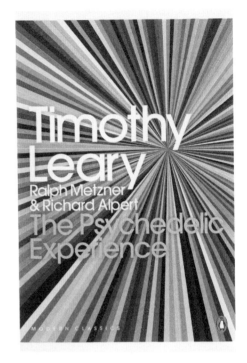

2008
intro. Daniel Pinchbeck, 2007
—
The Psychedelic Experience
is dedicated to Aldous Huxley
(65) and opens with an
epigraph from his *Doors of
Perception* (1954).

Ralph Metzner 1936–2019

Metzner was a psychotherapist who conducted psychedelic research with Timothy Leary and Richard Alpert. He later became Professor of Psychology at the California Institute for Integral Studies and was the President of the Green Earth Foundation, a non-profit organization dedicated to reconnecting humans and the environment.

Richard Alpert 1931–2019

Alpert was dismissed from Harvard University in 1963 along with Timothy Leary. In 1967, he travelled to India to study Hinduism and yoga with the guru Neem Karoli Baba, who gave him a new name, Ram Dass. Ram Dass then wrote the influential spiritual text *Be Here Now* (1971), which sold more than 1 million copies and helped to popularize eastern spirituality and yoga.

The Psychedelic Experience
A Manual Based on the Tibetan Book of the Dead 1964

This book is both a reinterpretation of the Tibetan Buddhist afterlife and a how-to manual for hosting a 'psychedelic session'. It was a founding text of the 1960s counterculture. In 1966, the authors released an LP of their readings from the book.

Counterculture

Inspired in part by the anti-establishment Beat Generation (491), a 'counterculture' emerged in mid-1960s America. Hippies were anti-technological and anti-materialist, with a philosophy of universal peace and love, a willingness to live communally and a proclivity for mysticism, rock music, drugs and sexual permissiveness. They wore clothes with beads and grew long hair, promoting ideas of 'flower power', 'beautiful vibes' and 'love-ins'. A key event was the Summer of Love in 1967, a gathering of 100,000 hippies in the San Francisco area, where Timothy Leary called on them to 'turn on, tune in, drop out'. Key literary figures of the counterculture were Richard Fariña (529), Kurt Vonnegut (523), Charles Webb (523), and Ken Kesey (520) with his entourage of 'Merry Pranksters'.

Donald Barthelme 1931–1989

Barthelme was raised in Texas, the son of an architecture professor. He studied journalism at the University of Houston and worked as a reporter for the *Houston Post*. He was drafted into the US army in 1953, arriving in Korea on the day the Korean War ended. He later served as director of the Houston Contemporary Arts Museum and taught at the University of Buffalo, Boston University, the City College of New York and the University of Houston. He was a long-time contributor to the *New Yorker*. 'Donald Barthelme may have influenced the short story in his time as much as Hemingway (428) or O'Hara (449) did in theirs,' wrote the *New York Times*. 'They loosened the story's grip on the security of plot, but he broke it altogether and forced the form to live dangerously.' In 1978, he was elected to the American Academy of Arts and Letters.

1993 Penguin Books
2005 Modern Classics
intro. David Gates, 2003

1989 Penguin Books
2005 Modern Classics
intro. Dave Eggers, 2005

Sixty Stories

1964–79, pub. 1981

These dark, playful, postmodern (505) stories feature a 35-year-old man who finds himself back at school due to a clerical error, King Kong as an adjunct professor of art history, and a vast balloon that expands over Manhattan. 'I'm enormously impressed by Beckett (20),' said Barthelme. 'I'm just overwhelmed by Beckett, as Beckett was, I speculate, by Joyce (8).'

Forty Stories

1968–87, pub. 1987

This companion volume to Barthelme's *Sixty Stories* comprises even shorter pieces than the other collection. Titles include 'Porcupines at the University', 'At the Tolstoy Museum' and 'Sentence', a seven-page story in only one sentence (and with no full stop). 'This is the best book you will read this year,' writes Dave Eggers in his introduction, 'so please begin.'

John Ball 1911–1988

Ball was born in Schenectady, New York, grew up in Milwaukee, Wisconsin, and lived most of his life in Encino, California. He was a nudist, an astronomer, a martial arts enthusiast and a semi-professional magician with the stage name 'Howduzi'. He worked as a part-time police officer in Los Angeles and wrote more than 30 novels.

In the Heat of the Night 1965

On a hot sultry night in South Carolina, a famous conductor is found dead in the middle of the highway with his head caved in. This is a case for Virgil Tibbs, the softly spoken African American homicide detective. Written at the height of the civil rights movement (502), *In the Heat of the Night* was made into a film in 1967 starring Sidney Poitier; it won five Academy Awards, including Best Picture. The novel has 'fizz and freshness that make most crime stories look dull', said the *Sunday Times*. '[…] Mr Ball's delicate treatment of several kinds of colour prejudice is what gives the book its bitter-sweet ironic flavour.'

2016
fwd. John Ridley
—
John Ridley is a screenwriter, film director and novelist. He won the Academy Award for Best Adapted Screenplay for *12 Years a Slave* (2013).

The Original Virgil Tibbs Novel

John Ball
In the Heat of the Night

Malcolm X 1925–1965

Malcolm Little was born in Omaha, Nebraska, the son of a Baptist preacher who was killed, possibly murdered, when Malcolm was six years old. Malcolm was placed in a foster home and then reform school, before making his way to New York, where he worked as a waiter and began selling marijuana. He soon became addicted to cocaine and turned to burglary. In 1946, he was sentenced to ten years in prison, during which time he became a disciple of Elijah Muhammad and joined the Nation of Islam sect, an organization within the 'Black Muslims' movement. After Malcolm was paroled in 1952, he gave up his surname, which he saw as a relic of slavery, becoming known as 'Malcolm X'. He spent ten years travelling the USA, during which he advocated segregation, black supremacy and violent protest, called for the demise of the white race and criticized the non-violence of the civil rights movement (502). He befriended the boxer Cassius Clay and, in 1964, persuaded him to join the Nation of Islam, after which Clay changed his name to Muhammad Ali. That same year, Malcolm split from the Black Muslims and founded his own protest group, the Organization of Afro-American Unity; he also met Martin Luther King, Jr. (502) for the first and only time. In 1965, he was murdered by Black Muslim assassins while addressing a rally in New York.

1968 Penguin Books
2001 Modern Classics
fwd. Alex Haley, 1965
intro. Paul Gilroy, 2001
—
James Baldwin (492) collaborated with Arnold Perl on an unfilmed screen adaptation of the autobiography, which Spike Lee used as the basis for his 1992 biopic *Malcolm X*, starring Denzel Washington.

The Autobiography of Malcolm X

with the assistance of Alex Haley 1965

In 1963, Malcolm X began collaborating with the journalist Alex Haley, who would go on to write the bestselling novel *Roots* (1973). 'If I'm alive when this book comes out,' Malcolm said, 'it will be a miracle.' The book was published a few months after his death. It sets out his ideas of black pride, black nationalism and pan-Africanism, and it became an important influence on the Black Power and Black Arts movements (534) in the late 1960s. The *New York Times* called it 'a brilliant, painful, important book'.

Thomas Cullinan

1919–1995

Cullinan was born and raised in Cleveland, Ohio. He wrote novels, plays and television dramas, and he died in a theatre in Cleveland while judging a high-school playwriting festival.

The Beguiled 1966

'Miss Harriet had given me permission to hunt for mushrooms […] I didn't find very many mushrooms, but I did find him.' Set during the American Civil War, this is a sizzling Southern Gothic (433) tale of an injured Union soldier taken in by a girls' boarding school in Confederate Mississippi. Don Siegel made a film version in 1971, starring Clint Eastwood, and Sofia Coppola directed a 2017 adaptation, starring Nicole Kidman, Colin Farrell and Kirsten Dunst.

2017
—

Richard Fariña
1937 – 1966

Fariña grew up in Brooklyn, the son of a Cuban father and Irish mother. He studied at Cornell University, where he met Thomas Pynchon, and claimed that he spent time in Ireland working for the IRA and also in Cuba supporting Fidel Castro. He then became a regular at the White Horse Tavern in Greenwich Village, New York, falling in with poets, artists and folk singers, including Bob Dylan. Between 1959 and 1963, he moved between London and Paris, making a living from 'street-singing, script-writing, acting, a little smuggling'. While in France, he met the 17-year-old Mimi Baez, the sister of Joan Baez, and they married in 1963, with Thomas Pynchon as the best man. They lived in Carmel, California, where Fariña composed songs with Mimi – they recorded three successful folk-rock albums together – as well as writing poetry and stories for magazines. Fariña died in a motorcycle accident at the age of just 29, two days after the publication of *Been Down So Long It looks Like Up to Me*.

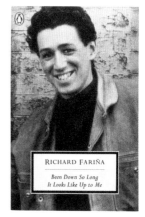

Been Down So Long It Looks Like Up to Me 1966

Fariña began writing his novel in Ithaca, upstate New York. It is the story of Gnossos Pappadopoulis, a modern Odysseus, who has a psychedelic, picaresque adventure around the USA and Cuba, encountering mescaline, women, eastern religion, a monkey demon and feta cheese. It became the cult novel of the 1960s counterculture (526). 'This book comes on like the Hallelujah Chorus done by 200 kazoo players with perfect pitch,' says Thomas Pynchon, '[…] hilarious, chilling, sexy, profound, maniacal, beautiful and outrageous all at the same time.'

1983 Penguin Books
1996 Twentieth-Century Classics
• intro. Thomas Pynchon, 1983
—
Thomas Pynchon is the author of novels including *V* (1963), *The Crying of Lot 49* (1965) and *Gravity's Rainbow* (1973). Pynchon dedicated *Gravity's Rainbow* to Fariña.

1997
• aftwd. William H. Gass

In 1958, Gass was working on the final chapter of this book, when the entire manuscript was mysteriously stolen. In his 1997 afterword, he recalled how he rewrote it from scratch and became increasingly suspicious of a colleague called Edward Drogo Mork.

William H. Gass 1924 – 2017

William Howard Gass was born in Fargo, North Dakota, and raised by an abusive father and an alcoholic mother. He served in the US navy during the Second World War and then studied philosophy at Cornell University, where he met Ludwig Wittgenstein. He taught philosophy at Purdue University and Washington University in St Louis and he wrote three postmodern (505) novels, three collections of short stories and seven volumes of essays. 'Language without rhythm, without physicality, without the undertow of that sea which once covered everything and from which the land first arose like a cautious toe – levelless language in short, voiceless type, pissless prose – can never be artistically complete,' declared Gass. 'Sentences which run on without a body have no soul.'

Omensetter's Luck 1966

Set in a small Ohio town in the 1890s, Gass's first novel describes the arrival of lucky Brackett Omensetter and his clash with unstable Reverend Furber. The *New Republic* announced it as 'the most important work of fiction by an American in this literary generation', and *Harper's* magazine called it 'a rich fever, a parade of secrets, delirious, tormented, terrifying, comic […] one of the most exciting, energetic and beautiful novels we can ever hope to read'.

Harry Harrison 1925–2012

Born Henry Maxwell Dempsey – his father later changed the family name – Harrison worked as a commercial illustrator and art director in New York until his science fiction writing began to sell, at which point he and his family set off to travel the world, living in Mexico, England, Italy, Denmark and Ireland. He is particularly well known for his 'Deathworld' trilogy and for his Stainless Steel Rat and his Bill the Galactic Hero series. He was a Damon Knight Grand Master of the Science Fiction Writers of America and he was also a cult hero in Russia, winning the 2008 Golden Roscon for lifetime achievement in science fiction. He was a close friend of Brian Aldiss (142), who called him 'a constant peer and great family friend'.

Make Room! Make Room! 1966

It is August 1999, the distant future, and the planet's population has exploded to 7 billion. The 35 million inhabitants of New York City run their televisions off pedal power, riot for water and loot food shops for soy-lentil 'steaks'. This chilling cautionary tale of overpopulation and stretched planetary resources was the basis for Richard Fleischer's 1973 film *Soylent Green*, starring Charlton Heston. It is dedicated to Harrison's children, Todd and Moira: 'For your sakes, children, I hope this proves to be a work of fiction.'

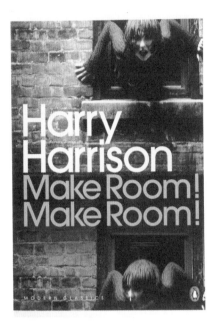

1967 Penguin Books
<u>**2008**</u> Modern Classics
aftwd. Harry Harrison, 2008
—
'We are now living in the world that I wrote about then,' said Harrison in his 2008 afterword: 'the future has arrived.'

Larry McMurtry 1936–2021

McMurtry was raised on a ranch outside Archer City, Texas, and lived there most of his life. He studied creative writing at Stanford University, where he met Ken Kesey (520) and was taught by Frank O'Connor (16), Wallace Stegner (459) and Malcolm Cowley (448). He was the author of 30 novels, most of which are set in 'Thalia', a fictional version of Archer City, and many of which have been adapted into Academy Award-winning films. He also wrote or co-wrote more than 40 screenplays, including that for *Brokeback Mountain* (2005), for which he shared the Academy Award for Best Adapted Screenplay. His novel *Lonesome Dove* (1985) won the Pulitzer Prize for Fiction in 1986 and was adapted in 1989 as an acclaimed TV series starring Tommy Lee Jones and Robert Duvall. McMurtry ran a second-hand bookshop in Archer City and was married to Faye, Ken Kesey's widow.

The Last Picture Show 1966

Teenagers Sonny and Duane drift between the pool hall, the picture house and the all-night café in Thalia, a small Texan town of tumbleweed, eccentrics and frittered dreams. McMurtry co-wrote the Academy Award-nominated screenplay for the 1971 Peter Bogdanovich film adaptation, which was shot in McMurtry's home town of Archer City, Texas.

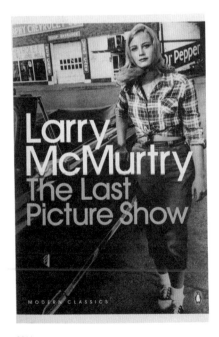

2011
intro. Mary Karr

Chaim Potok 1929–2002

Herman Harold Potok was born and raised in New York, the son of Polish Jewish immigrants. He was the eldest of four children, all of whom became or married rabbis. He decided to be a novelist after reading Evelyn Waugh's *Brideshead Revisited* (69) and began writing stories for the Yeshiva University literary magazine in New York. He was ordained a rabbi in 1954 and served with the US army in South Korea as a chaplain. He took a doctorate in philosophy at the University of Pennsylvania and lived in Jerusalem for six years in the 1970s. He wrote novels, children's books, plays and a history of the Jews.

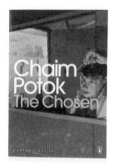

1970 Penguin Books
2009 Modern Classics
intro. Shalom Auslander, 2009

The Chosen 1966

Reuven Malter is injured during a baseball game by Danny Saunders, but nonetheless the two Orthodox Jewish boys become close friends. The setting is New York just as the Second World War is ending, the scale of the Holocaust is becoming apparent and the state of Israel is being founded. 'Anyone who finds *The Chosen* is finding a jewel,' wrote the *Wall Street Journal*. 'Its themes are profound and universal.' Potok's first novel spent 39 weeks in the *New York Times* bestseller list and was made into a film in 1981.

My Name is Asher Lev 1972

This semi-autobiographical novel tells the story of Asher Lev, a Hasidic Jew who longs to be an artist despite the disapproval of his family.

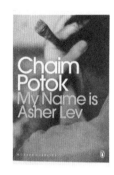

1974 Penguin Books
2009 Modern Classics
intro. Norman Lebrecht, 2009

Hunter S. Thompson 1937–2005

Hunter Stockton Thompson worked as a journalist in Florida, New York, Puerto Rico, Colombia and Brazil. In 1963, he returned to the USA with amoebic dysentery, and after a period of immersion in the Californian drug scene he moved to a fortified compound in Woody Creek, Colorado, where he lived for the rest of his life, hunting elk and breeding Dobermamn pinschers. In 1970, he narrowly missed being elected sheriff of Pitkin County on a 'Freak Power' ticket, and he went to Zaire in 1974 to cover the Rumble in the Jungle (497), but he was so drunk he missed the fight. 'I hate to advocate drugs, alcohol, violence, or insanity to anyone,' he apparently said, 'but they've always worked for me.' At the age of 67, he shot himself in the head. His ashes were fired from a cannon on top of a tower, in a ceremony funded by Johnny Depp. 'There are only two adjectives writers care about anymore,' said the New Journalist (464) Tom Wolfe: '"brilliant" and "outrageous" – and Hunter has a freehold on both.'

Hell's Angels The Strange and Terrible Saga of the Outlaw Motorcycle Gangs 1966

Thompson made his name with this insider account of the famous biker gang with their 'long hair in the wind, beards and bandanas flapping, earrings, armpits, chain whips, swastikas and stripped-down Harleys flashing chrome'. The marauding Hells Angels were widely feared in the 1960s, but Thompson spent a year living with the club's San Francisco chapter, alongside Charger Charley, Big Frank, Little Jesus and the Gimp, documenting their violent, sexual and gasoline-fuelled exploits until they treated him to a vicious beating, or 'stomping'. The account also includes a description of Ken Kesey's (520) Merry Pranksters and their 'Acid Tests'. The *New York Times* called *Hell's Angels* an 'angry, knowledgeable, fascinating, and excitedly written book'.

1967 Penguin Books
2003 Modern Classics
—

2012
ed. Jann S. Wenner, 2011
intro. Paul Scanlon, 2011
—
Jann Wenner co-founded
Rolling Stone magazine in 1967.

2003 Penguin Books
2015 Modern Classics
fwd. Timothy Ferris, 2003

Fear and Loathing at *Rolling Stone*
The Essential Writing of Hunter S. Thompson 1970–2004, pub. 2011

Thompson's first piece for *Rolling Stone* appeared in 1970. He was a regular contributor for the next 30 years and was instrumental in the magazine's success. This selection of his best writing for *Rolling Stone* includes his political reporting from presidential campaign trails, articles on the Vietnam War and diatribes against President Nixon. It also features extracts from *Fear and Loathing in Las Vegas*, which first appeared in *Rolling Stone* magazine in 1971. Thompson's most famous work is based on a trip to Las Vegas with his attorney, Oscar Zeta Acosta. Renamed 'Raoul Duke' and 'Dr Gonzo', the pair chronicle the death of the American Dream and mourn the failure of the 1960s counterculture movement (526) while ingesting 'two bags of grass, seventy-five pellets of mescaline, five sheets of high-powered blotter acid, a salt shaker half full of cocaine, and a whole galaxy of multi-colored uppers, downers, screamers, laughers … and also a quart of tequila, a quart of rum, a case of Budweiser, a pint of raw ether, and two dozen amyls'. The 1972 book publication of *Fear and Loathing in Las Vegas* was illustrated by Thompson's regular collaborator Ralph Steadman and it was adapted in 1998 as a cult film, directed by Terry Gilliam and starring Johnny Depp and Benicio del Toro. The phrase 'fear and loathing', which Thompson used in book and article titles throughout his career, appears in Thomas Wolfe's *The Web and the Rock* (438).

Kingdom of Fear
Loathsome Secrets of a Star-Crossed Child in the Final Days of the American Century 2003

What starts out as an uncensored memoir from the founder of Gonzo journalism descends into a fragmentary collection of random exploits, from crazed road trips and political campaigns to the time he was accidentally accused of trying to kill Jack Nicholson. 'Reviewers have despairingly characterised Thompson's persona as a coked-out prophet in the Book of Revelation, a hillbilly bookworm on speed, a psychopath with an arsenal of high-powered weapons, a paranoid gun junkie, a womaniser, a drunk and worse,' wrote Paul Theroux (543) in 2003. '[…] The truth is far weirder: most of the time Hunter Thompson is a strangely modest man, a serious thinker, a great wit, a superb satirist and a sports fan.'

Gonzo Journalism

In 1970, Thompson was commissioned to cover the Kentucky Derby. Up against his deadline, he began ripping pages out of his notebook and submitting them unedited: the result was a manic, disjointed, subjective narrative, which Thompson described as like 'falling down an elevator shaft and landing in a pool of mermaids'. The editor Bill Cardoso subsequently read the piece and said to Thompson: 'This is it, this is pure Gonzo. If this is a start, keep rolling.' Thompson adopted the word and wrote all his subsequent work in the same frenetic, subjective style. For the Kentucky Derby job, Thompson was paired with the illustrator Ralph Steadman, whose wild, blotchy, irreverent cartoons became an important aspect of Gonzo, and they continued to collaborate closely. Thompson's writing often dealt with the effects of recreational drugs and alcohol, which further distorted its subjective perspective. Sometimes considered a subgenre of New Journalism (464), Gonzo was described by Tom Wolfe as 'part journalism and part personal memoir admixed with powers of wild invention and wilder rhetoric'. 'You worthless scumsucking bastard,' Thompson wrote to Wolfe in 1971. 'I'll have your goddam femurs ground into bone splinters if you ever mention my name again in connection with that horrible "new journalism" shuck you're promoting.'

1997 Puffin Books
2007 Modern Classics
intro. Jodi Picoult, 2006

More COMING-OF-AGE NOVELS

John McPhee *Oranges*

2000
● pref. John McPhee

S. E. Hinton

b. 1948

Susan Eloise Hinton was born in Tulsa, Oklahoma. *The Outsiders* made her a household name when she was still a teenager and she has gone on to write other novels for young adults, as well as books for older and younger readers. She is sometimes credited with inventing the 'young adult' genre, and in 1988 she won the first Margaret A. Edwards Award, a prize for a lifetime's achievement given by the Young Adult Library Services Association. She still lives in Tulsa.

The Outsiders 1967

When Hinton was fifteen, she began writing a novel inspired by the rival gangs at her high school, the greasers and the rich-kid Socs. *The Outsiders* is written from the point of view of Ponyboy Curtis, a 14-year-old greaser, revealing a world of youthful rebellion, drive-ins, drag races and switchblades. It became an immediate sensation and it is still one of the bestselling young adult novels of all time. In 1983, Francis Ford Coppola directed a film adaptation with a young cast including Tom Cruise, Patrick Swayze, Rob Lowe and Matt Dillon, in which Hinton has a cameo appearance.

John McPhee

b. 1931

McPhee worked as a television playwright and a contributing editor for *Time* magazine before becoming a staff writer for the *New Yorker* in 1965. He is a pioneer of creative non-fiction, writing on such varied subjects as geology, aircraft, nuclear engineering, farmers' markets, the transport of coal, the shifting flow of the Mississippi River, the Alaskan wilderness, the forests in New Jersey and the Hebridean island of Colonsay. As Robert Macfarlane says, 'McPhee's genius is that he can write about anything.' Since 1974, McPhee has been the Ferris Professor of Journalism at Princeton University, and in 1988 he was elected to the American Academy of Arts and Letters.

Oranges 1967

'A classic of American reportage,' writes Julian Barnes, '[…] a meeting point of zest, pith, colour, fruit, sweetness and acid.' McPhee weaves together history, anecdote and science in this sensuous, quirky tour of the world of oranges.

Audre Lorde 1934–1992

Audrey Geraldine Lorde was born in New York, the daughter of Caribbean migrants from Barbados and Carriacou; as a child, she dropped the 'y' from Audrey so that both her names would end with an 'e'. She worked as a librarian and began to publish poetry in the 1960s, protesting against the injustices of racism, sexism, classism, heterosexism and homophobia. 'Poetry is the way we help give name to the nameless so it can be thought,' she wrote. Her 1976 collection, *Coal*, established her as a major figure in the Black Arts Movement, and in 1991 she was appointed Poet Laureate of New York State. She died of cancer at the age of 58.

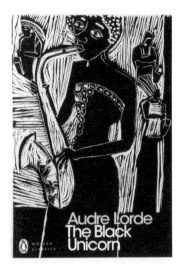

2019
—

The Black Unicorn 1968–78, pub. 1978

'Audre Lorde writes as a black woman, a mother, a daughter, a lesbian, a feminist, a visionary,' said the poet Adrienne Rich; 'poems of elemental wildness and healing, nightmare and lucidity […] which blaze and pulse on the page.' This is Lorde's most acclaimed poetry collection.

2019
—

Sister Outsider 1976–83, pub. 1984

'It hurts when even my sisters look at me in the street with cold and silent eyes,' wrote Lorde. 'I am defined as other in every group I'm a part of. The outsider, both strength and weakness.' This volume of her essential prose comprises essays, speeches, letters and interviews. It includes her most famous piece, 'The Master's Tools Will Never Dismantle the Master's House', in which she exhorts women to embrace difference: 'In our world,' she urges, 'divide and conquer must become define and empower'.

The Cancer Journals 1980

When Lorde was 44, she discovered a lump in her right breast, and this slim volume describes her experience of cancer from diagnosis to surgery. It is 'a brave, beautiful book', writes the poet Jackie Kay, 'that could double as a handbook to accompany anyone on their journey through cancer.'

2020
—

Zami: A New Spelling of My Name →
A Biomythography 1982

'Zami,' Lorde explains: 'a Carriacou name for women who work together as friends and lovers.' This rapturous blend of history, autobiography and myth is both a fictionalized memoir and a celebration of the women who inspired and encouraged Lorde throughout her life. 'Excellent and evocative,' wrote the *New York Times*. '[…] Her experiences are painted with exquisite imagery.'

Black Arts Movement

In New York in 1965, the poet Amiri Baraka established the Black Arts Repertory Theatre School in Harlem, which became the focus of the Black Arts Movement. Inspired by the Harlem Renaissance (413), the civil rights movement (502) and Malcolm X (528) in particular, exponents of the Black Arts Movement believed that art should inspire, educate, delight, and move people to action. They worked to establish black cultural institutions and encourage black pride. Larry Neal, the theorist of the movement, described it as the 'aesthetic and spiritual sister of Black Power'. Artists and writers associated with the movement include Maya Angelou, James Baldwin (492), June Jordan, Audre Lorde and Ishmael Reed (539).

MODERN
CLASSICS

Audre Lorde

Zami: A New Spelling of My Name
A Biomythography

2018
—
The artwork on the cover is *Revolutionary Sister* (1971) by the Harlem-born
artist Dindga McCannon. 'In the 60s and 70s we didn't have many women
warriors,' says McCannon, '[…] so I created my own.'

Robert Coover b. 1932

Coover is 'a marvelous magician', wrote William H. Gass (529), '[...] a maker of miracles, a comic, a sexual tease'. He won the William Faulkner (433) Award for his first novel, *The Origin of the Brunists* (1966), and he has gone on to write ten more novels, eight novellas and four collections of short stories, many of which are subversive experiments in metafiction. 'All the fiction tricks we think are new,' says the novelist Ben Marcus, 'were built in Coover's backyard shed.' He taught at Brown University for 30 years, leading workshops in electronic writing, mixed media, and 'CAVE writing' in an immersive virtual reality. In 1999, he co-founded the Electronic Literature Organization.

Pricksongs & Descants 1969

'Pricksongs' and 'descants' are both terms for sung lines that embellish existing melodies, and many of Coover's dark short stories riff on familiar fairy tales. This landmark collection also includes the nightmarish 'The Elevator', 'Seven Exemplary Fictions' – a tribute to Borges (572) – and the fragmentary masterpiece 'The Babysitter'. Coover 'is unfair, rude, cruel and murderously funny', wrote Angela Carter (156). 'A master.'

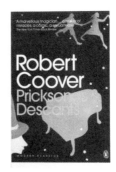

2011
intro. Kate Atkinson
—
The covers of the Modern Classics editions of Coover's books feature paintings by the artist Jonathan Huxley, who won the 2009 Penguin Classics Prize for Cover Art awarded by the Royal Watercolour Society.

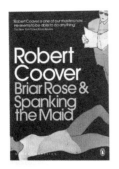

2011
intro. John Banville

Briar Rose and Spanking the Maid 1982–96

Spanking the Maid (1982), the earlier of these two comic novellas, is about a maid and her master, locked in an intense sadomasochistic relationship. She attempts to perform simple household duties without error; he punishes her with a rod, belt, hairbrush, whip, cane or slipper when she inevitably fails. *Briar Rose* (1996) enters the dreams of Sleeping Beauty, trapped in an enchantment for a hundred years. She fantasizes about waking up in various disappointing and traumatic ways, while the bodies of princes accumulate on the thorns outside her window.

Gerald's Party 1986

Set over the course of a single night, Gerald describes the party to end all parties. It starts with the murder of Ros, a beautiful actress, and soon turns into an orgiastic carnival as brutal detectives attempt to solve the murder and drunken guests continue to chatter and engage in various increasingly graphic forms of intercourse. The *New York Times* called it 'a hallucinogenic phantasmagoric nightmare of mayhem and ecstasy'.

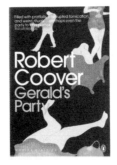

2011
—
Gerald's Party is dedicated to John Hawkes (519), 'who, standing beside me in a dream one night long ago, long before we'd become friends, and remarking upon another author's romanticization of autumn (there seemed to be hundreds of them actually, stooped over, on the endless tree-lined streets before us), observed wistfully: "It's so true, people still do that, you know, count the dead leaves."'

Hypertext Fiction

The philosopher Ted Nelson coined the term 'hypertext' in 1965 to describe stories with non-sequential narratives. Jorge Luis Borges had already extrapolated the idea to an extreme in 'The Garden of Forking Paths' (573) in 1941 and other writers have experimented with non-linear narratives, including William S. Burroughs (481), Italo Calvino (218), James Joyce (8) and Vladimir Nabokov (304), but in the late 1960s the advent of platforms for reading literature electronically greatly expanded the potential for hypertext fiction. 'Paper is a crutch,' declared Nelson, 'an old-fashioned idea that is holding us back.' In theory, electronic texts can be hyperlinked indefinitely to create infinitely labyrinthine narratives; in 1999, Robert Coover co-founded the Electronic Literature Organization to promote the creation and appreciation of these works.

MODERN CLASSICS

Don DeLillo
Americana

Don DeLillo b. 1936

Donald Richard DeLillo was born into an Italian American family in New York City. He grew up reading Joyce (8), Faulkner (433) and Hemingway (428), listening to jazz and watching European cinema. In 1958, he took a job as a copywriter for an advertising firm and published his first short story in 1960. He went on to write not only more short stories, plays, screenplays and essays but also seventeen novels: *White Noise* (1985) won the National Book Award, *Mao II* (1991) won the PEN/Faulkner Award and *Underworld* (1997) won the Jerusalem Prize. In 2010, he won the PEN/Saul Bellow (477) Award for Achievement in American Fiction, and the Norman Mailer (496) Prize for Lifetime Achievement in 2014. 'He's a writer, who, once you read him, makes you want to read everything he's done,' says Martin Amis (160).

Americana 1971

1990 Penguin Books
2006 Modern Classics
—

DeLillo's first novel is about a New York television executive, trapped in a vacuous lifestyle. He quits his job and travels to the Midwest in search of the 'big picture', filming an autobiographical road movie along the way, only to discover that the heart of his homeland is just as devoid of meaning. 'Nearly every sentence of *Americana* rings true,' says Joyce Carol Oates.

Libra 1988

1989 Penguin Books
2006 Modern Classics
—

Kennedy's assassination 'marked the real beginning of the 1960s,' says DeLillo. 'It was the beginning of a series of catastrophes: political assassinations, the war in Vietnam, the denial of Civil Rights (502) and the revolts that occasioned, youth revolt in American cities, right up to Watergate. When I was starting out as a writer it seemed to me that a large part of the material you could find in my novels – this sense of fatality, of widespread suspicion, of mistrust – came from the assassination of JFK.'

DeLillo tells the story of Lee Harvey Oswald as he prepares to assassinate President John F. Kennedy on 22 November 1963. The narrative is based on the 888-page report of the Warren Commission, a document DeLillo describes as 'the megaton novel James Joyce (8) would have written if he'd moved to Iowa City and lived to be a hundred', but it also incorporates a fictional CIA conspiracy. It 'reads like a cross between Theodore Dreiser (407) and William Burroughs (481)', wrote Philip Roth. 'This you feel is America,' said the *Sunday Times*, 'and the bad news starts here.'

MODERN CLASSICS

Don DeLillo
Libra

E. L. Doctorow 1931–2015

Edgar Lawrence Doctorow was named after Edgar Allan Poe. After serving with the US army in West Germany he became an editor with New American Library and the Dial Press, working with Ayn Rand (450), James Baldwin (492) and Norman Mailer (496), among others. He left in 1969 to pursue his own writing career and produced twelve novels, three volumes of short stories and a play. In 1998, President Bill Clinton awarded him the National Humanities Medal and, when he died, President Barack Obama called him 'one of America's greatest novelists'.

The Book of Daniel 1971

Daniel Isaacson's parents were arrested and executed for conspiring to pass atomic secrets to the Soviet Union during the Cold War. Now he is married with a son of his own and he is trying to piece together the truth behind his parents' actions. Doctorow's novel was inspired by the real trial and execution of Julius and Ethel Rosenberg in the early 1950s. '*The Book of Daniel* not only compels a reader to read it – eagerly, fearfully, perhaps desperately – but to assimilate its terrible wisdom into the reader's life, so that life itself seems altered,' wrote Joyce Carol Oates. 'I can think of no higher praise for a work of fiction.'

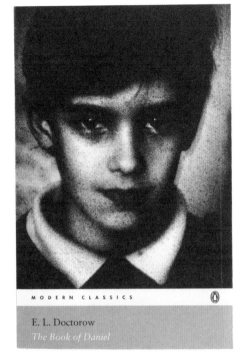

2006
intro. Jonathan Freedland

2006
intro. Al Alvarez
—
Doctorow takes his epigraph from the composer Scott Joplin: 'Do not play this piece fast. It is never right to play Ragtime fast…'

Ragtime 1975

This sweeping portrait of early 20th-century America incorporates historical figures such as Theodore Dreiser (407), Henry Ford, Sigmund Freud (265), Harry Houdini, Carl Jung (262), J. P. Morgan and Emiliano Zapata (444), as well as the former chorus girl Evelyn Nesbit, who inspired a mad millionaire to murder the architect Stanford White. Around these people and events, Doctorow orchestrates three fictional families, one black, one Jewish and one white, in a narrative that spans dire poverty and fabulous wealth. 'An extraordinary fictional tapestry,' said the *New Republic*, 'completely absorbing because once in, there is no possible way out except through the last page.' *Ragtime* won a National Book Critics Circle Award and Miloš Forman directed a 1981 film adaptation. In 1998, the Broadway musical adaptation won four Tony Awards.

Billy Bathgate 1989

Billy 'Bathgate' Behan is a 15-year-old New York street kid who can juggle, somersault and run like the wind. He is taken under the wing of the gangster Dutch Schultz as his 'good-luck kid', but Billy's newfound world of glamour and money is also deadly dangerous. 'Huck Finn and Tom Sawyer with more poetry, Holden Caulfield (499) with more zest and spirit,' wrote the *New York Times*. '[…] The kind of book you find yourself finishing at three in the morning.' It won a National Book Critics Circle Award and the PEN/Faulkner (433) Award and was adapted as a film in 1991 starring Dustin Hoffman. John le Carré (143) called it 'a modern American masterpiece'.

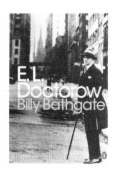

2016
—

Ishmael Reed b. 1938

Reed grew up in the working-class neighbourhoods of Buffalo, New York. In 1962, he co-founded the underground magazine *East Village Other* and he published his first novel in 1967. He has written novels, poetry, plays, song lyrics and essays. He taught for 35 years at the University of California, Berkeley. 'I've probably been more influenced by poets than by novelists,' says Reed – 'the Harlem Renaissance (413) poets, the Beat (491) poets, the American Surrealist (176) Ted Joans. Poets have to be more attuned to originality, coming up with lines and associations the ordinary prose writer wouldn't think of.' He himself has influenced writers including Thomas Pynchon, Paul Beatty and Colson Whitehead, and musicians from George Clinton and David Murray to Tupac Shakur. James Baldwin (492) called Reed 'a great writer'.

Mumbo Jumbo

1972

An epidemic is spreading across 1920s America: the 'Jes Grew' virus makes people want to dance and be happy, and it's raging from New Orleans to New York. The sinister Wallflower Order is trying to suppress the outbreak, but they have not reckoned with PaPa LaBas, the voodoo priest from Harlem. This anarchic postmodern (505) satire features real figures, such as James Weldon Johnson (412), W. E. B. Du Bois (408) and Malcolm X (528), and uses a unique typography and format with fade-ins, freeze frames, drawings and photographs. 'Wholly original,' wrote the *New York Times*, 'his book is an unholy cross between the craft of fiction and witchcraft.'

Flight to Canada

1976

This novel 'always was, and will always be the most fearlessly original, most viciously political, most rambunctiously funny epic of slavery ever written', says the Booker Prize-winning novelist Marlon James. 'America almost doesn't deserve it.' *Flight to Canada* is set in a version of 19th-century America with limousines, waterbeds, pornographic movies and jumbo jets that can fly escaped slaves to Canada. 'The book explodes,' said the *New York Times*. 'Reed's special grace is anger. […] *Flight to Canada* is a hellish book with its own politics and a muscular, luminous prose.'

2017
—

2018
—

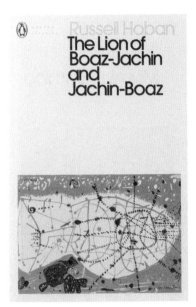

2021
—
The covers of the Modern
Classics editions of Hoban's
novels feature paintings
by the Scottish pop artist
Eduardo Paolozzi.

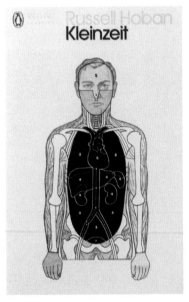

2021
—
On Hoban's birthday each
year, 4 February, dedicated
fans write favourite quotations
on sheets of yellow paper and
leave them in public spaces.
This annual international
occurrence is known as
the Slickman A4 Quotation
Event (SA4QE).

Russell Hoban 1925–2011

Russell Conwell Hoban was born in Pennsylvania, the son of Ukrainian Jews; his father was the advertising manager of Abraham Cahan's (318) *Jewish Daily Forward* and his mother tended a flock of 2,000 pigeons. Hoban served as a radio operator during the Second World War, in the Philippines and Italy, and then worked as a magazine illustrator and advertising copywriter, while also writing a series of bestselling children's books about an endearingly odd little girl called Frances – whom his wife Lillian, another illustrator, drew as a badger – and a philosophical children's novel, *The Mouse and His Child* (1967), about a pair of conjoined mechanical toys. In 1969, the Hoban family moved to England. The marriage dissolved and Lillian took the children back to the USA, but Russell stayed in London for the rest of his life, writing a number of fantastically peculiar novels for adults, involving lions, sheets of yellow paper, alternate realities, mythology, science fiction and humour. When he died, *The Times* described him as 'perhaps the most consistently strange writer of the late 20th century'.

The Lion of Boaz-Jachin and Jachin-Boaz 1973

In Hoban's first book for adults, the mapmaker Jachin-Boaz abandons his family and leaves a note that reads: 'I have gone to look for a lion.' He is pursued on his quest by his son, Boaz-Jachin, and a mysterious creature with amber eyes. 'Mr Hoban is unclassifiable, thank goodness,' wrote the *Sunday Times*. '[…] His narrative is so minutely and compellingly realistic that after a time you cease to notice that he has stood reality on its head.'

Kleinzeit 1974

'I think there's most of me in *Kleinzeit*,' said Hoban. This surreal, metaphysical novel is about an advertising copywriter called Kleinzeit ('Small-time'), who finds himself on hospital ward A4, where patients suffer from skewed hypotenuses, blocked stretti, imbricated noumena and hendiadys. Through intimate relations with a blank sheet of yellow paper, Kleinzeit explores his own creativity, conversing with various abstract concepts such as Word, Death, Hospital, the Underground and God. 'Kleinzeit is a sort of holy fool, a fierce, lonely intelligence desperately trying to make sense of a hopeless world,' wrote Auberon Waugh.

Turtle Diary 1975

Two lonely people – a bookseller and a children's illustrator – come together to rescue and release the giant sea turtles at London Zoo. 'This lovely human fable seems to me one of the best things of its kind,' said the novelist John Fowles – 'a fine and touching achievement.' Harold Pinter wrote the screenplay for a 1985 film adaptation starring Glenda Jackson, Ben Kingsley and Michael Gambon.

2021
—

Riddley Walker 1980

'Walker is my name and I am the same. Riddley Walker. Walking my riddels where ever theyve took me and walking them now on this paper the same.' Hoban's masterpiece was inspired by the late-medieval wall painting of the legend of Saint Eustace at Canterbury Cathedral. It is set in a post-nuclear Iron Age, in which ancient machines are salvaged for scrap metal, religion is disseminated through Punch and Judy shows, and the language is a phonetic descendant of the Kentish accent. It is 'the strongest, most desolate and bewildered voice in modern fiction,' ran the *Cosmopolitan* review. 'In the mental silence that followed the closing of the last page, I wanted to applaud, through tears.' It won the 1982 John W. Campbell Memorial Award for best science fiction novel. 'This is what literature is meant to be,' said Anthony Burgess (148).

2021
—

Pilgermann 1983

2021
—

In 1097, the age of the First Crusade (121), a castrated German Jewish wanderer, Pilgermann, makes a picaresque journey across medieval Europe and the Mediterranean. On his grim pilgrimage towards Jerusalem, he is joined by his own Death, is captured by pirates, sold into slavery in Antioch and granted a vision of a mystical geometric design. Hoban drew inspiration from Hieronymus Bosch, tarot cards and the Kabbalah. 'Those who find the very fact of existence troubling,' writes the critic Victoria Glendinning, 'will find *Pilgermann* both frightening and comforting.'

The Medusa Frequency 1987

2021
—

Herman Orff is a freelance writer in London. When he receives a leaflet through the door, offering a cure for writer's block, he finds himself entering 'those places in your head that you can't get to on your own'. His hallucinatory trip involves dreams, Vermeer, his ex-girlfriend Luise von Himmelbett, the talking severed head of Orpheus and a lurking Kraken. 'Russell Hoban's *The Medusa Frequency* is the sort of hyper-kinetic feat of the imagination that runs on high-octane fuel and thunders across its surreal landscape at a dangerously toxic speed,' wrote the *Listener*.

Fremder 1996

2021
—

On the planet of Badr-al-Budur in the Fourth Galaxy, Fremder Gorn is being examined by the Physio/Psycho Unit. How has he miraculously survived the disappearance of his spaceship, the *Clever Daughter*? As Dr Caroline Lovecraft peers into Fremder's memories and dreams, she gets lost among the unknowable fragments of his mind. The *Guardian* compared *Fremder* to both George Orwell's *Nineteen Eighty-Four* (84) and H. G. Wells's *The Time Machine* (26). *Fremde* in German means 'stranger'.

2021
—

Mr Rinyo-Clacton's Offer 1998

When Jonathan Fitch bumps into the devilish Mr Rinyo-Clacton in Piccadilly Circus underground station, he is offered a Faustian pact: Mr Rinyo-Clacton will give Jonathan £1 million, if he agrees to die in a year's time. 'Nothing is accidental or optional in this jewelled clockwork egg of a book,' wrote the *Times Literary Supplement*. '[…] In this hugely skilled, moving and endlessly entertaining writer, you can be sure of that.'

Edward Abbey 1927-1989

At the age of seventeen, Abbey set off to explore the American southwest and fell in love with the desert country. After studying philosophy at the University of New Mexico, he spent many years working as a ranger and fire lookout in southwestern national parks, maintaining trails, greeting visitors and collecting campground fees. He also taught creative writing at the universities of Utah and Arizona, where he devised four rules for aspiring novelists: 'Write right. Write good. Right wrong. Write on!' He became one of America's most prominent anarchists and environmentalists, perhaps most famous for *Desert Solitaire* (1968), a book of lyrical nature writing that has been compared to Henry David Thoreau's *Walden* (1854) and Aldo Leopold's *A Sand County Almanac* (1949). 'Edward Abbey was like stone,' says Robert Redford, '[...] a man of great passion and love of the natural order'. Abbey asked to be buried in the desert in an old sleeping bag. 'I want my body to help fertilize the growth of a cactus or cliff rose or sagebrush or tree,' he wrote.

The Monkey Wrench Gang 1975

'This book, though fictional in form, is based strictly on historical fact,' explained Abbey. 'Everything in it is real or actually happened.' It tells the story of an eccentric band of eco-warriors – a boozy Vietnam veteran, a wealthy, billboard-burning doctor, a Jewish feminist revolutionary and a polygamist riverboat guide – who disrupt the construction of the Glen Canyon Dam on the Colorado River through various forms of sabotage. This provocative novel helped to inspire the creation of Earth First!, an international environmental organization that advocates eco-sabotage and 'monkeywrenching'. It is 'a sad, hilarious, exuberant, vulgar fairy tale', wrote the *National Observer*. '[...] It'll make you want to go out and blow up a dam.'

2004
pref. Robert Redford
intro. Eric Schlosser

Paul Theroux b. 1941

After graduating from the University of Massachusetts Amherst in 1963, Theroux travelled to Italy and then Africa, working as a teacher in Malawi and then as a lecturer at Makerere University in Uganda, where he met and befriended V. S. Naipaul (555). He taught English at the University of Singapore for three years and then moved to the UK in 1971 and began writing the novels and travel books for which he is known. In 1990, Theroux returned to the USA and now divides his time between Hawaii and Cape Cod, Massachusetts. As William Golding (131) put it, 'he has done our travelling for us brilliantly'. Theroux's two sons are the authors and film-makers Marcel and Louis Theroux. He is a Fellow of the Royal Geographical Society, the Royal Society of Literature and the American Academy of Arts and Letters.

1977 Penguin Books
2008 Modern Classics
pref. Paul Theroux, 2008
—
In 2006, Theroux retraced his journey and wrote about the experience in *Ghost Train to the Eastern Star* (2008).

The Great Railway Bazaar
By Train through Asia 1975

Theroux's first travel book is an account of his four-month journey by rail through Europe and Asia, taking the Direct-Orient Express, the Khyber Pass Local, the Delhi Mail from Jaipur, the Golden Arrow to Kuala Lumpur and the Hikari Super Express to Kyoto, before returning to London on the Trans-Siberian Express. It is written in what Graham Greene (88) called 'the fine old tradition of purposeless travel for fun and adventure'.

More TRAINS

The Old Patagonian Express
By Train through the Americas 1979

Theroux's second adventure was another train journey, this time travelling the length of North and South America, from the subway in Boston, Massachusetts, to the furthest tip of Argentina, via Texas, Machu Picchu and Buenos Aires, where he paused to read some of Kipling's poems (22) to Jorge Luis Borges (572). The *Financial Times* called it 'one of the most entrancing travel books written in our time'.

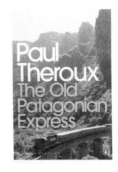

1980 Penguin Books
2008 Modern Classics
pref. Paul Theroux, 2008
—
The 'Old Patagonian Express' of Theroux's title is known in Spanish as 'La Trochita'. It is a narrow-gauge steam railway that runs for 250 miles through the southern foothills of the Argentinian Andes, between El Maitén and Ingeniero Jacobacci.

Andy Warhol 1928 – 1987

Andrew Warhola was the son of Lemko migrants from the Austro-Hungarian Empire. As a child, he suffered from St Vitus's dance and was bedridden for long periods, during which he would draw pictures and collect images of movie stars. He trained as an illustrator, and spent the 1950s drawing shoe advertisements, before emerging in the sixties as the leader of the pop art movement, with his iconic images of American objects such as dollar bills, electric chairs, Coca-Cola bottles and his famous Campbell's soup cans. His New York studio, where he worked with a team of collaborators, became known as 'the Factory'. Its walls were covered with aluminium foil and silver paint and it attracted an eclectic crowd of intellectuals, drag queens, playwrights, musicians and actors. Warhol made experimental films – such as *Chelsea Girls* (1966), *Blow Job* (1964) and *Eat* (1963), in which a man eats a mushroom for 45 minutes – with members of his entourage, whom he promoted as 'superstars'. In 1968, he was shot and nearly killed by an actress in his film, *I, a Man* (1967). He also produced the rock band The Velvet Underground and founded *Interview* magazine. He was openly gay, a practising Ruthenian Catholic and, when he died, he was buried in a solid bronze casket with gold-plated rails and white upholstery.

The Philosophy of Andy Warhol
(From A to B and Back Again) 1975

Warhol's flamboyantly zany autobiography includes reflections on his life, spliced with self-consciously ironic aphorisms on love, sex, food, beauty, fame, work, money, underwear and death. 'I would rather watch somebody buy their underwear than read a book they wrote,' he declares. 'Acute. Accurate. Mr Warhol's usual amazing candor,' summarized Truman Capote (463). 'A constant entertainment and enlightenment.'

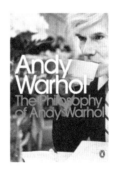

2007
—
The Philosophy of Andy Warhol was ghost-written by Pat Hackett, Warhol's friend and collaborator for almost 20 years. She based the text on taped interviews, including conversations between Warhol and his 'superstar' Brigid Berlin, the 'B' of the subtitle.

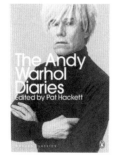

2010
ed. Pat Hackett, 1989

The Andy Warhol Diaries 1976 – 87, pub. 1989

In 1976, Warhol began calling Pat Hackett every weekday morning at nine o'clock and speaking a 'diary entry' aloud for at least an hour. Hackett would transcribe his monologue and type it up, eventually amassing 20,000 typewritten pages. This book is the 1,200-page abridged version, with descriptions of Warhol's trips to London and Paris, portraits of Calvin Klein, Shirley Bassey, Estée Lauder and Muhammad Ali, and an exact account of each day's spending. The *Guardian* called it 'a dream of Manhattan touched by movie stars and pop celebrities [who] flare briefly through a prose as soft and depthless as his screen prints of car crashes and electric chairs. […] In many ways Warhol is the Walt Disney of the amphetamine age.'

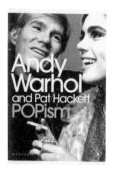

2007
—

POPism
The Warhol Sixties
with Pat Hackett 1980

'This is my personal view of the Pop phenomenon in New York in the 1960s,' explains Warhol. 'In writing it, Pat Hackett and I have reconstructed the decade, starting in '60 when I began to paint my first Pop canvases. It's a look back at what life was like then for my friends and me – at the paintings, movies, fashions, and music, at the superstars and the relationships that made up the scene at our Manhattan loft, the place known as the Factory.' 'It is as absorbing as the best telephone gossip', wrote Christopher Isherwood (103), 'funny yet full of insights'.

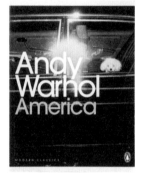

2011
• —
America is an unusual format for a Penguin Modern Classic, because the page size is necessarily determined by Warhol's design. It is 198 millimetres tall as usual, but 152 wide, which is 23 millimetres wider than most other editions.

More FACTORIES

The Grim Smile of the Five Towns
by Arnold Bennett   37

Half a Lifelong Romance
by Eileen Chang   347

Charlie and the Chocolate Factory
by Roald Dahl   113

All My Sons
by Arthur Miller   486

The Jungle
by Upton Sinclair   409

America 1985

'America really is The Beautiful.' This artist's book is a blend of text and photography. It features images of wrestlers and politicians, the glamorous wealthy and the disenfranchised poor, Truman Capote (463) with the fresh scars of a facelift, babies in prams and men in pig's-head masks. It is a reverie on commercialism, fame and beauty. 'I love Los Angeles. I love Hollywood,' Warhol once said. 'They're so beautiful. Everything's plastic, but I love plastic. I want to be plastic.'

John Cheever 1912–1982

Cheever was born in Massachusetts. His father was a prosperous shoe salesman and his mother owned a gift shop, but the family money evaporated in the 1929 Wall Street Crash and his father turned to drink. Cheever dropped out of education and moved to the Yaddo artists' colony in Saratoga Springs, New York. He published a short story in the *New Yorker* in 1935 and went on to write many more, becoming known as 'the Chekhov of the suburbs'. For five years after the Second World War, he left his Manhattan apartment each morning in a suit, took the elevator down to a basement room, stripped to his boxer shorts and typed until lunch. His first novel, *The Wapshot Chronicle* (1957), won the National Book Award, and his collection *The Stories of John Cheever* (1978) won a National Book Critics Circle Award and the Pulitzer Prize for Fiction. He struggled with his bisexuality and fought with his wife, nearly drinking himself to death while teaching at both Boston University and Sing Sing maximum-security prison.

Falconer 1977

Ezekiel Farragut, a college professor and heroin addict, is sent to Falconer Correctional Facility for the murder of his brother. In his filthy cell, he recalls his traumatic childhood and troubled marriage and finds himself falling in love with a fellow inmate. 'It is rough, it is elegant, it is pure,' said Saul Bellow (477). 'It is also indispensable, if you earnestly desire to know what is happening to the human soul in the USA.'

1978 Penguin Books
2005 Modern Classics
• intro. A. M. Homes, 2005

Leslie Marmon Silko b. 1948

Leslie Marmon grew up on the Laguna Pueblo Reservation
in New Mexico, learning the stories of the Laguna people from her
great-grandmother. After studying at the University of New Mexico,
she married John Silko and began writing short stories and poetry.
In 1973, she moved to Ketchikan, Alaska, where she wrote *Ceremony*.
The *New York Times Book Review* calls her 'the most accomplished
Native American writer of her generation'. She currently lives on
a ranch outside Tucson, Arizona.

Ceremony 1977

Tayo returns to the Laguna Pueblo Reservation after the Second
World War, suffering from post-traumatic stress, and he eventually finds
peace through the ancient traditions, stories and ceremonies of his
ancestors. Silko herself was struggling with depression as she wrote this
novel and has described the book itself as 'a ceremony for staying sane'.
She interweaves through its narrative various stories, timelines, oral
traditions, and mythologies in a mixture of prose and poetry. 'Ceremony
is the greatest novel in Native American literature,' writes the author
Sherman Alexie. 'It is one of the greatest novels of any time and place.'

1986 Penguin Books
2011 Deluxe Classics
● intro. Larry McMurtry (530),
2006
<u>2020</u> Modern Classics
pref. Leslie Marmon Silko,
2006

Angela Y. Davis b. 1944

Angela Yvonne Davis was born in Birmingham, Alabama, 'the most segregated city in America'.
She won a scholarship to study French at Brandeis University, Massachusetts, and then philosophy
at the University of Frankfurt in Germany. On her return to America, she joined the Black Panther
Party and the Communist Party USA and became a prominent activist campaigning for black
and women's liberation and against the Vietnam War and the 'prison-industrial complex'.
In 1969, she went to teach philosophy at the University of
California, Los Angeles, but was repeatedly fired over her
political beliefs, and in 1970 she was jailed for two years
for supplying guns to a violent protester. In 1991, she joined
the feminist studies department at the University of California,
Santa Cruz, and eventually became department director,
a post she held until her retirement in 2008. She continues
to be an inspirational activist and speaker, and was included
in *Time* magazine's '100 Most Influential People of 2020'.

Women, Race and Class 1981

In these thirteen essays, Davis traces both the 20th-century history
of women's liberation movements and the longer history of slavery
and abolitionism in the USA. It provides a nuanced view of female
struggles for liberation, analysing the relationships between gender,
race and class inequality and criticizing the racism and class prejudice
inherent in some forms of white feminism. 'The power of her
historical insights and the sweetness of her dream cannot be denied,'
wrote the *New York Times*.

2019
—

Kathy Acker 1947–1997

Karen Lehman, known as Kathy, studied at Brandeis University in Massachusetts and married Robert Acker in 1966. In her twenties, she broke ties with her family and worked as a stripper in New York, writing and publishing in the punk literary scene under the pseudonym 'Black Tarantula'. She lived between San Diego, San Francisco, New York and London, and once interviewed the Spice Girls for the *Guardian*. In 1996, she was diagnosed with breast cancer and after a failed surgical procedure abandoned western medicine. She died in an alternative cancer treatment centre in Mexico, in Room 101 (84). 'There's nothing that woman can't turn into a literary reference,' said her friend the graphic novelist Alan Moore.

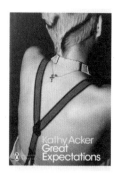

2018
—

Great Expectations 1982

This anarchic reimagining of Charles Dickens's novel gives its protagonist Pip a new sex and a new century, transplanting the orphaned narrator to 1980s New York. Picaresque adventures ensue, involving sadism, pornography, art and a semi-autobiographical account of Acker's mother's suicide. William S. Burroughs (481) called Acker 'a postmodern (505) Colette (170) with echoes of Cleland's *Fanny Hill*'.

2017
—

Blood and Guts in High School 1984

This punk collage novel is about Janey, a ten-year-old girl. When the book opens, she is in Mexico having an incestuous relationship with her father, who acts as her 'boyfriend, brother, sister, money, amusement, and father'. Then we follow her to New York, where she is sold to a Persian slave trader and develops cancer, before fleeing to Morocco and encountering Jean Genet (190). The narrative is told through a mash-up of poems, letters, dramatic dialogues, dream maps, unusual typography and sexually explicit drawings. It caused a sensation when it was first published and was immediately banned in several countries. The *New York Times* described it as 'a combination of the early Sex Pistols' raging repetition and the drugged synthesizer tonalities of Laurie Anderson's mantric songs'.

Cedric J. Robinson

1940–2016

Robinson studied social anthropology at the University of California, Berkeley and at Stanford. In 1978, he joined the faculty at the University of California, Santa Barbara, where he became the director of the Center for Black Studies Research and led the departments of both black studies and political science.

Black Marxism
The Making of the Black Radical Tradition 1983

'This work is about our people's struggle, the historical Black struggle,' writes Robinson. 'It takes as a first premise that for a people to survive in struggle it must be on its own terms.' Robinson repurposes Marxism to describe the history of Black African resistance as a revolt against 'racial capitalism'. He discusses European radicalism and examines key figures of black radicalism, such as W. E. B. Du Bois (408) and Richard Wright (462). 'I have learned a great deal from Cedric Robinson regarding the uses of history,' writes Angela Y. Davis (545). '[…] I have felt kinship with his approach since I first read *Black Marxism*.'

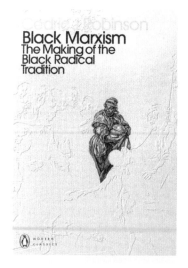

2021
fwd. Robin D. G. Kelley, 2020
pref. Damien Sojoyner & Tiffany
Willoughby-Herard, 2020

James Wilcox b. 1949

Wilcox has written nine comic novels, most of which are set in the fictional town of Tula Springs, Louisiana. In 1994, he was the subject of a *New Yorker* article, 'Moby Dick in Manhattan', about his struggle to make a living from literary fiction, eking three meals out of 'chicken he bought at Key Food for three dollars and forty cents'. Since 2004, he has taught at Louisiana State University in Baton Rouge.

Modern Baptists 1983

When the devilish and dissolute F.X. gets released on parole from Angola Prison, he moves in with his half-brother Bobby Pickens, the middle-aged, middle-class assistant manager of Sunny Boy Bargain Store in Tula Springs. As F.X. turns his life upside down, Bobby struggles to maintain his respectability, and the narrative climaxes with a Christmas Eve party in a cabin in a poisoned swamp. 'James Wilcox has made a tale that is realistic and fantastic, painfully comic, and, in a strange way, psychologically penetrating,' wrote Robert Penn Warren (489). '*Modern Baptists* is an impressive achievement, and its author a writer of impressive promise. There is no writer exactly like him. He is an original.'

1985 King Penguin
2005 Modern Classics
• intro. Jim Crace, 2005

Charles Willeford 1919 – 1988

Both Willeford's parents had died of tuberculosis by the time he was nine, and at thirteen he ran away from his grandmother's house. He served as a tank commander during the Second World War and then held various jobs as a horse trainer, boxer, actor, radio announcer and painter. He is most famous for his four Miami detective stories featuring Hoke Moseley.

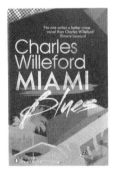

2012
• —

Miami Blues 1984

Hard-boiled homicide detective Hoke Moseley is on the trail of ex-con Freddy 'Junior' Frenger, chasing him through the Cuban ghettos, luxury hotels and seedy suburban sprawl of Miami. The novel was made into a film in 1990 starring Alec Baldwin.

Sideswipe 1987

Detective Hoke Moseley needs a holiday: his daughters want to quit school, his ex-wife has just remarried and his beat partner is eight months pregnant. Then a restorative trip to Singer Island in Palm Beach coincides with a cowboy-hatted psychopath on an armed robbery spree. One of the novel's epigraphs is by William Carlos Williams (418): 'There's a lot of bastards out there!'

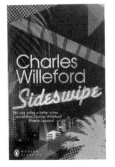

2012
• —

New Hope for the Dead 1985

'Drugs, beaches, crazed immigrants, rednecks, cults, alligators and crooked cops,' lists the crime writer Maxim Jakubowski, 'it's all here in abundance.' Detective Hoke Moseley is investigating the death of a young junky while looking after his own teenage daughters and liaising with his ex-wife.

The Way We Die Now 1988

Detective Hoke Moseley goes undercover in Collier County as a migrant worker to investigate a murder and human trafficking case. The previous Moseley novels had been so successful, they earned Willeford a $225,000 advance for this fourth instalment; sadly it was his final novel.

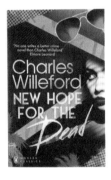

2012
• —

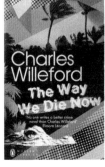

2012
• —

Mary Gaitskill b. 1954

Gaitskill sold flowers as a teenager and worked as a stripper and a call girl before she became a writer. She has since taught at universities in California, Texas, New York, Rhode Island and Pennsylvania, and is currently a visiting professor at Claremont McKenna College in California. Her stories have appeared in the *New Yorker*, *Harper's*, *Artforum* and *Granta*. In 2020, she was elected to the American Academy of Arts and Letters. 'What makes her scary, and what makes her exciting,' said the *New York Times*, 'is her ability to evoke the hidden life, the life unseen, the life we don't even know we are living.'

Bad Behavior 1988

Half of these tales of desire in 1980s New York are told from a male perspective and half from a female. They deal with friendship, romance, love, dominance, submission, sex work and drug addiction. 'An air of Pinteresque menace hangs over these people's social exchanges like black funereal bunting,' wrote the *New York Times*. The 2002 film *Secretary*, starring Maggie Gyllenhaal and James Spader, was inspired by Gaitskill's sadomasochistic story of the same name: the movie is 'the *Pretty Woman* version', says Gaitskill, 'heavy on the charm (and a little too nice)'.

2019
—

Two Girls, Fat and Thin 1991

Gaitskill's first novel is about thin Justine Shade, a freelance journalist and inveterate masochist, who interviews fat Dorothy Never, a reclusive proof-reader and former devotee of Anna Granite, a thinly fictionalized version of Ayn Rand (450). When the two women meet, they are immediately drawn to each other and gradually reveal their separate childhood traumas. 'Uncompromisingly brilliant,' wrote *New Woman*. '[…] Her ability to lay bare intense, often raw emotions will knock you off your feet.' The epigraph is taken from Vladimir Nabokov's *Speak, Memory* (308).

Because They Wanted To
1993–97, pub. 1997

This collection of compelling and quietly devastating tales was nominated for the PEN/Faulkner (433) Award. The *Independent* called it 'a perfectly formed set of stories about alienation in modern times'. Gaitskill's epigraph comes from Carson McCullers's *The Ballad of the Sad Café* (454).

2020
—

2021
—

Oscar Hijuelos 1951–2013

Oscar Jerome Hijuelos was born in New York, the son of Spanish-speaking Cuban parents. As a child, he spent a year in hospital suffering from nephritis, during which he learned English and lost his Spanish. He studied creative writing at the City College of New York, where he was taught by William S. Burroughs (481), Susan Sontag (524) and Donald Barthelme (527), who became his mentor. He then made a living installing advertising displays, but he began to write short stories as well, and his first novel was published in 1983. He died while playing tennis in Manhattan, at courts that have since been renamed after him.

The Mambo Kings Play Songs of Love 1989

Cesar Castillo listens to old recordings and recalls how he and his brother Nestor left Havana in 1949 and travelled to New York. The musician brothers became the Mambo Kings, packing out dance halls and theatres with their sensuous Latin rhythms. Hijuelos evokes a world of smoky clubs, sharp suits and stiletto heels, with cameos from real-life mambo stars such as Desi Arnaz, Pérez Prado and Machito. The novel won the Pulitzer Prize for Fiction and was filmed in 1992 as *The Mambo Kings*, starring Armand Assante and Antonio Banderas. 'It makes you want to get up and dance,' said the *Sunday Times*.

1558 Penguin Books
2009 Modern Classics
—

Dorothy Allison b. 1949

Allison grew up in Greenville, South Carolina, the daughter of a 15-year-old unmarried waitress. When her mother remarried, Allison's stepfather began to abuse her sexually. After seven years, she told a relative, who told her mother; the abuse stopped briefly, but then it resumed for another five years. Once Allison graduated from high school, she cut ties with her family and went to study anthropology at the New School for Social Research in New York. In the 1970s, she worked as a maid, a nanny and a substitute teacher, as well as at a child-care centre and a rape-crisis phone line. In the early 1980s, she met Audre Lorde (534), who encouraged her to write. She made contact with her mother again and began publishing poetry and short stories. In 2007, she won the Robert Penn Warren (489) Award and was elected to the Fellowship of Southern Writers in 2014.

Bastard Out of Carolina 1992

Allison's raw, semi-autobiographical first novel tells the story of Ruth Anne 'Bone' Boatwright, who is horribly abused by her stepfather. It was a finalist for the National Book Award and won the Ferro-Grumley Prize and the ALA Award for Lesbian and Gay Writing. The *New York Times* review compared it to J. D. Salinger's *Catcher in the Rye* (499) and Harper Lee's *To Kill a Mockingbird* (1960). Anjelica Houston directed an award-winning film adaptation in 1996. 'For anyone who has ever felt the contempt of a self-righteous world, this book will resonate within you like a gospel choir,' says Barbara Kingsolver. 'For anyone who hasn't, this book will be an education.'

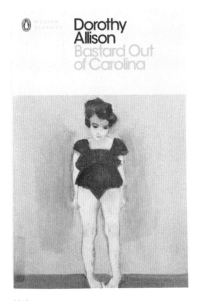

2012
—
Allison dedicates her book to 'Mama, Ruth Gibson Allison, 1935–1990'.

William Langewiesche b. 1955

Langewiesche is the son of the pilot Wolfgang Langewiesche, author of the classic aviation reference text *Stick and Rudder* (1944). Langewiesche worked as a pilot for fifteen years and contributed to the magazine *Flying* before making his name in the early 1990s writing for *Atlantic Monthly*, where he was nominated for eight consecutive National Magazine Awards. Since 2006, he has been *Vanity Fair*'s international correspondent. He has been described as a leading writer of the 'New New Journalism' (464).

Aloft 1993–2009

In graceful prose, Langewiesche's essays describe the thrilling and unnerving experience of flight and the ways in which it has changed our view of the world over the past hundred years. 'These are wonderful essays,' writes the novelist John Banville in his introduction, 'at once thrilling and informative, awe-inspiring and exact, in places frightening, in others reassuring, and always elegant.'

2010
intro. John Banville

More FLYING

Over to You
by Roald Dahl — 113

A Kestrel for a Knave
by Barry Hines — 155

Tales of Pirx the Pilot
by Stanisław Lem — 594

Wind, Sand and Stars
by Antoine de Saint-Exupéry — 179

The Hunters
by James Salter — 508

THE CARIBBEAN

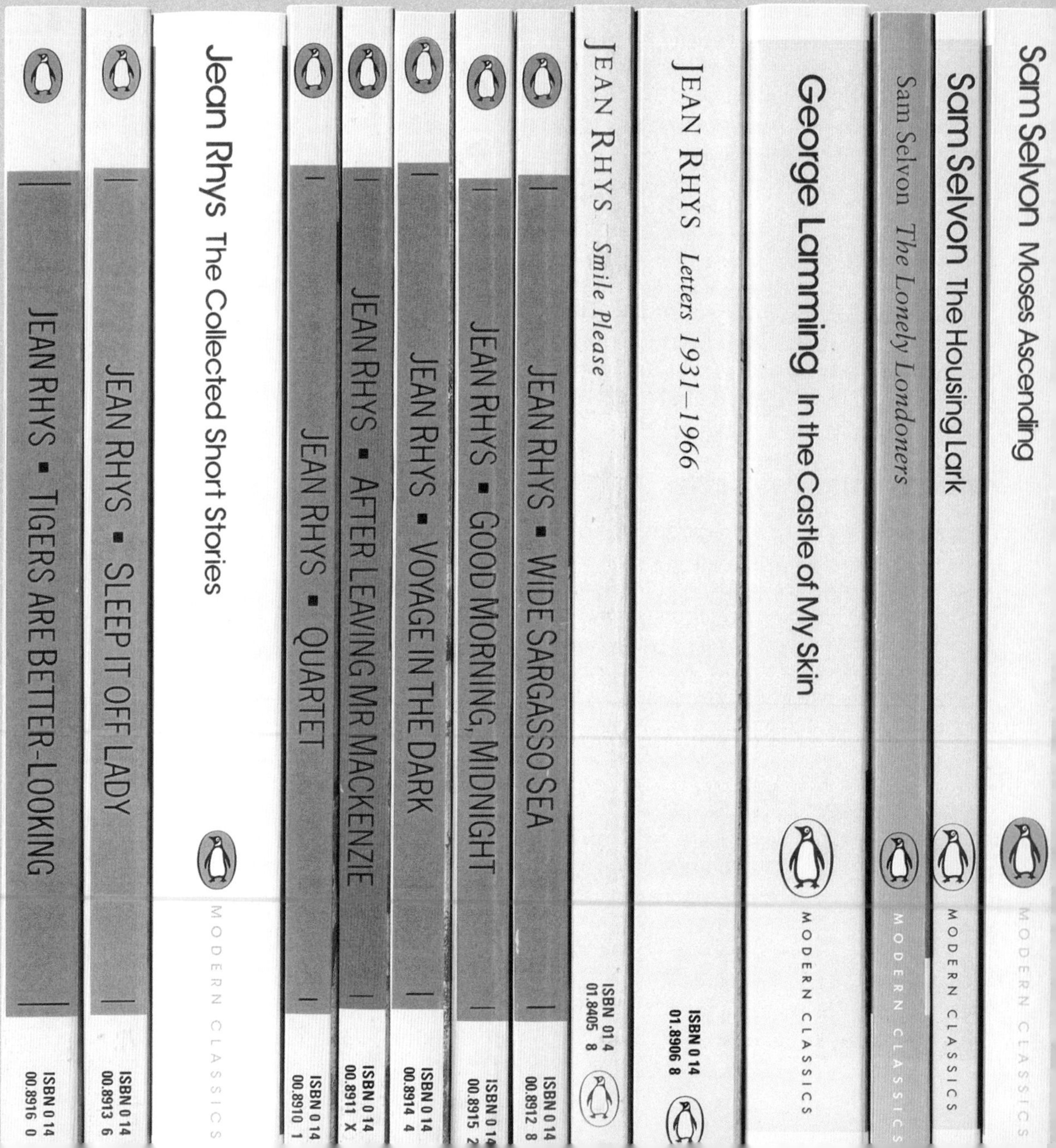
JEAN RHYS ▪ TIGERS ARE BETTER-LOOKING
ISBN 0 14 00.8916 0
JEAN RHYS ▪ SLEEP IT OFF LADY
ISBN 0 14 00.8913 6
Jean Rhys The Collected Short Stories
MODERN CLASSICS
JEAN RHYS ▪ QUARTET
ISBN 0 14 00.8910 1
JEAN RHYS ▪ AFTER LEAVING MR MACKENZIE
ISBN 0 14 00.8911 X
JEAN RHYS ▪ VOYAGE IN THE DARK
ISBN 0 14 00.8914 4
JEAN RHYS ▪ GOOD MORNING, MIDNIGHT
ISBN 0 14 00.8915 2
JEAN RHYS ▪ WIDE SARGASSO SEA
ISBN 0 14 00.8912 8
JEAN RHYS Smile Please
ISBN 014 01.8405 8
JEAN RHYS Letters 1931–1966
ISBN 0 14 01.8906 8
George Lamming In the Castle of My Skin
MODERN CLASSICS
Sam Selvon The Lonely Londoners
MODERN CLASSICS
Sam Selvon The Housing Lark
MODERN CLASSICS
Sam Selvon Moses Ascending
MODERN CLASSICS

Dominica, Barbados, Trinidad & Jamaica

Jean Rhys 1890–1979

Ella Gwendoline Rees Williams was born in Dominica, in the Lesser Antilles, the daughter of a Welsh doctor and a third-generation creole mother. She regularly visited her mother's family estate, a former slave plantation, until she was sixteen, when she went to school in England. She found England frightening and cold. After training briefly as an actress, she was a chorus girl, a fashion mannequin and an artist's model, before becoming the mistress of a wealthy stockbroker and narrowly surviving a back-street abortion. To escape her circumstances, she married a Dutch spy and songwriter, with whom she lived in Paris until he was arrested for currency speculation. While filing for divorce, she had an affair with Ford Madox Ford (46), who encouraged her to write and suggested her pen name, 'Jean Rhys'. In 1924, Ford published her first short story, 'Vienne', in his magazine, the *Transatlantic Review*. Her second husband was Leslie Tilden-Smith, a freelance literary agent, and her third was Max Hamer, Leslie's cousin, who was convicted of fraud and spent two years in prison. After 1939, Rhys disappeared from the literary scene: her works fell out of print and she was widely assumed to be dead. In fact, she was living in Bude, in Cornwall – she called it 'Bude the Obscure'. She was eventually contacted by the writers Selma Vaz Dias and Francis Wyndham, both of whom encouraged her to return to writing. The result was her masterpiece, *Wide Sargasso Sea* (552), her first book in more than a quarter of a century. It won several awards and brought her fame; but, as Rhys said, 'It has come too late.' She was 76 and never published another novel.

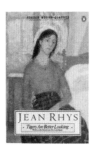

1973 Penguin Books
1987 Modern Classics
• —

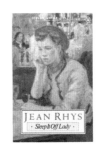

1979 Penguin Books
1987 Modern Classics
• —

2017
intro. Diana Athill, 1987
—

The Collected Short Stories gathers Rhys's three anthologies, and is introduced by Diana Athill, Rhys's editor at André Deutsch. 'I knew her only for the last fifteen years of her life,' Athill wrote, 'but even as an old woman her voice, her look, her manner, her way of laughing until the tears ran down her face, made her unusually attractive. Because she had learnt to pare everything extraneous away from her prose, it expressed the essence of how she saw things – and therefore, the essence of how she was.'

Stories 1924–79

Rhys published three volumes of short stories in her lifetime. Her first was *The Left Bank* (1927), with an introduction by Ford Madox Ford (46): 'coming from the Antilles, with a terrifying insight and a terrific – an almost lurid! – passion for stating the case of the underdog, she has let her pen loose on the Left Banks of the Old World,' wrote Ford. The frank, semi-autobiographical stories describe seedy hotels, ruinous love affairs, lonely London bedsits, genteel poverty and the temporary oblivion of alcohol. Following the late success of *Wide Sargasso Sea* (552), she published *Tigers Are Better-Looking* (1968), with eight new stories, and a decade later she gathered sixteen more in *Sleep It Off Lady* (1976).

Quartet 1928

Marya Zelli lives in bohemian Paris with her husband Stephan, a nefarious art-dealer. When he is arrested for selling stolen goods, she is left isolated and penniless, until she finds herself supported and then gradually tyrannized by a sophisticated English couple, the Heidlers, who are transparent ciphers for Ford Madox Ford (46) and his common-law partner, the Australian artist Stella Bowen.

1973 Penguin Books
1987 Modern Classics
aftwd. Katie Owen, 2000
—

Quartet was first published in the UK as *Postures*. In the USA it was called *Quartet*, which Rhys preferred, so she changed the title when the novel was republished in the UK in 1969.

After Leaving Mr Mackenzie
1930

Julia Martin is the second incarnation of what the writer Francis Wyndham called Rhys's semi-autobiographical 'composite heroine'. She finds herself adrift in Paris and London after Mr Mackenzie abandons her. One scene was inspired by the funeral of Rhys's own mother at Golders Green Crematorium, in north London, in 1927. 'It is doubtful if one should open this volume unless one is happily married, immensely rich, and in robust health,' wrote the author Rebecca West.

1971 Penguin Books
1987 Modern Classics
aftwd. Lorna Sage, 2000

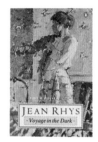

Voyage in the Dark 1934

Anna Morgan moves from the West Indies to grey, chilly England and works as a chorus girl, eventually becoming the mistress of a much older man. The novel is based on Rhys's own experiences of the London demi-monde. Rhys 'is the obverse of Colette (170)', said the *New York Times*. '[…] Open a book by Colette and you walk into light. In Jean Rhys it is always the hour of the wolf and it is always cold. Colette's women love their lives; Jean Rhys's women only inhabit theirs.'

1969 Penguin Books
1987 Modern Classics
2000 Modern Classics
aftwd. Carole Angier, 2000
—
Carole Angier wrote the biography *Jean Rhys: Life and Work* (1990), which won the Writers' Guild award for non-fiction.

Good Morning, Midnight
1939

Ageing Sasha Jansen, alone in 1930s Paris, decides to dye her hair blonde and embrace her independence. Emancipation, however, proves to be more complicated than she expected. 'The world of Jean Rhys's fiction is both strange and unnervingly familiar,' writes the novelist A. L. Kennedy in her introduction. 'Anyone who has ever been lonely, uncertain, afraid will find something of themselves here; something of the insidious, banal horror of a simply unhappy life.'

1969 Penguin Books
1987 Modern Classics
2000 Modern Classics
aftwd. A. L. Kennedy, 2000

Wide Sargasso Sea 1966 →

Rhys began contemplating a Caribbean novel as early as 1936, after a return visit to Dominica. *Wide Sargasso Sea* is her response to Charlotte Brontë's *Jane Eyre* (1847), her attempt to rehabilitate the madwoman in the attic. Antoinette Cosway is a creole heiress from Jamaica, wooed and ultimately undone by Edward Rochester, in a novel shot through with Caribbean mythology, menacing vegetation and the shadows of ghosts. Doris Lessing considered it 'a masterpiece, surely one of the best novels of the century'.

1968 Penguin Books
1987 Modern Classics
2000 Modern Classics
aftwd. Andrea Ashworth, 2000

Smile Please 1979
An Unfinished Autobiography

'This time I must not blot a line,' wrote Rhys. 'No revision, no second thoughts. Down it shall go. Already I am terrified.' She began dictating her memoirs just months before she died. She managed to complete one section, about her childhood on Dominica. In this edition, Diana Athill also includes the notes Rhys made about her adult life and excerpts from her diary, 'at the Ropemakers' Arms', which she wrote in the 1940s in Maidstone, Kent.

1981 Penguin Books
1990 Twentieth-Century Classics
ed. Diana Athill, 1979

Letters 1931–66, pub. 1984

Rhys's letters are organized into six periods: 'Leslie' and 'Max', her second and third husbands; 'Maryvonne Moerman', her daughter; 'Selma Vaz Dias', the writer who helped 'rediscover' her; 'Cheriton Fitzpaine', her last home in Devon, which she described as 'a dull spot which even drink can't enliven much'; and *Wide Sargasso Sea*, the title of her breakthrough masterpiece. 'Her letters are eloquent and invaluable revelations,' says Marina Warner.

1985 Penguin Books
1995 Twentieth-Century Classics
● ed. Francis Wyndham & Diana Melly, 1984

JEAN RHYS

Wide Sargasso Sea

1997
ed. Angela Smith

Angela Smith's annotated edition reprints as an appendix Francis Wyndham's
introduction from the 1966 first edition. The artwork on the cover is a detail from
Landscape Near Kingston, Jamaica (1950) by John Minton.

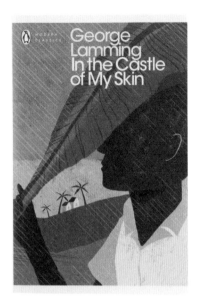

2017
intro. George Lamming, 1983
—
Lamming's title comes
from a Derek Walcott poem,
Epitaph for the Young (1949).

George Lamming b. 1927

Lamming was born on Barbados, but travelled to Trinidad as a teenager, where he taught and wrote poetry. In 1950, he sailed to England on the same boat as Sam Selvon and began contributing to the BBC's *Caribbean Voices* radio programme. The success of his first two novels, *In the Castle of My Skin* and *The Emigrants* (1954), established his reputation and in 1967 he began an academic career. He has taught at universities around the world and is currently an honorary professor at the University of the West Indies. 'He evoked, for me, an unforgettable picture of a peasant revolt in a white-dominated world,' writes Ngũgĩ wa Thiong'o (365). 'And suddenly I knew a novel could be made to speak to me, could, with a compelling urgency, touch chords deep down in me.'

In the Castle of My Skin 1953

'In the desolate, frozen heart of London, at the age of twenty-three,' recalls Lamming, 'I tried to reconstruct the world of my childhood and early adolescence.' Nine-year-old G. grows up in a sleepy village on the coast of Barbados, overseen by an English landlord, and he is only dimly aware of a distant mother country across the sea. This lyrical coming-of-age novel is also a story of historical injustice and the crumbling of colonial power. It won the Somerset Maugham (32) Award and was praised by Jean-Paul Sartre (185) and Richard Wright (462).

Sam Selvon 1923–1994

Samuel Dickson Selvon was born in San Fernando on Trinidad, to Indian parents. During the Second World War, he served as a telegraphist on a minesweeper, and then he worked as a journalist in Port of Spain, publishing stories in local magazines and submitting poems to the BBC's *Caribbean Voices* radio programme. In 1950, he travelled to London on the same boat as George Lamming and published his first novel, *A Brighter Sun* (1952). He wrote novels and stories set in London and Trinidad until 1978, when he left the UK and moved to Calgary in Canada. Lamming calls him 'the best folk poet the British Caribbean has yet produced'.

The Lonely Londoners 1956

Selvon's poignant portrait of the West Indian community in 1950s Bayswater is written in Trinidadian dialect peppered with creole vocabulary. It follows Moses Aloetta as he welcomes a new arrival nicknamed 'Galahad' to the cold, foggy city, interspersed with digressions to describe the humorous and heartbreaking activities of the rest of the 'boys'. 'Selvon's meticulously observed narratives of displaced Londoners' lives,' says the novelist and playwright Caryl Phillips, '[...] created a template for how to write about a migrant, and postmigrant, London for countless writers who have followed in his wake, including Hanif Kureishi and Zadie Smith.'

2006
intro. Susheila Nasta
—
Susheila Nasta is the founder
of the international literary
journal *Wasafiri*.

2020
—

The Housing Lark 1965

Squeezed by heartless Brixton landlords, 'Bat' Battersby and his motley group of friends decide to save up and buy a house of their own in London. But in the face of social ostracism and expensive temptations, getting the money together is not straightforward. 'His is a world like Damon Runyon's (439),' says A. S. Byatt, 'where tarts are warm-hearted girls whose main fear is "pewmonia" from cold grass, dope-pedlars are vaguely sinister figures of fun and rent-collectors pathetically pompous but lonely at heart.'

Moses Ascending 1975

Moses and Galahad from *The Lonely Londoners* (554) return, this time in 1970s Shepherd's Bush. Moses is now a landlord, living on the top floor of an apartment block and overseeing a motley crew of incendiary tenants with the assistance of his handyman Bob. 'I have weathered many a storm in Brit'n,' says Moses, 'and men will tell you that in my own way I am as much part of the London landscape as little Eros with his bow and arrow in Piccadilly, or one-eye Nelson with his column in Trafalgar Square, not counting colour.'

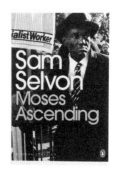

2008
intro. Hari Kunzru

V. S. Naipaul 1932–2018

Vidiadhar Surajprasad Naipaul was born in Trinidad and won a scholarship to study in England in 1950. He met his future wife, Patricia Ann Hale, at Oxford University, before moving to London and working for the BBC's *Caribbean Voices* radio programme. His first novel, *The Mystic Masseur* (1957), won the John Llewellyn Rhys Prize and he went on to write a series of comic novels set in Trinidad. He travelled widely and wrote politically engaged travel books and novels, such as *In a Free State* (1971), which won the Booker Prize. In 1990, he was awarded a knighthood, and in 2001 he won the Nobel Prize for Literature (576).

A House for Mr Biswas 1961

Mr Mohun Biswas is an Indo-Trinidadian based partly on Naipaul's own father, Seepersad. Biswas struggles valiantly at various vocations, including Hindu priest, sign-painter, shop owner and journalist, but finally he sets his sights on building his own house. This is the novel that made Naipaul's reputation and it is still considered his greatest achievement. It has 'the Dickensian largeness and luxuriance', writes Paul Theroux (543), 'without any of the Dickensian sentimentality, apostrophizing or preaching'.

1969 Penguin Books
1992 Twentieth-Century Classics
• intro. Ian Buruma, 1992

—

In 1961, *A House for Mr Biswas* was adapted by Monty Norman into a stage musical that was to have been directed by Peter Brook (155). The musical was never produced but Norman recycled the rhythm and tune of one of its songs, 'Bad Sign, Good Sign', for the James Bond theme, which he wrote for *Dr No* (128) in 1962.

V. S. NAIPAUL
A House for Mr Biswas

Shiva Naipaul 1945–1985

Shivadhar Srinivasa Naipaul was the younger brother of V. S. Naipaul (555). Like him, he won a scholarship to study at Oxford University and met his wife there. As Vidiadhar's brother, Shiva felt an 'intimidating burden of expectation', but nonetheless produced several prize-winning works of fiction and non-fiction himself. He died at the age of 40, at his writing desk. He 'was one of those people who caused your heart to lift when he entered a room', wrote Martin Amis (160). '[. . .] In losing him, we have lost 30 years of untranscribed, unvarnished genius.'

1971 Penguin Books
1995 Twentieth-Century Classics
2012 Modern Classics
fwd. Amit Chaudhuri, 2012

Fireflies 1970

The Khojas are an old Hindu family on Trinidad, living on a ramshackle estate and bumbling through life – all except 'Baby' Khoja, Naipaul's resourceful heroine. Margaret Forster described *Fireflies* as 'one of the funniest, one of the saddest and one of the most beautifully written novels I have ever read'.

The Chip-Chip Gatherers 1973

Egbert Ramsaran is the owner of the Ramsaran Transport Company in a large Trinidadian village. He is a rich and eccentric tyrant, who controls the lives of everyone around him. The novel ends with an image of a bleached driftwood tree on the beach, ignored by the stray dogs and villagers gathering 'chip-chip' molluscs at low tide. The *Times Literary Supplement* called it a novel 'about rootlessness, rather than roots'.

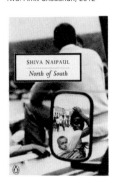

1976 Penguin Books
1997 Twentieth-Century Classics
2012 Modern Classics
fwd. Amit Chaudhuri, 2012

North of South
An African Journey 1978

In the 1970s, Naipaul spent several months in Kenya, Tanzania and Zambia, visiting the Asian populations in those newly independent countries. Graham Greene (88) described his account as 'very sad, very funny'.

1980 Penguin Books
1996 Twentieth-Century Classics
—

A Man of Mystery and Other Stories

1969–74, pub. 1984

'Naipaul shares with Evelyn Waugh (67) the same eye for the ridiculous, the same dark humour, the same ultimate cynicism about the human race,' wrote Elspeth Huxley (365). This collection of eight short stories ranges from the comedy of 'The Beauty Contest' to the tragedy of 'The Dolly House'. 'A Man of Mystery' is about the downfall of a cobbler who cannot compete with commercialization. 'Mr Naipaul goes to a lot of bad places,' wrote Anthony Burgess (148), 'and even lives in them. Some, like Earls Court, Brixton and Liverpool, are cold, but they still pullulate with squalor and wretchedness.'

1995
• —
The stories in *A Man of Mystery* were first collected in *Beyond the Dragon's Mouth* (1984), a selection of fiction, memoir and journalism.

A Hot Country 1983

The fictional South American country of Cuyama is falling into a post-independence malaise and the nation's fate is mirrored by the crumbling relationship between Aubrey St Pierre, a bookseller, and his wife Dina. 'He uses language like an epicure,' wrote the *Times Literary Supplement*: 'with relish and precision. *A Hot Country* is a sad book about waste, but a work of art that delights with its craft as it dismays with its vision.'

1985 Penguin Books as *Love and Death in a Hot Country*
1995 Twentieth-Century Classics
• —
Naipaul's epigraph is taken from D. H. Lawrence's *The Plumed Serpent* (55): 'In this country she was afraid. But it was her soul more than her body that knew fear. She had thought that each individual had a complete self, a complete soul, an accomplished I. And now she realised … that this was not so.'

Linton Kwesi Johnson b. 1952

Johnson was born in Jamaica. His middle name, 'Kwesi', is given to Ghanaian boys born on a Sunday. In 1963, he travelled to London to join his mother in Tulse Hill. At school, he joined the Black Panthers and organized a poetry workshop within the movement. He went on to study at Goldsmiths' College, University of London, where he began to write and perform his poetry, reciting and improvising over dub-reggae music. *Dread Beat an' Blood* (1975) established his reputation, and today he continues to perform internationally. He has his own music label, LKJ Records.

Mi Revalueshanary Fren
Selected Poems 1975–2000

'Writing was a political act and poetry was a cultural weapon,' said Johnson in 2008. This landmark selection charts black experiences in Britain, with angry protests against racism and playful celebrations of urban life. Titles include 'Inglan is a Bitch', 'Tings an Times' and 'If I Woz a Tap Natch Poet'. Johnson uses Caribbean creole and reggae rhythms to create his unique oral literature, which the poet Fred D'Aguiar describes as the 'most original poetic form to have emerged in the English language in the last quarter century'. *Time Out* calls Johnson 'the alternative poet-laureate'.

2002
• intro. Fred D'Aguiar

Martinique & Guadeloupe

Frantz Fanon 1925–1961

Frantz Omar Fanon was born on Martinique, a French colony at the time. He was taught by the writer Aimé Césaire and joined the Free French Forces in 1943, serving in the last years of the Second World War. Afterwards he studied medicine in France, specializing in psychiatry. Working in a hospital in Algeria in 1953, he felt compelled to side with the 'rebels' during the country's revolution against French rule, so he joined the Algerian National Liberation Front and became one of its most articulate spokesmen. He was diagnosed with leukaemia, however, and died a year before the country saw independence. He is buried in a martyrs' graveyard in eastern Algeria.

2021
trans. Richard Philcox, 2008

Black Skin, White Masks 1952

In this landmark, postcolonial (335) study, Fanon examines the effects of racism on the psyche, demonstrating the ways in which the subjects of colonialism internalize its prejudices, eventually emulating the 'white masks' of their oppressors. His urgent critique has influenced civil rights (502), anti-colonial and black consciousness movements around the world, and it remains one of the most radical and influential essays ever written about race and racism. 'Fanon is our contemporary,' says the novelist Deborah Levy. '[…] In clear language, in words that can only have been written in the cool heat of rage, Fanon showed us the internal theatre of racism.'

The Wretched of the Earth
1961

Fanon wrote this classic anti-colonial text at the height of the Algerian war for independence. As a psychotherapist, Fanon details the deleterious psychological effect of colonization and insists on revolutionary violence as the means of rebuilding a dignified national culture. His passionate polemic has inspired anti-colonial movements around the world. 'When you have read Fanon's last chapter,' wrote Jean-Paul Sartre (185) in his preface, 'you will be convinced that it would be better for you to be a native at the uttermost depths of misery than to be a former settler.'

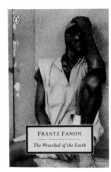

1967 Penguin Books
1983 Pelican Books
1990 Twentieth-Century Classics
pref. Jean-Paul Sartre, 1961
trans. Constance Farrington, 1963

Maryse Condé b. 1937

Maryse Boucolon was born in Pointe-à-Pitre on Guadeloupe, and wrote her first play before she was twelve. She travelled to study in Paris, where she married the Guinean actor Mamadou Condé. She then lived and taught in West Africa – in Guinea, Ghana and Senegal – before publishing her first novel, the controversial *Hérémakhonon* (*Waiting for Happiness*, 1976), at the age of 39. After the success of *Segu*, her third novel, she moved to the USA and taught French and francophone literature at several universities. In 2018, she was awarded the 'alternative Nobel Prize for Literature' (577).

2017
trans. Barbara Bray, 1987

Segu 1984

Set in 1797, in the historical West African kingdom of Segu, Condé's epic novel revolves around Dousika Traore, the king's most trusted advisor, as his family is torn apart by the influences of Islam from the east and the slave trade from the west. It is 'rich and colourful and glorious', wrote Maya Angelou. 'It sprawls over continents and centuries to find its way into the reader's heart.'

Négritude

The *négritude* cultural movement was launched in 1935 by three black students in Paris: Léon Damas from French Guiana; Léopold Sédar Senghor (359), later the first President of Senegal; and the Martiniquan poet Aimé Césaire. They founded a magazine, *L'Étudiant Noir* (*The Black Student*), and Césaire wrote a passionate tract against colonial assimilation, calling for a movement to reclaim African culture and assert the value of blackness. Césaire's book-length poem *Notebook of a Return to My Native Land* (1939) is considered the masterpiece of the *négritude* movement; André Breton (176) called it 'nothing less than the greatest lyrical monument of this time'. Frantz Fanon (557) referred frequently to *négritude* in his writings, and the leading pan-African journal *Présence Africaine*, founded in 1947, continued to promote it. Léopold Sédar Senghor defined *négritude* as 'the sum total of the values of the civilization of the African world', although some black writers have subsequently pushed for a more radical movement. 'The tiger does not proclaim his tigritude,' Wole Soyinka is said to have quipped – 'he pounces.'

More
BOOKS ABOUT SLAVERY

The Woman in the Dunes by Kobo Abe — 352

The Kingdom of This World by Alejo Carpentier — 559

Juneteenth by Ralph Ellison — 458

Flight to Canada by Ishmael Reed — 539

The Slave by Isaac Bashevis Singer — 290

Cuba

Alejo Carpentier 1904–1980

Carpentier was born in Switzerland, the son of a French architect and a Russian-language teacher, but he grew up in Havana and always considered himself Cuban. He studied architecture at the University of Havana, but became more interested in musicology. He was the editor of *Carteles* from 1924, the most influential magazine in Cuba, and his left-leaning journalism supported the foundation of the Cuban Communist Party. He was briefly imprisoned in 1927 for criticizing the government, and he subsequently escaped to Paris, where he immersed himself in Surrealism (176) and made contact with Pablo Neruda (569), Miguel Ángel Asturias (562) and Pablo Picasso. He returned to Cuba in 1939, but moved to Venezuela for fourteen years, running a radio station and working at the Central University of Caracas. When Fidel Castro led the successful Cuban Revolution in 1959, Carpentier returned and was appointed Vice-President of the National Council of Culture. He became the director of the Cuban State Publishing House in 1962 and Cuba's ambassador to France in 1966. He wrote novels, short stories, plays, poems, musical scores and the first history of Cuban music. In 1977, he was awarded the prestigious Cervantes Prize.

1975
• trans. Harriet de Onís, 1957
—
In his original prologue to *The Kingdom of This World*, Carpentier formulated the concept of 'lo real maravilloso', 'the marvellous real': real events that are extraordinary but nonetheless true.

The Kingdom of This World 1949

This slim historical novel recreates the events of the Haitian Revolution of 1791, when the slave leader Toussaint Louverture staged a successful insurrection against his French colonial masters and established a short-lived black republic. It was inspired by a trip Carpentier made to Haiti in 1943. 'Carpentier's writing has the power and range of a cathedral organ on the eve of the Resurrection,' wrote the *New Yorker*.

The Lost Steps 1953

1968
• trans. Harriet de Onís, 1956

A musicologist abandons his wife and travels to the jungles of South America to search for primitive musical instruments on the upper Orinoco. In a reversal of Conrad's *Heart of Darkness* (29), he finds himself increasingly enlightened as he travels up the river. J. B. Priestley (87) called it 'one of the major works of our time'.

Explosion in a Cathedral 1962

Victor Hugues was a French revolutionary who brought radical ideas to the Caribbean and governed French Guadeloupe from 1794 to 1798. Through different narrators, and recurring images of the printing press and the guillotine, Carpentier paints a portrait of Hugues and explores how his ideals evolved around the Caribbean. The *Observer* called *Explosion in a Cathedral* 'the veritable godmother of all those magic-realist (563) historical novels, which have made us love or loathe Latin-American fiction'. The original Spanish title, *El Siglo de las Luces*, literally translates as *The Age of Enlightenment*.

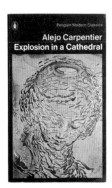

1971
• trans. John Sturrock, 1963
—
When Gabriel García Márquez read *Explosion in a Cathedral*, he abandoned his draft of *One Hundred Years of Solitude* (562) and started again from scratch.

LATIN AMERICA

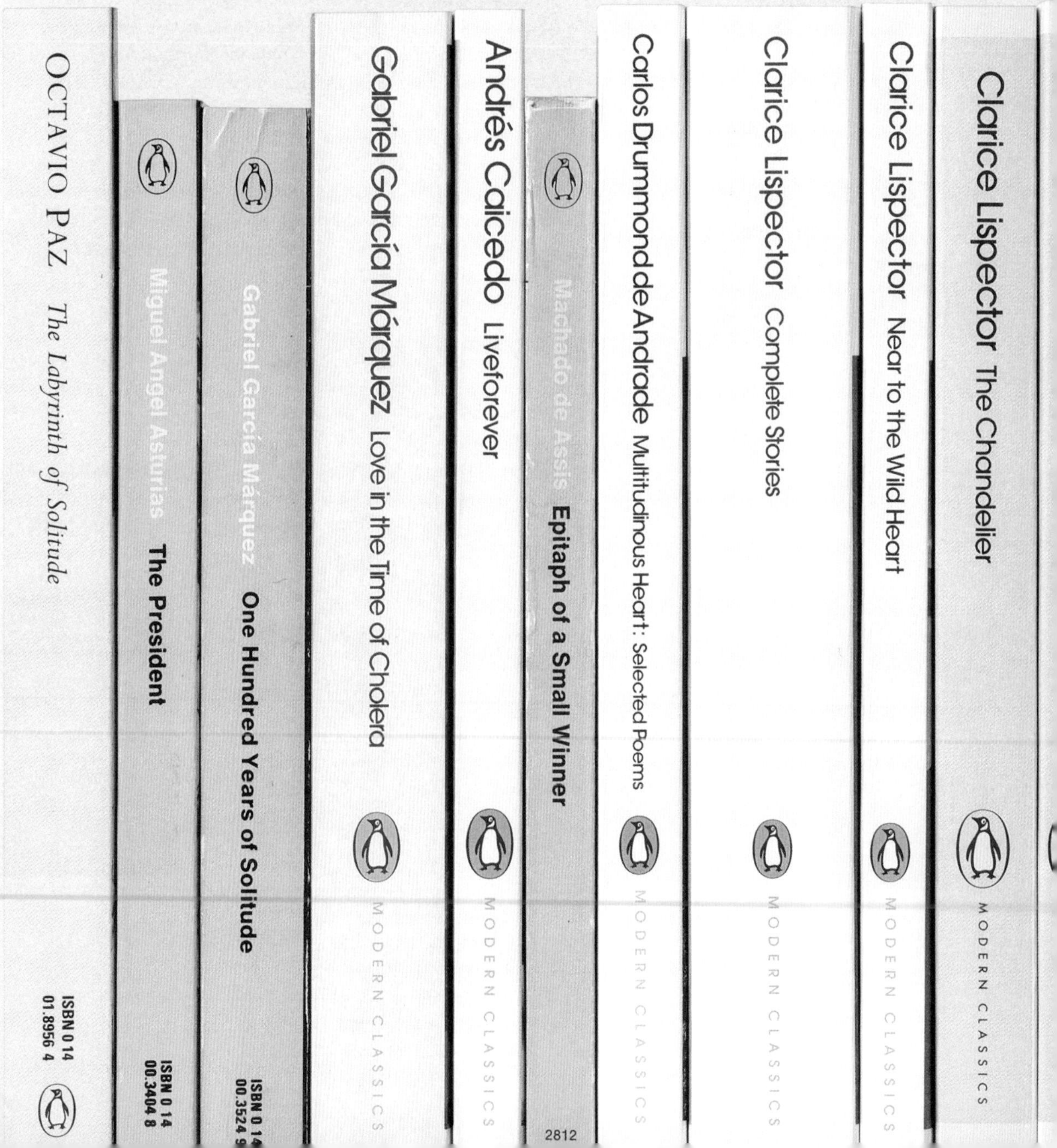

OCTAVIO PAZ The Labyrinth of Solitude
ISBN 0 14 01.8956 4
Miguel Angel Asturias The President
ISBN 0 14 00.3404 8
Gabriel García Márquez One Hundred Years of Solitude
ISBN 0 14 00.3524 9
Gabriel García Márquez Love in the Time of Cholera
MODERN CLASSICS
Andrés Caicedo Liveforever
MODERN CLASSICS
Machado de Assis Epitaph of a Small Winner
2812
Carlos Drummond de Andrade Multitudinous Heart: Selected Poems
MODERN CLASSICS
Clarice Lispector Complete Stories
MODERN CLASSICS
Clarice Lispector Near to the Wild Heart
MODERN CLASSICS
Clarice Lispector The Chandelier
MODERN CLASSICS

Mexico

Octavio Paz

1914–1998

Paz was born in Mexico City and grew up reading in his grandfather's extensive library. He abandoned his law degree in 1937 and moved to the Yucatán peninsula to teach and write poetry. That same year, he married Elena Garro, another Mexican writer, and attended the Second International Congress for Anti-Fascist Writers in Spain, during the Spanish Civil War, along with Ernest Hemingway (428), André Malraux (184) and Pablo Neruda (569). On his return to Mexico, he founded a literary magazine, *Taller* (*Workshop*), and joined the Mexican diplomatic service. His first posting was Paris, where he wrote *The Labyrinth of Solitude* in 1950, and mixed with the Surrealists (176). Subsequent postings included Tokyo and Geneva, and in 1962 he became the Mexican ambassador to India, all the while writing poetry. In 1968, he resigned in protest against his government's massacre of students in Mexico City. He returned to Mexico and founded the magazines *Plural* and *Vuelta* (*Return*). He won the Cervantes Prize in 1981, the Neustadt International Prize in 1982 and the Nobel Prize for Literature (576) in 1990.

The Labyrinth of Solitude

1950–79, pub. 1950–85

The book-length title essay in this anthology of Paz's prose considers what it means to be Mexican, analysing Mexican culture, history and psychology. In nine sections, with titles such as 'Mexican Masks', 'The Day of the Dead' and 'The Conquest and Colonialism', Paz argues that Mexicans hide behind a 'mask of solitude', which is the reason for their unique perspectives on death and identity. Subsequent editions included later pieces, such as *The Other Mexico* (1972), Paz's response to the student massacre in Mexico City in 1968, and 'Return to the Labyrinth of Solitude', a conversation with the French critic Claude Fell about his famous essay.

Latin American Boom

In the 1960s, a young generation of South American writers began experimenting with modernism (11) and magical realism (563), inspired by contemporary politics and the *vanguardia* movement (569). Their writing coincided with the first widespread publication of South American writers in Europe, leading to an explosion of international interest in the literature of the continent. The key figures of the 'boom' were Julio Cortázar from Argentina, Carlos Fuentes from Mexico, Gabriel García Márquez (562) from Colombia and Mario Vargas Llosa from Peru. Their novels combine historical fiction with political allegory, occasional fantasy and unusual formats. Cortázar's novel *Hopscotch* (1963), for example, has 155 chapters, designed to be read in a number of different orders.

1985 King Penguin
1990 Twentieth-Century Classics trans. Lysander Kemp, Yara Milos & Rachel Phillips Belash, 1961–85
—
The first UK hardback edition of *The Labyrinth of Solitude* was published in 1967, one of the earliest titles in Penguin's 'Allen Lane The Penguin Press' series of hardbacks.

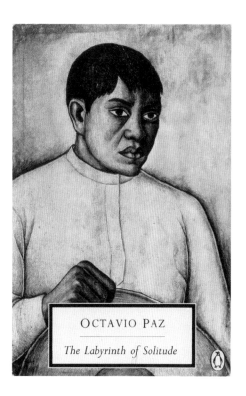

OCTAVIO PAZ

The Labyrinth of Solitude

Guatemala

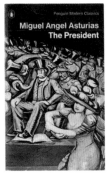

Miguel Ángel Asturias 1899–1974

Asturias studied law before travelling to Paris in 1923 to research the Maya civilization at the Sorbonne. He lived in Paris for ten years, where he mixed with the Surrealists (176) and published his first book, *Leyendas de Guatemala* (1931), poetic retellings of Guatemalan myths with a preface by Paul Valéry. He then joined the Guatemalan diplomatic service, taking posts in Mexico, Argentina and France, before becoming ambassador to El Salvador in 1953. After the Guatemalan *coup d'état* in 1954, however, Asturias was stripped of his citizenship and went into exile in Argentina, Chile and then Italy. When President Méndez was elected democratically in 1966, Asturias was rehabilitated and appointed ambassador to France. The critic Gerald Martin lists him as one of the 'ABC writers' of Latin American modernism (11): Asturias, Borges (572) and Carpentier (559). In 1967, he won the Nobel Prize for Literature (576).

The President
1933, pub. 1946

Asturias's most famous novel is a portrait of an anonymous Latin American state overseen by a brutal dictator, the President, whose subjects squirm as they meet his corrupt whims and avoid his displeasure. Asturias's dreamlike, fragmentary, stream-of-consciousness style has been compared with both James Joyce (8) and William Faulkner (433). The novel draws on memories of Manuel Estrada Cabrera's dictatorship, under which Asturias grew up.

1972
● trans. Frances Partridge, 1967

—

Asturias completed this novel in 1933, but he felt unable to publish it during the dictatorship of Jorge Ubico (1931–44). Eventually he published the novel privately in Mexico.

Colombia

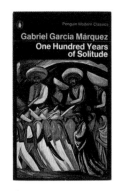

Gabriel García Márquez 1927–2014

García Márquez was raised by his grandparents in Aracataca, a tropical town near the Caribbean coast of Colombia. After studying law in Bogotá, where he read Franz Kafka's 'Metamorphosis' (280) translated by Jorge Luis Borges (572), he became a journalist, writing for *El Universal*, *El Heraldo* and then *El Espectador*, for whom he travelled as a foreign correspondent to Rome, Paris, Barcelona, Caracas and New York. The publication of his second full-length novel, *One Hundred Years of Solitude*, made him an international celebrity, known affectionately as 'Gabo'. He was a leading figure of the Latin American Boom (561), along with his literary rival, the Peruvian Mario Vargas Llosa, who once punched him in the face. García Márquez was awarded the Neustadt International Prize in 1972 and the Nobel Prize for Literature (576) in 1982. When he died, the President of Colombia, Juan Manuel Santos, described him as 'the greatest Colombian who ever lived'.

One Hundred Years of Solitude 1967

García Márquez's masterpiece traces seven generations of the Buendía family in Macondo, the 'city of mirrors'. Macondo, a fictionalized version of Aracataca, is both a typically isolated Colombian town and a microcosm of Colombia as a whole. It is swept by war, disaster and genuine historical events, but it is also the setting for wondrous miracles. Pablo Neruda (569) called *One Hundred Years of Solitude* 'the greatest revelation in the Spanish language since the *Don Quixote* of Cervantes'; Salman Rushdie considered it 'the greatest novel in any language of the last fifty years'; and the novelist William Kennedy hailed it as 'the first piece of literature since the Book of Genesis that should be required reading for the entire human race'.

1972
trans. Gregory Rabassa, 1970

Love in the Time of Cholera

1985

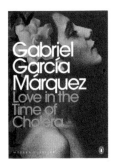

1989 Penguin Books
2007 Modern Classics
trans. Edith Grossman, 1988

In Spanish, *cólera* means both 'cholera' and 'intense passion'. This is the story of a lifelong romance between Florentino Ariza and the beautiful Fermina Daza, who nevertheless marries the distinguished Dr Urbino, who dedicates himself to fighting a cholera epidemic. Fifty years later, when Florentino and Fermina are in their seventies, they have a second chance of happiness. 'Oh boy – does [García Márquez] write well,' exclaims Thomas Pynchon. 'He writes with impassioned control, out of a maniacal serenity: the Garciamarquesian voice [...] can at once be classical and familiar, opalescent and pure, able to praise and curse, laugh and cry, fabulate and sing and when called upon, take off and soar.'

Magical Realism

'Magical realism' is a broad term for otherwise realistic works that incorporate elements of fantasy. It was first used in Germany, to describe certain artworks in the New Objectivity movement (255), but today it is usually associated with the Latin American Boom (561) and writers such as Miguel Ángel Asturias (562), Alejo Carpentier (559) and especially Gabriel García Márquez (562). In *One Hundred Years of Solitude* (562), for example, a character ascends to Heaven while hanging out the laundry. In 1955, the critic Angel Flores identified *A Universal History of Infamy* (573) by Jorge Luis Borges as the origin of magical realism in Latin America.

Andrés Caicedo

1951 – 1977

Luis Andrés Caicedo Estela lived his whole life in Cali, 'the world capital of salsa'. As a teenager, he acted with the Teatro Experimental de Cali, founded the Cineclub de Cali and launched a film magazine, *Ojo al Cine* (*Eye on Cinema*). He began writing short stories at the age of thirteen and by fifteen he had written several award-winning plays. He wrote one novel: *Liveforever*. On the same afternoon that he received the first printed copy, he took an overdose of sleeping pills and died at the age of 25.

Liveforever 1970 – 75, pub. 1977

María del Carmen Huerta is a respectable teenage girl who drops out of high school to pursue her passion for dancing. She embarks on an odyssey around the city of Cali, encountering car park *rumbas* and a concert of 'the kings of salsa', Richie Ray and Bobby Cruz, experimenting with different aspects of the counterculture (526) and seeking meaning amidst a hedonistic whirl of music and debauchery. Though strange and hallucinogenic in places, *¡Que viva la música!* (literally *Long Live Music!*) is determinedly realistic, in opposition to the vogue for magical realism.

2014
trans. Frank Wynne
intro. Juan Gabriel
Vásquez

—

'This book is no longer dedicated to Clarisolcita,' wrote Caicedo in place of a dedication, about a girl he once met in 1972, 'since, when she grew up, she became so much like my heroine that she no longer deserved it.'

Brazil

1968 Modern Classics
● trans. William
L. Grossman, 1952
2021 Penguin Classics
*The Posthumous Memoirs
of Brás Cubas*
trans. Flora Thomson-
DeVeaux, 2020
fwd. Dave Eggers, 2020

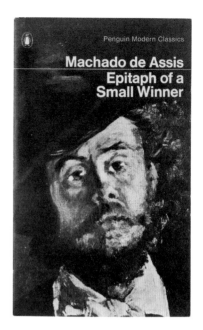

Machado de Assis 1839–1908

Joaquim Maria Machado de Assis was born in Rio de Janeiro,
the son of a house painter and a Portuguese washerwoman.
He was raised by his stepmother, who made sweets for a girls'
school, so he scrounged an education by listening to the girls'
lessons and picking up French from the baker next door. Epileptic,
myopic and stammering, he worked as a typesetter, a journalist
and a public official in the Ministry of Agriculture; but he also wrote
prolifically, producing nine novels and more than 200 short stories,
eventually becoming the most celebrated author in Brazilian literature.
He was the President of the Brazilian Academy of Letters from
its foundation in 1897 until his death. 'If Borges (572) is the author
who made García Márquez (562) possible,' wrote Salman Rushdie,
'then it's no exaggeration to say that Machado is the author who
made Borges possible.'

Epitaph of a Small Winner 1881

Machado spent 1879 convalescing at a health resort, where he dictated
Memórias Póstumas de Brás Cubas to his wife. This eccentric, experimental
novel is narrated from beyond the grave by the dead Brás Cubas, who
dedicates his life story to 'the worm that first gnawed at the cold flesh
of my cadaver'. He evaluates his life, his adulterous affairs and his lack of
children as a series of theoretical profits and losses, finally calculating that
he is 'a small winner'. 'It's a very, very original piece of work,' wrote Woody
Allen. 'It rang a bell in me, in the same way that *The Catcher in the Rye* (499)
did. It was about subject matter that I liked and it was treated with great
wit, great originality and no sentimentality.'

More AFTERLIVES

2015
trans. Richard Zenith

Carlos Drummond de Andrade

1902–1987

Drummond was born in a mining village
in southeastern Brazil. He worked as a
civil servant for most of his life and briefly
edited the Brazilian Communist Party's
newspaper. He was also Brazil's greatest
poet, renowned and loved for his prolific
body of innovative, modernist (11) verse.

Multitudinous Heart
Selected Poems

1930–87

Drummond said that he wrote
poetry in order to 'express sensations
and emotions that troubled my spirit
and caused me anguish'. This selection
spans his near 60-year career, with titles
including 'International Symposium
of Fear', 'Death of the Milkman',
'Sponge Song' and 'Threesome in a Café'.

2015
trans. Katrina Dodson
intro. Benjamin Moser
—
The cover shows a portrait
of Lispector painted in Rome
in 1945 by Giorgio de Chirico;
the jackets of her other works
in Modern Classics also feature
paintings by De Chirico. She cut
a famously glamorous figure:
when the translator Gregory
Rabassa was introduced
to her in the 1960s, he was
'flabbergasted to meet that rare
person who looked like Marlene
Dietrich and wrote like Virginia
Woolf (42)'. Benjamin Moser
is the author of *Why This World:
A Biography of Clarice Lispector*
(2009) and the general editor
of the Penguin Modern
Classics editions of Lispector's
works. In his introduction to
the *Complete Stories*, he calls
her 'the unforgettable Clarice
Lispector: a female Chekhov
on the beaches of Guanabara'.

Clarice Lispector 1920 – 1977

Chaya Pinkhasova Lispector was born in Ukraine, to a Jewish family who fled the Russian Civil War and settled in rural Brazil when she was less than a year old. On arrival, they changed their names and 'Chaya' became 'Clarice'. After her mother died, she moved with her father to Rio de Janeiro, where she studied law, began writing short stories and worked as fashion journalist. The publication of her first novel, *Near to the Wild Heart*, caused a sensation and made her an instant literary celebrity. She married a diplomat in 1944 and they moved around the world, living in Italy, Switzerland, the UK and the USA, before returning to Brazil in 1959. In 1966, she took a sleeping pill and fell asleep with a lit cigarette; the ensuing fire scarred her legs permanently and almost necessitated the amputation of her right hand. It caused her pain for the last ten years of her short life. The novelist Edmund White calls her 'an emblematic twentieth-century artist who belongs in the same pantheon as Kafka (280) and Joyce (8)'.

Complete Stories 1940 – 77

'In painting as in music and literature,' wrote Lispector, 'what is called abstract so often seems to me the figurative of a more delicate and difficult reality, less visible to the naked eye.' This volume collects all 85 of her short stories, from her juvenilia to the unfinished pieces on which she was working when she died. They are stylistically innovative, psychologically scorching tales, with titles such as 'Pig Latin', 'The Crime of the Mathematics Teacher' and 'The Smallest Woman in the World'. When the writer Érico Veríssimo read *Family Ties* (1960), her first major volume of tales, he declared it 'the most important story collection published in this country since Machado de Assis (564)'.

Near to the Wild Heart 1943

Lispector published her first novel when she was 23 and its instant success earned her the nickname 'Hurricane Clarice'. Critics were astounded by her impressionistic style, interior monologues and idiosyncratic vocabulary. Through flashes of memory, the novel reveals an inner portrait of Joana, a young woman recalling a wild childhood, her first attempts at poetry and her unfaithful marriage to Otávio.

2014
trans. Alison Entrekin, 2012
intro. Benjamin Moser, 2012
—
This novel's title and epigraph
come from James Joyce's
*A Portrait of the Artist as a Young
Man* (8): 'He was alone.
He was unheeded, happy, and
near to the wild heart of life.'

2019
trans. Johnny Lorenz
ed. Benjamin Moser
—
Lispector wrote *The Besieged
City* while living in Bern, which
she hated. 'This Switzerland,'
she wrote to her sister,
'is a cemetery of sensations.'

The Chandelier 1946

Lispector's second novel, which she wrote partly in Naples, is the interior monologue of Virginia, recalling her idyllic childhood on Quiet Farm and her formative transition into adulthood. Colm Tóibín calls it 'utterly original and brilliant, haunting and disturbing'.

The Besieged City
1948

As Lucrécia Neves grows up, so does her small town of São Geraldo, which transforms from a backwater into an urban hub. Lucrécia is vain, superficial and beautifully dressed, and the book is peppered with metaphors of sight and surfaces.

2019
trans. Benjamin Moser
& Magdalena Edwards, 2018

MODERN
CLASSICS

'One of the hidden geniuses of the
twentieth century' Colm Tóibín

Clarice Lispector
The Passion According to G.H.

2014
trans. Idra Novey, 2012
intro. Caetano Veloso, 2012
ed. Benjamin Moser, 2012

The Passion According to G.H. is divided into multiple fragmentary
sections. The last sentence of each section becomes the first sentence
of the next. The artwork on the cover is a detail from *The Silent Statue
(Ariadne)* (1913) by Giorgio de Chirico.

← **The Passion According to G.H.**

1964

In Lispector's most famous, most shocking novel, G.H. is a wealthy sculptress from Rio de Janeiro whose maid has recently left her service. Entering the maid's vacated quarters, G.H. discovers 'an entirely clean and vibrant room as in an insane asylum' and sees a cockroach crawling out of the wardrobe. Panicking, she slams the wardrobe door on the insect, but then becomes irresistibly fascinated by the oozing carcass, experiencing an unexpected existential epiphany that encompasses the cosmos and her own identity and leads to her putting the insect's gungy exudate into her own mouth. 'This book is like any other book,' wrote Lispector in her preface. 'But I would be happy if it were only read by people whose souls are already formed.'

A Breath of Life

Pulsations 1974–7, pub. 1978

Lispector's final, unfinished novel was 'written in agony' and pieced together posthumously by her amanuensis Olga Borelli. It consists of a mystical dialogue between a godlike male author and his own literary creation, Angela Pralini, a character from one of Lispector's short stories, 'The Departure of the Train'. The film director Pedro Almodóvar calls it 'a thrilling book'.

2014
trans. Johnny Lorenz, 2012
intro. Olga Borelli, 1978
pref. Pedro Almodóvar
& Benjamin Moser, 2012
ed. Benjamin Moser, 2012

Hour of the Star 1977

Macabéa has moved from rural Alagoas, the district where Lispector lived as a child, to the slums of Rio de Janeiro, where she attempts to make a living as a typist. Though she is ugly, underfed and unloved, within herself she is innocent and free. 'It's an unfinished book because it's still waiting for an answer,' Lispector wrote in the novel's dedication. 'An answer I hope someone in the world can give me. You?'

2021
trans. Stefan Tobler
ed. Benjamin Moser
aftwd. Sheila Heti

Água Viva 1973

The Portuguese title *Água Viva* means both 'living water' and 'jellyfish'. Like a floating invertebrate, Lispector's slim masterpiece has no backbone of plot. It consists of hypnotic confessions about life, time and sleep, intricately composed like a piece of music with recurring themes and patterns, in an attempt to 'capture the present'. The celebrated Brazilian singer-songwriter Cazuza read the book III times.

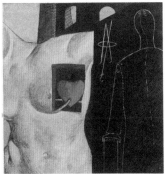

2014
trans. Benjamin Moser, 2011
intro. Colm Tóibín, 2011

An Apprenticeship
or, The Book of Pleasures

1969

Lóri is a lonely primary school teacher in Rio de Janeiro when she meets Ulisses, a professor of philosophy. She yearns for love, but finds herself trapped in her own interior world. This is the novel with which, Lispector said, 'I humanized myself.'

2014
trans. Stefan Tobler, 2012
intro. Benjamin Moser, 2012
—
In composing *Água Viva*, Lispector was assisted by Olga Borelli, a former nun, who became her amanuensis for the last eight years of her life.

Lispector composed this novel on scraps of paper, which she pieced together with the help of her amanuensis Olga Borelli; it was the last novel she published in her lifetime. She included in it a list of alternative titles: 'IT'S ALL MY FAULT, *or* THE HOUR OF THE STAR, *or* LET HER DEAL WITH IT, *or* THE RIGHT TO SCREAM, [*or*] AS FOR THE FUTURE, *or* SINGING THE BLUES, *or* SHE DOESN'T KNOW HOW TO SCREAM, *or* A SENSE OF LOSS, *or* WHISTLING IN THE DARK WIND, *or* I CAN'T DO ANYTHING, *or* ACCOUNT OF THE PRECEDING FACTS, *or* CHEAP TEARJERKER, *or* DISCREET EXIT THROUGH THE BACK DOOR'.

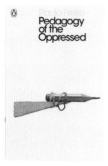

1972 Pelican Books
1990 Penguin Books
2017 Modern Classics
trans. Myra Bergman Ramos,
1970
—
Freire dedicated his book
'to the oppressed, and to
those who suffer with them,
and fight at their side'.

Paulo Freire 1921–1997

Paulo Reglus Neves Freire spent his childhood in poverty, playing street football in northeastern Brazil. He studied law at the University of Recife and took classes in philosophy and the psychology of language. He then became a teacher and campaigned for improved adult literacy, developing a reputation as a revolutionary educational theorist. Following the Brazilian *coup d'état* of 1964, Freire was imprisoned as a traitor. He escaped after 70 days and fled into exile in Chile, where he wrote *Pedagogy of the Oppressed*. Its international success led to appointments at Harvard University and the World Council of Churches. He returned to Brazil in 1980 and joined the Workers' Party in São Paulo.

Pedagogy of the Oppressed
1968

In this landmark work, Freire argues that 'education is freedom'. Inspired by Hegel, Marx and especially Frantz Fanon's *The Wretched of the Earth* (558), he criticizes the traditional educational model, which treats students as passive recipients of knowledge, and advocates instead a 'critical pedagogy': a cooperative teaching style that encourages students to take ownership of their newfound knowledge. It is 'the foremost work on the key democratic task', writes George Monbiot: 'helping people to identify and challenge the sources of their oppression'.

Raduan Nassar b. 1935

Nassar was born on a small Brazilian farm, the son of a Lebanese immigrant family. He studied law and philosophy at the University of São Paulo, before working as a journalist and founding a newspaper with his brothers. He is best known for his two acclaimed novellas, *Ancient Tillage* and *A Cup of Rage*. In 1984, however, Nassar gave up writing and dedicated himself to livestock farming. In 2011, he donated his farm to the agricultural departments of the Federal University of São Carlos and retired to a smaller farmstead. In 2016, he won the Camões Prize, the most prestigious award for writers of Portuguese.

2015
trans. K. C. S. Sotelino

More FARMERS

The Worm Forgives the Plough
by John Stewart Collis   19

Tarry Flynn
by Patrick Kavanagh   15

The Octopus
by Frank Norris   406

Virgin Soil Upturned
by Mikhail Sholokhov   312

The Tree of Man
by Patrick White   382

Ancient Tillage 1975

In this lyrical novella, André is a boy growing up on a small Brazilian farm. He loves the earth and the wheat, but he dreads his pious father and hates himself for the feelings he has towards his sister Ana.

A Cup of Rage 1978

Two lovers – one a young female journalist, the other an older landowner – spend the night together on the man's isolated farm. But the next day they attack each other with insults as their erotic adventure transforms into a vicious power game. It is 'a savagely short novel of immeasurable ambition and violent beauty', writes the Mexican novelist Juan Pablo Villalobos. 'This is the language of genius.'

2015
trans. Stefan Tobler

Chile

Pablo Neruda 1904–1973

'I have never thought of my life as divided between poetry and politics,' wrote Ricardo Eliécer Neftalí Reyes Basoalto. He grew up in the southern town of Temuco, in the 'wild west' of Chile, and at fourteen he became the literary editor of a local newspaper, *La Mañana* (*The Morning*). He published his first book of poetry at seventeen, under the pseudonym 'Pablo Neruda', and achieved widespread recognition for *Twenty Love Poems and a Song of Despair*, which remains his most popular collection. For 20 years, he wrote poetry while serving as Chilean consul in Rangoon, Colombo, Batavia, Singapore, Buenos Aires, Barcelona, Madrid, Paris and Mexico City. Following the death of Federico García Lorca (230) in the Spanish Civil War, however, he joined the Chilean Communist Party and dedicated himself to writing poetry for the benefit of the people in his 'thin country'. From 1970, he served as the Chilean ambassador to Paris, on behalf of the socialist administration of President Salvador Allende, and won the Nobel Prize for Literature (576) in 1971. He died in 1973, under mysterious circumstances, shortly after Allende was ousted in a coup by General Augusto Pinochet. Gabriel García Márquez (562) called Neruda 'the greatest poet of the twentieth century, in any language'.

1975 Penguin Poets
1992 Twentieth-Century Classics
• ed. Nathaniel Tarn, 1975
trans. Anthony Kerrigan et al., 1970–75
intro. Jean Franco, 1975
—
The *Selected Poems* is a parallel-text edition.

1976 Penguin Poets
1993 Twentieth-Century Classics
• trans. W. S. Merwin, 1969

Vanguardia

The *vanguardia* was a Latin American movement in arts and literature which reflected contemporary European avant-garde movements such as Surrealism (176) and which remained highly influential throughout the 20th century. One of the first *vanguardia* poets was the Nicaraguan José Coronel Urtecho; other key figures include Octavio Paz (561), Gabriela Mistral – the first Latin American author to win the Nobel Prize for Literature (576) – Pablo Neruda and Jorge Luis Borges (572). Urtecho's 1931 *vanguardia* manifesto stated the movement's aim to 'initiate a struggle to get the public attention through artistic expressions, intellectual scandal, and aggressive criticism'.

Poems 1924–67

Neruda believed that poetry should achieve a balance 'between solitude and solidarity, between feeling and action, between intimacy of one's self, the intimacy of mankind, and the revelation of nature'. His popular early collection *Twenty Love Poems and a Song of Despair* (1924) is a sensuous celebration of nature, the universe and erotic love. The masterpiece of his later years is *Canto General* (1950), an epic verse history of Latin America, tracing the landscape of the continent and its turbulent politics; it includes the sequence *The Heights of Machu Picchu*.

Memoirs 1972–3, pub. 1974

'In these memoirs or recollections there are gaps here and there, and sometimes they are also forgetful, because life is like that,' wrote Neruda. 'Intervals of dreaming help us to stand up under days of work. Many of the things I remember have blurred as I recalled them, they have crumbled to dust, like irreparably shattered glass. Perhaps I didn't just live in my self, perhaps I lived the lives of others.' He recalls his childhood, his vocation for politics as well as poetry, his years of self-exile and his meetings with figures such as Federico García Lorca (230), M. K. Gandhi (340), Fidel Castro and Salvador Allende.

1978 Penguin Books
1989 Twentieth-Century Classics
• trans. Hardie St. Martin, 1977

Uruguay

Mario Benedetti 1920–2009

Mario Orlando Hamlet Hardy Brenno Benedetti Farrugia was a leading member of the Generación del 45. He was a journalist, a novelist and a poet, and he translated Kafka (280). He wrote for the weekly newspaper *Marcha* for almost 30 years, serving as its literary editor for 20. When the military government forcibly closed the paper in 1973, however, he went into exile in Argentina, Peru, Cuba and Spain, only returning to Uruguay in 1985. In one of his last poems, he wrote, 'When I'm buried / don't forget to put a Biro in my coffin.'

Who Among Us? 1953

Eleven years into a creaking marriage, Miguel and Alicia allow their old friend Lucas back into their lives, resurrecting a teenage love triangle. The story is told through Miguel's diary entries, a letter written to Alicia and a short story by Lucas. 'The novel is a jewel,' said the reviewer in the *Huffington Post*, '[…] one of those books that enter the soul, which it is impossible not to be conquered by. It is a masterpiece like few others.'

The Truce
The Diary of Martín Santomé 1960

When Martín Santomé, a widowed, 49-year-old accountant, falls unexpectedly and passionately in love with Laura Avellaneda, the joy he experiences feels like a fleeting 'truce' with the hardships of his life. In this novel, 'all the emotions of your life are identified, named and renamed', says the writer Roberto Saviano.

> ### Generación del 45
>
> The Generación del 45 was an intellectual and literary movement among Uruguayan writers who had emerged shortly after the Second World War, including Mario Benedetti and Juan Carlos Onetti, who won the Uruguay National Literature Prize in 1962. Onetti left Uruguay in 1974 after he had been incarcerated for six months in a mental institution by the authoritarian regime of President Juan María Bordaberry for having awarded a literary prize to a controversial short story.

2019 trans. Nick Caistor

2015 trans. Harry Morales

Springtime in a Broken Mirror 1982

Santiago is a political prisoner in the Uruguayan capital, Montevideo, after a brutal military coup. We piece together his story through splintered glimpses of his cell in Libertad jail, and of the lives of his family as they adjust to the terrors and temptations of exile in a distant country.

More PRISONS

Falconer
by John Cheever   544

Miracle of the Rose
by Jean Genet   190

Darkness at Noon
by Arthur Koestler   278

Invitation to a Beheading
by Vladimir Nabokov   307

The Tunnel
by Ernesto Sábato   575

2019
trans. Nick Caistor,
2018

Eduardo Galeano 1940–2015

Galeano was a journalist who wrote for several national Uruguayan newspapers and magazines. His first book, *Open Veins of Latin America* (1971), was a passionate history and social analysis of the region. In 1973, he was briefly imprisoned during the country's military coup, after which he fled into exile. He lived in Argentina and Spain and wrote novels, the best known of which is his *Memory of Fire* trilogy (1982–6).

Football in Sun and Shadow
1995, rev. 2013

'Like all Uruguayan children, I wanted to be a football player,' wrote Galeano at the start of this passionate history of the sport. He tells tales of drama, heartbreak, tragedy, spectacle and the seething emotions of the 'great pagan mass' in the stands. The book is dedicated to 'the children who once upon a time, years ago, crossed my path on Calella de la Costa. They had been playing football and were singing: We lost, we won, either way we had fun.' The *Financial Times* calls it 'sport's answer to *One Hundred Years of Solitude* (562).'

2018
trans. Mark Fried,
1997–2013

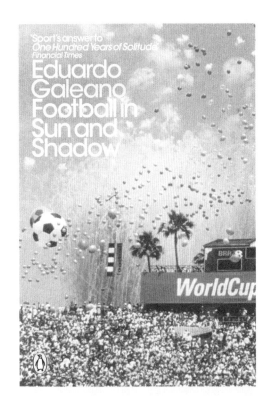

Argentina

Jorge Luis Borges 1899–1986

Jorge Francisco Isidoro Luis Borges Acevedo, known as 'Georgie' to his family, was born in Buenos Aires, into a home with an extensive library. At the age of nine, he translated Oscar Wilde's story 'The Happy Prince' (3) into Spanish, and in 1914 the family moved to Europe for seven years, where he immersed himself in English literature, German philosophy and Spanish ultraist (573) poetry. Returning to Argentina, Borges began contributing poems and essays to avant-garde journals, including *Martín Fierro* and *Sur*. He started publishing stories in the 1930s, while also translating Rudyard Kipling (22), Virginia Woolf (42), André Gide (164), Hermann Hesse (247) and Franz Kafka (280), lecturing on Old English literature and working as a municipal librarian. In 1946, when the authoritarian Juan Perón became president, the subversive Borges was 'promoted' to poultry inspector at the municipal wholesale market, a deliberate snub. When Perón fell in 1955, however, Borges was appointed director of the Argentine National Library, a post he held for 20 years, despite the 'splendid irony' that he went blind soon afterwards, surrounded by books he would never read with his own eyes. Apart from a short and unsuccessful first marriage, Borges lived with his mother for most of his life. She cared for him after he went blind and acted as his secretary until she died at the age of 99; after that he travelled extensively with his assistant, María Kodama, whom he married a few months before his death. He gained international recognition only after winning the Prix Formentor jointly with Samuel Beckett (20) in 1961. He won the Jerusalem Prize in 1971 and the Cervantes Prize in 1980, but never the Nobel Prize for Literature (576). 'Not granting me the Nobel Prize has become a Scandinavian tradition,' he quipped; 'since I was born they have not been granting it to me.'

Borges in Penguin

One of the first appearances of Borges in English was Anthony Boucher's 1948 translation of 'The Garden of Forking Paths' (573), which was published in *Ellery Queen's Mystery Magazine* in the USA. But it was not until 1970 that Borges first appeared in Penguin, in the landmark anthology *Labyrinths* (574), edited by Donald A. Yates and James E. Irby. Later in the 1970s, Borges collaborated with the American translator Norman Thomas di Giovanni on a more complete set of English translations, many of which were published by Penguin and found their way into Penguin Modern Classics a few years later. In a somewhat controversial manoeuvre in the 1990s, however, Borges's widow María Kodama rescinded the rights to the di Giovanni editions and commissioned new translations of his fiction from the academic Andrew Hurley. Penguin published these new translations as a single hardback entitled *Collected Fictions* in 1998, and they were later reintroduced separately to Penguin Modern Classics.

The Total Library
Non-Fiction 1922–86

This anthology draws together more than six decades of Borges's non-fiction writing, from juvenilia and 'capsule biographies' written for the women's magazine *El Hogar* (*Home*), to film reviews, philosophical essays, commentaries on Nazi propaganda, extempore lectures delivered after he went blind, and literary criticism on authors such as Lady Murasaki, Dante, H. G. Wells (26), James Joyce (8) and William Faulkner (433). 'Like the best fiction, his essays tantalize and probe,' writes the author Geoff Dyer. 'They open up a textual and metaphysical world whose possibilities are as limitless as those of poetry.'

2001
ed. Eliot Weinberger, 1999
trans. Esther Allen,
Suzanne Jill Levine
& Eliot Weinberger, 1999

Jorge Luis Borges The Total Library
Non-Fiction 1922-1986

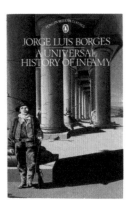

A Universal History of Infamy

1933–4, pub. 1935, rev. 1954

These fictionalized sketches of historical criminals were originally written for the newspaper *Crítica*. They are portraits of gunslingers, gentlemanly scoundrels, evil wizards and false prophets, including 'The Widow Ching, Lady Pirate' and 'The Masked Dyer, Hakim of Merv'. Borges later described them as 'the irresponsible game of a shy young man who dared not write stories'. The volume does, however, include his first published work of fiction: a 1933 story called 'Streetcorner Man', about a duel between two knife-fighters.

1975 Penguin Books
1985 Modern Classics
• trans. Norman Thomas di Giovanni, 1972
2001 Modern Classics
A Universal History of Iniquity
trans. Andrew Hurley, 1998

Selected Poems 1923–85

Borges began his literary career by writing verse and he continued throughout his life, especially once he was blind, after which he would carefully compose poems in his mind and dictate them whole. The Penguin parallel text editions contain selections from all his major poetry collections, including *The Maker* (1960), *The Self and Other* (1964), *In Praise of Darkness* (1969) and *The Gold of the Tigers* (1972).

1985 Modern Classics
• trans. Norman Thomas di Giovanni, 1972
2000 Modern Classics
ed. Alexander Coleman, 1999
trans. María Kodama et al., 1999

2000
trans. Andrew Hurley, 1998
—
'Like most overnight successes,' writes Hurley, 'this one was a long time coming.' *Ficciones* reprinted an earlier collection of eight stories, *The Garden of Forking Paths* (1941), adding six further stories in a new section called *Artifices*. Nearly all of these fourteen tales had been published previously in magazines. Borges expanded *Artifices* with another three new stories in the revised 1956 edition of *Ficciones*, and it was this version that was first translated into English by Anthony Kerrigan in 1962.

Fictions 1936–44, pub. 1941–44, rev. 1956

'I love his work,' wrote Italo Calvino (218), 'because every one of his pieces contains a model of the universe or an attribute of the universe.' The collection *Ficciones* (1944) was an overnight success for Borges, announcing a prose style that blurred fiction and reality, blended philosophy with humour and played 'games with infinity'. His 'fictions' are presented as detective stories, biographies or fragments of literary criticism, but in a few pages they manage to expand the mind, explode reality and embrace the cosmos. Two of the most famous stories are 'The Garden of Forking Paths', in which Borges invented the concept of parallel universes, and 'The Library of Babel', in which he imagines the universe as an infinitely cyclical library of hexagonal rooms. 'He has lifted fiction away from the flat earth where most of our novels and short stories still take place,' declared John Updike (514).

Ultraísmo

This Spanish avant-garde literary movement began in 1919, in Madrid's Café Colonial. Led by the poet Guillermo de Torre, it was a reaction against *modernismo*, the dominant mode of Spanish poetry since the late 19th century. It had similarities to Surrealism (176), Expressionism (269) and Imagism (61), aiming to liberate poetry from formal and logical structures and relying instead on evocative images, startling metaphors and references drawn from the modern world. Jorge Luis Borges (572) brought the movement to Argentina, where he summarized its goals as:

1. Reduction of the lyric element to its primordial element, metaphor.

2. Deletion of useless middle sentences, linking particles and adjectives.

3. Avoidance of ornamental artefacts, confessionalism, circumstantiation, preaching and far-fetched nebulosity.

4. Synthesis of two or more images into one, thus widening its suggestiveness.

1970
trans. Donald A. Yates et al.,
1956–62
ed. Donald A. Yates
& James E. Irby, 1962
pref. André Maurois, 1962
—

'I first read Jorge Luis Borges'
Labyrinths in an armchair
upholstered with a smooth
lettuce-green brocade,
patterned with leaves that were
themselves not unlike lettuce,'
recalls the novelist William
Gibson. '[…] I sat, changed,
in the green chair, and regarded
a different world, one whose
underpinnings had been
revealed to be at once infinitely
more mysterious and far
more interesting than I could
previously have imagined.
When I left that room, I took
Borges with me, and my life has
been better for it, much better.'

Labyrinths
Selected Stories and Other Writings
1939–59, pub. 1962

In 1962, two volumes appeared in English that
helped to popularize Borges in the anglophone world:
Anthony Kerrigan's translation of *Fictions* (573) and
this anthology, *Labyrinths*, a title chosen by Borges.
Labyrinths are a recurring motif for Borges, representing
both the complexity of the universe and the intricacies
of the human mind. This collection gathers stories
from *Fictions* and *The Aleph*, as well as a sprinkling
of *essays* (572) and prose parables from *The Maker*.
'He creates, outside time and space, imaginary and
symbolic worlds,' wrote André Maurois in his preface.
'[…] He is akin to Kafka (280), Poe, sometimes to
Henry James (397) and Wells (26), always to Valéry
by the abrupt projection of his paradoxes in what
has been called "his private metaphysics".'

The Aleph
Including the Prose Fictions from *The Maker*
1944–9, pub. 1949, rev. 1952

The Aleph (1949) is a further collection of paradoxical, philosophical
stories, including tales of an unrepentant Nazi, a demented mythological
beast, and a shape-shifting obsession. The title story is about a point
in space, located in the basement of a house in Buenos Aires, which
contains all other spaces at once. This edition also includes the prose
pieces from *El Hacedor* (*The Maker*), a 1960 collection of haunting vignettes,
poems and literary sketches, which Borges wrote soon after losing his
sight. Some critics consider *The Maker* to be Borges's masterpiece. 'Of all
the books I have delivered to the printer,' Borges said of it, 'none, I think,
is as personal as this unruly jumble, this florilegium.'

2000
trans. Andrew Hurley,
1998
—

Most of the poems from
The Maker are included
in the current Modern
Classics edition of the
Selected Poems (573).
The Maker has also been
translated into English
as *Dreamtigers*.

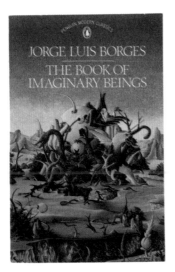

1974 Penguin Books
1987 Modern Classics
● trans. Norman Thomas
di Giovanni, 1969
—

The original 1957 edition
contained 82 entries.
Borges and Guerrero added
34 new pieces for the revised
1967 edition, and when they
collaborated with the American
translator Norman Thomas
di Giovanni, they altered some
entries and added new ones,
bringing the total to 120.
*The Book of Imaginary
Beings* is not meant to be
read straight through,' wrote
Borges; 'rather, we should
like the reader to dip into these
pages at random, just as one
plays with the shifting patterns
of a kaleidoscope.'

The Book of Imaginary Beings
with Margarita Guerrero 1957, rev. 1967–9

Borges compiled this inventory of fabulous mythological
and literary creatures with his friend Margarita Guerrero.
It includes entries on Burak, Fastitocalon, Humbaba,
Kujata and the Squonk. 'There is a kind of lazy pleasure
in useless and out-of-the-way erudition,' Borges wrote.
'The compilation and translation of this volume have
given us a great deal of such pleasure; we hope the reader
will share something of the fun we felt when ransacking
the bookshelves of our friends and the mazelike vaults
of the Biblioteca Nacional in search of old authors
and abstruse references.'

Doctor Brodie's Report 1966–70, pub. 1970

At the age of 70, after a gap of 20 years, Borges returned to writing short stories. In this collection he revisits the brutality, bloodshed and violence of A Universal History of Infamy (573), incorporating ideas of fate, free will and memory. 'I have done my best – I don't know with what success – to write straightforward stories,' said Borges in his preface. 'I do not dare state that they are simple; there isn't anywhere on earth a single page or a single word that is, since each thing implies the universe.'

1977 Penguin Books
1985 Modern Classics
● trans. Norman Thomas di Giovanni, 1972
2000 Modern Classics
Brodie's Report
trans. Andrew Hurley, 1998
—
Andrew Hurley's edition also includes the prose fiction from *In Praise of Darkness* (573).

1979 Penguin Books
1986 Modern Classics
● trans. Norman Thomas di Giovanni, 1977
2001 Modern Classics
with Shakespeare's Memory
trans. Andrew Hurley, 1998
—
The 1986 edition does not include *Shakespeare's Memory*, but it does incorporate poems (573) selected from *The Gold of the Tigers* (1972) and *The Unending Rose* (1975) and translated by Alastair Reid.

The Book of Sand 1971–5, pub. 1975

The title story in *The Book of Sand* describes a book with an infinite number of infinitely thin pages. The collection also includes 'The Congress', which, at nineteen pages, is Borges's longest single work. 'If of all my stories I had to save one,' he once said, 'I would probably save "The Congress".' The current Modern Classics (ix) edition also includes *Shakespeare's Memory* (1983), Borges's final story collection, a sequence of four mysterious parables; the title story, the last he ever wrote, was inspired by a dream.

Ernesto Sábato 1911–2011

After studying physics, Sábato moved to Paris and worked on atomic radiation at the Curie Institute. 'I buried myself with electrometers and graduated cylinders during the morning,' he recalled, 'and spent the nights in bars, with the delirious surrealists (176).' After the Second World War he abandoned science, returning to Argentina and dedicating himself to painting and writing. He wrote three novels and won the Cervantes Prize in 1984. He also led the commission investigating the thousands of political 'disappearances' and extrajudicial executions that occurred during the Argentinian Dirty War. When Sábato died two months before his 100th birthday, *El País* called him the 'last classic writer in Argentine literature'.

The Tunnel 1948

In his prison cell, the deranged painter Juan Pablo Castel recalls his obsession with María Iribarne, which ultimately led to her murder. This dark, existential novel was first published in the avant-garde literary journal Sur. Albert Camus (181) commissioned a translation for the French publisher Gallimard, and it was highly praised by Thomas Mann (245) and Graham Greene (88).

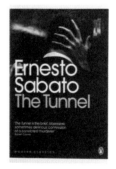

2011
trans. Margaret Sayers Peden, 1988
intro. Colm Tóibín, 2011

On Heroes and Tombs 1961

This strange novel tells the story of 19-year-old Martín, who falls in love with the beautiful but unbalanced Alejandra Vidal Olmos, whose father Fernando is a criminal lunatic. The narrative is interspersed with a biography of Juan Lavalle, the historical 19th-century Argentine military hero; it also includes a nightmarish 'Report on the Blind', which details Fernando's obsession with, and fear of, losing his sight. Salman Rushdie has described the book as 'a rich motherlode of imagery, language and haunting scenes'.

2017
trans. Helen R. Lane, 1981
intro. David William Foster, 1981

For thirteen years after the publication of *The Tunnel*, 'I continued to explore that dark labyrinth that leads to the central secret of our life,' Sábato wrote, '[...] until I grew discouraged at the poor results and ended up destroying the majority of my manuscripts.' One of the few to escape the flames was *On Heroes and Tombs*. It is now considered Sábato's masterpiece.

The Nobel Prize

Alfred Nobel, the Swedish inventor of dynamite, read his own obituary in 1888, in which he was described as 'the merchant of death'. Concerned about his posthumous reputation, he immediately rewrote his will, bequeathing his substantial fortune to the establishment of five international prizes in the fields of Physics, Chemistry, Physiology (or Medicine), Literature and Peace, to be awarded annually to individuals or organizations that conferred the 'greatest benefit on mankind'.

Since 1901, the Nobel Prize for Literature has become the world's most esteemed literary prize, and many of the 20th and 21st centuries' greatest authors have travelled to Stockholm to receive the award. There have been 117 literature laureates so far, listed here, 48 of whom have become Penguin Modern Classics authors. The series also includes winners of the Peace Prize – Martin Luther King, Jr. (502), Nelson Mandela (372) and Elie Wiesel (325) – and one physics laureate, Werner Heisenberg (260).

The literature prize is awarded to living authors only, so there have been several notable omissions. *The Economist* once said that Jorge Luis Borges (572) was 'probably the greatest twentieth-century author never to win the Nobel Prize'; other eminent non-winners include Chinua Achebe (359), Karen Blixen (240), Italo Calvino (218), F. Scott Fitzgerald (422), Graham Greene (88), James Joyce (8), Vladimir Nabokov (304), Arthur Miller (486), Ezra Pound (11), Marcel Proust (166) and John Updike (514).

Over the years, there have been a few fictional winners, such as Andrew Craig in Irving Wallace's *The Prize* (1962), John Updike's Henry Bech (515) and Joe Castleman in Meg Wolitzer's *The Wife* (2003). Bookmakers' predictions for future winners include Adonis (334), Maryse Condé (558), Don DeLillo (537), Nuruddin Farah (366), Javier Marías (233) and Ngũgĩ wa Thiong'o (365).

1901	Sully Prudhomme	France
1902	Theodor Mommsen	Germany
1903	Bjørnstjerne Bjørnson	Norway
1904	Frédéric Mistral	France
1904	José Echegaray	Spain
1905	Henryk Sienkiewicz	Poland
1906	Giosuè Carducci	Italy
1907	Rudyard Kipling (22)	Britain
1908	Rudolf Christoph Eucken	Germany
1909	Selma Lagerlöf*	Sweden
1910	Paul von Heyse	Germany
1911	Maurice Maeterlinck	Belgium
1912	Gerhart Hauptmann	Germany
1913	Rabindranath Tagore (337)	India
1915	Romain Rolland	France
1916	Verner von Heidenstam	Sweden
1917	Karl Adolph Gjellerup	Denmark
1917	Henrik Pontoppidan	Denmark
1919	Carl Spitteler	Switzerland
1920	Knut Hamsun†	Norway
1921	Anatole France (173)	France
1922	Jacinto Benavente	Spain
1923	W. B. Yeats (4)	Ireland
1924	Władysław Reymont*	Poland
1925	George Bernard Shaw (4)	Ireland
1926	Grazia Deledda	Italy
1927	Henri Bergson	France
1928	Sigrid Undset†	Norway
1929	Thomas Mann (245)	Germany
1930	Sinclair Lewis (421)	USA
1931	Erik Axel Karlfeldt	Sweden
1932	John Galsworthy (47)	Britain
1933	Ivan Bunin (304)	Russia
1934	Luigi Pirandello (215)	Italy
1936	Eugene O'Neill (415)	USA
1937	Roger Martin du Gard	France
1938	Pearl S. Buck	USA
1939	Frans Eemil Sillanpää	Finland
1944	Johannes Vilhelm Jensen	Denmark
1945	Gabriela Mistral	Chile
1946	Hermann Hesse (247)	Germany
1947	André Gide (164)	France
1948	T. S. Eliot†	USA
1949	William Faulkner (433)	USA

1950	Bertrand Russell	Britain		1992	Derek Walcott	St Lucia
1951	Pär Lagerkvist	Sweden		1993	Toni Morrison	USA
1952	François Mauriac (174)	France		1994	Kenzaburo Oe	Japan
1953	Winston Churchill*	Britain		1995	Seamus Heaney	Ireland
1954	Ernest Hemingway (428)	USA		1996	Wisława Szymborska	Poland
1955	Halldór Laxness	Iceland		1997	Dario Fo	Italy
1956	Juan Ramón Jiménez	Spain		1998	José Saramago	Portugal
1957	Albert Camus (181)	France		1999	Günter Grass	Germany
1958	Boris Pasternak (302)	Russia		2000	Gao Xingjian	China and France
1959	Salvatore Quasimodo	Italy		2001	V. S. Naipaul (555)	Britain
1960	Saint-John Perse	Guadeloupe and France		2002	Imre Kertész	Hungary
1961	Ivo Andrić	Yugoslavia		2003	J. M. Coetzee	South Africa
1962	John Steinbeck (440)	USA		2004	Elfriede Jelinek	Austria
1963	George Seferis	Greece		2005	Harold Pinter	Britain
1964	Jean-Paul Sartre (185)	France		2006	Orhan Pamuk	Turkey
1965	Mikhail Sholokhov (312)	Russia		2007	Doris Lessing	Zimbabwe and Britain
1966	S. Y. Agnon (274)	Austria		2008	J. M. G. Le Clézio (199)	France
	Nelly Sachs	Germany and Sweden		2009	Herta Müller	Romania and Germany
1967	Miguel Ángel Asturias (562)	Guatemala		2010	Mario Vargas Llosa	Peru
1968	Yasunari Kawabata (348)	Japan		2011	Tomas Tranströmer (239)	Sweden
1969	Samuel Beckett (20)	Ireland		2012	Mo Yan	China
1970	Aleksandr Solzhenitsyn (314)	Russia		2013	Alice Munro	Canada
1971	Pablo Neruda (569)	Chile		2014	Patrick Modiano (200)	France
1972	Heinrich Böll†	Germany		2015	Svetlana Alexievich (320)	Belarus
1973	Patrick White (382)	Australia		2016	Bob Dylan	USA
1974	Eyvind Johnson	Sweden		2017	Kazuo Ishiguro	Britain
	Harry Martinson	Sweden		2018	Olga Tokarczuk	Poland
1975	Eugenio Montale (215)	Italy		2019	Peter Handke (277)	Austria
1976	Saul Bellow (477)	USA		2020	Louise Glück‡	USA
1977	Vicente Aleixandre	Spain				
1978	Isaac Bashevis Singer (288)	Poland				
1979	Odysseus Elytis	Greece				
1980	Czesław Miłosz (287)	Poland				
1981	Elias Canetti (328)	Bulgaria				
1982	Gabriel García Márquez (562)	Colombia				
1983	William Golding (131)	Britain				
1984	Jaroslav Seifert	Czechoslovakia				
1985	Claude Simon	France				
1986	Wole Soyinka	Nigeria				
1987	Joseph Brodsky (316)	Russia				
1988	Naguib Mahfouz	Egypt				
1989	Camilo José Cela	Spain				
1990	Octavio Paz (561)	Mexico				
1991	Nadine Gordimer	South Africa				

No prizes were awarded in 1914, 1918, 1935 or between 1940 and 1943. Jean-Paul Sartre (185) declined the award, as did Boris Pasternak (302), who was forced to do so by the Soviet government, but the Swedish Academy considers both of them to be laureates nonetheless. In 2018, following a corruption scandal, the Academy postponed its announcement of that year's winner (Olga Tokarczuk) until 2019. An 'alternative Nobel Prize' was crowd-funded independently in 2018 and awarded to the Guadeloupean novelist Maryse Condé (558).

* Authors published – or soon to be published – in Penguin Classics, but not in Penguin Modern Classics.

† Available at some point in Penguin Modern Classics, but never in the UK.

‡ Forthcoming in Penguin Modern Classics.

Timeline

This is a list of the titles in this book, organized by original publication date.

1879

– *The Diary of Mademoiselle D'Arvers*
   by Toru Dutt† 337

1880

– *Washington Square* by Henry James 398

1881

– *Epitaph of a Small Winner*
   by Machado de Assis 564
– *The Portrait of a Lady*
   by Henry James 398

1883

– *The Story of an African Farm*
   by Olive Schreiner 368
– *Little Novels of Sicily*
   by Giovanni Verga 213

1889

– *Mastro-Don Gesualdo*
   by Giovanni Verga 213

1890

– *The Tragic Muse* by Henry James 399
– *The Picture of Dorian Gray*
   by Oscar Wilde 3

1891

– *The Light That Failed*
   by Rudyard Kipling 23
– *John Sherman* by W. B. Yeats 5

1892

– *The Diary of a Nobody*
   by George & Weedon Grossmith 25
– *Barrack-Room Ballads*
   by Rudyard Kipling 22
– *A Life* by Italo Svevo 214
– *The Countess Cathleen* by W. B. Yeats 6

1895

– *Almayer's Folly* by Joseph Conrad 28
– *Studies in Hysteria* by Sigmund Freud
   & Joseph Breuer 265
– *The Second Jungle Book*
   by Rudyard Kipling 23
– *The Time Machine* by H. G. Wells 26

1896

– *An Outcast of the Islands*
   by Joseph Conrad 28
– *A Shropshire Lad* by A. E. Housman 31
– *The Spoils of Poynton*
   by Henry James 399
– *The Island of Doctor Moreau*
   by H. G. Wells 26

1897

– *Fruits of the Earth* by André Gide 164
– *What Maisie Knew* by Henry James 399
– *Liza of Lambeth*
   by W. Somerset Maugham 32
– *The Invisible Man* by H. G. Wells 26

1898

– *Tales of Unrest* by Joseph Conrad 28
– *The Turn of the Screw*
   by Henry James 397
– *The Day's Work* by Rudyard Kipling 23
– *As a Man Grows Older* by Italo Svevo 214
– *The War of the Worlds* by H. G. Wells 22

1903

– *The Riddle of the Sands*
   by Erskine Childers 7
– *Claudine and Annie* by Colette 170
– *The Souls of Black Folk*
   by W. E. B. Du Bois 408
– *The Ambassadors* by Henry James 400
– *The Call of the Wild* by Jack London 405
– *Tonio Kröger* by Thomas Mann 245
– *Tristan* by Thomas Mann 245
– *The Pit* by Frank Norris† 406

1904

– *The Napoleon of Notting Hill*
   by G. K. Chesterton 41
– *Nostromo* by Joseph Conrad 29
– *Cabbages and Kings* by O. Henry 409
– *Peter Camenzind* by Hermann Hesse 247
– *The Golden Bowl* by Henry James 400
– *Ghost Stories of an Antiquary*
   by M. R. James 40
– *Traffics and Discoveries* by Rudyard
   Kipling 24
– *The Sea-Wolf* by Jack London 405
– *The Merry-Go-Round* by W. Somerset
   Maugham 32
– *Hadrian the Seventh* by Fr. Rolfe 40

1905

– *The Club of Queer Trades*
   by G. K. Chesterton 41
– *Where Angels Fear to Tread*
   by E. M. Forster 38
– *The Joke and Its Relation to the
   Unconscious* by Sigmund Freud 266
– *Three Essays on Sexual Theory*
   by Sigmund Freud 266
– *The Prodigy* by Hermann Hesse 248
– *The Jungle* by Upton Sinclair 409
– *The Little Demon* by Fyodor Sologub 299
– *The House of Mirth*
   by Edith Wharton 401

1906

– *A Woman* by Sibilla Aleramo 215
– *The Mirror of the Sea*
   by Joseph Conrad 29
– *The Fifth Queen* by Ford Madox Ford 46
– *The Man of Property*
   by John Galsworthy 47
– *Puck of Pook's Hill*
   by Rudyard Kipling 24
– *White Fang* by Jack London 405
– *Traveller to the East*
   by Thomas Mofolo 368
– *The Confusions of Young Torless*
   by Robert Musil 270
– *Love Among the Chickens*
   by P. G. Wodehouse 48

1911

– *Zuleika Dobson* by Max Beerbohm 60
– *The Card* by Arnold Bennett 37
– *The Devil's Dictionary*
   by Ambrose Bierce 411
– *The Secret Garden*
   by Frances Hodgson Burnett 60
– *The Innocence of Father Brown*
   by G. K. Chesterton 41
– *Under Western Eyes*
   by Joseph Conrad 30
– *Jennie Gerhardt* by Theodore Dreiser 407
– *Memories and Impressions*
   by Ford Madox Ford 46

– *The Celestial Omnibus* by E. M. Forster 38
– *The Schreber Case* by Sigmund Freud 267
– *Isabelle* by André Gide 165
– *The Outcry* by Henry James 400
– *The White Peacock*
   by D. H. Lawrence 51
– *In a German Pension*
   by Katherine Mansfield 388
– *The Chronicles of Clovis* by Saki 35
– *The New Machiavelli* by H. G. Wells 27
– *Ethan Frome* by Edith Wharton 401

1912

– *The Promised Land* by Mary Antin 319
– *A Personal Record*
   by Joseph Conrad 29
– *'Twixt Land and Sea*
   by Joseph Conrad 30
– *The Gods Will Have Blood*
   by Anatole France 173
– *Grania* by Lady Gregory 6
– *Riders of the Purple Sage*
   by Zane Grey 411
– *The Autobiography of an Ex-Colored Man*
   by James Weldon Johnson 412
– *The Trespasser* by D. H. Lawrence 51
– *Death in Venice* by Thomas Mann 245
– *The Unbearable Bassington* by Saki 35
– *The Reef* by Edith Wharton 403

1913

– *Le Grand Meaulnes* by Alain-Fournier 173
– *Petersburg* by Andrei Bely 302
– *O Pioneers!* by Willa Cather 414
– *The Captive* by Colette 171
– *Chance* by Joseph Conrad 30
– *Villa des Roses* by Willem Elsschot 201
– *Totem and Taboo* by Sigmund Freud 267
– *A Boy's Will* by Robert Frost 415
– *My Childhood* by Maxim Gorky 300
– *Sons and Lovers* by D. H. Lawrence 51
– *Stone* by Osip Mandelshtam 301
– *The Way by Swann's*
   by Marcel Proust 169
– *When William Came* by Saki 35
– *Mother and Son* by Arthur Schnitzler 270
– *Unconventional Reminiscences*
   by William Scully 370
– *The Custom of the Country*
   by Edith Wharton 403

† Posthumous publication.

1914

- The Vatican Cellars by André Gide 165
- Dubliners by James Joyce 8
- The Prussian Officer and Other Stories
  by D. H. Lawrence 50
- The Widowing of Mrs Holroyd
  by D. H. Lawrence 51
- Sinister Street
  by Compton Mackenzie 61
- The Ragged Trousered Philanthropists
  by Robert Tressell† 12

1915

- The Song of the Lark by Willa Cather 414
- Victory by Joseph Conrad 31
- Within the Tides by Joseph Conrad 30
- The Good Soldier
  by Ford Madox Ford 46
- Metamorphosis by Franz Kafka 280
- The Rainbow by D. H. Lawrence 52
- Of Human Bondage
  by W. Somerset Maugham 33
- The Voyage Out by Virginia Woolf 42

1916

- Under Fire by Henri Barbusse 174
- Greenmantle by John Buchan 62
- My Apprenticeship by Maxim Gorky 300
- A Portrait of the Artist as a Young Man
  by James Joyce 8
- You Know Me Al by Ring Lardner 416
- Twilight in Italy by D. H. Lawrence 53
- The Farmer's Bride by Charlotte Mew 61
- The Home and the World
  by Rabindranath Tagore 338

1917

- White Flock by Anna Akhmatova 301
- The Rise of David Levinsky
  by Abraham Cahan 318
- The Shadow-Line by Joseph Conrad 31
- South Wind by Norman Douglas 63
- A Son of the Middle Border
  by Hamlin Garland 416
- A Diversity of Creatures
  by Rudyard Kipling 24
- The State and Revolution by V. I. Lenin 299

1920

- Glinda of Oz by L. Frank Baum† 408
- Chéri by Colette 171
- The Rescue by Joseph Conrad 31
- Flappers and Philosophers
  by F. Scott Fitzgerald 422
- This Side of Paradise
  by F. Scott Fitzgerald 422
- Beyond the Pleasure Principle
  by Sigmund Freud 268
- In Chancery by John Galsworthy 47
- If It Die by André Gide 165
- Storm of Steel by Ernst Jünger 250

- The Lost Girl by D. H. Lawrence 53
- Women in Love by D. H. Lawrence 52
- Main Street by Sinclair Lewis 421
- Bliss and Other Stories
  by Katherine Mansfield 388
- A Few Figs from Thistles
  by Edna St Vincent Millay 412
- Anna Christie by Eugene O'Neill 416
- The Emperor Jones by Eugene O'Neill 416
- The Age of Innocence
  by Edith Wharton 403
- Hungry Hearts by Anzia Yezierska 421

1921

- Three Soldiers by John Dos Passos 426
- To Let by John Galsworthy 47
- The Good Soldier Schweik
  by Jaroslav Hašek 284
- Crome Yellow by Aldous Huxley 65
- The Big Town by Ring Lardner 412
- Psychoanalysis and the Unconscious
  by D. H. Lawrence 53

- Sea and Sardinia by D. H. Lawrence 53
- Second April
  by Edna St Vincent Millay 412
- Six Characters in Search of an Author
  by Luigi Pirandello 215
- The Guermantes Way
  by Marcel Proust 169
- Queen Victoria by Lytton Strachey 64

1924

- Sorrow in Sunlight
  by Ronald Firbank 65
- Some Do Not... by Ford Madox Ford 46
- A Passage to India by E. M. Forster 39
- The White Monkey
  by John Galsworthy 47
- Fragments from My Diary
  by Maxim Gorky 300
- Padmarag
  by Rokeya Sakhawat Hossain 338

- The Boy in the Bush by D. H. Lawrence
  & M. L. Skinner 55
- The Magic Mountain
  by Thomas Mann 246
- The Rector's Daughter by F. M. Mayor 73
- The Spanish Farm by R. H. Mottram 73
- Twenty Love Poems and a Song
  of Despair by Pablo Neruda 569
- Playground by Premchand 340
- We by Yevgeny Zamyatin 303

1925

- Manhattan Transfer
  by John Dos Passos 426
- The Great Gatsby
  by F. Scott Fitzgerald 424
- No More Parades
  by Ford Madox Ford 46
- An Autobiography by M. K. Gandhi 340
- The Counterfeiters by André Gide 165
- In Our Time by Ernest Hemingway 428
- Those Barren Leaves
  by Aldous Huxley 65
- The Trial by Franz Kafka† 282
- St Mawr and Other Stories
  by D. H. Lawrence 55
- Gentlemen Prefer Blondes
  by Anita Loos 432

- Sangschaw by Hugh MacDiarmid 72
- The Painted Veil
  by W. Somerset Maugham 34
- The Desert of Love
  by François Mauriac 174
- Cuttlefish Bones by Eugenio Montale 215
- Sixty-Four, Ninety-Four
  by R. H. Mottram 73
- The Fugitive by Marcel Proust† 169
- The Way Home
  by Henry Handel Richardson 380
- In the American Grain
  by William Carlos Williams 418
- The Common Reader
  by Virginia Woolf 42
- Mrs Dalloway by Virginia Woolf 44

1928

- Story of the Eye by Georges Bataille 176
- John Brown's Body
  by Stephen Vincent Benét 429
- Undertones of War
  by Edmund Blunden 78
- Nadja by André Breton 176
- Armed with Madness by Mary Butts 78
- The Last Post by Ford Madox Ford 46
- The Eternal Moment by E. M. Forster 38
- Swan Song by John Galsworthy 47
- The Well of Loneliness
  by Radclyffe Hall 79
- Point Counter Point by Aldous Huxley 66
- Quicksand by Nella Larsen 437
- Lady Chatterley's Lover
  by D. H. Lawrence 56
- The Woman Who Rode Away and Other
  Stories by D. H. Lawrence 50

- Gypsy Ballads
  by Federico García Lorca 230
- Poems by Osip Mandelshtam 301
- King, Queen, Knave
  by Vladimir Nabokov 306
- Quartet by Jean Rhys 551
- The Letters of Sacco and Vanzetti† 425
- The Intelligent Woman's Guide
  to Socialism and Capitalism
  by George Bernard Shaw 4
- Journey's End by R. C. Sherriff 87
- And Quiet Flows the Don
  by Mikhail Sholokhov 312
- Elizabeth and Essex
  by Lytton Strachey 64
- Decline and Fall by Evelyn Waugh 67
- Orlando by Virginia Woolf 44
- The Tower by W. B. Yeats 5

1929

- The Last September
  by Elizabeth Bowen 13
- Cattle Thief by Frank Brownlee 370
- Les Enfants Terribles by Jean Cocteau 178
- The Other One by Colette 172
- Sido by Colette 171
- Berlin Alexanderplatz
  by Alfred Döblin 253
- The Sound and the Fury
  by William Faulkner 433
- Goodbye to All That by Robert Graves 57
- The Man Within by Graham Greene 88
- A Farewell to Arms
  by Ernest Hemingway 428
- A High Wind in Jamaica
  by Richard Hughes 86
- Mr Ma and Son by Lao She 346
- The Escaped Cock by D. H. Lawrence 54
- The Middle Parts of Fortune
  by Frederic Manning 381

- The Bedbug by Vladimir Mayakovsky 313
- The Rambling Sailor
  by Charlotte Mew† 61
- Wolf Solent by John Cowper Powys 86
- The Good Companions
  by J. B. Priestley 87
- Ultima Thule
  by Henry Handel Richardson 380
- Southern Mail
  by Antoine de Saint-Exupéry 178
- Cup of Gold by John Steinbeck 440
- The True Heart
  by Sylvia Townsend Warner 76
- Summer Lightning
  by P. G. Wodehouse 48
- Look Homeward, Angel
  by Thomas Wolfe 438
- A Room of One's Own
  by Virginia Woolf 45

1918

- *Tarr* by Wyndham Lewis 62
- *Renascence and Other Poems*
  by Edna St Vincent Millay 412
- *So It Is (If You Think So)*
  by Luigi Pirandello 215
- *Australia Felix*
  by Henry Handel Richardson 380
- *A Confirmed Bachelor*
  by Arthur Schnitzler 270
- *Summer* by Edith Wharton 403

- *My Ántonia* by Willa Cather 414
- *Exiles* by James Joyce 8
- *Man of Straw* by Heinrich Mann 250
- *Beyond the Horizon*
  by Eugene O'Neill 415
- *Eminent Victorians*
  by Lytton Strachey 64

1919

- *Winesburg, Ohio*
  by Sherwood Anderson 420
- *Valmouth* by Ronald Firbank 64
- *La Symphonie Pastorale*
  by André Gide 165
- *Demian* by Hermann Hesse 248
- *Strange News from Another Star*
  by Hermann Hesse 248
- *A Country Doctor* by Franz Kafka 280
- *The Butterfly's Evil Spell*
  by Federico García Lorca 230

- *The Moon and Sixpence*
  by W. Somerset Maugham 33
- *The Straw* by Eugene O'Neill 415
- *In the Shadow of Young Girls in Flower*
  by Marcel Proust 169
- *Ten Days That Shook the World*
  by John Reed 420
- *South* by Ernest Shackleton 12
- *Night and Day* by Virginia Woolf 42

1922

- *The Enchanted April*
  by Elizabeth von Arnim 380
- *My Mother's House* by Colette 171
- *The Enormous Room*
  by e e cummings 427
- *The Beautiful and Damned*
  by F. Scott Fitzgerald 424
- *Tales of the Jazz Age*
  by F. Scott Fitzgerald 422
- *The Golden Bough* by James Frazer 27
- *Futility* by William Gerhardie 72
- *Siddhartha* by Hermann Hesse 248
- *Ulysses* by James Joyce 10
- *Aaron's Rod* by D. H. Lawrence 54

- *England, My England*
  by D. H. Lawrence 50
- *Babbitt* by Sinclair Lewis 421
- *Tristia* by Osip Mandelstam 301
- *The Garden Party and Other Stories*
  by Katherine Mansfield 390
- *The Hairy Ape* by Eugene O'Neill 415
- *Henry IV* by Luigi Pirandello 215
- *Sodom and Gomorrah*
  by Marcel Proust 169
- *A Short History of the World*
  by H. G. Wells 27
- *Jacob's Room* by Virginia Woolf 44

1923

- *Odessa Tales* by Isaac Babel 321
- *Riceyman Steps* by Arnold Bennett 37
- *Encounters* by Elizabeth Bowen 13
- *Ripening Seed* by Colette 172
- *The Flower Beneath the Foot*
  by Ronald Firbank 65
- *New Hampshire* by Robert Frost 415
- *The Prophet* by Khalil Gibran 334
- *My Universities* by Maxim Gorky 300
- *Antic Hay* by Aldous Huxley 65
- *The Captain's Doll, The Fox, Kangaroo,*
  The Ladybird & Studies in Classic
  American Literature
  by D. H. Lawrence 54

- *The Prisoner* by Marcel Proust[†] 169
- *The Devil in the Flesh*
  by Raymond Radiguet 174
- *The Duino Elegies*
  by Rainer Maria Rilke 269
- *The Sonnets to Orpheus*
  by Rainer Maria Rilke 269
- *Confessions of Zeno* by Italo Svevo 214
- *Spring and All*
  by William Carlos Williams 418

1926

- *Red Cavalry* by Isaac Babel 321
- *Moravagine* by Blaise Cendrars 263
- *The Last of Chéri* by Colette 171
- *Soldiers' Pay* by William Faulkner 433
- *Concerning the Eccentricities of Cardinal*
  Pirelli by Ronald Firbank[†] 64
- *A Man Could Stand Up —*
  by Ford Madox Ford 46
- *Payment Deferred* by C. S. Forester 75
- *The Silver Spoon* by John Galsworthy 47
- *The Castle* by Franz Kafka[†] 283
- *Debits and Credits* by Rudyard Kipling 25
- *The Plumed Serpent*
  by D. H. Lawrence 55
- *Seven Pillars of Wisdom*
  by T. E. Lawrence 74

- *The Case of Mr Crump*
  by Ludwig Lewisohn 432
- *A Drunk Man Looks at the Thistle*
  by Hugh MacDiarmid 72
- *Penny Wheep* by Hugh MacDiarmid 72
- *The Crime at Vanderlynden's*
  by R. H. Mottram 73
- *Mary* by Vladimir Nabokov 306
- *Enough Rope* by Dorothy Parker 419
- *Dream Story* by Arthur Schnitzler 270
- *Religion and the Rise of Capitalism*
  by R. H. Tawney 71
- *Lolly Willowes*
  by Sylvia Townsend Warner 75
- *My Apprenticeship* by Beatrice Webb 73

1927

- *The Hotel* by Elizabeth Bowen 13
- *Death Comes for the Archbishop*
  by Willa Cather 414
- *Aspects of the Novel* by E. M. Forster 39
- *Steppenwolf* by Hermann Hesse 248
- *God's Trombones*
  by James Weldon Johnson 413
- *Pomes Penyeach* by James Joyce 8
- *America* by Franz Kafka[†] 282
- *Dusty Answer*
  by Rosamond Lehmann 77
- *The Wild Body* by Wyndham Lewis 63
- *But Gentlemen Marry Brunettes*
  by Anita Loos 432
- *Thérèse Desqueyroux*
  by François Mauriac 175

- *Mr Weston's Good Wine*
  by T. F. Powys 77
- *Finding Time Again*
  by Marcel Proust[†] 169
- *The Left Bank* by Jean Rhys 551
- *Mr Fortune's Maggot*
  by Sylvia Townsend Warner 76
- *The Bridge of San Luis Rey*
  by Thornton Wilder 436
- *Tarka the Otter*
  by Henry Williamson 77
- *To the Lighthouse* by Virginia Woolf 44
- *The Case of Sergeant Grischa*
  by Arnold Zweig 253

1930

- *My Life* by Marc Chagall 319
- *The Diary of a Provincial Lady*
  by E. M. Delafield 95
- *The 42nd Parallel* by John Dos Passos 426
- *As I Lay Dying* by William Faulkner 434
- *Plain Murder* by C. S. Forester 75
- *Civilization and Its Discontents*
  by Sigmund Freud 268
- *On Forsyte 'Change*
  by John Galsworthy 47
- *Narziss and Goldmund*
  by Hermann Hesse 249
- *Brief Candles* by Aldous Huxley 66
- *Love Among the Haystacks and Other*
  Stories by D. H. Lawrence[†] 50
- *The Virgin and the Gipsy*
  by D. H. Lawrence[†] 55

- *The Apes of God* by Wyndham Lewis 63
- *The Shoemaker's Prodigious Wife*
  by Federico García Lorca 230
- *Cakes and Ale*
  by W. Somerset Maugham 34
- *The Eye* by Vladimir Nabokov 307
- *The Luzhin Defense*
  by Vladimir Nabokov 306
- *Angel Pavement* by J. B. Priestley 87
- *After Leaving Mr Mackenzie*
  by Jean Rhys 552
- *Pietr the Latvian* by Georges Simenon 202
- *History of the Russian Revolution*
  by Leon Trotsky 322
- *Labels* by Evelyn Waugh 67
- *Vile Bodies* by Evelyn Waugh 68

1931

- *Mapp and Lucia* by E. F. Benson 95
- *Friends and Relations*
  by Elizabeth Bowen 13
- *The Anarchist* by Hermann Broch 272
- *The Romantic* by Hermann Broch 272
- *A Small Circus* by Hans Fallada 251
- *Sanctuary* by William Faulkner 434
- *Maid in Waiting*
  by John Galsworthy 47
- *An Essay on Typography* by Eric Gill 96
- *Boy* by James Hanley 97
- *The Great Wall of China*
  by Franz Kafka[†] 280
- *Gilgi, One of Us* by Irmgard Keun 254
- *Life Is a Dream* by Gyula Krúdy 277
- *Apocalypse* by D. H. Lawrence[†] 56
- *Juan in America* by Eric Linklater 96

- *The Love of Don Perlimplín*
  and Belisa in the Garden
  by Federico García Lorca 230
- *Death and Taxes* by Dorothy Parker 419
- *Night Flight*
  by Antoine de Saint-Exupéry 178
- *A Crime in Holland, The Dancer at the*
  Gai-Moulin, The Grand Banks Café,
  The Hanged Man of Saint-Pholien,
  The Late Monsieur Gallet, Lock 14,
  A Man's Head, Night at the Crossroads
  & The Yellow Dog
  by Georges Simenon 202–3
- *Remote People* by Evelyn Waugh 68
- *The Dream Life of Balso Snell*
  by Nathanael West 446
- *The Waves* by Virginia Woolf 45

1932

- *Hindoo Holiday* by J. R. Ackerley 99
- *Mount Zion* by John Betjeman 88
- *To the North* by Elizabeth Bowen 13
- *The Realist* by Hermann Broch 272
- *Journey to the End of the Night* by Louis-Ferdinand Céline 180
- *The Pure and the Impure* by Colette 172
- *The Provincial Lady Goes Further* by E. M. Delafield 95
- *Nineteen Nineteen* by John Dos Passos 426
- *Little Man, What Now?* by Hans Fallada 252
- *Young Lonigan* by James T. Farrell 447
- *Light in August* by William Faulkner 434

- *Save Me the Waltz* by Zelda Fitzgerald 447
- *Flowering Wilderness* by John Galsworthy 47
- *Sunset Song* by Lewis Grassic Gibbon 100
- *Cold Comfort Farm* by Stella Gibbons 99
- *Stamboul Train* by Graham Greene 89
- *Brave New World* by Aldous Huxley 66
- *The Artificial Silk Girl* by Irmgard Keun 254
- *Limits and Renewals* by Rudyard Kipling 25
- *Sketches of Etruscan Places* by D. H. Lawrence[†] 53

- *The Futurist Cookbook* by Filippo Tommaso Marinetti 216
- *The Narrow Corner* by W. Somerset Maugham 34
- *The Knot of Vipers* by François Mauriac 175
- *Glory* by Vladimir Nabokov 307
- *Laughter in the Dark* by Vladimir Nabokov 307
- *Midsummer Night Madness and Other Stories* by Sean O'Faolain 17
- *Second Birth* by Boris Pasternak 302
- *The Radetzky March* by Joseph Roth 273
- *Guys and Dolls* by Damon Runyon 439

- *Virgin Soil Upturned* by Mikhail Sholokhov 312
- *The Bar on the Seine, The Flemish House, Liberty Bar, The Madman of Bergerac, The Misty Harbour, The Saint-Fiacre Affair & The Shadow Puppet* by Georges Simenon 203–4
- *The Pastures of Heaven* by John Steinbeck 440
- *Cheerful Weather for the Wedding* by Julia Strachey 100
- *Black Mischief* by Evelyn Waugh 68
- *The Common Reader: Second Series* by Virginia Woolf 42

1935

- *Requiem* by Anna Akhmatova 301
- *Untouchable* by Mulk Raj Anand 341
- *A Universal History of Infamy* by Jorge Luis Borges 573
- *The House in Paris* by Elizabeth Bowen 14
- *Auto da Fé* by Elias Canetti 328
- *A House and Its Head* by Ivy Compton-Burnett 104
- *Judgement Day* by James T. Farrell 447
- *Later Fruits of the Earth* by André Gide 164
- *Claudius the God* by Robert Graves 58
- *England Made Me* by Graham Greene 99

- *The Furys* by James Hanley 97
- *Mr Norris Changes Trains* by Christopher Isherwood 103
- *Saint Peter Relates an Incident* by James Weldon Johnson 413
- *It Can't Happen Here* by Sinclair Lewis 421
- *Lament for Ignacio Sánchez Mejías* by Federico García Lorca 230
- *La Fin de la Nuit* by François Mauriac 175
- *Aller Retour New York* by Henry Miller 451
- *Invitation to a Beheading* by Vladimir Nabokov 307

- *A Clergyman's Daughter* by George Orwell 82
- *The Green Child* by Herbert Read 103
- *Money from Home* by Damon Runyon 439
- *The Pitards* by Georges Simenon 210
- *Tortilla Flat* by John Steinbeck 441
- *The Maker of Heavenly Trousers* by Daniele Varè 216
- *Edmund Campion* by Evelyn Waugh 68
- *Of Time and the River* by Thomas Wolfe 438

1936

- *Locos* by Felipe Alfau 231
- *Coolie* by Mulk Raj Anand 341
- *Language, Truth and Logic* by A. J. Ayer 106
- *War with the Newts* by Karel Čapek 283
- *The Rock Pool* by Cyril Connolly 107
- *The Big Money* by John Dos Passos 426
- *Absalom, Absalom!* by William Faulkner 435
- *The Ego and the Mechanisms of Defence* by Anna Freud 274
- *Of Mortal Love* by William Gerhardie 72
- *A Gun for Sale* by Graham Greene 90

1938

- *Cause for Alarm* by Eric Ambler 109
- *Epitaph for a Spy* by Eric Ambler 109
- *The Death of the Heart* by Elizabeth Bowen 14
- *Enemies of Promise* by Cyril Connolly 107
- *Iron Gustav* by Hans Fallada 252
- *The Unvanquished* by William Faulkner 434
- *Count Belisarius* by Robert Graves 58
- *Brighton Rock* by Graham Greene 90
- *The Age of the Fish* by Ödön von Horváth 277
- *The Green Fool* by Patrick Kavanagh 15
- *Child of All Nations* by Irmgard Keun 254

- *If I Die Before I Wake* by Sherwood King 458
- *The Summing Up* by W. Somerset Maugham 34
- *The Gift* by Vladimir Nabokov 308
- *Homage to Catalonia* by George Orwell 83
- *Anthem* by Ayn Rand 450
- *Furthermore* by Damon Runyon 439
- *Take It Easy* by Damon Runyon 439
- *Nausea* by Jean-Paul Sartre 185
- *The Man Who Watched the Trains Go By* by Georges Simenon 210
- *The Long Valley* by John Steinbeck 441

- *The Fathers* by Allen Tate 459
- *Journey to the Border* by Edward Upward 79
- *After the Death of Don Juan* by Sylvia Townsend Warner 76
- *Scoop* by Evelyn Waugh 69
- *The Buccaneers* by Edith Wharton[†] 403
- *Our Town* by Thornton Wilder 49
- *The Code of the Woosters* by P. G. Wodehouse 49
- *Three Guineas* by Virginia Woolf 45

1939

- *The Mask of Dimitrios* by Eric Ambler 109
- *Nuptials* by Albert Camus 191
- *Mister Johnson* by Joyce Cary 18
- *The Big Sleep* by Raymond Chandler 461
- *A Family and a Fortune* by Ivy Compton-Burnett 105
- *The Wild Palms* by William Faulkner 435
- *The Confidential Agent* by Graham Greene 90
- *The Lawless Roads* by Graham Greene 90
- *After Many a Summer* by Aldous Huxley 66
- *Red Strangers* by Elspeth Huxley 365
- *Goodbye to Berlin* by Christopher Isherwood 104

1941

- *Let Us Now Praise Famous Men* by James Agee & Walker Evans 465
- *Madame Edwarda* by Georges Bataille 177
- *The Garden of Forking Paths* by Jorge Luis Borges 573
- *Herself Surprised* by Joyce Cary 18
- *Julie de Carneilhan* by Colette 172
- *Parents and Children* by Ivy Compton-Burnett 105
- *The Last Tycoon* by F. Scott Fitzgerald[†] 425

- *Hangover Square* by Patrick Hamilton 112
- *The Case of Charles Dexter Ward* by H. P. Lovecraft[†] 417
- *Reflections in a Golden Eye* by Carson McCullers 454
- *A Woman of the Pharisees* by François Mauriac 175
- *The Colossus of Maroussi* by Henry Miller 452
- *The Real Life of Sebastian Knight* by Vladimir Nabokov 308
- *The Lion and the Unicorn* by George Orwell 83

- *The Log from the Sea of Cortez* by John Steinbeck 442
- *Over to Candleford* by Flora Thompson 111
- *Curtain of Green* by Eudora Welty 457
- *The Living and the Dead* by Patrick White 382
- *Between the Acts* by Virginia Woolf[†] 45
- *The Royal Game* by Stefan Zweig 271

1942

- *The Myth of Sisyphus* by Albert Camus 182
- *The Outsider* by Albert Camus 182
- *To Be a Pilgrim* by Joyce Cary 18
- *The High Window* by Raymond Chandler 462
- *Winter's Tales* by Isak Dinesen 240
- *Go Down, Moses* by William Faulkner 435
- *A Witness Tree* by Robert Frost 415
- *The Great Hunger* by Patrick Kavanagh 15

1933

- *Marya* by Isaac Babel 313
- *The Cat* by Colette 172
- *Over the River* by John Galsworthy† 47
- *Cloud Howe* by Lewis Grassic Gibbon 100
- *Love on the Dole*
    by Walter Greenwood 101
- *Winner Takes Nothing*
    by Ernest Hemingway 428
- *Along This Way*
    by James Weldon Johnson 413
- *Cat Country* by Lao She 346
- *Blood Wedding*
    by Federico García Lorca 231
- *Ultramarine* by Malcolm Lowry 101
- *Man's Estate* by André Malraux 184
- *The Tales of Jacob* by Thomas Mann 246
- *The Frontenac Mystery*
    by François Mauriac 175

- *Down and Out in Paris and London*
    by George Orwell 81
- *Lock No. 1* by Georges Simenon 204
- *Mr Hire's Engagement*
    by Georges Simenon 201
- *Satan in Goray*
    by Isaac Bashevis Singer 288
- *The Autobiography of Alice B. Toklas*
    by Gertrude Stein 410
- *To a God Unknown*
    by John Steinbeck 440
- *The Forty Days of Musa Dagh*
    by Franz Werfel 273
- *Miss Lonelyhearts* by Nathanael West 446
- *Heavy Weather* by P. G. Wodehouse 49
- *Flush* by Virginia Woolf 45

1934

- *Novel with Cocaine* by M. Ageyev 313
- *Threepenny Novel* by Bertolt Brecht 255
- *Exile's Return* by Malcolm Cowley 448
- *The Provincial Lady in America*
    by E. M. Delafield 95
- *Seven Gothic Tales* by Isak Dinesen 240
- *Once a Jailbird* by Hans Fallada 252
- *The Young Manhood of Studs Lonigan*
    by James T. Farrell 447
- *Tender is the Night*
    by F. Scott Fitzgerald 424
- *Grey Granite* by Lewis Grassic Gibbon 100
- *I, Claudius* by Robert Graves 58
- *It's a Battlefield* by Graham Greene 89
- *The Thin Man* by Dashiell Hammett 448
- *Mr Noon* by D. H. Lawrence† 53
- *Yerma* by Federico García Lorca 231
- *Young Joseph* by Thomas Mann 246
- *Tropic of Cancer* by Henry Miller 451

- *Despair* by Vladimir Nabokov 307
- *Appointment in Samarra*
    by John O'Hara 449
- *Burmese Days* by George Orwell 82
- *The Last Summer* by Boris Pasternak 302
- *Voyage in the Dark* by Jean Rhys 552
- *Call It Sleep* by Henry Roth 449
- *For Two Thousand Years*
    by Mihail Sebastian 323
- *Maigret* by Georges Simenon 204
- *The Man from London*
    by Georges Simenon 210
- *The Quest for Corvo*
    by A. J. A. Symons 102
- *My First Wife*
    by Jakob Wassermann† 249
- *A Handful of Dust* by Evelyn Waugh 68
- *Ninety-Two Days* by Evelyn Waugh 68
- *A Cool Million* by Nathanael West 446

1937

- *Journey Without Maps*
    by Graham Greene 90
- *Eyeless in Gaza* by Aldous Huxley 66
- *The Mint* by T. E. Lawrence† 74
- *The Weather in the Streets*
    by Rosamond Lehmann 78
- *The House of Bernarda Alba*
    by Federico García Lorca 231
- *At the Mountains of Madness*
    by H. P. Lovecraft 417
- *Mephisto* by Klaus Mann 256
- *Joseph in Egypt* by Thomas Mann 246
- *Posthumous Papers of a Living Author*
    by Robert Musil 270

- *The Diary of Vaslav Nijinsky* 321
- *Keep the Aspidistra Flying*
    by George Orwell 82
- *We the Living* by Ayn Rand 450
- *The Brothers Ashkenazi* by I. J. Singer 291
- *Novel on Yellow Paper*
    by Stevie Smith 108
- *In Dubious Battle* by John Steinbeck 441
- *Summer Will Show*
    by Sylvia Townsend Warner 76
- *Waugh in Abyssinia* by Evelyn Waugh 69

- *Uncommon Danger* by Eric Ambler 108
- *Out of Africa* by Karen Blixen 240
- *The Wrong Side and the Right Side*
    by Albert Camus 181
- *Ferdydurke* by Witold Gombrowicz 292
- *To Have and Have Not*
    by Ernest Hemingway 429
- *After Midnight* by Irmgard Keun 254
- *Something of Myself*
    by Rudyard Kipling† 25
- *The Revenge for Love*
    by Wyndham Lewis 63
- *Days of Hope* by André Malraux 184
- *The Road to Wigan Pier*
    by George Orwell 82

- *I Have Been Here Before*
    by J. B. Priestley 88
- *Time and the Conways* by J. B. Priestley 88
- *Weights and Measures*
    by Joseph Roth 273
- *More Than Somewhat*
    by Damon Runyon 439
- *Of Mice and Men* by John Steinbeck 441
- *The Red Pony* by John Steinbeck 440
- *South African Eden*
    by James Stevenson-Hamilton 370
- *He* by Rabindranath Tagore 338
- *White Mule*
    by William Carlos Williams 418
- *The Years* by Virginia Woolf 415

1940

- *Finnegans Wake* by James Joyce 11
- *On the Marble Cliffs* by Ernst Jünger 250
- *How Green Was My Valley*
    by Richard Llewellyn 110
- *Lotte in Weimar* by Thomas Mann 246
- *The Unknown Sea*
    by François Mauriac 175
- *Tropic of Capricorn* by Henry Miller 451
- *At Swim-Two-Birds* by Flann O'Brien 19
- *Coming Up for Air* by George Orwell 83
- *Pale Horse, Pale Rider*
    by Katherine Anne Porter 427
- *Good Morning, Midnight*
    by Jean Rhys 552
- *Wind, Sand and Stars*
    by Antoine de Saint-Exupéry 179

- *The Hopkins Manuscript*
    by R. C. Sherriff 87
- *The Krull House* by Georges Simenon 210
- *The Grapes of Wrath*
    by John Steinbeck 442
- *Lark Rise* by Flora Thompson 111
- *Johnny Got His Gun*
    by Dalton Trumbo 461
- *Work Suspended* by Evelyn Waugh 67
- *The Day of the Locust*
    by Nathanael West 446
- *The Web and the Rock*
    by Thomas Wolfe† 438
- *Beware of Pity* by Stefan Zweig 271

- *Poem Without a Hero*
    by Anna Akhmatova 301
- *Journey into Fear* by Eric Ambler 109
- *Guilty Men* by 'Cato' 111
- *Farewell My Lovely*
    by Raymond Chandler 461
- *Chance Acquaintances* by Colette 172
- *The Provincial Lady in Wartime*
    by E. M. Delafield 95
- *An Outline of Psychoanalysis*
    by Sigmund Freud† 268
- *Sergeant Lamb of the Ninth*
    by Robert Graves 59
- *The Power and the Glory*
    by Graham Greene 91
- *For Whom the Bell Tolls*
    by Ernest Hemingway 429
- *Darkness at Noon* by Arthur Koestler 278

- *Poet in New York*
    by Federico García Lorca† 230
- *The Heart is a Lonely Hunter*
    by Carson McCullers 453
- *Inside the Whale and Other Essays*
    by George Orwell 81
- *The Don Flows Home to the Sea*
    by Mikhail Sholokhov 312
- *The Strangers in the House*
    by Georges Simenon 210
- *The Man Who Loved Children*
    by Christina Stead 381
- *In the Money*
    by William Carlos Williams 418
- *You Can't Go Home Again*
    by Thomas Wolfe† 439
- *Native Son* by Richard Wright 462

1943

- *Flight to Arras*
    by Antoine de Saint-Exupéry 179
- *Cécile is Dead, The Hotel Majestic*
    & The Judge's House
    by Georges Simenon 204
- *The Moon is Down*
    by John Steinbeck 442
- *Put Out More Flags* by Evelyn Waugh 69
- *The Skin of Our Teeth*
    by Thornton Wilder 436
- *The Death of the Moth and Other Essays*
    by Virginia Woolf† 42

- *Betrothed* by S. Y. Agnon 274
- *Madonna in a Fur Coat*
    by Sabahattin Ali 329
- *Western Star*
    by Stephen Vincent Benét† 429
- *Two Serious Ladies* by Jane Bowles 474
- *The Good Woman of Setzuan*
    by Bertolt Brecht 255
- *The Lady in the Lake*
    by Raymond Chandler 462
- *Wife to Mr Milton* by Robert Graves 59

- *The Ministry of Fear*
    by Graham Greene 91
- *Bound for Glory* by Woody Guthrie 474
- *The Glass Bead Game*
    by Hermann Hesse 249
- *Arrival and Departure*
    by Arthur Koestler 278
- *Near to the Wild Heart*
    by Clarice Lispector 565
- *The Dream-Quest of Unknown Kadath*
    by H. P. Lovecraft† 417

- *The Ballad of the Sad Café*
    by Carson McCullers 454
- *Joseph the Provider* by Thomas Mann 246
- *Malgudi Days* by R. K. Narayan 342
- *The Fountainhead* by Ayn Rand 450
- *The Little Prince*
    by Antoine de Saint-Exupéry 179
- *The Flies* by Jean-Paul Sartre 185
- *The Big Rock Candy Mountain*
    by Wallace Stegner 459
- *Candleford Green* by Flora Thompson 111

1944

- *Fair Stood the Wind for France*
  by H. E. Bates 116
- *Dangling Man* by Saul Bellow 477
- *Fictions* by Jorge Luis Borges 573
- *Cross Purpose* by Albert Camus 182
- *The Horse's Mouth* by Joyce Cary 18
- *Gigi* by Colette 172
- *The Unquiet Grave* by Palinurus 107
- *The Golden Fleece* by Robert Graves 59
- *Story of a Secret State* by Jan Karski 292
- *The First Lady Chatterley* by
  D. H. Lawrence[†] 56

- *The Razor's Edge*
  by W. Somerset Maugham 34
- *Nikolai Gogol* by Vladimir Nabokov 309
- *The Portable Dorothy Parker* 419
- *Huis Clos* by Jean-Paul Sartre 185
- *The Dragon* by Yevgeny Schwartz 313
- *Félicie, Inspector Cadaver & Signed,
  Picpus* by Georges Simenon 204
- *The Glass Menagerie*
  by Tennessee Williams 455

1945

- *The Blood of Others*
  by Simone de Beauvoir 187
- *The Death of Virgil*
  by Hermann Broch 272
- *The Tartar Steppe* by Dino Buzzati 217
- *Caligula* by Albert Camus 182
- *Apocryphal Stories* by Karel Čapek[†] 283
- *London Belongs to Me*
  by Norman Collins 116
- *Prater Violet*
  by Christopher Isherwood 104
- *Christ Stopped at Eboli* by Carlo Levi 222
- *Focus* by Arthur Miller 486
- *Rescue* by Czesław Miłosz 287

- *The Pursuit of Love* by Nancy Mitford 117
- *Animal Farm* by George Orwell 84
- *An Inspector Calls* by J. B. Priestley 88
- *The Age of Reason*
  by Jean-Paul Sartre 186
- *The Reprieve* by Jean-Paul Sartre 186
- *Monsieur Monde Vanishes*
  by Georges Simenon 210
- *Cannery Row* by John Steinbeck 442
- *The Thurber Carnival*
  by James Thurber 446
- *Brideshead Revisited*
  by Evelyn Waugh 69

1948

- *This Way for the Gas, Ladies and
  Gentlemen* by Tadeusz Borowski 293
- *The Heat of the Day*
  by Elizabeth Bowen 14
- *The Caucasian Chalk Circle*
  by Bertolt Brecht 255
- *The Military Orchid*
  by Jocelyn Brooke 120
- *Other Voices, Other Rooms*
  by Truman Capote 463
- *All About H. Hatterr* by G. V. Desani 344
- *Intruder in the Dust*
  by William Faulkner 435
- *Concluding* by Henry Green 119

- *The Heart of the Matter*
  by Graham Greene 91
- *The Third Man* by Graham Greene 89
- *The Road Through the Wall*
  by Shirley Jackson 466
- *Tarry Flynn* by Patrick Kavanagh 15
- *Snow Country* by Yasunari Kawabata 348
- *The Besieged City*
  by Clarice Lispector 565
- *The Naked and the Dead*
  by Norman Mailer 496
- *Under a Glass Bell* by Anaïs Nin 430
- *Cry, The Beloved Country*
  by Alan Paton 371

- *The Tunnel* by Ernesto Sábato 575
- *Maigret's Dead Man, Maigret's Holiday
  & The Snow Was Dirty*
  by Georges Simenon 205, 211
- *A Russian Journal* by John Steinbeck 444
- *The Corner That Held Them*
  by Sylvia Townsend Warner 76
- *The Loved One* by Evelyn Waugh 70
- *The Aunt's Story* by Patrick White 382
- *The Ides of March*
  by Thornton Wilder 436
- *Summer and Smoke*
  by Tennessee Williams 455

1949

- *Usurpers* by Francisco Ayala 232
- *The Second Sex*
  by Simone de Beauvoir 187
- *The Aleph* by Jorge Luis Borges 574
- *The Sheltering Sky* by Paul Bowles 480
- *Beautiful Antonio*
  by Vitaliano Brancati 224
- *A Mine of Serpents*
  by Jocelyn Brooke 120
- *The Just* by Albert Camus 182
- *The Kingdom of This World*
  by Alejo Carpentier 559
- *The Little Sister*
  by Raymond Chandler 462
- *A Short History of Decay*
  by E. M. Cioran 323

1951

- *The Origins of Totalitarianism*
  by Hannah Arendt 258
- *Malone Dies* by Samuel Beckett 20
- *The Rebel* by Albert Camus 103
- *The Grass Harp* by Truman Capote 465
- *Tempest-Tost* by Robertson Davies 395
- *Requiem for a Nun*
  by William Faulkner 435
- *Miracle of the Rose* by Jean Genet 190
- *The End of the Affair*
  by Graham Greene 92
- *The West Pier* by Patrick Hamilton 112
- *A World Apart* by Gustav Herling 293
- *The Lesson* by Eugène Ionesco 324

- *Hangsaman* by Shirley Jackson 468
- *From Here to Eternity*
  by James Jones 500
- *The Holy Sinner* by Thomas Mann 247
- *Forbidden Colours* by Yukio Mishima 351
- *The Blessing* by Nancy Mitford 117
- *Speak, Memory* by Vladimir Nabokov 308
- *Mittee* by Daphnee Rooke 372
- *The First Crusade*
  by Steven Runciman 121
- *The Catcher in the Rye*
  by J. D. Salinger 499
- *Lucifer and the Lord*
  by Jean-Paul Sartre 185

- *Maigret and the Tall Woman,
  Maigret at Picratt's, Maigret Takes
  a Room & Maigret's Memoirs*
  by Georges Simenon 205–6
- *An Integrated Man* by Julia Strachey 100
- *The Goshawk* by T. H. White 106
- *The Rose Tattoo*
  by Tennessee Williams 456
- *The Day of the Triffids*
  by John Wyndham 122
- *Memoirs of Hadrian*
  by Marguerite Yourcenar 191

1952

- *Let It Come Down* by Paul Bowles 480
- *The Cardboard Crown*
  by Martin Boyd 384
- *Invisible Man* by Ralph Ellison 458
- *Black Skin, White Masks*
  by Frantz Fanon 557
- *In the Making* by G. F. Green 124
- *Go* by John Clellon Holmes 501
- *The Chairs* by Eugène Ionesco 324
- *Thousand Cranes*
  by Yasunari Kawabata 348
- *The Natural* by Bernard Malamud 475
- *The Man on a Donkey*
  by H. F. M. Prescott 124

1954

- *Lucky Jim* by Kingsley Amis 132
- *The Amen Corner*
  by James Baldwin 493
- *Into the War* by Italo Calvino 218
- *Summer* by Albert Camus 191
- *Italian Food* by Elizabeth David 131
- *Leaven of Malice*
  by Robertson Davies 395
- *Live and Let Die* by Ian Fleming 127
- *I'm Not Stiller* by Max Frisch 263
- *Lord of the Flies* by William Golding 131
- *Amédée, or How to Get Rid of It*
  by Eugène Ionesco 324

- *The Bird's Nest* by Shirley Jackson 468
- *The Master of Go*
  by Yasunari Kawabata 350
- *The Sound of the Mountain*
  by Yasunari Kawabata 348
- *Death in Rome* by Wolfgang Koeppen 259
- *Unknown Soldiers* by Väinö Linna 239
- *Confessions of Felix Krull, Confidence
  Man* by Thomas Mann 247
- *A Spy in the House of Love*
  by Anaïs Nin 431
- *Against Sainte-Beuve and Other Essays*
  by Marcel Proust[†] 166

- *The Kingdom of Acre*
  by Steven Runciman 121
- *Bonjour Tristesse* by Françoise Sagan 192
- *Maigret and the Dead Girl, Maigret and
  the Minister & Maigret Goes to School*
  by Georges Simenon 206–7
- *Sweet Thursday* by John Steinbeck 445
- *The Flint Anchor*
  by Sylvia Townsend Warner 76
- *The Matchmaker* by Thornton Wilder 436
- *How to be Topp* by Geoffrey Willans
  & Ronald Searle 125

1955

- *That Uncertain Feeling*
  by Kingsley Amis 132
- *Notes of a Native Son*
  by James Baldwin 492
- *The Expelled, The Calmative & The End*
  by Samuel Beckett 20
- *A World of Love* by Elizabeth Bowen 14
- *The Spider's House* by Paul Bowles 481
- *A Difficult Young Man* by Martin Boyd 384
- *The Edge of the Sea*
  by Rachel Carson 504
- *Cards of Identity* by Nigel Dennis 135
- *Auntie Mame* by Patrick Dennis 503
- *Moonraker* by Ian Fleming 127
- *The Recognitions* by William Gaddis 505

1946

- *The President*
  by Miguel Ángel Asturias 562
- *While Following the Plough*
  by John Stewart Collis 19
- *Over to You* by Roald Dahl 113
- *The Angelic Avengers*
  by Isak Dinesen 242
- *Alamein to Zem Zem*
  by Keith Douglas[†] 116
- *King Jesus* by Robert Graves 59
- *Hiroshima* by John Hersey 488
- *The Chandelier* by Clarice Lispector 565
- *The Member of the Wedding*
  by Carson McCullers 454
- *Auschwitz* by Miklós Nyiszli 279

- *Titus Groan* by Mervyn Peake 118
- *Men Without Shadows*
  by Jean-Paul Sartre 185
- *The Respectable Prostitute*
  by Jean-Paul Sartre 185
- *The Mahé Circle* by Georges Simenon 211
- *Three Bedrooms in Manhattan*
  by Georges Simenon 211
- *The Stones of the Field*
  by R. S. Thomas 119
- *All the King's Men*
  by Robert Penn Warren 489
- *When the Going Was Good*
  by Evelyn Waugh 69
- *Paterson* by William Carlos Williams 418

1947

- *The Victim* by Saul Bellow 477
- *The Path to the Spiders' Nests*
  by Italo Calvino 218
- *The Plague* by Albert Camus 183
- *Down to Earth* by John Stewart Collis 19
- *Alone in Berlin* by Hans Fallada[†] 252
- *The Diary of a Young Girl*
  by Anne Frank[†] 256
- *The Slaves of Solitude*
  by Patrick Hamilton 112
- *In a Lonely Place*
  by Dorothy B. Hughes 489
- *If This is a Man* by Primo Levi 222
- *Under the Volcano* by Malcolm Lowry 102
- *Of Love and Hunger*
  by Julian MacLaren-Ross 119
- *Doctor Faustus* by Thomas Mann 246

- *All My Sons* by Arthur Miller 486
- *Bend Sinister* by Vladimir Nabokov 309
- *The Harp in the South* by Ruth Park 391
- *The Linden Tree* by J. B. Priestley 88
- *Fortress Besieged* by Qian Zhongshu 132
- *Berlin Finale* by Heinz Rein 258
- *Maigret Gets Angry*
  by Georges Simenon 204
- *Maigret in New York*
  by Georges Simenon 205
- *The Pearl* by John Steinbeck 442
- *The Wayward Bus* by John Steinbeck 444
- *The Middle of the Journey*
  by Lionel Trilling 489
- *Froth on the Daydream* by Boris Vian 190
- *Gravity and Grace* by Simone Weil[†] 180
- *A Streetcar Named Desire*
  by Tennessee Williams 455

- *The Thief's Journal* by Jean Genet 190
- *Seven Days in New Crete*
  by Robert Graves 59
- *The Girl on the Via Flaminia*
  by Alfred Hayes 498
- *The Lottery and Other Stories*
  by Shirley Jackson 466
- *A Writer's Notebook*
  by W. Somerset Maugham 34
- *Death of a Salesman* by Arthur Miller 486
- *Sexus* by Henry Miller 452
- *Confessions of a Mask*
  by Yukio Mishima 350
- *Love in a Cold Climate*
  by Nancy Mitford 117
- *Cock-a-Doodle Dandy* by Sean O'Casey 6

- *Olivia* by 'Olivia' 97
- *Nineteen Eighty-Four*
  by George Orwell 84
- *Poor Man's Orange* by Ruth Park 391
- *The Concept of Mind* by Gilbert Ryle 121
- *Iron in the Soul* by Jean-Paul Sartre 186
- *The Case of Comrade Tulayev*
  by Victor Serge[†] 313
- *Maigret at the Coroner's,*
  Maigret's First Case & My Friend
  Maigret by Georges Simenon 205
- *Life with a Star* by Jiři Weil 284
- *The Golden Apples* by Eudora Welty 457
- *The Mating Season*
  by P. G. Wodehouse 49

1950

- *Edo and Enam* by S. Y. Agnon 274
- *L'Abbé C* by Georges Bataille 177
- *The Goose Cathedral*
  by Jocelyn Brooke 120
- *Half a Lifelong Romance*
  by Eileen Chang 347
- *The Town and the City*
  by Jack Kerouac 469
- *Ferdinand, the Man with the Kind Heart*
  by Irmgard Keun 254
- *The Drowning Pool*
  by Ross Macdonald 498
- *An Enemy of the People*
  by Arthur Miller 487
- *Thirst for Love* by Yukio Mishima 350

- *Canto General* by Pablo Neruda 569
- *Shooting an Elephant and Other Essays*
  by George Orwell[†] 81
- *The Labyrinth of Solitude*
  by Octavio Paz 561
- *Gormenghast* by Mervyn Peake 118
- *The Friend of Madame Maigret*
  by Georges Simenon 205
- *Maigret and the Old Lady*
  by Georges Simenon 205
- *The Family Moskat*
  by Isaac Bashevis Singer 289
- *Burning Bright* by John Steinbeck 444
- *Helena* by Evelyn Waugh 70

1953

- *Jean Santeuil* by Marcel Proust[†] 116
- *The Kingdom of Jerusalem*
  by Steven Runciman 121
- *The Terror of St Trinian's*
  by Ronald Searle 120
- *Maigret, Lognon and the Gangsters*
  by Georges Simenon 206
- *Maigret's Revolver*
  by Georges Simenon 206
- *The Manor* by Isaac Bashevis Singer 289
- *East of Eden* by John Steinbeck 444
- *Men at Arms* by Evelyn Waugh 70

- *Professor Taranne* by Arthur Adamov 324
- *Go Tell It on the Mountain*
  by James Baldwin 492
- *The Adventures of Augie March*
  by Saul Bellow 478
- *Who Among Us?* by Mario Benedetti 570
- *Junky* by William S. Burroughs 482
- *The Lost Steps* by Alejo Carpentier 559
- *The Long Goodbye*
  by Raymond Chandler 585
- *The Present and the Past*
  by Ivy Compton-Burnett 105
- *Someone Like You* by Roald Dahl 113

- *Casino Royale* by Ian Fleming 126
- *Mr Stimpson and Mr Gorse*
  by Patrick Hamilton 112
- *The Go-Between* by L. P. Hartley 125
- *In Love* by Alfred Hayes 498
- *Life Among the Savages*
  by Shirley Jackson 466
- *One* by David Karp 501
- *In the Castle of My Skin*
  by George Lamming 554
- *The Echoing Grove*
  by Rosamond Lehmann 78
- *The Crucible* by Arthur Miller 487

- *Plexus* by Henry Miller 452
- *The Captive Mind* by Czesław Miłosz 287
- *Jules et Jim* by Henri-Pierre Roché 191
- *Maigret is Afraid, Maigret's Mistake*
  & The Man on the Boulevard
  by Georges Simenon 206
- *Under Milk Wood* by Dylan Thomas 98
- *Hurry on Down* by John Wain 124
- *Love Among the Ruins*
  by Evelyn Waugh 71
- *Down with Skool!* by Geoffrey Willans
  & Ronald Searle 125
- *Camino Real* by Tennessee Williams 456

1956

- *Homer's Daughter* by Robert Graves 59
- *Loser Takes All* by Graham Greene 92
- *The Quiet American*
  by Graham Greene 92
- *Unknown Assailant*
  by Patrick Hamilton 112
- *Tristes Tropiques*
  by Claude Lévi-Strauss 194
- *A View from the Bridge*
  by Arthur Miller 487
- *The Issa Valley* by Czesław Miłosz 288
- *The World and the Cattle*
  by A. S. Mopeli-Paulus 369
- *Lolita* by Vladimir Nabokov 309
- *The Shiralee* by D'Arcy Niland 385

- *A Certain Smile* by Françoise Sagan 192
- *Maigret and the Headless Corpse*
  by Georges Simenon 207
- *Maigret Sets a Trap*
  by Georges Simenon 207
- *The Estate* by Isaac Bashevis Singer 289
- *Officers and Gentlemen*
  by Evelyn Waugh 70
- *The Tree of Man* by Patrick White 382
- *Cat on a Hot Tin Roof*
  by Tennessee Williams 456
- *The Man in the Gray Flannel Suit*
  by Sloan Wilson 503
- *The Chrysalids* by John Wyndham 122

- *Giovanni's Room* by James Baldwin 493
- *Within the Walls* by Giorgio Bassani 224
- *A Legacy* by Sybille Bedford 260
- *Seize the Day* by Saul Bellow 478
- *Italian Folktales* by Italo Calvino 219
- *The Fall* by Albert Camus 183
- *The Muses Are Heard*
  by Truman Capote 465
- *The Death of Grass* by John Christopher 135
- *Diamonds are Forever* by Ian Fleming 127
- *Howl and Other Poems*
  by Allen Ginsberg 490
- *Lady Sings the Blues* by Billie Holiday
  & William Dufty 506
- *Madame Solario* by Gladys Huntington 506

- *The Sweet Science* by A. J. Liebling 500
- *Venice Observed* by Mary McCarthy 507
- *Quiet Days in Clichy* by Henry Miller 452
- *The Temple of the Golden Pavilion*
  by Yukio Mishima 351
- *Boy in Darkness* by Mervyn Peake 118
- *The Hunters* by James Salter 508
- *The Lonely Londoners* by Sam Selvon 554
- *The Little Man from Archangel*
  by Georges Simenon 211
- *Maigret's Failure*
  by Georges Simenon 207
- *Whizz for Atomms* by Geoffrey Willans
  & Ronald Searle 125
- *Baby Doll* by Tennessee Williams 456

1957

- *A Death in the Family* by James Agee[†] 465
- *On Leave* by Daniel Anselme 195
- *Blue of Noon, Eroticism & Literature and Evil* by Georges Bataille 177
- *The Book of Imaginary Beings* by Jorge Luis Borges & Margarita Guerrero 574
- *Outbreak of Love* by Martin Boyd 384
- *South from Granada* by Gerald Brenan 135
- *Exile and the Kingdom* by Albert Camus 183

- *Reflections on the Guillotine* by Albert Camus 182
- *The God Boy* by Ian Cross 391
- *Last Tales* by Isak Dinesen 240
- *From Russia with Love* by Ian Fleming 127
- *Homo Faber* by Max Frisch 264
- *The Hireling* by L. P. Hartley 126
- *A Rage in Harlem* by Chester Himes 509
- *The Uses of Literacy* by Richard Hoggart 136
- *The Black Cloud* by Fred Hoyle 136
- *Raising Demons* by Shirley Jackson 468

- *On the Road* by Jack Kerouac 470
- *The Star Diaries* by Stanisław Lem 294
- *Memories of a Catholic Girlhood* by Mary McCarthy 507
- *The Assistant* by Bernard Malamud 475
- *A Treatise on Poetry* by Czesław Miłosz 287
- *Dojoji* by Yukio Mishima 351
- *The Dock Brief* by John Mortimer 139
- *The Elephant* by Sławomir Mrożek 295
- *Pnin* by Vladimir Nabokov 309
- *The Merchant of Prato* by Iris Origo 137

- *Parkinson's Law* by C. Northcote Parkinson 137
- *The Wit to Woo* by Mervyn Peake 118
- *Atlas Shrugged* by Ayn Rand 450
- *Maigret Enjoys Himself* by Georges Simenon 207
- *Maigret Travels* by Georges Simenon 207
- *The Short Reign of Pippin IV* by John Steinbeck 445
- *The Birds* by Tarjei Vesaas 237
- *The Ordeal of Gilbert Pinfold* by Evelyn Waugh 71

1959

- *The Zoo Story* by Edward Albee 324
- *Henderson the Rain King* by Saul Bellow 478
- *Naked Lunch* by William S. Burroughs 483
- *The Possessed* by Albert Camus 182
- *The Captive and the Free* by Joyce Cary[†] 19
- *Mrs Bridge* by Evan S. Connell 512
- *Goldfinger* by Ian Fleming 128
- *All Shot Up* by Chester Himes 509
- *Rhinoceros* by Eugène Ionesco 324
- *The Haunting of Hill House* by Shirley Jackson 468

- *Doctor Sax, Maggie Cassidy & Mexico City Blues* by Jack Kerouac 471
- *The Sleepwalkers* by Arthur Koestler 272
- *Cider with Rosie* by Laurie Lee 114
- *The Stones of Florence* by Mary McCarthy 507
- *The Galton Case* by Ross Macdonald 498
- *Advertisements for Myself* by Norman Mailer 496
- *The Island* by Ana María Matute 232
- *Native Realm* by Czesław Miłosz 288

- *Children of the Albatross* by Anaïs Nin 431
- *Titus Alone* by Mervyn Peake 118
- *Zazie in the Metro* by Raymond Queneau 196
- *The Apprenticeship of Duddy Kravitz* by Mordecai Richler 396
- *Altona* by Jean-Paul Sartre 185
- *The Last of the Just* by André Schwarz-Bart 195
- *Maigret and the Reluctant Witnesses* by Georges Simenon 207

- *Maigret's Secret* by Georges Simenon 207
- *The Magician of Lublin* by Isaac Bashevis Singer 289
- *The Hustler* by Walter Tevis 513
- *The Poorhouse Fair* by John Updike 514
- *The Life of Right Reverend Ronald Knox* by Evelyn Waugh 71
- *Back in the Jug Agane* by Geoffrey Willans[†] & Ronald Searle 125
- *Sweet Bird of Youth* by Tennessee Williams 457

1961

- *Songs of Mihyar the Damascene* by Adonis 334
- *Hothouse* by Brian Aldiss 142
- *Nobody Knows My Name* by James Baldwin 493
- *The Soft Machine* by William S. Burroughs 484
- *What is History?* by E. H. Carr 142
- *Jagua Nana* by Cyprian Ekwensi 362
- *The Wretched of the Earth* by Frantz Fanon[†] 558
- *The Memoir of an Anti-Hero* by Kornel Filipowicz 297
- *Thunderball* by Ian Fleming 128
- *Kaddish and Other Poems* by Allen Ginsberg 490

- *A Burnt-Out Case* by Graham Greene 92
- *In Search of a Character* by Graham Greene 91
- *The Lime Twig* by John Hawkes 519
- *The Heat's On* by Chester Himes 509
- *Call for the Dead* by John le Carré 143
- *The Children of Sánchez* by Oscar Lewis 518
- *Hear Us O Lord from Heaven Thy Dwelling Place* by Malcolm Lowry[†] 101
- *Clock Without Hands* by Carson McCullers 454
- *A New Life* by Bernard Malamud 475
- *The Frolic of the Beasts* by Yukio Mishima 351

- *A House for Mr Biswas* by V. S. Naipaul 555
- *The Man-Eater of Malgudi* by R. K. Narayan 343
- *Seduction of the Minotaur* by Anaïs Nin 431
- *An Only Child* by Frank O'Connor 16
- *One Moonlit Night* by Caradog Prichard 142
- *A Hundred Thousand Billion Poems* by Raymond Queneau 197
- *On Heroes and Tombs* by Ernesto Sábato 575
- *Maigret and the Idle Burglar* by Georges Simenon 208

- *The Prime of Miss Jean Brodie* by Muriel Spark 141
- *A Shooting Star* by Wallace Stegner 460
- *The Winter of Our Discontent* by John Steinbeck 445
- *The Time Regulation Institute* by Ahmet Hamdi Tanpinar 329
- *Unconditional Surrender* by Evelyn Waugh 70
- *Riders in the Chariot* by Patrick White 383
- *The Night of the Iguana* by Tennessee Williams 457

1964

- *On Her Majesty's Secret Service* by Ian Fleming 129
- *The Feminine Mystique* by Betty Friedan 522
- *The Experience of Pain* by Carlo Emilio Gadda 217
- *Visions of Gerard* by Jack Kerouac 472
- *Strength to Love* by Martin Luther King, Jr. 502
- *The Spy Who Came in from the Cold* by John le Carré 143
- *The Truce* by Primo Levi 222
- *The Assassination Bureau, Ltd.* by Jack London[†] & Robert L. Fish 405
- *Lunar Caustic* by Malcolm Lowry[†] 101
- *The Group* by Mary McCarthy 507
- *The Sailor Who Fell from Grace with the Sea* by Yukio Mishima 351
- *Blame Me On History* by Bloke Modisane 374

- *Chaos and Night* by Henry de Montherlant 198
- *Self-Portrait* by Man Ray 521
- *Maigret and the Tramp* by Georges Simenon 208
- *Maigret's Anger* by Georges Simenon 208
- *In My Father's Court* by Isaac Bashevis Singer 290
- *The Benefactor* by Susan Sontag 524
- *The Man Who Fell to Earth* by Walter Tevis 513
- *The Making of the English Working Class* by E. P. Thompson 149
- *The Centaur* by John Updike 515
- *The Ice Palace* by Tarjei Vesaas 238
- *Cat's Cradle* by Kurt Vonnegut 523
- *The Graduate* by Charles Webb 523
- *The Milk Train Doesn't Stop Here Anymore* by Tennessee Williams 456

- *The Face of Another* by Kobo Abe 352
- *Arrow of God* by Chinua Achebe 361
- *Behind the Door* by Giorgio Bassani 226
- *A Very Easy Death* by Simone de Beauvoir 189
- *Herzog* by Saul Bellow 478
- *The Self and Other* by Jorge Luis Borges 573
- *The Little Girls* by Elizabeth Bowen 14
- *Nova Express* by William S. Burroughs 484
- *My Autobiography* by Charles Chaplin 149
- *Charlie and the Chocolate Factory* by Roald Dahl 113
- *Funeral in Berlin* by Len Deighton 147
- *You Only Live Twice* by Ian Fleming 129
- *Second Skin* by John Hawkes 519
- *Cotton Comes to Harlem* by Chester Himes 509
- *The Lucky Country* by Donald Horne 385
- *Beauty and Sadness* by Yasunari Kawabata 350

- *The Perfect Murder* by H. R. F. Keating 150
- *Why We Can't Wait* by Martin Luther King, Jr. 502
- *The Psychedelic Experience* by Timothy Leary, Ralph Metzner & Richard Alpert 526
- *Pedro Martínez* by Oscar Lewis 518
- *The Passion According to G.H.* by Clarice Lispector 567
- *The Chill* by Ross Macdonald 499
- *After the Fall* by Arthur Miller 487
- *Incident at Vichy* by Arthur Miller 487
- *Words* by Jean-Paul Sartre 186
- *Last Exit to Brooklyn* by Hubert Selby Jr. 510
- *The Royal Hunt of the Sun* by Peter Shaffer 151
- *The Blue Room, Maigret and the Ghost & Maigret Defends Himself* by Georges Simenon 208, 211
- *A Little Learning* by Evelyn Waugh 71

1958

- *Voss* by Patrick White 382
- *Orpheus Descending*
  by Tennessee Williams 456
- *The Child and the Family*
  by D. W. Winnicott 138
- *The Child and the Outside World*
  by D. W. Winnicott 138
- *The Midwich Cuckoos*
  by John Wyndham 122
- *Family and Kinship in East London* by
  Michael Young & Peter Willmott 138

- *Things Fall Apart* by Chinua Achebe 359
- *The Two Executioners*
  by Fernando Arrabal 324
- *The Gold-Rimmed Spectacles*
  by Giorgio Bassani 224
- *Memoirs of a Dutiful Daughter*
  by Simone de Beauvoir 187
- *Breakfast at Tiffany's*
  by Truman Capote 464
- *A Mixture of Frailties*
  by Robertson Davies 395
- *Anecdotes of Destiny* by Isak Dinesen 242
- *The Rack* by A. E. Ellis 140

- *Dr No* by Ian Fleming 128
- *Our Man in Havana*
  by Graham Greene 92
- *My Face for the World to See*
  by Alfred Hayes 498
- *The Real Cool Killers*
  by Chester Himes 509
- *The Sundial* by Shirley Jackson 468
- *The Best of Everything* by Rona Jaffe 512
- *The Dharma Bums* by Jack Kerouac 472
- *The Subterraneans* by Jack Kerouac 471
- *What Shall We Tell Caroline?*
  by John Mortimer 139

- *Nabokov's Dozen*
  by Vladimir Nabokov 305
- *The Guide* by R. K. Narayan 343
- *Maigret's Doubts*
  by Georges Simenon 207
- *The Cowards* by Josef Škvorecký 285
- *Once There Was a War*
  by John Steinbeck 442
- *Night* by Elie Wiesel 325
- *Suddenly Last Summer*
  by Tennessee Williams 456

1960

- *No Longer at Ease* by Chinua Achebe 361
- *New Maps of Hell* by Kingsley Amis 133
- *Take a Girl Like You* by Kingsley Amis 133
- *The Prime of Life*
  by Simone de Beauvoir 187
- *The Truce* by Mario Benedetti 570
- *The Maker* by Jorge Luis Borges 574
- *Crowds and Power* by Elias Canetti 328
- *French Provincial Cooking*
  by Elizabeth David 131

- *Shadows on the Grass*
  by Isak Dinesen 242
- *For Your Eyes Only* by Ian Fleming 128
- *Promise at Dawn* by Romain Gary 197
- *Pornografia* by Witold Gombrowicz 292
- *Meetings with Remarkable Men*
  by G. I. Gurdjieff[†] 333
- *Facial Justice* by L. P. Hartley 126
- *Road to Ghana* by Alfred Hutchinson 373
- *Lonesome Traveler* by Jack Kerouac 472

- *Tristessa* by Jack Kerouac 472
- *The Divided Self* by R. D. Laing 140
- *Family Ties*
  by Clarice Lispector 565
- *Nexus* by Henry Miller 452
- *Peterley Harvest* by David Peterley 94
- *To Bedlam and Part Way Back*
  by Anne Sexton 518
- *Harvest on the Don*
  by Mikhail Sholokhov 587

- *Maigret and the Old People*
  by Georges Simenon 208
- *Maigret in Court* by Georges Simenon 207
- *The Slave* by Isaac Bashevis Singer 290
- *The Ballad of Peckham Rye*
  by Muriel Spark 141
- *Rabbit, Run* by John Updike 514
- *Period of Adjustment*
  by Tennessee Williams 457

1962

- *The Woman in the Dunes*
  by Kobo Abe 352
- *Portrait in Brownstone*
  by Louis Auchincloss 519
- *Another Country* by James Baldwin 493
- *The Garden of the Finzi-Continis*
  by Giorgio Bassani 225
- *Labyrinths* by Jorge Luis Borges 574
- *When Blackbirds Sing* by Martin Boyd 384
- *A Clockwork Orange*
  by Anthony Burgess 148
- *The Ticket That Exploded*
  by William S. Burroughs 484
- *Explosion in a Cathedral*
  by Alejo Carpentier 559
- *Silent Spring* by Rachel Carson 504
- *The IPCRESS File* by Len Deighton 147
- *The Man in the High Castle*
  by Philip K. Dick 520

- *Conversations with Stalin*
  by Milovan Djilas 327
- *My Happy Days in Hell*
  by György Faludy 279
- *The Reivers* by William Faulkner[†] 435
- *The Spy Who Loved Me*
  by Ian Fleming 129
- *Physics and Philosophy*
  by Werner Heisenberg 260
- *We Have Always Lived in the Castle*
  by Shirley Jackson 468
- *The Thin Red Line* by James Jones 500
- *Nobody Leaves*
  by Ryszard Kapuściński 296
- *Big Sur* by Jack Kerouac 472
- *One Flew Over the Cuckoo's Nest*
  by Ken Kesey 520
- *A Murder of Quality*
  by John le Carré 143

- *Seven Days at the Silbersteins*
  by Etienne Leroux 374
- *The Pumpkin Eater*
  by Penelope Mortimer 146
- *Pale Fire* by Vladimir Nabokov 311
- *All My Pretty Ones* by Anne Sexton 518
- *Maigret and the Good People of
  Montparnasse* by Georges Simenon 208
- *Maigret and the Saturday Caller*
  by Georges Simenon 208
- *One Day in the Life of Ivan Denisovich*
  by Aleksandr Solzhenitsyn 314
- *Wolf Willow* by Wallace Stegner 460
- *Travels with Charley*
  by John Steinbeck 445
- *Pictures from Brueghel*
  by William Carlos Williams 418

1963

- *One Fat Englishman* by Kingsley Amis 133
- *Eichmann in Jerusalem*
  by Hannah Arendt 259
- *On Revolution* by Hannah Arendt 259
- *The Fire Next Time* by James Baldwin 495
- *Force of Circumstance*
  by Simone de Beauvoir 189
- *A Favourite of the Gods*
  by Sybille Bedford 225
- *Planet of the Apes* by Pierre Boulle 198
- *Inside Mr Enderby*
  by Anthony Burgess 148
- *The Yage Letters* by William S. Burroughs
  & Allen Ginsberg 482
- *A God and His Gifts*
  by Ivy Compton-Burnett 105
- *Horse Under Water* by Len Deighton 147
- *Ehrengard* by Isak Dinesen[†] 242

1965

- *Going to Meet the Man*
  by James Baldwin 492
- *In the Heat of the Night* by John Ball 527
- *Cosmicomics* by Italo Calvino 221
- *In Cold Blood* by Truman Capote 464
- *117 Days* by Ruth First 375
- *The Man with the Golden Gun*
  by Ian Fleming[†] 129
- *Closely Watched Trains*
  by Bohumil Hrabal 285
- *Desolation Angels* by Jack Kerouac 472
- *The Looking Glass War*
  by John le Carré 143
- *Fever* by J. M. G. Le Clézio 199
- *The Cyberiad* by Stanisław Lem 294
- *An American Dream*
  by Norman Mailer 497

- *No Easy Walk to Freedom*
  by Nelson Mandela 372
- *Spring Snow* by Yukio Mishima 351
- *The River Between*
  by Ngũgĩ wa Thiong'o 365
- *The Housing Lark* by Sam Selvon 555
- *Maigret's Patience*
  by Georges Simenon 208
- *The Merry-Go-Round in the Sea*
  by Randolph Stow 386
- *Of the Farm* by John Updike 515
- *In Praise of Older Women*
  by Stephen Vizinczey 279
- *The Autobiography of Malcolm X*[†] 528

1966

- *A Man of the People*
  by Chinua Achebe 361
- *The Anti-Death League*
  by Kingsley Amis 133
- *My Mother* by Georges Bataille[†] 117
- *Plain Pleasures* by Jane Bowles 474
- *Up Above the World* by Paul Bowles 481
- *The Master and Margarita*
  by Mikhail Bulgakov[†] 322
- *The Beguiled* by Thomas Cullinan 528
- *Billion-Dollar Brain* by Len Deighton 147
- *Been Down So Long It looks Like
  Up to Me* by Richard Fariña 529
- *Octopussy and The Living Daylights*
  by Ian Fleming[†] 128
- *Omensetter's Luck*
  by William H. Gass 529
- *The Comedians* by Graham Greene 92
- *Make Room! Make Room!*
  by Harry Harrison 530
- *Satori in Paris* by Jack Kerouac 473

- *The Flood* by J. M. G. Le Clézio 199
- *The Third Eye* by Etienne Leroux 374
- *The Last Picture Show*
  by Larry McMurtry 530
- *The Fixer* by Bernard Malamud 476
- *Design as Art* by Bruno Munari 226
- *Nairn's London* by Ian Nairn 153
- *The Chosen* by Chaim Potok 531
- *Wide Sargasso Sea* by Jean Rhys 552
- *Season of Migration to the North*
  by Tayeb Salih 357
- *Live or Die* by Anne Sexton 518
- *Maigret and the Nahour Case*
  by Georges Simenon 208
- *Enemies: A Love Story*
  by Isaac Bashevis Singer 290
- *Against Interpretation*
  by Susan Sontag 524
- *Hell's Angels* by Hunter S. Thompson 531
- *The Solid Mandala* by Patrick White 383

1967

- *The Ruined Map* by Kobo Abe 352
- *The Dead Man* by Georges Bataille† 177
- *Time and the Hunter* by Italo Calvino 220
- *Childhood* by Tove Ditlevsen 243
- *Youth* by Tove Ditlevsen 243
- *Jerusalem the Golden*
  by Margaret Drabble 152
- *One Hundred Years of Solitude*
  by Gabriel García Márquez 562
- *May We Borrow Your Husband?*
  by Graham Greene 89
- *The Mersey Sound* by Adrian Henri,
  Roger McGough & Brian Patten 153
- *The Outsiders* by S. E. Hinton 533
- *Ice* by Anna Kavan 154
- *Terra Amata* by J. M. G. Le Clézio 199

- *The Medium is the Massage* by Marshall
  McLuhan & Quentin Fiore 396
- *Oranges* by John McPhee 533
- *Runaway Horses* by Yukio Mishima 351
- *In Corner B* by Es'kia Mphahlele 371
- *The Vendor of Sweets* by R. K. Narayan 343
- *A Grain of Wheat*
  by Ngũgĩ wa Thiong'o 366
- *Maigret's Pickpocket*
  by Georges Simenon 209
- *The Certificate* by Isaac Bashevis Singer 290
- *Scum* by Isaac Bashevis Singer 290
- *Death Kit* by Susan Sontag 524
- *All the Little Live Things*
  by Wallace Stegner 460
- *The Eighth Day* by Thornton Wilder 436

1968

- *I Want It Now* by Kingsley Amis 153
- *Tell Me How Long the Train's Been Gone*
  by James Baldwin 495
- *The Heron* by Giorgio Bassani 225
- *A Compass Error* by Sybille Bedford 261
- *Mosby's Memoirs* by Saul Bellow 477
- *Eva Trout* by Elizabeth Bowen 14
- *Gorbunov and Gorchakov*
  by Joseph Brodsky 316
- *The Empty Space* by Peter Brook 155
- *Enderby Outside* by Anthony Burgess 148
- *World Memory and Other Cosmicomic
  Stories* by Italo Calvino 220
- *The Voices of Marrakesh*
  by Elias Canetti 328
- *Belle du Seigneur* by Albert Cohen 264

- *The Faces* by Tove Ditlevsen 243
- *Pedagogy of the Oppressed*
  by Paulo Freire 568
- *A Kestrel for a Knave* by Barry Hines 155
- *Vanity of Duluoz* by Jack Kerouac 473
- *A Small Town in Germany*
  by John le Carré 143
- *Tales of Pirx the Pilot*
  by Stanisław Lem 294
- *One for the Devil* by Etienne Leroux 374
- *An Apprenticeship*
  by Clarice Lispector 567
- *Dark as the Grave Wherein My Friend
  is Laid* by Malcolm Lowry† 102
- *The Armies of the Night*
  by Norman Mailer 497

1971

- *Fireflies* by Shiva Naipaul 556
- *Maigret and the Wine Merchant,
  Maigret's Madwoman & When I Was
  Old* by Georges Simenon 209, 211
- *The Driver's Seat* by Muriel Spark 141
- *The Ogre* by Michel Tournier 199
- *Bech: A Book* by John Updike 515
- *The Vivisector* by Patrick White 383

- *Girl, 20* by Kingsley Amis 133
- *Malina* by Ingeborg Bachmann 275
- *M/F* by Anthony Burgess 148
- *The Wild Boys*
  by William S. Burroughs 485
- *A Happy Death* by Albert Camus† 181
- *The Last and the First*
  by Ivy Compton-Burnett† 105
- *Americana* by Don DeLillo 537
- *Dependency* by Tove Ditlevsen 243
- *The Book of Daniel* by E. L. Doctorow 538
- *Don't Look Now*
  by Daphne du Maurier 150

- *Maurice* by E. M. Forster† 39
- *A Sort of Life* by Graham Greene 93
- *Pic* by Jack Kerouac† 470
- *The Naive and Sentimental Lover*
  by John le Carré 144
- *The Futurological Congress*
  by Stanisław Lem 294
- *The Mortgaged Heart*
  by Carson McCullers† 453
- *The Underground Man*
  by Ross Macdonald 499
- *A Fire on the Moon*
  by Norman Mailer 497

- *The Tenants* by Bernard Malamud 476
- *The Decay of the Angel*
  by Yukio Mishima† 351
- *The Room* by Hubert Selby Jr. 511
- *Maigret and the Informer*
  by Georges Simenon 209
- *Maigret and the Loner*
  by Georges Simenon 209
- *Angle of Repose* by Wallace Stegner 460
- *Black List, Section H*
  by Francis Stuart 21
- *Rabbit Redux* by John Updike 514

1974

- *Água Viva* by Clarice Lispector 567
- *A Russian Beauty and Other Stories*
  by Vladimir Nabokov 305
- *Strong Opinions* by Vladimir Nabokov 305
- *The Chip-Chip Gatherers*
  by Shiva Naipaul 556
- *The Ramayana* by R. K. Narayan 343
- *Equus* by Peter Shaffer 151
- *A Crown of Feathers and Other Stories*
  by Isaac Bashevis Singer 289
- *The Penitent* by Isaac Bashevis Singer 290
- *The Eye of the Storm*
  by Patrick White 383

- *Ending Up* by Kingsley Amis 134
- *If Beale Street Could Talk*
  by James Baldwin 495
- *A Nip in the Air* by John Betjeman 88
- *The Clockwork Testament*
  by Anthony Burgess 148
- *The Hearing Trumpet*
  by Leonora Carrington 158
- *My Poems Won't Change the World*
  by Patrizia Cavalli 228
- *Kleinzeit* by Russell Hoban 540
- *Tinker Tailor Soldier Spy*
  by John le Carré 144

- *History: A Novel* by Elsa Morante 228
- *Look at the Harlequins!*
  by Vladimir Nabokov 311
- *Memoirs* by Pablo Neruda† 569
- *How I Came to Know Fish*
  by Ota Pavel† 286
- *Species of Spaces* by Georges Perec 196
- *The Death Notebooks*
  by Anne Sexton 518
- *A Little Boy in Search of God*
  by Isaac Bashevis Singer 291
- *Shosha* by Isaac Bashevis Singer 291
- *The Cockatoos* by Patrick White 383

1975

- *The Monkey Wrench Gang*
  by Edward Abbey 542
- *Humboldt's Gift* by Saul Bellow 479
- *The Book of Sand*
  by Jorge Luis Borges 575
- *The Unending Rose*
  by Jorge Luis Borges 575
- *Answered Prayers* by Truman Capote 464
- *How Steeple Sinderby Wanderers Won
  the FA Cup* by J. L. Carr 159
- *World of Wonders*
  by Robertson Davies 395

1977

- *Secret Rendezvous* by Kobo Abe 352
- *Liveforovor* by Andrés Caicedo 663
- *The Fairy Tales of Charles Perrault*
  by Angela Carter 156
- *Falconer* by John Cheever 544
- *Monkey Grip* by Helen Garner 386
- *The Left-Handed Woman*
  by Peter Handke 275
- *The Honourable Schoolboy*
  by John le Carré 144
- *Hour of the Star* by Clarice Lispector 567
- *The Danger Tree* by Olivia Manning 159
- *Petals of Blood* by Ngũgĩ wa Thiong'o 366
- *Delta of Venus* by Anaïs Nin† 431
- *Ceremony* by Leslie Marmon Silko 545
- *On Photography* by Susan Sontag 525

1978

- *Badenheim 1939*
  by Aharon Appelfeld 326
- *The Human Factor* by Graham Greene 93
- *The Emperor* by Ryszard Kapuściński 296
- *A Breath of Life* by Clarice Lispector† 567
- *The Black Unicorn* by Audre Lorde 534
- *The Battle Lost and Won*
  by Olivia Manning 159
- *House of Hunger*
  by Dambudzo Marechera 377
- *Missing Person* by Patrick Modiano 200
- *Rumpole of the Bailey*
  by John Mortimer 139

- *North of South* by Shiva Naipaul 556
- *The Mahabharata* by R. K. Narayan 344
- *A Cup of Rage* by Raduan Nassar 568
- *Orientalism* by Edward W. Said 335
- *Requiem for a Dream*
  by Hubert Selby Jr. 511
- *Lost in America*
  by Isaac Bashevis Singer 291
- *Illness as Metaphor* by Susan Sontag 525
- *Child of Fortune* by Yuko Tsushima 353
- *The Coup* by John Updike 516

1979

- *Just Above My Head*
  by James Baldwin 495
- *Say a Little Mantra for Me*
  by Yvonne Burgess 376
- *Handcarved Coffins*
  by Truman Capote 465
- *Smiley's People* by John le Carré 144
- *Dubin's Lives* by Bernard Malamud 476
- *The Trials of Rumpole*
  by John Mortimer 139
- *Little Birds* by Anaïs Nin† 431
- *And Again?* by Sean O'Faolain 17
- *Smile Please* by Jean Rhys† 552
- *Solo Faces* by James Salter 508
- *Amadeus* by Peter Shaffer 151
- *Recapitulation* by Wallace Stegner 460
- *The Old Patagonian Express*
  by Paul Theroux 543
- *Territory of Light* by Yuko Tsushima 353
- *The Twyborn Affair* by Patrick White 384

1969

- *Miami and the Siege of Chicago*
  by Norman Mailer 497
- *The Price* by Arthur Miller 488
- *Life for Sale* by Yukio Mishima 351
- *The Temple of Dawn*
  by Yukio Mishima 351
- *My Father's Son* by Frank O'Connor[†] 16
- *Tigers Are Better-Looking*
  by Jean Rhys 551
- *The Hand, Maigret Hesitates, Maigret
  in Vichy & Maigret's Childhood Friend*
  by Georges Simenon 209, 211
- *Cancer Ward*
  by Aleksandr Solzhenitsyn 314
- *Couples* by John Updike 515
- *Chocky* by John Wyndham 122

- *Scent of a Woman*
  by Giovanni Arpino 227
- *Akenfield* by Ronald Blythe 155
- *Familiarity is the Kingdom of the Lost*
  by Dugmore Boetie[†] 375
- *In Praise of Darkness*
  by Jorge Luis Borges 573
- *The Job* by William S. Burroughs
  & Daniel Odier 484
- *Kafka's Other Trial* by Elias Canetti 328
- *Heroes and Villains* by Angela Carter 156
- *Mr Bridge* by Evan S. Connell 512
- *Pricksongs & Descants*
  by Robert Coover 536
- *Travels with My Aunt*
  by Graham Greene 93

- *As I Walked Out One Midsummer
  Morning* by Laurie Lee 114
- *A Death in the Sánchez Family*
  by Oscar Lewis 518
- *The Goodbye Look*
  by Ross Macdonald 499
- *Ada or Ardor* by Vladimir Nabokov 311
- *Poems and Problems*
  by Vladimir Nabokov 304
- *Maigret and the Killer*
  by Georges Simenon 209
- *Styles of Radical Will*
  by Susan Sontag 524

1970

- *Old Age* by Simone de Beauvoir 189
- *First Love* by Samuel Beckett 20
- *Mr. Sammler's Planet* by Saul Bellow 478
- *Doctor Brodie's Report*
  by Jorge Luis Borges 575
- *Fifth Business* by Robertson Davies 395
- *From a Crooked Rib*
  by Nuruddin Farah 366
- *The Goalkeeper's Anxiety at the Penalty
  Kick* by Peter Handke 274
- *Inspector Ghote Breaks an Egg*
  by H. R. F. Keating 150
- *October Ferry to Gabriola*
  by Malcolm Lowry[†] 102
- *A Voyage Round My Father*
  by John Mortimer 139

1972

- *Watership Down* by Richard Adams 158
- *The Smell of Hay* by Giorgio Bassani 225
- *All Said and Done*
  by Simone de Beauvoir 189
- *Ways of Seeing* by John Berger 154
- *The Gold of the Tigers*
  by Jorge Luis Borges 573
- *The Infernal Desire Machines of Doctor
  Hoffman* by Angela Carter 156
- *The Manticore* by Robertson Davies 395
- *The Needle's Eye*
  by Margaret Drabble 152

- *The Life to Come and Other Stories*
  by E. M. Forster[†] 38
- *Dandelions* by Yasunari Kawabata[†] 350
- *Inspector Ghote Trusts the Heart*
  by H. R. F. Keating 150
- *Visions of Cody* by Jack Kerouac[†] 470
- *John Thomas and Lady Jane*
  by D. H. Lawrence[†] 56
- *Journey Through a Small Planet*
  by Emanuel Litvinoff 158
- *Transparent Things*
  by Vladimir Nabokov 311

- *The Combat* by Kole Omotoso 362
- *The Other Mexico* by Octavio Paz 561
- *My Name is Asher Lev*
  by Chaim Potok 531
- *Shadow Game* by Michael Power 376
- *Mumbo Jumbo* by Ishmael Reed 539
- *Maigret and Monsieur Charles*
  by Georges Simenon 209
- *Small Craft Warnings*
  by Tennessee Williams 456

1973

- *The Box Man* by Kobo Abe 352
- *The Riverside Villas Murder*
  by Kingsley Amis 133
- *Exterminator!*
  by William S. Burroughs 485
- *The Trouble with Being Born*
  by E. M. Cioran 324
- *The Honorary Consul*
  by Graham Greene 93
- *A Question of Power* by Bessie Head 377
- *The Lion of Boaz-Jachin and Jachin-Boaz*
  by Russell Hoban 540
- *The Little Town Where Time Stood Still*
  by Bohumil Hrabal 285

- *Ragtime* by E. L. Doctorow 538
- *Discipline and Punish*
  by Michel Foucault 193
- *J R* by William Gaddis 505
- *Turtle Diary* by Russell Hoban 540
- *Dread Beat an' Blood*
  by Linton Kwesi Johnson 557
- *I Can't Stay Long* by Laurie Lee 114
- *The Periodic Table* by Primo Levi 223
- *The Fight* by Norman Mailer 497
- *Tyrants Destroyed and Other Stories*
  by Vladimir Nabokov 305

- *Ancient Tillage* by Raduan Nassar 568
- *A Woman Speaks* by Anaïs Nin 431
- *Light Years* by James Salter 508
- *Moses Ascending* by Sam Selvon 555
- *Zapata* by John Steinbeck[†] 444
- *The Great Railway Bazaar*
  by Paul Theroux 542
- *A Month of Sundays* by John Updike 516
- *The Philosophy of Andy Warhol* 543
- *Memoirs* by Tennessee Williams 457

1976

- *To Jerusalem and Back*
  by Saul Bellow 479
- *The Will to Knowledge*
  by Michel Foucault 193
- *Travesty* by John Hawkes 519
- *Cutting It Short* by Bohumil Hrabal 286
- *Another Day of Life*
  by Ryszard Kapuściński 296
- *Details of a Sunset and Other Stories*
  by Vladimir Nabokov 305
- *The Painter of Signs* by R. K. Narayan 343
- *In Favour of the Sensitive Man*
  by Anaïs Nin 431

- *Flight to Canada* by Ishmael Reed 539
- *Sleep It Off Lady* by Jean Rhys 551
- *The Demon* by Hubert Selby Jr. 511
- *A Young Man in Search of Love*
  by Isaac Bashevis Singer 291
- *The Spectator Bird*
  by Wallace Stegner 460
- *The Acts of King Arthur and His Noble
  Knights* by John Steinbeck[†] 445
- *The Children of Dynmouth*
  by William Trevor 21
- *Marry Me* by John Updike 516
- *A Fringe of Leaves* by Patrick White 383

1980

- *How German Is It* by Walter Abish 275
- *Earthly Powers* by Anthony Burgess 149
- *Music for Chameleons*
  by Truman Capote 465
- *A Month in the Country* by J. L. Carr 159
- *The Shooting Party* by Isabel Colegate 160
- *The Samurai* by Shusaku Endo 353
- *Honour and Other People's Children*
  by Helen Garner 387
- *The Kites* by Romain Gary 197
- *Doctor Fischer of Geneva*
  by Graham Greene 93

- *Ways of Escape* by Graham Greene 93
- *Riddley Walker* by Russell Hoban 541
- *The Cancer Journals* by Audre Lorde 534
- *The Sum of Things*
  by Olivia Manning[†] 159
- *Under the Sign of Saturn*
  by Susan Sontag 524
- *A Confederacy of Dunces*
  by John Kennedy Toole[†] 521
- *POPism* by Andy Warhol
  & Pat Hackett 544
- *Collected Stories* by Eudora Welty 457

1981

- *Sixty Stories* by Donald Barthelme 527
- *Adieux* by Simone de Beauvoir 189
- *Cities of the Red Night*
  by William S. Burroughs 485
- *The Sky* by Patrizia Cavalli 228
- *Women, Race and Class*
  by Angela Y. Davis 545
- *Moments of Reprieve* by Primo Levi 223
- *The Search for Roots*
  edited by Primo Levi 223
- *Rabbit is Rich* by John Updike 514
- *Flaws in the Glass* by Patrick White 384

1982

- *Great Expectations* by Kathy Acker 546
- *The Dean's December* by Saul Bellow 479
- *Springtime in a Broken Mirror*
  by Mario Benedetti 571
- *Spanking the Maid* by Robert Coover 536
- *Bluebeard* by Max Frisch 264
- *Monsignor Quixote*
  by Graham Greene 93
- *Shah of Shahs*
  by Ryszard Kapuściński 296
- *If Not Now, When?* by Primo Levi 223
- *Zami* by Audre Lorde 534
- *God's Grace* by Bernard Malamud 476
- *Clinging to the Wreckage*
  by John Mortimer 139
- *The Book of Disquiet*
  by Fernando Pessoa[†] 235
- *The Wall Jumper* by Peter Schneider 261
- *Bech is Back* by John Updike 515

1983

- *Shakespeare's Memory*
  by Jorge Luis Borges 575
- *The Place of Dead Roads*
  by William S. Burroughs 485
- *Fantastic Tales* edited by Italo Calvino 222
- *The Sorrow of Belgium*
  by Hugo Claus 212
- *French and Germans, Germans and
  French* by Richard Cobb 160
- *Paris* by Julian Green 200

- *Pilgermann* by Russell Hoban 541
- *The Encyclopedia of the Dead*
  by Danilo Kiš 327
- *The Little Drummer Girl*
  by John le Carré 144
- *A Hot Country* by Shiva Naipaul 556
- *A Tiger for Malgudi* by R. K. Narayan 344
- *Black Marxism* by Cedric J. Robinson 546
- *The Queen's Gambit* by Walter Tevis 513
- *Modern Baptists* by James Wilcox 547

1984

- *Blood and Guts in High School*
  by Kathy Acker 546
- *Money* by Martin Amis 160
- *Him with His Foot in His Mouth*
  by Saul Bellow 477
- *Enderby's Dark Lady*
  by Anthony Burgess 148
- *Collection of Sand* by Italo Calvino 221
- *Segu* by Maryse Condé 558
- *The Care of the Self*
  by Michel Foucault 193
- *The Use of Pleasure*
  by Michel Foucault 193

- *Getting to Know the General*
  by Graham Greene 94
- *According to Mark* by Penelope Lively 161
- *Sister Outsider* by Audre Lorde 534
- *Circles in a Forest* by Dalene Matthee 576
- *Beyond the Dragon's Mouth*
  by Shiva Naipaul 556
- *Ideal* by Ayn Rand[†] 450
- *The Witches of Eastwick*
  by John Updike 516
- *Miami Blues* by Charles Willeford 547

1987

- *Anthills of the Savannah*
  by Chinua Achebe 361
- *Forty Stories* by Donald Barthelme 527
- *More Die of Heartbreak*
  by Saul Bellow 479
- *The Western Lands*
  by William S. Burroughs 485
- *The Medusa Frequency*
  by Russell Hoban 541
- *Moon Tiger* by Penelope Lively 161
- *Crossing to Safety*
  by Wallace Stegner 460
- *Sideswipe* by Charles Willeford 547

1988

- *Difficulties with Girls*
  by Kingsley Amis 134
- *To Urania* by Joseph Brodsky 316
- *The Marriage of Cadmus and Harmony*
  by Roberto Calasso 229
- *Six Memos for the Next Millennium*
  by Italo Calvino[†] 221
- *Libra* by Don DeLillo 537
- *Bad Behavior* by Mary Gaitskill 548
- *The Captain and the Enemy*
  by Graham Greene 94

- *The Grass Arena* by John Healy 161
- *Among Friends*
  by Ludmilla Petrushevskaya 317
- *The Death of Methuselah and Other
  Stories* by Isaac Bashevis Singer 289
- *The King of the Fields*
  by Isaac Bashevis Singer 291
- *S.* by John Updike 516
- *The Way We Die Now*
  by Charles Willeford 547

1989

- *Boys in Zinc* by Svetlana Alexievich 320
- *Jigsaw* by Sybille Bedford 261
- *Interzone* by William S. Burroughs 483
- *Nostalgia* by Mircea Cărtărescu 326
- *Billy Bathgate* by E. L. Doctorow 538
- *The Mambo Kings Play Songs of Love*
  by Oscar Hijuelos 548
- *The Russia House* by John le Carré 145
- *All Souls* by Javier Marías 233
- *The Snows of Yesteryear*
  by Gregor von Rezzori 276
- *AIDS and Its Metaphors*
  by Susan Sontag 525
- *The Andy Warhol Diaries*[†] 343

1994

- *It All Adds Up* by Saul Bellow 477
- *Hermit in Paris* by Italo Calvino[†] 219
- *The First Man* by Albert Camus[†] 183
- *Cosmopolitan Greetings*
  by Allen Ginsberg 490
- *Oleander, Jacaranda*
  by Penelope Lively 161
- *Tomorrow in the Battle Think on Me*
  by Javier Marías 234
- *Meshugah* by Isaac Bashevis Singer[†] 291
- *Brazil* by John Updike 517

1995

- *On Grief and Reason*
  by Joseph Brodsky 316
- *My Education*
  by William S. Burroughs 483
- *Football in Sun and Shadow*
  by Eduardo Galeano 571
- *Our Game* by John le Carré 145
- *No Truce with the Furies*
  by R. S. Thomas 119

1996

- *Ka* by Roberto Calasso 229
- *Briar Rose* by Robert Coover 536
- *Fremder* by Russell Hoban 541
- *The Tailor of Panama* by John le Carré 145
- *Heat Wave* by Penelope Lively 161
- *The Scent of Dried Roses* by Tim Lott 162
- *When I Was Mortal* by Javier Marías 233
- *In the Beauty of the Lilies*
  by John Updike 517

1997

- *Chernobyl Prayer*
  by Svetlana Alexievich 320
- *The King's English* by Kingsley Amis[†] 134
- *The Actual* by Saul Bellow 479
- *Because They Wanted To*
  by Mary Gaitskill 548
- *Just an Ordinary Day*
  by Shirley Jackson[†] 466
- *Toward the End of Time*
  by John Updike 517

2002

- *K.* by Roberto Calasso 229
- *The Seven Sisters*
  by Margaret Drabble 152
- *Mi Revalueshanary Fren*
  by Linton Kwesi Johnson 557
- *Fever and Spear* by Javier Marías 234
- *Resurrection Blues* by Arthur Miller 488
- *Chocolates with Liqueur*
  by Ludmilla Petrushevskaya 317
- *Waiting Period* by Hubert Selby Jr. 511

2003

- *Reading Lolita in Tehran*
  by Azar Nafisi 335
- *Kingdom of Fear*
  by Hunter S. Thompson 532

2004

- *Absolute Friends* by John le Carré 146
- *Dance and Dream* by Javier Marías 234

2005

- *Summer Crossing*
  by Truman Capote[†] 463

2010

- *Aloft* by William Langewiesche 549
- *The Blizzard* by Vladimir Sorokin 318

2011

- *The Pursued* by C. S. Forester[†] 75
- *The Sea is My Brother*
  by Jack Kerouac[†] 469

2013

- *Autobiography* by Morrissey 162

2014

- *The Haunted Life* by Jack Kerouac[†] 469

1985

– *Last Witnesses*
   by Svetlana Alexievich 320
– *The Unwomanly Face of War*
   by Svetlana Alexievich 320
– *Old Masters* by Thomas Bernhard 276
– *Queer* by William S. Burroughs 482
– *Love in the Time of Cholera*
   by Gabriel García Márquez 563
– *The Tenth Man* by Graham Greene 91

– *Paradise Postponed*
   by John Mortimer 140
– *Under the Banyan Tree and Other Stories*
   by R. K. Narayan 343
– *Missus* by Ruth Park 391
– *Perfume* by Patrick Süskind 261
– *America* by Andy Warhol 544
– *New Hope for the Dead*
   by Charles Willeford 547

1986

– *Extinction* by Thomas Bernhard 276
– *Less Than One* by Joseph Brodsky 316
– *The Cat Inside*
   by William S. Burroughs 495
– *Under the Jaguar Sun* by Italo Calvino[†] 222
– *Gerald's Party* by Robert Coover 536
– *The Bodysurfers* by Robert Drewe 387
– *White Shroud* by Allen Ginsberg 490
– *Potiki* by Patricia Grace 391
– *Repetition* by Peter Handke 275
– *All My Cats* by Bohumil Hrabal 286
– *The Well* by Elizabeth Jolley 387
– *Under a Monsoon Cloud*
   by H. R. F. Keating 150

– *Search Sweet Country* by Kojo Laing 363
– *A Perfect Spy* by John le Carré 144
– *Fiasco* by Stanisław Lem 295
– *The Man of Feeling* by Javier Marías 233
– *The Enchanter* by Vladimir Nabokov[†] 308
– *Talkative Man* by R. K. Narayan 344
– *Song of the Silent Snow*
   by Hubert Selby Jr. 510
– *The Image and Other Stories*
   by Isaac Bashevis Singer 289
– *I'm Dying Laughing*
   by Christina Stead[†] 381
– *Roger's Version* by John Updike 516

1990

– *The Folks That Live on the Hill*
   by Kingsley Amis 134
– *Something to Remember Me By*
   by Saul Bellow 477
– *The Road to San Giovanni*
   by Italo Calvino[†] 219
– *The Last Word and Other Stories*
   by Graham Greene 89
– *The Secret Pilgrim* by John le Carré 145
– *Titmuss Regained* by John Mortimer 140
– *Rabbit at Rest* by John Updike 514

1991

– *Wartime Lies* by Louis Begley 297
– *Why Read the Classics?*
   by Italo Calvino[†] 218
– *Two Girls, Fat and Thin*
   by Mary Gaitskill 548
– *A Moment of War* by Laurie Lee 114
– *The Ride Down Mt Morgan*
   by Arthur Miller 488

1992

– *Bastard Out of Carolina*
   by Dorothy Allison 549
– *Watermark* by Joseph Brodsky 316
– *Fever Pitch* by Nick Hornby 162
– *A Heart So White* by Javier Marías 233
– *The Time Is Night*
   by Ludmilla Petrushevskaya 317
– *The Volcano Lover* by Susan Sontag 525
– *Memories of the Ford Administration*
   by John Updike 517

1993

– *Numbers in the Dark*
   by Italo Calvino[†] 218
– *Wake Up* by Jack Kerouac[†] 471
– *The Night Manager* by John le Carré 145

1998

– *The Mountains of My Life*
   by Walter Bonatti 226
– *Mr Rinyo-Clacton's Offer*
   by Russell Hoban 541
– *Dark Back of Time* by Javier Marías 234
– *The Sound of Trumpets*
   by John Mortimer 140
– *The Art of Joy* by Goliarda Sapienza[†] 227
– *The Willow Tree* by Hubert Selby Jr. 511
– *Bech at Bay* by John Updike 515

1999

– *Juneteenth* by Ralph Ellison[†] 458
– *Death & Fame* by Allen Ginsberg[†] 490
– *Single & Single* by John le Carré 145

2000

– *Ravelstein* by Saul Bellow 479
– *The Jungle Play* by Rudyard Kipling[†] 23
– *Written Lives* by Javier Marías 234
– *In America* by Susan Sontag 525

2001

– *The Constant Gardener*
   by John le Carré 146
– *Where the Stress Falls*
   by Susan Sontag 525

2006

– *Tiepolo Pink* by Roberto Calasso 229
– *Lazy Gods, Lazy Fate*
   by Patrizia Cavalli 228
– *The Mission Song* by John le Carré 146
– *Day of the Oprichnik*
   by Vladimir Sorokin 318

2007

– *A Tranquil Star* by Primo Levi[†] 223
– *Poison, Shadow and Farewell*
   by Javier Marías 234

2008

– *And the Hippos Were Boiled in Their
   Tanks* by William S. Burroughs[†]
   & Jack Kerouac[†] 481
– *A Most Wanted Man* by John le Carré 146
– *The Tragedy of Mister Morn*
   by Vladimir Nabokov[†] 306

2009

– *The Education of a British-Protected Child*
   by Chinua Achebe 361
– *The Original of Laura*
   by Vladimir Nabokov[†] 311

2015

– *Let Me Tell You*
   by Shirley Jackson[†] 466

2016

– *Confabulations* by John Berger 154
– *Wait Till I'm Dead* by Allen Ginsberg[†] 490

2017

– *The Best Minds of My Generation*
   by Allen Ginsberg[†] 491

2018

– *Confessions of the Flesh*
   by Michel Foucault[†] 193

Index

INDEX

Mersey Sound, The 153, 588

Meshugah 291, 590

Metamorphosis and Other Stories 280–81, 302, 562, 580

Metzner, Ralph 526, 586

Mew, Charlotte 61, 580

Mexico City Blues 471, 586

Mi Revalueshanary Fren 557, 590

Miami and the Siege of Chicago 497, 589

Miami Blues 547, 590

Middle of the Journey, The 489, 585

Middle Parts of Fortune, The 381, 580

Midsummer Night Madness and Other Stories 17, 582

Midwich Cuckoos, The 122, 587

Military Orchid, The 120, 584

Milk Train Doesn't Stop Here Anymore, The 456, 586

Millay, Edna St Vincent 412, 580–81

Miller, Arthur 240, 264, 283, 323, 441, 448, 455, 486–9, 516, 544, 576, 584–6, 589–91

Miller, Henry 80, 83–4, 263, 289, 420, 430, 451–2, 522, 582–3, 585, 587

Miłosz, Czesław xvii, 287–8, 292–3, 316, 328, 335, 577, 584–6

Milton, John 59, 66; Paradise Lost 327, 337, 404–5

Mind of an Outlaw 496

Mine of Serpents, A 120, 584

Ministry of Fear, The 91, 583

Mint, The 74, 583

Miracle of the Rose 190, 571, 584

Mirror of the Sea, The 29, 234, 579

Mishima, Yukio 56, 129, 177, 234, 348, 350–51, 372, 285, 503, 584–9

Miss Lonelyhearts ix, 446, 583

Missing Person 41, 200, 588

Mission Song, The 146, 591

Missus 391, 591

Mister Johnson 18, 582

Mister Paradise and Other One-Act Plays 455

Mistral, Gabriela 569, 576

Misty Harbour, The 200, 203, 582

Mitford, Nancy 70, 107, 117, 260, 387, 584–5

Mittee 372, 584

Mixture of Frailties, A 395, 587

Modern African Poetry, The Penguin Book of 359

Modern Baptists 547, 590

Modern Comedy, A 47

Modern Times 185

modernism xviii–xix, 3, 11, 42, 44, 59, 72, 78, 214–15, 263, 266, 269–72, 301–2, 312, 319, 334, 348, 400, 410, 418, 426–7, 433, 449–50, 465, 474, 484, 490, 505, 524, 561–2, 564

Modiano, Patrick 41, 200, 577, 588

Modigliani, Amedeo 174, 178, 301

Modisane, Bloke 371, 374, 586

Mofolo, Thomas 362, 368, 579

Molesworth 120, 125, 235

Molière 173, 228

Moment of War, A 114, 591

Moments of Reprieve 223, 589

Monbiot, George 284, 568

Money xi, 160, 590

Money from Home 439, 582

Monkey Grip 386, 482, 588

Monkey Planet 198

Monkey Wrench Gang, The 542, 588

Monkey's Paw, The xiv, 36

Monroe, Marilyn 240, 453, 465, 486–7, 496

Monsieur Monde Vanishes 210, 584

Monsignor Quixote 93, 589

Montale, Eugenio 214, 215, 218, 577, 580

Month in the Country, A xi, 159, 589

Month of Sundays, A 353, 516, 589

Montherlant, Henry de 172, 189, 194, 198, 586

Moon and Sixpence, The 33, 581

Moon is Down, The 252, 441, 442, 583

Moon Tiger 161, 361, 590

Moonraker 127, 584

Mopeli-Paulus, A. S. 369, 585

Morante, Elsa 228, 588

Moravagine 224, 263, 581

More Die of Heartbreak 479, 590

More Than Somewhat 439, 583

Morris, William 46, 149, 397

Morrison, Blake 51, 148, 162, 296, 465

Morrison, Toni vi, 458, 492, 577

Morrissey 162, 590

Mortal Coil and Other Stories, The 50, 598

Mortal Engines 295, 598

Mortgaged Heart, The 453, 588

Mortimer, John 49, 65, 132, 139–40, 146, 397, 510, 586, 588–91

Mortimer, Penelope 139, 146, 382, 587

Mosby's Memoirs and Other Stories 477, 588

Moses Ascending 555, 589

Moss, Rose Rappoport 375

Most Wanted Man, A 146, 591

Mother and Son 270, 579

Motion, Andrew 57, 81

Mottram, R. H. 73, 580–81

Mount Zion 88, 582

Mountains of My Life, The 226, 246, 591

Movement, The 86, 124

Mphahlele, Es'kia 303, 371, 373, 586

Mr Bridge 512, 589

Mr Fortune's Maggot 76, 523, 581

Mr Hire's Engagement 201, 583

Mr Ma and Son 346, 580

Mr Noon 53, 583

Mr Norris Changes Trains 103, 582

Mr Sammler's Planet 476, 478, 589

Mr Stimpson and Mr Gorse 112, 585

Mr Weston's Good Wine 77, 581

Mrożek, Sławomir 295, 586

Mrs Bridge 512, 589

Mrs Craddock 32, 578, 586

Mrs Dalloway 10, 44, 580

Muir, Edwin 72, 272, 280–83

Muir, Willa 272, 280–83

Multitudinous Heart 564

Mumbo Jumbo xii, 396, 539, 589

Munari, Bruno xvii, 226, 587

Munro, Alice 19, 577

Munro, H. H. see Saki

Murder of Quality, A 143, 587

Murdoch, Iris vii, 13, 185, 328

Murray, Les 382, 385

Muses Are Heard, The 465, 585

Muse's Tragedy and Other Stories, The 401

Music for Chameleons 464, 465, 589

Musil, Robert 235, 253, 270, 272–3, 579, 583

Mussolini, Benito 215, 228, 259

My Ántonia 414, 581

My Apprenticeship (Gorky) 300, 580

My Apprenticeship (Webb) 73, 581

My Autobiography (Chaplin) 149, 587

My Childhood (Gorky) 300, 579

My Country Right or Left (Orwell) 81

My Education (Burroughs) 483, 590

My Face for the World to See 498, 587

My Father's Son (O'Connor) 16, 589

My First Wife (Wassermann) 249, 583

My Friend Maigret 205, 585

My Happy Days in Hell (Faludy) 279, 587

My Life (Chagall) 319, 581

My Mother (Bataille) 177, 587

My Mother's House (Colette) 171, 581

My Name is Asher Lev 531, 589

My Oedipus Complex and Other Stories 16

My Poems Won't Change the World 228, 588

My Universities (Gorky) 300, 581

Myth of Sisyphus, The 182, 184, 324, 582

N

Nabokov, Vladimir xi, xvi, 10–11, 20, 132, 168, 231, 233–4, 299, 302–3, 304–11, 313, 419, 427, 460, 505, 513, 536, 548, 571, 576, 580–89, 591; PEN/Nabokov Award 334

Nabokov's Dozen 305, 587

Nadja 176, 580

Naess, Arne 238

Nafisi, Azar 335, 590

Naipaul, Shiva 99, 556, 588, 590

Naipaul, V. S. 14, 32, 94, 343, 525, 542, 555, 556, 577, 586

Nairn, Ian 153, 587

Nairn's London 153, 587

Naive and Sentimental Lover, The 144, 588

Naked and the Dead, The 496, 584

Naked Lunch 242, 482, 483, 484–5, 491, 586

Napoleon Bonaparte 29, 283

Napoleon of Notting Hill, The 41, 579

Narayan, R. K. 42, 286, 342–4, 448, 562, 565, 577, 586

Narrow Corner, The 34, 582

Narziss and Goldmund 249, 387, 581

Nassar, Raduan 568, 588–9

National Association for the Advancement of Colored People, the 407–8, 412, 419, 502

Native Realm 288, 586

Native Son 376, 462, 492, 509, 583

Natural, The 475, 584

Nausea 181, 185, 477, 582

Neal, Larry 534

Near to the Wild Heart 565, 583

Needle's Eye, The 152, 589

négritude xix, 558

Neruda, Pablo 559, 561–2, 569, 577, 580, 585, 588

New and Collected Poems (Miłosz) 287

New Apocalypse, the 98, 103, 124

New Criticism, the 459, 489

New Hampshire 415, 581

New Hope for the Dead 547, 591

New Journalism 463, 464, 488, 496–7, 519–20, 531–2, 549

New Life, A 132, 475, 586

New Machiavelli, The 27, 73, 579

New Maps of Hell 133, 587

New Objectivity, the 255, 563

New York Intellectuals, the 489, 507

Newman, Paul 456, 498, 512–13

Nexus 452, 587

Ngũgĩ wa Thiong'o 335, 362, 365–6, 554, 576, 587–8

Nicholson, Jack 516, 532

Nicolson, Harold 44, 96

N— of the 'Narcissus', The 28

Night 325, 587

Night and Day 42, 581

Night at the Crossroads 202, 581

Night Flight 178, 581

Night Manager, The 36, 145, 591

Night of the Iguana, The 36, 456–7, 586

Nijinsky, Vaslav 321, 583

Nikolai Gogol 309, 584

Niland, D'Arcy 385, 585

Nin, Anaïs 53, 451, 430–31, 451, 584, 586, 588–9

Nineteen Eighty-Four 66, 80, 82–3, 84–5, 258, 278, 287, 303, 346, 501, 514, 541, 585

Nineteen Nineteen 404, 426, 582

Ninety-Two Days 68, 69, 496, 583

Nip in the Air, A 88, 588

Nixon, Richard 497, 526, 532

No Easy Walk to Freedom 372, 587

No Exit 185

No Longer at Ease 361, 587

No More Parades 46, 580

No Truce with the Furies 119, 590

Nobel Prize for Literature, the 4, 20, 22, 25, 47, 131, 164, 173–4, 180–82, 185, 199–200, 215, 239, 245, 247, 274, 287–8, 293, 297, 302, 304, 312, 314, 316, 320, 328–9, 334, 337, 348, 350, 362, 382–3, 415, 421, 428, 433–4, 440, 448–9, 474, 477, 515, 555, 558, 561–2, 569, 572, 576–7

Nobody Knows My Name 135, 493, 586

Nobody Leaves 296, 587

Norris, Frank 406, 407, 568, 578–9

North of South 556, 589

Northland Stories 154, 404

Nostalgia 326, 590

Nostromo 29, 579

Notes of a Native Son 376, 492, 584

Nova Express 363, 484, 586

Novel of Ferrara, The 224–5

Novel on Yellow Paper 99, 108, 583

Novel with Cocaine 313, 482, 583

Numbers in the Dark 218, 591

Nuptials 181–2, 582

Nyiszli, Miklós 224, 279, 585

O

O Pioneers! 414, 579

Oates, Joyce Carol 152, 468, 478, 480, 495, 514, 577

Obama, Barack 441, 458, 502, 538

Objectivism 418

O'Brian, Patrick 189–90

O'Brien, Flann 13, 18, 231

O'Casey, Sean 6, 87, 585

O'Connor, Flannery 433, 475, 519

O'Connor, Frank 6, 16, 17, 520, 530, 586, 589

October Ferry to Gabriola 102, 589

Octopus, The 406, 568, 578

Octopussy 128, 587

Odessa Tales 321, 581

Odier, Daniel 484, 589

Oedipus 101, 148, 247, 324; Oedipus complex 16, 53, 265, 270

Of Human Bondage 33, 372, 580

Of Love and Hunger 119, 585

Of Men and Their Making 441

Of Mice and Men 387, 441, 442–3, 583

Of Mortal Love 72, 582

Of the Farm 515, 587

Of Time and the River 438, 582

O'Faolain, Sean 13, 17, 18, 26, 403, 582, 588

Officers and Gentlemen 70, 585

Ogre, The 199, 588

O'Hara Frank 79, 519

O'Hara, John 449, 527, 583

Okri, Ben 359

Old Age 189, 589

Old Masters 189, 276, 591

Old Patagonian Express, The 543, 588

Old Wives' Tale, The 37, 578

Oleander, Jacaranda 161, 590

Olivia 79, 97, 585

'Olivia' see Bussy, Dorothy

Omensetter's Luck 529, 587

Omotoso, Kole 362, 589

On Broadway 439, 598

On Forsyte 'Change 47, 581

On Grief and Reason 316, 590

On Her Majesty's Secret Service 128, 129, 586

On Heroes and Tombs 575, 586

On Leave 195, 463, 586

On Mourning and Melancholia 267

On Photography 154, 525, 588

On Revolution 259, 587

On the Marble Cliffs 250, 583

On the Road xi, 147, 363, 448, 469, 470, 472–3, 49, 514, 586

Once a Jailbird 252, 583

Once There Was a War 442, 587

One 501, 585

One Day in the Life of Ivan Denisovich 293, 314–15, 316, 587

One Fat Englishman 133, 587

One Flew Over the Cuckoo's Nest 151, 448, 520, 587

One for the Devil 374, 588

One Hundred Years of Solitude 47, 559, 562, 563, 571, 588

One Moonlit Night 142, 586

One-Way Street and Other Writings 251

O'Neill, Eugene 415, 455, 576, 580–81

Only Child, An 16, 586

Oranges 242, 533, 588

Ordeal of Gilbert Pinfold, The 71, 200, 586

Orient Express, the 89, 127, 265, 542

Orientalism 39, 335, 588

Original of Laura, The 20, 311, 591

Origins of Totalitarianism, The 258, 584

Origo, Iris 137, 586

Orlando 26, 44, 156, 580

Ornament and Crime 269

Orpheus 269, 353, 456, 541

Orpheus Descending 456, 587

Orwell, George 11, 22, 28, 34, 58, 61, 65–6, 80–85, 86, 104, 106–8, 161, 184, 200, 278, 287, 296, 303, 340–41, 346, 404, 428, 451, 470, 489, 541, 582–5

Orwell and Politics 84

Orwell and the Dispossessed 81

599

Acknowledgements

Firstly, many thanks to the three editors who have steered this book to completion – Helen Conford, Cecilia Stein and Richard Atkinson. I am hugely grateful for their vision, their humour and the sanity they have brought to this unruly project. Thanks to Rebecca Lee for wrangling the schedule, Katy Banyard for overseeing the production, Annabel Huxley for publicity pyrotechnics, Sam Voulters for marketing magic and to all my other Penguin colleagues who have helped to make this book happen: Maria Bedford, Bianca Bexton, Thi Dinh, Sam Fulton, Donald Futers, Rosie Glaisher, Jessica Harrison, Nicola Hill, Edward Kirke, Ingrid Matts, Stefan McGrath, Jon Parker, Zia Rahman, Di Riley, Jon Roberts, Ben Rolfe, Ilaria Rovera, Jim Stoddart, Anna Wilson, Dahmicca Wright and Emmy Yoneda.

Many thanks to the staff at the Penguin Random House Archive in Rushden, especially Nicki Carter, Louise King and Catherine Flynn, who have patiently assisted with incessant book requests and lengthy photography visits. Thanks to Theo Inglis and Jouve India for their help with the typesetting and Alta for their work on the images. Thanks to Ian Daley, Keith Ferguson, Tim Graham and especially James Mackay, as well as other members of the Penguin Collectors Society, for their kind comments and their excellent *Companion to the Study of Penguin Books* (2020). Thanks also to Alec Spencer, creator (and curator) of the invaluable Penguin First Editions website, James Pardey and his Art of Penguin Science Fiction website and Steve Trussel for his Penguin Maigret (202) webpage.

Particular thanks are due to four individuals who have given their attention, expertise and flair to every page of this book:
to David Post, for taking most of the 2,000 and more cover photographs at the Penguin Random House Archive;* to Kit Shepherd, for his erudite, witty and always scrupulous copy-editing; to Matthew Young, for another spectacular feat of design, transforming base text into typeset gold; and to Stephen Ryan, for meticulous proof-reading. All four have contributed enormously to the book you hold in your hands and I am extremely grateful to them. Matt also designed the cover and selected the three typefaces used in this volume: Avant Garde (xii), Univers (154) and Joanna (ix).

Thanks to my friends Matt Lloyd-Rose, Ed Posnett and Andy Wimbush for their support as always; to my parents Olivia and Simon and sister Georgina for a loving home full of books; and to Georgie for the wonderful chapters we have shared so far and all the ones we are still to write together. *The Penguin Classics Book* was dedicated to the teachers who inspired my love of literature; this volume is dedicated to Toby, who arrived just as it was finished, and who is finding new ways to inspire me every day.

Finally, I would like to thank all the Penguin editors, past and present, who have stewarded the Modern Classics series over the last 60 years, especially Tony Godwin (ix), whose idea it was in the first place, and also my friend and colleague Simon Winder (xi), who has been involved in the list for more than a third of its existence and continues to guide its evolution. The Penguin Modern Classics comprises a remarkable collection of authors and titles. The books are experimental and exhilarating and it has been a joy and a privilege to write about them.

* It may be of interest to know that at least two artworks were reused on different book covers that appear in this volume. One is a painting by William John Leech called *The Sunshade* (c.1913) – you can find it on p.45 and p.551 – and the other is Salvador Dalí's *Tête Raphaëlesque éclatée* (1951), which appears on p.266 and p.559.